VAT Planning 2012–13

VAT Planning 2012–13

CCH
a Wolters Kluwer business

Legislative and other material

Telephone Helpline Disclaimer Notice

© 2012 Wolters Kluwer (UK) Ltd

Wolters Kluwer (UK) Ltd
145 London Road
Kingston upon Thames
KT2 6SR
Telephone: 0844 561 8166
Facsimile: 020 8247 2637
email: cch@wolterskluwer.co.uk
website: www.cch.co.uk

ISBN 978-1-84798-511-8

British Library Cataloguing-in-Publication Data

A catalogue record for this book is available from the British Library.

Typeset by Innodata Inc., India
Printed and bound in the UK by Hobbs the Printers Ltd

About the author

John Davison FCCA, CTA (Fellow) is an independent indirect tax consultant. He has been a partner in several mid-tier firms in the UK and Australia, and has written several VAT books and numerous articles. He has lectured around the world and also been an examiner for three tax institutes. John is a Fellow of the Chartered Institute of Tax and the Association of Chartered Certified Accountants.

Preface

I would like to express my thanks to the previous editors and contributors, particularly Neil Owen and Vaughn Chown. Without their dedication and effort *VAT Planning* would not be what it is today, a reference book that should be included in all VAT advisers' and practitioners' library.

VAT Planning contains many VAT planning tips and ideas. This will help practitioners and advisers to deal with the numerous VAT problems and issues that are encountered on a daily basis. As VAT constantly changes, there are numerous alterations to the book each year. The last couple of years have seen many changes that have required *VAT Planning* to be updated. For example, there have been several changes to the VAT rate, changes to the way protected buildings are dealt with, alterations to the way private use is taxed as well as numerous Tribunal and Court decisions.

Although no book can include all aspects of VAT or the situations that a business may encounter, *VAT Planning* aims to cover the most commonly encountered situations and also the common pitfalls. This year the book has been revamped to alter the way it presents the information. It has been restructured to cover many of the situations that a business could encounter, such as registration, partial exemption, special schemes, avoidance, appeals, etc. In addition, the book has further chapters on specific topics, such as property, agents, motor vehicles, imports, exports and electronic supplies. This will be expanded over the next few years to cover further topic areas.

It is hoped that all readers will find this a useful and practical aid to their working life.

John Davison FCCA, CTA (Fellow)
Author, *VAT Planning*
December 2012

Contents

Contents

Contents

Contents

Contents

Contents

Abbreviations

The following abbreviations are commonly used throughout this publication.

AAD	accompanying administrative document
All ER	All England Law Reports, from 1936–(current)
art.	article
BETA	British Equestrian Trade Association
BV	Besloten Vennootschap
BVC	British VAT Cases (CCH)
CC	county council
CGAS	capital goods adjustment scheme
CGS	capital goods scheme
CIF	cost, insurance and freight
Co	Company
CSF	charitable schools foundation
CT	corporation tax
C & E Commrs	Customs and Excise Commissioners
DDU	delivered duty unpaid
DGT	daily gross takings
DIY	do-it-yourself
DMU	Debt Management Unit
ECHR	European Convention on Human Rights
ECJ	European Court of Justice
ECR	European Court Reports
EDI	Electronic Data Interchange
EPOS	electronic point of sale
ESCs	extra-statutory concessions
ESF	European Social Fund
ESLs	EC sales lists
ESPs	expected selling prices
EU	European Union
EXW	ex-works
FICO	Financial Intermediaries and Claims Office
FOB	free on board
Grp	group
HMRC	Her Majesty's Revenue and Customs
HP	hire purchase
ICTA 1988	Income and Corporation Taxes Act 1988
IPT	insurance premium tax
J	Justice
LA	local authority
LJ	Lord Justice
LLP	limited liability partnership

Abbreviations

Ltd	Limited
MBI	motor breakdown insurance
MOT	Ministry of Transport
MP	Member of Parliament
NETPs	non-established taxable persons
NHS	National Health Service
NIC	National Insurance contributions
No.	number
OECD	Organisation for Economic Co-operation and Development
para.	paragraph
PAYE	pay as you earn
plc	public limited company
Pt.	Part
QC	Queen's Counsel
R	Rex or Regina
RCP	relevant charitable purpose
reg.	regulation
RES	retail export scheme
s.	section
SAD	single administrative document
Sch.	Schedule
SDLT	stamp duty land tax
SDs	supplementary declarations
SIVA	simplified import VAT accounting
SOR	sale or return
SPIC	simplified procedure for import clearance
SSDs	supplementary statistical declarations
t/a	trading as
TC	Tax Cases, from 1875 – (current)
TOGC	transfer of business as a going concern
TOMS	tour operators' margin scheme
TUPE	Transfer of Undertakings (Protection of Employment) Regulations
TURN	Traders unique reference number
UK	United Kingdom
UN	United Nations
US	United States
v	versus
VATA 1983	Value Added Tax Act 1983
VATA 1994	Value Added Tax Act 1994
VATTR	Value Added Tax Tribunal Reports
VCU	VAT Central Unit
VED	Vehicle Excise Duty
VIES	VAT Information Exchange System
VRO	Vehicle Registration Office

Introduction

1.1 Introduction

Is VAT planning worth doing? This is the obvious question. One can answer this by saying that there are many examples of businesses not even planning to achieve compliance, which has ultimately cost them dear. Where a tax is imposed at 20 per cent of gross transaction values it would be foolhardy to ignore it. VAT rates are so high that the tax itself may be far higher than any net, or even gross, profit to be made. This theoretical view is backed up by practical experience.

The amount of effort which should be devoted to VAT planning will vary, depending on the type of business concerned, the extent to which it is drawn into the more complex areas of VAT (or may benefit from drawing itself into them) and the particular transactions in which it finds itself involved.

Even basic compliance (meeting the requirements of HMRC) will not be achieved without a little planning in its widest sense (such as checking out the liabilities and procedures, and making sure that there are resources in place to implement these). Planning can be as simple as making sure that the business complies with the legislation and avails itself of the available reliefs. No sensible business should miss these opportunities; indeed HMRC spends a considerable amount of time and effort to try and persuade businesses to use the available reliefs and simplification (such as cash and annual accounting).

The very nature of VAT makes a wider form of planning desirable. VAT is charged and recovered on individual transactions along a chain of production and distribution, which may be long or short. The position of the parties at each link in that chain depends upon their own contractual and pricing arrangements. Any break in the chain of charging and recovering VAT will have an effect on final prices and/or the profit margins of those in the chain (or at least one or two of them) with obvious commercial implications.

In a sense, it is fair to say that almost any contract apparently involving two parties actually involves three, the third being HMRC, who will feel it is their duty to insist upon any benefits they are able to obtain under the agreement.

> **Planning point**
>
> It is impossible for any business (whether dealing with final consumers entities within the chain of transactions) to do such a basic thing as set its prices safely unless it understands its VAT position and ensures that this is reflected in those prices, terms of contracts, etc.

1.2   What is VAT planning?

VAT planning embraces all sorts of things. It may simply involve an adviser, with no particular specialism in VAT, advising a client setting up a new business that it may be necessary to register. Or it may involve a VAT specialist looking at a particular business scenario, identifying the detail of the relevant legislation (perhaps noting inconsistencies between UK and EU law) and devising special structures to get a particularly advantageous VAT result. It most commonly involves compliance, avoiding unnecessary costs within the spirit of the system and, on occasion, setting up special arrangements to minimise administration costs, rather than making raids on the revenue.

Its essential characteristic is that it involves having a proactive attitude, avoiding problems before they arise or else grasping opportunities that exist (or sometimes creating opportunities), rather than merely reacting to visits from HMRC or assuming that everything is satisfactory. It is as much to do with ensuring that contractual arrangements between commercial counterparties are satisfactory for all concerned, and that VAT consequences are properly factored into commercial decisions before they are made, as it is with direct relations with HMRC.

> **Planning point**
>
> It is certainly planning in the proper sense to consider the VAT position of a transaction, in that it generally needs to be done in advance of the transaction occurring, let alone before the end of the periods in which they occur. Once a contract has been entered into without thought for the VAT consequences, the damage may already have been done; the VAT consequences will have been set by the transaction and cannot be altered at a later date.

Perhaps its most important characteristic is that, while it is largely based on a body of tax law, most of the time it is a specialised aspect of ordinary commercial planning and decision making rather than being a taxation matter in the traditional sense.

1.3   How can this book help?

This volume certainly cannot help by providing instant answers to the VAT intricacies of every commercial transaction that can be devised. What it can do is provide indications of the general approaches available to VAT planning, and help to develop thought processes to identify and deal with VAT opportunities and problems, and outline information and aide-memoires on some specific areas where VAT planning is particularly relevant in practice.

1.4 Objectives of VAT planning

1.4.1 Introduction

The main objectives of VAT planning (some of which overlap) are:

- compliance;
- business planning;
- avoiding unnecessary tax costs;
- avoiding penalty and interest costs;
- improving cash flow;
- improving competitive position, and
- minimising administration.

The weight given to different aspects will vary considerably between organisations, depending on the general ethos, attitudes to risk taking, etc.

1.4.2 Compliance

Compliance with the VAT legislation is a statutory obligation and does not just happen on its own. It requires planning and forethought, even at the very basic level of putting arrangements in hand to collect and retain the necessary information, ensuring returns are submitted and paid on time and evidence to support input tax claims such as tax invoices, import documents, etc. is retained. Good compliance, in itself, requires good planning.

> **Planning point**
>
> Sensible planning includes ensuring systems are in place to enable returns are submitted on time and cash flow is managed to enable VAT liabilities to be met.

1.4.3 Business planning

Planning, in the sense of analysing the VAT consequences of transactions and structures so as to be able to forecast their impact on the overall position, is required so that these can be incorporated in the overall planning of the business. By the same token, those responsible for VAT planning need to be brought into the overall business planning, so that they are aware of likely events before they happen and can factor these into the VAT planning.

> **Planning point**
>
> Whenever a complex or new transaction is to be undertaken, the VAT consequences must be considered. This can include transactions such as property transactions, financial transactions, exports, imports, and transactions with or in other member states of the EU. Errors are frequently made, and unexpected VAT liabilities incurred, when undertaking a transaction that is different from the usual transactions of the business as the VAT implications are not fully understood.

1.4.4 Avoiding unnecessary tax costs

The most obvious objective of VAT planning is the avoidance of unnecessary VAT costs.

This can take a number of forms and, notwithstanding the use of the word avoidance, does not generally involve trying to get out of liabilities that ought to arise. Often, it is a matter of preventing the artificial or unnecessary generation of liabilities. Proper VAT planning permits avoiding VAT where the avoidance is within the spirit and intent of the VAT legislation. HMRC rarely objects to this type of planning (although there may be some differences of opinion as to what is within the spirit and intent of the law). HMRC objects and combats the creation of artificial schemes to reduce VAT liabilities and this book does not concern itself with artificial schemes to avoid VAT.

For example, a developer who builds a house and then lets it on a 20-year lease will make an exempt supply, and suffer disallowance of the input tax on the construction costs. If a 22-year lease had been granted, then the supply would have been zero-rated and the input tax recoverable. Also, a sale of the house (but only the first sale as subsequent sales are exempt from VAT) would have been zero-rated and this would permit VAT on expenses to be reclaimed. However, this highlights direct tax considerations which must also be considered when VAT planning. A sale may generate a capital gain that would be taxed. VAT planning must never be conducted in isolation of direct tax planning or overall business planning.

In housing recessions or slow downs developers that have had great difficulty selling new houses, often wished to let them on short leases to generate much needed cash flow, which would have involved a substantial VAT cost. Instead of doing this directly, many formed separate companies (not within the same VAT group) and sold the properties to these associated companies, which then granted the short lets. The effect was to sacrifice the VAT on the ultimate selling costs (as these would be exempt sales, not being the first sale of the house), but preserve the recovery of far larger amounts of VAT on the construction costs. While the structures adopted were put in place solely for VAT reasons, many would not believe that this was subverting the purpose of the legislation. This was planning which maintained the objective of relieving the construction of new housing from VAT, in circumstances which had not been envisaged when the legislation was drafted.

In the recession that started in 2008/09, the structures have been adopted again, selling the houses to an associated non-VAT group company, which enters into the short-term lets. The sales enabling the retention of previous VAT claimed. HMRC have offered assistance in this regard with the issue of guidance contained in *Revenue & Customs Brief* 54/08, issued 28 October 2008. This is an indication that an artificial structure that is entered into to enable VAT to be reclaimed can be regarded as acceptable. The dividing line between acceptable and unacceptable planning can, however, be very difficult to distinguish.

In these and any other circumstances where steps are deliberately taken to achieve a preferential VAT outcome, regard must now be had to the rules on disclosure of schemes (see **Chapter 32**) in case there is a requirement to draw the facts of the case to HMRC's attention.

> ### Planning point
>
> When a transaction is being entered into that reduces the VAT liability, it is necessary to consider how this will be viewed by HMRC and it may be worth considering obtaining a ruling on this matter.

It is also worth noting that the purpose of planning to save tax is not necessarily to affect the amount collected by the Exchequer. As noted earlier, HMRC are just one of at least three parties involved in any contract. A supplier who enters into a contract to make supplies for a consideration of £X, with no further provisions relating to VAT, is entitled to receive a consideration of £X. If the supply happens to be taxable, then the VAT due must be paid out of the agreed consideration. The supplier has no entitlement to add VAT to the consideration unless it is explicitly stated that VAT is due in addition to any amount advertised or contracted for.

> ### Planning point
>
> Planning, in this context, involves thinking about the VAT position before signing the contract. It is really about making sure that the parties properly understand the implications of what they are setting out to do, and can still reach agreement.

It is a necessary consequence of a transaction-based tax that different ways of achieving a particular economic effect can result in different tax liabilities, and it is to be expected that businesses will seek to identify the ways which give the least ultimate liability particularly when the standard rate of the tax is at such a high rate of transaction values, which can readily exceed the profit element. In such cases, eliminating a VAT liability can more than double the profit.

> ### Planning point
>
> More elaborate planning approaches are sometimes taken, devised purely for tax reasons and aimed at eliminating or reducing VAT costs despite the presumed intention of the legislation. These need to be approached with a degree of caution, as the courts will be inclined to find against them if possible, and a judge worth his salt can usually find ways of taxing a transaction even where the planning scheme may indicate no tax was due. In addition, such techniques may now need to be disclosed to HMRC as soon as they are implemented, leading to a greater degree of likelihood that they will be challenged by the authorities (see **Chapter 32**).

1.4.5 Avoiding penalty and interest costs

The existence of VAT penalties and interest provide further reasons for planning to achieve proper compliance. Even where it is possible to send money in a circle so that no ultimate VAT cost arises from errors there is still the risk of penalties, although interest should not normally be in point in these circumstances, following HMRC's undertaking not to impose default interest except where this is necessary to achieve commercial restitution, bearing in mind customers' ability to recover the tax as input tax (see *Customs News Release* 34/94 (7 September 1994) and para. 2.3ff of *VAT Notice 700/43* (February 2003)).

1.4.6 Improving cash flow

Cash flow is an important element of all business planning. In the case of VAT, there are ultimately payments to be made or repayments to be received. Even where it is not possible to affect the overall VAT position, the timing of these payments and repayments can be important.

For instance, assume that there are two fully taxable businesses under common control. As a matter of administrative convenience, one of them employs all the staff and makes charges to the other for its use of them. On the face of it, this gives a VAT-neutral result. The supplier company must charge VAT, while the customer recovers it in full.

However, consider the position if the supplier company makes its returns for calendar quarters, ending on 31 March, etc., while the customer makes quarterly returns to 30 April, etc. If the supplier bills quarterly, during April and corresponding months, the customer should have its input tax credit by the end of May, while the supplier does not have to account for output tax until the end of July giving a cash flow advantage. Conversely, if the supplier invoices quarterly in March and equivalent months, it will have to account for the tax by the end of April while the customer will not obtain its repayment until the end of May causing a cash flow disadvantage.

> ⚠ **Warning!**
>
> There are indications that HMRC now consider this to be unacceptable; it is not wrong, but there is a risk that a change in VAT periods will be imposed. HMRC are more likely to accept this practice where the differing VAT periods have historic or business reasons. They are less likely to accept it where the associate company is especially formed to create a cash flow advantage.

There are many instances in practice where cash flow is important. Not least of these is the position where planning has failed (or simply not been undertaken) and misdeclarations have occurred. In such cases, counter-parties to the transactions are often prepared to cooperate in rectifying the position, so that there is no ultimate VAT cost. However, they are not usually prepared to bear any carrying costs of the cash flows involved in this process. A common result is that a supplier company must, at the least, bear unexpected carrying costs in the form of interest, etc. Sometimes there can be great difficulty in obtaining short-term finance needed to put things right.

1.4.7   Improving competitive position

The improvement of a competitive position overlaps with the elimination of VAT arising on supplies to final consumers. There are two ways of using the saving. One is to maintain prices and pocket the saving. Another is to maintain the existing margin, but be able to reduce prices and expand market share. Usually a mixture of the two is used.

1.4.8   Minimising administration

For a fully taxable business, the administration involved in complying with the basic VAT system should not be underestimated. It involves recording each transaction, preserving evidence, generating VAT-related documents, etc. For some there are considerable further requirements. Careful planning combined with the specific agreement of easements with HMRC can occasionally help to reduce this burden without affecting the operation of the VAT system as a whole.

1.5   General approach to VAT planning

1.5.1   Planning process: the four As

The precise planning process varies considerably depending on the circumstances of the entities involved and the transaction, but it always has the same basic characteristics (the four As), as follows.

7

Ascertainment

This means finding out the facts of the case, including:

- the general context, whether the objective is to consider planning in its widest sense or mainly in relation to a particular transaction, project, etc.;
- the entities involved (or potentially involved);
- the facts generally; and
- the commercial background and objectives.

Analysis

The facts need to be analysed in VAT terms and the VAT consequences of proposals analysed, paying particular attention to:

- the identification of supplies (and non-supplies) and other chargeable events (e.g. importations or acquisitions of goods);
- the supply path;
- the characterisation and VAT liability of the supplies involved;
- the commercial terms of the transactions concerned from a VAT viewpoint (e.g. if there is a liability, which party will bear it);
- the VAT status of the entities involved;
- the extent of uncertainties in the analysis; and
- the likely VAT consequences.

Alternatives

It may be that the outcome of the analysis stage is that the VAT consequences are satisfactory. For instance, if no output tax liabilities arise and all input tax is fully recoverable, it is unlikely that there is much to be done in the way of planning, apart from compliance planning to ensure that appropriate evidence is held to support this happy state of affairs and, perhaps, considering whether any steps can be taken to accelerate input tax recoveries. Otherwise, it is necessary to consider whether anything can be changed to improve the position, including such matters as:

- the entities involved (perhaps including the creation of new entities);
- the supply path;
- terms of agreement and methods of carrying out transactions in so far as they may affect the VAT status;
- terms of agreement as they affect relations between the parties; and
- if there are promising alternatives, it is then necessary to revisit the ascertainment and analysis stages to reach a proper assessment of these and arrive at a plan.

Action

Once a plan has been arrived at, action is needed to implement it. This may include such matters as:

- changing draft contracts and agreements and/or putting these in place for commercial actions other than those initially intended;
- ensuring that appropriate compliance measures are in place (obtaining evidence for input tax recovery, certificates needed to qualify for zero-rating, etc.); and
- entering into negotiations with HMRC to resolve uncertainties which have been identified.

A fifth 'A' may also be considered: Advice. Obtaining advice at the appropriate time, either from the business's general advisor, a VAT specialist or even from HMRC may greatly assist with VAT planning.

1.5.2 Interaction

The alternative stage is the one most commonly associated with VAT planning as a positive activity. However, reaching the conclusion that there are no sensible alternative ways of approaching transactions can be equally valuable. The action stage remains important. The nature of VAT is such that good housekeeping is indispensable, and good compliance is good planning.

1.5.3 Documentation

It is important to document as much as possible. A business should keep a VAT folder detailing:

- VAT liabilities for supplies made;
- procedures for completing the VAT return and payment (that is how is the return completed, who checks it, what accounts are used, etc.);
- agreements reached with HMRC (for example the liability of supplies, any partial exemption agreement, agreements on how to account for VAT);
- documentation and correspondence with HMRC;
- any documentation concerning options to tax, capital items scheme adjustments, partial exemption adjustments;
- names and contact details of persons to contact about VAT within the business and where appropriate at HMRC; and
- processes for dealing with VAT.

In addition, where complicated matters are dealt with a specific VAT manual should be completed. For example, a property company may wish to include in the manual what types of invoices or architect's certificates are appropriate and satisfactory evidence for input tax deduction. It may also want to detail how VAT liability is determined on transactions, procedures for opting to tax (who has the authority to do so, etc.) and record which properties are subject to the option.

1.6 VAT planning considerations

1.6.1 Planning in advance

Obviously, any form of planning needs to be done in advance. In the case of VAT, this means that planning needs to be done in advance of individual transactions, not just in advance of the end of a tax period of some sort or the completion of a large project (as planning for intermediate steps is also important). Furthermore, it needs to be undertaken before the transactions are even contracted, not merely before they take place.

> **Planning point**
>
> This is because VAT is levied at the level of individual transactions and on the transactions themselves rather than on the financial results stemming from them. In many cases, the VAT treatment will depend upon the precise structure of the transactions, which may be impossible to change once contracted for.

Frequently, obtaining a favourable VAT treatment depends upon the taking of actions, or the obtaining of evidence, that must be carried out, or at least planned for, in advance as the following examples demonstrate.

1. Zero-rating for the construction of a building for relevant residential or charitable use is not available unless the customer provides the contractor with a certificate of use before the supply takes place.

2. Input tax recovery on the importation of goods is only available to the person named as the importer in the import documentation, which must be completed before the goods can enter the territory. It is therefore essential to identify a valid importer who is in a position to recover the tax, and ensure that person obtains and retains the required documentation.

3. The option for taxation in respect of land transactions cannot be exercised retrospectively (although a period of 30 days is allowed for the provision of written notification to HMRC). If it is desired that such a transaction should be taxed, therefore, the supplier needs to exercise the option before the transaction takes place. In certain cases the permission of HMRC must be sought for the option to be exercised.

4. Non-supply treatment for taxable land included in a transfer of a going concern is not available unless the customer both opts for taxation and notifies HMRC before the first tax point arises in respect of the transaction (which could be at exchange of contracts if the vendor's solicitor receives a deposit as agent rather than as stakeholder) and also makes the required notification to the vendor regarding the non-applicability of the disapplication of the option to tax.

1.6.2 Organisation and resources

It goes without saying that VAT planning is unlikely to be carried out satisfactorily unless the business organises it. Just what form this takes will depend very much on the size and structure of the business. It is important, however, that someone should take overall responsibility for VAT planning, and that person should be brought into the more general business planning process before transactions are committed to (for the reasons outlined above).

Whomever is responsible for VAT planning also needs appropriate resources, in the form of sources of information and, often, advice.

1.6.3 Political considerations

The precise approach to VAT planning will vary significantly between businesses. Clearly, most businesses will wish to avoid generating unnecessary liabilities and also to take advantage of reliefs that are available to them. Sometimes businesses will also wish to seek out VAT advantages that might be seen by other eyes (those of HMRC, for instance) as not being applicable to their circumstances. Much will depend upon the culture of the business and its attitude to risk taking.

The relationship of the business with HMRC is an important factor to be taken into account. A good relationship can be of great benefit, both in minimising the administrative effort expended in dealing with control visits, etc. and in maximising the likelihood of securing agreement to special treatments and the overlooking of mere technical errors, such as minor shortcomings in tax invoices for inputs.

This is not to say that it is necessarily harmful to proceed with plans which may be challenged by HMRC, or to get into disputes with them. What is most important is to deal with them openly and fairly.

That said, there is an increasing tendency on HMRC's part to take an aggressive line on many issues (possibly in part due to pressure to increase the tax take), which has complicated the process of open debate and negotiation in a proportion of cases. There is a case to be made for avoiding making an approach or deliberately drawing matters to their attention, where this is an entirely legitimate option (e.g. where no disclosure needs to be made). The approach taken is dependent upon the risk appetite of the business concerned and the relationship between the business and HMRC.

Experience suggests that the best way to deal with unnecessarily obstructive officers and/or offices is to confront them. The difficulty is that, in practice, this option is only available to larger businesses with deep pockets. The details of the VAT legislation are such that most businesses are unable to comply in every particular (one large business found, on analysis, that over a third of its input tax invoices were incomplete in some particular), and officials will usually be able to claim, and be supported by their department in this, that they are merely seeking to protect the revenue, even

11

if the actions they use for this are considerably more restrictive than those found necessary by some of their colleagues. Most officers are, however, helpful and do want to help businesses whilst still having the prime aim of collecting the revenue. This can be where establishing a good relationship with the visiting officers can be beneficial; creating a relationship where there is respect and trust on both sides.

1.6.4 Disclosure of schemes

There is a requirement to notify avoidance 'schemes'. This applies not only to arrangements designed purely to reduce the amount of VAT payable and for which there is very little other commercial purpose, but also to many commercial choices affected by VAT considerations.

Businesses with a turnover of less than £10 million are only affected if:

- their turnover is greater than £600,000; and
- they implement a specific scheme appearing in a list published by HMRC.

It is therefore only businesses with an annual turnover greater than £10 million that need to be greatly concerned by these rules unless a specifically listed scheme is implemented. For such businesses, establishing whether or not disclosure needs to be made is a necessary part of considering any planning of the sort described in this book (see **Chapter 32**).

1.6.5 Interactions

VAT planning cannot be considered in isolation.

Businesses exist for their own purposes (whether to maximise profits or some other purpose) and these rarely include the creation of interesting VAT problems. The implications of VAT planning steps for these other purposes must always be considered. In particular, different structures and approaches can affect relations with customers and suppliers. Also, the incidence of VAT needs to be taken into account when concluding contracts, particularly to ensure that it is clear whether any VAT due is to be added to the consideration or is already included in it.

VAT also interacts with other taxes. For instance, if it is desired for VAT purposes to have a separate property-holding company letting property to an operating company, as opposed to the operating company holding the property directly, this may have an impact on the incidence of corporation tax.

Another example is that, if the option to tax is exercised so that a property transaction which would otherwise be exempt becomes subject to the standard rate of VAT, this will increase the consideration for stamp duty land tax purposes and hence the SDLT liability.

Of course, steps taken for other tax purposes can also have an effect on the VAT position. For instance, the sale of the whole of a company's assets as a going concern is normally outside the scope of VAT. However, it may be desired to sell an asset via a different company in the commercial group (which may or may not also be a VAT group) in order to utilise capital losses. If the intermediary company is outside the VAT group, the supply of that asset is unlikely to qualify for non-supply treatment and this needs to be taken into account. Any relief from VAT is tightly drawn and any transaction that is outside the specific terms of the relief will not benefit from it even if, in substance, it has the same effect as a transaction within the relief.

1.6.6 Risk management

A significant element of VAT planning concerns the management of risk. The fact that there have been some 20,000 tribunal decisions and over 3,500 Court decisions since the inception of VAT in 1973 is a good indicator that the operation of the tax in practice is littered with areas of uncertainty. These need to be identified and appropriate action taken to deal with them.

Sometimes the VAT treatment will be of little final significance for transactions within the supply chain, provided that everyone is aware of the treatment and makes arrangements accordingly. In those cases it is often sufficient to reach formal written agreement with HMRC as to the treatment. In the event that the treatment proves to be incorrect (perhaps following a court judgment in a different case) the parties may be able to rely upon the advice from HMRC contained in their publication *When You Can Rely On Advice Provided By HMRC, VAT Notice 700/06*. HMRC will abide by any advice or decisions given if they have the full facts of the case and the transaction actually reflects the facts they were given.

It is also probable that a decision by HMRC to resile retrospectively from such a ruling could in any case be successfully challenged via the judicial review process, although this can be an expensive procedure.

In other cases it will often be advisable to initiate disputes at an early stage, before the sums of money at stake become unmanageably large. In particular, if it is considered that an overpayment of tax has taken place, this should be claimed as early as possible to prevent the amount repayable being limited by the four-year capping provisions.

As a general rule it is better, while a dispute is in progress, to make returns on the preferred basis (and notify HMRC of this) rather than cooperating with their requested treatment, as this reduces the risk of a subsequent repayment being restricted under the four-year capping provisions (three years before 1 April 2010) and the unjust enrichment provisions. However, this needs to be considered carefully in the light of any effects on relations with suppliers or customers. The mismatch between the amount of statutory interest due on repayments compared with the amount of default interest payable on underdeclared VAT also needs to be taken into account.

As well as the need to determine how to proceed with HMRC pending the resolution of uncertainties, it is also necessary to take the uncertainties into account in formalising commercial relationships. Often it will be desirable to include provisions in contracts to cover the position whatever the outcome in VAT terms. In some cases it may be prudent to arrange for VAT amounts whose treatment is considered doubtful to be paid into some form of holding arrangement, such as an escrow account, until the position is resolved.

It should be borne in mind that the four-year capping rules (three years before 1 April 2010) may have different effects on suppliers and customers because of different timing rules for the application of these provisions to payments and repayments, and because of different VAT accounting periods of the parties.

In addition, it should be noted that there is no statutory provision for four-year capping (three years before 1 April 2010) as between the parties to an agreement. Whether there is some general legal principle of unjust enrichment which might prevent one party being liable to pay a VAT amount to the other once the other was no longer obliged to pass it on to HMRC because of four-year capping (three years before 1 April 2010), is a matter for conjecture.

1.6.7 VAT-only arrangements and abuse of right

The ECJ decision in *Halifax plc* [2006] BVC 377 introduced a new area of uncertainty.

This case gave rise to a reference to the ECJ on the matter of whether or not transactions entered into purely for VAT mitigation reasons did amount to supplies for VAT purposes, or are not done in the course of a business activity (as the tribunal had originally decided) and should therefore be ignored. This approach did not meet with the approval of the Court, which held that each transaction must be considered in isolation and cannot be looked at in combination with others to determine its legitimacy as a supply. However, the Court also held (supporting HMRC's alternative submission) that a business may not use VAT provisions to obtain an abusive result.

The Advocate-General expressed the view opinion that a person that relies upon the literal interpretation of a community provision to claim a right that runs counter to its purposes does not deserve to have that right upheld. In such circumstances the legal provision must be interpreted contrary to its literal interpretation and not to confer the right. Tax law is not to become some form of 'legal wild west' where opportunistic behaviour can be tolerated so long as it conforms to a strict formalistic interpretation of the tax law. The ECJ held that the application of Community law was not to cover transactions not carried out in the context of normal commercial operations but solely for the purpose of wrongfully obtaining advantages provided for by Community

14

Law. It was, however, for the national courts to determine what actions were to be considered abusive but that any action that was seen as being abusive must be redefined so as to re-establish the position that would have prevailed in the absence of the abusive transactions. At the same time, the Court stated that taxpayers may 'choose to structure their business so as to limit their tax liability' and that 'in the sphere of VAT an abusive practice could be found to exist' only if it resulted in an advantage contrary to the normal scheme of the tax and had as its essential aim the obtaining of a tax advantage. In essence, the Court struck down the arrangements in *Halifax* on these grounds but, in doing so, upheld the general taxpayer's right to organise their affairs so as to mitigate their VAT liability. It is not difficult to see the distinction between these two situations becoming fertile ground for future litigation. The Courts will, however, strike down arrangements that whilst legitimate are seen as abusing the provisions of the legislation to give an unintended result.

Although the decision was directed at highly complex arrangements entered into with a view to producing a result which appears contrary to the scheme of the tax, arguably the principles could equally be applied to many ordinary transactions, where it could be alleged that a transaction has taken place solely to gain a tax advantage. For instance, a person who builds a house, then sells it to a separate entity (such as a wholly-owned subsidiary) in order to create a zero-rated supply before exempt letting on short tenancies could well have problems as a result of this decision. The sale to the separate entity is, in all probability, carried out solely for VAT reasons, but, on the other hand, can be argued not to distort the general principles of the tax, which relieve of VAT the sale of a new dwelling. It is not easy to see which side of the line such a transaction falls.

HMRC have confirmed however that as the circumstances have been created outside of the supplier's control, the supply of new houses to an associated non-VAT group registered company to preserve input tax recovery is not considered by HMRC as abusive (*Revenue & Customs Brief* 54/08).

As an illustration of the potential for these issues to give rise to disputes, of the uncertain scope of the parameters for abusive transactions and of HMRC's intention to use the new doctrine to their advantage, one needs to look no further than the case of *R & C Commrs v Weald Leasing Ltd* [2008] BVC 205, decided in the High Court. Weald Leasing Ltd, a member of the Churchill corporate group, but not its VAT group, purchased assets for use by the group, and leased them to an independent third party which in turn leased them to Churchill group companies. HMRC unsuccessfully sought to have the arrangement struck down and to allow Weald only the amount of input tax that would have been claimable by the Churchill group companies had the supply been directly to them. On the face of it, this looks more like choosing to structure their business to limit a tax liability, rather than implementing an abusive practice, making HMRC's prospects on appeal poor, but it does illustrate the fact that HMRC are willing to extend their view of abusive avoidance to arrangements aimed purely at cash flow saving, as well as outright tax saving and HMRC clearly regarded the insertion of an independent third party as being abusive. There is clearly much more to come in the future on this front.

If HMRC are likely to be hostile to the arrangements, there is much to be said for avoiding contact with them and making returns on the basis of the treatment considered to be correct. After four years (three years before 1 April 2010), HMRC cannot disturb the position unless fraud is involved. However, the freedom to take this course has been severely limited in some situations by the introduction of the disclosure rules. This, however, also has the advantage of starting another 'clock ticking'. HMRC are restricted by time limits when they issue assessments. One of these time limits is one year after full information has been provided to HMRC (and two years from the end of the relevant VAT period). Thus, disclosure to HMRC has the advantage of forcing them to act, or if they do not act of providing certainty.

Regrettably, the terms of the *Halifax* litigation may also encourage traders to be less than honest (or at least to manipulate the strict truth) by emphasising, and creating evidence to support, commercial reasons for elements of transactions that may not exist in reality. There can be attempts to 'dress-up' transactions as being undertaken for commercial reasons when they are, in reality, undertaken for VAT purposes only.

In any case, where it might be said that any transaction is done for VAT purposes only it is important to have specialist VAT advice based on the most up-to-date position.

1.6.8 Basic tactical aims: output tax

In the case of supplies to final consumers, for whom any VAT charge represents an actual cost, the basic aim is usually to reduce or eliminate the VAT due. Failing this there may be scope for deferring payment of it.

In the case of supplies to taxable businesses, the first aim must be to ensure that any VAT chargeable is, in fact, recoverable as input tax. There may also be a cash flow benefit to be obtained by the timing of significant transactions where the businesses concerned have different prescribed accounting periods.

Example 1.1

A Ltd makes VAT returns for quarters ending on 31 March, etc. B Ltd makes returns for quarters ending on 30 April, etc.

On 25 March, A and B exchange contracts for A to supply a taxable building to B for £5 million plus VAT of £875,000. The deposit is held by A's solicitor as stakeholder. Completion is to take place on 5 May.

In the normal course of events the tax point for the supply would arise on 5 May. A would be obliged to account for the tax on its June return, making payment by 31 July. B would recover the input tax on its July return.

However, if A issues a tax invoice for the supply during April, this will create a tax point and enable B to recover the input tax on its April return, while A would still account for the output tax on its June return.

Planning point

The kind of cash-flow benefit illustrated in the above example is frequently missed in practice simply because the parties are unaware of each other's VAT periods. In the case of substantial transactions, it can be well worth asking the other side for this information which can be used to the benefit of both parties. The provisions concerning disclosure of schemes must, however, now be taken into account in such situations.

1.6.9   Basic tactical aims: input tax

The basic aim with input tax is to be in a position to recover it from HMRC. In the case of a fully taxable business this is generally an administrative matter, making sure that proper evidence is held to support claims (and, of course, that the tax on inputs is properly chargeable, since incorrectly charged VAT is not input tax and is therefore not, in principle, recoverable as such). It is also necessary to ensure that, where possible, it can be clearly demonstrated that the tax is properly referable to the business and not to some non-business activity.

A partly exempt business will wish to make sure that it has a suitable partial exemption method which is easy to operate and which does not attribute unreasonably high amounts to its exempt activities. (HMRC, of course, will be concerned to ensure that it does not attribute unreasonably high amounts of input tax to taxable supplies.)

1.6.10 Flexibility

It is a fact of life that things change, and businesses need to be able to change their structures and operations in response to this.

It follows that effective VAT planning must leave room for future flexibility, particularly as it is a reasonable prediction that one thing which will change, in response to VAT schemes which go against the basic grain of the tax, is the VAT legislation itself.

Planning point

Sometimes it is possible to achieve VAT objectives by putting in place complex structures, which then have to be maintained for a considerable period. This tends to be a bad idea, not only because it is vulnerable to subsequent changes in the law, but also because it makes it much more difficult for the business to adapt to future changes generally. Limiting flexibility in this way can endanger the business itself.

1.6.11 Simplicity

Complexity cannot always be avoided, but the best VAT planning tends to be simple, to the extent that it might even be better described as positive compliance.

An example concerns the VAT treatment of associations of various kinds charging subscriptions to their members. The ones which can benefit from a little positive action are:

- those whose subscriptions are exempt from VAT (whether or not their members are final consumers); and
- those whose subscriptions are not exempt but whose members are final consumers and so cannot recover any VAT charged.

In either case there is a strong likelihood that a significant proportion of the services provided to members are actually delivered in the form of printed publications.

It is generally possible to agree with HMRC that the supplies made by the body in return for the subscriptions include a zero-rated element, and to agree a suitable proportion of the subscription to be treated as such. In the case of the originally standard-rated body, this enables a reduction in the subscriptions charged to the final consumer members. In the case of the exempt body, it reduces costs by enabling the body to recover some part of its input tax. HMRC will not, however, agree to unrealistic apportionment, nor will HMRC agree to treat as separate zero-rated transactions publications that are part of a composite single supply of membership.

1.6.12 Tensions

Because of its origins, UK VAT is subject to a number of tensions that create uncertainties and interesting problems of interpretation.

The basic principles of the tax are set out in the Principal VAT Directive (Directive 2006/112 on the common system of value added tax), which is a consolidation of earlier directives, namely Directive 67/227, the First VAT Directive, and Directive 77/388, the Sixth VAT Directive. As a general rule, the principles are a useful aid for interpreting the provisions concerning mechanisms. However, where there has been an absolute conflict between the principle of exact proportionality set out in what was art. 2 of the First VAT Directive, and the mechanisms laid down by what was the Sixth VAT Directive, the European Court of Justice has held that the basic principle should prevail (*Elida Gibbs Ltd v C & E Commrs* (Case C-317/94) [1997] BVC 80).

There are also tensions between the Directives and the UK law implementing them. In the case of conflict, the EU provisions should generally prevail, either as an aid to interpretation of the UK provision or as having direct effect. However, the State (meaning the UK and by implication, HMRC) cannot rely on the EU provisions as having direct effect so, if the UK provisions cannot simply be interpreted as having the same effect as intended by the Directive, the UK trader can choose to rely on the UK law and ignore the Directive.

1.6.13 Misleading terminology

In common with any other tax planner, the VAT planner needs to be very careful in ascertaining the facts of a case before advising. This is exacerbated for VAT because so much depends on the narrow classification of transactions, exceptions to the general rule of taxing transactions (that is zero-rating and exemption) will, for instance, always be interpreted narrowly. Thus, it is vital to ensure that any relief that is being relied on falls squarely within the interpretation of the exception. Words used in a natural sense (by clients, for instance) may not mean quite the same as when used in the context of VAT.

For instance, if someone says that they have constructed a new factory in the last year or two, and are now going to sell it, it would be easy to say that this will give rise to a standard-rated supply. However, if their interest in the building is a 999-year lease, rather than a freehold interest then, although it may be correct to say that they are selling their entire interest in the building, this will not be a supply of the freehold and so will be intrinsically exempt. Depending on the precise circumstances such advice may leave them with only the net-of-VAT sale proceeds but with a catastrophic effect on the input tax recovery on the construction costs.

1.6.14 Reversals

An interesting approach to VAT planning (indeed to any tax planning) can be simply to turn things round. This sort of approach first came to prominence a number of years ago when, after the judgment in a case involving a company called Nairn Williamson had been published, references were made to a tax planning scheme as a 'reverse Nairn Williamson'.

The idea is simple. The particular decision had been in favour of the Inland Revenue (as it then was) in the circumstances of that specific case. However, there were other taxpayers whose circumstances were different, and who could benefit considerably from the view of the law put forward by the Revenue, and approved of by the court, in the original case.

The structure of VAT, with passing on of tax and input tax recovery, makes this sort of reversal particularly likely to apply. It is not unusual to come across the odd spectacle of a trader in the middle of a supply chain arguing furiously that his supplies are taxable, and HMRC equally furiously maintaining that they are exempt from VAT. Similar businesses whose customers are final consumers can clearly benefit from the success of HMRC's arguments.

1.7 Planning triggers

1.7.1 The triggers

There are several general non-technical areas which for one reason or another, frequently give significant problems for VAT purposes (and, indeed, for other tax purposes). These are:

- land;
- transactions involving large amounts;
- international transactions;
- associated party transactions;
- one-off transactions; and
- changes in trading pattern.

It is valuable to summarise the reasons for the importance of these areas, all of which are covered in individual chapters of this publication.

1.7.2 Land

The UK law relating to land has evolved over a very long period. In the process it has become extremely complex. What might appear to the layman to be a single practical effect can often be achieved, in law, by any of a number of different mechanisms. Each will, of course, have differing legal effects.

Any tax system in the UK, however simple, still has to tie itself in with the whole body of UK law, including the law relating to land. It follows that, where different legal mechanisms for achieving a commercial effect have different legal results there will often be different tax effects, and these may not be immediately obvious.

It is vital, therefore, to ensure that the VAT and other tax consequences of land transactions are considered carefully before proceeding with the transaction. This is especially the case given that land transactions typically involve large sums of money (see **1.7.3**), and have effects reaching far into the future. For many businesses they also fall into the category of one-off transactions (see **1.7.6**), another danger signal.

The impact of VAT on land transactions has been accentuated by the introduction of standard-rating for many supplies which were previously exempt or zero-rated, and of the option for taxation. The whole area of VAT and property is now extremely complex and uncertainties abound. The businessman who proceeds with even the simplest of land transactions without first researching the VAT implications is foolhardy indeed.

1.7.3 Large sums

By definition, the larger the sums involved in a transaction, the larger the potential cost if it is mishandled. In dealing with VAT, it should be noted that the sums of money which are relevant are the gross money flows arising from the transaction, not the net profit which is intended to result from it.

Before committing large amounts, it is worth ensuring that the VAT aspects have been fully taken into account. While it might be acceptable to take a guess on a single transaction involving, say, £20, this course of action would be foolish if the amount of money involved was, say, £1 million.

⚠ *Warning!*

As will have become apparent, the VAT position is generally crystallised at the point where the contracts are made and certainly when the supplies are made. The VAT position might only be considered when it is necessary to render a VAT return (or when a visiting officer raises the question), by which time it is too late to change the VAT nature of the transaction. It is essential to ensure that large transactions are fully considered in advance.

1.7.4 International transactions

For all taxes, special problems arise with international transactions. Any tax is levied in relation to a particular territory or national jurisdiction, and so that jurisdiction must be defined.

In their very nature, international transactions cross the borders of the jurisdiction, so there are matters of definition to be considered to determine whether the transaction falls within the jurisdiction or outside of it. International VAT truly involves a great number of borderline cases.

As far as UK VAT is concerned, many supplies sourced in (or supplied from) the UK are relieved from tax, because the goods or services concerned are actually consumed outside of the territory. As usual with VAT reliefs, there is a need to obtain and retain appropriate evidence to substantiate the relief.

In the case of supplies coming into the UK, there is often a tax charge levied on the recipient of the supply. In the case of imports of goods from outside the EC, the tax is automatically levied at the point of importation but proper evidence is needed to enable the importer to obtain a refund of the tax as input tax. For imports of certain services, and for intra-EU acquisitions of goods, the customer must take the initiative in accounting for the tax.

A further difficulty in relation to international transactions is that the business is dealing with overseas entities which may have no understanding of the VAT system, and its requirements. Where action is needed by the overseas entity (e.g. in the provision of documents as evidence) this needs to be clearly agreed at the outset.

1.7.5 Associated party transactions

Transactions between persons who are closely linked with one another are frequently carried out with less forethought and formality than transactions with complete outsiders. This can lead to problems in proving exactly what transactions have occurred and the form that they took. It can also mean that transactions are inappropriately structured, giving rise to unnecessary liabilities.

For instance, a business might lend employees to an associated business and receive reimbursement of the related payroll costs. This reimbursement represents consideration for a taxable supply of staff services and is liable to VAT at the standard rate. If the business borrowing the staff is not fully taxable, it may be unable to recover all or part of the tax due. In the case of a transaction between outsiders, the VAT position would, in all probability, be recognised at the outset and dealt with correctly. Where the transaction is between associates, the VAT position, and any cost implications, may well go unrecognised at the time of the transaction and only be picked up when it is too late to take any action.

Examples of associated parties include:

- companies under common ownership;
- businesses run by members of the same family;
- a business and its proprietors;
- a business and its employees; and
- joint owners of land.

1.7.6 One-off transactions

The people running a business are likely, over a period of time, to become fairly familiar with the treatment necessary for transactions undertaken frequently, in the normal course of business. Even if they get things wrong at first, after a few years when there have been several audits by independent accountants, and visits have been made by HMRC, it is likely that most major mistreatment of day-to-day transactions will have been identified.

> **Planning point**
>
> Where there is a one-off transaction (e.g. sale of premises, sale of know-how, issue of shares), this is by definition something of which the business has little experience. It is an occasion to assume that advice is needed, rather than to assume that the most obvious treatment is the correct one. Businesses that undertake a one-off transaction, particularly one with a large value, should ensure that their advisors are instructed to consider the VAT implications of the transaction.

1.7.7 Changes in pattern

Business does not remain static but responds to changes in its environment. A change in the pattern of a business, such as the introduction of a new product, entry into a whole new market or merely a change in the terms on which the business trades with its suppliers or customers, needs attention for the same reasons as a one-off transaction. Because that which is being done differs from that which has been done before, it may well need treating differently for VAT purposes.

Planning point

Since the effects of a change in the pattern of the business's activities will continue down the years, rather than being restricted to a single occasion, it is doubly important to ensure that the correct treatment is identified from the outset.

1.7.8 Combination of triggers

Each of the trigger points dealt with above can give a useful warning of the need to check the VAT position. When several appear at once, complications are guaranteed. For instance, if joint owners of land propose a one-off transaction (such as a sale and leaseback), which almost inevitably involves large sums, the combination of four triggers (land, large sums, associated parties, and one-off transactions) is a good indicator that it would be most unwise – some would say, pure folly – to proceed without first taking VAT advice.

1.8   Regular review

1.8.1   Introduction

Strictly speaking, regular review is a non-subject, as effective VAT planning needs to be a constant process, or continual revolution, as someone once put it.

However, this is a counsel of perfection and unlikely to be achieved in the real world. It is therefore well worth setting up a programme of regular review of the VAT position and possible planning steps, with an eye both to compliance and to obtaining any VAT advantages which are available. More details can be found on this topic in **Chapter 28, Review of business for VAT issues**.

1.9 Disclosure of schemes

1.9.1 Introduction

Businesses in certain circumstances must notify their use of tax mitigation arrangements. No VAT planning can now be undertaken without consideration of them (unless the business concerned has an annual turnover of £600,000 or less).

The purpose of the rules is to bring arrangements to the attention of HMRC and should not be construed as making any notifiable arrangement(s) illegal.

Penalties apply to the failure to notify schemes in accordance with the requirements of the new legislation. These are a fixed sum for 'hallmarks of avoidance' schemes (£5,000) and a tax-geared penalty in respect of the specific notifiable schemes (15 per cent of the saving).

This subject is considered in detail in **Disclosure of VAT avoidance schemes**.

1.9.2 How the disclosure rules work

There are effectively three sets of rules (or lack of rules) applying to three sets of businesses, namely:

- those with a turnover below £600,000;
- those with a turnover between £600,000 and £10 million; and
- those with a turnover over £10 million.

For ease, these can for this purpose be termed small, medium-sized and large businesses respectively.

1.9.3 Small businesses

Small businesses, as defined, have no additional responsibilities or considerations in the light of the changes.

1.9.4 Medium-sized businesses

Medium-sized businesses, those with a turnover exceeding £600,000 must notify HMRC if they implement a scheme appearing on a list published by way of statutory instrument by HMRC. At the time of writing, there are ten items on the list, all of which are very specific known schemes. Turnover includes both taxable and exempt income.

Most of the planning principles described in this chapter can therefore be applied by such businesses without the need to consider the disclosure rules.

1.9.5 Large businesses

Large businesses, businesses with a turnover in excess of £10million are obliged to notify any of the schemes on the list mentioned above (by virtue of having a turnover exceeding £600,000). In addition, they must also advise HMRC of any arrangements that they put in place, which have as the sole or one of the main purposes a saving of VAT and exhibit at least one of the designated 'hallmarks of avoidance'.

In such cases, the 'tax advantage' must be notified. This means any 'arrangements, transaction, or series of transactions' which have the result that:

- in the case of a payment trader, the VAT payable in any given VAT period is less than it would otherwise have been;
- in the case of a repayment trader, the VAT repayable is greater than it would otherwise have been; or
- in the case of the recipient of a supply, the difference in the time when he accounts for input tax and the supplier accounts for output tax is greater than it would otherwise have been.Example 1.1

Pre-registration Issues

2.1 Introduction

2.1.1 Initial steps

The initial steps that need to be considered are:

- the various structures that can be utilised for the economic activity;
- whether an activity is an economic activity for VAT purposes;
- if there is an economic activity, whether there is a requirement to register;
- the advantages and disadvantages of registration; and
- input tax credits that can be claimed.

2.1.2 VAT Jargon and concepts

There is a considerable amount of jargon used in VAT and anybody that is starting in business will need to understand these terms and principles. It is in these early days of a business that structures are set up and the seeds laid for success and failure. Not understanding the requirements of VAT can be a factor in a business's failure and, many problems can be avoided if these simple concepts are understood at the outset. It should be noted that VAT is a European tax; the UK is required, as a condition of membership of the European Union, to impose the tax and the UK legislation is meant to reflect the European VAT Directive. Some European concepts differ from UK legal concepts and this can cause some of the difficulties within the tax.

The first matter to consider is 'economic activity'. Economic activity is an EU concept. VAT is charged on the economic activity of an entity. Economic activity has a wider meaning than business. It is the carrying on of transactions in the course or furtherance of a business for consideration. This can include activity that is not normally regarded as business in the UK and will include trading in shares, mutual trading and the activities of a not-for-profit organisation or government body. In this book, activities are usually described as business for simplicity, but the wider meaning must be borne in mind. VAT is not a tax on business. Although the business collects and pays the tax to the revenue authority, it is not a burden upon the business (other than for administration). VAT is a tax on the final consumer; this is the person at the end of the supply chain, usually a member of the public who cannot reclaim the VAT that has been charged to them. A business can be a final consumer where it cannot reclaim VAT (such as an exempt financial institution). The business will normally be termed the taxable person, the person that makes the taxable supplies. For VAT purposes, 'person' includes both legal persons and natural persons such as sole proprietors, partnerships, limited companies, charities, LLPs, joint ventures, professional bodies, clubs, associations, trustees, European Economic Interest Groupings and any other entity. A taxable person is a person that makes the taxable supplies that are subject to VAT and, is or must be registered for VAT. VAT is due on taxable supplies; that is supplies that are not exempt or outside the scope of VAT. Supplies are the VAT transactions of a taxable person and are made and received by the taxable person. When determining the VAT liability it is necessary to consider the supplies that are made rather than looking at the cash payments made (although there is no VAT where there is no consideration). Supplies include anything done by the business and will also include things not done, acts of forbearance, barter, etc.

Whilst most businesses think of the income they receive, in VAT it is the consideration that is the important factor. This again has a wider meaning than normal business income. Consideration is the value received by a taxable person for the supplies that he makes. This is most frequently the cash the taxable person receives, but consideration can take many other forms including the items or services exchanged in a barter transaction, amounts received from third parties and other amounts. In VAT a taxable person has to consider his outputs (the supplies made) and the output tax (the VAT on the outputs, as well as its inputs (the supplies received; purchases and other acquisitions) and the input tax (the VAT incurred on the inputs). When reviewing a VAT transaction it is necessary to examine the supplies rather than the cash movements. This is not to say that cash is not important, as there is no taxable supply without consideration. Consideration is wider than cash, it is the value received by a taxable person for the supplies made. This is most frequently the cash the taxable person receives, but consideration can take many other forms including the items or services exchanged in a barter transaction, amounts received from third parties and other amounts.

2.2 Starting a business activity

2.2.1 Starting a business activity: overview

The commencement of a business is generally a busy, stressful and sometimes exciting time. It is also a time at which many other issues arise which can detract from consideration of the VAT position.

While a VAT specialist might instinctively feel that getting the VAT position right is the overall priority, this is clearly wrong. VAT is not terribly important to the world generally until there is a viable business with ongoing activities (although it may be of great importance to the business in reaching this stage).

Once in a while, the VAT treatments may be of critical importance to a new business getting started. More often, they are less important at the very outset. However, they will become important and considering the VAT position from the start can save subsequent time and effort.

There are many things which will concern a new business before VAT heaves its way above the horizon, many of which will affect the VAT position, including:

- who is involved in the enterprise;
- ownership structures and legal entities involved;
- sources and manner of financing;
- ownership of assets;
- other commercial/regulatory considerations;
- direct tax considerations (including inheritance tax/capital gains tax, etc. for proprietary businesses); and
- future plans or hopes, such as the (prosperous) exit of some of the parties from the business.

All of these factors need to be taken into account in setting up the new business. VAT also needs to be taken into account.

It is then necessary to consider the VAT position of the business entity (or entities) as finally constituted.

> **Planning point**
>
> Experience suggests that the best plan is to consider the non-VAT factors first, then see what are the VAT implications of the preferred position (provided that the VAT position is considered before arrangements are finalised). This is because the nature of VAT, as a general tax on consumption, is such that it is usually possible to adapt the VAT arrangements to fit with the arrangements adopted for other purposes.
>
> In some cases there will be insuperable VAT problems which make it necessary to alter the basic arrangements, but this is not usually the case.

2.2.2 Introduction to the VAT issues

Once the preferred commercial structure, ignoring VAT, is known, it is time to consider the VAT implications of that preferred position, both for the short term and for the long term.

This may involve identifying unacceptable VAT costs and a need to find alternative arrangements which will still meet the basic requirements in other fields. The main danger areas in VAT terms are:

- unnecessary VAT liability on supplies to final consumers;
- unnecessary block points created by the proposed structure; and
- uncertainty of treatment anywhere along the line.

It is essential that these dangers be avoided if at all possible.

Depending on the entities involved, there may then be scope for fine-tuning to improve cash flow, etc. The various non-VAT factors mentioned above will inevitably affect the details of the VAT position.

> ### Planning point
>
> Although the non-VAT factors are necessarily considered separately elsewhere, it is really only at the point where they are all brought together that sensible decisions can be made on how best to proceed.

2.2.3 Persons involved

The general shape of the business depends, of course, on the people who are setting it up and their wishes and hopes. This is not, at least in the first instance, a VAT matter.

In the case of a business set up by one individual, then the likelihood is that the business will be operated by that individual as a sole trader. Another possibility is that the individual will choose to form a limited company to operate the business. This sort of choice is unlikely to be made by reference to VAT considerations. Factors such as the risks inherent in the venture, and the treatment for direct taxes, are likely to be much more relevant.

A new business set up by an existing company, or several companies, will more than likely be constituted as a company itself. Again, this has little to do with the VAT considerations, and the VAT considerations should not usually influence the basic choice of vehicle.

Where there are several individuals involved in setting up a business the likely choices become more complex. The most obvious approach is to form a partnership, although a corporate structure may be preferred.

As a general rule, the nature of the persons involved in setting up a new business will have a great bearing on the best decisions to make concerning the vehicle(s) used, but this will be based on commercial and direct tax considerations. From a VAT point of view the most important aspects are the liability of the supplies made by the business as a whole and whether the customers are final consumers or taxable persons who can reclaim any VAT charged. These matters are rarely affected by the particular choice of legal vehicle for the business.

2.2.4 Ownership of assets

The ownership of the business assets (an area which crosses over with the financing of the business) can have a significant effect on the structures desired for non-VAT purposes, and consequently on the VAT related decisions which need to be made.

The most obvious example is that where there are several parties wishing to set up a business, one of whom owns suitable premises. An obvious option is to form a partnership, and introduce the premises concerned as capital, becoming an asset of the partnership. However, the owner of the property may well be reluctant to do this, especially if the property is considerably more valuable than any capital to be introduced by the other parties. It may be decided, therefore, that a partnership (or company) be formed and that this should rent the premises from the property owner. In this case it will then be necessary to decide how to handle, for instance, necessary costs concerned with altering the property and any future costs connected with the property for the intended business use. One option would be for the newly formed business to meet such costs. Another would be for the property owner to meet them and for the rent charged to reflect this. In the latter case the further question would then arise regarding whether the property owner should register for VAT and opt to tax the rents.

Planning point

The important point is that if there is any separation between the main business activity and the ownership of assets used for business purposes, as will often be required for non-VAT reasons, then this will involve the existence of further entities and the VAT consequences which follow. These should not generally cause significant problems if they are addressed from the outset. If they are ignored, they almost certainly will cause problems and often give rise to potentially unnecessary costs.

⚠ Warning!

Where the business is run as a sole proprietor it is not possible to separate any assets from the business unless they are held in a separate entity. All the business activities of a sole proprietor are encompassed within its VAT registration. Thus, an asset owned by the sole proprietor is at risk if used in the business. For example, a sole proprietor may not wish for his property or other assets to be included within his VAT registered business. He will, therefore need to ensure these assets are owned by a separate entity (for example a partnership with the spouse, or in a company or trust). These assets, if used in the business will then need to be supplied to the sole proprietor and consideration given to VAT registering that entity for the purpose of its supplies. Similarly, an asset owned by an individual will not be part of the VAT registered business if the VAT registered business is a trust, company or partnership.

2.2.5 Financing

A new business needs to be financed. The source of finance can in itself have VAT implications.

Where the finance is provided by way of a loan or introduction of capital by the parties themselves, or by simple borrowing from a bank or some other source of ordinary loan finance, this will generally have no VAT implications. Obtaining finance by the issue of shares or of loan stock, on the other hand, was historically seen by HMRC as involving exempt supplies made by the person obtaining the finance.

This was always a controversial view, and one with which many advisers disagreed. It held sway for very many years until the case of *Kretztechnik* (Case C-465/03) [2006] BVC 66 was decided in the ECJ in early 2005. The court's judgment held that the issue by a company of its own shares is not a supply at all. Consequently, the matter of the share issue is irrelevant, and any input tax incurred in connection with the share issue were general overhead costs and should be treated as applicable to the general activities of the company. It follows that such input tax can be deducted, in full by fully taxable businesses, and in part by partly exempt ones, in the same way as other residual input tax.

Costs of financing, however, may not be costs of the business. For example, where a bank obtains a report on the business to determine if it is viable to loan it money, the bank will often require the business to pay for the report. As the bank is the recipient of the supply of the report, only the bank can reclaim the VAT incurred. As a bank is exempt or partially exempt it cannot recover any or much of the VAT incurred. Consequently, the business will usually incur the full VAT inclusive cost, but it is not able to reclaim the VAT incurred as it is not the recipient of the supply.

2.2.6 Structures and legal entities

The factors mentioned above will give rise to the basic plan for the structures and legal entities involved with the new business. These then need to be reviewed from a VAT point of view, and the possibility of changes considered. Possible types of entity, and their basic characteristics are set out below.

Sole trader

As applies for all types of VAT entity, the registration of a sole trader will cover all activities carried on by that individual. However, in the case of a sole trader it is possible that there will be business activities not included in the main business accounts. A particularly common example is that of a property-letting activity. In the case of holiday lettings, this may bring into the charge to VAT an activity which might otherwise escape VAT on the basis that the rentals, taken alone, are below the turnover limits. If the holiday lettings are conducted as a business (which HMRC will inevitably conclude that they are) the turnover of these lettings must be included in the turnover of the VAT registered sole proprietor and VAT charged on the income received. (Consider operating one activity or the other in partnership with a spouse to avoid this.) In the case of exempt property letting it may enable the proprietor to recover input tax relating to the property letting, provided that this falls below the partial exemption *de minimis* limits, thus producing a saving.

> ## Planning point
>
> All of the business activities of a sole proprietor are included within that person's VAT registration; the registration is not per business, but by entity. Ensure all activities are included when accounting for VAT. To avoid the need to account for VAT on subsidiary activities, it may be necessary to include these activities in another entity (a partnership, another sole proprietor, in a corporate body). Where the income is incurred in another entity, however, no input tax can be claimed as a credit in relation to these subsidiary activities in the sole proprietor's activities.

Where a business splits its activities artificially, HMRC can join these activities together in one VAT registration using the 'disaggregation' provisions – see **3.6**.

Partnership

A partnership exists where persons carry on a business in common with a view to profit. The partners may be individuals or corporate bodies. In Scotland, a partnership has legal personality but in England and Wales it does not.

It is the partners that are registered for VAT, but in the name of the partnership (VATA 1994, s. 45). If there is a change in the partners, this must be notified to HMRC and the register amended accordingly. However, the registration of the firm continues. This should be contrasted with the case where a sole trader takes in a partner, or one person leaves a partnership of two, so that a sole trader remains. In either of these cases, the former entity is deregistered and a fresh registration is required (although it may be possible to continue using the same registration number). Two partnerships having identical partners are treated as the same entity for VAT purposes and have a single VAT registration (*C & E Commrs v Glassborow* (1974) 1 BVC 4).

Partners will be jointly and severally liable for the debts of the members of the partnership. This emphasizes the importance of informing HMRC of changes in the partnership as a partner that leaves a partnership will remain liable for VAT debts even after he or she leaves the partnership until HMRC are informed of the change.

> ## ⚠ Warning!
>
> It may be advisable where there are changes from a partnership to a sole proprietor or from a sole proprietor to a partnership to ensure that the VAT number is changed and that no application is made to continue to use the old VAT number. The benefit of doing this is that all potential VAT liabilities (known and unknown) will be left with the old registration and the new registration will be starting with a *clean slate*. Failure to do so will mean that any past liabilities will remain with the new owner or owners of the business. In addition, if a partnership continues following a partner leaving the partnership, the partner that has left remains liable for the debts of the partnership during his period of partnership, and new partners joining remain liable for all VAT debts of the partnership even those that arose before they joined. Consequently, it is advisable, where possible, for the partnership to be dissolved and transferred as a going concern to a new partnership if at all possible.

Limited partnership

A limited partnership consists of one or more general partners and one or more limited partners. Any of these may be either an individual or a corporate body.

A limited partnership is registered for VAT in the same way as an 'ordinary' partnership. However, the partnership is identified by its general partner or partners and any limited partners are ignored for this purpose (*Saunders & Sorrell* (1980) 1 BVC 1,133).

Limited liability partnership (LLP)

An LLP has a legal status as a corporate body and is distinct from its members. Individual members of the LLP are not responsible for other members' debts/liabilities. An LLP can join a VAT group provided the VAT group control requirements are met.

Limited company

A limited company is a legal entity in its own right.

A limited company will generally be registered in its own right. However, it may instead be included in a VAT group.

Members (shareholders) and directors do not have any VAT liability for the VAT debts of the company unless there is fraud or insolvent trading.

Group of companies

UK established companies under common ownership may choose to be included in a VAT group; this is an optional registration option for the company and its associated companies.

Where a VAT group exists, the registration of all of the companies in the VAT group is in the name of a representative member; supplies between members of the group (generally) are ignored, although there are some exceptions to this rule. Supplies by or to members of the group are treated as made by or to the representative member; and the representative member is responsible for accounting for VAT on behalf of the group. However, each company in the group is jointly and severally liable for VAT liabilities arising during its membership of the VAT group. VAT groups can play an important part in VAT planning, and are covered in more detail in **Chapter 4**.

Unincorporated association

An unincorporated association (such as a club) has no legal personality separate from that of its members.

An unincorporated association is regarded as a separate entity for VAT purposes and may be registered in its own name (VATA 1994, s. 46(2) and (3)). Responsibility for its VAT affairs rests jointly and severally with the members holding office as president, chairman, treasurer, secretary, etc. or, failing that, with members holding office as committee members or, failing that, all of the members (VAT Regulations 1995 (SI 1995/2518), reg. 8).

Trust

A trust is a form of property ownership, rather than a person as such. The property of a trust is owned by its trustee(s) subject to the terms of the trust.

Generally, persons acting as trustees are regarded as acting in a different capacity from their 'ordinary' capacity, and a trust may be registered in the names of the trustees (although there is no specific legislation on this). However, in the case of an employer acting as sole trustee for its own pension fund, HMRC see the fund activity as part of the employer's overall business activity. Trustees are registered as if they are partnerships (where there is more than one trustee) and as a sole proprietor where there is one trustee. HMRC then treat them as partnerships/sole proprietors although they will generally allow separate registration of the trust from another partnership with the same partners or from a sole proprietor with its own VAT registered business. The proper treatment of trusts and trustees must be regarded as doubtful and it is therefore an important matter of risk management to clear the treatment with HMRC.

Joint venture

A joint venture falling short of being a partnership has no separate legal personality in the UK.

The correct VAT treatment of a joint venture arrangement will depend on the exact terms of agreement, and course of dealing, between the parties. The form of arrangements can vary considerably. The mere fact that the arrangements are referred to as a joint venture may mean that the parties have not fully thought through the nature of their relationship. This should be regarded as a danger signal and an indication that the arrangements need to be looked at objectively and the VAT treatment agreed with HMRC. Often the arrangement is of partnership (the sharing of profit) although there may be a lead joint venturer that has to register, and the other joint venturers are treated for VAT purposes as making supplies to and receiving supplies from the lead joint venturer.

Joint property owners

The mere joint ownership of property does not necessarily create a partnership (although there may be one), nor does it bring into being any recognisable legal entity other than the joint owners themselves.

In practice, joint owners are treated for VAT purposes as if they were a partnership, although legally this is not the case.

35

> **Planning point**
>
> The proper consideration of the legal entity that has been formed, the extent of the activities that it covers, and the impact this has for VAT is an essential building block when considering VAT.

2.3 Economic activity

2.3.1 Economic activity – UK considerations

Economic activity has a wider meaning than business. It includes mutual trading, charitable activities and some Government activities. In addition, activities prior to commencing business, such as feasibility studies, are economic activity but, the concept of being in business is usually sufficient to understand what is required for VAT. Section 94 of the Value Added Tax Act 1994 states that 'VAT shall be charged on any supply of goods or services made in the UK, where it is a taxable supply made by a taxable person in the course or furtherance of any business carried on by him'. One of the first matters to consider is whether the activities of an entity is business, (or economic activity) as an entity not undertaking economic activity will not be able to register for VAT, cannot charge VAT, nor reclaim VAT incurred.

Business is defined at section 94 VATA 1994 as including any trade, profession or vocation. It mentions a few specific activities (such as admission fees and the provision of services by a club to members), but gives no further assistance in defining the term. It is necessary to go further than this and consider the 'business test'. HMRC have stated (Notice 701/1 para 4.1) that:

> 'An organisation that is run on a not-for-profit basis may still be regarded as carrying on a business activity for VAT purposes. The normal questions which need to be considered when determining whether an activity is business for VAT purposes or not are:
>
> - is the activity a serious undertaking earnestly pursued? (This considers whether the activity is carried on for business or daily work rather than pleasure or daily enjoyment.)
> - is the activity an occupation or function which is actively pursued with reasonable or recognisable continuity? (When considering this test you should consider how frequently the supplies will be made.)
> - does the activity have a certain measure of substance in terms of the quarterly or annual value of taxable supplies made?
> - is the activity conducted in a regular manner and on sound and recognised business principles?
> - is the activity predominately concerned with the making of taxable supplies for a consideration?
> - are the taxable supplies that are being made of a kind which, subject to differences of detail, are commonly made by those who seek to profit from them?'.

Whilst this notice concerns charities the points are based upon the questions raised in a leading VAT decision on business *Lord Fisher* (1981) 1 BVC 392. These points are only guidance as each case will be decided on its merits. Not all of these factors need be present for there to be a business, nor does the absence of a factor mean that the activity is not a business.

It should also be noted that the absence of profit does not mean that the activity is not a business for VAT purposes. An activity that would normally be regarded as being business will be a business activity for VAT purposes even where no profits are made or the profit motive is absent. A hobby will not normally be regarded as economic activity, but one that is carried on earnestly and in a business like manner will be. Factors that may be taken into account will be the way an activity is advertised, is income received just to defray costs or is there an intention to profit, is there a prospect of profit, how is the activity organised?

A one-off activity may not be considered a business activity, but where it is a significant event (such as the disposal of a large capital item, it may be regarded as an economic activity if organised in a business-like manner. It has been held that the hiring of a single asset to a single customer did not constitute a business activity, so the input tax could not be reclaimed – *Three H. Aircraft Hire* (1982) 1 BVC 480. The motives and potential private use of the asset may have had a bearing on this decision. In contrast, it was held in *Staatssecretaris van Financiën v J Heerma* (Case C-23/98). [2003] BVC 97 that the letting of a single item to a single customer was economic activity for VAT purposes. The distinction is in the way the transactions are structured and the manner the activity is undertaken.

The fact that no supplies have been made does not mean there is no economic activity nor that the person concerned should not register for VAT (indeed, the person may frequently be best advised to register for VAT so that they can reclaim the VAT incurred on expenditure). Preparatory activities (such as drawing up business plans, feasibility studies and testing) will be regarded as economic activity. This allows the entity to register for and reclaim VAT on expenditure even if supplies have not been made, or will not be made for many years to come. HMRC will not register the entity when there is no continued activity and no prospect of future taxable supplies even when HMRC would have registered the entity if an earlier application had been made when the preparatory works were being undertaken; this highlights the importance of timing the registration for VAT correctly. See *Merseyside Cablevision Ltd* (SI 1989/2034) and *Intercommunale voor Zeewaterontzilting (INZO) v Belgian State* (Case C-110/94). [1996] BVC 326.

A number of activities are deemed to be business. Thus, these activities will be subject to VAT (assuming the VAT registration threshold is met and are to be included in a VAT registration. These include:

- membership subscriptions (to clubs, organisations societies, etc.);
- admission fees (including to one off events, testimonials, fund raising events, etc.);

- office holders – for example a solicitor that acts as a Town Clerk. Where the office is held due to the professional qualifications or professional abilities of the individual it will be regarded as consideration for professional services and attributable to that person's VAT registration (including a partnership registration). Where the office is given to a person due to their personal attributes the income is not regarded as being subject to VAT;
- termination of a business;
- transfer of a business as a going concern;
- disposal of the assets or liabilities of a business; and
- the use of business assets for a private purpose.

2.3.2 International issues

It is also necessary to consider international matters such as cross-border trading. There is a requirement to consider VAT registration in the UK when the person is not registered and goods are acquired from EU suppliers, or an EU supplier without a place of establishment in the UK makes supplies of goods to UK customers that are not VAT registered (distance sales), or there are the sale of goods where VAT has been reclaimed by the vendor under the 8th or 13th VAT Directive. In addition, some supplies that are deemed to be made in the UK (this may apply to UK persons that may otherwise not be required to be registered or to overseas persons that are deemed to be making supplies in the UK). This will include goods that are physically in the UK, or services that are regarded as having a nexus with the UK (such as services physically performed in the UK or supplies that relate to land in the UK). In addition it may be necessary to register for VAT either using an EU where there are electronically supplied services into the EU. These matters are considered in **Chapter 21, Supplying or receiving services within the EU**.

2.3.3 Voluntary and intending registrations

There are often advantages to registering early for VAT or on a voluntary basis. This is considered in more detail in **Chapter 3, VAT Registration**.

2.4 Pre registration planning

2.4.1 Planning stages

The planning process can be divided into four basic stages:

- ascertainment;
- analysis;
- alternatives; and
- action.

This is as true at the commencement of a business as at any other time.

> **Planning point**
>
> Planning is particularly important at this stage, as this is the time when the basic business structures can most readily be affected. Particularly important information will be the entities involved, and the supply paths and liability of supplies.

Matters to be particularly alert for are:

- positive-rated supplies made to final consumers; and
- input tax block points.

Bear in mind also that at this special time it is necessary to balance:

- the likely ongoing position; and
- the treatment of start-up costs, which can be substantial in themselves.

For instance, it may be considered that use of the cash accounting scheme will be of long-term benefit. However, this may defer the obtaining of input tax recovery in respect of start-up costs.

> **Planning point**
>
> The balance of advantage may lie in opting for the ordinary VAT scheme to begin with, and switching to cash accounting once the start-up costs have been paid for.

2.4.2   Basic planning priorities

The basic planning priorities for the organisation as a whole, whether it consists of one entity or several, will generally be determined by the liability of the supplies made to third-party customers and the status of those customers. Likely planning priorities are summarised below.

Positive-rated supplies to final consumers

Priorities are likely to be:

- avoiding/deferring registration;
- obtaining exemption/zero-rating;
- reducing taxable value (e.g. use of second-hand goods scheme);
- eliminating block points; and
- cash flow measures.

Zero-rated supplies to final consumers

Priorities are likely to be:

- seeking registration;
- eliminating or minimising input tax block points; and
- cash flow.

Exempt supplies to final consumers

Priorities are likely to be:

- eliminating VAT on intra-business costs (the final supplier is a block point);
- cash flow; and
- partial exemption planning if taxable supplies also take place.

Taxable (positive-rated or zero-rated) supplies to businesses

Priorities are likely to be:

- eliminating or minimising input tax block points; and
- cash flow.

Exempt supplies to businesses

Priorities are likely to be:

- achieving taxability;
- eliminating VAT on intra-business costs (the final supplier is a block point); and
- cash flow.

Preparing for VAT registration

Once the decision has been made to register for VAT, there are a number of matters that need to be dealt with. The following notes are not exhaustive and each business needs to consider their own personal circumstances.

Can the accounting system identify VAT adequately? It is best practice to use three VAT accounts: one for input tax, another for output tax and a final clearing account. The clearing account is used to transfer the input tax and output tax into at the end of each VAT period. Separate input and output accounts are used so that it is easy to identify credit notes in both the input tax and output tax accounts; failure to do so creates confusion when trying to determine if the matter is a credit or not. At this point consideration should be make to see if there is a need to set a schedule for regular reviews, see **Chapter 28, Review of business for VAT issues**.

Calculate when VAT will be payable to HMRC and when VAT will be payable to suppliers and received from customers. Can the cash flow of the business sustain the delay in obtaining VAT from customers before it is paid to HMRC? A spreadsheet should be used to determine when VAT payments are due to be made and what will be available to make this payment. HMRC are not forgiving regarding late payments.

Do the contracts with customers allow VAT to be added to the price of the goods or services supplied? Will customers accept an increase due to VAT; can they reclaim the VAT? If the customer cannot reclaim VAT (the public or exempt persons such as the health, education and finance sector) they may not pay an increased price due to VAT.

Prepare stationary for VAT, but do not issue any invoice showing VAT until registered for VAT (if it is necessary to raise an invoice, show the gross amount, state that a VAT invoice will be issued once your VAT number has been received and then issue the VAT invoice at a later date). Conversely, ensure that all invoices issued after registration are proper VAT invoices and that proper VAT invoices are obtained for all purchases to support claims for input tax credits.

Determine if any of the small scheme reliefs for VAT are available to be used, such as cash accounting, annual accounting, the flat rate scheme, etc. Also, would there be a benefit in using other VAT accounting schemes that are available to the business (such as retail schemes, second hand goods schemes, etc.) ensure that these schemes are understood to ensure that the rules are complied with and best advantage is obtained. All of these schemes are discussed in this book.

It is also advisable to obtain professional advice prior to registration to ensure that all matters have been considered, that the accounts are being set up correctly and the appropriate reliefs are being obtained and VAT is being correctly charged and claimed (and VAT is not charged or claimed on supplies that do not bear VAT). If complex VAT matters are dealt with, professional advice must be obtained. Complex matters include, but are not limited to, land and property, imports, exports, sales (dispatches) and purchases (acquisitions) into and from the EU and exempt transactions (such as finance, insurance, property transactions, health, education, etc.)

2.4.3 Pre-registration input tax

VAT can be reclaimed on certain expenditure incurred prior to registration. What can be claimed depends on whether the VAT was incurred on goods or services, the date of the expenditure and also the proposed use of the expenditures.

VAT on goods bought or imported less than four years before your registration can be reclaimed where:

- the goods were purchased by the entity that is registered for VAT and not another person;
- the goods are to be used in the taxable business; and
- the goods are on hand at the date of registration or have been incorporated into other goods that are on hand.

41

VAT cannot be reclaimed on goods:

- consumed, destroyed, supplied or otherwise disposed of prior to the date of registration;
- that relate to exempt supplies made or to be made; and
- used or to be used for private purposes.

VAT can be claimed on services acquired up to six months prior to the date of registration if the services relate to the taxable business. VAT cannot be claimed if the services were used on goods that have been disposed of prior to registration, where the service relates to exempt supplies or is used for private purposes. In *Jerzynek* [2005] BVC 2,078, Customs sought to argue that rent paid on premises was totally absorbed into supplies made before registration, but the tribunal held that this was not the case and that rent (for example, telephone bills and accountancy fees), was more in the nature of a general overhead of the business and that the VAT was therefore eligible for recovery.

The input tax incurred on pre-registration expenses that are linked exclusively or partly to exempt supplies is not recoverable. Pre-registration residual input tax is not allowed by HMRC to be included in the partial exemption calculations for the first return.

Douros (t/a Olympic Financial Services) [1995] BVC 1,132 attempted to reclaim the input tax on pre-registration supplies that were used in the making of predominantly exempt supplies on the grounds that the exempt input tax was below the *de minimis* limits. The tribunal upheld the right of HMRC to use their discretion not to allow this repayment.

To reclaim the VAT incurred on goods or services acquired prior to registration a stock list for goods and a list of services must be created. The stock list must record the quantities of goods, description of the services and the date they were acquired. It is necessary to detail what goods have been disposed of after registration. HMRC also expect to be able to see evidence that VAT has been paid on the goods and services; evidence would include VAT invoices and import VAT certificates (form C79). The VAT on goods and services bought before registration is to be included in box 4 of the first VAT Return.

Planning point

The restriction on expenditure incurred prior to the date of registration is to take account of the consumable nature of services and, unless the VAT was clearly not incurred in the making of taxable supplies, there is no need to examine the claim further from this point of view.

Planning point

When looking at recovery of pre-registration expenditure it is important, because of the time limits, to ensure that the date of registration is the most beneficial for recovery of VAT. Although many businesses wait until a compulsory registration is necessary, it is possible to register on a voluntary basis providing that taxable supplies are being made or are intended. A registration date that maximises input tax recovery can therefore be arranged. If the registration is on a voluntary basis, once the date for registration is selected it cannot be backdated further. It is therefore important to get this right first time. In addition, where output tax values would be low but input tax values high, it is possible to back date the date of VAT registration by up to four years, giving a maximum claim period for goods of eight years. If the output tax which would be payable by backdating, exceeds the input tax to be claimed this is obviously not worthwhile.

Planning point

If taxable supplies have not yet commenced and the business is intending to trade, it may be possible to request an earlier date of VAT registration to capture input tax incurred more than four years or six months prior to the current date.

⚠ Warning!

Where exempt input tax is incurred prior to the date of registration it is not recoverable in any circumstances, no matter how small the amount, because the *de minimis* limits do not apply to periods before the date of registration.

Law: VAT Regulations 1995 (SI 1995/2518), reg. 111

Other guidance: VAT Notice 700, s. 11

2.4.4 Pre-incorporation expenses

Where the new business is a limited company, a difficulty arises in that a tax invoice in the name of the company will not exist for pre-incorporation expenditure. In such cases, HMRC allow by concession that if the tax invoice is in the name of an officer of the company (a director or secretary), member or employee, then VAT incurred pre-incorporation may be claimed, providing that the officer was not himself a taxable person in his own right at the time the VAT was incurred, and the officer is reimbursed by the company for the expense.

It should be noted that although a claim for input tax on an invoice made out to an officer, member or employee of the company dated after incorporation may be allowed, in practice, the concession does strictly relate to pre-incorporation supplies and officers should ensure that suppliers are informed of the correct billing details as soon as possible.

2.5　Checklist

2.5.1　Pre-registration checklist

Is there a registrable business? [*Sch. 1*]

Note: A registrable business may include: sole traders; partnerships; joint ventures; racehorse owners; limited companies; groups of companies; companies in divisions; clubs; associations; charities; businesses taken over as a going concern; traders from overseas, and non-profit making organisations.

Are there:

(a) standard-rated supplies;
(b) zero-rated supplies – certain specified goods and services; and [*Table 4*]
(c) reduced-rated supplies – certain specified goods and services?

Note: These are 'taxable' supplies.

Have the following been excluded from the taxable supplies:

(a) exempt supplies – certain specified goods and services; [*Table 4*]
(b) capital items – goods or services which are capital assets; and
(c) supplies which are outside the scope of VAT?

Taxable supplies less the items that can be excluded will count towards the registration threshold. The full value of margin scheme supplies (such as second-hand goods), other than tour operator supplies need to be included towards the VAT registration threshold. Tour operators can use just their margin but the full value of any in-house supplies made and commissions received as their taxable turnover for registration purposes.

Note: Supplies made outside the UK are not included in the turnover figure for calculating VAT registration.

Has the business checked the requirements for compulsory or voluntary registration?

Note: The disaggregation rules will apply to artificially split business activities.

VAT Registration

3.1 Introduction

3.1.1 General background

Registration is a key aspect of VAT law and practice. It is through the route of registration that the person joins the register of taxpayers held by HMRC. It is also through this registration that a person's returns and payments are made.

Each registered person has a unique nine-digit VAT registration number. In relation to intra-Community trade (and in any other context, should the taxpayer desire), this should be prefixed by 'GB'.

3.1.2 European background

The Principal VAT Directive (EU Directive 2006/112) art. 9 defines what is meant by 'taxable person'. For discussion of the scope of this definition, see *Polysar Investments Netherlands BV v Inspecteur der Invoerrechten en Accijnzen, Arnhem* (Case C-60/90) (Case C-60/90) [1993] BVC 88; *Enkler v Finanzamt Homburg* (Case C-230/94) [1997] BVC 24; *C & E Commrs v Yarburgh Children's Trust* [2002] BVC 141 and **3.1.5** below.

Essentially, however, a taxable person is regarded as anybody that undertakes 'economic activity'. Economic activity is often equated to business, but its definition is much wider than this. This means that a person that is not in business can register for VAT, reclaim VAT incurred on expenses and will have to pay VAT on supplies made even if he is not regarded as being in business. For example, a person that is incurring costs preparatory to registration can register even though he is not in business. Mutual trading organisations and clubs, government bodies and charities will all be regarded as undertaking economic activity for some or all of their activities even if they would not normally be regarded as being in business.

3.1.3 UK Legislation

VATA 1994, s. 3 defines a 'taxable person' as a person who is, or who is required to be, registered.

Schedules 1, 2, 3, 3A and 3B provide detailed provisions in respect of registration in various circumstances. There are also provisions contained in the VAT Regulations 1995 (SI 1995/2518), reg. 5–10.

3.1.4 HMRC Notice

Notice 700/1 is published by HMRC, providing information regarding registration in respect of taxable supplies, distance sales, acquisitions and non-established taxable persons, as well as providing a Statement of Practice in respect of disaggregation. HMRC's website (*www.hmrc.gov.uk*) also provides details in respect of registration, rates, thresholds and how to register. All the forms necessary to register are available to download from this website and it is also possible to register on-line through the website.

3.1.5 Taxable person

A taxable person is any person who independently carries out an economic activity, as defined, irrespective of the purpose or results of that activity. This definition relates to a business, or economic activity, rather than registration for VAT. The definition is thus wider than that contained in UK legislation. The European definition is closer to the UK definition of 'business' in VATA 1994, s. 94. Economic activity is wider than business as it includes non-profit activities, activities in preparation for business activities and failed business activities.

For the purpose of this chapter, the UK definition is relevant. It is a taxable person (VATA 1994, s. 3) who is required to be registered for VAT. The Interpretation Act 1978 (Sch. 1) provides that a 'person' includes a body of persons corporate or unincorporate. Thus a person may be a natural person or a legal person.

Examples of natural persons include a sole trader, a partnership and an unincorporated association. Examples of legal persons include limited companies, European Economic Interest Groupings, local authorities and Crown bodies.

(In Scotland, a partnership is treated as a legal entity, a body separate to the partners, whereas in England and Wales a partnership has no existence separate from its partners.)

Where a person undertakes a number of business activities, the question to be addressed is whether the person should be registered for VAT, not whether each of the separate businesses should be registered. This matter was raised in the early case of *C & E Commrs v Glassborow* (1974) 1 BVC 4. The case concerned a married couple, Mr and Mrs Glassborow, who traded as estate agents and as land developers. To this end, two separate partnership agreements were in place and each partnership sought separate registrations for VAT. The court held that the 'person' trading as estate agents was the same person as that trading as land developers, and thus only one registration for VAT was permissible. A number of tribunal cases have followed this precedent. In particular, it must be noted that all the economic activity, or business activities, of a sole proprietor are included in the single VAT registration. Where a person registers as a sole proprietor, all his economic activity (including what that person may regard as separate or subsidiary activities) is included in the single registration. To prevent the activity being included, it will need to be undertaken in a separate legal entity (in a spouse's name, in a partnership or in a separate corporate entity). Also, care needs to be taken that what the individual regards as a hobby or pastime is not included as part of the registration. Where it is a hobby or pastime, no input tax credits should be claimed as HMRC will either disallow the credits or require VAT to be accounted for on any income received.

There are circumstances where there is doubt as to whether a person is employed or self-employed. An employed person does not make taxable supplies to his employer, and therefore cannot be registered in respect of those activities. However, a person may be self-employed in respect of some services, and may be required to be registered for VAT and, at the same time, be employed, which activities would remain outside the scope of his VAT registration.

This chapter only considers registration in the UK. A taxable person should also be aware of the possible requirement to be registered in another EU member state or, indeed, in any state which requires registration in respect of indirect tax on supplies. Further details concerning economic activity and taxable persons is given at **3.1.5.**

⚠ *Warning!*

As a 'rule of thumb' if a person is not required to be registered or account for VAT in the UK for supplies that are made then it is likely that VAT will have to be accounted for elsewhere. For example, a real estate agent selling hotels on a world-wide basis will not be regarded as making a supply in the UK if he sells a hotel in, say, New Zealand. He would, however, be regarded as making a supply in New Zealand and be required to register and account for New Zealand's equivalent of VAT (GST). In business to business transactions it is sometimes possible to transfer the liability to account for VAT to the customer who can then reclaim the VAT incurred subject to the normal rules of VAT of that jurisdiction.

3.2   Registration for VAT

3.2.1 Compulsory registration

A person is liable for registration under any of the following circumstances.

1.   If, at the end of any month, the value of his taxable supplies for the period of 12 months then ending has exceeded the specified limit ('historical turnover' rule).

2.   If at any time, the person expects that the value of his taxable supplies for the next 30 days will exceed the specified limit ('future turnover' rule).

3.   Where a business is transferred as a going concern, the transferee will become liable to register if, at the time of the transfer, the value of taxable supplies for

the period of 12 months then ending has exceeded the specified limit. Under this rule, the turnover of the transferred business prior to transfer must be added to the turnover, if any, of the transferee.

4.   Where a business is transferred as a going concern, the transferee will become liable to register if, at the time of the transfer, he expects that the value of his taxable supplies for the next 30 days will exceed the specified limit.

The 'specified limit' is, with effect from 1 April 2012, £77,000. This limit is usually increased at the time of the Budget. Previous thresholds can be found in the Registration Thresholds table at the end of this chapter and in HMRC's supplement to *Notice 700/1* or *Hardman's Tax Rates and Tables*.

When calculating the turnover of a business for the purposes of VAT registration it is only necessary to consider the value of the taxable supplies. Taxable supplies include supplies that would be taxed at the standard rate, the reduced-rate or the zero-rate. Where margin-scheme goods are sold (for example, second-hand goods) the value of the supply for the purpose of registration is the full value of the sale and not just the margin. Under the Tour Operators Margin Scheme, however, the value for registration is the taxable margin plus any in-house supplies and commissions and not the full selling price of the tour.

Revenue or income that can be ignored when calculating the VAT registration threshold includes:

- exempt income (financial services, certain property transactions, insurance, health, education etc.);
- capital assets (other than land, which may be exempt and excluded under that heading), see **3.2.5**);
- distance sales that are treated as supplied in another EU country;
- supplies of distance sales made by an overseas person in the UK (but see below in respect of supplies made by overseas persons;
- supplies made outside the UK that are outside the scope of UK VAT;
- supplies made when previously VAT registered;
- certain supplies subject to the fiscal warehousing rules; and
- a proportion of the income received from individuals staying in hotel type accommodation for over four weeks (the non-taxable element).

Planning point

When calculating the liability to register for VAT, always exclude exempt supplies or supplies which are outside the scope of UK VAT, as in some cases this makes the difference between an obligation to register and a choice over registration. It should also be noted that a person who only makes exempt supplies (or whose income is not regarded as being a supply for VAT purposes, such as some grant income) cannot register for VAT and, therefore, cannot reclaim VAT incurred on expenditure.

> **⚠ Warning!**
>
> The requirement to include the value of reverse chargeable services received from overseas can cause an otherwise wholly exempt trader to be obliged to register for VAT in order to account for VAT on the value of the relevant services, which is not then recoverable as input tax.

Whether the disposal of certain goods constituted the disposal of capital assets, and should therefore be excluded from the value of taxable supplies made, was the subject of *Harbig Leasing Two Ltd* [2001] BVC 2,134. In that case at para. 51 the following principles were laid down in considering whether goods should be treated as capital assets:

- durable nature;
- value;
- whether the goods are sold immediately or retained for a number of years;
- whether the transactions are unusual and make a drastic change in the turnover for one year; and
- whether the transactions reflect the actual size of the undertaking.

Individuals also need to consider whether they are employees or self-employed and, if self-employed, whether they are making supplies as principals or acting as agents. If they are employees, they will not have any liability to register for the income earned as an employee. Where self-employed as a principal, the income earned (gross before any costs or commissions are deducted) needs to be counted towards the VAT registration threshold. This has often given problems where people act as representatives under 'party plan' or similar arrangements. For persons working under party plan arrangements or other commission type agency agreements, regard must be given to whether the value of their supplies is the total amount paid by the customer or only the mark-up amount retained. Where a person is acting as an agent only, the principal supplies the goods and the taxable income for VAT purposes is the commission element only. Where the self-employed person is acting as a principal then the value of the goods needs to be included in the taxable value when determining the VAT value and also when considering the VAT registration threshold.

Where a person makes supplies under TOMS the value of a 'designated travel service' is the margin, being the difference between the cost price and the selling price.

> **Planning point**
>
> When deciding whether or not registration is required, a person making supplies covered by the TOMS only needs to count the margin on any bought-in supplies sold on unchanged and not the full value of those elements of the package.

A person may become liable to be registered in respect of a one-off event, where the turnover exceeds the specified limit, for example an annual event such as a concert or sports event, or a one-off disposal of stock by an unregistered business. The rules explained here apply equally to such a situation. Such a person may be entitled to deregister after the event.

3.2.2 Requirement to notify

Where a person is liable to be registered under the historical turnover rule, he is required to notify HMRC within 30 days of the end of the 12-month period. That person is then registered with effect from the first day of the next but one month, or an earlier date agreed with HMRC.

> ### Example 3.1
>
> Turnover exceeds specified limit: May 2011.
>
> Liability to notify: before the end of June 2011.
>
> Registration with effect from: 1 July 2011.

Where a person is liable to be registered under the future turnover rule, he is required to notify HMRC before the end of the 30-day period. That person is then registered from the beginning of that period.

> ### Example 3.2
>
> Turnover expected to exceed the specified limit, in the 30 days beginning 15 May 2011.
>
> Liability to notify: before 14 June 2011.
>
> Registration with effect from: 15 May 2011.

Where a person is liable to be registered in respect of a transfer of a business as a going concern, he is liable to notify HMRC within 30 days of the transfer. That person is then registered from the date of transfer.

> ### Example 3.3
>
> Date of transfer: 20 June 2011.
>
> Liability to notify: before 20 July 2011.
>
> Registration with effect from: 20 June 2011.

> ### ⚠ *Warning!*
>
> When taking over the business of someone who is, or is liable to be, VAT registered (a transfer of a going concern), the new owner 'inherits' the former owner's taxable turnover and cannot choose to wait until turnover under his ownership exceeds the VAT threshold before registering. However, when taking on a business from someone who is neither registered nor liable to be registered, the new owner does not 'inherit' the turnover, and commences with a 'clean sheet'.

Where a person is liable to be registered under more than one rule, the earlier date of registration will always apply.

> ### *Example 3.4*
>
> John commences in business in January 2011. During May 2011, his cumulative turnover exceeds £77,000, necessitating registration with effect from 1 July 2011. However, on 20 May 2011, he agrees a single order worth £78,000, to be delivered and invoiced within 30 days. This necessitates registration with effect from 20 May under the future turnover rule, overriding the 1 July date.

Where a person is liable to be registered under the historic turnover rule, and he had previously been registered and that registration ceased, any supplies made when previously registered are to be disregarded for the purposes of ascertaining the value of the person's taxable turnover. This rule shall not apply if his registration was cancelled as void, nor if HMRC are not satisfied that, when he cancelled the previous registration, they were given full information about the cancelling of the registration. When applying for registration, a person is required to give the VAT number of any business in which he had previously been involved.

> ### *Planning point*
>
> Until March 1990, the future turnover rule applied to supplies to be made in the succeeding year. This was abolished in the 1990 Budget, since when the law has made no reference at all to future turnover expectations calculated annually. This remains an issue as the effective date of registration is not capped, so if a person was caught by this rule but had not applied it, it is possible for HMRC to amend the VAT registration date and collect any VAT due.

A person needs register for VAT in the UK when they are not registered and:

- supplies are made in the UK (including exports); or
- goods are acquired from EU suppliers; or
- an EU supplier without a place of establishment in the UK makes supplies of goods to UK customers that are not VAT registered (the so-called distance sales); or

- supplies that are deemed to be made in the UK (this may apply to UK persons that may otherwise not be required to be registered or to overseas persons that are deemed to be making supplies in the UK by the place of supply rules); and
- the sale of goods where 8th or 13th Directive claims have been made.

⚠ *Warning!*

If supplies are made that are not subject to VAT in the UK it is likely that these supplies will be subject to VAT elsewhere. A person based in the UK that sells into another country must consider if the supply is subject to local VAT.

Example 3.5

Venice Mountby is a real estate agent specialising in selling international hotels. Venice is registered for VAT in the UK and accounts for VAT on the commission he receives on the sale of UK hotels. No UK VAT has been accounted for on the commission he has charged on the sale of hotels in France or Australia. Venice employs a VAT adviser who tells him that the VAT on the sale of the French hotel can be accounted for through the reverse charge if the supply was made to a person registered in France, otherwise he will be required to account for VAT in France. Venice will also have to account for Australian GST on the commission received for the sale of the Australian hotel, subject to any GST relief that may be available.

As has been detailed above, a person established in the UK must look at future supplies as well as past supplies to determine if it is required to be registered for VAT. When either the future or historic threshold is exceeded the person is required to be registered. It should be noted that registration can be required under the distance sales test or the acquisitions test (sales or purchases from other EU member states) or reverse charged supplies are received even when received by an unregistered person.

Planning Point

The historic test requires a business to monitor taxable turnover at the end of each month on a rolling 12-month basis. Where taxable turnover for the previous 12 months (or since trading commenced if a shorter period exceeds the VAT registration threshold) the person must register for VAT and HMRC are required to register the person. The date of registration will be the first day of the month following notification (notification is required within 30 days of breaching the threshold) or at a mutually agreed earlier date (an earlier date would be requested by the business to permit input tax incurred before the date of compulsory registration to be claimed).

Example 3.6

Pria is a sole proprietor who commenced trading in January 2011. At the end of June 2012, her taxable turnover reached £78,000. Pria is required to notify HMRC by 30 July 2012 and HMRC will register the business from 1 August 2011 or on a mutually agreed earlier date. As Pria has incurred substantial costs in purchasing equipment to establish her business, she wishes to agree an earlier date of registration. Pria can choose to back date the registration by up to four years with HMRC's agreement, to reclaim the VAT incurred, or she may choose to claim back the VAT incurred prior to registration. Pria can reclaim VAT incurred on services used in the six months prior to registration (subject to certain exceptions) and on goods acquired in the previous four years if the goods remain on hand at the date of registration.

⚠ **Warning!**

It is important for an unregistered person to monitor taxable turnover every month to ensure that the turnover limit is not breached. If the turnover is only examined and compared to the registration threshold at the financial year-end it is possible that the threshold could have been breached some time earlier and this may render the business liable to penalties for late registration.

⚠ **Warning!**

VAT registration is not only required for transactions between UK suppliers and UK customers. Registration is also required where there are acquisitions from the EU, distance sales into the UK, where goods are supplied into the UK that have been subject to 8th or 13th Directive reclaims, and where reverse charge supplies are received by certain businesses from outside the EU.

A UK person that acquires from a business in another EU member state may be required to register for VAT; registration is required if the value of the goods acquired exceeds the acquisitions threshold. There are both historic and future tests for the acquisition threshold and it does not operate on a rolling basis but rather uses the calendar year. The turnover still needs to be checked regularly as registration is required as soon as the VAT registration threshold is breached.

Example 3.7

A UK non-VAT registered business purchases goods from various suppliers in the EU. Between 1 January 2012 and 12 July 2012 £78,000 of goods has been acquired. The business is therefore required to register for VAT by 31 July 2012 and must notify HMRC by 31 August 2012. HMRC will register the person on 1 September 2012.

Where supplies of goods are made into the UK for a person that is based overseas the overseas person may be required to register for VAT in the UK. Where the person is based outside the EU the overseas person will only be required to register if they supply goods that are in the UK when the supply is made. For example, if the overseas person imports the goods into the UK and then sells them to a third party the goods will be supplied in the UK and the overseas person will be required to register (it should be noted that the VAT registration threshold does not apply to overseas persons and registration is required if any supplies are made). The overseas person will also be liable to pay the import duty and VAT.

Where an EU person makes sales of goods to the UK from the EU (distance sales) to persons who are not registered for VAT (and are not required to be registered) the EU person is required to register for VAT when the value of the UK supplies exceed the distance sales threshold (currently £70,000) during the calendar year. Note that if the distance sales are sales of excise goods (tobacco or alcohol) registration is required immediately whatever the value of the sales. More detail is provided in **3.5**.

⚠ *Warning!*

A UK person also has to register for VAT in the EU member state where he makes distance sales (sales to non-registered persons; that is individuals or entities that do not need to register or are not in business such as government bodies) and the value of the sales exceed the individual member state's distance selling threshold. There are separate thresholds for distance sales for each EU member state. When the distance selling threshold has not been breached, the UK supplier will account for UK VAT on the sale. The threshold is breached on a member state by member state basis (i.e. the threshold may be breached in France and the UK person will have to register in France and account for French VAT, but not breached in Germany and the UK person will still account for UK VAT on German supplies). The member state's distance selling thresholds differ but are usually either EUR70,000 or EUR35,000 or the equivalent in the national currency.

There are a variety of supplies that are treated as being made in the UK by the place of supply rules by overseas suppliers. Most of these supplies do not require the supplier to register for VAT as the VAT is accounted for under the reverse charge when made to a VAT registered person in the UK. Registration is, however, required when the supply is made to a person that is neither registered nor required to be registered. The supplier will be required to register for VAT if it makes supplies in the UK that are not subject to the reverse charge even if the value of the supplies does not exceed the VAT registration limit. A single small value supply could require the person to register for VAT in the UK.

Where a UK person makes these supplies in other member states of the EU it may also be liable to register for VAT in that member state. Indeed, there may be a liability to register if the supplies are made to persons outside the EU, but that will be subject to local VAT or GST rules.

A person is required to account for VAT in the UK if it makes a supply of goods on which an 8th or 13th Directive claim has been made or is going to be made. If the person making the supply is not VAT registered the value of the supply counts towards the VAT registration threshold.

There are various special registration schemes and accounting methods for flat rate farmers, race horses, telecommunications and electronically supplied services. These are dealt with in separate chapters and sections.

3.2.3 Exception from registration

Once a person becomes liable to be registered, he ceases to be liable if he satisfies HMRC that he does not expect his turnover in the 12-month period then beginning to exceed the deregistration limit. This limit is set at £2,000 below the limit for registration.

Example 3.8

Bob's cumulative turnover has exceeded £77,000. He is thus liable to notify HMRC of his liability to register for VAT.

However, he expects that his turnover in the next year will be below £75,000. He may therefore ask HMRC not to register him.

In this situation, the person is still required to notify HMRC that his turnover has exceeded the specified limit. At the same time, the person may apply not to be registered. The VAT Regulations 1995 (SI 1995/2518), reg. 5(1) provides that a person notifies liability on form VAT 1, although HMRC have indicated that a VAT 1 is not required where the person is seeking exception from registration. They will, however, require details of the business activities. Thus, a person may prefer to submit a VAT 1 with a covering letter explaining the full circumstances of the application.

Where a person seeks exception as set out in this section, if he expects to cease making taxable supplies, or he suspends making taxable supplies for 30 days or more, he will not be entitled to exception.

If a person is granted exception from registration, he will be notified that the specific exceptional supplies which caused him to exceed the threshold on a temporary basis may be ignored in computing the level of turnover for registration purposes thereafter. (Without this provision, the exceptional turnover could cause the person to be liable to notify a value of taxable supplies above the registration threshold every month for 11 months after the event.) However, if turnover increases after the granting of exception, a liability to register may later arise. That is to say, the person granted exception cannot treat it as a blanket relief from the normal requirement to register for any given period of time; it is specific to the circumstances giving rise to the request.

> ⚠ **Warning!**
>
> Exception from registration requires HMRC's approval and cannot be assumed.
> Failure to notify leaves open an indefinite liability to register for VAT.

In a case where notification is late, the question may be asked whether a person may then be excepted from registration. This question was considered in *Gray v C & E Commrs* [2000] BVC 396. The case concerned a person who notified his liability to registration late. Upon application, he also requested that, since his taxable turnover subsequently fell below the prescribed limit, he should be excepted from registration. Consideration was given to two questions.

1. At what date should HMRC look at the position in deciding whether or not they are satisfied as mentioned in para. 1(3)?

2. In the case of a late registration, should HMRC consider only the knowledge of the facts which they actually had at that date, or should there be attributed to them knowledge which they acquired only at a later date?

Paragraph 1(3) is directed primarily to the circumstance where a person notifies HMRC timeously with respect to his registration. Its application is of short duration, as it relates to the process of notification. In practice a person notifying liability to registration will at the same time notify his application for exception from registration.

The conclusion given was that HMRC, in cases of late registration, must give effect to para. 1(3) by considering the facts of the case at the time when registration would otherwise have taken effect, and by looking forward from that historical time. Further, they must only give weight to evidence that was available at that time, not information which subsequently became available. The alternative would be that the person notifying late would actually be at an advantage over a person notifying at the correct time.

> **Planning point**
>
> Possibly as a result of this case, HMRC have, in recent years, become more amenable to the possibility of granting retrospective exception. Where past occurrences of short-term and exceptional breaches of the threshold are discovered, they should be notified. Exception will be granted if HMRC are satisfied that the person, at the time, had sufficient knowledge that his turnover would fall back below the limits. That is to say, hindsight may not be used. HMRC will not, however, backdate registration once the date of registration has been agreed (or if back dating was not requested and the person became compulsorily registered). If a person has incurred VAT prior to registration serious consideration must be given to backdating registration to enable the VAT incurred to be reclaimed.

VATA 1994, Sch. 1, para. 1(3) excludes reference to a person who believes his turnover will exceed the specified limit within 30 days. Thus if a person is liable to be registered under the future turnover rule, he cannot be granted exception from registration. This provides that a person who arranges a one-off event, which makes him liable for registration where the turnover exceeds the specified limit, cannot then be exempted from registration because his anticipated future turnover, for the 12 months after the event, will fall below the specified limit.

3.2.4 Exemption from registration

A person may also seek exemption from registration where his taxable supplies are wholly or predominantly zero-rated. Granting a request for exemption of course deprives the applicant of input tax incurred on his purchases. An application for exemption may be made on a form VAT 1 and a box ticked to indicate that it is requested. HMRC usually permit this where input tax credits available exceed any output tax payable. This, however, is to the disadvantage of the business as it loses the input tax that it can claim.

> **Planning point**
>
> Exception from registration (see **3.2.3**) and exemption from registration are often confused. In particular, exception is often described as exemption. This is incorrect, and caution should be exercised in using the correct terminology when communicating with HMRC.

> **Planning point**
>
> If the business would predominantly be in receipt of repayments of VAT, exemption from VAT registration can be applied for. Repayments of VAT, however, will be lost and businesses should consider this very carefully. To apply for exemption it is necessary for the business to notified HMRC of its registration details on form VAT 1 (and form VAT 2 for partnerships) with a request for exemption to the appropriate VAT registration unit.

3.2.5 Entitlement to be registered

Where a person is not obliged to be registered, he may in certain circumstances choose to be registered. There are two specific scenarios, generally referred to as intending trader registration and voluntary registration.

Where a person seeks registration under these conditions, the effective date of registration can be backdated. However, with effect from 1 April 1997, such a registration may only be backdated for a maximum of four years (VATA 1994, s. 80(4); *Business Brief 8/97* (25 March 1997)).

Intending trader registration

Where a person intends to make taxable supplies in the future, and is incurring input tax in relation to certain 'preparatory acts', he may apply to be registered. The person is required to satisfy HMRC that he intends to make taxable supplies, by providing, for example (list extracted from *Notice 700/1*):

- details of the arrangements he has made;
- copies of contracts he has in the pipeline;
- planning permission;
- details of what he has bought for the business;
- details of any patents he has applied for, or
- a statement with an option to tax certain land or buildings.

Whether a person is entitled to be registered was considered in the tribunal case, *Merseyside Cablevision Ltd* (1987) 3 BVC 596, (applying *Rompelman v Minister van Financiën* (Case 268/83) (1985) 2 BVC 200,157). It was held that a person carrying out preparatory acts was a taxable person within the meaning of Directive 2006/112, art. 9, and therefore the company could be registered for VAT and recover its input tax prior to the making of taxable supplies. There is no obligation upon a person to state a date by which he intends to make taxable supplies, nor is the person required to estimate the value of those supplies (although HMRC expect to be given this information for the protection of the Revenue).

Individual HMRC officers sometimes appear to take the view (entirely unjustified in the light of the relevant case law) that, until taxable supplies have been carried out, any input tax deduction is provisional. In addition, upon receipt of an application for registration and allocation of a registration number, HMRC generally inform a person registering under the intending trader provisions of the requirement in certain circumstances of input tax claimed. HMRC can make this claim for repayment where there is no economic activity or the acquisitions are applied to a private or domestic use.

Planning point

It can sometimes be difficult to persuade HMRC to grant intending trader registration, particularly where it is at such an early stage that there is little evidence available unequivocally to support the application. Since an intending trader registration can be backdated, as long as this is requested at the time the application is made, it can sometimes be more effective to delay an application until more evidence is available and then apply for an earlier date of registration.

Voluntary registration

Where a person makes taxable supplies in the course of a business, even though the value of those supplies is below the registration threshold, he may apply to be registered. HMRC often do not appear to require evidence of business activities carried on.

> **Planning Point**
>
> Where the client base is mainly consumers or persons that cannot reclaim VAT there is an advantage in not charging VAT on supplies, thus VAT registration should be delayed as long as possible. Where the customers can reclaim VAT there is an advantage in registering early (as long as the supplier can add VAT to the supply; contracts and agreements must be checked to ensure that VAT can be added to the price and that the agreement is not for a VAT inclusive price). Where the customer can reclaim VAT the VAT charged is not an additional cost to the customer and the supplier can reclaim the VAT incurred on expenses.

> **Planning Point**
>
> When considering VAT registration it is vital to consider the amount of VAT that can be reclaimed. Registering for VAT requires VAT to be accounted for on supplies made but input tax, the VAT incurred on expenses, cannot be claimed unless the person registers for VAT. VAT can, however, be incurred on some services and goods acquired before registration, but limits are applied to the VAT that can be reclaimed (mainly concerning the time period of the claim).

Where a person has a business establishment or his usual place of residence in the UK, but makes supplies outside the UK and those supplies would be taxable supplies if made in the UK, he can apply for registration even if the value of these supplies is below the VAT registration threshold.

> **Planning point**
>
> Where an organisation has an entitlement to register in the UK under these provisions, it is often a preferable course, as it makes the recovery of input tax considerably simpler than the regular submission of Eighth or Thirteenth Directive refund claims.

3.2.6 Notification of liability to register

Where a person is required to notify HMRC of his liability to register for VAT, he must use form VAT 1. For convenience, where a person who is not required to notify HMRC wishes to register, he will also use form VAT 1. This form appears within the VAT Regulations 1995 (SI 1995/2518), Sch. 1, form 1. Where the person is a partnership, a list of partners is also required, on form VAT 2. This form appears within the VAT Regulations 1995 (SI 1995/2518), Sch. 1, form 2. Forms are also available from www.hmrc.gov.uk, and by calling the help line: 0845 010 9000 (open 0800 to 2000 Monday to Friday).

Upon receipt of a valid application for registration, HMRC issue a VAT registration number, unique to that person, and a Certificate of Registration, showing the registered person's details.

In particular, the Certificate of Registration indicates the periods for which the person will be required to submit VAT returns.

> ### ⚠ *Warning!*
> In the absence of any request to the contrary, an applicant will be allocated VAT periods on an entirely random basis; VAT periods are usually quarterly periods but may not end on calendar quarters. HMRC allocate period ends to 31 January, 28 February as well as 30 March (and quarterly thereafter) to spread the flow of VAT returns submitted. If specific VAT periods are desired, for example to coincide with the accounts year or, in the case of a repayment trader, to facilitate more frequent refunds through monthly VAT returns, this should be requested at the time of registration in a letter accompanying form VAT 1.

In the circumstance where a person is registered late, he will be required to complete a VAT return from the date he was originally required to be registered. HMRC are entitled to issue such a return, see *Bjellica (t/a Eddy's Domestic Appliances) v C & E Commrs* [1995] BVC 139. In that case, the taxpayer registered with effect from 1 November 1987. Subsequently, Customs discovered that he should have been registered from 21 April 1975 and issued a VAT return for the period 21 April 1975 to 31 October 1987. The Court of Appeal upheld their power so to do.

An application for registration where such registration is not compulsory does not require the completion of form VAT 1. This is because reg. 5 only refers to compulsory registration. However, in practice HMRC request that such an application be completed.

There may be dispute with HMRC as to whether a form VAT 1 has actually been submitted. There have been a number of cases where a person has claimed to have posted the form to HMRC but they have claimed not to have received it. See section **3.2.10** for a discussion of this issue. The person applying for registration is best advised to take a copy of the completed form, note the date when it was posted, and remind HMRC if an acknowledgement is not received within 30 days.

HMRC have indicated that application forms are frequently submitted inaccurately or incomplete. This may delay the issue of a VAT registration number whilst further information has to be provided.

> ### *Planning point*
> Where a particular date of registration is required, or the registration is compulsory and time to gather information and complete returns is short, it is advisable to submit the VAT 1 as soon as possible to establish the application and notification of registration with HMRC. Other required information can be submitted later. Where, however, it is possible to gather all information and the time limits are not pressing, it is advisable to send all the necessary information together as this makes the processing of the application simpler and quicker.

> ### ⚠ *Warning!*
>
> HMRC aims to process 70 per cent of VAT registration applications within ten working days. HMRC claim that the vast majority of VAT registration applications are processed within a month. Where HMRC need to carry out additional checks there may be further delays. To ensure that there are not delays with an application, care should be taken in completing the form and HMRC should be provided with as much information as possible. Where the need for a VAT number is urgent it is recommended that early application is made to enable HMRC to process the application as soon as possible. It is difficult for HMRC to process applications urgently as they may not know where the application is within their system and HMRC also claim, rightly, that to treat some applications differently is unfair to other applicants.

3.2.7 Effective date of registration

In most circumstances, the date set within the legislation will suffice as the date from which registration is to take effect. However, a person may agree an earlier date with HMRC.

It may be advantageous to apply for a retrospective registration, particularly where the amount of input tax to be recovered exceeds the amount of output tax payable or where there is input tax that is to be reclaimed in earlier periods; the rules regarding the capping of claims needs to be considered. In such circumstances, a person may only backdate their registration for a maximum of four years (three years before 1 April 2010).

> ### *Example 3.9*
>
> A business has not exceeded the VAT registration threshold for the past four years. It is, however, expected to exceed the threshold shortly. The business has incurred a substantial amount of input tax on goods used in the business (goods that still remain in the business – for example, equipment used in manufacture).
>
> The majority of this equipment was acquired five years ago. The business makes mainly zero-rated supplies and will be in a repayment position. It requests that its VAT registration is backdated four years and on its first VAT return it reclaims the VAT incurred on the goods acquired five years ago, as these goods were on hand at the effective date of registration and were acquired less than four years before the date of registration. The ability to back date a registration by four years and reclaim the VAT incurred on goods on hand that were acquired up to four years earlier gives a window of opportunity to reclaim VAT on goods for up to eight years.

Applications for backdating a registration must be made at the time of application for registration. HMRC will not backdate a registration once the effective date of registration has been agreed or allocated.

Compulsory registrations can be backdated indefinitely and are not subject to the four-year cap (three years before 1 April 2010).

Rules apply which allow a person to claim input tax incurred prior to registration. A person may find it preferable to use this means to reclaim input tax, rather than backdate his registration as when the VAT registration is backdated the taxpayer becomes liable to pay output tax on supplies made in the period when the registration is backdated.

A legal person has no existence prior to its incorporation, or equivalent. It can therefore only be registered on or after its date of incorporation. Expenses incurred by an individual on behalf of a company can be reclaimed by the company, subject to a number of limitations (for example the individual must become an officer, member or employee of the company). (See **9.3.1.**) Details of how to register are shown at the end of this chapter.

3.2.8 Changes of circumstances

A person is required to notify HMRC of any change in the name, constitution or ownership of his business, or any event which requires a change in the register. Such notification must be within 30 days of the change occurring.

Where a person has been granted exemption from registration on the basis that he makes zero-rated supplies, the person is required to notify any material change in the supplies he makes. In particular, where the proportion of zero-rated supplies changes materially, he is required to notify HMRC.

A registered person is required to notify HMRC of any intention to cease making taxable supplies. A registered person who only makes supplies outside the UK is required to notify HMRC of any intention to make taxable supplies in the UK.

The requirement is that the registered person notifies HMRC in writing of such changes.

> **Planning point**
>
> Although there are statutory penalties for failure to notify changes in circumstances, these are in practice only levied when tax has been lost as a result of the failure, which in most circumstances is not the case. There is therefore no real need for apprehension when notifying changes, even many years after the event.

3.2.9   Failure to notify registration

In certain cases of failing to register, HMRC may regard the failure as particularly serious and apply the 'civil fraud' provisions and consider that a dishonesty penalty may be appropriate. For example, in the case of *Stevenson and Telford Building & Design Ltd v C & E Commrs* [1996] BVC 428, a penalty was imposed under what is now VATA 1994, ss. 60 and 61, where the person traded without registering for VAT. The court stated that a failure to register for VAT was conduct that could give rise to a penalty under those sections. Thus, while most cases of a failure to register or, strictly, a failure to notify liability to register, may be dealt with under the civil penalty regime for failure to register for VAT, HMRC may deem that the facts demand the more severe penalties available under ss. 60 and 61. These penalties only applied to periods occurring before 1 April 2010. After this date the new 'harmonised' regime applies (see **Chapter 31**).

A new penalty regime also applies to the late registration penalty. Finance Act 2008, s. 123, Sch. 41 applies a new regime of penalties to the failure to notify obligations. The penalty that is applied is:

- 100 per cent of the potential lost revenue due to a deliberate or concealed act or failure;
- 70 per cent of the potential lost revenue due to a deliberate but not concealed act or failure; and
- 30 per cent of the potential lost revenue in any other case.

The amount of penalty due may be reduced in respect of other penalties or surcharges due that have been determined in respect of the same VAT liability. Furthermore, the penalty may be reduced due to disclosure or other factors (see **3.2.10** below).

The potential lost revenue is the VAT that the person is liable for in the period from the date that the person is liable to be registered to the date that HMRC is notified, or otherwise became aware, of the liability to register for VAT. This is the total output tax due less any input tax credit for which the person may be eligible.

It should be noted that the same regime applies to failure to notify HMRC of changes that mean the person is no longer exempt from registration, obligation to register due to acquisitions from other member states, an obligation to register due to a transfer of a going concern, or any of the other registration requirements. In addition, a similar penalty applies to the issue of an invoice by an unauthorized person (that is an unregistered person).

Example 3.10 (Based on a standard rate of 20 per cent)

Joe was required to be registered on 1 April 2011. HMRC discovered his liability on 30 November 2011. Joe failed to register as his business had been expanding rapidly and had fallen behind with his bookkeeping. His gross income during that period was £100,000, and the allowable input tax was £6,000.

The output tax amount is £100,000 × 1/6 = £16,666.

The 'potential revenue lost' is £16,666 − £6,000 = £10,666.

The penalty percentage is 30 per cent as there was no deliberate or concealed act or failure.

The penalty amount is therefore £10,666× 30 per cent = £3,200.

The penalty regime that applied before 1 April 2010 is detailed below. A penalty was applied in respect of the 'relevant VAT' due. The amount of 'relevant VAT' is the net amount due for the period:

- beginning on the date the person was required to be registered; and
- ending on the date on which HMRC received his notification, or otherwise became aware of his liability to be registered.

Thus, where HMRC discover the person to be registerable without having notified them, the amount of relevant VAT will be calculated up to the date of discovery.

The length of that period determines the penalty percentage that is applicable:

- where the period is less than 9 months, a 5 per cent penalty applies;
- where the period is between 9 and 18 months, a 10 per cent penalty applies; and
- where the period exceeds 18 months, a 15 per cent penalty applies.

Example 3.11 (Based on a standard rate of 17.5 per cent)

Sarah was required to be registered on 1 January 2005. HMRC discovered her liability on 1 January 2006. Her gross income during that period was £100,000, and her allowable input tax was £6,000.

The output tax amount is £100,000 × 7/47 = £14,894.

Her 'relevant VAT' is £14,894 − £6,000 = £8,894.

The penalty percentage for 12 months is 10 per cent.

The penalty amount is therefore £8,894 × 10 per cent = £889.

HMRC have, however, indicated that a penalty will not generally be imposed at all if the period of belatedness is less than three months.

> **Planning point**
>
> As illustrated by the above example, output tax must be calculated as if included within t he value of supplies made during the period of belatedness. If the person, once registered, is able to charge customers VAT retrospectively on top of that value, the output tax for the belatedness period is still calculated in the same way. The difference between the VAT so charged and the amount retrospectively due becomes a liability in the period in which the supplementary invoice is issued. The penalty will be needlessly increased if the full amount of VAT is attributed to the belatedness period.

> **Planning point**
>
> HMRC ordinarily use a person's invoices as the basis for calculating his date of registration and therefore any penalty. For some businesses, the invoice date is not the same as the tax point, and thus either the date of registration or the amount of the penalty may be incorrect. An adviser should bear this in mind when reviewing a penalty under this chapter.

Where a person is exempted from registration on the basis that his supplies are mainly zero-rated, and there is a 'material change' in those supplies, the person is required to notify HMRC within 30 days of that change or, if there is no identifiable date on which the change occurred, within 30 days of the end of that quarter. Failure to do so will render the person liable to a penalty under s. 67.

HMRC have indicated that serious cases of avoiding registration for VAT will be investigated and even criminal charges may be considered (*Notice 700/1*, para. 13.3).

3.2.10 Cancellation and reduction of penalty

A penalty issued under both the old and the new provisions can be cancelled where the person can establish a 'reasonable excuse' for the failure to register. HMRC or the Tribunal has, in the past, accepted a variety of reasonable excuses, such as the complexity of the tax or the person not being expected to understand the requirement to register (for example a very young person – an older person or an experienced business person would not be able to avail themselves of this excuse).

A penalty arising after 1 April 2010 can be reduced where there is a disclosure. The penalty is reduced as follows:

(1) Where the penalty applied was 100 per cent, where there is an unprompted disclosure the penalty can be reduced to a percentage not below 30 per cent.

(2) Where the penalty applied was 100 per cent, where there is a prompted disclosure the penalty can be reduced to a percentage not below 50 per cent.

(3) Where the penalty applied was 70 per cent, where there is an unprompted disclosure the penalty can be reduced to a percentage not below 20 per cent.

(4) Where the penalty applied was 70 per cent, where there is a prompted disclosure the penalty can be reduced to a percentage not below 35 per cent.

(5) Where the penalty applied was 30 per cent, where there is an unprompted disclosure the penalty can be reduced to:

    (a) any percentage, including nil, if HMRC become aware of the failure to register within 12 months of the due date; or

    (b) in any other case to an amount not below 10 per cent.

(6) Where the penalty applied was 30 per cent, where there is a prompted disclosure the penalty can be reduced to:

    (a) any percentage, not below 10 per cent, if HMRC become aware of the failure to register within 12 months of the due date; or

    (b) in any other case to an amount not below 20 per cent.

Where HMRC think it is right, they may also apply a special reduction (at their discretion and an amount of their choosing). Special circumstances do not include an inability to pay or if the potential loss of revenue is balanced by a potential overpayment by another person.

Further, in respect of s. 67 penalties (applying before 1 April 2010), a penalty may be mitigated where circumstances fall short of a 'reasonable excuse'.

HMRC have indicated four areas where a reasonable excuse may be considered.

(1) Compassionate circumstances.

(2) Transfer of a business as a going concern.

(3) Doubt about the liability of supplies.

(4) Uncertainty of employment status.

The existence of such circumstances cannot automatically ensure a defence. A person is expected to have acted as a conscientious business person in the circumstances and be able to demonstrate that fact, with documentation as appropriate.

For a further explanation of these issues, see **Chapter 31**.

3.2.11 Appealable matters

A person may appeal to the VAT and Duties Tribunal with respect to registration and the cancellation of registration. Appeals are also permitted where a person applied for registration as an intending trader where this application is refused by HMRC (*Dewhirst* [1996] BVC 4,228). Similarly, Customs' decision to cancel a registration on the grounds that the person was not carrying on a business was also a matter the tribunal could consider (*Brookes* [1995] BVC 681).

There is no appeal regarding the length of a prescribed accounting period as notified on a VAT registration Certificate (*Punchwell Ltd* (1981) 1 BVC 1,153).

A person may also appeal against any liability to a penalty, and against the quantum of that penalty. This includes the circumstances resulting in the default penalised and the calculation of the penalty.

3.2.12 Registration in respect of self-supplies and deemed supplies

In certain circumstances, a person may become registrable in respect of specified self-supplies and deemed supplies. The main areas to be considered are 'reverse charge' services, the change of use of certain buildings where zero-rated supplies had previously been made, certain in-house construction services, and the supply of a building or land which is a capital asset.

A person who is the recipient of certain services, where those services are received in the course of a business carried on by him, is deemed to make a supply of those services. These 'reverse charge' services are also called 'Schedule 5' services, as they are listed in VATA 1994, Sch. 5.

Since registration depends upon both the value of supplies made, or deemed to have been made, and the time those supplies were deemed to have been made, consideration must be given to both the value and time of supply. Where the services are paid in money, the value of the supply is the amount paid, and the time of supply is the date the money is paid. Where the services are paid by any other means, the value of the supply is the amount of money being equivalent to the consideration actually paid. The time of supply is the last day of the prescribed accounting period, being 31 March, 30 June, 30 September, or 31 December, whichever is the case (VATA 1994, Sch. 6, para. 8; VAT Regulations 1995 (SI 1995/2518), regs. 25(1), 82).

Where a person benefits from a zero-rated supply in relation to a building intended for use solely or partly for relevant residential and relevant charitable purposes and:

- within ten years, there is a grant of the building or any part to which zero-rating applied; or
- within ten years, there is a use of the building, or any part to which zero-rating applied, which is for a purpose which is neither relevant residential or relevant charitable use,

there is a deemed taxable supply. See VATA 1994, Sch. 10, para. 1.

The value of the deemed supply was, before 1 June 2002, the value of the original zero-rated supply. From 1 June 2002, the value of the supply reduces by 10 per cent for each complete year of relevant residential or relevant charitable use (VAT (Buildings and Land) Order 2002 (SI 2002/1102)).

The ten-year period commences when the person completes the building, or the person leases the building or relevant part of it. From that point in time, there remains a theoretical risk that a taxable supply will occur, with the necessity to register, where the specified limit is breached.

A supply occurs where a person undertakes construction work on his own behalf and where the value of such work exceeds £100,000. For this rule to apply, the person has to perform any of the following:

- the construction of a building;
- the extension of a building, or the construction of an annex, where the floor area of the original building is increased by at least ten per cent;
- the construction of a civil engineering work; or
- any demolition work, which is either preparatory to, or carried out contemporaneously with any of the previous work (VAT (Self-Supply of Construction Services) Order 1989 (SI 1989/472)).

Where a registered person who is fully taxable undertakes such work, there is no loss of tax. However, a non-registered person who is in business may find that he is required to register, and charge output tax on the deemed supply, but not be able to reclaim that amount as input tax.

Ordinarily, the supply of a capital asset is excluded from the value of supplies in ascertaining whether a person has exceeded the registration limit or will during the following 30 days. However, a supply of land or a building which would otherwise be positive-rated (i.e. at the standard rate or the lower rate) has to be included in the value of taxable supplies. A person making no other taxable supplies may be required to be registered in such circumstances.

Law: VATA 1994, Sch. 1, para. 1(8)

3.2.13 Registration in respect of acquisitions

Where goods are acquired by a UK business from a business established in another EU member state, the UK business will be required to register for VAT if the value of the goods acquired exceeds the acquisitions threshold, then the UK business is liable to register for VAT. This operates in a similar manner to the normal VAT registration tests as there are both historic and future tests for acquisitions. The historic test, however, is not on a rolling basis, but operates on a calendar year basis. This does not mean that the turnover is only checked once a year (at the end of December), but throughout the year. HMRC must be notified as soon as the turnover level is breached in the calendar year. For example, if on 20 July 2012 Jones Ltd, a UK non-VAT registered business had purchased goods worth £80,000 since 1 January 2012 from businesses established in France, Germany and Italy, then Jones Ltd would be liable to register for VAT by 31 July 2012 and must notify HMRC by 31 August 2012. Jones Ltd will become registered on 1 September 2012. This registration rule applies to both UK entities and persons based overseas where the overseas person has acquired goods in the UK from EU suppliers.

3.2.14 Supplies deemed to be made in the UK

Where a supply is deemed to be made in the UK the person deemed to be making the supply has to register for VAT if the VAT registration threshold is exceeded. This includes reverse charge services and supplies that are supplied where performed hired goods, etc.

Reverse charge supplies include services such as those that are supplied where performed, hired goods, telecommunication services, electronically supplied services or services relating to land. Where an unregistered person receives these services that person treats them as being both supplied to and from himself. The value of the supply is the consideration and VAT is due in addition to this value. If the recipient is unregistered, the value of the services will be included in the turnover of the business and will count towards the VAT registration threshold.

Other services are regarded as being supplied where performed. Where these are supplied in the UK and the VAT registration threshold is breached the person making the supply must register for VAT. This includes supplies relating to land and property, entertainment, exhibition, educational services, passenger transport services and services in respect of the letting of goods on hire. Similar rules also apply to non-UK intermediary that arrange a supply in the UK and the customer is not VAT registered. The intermediary is responsible for accounting for VAT on the supply. If the intermediary is not VAT registered in the UK, he becomes liable to register if the supplies he makes (including any other supplies made in the UK) exceed the VAT registration threshold.

3.2.15 Supplying goods in the UK on which an 8th or 13th Directive refund has been claimed

The value of a supply (sale, or otherwise disposing of an asset) of goods on which someone has claimed – or intends to claim – an 8th or 13th Directive refund counts towards the VAT registration threshold. Where the threshold is breached registration is compulsory.

3.2.16 Electronic supplies

A special scheme applies where non-EU businesses supplying electronic services (but not goods) to EU consumers. Services included in this scheme include website supply or web hosting services, the maintenance of programs and equipment, the supply of software, images, text and information and making available databases, the supply of music, films and games, distance teaching and political, cultural, artistic, sporting, scientific, educational or entertainment broadcasts. There is no registration threshold and registration and payment of VAT due is undertaken electronically. Further details are included in **Chapter 26**.

3.3   Registration

3.3.1 Registration planning decisions

Prior to registration, or when registration is considered, it is necessary to consider some general VAT planning or housekeeping.

3.3.2 Registration: taxable supplies to final consumers

The main reason for wishing not to register, or to defer registration, arises where the business makes positive-rated supplies to final consumers. In this case the VAT chargeable on the supplies is effectively a cost to the business. Assuming that the tax on inputs is less than that on outputs, an advantage will be gained by not having to register.

3.3.3 Smaller businesses

The main possible ways of avoiding needing to register are as follows.

1.   Keeping the business small, so that the turnover threshold is never exceeded. The disadvantage of this approach is that it puts a definite restriction on the level of income which can ever be derived from the business.

2.   Having several businesses, each operated by a different entity and having turnover below the turnover threshold. The disadvantages of this approach are:

   (a)   complexity of accounting, and need to avoid supplies between the businesses which might trigger a registration requirement;

   (b)   risk of failing to achieve an effective separation of activities, with retrospective registration and possible penalties;

   (c)   risk of an anti-disaggregation direction treating the various entities as being one for VAT purposes (although this would not have retrospective effect); and

   (d)   the structure is unlikely to be ideal commercially or for direct tax purposes.

3.   Finding a way to recharacterise the supplies so that they are properly treated as being exempt from VAT. This is an advantage where the customers of the business are final consumers or other persons that cannot reclaim VAT (banks, education sector, health sector, etc.). Where the customer can reclaim VAT it is a disadvantage to make exempt supplies as the person making exempt supplies cannot reclaim VAT incurred on its expenditure.

Planning point

Even if registration will eventually be necessary, a business supplying final consumers can, depending on the balance between input tax and output tax, make significant savings by deferring registration until the registration threshold is exceeded.

Example 3.12

A business expects to turn over up to £45,000 per month and this proves to be the actual level of turnover.

At the end of month 1 its turnover has not exceeded the registration threshold.

At the end of month 2 its turnover has exceeded the turnover limit (£77,000 from 1 April 2012), and notification of liability to register must be made within 30 days. The business is then registered from the first day of month 4.

Over the first three months of trading the business has turned over £135,000 free of VAT, saving output tax of £22,500, as this amount would otherwise be VAT at 20 per cent (1/6th of £135,000). Against this must be set any loss of input tax. This is on the assumption that no customers can reclaim any VAT charged to them and that the business could not increase its prices by the 20 per cent VAT rate.

Planning point

The deferment of registration may not be particularly valuable for businesses with high levels of input tax, such as those dealing in standard-rated goods, who may prefer to accept a slight cost for greater administrative simplicity and elimination of risk, by registering early. High levels of input tax will certainly be incurred if there are high set-up costs, although it must be remembered that the VAT incurred on most goods that remain on-hand at the date of registration and certain services incurred in the six months prior to registration can be reclaimed.

Delaying VAT registration will be of most benefit to suppliers of final consumers who have low inputs, such as:

- service industries supplying consumers, such as hairdressers;
- service industries serving exempt businesses, such as a consultant to certain financial sector businesses; and
- businesses with standard-rated outputs but zero-rated inputs, such as restaurants.

3.3.4 Larger businesses

Notwithstanding the advantages of deferring registration, these are likely to be irrelevant to larger businesses unless they can do so by finding some way of entirely recharacterising the supplies made so as to become exempt from VAT (or zero-rated, in which case registration will be an advantage).

> ### *Planning point*
>
> A larger business will usually benefit by registering as early as possible, to minimise uncertainties, ease administration and obtain the most rapid recovery of input tax on costs, including start-up costs.

3.3.5 Pre-registration input tax

Any business delaying registration but which may ultimately wish, or need, to register needs to bear in mind the treatment of pre-registration input tax. This can be recovered where it relates to goods still on hand at registration or services that have not effectively been incorporated into onward supplies before registration. However, it is not possible to recover input tax on:

- services obtained more than six months before registration; or
- goods obtained more than four years (three years before 1 April 2010) before registration. For further details see **2.4.3**

> ### *Planning point*
>
> It is essential in considering the timing of registration to have proper regard to these pre-registration inputs, which can be disproportionately large when there are significant start-up costs.

> ### ⚠ *Warning!*
>
> Where an entity registers late for VAT it cannot reclaim any VAT incurred before these time limits. This may be a significant disadvantage to any business that is not making any supplies for a long period (for example, it may be undertaking considerable development of a product, or undertaking research that may, or may not lead to taxable supplies). Where the business is actively undertaking *economic activity* it can register for VAT and claim back VAT on its expenditure as long as it hopes and expects there to be taxable supplies. Once that expectation ceases it will no longer be able to claim the VAT incurred on expenditure as it no longer expects to make taxable supplies; thus, early registration is advisable.

3.3.6 Registration: taxable supplies to taxable persons

A business making taxable supplies to persons who can recover the tax charged will almost certainly wish to register from the earliest possible moment, since the liability to charge output tax will cause no difficulties and the prompt registration will protect input tax recovery.

3.3.7 Voluntary registration and intending trader registration

A business that is making taxable supplies falling below the registration limit is entitled to register for VAT voluntarily if it wishes.

A business which does not yet make taxable supplies but intends to do so can register for VAT as an intending trader if it satisfies HMRC of its business activity and its intention to make supplies.

> **Planning point**
>
> This can be extremely useful to businesses with substantial preparatory activities, enabling them to recover tax on the costs incurred as they arise.

In the case of an intending trader, the State is entitled to objective evidence of the existence of the business activity and the intention to make taxable supplies but cannot refuse the registration and input tax recovery once these factors are established (*Rompelman v Minister van Financiën* (Case 268/83) (1985) 2 BVC 200,157).

3.3.8 Abortive business activity

It should be noted that, once the right to intending trader registration and consequent input tax recovery has been established, the input tax cannot be recouped from the taxable person if the business activity ultimately proves abortive, so that no taxable supplies are ever in fact made (*Intercommunale voor Zeewaterontzilting (INZO) v Belgian State* (Case C-110/94) [1996] BVC 326). If supplies are made, but are exempt rather than taxable, the input tax must be recharacterised as exempt and in those circumstances will become repayable to HMRC.

3.3.9 Eliminating block points

Once it is decided that the entity making supplies to third parties is to register for VAT, either because this is advantageous or because it is compulsory, it is necessary to review the position of any other entities involved with the overall business activity to see that no block points are unnecessarily created.

The most obvious case in which this might happen is where it is decided that the business premises should be held in a separate entity from the main operating business. If this entity incurs significant input tax in respect of the property but its supplies of letting the property to the main operating business are exempt, then this creates a block point and the input tax is lost.

The most obvious way around this is for the property-owning business to opt to tax, register for VAT and charge VAT on the rents. Where the operating business, however, is partly exempt rather than fully taxable this may be undesirable or even prevented by anti-avoidance provisions (see **17.11**). The full ramifications of opting to tax must in any case be considered before reaching a decision on this.

Another possibility might be for the property-owning entity to occupy the premises and employ the staff itself, and provide the operating entity with general business services rather than a lease or licence to occupy the property.

If the entities concerned are limited companies and the ownership requirements are met, it might be desirable to obtain group treatment so that supplies between them are ignored and the input tax concerning the property can be linked directly with the taxable supplies to third parties.

If the operating entity is a partnership but the property is to be owned by one of the partners, consideration might be given to constituting the property-owning entity as a separate partnership, with the other partners in the operating partnership owning some minuscule share in it. This could achieve a very similar commercial result but with the entities being identical for VAT purposes and so eliminating the internal property supplies and creating a direct link between the property input tax and taxable supplies to third parties.

3.3.10 Cash flow

Where there are going to be recurring taxable supplies between taxable entities forming part of the overall operation, it is worth considering applying for different VAT accounting periods in order to optimise cash flow, although HMRC are increasingly resistant to this form of simple planning.

This may, however, be regarded as avoidance and may require disclosure to HMRC **Chapter 32**.

3.3.11 Exempt supplies

A business making only exempt supplies has no need or entitlement to register for VAT. An entity making both taxable and exempt supplies may need to register or otherwise be able to do so voluntarily.

> **Planning point**
>
> It is important to ensure that irrecoverable input tax is not *generated* in the hands of the exempt or partly exempt entity due to VAT arising on a recharge or charge by an associate relating to costs which did not bear VAT in the first instance.

The most common example of this is where the staff working in the business are employed by an associate which makes a charge for their services. In this case it may be preferable for the operating entity to employ the staff directly or for there to be joint contracts of employment. Where the employees are paid by the taxable entity it is important to show that the employees are actually employed and working for the exempt entity and that the taxable entity is only acting as a *paymaster*. When the entity operating the payroll charges the other for the services of the staff then, provided this merely represents an exact recharge of the employment costs for the staff's work for that entity, it is not regarded as consideration for a supply and no VAT charge arises. Any additional charge for operating the payroll will be subject to VAT in the ordinary way.

As noted above regarding properties, an alternative in the case of companies is to apply for a group treatment while, in the case of partnerships, it may be possible to bring about a position where the partners are identical so that the entities are treated as one for VAT purposes.

Other guidance: VAT Notice 700/34 Staff

3.3.12 Start-up costs

It is necessary to distinguish between transactions involved in setting up the various entities and in raising necessary finance, and those connected with the development of the business itself. The input tax on the latter should normally be directly attributable to the ongoing supplies of the business, or at worst treated as residual for partial exemption purposes. The former may involve one-off supplies in themselves, which could lead to potential complications.

For instance, if the start-up results from some kind of restructuring of a previous business, the matters discussed above at **2.2.5** may be relevant.

It is also not uncommon for cash to be raised by a sale and leaseback of assets such as land. This again involves specific supplies by and to the business and the position needs to be examined carefully before proceeding. For example, are the sales taxable or exempt? If exempt, can they be made taxable by opting to tax, and if so, is this desirable or not? Is the leaseback taxable or exempt, and again would it be desirable to make an exempt leaseback taxable?

The implications of these transactions need to be considered for VAT to be charged and reclaimed as well as the SDLT and direct tax implications.

> **Planning point**
>
> In planning the commencement of a business it is essential to remember that the treatment at the start may vary significantly from the ongoing position.

3.3.13 Uncertainties, special schemes, etc.

The commencement of a business is the best time for identifying and resolving any uncertainties of treatment of its expected activities (possibly by formal agreement with HMRC). It is possible to address such matters before there are existing risks and while there may still be time to mitigate any likely future loss by altering the proposed arrangements, without causing undue disruption. Once agreement has been reached HMRC should be asked to confirm the position in writing.

Where any special schemes, optional or compulsory, apply there may be formalities to comply with or a need to agree with HMRC the details of their use.

> **Planning point**
>
> It is advisable to make a record, for each entity, of the major classes of supplies to and by it, their treatment, special schemes in use and any agreements reached with HMRC. This can then be used as a basis for periodic review of the position.

3.4 The registered person

3.4.1 Registration of natural persons

The following fall into this category:

- sole trader (or sole proprietor);
- partnership;
- trust; and
- members of a club or association, or organisation.

A partnership will be registered in the name of the firm, and no account shall be taken of any change in the partnership, where individuals leave or join the partnership. Although a partnership is not a legal person distinct from the persons constituting the partnership, VAT law effectively treats the partnership as a person. An individual is treated as a member of a partnership until HMRC are notified that he has ceased to be a member. Thus, the person remains liable for any VAT due for the period during which he was a member.

In the event of any change in the constituent members of a partnership, no account is made of that, except the addition or removal or both, of individual partners (VATA 1994, s. 45).

A trust is registered in the name of the trustees. There is no specific provision for the registration of a trust and they are dealt with by HMRC as if they are partnerships.

A 'club, association or organisation' managed by its members or by a committee of its members may be registered in its own name. Any change in membership is not required to be notified to HMRC. There is, however, a joint and several liability which falls upon the following.

1.   Every officer of the club or association or organisation, i.e. president, chairman, treasurer, secretary or similar officer.

2.   In default of those above, every member of a committee.

3.   In default of those above, every member of the club or association or organisation.

Law: VATA 1994, ss. 45–46; VAT Regulations 1995 (SI 1995/2518), reg. 8

3.4.2   Registration of legal persons

The following fall into this category:

*   limited company (body corporate), whether private or public;
*   limited liability partnership (see Limited Liability Partnership Act 2002; *Business Brief 3/01*);
*   corporate trustees;
*   co-owners of land; and
*   European Economic Interest Grouping.

Such a body is an association of individuals. Where it is incorporated, it is then a legal person distinct from its members. Commonly, such bodies are incorporated under the Companies Acts; however, bodies may also be incorporated under:

*   the Further and Higher Education Act 1992;
*   the Building Societies Act 1986;
*   the Credit Unions Act 1979; or
*   the Industrial and Provident Societies Act 1967.

A number of companies may be registered as a group. This is covered in **Chapter 4** on VAT groups.

Note that a European Economic Interest Grouping is an association formed by businesses or enterprises from at least two EU member states, established to encourage cooperation across national boundaries and between similar businesses. Under the European Economic Interest Groupings Regulations 1989 (SI 1989/638), where a Grouping has its official address in the UK, it is required to be registered with Companies House. Similar arrangements exist in some, but not all, EU member states.

3.4.3   Registration of co-owners of land

The legislation provides for the registration where there is a supply consisting of the grant, or assignment or surrender, of any interest in or right over land, including a licence to occupy land, where that grant, assignment or surrender is made by more than one person. The section provides that co-owners are treated as 'the property owner', which is treated as a taxable person in its own right. The persons shall be individually liable for any obligations of the property owner.

> **Planning point**
>
> To all intents and purposes, co-owners of land are treated for VAT purposes as a partnership. Although this is an effective legal fiction, it is sensible to think in these terms when dealing with the property affairs of co-owners.

Regulations have yet to be made under this section.

Law: VATA 1994, s. 51A

3.4.4 Registration of government bodies

Directive 2006/112, art. 13(1) excludes from its definition of taxable persons, 'states, regional and local government authorities and other bodies governed by public law' in respect of activities or transactions in which they engage as public authorities.

Such a body shall not be excluded from the definition where it undertakes activities that may lead to significant distortion of competition. This matter was addressed in *Metropolitan Borough of Wirral* [1997] BVC 2,211. It was held that to treat its activities as non-taxable:

> 'would bear unfairly on private organisations which would be accountable for VAT on similar work, and the distortive effect of such treatment would be significant within the meaning of Article 60-081.'

Such a body shall also not be excluded from the definition where it undertakes activities falling within a specified list (Directive 2006/112, Annex I). Thus, where a public body carries out such activities, it may be liable to be registered.

VATA 1994, s. 41 provides that a government department may be registered for VAT. Such a body may claim refunds of VAT paid in respect of non-business activities.

A local authority (as defined in VATA 1994, s. 96(4)) shall be registered if it makes any taxable supplies.

VATA 1994, s. 33 provides that certain statutory bodies may claim a refund for VAT paid in respect of non-business activities.

3.4.5 Registration of terminal markets

VATA 1994, s. 50 provides for simplification measures in respect of persons involved in terminal markets (or commodity markets). Special rules apply to a person making supplies of investment gold but who is not a member of the London Bullion Market Association. A detailed explanation of these rules is beyond the scope of this publication.

3.4.6 Registration under the agricultural flat rate scheme

Although often thought of as a kind of quasi-VAT registration, the agricultural flat rate scheme is an altogether different provision, which is considered at **Sch6.15**. To register under the flat rate scheme it is first necessary to be registered for VAT (although application can be made simultaneously).

3.4.7 Registration of racehorse owners

Under an agreement with the thoroughbred horseracing and breeding industry, and with effect from 16 March 1993, horse owners who seek income through sponsorship and appearance money are treated as carrying on a business activity and may be registered for VAT purposes. Changes were made to the scheme, taking effect from 1 January 1998. Details of the scheme are in HMRC *VAT 700/67*.

It is not necessary to register under this scheme if the owner is registered for other activities (such as breeding or training) as the registration would be available for these other activities. If the owner is not VAT registered for other activities this scheme must be used to enable the race horse owner to register for VAT. This is essentially a scheme to permit race horse owners to register and reclaim VAT even though there may not be a large amount of output tax payable on sponsorship and prize money. Registration is permitted where the racehorse owner can either show that he has or will receive business income (such as sponsorship or appearance money) or the horse or horses are covered by a sponsorship arrangement registered at Weatherbys or by a trainer's sponsorship agreement registered at Weatherbys and the person is registered as an owner at Weatherbys.

Where the sponsorship for the horse is lost, the horse must be deregistered form the scheme unless the owner is actively seeking new sponsorship. HMRC usually allow six months to obtain new sponsorship.

The VAT registration process is the same as the normal process but one of two forms must also be submitted. These are form D1 (owners not in partnership) or D2 (owners in partnership). These forms can be obtained from and are to be returned to:

VAT Declarations
Weatherbys
Sanders Road
Wellingborough
Northants
NN8 4BX

Where a horse is part owned, the owner can register in his own name if he owns at least 50 per cent of the horse, but if less the registration must be a partnership with other joint owners.

VAT is due on any sponsorship received as well as appearance and prize money (distributed through Weatherbys). When a horse is disposed of VAT is due on the proceeds, but the second hand goods scheme can be used if no VAT was incurred on acquisition. A horse that is given away or put to a non-business use is subject to VAT on the open market value of the horse at the time it is given away. Input tax credits on expenditure relating to the horse can be reclaimed in the normal manner.

Special rules also apply to point-to-point horses. These can be registered for VAT the hunter chasing season only (January to June). The registration is available for a horse with a sponsorship agreement that is entered in a hunter chase. Fifty per cent of the VAT incurred can be claimed (as the registration is for 50 per cent of the year. The registration can be retained throughout the year if it can be demonstrated that the horse is to be entered into hunter chases in the following season and there is either existing sponsorship, or further sponsorship is to be obtained.

3.5 Registration of overseas persons

3.5.1 Registration in respect of distance sales

A person who makes supplies of specified description which involve the removal of the goods into the UK from another EU member state may be required to be registered in the UK. Such supplies are known as 'distance sales', although the phrase does not appear in the legislation. VATA 1994, Sch. 2 provides for registration for such persons. (Persons established in the UK may be liable to be registered in other EU member states in similar circumstances.)

Distance sales are defined as follows, where:

- the removal of the goods to the UK is under direction of the supplier;
- the supply does not involve the assembly or installation of the goods;
- the goods are acquired in the UK by a non-taxable person;
- the person supplying the goods is established in another member state;
- the supplies are made in the course of that person's business;
- deemed supplies are excluded where the goods are treated as being supplied for private or non-business use;
- goods removed from a place in one EU member state to a place in another EU member state are also excluded where that removal is in the course of the supplier's business; and
- sales of new means of transport are also excluded.

Where a person makes distance sales, a range of options must be considered as follows.

1. If a person is already registered in the UK under VATA 1994, Sch. 1, then any distance sales made into the UK are deemed to be made in the UK (VATA 1994, s. 7(4)).

2. If a person is not registered in the UK but makes distance sales of goods subject to excise duty, such as tobacco and alcohol, then he is liable to register, whatever the value of goods removed (Sch. 2, para. 1(3)).

3. If a person is not registered in the UK, and makes distance sales of goods not subject to excise duty, then he is liable to register once the cumulative value of those supplies in a calendar year exceeds the prescribed limit (Sch. 2, para. 1(1)). VAT charged in another EU member state on such supplies shall not be treated as part of the value of those supplies made.

4. If a person is not registered in the UK, but makes distance sales of goods not subject to excise duty, and he has opted in his home member state to treat those supplies as being made in the UK, then the person is liable to register in the UK, whatever the value of goods removed (Sch. 2, para. 1(2)).

5. A person not liable to be registered under Sch. 2 may request to be so registered. He must satisfy HMRC that:

    (a) he intends to make distance sales of goods subject to excise duty;
    (b) he intends to opt that his distance sales will be treated as being made in the UK; or
    (c) he intends to make supplies to which such an option has already been made (Sch. 2, para. 4).

Example 3.13

Anita is a person established in Italy who sells goods of value £75,000 to non-business customers in the UK, and who charges Italian VAT at the rate of 20 per cent. She accounts for £15,000 VAT in Italy, and her total income is therefore £90,000. Anita's taxable turnover for the purposes of para. 1(1) is £75,000, and she is therefore not obliged to register for VAT in the UK.

Subject to the discretion of HMRC, and subject to such conditions as they may impose, the person making distance selling supplies into the UK but under the registration threshold may be registered in the UK. HMRC would expect to see written evidence of the option to make distance sales and written evidence of the option to tax supplies in the UK. A person who makes such an option shall be registered for a minimum of two years, running from 1 January after he is registered (Sch. 2, para. 7(3)).

Such a person is also required to notify HMRC within 30 days of making the option to treat his distance sales as being made in the UK, or that he has made a supply in the UK (Sch. 2, para. 5).

The registration limit for distance sales is £70,000 and is based upon the calendar year, running from 1 January each year. This limit has not changed since 1993.

Liability to registration under this section must be on form VAT 1A. The application must be submitted to the Aberdeen VAT Office, Custom House, 28 Guild Street, Aberdeen AB9 2DY.

Law: VAT Regulations 1995 (SI 1995/2518), Sch. 1, form No. 6

Changes to registration particulars

A person registered in respect of distance sales is required to notify any change in the name, constitution or ownership of his business, or any event which requires a change in the register. Such notification must be within 30 days of the change occurring.

A person registered under this section is required to notify when he ceases to be registrable.

Deregistration

A person who ceases to be liable to be registered under this section may be deregistered. This shall take effect from a date agreed with HMRC.

Where a person was not liable to be registered, but chose to be registered, he shall cease to be registrable if he no longer intends to make an option to treat distance sales as being made in the UK, or he no longer intends to make such supplies as would be so opted. If such a person has contravened a condition of his registration, the registration may be cancelled from the date that the condition was contravened.

A distance selling registration can be cancelled if distance sales are expected to be less than £70,000 in the current year.

Penalties in respect of distance sales registration

The penalties for failing to register for distance sales are the same as for failing to register (see **3.2.9**). In addition, there are penalties for breach of regulatory provisions (see **Chapter 31**).

3.5.2 Registration in respect of acquisitions

Subject to certain minor exceptions, a UK business or organisation which purchases goods from a registered person in another EU member state, for removal into the UK, makes a taxable acquisition.

> ### *Planning point*
>
> An organisation which is not a taxable person in respect of its ordinary activities may find that it is liable to register under this section. Such an omission is understandable, given that, to a layman, an acquisition is not the same as a supply. This may leave the organisation liable to a penalty for failure to notify its liability for registration.

Having established that a person is making acquisitions which are taxable in the UK, a person is liable to be registered in respect of his taxable acquisitions when:

- at the end of any month, beginning at the start of January that year, the value of his taxable acquisitions has exceeded the specified limit ('historic turnover' rule); or
- at any time, the person expects that the value of his taxable acquisitions for the next 30 days will exceed the specified limit ('future turnover' rule).

The specified limit is the same as that for registration in respect of UK taxable supplies. Thus, with effect from 1 April 2012, the specified limit is £77,000.

In ascertaining the value of taxable acquisitions, the amount of any VAT charged on the transaction in another EU member state shall be excluded; also excluded shall be the last acquisition or supply of goods before removal from fiscal warehousing, under VATA 1994, s. 18.

A person shall not be liable to be registered if the value of the taxable acquisitions made in the previous full calendar year was below the specified limit and HMRC are satisfied that the value of the taxable acquisitions in the following year will not exceed that limit. However, this rule does not apply where a person expects to make taxable acquisitions exceeding the specified limit in the immediately-succeeding 30 days.

> ### Example 3.14
>
> David made taxable acquisitions of £45,000 in 2010. He makes taxable acquisitions of a similar value during 2011. However, on 1 May 2012, he secures a contract which involves taxable acquisitions worth £79,000 during May 2012. He then expects his taxable acquisitions to return to below £50,000 in 2013.
>
> David is liable to registration in respect of his acquisitions under para. 2(2).

A person liable to registration in respect of his taxable acquisitions is required to notify his liability within 30 days of the end of the month when he exceeded the specified limit. The person will be registered with effect from the end of the next month.

Where a person is registered under the future turnover rule, he must notify HMRC within the 30-day period. The person will be registered from the beginning of that 30-day period.

> ### *Planning point*
> In cases such as that highlighted by the example above, advance planning is required if at all possible. In order to obtain the goods VAT-free in the country of origin, it is necessary to quote a UK VAT number. Since it can take a number of weeks to go through the registration process, an early start is advisable.

Where a person makes taxable acquisitions but is not obliged to be registered, he may apply to be registered. The person is required to satisfy HMRC that he intends to make such acquisitions; written orders would normally suffice. HMRC may register such a person from an agreed date, although they may impose conditions on the registration. In particular, he is required to notify HMRC within 30 days of the first taxable acquisition he makes after registration. If registered, he is required to remain registered for a minimum of two years, from 1 January after the effective date of registration.

Liability to registration under this section must be notified on form VAT 1B, VAT Regulations 1995 (SI 1995/2518), Sch. 1, form 7. The application must be submitted to the Aberdeen VAT Office (see **3.5.1**).

Law: VATA 1994, Sch. 3, para. 2

Changes to registration particulars

A person registered in respect of acquisitions is required to notify any change in the name, constitution or ownership of his business, or any event which requires a change in the register. Such notification must be within 30 days of the change occurring.

A person registered under this section is required to notify when he ceases to be registrable.

Deregistration

A person who ceases to be liable to be registered under this section may be deregistered and is required to notify HMRC within 30 days of ceasing to be registrable. The deregistration shall take effect from the date he ceased to be so liable, or from a date agreed with HMRC.

Where a person was registered under this section, but was not required to be registered, the registration may be cancelled with effect from the date on which he was so registered.

Where a person who was not liable to be registered, but who was registered with the intention to make taxable acquisitions, either does not make such acquisitions or contravenes the conditions imposed by HMRC, his registration shall be cancelled. The registration may be cancelled from the date he expected to make an acquisition, although he did not do so, or from the date he contravened a condition imposed upon him, or from such later date as may be agreed.

Where a person was not registrable or makes no taxable acquisitions or contravenes the conditions imposed upon him, he will not be required to be registered for the two-year minimum normally applicable to voluntary registrations and will be deregistered by HMRC.

A person may cancel their registration for acquisitions if they expect their sales to fall below the registration limit, currently £77,000.

Penalties in respect of acquisitions registration

The penalties for failing to register in respect of acquisitions are the same as for failing to register (see **3.2.9**). In addition, there are penalties for breach of regulatory provisions (see **Chapter 31**).

3.5.3 Registration in respect of disposal of assets

This section was added with effect from 20 March 2000. It was designed as a measure to counter certain VAT avoidance schemes which took advantage of the fact that any disposal of assets is disregarded when ascertaining whether a person should be registered for VAT.

A UK person could not benefit from the scheme on the basis that he could not recover input tax. However, a person outside the UK could recover input tax through the Eighth or Thirteenth VAT Directives. He could then dispose of those goods VAT-free in the UK. This section creates a liability to register in this circumstance.

The legislation is based around the concept of a person making 'relevant supplies', being:

- taxable supplies of goods which were assets of the business; and
- supplies where the person, or a predecessor of the person, recovered VAT on the purchase of those goods, or of anything comprised in them.

This wording is designed to be relevant where one person makes the claim for repayment of goods and his business is sold as a going concern to another person before sale of those goods. It is also designed to be relevant where the goods purchased are made into different goods before resale.

There is no minimum value of supplies made or to be made before the person is liable to be registered. He is liable to be registered:

- if he has made any such supplies, in which case, the person is required to notify HMRC that he has made such supplies; and he will be registered from that date; or
- he intends to make such supplies within the next 30 days, in which case the person is required to notify HMRC before making such supplies, and he will be registered from the beginning of the 30-day period.

Where the person can satisfy HMRC that the relevant supplies would be zero-rated, then he may be exempted from registration under this section, if they think fit. HMRC may reject any request for exemption, either at the time the application is made or at any later time (VATA 1994, Sch. 3A, para. 7(1) and (4)).

Changes to registration particulars

Where a person is registered under this section and he then ceases to have the intention of making relevant supplies, he is required to notify HMRC within 30 days of such intention.

A person registered in respect of such supplies is required to notify any change in the name, constitution or ownership of his business, or any event which requires a change in the register. Such notification must be within 30 days of the change occurring.

A person who is exempted from registration is required to notify HMRC of any material change in the nature of the supplies he makes, or any material change in the proportion of zero-rated supplies that he makes.

Deregistration

A person may only be deregistered under this section where he satisfies HMRC that he has ceased to be liable to be so registered.

Penalties in respect of registration in relation to disposal of assets

The penalties for failing to register in respect of the disposal of assets are the same as for failing to register (see **3.2.9**). In addition, there are penalties for breach of regulatory provisions (see **Chapter 31**).

3.5.4 Non-established taxable persons

A Non Established Taxable Person (NETP) is a person who:

- is not normally resident in the UK;
- does not have a business establishment in the UK; or
- in the case of a limited company, is not incorporated in the UK.

An NETP may be liable to be registered for VAT under any of the above sections:

- if he makes taxable supplies;
- if he makes distance sales;
- if he makes taxable acquisitions; or
- if he makes a disposal of assets.

The person may also be registered on a voluntary basis, under any of the first three sections.

Prior to 1 January 2002, HMRC could direct that any NETP appoint a VAT representative. From that date the rules were relaxed, as they were throughout the EU, such that if the NETP is established either in the EU or in any state which has a 'mutual assistance' agreement with the UK, then HMRC cannot direct such a person to appoint a VAT representative. An NETP can, of course, choose to appoint a VAT representative.

An NETP, preferring not to appoint a VAT representative, can handle his own VAT affairs, including registration and related matters. The NETP's VAT affairs will be controlled from the Aberdeen VAT Office.

An NETP registering for VAT is required to complete the relevant form. If he appoints a VAT representative, he is required to complete form VAT 1TR.

An NETP can also appoint an agent to fulfil his responsibilities as regards UK VAT without taking on the obligations of a VAT representative. In these circumstances, the NETP is required to sign a form of authority appointing the agent. A copy of this must accompany any registration application where the agent's address is used as the NETP's UK address for VAT purposes (where the NETP has no other place of establishment in the UK, for example).

⚠ **Warning!**

Becoming a VAT representative involves taking on joint and several liability for VAT debts. It should therefore be avoided in favour of becoming an agent wherever possible.

Other guidance: HMRC *VAT Notice 700/1, s. 8*

3.5.5 Registration in other states

A UK-based organisation making supplies in the course of its business must be aware of the possibility of registration outside the UK. For example, if a person makes sales of goods to private persons in another EU member state, he may be required to be registered under the distance sales provisions in that state. Alternatively, a UK business may provide specified services which are determined as supplied where they are performed, or where the customer is based, and may therefore be liable to be registered in another state, see VATA 1994, s. 7A and Sch. 4A. Before 1 January 2010, the law on the place of supply of services was generally in VAT (Place of Supply of Services) Order 1992 (SI 1992/3121). The power conferred on the Treasury to make such an order was given under VATA 1994, s. 7(11). The omission of the words 'or services' from s. 7(11) by FA 2009, s. 76 and Sch. 36, para. 3(2), with effect in relation to supplies made on or after 1 January 2010, means that s. 7(11) no longer confers power on the Treasury to make statutory instruments relating to services (although the power continues in relation to supplies of goods).

Registration outside the UK is beyond the scope of this publication.

3.6 Disaggregation

3.6.1 Definition of disaggregation

The existence of a VAT registration limit creates a situation where a person trading just below the limit may be more competitive than a person operating a similar business but trading just over the limit. This is especially true where the customers are private persons and therefore unable to reclaim VAT, where there is little deductible input tax for the business and where the principal cost to the business is wages. A typical example is a restaurant within a pub.

One 'solution' to this situation is to disaggregate the business into two or more separate entities, such that each one trades below the registration limit. HMRC take the view that such avoidance is not only a loss to the public purse, but it creates a situation of unfair competition. They therefore have powers to aggregate the taxable turnover of such entities, so that they become registered for VAT. HMRC's powers are based on art. 10 of Directive 2006/112, which allows EU member states to treat as a single taxable person any number of persons who, although legally independent, are closely bound by financial, economic, and organisational links.

Prior to 19 March 1997, Customs had to be satisfied that a 'main reason' for the business separation was the avoidance of a VAT liability. From that date, the avoidance of VAT is only required to be an effect of the separation, rather than a reason for it.

HMRC's powers target 'artificial separation'. The intention is that a separation of an existing business for genuine reasons should not be caught. Similarly, where two or more businesses which were established separately, operate very closely, they should not be caught. However, the wording of the current legislation, and the restrictions relating to a successful appeal, mean that genuine arrangements may still be caught.

HMRC may issue a direction under this section when the following conditions are fulfilled, that:

- the person is making, or has made, taxable supplies;
- the activities in which he is involved form only part of certain activities, the other activities being carried on concurrently or previously, or both; and
- if all those taxable supplies were taken into account, the person would be liable to be registered for VAT.

The second condition above does not restrict the circumstances to a situation where activities are carried on concurrently but will include an arrangement where a person operates a series of separate businesses. The third condition provides a 'strict liability' such that where the cumulative taxable turnover exceeds the registration limit, then a direction may be issued.

A direction must be served on each person named in it. A supplementary direction may be issued where HMRC identify other persons who are involved in the activities in question. As a result of a direction, the 'single taxable person' will be liable to register for VAT. The 'single taxable person' is treated as a partnership and each partner is jointly and severally liable for the debts of the partnership.

Registration as a result of a direction can only apply from the date of the direction or, where specified, a later date. A direction cannot be backdated.

⚠ *Warning!*

Although HMRC cannot backdate a direction under this section, they may register a person from an earlier date on the basis that there only ever existed a single person from that date and throughout that period. That is to say, there was only ever one business run as a partnership between the various parties concerned. Thus, an assessment for back tax and a penalty may also be issued. It has to be said that HMRC sometimes choose this option, and do not issue a direction at all.

In addition, if a person has been subject to a disaggregation order, and HMRC believe that there is a further split in the business with a 'new' person making supplies, HMRC can issue an order that adds the new person to the registration from the date of the original order.

Example 3.15

Phil operates a fly fishing business. Phil registered for VAT on 1 January 2003. Phil's wife, Alice, runs a catering business that provides food for Phil's customers and has provided this service since 2003. HMRC form the view that this is essentially one business and issues a disaggregation order that joins the businesses together with effect from 1 July 2010. HMRC later observe, in 2011, that Roy, Phil's son, now provides a catering service. A further disaggregation notice is served on Phil and Roy, and Roy's business is joined to Phil's with effect from 1 July 2010.

HMRC have produced a Statement of Practice pertaining to disaggregation, which can be found in HMRC *VAT Notice 700/1*.

Law: VATA 1994, Sch. 1, para. 1A and 2

Other guidance: HMRC *VAT Notice 700/1, s. 14*

3.6.2 Appeals and cases

An appeal can be made against a direction but a tribunal will only allow such an appeal where it considers that HMRC have acted unreasonably (VATA 1994, ss. 83(u), 84(7)). This presents a stiffer challenge to the appellant. Where HMRC backdate a registration and issue an assessment then the ordinary grounds of appeal will apply.

Osman v C & E Commrs (1989) 4 BVC 132 considered the validity of Customs' jurisdiction, although it related to the law as it stood before 19 March 1997. The High Court held that the UK legislation does fairly reflect Directive 2006/112, art. 10.

In *Garton (t/a The Dolly Tub)* [2000] BVC 4,026, Customs chose not to issue a direction under this section (see para. 40, 50 and 54, of the decision) and backdated the registration, taking in four separate businesses (three limited companies and one partnership). The Tribunal held that the activities were independent and allowed the appeal. Comment was made that had Customs issued a direction, the outcome may have been different. Indeed, the appellant's representative admitted that he thought that an appeal against a direction would not have been successful.

One appeal succeeded against a direction on the basis that it was backdated, albeit by mistake. The error could not be considered to be immaterial to the direction, and the Tribunal held that it was therefore invalid, (*Elder* [1999] BVC 4,052).

In the case of *Trippitt* [2001] BVC 4,173, Customs issued a direction where a bed and breakfast business was operated in the same premises as a public house, a husband running the public house, and his wife running the bed and breakfast. The case may be considered a typical example of the review of a direction under this section.

The public house was registered for VAT in its own right, in Mr Trippitt's name. Mrs Trippitt ran the bed and breakfast and, for a period, provided bar snacks. Later, the kitchen was refurbished so that a full meal service could be offered, from which time the catering sales were included on the public house VAT returns. Mrs Trippitt's business continued to use the kitchen facilities. There was no formal written agreement between the parties, although Mrs Trippitt paid 35 per cent of her income to Mr Trippitt in payment for rent and the use of facilities. Mr Trippitt accounted for output tax on this amount.

In reviewing the whole arrangement, the Tribunal noted that some factors pointed in favour of a single business, and other factors in favour of separate businesses. Since a direction had been issued, the Tribunal could only allow the appeal if it considered that Customs had failed to come to a reasonable decision on the facts.

Those factors in favour of a single business are financial, economic or organisational links, including:

- that the businesses operated from the same premises;
- that all utility bills were paid by Mr Trippitt;

- that the lease for the property was in Mr Trippitt's name and there was no separate lease for Mrs Trippitt;
- that there was only one business insurance policy, one rates bill, and one telephone bill; and
- that some advertising material gave the impression of a single business.

In contrast, other factors in favour of there being separate businesses were that:

- there were separate business records and bank accounts;
- there were separate staff;
- the bed and breakfast business used the public house premises for meals, but only when the public house was not open;
- the previous owners had also operated two separate businesses from the same premises;
- Mrs Trippitt did make a contribution towards overheads, by her 35 per cent payment to Mr Trippitt; and
- there was a separate entrance for bed and breakfast guests, and a separate sign.

The tribunal held that Customs had failed to give sufficient weight to those factors which favoured the taxpayers' argument, and they should have reached a different decision. Thus, the separation was held not to have been artificial.

Although each case will necessarily turn on its own particular facts, this case demonstrates the tribunal's approach to such appeals. It also demonstrates that Customs' powers, although stronger since 1997, can be successfully challenged.

3.7   Transfer of a business as a going concern

3.7.1   Introduction

This is an area which causes some difficulty. In addition, since it is also an area with which some VAT avoidance has been associated, there are complex rules which may affect the unwary.

(See **13.3** for further details of this complex area.)

A TOGC occurs where the assets of a business are transferred from one person to another. The definition is provided by the VAT (Special Provisions) Order 1995 (SI 1995/1268), art. 5, which order is made under VATA 1994, s. 5(3).

The existing VAT registration number may be transferred to the new owner, under conditions found in the VAT Regulations 1995 (SI 1995/2518), reg. 6, which order is made under VATA 1994, s. 49. In such a case, both parties are required to complete a form VAT 68, which is their joint application for the transfer of a VAT registration number. (This form is at VAT Regulations 1995 (SI 1995/2518), Sch. 1, form 3.) There is no obligation to make such a transfer and, in most cases, the new owner may prefer to have a new VAT registration number.

> ### ⚠ *Warning!*
>
> Accepting the transfer of the VAT number involves accepting all previous VAT liabilities and entitlements. It is suggested therefore that only in the case of connected persons (husband taking wife into partnership, partnership incorporating, etc.) where there is no real transfer of risk, should the VAT 68 procedure be used. It has, however, been held at Tribunal that this liability only applies where the transferor has outstanding returns, and does not apply to errors on returns that have been submitted.

3.7.2 Definition of a TOGC

A TOGC is a transaction which is treated as neither a supply of goods nor a supply of services.

The conditions for a TOGC are that:

- the assets to be transferred must be used in carrying on the same type of business;
- the business, or part of the business, to be transferred must be capable of separate operation; and
- where the transferor is a taxable person, the transferee must become a taxable person as a result of the transfer, or already be a taxable person.

The leading VAT case related to this matter appears to be *Dearwood Ltd v C & E Commrs* (1986) 2 BVC 200,222. A number of other cases have been heard. These cases have provided other guidance as to whether a transfer should be treated as a TOGC.

Where the assets include a grant of an interest in, a right over or a licence to occupy land or property, and that grant has been 'opted to tax', then the TOGC will only include the land or property where the transferee also opts to tax the same land or property, confirms that their option to tax will not be disapplied, and notifies HMRC, accordingly, no later than the date of proposed transfer and fulfils certain other conditions. These are considered in greater detail at **14.4**.

Note that a transfer of a business can include a non-supply and a taxable supply. For example, where the transfer itself fulfils the above conditions, it is a non-supply. Where an opted property is included within the transfer but the new owner chooses not to opt to tax, then output tax will be chargeable for that part of the transfer only.

Where the business to be transferred consists of a property rental business, see **14.4**.

Special rules also apply where a business is transferred as a TOGC into a VAT group.

3.8 Registration Procedures

3.8.1 How to register for VAT

Notification of a liability to register or to voluntarily register can be made over the internet using HMRC's website (*www.hmrc.gov.uk*). It is necessary to create an account with HMRC to do this. There is a time delay between creating an account and being able to use electronic services so it is advisable to create an account a few days before registration is required or desired. To register for VAT, the business/taxable person must complete one or more forms and submit them to HMRC for approval. The form used and the number needed will depend on the business's particular circumstances. Most businesses only need to complete one form. Exceptions include partnerships, where you need to complete one extra (simple) form listing details of the partners, and registering a group of companies (see **Chapter 4**).

Most applications for VAT registration can be completed online (but see **3.8.3.1** below if you wish to register a group of companies or **3.8.4** for businesses trading internationally). All other VAT registration forms are available on the HMRC website. These need to be printed, completed by hand and posted to HMRC. To register for VAT Online or use other VAT online services, it is necessary to register with HMRC Online Services or the Government Gateway at: *https://online.hmrc.gov.uk/registration/* or go to *www.hmrc. gov.uk/vat/index.htm* and on the right hand side there is a link to register online. If this is clicked this allows the account to be created. Electronic registration is not mandatory and only Form VAT 1 is available for submission online. All the other supplementary forms required for VAT registration must be sent by post, though they can be downloaded from HMRC's website. Electronic registration does, however, have advantages; it is, for example, quicker, a guide is given to help completion of the form and feedback is provided by HMRC on the screen acknowledging receipt of the application.

A significant disadvantage of the online registration system is that only the VAT 1 can currently be lodged electronically. All other forms and information have to be sent to HMRC in hard copy format. HMRC are, however, looking to make amendments to their system shortly to add further facilities and allow other documents and forms to be lodged online.

A variation of the VAT 1 needs to be completed by all businesses that are required or wish to register for VAT in the UK and there are also certain other forms that may need to be submitted. These are:

(1)   VAT 1 – The VAT registration form for most businesses.

(2)   VAT 1A – Application form for distance selling into the UK.

(3)   VAT 1B – Application form for registration when acquisitions are made from other EU States and the goods are brought to the UK.

(4)   VAT 1C – Application form for VAT registration when a person that has made 8th or 13th Directive claims supplies goods in the UK.

(5)   VAT 1TR – Application form for distance selling into the UK and a tax representative is to be appointed.

(6)   VAT 2 – Application form for partnerships; this lists all the partners to be included in the registration (VAT 1 is also required).

(7)   VAT 50 & 51 – Application forms for Group Registration (VAT 1 is also required on the first registration of a group) VAT 51 gives the details of all the companies, VAT 50 is the application to group and amend the group.

(8)   VAT 68 – for transfer of a going concern transactions (TOGCs), where the transferee is taking on the transferor's VAT number.

Even where a person registers electronically they will still need to send supporting documentation to HMRC by post. The reference number given online must be noted on the supplementary information and it this reference number is put on every page submitted to HMRC to ensure no documentation is lost. Where it is decided to use paper forms these can be downloaded from HMRC's website and sent to:

Wolverhampton Registration Unit
HMRC
Deansgate
62-70 Tettenhall Road
Wolverhampton
WV1 4TZ

Wolverhampton also deals with VAT registrations where goods are acquired from other EU countries and for EU businesses making distance sales into the UK. These applications cannot be completed online.

The date of receipt by HMRC is treated as the date of notification.

A person that has not a place of establishment in the UK or where goods on which 8th or 13th Directive reclaims have been made must register at the Non Established Taxable Persons Unit. Online registration is not available for an overseas taxpayer.

Non Established Taxable Persons Unit
HMRC
Custom House
28 Guild Street
Aberdeen
AB11 6GY

A non-established person may, but does not have to, appoint a tax representative to act for them. The representative will keep records for the non-established business and will also be jointly and severally liable for any VAT owing by the non-established business. There is a clear risk in this for the representative, but it does, of course, provide HMRC with a degree of comfort that they can deal with a local representative that is liable for the VAT due. A non-established person can only appoint one representative (but the representative can act for several businesses). VAT form VAT 1TR needs to be completed to appoint a representative. HMRC can require that a tax representative is appointed, but only for countries where there is no mutual assistance agreement. Most 'western' countries have such an agreement. If the country where the business is established does not have such an agreement with the UK then form VAT 1TR must be completed to enable the application to be processed. An agent can be appointed instead of a representative but an agent is not liable for VAT debts, so HMRC may still require a tax representative to be appointed. Where a tax representative or agent is appointed:

- only one person at a time is to act as the business's tax representative of agent (although an agent or representative may act for more than one principal);
- the appropriate form must be completed to apply for registration; and
- the agent or representative requires to be authorised to act in VAT matters and this needs to be provided to HMRC before they will deal with the representative or agent.

Authorisation for an agent can be provided using the following form of words:

(Principal's name) of (Principal's address) appoints (name of UK agent) of (address of UK agent) to act as agent for the purpose of dealing with all their legal obligations in respect of VAT. This letter authorises the above named agent to sign VAT returns and any other document needed for the purpose of enabling the agent to comply with the VAT obligations of the principal.

Signed (by principal)   Date

For a business opting to tax a property, including TOGCs of a property rental business, a copy of Form VAT 1614, is required. Whilst it is not strictly necessary to send this to the Option to Tax Unit (the VAT registration unit will forward it on) it is recommended that this is sent to the Option To Tax Unit to ensure that both offices obtain a copy of the form. The Option To Tax Unit address is:

HMRC
Option to Tax Unit
Cotton House
7 Cochrane Street
Glasgow
G1 1GY

When applying for registration, the applicant must tell HMRC if they have been or are currently involved in any other VAT registration. This is so HMRC can assess the risk of any tax it may lose due to a default. If HMRC believe that there is a risk of default they have the power to ask for a security payment in advance or a guarantee. This is usually between 150 and 200 per cent of the estimated VAT due in a VAT period. The amount can be reduced by requesting monthly returns to reduce the amount that will be outstanding at any one time.

HMRC aims to process 70 per cent of applications within ten working days and most applications are actually processed within a month. HMRC have stated that they processed about 80 per cent of applications within ten days in the past year (67.5 per cent in 2010/11). Most delays are caused by forms being incomplete or by HMRC needing to make additional checks. Applicants are notified when further enquiries are being made in respect of their application, so if no notification or if the registration is not completed within two weeks HMRC should be contacted. HMRC expect additional checks to be completed within three months and have stated that only a handful of applications are actually taking longer than 50 days.

Delays can be reduced by ensuring that the VAT registration form is completed accurately and that it is complete (bank details, national insurance numbers, signed, etc). In addition, all required forms (such as VAT 2 for partnerships, VAT 50 and 51 for group registrations need to be sent in at the same time). Delays may arise where there is a complicated issue for example, property and construction businesses, Transfers of Going Concerns, commencing a business involved in a risk area such as mobile phones or micro chips, 'intending traders', finance companies, businesses where directors or officers have been involved in failed businesses in the past, businesses with no UK presence and where agents are involved.

3.8.2 Accounting for VAT before you receive your VAT registration number

A person that requests to be registered or is required to be registered from a certain date, must account for VAT from that date, even before the application is processed. VAT incurred in this period, plus VAT incurred before registration as appropriate can also be reclaimed once the registration is processed. Do get information about when you must register for VAT.

Until the VAT registration number is received, the business cannot actually charge VAT, or show VAT as a separate item on an invoice. Thus, the price of supplies made must be increased by an equivalent amount of the VAT that is going to be charged. When the VAT registration number is received, invoices can be reissued and amended to show the VAT registration number and the VAT charged.

3.8.3 Addresses

Where form VAT 1 (and a VAT 2 if appropriate) is printed and completed (rather than completed online) it should be sent to:

HM Revenue & Customs
Deansgate
62-70 Tettenhall Road
Wolverhampton
WV1 4TZ

For businesses opting to tax a property, including TOGCs of a property rental business, a copy of form VAT 1614 is required. HMRC state that it is not necessary to send this to the Option to Tax Unit as the VAT registration unit will forward this on, but many taxpayers and advisors prefer to ensure that both offices obtain a copy of the form (or the VAT 1 is submitted electronically and followed up with a postal VAT 1614 to both the registration unit and the Option to Tax Unit). If the person has already made an exempt supply of the land or building (sale, leasing or letting) before the date of the option, it is necessary to first obtain HMRC's written permission to opt to tax. However, this is not necessary if the conditions for automatic permission are met and HMRC is notified of the option to tax.

3.8.3.1   Group registration forms

Group registration forms cannot be completed online and the VAT 1, VAT 50 and VAT 51 must be sent to:

HM Revenue & Customs
Imperial House
77 Victoria Street
Grimsby
DN31 1DB

Similarly, applications for distance selling, acquisitions and dispatches cannot be completed online. These forms (VAT 1A, VAT 1B and VAT 1TR) should be sent to the Wolverhampton address above.

3.8.4   How to register for VAT if you do business internationally

A business that makes supplies in the UK (trades in the UK) but does not have any place of establishment in the UK must register with an office that is dedicated to Non-Established Taxable Persons (NETP) in Aberdeen. This office does not accept online applications and the VAT 1 must be downloaded, completed manually and posted to:

The Non Established Taxable Persons Unit (NETPU)
HM Revenue & Customs
Ruby House
8 Ruby Place
Aberdeen
AB10 1ZP

Similarly, a person disposing of 8th and 13th Directive goods must manually complete form VAT 1C and send this to the NETP office in Aberdeen.

3.8.5 Variations

HMRC are also to be informed of changes of details including the name or trading name of the business, the principal address of the business, where there is a change to the legal status of your business (for example a change from sole trader to partnership or limited company), bank account details, the main business activity, or the composition of the partnership. These details are to be sent to the Grimsby unit.

HM Revenue & Customs
Imperial House
77 Victoria Street
Grimsby
DN31 1DB

HMRC's administrative requirements change frequently and further information can be obtained from the National Advice Service on 0845 010 9000 or from HMRC's website.

3.9 Pre Registration Input Tax

3.9.1 Outline

Details of the VAT that can be reclaimed on expenditure prior to registration is given at **2.4.3**.

3.9.2 Re-Registration

A business that de-registers for VAT has to account for VAT on a deemed supply of any goods on hand, subject to a de minimis limit upon which it has claimed input tax (no matter how small that input tax credit is). If the business re-registers and it has, on re-registration, any of the goods on hand upon which it has made a deemed supply due to de-registration, it is not immediately apparent that an input tax credit can be claimed. This is because when the deemed supply was made no tax invoice was issued, so there is no tax invoice to support the claim for input tax on registration. HMRC had, however, previously allowed an 'input tax credit' to be claimed by concession and now permits a claim, not by concession, but because HMRC believe that it has discretion to allow such a claim for an input tax credit under the VAT Regulations 1995 (SI 1995/2518), reg. 29 to allow alternative evidence (documents that show that VAT was paid on the deemed supply on de-registration) under reg. 111. Consequently, where there is proof that VAT was paid to HMRC on the deemed supply on de-registration, this will be accepted as alternative evidence to support a claim for input tax. Due to this change the previous concession is no longer required and has been withdrawn.

3.10 Case law regarding registration

1. Property letting: *C & E Commrs v Morrison's Academy Boarding Houses Association* (1977) 1 BVC 108.

    The Association was a company limited by guarantee and although not a registered charity, was accepted as a charity by the Inland Revenue. It let accommodation to children boarding at the Academy and parents were invoiced separately from the school fees. The activities of the company were carried out without a view to making a profit, and it claimed it was not carrying on a business. The court ruled in favour of Customs, holding that the lack of profit motive was irrelevant. The meaning of the word 'business' was wide enough to encompass any actively pursued occupation or function with reasonable continuity.

2. Religion: *Church of Scientology of California v C & E Commrs* (1980) 1 BVC 343.

    The Church of Scientology was incorporated in California and had the objects of propagating the faith of scientology. From premises in Sussex it provided training and auditing courses and made sales of books, E meters and other equipment. It appealed against Customs' contention that it was making taxable supplies, contending that a body which propagated religious philosophy should not be treated as carrying on a business. The court rejected this contention and ruled in favour of Customs.

3. Statutory body: *Institute of Chartered Accountants in England and Wales v C & E Commrs* [1999] BVC 215.

    The Institute is a recognised supervisory body, issuing certificates authorising or licensing its members to carry on investment business, insolvency and audit work. In this case, Customs argued that the Institute was not in business so it should not account for output tax on its income, nor recover input tax on its expenditure. The tribunal and on appeal the High Court and House of Lords all agreed that the predominant concern of licensing activities was the implementation of the statutory policy of protecting the public interest through self-regulation of the relevant practitioners, and did not amount to the carrying on of a business.

4. Legal aid and assistance: *Hillingdon Legal Resources Centre Ltd* (1990) 5 BVC 837.

    The company was a registered charity and provided legal aid and assistance free of charge to poor people in the borough of Hillingdon. It had recovered all of its input tax and Customs raised an assessment on the basis that the VAT incurred on the services provided free of charge was not recoverable. The tribunal upheld the assessment, holding that the services provided for no consideration were not carried on in the course or furtherance of a business.

5. Children's day nursery: *C & E Commrs v Yarburgh Children's Trust* and *St Paul's Community Project* [2005] BVC 12.

Both Yarburgh Children's Trust and the organisation running the playgroup, Yarburgh Community Playgroup, were registered charities. A building was constructed by the Trust, with help from Lottery funding, which let it to the Playgroup at a rent that was less than market value. The court determined that under the circumstances, the lease merely provided for the use of the building by the second charity and did not constitute a business activity. Furthermore, in common with *St Paul's*, it determined that the activities of the Playgroup were not by way of a business because it was operated on a voluntary basis and the charges were set merely to meet operating costs, not with a view to making a profit. The building therefore enjoyed the benefit of zero-rating as a charitable, non-business building.

From case law there are a number of guidelines which must be considered in determining whether an organisation is in business or not.

1. Is the activity a serious undertaking earnestly pursued?

2. Is the activity an occupation or function that is actively pursued with reasonable and recognisable continuity?

3. Does the activity have a certain measure of substance in terms of the quarterly or annual value of taxable supplies?

4. Is the activity conducted in a regular manner and on sound and recognised business principles?

5. Is the real nature of the activity predominantly concerned with the making of supplies for a consideration?

6. Are the taxable supplies that are being made of a kind which, subject to differences in detail, are commonly made by those who seek to profit from them?

3.11 Registration records

The following section examines the details that need to be checked on registration.

Note: The certificate of VAT registration, form VAT 4, will be sent to the business following notification that registration has been allowed.

Check that the correct registration number and business details are shown:

(a) name and address;
(b) bank details;
(c) legal entity; and
(d) trade classification.

The business must notify HMRC of changes in circumstances for the amendment of registration details, including:

(a) to the business:

  (i)   the name or trading name;
  (ii) the address of the place of business or any partner;
  (iii) the trade classification;

(b) to the legal entity:

  (i)   the composition of a partnership;
  (ii) the liability status from unlimited to limited or vice versa; and

(c) to the bank details:

  (i)   the bank or National Giro account number or sorting code.

Planning point

The provision of bank details normally means speedier repayments from HMRC.

Note: Other changes may require the cancellation of registration.

Has the business notified HMRC on form VAT 902 or by letter within 30 days of the change?

If the business is using the annual accounting scheme, have the following been notified of any relevant changes:

(a) the bank; and
(b) the VAT central unit annual accounting section?

3.12 Overseas traders in the UK

If an overseas business makes supplies of goods or services in the UK (or which would be taxable if supplied in the UK) and either:

(a) has a business establishment in the UK; or
(b) makes supplies to EU customers upon receipt of evidence of business status,

then in order to recover UK VAT input tax on purchases the business may either:

(a) require to register in the UK; or
(b) choose to be registered.

Has the overseas business checked whether compulsory registration is required in respect of its UK business activities?

Does the overseas business make supplies of services over the internet to private individuals? If so, is it correctly accounting for VAT either through an EU VAT registration or under the special VAT accounting scheme for overseas businesses?

3.13 Registration thresholds

Previous registration limits

17 March 1993–30 November 1993	£37,600
1 December 1993–29 November 1994	£45,000
30 November 1994–28 November 1995	£46,000
29 November 1995–26 November 1996	£47,000
27 November 1996–29 November 1997	£48,000
30 November 1997–31 March 1998	£49,000
1 April 1998–31 March 1999	£50,000
1 April 1999–31 March 2000	£51,000
1 April 2000–31 March 2001	£52,000
1 April 2001–24 April 2002	£54,000
25 April 2002–9 April 2003	£55,000
10 April 2003–31 March 2004	£56,000
1 April 2004–31 March 2005	£58,000
1 April 2005–31 March 2006	£60,000
1 April 2006–31 March 2007	£61,000
1 April 2007–31 March 2008	£64,000
1 April 2008–30 April 2009	£67,000
1 May 2009–31 March 2010	£68,000
1 April 2010–31 March 2011	£70,000
1 April 2011–31 March 2012	£73,000
1 April 2012 to date	£77,000

VAT Implications of Different Structures (Groups, Divisions, Partnerships etc)

4.1 Groups of companies

There are special rules for groups of companies that, in broad terms, enable a group to be treated as a single entity for VAT purposes. This helps to recognise the fact that, in many cases, the companies in a group are so interlinked as to amount, in reality, to a single business entity. The same sort of economic and financial linkage can, of course, occur between entities that are not limited companies; however, there is no similar treatment available in such cases.

Group treatment of companies is not compulsory. It is an option the companies concerned can choose to exercise, subject to the consent of HMRC.

Application for group treatment between some or all of the companies in a potential VAT group can have a significant effect on the overall VAT liability of the group. It is particularly important where partial exemption is concerned, and especially if there are taxable supplies passing between members of the group.

> **Planning point**
>
> The group treatment rules therefore provide a powerful VAT planning tool. It should be noted, however, that the position is as with most VAT planning – the tools available can help to avoid unnecessary VAT costs without undue changes in the business structure but are not usually suited to the creation of schemes to avoid tax which is properly due.

4.2 Group treatment: General

There are special rules for groups of companies which, in broad terms, enable a group to be treated as a single entity for VAT purposes. This helps to recognise the fact that in many cases the companies in a group are so interlinked as to amount, in reality, to a single business entity. The same sort of economic and financial linkage can, of course, occur between entities that are not limited companies; however, there is no similar treatment available in such cases. Grouping is intended to be an administrative easement, as only one return needs to be submitted and VAT is not chargeable on supplies made between the group entities. It is also true, however, that VAT grouping can give distinct VAT advantages. Hence, HMRC are interested in 'controlling' grouping to protect the Revenue.

Group treatment of companies is not compulsory. It is an option that the companies concerned can choose to exercise, subject to the consent of HMRC.

Application for group treatment between some or all of the companies in a potential VAT group can have a significant effect on the overall VAT liability of the group. It is particularly important where partial exemption is concerned (see **Chapter 12**), and especially if there are taxable supplies passing between partially exempt members of the group.

Planning point

Group treatment provides a powerful VAT planning tool. It should, however, be noted that the position is as with most VAT planning – the tools available can help to avoid unnecessary VAT costs without undue changes in the business structure but are not usually suited to the creation of schemes to avoid tax which is properly due.

Law: VATA 1994, s. 43

Other guidance: VAT Notice 700/2

4.3　Eligibility for group treatment

Grouping is available only between corporate bodies, and only if each company concerned is either established in the UK or has a fixed establishment in the UK. Furthermore, the companies must be under common control, meeting one of the following tests:

- one of them controls each of the others;
- one person (either a body corporate or an individual) controls all of them; or
- two or more individuals carrying on business in partnership control all of them.

A person controls a company if that person is empowered by statute to control its activities, or is its holding company (or, in the case of an individual or partnership, meets the criteria of a holding company) within the meaning of the Companies Act 2006. In broad terms, this means that the controlling entity must:

- hold a majority of the voting rights in that company;
- be a member of it and have the right to appoint or remove a majority of its board of directors; or
- be a member of it and control alone under an agreement with other members, a majority of the voting rights in it.

A company is established in the UK if it has the main seat of its business in the UK. It has a fixed establishment if it has an establishment with the permanent human and technical resources in the UK needed to undertake its business activities.

> ⚠ **Warning!**
>
> Where control of the companies within a group rests with more than one individual, HMRC take the view that the conditions for group treatment are only met if the shares are in joint ownership. That is to say, two companies owned 50/50 by the same two people do not qualify.

Law: VATA 1994, s. 43A

4.4   Exempt companies, dormant companies and passive holding companies

There is no specific requirement for eligibility for group treatment and inclusion in a group registration other than the control/ownership conditions. There are no specific requirements that a company applying for group membership makes taxable supplies or indeed be active in any way. It follows that companies making exclusively exempt supplies or those making no supplies at all may be included within a VAT group. It must be stressed, however, that HMRC can deny an application to join a group for the protection of the Revenue. This can include denying eligibility of a potential member which is dormant, fully or partially exempt if HMRC believes that this will result in less VAT being collected (as the dormant/exempt company will not incur VAT that it cannot reclaim). There is currently a question as to whether a non-trading holding company can be a member of a VAT group. The European Commission is taking infraction proceedings against seven countries that allow this to occur (Finland, Ireland, the Netherlands, Spain, Denmark, the Czech Republic, and the UK). The UK is contesting the action. Thus, the eligibility rules for VAT grouping may change in the future. This problem can be avoided if the holding company provides genuine management services to some or all of the members of the VAT group, or makes other taxable supplies either to group members or to persons outside the group.

One of the major positive aspects of VAT group registration is it allows companies ineligible to be VAT-registered in their own right to procure goods and services from other group members without the addition of irrecoverable VAT. Where, however, this entity makes supplies that are exempt to persons outside the VAT group, this will mean that the VAT group is partially exempt and can cause an overall input tax restriction to apply to the VAT group. Great care needs to be exercised when including partially exempt VAT companies in a group to ensure that the adverse impact is minimised.

In practice, many existing UK groups include dormant companies, often because they were grouped while active, have since ceased their activities and may be reactivated at any time. There is no obvious reason why application should not be made to include a currently dormant company in a group treatment.

There are also some UK VAT groups which include holding companies carrying on no activity other than the holding of shares in their subsidiaries and the receipt of dividends. HMRC do not currently seek simply to disallow inputs of such grouped holding companies, provided that they are within a proper group rather than merely being grouped with a subsidiary providing management services to non-VAT group companies. This position may change following the EC's intervention mentioned above.

⚠ *Warning!*

On occasions, a VAT group may consist of one trading company and one or more dormant companies, usually subsidiaries. It must be remembered that if at any stage such a dormant company is struck off (perhaps for other commercial reasons or simply tidiness), leaving only one company, the group will cease to exist. This will have the effect of obliging the one remaining company to forfeit the registration number (since this is uniquely allocated to the group). This in turn will mean that all existing arrangements or agreements with HMRC will need to be renegotiated. It can sometimes be worthwhile to retain a dormant subsidiary indefinitely for VAT reasons.

4.5   Application for group treatment

To group register the members of the group must make an application to HMRC by completing a form VAT 1 (registration form), a form VAT 50 for the representative member and form VAT 51 for each member of the group. A new VAT registration form (form VAT 1) is required to create a VAT group even if the entities are already VAT registered. Any existing VAT registration number will be cancelled when the new group is formed. The particular matters in respect of which an application may be made are that:

(a)   specified companies be treated as members of the group;

(b)   a further company be added to the group treatment;

(c)   a different company be treated as the representative member of the group (see below);

(d)   a company be removed from the group treatment; and

(e)   the group treatment be cancelled.

As far as (a) and (b) are concerned, HMRC have long been able to refuse the application if they consider it necessary to do so for the protection of the revenue. Since 1 May 1995 they have also been able, where necessary for the protection of the revenue, to refuse the applications at (c) and (d) above, unless the control requirements for group treatment have ceased to be met.

Planning point

Although the power to refuse an application is used sparingly, it should not be ignored.

HMRC have issued guidelines indicating when they are likely to use the power and these include:

- where proposed group members have a poor compliance record (for example failure to pay VAT debts) which might pose a threat to HMRC's ability to collect the revenue due;
- if HMRC believe that the grouping facility is likely to be used in order to operate an avoidance scheme;
- if group treatment would alter the liability of the group's supplies from exempt to taxable with consequent increase in the recovery of input tax; and
- if group treatment would otherwise affect the liability of the group's supplies and lead to loss of revenue.

They emphasise that in considering an application they will have regard, not only to the VAT position of the proposed group, but also to those of its suppliers and customers.

It should be noted that the effect of a group treatment is restricted to the companies specified in the application.

Planning point

If HMRC refuse to group a member (usually on eligibility grounds) an appeal can be made to the Tax Tribunal.

Planning point

Once the necessary group relationship exists, the companies concerned can mix and match in arriving at the treatment best suited to their circumstances (subject to the approval of HMRC). For instance, if there are ten companies eligible for group treatment, it is perfectly acceptable to have three companies in one group treatment, four in another and the remaining three treated as entirely separate registrations in their own right.

4.6   Making the application

An application for group treatment should normally be made using forms VAT 50 and VAT 51. However, this is not essential, and it has even been held that such applications may legally be made orally (*Marine & General Print Holdings Ltd v The Treasury* (1986) 2 BVC 208,102). In practice, however, it is simplest to use the correct forms.

An application for group treatment, or a variation of it, has effect from the date the application is received by HMRC, or from such earlier or later date as they may allow.

Planning point

It is important when making an application to clearly indicate the date from which it is required to have effect.

⚠ Warning!

It is highly advisable to plan VAT group applications in advance as, in practice, HMRC are very reluctant to allow an inception date which pre-dates by more than 30 days the making of the application and there is no provision under which they can be obliged to do so. HMRC also need time to process the application – a minimum of 15 days and up to 30 days, under normal circumstances.

Once an application is submitted, it has immediate effect from the date requested. However, HMRC have power to refuse the application if they consider this necessary for the protection of the revenue, and they have 90 days from the date on which the application was received by them in which to do this. If they refuse the application it is deemed never to have had effect, and any necessary adjustments to the VAT accounting (including the liability of supplies) must be made to reflect this.

Planning point

If a proposed change is not particularly time critical, or in any case where there is advance warning of the proposed change, it may be considered that the application should be submitted more than 90 days before it is required to have effect. That will avoid the risk of some costly and time-consuming untangling of transactions if HMRC refuse the application.

Planning point

Notwithstanding the Planning Point immediately above, HMRC will usually process the application form within 15 days. Only a tiny minority of applications are refused and there is very little risk in making a run-of-the-mill application less than 90 days in advance. HMRC will, however, usually backdate the date of group registration to 30 days prior to the date of application on request (but usually to the date of the VAT period of the VAT group, if later). Backdating is entirely at the discretion of HMRC, but they will usually backdate the registration.

HMRC's policy is to respond to an application within 15 days, confirming that it has been received and processed and indicating whether they need to make further enquiries before deciding whether to accept it. If further enquiries are needed they aim to notify the result as soon as these are completed.

Enquiries by HMRC will include ascertaining the wider effects on the applicant (such as administrative costs) if the application is refused, so that these can be balanced against any perceived revenue risk.

Group registration applications, changes and deregistration are to be sent to:

HMRC
Imperial House
77 Victoria Street
Grimsby
DN31 1DB

4.7   The effect of grouping

4.7.1 Effect of group treatment

When application is made for group treatment, a company in the group must be nominated to act as the representative member of the group. If the application is accepted the VAT treatment which follows is very much as if all of the activities carried on by companies within the group treatment were actually carried on by the representative member. In particular:

- supplies between members of the group are disregarded as would be supplies between different departments of a single entity;
- all supplies by or to members of the group are treated as if they were made to or by the representative member; and
- importations of goods by members of the group are treated as if done by the representative member.

In one case, it was held that where a retailer supplied goods paid for by credit cards issued by a company in the same VAT group, the retail scheme should be applied as if the retailer was providing credit to its customers directly (*C & E Commrs v Kingfisher plc* [1994] BVC 3).

Example 4.1

Company A owns 100 per cent of the share capital of company B and company C. They decide to form a VAT group. This application was accepted and the group was formed on 1 April 2010. Company A makes management charges of £100,000 per year plus VAT, to both B & C.

B is a fully taxable company and makes supplies of £8m a year to third parties. C is a finance company. It is 50 per cent taxable. It makes taxable supplies of £1 million plus VAT, and £1 million of interest charges to third parties. VAT on overheads for each company is £100,000 plus VAT per annum.

Prior to grouping, A & B could reclaim all the VAT it incurred as both were fully taxable. C could only claim 50 per cent of the VAT on the management charge

---

and also its overheads. With VAT at 20 per cent this meant that it lost 50 per cent: £20,000 + £20,000 (£40,000) - £20,000 = £20,000.

After grouping, the supplies by A to B & C are ignored for VAT purposes. Thus, C only has to restrict the VAT incurred on its overheads. A & B also has to restrict the VAT that they incur on overheads. It may be arguable that as the group as a whole is 10 per cent partially exempt that 10 per cent of the VAT incurred on all overheads has to be restricted; the figure is 10 per cent as the total supplies of the group are £10 million, with exempt supplies of £1 million. This would be 10 per cent x (£20,000 x 3) = £6,000. Alternatively, HMRC may argue that the overheads that need to be restricted are those that relate to C only (that is 50 per cent of £20,000 = £10,000). In addition, HMRC may argue that a proportion of the VAT incurred by A in managing C should also be restricted, perhaps 50 per cent of 50 per cent of £20,000 (that is the overheads relate to two companies being managed, one of which has a 50 per cent restriction, and that leads to an apportionment of the VAT incurred by A); an extra restriction of £5,000. Either of these scenarios provides less of a VAT loss than that when not grouped, as when grouped no VAT is charged, incurred or restricted on the management charges.

The precise restriction will depend on what is fair and reasonable, the precise circumstances of the various companies and what can be agreed with HMRC. As can be seen, grouping is not a matter to be entered into lightly when there are companies that cannot reclaim all of their VAT, even though it is probable that the outcome will be beneficial. Finally, HMRC may not permit grouping, for protection of the revenue reasons, as they believe that the loss of the input tax restricted on the management charge from A is unacceptable.

4.7.2 Special status companies

In some instances, the VAT liability of a supply depends upon the status of the person making the supply. For instance, most supplies of education only qualify for exemption when made by an 'eligible body'; a school, university or some such similar body. In such cases, the liability is to be determined by reference to the status of the company actually making the supply and not by reference to the status of the representative member of the group (which is deemed to make the supply for VAT accounting purposes).

4.7.3 Joint and several liability

VAT returns are made by the representative member and cover supplies made by or to all members of the VAT group. Although the representative member is liable, in the first instance, to account for any tax due, all members of the group are in the end jointly and severally liable for such tax.

⚠ *Warning!*

Sometimes this can be a reason for excluding one or more companies from a VAT group, e.g. the property-holding company where there is a desire not to put the assets at risk, or there is a substantial minority shareholder of one eligible company who is unwilling to accept the potential liability.

4.8 Ceasing to be eligible/termination of membership

If a company within a VAT group ceases to be eligible for group treatment because it no longer meets the control requirements, HMRC may exclude it from the group treatment from a date specified by them in a notice excluding the company.

In *C & E Commrs v Barclays Bank plc* [2001] BVC 606 it was decided that Customs (as they then were) were not obliged to exclude a company from a group as soon as the company ceased to be controlled by the group-holding company. Customs issued *Business Brief 30/02* to clarify the position. The normal practice will be for HMRC to agree to the date of termination suggested by the group. They will only specify a later date if VAT avoidance is involved or likely to arise through obtaining a later date.

HMRC also have power to exclude a company from a VAT group if it appears to them to be necessary for the protection of the revenue. HMRC must give notice to the company concerned and exclusion takes effect from a date specified in the notice (but which cannot be before the date of the notice).

If HMRC consider that a group company may pose a revenue risk, it is their normal policy to notify the group that they are making enquiries and to request any information needed in connection with their enquiries. Such enquiries occur particularly on the application to registration (although they arise fairly infrequently). When they decide to exclude a company from a group it is their normal policy to provide sufficient advance notification to enable the group to reorganise its affairs, but they do not undertake to do this in all cases.

4.9 Summary of main uses of group treatment

4.9.1 Administrative convenience

Where the activities of a group are closely interlinked and centrally administered, it may be easier to deal with a central VAT return which excludes intra-group transactions.

> **Planning point**
>
> At a very basic level, group treatment avoids the need to examine each and every inter-company journal for its VAT consequences.

4.9.2 Internally generated input tax

A frequently occurring position is that in which a company making exempt supplies acquires resources from companies in the same group by way of taxable supplies.

111

Typically, this might involve management charges or recharges of staff costs. The tax on such supplies is irrecoverable and, if the resources concerned did not bear VAT when first acquired into the commercial group (e.g. labour costs), this is a completely unnecessary and artificial loss.

> ### *Planning point*
>
> If the companies are within the same VAT group, no charge to tax arises on the intra-group supplies so that the artificial loss of internally generated tax is avoided.

4.9.3 Exempt intra-group supplies

Another instance where loss can arise without group treatment is where functions are separated between companies in the commercial group, giving rise to exempt supplies within the group. A typical example is that of a group property-holding company letting premises, by way of exempt supplies, to operating companies involved in making taxable supplies. Similarly, a group finance company will generate exempt financial supplies. Without group treatment such a company will be exempt or partly exempt and so unable to recover input tax on expenses relating to the properties. This is an unnecessary loss as the tax ultimately relates to the taxable supplies made by the tenant.

> ### *Planning point*
>
> If the companies are included in a group treatment, then the intra-group supply will be ignored and the input tax relating to the property will be attributed to the onward taxable supplies by the tenant. In this way, the loss of input tax is avoided.

> ### *Planning point*
>
> The usefulness, or otherwise, of group treatment depends upon the precise facts of the particular case, and a detailed analysis of the circumstances is always necessary to determine the best treatment.

4.10 Partial exemption

Although a VAT group of companies is effectively treated as a single entity for most VAT purposes, an exception is made for some partial exemption purposes. For instance, in determining whether certain exempt supplies can be treated as taxable for these purposes, the businesses carried on by different companies in the VAT group are looked at separately (*VAT Notice 706, para. 12.1*(2006 edn)).

Input tax recovery is determined by the way in which supplies to the group are used to generate supplies outside the group. This is significant when dealing with partly exempt groups.

There will only be one partial exemption method. This will be either the standard method or an agreed special method. The method is applied to the group as a whole. The special method can, however, be applied on a company-by-company basis or on a sector-by-sector basis within the group.

It is not possible to apply the *de minimis* tests on a company-by-company basis and therefore gain an input tax advantage. The VAT group is one single entity for partial exemption purposes and therefore the *de minimis* tests are applied to the group as one unit.

The partial exemption method in use determines the way in which input tax incurred by members of the group is attributed to supplies made to persons outside the group. It is possible that the transfer of a going concern to a VAT group which is partly exempt may trigger an anti-avoidance measure.

When the measure applies, the receiving VAT group triggers a self-supply charge and must account for output tax on the incoming business. There is therefore an output tax charge and input tax credit as with other self-supplies (VATA 1994, s. 44).

When companies are grouped, it is necessary to consider what input tax relates to an individual company and needs to be considered in the light of the taxable and exempt supplies made by that company, and which input tax is group input tax and needs to be considered in the light of the total taxable and exempt supplies made by the group. In addition, it is necessary to consider what input tax is incurred by one group member that could be regarded as relating to exempt supplies made by another group company. See example 4.1 above.

4.10.1 Partially exempt group acquisition of a business

If a VAT group acquires a business as a going concern, and the group is partly exempt during the return period or longer period (usually a VAT year) concerned, then a reverse charge of VAT arises on the acquisition. The group is deemed to have supplied those assets acquired which attract VAT at a positive rate, at market value, on the day of the transfer. The group is also deemed to have received a supply of these assets, so that the tax also qualifies for treatment as input tax. However, the fact that the group is partly exempt means that it may not be able to recover as input tax the whole of the tax which it must account for as output tax.

This provision does not apply if it can be shown that the transferor acquired the assets concerned more than three years before the day of the transfer. Also, HMRC have power to reduce the tax due if they are satisfied that the transferor did not obtain full input tax credit on the acquisition of them (eg because the transferor was itself partly exempt).

4.11 Capital Goods Scheme

The Capital Goods Scheme (CGS) provisions should always be considered when a VAT group is formed or disbanded or there is a change in the membership of a VAT group.

Computers, land and buildings which are subject to the provisions of the scheme are known as 'capital items'. The purpose of the scheme is to provide adjustments, over a fixed period, to the input tax incurred on capital items where there is a change in the extent to which they are used to make taxable supplies.

If a company which owns a 'capital item' joins or leaves a VAT group, there may be a change in the way in which the item is used in the business, and adjustments under the scheme may be necessary. For example, a leasing company has a computer (a 'capital item') which is used for the taxable leasing activities of the business. The company joins a VAT group and the computer is leased to another group member which uses it, in turn, to make exempt supplies outside the group. The representative member would then be required to make the necessary adjustments under the CGS to take account of this change in use of the item.

If a company owns a 'capital item' and it joins or leaves a VAT group, this can also have an effect on the time when adjustments have to be made under the scheme. Normally the CGS adjustment intervals are the same as a company's VAT tax year. However, these intervals can change if it joins or leaves a VAT group. For example, if it joins a VAT group, the interval then applying to its capital item ends on the day before it joins the group, and any adjustment required must be made on the final return of its old registration.

The representative member will take over responsibility for making future adjustments under the scheme, and all remaining intervals will run for 12 months from the date the company joined the VAT group. These intervals will remain fixed until the adjustment period for the capital item has expired – even if it subsequently leaves the group or joins another VAT group.

4.11.1 Interaction of the Capital Goods Scheme with reverse charge liability on VAT grouping

Under VATA 1994, s. 44(4), the reverse charge on chargeable assets imposed when a business is transferred as a going concern to a member of a VAT group does not apply to assets coming within the CGS.

4.12 Anti-avoidance

4.12.1 Power to make directions

HMRC have powers to counter avoidance schemes involving the use of VAT groups. These are in addition to the general power to exclude a company from a group, covered above.

HMRC can make various directions:

- that an intra-group supply which would normally be disregarded under VATA 1994, s. 43(1)(a) is not to be disregarded;
- that a company which was (or is) a member of a group during a specified period is to be treated as if it were not a member of the group; or
- that a company which was not (or is not) a member of a group during a specified period, but was (or is) eligible to be a member of it, is to be treated as if it were a member of the group.

(A direction may also specify which company is to be assumed to be the representative member of the group in question.) It appears, therefore, that, in theory at least, HMRC can in effect direct into existence a VAT group which would not otherwise exist at all.

A direction can vary an earlier direction. The power to make a direction is not affected by HMRC's earlier refusal or non-refusal of an application under VATA 1994, s. 43 (i.e. an application to form, vary or disband a group, etc.).

Law: VATA 1994, Sch. 9A

4.12.2 Conditions for making a direction

A direction may only be made in the following instances.

1. A 'relevant event' occurs.

2. There is or may be a positive-rated supply which falls to be taxed by reference to an amount less than its full value and in respect of which:

    (a) a person becomes entitled to credit for input tax allowable as attributable to the supply; or
    (b) a person becomes entitled to a repayment in respect of the supply under the provisions relating to repayments to overseas traders.

The input tax appears to be input tax in the hands of the person making the undervalue supply. While that at (2)(b) appears to be tax on the supply itself, it seems more likely that it is intended once more to be input tax in the supplier's hands.

A 'relevant event' occurs when a company joins or leaves a VAT group, or enters into any transaction. However, in respect of the relevant event concerned, HMRC cannot make a direction if they are satisfied that its main purpose (or, if there was more than one main purpose, each of them) was a genuine commercial purpose unconnected with bringing about the circumstances whereby the supply is taxed at an undervalue, etc.

4.12.3 Directions: time limits and notification

A direction must be made within six years after the later of:

- the relevant event which triggers the direction; or
- the end of the prescribed accounting period at the end of which the entitlement to deduct input tax relating to the undervalue supply arose.

A direction in respect of a supply may be given to the person who made the supply or to any body corporate which is then the representative member of the group of which the supplier was a member at the time of the supply. It seems that if, by the time HMRC seek to make a direction, the supplier has ceased to exist and the group has disbanded, there will be no one left on whom a direction can be served under this head.

A direction relating to a company (i.e. a direction to treat it as grouped or degrouped for a specified period) may be served on that company or on the person who is, or is treated as, the representative member of the group concerned at the time when the direction is made.

4.12.4 Effects and assessments

Once a direction has been made those affected by it must account for VAT on the assumptions contained in the direction.

For earlier periods, HMRC may assess, to the best of their judgement, so as to collect any unpaid tax arising as a result of the assumptions as to grouping, etc. contained in the direction, being any output tax due as a result of it plus any input tax credit or repayment which has been obtained but would not have been due on the assumptions contained in the direction.

An assessment may be made on the person to whom the direction is given or on any other relevant person (being the representative member of any group of which the person receiving the direction has been, or been treated as, a member, or which is treated under the direction as being the representative member of that group). An assessment must be made within one year of the making of the direction and notification of it may be incorporated into the direction itself.

Amounts assessed can be recovered from the person assessed or, if that person is treated as a member of a VAT group, from the representative member of the group; where more than one person is liable to pay the tax they are to be treated as jointly and severally liable.

116

Default interest may be due on amounts assessed under these provisions but runs only from the date when the assessment is notified.

4.12.5 Appeals against a direction

There is a right of appeal against the making of a direction under these provisions, and against any resultant assessment.

However, a tribunal can only allow an appeal against a direction if it is satisfied that HMRC could not reasonably have been satisfied that the conditions for making a direction had been met or if it is itself satisfied, in respect of the relevant event concerned, that its main purpose (or, if there was more than one main purpose, each of them) was a genuine commercial purpose unconnected with bringing about the circumstances whereby the supply is taxed at an undervalue, etc.

Presumably, once it is established that the direction is properly made, an appeal against an assessment must come down to argument about the numbers or about who is liable.

4.12.6 Guidance from HMRC

HMRC have issued guidance on how they intend to apply these anti-avoidance provisions (see *Statement of Practice* 6/96 (24 June 1996), reproduced in *VAT Notice 700/2*, s. 8).

4.12.7 Anti-avoidance: imported services

There are special provisions which apply where a member of a VAT group has an overseas branch, the overseas branch receives supplies of services falling within VATA 1994, Sch. 5 (i.e. services treated as supplied where received) which are then resupplied to another member of the group. Under these provisions the intra-group supply is not disregarded. The representative member is treated as supplying the services to itself, and that supply is treated as made in the UK. There are additional provisions to prevent this measure being avoided by such devices as an intra-group transfer of a going concern.

Legislation is to be introduced in *Finance Bill 2012* to give statutory effect to a VAT extra statutory concession (ESC 3.2.2). This applies to VAT groups with an overseas member that supplies services to the UK VAT Group. The concession allows the value of an anti-avoidance VAT charge to be capped at the value of services purchased by the overseas group member. The VAT due, without the concession, would be the VAT on the total value of the supply from the overseas group member to the UK member, including any services sourced in-house; this was applied through a reverse charge on the value of the supply if the supply incorporated services bought by the overseas member that would be treated as supplied here if bought by the UK members of the group and the supply would have been taxable if supplied in the UK.

The concession ensures that VAT does not apply to any in-house services that are supplied. HMRC commenced a consultation in May 2011 and has issued *Revenue & Customs Brief 16/11* regarding this matter.

It should be noted that on 1 January 2010 the place of supply rules changed. The general rule determining where a supply was made for business to business transactions changed from the place where the supplier belongs to the place where the customer belongs. As a result of this change, VATA 94, Sch. 5 became redundant and was repealed. Until the legislation is enacted, the reference to Sch. 5 should be read as a reference to the new general rule for supplies to businesses, in VATA 1994, s. 7A(2)(a). The ESC will continue to allow VAT groups to value the tax charge by reference to the services the overseas member has bought in that would now be treated as subject to UK VAT if the UK group member bought them direct. HMRC expect (both before the date of this change and subsequent to the change) that evidence of the value of the services bought in is retained. The evidence should show that the services bought in have not been undervalued.

4.13 Joint ventures

4.13.1 Joint ventures: general

Special problems can arise where two or more persons carry on a business venture jointly but under terms not intended to create a formal partnership. In a classic joint venture, different aspects of the venture, in terms of obtaining supplies and making supplies, may be handled by the different parties but a final settlement between them is then made. As noted below, this may well create a partnership.

The term joint venture may be (and is) also used to describe such arrangements as:

- one party carrying on a business activity and the other acting as an independent contractor to provide some or other resource;
- independent business organisations setting up a jointly-owned joint venture company to carry on some business activity or project which is of interest to each; or
- some loose understanding between parties interested in a common objective, which may not even create any legal or commercial relationship between them other than mutual acknowledgement of that common objective.

> ⚠ **Warning!**
>
> The important point from a VAT planning viewpoint is that it is not possible to ascertain what is actually going on or to determine the correct VAT analysis from the use of the term 'joint venture'.

Determining the true nature of the enterprise, and the VAT treatment that flows from this, can be tremendously tricky and varies depending upon the precise terms of the agreement and the way in which it is implemented. Often there is no formal agreement and the course of dealing that takes place may be open to a number of interpretations.

4.13.2 Partnership

If the terms are such that the parties share in any losses as well as profits, it may well be that a partnership exists, even though the parties did not intend this and may have sought to avoid it (*George Hall & Son v Platt (HMIT)* (1954) 35 TC 440). That case involved the joint growing of a crop of carrots by a farmer and a merchant on land occupied by the farmer. Each party contributed certain of the resources (land, seed, fertiliser, labour, machinery, transport, marketing, etc.) at its own expense, and the gross proceeds of the crop were to be divided according to an agreed formula.

In many cases there is an agreement between the parties which explicitly states that the agreement does not create a partnership.

> ### ⚠ *Warning!*
>
> It is an arguable view that this gives a reasonably clear indication that at least one of the lawyers involved in drawing up the agreement had an idea that it might do exactly that. Since HMRC are not a signatory to the agreement they cannot be bound by any such declaration; a declaration that the arrangement is not a partnership does not prevent a partnership being created if the actions of the parties and circumstances of their operation mean that a partnership is, in fact, in operation.

In some cases it may be that each party makes and receives supplies independently and supplies also flow between the parties. For cases in which significantly different VAT consequences have been held to arise from transactions which were fundamentally similar to one another, see the cases of *Theatres (Consolidated) Ltd* (1974) 1 BVC 1,030, *Mike Parker Promotions Ltd* (1976) VATTR 115 and *Greater London Council* (1982) VATTR 94.

4.13.3 Joint venture and joint venture accounting

The *Greater London Council* case referred to above is particularly interesting in that, having found that the arrangements amounted to a joint venture but not to a partnership, the tribunal indicated that it was possible that the venture ought to be registered separately from the parties to it. However, the point had not been raised before the tribunal, so it declined to consider this issue in any depth. This matter has not, at the time of writing, been raised in any subsequent tribunal case.

In practice, there are cases where HMRC are prepared to accept that there is a joint venture not amounting to a partnership and, where each party is registered for VAT, to permit joint venture accounting for VAT whereby each venturer accounts for and reclaims output and input tax on supplies passing through his hands, and settlement payments between the venturers are ignored for VAT purposes.

Planning point

There does not seem to be any particular basis in law for this last treatment but, pragmatically, it is often the most convenient approach and gives the right net answer. It is wise to obtain agreement from HMRC before using it. Indeed, it would be foolish to adopt a treatment having no explicit backing either in law or in HMRC's published material without obtaining explicit approval to it.

There are some comments about joint ventures in HMRC *Guidance Manual*, Vol. 1-5, Ch. 2, s. 3. These are fairly general and not reproduced here. However, they do appear to warn officers that the sky may fall in if they allow joint venture treatment without being certain that there is no risk of revenue loss (an indication that the joint venture accounting described above is not regarded as being available as of right).

4.13.4 Clarification

Frequently it will have little effect on the venturers which treatment applies, provided that it is known from the outset.

Planning point

If an incorrect treatment (or one which is open to challenge) is followed at the start, then it may be costly to correct later.

There may be penalties if a new registration is needed but not implemented, since there may be tax due on supplies not recognised at the time, and input tax may be lost because invoices are not made out in the right name. Such losses can be avoided if the uncertainties are recognised at the outset and if appropriate a ruling sought from HMRC as to the VAT treatment.

Planning point

Where possible, the VAT aspects of a joint venture should be covered in the agreement. On some occasions, a ruling should be sought from HMRC as to the VAT treatment of the venture at the outset to avoid loss of input tax on purchases and penalties being incurred due to tax payable on supplies not being levied at the time.

4.13.5 Commercial considerations

In some cases, the true nature of the arrangements may be crucial. For instance, in share farming agreements it would often be disadvantageous to draw up the terms in such a way that the underlying transaction was the exempt grant of a right over land, or licence to occupy land, by the landowner in return for a share of the net proceeds of the farming activities carried on by the farmer who joins in the venture. Input tax on supplies attributable to the exempt supply would be exempt input tax in the landowner's hands.

> ### *Planning point*
>
> In such cases where a particular result is desired, great care is needed to ensure that the result is in fact achieved and an acceptable VAT treatment is negotiated with HMRC, also with due regard for the disclosure provisions (see **Chapter 32**), if these are relevant.

4.13.6 Planning for joint ventures

In practice, the money flows, etc. are not infrequently inconsistent with the apparent supply paths, which makes it particularly difficult to reach a conclusion on the VAT position.

> ### *Planning point*
>
> Before deciding an approach to HMRC about an arrangement described as a joint venture, a good start can be made by going through all agreements and accounting arrangements to identify the parties involved, the supply paths, and the resultant money flows and calculations of payments.
>
> Importantly, it is often a first sign that the agreements read as a whole are internally inconsistent and potentially unenforceable.

Once some clarity is reached about what is actually meant by the commercial and legal arrangements, it is usually possible to arrive at a mutually satisfactory VAT treatment and, if necessary, take this to HMRC for approval. If the natural VAT treatment appears disadvantageous, it is often possible to vary the arrangements to give a similar commercial result with more acceptable VAT consequences. Once again, regard must now be had to the potential applicability of the rules on disclosure of avoidance schemes.

> ### *Planning point*
>
> Of course, this process really needs to be gone through before the agreements are entered into, although it may be difficult to persuade HMRC to commit themselves in advance, on the basis that the transaction is at that stage merely hypothetical.

4.14 Divisional registration

A body corporate that conducts its business through divisions can register for VAT in the names of the Divisions. Thus, each division will have its own VAT number and will account for VAT separately on its own VAT return, although these returns must be for the same VAT period for all divisions. This is permitted where the divisions are self-accounting units that are either geographically separate, or supply different commodities or carry out different functions. The body corporate, however, remains a single taxable person and it remains liable for the VAT debts of all the divisions.

HMRC requires all divisions to be registered, even if a division has a turnover below the VAT registration threshold. HMRC does not allow divisional registration unless the body as a whole is fully taxable.

HMRC permits divisional registration where it can be convinced that there would be difficulties in submitting a single VAT return for the body corporate. This is a little used facility and it is suggested will be used even less now that computers and electronic communication is widespread.

4.15 Partnership

4.15.1 Sole trader taking in a partner

When a sole trader takes in a partner, the partnership represents a new VAT entity and a new registration is required. The new owner may elect to continue with the VAT registration number of the sole trader.

The position is unsatisfactory in that there is generally no formal transfer of business assets from one entity to another, merely a change in the ownership of what looks like an existing entity. In theory (even where the VAT number is transferred) there could be liabilities arising in respect of goods on hand at the deregistration of the sole trader business (with no obvious mechanism for an input tax refund to the new partnership), and capital goods scheme (CGS) clawbacks in respect of property (other than a new freehold building) subject to the scheme.

> **Planning point**
>
> In practice, the change is likely to be treated as involving a transfer of a business as a going concern (TOGC), in which case care is needed in the case of new freeholds and opted property, where the partnership may need to opt to tax to allow the TOGC provisions to operate.

Because the partnership represents a different VAT entity, written rulings given by HMRC to the sole trader should be refreshed. This is a good opportunity to seek formal rulings in respect of any further areas of uncertainty which may be identified. Although in theory this applies where the VAT number is retained, in practice, HMRC regard rulings as applicable to the VAT number rather than the legal entity, rendering it unnecessary in such circumstances.

It should be noted that the sole trader registration may have covered other business activities which continue to be carried on by the individual concerned. In the case of exempt property letting, these will cease to be covered by a registration and any previous restriction of input tax recovery at the registered business will cease and if input tax had previously been claimed as being below the *de minimis* limits in relation to the exempt activities, this input tax is no longer claimable. In the case of taxable activities that are below the VAT registration threshold, a decision is needed whether to maintain the registration, taking into account any deemed supply on deregistration.

Similar considerations to the above apply if one or more partners leave a partnership, so that only one of the former partners remains and continues in business as a sole trader.

4.15.2 Change of partners

Where partners join or leave a partnership, but the partnership continues, this does not give rise to a new business entity. The transactions between the partners, in contributing or extracting capital or making payments between themselves outside the partnership accounts, are regarded as not being done in the course of business and so outside the scope of VAT.

It is necessary to notify HMRC of the change, so that the VAT register can be amended accordingly.

> **Planning point**
>
> It is particularly important for an outgoing partner to ensure that proper notification is made, as his joint and several liability for VAT (and penalty) debts of the partnership will otherwise continue until such time as notification is eventually made.

Care is also needed to see whether the change will create (or terminate) commonality of identity with another partnership having (or ceasing to have) the same partners, and to consider the effects that this may have on the VAT position.

This is particularly likely to be relevant where the business is structured so that the business property is owned by a separate land-owning partnership and let to the operating partnership.

4.16 Incorporation of a non-incorporated business

4.16.1 Incorporation of a non-incorporated business

The incorporation of a non-incorporated business involves the transfer of the business assets to the company, generally in return for shares. This will usually be a non-supply under the rules for the transfer of a going concern. All of the considerations concerning the purchase or sale of a business apply (see **13.2** and **14.1**). Again, the VAT number may be transferred.

> ### *Planning point*
>
> Special care is needed to take account of any changes in the business structure and the number of VAT entities.

For instance, it is often considered desirable to keep the business property (or other business assets) outside the company, retaining it in the hands of former partners or transferring it to a pension fund. This can have considerable VAT implications, particularly where there has been (or will be) significant VAT-bearing expenditure on the property, and it may be necessary for the property owner(s) to waive exemption. It will generally be unwise for the property owner(s) to allow the company to occupy the property rent-free, as they can then hardly be said to be carrying on a business, with consequential effects on their ability to remain registered for VAT or recover input tax.

> ### *Planning point*
>
> Because the company represents a different VAT entity, written rulings given by HMRC to the unincorporated business should be refreshed (unless the same VAT number has been retained). This is a good opportunity to seek formal rulings in respect of any further areas of uncertainty which may be identified.

4.17 Special circumstances for partially exempt structures

4.17.1 Capital goods scheme

A capital goods scheme interval comes to an end when a corporate body joins or leaves a VAT group during the adjustment period. A new interval then starts and ends 12 months later.

When a corporate body joins a group the representative member is responsible for making adjustments arising after the event. A corporate body leaving a VAT group is responsible for subsequent adjustments.

4.17.2 Divisional registrations

A divisional registration is a facility by which divisions of the same corporate body may be registered separately. It is intended to ease administration.

Divisional registrations and group registrations are incompatible. They cannot be used together. A corporate body registered under the divisional registration facility must terminate the divisional registration if it wants to join a VAT group.

4.17.3 Limited liability partnership

For the purposes of VAT group legislation, an LLP is treated in exactly the same way as any other corporate body (see Customs *Business Brief 03/01* (20 February 2001).

4.17.4 No taxable supplies outside the group

It is possible that as a result of the formation of a group, there are no taxable supplies made outside the group. In order for such a group to be formed, at least one of the members must be making taxable supplies that would mean it is eligible or liable to be registered for VAT if it were on its own.

However, a group of wholly exempt companies is entitled to register as a VAT group, in order to avoid the need to register for VAT and account for VAT in respect of inter-company management charges, etc. Such a group will have no entitlement to recover input tax. Although there are no taxable supplies outside the group, VAT returns must still be completed – even though they will be nil returns.

4.17.5 Partial exemption

The normal rules of VAT group registrations apply to partly exempt VAT groups. As all inter-group supplies are usually disregarded, input tax recovery is determined by how supplies to the group are used to generate supplies to outside the group.

The VAT group will only have one partial exemption method that will be applied to the group as a whole. Input tax incurred by members of the group must be attributed to supplies made to persons outside the group in accordance with the partial exemption method in use.

As with other threshold limits, the *de minimis* tests are applied to the group as one unit. It is not possible to apply the tests on a company-by-company basis and therefore gain an advantage.

> **Planning point**
>
> The application of one *de minimis* limit to a group registration can be a potential advantage, in that a single wholly exempt company ineligible for registration in its own right may possibly benefit from the limit available to a VAT group of which it is entitled to be a member, thus becoming eligible for input tax deduction.

4.17.6 Retailers

The turnover limits apply to the VAT registration as a whole, not on a business-by-business basis. In order to ascertain whether a bespoke scheme must be drawn up it is necessary to look at the retail turnover of the whole group.

Other guidance: VAT Notice 727

4.17.7 Tour operators' margin scheme (TOMS)

A corporate body operating TOMS is not always eligible to be a member of a VAT group. The corporate body concerned is disqualified from belonging to a group if any other member of the group:

- has an overseas establishment;
- makes supplies outside the UK which would be taxable supplies if made within the UK; or
- supplies goods or services which will become, or are intended to become, a designated travel service.

When these conditions apply, the corporate body operating TOMS may not belong to a VAT group.

Law: Value Added Tax (Tour Operators) Order 1987 (SI 1987/1806), art. 13

Other guidance: VAT Notice 709/5

4.18 Checklists

4.18.1 Group Registration

Note: HMRC have extensive powers in respect of VAT groups. These powers will be invoked by HMRC if they perceive any revenue loss deemed greater than should follow from the 'normal operation of grouping', which HMRC widely define and upon which further guidance is recommended.

A group of two or more UK-resident companies can be treated as a group with a single VAT registration provided:

(a)   one company controls the others;
(b)   an individual or another company controls all of them; and
(c)   a business partnership controls all of them.

Has the group:

(a)   if new, determined which company is to be the representative member and prepared and submitted form VAT 1 to HMRC; and
(b)   if new or existing, prepared and submitted form 50 for the group and form 51 for each company (joining or leaving) to HMRC?

Note: Group applications are given immediate provisional effect by HMRC when received. HMRC then have 90 days to decide whether to accept or refuse the application for the 'protection of the revenue'.

A group registration will mean that for VAT purposes:

(a)   there is a single VAT registration which is the responsibility of the representative member;
(b)   inter-company transactions are ignored;
(c)   all members are jointly and severally liable for any VAT due; and
(d)   the group may have a partial exemption restriction if a company is making VAT-exempt supplies. [*Table 4*]

Note: HMRC have the power to refuse applications for new groups or changes (including disbanding) to existing groups. HMRC have the power to refuse a group application or to remove a company from an existing VAT group for the 'protection of the revenue'.

Accounting for VAT

5.1 Introduction

This chapter considers the way that VAT should be accounted for and a number of opportunities to improve VAT accounting. It does not consider VAT special accounting schemes (such as cash accounting or annual accounting nor cash flow planning as these are dealt with in separate chapters. This chapter reviews the systems required when VAT is due to be accounted for (including bad debt relief) and also error correction.

5.1.1 VAT Systems

A VAT registered person is obliged to maintain certain records and also to manage VAT adequately. There are regulations that determine the format of VAT invoices and the completion of VAT returns. Furthermore, best practice will determine how VAT accounting records should be kept.

Is the VAT-registered business keeping the required books and records as evidence of all VAT transactions on a day-to-day basis and ready for inspection from time to time by HMRC?

> **Planning point**
>
> Special records are required where a VAT scheme is being used, e.g. sales under the second-hand margin scheme, flat rate scheme, etc.

5.1.2 VAT periods

A taxable person must account for VAT by reference to the VAT period allocated to that person. These periods are usually quarterly periods. VAT periods are allocated to even out the flow of the receipt of VAT returns, so may finish at the end of January, February or March (and quarterly thereafter). A taxable person may request for the periods allocated to be altered if this suits the taxpayer. Since 1 April 2012 all returns must be submitted electronically. Payments must also be made electronically where an electronic return is submitted. This is usually by direct debit or direct credit. An exception to electronic returns is made for persons subject to an insolvency procedure and those who have a religious objection to using computers. The return is due to be submitted on the last day of the month following the VAT period end and must be paid at the same time, or seven days later if paid electronically. Details of how to register to account for VAT electronically can be found at *www.hmrc.gov.uk/vat/vat-online/moving.htm*.

Where a business expects to be in receipt of repayments (for instance when a business commences and is stocking up or incurring large costs for construction) or makes predominantly zero-rated supplies but receives standard-rated supplies, it may apply to move to monthly returns to enable it to reclaim VAT more quickly. Small businesses (turnover less than £1,350,000) can apply to account for VAT on an annual basis, although payments on account must be made throughout the year – see **Chapter 6, Schemes to help small businesses**.

Where a taxpayer has annual VAT payments in excess of £2 million, HMRC will require that business to make monthly VAT payments on account. Quarterly VAT returns are required to be made, but in the second and third months of the VAT period an estimate of the VAT payable (provided by HMRC) must be paid with the balancing payment being made at the usual time, the month following the VAT period end. As the payments are made electronically the payment can be made seven days after the month end. Thus, if the business was on calendar quarterly periods, the first payment on account for the March period will be due on 7 March, the second will be due on 7 April and the balancing payment will be due on 7 May. The return will be due on 30 April.

5.1.3 VAT return

At the end of each VAT period a VAT return must be completed. This must be submitted to HMRC (electronically, even if it is a nil return. There are penalties for non-submission and late returns. The business should consider if changing the return periods to more convenient accounting quarters or periods is beneficial. Also, has the business received a VAT return for the correct period; it is essential that the correct period is accounted for on the return? Businesses should be aware that it is their responsibility to go online and render the return. When reviewing the return the following points should be considered:

- Does the return show the correct details including: address, return period, due date?
- Has the business calculated the totals for boxes 1 to 9? If there are no entries, has 'none' been entered in boxes 1 to 9?
- If a first return, has allowable pre-registration input tax been claimed.
- If a final return, is the business required to account for VAT, if more than £1,000, on goods on hand at the close of business.
- Have any partial exemption and/or capital goods scheme adjustments been mad.
- Have one or more errors been discovered on any earlier returns, subject to the general four-year time limit? If so, have the errors been recorded and verified, are the errors required to be disclosed to HMRC (certain adjustments may be made on the relevant return, including credit and debit notes, bad-debt relief claims and partial exemption annual adjustments, without disclosure), and has the amount of the net errors discovered (amounts payable to HMRC less amounts repayable to the business) been calculated, and if so are they permitted to be adjusted on the return?

- Has the declaration been authorised and reviewed by an authorised person?
- If a payment is due have the arrangements been made to make the payment?

The return is to be completed as follows:

Box 1: This is the total of the output tax on sales and other outputs for the prescribed accounting period. Has VAT been included on all:

- taxable business activities,
- private use,
- fuel scale charges,
- imported services under the 'reverse charge' procedure,
- sales of business assets,
- self-supplies,
- goods taken out of the business,
- supplies to staff,
- hire or loan of goods,
- gifts of goods costing more than £50,
- supplies to unregistered EU customers,
- errors from previous returns that can be corrected on a later return,
- commission received, and
- vending machine income?

Has VAT been calculated under the correct accounting method;

- cash accounting,
- invoice basis,
- annual accounting,
- retail scheme,
- second-hand goods margin scheme,
- flat-rate scheme, or
- continuous supplies of services?

Has VAT been reduced for:

- credit notes issued to customers, and
- errors from previous returns that can be corrected on the return?

Box 2: Total the VAT due on acquisitions from other EU member states.

- Has UK VAT been calculated and included on goods and related services on acquisitions from the EU?
- Have the acquisitions for the correct period been taken into account?

Note: The tax point is the earlier of either the date of issue of supplier's invoice or the 15th day of the month following goods acquired.

Box 3: Total of the VAT due on sales and other outputs and acquisitions from other EU countries. Have boxes 1 and 2 been totaled?

Box 4: Total of the VAT input tax to reclaim in the prescribed accounting period. Has VAT on the following been included:

- allowable business expenditure, making any necessary adjustments for partial exemption,
- the acquisition of goods from other EU member states,
- imported services under the reverse charge procedure,
- imports or removals from customs warehouses/free zones,
- errors that can be corrected on a return,
- bad-debt relief,
- credit notes received from suppliers,
- deduction for VAT input tax previously recovered on unpaid invoices where six months has elapsed, and
- share issues as a means of raising capital where these are attributable to the taxable supplies of the business?

Has the business excluded the following VAT from the claim:

- VAT on motor cars purchased which are not wholly for business use,
- 50 per cent of the VAT on the rental charges of leased business cars used privately or partly privately,
- business entertainment (except the entertainment of overseas customers),
- personal or private purchases, private use of domestic accommodation of directors or proprietors,
- goods under a second-hand VAT scheme, and
- other non-business or non-allowable items?

Box 5: Total of the VAT due to be paid or repaid. Has the difference between box 3 and 4 been calculated?

Box 6: Total of the value of outputs. Has the value of the following been included:

- standard-rated and reduced-rated supplies,
- road fuel scale charges,
- zero-rated supplies including exports,
- supplies to VAT-registered traders in other EU member states,
- supplies of services which are outside the scope of UK VAT under the place of supply rules,
- exempt supplies,
- reverse charge transactions on services from outside the UK,
- distance sales to non-VAT-registered or private individuals in EU member states if below the threshold in country of receipt,
- own goods transferred to other EU member states,
- supplies to customers in EU member states on a sale or return basis, deposits, any other business income, and
- the full selling price of second-hand margin scheme eligible goods, less any VAT?

Has the value of the following been deducted:

- the VAT itself,
- money put into the business,
- loans received or gifts of money,

- dividends received,
- insurance claims recovered,
- Stock Exchange dealings (other than by a financial institution),
- motor vehicle licence duty refunds,
- income or receipts outside the scope of VAT?

Note: the value of box 6 should always be equal to or greater than the net value of the output tax box (box 1); that is box 1 multiplied by six. Box 1 should usually be 20 per cent or more of the value of box 6.

Box 7: The total of the values of inputs. Has the value of the following been included:

- business expenditure at the standard, reduced, zero and exempt rates,
- imports, acquisitions from other EU member states,
- reverse charge transactions of services from outside the UK,
- new motor cars, and
- eligible second-hand goods (purchase price including VAT)?

Has the value of the following been deducted:

- The VAT itself (except on second-hand goods),
- wages and salaries, PAYE and NIC,
- money taken out of the business,
- stock exchange dealings,
- motor vehicle licence duty and MOT certificates,
- local authority rates,
- customs duties, and
- payments which are outside the scope of VAT including amounts paid but where there is no supply?

Box 8: The total value of supplies of goods to VAT-registered customers in other EU member states. Has the value of the following supplies been included:

- goods dispatched from the UK to another EU member state,
- services directly related to (including freight and insurance charges) including supplies, with or without an actual sale, invoiced to person outside the EU,
- goods dispatched from the UK for installation or assembly in another EU member state, to customers in another EU member state including;
  - o distance sales exceeding the threshold,
  - o new means of transport, and transport of own goods to another EU member state including, good supplied on a call-off basis for customers,
  - o goods on a sale or return basis?

Has the value of the following been deducted:

- VAT itself,
- services not directly related, including legal and financial, for processed work, to the value of the goods, and
- distance sales to unregistered customers in another EU member state falling below threshold?

Has the total value been included in the amount shown in box 6?

Box 9: The total value of goods acquired from other EU member states. Has the value of the following acquisitions been included:

- goods acquired from another EU member state including,
    - o with or without an actual purchase,
    - o invoiced by a person outside the EU,
    - o goods dispatched from another EU member state for installation or assembly in the UK, and
    - o process work from other EU member states?

Have the acquisitions been included in the correct VAT return period (in which the tax point occurs)?

Has the value of the following been excluded:

- VAT itself, and
- for processed work, the value of the goods?

Has the total value been included in the amount shown in box 7?

5.1.4 Accounting systems

Most modern accounting systems will adequately deal with VAT. It is necessary, however, to ensure that the system will deal separately with input tax and output tax and it is recommended that three VAT accounts are used; one for input tax, another for output tax and a final clearing account. The clearing account is used to transfer the input tax and output tax into at the end of each VAT period. Separate input and output accounts are used so that it is easy to identify credit notes in both the input tax and output tax accounts; failure to do so creates confusion when trying to determine if the matter is a credit or not. Any other records required can be noted from **5.1.6**.

5.1.5 Tax invoices

Most VAT registered businesses are obliged to issue tax invoices? There are certain exceptions, such as businesses that use the margin scheme, who cannot issue a tax invoice and retailers who may issue an invoice if requested but are not obliged to issue an invoice for most transactions. The details that should be included on a full tax invoice are:

- Standard-rated supplies to a UK-registered person.
- Supplies (other than exempt) to an EU person.

The VAT invoices must contain the following information (unless special rules apply):

(a)   name and address of supplier;
(b)   VAT registration number of supplier;

(c) identifying number;

(d) time of the supply (the tax point);

(e) date of issue of the document;

(f) customer's name and address; and

(g) type of supply (this used to be compulsory but is now optional);

Note: Includes sale, HP, loan, exchange, hire, sale or return, process or commission.

(h) description of goods/services;

(i) for each supply describe:

  – the rate of VAT (optional from 1 January 2004);
  – the gross amount payable;
  – the rate of any discount offered; and
  – the amount of VAT chargeable (optional from 1 January 2004;
  – the total gross amount payable excluding VAT;
  – the total amount of VAT chargeable (if the invoice is issued in a foreign currency, including euros, is the total amount of VAT expressed in sterling?); and
  – the unit price with effect from 1 January 2004 (this applies to goods and services which can be counted in units).

Certain businesses issue tax invoices under special rules. These include:

(a) retailers;

(b) cash and carry wholesalers;

(c) petrol and derv;

(d) foreign currency invoices;

(e) second-hand scheme;

(f) the customer is either:

  (i) in another EU member state; or
  (ii) accounting for the VAT?

Note: The business must quote the customer's VAT number and country identifier if supplying goods to a VAT-registered person in another member state.

Where a retailers or less detailed tax invoice is issued it only needs to show the name, address and registration number of the supplier, the date of the supply, the goods or service supplied, the rate of VAT charged, and for each rate the gross amount payable. These less detailed tax invoices can only be issued when the total consideration does not exceed £250.

Planning point

Where continuous supplies of services are provided, pro forma invoices can be issued.

If the invoice is a pro forma, does it state: 'this is not a tax invoice'?

Note: The business is not required to account for VAT shown on a pro forma invoice. The VAT is accounted for when payment is received or a valid tax invoice is issued, or a period of 12 months has elapsed whichever is the sooner.

Where a reduction is given to a customer a credit note must be issued. To be valid for VAT purposes the credit note must be issued:

(a)   to give credit for a genuine error, mistake, overcharge or reduction;
(b)   within one month of the amount to be credited being discovered or agreed;
(c)   to give value for the amount overcharged either by refund or offset against future supplies; and
(d)   headed 'credit note' or 'debit note' with an identifying number and reference to the original invoice number.

The adjustment to the original VAT charge is made in the period in which the credit note is issued. (The rules for insolvent businesses are different – professional advice should be sought where there is an insolvency.) If both parties agree, there is no obligation to adjust the original VAT charged, providing the customer can reclaim the VAT charged.

5.1.6   Contract terms

Where a contract has been agreed, the contract will determine the VAT due on any payment or supply made. It is best to embark on the process of analysing the VAT position at an early stage in the negotiations, particularly where complex structures are likely to be involved, and prior to the contract commencing or the supplies being made. VAT consequences not appreciated until late in the proceedings can be a deal breaker and it may be necessary to settle for a less than optimum VAT position if, by the time VAT is considered, the structure of the deal is too far entrenched for it to be feasible to make alterations to improve the VAT treatment in the time available. The contract may state that any agreed price in the contract is inclusive or exclusive of VAT; this gives certainty.

> **Planning point**
>
> Early consideration of the VAT contract terms is important, but often forgotten.

Of course, getting the contract terms right can be difficult if the parties are unsure of the appropriate VAT treatment, such as whether the TOGC provisions apply or not.

In some cases this is so critical to the commercial viability of the deal that it is essential to obtain sufficient certainty before finalising the transactions, usually by providing full details of the proposals to HMRC before finalisation and seeking their written agreement to the desired treatment. It is essential in such cases to ensure that full information has been provided, that there is evidence of this and also that the written agreement from HMRC is clear and unambiguous.

Experience has shown that HMRC are highly variable in their willingness to provide speedy rulings on such business transfers, even where they realise the commercial importance of achieving certainty as to the VAT treatment. However, they cannot always meet the deadlines which are important to the parties and are sometimes reluctant to provide an advance ruling at all, on the basis that, until it happens, it is merely theoretical, or, more recently, that as VAT is a self-assessed tax and that the onus is therefore on the taxpayer to make the decision.

Planning point

In many cases the precise VAT treatment is not ultimately crucial, provided that appropriate terms between the parties can be embodied in the contract. In these cases it is not unusual to draft clauses to meet the position in either case, with an agreement between the parties to obtain appropriate rulings. For example an amount can be agreed with VAT being charged in addition if applicable. This can enable the transaction to proceed on schedule even though the final VAT result remains unknown for a while. In these cases it is also common for uncertain amounts of VAT to be secured by payment into an escrow account, to be released to one party or the other, with interest, depending on the ruling finally obtained from HMRC.

⚠ Warning!

It will be clear from the above that both buyer(s) and seller(s) need to analyse the proposed transactions carefully before finally committing themselves. They also need to ensure that the contract terms embody the transactions which they have finally settled upon and the VAT consequences of them and that both parties are satisfied with the result.

5.2 Tax point/time of supply

5.2.1 Single payment contract

In general, the normal tax point rules will apply to supplies of construction services, although there is a specific anti-avoidance provision in relation to certain supplies.

Where a service is performed and there will be a single payment in relation to the contract, the basic tax point for the services is the time when the services are performed. This is normally taken to be the date when all the work except any outstanding invoicing has been completed.

However, an actual tax point will be created when the supplier issues a VAT invoice or receives payment in respect of the supply before the basic tax point arises. The tax point will then be the date of issue of the invoice or the date payment is received. In addition, an actual tax point is created if the supplier issues a VAT invoice within 14 days after the basic tax point, unless HMRC have agreed to an extension of the 14-day rule.

5.2.2 Continuous supplies of services

Where a contract provides for periodic payments to the supplier (e.g. stage payments) a tax point will arise at the earliest of the following dates:

(a) the date a payment is received by the supplier;

(b) the date that the supplier issues a VAT invoice;

(c) where the parties are 'connected', no more than 12 months after the previous tax point under new legislative provisions introduced from 1 October 2003; or

(d) the day on which the services are performed where the building in question is to be occupied by a person who cannot recover all of the VAT that is incurred and the contractor is connected with either the occupier or has been financed by the occupier/someone connected to the occupier to carry out the construction services.

Other guidance: *VAT Notice 708*, s. 24

5.2.3 Retention payments

If the anti-avoidance provisions described at (c) or (d) above apply, the tax point will follow the relevant tax point provisions.

In all other cases, the tax point in respect of a retention will arise on the date a payment is received by the supplier or the date that the supplier issues a VAT invoice, whichever is earlier.

Planning point

There are two distinct ways in which retentions are invoiced. Sometimes, the VAT is added to the gross contract value before the retention is deducted, sometimes it is added to the net payment due and then to the retention at the time it is released. Contractors should be careful not to account twice for the VAT on retentions. The danger of this is increased where the transaction is self-billed by the customer.

5.3   Claims for overpaid VAT

5.3.1   Introduction

At under 40 years old, VAT is still a relatively new tax on the scene. Also, because it is governed from Europe, the UK has limited room for manoeuvre when it comes to writing the rules. These two factors result in frequent changes to the interpretation of the legal provisions, which often result in the realisation that VAT has consistently been overpaid in the past by some businesses. In such circumstances, claims can be made, subject to the three-year cap (four years with effect from 1 April 2009).

> ### Planning point
>
> At the time of writing, claims for the refund of VAT overpaid before the introduction of the three-year cap can be made. Litigation having proved that, in its then form, it did not have retrospective effect, HMRC have been forced to accept claims for input tax underclaimed up to 30 April 1997 and for output tax overpaid up to 4 December 1996, both going back to the introduction of VAT into the UK in 1973. However, the opportunity to make such claims expired on 31 March 2009, when the capping legislation will become effective for all overpayments arising more than three years (as defined) before the claim is made.

Such claims basically take the form of an error correction declaration and should be reported to HMRC as such. If the overpayment resulted from official error (including HMRC's failure to implement UK or EU law correctly), interest should also be paid by them.

> ### Planning point
>
> The payment of interest does not always happen automatically and sometimes needs to be specifically claimed.

Other guidance: VAT Notice 700/45

5.3.2   Unjust enrichment

If a claim is made for output tax overpaid, HMRC may seek to use the unjust enrichment provisions. These are aimed at ensuring that the claimant is not unfairly enriched by the refund, as the VAT accounted for may have been charged to the customer who has thereby effectively borne the burden of the tax. In such cases, HMRC are empowered to make it a condition of meeting the claim that the claimant repays some or all of the VAT concerned to those customers.

Somewhat regrettably, HMRC often do not make it clear when attempting to impose these conditions that there is a defence against them. If the trader can show that they, rather than the customer, bore the burden of the tax, then the restrictions do not apply. This can often be done, for example, by showing that unregistered competitors set the market rate or that the output tax claimed is offset by retrospectively lost exempt input tax.

5.4   Repayment supplement

Repayment supplement is an additional sum payable by HMRC to a VAT-registered person where delays arise in meeting a repayment claimed on a VAT return.

HMRC are obliged to pay the supplement, which is calculated at 5 per cent of the refund due, if more than 30 days are taken after receiving the return to make repayment (allowing for reasonable enquiries).

Essentially, the 30-day clock stops running at the point where HMRC first make contact with the trader and restarts when satisfactory responses have been received to any reasonable queries which they raise concerning the repayment.

HMRC are very aware of their responsibilities in regard to the prompt repayment of such VAT claims (something which regrettably cannot be said of refunds requested by voluntary disclosure, which are not subject to this regime). For this reason they take detailed notes of all action taken to verify claims before they are authorised, such as telephone calls, delays in arranging visits to check the records, etc., in order to demonstrate that they are not responsible for any slowness in making repayment.

Repayment supplement is not payable in circumstances where the return is rendered late or, as a result of HMRC's checks, it is established that the amount actually due to be repaid is less than the amount claimed by more than 5 per cent of the correct amount or £250, whichever is the greater.

> ### Planning point
> If a repayment supplement is due, it may not necessarily be paid automatically by HMRC. It is therefore advisable for a business making a repayment claim to maintain its own record of events and dates, so as to make a claim for the supplement if it is thought to be due.

5.5   Time-to-pay agreements

From time to time traders find themselves in a position where their full VAT liability cannot be paid. If approached properly at the right time, HMRC's debt management units (DMUs) – now centralised regionally – can be very helpful in agreeing time to pay. Initially, requests for assistance for payment problems must be made through the National Advice Service (0845 010 9000) who will direct the caller to the debt management unit.

> ### Planning point
>
> HMRC have, in the current economic downturn become more lenient with time to pay arrangements. The new Business Payment Support Service are very flexible. HMRC comment 'VAT default surcharges will not be charged if the business contacts us before the payment is due and agrees a time to pay arrangement. Entering into the time to pay arrangement will not be treated as a default so it will not extend the 12 month rolling period nor will the default percentage increase because of the time to pay arrangement, provided the terms of the arrangement are adhered to.'

As often as possible, some payment, as an earnest of good faith, should be made with the relevant return, voluntary disclosure, etc. A written proposal for set sums to be paid over a given period of time can then be sent to the DMU. HMRC appear to work to a normal 12-week maximum for the discharge of most debts, ensuring that the liability is discharged before the next return and payment are due, but an initial proposal will often request a longer timescale.

> ### Planning point
>
> Under normal economic circumstances HMRC expect to see firm evidence of the fact that there is no other available source of funding, i.e. copies of bank statements and a letter from the bank stating that it is unwilling to make a loan or extend the overdraft facility. Any taxpayer in default should seriously consider all other options before trying to gain long-term funding by way of a time-to-pay agreement with HMRC.

Any proposal should take into account future liabilities and perhaps suggest a longer gap between payments at the time the next return is due. Normally, a compromise is reached that is acceptable to both parties, and the time taken over the necessary exchanges of correspondence can provide a welcome breathing space itself.

> ### Planning point
>
> Although HMRC may enter into such agreements late in the day, when they have begun to enforce the debt, it is far better to take the initiative and start the ball rolling before this point is reached.

> ### *Planning point*
>
> If the gross debt exceeds £100,000, it will be dealt with by the national debt management office in Northampton, rather than a regional office. Experience current at the time of writing indicates that, assuming full cooperation and ready communication, they can be very flexible in negotiations.

5.6 Bad-debt relief

Bad-debt relief in the context of VAT is effectively a method of government compensation. Output VAT is due on supplies which have been made, regardless of whether or not payment is made for the supply. For any business not on cash accounting, therefore, a VAT liability arises in respect of every supply at a positive rate of VAT. By way of an exception to this basic principle, the government permits any VAT accounted for to be reclaimed from HMRC in the event of non-payment. This prevents the supplier suffering twice, once from non-receipt of the monies due to them and also from the need to account for VAT out of their own resources.

VAT relief is available six months after the due date for payment of the supply concerned. Thus, if terms are payment within 30 days bad-debt relief can be claimed after six months and 30 days. If terms are immediate payment, then bad-debt relief entitlement arises six months from the date of the invoice.

> ### *Planning point*
>
> In addition to any commercial reason for doing so, this represents a powerful reason to state payment terms on the face of the sales invoice, as this indisputably fixes the date of entitlement to VAT bad debt relief.

> ### *Planning point*
>
> It should be noted that there is no requirement that the debt be written off in the accounts, nor even provided for, in order for relief to be claimed. What is required is that the amount is transferred to a 'refunds for bad debts account'. This account can be created for VAT purposes only and does not have any effect over the usual accounting treatment for otherwise bad or doubtful debts.

The claim should be made by entering the amount of VAT claimable in box 4 of the VAT return for the period in which the entitlement arose (or such later return as the trader may choose, always accepting that no claim may be made more than three years and six months after the due date for payment).

Planning point

Strictly, a claim for relief can be made if the six months has elapsed by the time of submission of the VAT return on which the claim is made, since the claim is not for VAT as such but for 'relief' (effectively governmental compensation for the loss).

If payment is received subsequent to bad-debt relief having been claimed, then the VAT proportion of the consideration received must again be accounted for as output tax.

Prior to 1 January 2003, it was necessary for the customer (if VAT-registered) to be notified of the claim being made by way of a formal notice. However, for invoices raised on or after that date, a formal notice is no longer required. Failure to send these notifications prior to making a claim was the most common error in dealing with bad-debt relief and would result in the claim being clawed back by Customs.

Under current legislation, the customer is still required to adjust his claim to input tax, if any, six months after the due date for payment (see **5.7**).

Planning point

A system for making claims should be in place, allocating responsibility to an individual to monitor aged debtors and to ensure that claims are made on a timely basis.

⚠ Warning!

If a customer has paid part of an invoice, bad-debt relief can be claimed on the balance outstanding, calculated by how much VAT is included within the balance, i.e. applying the VAT fraction of 7/47ths (or 1/6th from 4 January 2011 and 3/23rds from 1 December 2008 to 31 December 2009; the fraction claimed will depend upon the period the invoice was issued in or when the supply was made), assuming the supply to have been standard-rated. If the customer has paid the net amount and left only the VAT amount outstanding, the same rule applies and only the VAT proportion (1/6th or whatever fraction is applicable) of the amount outstanding is claimable as bad debt relief. Thus, if a supply was made for £100 plus £20 VAT and the customer only paid £100 bad debt relief of £3.33 only can be claimed (£20/6). A seeming exception to this is where the customer did not pay a VAT only invoice. Although the net amount has been paid and the VAT element has not been paid the Upper Tier Tribunal has permitted the appellant's appeal to claim the whole amount as bad debt relief and not the VAT fraction element of the VAT amount not paid. (*Simpson & Marwick v R & C Commrs* [2012] BVC 1,533) The Upper Tier Tribunal considered that the bad debt relief provisions justified treating the whole amount of a VAT only invoice as unpaid VAT and eligible for refund. Where the consideration written off is all VAT the refund should be calculated accordingly as it was established case law that the amount of VAT to be collected by the tax authorities is not to exceed the amount that is actually paid by the final consumer.

For smaller businesses, instant bad-debt relief can of course be gained by use of the Cash Accounting Scheme. This is available to any business with an annual turnover of up to £1.35m and once using the scheme a business can go up to £1.6m before having to stop using the scheme.

It is now also possible to claim back bad-debt relief incurred after the transfer of a business as a going concern in respect of pre-transfer supplies, provided that the VAT registration number is transferred. The potential benefit of this should, however, be carefully weighed before the registration number is taken on by the purchaser as this can lead to responsibility for other liabilities incurred prior to the transfer.

When bad-debt relief is claimed and the customer becomes insolvent, the supplier should prove in the insolvency for the full amount of the debt. Under the terms of Extra-Statutory Concession 3.20 and *Notice 48*, an insolvency practitioner is not required to make a bad-debt relief adjustment for any bad debts relating to a supply made prior to the insolvency. However, adjustments are required if the supply was made during the insolvency appointment.

If a taxpayer assigns a debt prior to making a claim for bad-debt relief, then the payments received by the assignee must be taken into account when calculating the amount of the claim. However, if the debt is assigned after the making of a claim, no adjustment is required to the claim unless the debt is assigned to a connected party, in which case an adjustment is required (this adjustment came into force on 11 December 2003).

Law: VATA 1994, s. 36; VAT Regulations 1995 (SI 1995/2518), Part XIX–XIXA

Other guidance: VAT Notice 700/18

5.7   Aged creditors

When the bad-debt relief rules were last changed (affecting supplies made from 1 January 2003 onwards), HMRC lost the trigger which caused a VAT-registered debtor to repay any input tax claimed on the supply in respect of which the creditor was claiming bad-debt relief. A replacement mechanism was needed to ensure that this tax was brought to account. The easiest, most obvious and quite possibly the only way of doing this was to place an obligation on every debtor to repay input tax on any outstanding purchase balance remaining unpaid six months after the due date for payment. Simple such a scheme may be, but it has the effect of placing an obligation on the debtor whether or not the creditor has chosen to make a bad-debt relief claim. Although it is ostensibly the mirror image of bad debt relief, for this reason it is not a measure which restores balance, but one which tips the balance in favour of HMRC quite decisively.

> **⚠ *Warning!***
>
> No debtor can afford to be unaware of these rules. Indeed, unless the business is one which consistently pays all creditors on a timely basis, systems should be set up to monitor aged creditors to ensure that input tax is repaid as soon as the deadline arises, i.e. on the VAT return covering the relevant date.

All official announcements of these rules and all published guidance on them appear under the general heading of 'bad-debt relief', which is arguably very unhelpful. By their nature they affect many businesses which have no call to take account of bad debt relief, such as retailers, farmers and other repayment traders. Such businesses are often ignorant of these provisions for entirely understandable reasons.

> **⚠ *Warning!***
>
> HMRC are well aware of the lack of appreciation of these rules on the part of many businesses (although perhaps also sadly unaware of their own contribution to this ignorance by treating it as a bad-debt issue) and in some parts of the country have undertaken VAT visits specifically to look at this particular issue. It has also become a regular area for checking on more routine visits.

Of course, if input tax has been repaid correctly to HMRC in the event of a long-outstanding creditor, and payment is subsequently made, the input tax may be claimed a second time.

> **⚠ *Warning!***
>
> It is difficult to overemphasise the dangers and adverse impact of this provision. It is especially damaging for struggling businesses, where the very reason for delayed payment is adverse cash flow, which can only be made worse by the requirement to part with actual money to HMRC if the six-month limit is passed. Where possible, such businesses would be advised to agree revised payment dates with their creditors, which has the effect of forestalling the need to make repayment of the input tax.

Law: VATA 1994, s. 26A; VAT Regulations 1995 (SI 1995/2518), Part XIXB

Other guidance: VAT Notice 700/18

5.8 Error correction

This section deals with the correction of errors discovered in their own records by VAT-registered persons and disclosed unprompted to HMRC.

Two methods exist for making such a correction, namely an adjustment to the VAT return following discovery of the error, and separate notification of the mistake to HMRC. The first method is only available for the correction of errors up to a certain threshold; the second method must be used for all corrections greater than that in value.

When calculating the value of net errors, it is permissible to offset against each other all mistakes discovered in a given VAT period. It is important to read this statement correctly. That is to say, it is the VAT period of discovery of the errors which is important, rather than the period or periods in which they took place.

For corrections declared on VAT returns beginning on or after 1 July 2008, the threshold above which a separate notification must be made to HMRC is the greater of £10,000 or one per cent of the box 6 figure on the VAT return, subject to an overriding maximum of £50,000. Previously, the threshold stood at £2,000.

Such notifications were formerly referred to as voluntary disclosure, although HMRC have also indicated that they have now abandoned this term as an official designation.

HMRC used to apply a penalty (see **Chapter 31**) where they discovered an error that would, except for their intervention, have been corrected automatically on the next return; for example, where input tax is claimed in a period earlier than the entitlement arose. HMRC announced a change in policy in the way penalties are to be calculated on 6 April 2011 (see *R&C Brief 15/11*). A penalty will no longer be applied in these circumstances.

Planning point

The increase in the threshold is hugely beneficial, and will eradicate the need for a separate notification of errors in a significant proportion of cases, reducing compliance burdens for both business and HMRC. In addition, it allows for the correction of underpayments of some value without incurring a liability to interest. However, if the correction relates to output VAT overpaid as a result of official error, a separate notification may still be appropriate, in order to make a claim for statutory interest.

Example 5.1

Paul, whose VAT periods end on 31 March, 30 June, 30 September and 31 December, discovers in January 2009 that he has failed to claim any input tax on his leased car over the last two years, whereas he was entitled to 50 per cent of the VAT incurred. The underclaim amounts to £960. In March 2009, he is informed by his auditors that, as a result of the corruption of data on his computer system, he underdeclared his output tax for period 06/08 by £10,650. The box 6 figure on his 03/09 VAT return is £300,000.

> As the errors were both discovered in the same VAT period and amount to a sum no greater than £10,000, Paul is entitled to net them off against each other and make an adjustment in HMRC's favour on the 03/06 VAT return of £9,690.
>
> Paul may also choose to notify HMRC of the errors separately from his VAT return; if he does so, HMRC will charge no interest as none would have been due had he corrected the errors on his VAT return.

HMRC produce form VAT652 for the reporting of errors. There is no obligation to use the form, however, and a simple letter advising of the mistakes can be written instead.

Planning point

If an error results in a net sum due to HMRC, this will normally be processed routinely by HMRC without any enquiries being made. A very simple description of the errors on form VAT652 is often the best way of dealing with such situations. If the notification relates to an amount repayable to the trader, HMRC will normally require a much greater amount of information to justify releasing the money requested, and a detailed letter explaining the nature of the error(s) is likely to be appropriate, often accompanied by some documentary evidence of what has happened.

Under the provisions of the three-year cap, no voluntary disclosure can be made more than three years after the period in which the original error took place. However, the precise method of calculating this is not totally straightforward. The orthodox time limits for making voluntary disclosures vary according to the nature of the error and the status of the VAT return on which the original error took place.

If the error was an overdeclaration, resulting in too high a sum being actually paid to HMRC, in relation either to output tax or to input tax, the three years run from the date on which the payment due with the return on which the error arose was received by HMRC.

If the error was an overdeclaration, resulting in too small a sum being claimed by the trader on a net repayment VAT return, the three years runs from the last day of the VAT period in which the original error took place.

If the error was an underdeclaration, resulting in too small an amount being paid to HMRC or in too large a repayment being claimed, the three years runs from the last day of the VAT period in which the original error took place.

⚠ Warning!

The error correction regime is intended for use only to correct errors. It is not therefore applicable to adjustments which are required to be made on particular VAT returns, even where these have the effect of paying or claiming amounts previously declared on a provisional basis, such as annual adjustments for partial exemption, retail schemes and TOMS.

Error corrections not made on a VAT return must be sent to one of HMRC's regional units. Update 2 to *VAT Notice 700/45* (see *www.hmrc.gov.uk*) contains a list of postcodes and addresses for the relevant offices.

> ### Planning point
>
> If a disclosure is notifying tax due to HMRC, there is no requirement to send payment with the disclosure. Once it has been processed by HMRC a demand, together with interest if applicable, will be issued automatically to the registered person. However, it is permissible to send payment with the notification, which has the effect of stopping interest running; those who follow this method need to be aware that a demand for interest will subsequently be received.

> ### Planning point
>
> If a correction of errors relates to a failure to charge output tax on a standard-rated supply in circumstances where the recipient of the supply would have been able to claim the VAT back as input tax had it been correctly charged at the time, HMRC should not require interest to be paid (see *VAT Notice 700/43, para. 2.3*).

Other guidance: VAT Notice 700/45

5.9   Unjust enrichment

Where a business has overpaid VAT, HMRC can refuse to repay it if they can show that it would unjustly enrich the taxpayer (VATA 1994, s. 80).

This legislation was originally introduced in 1990. From 4 December 1996, regulations were introduced regarding reimbursement of customers who have borne the original VAT charge (VAT Regulations 1995 (SI 1995/2518), reg. 43A–43G). In such cases, suppliers must undertake to reimburse customers with the full amount of VAT and of any interest received by the supplier from HMRC within 90 days of receiving repayment. There is no provision for the making of a handling or other charge – all of the funds must be repaid to the customer that paid the original VAT charge or the refund received from HMRC must be repaid to them within 14 days of the end of the 90-day period. In such cases it is not in the supplier's interest to make a claim for a refund, unless under pressure from customers to do so, or if it can be utilised as a matter of customer care. Suppliers are required to keep a record of all repayments made.

From 19 March 1997, where the VAT has been borne by someone other than the claimant (as is the case where the customer has been charged and has paid the VAT) the claim is restricted to an amount that compensates the claimant for the loss or damage which he has or may incur as a result of mistaken assumptions regarding the operation of any VAT provisions.

The issue of unjust enrichment has been considered by the European Court in the joined cases of *Société Camateb v Directeur Général des Douanes et Droits Indirects* (Joined cases C-192/95 to C-218/95) [1997] ECR I-165. The court ruled that the tax authority of an EU member state could only refuse to repay a charge which had been wrongly levied if that charge had been borne in its entirety by another person and that reimbursement to the supplier would amount to unjust enrichment. But where only a part of the charge had been passed on, the supplier should be reimbursed to the extent of the part which was not passed on.

However, where prices are set at market level regardless of the impact of VAT, and VAT accounted for out of the charge made, then the taxpayer has a just argument for recovery of overpaid VAT. In the case of *King (t/a The Barbury Shooting School)* [2003] BVC 4,039, they started trading as The Barbury Shooting School in 1987 and set their prices according to what they thought customers would pay. They accounted for VAT on their income, but in January 2002 submitted a refund claim for supplies to individuals on the basis that these supplies were exempt from VAT under VATA 1994, Sch. 9, Grp. 6, item 2. Customs accepted that VAT had been overpaid but challenged the refund claim on grounds of unjust enrichment. In deciding that the appellants had not been enriched let alone unjustly, the tribunal reasoned that having received the repayment they would have been no better off than they would have been had they accounted for VAT correctly in the first place, their prices being set according to what the market would stand.

Law: VATA 1994, s. 80(3)–(3C)

Other guidance: VAT Notice 700/4, s. 145

5.10 Change of VAT rate

To ease the economic crisis the standard VAT rate was reduced from 17.5 per cent to 15 per cent with effect from 1 December 2008.

The standard rate is to return to 17.5 per cent with effect from 1 January 2010.

The standard rate is also due to increase to 20 per cent from 4 January 2011.

The VAT fraction is:

  15 per cent: 3/23.

  17.5 per cent: 7/47.

  20 per cent: 1/6.

> ### *Planning point*
>
> Pubs, clubs, hotels and other establishments whose busiest night of the year will be affected by the change in VAT rate, i.e. sell drinks at 11.59pm on 31 December 2010 at 15 per cent and 12:01am on 1 January 2010 at 17.5 per cent will be able to determine the VAT rate based upon a 'session'. This means that the 15 per cent VAT rate can be used until the session commencing immediately prior to midnight on the 31 December and ending one or two hours into the New Year is completed. This has been ratified in a Parliamentary question posed mid-2009.

5.10.1 Dealing with the change in rate

VAT is to be accounted for at 20 per cent for all takings received on or after 4 January 2011. Where, in a cash or retail business mainly dealing with non-business customers, goods were taken away before this date, but paid for after this date, VAT can be accounted for at 17.5 per cent. Where a retailer uses an apportionment or direct calculation scheme, it will be necessary to make a calculation up to 3 January 2011 and a further calculation for the period commencing 4 January 2011. Where sales are made through a coin operated machine that does not record when the sales are made, it is necessary to apportion the income received according to typical usage of the machine.

Where the customers are mainly business customers, VAT at 20 per cent needs to be accounted for on all invoices issued on or after 4 January 2011 that are issued within 14 days of the service being completed or goods delivered (or such longer period as agreed with HMRC).

> ### *Planning point*
>
> Issue invoices for all outstanding sales on 3 January or before to ensure that VAT can be charged at 17.5 per cent (see **5.10.2** regarding avoidance legislation). Where the customer is a business customer that can reclaim VAT this is not an important issue.

Credit notes need to identify the invoice that was issued to ensure that the correct VAT rate is adjusted. An invoice issued at 17.5 per cent needs a credit note for 17.5 per cent even if issued after 4 January 2011; all refunds also need to reflect the VAT originally charged. Similarly, if Bad Debt Relief is claimed, it must be claimed at the same rate as the VAT that was originally charged.

If a deposit is received before 4 January 2011, the deposit will be subject to 17.5 per cent VAT. If the balance is received on or after that date, it will be subject to 20 per cent VAT (although the issue of a tax invoice may override this). The supplier can, if it simplifies accounting, charge 20 per cent of the deposit and the balancing payment.

Continuous supplies that span the date of the rate change can be apportioned for the value supplied before and after the change in rate. A single supply that spans the rate change, however, will be subject to VAT at 20 per cent as it will not be completed until after the change in rate. It is possible to invoice for the value supplied up until the change in rate at 17.5 per cent for work done up to 3 January 2011 if an invoice is issued or payment received before the date of the change in rate. Similar rules apply to stage payments made for work in progress and work completed in the construction industry.

Where a ticket is sold, or a season ticket is sold, before 4 January 2011 the VAT rate for the supply will be 17.5 per cent even if the event does not take place until after 3 January 2011.

VAT will need to be claimed at the appropriate rate on invoices for supplies received. For example, the appropriate VAT fraction needs to be applied to less detailed tax invoices according to the date of issue. Supplies made over a period that provide a schedule with the invoice will be required to issue a new schedule for supplies after 4 January 2011.

The new scale charges that reflect the 20 per cent rate are shown in **Chapter 11**.

5.10.2 Anti-forestalling Legislation

HMRC have issued anti-forestalling legislation effective from 25 November 2008 to combat businesses that try and take advantage of the 15 per cent VAT rate for supplies which predominately take place after 1 January 2010 when the rate rises to 17.5 per cent (Finance Act 2009, Sch. 36). Similar legislation has been introduced in respect of the rate change on 4 January 2011. Effectively, the supplier tries to fix the VAT rate by issuing an invoice or receiving payment before the rate rises. This fixes the VAT due at the lower rate even though the goods or services are not delivered or performed until on or after the date of the rate rises.

The legislation that affects the 2011 change introduces a supplementary charge to VAT on the supply of goods or services (or the grant of the right to receive goods or services) where the customer cannot recover all of the VAT charged on the supply and one of the following conditions is met:

- the supplier and customer are connected parties;
- the supplier issues advance invoices to persons connected with the supplier for future supplies;
- prepayments are received or invoices are issued in advance in excess of £100,000 and this is not normal commercial practice;
- rights or options are supplied to receive goods or services free of charge or at a discount;
- the supplier funds the purchase of the goods or services or grant of rights; or
- a VAT invoice is issued by the supplier where payment is not due for at least six months.

A supplementary charge of 2.5 per cent will apply to transactions that meet these criteria.

5.11 Tables

5.11.1 Table 5.1 – Rates of tax

VAT Rates		
	Rate	*VAT fraction*
Standard rate:		
4 January 2011 to date	20%	1/6
1 January 2010–3 January 2011	17.5%	7/47
1 December 2008–31 December 2009	15%	3/23
1 April 1991–30 November 2008	17.5%	7/47
Reduced rate:		
1 April 1994–31 August 1997	8%	2/27
1 September 1997 to date	5%	1/21

5.11.2 Table 5.2 – VAT liability

Zero-rated supplies (Sch. 8)	
Bank notes	Gold
Books	Imports and exports
Caravans and houseboats	International services
Charities	Protected buildings
Clothing and footwear	Sewerage and water
Construction of buildings	Talking books (blind and handicapped) and wireless sets (blind)
Drugs and medicines, and aids for handicapped people	Transport
Food	

Reduced-rated supplies (Sch. 7A)	
Children's car seats	Residential renovations and alterations
Contraceptive products	Residential conversions
Domestic fuel and power	Smoking cessation products
Energy-saving materials: installation	Welfare advice or information
Heating equipment, security goods and gas supplies: grant funded installation or connection	Women's sanitary products

Exempt supplies (Sch. 9)	
Betting, gaming and lotteries	Insurance
Burial and cremation	Investment Gold
Cultural Services	Land
Education	Postal services
Finance	Sports, sports competitions and physical education
	Supplies of goods where input tax cannot be recovered
Fundraising events by charities and other qualifying bodies	Subscriptions to trade unions, professional and other public interest
Health and welfare	Works of art

Note: these are the group headings of zero-rated and exempt supplies in VATA 1994 and the liability of any specific items must be verified.

Schemes to Help Small Businesses

6.1   Introduction

6.1.1   The schemes covered

Various simplified schemes exist, designed for smaller businesses, to reduce the cost of their administration of VAT. This chapter outlines the three schemes: cash accounting, annual accounting and the flat rate scheme. It considers the benefits of using the schemes, including the benefits of using more than one scheme, and it considers the interaction with other aspects of VAT.

Cash accounting was introduced with effect from 1 October 1987, annual accounting from 1 July 1988, and the flat rate scheme with effect from 24 April 2002. All three schemes are voluntary. A taxable person may use the cash accounting scheme without prior approval from HMRC, whilst entry to both annual accounting and the flat rate scheme requires prior application.

6.1.2   Outline of the schemes

From a European perspective, art. 395(1) of the Principal VAT Directive (Directive 2006/112) allows EU member states to introduce special measures that simplify procedures for charging VAT, as long as the amount of VAT payable at the final consumption stage is affected to no more than a negligible extent.

Other guidance:

- VAT Notice 731;
- VAT Notice 732;
- VAT Notice 733;
- VAT Notice 04/SB/001;
- VAT Notice 04/SB/002;
- VAT Notice 04/SB/003; and
- VAT Notice 04/SB/004.

6.1.3   Turnover limits

Entry to the schemes is restricted to smaller businesses, as measured by annual taxable turnover of £1.35 million excluding VAT for both cash accounting and annual accounting. For entry to the flat rate scheme, the taxable turnover must be below £150,000 excluding VAT exempt income and sales of any capital assets.

6.1.4 Brief history of the schemes

The most obvious development of the cash accounting and annual accounting schemes has been the increase in turnover limits, from the original £250,000 to their current levels. The taxable turnover limit for the flat rate scheme has also increased from £100,000 to £150,000.

Planning point

The cash accounting scheme originally required the taxable person to apply to HMRC. This requirement was dropped with effect from 1 April 1993.

6.2 Cash accounting – joining the scheme

6.2.1 Conditions for joining the scheme

A taxable person may join the scheme as long as the following conditions are fulfilled:

- there are reasonable grounds for believing that the annual taxable turnover in the year then beginning will not exceed £1.35 million, excluding VAT (reg. 58(1) (a)), i.e. the person is required to predict his future turnover;
- all VAT returns have been submitted;
- all VAT payments, in respect of returns and assessments, have been made;
- if all VAT payments have not been made, an agreement has been reached with HMRC that the outstanding amount will be settled;
- in the previous year, the person has not been convicted of any offence in connection with VAT;
- in the previous year, the person has not made any payment to compound penalties under Customs and Excise Management Act 1979, s. 152;
- in the previous year, the person has not been assessed to any penalty under VATA 1994 s. 60; and
- in the previous year, the person has not ceased to be entitled to continue to operate the scheme, i.e. was expelled from the scheme under the provisions of reg. 64(1).

For the purposes of joining the scheme, the value of taxable supplies should include supplies made at the standard, reduced and zero rates, but exclude the value of any expected sales of capital assets.

> **Planning point**
>
> In a case where a taxable person is expected to exceed £1.35 million only by including the value of the sale of a capital asset, the person should make a note of his anticipated turnover and details of the expected sale(s) of capital assets. Should a dispute with HMRC arise later about his eligibility to join the scheme, such a note will enable the dispute to be resolved.

A taxable person is no longer required to apply to join the scheme. Once he has satisfied himself that he is entitled to use the scheme, he may do so from the start of any prescribed accounting period (reg. 58(1)).

Law: VAT Regulations 1995 (SI 1995/2518), reg. 58

6.2.2 Joining from the commencement of business

A person beginning in business may register for VAT and commence using cash accounting with effect from the same date.

Such a person may receive money for supplies made and invoices issued before registration. Such receipts are not chargeable to VAT, since the supplies were made before registration for VAT. The person must be careful to separate such receipts from those received in respect of supplies made after registration.

Equally, where payments are made for supplies received prior to registration, input tax is not deductible under the scheme, although it may be allowable under the pre-registration input tax rules.

6.2.3 Late notification of registration

A person who has notified his liability to register for VAT later than he was required to cannot use the cash accounting scheme for supplies made before the date he notified HMRC. Once the person has submitted his first return, and either made full payment or reached agreement with HMRC for making payment in instalments, he can join the scheme.

> **Planning point**
>
> In practice, however, it is unusual for HMRC to object to the use of cash accounting in these circumstances.

6.2.4 VAT accounting on joining the scheme

If a person is already registered for VAT and using conventional accounting, output tax will already have been accounted for on supplies made and invoices issued in previous periods. The cash accounting scheme does not apply to such supplies or their corresponding receipts. The person must be careful to separate such receipts from those received in respect of supplies made under the scheme.

Input tax incurred under conventional accounting should have been claimed before changing to cash accounting, even if payment has not yet been made. The person must be careful to separate such payments from those made in respect of supplies received under the scheme.

6.2.5 Retrospective use of the scheme

A person may not apply the scheme retrospectively to his business.

6.2.6 Refusal to allow use of the scheme

HMRC have powers, 'for the protection of the revenue', to prevent a person from joining the scheme (reg. 58(4)). Thus, they may act pre-emptively to prevent an abuse of the scheme which gives the taxable person greater advantage than is intended by the scheme.

Notice 731, para. 2.9, brings together HMRC's power to prevent a person from joining the scheme and their power to expel a person from the scheme. The two powers clearly complement each other, and appear to be designed for use against a person who deliberately manipulates the scheme or a person who acts negligently in using the scheme.

For details of the circumstances in which these powers may be used, see **6.3.7**.

Law: VAT Regulations 1995 (SI 1995/2518), reg. 58(4)

6.2.7 Change in VAT rate

VAT is due at 17.5 per cent on supplies made before 4 January 2011, even if payment is made after this date. It will be necessary to keep records to show that the supply was made before 4 January (for example, invoice being issued, service completed or goods delivered). Failure to do so will mean that VAT is due at 20 per cent. Similarly, purchases received before 4 January will only be eligible for a deduction of VAT at 17.5 per cent. Where a deposit is received before 4 January, VAT will be due on the deposit at 17.5 per cent. If the balance is paid after 4 January, it will be subject to VAT at 20 per cent (but note, special anti-avoidance rules can also apply). More information is in section **5.10**.

6.3 Cash accounting – using the scheme

6.3.1 Record-keeping requirements

Once a person has commenced using the scheme, he is required to issue invoices and maintain his records in common with other taxable persons. However, there are certain additional requirements.

Since cash accounting provides that VAT is accounted for on the date of payment or receipt, the scheme rules require that cross-references are made between invoices issued and payments received, and between invoices received and payments made. In particular, such cross-references must include bank statements, paying-in books and cheque stubs.

The exact way in which such cross-references are made is not laid down. What is required is that they are clear, complete and up to date.

Where the customer uses the scheme and makes payment in money (that is, in cash), the supplier must endorse the customer's copy of the sales invoice with the date and the amount paid. (The supplier is obliged to endorse an invoice in this way, whether or not he uses the scheme.) An invoice does not need to be receipted where there is an accompanying till receipt or similar, which clearly indicates 'cash sale'. Such a receipt should be attached to the customer's copy of the invoice. HMRC may question the veracity of any non-receipted cash purchases.

Law: VAT Regulations 1995 (SI 1995/2518), reg. 65(3)

Planning point

Although input tax may be claimed at the time payment is made, there remains an obligation to obtain a proper VAT invoice to substantiate the input tax claim. Cash accounting does not remove this obligation, even though in this circumstance it allows the person to claim input tax earlier than he would otherwise have done.

6.3.2 Date of receipts and payments

There are rules governing the date on which a payment is deemed to have been made or received. The date of payment by the customer and the date of receipt by the supplier are not necessarily the same.

Where the means of payment is in money (that is, cash), payment is received on the date the money is received; payment is made on the date the money is paid.

Where the means of payment is by cheque, payment is received on the date the cheque is received or, if later, the date on the cheque; payment is made on the date the cheque is sent or, if later, the date on the cheque. If the cheque is dishonoured, any entry should be adjusted.

Where the means of payment is by a bank transfer, direct debit or similar, payment is received on the date the bank account is credited with the amount; payment is made on the date the bank account is debited with the amount. It is assumed, therefore, that the taxable person will ensure that bank statements are received regularly, so that VAT can be accounted for correctly.

Where the means of payment is by debit or credit card, payment is received on the date the sales voucher is made out, not the date the money is debited to the bank account; payment is made on the date the sales voucher is made out, not when the credit card statement is received or settled. Where a payment is cancelled, an adjustment must be made.

6.3.3 Deposits and part payments

Where any payment is received in respect of a supply, then VAT output tax is due under cash accounting. Where a person using cash accounting pays a deposit, he should request that a VAT invoice be issued, to enable him to reclaim VAT input tax in respect of that amount. Subsequent partial payments are also treated in the same way.

A distinction needs to be made where a deposit is taken as security, for example, in respect of goods loaned. If only part of the deposit is returned, where goods loaned have been damaged, then a payment is deemed to have been made. (Since the payment is compensation, this may not be a consideration for a supply and thus may be outside the scope of VAT.)

Conversely, if the loan period is extended and the deposit is used to pay for the additional amount due, then payment has been made in respect of that additional amount.

6.3.4 Payments for supplies of different liabilities

Where a supplier using the scheme makes supplies of different VAT liabilities, then those items must be itemised clearly on the sales invoices.

Example 6.1

Description	Amount exclusive of VAT	VAT rate	VAT amount
Reference books	£200.00	0%	£0.00
Educational CDs	£400.00	20%	£80.00
		Net amount	£600.00
		VAT amount	£70.00
		Invoice amount	£680.00

Where a part payment is made for an invoice which includes supplies of different liabilities, then a fair and reasonable apportionment should be made.

Example 6.2

Using the invoice above, a payment of £204.00 is received.

Description	Amount invoiced	Amount received	
Reference books	£200.00	£200.00 × 204/680 =	£60.00
Educational CDs	£400.00	£400.00 × 204/680 =	£120.00
VAT	£780.00	£80.00 × 204/680 =	£24.00
Total	£680.00		£204.00

Thus, output tax of £24.00 is to be accounted for in respect of the payment.

Where payment is made covering more than one such invoice, then payments should be attributed to invoices in the order they were issued.

Example 6.3

A supplier issues two invoices.

Description	Amount exclusive of VAT	VAT rate	VAT amount
Reference books	£200.00	0%	£0.00
		Net amount	£200.00
		VAT amount	£0.00
Invoice dated 15 June 2012		Invoice amount	£200.00

Description	Amount exclusive of VAT	VAT rate	VAT amount
Educational CDs	£400.00	20%	£80.00
		Net amount	£400.00
		VAT amount	£80.00
Invoice dated 15 July 2012		Invoice amount	£480.00

The customer makes a payment of £435.00. The first invoice is paid in full, leaving £240.00 to be set against the second invoice. Of that amount, £40.00 represents VAT output tax.

However, where the parties have specifically agreed otherwise, they may depart from this rule. For instance, there may be a dispute about some goods or services, or the supplier may allow different settlement periods. It is advisable that, where payment is made in such circumstances, the customer provides a note indicating which invoices, or items, are being settled.

Example 6.4

A supplier issues two invoices, each identical to the first example above, but in the opposite order. There is a fault with the CDs, and the customer only pays £200.00 for the books. Since these goods are zero-rated, the supplier need account for no output tax.

6.3.5 Payments in a foreign currency

Special rules apply to payments made or received in a foreign currency. It is required that any conversion rate be calculated at the date of the invoice, not the date of a payment.

If the invoice shows amounts in sterling and in a foreign currency, and the full amount of foreign currency is paid, then the VAT amount shown is due. If a part payment of the foreign currency is made, then the amount of VAT due is calculated based on the proportion of foreign currency paid.

If the invoice is completed only in sterling, and the payment is made in a foreign currency, the conversion rate applicable on the invoice date must be used. If the resulting amount is lower than the amount shown on the invoice, then a correspondingly lower amount of output tax should be accounted for. If the resulting amount is higher than the amount shown on the invoice, it is assumed that a correspondingly higher amount of output tax will be accounted for. The conversion rates that can be used include HMRC's official rates and any well known commercial rate (such as a published bank rate or a rate in a newspaper).

Other guidance: *VAT Notice 700*, para. 3.1(f)

6.3.6 Completion of VAT returns

When a taxable person using cash accounting completes his VAT return, he must be careful to enter in the outputs box the value of payments received in respect of sales, and to enter in the inputs box the value of payments made in respect of purchases.

Where a person makes or receives supplies which must be accounted for outside the scheme, the VAT return should still be completed on the basis of the values of payments made and received. This means that, in respect of these supplies, the output tax and input tax is accounted for in the usual manner, but the values of outputs and inputs are based on payments made and received. (HMRC's publications should make this matter more explicit.)

6.3.7 Discretionary removal from the scheme

HMRC can expel a taxable person from the cash accounting scheme in certain circumstances. Their powers extend to expelling a person where the circumstances fall short of those described, but where HMRC consider it necessary for the 'protection of the revenue'.

Examples of circumstances in which this power may be used include:

- when a taxable person has defaulted on arrangements to settle VAT debts by instalments;
- when a taxable person incurs penalties not mentioned in reg. 64;
- when a taxable person consistently claims input tax before payment is made;
- where there is an incipient insolvency;
- where the compliance history of the individual or company suggests that there may be a further risk of tax loss; and
- where alleged supplies of services are artificial, and designed to manipulate cash accounting.

(These examples include circumstances which, before 3 July 1997, resulted in automatic expulsion from the scheme, and circumstances mentioned in HMRC's internal guidance.)

The above examples are also relevant when HMRC exercise their power not to allow a person to begin using cash accounting.

When notifying a taxable person of either his expulsion from the scheme, or that he is not entitled to begin using the scheme, HMRC will indicate a period, an 'exclusion period', during which that person may not use the scheme. Once that period has expired that person may then join, or rejoin, the scheme, subject to any conditions HMRC may set.

Law: VAT Regulations 1995 (SI 1995/2518), reg. 64

6.4   Cash accounting – particular circumstances

6.4.1   Supplies excluded from the scheme

Regulation 58(2)excludes a number of specific supplies from the scheme. This applies whether the supplies made or received by the taxable person are:

- agreements described as lease, hire purchases, conditional sale and credit sale agreements;
- supplies where a VAT invoice is issued, and full payment for the amount shown on the invoice is not due for a period longer than six months from the invoice date; and
- supplies where the VAT invoice is issued in advance of the time the supply is made (under this section, where there is a partial performance of the supply at the time the VAT invoice is issued, cash accounting does apply for that part of the supply (reg. 58(3)).

Example 6.5

A mail order business using the scheme receives an order for two lines of goods. One line is in stock and is delivered immediately. The second line is out of stock. An invoice sent with the first delivery includes both lines of goods. Cash accounting applies to the first line of goods but not to the second line.

Also excluded from the scheme are goods imported from outside the EU, acquired from a person registered for VAT in another EU member state, or removed from a customs warehouse or free zone. The scheme can be used for the onward supply of such goods in the UK.

6.4.2   Exports and removals

The scheme can be used for exports to a place outside the EU and for removals to another EU member state. Where evidence of export or removal is not received within the time limits provided for, output tax has to be accounted for in respect of payments received. Once evidence has been received, an adjustment can be made to claim back such output tax.

Details of time limits for exports and removals are found in HMRC *VAT Notice 703*, para. 1.12.

6.4.3   Acquisition tax

Where a taxable person receives a 'reverse charge' service, output tax must be accounted for. Since the tax point for such a supply is the date of payment, the reverse charge must be accounted for on the VAT return for the period in which payment is made.

There is an exception where the consideration for the supply is not in money. In this case the tax point is the last day of the prescribed accounting period in which the services are performed.

Law: VAT Regulations 1995 (SI 1995/2518), reg. 82

6.4.4 Debts and factored debts

With effect from 22 September 1997, a distinction was made between debts which are collected by a third party, and debts which are formally assigned to a third party.

In the first case, the person retains legal right to the debt, and output tax is only due when the third party receives the debt, or part of it. This remains true even if the third party provides a proportion of the debt as a loan.

In the second case, the debt is no longer the debt of the person using cash accounting. Such assigned debts are excluded from cash accounting, and output tax must be accounted for when the decision is made to assign the debt. The value to be accounted for is the value of the supply or supplies made to which the debt relates, not the amount for which the debt is assigned.

> ### Planning point
>
> Where a debt, which is assigned to a third party, is later reassigned to the person using cash accounting, output tax can be reduced to reflect that amount remaining outstanding.

6.4.5 Barter transactions and payments in kind

Special rules apply where a person provides goods or services as full or part payment for goods or services supplied to him.

Under the cash accounting rules, VAT is accounted for when payment is made or received, whether the payment is in money or something else. Thus, if a taxable person using the scheme receives a supply as payment for the supplies he made, output tax is due based on the value of supplies received, at the time those supplies are received. The time of supply is governed by the tax point rules, which apply irrespective of cash accounting considerations.

A tribunal considered a case where a person received share capital from a creditor company in satisfaction of a debt. At a later date, the company went into liquidation, rendering the shares worthless. The tribunal held that full payment for the debt, some

£30,000, was received when the shares were accepted and thus output tax was due on that amount (*A-Z Electrical* [1994] BVC 1,350).

Example 6.6

Peter, a taxable person, uses the cash accounting scheme. He receives a supply of goods as full consideration for a supply he has made. The tax point is the date those goods are made available to him, either by collection or delivery, or when a VAT invoice is issued in respect of those goods, as long as that is within 14 days of the date of collection or delivery. Peter must account for output tax on the value of the supplies he has made at the date those goods are delivered to him, or an invoice is received in respect of those goods. This holds true whether or not his customer uses cash accounting.

If his customer is not registered for VAT, he cannot issue a VAT invoice, therefore the time of supply is the date of collection or delivery of the goods. The taxable person is required to account for output tax at that date.

Where payment is made by the performance of services, the tax point is either the date those services are performed or the date a VAT invoice is issued. Output tax is due at the earlier of these occurrences.

⚠ *Warning!*

Since a taxable person making a supply, whether or not under cash accounting, is obliged to issue a VAT invoice, it is essential that, where a barter arrangement is to be used, the issue of invoices by both parties is agreed. This is relevant both to the value of supplies to be made and the dates on which such supplies are made.

6.4.6 Partial exemption

Where a taxable person makes supplies which are exempt, he will be required to restrict the input tax he can claim. Special rules apply to how the amount of input tax to be claimed is to be calculated.

In general, the partial exemption calculation is based on the proportion of taxable and exempt supplies made in the period concerned. Where a partially exempt person uses the cash accounting scheme, the calculation must be based on payments received.

A partial exemption calculation will require an annual adjustment. This adjustment will take into account receipts in respect of taxable and exempt supplies. The adjustment will reflect the value of receipts, not the value of supplies made in the year in question.

> ⚠ **Warning!**
>
> A person will lose all his input tax in the year if he receives money in that year only in respect of exempt supplies, even if he has made taxable supplies.

The cash accounting scheme entitles the taxable person to deduct input tax in the period in which payment or consideration is made (reg. 65(2)) and thus, application of the partial exemption rules must be to input tax where payment has been made, rather than input tax on supplies received. There was some discussion of this matter in the case of *CEB Ltd* [2001] BVC 4,097.

6.4.7 Use of computer accounting software

There is a particular difficulty where a taxable person uses an off-the-shelf PC accounting package which uses either conventional accounting or cash accounting in an accounting period but cannot account correctly for conventional invoice accounting and cash accounting transactions in the same period. Ideally, advice should be sought prior to purchase.

6.4.8 Annual accounts reconciliation

Visiting VAT officers generally check a taxable person's annual accounts, to compare the sales figures with those shown on the VAT returns. Where a taxpayer uses the cash accounting scheme, a reconciliation should be approached with caution, since the VAT returns show the value of payments received, whilst annual accounts show the value of sales made (assuming the accounts are made on the accruals basis).

Adjusting the value of sales, as per the annual accounts, by adding the opening and deducting the closing debtors will make reconciliation with the VAT returns possible.

6.4.9 Default surcharges

A default surcharge is applied where a registered person submits or pays his VAT return after the due date. There exists a statutory defence that a person will not be liable to a default surcharge where there is a 'reasonable excuse' for the return or the payment not being despatched in time (VATA 1994, s. 59(7)(b)). Although the reasonable excuse specifically excludes 'an insufficiency of funds' (VATA 1994, s. 71(1)(a)), the courts have held that it is possible to look behind the insufficiency of funds to the reason for that insufficiency. Where there is, in the words of the courts, 'unforeseeable and inescapable misfortune', a reasonable excuse may well be established. Examples have included dishonesty and persistent late settlement of invoices.

The relation between the cash accounting scheme and the default surcharge was raised in the Court of Appeal (*C & E Commrs v Steptoe* [1992] BVC 142) by Nolan LJ. His comment was that use of the cash accounting scheme 'will generally deprive such a trader from putting forward delays in payment by his customers as a reasonable excuse for non-payment of his tax'. (The tribunal has commented on this statement, for example, *Cohort Specialist Security Services Ltd* [1995] BVC 1,475; *J & G Precision Engineering Ltd* [1998] BVC 4,067.)

⚠ *Warning!*

Thus, where a taxable person using cash accounting incurs default surcharges, he may have an additional difficulty securing a 'reasonable excuse' defence.

6.5 Cash accounting – leaving the scheme

6.5.1 Voluntary decision to leave

A taxable person may choose to leave the scheme, for reasons of his own choosing, or he may be obliged to leave the scheme, in a variety of circumstances. *VAT Notice 731* refers to circumstances when the taxable person finds that the scheme is no longer of benefit, or his accounting system cannot cope with the requirements of the scheme.

A taxable person may choose to leave the scheme. He must do so at the end of a VAT period. There is no longer an obligation to remain in the scheme for a minimum of two years, nor a restriction that a person could only leave the scheme at the anniversary of joining.

With effect from 1 April 2004, a six-month option was introduced, to offset the impact of having to account for all outstanding output tax when ceasing to use the scheme. This allows the taxable person to account for the outstanding output tax up to six months after leaving the scheme.

This option allows VAT on debtors and creditors as at the date of leaving the scheme to be accounted for on a cash basis on the next two VAT returns, rather than being accounted for in full on the VAT return for the period in which the taxpayer ceases to use cash accounting. After the six-month period, the VAT on outstanding debtors needs to be accounted for, but this amount can be immediately set off by claiming bad debt relief.

Planning point

Although superficially attractive, this option only defers by three months the VAT due on debtors or claimable on creditors to the extent that these have not been paid for within three months of ceasing to use cash accounting. Except in the case of long-outstanding debtors, therefore, it has a trivial effect.

Regardless of the six-month option, there is almost always a cash flow impact of leaving the scheme. For most businesses, leaving the scheme will require a larger than usual VAT payment for the following period.

> **Planning point**
>
> If it is possible, a person may choose a quarter when outstanding debts are lower or he may defer the issuing of sales invoices, so as to minimise the impact of leaving the scheme. For some types of business, it may be possible to issue a pro forma invoice, or request for payment, rather than a VAT invoice. The effect is to defer the tax point until the date of payment, thus mitigating the cash flow disadvantage of leaving the cash accounting scheme.

6.5.2 Tolerance limit exceeded

Since its introduction, the cash accounting scheme has had a built-in tolerance limit. This limit is set 25 per cent higher than the turnover limit. Only once this higher limit has been exceeded is a person obliged to leave the scheme.

Thus, under current rules, where the turnover limit is £1.35 million, the tolerance limit is £1.6 million.

A person should calculate his turnover on a rolling basis. Thus, at the end of each quarter, he should add the totals of the taxable supplies made in that period and in the previous three periods. The person cannot exclude from the value of his taxable turnover the sale of any assets made within those periods. Note, a person is required to leave the scheme when the value of his taxable supplies, not the amount of cash received, exceeds the tolerance limit.

> **Planning point**
>
> Both the turnover limit and the tolerance limit represent the value of taxable supplies made. Thus, where a person makes a mixture of exempt and taxable supplies, he should only take into account the value of taxable supplies when considering whether he has exceeded either limit.

If a person is required to account for some transactions outside the scheme, the value of those transactions should still be taken into account when calculating taxable turnover.

It is advisable, once the turnover limit has been exceeded, that the person give thought to whether he should leave the scheme voluntarily before his turnover exceeds the tolerance limit, and take advantage of any planning opportunities as may exist.

6.5.3 Accounting for outstanding tax

Where a taxable person leaves the scheme, either voluntarily or because his turnover exceeds the limit, he has to account for VAT under conventional accounting from the beginning of the next prescribed accounting period. The person may also benefit from the six-month option, introduced with effect from 1 April 2004. The six-month option allows a person to operate the scheme for a further six months for supplies made while using the scheme (see **6.5.1**).

After the six-month period, the taxable person is required to account for any outstanding output tax and input tax on the next return.

Where a taxable person is expelled from the scheme by HMRC (see **6.5.8**), the 'transitional arrangements' do not apply.

6.5.4 Bad debt relief

When bringing VAT to account on debtors on ceasing to use the cash accounting scheme, bad debt relief may be claimed in respect of any qualifying debts, subject to the normal conditions, as follows if:

- it is six months since the debt became due or the supply was made, whichever was the later; and
- the debt has been written off to a 'refunds for bad debts' account in the person's records.

Where payment is later received in respect of any amount written off as a bad debt, output tax should then be accounted for.

6.5.5 One-off transaction

There may be circumstances where a person's taxable turnover exceeds the tolerance limit because of a one-off increase in sales. HMRC have power to allow such a person to remain in the scheme (VAT Regulations 1995 (SI 1995/2518), reg. 60(3)). In such circumstances, the person is expected to notify HMRC of the full facts and request to continue using the scheme. The person should address such issues as:

- that the sale was a one-off transaction, which had not occurred before and was not likely to recur, such as a sale of a capital asset;
- that there was a temporary increase in sales due to particular factors;
- that the increase arose due to genuine commercial activity;
- that the person will not gain an advantage over competitors; and
- that the person's taxable turnover in the succeeding 12 months is expected to fall below the turnover limit (not the tolerance limit).

It should be noted that the two scheme limits come into play in this situation. Thus, the question of a one-off transaction arises where the taxable turnover exceeds the tolerance limit (i.e. £1.6 million). The person will only be allowed to remain in the scheme if he can demonstrate to HMRC that his turnover is likely to fall below the turnover limit (i.e. £1.35 million).

Regulation 60(1) requires that a person leave the scheme immediately when his taxable turnover exceeds the tolerance limit. Regulation 60(3) grants HMRC power to allow the person to remain in the scheme. However, reg. 64(1)(c) states that the person shall not be entitled to continue using the scheme if he fails to leave the scheme as required by reg. 60(1). Thus, if HMRC decide that the person should not be entitled to continue using the scheme he cannot continue to use it, in breach of their direction. HMRC will assess such a person from the period he should have left the scheme.

If a dispute remains, the person should perhaps pursue the matter by means of an appeal.

6.5.6 Rejoining the scheme

A person who has left the scheme is entitled to rejoin it, subject to the rules for joining the scheme. He may rejoin the scheme at the beginning of any tax period.

Where a person was obliged to leave the scheme when his turnover exceeded the tolerance limit, he may rejoin it at a later date when his turnover is expected, during the succeeding 12 months, not to exceed the turnover limit.

However, that person may not rejoin the scheme if, within the previous year, he had been expelled from the scheme. Where HMRC write to a taxable person expelling him from the scheme, they should indicate a period during which he will not be entitled to use cash accounting. Typically that period is one year. The person is therefore not entitled to use the scheme until that period has elapsed.

6.5.7 Failure to leave the scheme

Where a person is required to leave the scheme, either because his turnover has exceeded the tolerance limit or because HMRC have directed him to do so, then he must begin accounting for output tax and input tax on the conventional invoice basis.

Where HMRC identify a person who has failed to leave the scheme, they should write, explaining the relevant facts and stating when the person should leave, or should have left, the scheme. They will also issue an assessment for any periods where cash accounting has been improperly used.

6.5.8 Compulsory expulsion from the scheme

Regulation 64(1) lays down four circumstances in which a taxable person is required to cease using the scheme:

- whilst using the scheme, the person has been convicted of an offence in relation to VAT, or he has made a compound payment, under Customs and Excise Management Act 1979, s. 152;
- whilst using the scheme, the person has been assessed for a penalty under VATA 1994, s. 60;
- the person has failed to leave the scheme when his turnover exceeded the tolerance limit; and
- HMRC consider that the person should leave the scheme 'for the protection of the revenue'.

Certain points should be noted.

1. Regulation 64(1)(a) does not restrict an offence in relation to VAT to an offence falling within VATA 1994, s. 72 (this is the offence section within VATA 1994). Thus, it is presumed, a conviction brought under the Theft Act 1968 in circumstances concerning VAT would also require expulsion from the scheme. (*VAT Notice 731* does refer to a VAT offence, apparently restricting the offence to one under VATA 1994, s. 72.)

2. The new penalty regime that started on 1 April 2010 will apply to the cash accounting scheme (see **Chapter 21**). This can apply penalties of up to 100 per cent of the potential lost VAT where the VAT has been lost due to deliberate and concealed actions. Penalties may be 70 per cent where the action was not concealed or otherwise as low as 30 per cent. Mitigation of these penalties is available where there has been disclosure (prompted or unprompted). This will reduce the penalty depending on the circumstances of the disclosure and the initial penalty.

Where a taxable person is expelled from the scheme under this regulation, he is required to account for all outstanding output tax on the return for the period in which he was expelled. The person should, of course, make any adjustment for input tax which remains unclaimed. HMRC have indicated that they will write to notify a person that his use of the scheme has been withdrawn (*VAT Notice 731*, para. 5.4 refers). Although such a letter should include the date from which the person must cease using the scheme, it should be noted that reg. 64 actually lays down the time at which the person must cease using the scheme.

> ### Example 6.7
>
> Sally uses cash accounting and is assessed for a penalty for evasion. Her VAT return period ends are March, June, September and December. The penalty assessment is issued on 10 March 2011. HMRC write to her on 13 April 2011 notifying that she must cease to use the scheme with effect from 30 June 2011.

> In this situation, reg. 64 requires that Sally cease to use the scheme with effect from 31 March 2011, and she must account for all outstanding output tax on the return for period ending 31 March 2011.

In contrast, if a person is required to leave the scheme under reg. 60(1), i.e. where their turnover exceeds the tolerance limit, HMRC may direct them to leave the scheme at a later date (reg. 60(3)).

6.5.9 Right of appeal

VATA 1994, s. 83(y) provides that a person may appeal to a tribunal in respect of a refusal of authorisation or termination of authorisation under the cash accounting scheme. Thus, a person may appeal where HMRC have not allowed him to begin using the scheme (reg. 58(4)), or where he has been expelled from the scheme (reg. 60(1); reg. 64).

Once an appeal has been submitted, the taxable person is not entitled to use the scheme until the appeal is concluded.

Notice 731, para. 2.10 states that if a person appeals on a separate issue, he will be entitled to continue using cash accounting unless they deem it necessary to withdraw use of the scheme 'for the protection of the revenue'.

The tribunal has held that HMRC's power (under what is now reg. 58(4) and reg. 64(1)(d)) to refuse or terminate authorisation to use the scheme is essentially a discretionary power. Therefore the tribunal could only allow an appeal against such a decision where HMRC had acted unreasonably, in this case, in withdrawing use of the scheme. (*Mainline Fabrications* [1992] BVC 1,389, applying *C & E Commrs v J H Corbitt (Numismatists) Ltd* (1980) 1 BVC 330). A number of other cases have been heard, and have followed this precedent.

Where the circumstances relate to matters of fact, such as whether or not a penalty has been assessed under VATA 1994, s. 60, or whether or not a person's taxable turnover has exceeded the tolerance limits, it is presumed that an appeal will be decided on those facts, rather than on HMRC's discretion.

6.5.10 Deregistration

When a taxable person deregisters for VAT, he is required to make a final return, accounting for all outstanding VAT output tax and adjusted for outstanding input tax. This return must be submitted and paid within two months of ceasing to be registered. The bad debt relief provisions may be used at the time of deregistration. This will be useful if the person is unlikely to receive payment for outstanding invoices.

There is a 'deemed supply' on deregistration in respect of goods forming part of the assets of the business: see VATA 1994, Sch. 4, para. 8. Such a supply applies to a person using cash accounting. Thus, where the person is deregistered and the VAT on the 'deemed supply' is more than £1,000, he is obliged to account for that amount of output tax on his final VAT return.

6.5.11 Ceasing to trade

When a person ceases to trade, he is required to notify HMRC (VATA 1994, Sch. 1, para. 11). The person will be deregistered for VAT. He will thus be required to submit a final return, and account for and pay outstanding VAT within two months of the date of deregistration. A person may continue to use cash accounting when disposing of any stocks and assets. Again, he may use the bad debt relief concession at the time of deregistration.

For the rules relating to the claiming of bad debt relief after the time of deregistration, see *VAT Notice 700/18*, para. 2.10.

6.5.12 Insolvency

If a taxable person becomes insolvent, he is required to make a final return, accounting for all outstanding output tax and adjusted for outstanding input tax. This return must be submitted within two months of the date of insolvency.

Where trading continues after insolvency, the person (office holder) responsible for the business may continue to use cash accounting. He will be required to maintain records as required by the scheme.

In addition, where trading continues after insolvency, the person responsible for the business must ensure that any payments received in respect of pre-insolvency trading are separated from other payments received. Output tax due on such receipts will have been accounted for on the final VAT return. Equally, if payments are made for supplies received (and invoices received) before insolvency, the person must separate such payments in his records. Input tax will have been claimed on the final VAT return.

6.5.13 Transfer of a business as a going concern

Regulation 63 provides for two distinct circumstances where a business is transferred as a going concern.

Where a person using cash accounting transfers his business and the new owner retains the same VAT registration number, the new owner is also required to account for VAT under the scheme, for both output tax and input tax. The previous owner is required to notify the new owner that he has been using cash accounting.

> ### ⚠ *Warning!*
>
> In these circumstances, all VAT outstanding at the time of transfer becomes the responsibility of the new owner. It may be said that form VAT 68 should include a statement relating to cash accounting, so that the position is made clear to both parties, but it does not.

The new owner can choose to leave the scheme. *VAT Notice 731*, para. 5.8 suggests that the new owner does this as soon as possible. This is not required by reg. 63, nor is it shown as an additional rule in the *Notice*, nor referred to in HMRC's internal guidance. It is suggested that the new owner can leave the scheme voluntarily. He is then required to account for all outstanding VAT, including any VAT outstanding from before the date of transfer.

If the parties do not agree, and the VAT registration number is not transferred, reg. 63(2) applies. Where the new owner does not retain the VAT registration number, the previous owner must follow the deregistration procedure. He must complete, submit and pay his final return within two months of the date of the transfer of the business including any VAT on supplies he has made that have not yet been paid (and reclaim input tax on supplies not yet paid for). The new owner may choose to use cash accounting, subject to the normal rules. This particular circumstance was addressed in the tribunal case of *Vaghela (t/a Vaghela Unadkat & Co)* [2001] BVC 4,170.

> ### ⚠ *Warning!*
>
> In this situation there remains the issue of payments and receipts outstanding. Whilst not strictly a VAT issue, it is advisable that the previous owner be aware, before the transfer, that he will be liable for outstanding output tax, less outstanding input tax, and that any consideration paid for the business reflect that.

6.6 Annual accounting – joining the scheme

6.6.1 Conditions for joining the scheme

A taxable person may join the annual accounting scheme as long as the following conditions are fulfilled, that:

- the person's predicted taxable turnover for the next year is less than £1,350,000, excluding VAT;
- the person has not ceased to use the scheme in the previous year;
- the person is not part of a group registration;

- the person is not part of a divisional registration; and
- any debt to HMRC is subject to a settlement agreement, see *VAT Notice 732*, para. 2.6.

HMRC may refuse an application where they consider it necessary for the protection of the revenue.

> ### ⚠ *Warning!*
>
> Since a person is required to apply to HMRC to use the scheme, he or she cannot backdate the use of the scheme.

Notice 732 contains an application form (VAT 600 AA), which the applicant is required to use. A separate form (VAT 600 AA/FRS) is also available where a person wishes to apply to join the flat rate scheme at the same time. The forms are available on the HMRC website.

Applications are processed by the Wolverhampton VAT registration unit (the address is shown at **3.8.3**).

The applicant is required to provide:

- the date he would like his annual accounting year to end; and
- the method of payment of the interim payments, since these are required to be made by electronic means.

Although a repayment trader is not prohibited from joining annual accounting, and would not make interim payments if he did, he would only be able to claim a repayment at the end of the year.

Law: VAT Regulations 1995 (SI 1995/2518), reg. 52

6.6.2 VAT accounting on joining the scheme

Where a person has been using conventional accounting, he will already have accounted for output tax and input tax on supplies made and received.

However, where the person subsequently discovers an error in his previous VAT returns, he may make an adjustment on a 12-month return. Alternatively, the person may use a voluntary disclosure form VAT 652.

> ### *Example 6.8*
>
> Francis has overstated his output tax on the final quarterly return before beginning to use annual accounting. He does not wish to wait a year before making the adjustment, even though it is below £2,000, and therefore uses a voluntary disclosure form.

Where a person has already been using cash accounting, then he may continue to do so. Outstanding output tax and input tax will be accounted for on the appropriate annual VAT return.

6.7 Annual accounting – using the scheme

6.7.1 Accounting periods

A person joining the scheme may be required to submit a VAT return for a period longer than three months but shorter than 12 months, to bring the accounting period into line with that selected. HMRC do not issue VAT returns for periods exceeding 12 months.

6.7.2 Interim payments

As long as the 'transitional accounting period' is four months or longer, an interim payment is, or payments are, required. An applicant can choose either nine monthly payments or three quarterly payments, in both cases leaving a final balancing payment due two months after the annual accounting year end. Monthly payments are set at 10 per cent of the overall liability, and quarterly payments are set at 25 per cent of the overall liability.

Where a person has been registered before using the scheme, the interim payments are based on the previous 12 months, although these can be changed by agreement. Where a person uses annual accounting immediately on registration, the interim payments have to be estimated.

The interim and final payments are made as shown in the table below.

Table 6.1

Month	Monthly payments	Quarterly payments
1		
2		
3		
4	Payment 1	Payment 1
5	Payment 2	
6	Payment 3	
7	Payment 4	Payment 2
8	Payment 5	
9	Payment 6	
10	Payment 7	Payment 3

Month	Monthly payments	Quarterly payments
11	Payment 8	
12	Payment 9	
13		
14	Balancing payment	Balancing payment
15		

A previous option, allowing a single annual payment where the overall liability was below £2,000, has now ceased.

6.7.3 Setting interim payments

It is important that the interim payments are set realistically. To overestimate means that excess VAT is paid during the year, to the detriment of cash flow. To underestimate means that a much higher balancing payment is due at the end of the year.

Planning point

In some cases, however, a person's trading pattern may suit such payments, and proper regard should be given to such a possibility.

6.7.4 Accounting

No additional accounting records are required for the annual accounting scheme. However, it should be noted that, since VAT returns are only submitted annually, adequate checks should be made on output tax and input tax accountable around the year end. Where an accounting system automatically includes any adjustment in the next accounting period, that will be a whole year later, and may generate a substantial interest charge if identified by a visiting VAT officer. Taxpayers using annual accounting still also need to be aware of the usual VAT requirements, such as the fuel scale charge, partial exemption and the capital items scheme.

6.8   Annual accounting – particular circumstances

6.8.1 Change of circumstances

A person using the scheme is required to notify HMRC immediately if there is a significant change of circumstances. This is especially relevant if the change will affect the amount of VAT due for the year.

> **Planning point**
>
> The amounts payable as interim payments can be changed during the year (*VAT Notice 732*, para. 6.6). This may be advisable, for example, if a taxable person's business grows substantially during the year.

A change of circumstances includes purchasing a business as a going concern. Similarly, a person will need to notify HMRC if his banking arrangements change.

6.8.2 Voluntary payments

A person can make voluntary payments, as long as they are in multiples of £5. These may be useful if a business generates one or more large, one-off contracts. An increase in interim payments may not be applicable but it may be useful simply to pay the net VAT due in respect of the contract.

6.8.3 Partial exemption

A partly exempt person can also use annual accounting. The specific requirement is that the partial exemption year coincides with the annual accounting year end.

6.8.4 Change of year end

A person using annual accounting can change his year-end by notifying HMRC in writing. A transitional accounting period, shorter than 12 months, will bring the year-end into line. It is recommended that any adjustment to payment dates and amounts is made correctly.

6.8.5 Default surcharge

A taxable person using annual accounting may be subject to the default surcharge, for a failure either to submit a return, or to make a payment. Two tribunal cases have been heard in relation to such circumstances: *IPMC Ltd* (1988) 3 BVC 761 and *Lineplan Ltd* [1993] BVC 1,424.

6.9 Annual accounting – leaving the scheme

6.9.1 Voluntary decision

A person may choose to leave the annual accounting scheme at any time, although to simplify accounting a month end date should be chosen. The person must notify

HMRC in writing. He will leave the scheme on the date they receive the letter. He will receive a VAT return for a transitional accounting period, ending on that date. The person has two months from that date to submit the return and make the balancing payment. He should also ensure the electronic payments to HMRC are stopped.

Law: VAT Regulations 1995 (SI 1995/2518), reg. 53–55

6.9.2 Turnover limit breached

Where a taxable person expects his taxable turnover to exceed £1,600,000 in the current accounting period (or current transitional accounting period), he is required to notify HMRC within 30 days. Although the published guidance is silent on when the person would be required to leave the scheme under such circumstances, it is understood that he would be required to leave the scheme at the end of the current accounting period.

When a person reaches the end of an annual accounting period or the end of a transitional accounting period, and his turnover has exceeded £1,600,000, he is required to leave the scheme at the end of that period. The person must submit and pay the VAT return within the normal two months. HMRC will conduct their own checks of the turnover of traders using annual accounting, and will notify them that they cannot continue to use the scheme if their turnover has exceeded £1.6 million.

There is no provision in *Notice 732* for a taxable person staying in the scheme where a one-off transaction takes him over the tolerance limit.

6.9.3 Cessation of trade, etc.

Where a taxable person using the scheme ceases to trade, ceases to be registered, becomes insolvent, becomes bankrupt, becomes incapacitated or dies, he has to leave the scheme immediately. The person will receive a VAT return for a transitional accounting period, ending on that date. He has two months from that date to submit the return and make the balancing payment.

6.9.4 Expulsion from the scheme

HMRC may expel a person from the scheme in a number of circumstances:

- if there has been a false statement made either by the taxable person or on his behalf in relation to his application;
- if the taxable person fails to submit a VAT return by the due date;
- if the taxable person fails to make a payment of money due from before he joined the scheme;

- if the taxable person fails to make either an interim payment or a balancing payment;
- if the taxable person fails to pay any assessment for VAT, for default surcharge, penalty or interest;
- if HMRC consider that, at any time, they have reason to believe that the value of the taxable person's taxable turnover will exceed £1.6 million in that current accounting period or transitional accounting period; and
- if it is necessary to do so for the protection of the revenue.

In circumstances where there has been failure to pay money due to HMRC, it is understood that they will generally issue a warning letter before expelling the taxable person from the scheme.

In all other cases, an expulsion may be immediate.

There is no right of appeal to a tribunal against either a refusal or termination of authorisation to use the scheme.

6.9.5 Change in VAT rate

HMRC will not change the instalment already notified.

> **Planning point**
>
> When the VAT rate decreases HMRC should be contacted and revised calculations provided to reduce the amounts payable. When the VAT rate increases, the instalments will remain the same with a benefit to cashflow. The business must, however, plan to have the increased VAT payable at the end of the annual accounting period.

6.10 Flat rate scheme – joining the scheme

6.10.1 Conditions for joining the scheme

The Principal VAT Directive (Directive 2006/112), art. 296 provides for an alternative registration for 'agricultural, forestry or fisheries undertakings' as listed in Directive 2006/112, Annexes VII and art. 295(1). UK legislation is in VATA 1994, s. 54; VAT (Flat-rate Scheme for Farmers) (Designated Activities) Order 1992 (SI 1992/3220); VAT (Flat-rate Scheme for Farmers) (Percentage Addition) Order 1992 (SI 1992/3221); VAT Regulations 1995 (SI 1995/2518), reg. 202–211.

A person may register under this scheme in the following cases:

(1)   He satisfies HMRC that he is carrying out a 'designated activity'.

(2)   His registration for VAT is cancelled (where the person carries out activities which fall outside those designated, he must not be liable to register for VAT in respect of those activities).

(3)   In the three years prior to certification, the person has not been assessed for a civil evasion penalty (VATA 1994, s. 60), nor been convicted of a VAT offence, nor made any payment to compound proceedings in respect of VAT.

(4)   He applies using form VAT 98.

(5)   He satisfies HMRC that the amounts of the flat-rate additions charged will not exceed the amount of input tax to which he would otherwise have been entitled by £3,000 or more. This effectively allows small farmers, with relevant annual turnover below £75,000, to register for the scheme.

Other guidance: *VAT Notice 700/46*

In addition to the conditions above, a taxable person may apply to use the flat rate scheme where his taxable activities meet the following conditions, that:

- the person's predicted taxable turnover for the next year is below £150,000, excluding VAT, capital goods and exempt income;
- the person is not required to use the tour operators' margin scheme;
- the person is not required to operate the capital goods scheme;
- the person does not intend to account for output tax under the margin scheme, global accounting or the auctioneers' scheme;
- the person has not stopped using the scheme in the previous 12 months;
- in the past 12 months, the person has not been convicted of an offence in relation to VAT, has not accepted a compound penalty or has not been assessed for a penalty for conduct involving dishonesty; and
- in the past 24 months, the person has not been eligible to be registered as part of a group, has not been registered as part of a divisional registration, has not been 'associated' with another person; although HMRC may grant the person's application if they are satisfied that use of the scheme would pose no risk to the revenue.

For the definition of 'associated', see reg. 55A(2). See also the explanation in *Notice 733*, paras. 13.5–13.8. HMRC indicate that they are looking at commercial reality rather than legal form.

A person may apply for the flat rate scheme immediately from his date of registration for VAT. Alternatively, the person can start using the scheme from the beginning of any VAT period. Regulation 55B(1) suggests that a taxable person can use any date, and he is not obliged to begin using the scheme from the beginning of a prescribed accounting period, although it seems that HMRC would prefer them to do so.

> ### ⚠ *Warning!*
>
> Since a person is required to apply to HMRC to use the scheme, he cannot backdate the use of the scheme beyond the beginning of the VAT period which is current at the time of application. This does, however, include the first, long VAT return of someone registering belatedly for VAT.

Notice 733 contains an application form (VAT 600 FRS) which the applicant should use. *Notice 733*, para. 5.1 indicates that an application can also be made by telephone. If a telephone application is made by a representative, then a copy of the application form is sent to the taxable person for checking.

Application forms must be sent to the appropriate registration unit for the taxable person.

Where a person is already registered for VAT, use of the scheme takes effect by default at the beginning of the accounting period starting when HMRC receive the application, unless another date has been specified. It is therefore advisable to retain a copy of the form and adequate proof of posting.

> ### *Planning point*
>
> Experience has shown that HMRC are willing to accept applications to join the scheme with effect from a past date, where this is the beginning of the current VAT period.

Notice 733, para. 4.8 indicates that the flat rate scheme is unsuitable for a repayment trader.

For a person not already registered for VAT, choosing a start date can provide some planning opportunities.

> ### *Planning point*
>
> It may be sensible for a newly registered trader to remain on conventional accounting during the time of start-up, when additional costs are being incurred and sales are modest, before joining the flat rate scheme once expenditure drops and income increases.

Law: VAT Regulations 1995 (SI 1995/2518), reg. 55L

Other guidance: VAT Notice 733

6.10.2 The cash benefit of using the scheme

Although the major benefit of using the flat rate scheme is in reduced administration time, it is clearly wise to review the cash benefit of moving from conventional accounting to using the scheme. A taxable person may review past VAT returns and compare his net VAT payments with the appropriate flat rate percentage prior to applying for the scheme.

> ### *Planning point*
>
> If a person will be worse off under the scheme, it is likely that he will see this as an unacceptable trade-off for simpler accounting, whereas a person who benefits financially is likely to have this as a major incentive, rather than simplicity. Only those for whom it makes little difference are likely to choose the flat rate scheme for the benefit of reduced administration.

6.11 Flat rate scheme – using the scheme

6.11.1 Treatment of pre-registration input tax

Input tax claims are not available to taxable persons using the flat rate scheme. However, a claim for pre-registration input tax is allowed. The normal rules applicable to such a claim apply.

Where assets on which input tax was claimed are subsequently sold, output tax must be accounted for outside the flat rate scheme.

> ### *Planning point*
>
> Those joining the scheme from the date of registration should be especially careful not to fail to claim under these provisions.

6.11.2 Choosing a flat rate

The taxable person calculates his effective net VAT liability using a percentage. This varies according to the type of business operated. The list is statutory, being found in reg. 55K. It is also reproduced in *Notice 733*, to which reference should be made when choosing an appropriate flat rate. Also, note that the tables for 2010 and 2011 (17.5 per cent and 20 per cent VAT rate) are shown in **6.14.1** and **6.14.2.**

It is expected that, for most small businesses, there will be only one available category from the list. However, a business may be borderline, or may include two or more categories. Where the business is borderline, a judgment must be made. Regrettably, HMRC will refuse to confirm in writing if the correct rate has been chosen even where they have been given the information in writing. However, at para. 4.2 of

Notice 733 (March 2007 edn), HMRC make clear that they will take no retrospective action at any later date in the event that they consider the wrong rate to have been chosen, provided that the reasoning for deciding on the rate chosen has been recorded in writing and that reasoning is not unreasonable.

> ### Planning point
>
> Where there is doubt as to the correct rate, it is recommended that a written record is made of the business's activities and the rationale for choosing the rate to be used, and is kept on file. Provided that this has been done, it is difficult, in the light of their published policy, to see how HMRC could then at a later date enforce a different percentage retrospectively.

Where there are multiple categories, the rate applicable to the more significant activity, judged by turnover, must be used. This is done annually on the basis of expectation.

> ### ⚠ Warning!
>
> Care should be taken here and a note made of how any decision is reached.

Additionally, where the type of business changes, a different category may become appropriate. Any change of rate must be notified to HMRC in writing. See *Notice 733*, s. 6 for details.

> ### Example 6.9
>
> A rural public house generates income from bar sales (flat rate percentage 5.5 per cent), and a restaurant (flat rate percentage 12 per cent). Careful thought should be given, firstly to whether the scheme is appropriate in any case, which is unlikely if restaurant income is expected to exceed bar sales. Where the flat rate scheme is regarded as appropriate, a careful choice of the flat rate that is to be used needs to be made. This choice will be governed by the predominant activity of the business.

A taxable person using the flat rate scheme must maintain, with his other accounting records, a record of his flat rate calculation for each prescribed accounting period.

6.11.3 Turnover methods

Notice 733 explains three methods of calculating the turnover on which the flat rate percentage is to be applied. The taxable person is not allowed repeatedly to switch between methods.

The basic turnover method follows conventional accrual VAT accounting. It takes the value of supplies made during the period. The ordinary tax point rules apply.

The cash-based turnover method follows cash accounting. It takes the value of money received for supplies during the period. It also takes into account other methods of payment, such as set-off and barter.

The retailer's turnover method (see *Notice 733*, s. 11) is based on the method of calculating gross takings for a retailer. This includes payment received in the period, plus credit sales, vouchers redeemed, etc.

Planning point

Except in the case of retailers, who have no choice but to use the gross takings calculation, it is difficult to see why anyone would not wish to choose the cash method. This improves cash flow, is consistent for many with reducing the business records to a simple cashbook, and provides automatic partial bad debt relief (but see **6.12.3** for further relief in the event of bad debts).

6.11.4 Invoicing

A taxable person using the flat rate scheme is still required to issue tax invoices for his supplies, with output tax itemised. These invoices must contain all the usual information. However, as far as the person using the flat rate scheme is concerned, his output tax is not calculated directly from the individual amounts of output tax shown on the invoices. Similarly, the person is not required to analyse purchase invoices for input tax purposes but he will need to maintain records for direct tax and other purposes.

6.11.5 Reduction in first year

Any person using the scheme can deduct a further one per cent from the flat rate percentage from the date of starting to use the scheme until the date of the first anniversary of their registration for VAT. This does not apply to the period of belatedness for any trader late in notifying their liability to be registered (although, on application, the flat rate scheme itself may be used from the effective date of registration provided that this does not pre-date the introduction of the flat rate scheme).

6.11.6 Reporting for direct tax purposes

A number of small businesses and their advisers regularly enquire about how, for example, a self-assessment tax return should be completed when the taxpayer is using the flat rate scheme. There is helpful information on the HM Revenue and Customs website, at BIM31585 (*VAT: Flat Rate Scheme*). This includes the treatment of capital allowances, and IR35 service companies. (See also *Tax Bulletin*, issue 61, pp. 973–974 and the joint statement issued by the then Customs and the Inland Revenue in *VAT Information Sheet* 17/03, Annex B.)

More generally, it also provides guidance on the completion of sales and expenses figures. For a flat rate scheme taxpayer the usual method is to treat the sales figure as the gross sales less the flat rate percentage, and to include all expenses gross of VAT.

Planning point

Note that a taxpayer is required to maintain adequate records to complete direct tax returns, in spite of the simplified approach offered by the scheme.

6.11.7 Input tax claims

Ordinarily, a taxable person using the flat rate scheme cannot claim any input tax.

However, input tax may be claimed on 'any relevant purchase of capital expenditure goods' of more than £2,000, VAT-inclusive, in any prescribed accounting period. *Notice 733*, para. 15.3 indicates that the £2,000 amount refers to a single capital asset. It also excludes goods purchased for resale, hire, let or lease, goods which will be consumed within one year and goods subject to the capital goods scheme.

⚠ Warning!

The legislation is specific in referring to goods; input VAT may not be claimed on services, even if they represent capital purchases (e.g. improvements to property, franchise fees).

This provision does not entitle the person to input tax deduction on an item for which he would not ordinarily be entitled to claim, for example the purchase of a motor car or an asset to be used for business entertainment.

6.11.8 Appeals

The first area where an appeal may be made is when HMRC either refuse authorisation or withdraw authorisation.

The grounds under which HMRC may refuse an application are in *Notice 733*, s. 3. These relate largely to matters of fact, although there is also a 'protection of the revenue' clause. HMRC may also withdraw authorisation where the taxpayer gave a false statement in his original application. In addition, where a taxpayer is no longer authorised to use the scheme, but fails to leave the scheme, then presumably HMRC will backdate the withdrawal.

The second area of appeal is the level of percentage appropriate for the trader. For most small businesses carrying on a single activity, this should present no problem as the business category will be clear and no dispute will arise about the appropriate percentage. However, disputes will arise.

A further concern with respect to appeals is that the tribunal can only allow an appeal where it considers that HMRC have acted unreasonably. This means that, even where the tribunal disagrees with HMRC's conclusion, they cannot allow the appeal unless the reasoning that led to that conclusion was improper in some way. For a small business such an approach to appeals may seem harsh. *Notice 733*, s. 16 refers to appeals, but makes no reference to this important restriction.

> ### ⚠ *Warning!*
>
> Note also that, where HMRC's decision relates to the use of the flat rate scheme, the taxpayer has to stop using the scheme until the appeal is decided. If the taxpayer originally opted to use the scheme at least partly because there was a clear cash benefit, then that benefit will be lost while the taxpayer awaits the decision. It may be advisable to include within the appeal, an application that HMRC repay the successful appellant the additional amount of VAT he paid during that period. Suppose the taxable person wins the appeal, and reapplies to join the scheme. Unfortunately, he cannot be admitted to the scheme if he has ceased to operate the scheme in the previous 12 months. A letter of explanation should therefore accompany the reapplication.

6.12 Flat rate scheme – particular circumstances

6.12.1 Partial exemption

The scheme includes businesses that generate exempt income. However, the flat rate percentage is designed to take into account exempt income. Such income must be included in the value of supplies made. No adjustment is made in respect of input tax, since none is claimed in any case.

6.12.2 Sale of assets

Where a taxable person using the flat rate scheme sells an asset for which input tax was claimed under the rules of the scheme, then the sale of the asset is excluded from the flat rate calculation. Output tax, assuming it is applicable, must be charged in the normal way and accounted for outside the scheme. This may well be an area in which errors occur and checks should be made in relation to all disposals of assets.

6.12.3 Bad debts

A taxable person using the flat rate scheme can make a claim for bad debt relief subject to the normal rules. Once an invoice is unpaid for six months from the time of supply, a claim can be made in the normal way. Note that the full amount of output tax shown on the invoice(s) can be reclaimed.

Where the taxable person uses the cash-based turnover method, he gains automatic relief on an amount equal to the flat rate percentage of the debt. *Notice 733*, s. 14 explains that the person can also make an adjustment, equal to difference between the amount of output tax chargeable on the supply and the amount calculated by the flat rate percentage. Thus the overall amount reclaimed is the same, whatever turnover method is used.

6.12.4 Change in rate of VAT

HMRC will issue a new table of flat rates applicable from the date of the change in rate of VAT.

Businesses which use the cash based turnover method to account for VAT when payment is received are required to account for VAT at the flat rate extant at the tax point of the supply. The flat rate in place at the tax point date should be used to determine the correct VAT liability.

6.13 Flat rate scheme – leaving the scheme

6.13.1 Voluntary departure from the scheme

A taxable person can leave the scheme at any time, by writing to HMRC. He can leave from any current date. However, HMRC prefer a person to leave from the end of a prescribed accounting period. When a person leaves part way through a prescribed accounting period, then the VAT return for that period requires two separate calculations: one under the flat rate scheme, and one under conventional accounting.

Other guidance: *VAT Notice 733*, para. 8.7

6.13.2 Turnover limit breached

When a person's expected turnover during the next 30 days will exceed £225,000, or when his actual turnover for 12 months beginning on the date he began using the scheme, or an anniversary of that date, has exceeded £225,000, then the person must leave the scheme unless there has been a one-off large transaction and it is expected that turnover in the next year will be below £187,500. These turnover figures are VAT-inclusive, on the basis that the person using the scheme will be used to using his inclusive figure in preparation of his VAT returns.

Under the future turnover rule, the person must leave the scheme at the beginning of that 30-day period. Under the past turnover rule the person must leave the scheme at the end of the VAT period containing the anniversary of his start date. If the person is using annual accounting as well, then he must leave from the earlier of the end of the annual accounting period and the month after the month containing the anniversary of joining the scheme.

From 4 January 2011, a person must leave the scheme when their income exceeds £230,000 (unless that is due to a one-off transaction and it is expected that income will fall back below £191,500 in the following year). A person must also leave the scheme if it is expected that turnover in the next 30 days will exceed £230,000.

> **Planning point**
>
> Unless turnover rises astronomically (to the point where the next 30 days' turnover on its own will exceed £225,000) there is no requirement to review it or to cease using the scheme until an anniversary of the start date.

There is no provision in *Notice 733* for a taxable person staying in the scheme where a one-off transaction takes him over the tolerance limit.

6.13.3 Expulsion from the scheme

A taxable person will be expelled from the flat rate scheme in certain circumstances.

1. If the person becomes a tour operator.

2. If the person intends to acquire, construct, or otherwise obtain a capital item within the capital goods scheme.

3. If the person makes supplies under the margin scheme, global accounting or the auctioneers' scheme.

4.   If the person becomes eligible to be registered as part of a group registration.

5.   If the person is registered as a divisional registration.

6.   If the person becomes associated with another person (in the specific terms meant by those words in this context).

7.   If the person has his authorisation terminated by HMRC, for the protection of the revenue or because he has made a false statement in relation to his original application.

In all cases, the person is obliged to leave the scheme with immediate effect; in relation to use of a margin scheme, this means the beginning of the period in which this will be used.

6.13.4 Accounting for VAT on leaving the scheme

When leaving the flat rate scheme, users of the cash-based turnover method must make an adjustment to reflect supplies made and received before leaving the scheme, but where payment has not been received or made until after leaving the scheme. This adjustment is calculated by adding the value of supplies made, but unpaid, and applying the flat rate percentage. This adjustment is not required if the person begins to use the cash accounting scheme immediately on leaving the flat rate scheme.

Planning point

Where a taxable person leaves the scheme and has on hand more stock than when he began to use the scheme, and he has not claimed input tax on that stock, the person may make a claim for input tax based on the value of stock on hand when he leaves the scheme. The person is not required to do a detailed stock take but simply to provide a reasonable calculation of its value. See *Notice 733*, s. 12.

6.13.5 Output tax on assets

If the taxable person has recovered input tax on a qualifying asset while using the scheme and has not accounted for output tax on it, then he makes a self-supply on leaving the scheme. In practice, this will only affect partly exempt persons, since they will not be entitled to recover all of the input tax on the self-supply.

6.14 Flat rate scheme

Changes to flat rate schemes are detailed below.

191

6.14.1 Flat rate scheme: percentage rates from 1 January 2010 to 3 January 2011

Table 6.2: percentage rates from 1 January 2010 to 3 January 2011

Category of business	Appropriate percentage
Accountancy or bookkeeping	13
Advertising	10
Agricultural services	10
Any other activity not listed elsewhere	10.5
Architect, civil and structural engineer or surveyor	13
Boarding or care of animals	10.5
Business services that are not listed elsewhere	10.5
Catering services including restaurants and takeaways	11
Computer and IT consultancy or data processing	13
Computer repair services	9.5
Dealing in waste or scrap	9.5
Entertainment or journalism	11
Estate agency or property management services	10.5
Farming or agriculture that is not listed elsewhere	6
Film, radio, television or video production	11.5
Financial services	12
Forestry or fishing	9.5
General building or construction services*	8.5
Hairdressing or other beauty treatment services	11.5
Hiring or renting goods	8.5
Hotel or accommodation	9.5
Investigation or security	10.5
Labour-only building or construction services*	13
Laundry or dry-cleaning services	10.5
Lawyer or legal services	13
Library, archive, museum or other cultural activity	8.5
Management consultancy	12.5
Manufacturing fabricated metal products	9.5
Manufacturing food	8
Manufacturing that is not listed elsewhere	8.5
Manufacturing yarn, textiles or clothing	8
Membership organisation	7
Mining or quarrying	9
Packaging	8
Photography	10
Post offices	4.5

Category of business	Appropriate percentage
Printing	7.5
Publishing	10
Pubs	6
Real estate activity not listed elsewhere	12.5
Repairing personal or household goods	9
Repairing vehicles	7.5
Retailing food, confectionary, tobacco, newspapers or children's clothing	3.5
Retailing pharmaceuticals, medical goods, cosmetics or toiletries	7
Retailing that is not listed elsewhere	6.5
Retailing vehicles or fuel	6
Secretarial services	11.5
Social work	10
Sport or recreation	7.5
Transport or storage, including couriers, freight, removals and taxis	9
Travel agency	9.5
Veterinary medicine	10
Wholesaling agricultural products	7
Wholesaling food	6.5
Wholesaling that is not listed elsewhere	7.5

* 'Labour-only building or construction services' means building or construction services where the value of materials supplied is less than ten per cent of relevant turnover from such services; any other building or construction services are 'general building or construction services'.

6.14.2   Flat rate scheme: percentage rates from 4 January 2011

Table 6.3: percentage rates from 4 January 2011

Category of business	Appropriate percentage
Accountancy or book-keeping	14.5
Advertising	11
Agricultural services	11
Any other activity not listed elsewhere	12
Architect, civil and structural engineer or surveyor	14.5
Boarding or care of animals	12
Business services that are not listed elsewhere	12

Category of business	Appropriate percentage
Catering services including restaurants and takeaways	12.5
Computer and IT consultancy or data processing	14.5
Computer repair services	10.5
Dealing in waste or scrap	10.5
Entertainment or journalism	12.5
Estate agency or property management services	12
Farming or agriculture that is not listed elsewhere	6.5
Film, radio, television or video production	13
Financial services	13.5
Forestry or fishing	10.5
General building or construction services*	9.5
Hairdressing or other beauty treatment services	13
Hiring or renting goods	9.5
Hotel or accommodation	10.5
Investigation or security	12
Labour-only building or construction services*	14.5
Laundry or dry-cleaning services	12
Lawyer or legal services	14.5
Library, archive, museum or other cultural activity	9.5
Management consultancy	14
Manufacturing fabricated metal products	10.5
Manufacturing food	9
Manufacturing that is not listed elsewhere	9.5
Manufacturing yarn, textiles or clothing	9
Membership organisation	8
Mining or quarrying	10
Packaging	9
Photography	11
Post offices	5
Printing	8.5
Publishing	11
Pubs	6.5
Real estate activity not listed elsewhere	14
Repairing personal or household goods	10
Repairing vehicles	8.5
Retailing food, confectionary, tobacco, newspapers or children's clothing	4

Category of business	Appropriate percentage
Retailing pharmaceuticals, medical goods, cosmetics or toiletries	8
Retailing that is not listed elsewhere	7.5
Retailing vehicles or fuel	6.5
Secretarial services	13
Social work	11
Sport or recreation	8.5
Transport or storage, including couriers, freight, removals and taxis	10
Travel agency	10.5
Veterinary medicine	11
Wholesaling agricultural products	8
Wholesaling food	7.5
Wholesaling that is not listed elsewhere	8.5

* 'Labour-only building or construction services' means building or construction services where the value of materials supplied is less than ten per cent of relevant turnover from such services; any other building or construction services are 'general building or construction services'.

6.15 Interrelationship of schemes

6.15.1 Interaction between small business schemes

A taxable person can use cash accounting with annual accounting. The person has to be eligible to join both schemes, and must fulfil the various additional accounting requirements. Since each scheme provides for an improved cash flow, the use of both schemes will necessarily improve cash flow further. Conversely, leaving both schemes due to increased turnover may create a more severe cash flow problem.

A taxable person can use annual accounting with the flat rate scheme; indeed, the existence of a joint application form provides for this. The value of interim payments will depend on the previous or expected turnover and also on the flat rate percentage applicable.

> **Planning point**
>
> Care should be given to ensure that the interim payments are reasonable and realistic.

Notice 732, s. 10 provides fuller details on this combination. Ideally, the two schemes will run concurrently but this is not obligatory. If the type of business changes during the year, a new flat rate percentage will apply for the rest of the year.

Where two schemes are in use, a person may become ineligible for one but not the other, in which case he can still remain in one after leaving the other. The person is required to be aware of the different but overlapping rules pertaining to the schemes.

A taxable person cannot use the flat rate scheme with cash accounting, since they represent mutually incompatible methods for calculating the VAT liabilities to be declared on the VAT return. The flat rate scheme has a cash-based turnover method, however, which is the effective equivalent.

6.15.2 Cash accounting and VAT group treatment

There is no restriction on a group of companies using the cash accounting scheme, above and beyond the ordinary restrictions of the scheme. The turnover and tolerance limits must be applied to the group as a whole, not just to one or more companies in the group. Equally, companies within a group must either all use the scheme, or all use conventional invoice accounting.

Additional difficulties may arise when a company joins a group, and either or both are using the scheme. There are a number of possible scenarios.

If the company is using the scheme, it must leave the scheme on joining the group, since it will be effectively deregistered at that date. (This is true even if the company and the group are both using the scheme.) It must therefore account for all outstanding VAT on its final return. Where payments are made and received after joining the group in respect of supplies received and made before joining the group, no additional VAT need be accounted for by the group.

If the group is using the scheme, it can continue to use the scheme, subject to the turnover and tolerance limits. It need only include the new company's turnover in its turnover from the date it joined the group.

Similarly, when a company leaves a group, there are a number of possible scenarios.

Where a company leaves a cash accounting group, the group will retain its VAT registration number and thus continue using the scheme.

Where supplies are made by the company before leaving the group, and the company receives payment for those supplies after leaving the group, the company is liable to account for and pay any outstanding VAT:

- if the company becomes registered in its own right and uses the scheme, when payments are made and received;
- if the company becomes registered in its own right; and does not use the scheme, at the date it leaves the group; or
- if the company does not become registered, at the date it leaves the group.

6.15.3 Annual accounting and VAT group treatment

Notice 732 is silent on groups. There is no statutory prohibition on a group of companies using the annual accounting scheme. The turnover limit must apply to the whole group, not just to a single member, and the whole group would have to use the scheme.

6.15.4 Flat rate scheme and VAT group treatment

A person who has been, in the previous 24 months, eligible for group membership is prohibited from using the flat rate scheme, unless HMRC are satisfied he presents no risk to the revenue.

If a person using the flat rate scheme becomes eligible for group membership, whether he exercises that option or not, he is required to notify HMRC, and he will be required to cease using the scheme with immediate effect.

6.15.5 Retail schemes

Whilst there is no restriction on a taxable person using cash accounting and a retail scheme, it may not provide that person with any great advantage. Indeed, it may prove an additional burden as the person will be required to fulfil the various additional accounting requirements.

> **Planning point**
>
> A person using cash accounting and a retail scheme will be obliged to account for output tax on sales as they are made since he would ordinarily receive full payment for goods or services as they are provided (output tax due in respect of credit sales will not become due until payment is received) but will not be allowed to claim input tax until he makes payment.

A person may use the annual accounting scheme with a retail scheme. He will only need to carry out his retail scheme calculation once each year, using the ordinary quarterly method. The only difference is where he wishes to use the second direct calculation scheme (ESP2), in which case his annual calculation replaces both the ordinary scheme calculations and the annual adjustment.

A person may not use the flat rate scheme with a retail scheme. The retailer's turnover method for the flat rate scheme effectively combines the method of recording daily gross takings. The flat rate percentage replaces the retail scheme calculation.

6.15.6 Margin schemes and global accounting

These schemes provide VAT relief for taxable persons dealing in second-hand goods. There are various restrictions to the schemes and additional record-keeping requirements, particularly the maintenance of a stock book and the issuing of invoices containing certain information.

Under margin schemes and global accounting the dealer does not issue VAT invoices when he makes sales of eligible goods. Thus, the dealer's tax point is the earlier of the date of delivery or collection of the goods and receipt of payment. Were he to use cash accounting also, he would simply be required to account for output tax on the date payment was received. This would provide little benefit if he made no sales on credit. As far as a dealer selling margin scheme goods on hire purchase (such as a motor dealer) is concerned, such sales are excluded from cash accounting in any case.

A margin scheme dealer can use annual accounting.

A dealer in second-hand goods is unlikely to find the flat rate scheme of any benefit. The two possible categories, 'retailing vehicles or fuel' at seven per cent, and 'retailing that is not listed elsewhere' at six per cent would most likely result in a higher output tax charge than using the margin scheme. Further, a taxable person cannot use a margin scheme and the flat rate scheme.

6.15.7 Cash accounting and the tour operators' margin scheme

There are two issues that are relevant for a taxable person considering using cash accounting and TOMS.

The first is the value of the person's taxable turnover. Under TOMS, the taxable turnover is the sum of the total margin of the person's 'margin scheme supplies', which are supplies bought in from a third party and supplied on to his customers, and the total value of other supplies made, including 'in-house supplies', provided from his own resources.

Example 6.10

Andrea arranges UK holidays using a third-party coach operator and third-party hotels. Suppose the total cost in a year of transport is £1,600,000 and of accommodation is £3,200,000; her total income is £5,400,000.

The amount of VAT due is calculated:

(£5,400,000 − £3,200,000 − £1,600,000) × 1/6 = £100,000.

The value of her margin scheme supplies is calculated:

£5,400,000 − £3,200,000 − £1,600,000 − £100,000 = £500,000.

Thus, although the cash throughput of her business is £5.4 million, Andrea's taxable turnover is £500,000. She is therefore eligible to use cash accounting.

The benefit of using cash accounting may not be in a taxable person's TOMS supplies, for the reasons explained below, but they may be entitled to use the scheme for another part of their business, not using TOMS.

In contrast, where supplies are provided from the taxable person's own resources, then they are called 'in-house' supplies, and their value has to be taken into account in ascertaining the person's turnover.

Example 6.11

Alternatively, Andrea arranges UK holidays but she uses her own transport. Using the same values (and assuming the cost of in-house transport is £1,600,000):

The amount of VAT is the same: £100,000.

The value of her taxable supplies is, however, £1,600,000 + £500,000 = £2,100,000. She is, therefore, not eligible to use cash accounting.

The second issue is that of tax point. Since there are special tax point rules covering TOMS supplies, cash accounting cannot be used for margin scheme supplies or for in-house supplies sold with margin scheme supplies as a package. In fact, for most circumstances, the tax points under TOMS are more attractive than those under cash accounting.

However, cash accounting may be used for in-house supplies sold without margin scheme supplies or for supplies falling outside TOMS. It is for this reason that a person using TOMS may consider the benefits of cash accounting.

6.15.8 Annual accounting and the tour operators' margin scheme

A tour operator may also use annual accounting. The guidance above in relation to the value of TOMS supplies is relevant here in ascertaining whether the person is eligible for the annual accounting scheme.

Although the relevant HMRC *Notices* are silent on the issue, it is convenient to ensure that the annual accounting year is the same as the accounting year for the TOMS calculation.

6.15.9 Flat rate scheme and the tour operators' margin scheme

A tour operator cannot use the flat rate scheme. A person already using the flat rate scheme must leave the scheme if he becomes a tour operator.

6.16 The agricultural flat rate scheme

The Principal VAT Directive (Directive 2006/112), art. 296 provides for an alternative registration for 'agricultural, forestry or fisheries undertakings' as listed in Directive 2006/112, Annexes VII and art. 295(1). UK legislation is in VATA 1994, s. 54; VAT (Flat-rate Scheme for Farmers) (Designated Activities) Order 1992 (SI 1992/3220); VAT (Flat-rate Scheme for Farmers) (Percentage Addition) Order 1992 (SI 1992/3221); VAT Regulations 1995 (SI 1995/2518), reg. 202–211.

A person may register under this scheme in the following cases.

1. He satisfies HMRC that he is carrying out a 'designated activity'.

2. His registration for VAT is cancelled (where the person carries out activities which fall outside those designated, he must not be liable to register for VAT in respect of those activities).

3. In the three years prior to certification, the person has not been assessed for a civil evasion penalty (VATA 1994, s. 60), nor been convicted of a VAT offence, nor made any payment to compound proceedings in respect of VAT.

4. He applies using form VAT 98.

5. He satisfies HMRC that the amounts of the flat-rate additions charged will not exceed the amount of input tax to which he would otherwise have been entitled by £3,000 or more. This effectively allows small farmers, with relevant annual turnover below £75,000, to register for the scheme.

Other guidance: VAT Notice 700/46

Margin Schemes

7.1 Margin scheme of second-hand goods

Ordinarily the supply of any goods by a taxable person attracts VAT at the standard rate, as calculated on the full selling price. However, rules exist which allow a dealer in specified goods to account for VAT calculated on the profit margin achieved by him on those goods. The European *vires* is the Directive 2006/112, art. 313(1). This was incorporated into UK Law by VATA 1994, s. 50A, which replaced s. 32 with effect from 1 June 1995. Previous schemes, which applied only to specified goods, were effectively subsumed within the new 'margin scheme'.

The margin scheme is designed primarily to benefit those taxable persons who, in buying goods from private individuals rather than other taxable persons, are thereby barred from input tax deduction on those goods and where, because the former owner was unable to claim input tax on purchase, there would be effective double taxation if output tax were imposed on the full value of any subsequent resale at a profit.

The scheme includes purchases made from 'margin scheme dealers' in other EU member states, and sales made to persons in other member states.

It should be noted that in this chapter the current standard rate of VAT is used, 20 per cent and the VAT fraction for this rate, 1/6th is used. Prior to 4 January 2011, a new rate of VAT applied, that is 17.5 per cent and the VAT fraction was 7/47ths.

Example 7.1

George, a taxable person, purchases an item for £100 from a private person; there is therefore no input tax to deduct. He sells it for £150.

Under the 'conventional' VAT system, based on a standard rate of 20 per cent he will be liable for VAT of £150 × 1/6 = £25.00

Under the margin scheme, he will be liable for VAT of (£150 − £100) × 1/6 = £8.33, a 'saving' of £16.67, i.e. in this example around 10 per cent of the total selling price.

Thus, from a very simple example, the benefit of the margin scheme is clearly illustrated.

> ### Planning point
>
> The margin scheme is not compulsory for sales of second-hand goods. Thus, a taxpayer may opt to account for VAT on the full selling price. This may occur where the taxpayer's customer identifies himself as a taxable person eligible for input tax recovery.

The margin schemes are governed by law, and by parts of HMRC's publication, Notice 718, on the subject (the latter having the force of law where specified in the Notice).

Law: VATA 1994, s. 50A(2)(c); VAT (Special Provisions Order) 1995 (SI 1995/1268), art. 12(2)(b); VAT (Cars) Order 1992 (SI 1992/3122)

Other guidance: VAT Notice 718

7.2   Profit margin

A key concept in using the margin scheme is the profit margin. This is defined as the amount by which the price at which the person obtained the goods is exceeded by the price at which he supplied them. Where this is a negative amount, where the purchase price exceeded the selling price, no output tax is due, and no credit for that loss can be claimed (although under the global accounting scheme (see **7.5**), there is an effective credit for such losses).

The price at which goods are obtained may be paid to more than one person; and the price at which goods are supplied may be paid by more than one person. For a discussion about how this can affect supplies under the margin scheme, see *Daron Motors Ltd* [1995] BVC 651.

> ### Planning point
>
> Once the profit margin has been calculated, this is treated as VAT inclusive. The VAT amount is calculated at 7/47ths of the profit margin. If the VAT rate is used instead of the VAT fraction, then the dealer will pay too much VAT on the transaction.

> ### ⚠ Warning!
>
> Although VAT is calculated on the profit margin, the value of the supply is the gross sales value, less any VAT accounted for on the margin. This is relevant in respect of the registration or deregistration of the taxable person, or in relation to partial exemption, or the cash accounting or annual accounting schemes.

> **Example 7.2**
>
> Samantha has made sales of second-hand goods totalling £2 million. She has accounted for £60,000 in output VAT. The value of her supplies is £1,940,000.
>
> If these sales were made in one year, then she will not be eligible for the cash accounting scheme or for the annual accounting scheme.

7.3   Eligible goods

The margin scheme treatment can be applied to all second-hand goods. The definition of second-hand goods for this purpose is:

> 'tangible moveable property that is suitable for further use as it is or after repair.'

Excluded from the definition are certain works of art, collectors' items and antiques.

Goods are eligible for the margin scheme where the dealer took possession of them through a supply in respect of which no VAT was chargeable; or a supply under the margin scheme. For restrictions in relation to goods obtained as part of a TOGC, see below.

Goods are not eligible for the margin scheme if the purchase invoice shows an amount attributable to VAT.

Where goods were sold at the zero rate, they may also be eligible for the margin scheme. See *Peugeot Motor Co plc* [1998] BVC 2,111 where the taxpayer purchased cars which were zero-rated under VATA 1994, Sch. 8, Grp. 12, item 15.

> ⚠ **Warning!**
>
> A dealer cannot simply forego the input tax and make non-eligible goods eligible. This applies equally to imported goods or goods acquired from a VAT-registered supplier in another EU member state (unless in the latter case, it is a dealer using the margin scheme in their country).

New goods generally become second-hand either when sold to a member of the public or to a person for non-taxable use.

7.4   Conditions of using the margin scheme

7.4.1 Record-keeping requirements

One of the most important conditions of using the margin scheme is the maintenance of specified records. That these requirements cause difficulties for some taxpayers is beyond question, since the tribunals have heard a number of cases where taxpayers have been debarred from using the margin scheme because they have failed to comply with these requirements.

Margin scheme records must be maintained for six years from the date of the sale of the goods. Where goods were previously transferred as a TOGC, evidence for longer than six years may be required to be kept, so as to substantiate the purchase prices; indeed it is prudent to keep records for as long as is necessary to substantiate a purchase price.

> ### ⚠ *Warning!*
>
> Anyone intending to use the margin scheme would be well advised to ensure that they become thoroughly familiar with these requirements, not least because there are circumstances where HMRC will seek to recover output tax on the full value of supplies made if they are not met.

7.4.2 Invoices

The taxpayer purchasing goods under the margin scheme is required to issue a purchase invoice which must contain certain specified information. The exception is where the taxpayer is purchasing from another taxable person, in which case that person's sales invoice serves as the purchase invoice.

Where the taxpayer purchases from an unregistered dealer, that dealer's sales invoice will suffice, as long as it contains all the information required. Otherwise the taxpayer must issue the invoice.

The information in the table below must always appear on the invoices received or issued for margin scheme goods. Where the goods are purchased from a private individual, the invoice is created by the second-hand goods dealer.

Purchase invoices	Sales invoices
Seller's name and address	Dealer's name, address and VAT registration number
Dealer's name and address	The Purchaser's name and address
A cross-reference between the sales system and the stock book, for example, the stock book number	A cross-reference between the sales system and the stock book, for example, the stock book number
Invoice number (unless the dealer made out the purchase invoice yourself)	Invoice number (based upon sequential number that enable the invoice to be identified)
Date of transaction	Date of transaction
A full description of the item that enables it to be identified	A full description of the item that enables it to be identified
Total price of the item purchased, but excluding any other costs	Total price – VAT is not to be shown
If the purchase price shows VAT then it is ineligible for the margin scheme	
When purchased from another VAT-registered business, any of the following (the last point is recommended): • a reference to Article 313 of Council Directive 2006/112/EC, or • a reference to section 50A of the VAT Act 1994 and the VAT (Special Provisions) Order 1995, or • any other indication that the Margin Scheme has been applied, for example, 'This invoice is for a second-hand margin scheme supply'.	Any of the following (the last point is recommended): • a reference to Article 313 of Council Directive 2006/112/EC, or • a reference to section 50A of the VAT Act 1994 and the VAT (Special Provisions) Order 1995, or • any other indication that the Margin Scheme has been applied, for example, 'This invoice is for a second-hand margin scheme supply'.

⚠ **Warning!**

Difficulty may arise where the 'margin scheme trader' purchases goods from another taxable person who does not use the margin scheme. Ordinarily, such supplies would not be eligible for the margin scheme, as output tax would be chargeable.

Where a person purchases a number of items at the same time, he is required to attribute a value to each item at the time of purchase and those values must be indicated on the invoice.

The taxpayer selling goods under the margin scheme is required to issue a sales invoice which is required to contain certain information. Much of that information would be required by any taxable person providing a VAT invoice. However, in addition, the invoice must show the stock book number; must not show a VAT amount separately; and must incorporate a declaration: 'This is a second-hand margin scheme supply' or 'This invoice is for a second-hand margin scheme supply' or an equivalent to one of these. Where more than one item is sold on an invoice, separate values must be attributed to each item.

> ### Planning point
>
> It should be noted that, with effect from the January 2002 edition of *VAT Notice 718*, invoices no longer require signatures. Some dealers retain this provision, so that the contract for sale is properly evidenced.

Other guidance: VAT Notice 718, s. 3, HMRC VAT Information Sheet 10/07

7.4.3 Stock book

A margin scheme dealer is required to maintain a stock book, in which all his eligible goods are recorded. Despite the fact that the dealer is no longer required to include the seller's or purchaser's address in the stock book (although the address is required on the purchase and sales invoices), many dealers do include the address.

The margin scheme dealer is required to enter the information from the invoices into his stock book. His VAT calculation is also carried out in the stock book.

Where a taxable person makes occasional sales of margin scheme goods, he is not required to prepare and retain the full records as required by the scheme. A person is required to hold evidence of both purchase price and selling price. Good practice would mean that the person cross-referenced the purchase to the sale.

Other guidance: VAT Notice 718, s. 3

7.4.4 Penalties and concessions

Since use of the margin scheme requires that the taxpayer maintain certain records, failure to maintain such records will make him ineligible for using the scheme. The taxpayer will thus be required to account for output tax on the full selling price of the goods sold.

> ### *Example 7.3*
>
> Tony, a dealer, has sold £20,000 worth of margin scheme goods and has accounted for £600 VAT (based on a mark-up of around 20 per cent). HMRC take the view that his records are insufficient to satisfy the requirements of the scheme. Therefore, they assess him for VAT at 1/6th of the full selling price, being £3,333.33, less £600 already paid. He is therefore liable to pay an additional £2,733.33.
>
> This amount represents more than half Tony's profit on those transactions.

> ### ⚠ *Warning!*
>
> Since the figures in the above example are based on generous margins, it is clear that the VAT liability could in some cases exceed the profit achieved on the items concerned.

The VAT (Special Provisions) Order 1995 (SI 1995/1268) provides that HMRC publish in a *Notice* the details of those records required by margin scheme dealers. There is no discretion for HMRC to accept records which fall short of those required (see *VAT Notice 718*, para. 2.4).

> ### *Planning point*
>
> Notwithstanding HMRC's apparent power to assess for VAT on the full value of the sales made (which power should by no means be ignored), in practice they often prove surprisingly reluctant to do so. Any suggestion that they might do so should therefore be firmly resisted; in such cases, it is worth putting much effort into finding alternative forms of supporting evidence to back up the VAT declared.

7.4.5 Part-exchange transactions

It is not uncommon for a margin scheme dealer to take a customer's goods as part payment for goods he is selling (part exchange). In such a situation the margin scheme dealer is still required to issue a purchase invoice for the part-exchange goods. This can be part of the sales invoice, as long as the full details as required by the margin scheme are fulfilled.

Further, at the time of sale, separate values must be attributed to items being sold and purchased. The margin scheme dealer is not allowed simply to indicate a net figure on his invoice.

> ### Example 7.4
>
> Bill's Trading emporium sells an article of furniture for £5,000. The customer paid Bill with £4,000 cash and a picture that was valued at £1,000 in part exchange.
>
> The cost of this article of furniture was £2,000. Bill made a profit of £3,000.
>
> VAT is due at £3,000 × 1/6 = £500.00.
>
> Bill later sells the picture for £1,600. He has made a £600 profit on the picture over its part-exchange valuation. VAT is to be accounted for on the profit.
>
> VAT is due at £600 × 1/6 = £100.00
>
> If the part-exchange item is sold in the later VAT period, then the output tax is deferred until that later tax period.
>
> Bill cannot adjust margins to ensure that a profit is made (rather than a loss) or to attempt to defer VAT until a later period. Manipulation of margins can be seen as an offence by HMRC. The amounts to be entered into the accounts are the agreed valuations between the parties for the sale and purchase of the items.

It is important that any adjustment of prices in this way is agreed with the customer and documentation signed by him.

Where a transaction is subject to hire purchase finance, available goods are actually sold to the finance company. The value for the transaction is, therefore, the amount financed and not any other amount that may be agreed with the purchaser. There have been problems where second-hand goods dealers have 'bumped' the price up to enable the purchaser to obtain a larger amount on finance to facilitate the deal. This has resulted in VAT being accounted for on the higher financed price. Where the finance is a personal loan, the finance arrangements are not relevant to the selling price as the goods are sold to the purchaser not the finance company.

7.5 Global accounting

7.5.1 Introduction

Global accounting is a variation of the margin scheme, and may be used for goods which have a purchase price of up to £500. It is beneficial for a business which deals in large numbers of low-value items, where the maintenance of a stock book listing for each item individually would be impractical.

> ### ⚠ *Warning!*
> Global accounting cannot be used for certain categories of goods, namely cars and other vehicles (unless being broken up for scrap), caravans and motor caravans, aircraft, boats and outboard motors, and horses and ponies.

Law: EC Directive 2006/112, art. 318(1); VATA 1994, s. 50A(7); VAT (Special Provisions) Order 1995 (SI 1995/1268), art. 13.

Other guidance: VAT Notice 718, ss. 5 and 6

7.5.2 Goods not eligible for the scheme

Global accounting cannot be used for certain goods, irrespective of their purchase price. These are broadly some (but not all) of the categories of goods for which separate second-hand schemes used to be in place, as follows:

- motor vehicles (the former scheme applied only to motor cars);
- aircraft;
- boats and outboard motors;
- caravans and motor caravans; and
- horses and ponies.

The non-global margin scheme remains appropriate for sales of such goods.

However, where such goods are purchased to be broken up as scrap, then, even where the purchase price exceeds £500, global accounting may be used as long as the component parts of the broken up item are less than £500 each.

7.5.3 Sales and purchase invoices

Invoices required under global accounting are essentially a simplified version of those required for the margin scheme. There are some differences: no stock-book reference is required and the invoice must be endorsed 'Global accounting invoice'.

The information in the table below must always appear on the invoices received or issued for margin scheme goods. Where the goods are purchased from a private individual the invoice is created by the second hand goods dealer.

Purchase invoices	Sales invoices
Seller's name and address	Dealer's name, address and VAT registration number
Dealer's name and address	The Purchaser's name and address
Invoice number (unless the dealer made out the purchase invoice yourself)	Invoice number (based upon sequential number that enable the invoice to be identified)
Date of transaction	Date of transaction
A full description of the item that enables it to be identified	A full description of the item that enables it to be identified
Total price of the item purchased, but excluding any other costs	Total price – VAT is not to be shown
If the purchase price shows VAT then it is ineligible for the margin scheme	
When purchased from another VAT-registered business, any of the following (the last point is recommended): • a reference to Article 318 of Council Directive 2006/112/EC, or • a reference to section 50A of the VAT Act 1994 and the VAT (Special Provisions) Order 1995, or • any other indication that the Margin Scheme has been applied, for example, 'This invoice is for a second-hand margin scheme supply'.	Any of the following (the last point is recommended): • a reference to Article 318 of Council Directive 2006/112/EC, or • a reference to section 50A of the VAT Act 1994 and the VAT (Special Provisions) Order 1995, or • any other indication that the Margin Scheme has been applied, for example, 'This invoice is for a second-hand margin scheme supply'.

In particular, the description of the goods must be sufficient to allow HMRC to check the items described. Such descriptions as 'assorted goods' or 'four chairs' are not acceptable.

When a person using global accounting purchases goods from a private person, he should make out the purchase invoice. Similarly, if a person purchases from an unregistered dealer, he must ensure that the invoice contains the information required; otherwise he should make out the invoice himself.

7.5.4 Calculations

Global accounting dispenses with the need to identify the profit margin achieved on each item. Instead it calculates output tax based on the overall (or global) margin achieved for each prescribed accounting period.

Where the purchases in one period exceed the sales, the dealer can carry the negative margin forward to the next period.

Example 7.5

In period 03/07, Frances, a taxable person, makes purchases of £14,500, and sales of £18,260.

In period 06/07, she makes purchases of £21,400, and sales of £19,800.

In period 09/07, she makes purchases of £13,000 and sales of £19,300.

She accounts for output tax as follows:

P03/07: global margin = £18,260 − £14,500 = £3,760

  Output tax = £3,760 ×1/6 = £626.67.

P06/07: global margin = £19,800 − £21,400 = (£1,600), negative margin

  Output tax = nil.

P09/07: global margin = £19,300 − £13,000 − £1,600 = £4,700

  Output tax = £4,700 × 1/6 = £783.33.

In the first period in which the person uses global accounting, he is entitled to add any stock in hand at the start of the period to his purchases in that period. Similarly, in the final period in which the person uses global accounting, he must add the purchase price of his closing stock to his sales figures for the final prescribed accounting period.

Example 7.6

First period of trading: stock in hand £24,000, plus purchases of £14,500, sales of £18,260.

Global margin = £18,260 − £24,000 − £14,500 = (£20,240).

A negative margin carried forward to the next period; no output tax to be accounted for.

Planning point

If a significant amount of stock is on hand on starting to use the scheme (e.g. a long-established dealer who has only just exceeded the VAT threshold and registered for VAT), the negative margin can easily be available to carry forward, gradually reducing, over a large number of VAT periods, significantly reducing the immediate impact for the dealer of registering.

Example 7.7

Final period of trading: purchases of £13,000, sales of £19,300, closing stock (at cost price) £11,560.

Global margin = £19,300 + £11,560 − £13,000 = £17,860

Output tax = £17,860 × 1/6 = £2,976.67

Planning point

Where the person deregisters for VAT and has stock in hand which he had purchased for sale under global accounting, the person must make an adjustment as in **Example 7.7**. However, if the output tax due in respect of total of stock and other goods on hand would be less than £1,000, then no output tax need be accounted for.

Example 7.8

Using the closing stock figure from **Example 7.7**, output tax due in respect of closing stock is £11,560 × 1/6 = £1,926.67. The trader must account for this amount on his final VAT return. This is included in the output tax figure of £2,976.67.

Example 7.9

Final period of trading: purchases of £13,000, sales of £19,300, closing stock (at cost price) £5,780.

Global margin = £19,300 + £5,780 − £13,000 = £12,080.

Output tax due in respect of stock in hand = £5,780 × 1/6 = £963.33. Since this is less than £1,000, the dealer may deduct this amount from his final period output tax:

Output tax = (£12,080 × 1/6 − £963.33 = £1050.00

This assumes that VAT on other assets on hand (e.g. office equipment) is less than £36.67.

Similarly, where part or all of a business is transferred as a TOGC, then the cost price of those items transferred must be added to the global sales in that period. This may, of course, be different to the amount actually received in respect of the transfer.

Further adjustments must also be made for any goods sold outside global accounting. This includes goods sold with output tax charged to other taxable persons and goods exported to a place outside the EU. In such cases, the trader should reduce his purchase value by the cost (or estimated cost) of those items sold outside the scheme. Such adjustment should be made in the period in which the goods were sold, not in the period in which they were purchased.

The exact method that a dealer must use in calculating his output tax is not set down. HMRC simply state that it must be reasonable, and the relevant records complete. Where estimates are made, the trader must be able to demonstrate how they were made. Where a dealer makes sales outside of global accounting, his records must clearly indicate which sales are within global accounting and which are outside.

Planning point

Global accounting is only available for items with a purchase value to the dealer of £500 or less. Many dealers will therefore have to keep separate records as required by the normal margin scheme accounting arrangements for items over £500 in value.

Planning point

The sale value of an item is irrelevant to global accounting. Thus an item purchased at £450 and sold at £600 will be eligible for global accounting treatment. An item purchased at £505 and sold at a loss for £475 will not be eligible and the dealer will get no relief for the loss made in such a case.

7.6   Special circumstances

7.6.1   Bad debts and deposits

Before 1 May 1997, there was no explicit provision for a taxpayer using either the margin scheme or global accounting to make a claim for bad-debt relief. However, provision was made in the 1996 Budget, and announced in *Business Brief 9/97* (27 March 1997). (This followed the decision of *Goldsmiths (Jewellers) Ltd v C & E Commrs* (Case C-330/95) [1997] BVC 494.) With effect from 1 May 1997, reg. 172A provided that relief can be claimed but the amount of VAT reclaimed cannot exceed the amount of output tax originally accounted for on that supply.

Although *Notice 718* makes no explicit reference to bad-debt relief for global accounting sales, it is clear that reg. 172A does provide for this. The amount of VAT to be reclaimed is taken as 7/47ths of the amount underpaid.

Where, after making a claim for bad-debt relief, the customer makes a further payment, the appropriate amount of VAT must be repaid to HMRC.

Where a customer pays a deposit for goods sold under the margin scheme, output tax is only payable if the deposit exceeds the cost price of that item. In this case, output tax is payable at 7/47ths of the excess.

Where a customer pays a deposit for goods sold under global accounting, the whole amount of the deposit must be recorded as a global accounting sale and taken into account when calculating the global margin for that prescribed accounting period.

Example 7.10

Phil purchases an item for £1,500 and sells it for £2,750.

The customer pays £1,000 deposit when the sale is agreed and another £1,250 when he collects the goods, with an agreement to pay the £500 balance one month later.

Phil's VAT return period ends after the sale but before the balance is paid.

On that VAT return, his margin is £2,750 − £1,500 = £1,250, and his output tax £1,250 × 1/6 = £208.33.

Suppose the customer omits to pay the £500 balance. Bad-debt relief can be claimed six months after the one-month period agreed. Since the margin was greater than £500, Phil can claim bad-debt relief of £500 × 1/6 = £83.33.

Suppose the customer makes a payment of £360 later. The dealer is then required to repay part of the bad-debt relief, £360 ×1/6 = £60.

7.6.2 Gifts of eligible items

Where an item bought under either the margin scheme or global accounting is given away, no output tax is due.

Under the margin scheme, the stock book should show the name and address of the person receiving the gift.

Under global accounting, the cost price of the item should be deducted from the total of purchases for that prescribed accounting period.

7.6.3 TOGC implications

There have been a number of changes to the margin scheme in relation to TOGCs. These appear to have been a response to abuse or potential abuse of the scheme.

Where a taxable person obtains goods under a TOGC, those goods are only eligible for the margin scheme if they were eligible in the hands of the previous owner. Further, the purchase price to be allocated to each item is the price paid by the previous owner. Thus, in the event of a TOGC, the transferor is obliged to notify the transferee of the eligibility and the purchase price of relevant goods. (These changes are reflected in the VAT (Special Provisions) Order 1995 (SI 1995/1268), arts. 12(3)(iii) and (iv) and 12(5)(v), and the corresponding articles of the VAT (Cars) Order 1992 (SI 1992/3122), art. 8.)

More recently, the same provision was applied to financial institutions who were assigned the rights to goods under finance agreements, and where those goods were transferred as a TOGC. Again, those businesses are only able to use the margin scheme for goods where the original owner was eligible to use the margin scheme. For details, see *Business Brief 16/02* (10 June 2002).

7.6.4 Finance transactions and documentation

Under hire purchase, or similar, agreements, the goods are sold to the finance company and then sold on to the customer. The finance company forwards the full price to the dealer and the customer pays the finance company by instalments.

Where margin scheme goods are sold subject to hire purchase, the dealer may use the hire purchase document as his sales invoice, as long as it includes the relevant information. Whether or not he does so, the dealer is required to retain a copy of the hire purchase document, either attached to the sales invoice or cross-referenced to it (*Notice 718*, para. 24.10).

Part of the reasoning behind this requirement is the practice, particularly in the motor trade, of dealers inflating prices on the finance agreement in order to secure finance on behalf of the customer. The matter has reached the Court of Appeal in *Lex Services plc v C & E Commrs* [2004] BVC 53. The court followed the decisions of the tribunal, that the prices indicated on the hire purchase agreements must represent the valuation for the sale and therefore that price must be shown in the dealer's stock book. Any lower price entered on a sales invoice is to be ignored.

A distinction may be made with a credit sale agreement, or loan agreement, where title passes directly to the customer. Again, the customer will pay by instalments. In this case there appears to be no such requirement for the dealer to retain a copy of the agreement.

Where a dealer receives commission in respect of finance which he has arranged on behalf of his customer, that commission is exempt.

7.6.5 Sale or return transactions

Under sale or return (SOR) transactions, a dealer holds goods in stock on behalf of a third party seller. Once a sale is agreed, the dealer sells the goods to the customer, and passes an agreed sum back to the third party. The dealer is deemed to act as principal, not agent, in such circumstances.

If the dealer is unable to sell the goods, they are either returned to the third party or, on occasion, passed on to another dealer.

The dealer is required to maintain a record of all goods held on an SOR basis. He must include within that record the date the goods were physically transferred to him and the date the goods were either sold or physically transferred away. Such a record may be within the dealer's stock book, or he may maintain a separate record. Although this legal requirement was only introduced with effect from 1 January 2002, good accounting practice would require that a dealer maintain such records in any case.

In one case, a dealer was assessed to VAT on goods claimed as being held on an SOR basis but not sold, but where he had no evidence of the SOR arrangement (*HA Wright Motors Ltd* (1989) 4 BVC 759).

7.6.6 Agents

A dealer may sell goods on behalf of a third party as agent, and never take title in those goods. The dealer must treat the sale as a supply to himself, and a supply by himself.

Such an arrangement will generally provide for the dealer to make a charge for selling the goods or retaining a portion of the selling price. There are two methods of calculation depending on whether the dealer makes a separate charge to the seller.

The selling price is the total amount charged, including any additional amounts paid by the buyer. Other optional items, such as insurance or transport, are separate supplies and should be invoiced separately.

The purchase price is either:

- where the dealer invoices the seller separately, the gross amount realised; or
- where the dealer retains a commission, the gross amount realised less the commission.

The margin is calculated in the usual way, i.e. the selling price less the purchase price. The output tax is calculated by multiplying the margin by 7/47.

The dealer must retain adequate documentation to indicate the nature of agency sales.

Where a person acts as auctioneer, see **7.8.1**.

7.6.7   Intra-EU transactions

The margin scheme and global accounting are EU-wide schemes. They are designed to facilitate supplies between dealers throughout the EU. This means that each member state has a margin scheme, based on the Directive 2006/112, art. 311(1).

In purchasing goods from a dealer in another EU member state, a UK dealer is required to ensure that the goods are eligible for the margin scheme in the usual way and that he is not being charged VAT.

Similarly, in selling margin scheme goods within the EU, a UK dealer is required to complete his invoice in the usual way.

Each EU member state has an 'input tax declaration', and these are listed in *Notice 718*, para. 16.1. That paragraph also indicates that, in some States, the declaration is not mandatory. The purchasing dealer is therefore advised to check that the goods are being sold under the margin scheme.

Notice 718, para. 15.5 indicates that margin scheme supplies should not be included on EC sales lists. *Notice 60* suggests that supplies under the margin scheme need not be entered on an Intrastat Supplementary Declaration.

> **Planning point**
>
> A dealer may choose not to use the scheme for intra-EU transactions. He may prefer to zero rate the goods. The invoice will not show the input tax declaration but will have a note of the customer's VAT number. The purchaser will therefore be required to account for acquisition tax and will not be entitled to use the margin scheme for those goods.

7.6.8   Imports and exports

A dealer cannot use the margin scheme for imported goods. This is because, at import, VAT is charged at 17.5 per cent on the full price of the goods (20 per cent from 4 January 2011). The dealer is, of course, entitled to deduct that amount of VAT but he must sell the goods outside the margin scheme.

Where a dealer exports margin scheme goods to a place outside the EU, he may zero rate the goods, subject to the rules for export. *VAT Notice 703* provides further details.

7.6.9   Pawnbrokers

Pawnbrokers may use the margin scheme of global accounting for unredeemed pledges, provided they maintain records required by the scheme. Further conditions are:

- the original loan did not exceed £75, with the statutory six-month redemption period (prior to 1 May 1998 this limit was £25); and
- the pawnbroker has taken title in the goods.

The purchase price for the margin scheme is the amount of the loan plus the initial six-months interest payable, less any payments received. The purchase invoice is either the credit agreement or pawn receipt, as long as the contract number is entered in the stock book.

Where the original loan amount exceeds £75 (£25 before 1 May 1998) the margin scheme cannot be used.

7.6.10 Optional extras and disbursements

A dealer using the margin scheme may sell other goods or services as optional extras.

Most commonly, a dealer may sell insurance:

- the insurance must be a contract between the insurer and the customer, and the customer's own risk must be covered, not the dealer's; and
- the amount of any premium and related fee must be itemised on the sales invoice.

In such circumstances, the dealer may treat the charge as exempt from VAT.

Other optional extras, or disbursements, are treated as separate supplies, and must be accounted for outside the scheme.

For optional extras and disbursements related to second-hand car sales, see **7.7.3**.

7.6.11 Flat rate scheme

This scheme was introduced for businesses with annual taxable turnover below £150,000 with effect from 25 April 2002. A margin scheme dealer cannot also use the flat rate scheme.

7.6.12 Joint ownership of goods

Notice 718, s. 14 deals with the arrangements to be followed where two or more taxable persons purchase and later sell an eligible item. Essentially, HMRC look to one of the parties to be responsible for a stock-book entry and for any output tax due.

7.6.13 Caravans

Where a caravan qualifies for zero-rating, under VATA 1994, Sch. 8, Grp. 9, item 1, the removable contents are standard-rated. The sale of a second-hand caravan will require that the output tax only be due in respect of the margin achieved on the removable contents. The dealer may either calculate the actual value of these contents or attribute 10 per cent of the margin to the contents (see *Notice 701/20*).

7.7   Motor vehicles

7.7.1   Background

Although the VAT (Special Provisions) Order 1995 (SI 1995/1268) does not specifically exclude motor cars from the general provisions relating to second-hand goods, a separate Order provides for a margin scheme for the sale of second-hand motor cars. A definition of a motor car appears in the VAT (Cars) Order 1992 (SI 1992/3122), art. 2 (see **Chapter 11**). Changes in the design and adaptability of car-derived vans resulted in HMRC issuing revised guidance in *Business Brief 16/04*. This affects such vehicles purchased from 1 October 2003.

Notice 718 includes a separate paragraph (s. 19) which deals specifically with second-hand motor vehicles. Sections 20 and 21 also relate to supplies linked to supplies of second-hand motor vehicles. No actual definition of motor vehicle appears in the notice or in the legislation. The use of the term 'vehicle' appears to be a mechanism for indicating that qualifying commercial vehicles are eligible for the margin scheme and that, to the extent that they share some characteristics in common with cars, the same broad principles (regarding motor breakdown insurance (MBI), for example, or extras) apply to them. It should also be noted that the exclusion from global accounting applies to motor vehicles, not to motor cars.

7.7.2   Definition of a second-hand vehicle

Whether a vehicle is deemed to be 'used' or 'second-hand' was the subject of *Lincoln Street Motors (Birmingham) Ltd* (No. 1100). The tribunal held that:

'In our judgment the essential qualification of a used motor car is:

* that it shall have been driven on the road by or at the direction of the person who has purchased it; or
* has been appropriated and used by a dealer for the purposes of his business before becoming the subject of a retail sale.'

Thus, minimal delivery mileage, or registration by the dealer, did not render a car 'used' for VAT purposes. (It should be noted that case law relating to the Trade Descriptions Act 1968 does not follow this definition of 'used'.)

Since 1 December 1999, this definition has been amended, so that where a car is a 'stock in trade' car it is not 'used' for VAT purposes (see **Chapter 11**).

7.7.3 Optional extras and disbursements

If a taxable person pays amounts to third parties as the agent of his client and debits his client with the precise amounts paid out, then the person may be able to treat them as disbursements for VAT purposes and exclude these amounts when he calculates any VAT due on the main supply. *Notice 700*, para. 25.1 describes in further detail whether certain payments can be treated as disbursements and the conditions which must be fulfilled to enable a person to treat payments made in this way.

Within the motor trade, a variety of 'extras' may be negotiated in a transaction. Whether any can be treated as disbursements, or separate supplies, has been the subject of some litigation. *Notice 718* contains specific guidance in relation to some of these.

Planning point

Where accessories are fitted to a car, they cannot be treated as a separate supply, even if invoiced separately. See *A Thompson & Sons Ltd* [1992] BVC 1,532. Thus, the selling price of a second-hand car must include the price of any accessories, even if they are itemised separately on the sales invoice. The dealer selling the vehicle, however, can claim an input tax deduction for the VAT incurred on the purchase of the accessory. A taxable person purchasing a second-hand car with accessories will not be entitled to deduct VAT charged on the accessories as input tax.

Following *C & E Commrs v British Telecommunications plc* [1999] BVC 306, delivery charges should not normally be treated as a separate supply. However, *Notice 718*, para. 2.8 allows that optional extras may be treated as disbursements in respect of sales of second-hand goods, subject to strict conditions (that is that the dealer is only acting as the agent in acquiring the goods).

7.7.4 Motor breakdown insurance (MBI)

An MBI describes a contract of insurance provided to the purchaser of a second-hand motor vehicle. The policy covers the customer for breakdown of specified components within a certain time period, up to a certain value and subject to specified conditions.

Some dealers used so-called 'value shifting' whereby the margin on the car was transferred to the MBI. Being insurance, no output tax was due on the MBI portion of the transaction. The decision in *Centurions* [1993] BVC 1,346 describes the process of value shifting. The Tribunal, in this case, accepted HMRC's revalued margin, preventing the value of the vehicle being shifted to the MBI. For a contrasting decision, see *Geddes* (1989) 4 BVC 573.

As a disincentive to value shifting, the rate of IPT (Insurance Premium Tax) on MBIs was imposed at 17.5 per cent with effect from 1 April 1997.

Where a dealer provides an MBI free of charge to the customer, the invoice should not show a separate amount for the MBI.

Where the dealer makes a separate charge for the MBI, then that is treated as a separate supply as long as:

- the MBI is a contract of insurance between the insurer and the customer;
- the customer is entirely free to purchase the car with or without the MBI; and
- the invoice identifies separately the premium charged and any related fee.

Planning point

Where the dealer does not identify the separate MBI charge, then he may only treat the net amount that the dealer paid for the MBI as an exempt supply.

Notice 718, ss. 20–21, refer to the treatment of MBIs.

7.7.5 Warranties

A warranty is distinguished from MBI since the premium is paid into a fund from which claims are paid. Thus, it is a guarantee made by the dealer, or person acting on the dealer's behalf, rather than an insurance product. Output tax is due at 17.5 per cent on such a supply.

A dealer may itemise the amount on his invoice, or he may include the amount due within the selling price. Any amount charged represents a separate supply and output tax should be accounted for outside the dealer's stock book. (For convenience, some dealers include the warranty selling price within the car selling price, so that output tax is accounted for through their stock book.)

7.7.6 Vouchers

A detailed treatment of vouchers is beyond the scope of this chapter. VATA 1994, Sch. 6, para. 5 provides that a face-value voucher may be provided without VAT being charged.

7.7.7 Road tax

Where a dealer surrenders a road fund licence from a car he buys, the refund is outside the scope of VAT. The dealer should not adjust the purchase price by the refund amount.

> **Planning point**
>
> Where a dealer agrees to purchase a road fund licence on behalf of his customer, then that may be treated as a disbursement, provided the necessary conditions are fulfilled (*Notice 700*, para. 25.1). See *DE Siviter (Motors) Ltd* (1989) 4 BVC 1,340).

> **Planning point**
>
> Where a dealer offers the road fund licence either free of charge or within an agreed sale price, then he is making a single supply and the car selling price must include the value of the licence. Where the dealer supplies a car with an unexpired licence, then that remains a single supply and the value of the licence cannot be itemised on the invoice.

7.7.8 MOTs

Where a dealer provides a new MOT with a used motor car that cannot be treated as a disbursement. The selling price must include the value of the MOT. The position, when taken by HMRC, has been upheld in the tribunal (see *Depot Corner Car Sales* [2001] BVC 4,064 for an example).

7.7.9 Qualifying cars

A motor dealer cannot use the margin scheme for qualifying cars. A qualifying car is one on which input tax deduction has not been disallowed or where the dealer chooses to treat it as such.

Where the car was sold by the original supplying dealer to a taxable person who was entitled to input tax deduction (such as a lease company), then that person would sell the car as a qualifying car. A motor dealer purchasing the car would therefore be charged output tax. The car is a qualifying car and ineligible for the margin scheme.

> ⚠ **Warning!**
>
> The dealer is not entitled to forego the input tax and include the car in the margin scheme. He is obliged to sell the car as a qualifying car. Where the purchaser is a taxable person, the motor dealer must issue a VAT invoice, identifying output tax on the invoice.

> ⚠ **Warning!**
>
> Where the purchaser is not a taxable person, a motor dealer will issue an invoice in any case. It is suggested that to itemise output tax separately may cause some confusion, and that the price indicated on the invoice should include output tax. The 'input tax declaration' should also be deleted, since the motor dealer has deducted input tax.

The legal position related to qualifying cars is in the VAT (Input Tax) Order 1992 (SI 1992/3222).

7.7.10 Stock-in-trade cars

With effect from 1 December 1999, a new category of car was introduced, the 'stock-in-trade' car. This is defined in the VAT (Input Tax) Order 1992 (SI 1992/3222), art. 2. Where a motor dealer purchases (or acquires or imports) a new or qualifying car, with the intention of resale within 12 months and, in the interim, uses that car within his business and/or puts the car to temporary private use, then the dealer can claim input tax deduction (see *Notice 700/64*, s. 3).

The private use of a stock-in-trade car gives rise to an output tax charge. An agreement has been reached between HMRC and the Retail Motor Industry Federation over a simplified method of calculating output tax in the free private use of stock-in-trade cars.

> **Planning point**
>
> When a dealer sells a stock-in-trade car, he is obliged to treat it as a qualifying car and account for output tax on its full selling price.

7.7.11 Imported cars

Cars imported from outside the EU are not eligible for the margin scheme. Input tax charged on importation may be deducted by the dealer but he must sell the car as a qualifying car.

Some difficulty has arisen where dealers have not claimed VAT charged on importation, or have purchased cars from other taxable persons who have not claimed VAT charged on importation, and have sought to resell them through the margin scheme. In such circumstances, the cars are still not eligible for the margin scheme. This matter was discussed in *Ball* [2002] BVC 4,073.

7.7.12 Repossessions/insurance sales

The VAT (Cars) Order 1992 (SI 1992/3122), art. 4 provides that the disposal of a used motor car by a finance company which has repossessed it under the terms of a finance agreement, or the repossession by an insurance company which has taken it in settlement of an insurance claim, is a non-supply, as long as the car is disposed of in the same condition as it was when taken.

A motor dealer purchasing such a car may sell it under the margin scheme (*Notice 718*, para. 24.2).

7.7.13 Subsidised finance

Some finance agreements provide that the motor dealer 'subsidise' the amount otherwise payable as interest. Such an arrangement may be described as '0 per cent interest' or 'reduced finance'. Where the motor dealer effectively pays such amounts to the finance company, it has been held that the 'deemed interest' represents a separate supply, not a reduction in the selling price of the car. See *Grant Melrose & Tennent Ltd* (1985) 2 BVC 208,065. This approach is consistent with the decision in *C & E Commrs v Primback Ltd* (Case C-34/99) [2001] BVC 315.

A distinction was made in the case of *A & D Stevenson (Trading) Ltd* [2003] BVC 4,078, where the amount payable to the dealer under the hire purchase contract was not paid in full at the time of the delivery to the customer and where the amount payable to the dealer was subsequently reduced.

7.7.14 Incomplete records – 100 per cent rule

Where a motor dealer does not fulfil all the record-keeping requirements, he would ordinarily be required to account for output tax on the full selling price of each car sold.

However, there is a concession applying where a motor dealer holds either a sales invoice or a purchase invoice, but not both, and where HMRC are satisfied that the mark-up achieved on sale does not exceed 100 per cent. Subject to these conditions, the output tax is calculated either:

- if the dealer holds only the purchase invoice, on the price paid for the car; or
- if the dealer holds only the sales invoice, on half the selling price.

(*Notice 718*, para. 19.4. This concession also appears in *Notice 48*, Extra-Statutory Concession 3.8.)

7.8   Horses and ponies

7.8.1   Record-keeping requirements

A variation of the margin scheme applies for taxable persons dealing in second-hand horses and ponies. Details of the scheme appear in *Notice 718*, s. 22.

The dealer can opt to use three-part forms provided by the British Equestrian Trade Association (BETA). Examples of the forms appeared in *Notice 718* (March 1999 edition), Appendix G, but have been excluded from the current edition.

Essentially, the dealer retains parts A and B of the form, and uses part C as his sales invoice. This applies equally to a sale made at auction.

The dealer can alternatively opt to maintain conventional margin scheme records, as described in **7.4.1** above.

In either case, a failure to maintain proper records would mean that the dealer would be required to pay output tax on the full selling price of the horses or ponies.

7.8.2   Eligible horses and ponies

> **Planning point**
>
> The scheme applies only for second-hand horses and ponies. A person selling a horse or pony that he has bred himself cannot use the scheme. Also, a person cannot use the scheme for a horse or pony purchased on an invoice showing VAT.

However, where a non-taxable person has reared a horse or pony from birth, the auctioneers' scheme may be used for its first sale.

7.8.3 Descriptions

The margin scheme requires that each item be described sufficiently to identify it. This is equally true for horses and ponies. There are standard means by which this is done, as laid down by the Royal College of Veterinary Surgeons, and this is reflected in the three-part form.

Ordinarily a horse or pony is registered with a recognised Breed Society, or Stud Book or Register. If not, as long as the purchase price exceeds £500, the seller and a vet must sign the form to certify that the horse or pony is the one described. If the purchase price is less than £500, a vet's signature is not required.

Where the dealer uses the margin scheme, the description must include: colour, sex, type, age, height, stable name and any distinctive markings.

7.9 Works of art, etc.

7.9.1 Background

Special arrangements exist for the importation and sale of works of art, collectors' items and antiques. These goods are defined in *Notice 718*, s. 25 (reproduced at **7.10.4** below). Certain goods are specifically excluded from the definition; precious metals and precious stones are therefore eligible for neither the special scheme for works of art, nor for the standard margin scheme. A separate scheme exists for supplies of certain gold items (see *Notices 701/21* and *701/21A*).

With the introduction of the margin scheme with effect from 1 June 1995, a special method of valuation was introduced for works of art. Thus, works of art are eligible for sale under both the margin scheme and the auctioneers' scheme. Details are in *Notice 718*, s. 11 and s. 18.

The dealer or auctioneer can use the respective scheme for imported works of art and for works of art obtained from their creators or heirs. He must fulfil the following conditions:

- import or obtain the goods directly;
- notifies VAT Written Enquiries Team, 4th Floor West, Alexandra House, 21 Victoria Street, Southend-on-Sea, Essex, SS99 1BD of this intention;
- intend to use the scheme for at least two years;
- notify the Written Enquiries Office if he wishes to cease using the scheme;
- use the scheme for all eligible works of art; and

- if the dealer or auctioneer sells any eligible goods outside the scheme, he cannot claim input tax on those goods until the prescribed accounting period in which he accounts for output tax on them.

Notice 718 provides no guidance on how HMRC will process an application to use the scheme for works of art.

7.9.2 Purchase and selling prices – margin scheme

When a margin scheme dealer imports a work of art, the purchase price includes any import VAT charged, being at five per cent. The dealer cannot recover this amount as input tax.

When a margin scheme dealer purchases or acquires a work of art from another EU member state, he will be charged VAT at five per cent on the full selling price. Acquisition tax should be included in box 2 of his VAT return. The dealer cannot recover this VAT as input tax and so the corresponding amount cannot be included in box 4 of his VAT return.

> **Planning point**
>
> The VAT amount should be included within the purchase price for the purposes of the dealer's margin scheme calculation. By including the VAT amount in the purchase price, the dealer effectively obtains some credit for the VAT amount paid. See the example in *Notice 718*, para. 18.4.

7.9.3 Purchase and selling prices – auctioneers' scheme

When an auctioneer obtains a work of art, either imported from outside the EU, acquired from another EU member state or obtained directly from the creator or heirs in the UK, he cannot claim any VAT charged on the goods.

The purchase price is the hammer price less the auctioneer's commission charges. This may of course be quite different from the amount he actually paid for the goods.

The selling price is the hammer price plus any buyer's premium. An example of a calculation under this scheme appears in *VAT Notice 718*, para. 9.1, example 5.

An auctioneer may sell goods under the margin scheme. If so, the purchase price is the hammer price. Any commission charged to the seller is then invoiced separately and VAT itemised. The selling price will include any buyer's premium. Thus, the auctioneer will account for output tax on the commission charged to the seller, and on his margin. An example of this calculation appears in *Notice 718*, para. 9.1, example 4.

7.9.4 Definitions of works of art, collectors' items and antiques

In *Notice 718*, s. 25, HMRC provide detailed definitions of the items eligible for this margin scheme, as follows:

'Works of art

1. "Work of art" means, subject to subsections (2) and (3) below–

    (a) any mounted or unmounted painting, drawing, collage, decorative plaque or similar picture that was executed by hand;

    (b) any original engraving, lithograph or other print which:

        (i) was produced from one or more plates executed by hand by an individual who executed them without using any mechanical or photomechanical process; and

        (ii) either is the only one produced from the plate or plates or is comprised in a limited edition;

    (c) any original sculpture or statuary, in any material;

    (d) any sculpture cast which:

        (i) was produced by or under the supervision of the individual who made the mould or became entitled to it by succession on the death of that individual; and

        (ii) either is the only cast produced from the mould or is comprised in a limited edition;

    (e) any tapestry or other hanging which:

        (i) was made by hand from an original design; and

        (ii) either is the only one made from the design or is comprised in a limited edition;

    (f) any ceramic executed by an individual and signed by him;

    (g) any enamel on copper which:

        (i) was executed by hand;

        (ii) is signed either by the person who executed it or by someone on behalf of the studio where it was executed;

        (iii) either is the only one made from the design in question or is comprised in a limited edition; and

        (iv) is not comprised in an article of jewellery or an article of a kind produced by goldsmiths or silversmiths;

    (h) any mounted or unmounted photograph which:

        (i) was printed by or under the supervision of the photographer;

        (ii) is signed by him; and

        (iii) either is the only print made from the exposure in question or is comprised in a limited edition;

2.   The following do not fall within the definition of works of art–

   (a)   any technical drawing, map or plan;

   (b)   any picture comprised in a manufactured article that has been hand-decorated; or

   (c)   anything in the nature of scenery, including a backcloth.

3.   An item comprised in a limited edition shall be taken to be so comprised for the purposes of subsection 1(d) to (h) above only if–

   (a)   in the case of sculpture casts–

   (i)   the edition is limited so that the number produced from the same mould does not exceed eight; or

   (ii)   the edition comprises a limited edition of nine or more casts made before 1st January 1989 which the Commissioners have directed should be treated, in the exceptional circumstances of the case, as a limited edition for the purposes of subsection 1(d) above;

   (b)   in the case of tapestries and hangings, the edition is limited so that the number produced from the same design does not exceed eight;

   (c)   in the case of enamels on copper–

   (i)   the edition is limited so that the number produced from the same design does not exceed eight; and

   (ii)   each of the enamels in the edition is numbered and is signed as mentioned in subsection 1(g)(ii) above;

   (d)   in the case of photographs–

   (i)   the edition is limited so that the number produced from the same exposure does not exceed thirty; and

   (ii)   each of the prints in the edition is numbered and is signed as mentioned in subsection 6(h)(ii) above.

Collectors' items

Collections and collectors' pieces of zoological, botanical, mineralogical, anatomical, historical, archaeological, palaeontological, ethnographical, numismatic or philatelic interest.

A collector's piece is of philatelic interest if:

   (a)   it is a postage or revenue stamp, a postmark, a first-day cover or an item of pre-stamped stationery; and

   (b)   it is franked or (if unfranked) it is not legal tender and is not intended for use as such.

Note: unfranked stamps which are valid for postage are not collectors' items and cannot be included in the margin schemes: that is, stamps on which the value is:

- in decimal currency;
- currently valid for 1st or 2nd class postage; or
- £1, or a multiple of £1, of the present monarch's reign.

Antiques

Antiques means objects other than works of art or collectors' items which are more than 100 years old.'

Notice 718, s. 25 continues by listing goods which are not eligible for any margin scheme, and which therefore cannot be put through this scheme under the heading of works of art, collectors' items or antiques. The ineligible items are as follows:

'Precious metals

Goods (including coins) consisting in precious metals or any supply of goods containing precious metals where the consideration for the supply (excluding any VAT) is, or is equivalent to an amount which does not exceed the open market value of the metal contained in the goods.

For gold coins sold at or below the open market value (that is the daily "fix" price) the special accounting and payment system for gold transactions applies. Further details can be found in *VAT Notice 701/21* Gold.

Investment gold

With effect from 1 January 2000, gold coins which meet the definition of investment gold are not considered of numismatic interest and are not eligible for the margin schemes. Further details about investment gold can be found in *VAT Notice 701/21A* Investment gold coins.

Precious stones

Precious stones of any age which are not mounted, set or strung are excluded. For the purposes of the margin scheme, precious stones are diamonds, rubies, sapphires and emeralds.'

7.10 Auctioneers

7.10.1 Overview

The auctioneers' scheme is essentially a variation of the margin scheme. It was introduced with effect from 1 June 1995. The auctioneers' scheme provides for the sale of goods by the following classes of persons:

- private persons;
- taxable persons using the margin scheme;
- taxable persons using global accounting;
- insurance companies disposing of goods taken in as part of an insurance settlement; and
- finance companies disposing of repossessed goods.

Where other taxable persons wish to sell goods on which output tax is chargeable, the auctioneers' scheme cannot be used.

Notice 718, ss. 7–10 and s. 12 provide information on the auctioneers' scheme.

The auctioneers' scheme can only be used for goods that would be eligible for the margin scheme. This excludes goods grown, made or produced by the vendor, since they cannot be described as 'second-hand'. A concession was introduced with effect from 1 January 1999, that where such goods were sold by a non-taxable person, the auctioneers' scheme could be used. See *Business Brief 23/98*; *Notice 718*, s. 10; and *Notice 48*, Extra-Statutory Concession 3.27. This therefore includes livestock and bloodstock reared from birth by non-taxable persons.

Where goods are sold and bought under the auctioneers' scheme, the auctioneer is deemed to have bought and sold them. The tax point for both transactions is therefore the same and is the earlier of:

- the handing-over of the goods to the buyer; and
- receipt of payment by the auctioneer.

7.10.2 Profit margin

The auctioneer using the auctioneers' scheme accounts for output tax on his profit margin, which is the difference between the deemed sale price and the deemed purchase price of the goods.

The sale price for this purpose is the hammer price plus any premium charges payable by the buyer. The purchase price is the hammer price less any commission charges payable by the vendor.

Any other optional charges, such as insurance, delivery, storage, etc., must be invoiced separately.

Example 7.11

Mary, an auctioneer, sells an item at £2,000. Her commission is 7.5 per cent, plus VAT for the vendor; and 10 per cent, plus VAT for the buyer.

Vendor's commission = £2,000 × 7.5 per cent + VAT = £176.25.

Purchase price is £2,000 − £176.25 = £1,823.75.

Buyer's premium = £2,000 × 10 per cent + VAT = £235.00.

Selling price is £2,000 + £235.00 = £2,235.00.

The auctioneer's margin is £2,235.00 − £1,823.75 = £411.25.

This also equals the total of the commission charges, £176.25 + £235.00 = £411.25.

Mary's output tax is £411.25 × 1/6 = £68.54.

For VAT purposes, the auctioneer may not charge vendors a commission by way of an identifiable separate supply. The VAT, being a proportion of a 'profit margin', must not be itemised on the invoice.

For all purposes other than VAT, the auctioneer continues to act as agent, not principal, and the invoices issued by the auctioneer will reflect this.

Planning point

If the person using the margin scheme sells goods at auction, the selling price is the hammer price less the commission. If a person using the margin scheme buys goods at auction, the purchase price is the hammer price plus the commission. VAT-registered dealers using the margin scheme therefore get effective credit for what would otherwise be input tax on the auctioneer's commissions by way of a reduction of their own profit margin on the relevant goods (always assuming, if the goods are not eligible for global accounting, that they make a profit).

⚠ Warning!

Goods sold on behalf of VAT-registered vendors not using the second-hand margin scheme are not eligible for the auctioneers' margin scheme.

Example 7.12

Using the figures in the previous example:

The vendor's margin scheme selling price is £1,823.75.

The purchaser's margin scheme purchase price is £2,235.00.

7.10.3 Invoices

The auctioneers' scheme requires that the auctioneer maintain sales and purchase invoices for all transactions. These are similar to those required under the margin scheme, as noted at **7.4.2**.

In addition, his purchase invoice must also show:

- the hammer price;
- VAT-inclusive commission charges; and
- the net amount due to the vendor.

His sales invoice must also show:

- the hammer price;

- VAT-inclusive commission charges; and
- the net amount due from the buyer.

If either the vendor or buyer is also using the margin scheme or global accounting, the purchase and selling prices must be clear from the invoices.

An auctioneer may include a number of items on the same invoice. Unless they were sold as a single lot, he must indicate a separate price for each item.

An auctioneer may include eligible and non-eligible goods on the same invoice. He must ensure that the items sold under the auctioneers' scheme are clearly identified.

7.10.4 Stock records

A person using the auctioneers' scheme is not required to maintain a stock book in the same way as a dealer using the margin scheme. However, he is required to maintain all the information that would be required in a stock book. This may include sales catalogues, entry forms, etc. In addition, the auctioneer should retain copies of all purchase and sales invoices.

7.10.5 Intra-EU transactions

Transactions under the auctioneers' scheme to or from other EU member states are treated in the same way as any other transactions. The same eligibility rules apply in respect of a vendor from another EU member state selling goods in the UK under the auctioneers' scheme. Similarly, where goods are sold to a person in another EU member state, there is no additional evidence to be provided.

Transactions under the auctioneers' scheme do not attract acquisition tax. Transactions under the auctioneers' scheme are not required to be entered in boxes 8 or 9 of a VAT return, or on a EC sales list.

7.10.6 Imports and exports

Goods imported from outside the EU have VAT charged on them at import. They are thus ineligible for the auctioneers' scheme.

Where goods are sold to a buyer outside the EU, the auctioneer is required to obtain satisfactory proof of export (see *Notice 703*). The auctioneer can then enter 'nil' in the VAT column of his stock record.

7.11 Tour Operators Margin Scheme

7.11.1 Overview

For reasons which are not entirely clear, the Tour Operators Margin Scheme (TOMS) has attracted much mystique and is seen by many, including, it would appear, most VAT officers, as a no-go area. In fact, the basic principles underlying it are simple, and understanding these is the key to understanding the TOMS and its operation.

Tour operators combine various facilities for travellers into a single package, which is sold as such. VAT is a consumption tax and in principle therefore must be accounted for where enjoyment of the various elements of the package takes place. If the tour operator had to account for this VAT as output tax, there would be a requirement for that operator to register for VAT in every EU jurisdiction where any element of any package was supplied. This would inevitably involve multiple registrations for numerous tour operators.

As a simplification measure, therefore, the TOMS has been introduced and applies throughout the EU as an alternative means of bringing VAT to account in the correct jurisdictions. In essence, it works as set out below.

1. Tour operators are not obliged to register for VAT in every member state where they buy and (as part of a package) resell facilities for travellers.

2. Instead, they are precluded from claiming input tax on the purchase of any element of the package bought in for resale (even if this is within their own jurisdiction). In this way, VAT is brought to account in the place where that element is enjoyed, by way of output tax in the hands of the supplier (e.g. the hotel).

3. The profit margin achieved by the tour operator (e.g. the difference between the cost of the elements of the package and the selling price of the package) is taxed in the jurisdiction where the tour operator is established.

4. The profit margin is calculated in accordance with rules contained within the TOMS itself.

5. If a tour operator provides any elements of the package out of their own resources (e.g. owning a hotel or coaches), rather than buying them in for resale, they become liable to account for VAT on the full value of these within the package (also calculated according to the TOMS rules) which may then entail their registering for VAT in the jurisdiction(s) where these elements of the package are enjoyed.

> ⚠ **Warning!**
>
> It is essential to note that the term 'tour operator' in this context is not limited to those who hold themselves out as such, but includes any person who buys, packages and resells facilities for travellers, either regularly or on a one-off basis.

> ### ⚠ *Warning!*
>
> The Upper Tribunal decision in *Secret Hotels2 Ltd (formerly Med Hotels Ltd) v R & C Commrs* [2011] BVC 1,700 highlights the need to be certain of the relationship between the parties. In this Upper Tribunal decision it was held that *Secrets Hotels2* was acting as an agent in providing accommodation and did not, therefore, need to use TOMS; it could account for VAT in the normal manner. The First Tier Tribunal had, however, held that it was not acting as an agent and had to use TOMS. It is, therefore, necessary to consider the nature that the supplier is acting in to determine if it is acting as a principal and whether or not TOMS applies.

> ### *Warning!*
>
> The European Commission has brought infringement proceedings against the Czech Republic *(ECJ Case C-269/11)* and Greece *(ECJ Case C-293/11)* for applying TOMS in cases where the travel services have been sold to a person other than the traveller. The Commission is also pursuing similar cases against Finland, France, Italy, Poland, Portugal and Spain. This is a matter that will no doubt develop and the changing requirements need to be monitored.

Law: VATA 1994, s. 53, Sch. 8, Grp. 8, item 12 and Value Added Tax (Tour Operators) Order 1987 (SI 1987/1806).

Other guidance: VAT Notice 709/5

7.11.2 TOMS supplies

For the purpose of the TOMS, the following supplies are to be treated as falling within margin scheme treatment:

- accommodation;
- passenger transport;
- hire of a means of transport;
- use of special lounges at airports;
- trips or excursions; and
- the services of tour guides.

Other supplies will fall liable for TOMS treatment if supplied in conjunction with those listed above, such as catering, theatre tickets and sports facilities.

7.11.3 The margin

The 'margin' within the TOMS is, as mentioned above, defined within the scheme itself. It is the difference between the bought-in value of the TOMS supplies and the income derived from the sale of the package. No account may be taken of any costs incurred which are not bought-in components, such as employed representatives in holiday locations or office expenses. In accounting terms, it is perhaps more akin to gross profit than net profit, but will often not correlate even to this as certain gross profit items will not qualify to be taken into account.

This computed margin or profit is deemed to be inclusive of VAT in the country in which the tour operator is established. Thus, if this is the UK, the tour operator's output tax liability will be 7/47ths of the margin achieved (1/6th from 4 January 2011) – to the extent that the holidays are enjoyed within the EU, that is. For holidays enjoyed wholly outside the EU, the margin is zero-rated for VAT purposes and no output tax liability therefore arises.

Where the tour operator provides elements of the package from own resources (known for TOMS purposes as in-house supplies), these must be valued as a component of the package, including their own share of the margin. The tour operator must account for output tax on the full value of the relevant elements in the jurisdiction in which they are supplied. This may entail VAT registration in another country if those in-house supplies are provided there.

> ### ⚠ *Warning!*
>
> It is important to recognise that the rules of the scheme apply even where the entire package is enjoyed in the tour operator's own jurisdiction. Thus, for a package holiday taking place within the UK, the UK tour operator must still calculate the margin, accounting for VAT accordingly, and must not claim any input tax on bought-in supplies (the VAT-inclusive cost of which becomes a deduction from turnover in calculating the margin). Also see **7.11.5**.

7.11.4 Accounting for VAT

As with all margin schemes, suppliers using the TOMS are not permitted to issue VAT invoices, nor any sales document which identifies a VAT amount included within the sum paid.

Tour operators are not permitted within the rules of the TOMS to account for VAT on the computed profit margins of individual tour packages. Instead all income from TOMS supplies must be aggregated and all bought-in supplies likewise totalled, and a single margin calculated. The rules of the scheme contain provisions for the margin to be subdivided in certain situations, such as where some tours are enjoyed within the EU and others outside it (although in this specific circumstance, it is possible to elect to treat these separately, carrying out two TOMS calculations). Where a tour operator also provides in-house supplies, the calculations also provide for the correct valuation of these within the overall turnover obtained from packages.

The rules for the treatment of in-house supplies also changed at the end of 2009. The European Commission instructed the UK that it must apply the decision in *MyTravel plc v C & E Commrs* [2008] BVC 426. This has affected the way in-house supplies are supplied. An example of this would be an airline supplying a package of hotel accommodation with its own air flight. Prior to this decision, a business that made travel service supplies combining bought in supplies with in-house supplies could supply the in-house services under the normal VAT rules. In the past, the margin (and VAT liability) was determined by an apportionment of costs relating to the respective types of supply. The ECJ held, however, that the in-house supplies were to be valued by their open-market value. Some applied this from the date of the judgment. Other tour operators are required, from 1 January 2010, to apply the decision.

> ### Planning point
>
> *VAT Notice 700/5* contains detailed notes on the computations which must be carried out, but if it is remembered that their basic aim is as described above, it is perhaps easier to follow what they are seeking to achieve.

It follows from the above that the true margin cannot be computed until the end of the year (which for TOMS purposes is the accounts year of the tour operator). However, VAT must be brought to account throughout the year as holidays are supplied to travellers. The TOMS also contains rules to allow this to take place. Essentially, VAT must be accounted for through the year, using a provisional calculation based on the previous year's performance. This is then corrected by an annual adjustment, which must be declared in the first VAT period after the end of the year.

The provisional calculation is basically a percentage which must be applied to income from packages, representing the VAT content of the margin. Thus, if the margin in the previous year was, say, 20 per cent of the gross income, VAT at 7/47ths of that sum would have been 2.98 per cent of the gross turnover. Therefore, in the current year, 2.98 per cent of income will be treated as output tax, pending a calculation of the true percentage after the end of the year. If this turns out to be 2.64 per cent, then a claim can be made on the first return of the following year equivalent to 0.32 per cent of turnover.

The TOMS also has unique tax points. Output tax must be accounted for in one of two ways; the tour operator can elect for one or the other. The tax point will either be receipt of cash (but only once at least 20 per cent of the price of the package has been paid for by the traveller; up to this point, no liability to output tax arises) or the date on which the traveller departs.

> ### *Planning point*
>
> The tax point based on receipt of monies has the advantage of being easier to integrate into an existing accounting system, whereas the tax point based on departure date maximises cash flow. Each tour operator will therefore need to make their own decision as to which is most beneficial to them in their particular circumstances.

> ### *Planning point*
>
> For the purposes of VAT registration, it is a tour operator's margin which is treated as taxable turnover, not the gross value of packages sold.

7.11.5 Sales to businesses

The TOMS is designed to cater for packaged travel facilities sold to travellers; and therefore it does not apply to sales to businesses for resale. Such sales should, therefore, be excluded from the TOMS. Until 31 December 2009, HMRC had allowed by concession, for them to be included within it. From 1 January 2010, it is necessary for these supplies to be accounted for under the 'normal' international services VAT accounting rules (see **Chapter 21**). Where supplies are made of travel services to other businesses that take place in other member states, the supplier will be regarded as making the supplies in these member states. This will require the supplier to register for VAT and account for VAT in these member states.

Sales to businesses for their own consumption (as opposed to onward supply) do fall within TOMS. HMRC had, until 31 December 2009, allowed businesses to opt out of applying TOMS, but this is no longer the case. Such supplies must now be included in TOMS accounting.

7.11.6 Intermediary services

Where a tour operator acts as a disclosed agent for another supplier they cannot use the TOMS accounting rules. From 1 January 2010, they must apply the new place of supply rules. This means that a supply to a VAT registered person will be liable to VAT where the customer is based. When the supply is made to a non-taxable person (a final consumer) the supply will be taxed where the underlying supply takes place (although this is less likely to occur than a supply to a VAT registered person for an intermediary service). This will cause very complicated VAT accounting issues and will probably mean that tour operators will have to register for VAT in several member states.

7.11.7 Conclusion

Planning point

This represents no more than a sketchy outline of the TOMS, provided in an attempt to demystify its operation. Those seeking to apply it to specific circumstances should take heed to *VAT Notice 700/5*, which sets out the rules in much greater detail. It is to be hoped that that publication will be the more comprehensible to readers with the benefit of the introduction to TOMS contained within these pages.

Other guidance: VAT Notice 709/5

Cashflow Planning

8.1   Introduction

There are a number of ways that cash flow can be improved, or maximised; it is better for the money to be in the businesses bank account rather than in somebody else's bank account. Not all of the ideas will work for everybody. The idea is to account for VAT as late as possible, delay when output tax is due and claim input tax as early as possible. Some of these ideas will relate to other chapters in the book and the details of the scheme are not repeated in this chapter; the objective of this chapter is to highlight ideas and if they are appropriate the various rules and regulations for applying it can be found in other chapters.

8.2   VAT returns

The easiest way to improve cash flow used to be to submit electronic returns and make electronic payments. This gave a seven day extension for the payment of VAT. The VAT return had to be submitted by the due date, but the payment could be sent seven days later. As all businesses, with a few exceptions, have to submit electronic returns everybody has this facility. Too many businesses, however, do not make use of this facility. All businesses should ensure that they do not pay the VAT that is due until the seventh day. Electronic banking systems enable the business to 'book' the payment on the appropriate day, so there is no reason not to delay the payment.

8.3   Monthly returns

Where a business is in regular receipt of repayments it can apply to use monthly VAT returns. This accelerates the repayment by HMRC of the input tax credits the business is entitled to.

8.4   Zero-rate subsidiaries

Where a business makes a number of zero-rated supplies it may wish to consider make these supplies through a subsidiary and separately registering the subsidiary. The subsidiary will be making zero-rated supplies and will be in receipt of repayments of VAT from HMRC. It will, therefore, be able to make monthly VAT returns, accelerating the repayment of VAT to the business.

HMRC may regard the creation of a subsidiary making only zero-rated supplies as artificial. HMRC has challenged arrangements that appear artificial, where the subsidiary is a shell and only has paperwork passing through it. For a zero-rated subsidiary to be successful it should undertake real transactions.

8.5 Grouping

Grouping may be an advantage as VAT does not need to be accounted for on inter company supplies. It always takes HMRC a few days to make a repayment, so not charging VAT to other group members and having to complete a VAT return may be an advantage.

8.6 Cash accounting and retailers

A significant advantage can be gained by either cash accounting or using a retail scheme if the business is eligible to do so (turnover less than £1,350,000 for cash accounting and being a retailer to use a retail scheme).

Where a business uses cash accounting input tax can only be claimed when business pays for his purchases. Conversely, output tax only needs to be accounted for when the customer pays the business. As payment is usually made after the invoice is issued and output tax exceeds input tax (usually), the effect of cash accounting is to delay the date when VAT has to be paid to HMRC. Also, output tax is only paid to HMRC when the VAT amount has actually been received from the customer.

Retail schemes have the advantage of only accounting for output tax when payment is reeved from a customer, but being able to claim input tax when the invoice is received. This gives a considerable cash flow advantage.

8.7 Annual accounting

Using annual accounting, if eligible (turnover below £1,350,000) gives a small cash advantage. Only one VAT return needs to be sent to HMRC in the year, but payments on account need to be made. Even if the payments on account accurately reflect the VAT due, there is a slight cash flow advantage in using the annual accounting scheme. In addition, it is likely that there will be a further advantage as the business may be growing and the amount payable on account will probably be less than the VAT amount due. The balancing payment is made at the year end.

8.8 Continuous services

A cash flow advantage can be gained by making a request for a payment to a customer rather than raising an invoice. When not using cash accounting the tax point, the date when VAT becomes payable, is when an invoice is issued. Where no invoice is issued the tax point arises when goods are delivered or made available or when a service is completed. Thus, for a continuous service the tax point never arises. Thus, by issuing a request for payment no liability to account for output tax arises until payment is received. The disadvantage of issuing a request for payment is that the customer will want to be issued a tax invoice when they have made a payment to enable them to reclaim an input tax credit.

8.9   Invoice dates

If invoices are issued just after the VAT period end the VAT due to be paid will be delayed by three months (if the taxpayer is using quarterly VAT returns). The disadvantage of issuing the invoice in the following VAT period/month, is that a customer may pay the invoice a month later if its policy is to pay invoices according to the month shown on the invoice. This can be ameliorated by agreeing the payment date with customers. In addition, the tax point rules need to be considered, the tax point is the invoice date only when the actual tax point (the date the goods are delivered or the service is completed) is within 14 days of the invoice date. If the invoice is issued later than this the VAT needs to be accounted for on the date the service is completed or the goods delivered. HMRC, however, will usually give permission for the tax point to be the invoice date rather than the date the goods are supplied or the service is completed if they are assured that the accounts system can only cope with accounting for VAT on the invoice date (which is usually the case) and that invoices are issued monthly.

8.10   Self-billing

A cash flow advantage is obtained if supplies are made that can utilise self-billing. Self-billing is usually used where the supplier does not know what he will be paid, such as in the construction industry or commission agents. The customer knows what is to be paid and will raise the suppliers invoice. If the arrangement complies with the self-billing regulations the supplier does not need to account for output tax until the self-billing invoice is received (and the payment from the customer usually also arrives with the self-billing document).

8.11   Bad debt relief

Bad debt relief gives not only a cash flow advantage, but a real cash saving. Where an invoice has been issued and VAT accounted for but the invoice has remained unpaid for six months after the due date, bad debt relief can be claimed. The VAT accounted for to HMRC can be claimed back by reducing output tax on the next return. Unfortunately many businesses do not make use of this opportunity. All that needs to be done is to review aged debtors each time a VAT return is to be submitted and reclaim the VAT on invoices that are six months past their due date for payment. Note, this is not an invoice that is six months old, but is six months past the due date for payment. Thus, if the customer is given 30 days to pay the invoice, the VAT bad debt relief can only be claimed once the invoice is seven months old.

8.12 Processing purchase invoices

Although input tax can be claimed as soon as a purchase invoice is received, invoices are often left in the office and not processed. Accounting systems cannot claim input tax unless the invoice is processed. To accelerate the input tax claim all invoices should be processed as soon as they arrive at the business. The invoice can then be checked and authorised for payment. Alternatively, if this is not possible all unprocessed invoices can be listed at the period end and the input tax claimed. It must, however, be remembered to reverse the claim in the next period otherwise there will be a double claim for input tax when the invoice is processed.

8.13 Import VAT deferral

VAT is normally payable immediately on import. This can be deferred so that the VAT is paid on the return when the input tax claim is made. This provides a real cash flow benefit. In addition, there is the benefit that where the VAT is deferred the goods move through Customs quicker as where there is no deferral the goods will not be cleared until the VAT (and any duty) due is paid. Furthermore, where VAT is due to be paid on import rather than being deferred the import agent will often pay the VAT du for the business. Whilst this helps facilitate the import there is obviously a cost to this as the agent will charge a fee.

It is necessary to apply to HMRC for deferral and a guarantee of twice the expected import VAT has to be provided. The VAT that can be deferred is 50% of that guarantee. There is a cost to the deferral guarantee (usually provided by the business's bank or an insurance company) and this cost has to be set against the cash flow saving and the easier administration of the import.

8.14 Deregistration

Clearly there us an advantage in deregistering from VAT if at all possible. No VAT needs to be accounted for, providing a real as well as a cash flow saving. The disadvantage of doing this is that there will be a VAT charge on the value of assets and goods on hand at the date of deregistration.

8.15 Non-VAT cash flow planning

A cash flow advantage can be obtained, and capital freed up, if assets are acquired through leasing or renting rather than being purchased. Also, assets can be sold and leased back so that further capital can be obtained; where the sale and lease back is to an associated entity there may be VAT avoidance issues that need to be considered and care is required. There are no avoidance issues where a commercial leasing or finance company is used. Obviously there is a cost to this and this is a business planning decision rather than a VAT issue.

244

Maximising Input Tax Credits

9.1 Introduction

A taxpayer's prime aim in respect of input tax is to be in a position to recover it from HMRC as soon as possible. A secondary aim is to improve the speed of recovery (claiming the input tax credit earlier). For a fully taxable business this is usually an administrative matter, making sure that proper evidence is held to support claims and ensuring the VAT has been properly charged. Where there are exempt or non-taxable activities it is also necessary to ensure it can be clearly demonstrated that the VAT incurred is properly referable to the business and not to exempt or non-business activity.

A partly exempt business will also wish to make sure that it has a suitable partial exemption method which is easy to operate and which does not attribute unreasonably high amounts to its exempt activities. (HMRC, of course, will be concerned to ensure that it does not attribute unreasonably high amounts of input tax to taxable supplies.)

9.2 Input tax

9.2.1 General

Planning for VAT on business expenses essentially means ensuring the recovery of the maximum amount of input tax incurred at the earliest possible time. This may entail simply ensuring that the correct evidence is held in order to claim a deduction, or structuring the activities so that more input tax is recoverable than it otherwise might be. Some VAT planning for business expenses will simply improve cash flow, whilst other planning options may well produce a real saving.

9.2.2 What is input tax?

To qualify as input tax, the VAT paid must have been incurred on a supply that was properly taxable at a positive rate and made by a VAT-registered business in the UK. Just because the supplier has shown what purports to be VAT on their invoice it does not mean that this can be claimed, e.g. if the supply should have properly been zero-rated or outside the scope of VAT. With regard to the latter, this is a common error with buying and selling a business as a going concern (see **13.3.1**).

> **⚠ Warning!**
>
> HMRC are strict in assessing input tax reclaimed where output VAT has been charged incorrectly, even where it is clear that the supplier will have accounted for the VAT charged as output tax.

> **Planning Point**
>
> The main points for planning for input tax are:
>
> - claim input tax as soon as an invoice is held even if it is not paid (unless the business is cash accounting when the invoice must be paid even before claiming an input tax credit), invoices should be posted as soon as they are received even before authorised for payment to maximise input tax credits;
> - accrue for invoices on hand that have not been processed in the accounts system – perhaps agree a figure for this with HMRC for the method of doing this;
> - ensure that systems are in place to prevent input tax credits being claimed when no VAT can be claimed, for example on zero-rated purchases, exempt purchases, non-business activities or blocked input tax such as motor cars or purchases for the purposes of business entertainment other than entertainment of overseas customers. This can be aided by hard coding VAT recovery rates in the computer system for certain suppliers or supplies and the use of exception reports;
> - introduce exception reporting to ensure that the VAT credits claimed align with expenditure;
> - ensure staff are trained (especially in the accounts payable section, and renew training regularly to ensure that new staff are trained and older staff are refreshed) and that a VAT manual is available detailing what VAT can be claimed and in what circumstances;
> - where the business cannot reclaim VAT, or its VAT claims are restricted, ensure that VAT is charged correctly on supplies received and that VAT is not charged at the standard-rate when it should be charged at the zero- or reduced-rate;
> - ensure VAT is claimed on expenditure even when no VAT invoice is held where this is permitted (such as coin operated machinery);
> - introduce systems to maximise VAT input tax on expenditure of items such as petty cash, expenses and mileage claims; and
> - ensure that proper tax invoices are obtained, do not pay invoices until a proper tax invoice is obtained, and train staff to recognise what is acceptable as a proper tax invoice.

The supply must also have been made to the business and that business must have used or be intending to use the purchase in the course of making taxable supplies, subject to the partial exemption provisions (see **Chapter 12**).

To determine whether VAT incurred is recoverable or not, the courts tend to examine whether the expenditure was a cost component of a taxable supply made by the business. If so, the VAT is recoverable. If not, the VAT is not input tax and may not be recovered.

In the case of *Metropole Treuhand WirtschaftssteruhandgmbH v Finanzlandesdirekion für Steiermark and Stadler v Finanzlandesdirekion für Vorarlburg* (Case C-409/99) [2004] BVC 424; [2002] ECR I-81, the European Court reviewed the right to recover input tax specifically in relation to the national laws of EU member states where they block the recovery of input tax. The court held that the restrictions on the right to recovery should be strictly interpreted in that:

> 'Article 17(2) of the Sixth VAT Directive sets out in express and specific terms the principle of the taxable person's right to deduct the amounts invoiced as VAT for goods supplied or services rendered to him, in so far as such goods or services are used for the purposes of his taxable transactions.'

Whilst this might be a basic issue and unremarkable in itself, if combined with the European principle of VAT being applied to an economic activity (art. 9(1) of Directive 2006/112) rather than the UK's terminology of a supply in the course or furtherance of a business (VATA 1994, s. 4(1)), it is perhaps somewhat more far-reaching.

Law: VATA 1994, ss. 24–26

Other guidance: VAT Notice 700, s. 10

9.2.3 Blocked input tax

Even when VAT has been charged on a supply, there are certain occasions when this VAT is statutorily blocked for recovery purposes. The most common examples of this are:

- the purchase of a car which is not used/to be used wholly for business purposes;
- purchases of goods within the margin scheme for second-hand goods – a VAT invoice will not be received for a supply purchased as a second-hand item, and recovery of input tax on an item to be sold under a margin scheme is blocked because it is only necessary to account for VAT on the profit made when the item is sold;
- purchases for the purposes of business entertainment, although the entertainment of overseas customers is not blocked;
- purchases of goods or services to be sold under the tour operators' margin scheme (TOMS) – as for second-hand items above, VAT is only required to be accounted for on the profit margin on goods or services sold under the scheme;
- purchases by builders of certain items to be installed in residential/charitable buildings; and

- costs relating to the provision of domestic accommodation for directors or persons connected to them, including costs of the accommodation itself, repair, refurbishment, furnishing, legal and estate agents' fees. From 1 January 2011, this legislation becomes redundant following the introduction by HMRC of the technical amendments following the adoption of the EU Technical Directive (Council Directive 2009/162/EU). The VAT will remain blocked (as will other private use input tax on property, land, boats and aircraft). More information is detailed at **Chapter 10**.

VAT incurred in relation to exempt or non-business activities is also restricted.

Other guidance: VAT Notice 700, para. 10.3

9.2.4 Evidence

Proper tax invoice

It is necessary to hold evidence of VAT paid prior to making a claim for its recovery, and this usually takes the form of a proper tax invoice. A proper tax invoice must contain the items of information set down in the VAT Regulations 1995 (SI 1995/2518), reg. 14(1).

Less detailed tax invoice

If a purchase is up to £250 in value, a less detailed tax invoice is satisfactory evidence for input tax recovery. Such an invoice still requires certain items of information and a simple shop receipt will not necessarily contain this, although many have been adapted to do so.

A less detailed tax invoice does not specify the value of VAT included in the supply. To calculate this it is necessary to apply the VAT fraction to the gross value of the supply. With VAT at 17.5 per cent, the VAT fraction is 7/47 (this is the simplest form of the fraction 17.5/117.5) so that where the gross value of an invoice is £100, there will be £14.89 VAT included in this if the supply is standard-rated ($100 \times 7/47 = 14.89$). For any rate of VAT, the VAT fraction is calculated using the formula: rate of tax/100+rate of tax; when the 20 per cent rate is introduced on 4 January 2011 the VAT fraction is 1/6th.

Law: VAT Regulations 1995 (SI 1995/2518), reg. 16(1)

No invoice required

Where the total cost of a supply, in respect of a single transaction, is no more than £25, input tax may be claimed, in the absence of a tax invoice for coin-operated purchases. Common examples include:

- telephone calls from public or private telephones;
- purchases made from coin-operated machines;

- car parking (except on-street meter parking, which is outside the scope of VAT); and
- a single or return road toll (other than the many which are outside the scope of VAT).

Other guidance: VAT Notice 700, para. 19.7.5

Imports

The prime document for recovery of VAT on an import from a country outside the EU is the Certificate of VAT Paid on Import, Form C79. This is automatically sent by HMRC to the person cited as the importer on the EU single administrative document (SAD) for the entry. It is not sufficient to simply claim the VAT shown as paid on the deferment account – another importer may have been permitted to use this.

Problems can arise if the entry document has not been correctly completed, especially in cases where the actual importer uses someone else's deferment account. Replacement or amended certificates can be obtained by application to HMRC at the port of entry of the goods, although this sometimes takes a considerable time.

For bulk entries where an agent uses a single SAD for a number of importers, a copy of the entry stamped by HMRC should be received, certifying the VAT paid on the import.

For postal entries, postponed accounting (accounting for the VAT payable on import on the VAT return) is used for entries under £2,000. For entries over this value a copy of the postal entry will be sent as evidence of input tax deduction.

9.2.5 When to claim input tax

Input tax should be claimed on the VAT return for the period in which the tax point for the supply falls except if the cash accounting scheme is used, in which case payment must be made prior to the input tax being claimed. However, a claim cannot be made until the correct evidence to support the claim is held (the tax invoice, import documentation or other acceptable documentation). Input tax on imported goods should be claimed in the period in which the goods are imported.

Planning point

If a claim for input tax is for some reason delayed (e.g. obtaining the tax invoice or processing it), then a claim may be made within three years of the period in which it should have been made. In such circumstances HMRC make a distinction between circumstances where a claim could have been made and was not, and those where no claim could have previously been made. In the former case, they regard the failure to claim as an error, making a voluntary disclosure necessary to correct it. In the latter case, the claim is proper to the period in which the evidence sufficient for the making of the claim was received, meaning that the VAT should be claimed directly on the relevant VAT return. See *VAT Notice 700/45*, s. 6.

Where an assessment of input tax is made on the basis that the correct evidence is not held, the input tax may be reclaimed once the appropriate evidence is obtained. As the assessment was correct at the time it was made there is no question of the assessment subsequently being reduced once the evidence is held. This may give rise to interest charges that could have been avoided if the correct evidence were held at the date of the claim. If the correct evidence was held at the time of the claim but has subsequently been lost then the assessment should be reduced or withdrawn once the appropriate evidence is again to hand.

9.2.6 The three-year cap (see Four-year cap at 9.2.6.1)

Claims for overpaid VAT are capped so that a claim cannot be made for a period more than three years beforehand under s. 80(4) of VATA 1994. The three-year cap was introduced on 18 July 1996 and was initially applied to any claim that had not been paid by Customs prior to that date. Parliament did not approve the measures until 4 December 1996 but the three-year cap was applied retrospectively. However, Customs erred in the introduction of the legislation and claims for under-claimed input tax were not effectively subject to the three-year cap until the VAT Regulations 1995 (SI 1995/2518), reg. 29(1A) was introduced with effect from 1 May 1997.

For overpaid output tax a claim must be made within three years of the date when the output tax was paid over to HMRC. For example, if the VAT return for the VAT period to 31 December 2005 contained output tax paid over in error, and this return was submitted and paid on 26 January 2006, then a claim for the overpaid output tax must be made by 26 January 2009.

For underclaimed input tax the claim must be made within three years of the date which the return containing the underclaimed input tax was required to be submitted. For example, if the VAT on an invoice should have been claimed in the period ending 31 December 2005, it may be claimed at any time to 31 January 2009, three years after the date by which the VAT return for the period to 31 December 2005 was required to be submitted, namely 31 January 2006. If the claim for underclaimed input tax is made by way of a voluntary disclosure (for example if it is over £2,000 and cannot therefore be entered on the VAT return) it should be made by 31 January 2009.

Correction of errors is also capped under the VAT Regulations 1995 (SI 1995/2518), reg. 29(1A), so that any error cannot be corrected more than three years after the end of the prescribed accounting period in which it was made.

The manner in which the three-year cap was introduced was such that its legality and precise effects in particular circumstances have been subject to virtually continuous litigation ever since. In particular, it was held in early 2008 in the joined cases, *Fleming (t/a Bodycraft) v R & C Commrs; Conde Nast Publications Ltd v R & C Commrs* [2008] BVC 221, that the three-year cap did not have retrospective effect at the time of its introduction. Consequently, overpayments of VAT arising prior to its implementation continue to be capable of correction by the taxpayer (HMRC are limited by their older powers, which always restricted them to six years). Having learnt from their mistakes in 1996, HMRC (Customs at the time of course) have responded to this decision by giving prior notice of their intention to change the law in this respect. Such claims will no longer be possible after 31 March 2009, after which date the three-year cap will operate as described above without qualification. It should be noted that this decision has no effect on overpayments of VAT occurring after 1 May 1997 (for output tax errors 4 December 1996), since these will have arisen after the effective date of the three-year capping legislation.

Law: VATA 1994, s. 80; VAT Regulations 1995 (SI 1995/2518), reg. 29, 43A–43H

9.2.6.1 Four-year cap

The three-year cap has been extended to four years, which was introduced from 1 April 2009, subject to transitional provisions which ensure that the amendments do not bring claims or assessments that would have been time-barred by 31 March 2009 back within the four-year time limit. The new four-year time limit for claims and assessments will therefore take effect gradually and will not be fully effective until 1 April 2010. In all other respects, similar provisions apply.

9.2.7 Estimating input tax

If it is not possible to determine the exact amount of input tax claimable on any return, the amount may be estimated (the same is true of output tax). This should enable a return to be rendered on time even if evidence of the amount of input tax claimable for any particular period is being awaited.

Planning point

Where the amount of input tax claimed on any return is estimated, prior written agreement of HMRC must be obtained. Errors in estimated amounts can attract penalties under the usual system for misdeclarations if not voluntarily disclosed.

Estimation has often been used by local authority bodies because of the delays inherent in their system for processing/approving invoices, although improvements in their accounting systems over recent years means that this is now less common.

9.2.8 Pre-registration expenses

VAT incurred on certain expenditure prior to the date of registration can be recovered. Although strictly this is not input tax, it may be treated as such by means of being claimed on the first VAT return after registration.

Claims should usually be made on the first VAT return, although they can be made in any period up to four years (three years before 1 April 2010) after the first return should have been made, for example if the evidence required is not immediately to hand.

Goods

To be eligible for claim, goods must have been purchased within four years prior to the date of registration (three years prior to 1 April 2010).

The goods must be on hand and not disposed of prior to the date of registration and the purchase must be used in the making of taxable supplies (that is standard-, reduced- or zero-rated income after the date of registration). For example, petrol (goods) or other consumables purchased a month before the date of registration are likely to have been used prior to the date of registration and so input tax will not be recoverable. Where goods have been consumed in the manufacture of other goods, which are themselves on hand at the date of registration, then the VAT involved may be recovered. The usual evidence of tax invoices is required to support the claim.

For stock, a stock list should be prepared of stock on hand on the date of registration, backed by the purchase invoices detailing the VAT incurred. It may, of course, be that a proportion of the stock on some invoices has been sold before registration and the claim should then be limited to that part which remains on hand.

Services

For services, the legislation allows recovery of any services incurred up to six months prior to the effective date of registration, provided that those services have not been totally absorbed into sales made prior to that date. In *Jerzynek* [2005] BVC 2,078, Customs sought to argue that rent paid on premises was totally absorbed into supplies made before registration, but the tribunal held that this was not the case and that rent (like, for example, telephone bills and accountancy fees), was more in the nature of a general overhead of the business and that the VAT was therefore eligible for recovery.

A list of services on which VAT is claimed prior to registration must be produced.

> ### Planning point
>
> The restriction on expenditure incurred prior to the date of registration is to take account of the consumable nature of services and, unless the VAT was clearly not incurred in the making of taxable supplies, there is no need to examine the claim further from this point of view.

> ### *Planning point*
>
> When looking at recovery of pre-registration expenditure it is important, because of the time limits, to ensure that the date of registration is the most beneficial for recovery of VAT. Although many businesses wait until a compulsory registration is necessary, it is possible to register on a voluntary basis providing that taxable supplies are being made or are intended. A registration date that maximises input tax recovery can therefore be arranged. If the registration is on a voluntary basis, once the date for registration is selected it cannot be backdated further. It is therefore important to get this right first time. In addition, where output tax values would be low but input tax values high, it is possible to back date the date of VAT registration by up to four years, giving a maximum claim period for goods of eight years. If the output tax which would be payable by backdating, exceeds the input tax to be claimed this is obviously not worthwhile.

> ### *Planning point*
>
> If taxable supplies have not yet commenced and the business is intending to trade, it may be possible to request an earlier date of VAT registration to capture input tax incurred more than three/four years or six months prior to the current date.

> ### ⚠ *Warning!*
>
> Where exempt input tax is incurred prior to the date of registration it is not recoverable in any circumstances, no matter how small the amount, because the *de minimis* limits do not apply to periods before the date of registration.

Law: VAT Regulations 1995 (SI 1995/2518), reg. 111

Other guidance: VAT Notice 700, s. 11

9.2.9 Pre-incorporation expenses

Where the new business is a limited company, a difficulty arises in that a tax invoice in the name of the company will not exist for pre-incorporation expenditure. In such cases, HMRC allow by concession that if the tax invoice is in the name of an officer of the company (a director or secretary), member or employee, then VAT incurred pre-incorporation may be claimed, providing that the officer was not himself a taxable person in his own right at the time the VAT was incurred, and the officer is reimbursed by the company for the expense.

It should be noted that although a claim for input tax on an invoice made out to an officer, member or employee of the company dated after incorporation may be allowed, in practice, the concession does strictly relate to pre-incorporation supplies and officers should ensure that suppliers are informed of the correct billing details as soon as possible.

9.2.10   Post-deregistration expenses

VAT incurred on services received after the date of deregistration can be recovered, provided that the services on which it is incurred are used in respect of the business carried on prior to the deregistration taking place. For example, VAT on an accountant's bill for preparing the accounts and tax computation for the final period of trading will be recoverable. Claims are made on form VAT 427 and must be submitted with the original invoices. HMRC request that claims are made within six months; however, a claim can be made provided it is not more than four years (three years before 1 April 2010) after the date of registration and there is a reasonable explanation for any delay. The form can also be used to claim input tax on goods and services supplied prior to deregistration which has not already been recovered on a VAT return, e.g. if the correct evidence was not held at the time the final return was submitted.

> ### ⚠ *Warning!*
>
> One issue that has thwarted many claims is that the partial exemption *de minimis* limits (see **12.11**) do not apply post deregistration. This means that if VAT is incurred on an exempt supply, such as legal fees on the sale of the business premises, it is not recoverable. If possible, these types of expenses, when below the *de minimis* limits, should be incurred prior to deregistration.

VAT incurred on goods purchased after the date of deregistration is not recoverable. Also, purchasing goods prior to the registration cancelled is unlikely to be beneficial as any goods on hand will be subject to a VAT charge on deregistration.

9.2.11 Abortive supplies

When VAT is incurred in relation to a supply which never takes place, for example if VAT is incurred in attempting to gain planning permission that is never gained, and therefore the development is never actually started, recovery of the VAT depends upon what the VAT liability of the ultimate supply intended would have been. For example, if the supply would have been taxable (either standard-rated, reduced-rated or zero-rated) the VAT is fully recoverable, whereas if the supply would have been exempt the VAT is exempt input tax and not recoverable, subject to the partial exemption *de minimis* limits.

In the European case of *Intercommunale voor Zeewaterontzilting (INZO) v Belgian State* (Case C-110/94) [1996] BVC 326, the company incurred considerable expenses on a profitability study in relation to a water purification project that never actually went ahead. The court decided that the company had satisfied the tax authorities that it intended to make taxable supplies. As such the profitability study was an economic activity and the VAT incurred was recoverable.

If it is not known what the VAT liability of the supply would have been, the input tax is treated as non-attributable input tax under the partial exemption rules (see **Chapter 12**). This means that if supplies made by the business are wholly taxable then the input tax on the abortive supply will be fully recoverable.

When VAT is incurred in relation to a supply which is intended to be taxable (standard-rated, reduced-rated or zero-rated) but the supply actually made is exempt from VAT then, subject to the partial exemption rules, the VAT reclaimed must be paid back to HMRC, but only if the supply is made within six years of recovering the input tax. See also **12.12**.

When VAT is incurred in relation to an intended exempt supply but the supply actually made is taxable, then the input tax previously not claimed may be recovered on the current VAT return, provided the supply is made within six years of incurring the input tax (subject to the written agreement of HMRC). See also **12.2**.

Where advance payment is made for a supply that is never made, for example where the supplier becomes insolvent before the supply can be made, then even if the correct documentation is held, there is no right to recover the input tax and this must be repaid to HMRC if a claim has already been made.

HMRC *Information Sheet* 8/01 details the treatment of VAT incurred on abortive or speculative development costs. This confirms the above analysis where the nature of the potential project is known and the liability of the supplies which would be made is clear. It also confirms that if the costs relate to a speculative project which is aborted in circumstances where the VAT liability of the eventual proposed supplies remains uncertain, the input tax is to be treated as residual for partial exemption purposes. If the project does eventually come into being, the treatment of the input tax must, of course, be reviewed and an adjustment made according to the treatment of the supplies made resulting from the project.

Where the supplies which would have taken place would have been taxable only on account of the exercise of the option to tax but the option has not yet been exercised, the input tax may be seen as attributable to a taxable supply provided that evidence is on hand to demonstrate that the option to tax would have been exercised, had the aborted transaction gone ahead (see HMRC *Business Brief* 14/04, following the tribunal decision in *Beaverbank Properties Ltd* [2003] BVC 4,108).

9.2.12   Incorrectly charged VAT

If a supplier incorrectly charges VAT, then the purchaser has no right of recovery of the VAT involved as input tax. Even though an amount shown as VAT on an invoice is recoverable by HMRC from the person who issued the invoice (any amount identified on an invoice as VAT being a debt to the Crown) it cannot be input tax for the purchaser (*Shire Equip Ltd* (1983) 2 BVC 208,018) since it is not actually VAT.

For example, if a supplier charges VAT on a supply of food that should be zero-rated, the purchaser cannot recover the VAT as input tax. The correct course of action is for the purchaser to go back to the supplier and obtain a refund and credit note for the incorrectly charged VAT.

Planning point

VAT being charged on supplies that do not bear VAT often arises with a transfer of a going concern (see **13.3.1**), or where a person who is not registered charges an amount that purports to be VAT. Although HMRC may, by concession, allow the purchaser to retain such VAT claimed as if it were input tax, it is far better not to have to rely on concessions and to ensure that VAT is only paid when it is properly chargeable. This is especially the case as HMRC are increasingly less willing to exercise discretion in this way. In addition, a warranty should always be included in the contract to allow a transferee to obtain any VAT overpaid from a transferee.

⚠ *Warning!*

Where VAT is charged at the standard rate on a supply to which the reduced rate is applicable, the difference between the amount chargeable at the reduced-rate and the amount actually charged is not recoverable as input tax. HMRC may, by concession, allow the amount to be claimed as input tax especially if they believe that the supplier has accounted for the output tax, but this concessional treatment cannot be relied on. HMRC do not exercise this discretion in respect of claims made under the DIY Builders & Converters Scheme, where they are very strict about only paying the correct amount of input tax refund.

Organisations which are unable to recover VAT, perhaps because they are involved in exempt or non-business activities, should make sure that VAT is not charged (or overcharged) to them in error. Many suppliers who are not sure of the correct VAT rate to administer will charge VAT at the standard rate, even if a lower or zero rate of VAT should apply. Typically, this can happen with printing costs (due to the complexity of the legislation) and fuel and power (e.g. with student accommodation where a claim for reduced rate has not been made). Therefore a review of VAT incurred on purchases can be well worthwhile for any exempt business or charity.

A particular problem area for overcharging VAT is the 5 per cent rate for conversions of non-residential properties into dwellings, the conversion of houses to flats, etc. and the renovation of dwellings which have been empty for two years or more. Builders appear to be very reluctant to charge at the 5 per cent rate unless it is pointed out to them, on many occasions asking for a certificate (although there is no provision for this unless the building becomes a relevant residential institutional building).

9.2.13   Third-party expenses

There are numerous occasions where a business will agree to pay the expenses incurred by a third party. A typical example of this is when a tenant agrees to pay the landlord's legal fees on renegotiating a lease (see **9.2.16**). Simply because the VAT has been paid by the tenant does not mean that this VAT may be recovered by the tenant as input tax. The supply was made by the solicitor to the landlord, not the tenant, and therefore it is not VAT incurred by the tenant in the course or furtherance of his business.

If the landlord is VAT registered and the rent is taxable at the standard rate, then the landlord may recover the VAT and payment by the tenant should be for the legal costs net of VAT, otherwise the costs must be met inclusive of VAT and no one is able to recover the VAT charged.

The House of Lords decision in *C & E Commrs v Redrow plc* [1999] BVC 96 determined that more than one party can be the recipient of a supply of services. In this case, Redrow not only paid the estate agent's fees for persons purchasing one of their new houses but were also involved in instructing the estate agent. They were, therefore, entitled to recover the VAT incurred on the estate agent's charges as they contracted for them. It is not enough to simply pay the bill; the person claiming the VAT must be able to show that the supply was made to him.

It should be noted that this decision has met with a setback in the joined cases heard in the European Court of Justice, *Loyalty Management UK Ltd* (Case C-53/09) and *Baxi Group Ltd* (Case C-55/09). This has held that the VAT on costs incurred on goods (and presumably services as well) that are passed to a third party cannot be reclaimed as a credit (see **27.1.2**).

9.2.14   Legal expenses of employees

Where an employer agrees to fund the legal expenses of defending an employee, the VAT incurred is generally seen as not recoverable because the employee is not a taxable person and the supply is made to them rather than the employer. In particular, HMRC (and the Tribunals and Courts) will not usually permit input tax claims in respect of legal fees defending directors from speeding offences or similar offences, even if the director's ability to drive is vital to the business. In contrast, in the case of *P & O European Ferries (Dover) Ltd* [1992] BVC 955, the tribunal found that the employers as well as the employees were clients of the solicitors and that the supplies were made to the former; the employer had a business interest in the outcome. In that case, therefore, the VAT was recoverable. This type of circumstance can, however, be regarded as exceptional and there is a requirement for the supply to be made to the business as well as the employee.

9.2.15 Legal expenses of insurance claims

From 1 January 1995, special rules were agreed with HMRC that where legal fees are incurred in the course of an insurance claim the supply can be seen as made to the policyholder, rather than the insurance company. Accordingly, the policyholder can recover the VAT on such fees, even when they are paid by the insurance company, provided the other conditions in respect of evidence for input tax recovery are met.

9.2.16 Landlord's legal expenses paid by tenant and bank's expenses paid by borrowers

It is common practice for the tenant to be required to pay the landlord's legal expenses when a lease is varied, etc. From 1 December 1992, HMRC's policy is that the payment by the tenant is seen as additional consideration for the rights granted in cases where the landlord's consent cannot reasonably be withheld. The landlord, therefore, may recover the VAT on such expenses, subject to the partial exemption rules. A tax invoice for the payment should be raised by the landlord, if the rent is taxable, so that the tenant is able to recover the VAT as input tax.

In cases where the landlord has absolute discretion as to whether to grant consent to the tenant, the payment of the landlord's costs is seen as consideration for a separate supply by the landlord, subject to VAT, unless the right granted constitutes in itself a supply which is exempt from VAT. If appropriate, the landlord should issue a VAT invoice to the tenant so that the tenant can support his claim for input tax.

Similarly, where a bank commissions a report into a borrower or potential borrower it will often require the borrower to pay the costs. This VAT is not recoverable as it is the expense of the bank and as the bank is making an exempt supply of finance it cannot reclaim the VAT charged. Thus, the borrower is liable to pay the gross amount of the cost and no input tax credit can be claimed.

9.2.17 Costs of company reorganisations

Care should be taken in the area of company reorganisations, because often the services carried out are contracted for by the shareholders rather than the VAT-registered business. In such cases the VAT is not recoverable as the supply is not made to the taxable person.

9.2.18 Shared expenses

Where two or more businesses share expenses, the best VAT structure for these expenses depends upon whether the expenses are subject to VAT and whether all of the businesses concerned are VAT registered.

If all of the businesses are VAT registered the VAT can be recovered by the party incurring the expense and the portion of the expense relevant to the other parties can be recharged plus VAT. This enables all parties to hold the correct evidence so that they are able to recover their own portion of the VAT incurred.

Where one or more of the businesses that are sharing expenses is not registered for VAT it is important that the purchase of an item which is subject to VAT, whether goods or services, is initially purchased by a VAT-registered business. This enables this business to hold the correct evidence to recover in full the input tax incurred. This VAT-registered business can then recharge the expense as appropriate and the other businesses can recover the VAT or not depending on whether they are registered for VAT. If an expense bearing VAT is incurred by a non-registered business the VAT incurred will be completely lost and irrecoverable, even when recharged, as the VAT cannot be charged on by a non-registered business.

Conversely, where an expense that is not subject to VAT is incurred it is often best for the non-registered business to incur the expense, which can then be recharged to the other businesses as appropriate, without the addition of VAT (subject to the VAT threshold). For example, if a VAT-registered business employs staff that are also utilised by a non-registered business, the recharge for the use of the staff will have to carry VAT at the standard rate (whereas the salary cost, etc. will have carried no VAT). This creates a VAT cost if recharged to a non-registered or partly exempt/exempt business. However, this situation does require care because the recharge of staff is a taxable supply and would count towards a non-registered business's VAT registration threshold. If this is the case then other planning to avoid registration would be required.

The 2012 budget has introduced an exemption for cost sharing to remove a barrier to organisations that are exempt or work in the non-business sector to enable them to share costs on projects. The exemption applies to charities, housing associations, educational bodies as well as commercial organisations such as banks and insurance companies. Where bodies that are partially exempt or undertake non-business activities co-operate and form a group to further their aims any supplies that had been made to the group used to be subject to VAT, but no VAT could be reclaimed because of their exempt or non-business status. The new measures will, from Royal Assent, remove the VAT charge from the supplies made, but only where the services are supplied by the group to group members at cost and only if the relief from VAT does not distort competition.

9.2.19   Reverse charges on international services

Where certain services are received from overseas businesses, a reverse charge becomes accountable. The VAT generated by the reverse charge is also input tax for the business and may be recovered subject to the partial exemption rules (see **Chapters 12** and **Chapter 21** for further details).

The value of these reverse chargeable services will count towards the registration threshold. Where such transactions are identified by a person who is partly or wholly exempt from VAT, they should try to identify if their affairs can be rearranged to avoid a reverse charge occurring. For example, a dividend could be paid to an overseas holding company or staff could be employed by the UK business. Such planning should also take account of other taxes.

9.2.20 Self-supplies

The legislation provides for self-supplies to be accounted for in specified circumstances as follows.

1. Where a car has been manufactured by a business and put to the taxable person's own use. This includes conversion of a vehicle to a car (such as a van to a caravanette, etc.).

2. Where a car on which input tax has been claimed is put to private or other non-business use. This includes the position where a car dealer appropriates a car from stock for use as a demonstration vehicle, etc.

3. Where zero-rating has been granted for the construction of a building for relevant residential or relevant charitable use and the building is put to non-qualifying use within ten years of construction.

4. Where construction services are supplied in-house to a value of over £100,000.

The self-supply will only create a cost if the business is partly or wholly exempt from VAT. In such cases – from a compliance aspect – it is important to identify the self-supply and account for it so that penalties and interest do not become chargeable. It may be possible to delay the change in circumstances that lead to a self-supply, for example on change of use of property, until the time limit had lapsed.

9.2.21 Gifts

Gifts are often given to staff or to good customers, a typical example being a bottle or hamper at Christmas. The VAT incurred on such items is a legitimate business expense providing that it is given for business reasons and can be recovered in full. However, the gift itself is a supply for VAT purposes and output tax is due, normally at the cost of the item in question, so that the output tax accountable corresponds to the input tax claimed. Where a gift (or series of gifts) is under £50 in value, net of VAT, then no output tax is required to be accounted for.

> ### Planning point
>
> For ease of administration, many businesses do not recover the input tax on gifts over £50 in value. This has the same effect as claiming the input tax and accounting for the output tax and is accepted by HMRC. If this method is used, the business should take care that the input tax on gifts under £50 is recovered.

In the case of *West Herts College* [2001] BVC 2,068, the taxpayer successfully argued that the prospectuses it gave away to prospective students, etc. were gifts. As such it was entitled to recover the VAT incurred on their production. If they had not been seen as gifts, the expense would have been seen as directly attributable to the exempt supplies of education made by the college and therefore non-recoverable. The above could apply to other businesses, such as the financial sector, where exempt activity is promoted by means of taxable printed matter given free of charge. This was, perhaps, an unusual decision and one that is unlikely to be followed by HMRC.

9.2.22 Private/non-business use

Where goods or services are used wholly for private purposes there is no right to deduct any of the VAT paid. However, some goods or services are purchased for business use and then turned over to private use at a later date, or they may be purchased partly for business and partly for private purposes.

This can lead to some complex VAT accounting and the *block* on the input tax that can or cannot be claimed has altered in recent years. This matter is discussed in more detail in **Chapter 10**.

9.2.23 Pension funds

The income of many pension schemes takes the form of dividends or exempt financial dealings. However, the input tax incurred by the company in relation to the day-to-day administration of the fund may be recovered by the company (not the pension fund itself) provided that the usual rules for evidence are adhered to. Input tax incurred in relation to the investment of the scheme's funds is seen as not incurred in the course or furtherance of the employer's business and therefore is not recoverable by the company and these costs usually relate to the exempt activities of the pension fund and cannot be recovered by the fund. Where, however, the expenses relate to taxable activities (or activities that are input taxed with credit – such as overseas investments) the VAT can be reclaimed as input tax. An example of this would be property that is subject to the option to tax.

Recoverable items include, for example, drawing up and revision of rules of the scheme and administration of the payment of pensions.

If a pension fund manager is used, separate invoices for the administration and investment services provided should be requested. Alternatively, it may be possible to negotiate recovery of a proportion of the VAT on the whole invoice with HMRC. Historically, this has often been done on a 70/30 basis, with 30 per cent of the invoice value being attributed to administration. In *Business Brief* 15/05 (9 August 2005), HMRC state that this may no longer accurately reflect the split in many cases and that they will, in future, expect to see some form of justification for any apportionment used.

In any case, the invoice must be made out to the employer rather than the fund itself.

9.2.24 Structuring

It is sometimes possible to structure a business in such a way that more input tax than otherwise may be recoverable can be claimed. A classic example of this is a private school which runs a minibus for transporting students. Input tax related to this activity is generally not recoverable because the school is probably not registered for VAT and even if it is, the VAT incurred will be seen to be attributable to exempt educational activities unless a separate charge is made for use of the minibus.

By running the minibus through a separate company which also employs the driver (possibly under a joint contract of employment), the company is able to supply zero-rated transport services to the school. The minibus must seat at least ten passengers (including the driver). This enables the company to register for VAT and to recover input VAT incurred on purchase, maintenance and fuel expenses.

This would probably not be a viable proposition if the company was not already in existence, and if it is set up solely for the purpose of undertaking this activity, HMRC may argue that it is not a business activity on *Halifax* principles.

Another example of structuring being used for VAT planning is where a charity supplies welfare services below cost as a non-business supply. There are instances where a trading company, which is not a non-profit making entity, with profits being covenanted to the charity could provide the service. The supplies made would thus fall to be treated as taxable, therefore allowing recovery of input tax. This can be a particularly useful arrangement where the supplies are funded by the local authority which can recover the VAT charged.

A further possible example is to use a separate company that owns a boat or aircraft that leases this to the main business, directors, employees and third parties. For this type of arrangement to be viable it will need to be organised on commercial lines.

Planning point

Having a separate trading company can be useful for any exempt or partly exempt business, particularly for purchasing high-value assets and leasing on to the main business. This enables VAT on the capital cost to be recovered, although the VAT on the onward leasing charge is restricted.

⚠ Warning!

Use of an associated entity to purchase assets for leasing in such circumstances can now give rise to a requirement to disclose the arrangements as a VAT avoidance scheme. This does not render the scheme illegal, but there are penalties for failure to disclose a notifiable scheme (see **Chapter 32**). Furthermore, HMRC may wish to examine the arrangements carefully to ensure that a market charge is made, that the assets are being exploited on a commercial basis, and that the operation is, in fact, a business enterprise.

9.2.25 Share issues and raising finance

A business that wished to raise finance through a bank loan is usually able to reclaim all the VAT that it incurs. The expenditure is seen as relating to the economic activity (or the business) of the business. The one exception to this is where a bank undertakes due diligence and commissions reports or incurs other costs. The bank is unable to reclaim the VAT incurred on these costs as the bank is making an exempt supply of finance (the loan to the business). Banks will frequently require the business seeking the loan to pay the bank's costs. This does not mean that the business can claim the VAT incurred; although the business has paid for the costs incurred, the supply has been made to the bank and not the business. The only entity that can reclaim the VAT is the bank, and it is prevented from doing so as it has made an exempt supply.

Planning point

VAT incurred on supplies made to an entity raising bank finance is deductible.

⚠ **Warning!**

VAT on supplies made to a business can be reclaimed. Paying the costs of a third party does not give an entitlement to reclaim the VAT on that cost.

Finance can also be raised through an issue of shares. HMRC has, for many years, prevented businesses from reclaiming input tax credits on costs associated with the issue of shares; this has ultimately proved to be an incorrect position. This was a significant disadvantage to companies that wished to raise finance through the issue of shares, rather than using a bank facility as there was an additional burden of irrecoverable VAT on the costs incurred.

The position changed following the decision in *Kretztechnik AG v Finanzamt Linz* (Case C-465/03) [2006] BVC 66. The company, *Kretztechnik* , made an issue of shares. It reclaimed the VAT incurred but the Australian tax authority rejected the claim in the belief that *Kretztechnik* had made an exempt supply (the issue of shares). *Kretztechnik* appealed (ultimately to the European Court of Justice) on the basis that the issue of shares was not a taxable supply. The VAT incurred, therefore, should be treated as part of the general overheads of the business. The ECJ agreed with this view.

Any VAT incurred can be reclaimed in line with the share issuing company's partial exemption scheme; the costs were overhead or residual expenses. Thus, a fully taxable company can reclaim all the VAT incurred despite issuing shares.

Planning point

VAT incurred on supplies made to an entity issuing shares is deductible as an overhead expense. This applies whether the shares are issued solely to raise finance, to place the company on a stock exchange or for any other purpose.

⚠ **Warning!**

The sale, supply or trading in existing shares (as opposed to issuing new shares) is an exempt supply and any VAT incurred that relates to this activity is not deductible unless a relief is available (such as selling the shares to an overseas customer).

A further complication arises on acquisition costs. Are the costs of acquiring another company deductible? This matter has recently been examined in the Upper Tribunal decision of *R & C Commrs v BAA* [2011] BVC 1,664 (and the cross appeal of *BAA v R&C Commrs* [2011] UKUT 258 (TCC)). An attempt was made by the company that acquired the British Airports Authority (BAA) to reclaim the VAT it had incurred on its acquisition costs. Although BAA was unsuccessful in their appeal to the Upper Tribunal it has raised the question as to whether the VAT incurred was deductible input tax.

The acquiring entities created a new company, Airport Development and Investment Limited (ADIL), to acquire BAA. Subsequent to acquiring BAA, ADIL joined the BAA VAT group and changed its name to BAA Limited. The new company provided management services to the group, but it did not charge a fee. The First-Tier Tribunal decided that the acquisition costs (investment bank costs, legal fees and professional advisers) were mainly concerned with the takeover. Acquiring the BAA shares was not 'an end in itself'. It was to enable ADIL to acquire the airports. There was sufficient nexus between the acquisition costs and the supplies that would be made by the BAA group after the acquisition to permit the input tax to be deducted. As the supplies made by BAA were taxable, the VAT incurred was deductible.

The taxpayer raised this argument again in its appeal to the Upper Tribunal and further argued that it had incurred the VAT as preparatory costs to make taxable supplies of management services (or the supplies it would be treated as making after it joined the VAT group). HMRC countered that ADIL was a passive holding company as it had not made any charges for its supplies. All it had done was incur the costs to enable it to acquire the BAA shares. ADIL had not undertaken any economic activity nor had there been any intention to make taxable supplies. Furthermore, there was no link between the pre-acquisition costs and any taxable supply as no management charges had been made.

In what may have been a surprise finding (certainly to HMRC), the Upper Tribunal confirmed the First-Tier Tribunal's finding that ADIL had an economic activity as the purpose of acquiring shares was the first step of an investment in the airports and it involved the management of the group. At first glance, this would appear to give BAA (as ADIL had now become) cause to reclaim the VAT incurred. Unfortunately, for BAA, the Upper Tribunal also held that there was no 'direct and immediate link' between the costs incurred and any taxable supplies made by ADIL, neither before it joined the VAT group nor any supplies made subsequent to grouping. It had been fatal to ADIL/BAA's arguments that they had not made any taxable supplies either when it incurred the VAT or after the takeover had been completed. It was apparent that ADIL had only formed an intention to make taxable supplies subsequent to the acquisition; thus, the costs could not be seen as relating to any taxable supplies that were to be made as there was no such intention at the time the costs were incurred.

The Upper Tribunal also found that the input tax could not be reclaimed as a consequence of grouping. The acquisition costs were not a component of any taxable supplies that would have been made subsequent to grouping.

Planning point

A business that acquires another business may (see Warning! below) be able to reclaim the VAT incurred on acquisition costs where it can clearly demonstrate that there is an intention to make and charge for taxable supplies of management services to the target entity subsequent to the acquisition. This intention should be documented. In addition, the position will be improved if the acquiring entity makes taxable supplies in addition to these management services to the acquired entity. The costs incurred may be regarded as part of the general overheads of a management company and deductible in line with its partial exemption position.

⚠ Warning!

The Upper Tribunal made its decision based upon the facts as determined by the Lower-Tier Tribunal. Where the facts differ, the VAT position may also differ. Furthermore, HMRC may not accept these conclusions and could seek to challenge any such input tax recovery and seek to establish different facts, particularly in respect to economic activity being established by the acquiring entity.

9.3   Employee expenses

9.3.1   Introduction

Where an employee is acting on behalf of an employer in ordering goods for resale or services for the purposes of the business, it is easy enough to ensure that the correct documentation is provided for input tax evidence. However, with employee expenses such as hotel accommodation and subsistence expenses, the supply is often made to the employee and it is only as a concession that the employer is allowed to recover the VAT incurred as input tax and then providing that the actual costs only are reimbursed by the employer.

> ### Planning point
>
> VAT is not recoverable where round sum allowances are given.

9.3.2 Staff entertainment

Between 1993 and 1997 Customs operated a policy that 50 per cent of the VAT incurred on staff entertainment was disallowable on grounds that it was not business use. However, since the decision in *Ernst & Young* [1997] BVC 2,541, HMRC have accepted that the provision of entertainment to staff as a reward for good performance and to maintain staff morale, etc. is a legitimate business expense and the VAT is fully recoverable.

> ### ⚠ Warning!
>
> It should be remembered that prospective employees, shareholders, former employees or pensioners, self-employed subcontractors, relatives or partners or friends of employees, are not employees and free provision of hospitality to them will be treated as business entertainment. If third parties do attend the event then an apportionment, usually on a per capita basis, will be necessary (e.g. if 50 out of 100 attendees are employees, then 50 per cent of the VAT is recoverable).

The entertainment must be open to all employees to attend and not just a perk for say directors of the company. If the entertainment is provided for, say, directors of limited companies or sole proprietors or partners, then HMRC do not accept that the VAT is incurred for a business purpose. They consider the VAT to be a personal expense, as the question of motivation or reward should not be an issue with such persons.

> ### Planning point
>
> There is, however, no requirement for apportionment when directors, partners, etc. attend staff functions.

9.3.3 Relocation expenses

Where a round sum or fixed sum allowance is given there is no right for the business to recover input tax.

Where the business agrees to pay an employee's expenses on relocation, the VAT incurred may be recovered. This includes solicitors', estate agents' and surveyors' fees, removal and storage costs of furniture and other effects, and services such as plumbing-in washing machines, fixing TV aerials and even altering curtains.

If the business pays only a proportion of the costs involved then only a similar proportion of the VAT may be recovered.

At present, HMRC allows recovery of the VAT when the tax invoice is made out to the employee rather than the business. HMRC consider removal expenses for directors, partners and sole proprietors as primarily a personal expense rather than business and will look for the business reason behind the move before allowing the recovery of input tax.

> ### Planning point
>
> Clearly, a move of home to a flat above the business premises for security reasons would be eligible for VAT recovery, whereas a move simply to a larger house would not be allowed, although in such a case a proportion may be claimed if the additional space is to be used for business purposes.

9.3.4   Hotel accommodation

If an employee is required to go away from the usual place of business and stay overnight in hotel accommodation and the cost is borne by the business, then the VAT incurred is recoverable. It is also possible that occasions may arise where an employee is put up in hotel accommodation close to the place of business, for example because of a rail strike or an early meeting at the business premises. Providing that the cost is met by the business, VAT incurred on this expenditure may be recovered.

When an employee is paid a fixed allowance for overnight stays, then no VAT is recoverable. This is because the supply of accommodation is not to the business – the business having paid the fixed allowance and put control as to how the money is spent into the hands of the employee – and the employee may choose to stay at a place which is not VAT registered.

HMRC take a stricter view on hotel accommodation expenditure incurred by sole proprietors and partners. Whereas in the case of employees the fact of the business paying the cost will be sufficient evidence of business use, a sole proprietor or partner must be sure to provide evidence of the business use of the expense. Accommodation whilst away from home on business or in the case of a rail strike for example, would be recoverable expenditure.

Every effort should be made for the invoices to be made out in the name of the business. If the invoice is made out in the name of the employee, HMRC may not permit input tax recovery, although most officers will exercise their discretion to permit such a claim when the invoice is in the employees name.

9.3.5   Residential accommodation

Where accommodation in the home is used for business purposes, VAT may be recovered on the expenditure incurred for business purposes or a proportion of general expenditure incurred in relation to the accommodation.

For example, if an employee is supplied with accommodation, say in a flat above the business premises so that the employee is on hand and the security of the business is improved, VAT incurred in maintaining the premises will be recoverable. If a rent is charged, the input tax incurred will be exempt input tax and the partial exemption rules must be observed.

VAT incurred on the provision of domestic accommodation for directors or their families and close relatives has been specifically blocked from recovery from 26 July 1990 and will now be blocked by the new legislation from 1 January 2011 (see above). This applies even if the family member or relative is an employee of the company.

> ### *Planning point*
>
> However, this does not prevent the recovery of VAT in respect of residential premises which are used for business purposes. For example, a director of a limited company may work from home and have a room specifically set aside as an office. VAT incurred in respect of this room would be recoverable, provided it is invoiced to the company. However, if there is any private use of the room, apportionment would be necessary.

The restriction on input tax recovery applies to the director's main residence, second home, weekend retreat or to a flat available for business meetings, but not to hotel accommodation. In addition to a director, the restriction applies to any accommodation and associated expenses in relation to any person connected to the director such as family members.

VAT incurred on relocation expenses for directors is not covered by the blocking order and the rules at **9.3.3** may be applied.

9.3.6 Farmhouses

As farmers need to be available to the business at all times and the farmhouse itself is often used for business purposes such as lambing, preparing poultry for market, or storage of drugs and chemicals, HMRC accept that input tax incurred on a farmhouse is partly for business purposes. Apportionment will need to be made to take account of the domestic use of the premises and this will vary in each case.

Where the farm is a full-time activity, and the input VAT is incurred on general repairs and maintenance, HMRC have agreed with the National Farmers' Union that up to 70 per cent of the input tax may be recovered.

Where farming is only a part-time activity the business use may be more difficult to justify and HMRC tend to restrict claims to less than 40 per cent of the VAT incurred.

Where the work is an improvement, alteration or extension, the business use of the VAT incurred must be judged on the individual circumstances. For example, an extension to form a farm office where none existed before would be 100 per cent recoverable, whereas an extension to form a bedroom would probably attract no recovery at all.

There is no set method of apportionment to be used in determining the extent of recovery. Floor area is a method that has been popular in the past, but more recently tribunals have tended to look for a more subjective test, examining the dominant purpose for having the work done.

⚠ *Warning!*

If the farmhouse is occupied by directors of a farming limited company then the legislation does not prevent a proportion of the VAT being recovered where the farmhouse is used for business purposes, but the guideline proportions above do not apply. It is necessary to discriminate between the use of the farmhouse for accommodating directors and its use for the purpose of the business and to claim VAT on the proportion deemed to represent the latter.

9.3.7 Subsistence

VAT incurred on employee meal expenses can be reclaimed (subject to the normal rules regarding invoices, etc.). VAT can only be reclaimed where it is necessary for subsistence and is some distance from the normal working place of the individual. HMRC quote in their internal guidance at V1-13 Chapter 2A, section 18.2 subsistence, that:

> 'The Tribunal case of *DG Mutch* (2,559) is a useful precedent. It concerned a sole proprietor who was disallowed the VAT incurred on meals taken within two or three miles from his office. The Tribunal applied a test from *Strong and Co of Romsey Ltd v Woodfield* in which Lord Davey referring to the words "for the purpose of trade" said:
>
> > "These words are used in other rules, and appear to me to mean for the purpose of enabling a person to carry on and earn profits in the trade. It is not enough that the (expenditure) is made in the course of, or arises out of, or is connected with the trade, or is made out of the profits of the trade. It must be made for the purpose of earning the profits."
>
> The Tribunal stated that the onus is upon the taxpayer to show that the expenditure for personal meals was for the purpose of the business and not for the "natural daily requirements for nourishment".'

HMRC will not, therefore, allow meal expenses for a sole proprietor, partner and a director to be reclaimed unless it is away from their place of work on a business trip. HMRC officers often use, as an unofficial guide, a five-mile radius from the office.

9.3.8 Staff canteens

VAT is due at the standard rate on any takings from a staff canteen or vending machine provided for staff, and VAT on expenditure incurred in relation to the provision of these facilities is therefore recoverable as input tax.

If an external caterer operates a canteen service for a business, the position will be determined by the terms of the contract. If the caterer is acting as agent and supplying the catering in return for a fee chargeable to the business (rather than to employees) then the input tax on expenditure will normally be recovered by the business, and the caterer must arrange for bills to be made out in the business's name.

9.3.9 Staff rewards/perks

Perks such as membership of a club, a holiday or other reward gifts given to employees are a legitimate business expense and the input tax incurred on them is recoverable. However, if a free supply of goods or services has been made to the employee and if this is over £50 in value the output tax must be accounted for on the supply as appropriate.

9.3.10 Home telephone, etc.

VAT may be recovered on home telephone bills to the extent that the service is used for business purposes. A sustainable basis should be used for the percentage of VAT to be claimed, perhaps based on a sampling of a representative period, which may need to be justified to HMRC on a VAT visit.

HMRC issued a *Business Brief* (14/99, 2 July 1999) regarding mobile telephones, which includes the following points.

(a)   The VAT incurred on the cost of providing and connecting a mobile telephone for business use and any standing or rental charge is fully deductible (but see (b) below).

(b)   Where the rental charges allows for a certain amount of 'free' calls the VAT on the total package must be apportioned for business and private use.

(c)   Where a business does not allow employees to make private calls, all of the VAT incurred on the call charges is input tax and is recoverable. HMRC and Excise accept that in practice a small amount of private calls may be made and this will not prevent all the input tax from being reclaimed.

(d)   If a business charges its employees for any private calls they make, then it may treat the VAT incurred on the calls as input tax, but must account for output tax on the amounts it charges.

(e)   Where employees make private calls without a charge from the employer, then the input tax incurred must be apportioned. Any apportionment method may be chosen that produces a fair and reasonable result.

HMRC have, in the past, undertaken surveys of the costs of phone and text messages and raised substantial assessments for private calls and text messages made out of hours.

9.3.11   Clothing

VAT incurred on clothing is not generally considered to be a business expense and is not therefore recoverable, even if it is necessary for a high standard of dress to be maintained or to present a certain image depending on the business activity. However, VAT incurred on uniforms and protective clothing to be worn by a taxable person or their employees in carrying on the business is a recoverable expense. Uniforms to be worn by car salespersons would, for example, include blazers with a company logo embroidered on them.

There are specific cases where HMRC consider VAT on clothing to be recoverable in the following instances.

1. Wigs and gowns required to be worn by barristers in court. It is also necessary for specific trousers, waistcoat, etc. to be worn, and provided that these items of clothing would not have been purchased if they were not required to attend court, then VAT incurred on them may also be recovered. VAT incurred on a dark suit or dress would not be input tax as such items can be used privately and are required for mere modesty if nothing else.

2. Clothing purchased by entertainers or television personalities for use solely as stage costumes.

9.3.12   Recruitment costs

Costs incurred on recruitment of staff are generally recoverable. However, any hospitality (free food, drinks or hotel accommodation, etc.) provided to prospective employees must be treated as business entertainment, because the candidate is not yet a member of staff. This would apply to functions held to attract potential staff to a career.

9.4   Business entertainment

9.4.1   What is entertainment?

VAT incurred for the purposes of business entertainment is specifically blocked from recovery under the VAT (Input Tax) Order 1992 (SI 1992/3222), art. 5. Case law defines business entertainment as: the free provision of hospitality to persons who are not employees of the business, employees including directors of limited companies.

An input tax block on the entertainment of overseas customers has been found to be 'ultra vires'. thus, the input tax incurred on the entertainment of overseas customers (that is customers where there is the potential chance of an export, not a customer that happens to be resident overseas) is deductible. Where a business has not claimed this input tax this can now be claimed subject to the four year cap provisions, see **9.4.4** below.

To be non-recoverable expenditure the hospitality must be free of charge or obligation. In the case of *C & E Commrs v Kilroy Television Co Ltd* [1997] BVC 422, the participants in the talk show were provided with a buffet meal. The court found that the company had put itself in a contractual position to provide the buffet, which was the only payment the participants received for taking part in the show. Therefore, there was no business entertainment provided. In a similar case, a market research company provided sandwiches at product trials where the public were invited to sample alcoholic beverages and complete questionnaires on them. HMRC accepted that the alcoholic beverages were not business entertainment but assessed the VAT recovered on the provision of food. The tribunal found that the food was a necessary part of supplying the drinks and was not business entertainment (*DPA (Market Research) Ltd* [1997] BVC 4,071).

The ECJ judgment in the *Danfoss/Astra Zeneca* case has confirmed that working lunches provided to directors in the course of a business meeting (provided no other employees are present) may have a business purpose and therefore costs involved in providing such meals are deductible for VAT purposes. Current UK VAT legislation restricts the recovery of VAT on business entertainment, including in-house lunches that are provided free of charge to clients during business meetings. Under the *Danfoss/Astra Zeneca* cases there may be entitlement to recover VAT paid on the provision of working lunches.

9.4.2 Events

If an event is held by a business, the main purpose of which is entertainment of customers/potential customers or other third parties, then the attendance of employees as hosts at the event does not allow a proportion of the VAT to be recovered.

It can make sense to charge a nominal fee when holding events that would otherwise fall into the business entertainment category. The fee must at least equal the cost of the business entertainment provided. If HMRC can show that the fee is below cost they may seek to assess VAT on business entertainment grounds on the difference between the fee charged and the value of hospitality provided.

If a potential customer is entertained by an employee whilst they are away on a business trip, then provided that the sole reason for the trip is not business entertainment, the

VAT on the employee's meal can be recovered under the subsistence rules above. That proportion of VAT referable to the potential customer's meal is, however, business entertaining and is not recoverable.

9.4.3   Purchase of goods or services for business entertainment

The business entertainment blocking provisions apply to the purchase of goods as well as entertainment supplied at events. Where an asset is purchased for both business purposes and entertainment purposes, an apportionment of the input tax should be made. This treatment is derived from the decision in *Thorn EMI plc*, where the taxpayer had hospitality chalets at an air show. As well as entertainment, the chalets provided a place to hold confidential discussions regarding the company's electronic systems which it displayed and sold at the air show (*Thorn EMI plc v C & E Commrs* [1995] BVC 282).

9.4.4   Overseas customers

Input tax credits are available on costs associated with the business entertainment of overseas customers. HMRC has accepted that their 'input tax block' introduced in 1988 was contrary to EU legislation. Thus, there is the opportunity to make backdated reclaims for any input tax incurred in the past (subject to the capping rules) on the entertainment of overseas customers. Note, VAT incurred on the entertainment of UK customers is not deductible.

> **Planning point**
>
> Examine past expenses for input tax incurred on the entertainment of overseas customers to determine if any VAT can be reclaimed.

9.4.5   Trade fairs/exhibitions

Where non-employees are brought in to assist with the running of events at an exhibition, show or sporting event, then VAT on their subsistence expenses is also recoverable.

However, VAT incurred on free hospitality given to visitors, journalists or other persons not involved in running the event is subject to restriction under the basic business entertainment rules.

9.4.6 Consultants and other third parties

VAT incurred on expenses paid for self-employed consultants or other third parties is not recoverable where the supply is to the consultant rather than the VAT-registered business. Where free hospitality is provided to consultants, etc., this must be treated as business entertainment. This includes hotel accommodation, food and drinks, for example where self-employed sales consultants attend a seminar/conference hosted by the VAT-registered business (*C & E Commrs v Shaklee International* (1981) 1 BVC 444).

9.5 Conferences and seminars

9.5.1 Attending a conference/seminar

VAT incurred on the costs of attending a conference or seminar is fully recoverable provided that the content of the conference/seminar is for the purposes of the business. This includes the attendance fee, accommodation costs and subsistence meals. If any entertaining is carried out, this is not a recoverable expense. For example, if a director or sole proprietor attends a conference on business management and buys dinner for a prospective or existing client, the proportion of the bill in respect of the guest is not recoverable but the proportion of the bill in respect of the director/sole proprietor is recoverable as subsistence.

9.5.2 Arranging a conference/seminar

Conferences or seminars are often held as a promotional or marketing exercise. The VAT incurred on the cost of hiring the premises, equipment for use in the seminar and on guest-speaker fees, is recoverable. However, any provision of free food or drinks to guests is considered to be business entertaining and the VAT incurred is not recoverable. Also, when staff attend such an event for the sole purpose of entertaining the guests, all of the VAT incurred on food/drinks is considered to be business entertaining and non-recoverable.

Planning point

If a charge is made for attendance at a seminar and the invitation, ticket or invoice makes it clear that the payment covers the cost of food and refreshments provided, then the hospitality is no longer free and the VAT incurred may be recovered. Where staff attend the event to be entertained (as opposed to acting as hosts) the VAT on their proportion of the cost is recoverable.

9.6 Viability studies

9.6.1 What are viability studies?

Viability studies are usually required by a bank, in circumstances where either the business requires a loan or where the business is in financial difficulties and the bank needs to know if the business can be assisted to regain financial viability. The work itself is usually carried out by accountants or management consultants and paid for by the business concerned. However, the recovery of VAT incurred on the fees for this work depends upon to whom the supply is actually made.

9.6.2 Work commissioned by business

Where the work is commissioned by the business, which receives the report, the supply is to the business and it may recover the VAT incurred on fees. This is so even if the sole reason for commissioning the report is to make it available to the bank, or even if the accountant/consultant carrying out the work has a separate duty of care to the bank involved. If the work is commissioned by the business but the business does not receive the report, HMRC argue that the supply is not used for the purposes of the business and the VAT is therefore not recoverable.

> **Planning point**
>
> In order to avoid these circumstances arising, the business should always receive a copy of the report even if it is made available to a bank or other third party as well.

9.6.3 Work commissioned by bank/other third party

Where the bank commissions the work and receives the report, the supply is to the bank and the business cannot recover the VAT incurred on the fees even if it pays for the work done. In some cases, the accountant/consultant may receive instructions from both the bank and the business either separately or jointly. In such instances, separate invoices should be raised and the bank and business can recover VAT on their respective invoices. See HMRC *Business Brief 6/95*.

9.7 Promotion and sponsorship

9.7.1 Sponsorship versus donation

The term sponsorship must be differentiated from a donation. In the latter case the funds or gift is given free of obligation and is outside the scope of VAT, but in the former case sponsorship indicates that the donor expects to receive something in return for the funds or gift, usually in the form of advertising or some other benefit, and the sponsorship is therefore seen as a payment for a supply of services which are usually standard-rated (*C & E Commrs v Tron Theatre Ltd* [1994] BVC 14).

A VAT invoice should be obtained from the recipient if they are registered for VAT so that this can be recovered as input tax. Where the recipient is not VAT registered, sponsorship will count towards their turnover threshold for registration purposes. For example, a sportsperson given £75,000 in sponsorship by a sports clothing manufacturer will immediately become registrable for VAT.

HMRC have agreed that the following instances will not turn a donation into a taxable supply for VAT purposes:

- a flag or sticker received in return for a donation;
- being included on a list of supporters in a programme or notice;
- naming a building or university chair after a donor; and
- putting the donor's name on the back of a seat in a theatre.

Planning point

If a donation is given in addition to the sponsorship, this may be treated as outside the scope of VAT, provided it is clear that the donation is freely given and no additional benefit is received in return.

9.7.2 Sponsorship by a gift of money

Sponsorship by a gift of money in return for benefits such as advertising is payment for a standard-rated supply of services by the recipient. A VAT invoice should be obtained so that input tax may be recovered.

9.7.3 Sponsorship by a gift of goods

A gift of goods by way of sponsorship involves two supplies, one of the goods themselves and, in return, the advertising or other benefit. VAT must be applied to each of these supplies as appropriate. The advertising will be standard-rated and it is likely that the goods will also be standard-rated. The supplier of the goods must raise a tax invoice to the recipient and account for output tax on the value of the goods supplied and should obtain a tax invoice from the recipient for the services supplied, usually in the same amount.

9.7.4   Sponsorship by a gift of services

A free gift of services is not a supply for VAT purposes but, where a benefit is received in return, such as advertising, then this is seen as payment for the services. VAT must be accounted for as appropriate on these services and a VAT invoice should be obtained from the recipient so that input tax may be claimed.

9.7.5   Racehorse, yachts, etc.

Some businesses advertise and promote their goods or services through sporting activities, by purchase of a boat, car, etc. and inviting prospective customers to attend a race meeting. Whether or not the VAT incurred on purchase and upkeep of the asset is recoverable depends upon whether it is seen as advertising or entertaining, or merely as a hobby for the principals of the business. VAT incurred on entertaining at such events will in any case be restricted under the business entertainment rules (see **9.4.1**).

The key issues in deciding whether the VAT incurred is recoverable are as follows.

1.   What was in the mind of the taxpayer at the time the decision was made to purchase the item? (*Ian Flockton Developments v C & E Commrs* (1987) 3 BVC 23.) To answer this question minutes of board meetings evidencing the decision are very useful.

2.   Is there any evidence of the results of the investment producing additional sales? Have orders been won from customers/potential customers attending events?

3.   Is there any evidence of directors'/proprietors' personal interest in the activity?

HMRC have set out a list of questions to be asked to assist an officer to determine if VAT incurred on sporting or recreational activities is recoverable or not. It is clear from the questions and issues raised what necessary action must be taken for the VAT on such expenditure to be reclaimed. This list can be found in *HMRC Guidance Manual*, Vol. V1-13 (*VAT: Input tax s. 12*).

9.8   VAT incurred in another EU member state

9.8.1   Claiming a VAT refund

When a UK business incurs VAT from another EU member state, the claim for refund cannot be made on the UK VAT return. It is necessary for a separate claim to be made. Since 1 January 2010, refunds of VAT paid in other EU countries must now be claimed electronically on a standardised form. Claims are to be made through the UK Government Gateway or HMRC VAT Online services. Prior to 2010, the claim would have been a paper based claim and made direct to the tax authority of the EU country where the VAT had been incurred.

The business can claim the refund itself or it can ask an accountant or other agent to do it. There are differing rules in each country, but before an agent can act for the business it will normally have to give your agent either a power of attorney or a letter of authority.

There is no limit to the maximum amount you can claim, but each EU country has set a minimum amount that they will refund; this is usually quite low. A common minimum is 25 for a full year's claim or 200 for a claim for part of a year.

The claim must be made no later than nine months after the end of the calendar year when the VAT was incurred. This is usually the date on the invoice and not the date you paid the supplier. A claim cannot be for more than a calendar year or for a period of less than three months (unless that is all that is left in the calendar year).

Each EU country will only repay VAT for VAT that is input tax in that country. Thus, France will not repay VAT incurred on hotel costs, as the French authorities do not repay this VAT to French VAT registered businesses. Most business type costs, however, can be reclaimed, such as conference costs.

Example 9.1

Joe incurs VAT on conference costs in France. He has incurred VAT on a hotel bill for his accommodation, which cannot be claimed. Joe also has an invoice for attending the conference for 200. The date on the invoice is October 2009. This forms part of the claim for the year ending 31 December 2009. The claim for the VAT incurred must be submitted by 30 September 2010 at the latest.

9.8.2   Can I make a claim?

Claims are not allowed if the UK business has made taxable supplies or is established in the member state concerned (in which case the VAT may only be recovered by registering for VAT in that member state). The rules regarding recovery of VAT are different in each EU member state.

Planning point

A business does not have to claim all of the VAT it incurs in the member state concerned. For example, if it has not retained the necessary evidence it can leave that item out of the claim.

Tax invoices

Original tax invoices are generally required to support a claim made but, where the EU member state in question allows claims by businesses established in its territory to be made on copy invoices, this should also be allowed for a UK business. As the claim is now made electronically, the invoices do not have to be sent, but the EU country where the claim is made can request that the invoices are sent to them to substantiate the claim.

9.8.3 Payment

Most EU member states make payment by credit transfer and in most cases any charges must be borne by the payee. Alternative methods of payment in a few EU member states, may be available.

9.8.4 Appeals

If a claim is not accepted by the EU member state concerned they should give a reason why. It is then possible to appeal against their decision.

9.9 Examples of input tax deduction

9.9.1 Input tax available for specific expenditure

The points made here are in outline only. It is assumed that there is a business purpose and not a private purpose when the expenditure is incurred. 'Yes' indicates that the input tax incurred can be reclaimed, 'No' means the VAT cannot be reclaimed. Any input tax claimed is also subject to a partial exemption restriction.

Description	Employee	Spouse/partner of employee	Director	Sole proprietor or partner
Domestic Accommodation	Yes	Not if supplied separately	No	Apportionment usual
Hotel Accommodation	Yes	No	Yes	Yes
Removal Expenses	Yes	Not if supplied separately	Yes, apportionment may be necessary	Yes, apportionment may be necessary

Description	Employee	Spouse/partner of employee	Director	Sole proprietor or partner
Cars – subject to special rules for specific cars such as taxis and car hire vehicles	No	No	No	No
Petrol	Scale Charge	Scale Charge	Scale Charge	Scale Charge
Repairs & Servicing	Yes	Yes – if part of the employment package	Yes	Yes
Accessories fitted after acquisition of the car	Yes	Yes – if part of the employment package	Yes, if there is a business nexus	Yes, if there is a business nexus
Tolls and car parking	Yes if VAT charged	Yes if VAT charged and part of the employment package	Yes if VAT charged	Yes if VAT charged
Subsistence	Yes	No	Yes	Yes
Fixed Allowances	No	No	No	No
Home Telephones	Apportionment	Apportionment	Apportionment	Apportionment
Mobile Telephones	Business Use only	Business Use only	Business Use only	Business Use only
Clothing	No	No	No	No
Uniforms and protective clothing	Yes	No	Yes	Yes
Tools and Materials	Yes	No	Yes	Yes
Legal Expenses	Rarely	Rarely	Rarely	Rarely
Entertainment	Yes	No	Yes	No

VAT is not deductible on entertainment of non-employees, but where the entertainment is not hospitality but a subsistence expense of a partner or sole proprietor, the VAT can be reclaimed. Any entertainment of third parties is not deductible, unless a charge is made (that is not nominal). Where there is a small charge, or there is entertainment of both employees and non-employees, the VAT incurred has to be apportioned. VAT incurred on entertaining staff members acting as hosts at an entertainment event is not deductible.

9.10 Recovery of VAT incurred on land transactions

9.10.1 Recap – general rules

Input tax can be recovered where it relates to the making of any taxable supplies. Only certain interests in land are automatically taxable (see **17.10** and **17.12.1**). Where the grant of an interest in land is taxable (whether at the standard or zero-rate), the input tax referable to that supply will be deductible.

VAT will also be deductible where the grant or supply would normally be exempt but the taxpayer has exercised the option to tax and that option is effective. The general rule is that input tax relating to the grant of an interest in land can be recovered even if it was incurred prior to an option to tax being exercised in respect of that land.

However, where the input tax is incurred and an interest in the land is granted prior to the option being made, the taxpayer will be unable to exercise the option to tax without prior permission of HMRC, who will not grant permission unless they can agree with the taxpayer a fair and reasonable method of attributing the tax to the exempt supplies first made and the subsequent taxable supplies.

> ### ⚠ *Warning!*
> Permission to opt may still be required where exempt supplies have taken place even if no additional VAT is to be claimed.

9.10.2 Provisional deduction of input tax

There may be occasions when a developer makes purchases and does not know at that time which type of supply they will be used for. In such a case, the partial exemption provisions will be of relevance (see **Chapter 12**).

9.10.3 Goods installed in new non-commercial buildings

To avoid distortion of competition, a taxable person constructing or effecting works to any non-commercial building (where the sale or lease would be zero-rated) may not recover any input tax on goods incorporated in the building unless they are 'building materials'.

The supply of such goods to a developer is always standard-rated. Where such goods are incorporated in a building which is then sold as a zero-rated supply, there is no separate supply of the goods. The provisions ensure that the tax on the goods is reflected in the price of the building by disallowing the VAT charged by the supplier to the developer. Input tax on the related services of installing the goods can be reclaimed, provided that the services are separately identified on the supplier's invoice.

The provision ensures that the developer suffers the same VAT cost on goods which are not 'building materials' as any other person who receives a standard-rated supply of such goods.

In addition to any goods not ordinarily installed by a builder in a dwelling of the type concerned, the legislation specifically precludes recovery of input tax on the following items.

1. Prefabricated furniture or materials for the manufacture thereof.

2. Electrical or gas appliances, unless they are:

    (a) designed to heat space or water or to provide ventilation, air cooling, air purification or dust extraction;

    (b) a burglar alarm, fire alarm or fire safety equipment for summoning emergency aid; or

    (c) a lift or hoist.

3. Carpets and carpeting material.

VAT Notice 708 contains lists of items that they consider to be allowable and disallowable for different categories of building.

> **Planning point**
>
> HMRC's notice represents their view and should not therefore be seen as definitive. In cases of doubt or difficulty, sensible judgment or reference to the outcome of relevant tribunal cases may be called for.

9.10.4   Showhouses

HMRC take the view that input tax cannot be reclaimed on goods which have been installed in showhouses, apparently in any circumstances. Arguably, however, input tax should be deductible if the goods are for display purposes only and will be removed for use elsewhere, will be scrapped at the end of their useful life or will be the subject of a separate taxable supply (being sold separately from the dwelling in which they have been displayed, for example).

Other guidance: VAT Notice 708, para. 12.3

9.10.5   Landscaping

Following the tribunal decision in *Rialto Homes plc* [2000] BVC 2,161, HMRC accepted that certain soft landscaping in addition to the laying of turf can be zero-rated when supplied in the course of constructing a non-commercial building (*Business Brief 7/00*). However, HMRC maintain that the following landscaping supplies remain standard-rated:

- work not included on a landscaping scheme approved by a planning authority under the terms of a planning consent condition; and
- work performed after completion.

Other guidance: *VAT Notice 708*, para. 3.3.4

9.10.6 Capital items

From 1 April 1990 input tax incurred on land and buildings costing more than £250,000 is required to be adjusted over a period of ten years (or a lesser period if the interest held does not equal or exceed ten years) (VAT Regulations 1995 (SI 1995/2518), reg. 113).

The regulations apply to input tax incurred on the following:

- the acquisition of land and/or buildings;
- a developer's self-supply under the provisions outlined in **17.13**;
- a self-supply following a change in use of a qualifying building; and
- a self-supply of construction services where a building is extended by more than ten per cent.

A full discussion of this subject appears in **Chapter 12**.

9.10.7 Service charges

The VAT liability of a service charge will normally follow the VAT liability of the rent charge. This is because the service charge is seen, in the UK, as being further consideration for the rent. Thus, an exempt rent will have an exempt service charge. Where the landlord has opted to tax, the service charge will also be subject to VAT. This can result in a loss of input tax where a landlord has not opted to tax and the tenants who are fully taxable can reclaim the VAT on their costs. The landlord cannot reclaim VAT on the costs that they incur and the recharge through the service charge will include this irrecoverable VAT. The tenant, however, cannot reclaim the VAT that is included in the charge as the VAT element is a component of an exempt supply, no VAT has actually been charged to the tenant. This is called the cascading of VAT. It cascades through the VAT system and accumulates, rather than being available as a credit.

It has been argued in a recent VAT Tribunal *Field Fisher Waterhouse LLP* [2011] TC 01371 that the service charge is not linked to the supply of the land. Thus, the service charge should be subject to VAT even where the underlying rent is exempt. The appellants argued that their view was supported by the ECJ Judgement *RLRE Tellmer Property sro v Finančni ředitelstvi v Ústi nad Labem* (Case C-572/07) [2010] BVC 802 (*Tellmer*). *Tellmer* owned apartment blocks, charging tenants exempt rent. It also separately invoiced tenants for the cleaning of common parts. The tax authority regarded the cleaning services as separate taxable supplies and required VAT to be charged. *Tellmer* appealed and the case was referred to the ECJ. The ECJ was asked whether the letting of an apartment and the cleaning of common parts were separate supplies, and if they were not separate supplies was VAT to be charged on cleaning as a cleaning service is taxable. The ECJ held that in these circumstances the supplies could not be regarded as a single letting transaction. The cleaning service was supplied separately.

Field Fisher Waterhouse had been charged an exempt rent. It wished to recover the VAT on the service charge that it had incurred. In addition to the *Tellmer* decision, it argued that the service charge could not be related to the area it rented as the charge also applied to common areas and would be used by persons that were not even tenants of the building. HMRC did not believe that *Tellmer* supported the appellant's arguments. HMRC argued that the ECJ had only considered the single or multiple supply issue. This was not relevant to these circumstances as the service charge was part of the rent . In *Tellmer* the tenant could appoint a third party to provide the cleaning service and had chosen the landlord to provide this service. *Field Fisher Waterhouse* was not in this position as the rent agreement clearly stated that the service charge was part of the rent and did not allow a third party to be appointed.

HMRC agree that where the lease agreement permits a third party to provide a service, such as cleaning, that this is a separate supply. VAT would be charged on this supply (if appropriate) and the input tax could be claimed by the tenant according to the normal rules. The Lower-Tier Tribunal has, however, referred this case to the European Court of Justice to determine if such supplies are separate to the main supply of letting or merely ancillary and part of the same single supply of letting. In addition, the ECJ has been asked if it is necessary for the supplies to be supplied by a third party for the service charge or cleaning charge to be regarded as a separate supply.

Planning Point

A service charge is regarded as a separate supply where a third party from the landlord can make the supply. The service charge will then take the VAT liability of the supply made (usual standard rated unless a zero-rate, reduced-rate or exemption relief applies). Where a separate service charge is supplied the tenant can reclaim any VAT charged according to the normal rules and his partial exemption position.

Where a service charge is reserved in the rent agreement as part of the rent, the service charge will have the same liability as the rent. Whether any VAT can be reclaimed on the costs that make up the cost of the service charge (for example contractors to the landlord) will depend upon the ability of the landlord to reclaim VAT and not be determined by the tenant's VAT position (with the proviso that the ECJ decision in *Field Fisher Waterhouse* may change this).

Non-deductible Input Tax

10.1   Introduction

VAT is not meant to be a cost to the business. Consequently, the general rule is that any VAT incurred can be reclaimed by the business. There are, however, exceptions. First, where VAT relates to exempt supplies no VAT can be claimed. This is discussed in **Chapter 12**. VAT is also not claimable where it relates to a non-business use or the VAT credit is specifically blocked. These two matters are discussed in this chapter.

For VAT to be claimable, however, the person claiming the input tax must be a taxable person (registered for VAT). In addition, the VAT incurred must relate to an actual supply, acquisition or importation. If there is no supply no VAT should have been charged and the amount charged cannot be reclaimed as input tax. This VAT must also be the amount of VAT that is properly chargeable; if it is not properly chargeable the VAT cannot be reclaimed. A person must not only have received the supply (or acquisition or importation) but in order to claim the VAT credit that person must also hold a proper tax invoice to support the claim for the input tax claim. There are certain exceptions to this rule: a less detailed tax invoice can be held or where coin operated machines are used no invoice at all may be necessary. These matters are discussed previously in **Chapter 9, Maximising input tax credits**. At **9.2** it goes into further detail concerning the rules for input tax. As most items that are blocked are significant (such as cars or second-hand goods) these are dealt with in other chapters and the next section summarises the items where input tax credits are blocked. This chapter concentrates on input tax that may be used for private purposes as well as business purposes. The most important example of this is the VAT incurred on private use, and this chapter looks closely at these expenses. This includes expenditure on farmhouses, expenditure on employee benefits home use of computers, etc. In addition, the ability to reclaim VAT by pension funds is mentioned at the end of this chapter.

10.2   Blocked input tax

In order to claim an input tax credit the VAT incurred must qualify as input tax. As mentioned in **9.2.2** to qualify as input tax, the VAT paid must have been incurred on a supply that was properly taxable at a positive rate and charged by a VAT-registered business in the UK. If it is not VAT that has been properly charged the VAT shown on the invoice cannot be claimed. It is not blocked input tax, but the impact on the business is the same, the amount paid as VAT cannot be claimed as a credit.

Even when VAT has been correctly charged on a supply, there are certain occasions when this VAT is statutorily blocked for recovery purposes. The most common examples of this are:

- the purchase of a car which is not used/to be used wholly for business purposes;
- purchases of goods within the margin scheme for second-hand goods – a VAT invoice will not be received for a supply purchased as a second-hand item, and recovery of input tax on an item to be sold under a margin scheme is blocked because it is only necessary to account for VAT on the profit made when the item is sold;
- purchases for the purposes of business entertainment;
- purchases of goods or services to be sold under the tour operators' margin scheme (TOMS) – as for second-hand items above, VAT is only required to be accounted for on the profit margin on goods or services sold under the scheme;
- purchases by builders of certain items to be installed in residential/charitable buildings; and
- costs relating to the provision of domestic accommodation for directors or persons connected to them, including costs of the accommodation itself, repair, refurbishment, furnishing, legal and estate agents' fees. From 1 January 2011, this legislation becomes redundant following the introduction by HMRC of the technical amendments following the adoption of the EU Technical Directive (Council Directive 2009/162/EU). The VAT will remain blocked (as will other private use input tax on property, land, boats and aircraft). More information is detailed at **10.10.3.1**.

VAT on cars that are purchased (including hire purchase) is generally non-deductible. VAT is, however, claimable where the use of vehicles (such as cars used as taxis for driving schools or car hire) permits input tax deduction. VAT can also be claimed on cars purchased for resale. Where a business hires or leases a vehicle it is eligible to reclaim 50 per cent of the VAT on the lease (but a full credit is allowed for VAT on the maintenance and repair of the vehicle). Further details are given at **Chapter 11**.

In addition, VAT is not claimable on second-hand goods or tour operator supplies, both of which are subject to margin scheme rules, see **Chapter 7**. VAT that is restricted on the Tour Operator Margin Scheme is discussed at **7.11**. VAT that is restricted on land transactions is discussed at **9.10**.

Other items are not statutorily blocked, but are not permitted under other rules; in particular the private/non-business use of supplies received.

VAT incurred in relation to exempt or non-business activities is also restricted.

Other guidance: VAT Notice 700, para. 10.3

10.3 Private/non-business use

Where goods or services are used wholly for private purposes there is no right to deduct any of the VAT paid. However, some goods or services are purchased for business use and then turned over to private use at a later date, or they may be purchased partly for business and partly for private purposes. This expenditure may take a variety of forms. There may be accommodation acquired for directors or spouses (before 1 January 2011 this was specifically blocked, but now comes under the new amended rules), racing cars, race horses, boxes at sports grounds, etc. Many of these items will be regarded as wholly private and non-deductible unless there can be a proven link to the business. Input tax deduction may be possible through the use of sponsorship, and this is considered at **10.11**. Usually, however, HMRC will deny input tax credits as not relating to the business. Where a link can be established between the business a percentage of the input tax can be claimed. These rules have changed on 1 January 2011 and the new and old methods are detailed below.

Prior to 1 January 2011 a different treatment of the input tax was utilized, often called Lennartz VAT accounting after the decision in *Lennartz v Finanzamt Munchen III* [1993] BVC 202. Without going into detail (given that this method is becoming restricted and it is detailed in the following paragraphs) this permitted a taxpayer that incurred VAT for both business and non-business uses to reclaim all the VAT incurred as input tax and account for VAT on the private use of the item over a period of years. This was exploited by some by applying a low value to the private use and accounting for little output tax. Even if applied without any extravagant exploitation, it clearly gives a cash flow boost to taxpayers by permitting full input tax recovery on items that may not be expected to permit much, if any, VAT recovery.

It should be noted, however, that the rules have changed or are changing markedly in respect of recovering input VAT on goods acquired for private or non-business use. Paragraphs **10.4** to **10.5** below describe the input tax rules that apply prior to the changes. The subsequent paragraphs consider the new interpretation and the new rules that are to be introduced.

The changes have come about due to two matters. First, there is the *Vereniging Noordelijke Land-en Tuinbouw Organisatie v Staatssecretaris van Financiën*(Case C-515/07) (*VNLTO*) decision. This considered whether or not *Lennartz* accounting can be used by a taxpayer whose activities are non-business activities and, therefore, not within the scope of VAT. The Court's decision made it clear that EU VAT legislation does not permit, and never has permitted, input tax deduction in full where there is no business use. In the past, many charities or non-business organisations have claimed input tax in full on expensive items (such as buildings) where there is no taxable use and accounted for output tax on the use of the item over a period of years. This is no longer permitted and this position is described in **10.6**.

Secondly, HMRC introduced rules to prevent, from 1 January 2011, taxpayers that buy land, property, boats or aircraft that are used for both business and private purposes from benefiting from the Lennartz accounting arrangements. This follows the adoption by the UK of the Technical Directive (Council Directive 2009/162/EU). These changes are detailed in **10.7**.

A key factor to consider is whether the expenditure has been incurred for business purposes. This often arises where the expenditure has been incurred for employees of the business. After considering the general rules in respect of items purchased for mixed business and private use, business entertainment, then employee expenditure will be considered.

10.4 Purchases of goods partly for business use – prior to 1 January 2011

For most goods, there are two options when the goods are purchased and it is known at the time that they will be partly used for business purposes and partly used for private/non-business purposes.

All of the VAT incurred may be treated as input tax and recovered, but a deemed charge on the private use of the asset is accounted for on a period-by-period basis using the *Lennartz* mechanism.

Following the 2007 Budget, HMRC took steps to restrict the time period during which such an adjustment may be made to five years (ten years for land and buildings).

Example 10.1

If a yacht is purchased costing £200,000 plus VAT of £35,000 (note, the VAT rate at this time was 17.5 per cent), the taxpayer can choose to treat the whole of the £35,000 as input tax and reclaim it in full on the VAT return covering the period of purchase. The base cost of the deemed supply would be £40,000 per year or £10,000 per quarter calculated over a five-year period. If the yacht is used 50 per cent for business and 50 per cent for private/non-business purposes, in the first quarter, then VAT must be accounted for on 50 per cent of the £10,000 which equals £875.00. If the private/non-business use increases to 75 per cent in the next quarter, VAT must be accounted for on 75 per cent of £10,000, £7,500, which equals £1,312.50.

Once the five-year period is up, there is no longer any need to account for the deemed supply.

In calculating the percentage of private/non-business use it is the days used for business/private purposes that are utilised in the calculation, not the days used for private purposes over the total number of days in the period (unless the asset is wholly used for business purposes during that time). However, see the case of *Sangster Group Ltd* [1998] BVC 4,114 where the tribunal agreed with Customs that the denominator should be the total number of days in the year rather than being limited to the number of days of use. The case concerned a manor-house refurbishment which the tribunal considered was available for private use for the time it was not used for business purposes.

VAT incurred on related expenditure such as maintenance, repairs, etc. may also either be apportioned or recovered in full and form part of the above baseline cost for the above calculations.

Alternatively, an apportionment of the VAT incurred on the initial purchase price of the asset may be made. In cases of uncertainty, it may be prudent to agree the method used and amount to be recovered with HMRC, but essentially any fair and reasonable method should be acceptable, otherwise HMRC may review the calculation at a future inspection in the light of actual use of the purchase.

Example 10.2

Using the same example as above, a yacht costing £200,000 plus VAT of £35,000 is intended to be used 50 per cent for business purposes and 50 per cent for private/non-business purposes. The apportionment would allow recovery of 50 per cent of the VAT incurred or £17,500. There would be no need to account for VAT on the private use of the vessel each period.

Between 9 April 2003 and 9 August 2005, HMRC took the view that the option in **Example 10.1** was not available in respect of the purchase of land, buildings or civil engineering works (VATA 1994, Sch. 4, para. 5) and the option in **Example 10.2** was the only method available, amending UK legislation to this effect. In the ECJ case of *P Charles, T S Charles-Tijmens* (Case C-434/03), referred by the Dutch authorities, it was held that this restriction on the use of the 'Lennartz mechanism' was *ultra vires* the European legislation, and in *Business Brief 15/05* (9 August 2005), HMRC acknowledged that they could no longer rely on the UK provisions. This has the effect of restoring the use of the mechanism to land, buildings and civil engineering works (legitimating its use retrospectively by those operating it in defiance of HMRC's position).

Planning point

It used to be the case that, regardless of which method was adopted, if input tax was claimed in whole or in part on the purchase, then HMRC would maintain that the sale of the asset would attract VAT on the whole selling price and, on deregistration, the whole value of the asset should be taken into account for the deemed supply of goods on hand. More recently, however, they have acknowledged that only the proportion of the asset on which VAT has been claimed is acquired by way of business and that output tax is due on sale or deregistration only on that proportion (unless in the case of sale the business opts to charge VAT on the full selling price).

10.5 Purchases of services partly for business use – prior to 1 January 2011

For most services, the input tax incurred for both business and private/non-business purposes must be apportioned according to the use to which the services are put. Any fair and reasonable method of calculation may be used, and HMRC reserve the right to challenge any method at a future VAT inspection.

However, in cases where services are incorporated into goods used in the business and which substantially increase the value of those goods to the business, such as the major restoration of a business vehicle, then the taxpayer may choose to recover all of the VAT incurred and account for VAT on the deemed supply of the business asset, as at **Example 10.1** above for goods. This option may also be applied to construction services. If this option is used for services, HMRC request that the taxpayer telephone the National Advice Helpline on 0845 010 9000 to agree its use, although there is no statutory basis for this.

10.6 Purchases initially wholly for business purposes

When a purchase made wholly for business purposes is later turned over to private or other non-business use, the VAT position is different depending upon whether the purchase is of goods or services and whether the item is put wholly to private use or only partly to private use.

Where the goods or services are turned wholly to private use there is a deemed supply, the value of which is the cost of replacing the goods in their state at the date the goods are turned over to private use. Where the goods or services are only partly used for private purposes but continue to be used for business purposes as well, the deemed supply is calculated in a similar way to that in **Example 10.1**.

10.7 Purchases by non-business entities

Following the decision in the *VNLTO* case it has become apparent that non-business entities, such as charities, cannot recover input tax using the *Lennartz* method. In the past, the non-business entity would have claimed input tax in full on an asset (often a building) and then pay output VAT over a period of use based upon their use of the building. Even if this did not give an absolute cash saving, it would give a cash flow benefit, making large capital items more affordable.

Following this decision, HMRC issued a Brief 02/10, detailing how, from 22 January 2010, they believe VAT should be dealt with. VAT is recoverable by a business to the extent that the input VAT is incurred for a taxable business purpose. The brief states:

> 'If goods are used for both business and private/non-business purposes, there is a choice about how to treat them for VAT purposes, which must be made at the time they are acquired, namely:
>
> * as a wholly non-business or private asset, in which case the VAT is not deductible;
> * as a part business, part non-business asset, in which case the VAT incurred is only deductible to the extent that it relates to the taxable business activities (section 24(5) of the VAT Act 1994); or
> * as a wholly business asset (the "Lennartz" approach) in which case the VAT incurred is treated as input tax and is deductible in full, subject to any partial exemption restriction; however, output tax must then be declared in so far as the goods are used for private/non-business purposes.
>
> Lennartz accounting is not, therefore, available in cases where goods (including services used to create goods) are used wholly for business purposes.'

It goes on to state that *Lennartz* accounting is now restricted to certain limited instances. This includes where the goods are used both for taxable purposes (where input tax is permitted to be deducted under the 'normal' rules) and the goods are also used for private purposes by the business owner and his staff (and possibly, and exceptionally, for purposes outside the business's enterprise).

The impact of this decision means that *Lennartz* type accounting was never permitted. HMRC could have required entities to repay all input tax claimed (and presumably offset this by the output tax paid). HMRC will, however, by concession, permit existing schemes to continue as long as all the necessary output tax is paid on the non-business use for the remaining period of the scheme. HMRC will not permit any further schemes to be commenced but will exceptionally consider applications from taxpayers that have made binding commitments based upon their expectation to be able to use *Lennartz* type accounting.

10.8 Private use – post 31 December 2010

HMRC has introduced changes to the legislation governing input tax deductions to adopt the Technical Directive (Council Directive 2009/162/EU). HMRC has issued an Information Sheet (06/11) detailing how it believes VAT should be accounted for following the introduction of the Technical Directive on 1 January 2011. The Technical Directive prevents the recovery of VAT using the *Lennartz* mechanism in the majority of cases.

From 1 January 2011, VAT recovery is limited for many assets (land, property, buildings, ships, boats and aircraft) to the extent the asset is used to make business supplies for which there is a right to claim an input tax credit; other assets can still apply the *Lennartz* mechanism described above, but there are likely to be few instances where this is advantageous. The Directive also requires an adjustment to be made to deal with any changes in use of the asset over its economic life, through the capital goods scheme (see **12.18.1**).

The *Lennartz* method can still be used for other assets where there is private use. VAT can be claimed in full on acquisition of the asset (subject to any partial exemption restriction) and VAT accounted for on the private use element for the next ten years.

Planning point

Consider if using the *Lennartz* method provides a cashflow advantage when assets are used privately by employees, directors or the owners of the business.

There are some transitional issues to consider. Where a business has already used *Lennartz* accounting for an asset (which is no longer available for this method of accounting) acquired prior to 1 January 2011, it must continue to account for VAT on private use on that asset. Any VAT incurred on or after 1 January 2011, however, can only be claimed to the extent that the asset is used for making taxable supplies. Thus, the asset will be in a type of VAT twilight world where it is both in (for output tax) and outside (for input tax credits) *Lennartz* accounting.

A further transitional point to bear in mind is the change introduced on 22 January 2010. HMRC introduced restrictions on the ability to reclaim VAT under the *Lennartz* principal following the ECJ decision *VNLTO*. The *VNTLO* decision severely restricted the ability of businesses to reclaim VAT in full on assets that were to be partly used for private or non-business purposes. With effect from 22 January 2010, HMRC requires taxpayers to alter their VAT accounting for assets used in this manner. HMRC permitted taxpayers to opt to continue to use *Lennartz* accounting, although no VAT on costs can be reclaimed from 1 January 2011 and output tax must continue to be accounted for on the value of private or non-business use. A person that opted not to continue to use *Lennartz* type accounting needed to repay any input tax claimed and could reclaim the output tax accounted for under *Lennartz* accounting. HMRC have stated in Information Sheet 06/11 that these adjustments must be completed by 30 June 2011.

Planning point

Consider which method you are permitted to use, and then which gives the best cash advantage as well as the best cashflow advantage where you are permitted a choice.

> **Planning point**
> Review the capital goods scheme section in this book (**Chapter 12**) to determine how the scheme has been altered to include assets used for non-business activities.

It will, however, be possible for a business to acquire an asset and lease it to directors and employees. HMRC will expect this to be run in a similar manner as a commercial leasing entity. Where arm's length fees are not charged or the item is not available for use by third parties, HMRC can be expected to challenge the arrangement.

10.9 Business entertainment

10.9.1 What is entertainment?

VAT incurred for the purposes of business entertainment is specifically blocked from recovery under the VAT (Input Tax) Order 1992 (SI 1992/3222), art. 5. Case law defines business entertainment as: the free provision of hospitality to persons who are not employees of the business, employees including directors of limited companies. Entertainment of employees is considered at **10.10, Employee expenditure.**

To be non-recoverable expenditure the hospitality must be free of charge or obligation. In the case of *C & E Commrs v Kilroy Television Co Ltd* [1997] BVC 422, the participants in the talk show were provided with a buffet meal. The court found that the company had put itself in a contractual position to provide the buffet, which was the only payment the participants received for taking part in the show. Therefore, there was no business entertainment provided. In a similar case, a market research company provided sandwiches at product trials where the public were invited to sample alcoholic beverages and complete questionnaires on them. HMRC accepted that the alcoholic beverages were not business entertainment but assessed the VAT recovered on the provision of food. The tribunal found that the food was a necessary part of supplying the drinks and was not business entertainment (*DPA (Market Research) Ltd* [1997] BVC 4,071).

The ECJ judgment in the *Danfoss/Astra Zeneca* case has confirmed that working lunches provided to directors in the course of a business meeting (provided no other employees are present) may have a business purpose and therefore costs involved in providing such meals are deductible for VAT purposes. Current UK VAT legislation restricts the recovery of VAT on business entertainment, including in-house lunches that are provided free of charge to clients during business meetings. Under the *Danfoss/Astra Zeneca* cases there may be entitlement to recover VAT paid on the provision of working lunches.

10.9.2 Events

If an event is held by a business, the main purpose of which is entertainment of customers/potential customers or other third parties, then the attendance of employees as hosts at the event does not allow a proportion of the VAT to be recovered.

It can make sense to charge a nominal fee when holding events that would otherwise fall into the business entertainment category. The fee must at least equal the cost of the business entertainment provided. If HMRC can show that the fee is below cost they may seek to assess VAT on business entertainment grounds on the difference between the fee charged and the value of hospitality provided.

If a potential customer is entertained by an employee whilst they are away on a business trip, then provided that the sole reason for the trip is not business entertainment, the VAT on the employee's meal can be recovered under the subsistence rules above. That proportion of VAT referable to the potential customer's meal is, however, business entertaining and is not recoverable.

10.9.3 Purchase of goods or services for business entertainment

The business entertainment blocking provisions apply to the purchase of goods as well as entertainment supplied at events. Where an asset is purchased for both business purposes and entertainment purposes, an apportionment of the input tax should be made. This treatment is derived from the decision in *Thorn EMI plc*, where the taxpayer had hospitality chalets at an air show. As well as entertainment, the chalets provided a place to hold confidential discussions regarding the company's electronic systems which it displayed and sold at the air show (*Thorn EMI plc v C & E Commrs* [1995] BVC 282).

10.9.4 Overseas customers

Input tax credits are available on costs associated with the business entertainment of overseas customers. HMRC has accepted that their 'input tax block' introduced in 1988 was contrary to EU legislation. Thus, there is the opportunity to make backdated reclaims for any input tax incurred in the past (subject to the capping rules) on the entertainment of overseas customers. Note, VAT incurred on the entertainment of UK customers is not deductible.

Planning point

Examine past expenses for input tax incurred on the entertainment of overseas customers to determine if any VAT can be reclaimed.

10.9.5   Trade fairs/exhibitions

Where non-employees are brought in to assist with the running of events at an exhibition, show or sporting event, then VAT on their subsistence expenses is also recoverable.

However, VAT incurred on free hospitality given to visitors, journalists or other persons not involved in running the event is subject to restriction under the basic business entertainment rules.

10.9.6   Consultants and other third parties

VAT incurred on expenses paid for self-employed consultants or other third parties is not recoverable where the supply is to the consultant rather than the VAT-registered business. Where free hospitality is provided to consultants, etc., this must be treated as business entertainment. This includes hotel accommodation, food and drinks, for example where self-employed sales consultants attend a seminar/conference hosted by the VAT-registered business (*C & E Commrs v Shaklee International* (1981) 1 BVC 444).

10.10   Employee expenditure

10.10.1 Employee or employer

When considering claiming VAT the distinction between costs incurred for an employee or by the employer, the business, needs to be considered. For example, where an employee eats food as subsistence, uses a hotel room during an overnight stay or puts petrol into the employee's own car for fuel used during a business trip, has the supply been made to the employee or the business? Similar issues have arisen in direct tax. In *Richardson v Worrall* [1985] BTC 508 it was held that the employee had a liability to pay for the fuel when he put it in the car and a subsequent payment through the use of a company credit card discharged the liability of the employee and a re-imbursement was an emolument. This contention was upheld in *R v Department of Social Security, ex parte Overdrive Credit Card Ltd* [1991] BTC 8036.

There is, however, a distinction between direct tax and VAT. Although the supply may be regarded as being made to the employee, it may also be regarded as being made to the employer and being incurred for the purpose of the business. Thus, such expenditure is normally regarded as deductible. The following are examples of types of expenditure where the supply may be seen as being supplied to the employee but are accepted by HMRC as made to the employer provided the employer meets the full cost:

- road fuel and other motoring expense;
- subsistence costs i.e. meals and accommodation necessarily paid for whilst away from the normal workplace;

295

- removal expenses arising from company relocation or transfer of staff; and
- sundry items such as small tools, materials, etc. purchased 'on site'.

Where a tax invoice shows a supply is made to an employee of a VAT registered business (that is, the invoice is made out in the name of the employee), this invoice is satisfactory for input tax purposes provided the supplies were purchased for the purpose of the employer's business (see (VAT Public Notice 700 paragraph 19.7.9).

This section will also, for completeness, consider the expenditure on directors (who are employees) and certain non-employees such as spouses, sole proprietors and partners in a partnership.

10.10.2 Not an employee

Where an agents, contractors or self-employed person is used in the role of an employee that person should claim any deductible VAT incurred if VAT registered. This intermediary person can reclaim the VAT incurred, and make an onward charge plus VAT to the main business. Tribunals have disallowed the VAT recovery by a business where it has been incurred by an agent, contractor or self-employed person (see Berbrooke Fashions [1997] VATTR 168 (426)) and *R Wiseman & Sons* (1984) 2 BVC 208043 and *Stormseal (UPVC) Window Co Ltd; Probelook Ltd* (1990) 5 BVC 543). There was, however, an element of entertainment in these cases, and entertainment is specifically blocked.

There are instances where VAT incurred on non-employee expenses can be reclaimed. Where a business wishes to run a conference or training event for non-employees to promote its business, even though its business may be run through these non-employees the VAT would be recoverable if it can be regarded as being a supply for the purpose of that business and made to the business. In *Customs and Excise Commissioners v Shaklee International and Anor* (1981) 1 BVC 444, however, it was held that the food and accommodation supplied to trainee agents of a pyramid selling organisation was business entertainment and non-deductible. If the expenditure was not regarded as entertainment it may be deductible. In addition, the VAT may be non-deductible if the supply is made directly to the individual and not the business (see *Institute of Purchasing & Supply* (1987) 3 BVC 640.

HMRC do allow input tax to be reclaimed where a non-employee incurs the VAT. For instance, where a business reimburses subsistence, road fuel or other motoring costs incurred by self-employed persons working for the business, the VAT incurred is deductible where:

- the individual is employed on the same basis as an employee;
- the expense is in respect of their 'employment';
- the individuals receive no payment from the end customer;
- the reimbursement is at cost, including VAT; and
- the amount is dealt with in the accounts in the normal way.

In addition, where a self-employed person buys tools or materials to use for a specific job for a business, the VAT incurred is the business's input tax and not the self-employed person's input tax provided the conditions above are met and the tools remain the property of the business, or the materials are incorporated into and become a cost component of the business's supply to the end customer.

10.10.3 Specific employee expenses

This section reviews specific expenditure that may be incurred by employees and whether it is deductible by the business.

10.10.3.1   Domestic accommodation

The provision of domestic accommodation is regarded as a private rather than business expense and consequently VAT cannot normally be recovered in respect of such costs. The cost of acquisition of the property or the rent charge will either be zero-rated or exempt, but VAT is incurred on alterations, maintenance and repairs. Where, however, a business is required to provide domestic accommodation to employees or such accommodation is necessary for the running of the business, the VAT on expenditure incurred in providing the accommodation is regarded as having been incurred for a business purpose. For example, the farming (tied cottages) and hotel industries often provide accommodation to employees to ensure staff are on hand. Former employees may also be provided with accommodation, where this is a benefit of previous employment and traditional practice (particularly, in farming). Unusually, HMRC permit input tax to be claimed although usually expenditure on a past employee is non-deductible.

A further problem arises where businesses are operated from domestic premises. Where a sole proprietor or partner carries on a business from home and uses a particular room for business the VAT incurred can be reclaimed if it can be identified. VAT on domestic items is not recoverable.

Apportionment is likely to occur for costs such as heat and light, security systems and general maintenance as a proportion will be regarded as being for private use. It has been agreed with the NFU that sole proprietors and partnerships who are full-time farmers may normally claim 70 per cent of the VAT incurred on repairs and maintenance, but it may be a greater or lesser amount for alterations depending on the part of the building to be altered (see Business Brief 18/96 (27 August 1996)).

VATA 1994, Sch. 6, para. 10, states that where accommodation is supplied to an employee the value will be taken as nil so there is no question of VAT being due on the value of the accommodation provided to the employee.

10.10.3.2   Hotel accommodation

VAT incurred on hotel accommodation (and similar accommodation) is deductible (even when incurred by directors) where the expense is borne by the business, where it is incurred for the purpose of the business and a proper tax invoice is obtained. An overnight stay for personal reasons is not a deductible expense. Should, however, a director, sole proprietor, partner or employee stay in a hotel due to transport strikes or other transport disruptions and the business bears the cost as it is accepted as being for the purpose of the business, the VAT incurred is deductible.

It is important to consider if the expense incurred is for a business purpose. This is a subjective matter and it is necessary to determine what is in the taxable person's mind when incurring the expense (see **Chapter 5** and *Ian Flockton Developments Ltd. v Customs and Excise Commissioners* (1987) 3 BVC 23). It is also necessary to consider if an 'onward' supply is made to employees under *VAT (Supply of Services) Order* (SI1993/1507), article 3) when incurring expenses for staff incentive schemes; thus the input tax may be deductible, but there is an output tax due on the onward supply. Other types of personal expenditure such as bar drinks, videos, dry-cleaning are non-deductible as personal expenditure with insufficient nexus to the business.

It is also essential to ensure that a tax invoice is obtained. It is not necessary to have a tax invoice in the name of the business; it can be in the name of the employee (see Public Notice 700 paragraph 19.7). It is prudent, however, to obtain an invoice in the name of the business wherever possible. Also, hotels, on occasion, produce invoices that are not proper tax invoices. Most officers will exercise their discretion and allow input tax deduction, it is advisable to ensure a proper tax invoice is obtained.

10.10.3.3   Removal expenses

HMRC's internal guidance states that VAT incurred on the removal expenses of employees, directors, partners and sole proprietors is deductible as input tax on:

- estate agents' and solicitors' fees;
- storage and removal of household and personal effects; and
- services such as plumbing-in washing machines or altering curtains.

This guidance states that 'claims should not be rejected even if, as is usual, the relevant invoices are addressed to the employee rather than the taxable person.' Where a proportion of the expenditure is reimbursed a pro-rata proportion of the input tax can be claimed. No input tax can be claimed where a fixed rate allowance is paid.

10.10.3.4   Travel costs

Most travel costs (train, bus and airfares) do not bear VAT and no input tax deduction is available. VAT is due on car hire, leasing and purchase and their maintenance and running costs. These are considered in **Chapter 11**.

10.10.3.5   Subsistence, meal costs, etc.

VAT incurred on employee meal expenses can be reclaimed (subject to the normal rules regarding invoices, etc.), but is only deductible where it is necessary for subsistence and is some distance from the normal working place of the individual. In the Tribunal decision *Mutch* (1987) 3 BVC 1346 a sole proprietor was disallowed the VAT incurred on meals taken within two or three miles from his office. The Tribunal held that expenditure for the business is to mean for the purpose of enabling a person to carry on and earn profits in the trade. It must be made for the purpose of earning the profits rather than just connected with it. The onus is on the taxpayer to show that the expenditure for personal meals was for the purpose of the business and not for the *natural daily requirements for nourishment*. HMRC will not, therefore, allow meal expenses for a sole proprietor, partner or a director to be reclaimed unless it is away from their place of work on a business trip.

10.10.3.6   Fixed allowances

No VAT deduction is, generally permitted where a fixed cash allowance is paid. Even when a tax invoice is obtained to support the claim no VAT is payable.

10.10.3.7   Telephones

It is established practice that an employee, partner, sole proprietor or director uses a home telephone for business purposes. The VAT element that relates to business use can be reclaimed by the business, however, a reasonable apportionment needs to be made. Usually, the telephone invoice will not be in the name of the business but in the name of the employee or other third party but this is regarded as sufficient for input tax deduction.

In respect to mobile telephones, HMRC usually permit full deduction of any VAT where the phone is provided by the employer. HMRC again expect an apportionment for private use. Where, however, private calls are banned by the employer, all the VAT incurred can be claimed. If a charge is made to the employee for private calls, all the input tax incurred can be claimed but an output tax charge is due on the charge made to the employee.

10.10.3.8   Clothing

Clothing is a normal expense of the individual and the VAT incurred is not normally reclaimable. VAT can be claimed where a uniform, protective clothing, or clothing that is appropriate for a job is provided and there is no private use. It would be expected that a uniform would have the business's name or logo on it. The wig, gown and bands that a barrister is required to wear in Court are considered to be a uniform and the VAT recovered as input tax No VAT is deductible on clothing that can be worn on private occasions (such as suits for television presenters) (*Hill & Anor. t/a J.K. Hill & Co. v C & E Commrs* (1988) 3 BVC 297). In contrast, where an actor bought clothing (a dress suit) for a particular role and did not wear it other than when acting, the Tribunal held that the input tax was deductible when (*Pearce* [1992] BVC 1539). HMRC's internal guidance emphasises the non-deductibility of VAT incurred on clothing expenses and any claim for input tax is likely to be resisted.

10.10.3.9   Legal expenses

VAT on the legal expenses of employees, sole proprietors and partners is rarely deductible. Whilst the expense may have been incurred for a business purpose this is often regarded as insufficient to create a nexus between the expenditure and the business (*C & E Commrs v Rosner* [1994] BVC 31). In *Rosner*, the proprietor of an educational establishment had been convicted of a conspiracy to defraud. The proprietor believed there was a business purpose in defending himself as if he had been imprisoned the business would have closed. The Tribunal held that there was insufficient nexus between the expenditure and the business. It is extremely unlikely that any VAT will be deductible in cases of drink driving or other motoring offences no matter how important a person's driving licence is to the business.

The VAT on legal expenditure was held to be deductible in *P & O European Ferries (Dover) Ltd* [1992] BVC 1536. The company was allowed to claim input tax in respect of legal fees incurred in the defence of employees against criminal charges (following the Herald of Free Enterprise disaster at Zeebrugge). Input tax recovery was allowed as the company considered that a guilty verdict on any of their employees would lead to a similar verdict being found against the company. Thus, there was a clear nexus with the business. The terms of engagement with the solicitors had the effect of making the company the client and the recipient of the services even though the employee also received the benefit of the services. This case, however, was exceptional.

10.11 Sports and hobbies

Many people that have an influence in a business (directors, sole proprietors, partners, or their family members) either have an interest in sport, the arts or in other activities that HMRC may regard as being private rather than a business activity. HMRC believe, and may on occasion be justified, that the VAT on the costs of these activities are incurred for private purposes and is not deductible. For example, a businessman will not be able to claim a VAT deduction for a golf club subscription just because he obtains business contacts at the club. Also, a business will not be able to claim a deduction for a health club membership just because his doctor has told him to keep fit as this will enable him to continue running his business. In contrast, a business may pay for the subscription for all staff at a health club as it believes there is a nexus between a healthy and happy workforce and its business activity. In addition, a business that manufactures and sells saddlery and bridles may be able to justify a sponsorship of the local gymkhana as a business expense even if the owner's daughter attends the gymkhana; it will depend upon the circumstances.

HMRC have provided some guidance in this matter. The questions that HMRC expects its officers to ask are:

- Is the owner of the business actively partaking in the sport (or other activity)?
- Does a family member take part?
- Is there a connection between the sport and the business?
- Is there related advertising or promotional material?
- Does the business name appear on merchandise, equipment or the venue of the entity that receives the sponsorship?
- Can the business produce any evidence of research into the benefits obtained through the promotion or advertising?

For an input tax claim to be successfully made (when the business owner or family member takes part) it is necessary to establish a link between the business and the activity, ensure that there is substantial advertising and undertake research as to the benefits (and/or have a stall selling goods at the event).

A further opportunity would be to create a business out of the activity. For example, if the business was motor related and the owner was interested in motor sport, the owner could start a race team and raise sponsorship from the business. Whether this would be a successful strategy or not would depend upon the circumstances. If the motor racing activity was successful, obtained sponsorship from other sources, obtained sponsorship from the business owner which was seen as at a reasonable level and there were benefits obtained from the advertising/sponsorship, then there is the chance that the VAT incurred by the business would be deductible. If the costs incurred were seen as just subsidising the owner's hobby the VAT incurred would not be regarded as deductible.

10.12 Pension funds

A funded pension scheme is normally regarded as a separate entity from the business. It will normally be managed by trustees separate from the directors or owners of the main business. The management of a pension fund is deemed to be part of the employer's business and the employer can reclaim by the business. This is because there is a nexus between the business and the provision of pensions to the employees of the business. The business cannot, however, reclaim any VAT that relates to the investment activities of the fund. This would include costs such as brokerage charges, rents and service charges on properties owned, legal fees in connection with changes in pension fund arrangements, custodian fees, etc.

The pension fund may be required to register in its own right (if it has taxable activities, such as rents that are subject to the option to tax). If it does register for VAT the pension fund can reclaim the VAT incurred on expenses that relate to the taxable activities.

Motor Vehicles

11.1 Introduction

Ever since VAT was introduced into the UK in 1973, a restriction has applied to the recovery of VAT on the purchase of most business cars. This approach has been considered a simple way of taxing the private use of business cars (see *VAT Notice 700/64*).

Although the VAT implications of company cars are not overly complicated, mistakes are frequently made. VAT inspectors often find easy pickings from issues relating to cars and/or fuel, so assessments are common. For some businesses there will not be significant VAT at stake if there are only a few cars, but for organisations with large fleets of company cars, the potential of interest and penalties on large assessments presents a real risk.

Where reference is made to VAT recovery or partial recovery, this will be subject to any further restrictions to which an organisation may be subject, e.g. partial exemption and/or business/non-business apportionment.

In summary, the basic rules are as follows.

1. Businesses are able to recover the VAT payable on the purchase or lease of motor cars which: will be used **wholly** for business purposes (subject to strict conditions – see below); are to be primarily used as a mini-cab, for self-drive hire or for driving tuition; form part of the 'stock-in-trade' of a motor manufacturer or motor dealer; or are used under the motability scheme.

2. Businesses cannot recover any VAT on the purchase of other cars.

3. Businesses can recover 50 per cent of the VAT on leasing payments where the car is only used partly for business purposes.

4. VAT must be charged by a business on the full selling price of a motor car, where VAT has been fully recovered on its purchase.

5. An employee's contribution, through a salary sacrifice arrangement or where the employer was unable to recover the VAT on the purchase of the car, towards the use of a motor car is not subject to VAT (with some exceptions).

Since 1 August 1995, the issue of whether the VAT incurred on the purchase of a car is recoverable has been determined on the basis of whether the car is used or to be used exclusively for business purposes or not. VAT is recoverable in the specific circumstances of a person who deals in cars (purchase from manufacturer for resale or leasing), a driving school, private taxi firm or self-drive car hire firm. HMRC also accept that a pool car which is kept on the business premises overnight is also wholly business use, as are demonstrator and courtesy cars providing that they are not assigned to an individual salesperson who can take the car home, etc. From 1 December 1999, input tax may be recovered on demonstrator and courtesy cars even when they are assigned to an employee, but output tax must be accounted for on private use.

> ### ⚠ *Warning!*
>
> The hire-purchase of a car is treated in the same way as the outright purchase of a car for VAT purposes, as title to the asset passes to the customer by virtue of the terms of the agreement.
>
> In the case of a normal company car there will be few instances when the VAT is recoverable as it is likely to be available for private use, which includes home-to-office travel.

> ### *Planning point*
>
> It is necessary to show not only that the car is not intended to be used for other than business purposes, but that the car is effectively unavailable for use for private purposes.

Law: VAT (Cars) Order 1992 (SI 1992/3122); VAT (Input Tax) Order 1992 (SI 1992/3222)

11.2   What is a car for VAT purposes?

11.2.1   Definition

For VAT purposes 'a motor car' is any motor vehicle of a kind normally used on public roads which has three or more wheels and either:

- is constructed or adapted solely or mainly for the carriage of passengers; or
- has to the rear of the driver's seat roofed accommodation which is fitted with side windows or which is constructed or adapted for the fitting of side windows.

It does not include the following.

1.   Vehicles capable of accommodating only one person.

2.   Vehicles capable of carrying 12 or more seated persons (including the driver) and which meet the requirements of the Road Vehicles (Construction of Use) Regulations 1986 (SI 1986/1078), Sch. 6 (Road Safety Regulations). (Before 1 December 1999, the exclusion applied to all vehicles suitable for carrying

12 or more persons. The change removes any incentive to make unsafe conversions from vehicles that normally carry fewer than 12 persons.)

3. Vehicles of not less than three tonnes unladen weight (as defined in the Road Vehicles (Construction of Use) Regulations 1986 (SI 1986/1078)).

4. With effect from 1 December 1999, vehicles constructed to carry a 'payload' of one tonne or more. 'Payload' is the difference between a vehicle's kerb weight and its maximum gross weight, both terms as defined in Road Vehicles (Construction of Use) Regulations 1986. The effect of this is to exclude from the definition certain vehicles, such as many double-cab pickups, which would otherwise fall within the definition of a car, but are not predominantly private use vehicles. Care may need to be taken with vehicles that border the limit, as the addition of accessories, or the purchase of a higher trimmed model may reduce the payload; it is essential to check that the exact model purchased has a payload of one tonne or more.

5. Caravans, ambulances and prison vans.

6. Vehicles constructed for a special purpose other than the carriage of persons and having no other accommodation for carrying persons than such as is incidental to that purpose (e.g. ice-cream vans, mobile shops, hearses, bullion vans and breakdown and recovery vehicles).

Law: VAT (Cars) Order 1992 (SI 1992/3122), art. 2

11.2.2 Accommodation

In a case concerning provisions in the Car Tax Act 1983, similar to the current legislation in VAT (Cars) Order 1992 (SI 1992/3122), art. 2, it was held that in point 2 above 'accommodation' means only accommodation for passengers and if the space is unsuitable for this purpose, the vehicle is not within the definition even if there are side windows (*R v C & E Commrs, ex parte Nissan UK Ltd* [1988] BTC 8,003).

11.2.3 Vehicles regarded as motor cars

Many cases have been heard over the years regarding vehicles with special characteristics, where taxpayers have unsuccessfully sought to argue that the definition of 'car' does not apply. The following is a selection of such examples.

1. Imported versions of saloon cars even where they are 'normally used on public roads' which are outside the UK (*Withers of Winsford Ltd v C & E Commrs* [1988] 3 BVC 241).

2. Estate cars with the rear seat removed (*County Telecommunications Systems Ltd* [1993] BVC 1,578); used for business purposes by a builder (*Gardner* No. 588); and licensed as a goods vehicle and used by a garage and grocery store (*Howarth* No. 632).

3.   A Chevrolet K10 Blazer with removable hard top (*Yarlett* (1983) 2 BVC 208,021).

4.   A Daihatsu Fourtrak Estate (*Specialised Cars Ltd* [1994] BVC 1,445).

5.   A Ford Escort, regardless of the fact that the rear seats could be folded away (*Lucia* [1991] BVC 1,341).

6.   An Isuzu pick-up not suitable for carrying 12 or more people (*Kunz (t/a Wharfedale Finance Co)* [1996] BVC 4,158).

7.   A Land Rover converted into a 'motor car' by being fitted with a hard-top body with side windows and upholstered seats (*Chartcliff Ltd* No. 262).

8.   A Range Rover even though first registered and taxed as a heavy goods vehicle and not used for domestic purposes (*C & E Commrs v Jeynes (t/a Midland International (Hire) Caterers)* (1983) 1 BVC 586).

9.   A Suzuki jeep modified by the fitting of a rear seat. Although it had no rear windows, the Tribunal considered that it was adapted solely or mainly for the carriage of passengers (*Compton (t/a Stan Compton Electrical Engineers and Contractors)* [1993] BVC 1,586).

10.   A Toyota Previa with the middle and rear rows of seats removed for delivery purposes (*Gorringe Pine Ltd* [1996] BVC 4,279); and a Toyota Spacecruiser with the rear seats removed and a hanging rail for transporting clothes installed (*Gohil (t/a Gohil Fashions)* [1998] BVC 4,085).

11.2.4   Vehicles not regarded as motor cars

Of course, some vehicles have been shown not to be cars, as can be seen from the following examples.

1.   Ice-cream vans, mobile shops and offices, hearses (see *Davies* No. 831) and bullion vans (which are all regarded as falling under point 6 in **7.2.1**).

2.   Vehicles originally suitable for carrying 12 or more persons but with seating capacity reduced below 12 because of the provision of wheelchair space for disabled passengers (ESC 3.12, see *VAT Notice 48*). To benefit from this concession, the owner must make a written request to HMRC.

3.   Motor caravans provided they conform to criteria agreed with the SMMT. The agreement specifies that to be treated as a motor caravan the vehicle must incorporate: a permanently installed sink and cooking facilities; seating arrangements to enable diners to sit at the meal table; at least one bed with a minimum length of 1.82m; and a permanently installed fresh water tank with a minimum capacity of 10 litres (HMRC *Guidance Manual* V1-13, Ch. 2A, para. 11.5).

4.   A pick-up truck with an attached, removable canopy (*Batty* (1986) 2 BVC 208,115).

5. A Daihatsu Fourtrak Commercial Hard Top with two folding rear seats, as the load space was not significantly diminished when the seating was down (*AL Yeoman Ltd* (1990) 5 BVC 526). Note this is a similar (but slightly different) vehicle to the one detailed above that was regarded as a motor car.

6. A Ford van fitted with wooden benches but no side windows was held not be solely or mainly for the purpose of the carriage of passengers (*Chartcliff Ltd* (1976) VATTR 165).

7. A Peugeot van modified by adding a window on each side behind the driver's seat for safety reasons. This did not constitute accommodation for passengers (*John Beharrell Ltd* [1991] BVC 1,460).

⚠ Warning!

The definition of a car is highly inflexible and, as illustrated by the cases above, is difficult to escape.

11.3   Other Vehicles

11.3.1   Vans

VAT incurred on a van purchased for business purposes is fully recoverable. If the van is also to be used for private purposes then an apportionment should be used, not only for the purchase price but also for ongoing maintenance, repair and petrol costs. Alternatively, the VAT may be recovered in full on the purchase and output tax accounted for on the private use in each VAT quarter as it occurs. Private use is calculated on the cost to the business of making the van available, including depreciation for the period in question. The costs applicable should be added together for the period and multiplied by the proportion of private use to total use. Note that it is the days used which form the numerator in the proportion, not number of days in the period.

Example 11.1

Van purchased for £16,000 plus VAT of £3,200.

Running expenses for the quarter to 31 March 2003: £400 plus VAT of £80.

	£
Depreciation of van: £16,000 × 25% × 90/365 =	986.30
Plus running costs	400.00
Total	1,386.30

Number of days used privately: 4 (2 weekends)

Number of days used: 68 (not used for 11 weekends)

$4/68 \times £1,386.30 = £81.54$.

$£81.54 \times 20$ per cent $= £16.31$ VAT to account for.

11.3.2 Motorcycles

Motorcycles are treated in the same way as vans for VAT purposes – there is no blocking order as for cars, but apportionment must be made for private use.

> ### ⚠ *Warning!*
>
> For businesses other than, say, motorcycle couriers, HMRC will be very sceptical of any claim that use of a motorcycle is for 100 per cent business purposes. Where this is the case, adequate records should be retained to demonstrate the fact.

11.3.3 Commercial vehicles

Scale charges do not apply to commercial vehicles such as vans or trucks – note that most Land Rover-type four-wheel-drive vehicles are treated as cars for VAT purposes. If fuel is used for private purposes output tax must be charged at or above cost price. Alternatively, the input tax may be apportioned on a fair and reasonable basis. This should be agreed with the VAT office in writing.

> ### ⚠ *Warning!*
>
> VAT recovery is allowed on any vehicle constructed to carry a payload of one tonne or more. There are a number of pick-up trucks on the market which fall into this category, including some with twin cabs. Purchasers should beware – it is the payload that matters, the difference between the kerb weight and the maximum gross weight. This means that if certain accessories such as hard covers or toolboxes are fitted, which reduce the payload to under one tonne, the vehicle does not meet the requirements.

11.4 Input tax recovery

11.4.1 Is the car available for private use?

The entitlement to input tax recovery depends upon the use to which the car will be put. Input tax can be recovered in full on cars that are purchased, acquired or imported, or cars that are leased or hired, if they are to be for exclusive business use.

'Exclusively for a business purpose' means that it is not intended to make the car available for the private use of anyone, except where it is done in the course of a commercial leasing or rental operation.

This is a very restrictive test and the main beneficiaries are leasing companies because there is self-evidently no private use of the cars purchased by them, although there may be private use in the hands of their customers.

Just how restrictive was illustrated by the case of *C & E Commrs v Upton (t/a Fagomatic)* [2002] BVC 451, finally decided in the Court of Appeal. The Court distilled the test into a single question: 'have steps been taken to prevent private use?' If not, the car must be seen as available for private use, even if, as a matter of fact it is never used privately. If this is the case, then input tax deduction is not available.

Mr Upton, who used his car (a Lamborghini) in his business of cigarette sales from vending machines, had satisfied the tribunal that he did not use the car for private purposes at all. Having lost on HMRC's appeal to the High Court, Mr Upton appealed its judgment, only to find the Court of Appeal reinforcing the view which HMRC have maintained throughout the existence of the current legislative provisions. That is to say, whether or not private use actually takes place is irrelevant. What matters is the intention to make the car available for private use and private use can be presumed in the absence of evidence that something has been done actively to prevent it.

HMRC accept that genuine pool cars satisfy this test, provided that they are:

- normally kept at the principal place of business;
- not allocated to an individual; and
- not kept at an employee's home.

Research and development cars used by car manufacturers and other companies engaged in car research and development, e.g. component manufacturers, will also qualify for input tax recovery.

⚠ *Warning!*

A car cannot be treated as used for wholly business purposes simply because a charge is made to an employee for its use. It can only be treated as business use if the car is made available on the same basis as an arm's length commercial leasing. This is not the case where a charge is made for private motoring based upon the proportion of private use.

Planning point

To claim input tax for exclusive business use, there must be a genuine and demonstrable intention not to make the car available for private use at the time the VAT is incurred. Indicators would include the staff manual prohibiting private use, restrictions on where the car is to be kept at night and insuring (or attempting to insure) the car for business use only.

In the case of *Squibb & Davies (Demolition) Ltd* [2003] BVC 4,041, the cars in question were a Range Rover, which had effectively been kitted out as a mobile office, and a Jaguar used to pick up clients from the station, etc. Other quality cars were owned by each of the directors for private use (Mercedes sports, etc.). It was a condition of the directors' or managers' employment that they were not allowed to use the cars for private purposes, and the cars were kept at company premises at night. The cars had to be logged in and out when in use, the permission of the managing director to use the cars was required and the keys were kept secure in a box and logged in and out. Schedules were kept of the mileage of the Range Rover and Jaguar with details and dates of journeys undertaken. The cars were insured under a fleet policy, which included insurance for the company's commercial vehicles including a low-level loader and dumper trucks, but did also include use for social, domestic and pleasure purposes. The tribunal allowed VAT recovery as mileage logs were kept for cars showing they were only used for business purposes, and the keys and cars themselves had to be booked out by employees (directors). The employees' contracts of employment were also amended so that the employee would be in breach of them if they used the cars for other than business purposes. The directors were also able to show that they had their own cars for private purposes.

To this end, HMRC and the tribunals have looked at the issue of insurance. If the insurance includes private use, or the business has not at least attempted to have the insurance restricted to business use (some insurance companies are apparently unable to provide such a restriction), then the VAT on its purchase will be irrecoverable. This would even prevent, for example, a salesperson who is constantly on the road, doing 30,000 plus miles per year, from recovering VAT on the purchase price.

It can also help a claim for recovery of VAT on the purchase if there is alternative means of private transport available: if one car is used for business only and another is available for any private motoring to be done.

HMRC have provided a list of questions in their internal guidance manuals which their officers will be asking to determine if a car is available for private use. These are listed below.

(1) Who has access to the car and when?

(2) What is to prevent the person(s) who has/have access to the car using it to make private journeys during or outside normal working hours?

(3) For what types of business journey is the car used? What is the likelihood that the car will never be used for mixed business and private journeys?

(4) What vehicles are used to perform private journeys and what is the availability of these vehicles? What happens when these vehicles are unavailable – being serviced, used by others, etc?

(5) Does the user keep a log of journeys?

(6) Is the car insured for private use?

Within HMRC's internal guidance, officers are reminded that the test is one of availability for private use rather than actual private use. The HMRC guidelines go on to state:

'There is no one single "insulator" although the insurance cover has been held in many appeals to be important. A car insured for business use only is not easily legally driven on private journeys and this may help it meet the test. Alternatively a car that is insured for both business and domestic use has no legal impediment to being driven on private journeys and tribunals tend to see this as indicative that it is available for such use.

Insurance cover cannot be used as the sole indicator of availability. Other indicators might be:

- the location the car and its keys are kept;
- whether the car is taxed for use on public roads;
- who is insured to drive the car;
- if it replaces a previous car, what model it replaces;
- if it has been adapted in any way.

Before issuing an assessment on availability officers should ensure they have obtained a full picture of the use the car will be put to and considered the points referred to above. If the trader claims they undertake private journeys in another vehicle you should obtain details of the model and age.'

11.4.2   Case law – successful cases

In *C & E Commrs v Elm Milk Ltd* [2006] BVC 296 the Court of Appeal held that input tax was deductible on the purchase of a car by a company with a single director where there was a board resolution made to prohibit anyone from using the car for private journeys. The car was to be kept at the company's premises, which were adjacent to the director's home and the keys were to be kept in the office.

In *Lowe* [1998] BVC 4,005 the tribunal accepted that a large, four-wheel drive vehicle had been purchased exclusively for business use as the trader already owned two other vehicles, including a saloon car used for private journeys.

Similarly in *Thompson* [1997] BVC 4,077 the appellant successfully contended that four cars which he purchased were used exclusively for business purposes as he had insured them for business use only so that they would be uninsured if used for any private purpose.

11.4.3   Case law – unsuccessful cases

In *Martinez* [2000] BVC 4,038 the tribunal rejected a claim by a second-hand car dealer that a four-wheel drive Nissan, used to pull a trailer for collection and delivery of vehicles, had been purchased exclusively for business purposes, even though the appellant maintained that the trailer was kept permanently attached to the car. As the appellant's only other private car was not purchased until two months after the Nissan, the tribunal concluded that, at the time of acquiring the Nissan, the appellant could not have been sure of having another car available at all times for private use (despite being able to use any of the business stock of cars) and therefore had probably not intended the Nissan to have exclusive business use.

In *R & C Commrs v Shaw* [2007] BVC 854 a farmer and contractor purchased a car with the intention of using it only for business purposes, taking insurance which included social, domestic and leisure use only because this was the cheaper option (and incidentally mirrored the terms of the insurance policy for the combine harvester). Although there was no indication that it had ever been used for any private purpose, and the tribunal had allowed his appeal, the High Court found that he had not taken steps sufficient to put the vehicle beyond the possibility of private use and as a consequence overturned the tribunal's decision, disallowing his input tax claim.

Delivery charges

Following the House of Lords' decision in *C & E Commrs v British Telecommunications plc* [1999] BVC 306, July 1999, Customs issued *Business Brief 17/99* (5 August 1999) confirming that delivery charges form part of the cost of a single supply of a delivered car and the VAT incurred on them was therefore blocked together with the VAT on the purchase price.

11.4.4   Sole proprietors, partners, directors and employees who work from home

The HMRC guidance states:

> 'It is unlikely that a car kept at a trader's home premises will not be available for private use regardless of how many other cars the trader possesses.
>
> You should ensure you obtain and record comprehensive details of use. In dealing with appeals the following information has been found to be useful:
>
> * who has access to the car and when;
> * what is to prevent the person(s) who have access to the car using it to make private journeys during or outside normal working hours;
> * for what types of business journey is the car used. What is the likelihood that the car will never be used for mixed business and private journeys;
> * what vehicles are used to perform private journeys and what is the availability of these vehicles. What happens when these vehicles are unavailable – being serviced, used by others, etc.;
> * does the user keep a log of journeys;
> * is the car insured for private use.'

11.4.5 Pool cars

The HMRC guidance states:

'Pool cars that are kept at a trader's business premises, used only for business journeys and never taken home overnight by employees will meet the test. Incidental private use that may occur on such business journeys, e.g. lunch stops can be ignored.

Home to office journeys are always considered to be private journeys and consequently cars that are expected to be taken home by employees are likely to remain blocked. This is true even if an employee takes the car home overnight en route to a business appointment the next day.'

This is particularly harsh where an employee has to make an early start for business purposes.

11.4.6 Emergency services marked cars

Marked emergency service cars are by their nature not suitable for private use. HMRC have therefore agreed with the Home Office that if a marked emergency service (police, fire or ambulance service) car is taken home and kept overnight by an officer necessarily in order to carry out official duties the next day, that particular use will be treated as part of the relevant authority's non-business activity and will not affect its entitlement to recovery of tax under VATA 1994, s. 33.

11.5 VAT on purchase of company car

11.5.1 The general position

Apart from the special cases listed below, VAT cannot generally be reclaimed on the purchase (including acquisition or importation) of a motor car. Purchase means not only outright purchase but also any purchase under a hire-purchase agreement or any other agreement whereby property in the car eventually passes, e.g. a lease-purchase agreement.

VAT incurred on supplies integral to the supply of a motor car is only deductible where input tax on the motor car itself is deductible. This includes manufacturer's warranty (although VAT on the purchase of an extension of the period of warranty is deductible). It has been held to include manufacturer's delivery charges passed on by dealers to customers. See *Wimpey Construction UK Ltd* No. 808 and *C & E Commrs v British Telecommunications plc* [1999] BVC 306.

11.5.2 Special cases

VAT may be reclaimed on the purchase, acquisition or importation of a motor car in the following circumstances.

Exclusive business use

The motor car is a 'qualifying' motor car supplied to, acquired or imported by a taxable person who intends to use the motor car exclusively for business purposes. This condition is not satisfied if the taxable person intends to:

- let it on hire to any person either for no consideration or consideration less than would be payable in an arm's-length commercial transaction; or
- make it available, otherwise than by letting on hire, to any person (including where the taxable person is an individual him- or herself or where the taxable person is a partnership/partner) for private use (whether or not for a consideration).

Note that a 'qualifying car' is a car that has not been subject to the full input tax block.

> ⚠ ***Warning!***
>
> As illustrated by the Court of Appeal in *Upton* (see **11.4.1**), this is a very difficult test to fulfil.

Mini-cabs, self-drive hire, driving instruction

The motor car is a 'qualifying' motor car supplied to, acquired or imported by, a taxable person who intends to use the motor car primarily:

- to provide it on hire with the services of a driver for the purposes of carrying passengers;
- to provide it for 'self-drive hire'; or
- as a vehicle in which instruction in driving of a motor car is to be given by him.

Motor dealers and manufacturers

With effect from 1 December 1999, the motor car forms part of the 'stock-in-trade' of a 'motor manufacturer' or a 'motor dealer'.

'Stock-in-trade' means a new or second-hand motor car (other than a second-hand motor car which is not a qualifying motor car as defined below) which is:

- produced by a motor manufacturer for the purpose of resale and intended to be sold by that manufacturer within 12 months of its production; or
- supplied to, acquired from another EU country by, or imported by, a motor dealer for the purpose of resale and intended to be sold by that motor dealer within 12 months of their supply, acquisition or importation.

'Stock-in-trade' cars do not cease to be stock-in-trade where they are temporarily put to a use in the motor manufacturer's or motor dealer's business which involves making them available for private use, but output tax must be accounted for on the cost of providing the car for private use (VATA 1994, Sch. 4, para. 5(4)). Alternatively, dealers may use the optional simplified method that has been agreed by HMRC and the Retail Motor Industry Federation.

A set amount of VAT must be accounted for in each period for each individual who has used a stock-in-trade car for private journeys in that period. This should be done by identifying the list price of the car that the individual has typically used from the table below and including the relevant amount of VAT as output tax in the VAT return.

Table 11.1

List price band range £	Average price £	VAT due on annual return £	VAT due on quarterly return £	VAT due on monthly return £
0–9,000	7,500	80.00	20.00	6.67
9,001–12,000	10,300	106.00	26.50	8.83
12,001–16,000	14,200	142.00	35.50	11.83
16,001–21,000	18,650	184.00	46.00	15.33
21,001–26,000	23,400	236.00	59.00	19.67
Over 26,000	Actual or by local agreement with HMRC			

Note that this table shows VAT at the 17.5 per cent rate. This will need to be increased from 4 January 2011.

As no new table has been produced by HMRC the table below has extrapolated the increase in VAT using the Retail Motor Industry's agreed values for cars and these amounts should be used from 4 January 2011.

Table 11.2

List price band range £	Average price £	VAT due on annual return £	VAT due on quarterly return £	VAT due on monthly return £
0–9,000	7,500	91.43	22.86	7.62
9,001–12,000	10,300	121.14	30.29	10.09
12,001–16,000	14,200	162.29	40.57	13.52
16,001–21,000	18,650	210.29	52.57	17.52
21,001–26,000	23,400	269.71	67.43	22.48

List price band range £	Average price £	VAT due on annual return £	VAT due on quarterly return £	VAT due on monthly return £
Over 26,000	Actual or by local agreement with HMRC			

'Motor manufacturer' means a person whose business consists (in whole or part) of producing motor cars including producing a motor car by conversion of a vehicle (whether a motor car or not).

'Motor dealer' means a person whose business consists (in whole or in part) of obtaining supplies of, acquiring from another EU country or importing, new or second-hand motor cars for resale with a view to making an overall profit on the sale of them (whether or not a profit is made on each sale).

Motability scheme

The motor car is unused and is supplied to a taxable person whose only taxable supplies are predominantly concerned with the letting of motor cars on hire to another taxable person whose business consists predominantly of making supplies within VATA 1994, Sch. 8, Grp. 12, item 14.

11.5.3 'Qualifying' motor car

A 'qualifying' car is a car which has not been subject to the full input tax block. Any business in the chain of supply must have been entitled to full VAT recovery on the purchase, acquisition or import. A car ceases to be 'qualifying' once the full input tax block has been applied at any stage in the chain.

11.5.4 Change of use

If circumstances change and a qualifying car against which input tax recovery is made is subsequently made available for private use, output tax must be accounted for at the time of change on the full current value of the car. HMRC have indicated that they will look closely at all cases of purported change of intention and, in the case of incorrect claims, will charge interest and penalties where appropriate. This indicates that HMRC will question why the input tax was claimed in the first place and whether there was truly a change of use/availability.

The self-supply provisions in the VAT (Cars) Order 1992 (SI 1992/3122) ensure that a business which obtains input tax relief on a car, because the car is intended for a use that qualifies for relief (a 'qualifying use'), does not get an unfair advantage if it subsequently changes its intention and puts the car to a use which would not qualify for input tax relief (a 'non-qualifying use') if VAT were incurred at that time. If such a change occurs, the business must account for output VAT on a deemed self-supply of the car.

What triggers the self-supply is the change from a qualifying use to a non-qualifying use. The time of the self-supply is the date that the change of use takes place. For example, if a hire company removes a car from its hire fleet to use as an ordinary company car, a self-supply will take place at the time of the change of use.

> ### *Planning point*
>
> A self-supply does not take place if the business changes a car from one qualifying use to another qualifying use. For example, if a motor dealer removes a car from stock-in-trade to use primarily as a self-drive hire car, a self-supply would not take place because the second use is itself a qualifying use.

Remember that there are special rules for motor manufacturers and dealers so, for stock-in-trade cars a self-supply charge is not triggered simply because the dealer or manufacturer has not sold the car within 12 months from having obtained it. The car ceases to be stock-in-trade only if at any time the dealer ceases to have the intention to sell the car within the following 12 months. For example, if a dealer buys a car on 31 March 2002 and it is still on hand on 1 April 2003, it was and remains stock-in-trade provided that on 31 March 2002 and at all times subsequently, up to and including 1 April 2003, the dealer's intention was to sell it within the next 12 months (i.e. on 1 April 2003 he intends to sell the car by 31 March 2004).

> ### ⚠ *Warning!*
>
> HMRC instruct their officers to challenge situations where a manufacturer or dealer has kept 'stock-in-trade' cars on hand for more than 12 months after obtaining them, by seeking to confirm whether it really was their intention to sell those cars within the original time limit.

> ### *Planning point*
>
> Where a car is purchased and there is initial private use thus blocking input VAT recovery, and subsequently the car is used wholly for business purposes, there is no provision for recovering any of the VAT originally incurred on the purchase. Wherever possible, it is unwise to allow this situation to arise.

11.5.5 Charges for private use

Where the purchase of a car has been subject to the input tax block, any charges made to an employee for private use are not subject to VAT. The charges are treated as neither a supply of goods or services.

The input tax block is a simple way of taxing private use and there is no need for further adjustments to be made.

If a car benefited from full input tax recovery then there is likely to have been a change of use if charges are now being made to an employee for private use. The change of use will trigger a self-supply and thereafter the charges for private use will not be subject to VAT.

11.5.6 Private use of a car where VAT has been recovered

If VAT is recovered on the purchase of a car and it is subsequently used for other than business purposes, then a self-supply must be accounted for. The value to be used for the self-supply is the cost of an identical vehicle or, if this is not available, the cost of a similar vehicle. In practice, this often means that the VAT recovered initially is paid back to HMRC.

The European Court has ruled that even where VAT has not been recovered on the purchase price but there has since been recovery of some VAT on repairs and maintenance, etc, the self-supply applies to the extent that this VAT has been recovered at the value of the goods at the time of allocation.

> **Planning point**
>
> In cases where the private use is more than *de minimis*, the business should account for the private use on the basis of the principals outlined at **10.4**.

11.5.7 In-house leasing

One method that has been explored by a number of businesses is to purchase a car in an in-house leasing company. The car is purchased in a separate entity which reclaims all the VAT incurred on the purchase of the car. The vehicle is then provided on a lease to the employees of the company. VAT is charged on the lease and the lessor can claim a 50 per cent deduction for the lease charge (see **11.6** below). It is essential that the value of the supply will be the 'full cost' arm's length value of providing the service. This does not necessarily mean that the price has to be the same as a commercial leasing company, but any reduction has to be justified (for example, because it is known that the vehicle will not be treated harshly, etc.).

11.6   VAT on contract hire/leasing

11.6.1   The general position

Hire-purchase and lease-purchase arrangements are treated in the same way as purchases. Since ownership of the asset passes to the hirer, such agreements constitute supplies of goods, not services.

If a motor car is leased or hired, only 50 per cent of the input VAT on the rental charges is recoverable as input tax, except in the following circumstances when 100 per cent relief is available.

1. The motor car is a 'qualifying' motor car let on hire to a taxable person who intends to use the motor car exclusively for business purposes. This condition is not satisfied if the taxable person intends to:

    - let it on hire to any person either for no consideration or consideration less than would be payable in an arm's-length commercial transaction; or
    - make it available, otherwise than by letting on hire, to any person (including, where the taxable person is an individual or where the taxable person is a partnership/a partner) for private use (whether or not for a consideration).

2. The motor car is a 'qualifying' motor car let on hire to a taxable person who intends to use the motor car primarily:

    - to provide it on hire with the services of a driver for the purposes of carrying passengers;
    - to provide it for 'self-drive hire'; or
    - as a vehicle in which instruction in driving of a motor car is to be given by him.

3. The motor car is unused and is let on hire to a taxable person whose business consists predominantly of making supplies within VATA 1994, Sch. 8, Grp. 12, item 14 by a taxable person whose only taxable supplies are concerned with the letting on hire of motor cars to such taxable persons (motability scheme).

11.6.2   Challenge to legality of 50 per cent VAT recovery block

The validity of a fixed block on input tax recovery was considered by the European Court in the case of *Finanzamt Sulingen v Sudholz* (Case C-17/01) [2006] BVC 692. The German authorities were authorised to limit to 50 per cent the right to deduct the VAT incurred on the purchase of a motor car, regardless of the particular degree of business use in any given case. This is of course almost identical to the UK treatment of leased cars.

The court held that such a fixed deduction was valid in cases of items where extensive private use is likely to be involved, upholding the German treatment and, by implication, the UK rules.

The case is actually more significant for the Advocate General's Opinion, which was not followed by the court, but which had suggested that a fixed deduction was contrary to the fundamental principles of the tax. In the UK, this gave rise to a flood of protective claims from businesses whose cars had been used more than 50 per cent for business purposes, often encouraged by opportunistic advisers. Such claims of course came to nothing.

11.6.3   Leasing invoices

Invoices issued by leasing companies must clearly identify whether or not the car is a qualifying car and, if it is, the amount of VAT that is potentially subject to the 50 per cent input tax restriction. This requirement does not apply to self-drive hire cars.

11.6.4   Self-drive hire

If the car is hired purely to replace an ordinary company car that is off the road, the 50 per cent block will apply from the first day of hire. Hiring of ten days or more will be subject to the 50 per cent restriction, unless it can be shown that the car was used for business purposes only.

> **Planning point**
> HMRC accept more readily a claim that a car is specifically for business use if it is hired for up to ten days only.

Other guidance: VAT Notice 700/64, para. 4.4

11.6.5   What does the 50 per cent restriction apply to?

There are frequently two distinct elements of the rental: basic rental for the provision of the car (including depreciation, funding cost, Vehicle Excise Duty (VED) and a proportion of overheads/profit) and an additional charge (covering repairs, maintenance and roadside assistance and a proportion of overheads/profit).

> **Planning point**
> Provided the additional charges are separately described in the contract-hire agreement and periodic invoices, VAT on the basic rental is subject to the 50 per cent restriction but VAT on the maintenance charge is recoverable in full, subject to the normal rules.

VAT on an excess mileage charge is subject to these same provisions if it is similarly separated into two distinct elements on a basis identical to the split of the rental. If it is expressed as a single sum, the VAT will be subject to the 50 per cent block.

For full details, see the agreement between the British Vehicle Rental and Leasing Association and HMRC reproduced in *VAT Notice 700/57*.

11.6.6   Charges for private use

Where the car has been subject to the 50 per cent input tax restriction, any charges made to an employee for private use are not subject to VAT. The charges are treated as neither a supply of goods nor a supply of services.

> **Planning point**
> The 50 per cent input tax restriction is a simple way of taxing private use and there is no need for further adjustments to be made.

In-house leasing

It is possible to set up an in-house leasing company so that VAT on the purchase of a car is recoverable. The charge for leasing the vehicle to the main trading company must be at open market value and 50 per cent of this VAT will not be recoverable by the trading company. It is advisable to obtain agreement from HMRC in writing that they are satisfied with the charge being made in order to save later arguments. The cars must not be used privately by the in-house leasing company or this will invalidate the claim for recovery of input tax on them.

> **⚠ Warning!**
> Note that the effect of other taxes should be considered prior to putting these arrangements into effect.

11.6.7   Health authorities and government departments

Health authorities and government departments that lease cars are not subject to the 50 per cent restriction on input tax (VATA 1994, s. 41(3)). They are able to recover VAT on the hire of vehicles, including repair and maintenance, for their non-business activities. Consequently, most charges made to an employee for the private use of such a car will be subject to VAT. Usually, the 50 per cent input tax restriction acts as a simple way to tax private use, so some other way of taxing private use is needed where full input tax recovery is allowed.

Charges made to an employee for private use are subject to VAT unless the employee is given the choice between a particular wage/rate of pay or a lower rate and the right to private use of a car. The salary sacrifice element is not subject to VAT.

11.6.8   Rebates of rental

Where a lessor rebates monthly rental payments to the lessee (a common occurrence on termination), and that lessee suffered the 50 per cent input tax restriction on the rental charges, he only needs to adjust 50 per cent of the VAT on the credit note.

> ⚠ **Warning!**
> This is easier to miss than an invoice and failure to account correctly for VAT on such rebates will cost the business money. Purchase ledger staff should be adequately trained to recognise such situations.

11.6.9   Early lease termination

Where a lease is terminated early, the leasing company may treat both the termination payment and any rental rebate as taxable or treat both as outside the scope. If it chooses to tax, it will normally set off the termination payment against any rebate and issue a VAT invoice for the difference:

- where the termination payment exceeds the rebate, any VAT charged by the leasing company is not subject to the 50 per cent restriction; and
- where any rebate exceeds the termination payment, the leasing company must issue a credit note. A lessee who incurred a 50 per cent input tax restriction on the rental charges need only adjust for 50 per cent of the VAT on the credit note.

11.6.10   Interaction with other apportionments

Where the 50 per cent input tax restriction applies and there are both business and non-business activities and/or exempt supplies, the order for carrying out the various apportionments is:

1.   VAT incurred between business and non-business activities;

2.   50 per cent input tax restriction on the VAT amount which relates to business activities; and

3.   any necessary partial exemption calculation.

11.6.11 Fleet leasing bonuses

Receipt of such a bonus reduces the VAT recoverable by the customer (if any) on the lease payments. For example, where 50 per cent of the VAT incurred on lease payments can be recovered, VAT due on the bonus payment is:

$7/47 \times 50$ per cent gross bonus payment,

and from 4 January 2011:

$1/6 \times 50$ per cent gross bonus payment.

11.7   VAT on disposal of company cars

11.7.1   Input tax was wholly excluded from credit on the purchase of the car

With effect from 1 March 2000, following the decision in *EC Commission v Italy* (Case C-45/95) [1997] BVC 536, the onward sale of a motor car on which input tax was blocked on purchase is an exempt supply under VATA 1994, Sch. 9, Grp. 14, regardless of whether it is sold at a profit or loss. Any input tax incurred in making the sale (e.g. valeting fees) is exempt input tax and not recoverable, subject to the partial exemption *de minimis* limits.

11.7.2   Input tax recovered in full

Where input tax was deductible on the purchase of the car, output tax must be accounted for on the full selling price. A VAT invoice must be issued to a VAT-registered buyer who requests one. Such a car cannot be sold under the margin scheme for second-hand goods.

> ⚠ *Warning!*
>
> It follows from this that a second-hand car dealer may need two sets of records for second-hand cars, one containing those eligible for the margin scheme and one containing those on which VAT has been charged to him on a VAT invoice. Although this may be onerous, a cash flow advantage does arise in connection with the latter category as input tax is deductible on purchase and second-hand cars are always valued by reference to the gross price even when sold on a tax invoice.

11.7.3 A proportion of input tax recovered

A business will only dispose of a car that was subject to partial input tax recovery if it is one where there has been an apportionment between business and non-business use or a partial exemption restriction. The standard 50 per cent restriction on input tax recovery because of availability for private use is not a consideration, as this is only for leased cars.

Where there has been an apportionment of the input tax on the purchase of a dual-use asset because of non-business use then, on the subsequent sale, VAT will only be due on the business proportion (*Finanzamt Uelzen v Armbrecht* (Case C-291/92) [1996] BVC 50).

11.7.4 Second-hand margin scheme

When a business sells a car on which no VAT was charged when it was bought (e.g. acquired from a private individual or from a dealer who sold it under the second-hand margin scheme), VAT does not have to be accounted for on the full selling price. VAT only needs to be accounted for on the profit margin (if any), using the second-hand margin scheme.

VAT Notice 718, s. 19, gives details on the operation of the second-hand margin scheme and the conditions that must be satisfied.

11.8 Other expenses

11.8.1 Repairs and maintenance

Other expenditure in relation to cars will be recoverable if it is for the purpose of the business, subject to the normal rules.

> **Planning point**
> In this context, the 'normal rules' do not require apportionment for private use, because this is accounted for through the prohibition of input tax on the purchase of motor cars.

If a vehicle is used for business purposes, VAT on repairs and maintenance on cars, vans, etc. is deductible in full by companies even where there is substantial private use (HMRC Internal Guidance V1-13, Chapter 2A, s. 11.60). This applies even if the vehicle is used for private motoring and even if no VAT is reclaimed on any road fuel in order to avoid use of the scale charges.

VAT on repairs, etc. to a privately owned car that is covered by a mileage allowance or relating to a vehicle used by a sole trader or partner for private motoring only cannot be treated as input tax.

Planning point

If an employer agrees to pay the full cost of repair and maintenance of employees' private cars, the VAT incurred may be treated as input tax provided the costs are recorded in the business records and the employee is not paid a mileage allowance (See HMRC *Guidance Manual* V1–13, para. 20.1).

11.8.2   Accessories

If a car is subject to the input tax block, any VAT on accessories supplied with the car is also blocked. VAT on accessories subsequently purchased can only be treated as input tax if:

- the vehicle is owned by the business or used in the business but not owned by it (e.g. an employee's or director's own car); and
- the accessory has a business use.

HMRC may seek to argue that accessories such as a CD player do not have a business use but, if it is to be used during business journeys, the input tax can be, arguably, recoverable. If at a later date an accessory is fitted for business purposes the VAT may be recovered in full. HMRC will look closely at the business use of the item in question. Items such as sun-roofs, stereo systems – for the general comfort of a driver – or alarm systems will generally be accepted as recoverable, but an item such as a child seat would be unlikely to satisfy the business use test unless the business had to do with care of children (*Broadhead Peel & Co* (1984) 2 BVC 208,049).

11.8.3   Insurance

Car insurance, whether a single or block policy, is not subject to VAT. It is exempt from VAT. However, it is subject to insurance premium tax (IPT) which is a real cost to the policyholder. Amounts charged as IPT are not recoverable as input tax.

11.8.4   MOTs

An MOT purchased from an authorised test centre is not subject to VAT. It is outside the scope of VAT if it does not exceed the statutory maximum fee. Similarly, if an unapproved garage arranges to have a car MOT'd and charges on the exact amount paid to the authorised garage, this is not subject to VAT. It will be treated as a disbursement.

Unnecessary extra costs, including VAT, are incurred where an unapproved garage charges more to the customer than was charged by the authorised test centre. In this case, there will be VAT on the amount charged over and above the fee charged by the MOT centre, and if the onward charge for the MOT fee does not comply with the conditions for being treated as a disbursement, the unapproved garage will have to account for VAT on the full amount.

> ⚠ **Warning!**
>
> HMRC have shown a very close interest in this issue in the recent past, carrying out a nationwide trawl of motor vehicle repairers with specific reference as to how they treat MOTs. Any such business should therefore ensure that the charge to the customer for the MOT is exactly the amount incurred by the garage, with any profit being shown separately as an arrangement fee (standard-rated).

11.8.5   Car fuel

Any business car that has had full input tax recovery either on its purchase or lease will be for business purposes only and will not be made available for private use. The VAT incurred on fuel purchased for that car will be recoverable in full.

Where a car is available for private use and the business allows fuel to be used for private journeys, then there will need to be some adjustment or restriction on input tax recovery. It is not enough for the employees to purchase fuel themselves for the private journeys (for example, one tankful in four) but, instead, detailed records have to be kept.

Remember that a journey from home to normal workplace is a private journey, whether for an employee or a director.

The most frequently used method to account for the VAT on private use of fuel is to use the motoring expenses scale charges. This is fairly straightforward and there is no need for detailed records to be kept but it may not be the most cost-effective method.

11.8.6   Scale charges

Output tax must be accounted for using the scale charges set out below if a business:

- provides road fuel for private motoring free or for a charge which is less than it paid; or
- allows people to make private journeys using road fuel paid for by the business.

The output tax must be included in the total output figure, and entered in box 1 of the VAT return, and the net value of the scale charge must be included in the figure for box 6.

The fuel scale charges below are the new rates that apply from the start of the VAT period that begins on or after 1 May 2012 for a three month period.

Table 11.3: CO_2 bands – three month periods

CO_2 band scale charge 3 month	VAT fuel period, £ 3 month	VAT on charge, £ 3 month	VAT exclusive charge, £
120 or less	166.00	27.67	138.33
125	250.00	41.67	208.33
130	266.00	44.33	221.67
135	283.00	47.17	235.83
140	300.00	50.00	250.00
145	316.00	52.67	263.33
150	333.00	55.50	277.50
155	350.00	58.33	291.67
160	366.00	61.00	305.00
165	383.00	63.83	319.17
170	400.00	66.67	333.33
175	416.00	69.33	346.67
180	433.00	72.17	360.83
185	450.00	75.00	375.00
190	467.00	77.83	389.17
195	483.00	80.50	402.50
200	500.00	83.33	416.67
205	517.00	86.17	430.83
210	533.00	88.83	444.17
215	550.00	91.67	458.33
220	567.00	94.50	472.50
225 or more	583.00	97.17	485.83

Table 11.4: CO_2 bands – one month periods

120 or less	55.00	9.17	45.83
125	83.00	13.83	69.17
130	88.00	14.67	73.33
135	94.00	15.67	78.33
140	100.00	16.67	83.33
145	105.00	17.50	87.50
150	111.00	18.50	92.50
155	116.00	19.33	96.67
160	122.00	20.33	101.67
165	127.00	21.17	105.83

CO₂ band scale charge 3 month	VAT fuel period, £ 3 month	VAT on charge, £ 3 month	VAT exclusive charge, £
170	133.00	22.17	110.83
175	138.00	23.00	115.00
180	144.00	24.00	120.00
185	150.00	25.00	125.00
190	155.00	25.83	129.17
195	161.00	26.83	134.17
200	166.00	27.67	138.33
205	172.00	28.67	143.33
210	177.00	29.50	147.50
215	183.00	30.50	152.50
220	189.00	31.50	157.50
225 or more	194.00	32.33	161.67

Table 11.5: CO₂ bands – 12 month periods

120 or less	665.00	110.83	554.17
125	1,000.00	166.67	833.33
130	1,065.00	177.50	887.50
135	1,135.00	189.17	945.83
140	1,200.00	200.00	1,000.00
145	1,270.00	211.67	1,058.33
150	1,353.00	222.50	1,112.50
155	1,400.00	233.33	1,166.67
160	1,470.00	245.00	1,225.00
165	1,535.00	255.83	1,279.17
170	1,600.00	266.67	1,333.33
175	1,670.00	278.33	1,391.67
180	1,735.00	289.17	1,445.83
185	1,800.00	300.00	1,500.00
190	1,870.00	311.67	1,558.33
195	1,935.00	322.50	1,612.50
200	2,000.00	333.33	1,666.67
205	2,070.00	345.00	1,725.00
210	2,135.00	355.83	1,779.17
215	2,200.00	366.67	1,833.33
220	2,270.00	378.33	1,891.67
225 or more	2,335.00	389.17	1,945.83

For each table, where the CO_2 emission figure is not a multiple of five, the figure is rounded down to the next multiple of five to determine the level of the charge. For a bi-fuel vehicle which has two CO_2 emissions figures, the lower of the two figures should be used. For cars which are too old to have a CO_2 emissions figure, you should identify the CO_2 band based on engine size, as follows:

(1)   If its cylinder capacity is 1,400cc or less, use CO_2 band 140.

(2)   If its capacity exceeds 1,400cc but does not exceed 2,000cc, use CO_2 band 175.

(3)   If its cylinder capacity exceeds 2,000cc, use CO_2 band 225 or above.

> **Planning point**
>
> A sole proprietor must apply the scale charges if private journeys are made using fuel bought by the business. If fuel is used only for business mileage, there is no need to account for the scale charges but sufficient records must be kept to substantiate this.

Provided VAT is accounted for by applying the appropriate scale charge, VAT on all road fuel bought by the business can be treated as input tax. This includes all road fuel that directors or employees use for private mileage. Input tax recovery is subject to the normal rules and evidence must be retained for its recovery. This may be petrol receipts or invoices, but most credit card slips or statements are not sufficient.

Scale charges and partial exemption

If a partly exempt business is unable to separate business and private motoring, all input tax on fuel (including that for private motoring) must be apportioned in the partial exemption calculations. However, the scale charge for private motoring may be reduced to equal the percentage of input tax recovered under the partial exemption method. For example, if only 80 per cent of the input tax is recovered, only 80 per cent of the appropriate scale charge is to be paid. Where an annual adjustment is carried out, the scale charge must also be adjusted.

Alternatives to the scale charges

There are a number of ways of avoiding the scale charge.

1.   By not charging any fuel for private motoring to the business. That way there can be no supply by the business.

2.   The business charges the user the full cost of privately used fuel and accounts for output tax thereon.

3.   By not recovering input tax on any road fuel purchased by the business.

> ⚠ **Warning!**
>
> If a business decides to pay for privately used road fuel, it is important that it does so for all of it. A single tankful in a quarter will be sufficient to make a business liable to output tax on the full charge for the quarter. There is no percentage reduction in the scale charge. It is an all or nothing situation.

Points also to note in particular are that:

- credit-card vouchers do not usually provide the details required on a less-detailed tax invoice unless they have been adapted to show the details required; and
- the supply must be to a member of staff (beware of the unregistered business such as a self-employed person).

On the private motoring, do not confuse input and output tax. If the scale charge for output tax is applied, all input tax on privately used fuel can be recovered.

11.8.7 No private motoring paid for by the business

If the business funds only business mileage, the scale charges do not apply. It must be able to show that this is the case from the business records. For many businesses it is not possible to know how the road fuel will be used at the time of purchase. Claims that:

- the cost of the private mileage has not been included in the business accounts; or
- the input tax relates only to the cost of the business mileage,

will have to be supported by detailed records.

Somewhat curiously, *VAT Notice 700/64* (January 2002) suggests that if detailed mileage records are maintained such that the exact business proportion can be calculated for each VAT period, then a proportion of the input tax can be claimed based on those figures, without the need either to account for scale charges or to make private payment for the private element. This methodology is not permitted by the legislation, but appears to pass muster with HMRC.

These records must include the business and total mileage and the cost of all fuel bought, eg if the records show that the total mileage is 4,290 of which 3,165 is business mileage, and the total cost of the fuel is £250, the cost of the business mileage is:

$$£250 \times \frac{3,165}{4,290} = £184.44$$

the input tax is:

$$£184.44 \times \frac{1}{6} = £30.74 \text{ (when VAT is 20\%)}.$$

> **⚠ Warning!**
>
> Although not made clear by *VAT Notice 700/64*, it appears that, for this methodology to be acceptable, the cost of the private mileage must not be included in the business accounts (HMRC *Guidance Manual* V1–13, para. 19.7). If it is, output tax should be accounted for using scale charges regardless of the amount of input tax claimed.

11.8.8 Fuel used for private motoring charged at or above cost

Again, detailed records need to be kept, logging the mileage of the car for each journey, so that the private mileage can be identified and a charge made to the particular employee. The fuel is supplied to the individual for private motoring and output tax is calculated by multiplying the amount charged for petrol by the VAT fraction.

11.8.9 Business mileage allowance

If a business pays a mileage allowance to an employee because that employee pays for all the fuel for the car, the business can claim a proportion of that mileage allowance as input tax. With effect from 1 January 2006, it is necessary for the business to hold tax invoices provided by the employees in order to make the claim. Previously, the mileage claim itself was the only evidence required.

Mileage allowances are often paid at two rates, a higher rate for employee-owned cars and a lower rate for business-owned cars. The higher rate for employee-owned cars will contribute to running expenses other than just the fuel, including oil, servicing, repairs, insurance, etc. Any input tax claim must be calculated on the proportion of the mileage claim relating to road fuel only.

Where the mileage allowance covers road fuel only (usually because it is a company car and the other costs are paid directly, only the fuel being purchased by the employee, partner, etc), input tax may be claimed at 1/6th of the total amount reimbursed (when VAT is 20 per cent, previously 7/47ths of the total amount reimbursed when VAT was 17.5 per cent).

The business should also meet the following conditions.

1. Records must be kept for each employee, showing business mileage, the model or engine capacity of the vehicle, how reimbursement has been calculated (for example, 100 miles at 10p per mile = £10) and the VAT element of the reimbursement (£10 × 1/6 = £1.67 with VAT at 20 per cent). If the expense claims contain all these details, provided they are retained as evidence, they will be a sufficient basic record.

2. If a composite mileage allowance is paid which covers other motoring expenses (insurance, etc) it must be apportioned to identify the road fuel element. Allowances not related to business mileage – such as annual amounts paid weekly or monthly – may not be used to calculate input tax, even if held out to relate only to fuel.

3. Tax invoices must be held to support the deemed amount paid for the fuel for which the employees are being reimbursed.

4. Deduction of input tax may be subject to further apportionment under the partial exemption rules.

5. Where there is a change in the rate of tax and a mileage claim includes journeys made before and after the date of the change, the mileage should be divided into two parts and the input tax calculated accordingly. Alternatively, the new VAT fraction may be applied to the whole claim provided this method is consistently applied for further changes of rates.

The VAT element of a composite mileage allowance is calculated as follows:

$$\frac{\text{No. of business miles}}{\text{Miles per gallon/litre}} \times \text{price per gallon/litre} \times \text{the VAT fraction}$$

> **Planning point**
>
> Provided that a sensible and justifiable calculation has been carried out, HMRC are unlikely to challenge the basis of calculation of the fuel element of a mileage allowance.

11.8.10 European Court VAT expenses ruling

This method of recovering VAT was expected to become a thing of the past following the decision of the ECJ in the case of the *EC Commission v United Kingdom* (Case C-33/03).

This judgment resulted from infringement proceedings taken against the UK by the Commission, which alleged that the UK legislation that allows deduction of input tax on road fuel purchased by an employee who is then reimbursed either by direct reference to cost or through a mileage allowance, was contrary to Directive 2006/112.

Although the decision in this case went against the UK, the Government indicated a desire to modify the rules in the light of the judgment (which apparently placed a high reliance on the fact that there is no formal provision in the UK legislation to restrict claims to cases of business mileage only) and the new requirement to hold VAT invoices is the result.

Other guidance: HMRC VAT Information Sheet 08/05

11.8.11 No input tax recovery on road fuel

This is a concession intended for use by very small businesses with perhaps one or two cars that are used very little for business purposes.

> ⚠ **Warning!**
> The concession operates on a business-by-business basis, not (as is sometimes thought) on a vehicle-by-vehicle basis.

It follows that, when HMRC say any fuel, they mean any road fuel. It is not appropriate to use the concession if, say, the business owns a fleet of lorries and one car that is marginally used for business purposes. HMRC expect the business not to deduct input tax on the diesel for the lorries as well as on the petrol for the car if the business wants to use this concession! It is likely to be cheaper to claim VAT on the diesel and the petrol and suffer the scale charge on the car or to use one of the alternative methods of avoiding the scale charge.

> ⚠ **Warning!**
> The concession cannot realistically be used by businesses running vehicles other than cars, as it rapidly becomes uneconomic.

11.8.12 Chauffeurs/drivers

There are no specific VAT issues regarding chauffeurs and drivers.

The most likely question to arise will relate to input tax and uniforms. VAT incurred on uniforms worn by employees in the performance of their duties can be claimed as input tax, subject to the normal rules.

Remember that if a chauffeur takes a car home, this is private mileage and the VAT incurred on the purchase of the car will not be recoverable.

11.8.13 Car parking costs

Where VAT is incurred on parking for business purposes, it is recoverable as input tax, subject to the normal rules.

It is sometimes difficult to establish whether VAT has been charged on parking charges and to obtain an invoice or receipt.

Generally, on-street parking is not subject to VAT. Where a public authority imposes charges (including excess parking charges) for parking at meter bays on the public highway, it does so under statutory powers that nobody other than a public authority can exercise. This activity is non-business. On the other hand, in providing off-street parking in garages, buildings and open spaces, the authority is not acting under any special legal provisions that give it powers beyond those available to commercial organisations with which it is in direct competition. This activity is business and subject to standard rate VAT, although this matter is currently subject to litigation which may result in due course in a different interpretation.

> ### Planning point
>
> In certain circumstances there is no need to hold an invoice for car parking charges. A VAT invoice is not needed for some types of supply if the total expenditure for each taxable supply was £25 or less (including VAT). It is necessary to make sure that the supplier was registered for VAT. See *VAT Notice 700*, para. 19.7.5) for their endorsement of this.

11.8.14 London congestion charge

The London congestion charge is a statutory levy imposed by Transport for London. The levy is outside the scope for VAT, so input tax is not recoverable as no VAT is charged.

11.8.15 Road tolls

In the UK, tolls for roads, tunnels and bridges were for many years treated as exempt from VAT. However, an ECJ ruling determined that this treatment should only apply when the road/tunnel/bridge is operated by a public authority, and should otherwise be standard-rated. It follows that tolls for all privately operated toll bridges – and the M6 toll road – are now standard-rated. Input tax deduction is therefore available where use of the toll is for business purposes (often, without even the need to obtain a VAT invoice, less detailed or otherwise (see **9.2.4**)).

The full list of tolls affected (as detailed by *Business Brief 03/03* (28 March 2003) is as follows:

- Cleddau Bridge;
- Dartford Crossing;
- Erskine Bridge;
- Forth Road Bridge;
- Humber Bridge;
- Itchen Bridge;
- Mersey Tunnel;
- Tamar Bridge;
- Tay Bridge; and
- Tyne Tunnel.

As mentioned above, the M6 toll road is also covered.

11.8.16 Personalised number plates

The VAT incurred on the purchase of special or personalised number plates may be recoverable in certain circumstances but HMRC are likely to challenge recovery and each case is judged on its own merits. The usual rules apply and the VAT will only be recoverable if the expenditure is for business purposes.

> **Planning point**
>
> If the number plate shows the initials of a director, the input tax is unlikely to be recoverable, but where the number is related in some way to the business a stronger argument can be made for an input tax claim, eg a carpet retailer with number plate 'RUG 1' or a television shop with number plate 'TV 1', but HMRC are in principle opposed to allowing input tax to be claimed on personalised number plates.

Beware! If input tax is recovered on the purchase of a personalised plate, output tax will be due on its sale.

Input tax on personalised number plates has been disallowed in a considerable number of cases including *Ava Knit Ltd* (1983) 2 BVC 208,017 and *Jones* (1990) 5 BVC 1,373 but allowed in *Alexander* [1992] BVC 691; *Sunner and Son's* [1993] BVC 1,313 and *Hamlet's (Radio and TV) Ltd* [1995] BVC 1,564.

11.9 VAT Information Sheet 08/11

11.9.1 VAT Information Sheet

HMRC issued VAT Information Sheet 08/11 providing information to be applied when using the simplified method of calculating VAT on private use of company cars, demonstrator vehicles and rental cars; this is frequently termed the 'car averaging' method. This affects motor dealers, manufacturers, daily car rental companies and contract hire companies that are entitled to reclaim VAT on the purchase of motor cars but are required to account for output tax on the private use of the car or cars.

The information sheet provides tables for the calculation of the VAT due; different tables are provided for rental cars, manufacturers and dealer demonstrators. Tables are provided for both the 17.5 per cent VAT rate and the 20 per cent VAT rate, and are reproduced below. VAT returns that span the change in VAT rate are to be apportioned to reflect private use. The VAT on private use for each person is calculated by identifying the persons that have a vehicle for private use, for each person identify the list price of the vehicle typically used in the period and then identify the price band in the table to determine the amount of VAT payable on private use. Where a person has more than one vehicle it is necessary to determine which vehicle was typically used.

Table 11.6

Motor Manufacturers at 17.5 per cent

Price band No.	List price incl. VAT band range £	Average price incl. VAT £	VAT due on annual return £	VAT due on quarterly return £	VAT due on monthly return £
1	0.00–8,999.99	7,470.00	63.09	15.77	5.26
2	9,000.00–11,999.99	10,320.00	82.99	20.75	6.92
3	12,000.00–16,999.99	14,620.00	113.01	28.25	9.42
4	17,000.00–22,999.99	20,470.00	153.85	38.46	12.82
5	23,000.00–30,999.99	27,590.00	203.55	50.89	16.96
6	31,000.00–39,999.99	35,600.00	259.47	64.87	21.62
7	40,000.00–49,999.99	44,500.00	321.61	80.40	26.80
8	50,000.00–64,999.99	58,500.00	419.35	104.84	34.95
9	65,000.00–79,999.99	72,000.00	513.60	128.40	42.80
10	80,000.00 upwards	Individual calculation based on actual cost prices.			

Table 11.7

Motor Manufacturers at 20 per cent

Price band No.	List price incl. VAT band range £	Average price incl. VAT £	VAT due on annual return £	VAT due on quarterly return £	VAT due on monthly return £
1	0.00–8,999.99	7,470.00	70.86	17.71	5.90
2	9,000.00–11,999.99	10,320.00	93.12	23.28	7.76
3	12,000.00–16,999.99	14,620.00	126.72	31.68	10.56
4	17,000.00–22,999.99	20,470.00	172.42	43.11	14.37
5	23,000.00–30,999.99	27,590.00	228.05	57.01	19.00
6	31,000.00–39,999.99	35,600.00	290.62	72.66	24.22
7	40,000.00–49,999.99	44,500.00	360.16	90.04	30.01
8	50,000.00–64,999.99	58,500.00	469.53	117.38	39.13
9	65,000.00–79,999.99	72,000.00	575.00	143.75	47.92
10	80,000.00 upwards	Individual calculation based on actual cost prices.			

Table 11.8

Dealer demonstrators at 17.5 per cent

Price band No.	List price incl. VAT band range £	Average price incl. VAT £	VAT due on annual return £	VAT due on quarterly return £	VAT due on monthly return £
1	0.00–8,999.99	7,470.00	70.04	17.51	5.84
2	9,000.00–11,999.99	10,320.00	92.59	23.15	7.72
3	12,000.00–16,999.99	14,620.00	126.61	31.65	10.55
4	17,000.00–22,999.99	20,470.00	172.90	43.23	14.41
5	23,000.00–30,999.99	27,590.00	229.24	57.31	19.10
6	31,000.00–39,999.99	35,600.00	292.61	73.15	24.38
7	40,000.00–49,999.99	44,500.00	363.03	90.76	30.25
8	50,000.00–64,999.99	58,500.00	473.80	118.45	39.48
9	65,000.00–79,999.99	72,000.00	580.62	145.15	48.38
10	80,000.00 upwards	Individual calculation based on actual cost prices.			

Table 11.9

Dealer demonstrators at 20 per cent

Price band No.	List price incl. VAT band range £	Average price incl. VAT £	VAT due on annual return £	VAT due on quarterly return £	VAT due on monthly return £
1	0.00–8,999.99	7,470.00	78.64	19.66	6.55
2	9,000.00–11,999.99	10,320.00	103.87	25.97	8.66
3	12,000.00–16,999.99	14,620.00	141.95	35.49	11.83
4	17,000.00–22,999.99	20,470.00	193.74	48.44	16.15
5	23,000.00–30,999.99	27,590.00	256.79	64.20	21.40
6	31,000.00–39,999.99	35,600.00	327.71	81.93	27.31
7	40,000.00–49,999.99	44,500.00	406.51	101.63	33.88
8	50,000.00–64,999.99	58,500.00	530.47	132.62	44.21
9	65,000.00–79,999.99	72,000.00	650.00	162.50	54.17
10	80,000.00 upwards	Individual calculation based on actual cost prices.			

Table 11.10

Daily rental cars at 17.5 per cent

Price band No.	List price band range £	Average price incl. VAT £	VAT due on annual return £	VAT due on quarterly return £	VAT due on monthly return £
1	0.00–8,999.99	£	41.67	10.42	3.47
2	9,000.00–11,999.99	10,320.00	53.40	13.35	4.45
3	12,000.00–16,999.99	14,620.00	71.09	17.77	5.92
4	17,000.00–22,999.99	20,470.00	95.16	23.79	7.93
5	23,000.00–30,999.99	27,590.00	124.45	31.11	10.37
6	31,000.00–39,999.99	35,600.00	157.41	39.35	13.12
7	40,000.00–49,999.99	44,500.00	194.03	48.51	16.17
8	50,000.00–64,999.99	58,500.00	251.63	62.91	20.97
9	65,000.00–79,999.99	72,000.00	307.17	76.79	25.60
10	80,000.00 upwards	Individual calculation based on actual cost prices.			

Table 11.11

Daily rental cars at 20 per cent

Price band No.	List price incl. VAT band range £	Average price incl. VAT £	VAT due on annual return on £	VAT due quarterly return £	VAT due on monthly return £
1	0.00–8,999.99	7,470.00	46.89	11.72	3.91
2	9,000.00–11,999.99	10,320.00	60.01	15.00	5.00
3	12,000.00–16,999.99	14,620.00	79.81	19.95	6.65
4	17,000.00–22,999.99	20,470.00	106.75	26.69	8.90
5	23,000.00–30,999.99	27,590.00	139.53	34.88	11.63
6	31,000.00–39,999.99	35,600.00	176.41	44.10	14.70
7	40,000.00–49,999.99	44,500.00	217.39	54.35	18.12
8	50,000.00–64,999.99	58,500.00	281.84	70.46	23.49
9	65,000.00–79,999.99	72,000.00	344.00	86.00	28.67
10	80,000.00 upwards	Individual calculation based on actual cost prices.			

How to Deal with Partial Exemption

12.1 Why partial exemption?

12.1.1 Introduction

A VAT-registered business is normally allowed to claim credit for input tax incurred for the purposes of making taxable supplies of goods or services. There is no general right of recovery of input tax incurred either for non-business activities or in making exempt supplies. The issue in any partial exemption situation is the input tax or the amount of input tax that may be recovered by a VAT-registered business when making exempt supplies.

If the commercial world were uncomplicated and geared solely to the wishes and needs of VAT, there would only be businesses which generate taxable supplies and those which trade in exempt supplies. The first type of trader would be registered for VAT and would recover, subject to a few restrictions, the input tax related to the running of the business. The trader generating exempt supplies would not be registered for VAT and would not be able to recover input tax.

This is not the situation in the commercial world. Many traders make both exempt and taxable supplies resulting in potential input tax problems for the business. It is essential that each situation is looked at carefully and that help is sought in any case of uncertainty as soon as possible.

It is often found that a trader who normally only makes taxable supplies starts to generate ones which are exempt. If the business then continues to claim credit for input tax, regardless of the liability of the new supplies, it is possible that too much input tax may be reclaimed. A problem will occur that may have been avoided with careful thought and planning.

A business generating exempt and taxable supplies should be helped, through the careful planning of purchases and the monitoring of input tax, to claim credit for as much input tax as is rightly recoverable.

> ### ⚠ *Warning!*
>
> It must not be forgotten that partial exemption can arise as easily on a one-off basis as in the context of ongoing activities. The rules set out in this chapter must be applied to a trader who makes a single exempt disposal of land, as well as one who commences a new business activity that is exempt in nature.

Other guidance: VAT Notice 706

12.1.2 Taxable supplies

Taxable supplies in the UK are those supplies that are subject to the standard rate, 20 per cent (15 per cent from 1 December 2008 to 31 December 2009 and 17.5 per cent from 1 January 2010 to 3 January 2011 and prior to 1 December 2008), the reduced rate of 5 per cent, or 0 per cent VAT.

12.1.3 Exempt supplies

An exempt supply is a supply which is within the scope of VATA 1994, Sch. 9. These supplies are not liable to VAT. They are exempt supplies, not taxable supplies.

The main areas of exempt supplies are:

- land;
- insurance;
- postal services;
- finance;
- education;
- health and welfare;
- burial and cremation;
- trade unions and professional bodies;
- sport, sports competitions and physical education;
- works of art; and
- cultural services.

It is impossible to state that this list is absolute without further consideration. For example, the following may all be termed as supplies of 'land':

- the supply of new dwellings;
- the supply of new commercial property; and
- the supply of older property.

However, a little further consideration will reveal that the supply of new dwellings is zero-rated; the supply of new commercial property is standard-rated; and the supply of older property may be exempt.

> ⚠ **Warning!**
>
> The above list provides a summary of danger areas that affected businesses should investigate and regard with caution.

12.1.4 Non-business activities

Input tax incurred in making non-business supplies is not normally recoverable. This affects many charities, philanthropic and voluntary bodies as well as non-profit-making organisations, although these supplies are not exempt, but outside the scope of VAT. Whilst any VAT registered person that makes non-business supplies (this could include charities and government bodies; although both these also make business supplies) must restrict the input tax incurred in relation to these supplies. No specific rules apply to this restriction, unlike the partial exemption rules, but most persons generally follow the principals established for partial exemption as they lack any other guidance.

> **Planning point**
>
> Where VAT is incurred on expenditure related to non-business activities it is essential that this is eliminated before any partial exemption rules or calculations are applied.

Such organisations have activities including the provision of free services or information, the publicising of political or religious views or the maintenance of historic buildings, parks, etc. to which there is no admission charge. These free activities are normally considered to be non-business activities.

> ⚠ **Warning!**
>
> It should be noted that problems may arise when such an organisation starts an activity that is considered to be a taxable supply. For example, many charities sell goods to raise funds or charge admission fees to historic sites. These charges and the revenue from the sale of goods will normally be business supplies and the organisation should register for VAT according to the normal rules.

> **Planning point**
>
> There is no *de minimis* limit for input tax associated with non-business activities. It is important that non-business activities are not confused with exempt supplies.

12.2 Identifying a partly exempt situation

Although partial exemption affects the input tax that may be recovered, it is not identifiable by consideration of the business costs or expenditure.

Considering the liability of the goods or services supplied by the business is the only way to identify a partly exempt situation.

Any business that makes taxable and other supplies must consider its input tax recovery. Thus, a business should analyse the supplies made into taxable, exempt and non-business supplies in order to be aware of any potential restriction on input tax recovery.

12.3   Recoverable input tax

12.3.1   Taxable supplies

The right to deduct input tax stems from European legislation:

> 'In so far as the goods and services are used for the purposes of his taxable transactions the taxable person shall be entitled to deduct [input tax].'

Directive 2006/112, art. 168

Subject to the normal rules, a registered trader is entitled to claim credit for input tax incurred in respect of taxable supplies, except in a limited number of situations where there is no right for the recovery of input tax associated with the making of exempt supplies.

Recoverable input tax is defined in UK legislation. It is input tax incurred in connection with:

- taxable supplies;
- supplies outside the UK which would be taxable supplies if made in the UK; and
- such other supplies outside the UK and such exempt supplies as the Treasury may by order specify.

Law: VATA 1994, s. 26(2)

12.4   Quantifying recoverable input tax

12.4.1   The basic principle

A partly exempt trader needs to divide input tax between that incurred in making taxable supplies together with other supplies for which input tax is recoverable, and that incurred in making exempt supplies. This must be done in a particular manner unless special arrangements – a special method – are made with HMRC. Subject to certain conditions HMRC may impose a special method.

The method that may be used without prior authority from HMRC is commonly known as the 'standard method'. This is the method prescribed by the VAT Regulations 1995 (SI 1995/2518), reg. 101.

The objective with the standard method or an approved special method is to analyse and quantify input tax into the following:

- that attributable, both directly and indirectly, to taxable supplies and other supplies for which input tax is recoverable; and
- that attributable, both directly and indirectly, to exempt supplies.

12.4.2   Exempt input tax

The input tax attributable to the exempt supplies is not recoverable unless within certain limits. Only if it is *de minimis* may it be recovered. When exempt input tax is *de minimis* is explained below (**12.11**).

12.4.3   Quantified annually

The procedure of quantifying the recoverable input tax is initially done each VAT period. However, the final amount is determined each 'year'. The 'year' is a VAT year, not the trading or fiscal year. For these purposes a year may not always be a 12-month period (see **12.7** for more details).

> **Planning point**
>
> It is essential that input tax is correctly coded as relating to taxable activities, relating to exempt activities or as overhead or residual VAT. No coding creates serious problems in trying to unravel what input tax can be claimed. Incorrect coding leads to errors. Coding in advance saves both time and money

12.5   The date from which a taxpayer is partly exempt

12.5.1   A business already VAT registered

The first step is to decide the date or time from which the partial exemption regulations affect the business and thus the date from which a partial exemption method should be used. This is determined by when exempt input tax is first incurred. The partial exemption regulations apply from the start of the period in which exempt tax is first occurred.

Example 12.1

Dan Developer has been registered for a number of years, building new houses for sale, and does not make exempt supplies. His quarterly returns end on 31 March, etc.

In April 2006, Dan started negotiations to buy a block of flats. At that time he instructed a surveyor who first invoiced him in June 2006. The deal was completed in August 2007. The flats were refurbished and let from May 2008 on assured shorthold tenancies. The first exempt supplies made by Dan were in May 2008.

The first exempt input tax incurred by Dan was incurred on the surveyor's fees in June 2004. This was in the VAT period from 1 April 2006 to 30 June 2006 (period 06/06). The partial exemption regulations affect Dan from the start of this period.

Planning point

It is a common feature of land transactions that the start of the project is many months or even years before an actual supply takes place. It is essential that the past is reviewed to establish when exempt input tax was first incurred.

Law: VAT Regulations 1995 (SI 1995/2518), reg. 99(4)

12.5.2 A newly VAT-registered business

The partial exemption method applies from the beginning of the registration period or, if later, from the date during the registration period when input tax is first incurred. If the registration period is more than six months then, for partial exemption purposes, it is a special accounting period and may have to be broken down into shorter periods.

Example 12.2

Bide-by-Ere, a small hotel, exceeds the registration limit and registers for VAT with effect from 1 December 2003. Its first VAT period ends 30 April 2004.

On 10 January 2004, Bide-by-Ere decided to purchase a second property and incurred input tax in connection with this purchase. The second property is to be used as a registered nursing home, therefore the input tax incurred was in connection with intended exempt supplies and hence 'exempt' input tax. This exempt input tax was incurred during the registration period and therefore a partial exemption method must be applied with effect from 10 January 2004.

If the exempt input tax had been incurred outside the registration period the normal rules would have applied as in the previous example.

Law: VAT Regulations 1995 (SI 1995/2518), reg. 99(5)

12.5.3   In cases of belated registration

A very long registration period may be created by a belated registration. The partial exemption method is normally applied from the date when exempt input tax is first incurred. A long registration period will usually be a 'special accounting period' that has to be broken down into a number of 'annual' periods.

Law: VAT Regulations 1995 (SI 1995/2518), reg. 99(1)(c) and 99(5)

12.6   Standard method

12.6.1   Overview

As with all partial exemption methods, the standard method requires registered traders to analyse input tax into three headings, as shown below. This is after eliminating any input tax that is not normally reclaimable (e.g. input tax incurred on business entertainment or in connection with non-business activities).

Input tax must be analysed on a period-by-period basis. This is to determine how much may be provisionally reclaimed each period. The final deduction is computed by the annual adjustment (see **12.7**).

The headings into which input tax must be analysed are set out below.

12.6.2   Directly attributable taxable input tax

This is the tax on imports, acquisitions or other supplies that are received and used, or intended to be used, exclusively to make taxable supplies. Such input tax is wholly recoverable in all circumstances.

12.6.3   Directly attributable exempt input tax

This is the tax on imports, acquisitions or other supplies that are received and used, or intended to be used, exclusively to make exempt supplies. Such input tax is in principle non-deductible, but may in some cases be claimed if, together with the exempt proportion of non-attributable input tax, it falls below the *de minimis* limits (see **12.11**).

12.6.4 Non-attributable input tax

Also sometimes known as residual input tax, this is VAT that cannot be exclusively attributed to either taxable or exempt supplies. This is usually, but not always, the tax on supplies for general use.

Planning point

What belongs in this category is any VAT on expenditure which is neither exclusively related to taxable supplies made or to exempt supplies made. Consequently, expenditure incurred on a development project which will generate both exempt supplies and taxable supplies must be allocated to this category, just as much as VAT on the general office telephone or the audit fee.

Example 12.3

De'Ath is an undertaker and stone mason. The stone masonry side manufactures stone products. These are all sold to third parties, De'Ath does not use any for his funeral business. In one VAT period De'Ath incurs the following expenditure, which he allocates as shown.

	Net £	VAT £	Total £
Stone to produce stone products	4,000	800	4,800
Stationery	200	40	240
Coffin handles	600	120	720
Telephone	400	80	480
Advertising (funerals only)	800	160	960
New coffin bier	1,000	200	1,200
New stone masonry machine	6,000	1,200	7,200
Total	13,000	2,600	15,600

Note: The stationery is for general use; the same telephone system is used for funerals and stone masonry.

For partial exemption purposes De'Ath will analyse his input tax as follows.

	Taxable activity £	Exempt activity £	Remainder (residual tax) £
Stone	800		
Stationery			40
Coffin handles		120	
Telephone			80
Advertising		160	
New coffin bier		200	
New stone masonry machine	1,200		
Total	2,000	480	120

The residual input tax needs to be apportioned between taxable and exempt activities using a partial exemption method.

Planning point

When analysing input tax it must always be remembered that the nature of the received supply is not relevant. What matters is the liability of the goods or services made or to be made by the person incurring the input tax. The input tax must be analysed solely according to the use to which it will be put in making taxable or exempt supplies. This is not always straightforward.

Planning point

In *BLP Group plc v C & E Commrs* (Case C-4/94) [1995] BVC 159 the court ruled that the right to deduct input tax depended upon a 'direct and immediate link' between the cost incurred and the generation of taxable supplies. It follows that the same principle must be applied when analysing input tax to exempt supplies, etc. There must be a 'direct and immediate link' between the expenditure and the goods or services supplied to customers.

In *C & E Commrs v Midland Bank plc* (Case C-98/98) [2000] BVC 229 the court ruled that input tax was not wholly recoverable unless a cost component of making taxable supplies. It follows that input tax should not be treated as relating to taxable supplies unless the expenditure is directly and immediately linked to those taxable supplies and is not used in connection with exempt supplies. Any input tax incurred in connection with taxable and exempt supplies or as a consequence of making taxable supplies is residual input tax. Most overheads and administration costs fall into this category. Also, input tax should not be analysed as relating to exempt supplies unless there is a 'direct and immediate' link with those exempt supplies and the expenditure is a cost component only of those supplies.

12.6.5   Apportioning residual input tax

The residual input tax must be allocated between the making of taxable supplies, and therefore reclaimable, and the making of exempt supplies, and therefore potentially blocked.

The standard method calculation to apportion the residual tax is laid down by the VAT Regulations 1995 (SI 1995/2518), reg. 101(2)(d), (3) and (4). To carry it out, it is necessary to make reference to the value of outputs of the business. The fraction of residual input tax attributable to taxable supplies is ascertained as follows:

$$\frac{\text{Value of taxable supplies}}{\text{Value of taxable supplies} + \text{Value of exempt supplies}}$$

This figure must be expressed as a percentage and is then rounded up to the next whole number in order to calculate the amount of residual input tax reclaimable.

$$\frac{£50,500}{£50,500 + £27,500} = 64.74\% \text{ (This is rounded up to 65\%)}$$

In order that the calculation is not distorted, certain supplies must be excluded from the above fraction. These are:

- the disposal of capital goods (usually fixed asset disposals);
- incidental financial transactions;
- incidental real-estate transactions;
- self-supplies;
- reverse charges;
- the sale of any car upon which the input tax was blocked, unless there was a profit on the sale in which case the profit element is included; and
- anything which is not a supply, e.g. the transfer of a going concern.

The meaning of 'incidental' in two of these categories has been a matter of some controversy. Broadly speaking, it refers to something which is not a normal part of the business's activities, such as the sale by a manufacturing business of a redundant factory building or the receipt of interest from the business deposit account.

However, there is not always a clear-cut boundary between those things which are incidental and those which are not. Even the courts have found it impossible to define precisely.

In *Régie Dauphinoise-Cabinet A Forest SARL v Ministre du Budget* (Case C-306/94) [1996] BVC 447, Advocate General C O Lenz considered what constituted 'incidental transactions'. At para. 47 he suggested that 'an exact determination of the extent of incidental transactions is ... not possible'. He continued at para. 48 that in order to be 'incidental' transactions would:

> 'have a certain link with the taxable person's other activity but do not form a direct part thereof. They may require the use of the relevant business assets only to a slight extent. They may not exceed the extent of the actual activity.'

It was suggested by Advocate General Lenz that any incidental transaction should not exceed the extent of the actual activity. This may not be limited to merely financial terms. It sometimes happens that a trader has a large-valued one-off transaction which could still be considered to be incidental to the main business.

The rounding up of the proportion of residual input tax attributed to taxable supplies does not apply where the amount of such input tax exceeds £400,000 per month (i.e. the very biggest businesses using that method).

12.6.6   Changes to the standard method

With effect from 1 April 2009 changes were made to the standard partial exemption method relating to:

- the current year provisional recovery rate;
- an early annual adjustment;
- a use based option for new partly exempt businesses;

(all the above are optional changes); and

- a compulsory change which widens the scope of the standard method to supplies of services to customers outside the UK, certain financial supplies such as shares and bonds and supplies made from establishments located outside the UK.

These changes were introduced in HMRC *VAT Information Sheet* 04/09.

With effect from 1 April 2009 a business may use its previous year's VAT recovery percentage to determine the provisional recovery of residual input tax in each VAT return. This is then finalised by making an annual adjustment in the usual way.

A business may continue to operate the old rules and calculate separate recovery percentages for each of its VAT return periods. There is no need to notify HMRC, but the business must consistently apply either the changes from 1 April 2009 or the old rules in any given VAT tax year.

> ### *Planning point*
>
> One of the main risks of using the previous year's recovery percentage is that if the business's turnover fluctuates considerably the percentage used may be too high.

If a business calculates recovery of input tax by reference to the value of supplies made in that period the business will be deemed to have opted to calculate separate recovery percentages for each VAT return falling within that VAT tax year.

> ### *Planning point*
>
> If a business uses the provisional recovery percentage to determine its VAT recoverable for the current VAT tax year the fact that a business may be *de minimis* for VAT purposes in the previous year is irrelevant. Therefore a business will need to use the recoverable percentage even though it may have been fully taxable in the previous year. Businesses may find that using the provisional recovery percentage will be detrimental to cashflow.

Where a business is subject to the standard method override calculation in the previous tax year, the provisional recovery percentage in the current year is applied before the application of the override.

At the end of the year the business must consider the override and apply it as per normal.

12.6.7 Early annual adjustment

With effect from VAT years ending on or after 30 April 2009 a business may bring forward its annual adjustment to the period in which the VAT year ends. For example if a business has a partial exemption year ending 31 March the business would normally account for its annual adjustment in its 30 June VAT return period. Under these new rules, which are not compulsory, a business may account for its annual adjustment calculation in the VAT return for the period ending 31 March.

There is no need to notify HMRC if the annual adjustment is to be brought forward.

> **Planning point**
>
> Bringing the annual adjustment forward to the end of the tax year instead of the first VAT return following the end of its tax year may mean that businesses can recover VAT on annual adjustments in an earlier period than they would ordinarily be able to do.

12.6.8 Use based option for new partly exempt businesses

Businesses may recover input tax on the basis of use to which the expenditure on which the input tax is incurred is attributed in accordance with the use or intended use of input tax bearing costs in making taxable supplies.

This change enables a new partly exempt business to recover its input tax on the basis of use in the following situations, where:

- during its registration period running from the date a business is first registered for VAT to the day before the start of its first tax year, normally 31 March, 30 April or 31 May depending on the periods covered by the returns;
- during its first tax year, normally the first period of twelve months commencing on 1 April, 1 May or 1 June following the end of the registration period provided it did not incur input tax relating to exempt supplies during its registration period; and
- during any tax year provided it did not incur input tax relating to exempt supplies in its previous tax year.

HMRC require a business to examine its main categories of expenditure and determine the extent to which they relate to taxable supplies. HMRC consider that most business which embark upon a new activity which is exempt for VAT purposes will have carefully considered how costs will be used in accordance with cost accounting principles when preparing their business plan. HMRC consider that provided this is logical, objective and transparent it will form an ideal basis for a fair recovery of input tax.

Where a business adopts the recovery of input tax on the basis of use it is also required to calculate its annual adjustment from the basis of use to ensure consistency.

> **Planning point**
>
> Where a business has not recovered input tax on the basis of use but would nevertheless have been entitled to do so, it may still calculate a use based annual adjustment. This gives new partly exempt businesses maximum flexibility and ensures a fair amount of input tax is recovered.

Use of these rules is optional. A business can still recover input tax using the values based calculation or can seek approval of a special method from HMRC.

12.6.9   Widening the scope of the standard method

A change was introduced with effect from 1 January 2009. This widened the scope of the standard method and affects businesses that make:

- supplies of services to customers outside the UK;
- certain financial supplies such as shares and bonds; or
- supplies made from establishments located outside the UK.

Prior to the change, the standard method only dealt with the recovery of input tax relating to taxable supplies made in the UK. Businesses that made overseas supplies that carried the right of recovery (foreign and specified supplies) were required to carry out an additional calculation (known as a regulation 103 calculation). They could also, from 1 April 2007, seek approval of a combined special method to include these supplies.

The new method now ring-fences the input tax of financial supplies (VATA 1994, Sch. 9, Grp. 5, items 1 and 6) and supplies made from overseas establishments. These are excluded from the values-based standard method. Instead, input tax relating to these supplies is ring-fenced and recovered on the basis of use. This change widens the scope of the standard method so it includes input tax on all supplies unless dealt with separately under regulation 103A (Investment Gold).

HMRC provide the following examples in VAT Information Sheet 04/09:

> 'Example 1: A business provides consultancy services to customers within the UK and outside the UK. Under the current rules the business is required to calculate a recoverable amount of input tax relating to its services to customers outside the UK by

way of a separate regulation 103 calculation or alternatively seek approval of a special method. The new rules simplify this by requiring residual input tax to be recovered by reference to the values based which includes the consultancy services irrespective of their place of supply.

Example 2: A business makes supplies of insurance, shares and bonds to customers located inside and outside the EU. Under the current rules, the business would be required to calculate input tax recoverable as attributable to these supplies to customers located outside the EU by way of a separate regulation 103 calculation. The new rules simplify this so that while input tax relating to shares and bonds, irrespective of their place of supply, must be recovered on the basis of use (for example on a transactions count basis), input tax relating to insurance can be recovered by reference to the values based calculation which includes the supplies of insurance irrespective of their place of supply.

Example 3: A business makes supplies of management services from an establishment located within the UK and outside the UK. Under the current rules the business would be required to recover input tax relating to its supplies to customers outside the UK using a regulation 103 calculation. The remaining input tax would be recovered using the values based calculation including supplies made to customers in the UK from the establishment located outside the UK, which could be distortive. To reduce this risk of distortion, the new rules require input tax relating to supplies made from establishments located outside the UK to be recovered on the basis of use. The remaining input tax is recovered using the values based calculation (excluding supplies made from the establishment located outside the UK).'

This change does not affect VAT returns prior to 1 April 2009. Supplies made prior to this are dealt with under the old rules.

Input tax incurred in VAT periods that end before or which straddle 1 April 2009 and which falls to be attributed under regulation 103 remains undisturbed. Input tax incurred in VAT periods that end before or which straddle 1 April 2009 are subject to an annual adjustment under the old rules.

Input tax incurred in VAT periods commencing on or after 1 April 2009 and recovered on the basis of use as relating to supplies of financial instruments or supplies from overseas establishments is subject to an annual adjustment on the basis of use.

Input tax incurred in VAT periods commencing on or after 1 April 2009 is subject to an annual adjustment in accordance with the new rules.

12.7   Annual adjustment

12.7.1   Introduction

The standard method incorporates an annual adjustment. The annual adjustment is also normally a feature of an agreed special method.

The purpose of the annual adjustment is to ensure that the input tax deduction is considered on an annual basis. In this way the seasonal variations in the business do not adversely affect the amount of input tax that may be reclaimed.

The input tax reclaimed each period is provisional. The final reclaim is computed annually or in certain circumstances for a shorter period. The annual adjustment is the difference between the total recovered on a period-by-period basis and that which is reclaimable when the same computation is applied to the year as a whole.

Example 12.4

Using the standard method, Rankin's input tax recovery was £3,000, £4,000, £2,500 and £5,000 for the periods ending on 30 June 2003, 30 September 2003, 31 December 2003 and 31 March 2004. The total reclaimed on a period-by-period basis was therefore £14,500. When the computations were reworked for the year as a whole, the input tax which may be reclaimed was calculated to be £15,000. The annual adjustment is £500 (£15,000 – £14,500). Rankin may reclaim a further £500.

Planning point

The adjustment is made by way of an entry on the VAT return for the first VAT period of the next VAT year. Therefore, in the example above, the £500 would be claimed in the period ending June 2004. This would be done by adding it to the VAT to be claimed in box 4 of the return. If the adjustment results in an amount due to HMRC, this must be done by adding it to the VAT to be declared as output tax in box 1.

With effect from VAT years ending on or after 30 April 2009, a business may bring forward its annual adjustment to the period in which the VAT year ends. For example, if a business has a partial exemption year ending 31 March the business would normally account for its annual adjustment in its 30 June VAT return period. Under these new rules, which are not compulsory, a business may account for its annual adjustment calculation in the VAT return for the period ending 31 March. There is no need to notify HMRC if the annual adjustment is to be brought forward.

Law: VAT Regulations 1995 (SI 1995/2518), reg. 99

12.7.2 The partial exemption tax year

The partial exemption tax year (the tax year) is defined in the law and it is normally 12 months. In certain circumstances it is shorter and it may be varied by HMRC. HMRC also have the power to approve or direct variations in the partial exemption year.

> ### *Planning point*
>
> If the date set by the legislation does not align with the accounts year of the registered person, it is almost always beneficial to apply to HMRC for the VAT year to be varied to correspond with the accounts year. Such an application will normally be approved by HMRC as a matter of course, provided that they are satisfied it is not being done to achieve an unfair advantage.

Unless HMRC have approved or directed a different date the tax year ends on 31 March, 30 April or 31 May (VAT Regulations 1995 (SI 1995/2518), reg. 99(1)(d)). The appropriate year-end is that which corresponds with the registered person's VAT periods. For someone submitting monthly returns, the tax year ends on 31 March: see *VAT Notice 706*, para. 7.4. The position is varied for a deregistering business: see **12.7.5**.

The tax year usually starts on the day following the end of the last tax year. For example, the tax year for a business that has been partly exempt for several years and whose VAT periods end on 30 April is from 1 May to 30 April.

The start date is varied in the following circumstances:

- when a registered person first becomes partly exempt; and
- when a business is newly registered.

Law: VAT Regulations 1995 (SI 1995/2518), reg. 99(1)(d)

12.7.3   Registered business becoming partly exempt

A registered business that is not making exempt supplies may have a shorter first 'tax year' if it commences making exempt supplies. The first 'tax year' will begin at the start of the VAT period in which the business first incurs any input tax that is attributable to exempt supplies.

> ### *Example 12.5*
>
> John is a management consultant. He has been registered for VAT for several years. His quarterly VAT periods end on 31 May, etc.
>
> In January 2003 John lets part of his office accommodation. The rent is exempt because he does not make an election to waive the exemption. The solicitor's invoice for preparing the lease was issued in December 2002. This is the first input tax attributable to exempt supplies incurred by John.
>
> John's first tax year begins on 1 December 2002. This is the start of the period in which the first exempt input tax was incurred. The initial tax year ends on 31 May 2003. It is only six months.

> ⚠ **Warning!**
>
> The reduction in the length of the VAT year leads to a reduction in the *de minimis* limit for the year, since this is adjusted pro rata by month (see **12.11**). It is especially important to consider this when budgeting for the effects of partial exemption in the first year.

Law: VAT Regulations 1995 (SI 1995/2518), reg. 99(4)

12.7.4 Newly registered businesses

A business which is making exempt supplies when it registers will normally have an initial tax year/registration period beginning on the day of registration and ending on the following 31 March, 30 April or 31 May. This is because the business should already have incurred some input tax attributable to exempt supplies.

If the first input tax attributable to exempt supplies is incurred after registration but before the following 31 March, 30 April or 31 May the start date changes. Then the initial tax year/registration period is from date upon which this input tax is incurred to the following 31 March, 30 April or 31 May.

Frequently, belated registrations have a first VAT return of many months. It is a special accounting period if it is in excess of six months. A special accounting period has to be subdivided into tax years. The first tax year/registration period runs from the date of registration or, if later, the date upon which the first exempt input tax is incurred to the following 31 March, 30 April or 31 May according to when the person's periods end. The tax years are 12-monthly thereafter.

> **Planning point**
>
> The partial exemption rules do not apply to expenditure incurred prior to VAT registration. When claiming pre-registration input tax (see **9.2.8**), any VAT incurred in connection with exempt supplies must be totally ignored, no matter how small the amount.

See **12.6.8** for the new (since 1 April 2009) use based method that can be adopted by newly registered businesses.

Law: VAT Regulations 1995 (SI 1995/2518), reg. 99(5)

12.7.5   Deregistering businesses

When a partly exempt business deregisters, the final tax year is from the end of the last tax year until the date of deregistration.

Law: VAT Regulations 1995 (SI 1995/2518), reg. 99(6)

12.8   Anti-avoidance measure

12.8.1   Standard method override

An anti-avoidance measure commonly referred to as the 'standard method override' was introduced with effect from 18 April 2002. The principal features are that:

- it only applies to persons using the partial exemption standard method;
- it does not apply to everyone using the partial exemption standard method; and
- it only affects those whose residual input tax is above certain limits.

The purpose of the standard method override is to correct anomalies in certain circumstances. It is to put right situations when applying the standard method allows input tax recovery that:

> 'differs substantially from … the extent to which the goods or services are used or are to be used … in making taxable supplies.'

The measure is intended to thwart manipulation of the standard method so that registered persons reclaim no more input tax than is considered 'fair and reasonable'.

Law: VAT Regulations 1995 (SI 1995/2518), regs. 107A(1) and 107B(1)

12.8.2   Persons to whom the override does not apply

Standard-method users are not affected if their residual input tax is below certain limits (VAT Regulations 1995 (SI 1995/2518), reg. 107E(1)). The limits are as follows:

- £50,000 for a partial exemption period of 12 months; and
- proportionally less for periods of less than 12 months.

Example 12.6

Rita becomes partly exempt during the quarter to 30 September. Her first longer period is from 1 July to the following 31 March, i.e. nine months. The standard method override limit applicable to Rita's first partial exemption 'year' is £37,500 (£50,000 × 9/12).

> **Planning point**
>
> It is important to remember that the £50,000 limit applies to residual input tax only and not to the total input tax incurred; the amounts of directly attributable input tax are irrelevant.

12.8.3   Groups

There is a lower limit for 'group undertakings' that are not members of the same VAT group. The limits for such undertakings are:

- £25,000 for a partial exemption period of 12 months; and
- proportionally less for periods of less than 12 months.

'Undertaking' and 'group undertaking' have the same meaning as for Companies Act 2006.

Law: VAT Regulations 1995 (SI 1995/2518), reg. 107E(1)

12.8.4   Applying the override

At the end of a partial exemption year, when the override applies, it is necessary to review the attribution of residual tax to taxable and exempt supplies. The steps to be taken are as follows.

1.   Complete the normal annual adjustment.

2.   Review the apportionment of residual tax on the basis of how the relevant supplies were or will be used for making taxable supplies.

3.   Quantify the amount of input tax that may be reclaimed after reviewing the residual input tax apportionment.

4.   Compute the difference in input tax recovery.

5.   Determine if the difference is 'substantial'.

The important distinction is that residual input tax is normally apportioned in the ratio of taxable supplies to exempt supplies. When the override applies this apportionment must be done on a different basis, i.e. how the underlying costs are used or to be used in making taxable supplies.

12.8.5   Apportioning residual tax on the basis of use made of the underlying costs

There is no statutory method for determining how the relevant input tax is used in making taxable and exempt supplies. The advice provided by HMRC in *Notice 706* is as follows:

'Any calculation will be acceptable if it produces a fair and reasonable attribution of input tax according to the use, or intended use, of your purchases.'

This seems akin to devising a partial exemption special method for apportioning residual input tax. Thus it must be sensible to take note of and probably follow the advice given about devising special methods. Some further information is available in VAT *Information Sheet* 4/02.

Example 12.7

Junior Ltd has been partly exempt for several years. The company supplies management consultancy services and is an insurance agent. The insurance agency is due to expand and more space is required. They are currently occupying rented accommodation in respect of which the lessor has not made an election to 'waive the exemption'.

Junior's partial exemption year ends on 31 March. In February in the year in question Junior purchases a property costing £400,000 plus VAT. In May all Junior's operations and staff will move to the new property. The management consultants and insurance agency departments will occupy approximately one-third and two-thirds respectively.

For the year to 31 March the management consultancy fees and insurance commissions were £1,000,000 and £750,000 respectively.

Junior's routine annual adjustment calculation for the year to 31 March was as follows.

Input tax:	Exclusively used for taxable supplies	Exclusively used for exempt supplies	Residual input tax
	£	£	£
	10,000	15,000	90,000
Apportionment of residual tax:			
£1,000,000			
£1,000,000 + £750,000			
= 58% (rounded up)	52,200	37,800	(90,000)
	62,200	52,800	

Note: Residual tax includes £70,000 paid on new building.

Revising the workings on the basis of use, the calculations are as follows:

Input tax:	Exclusively used for taxable supplies	Exclusively used for exempt supplies	Residual input tax
	£	£	£
	10,000	15,000	90,000

Apportionment of residual tax:

New building input tax:			
(£70,000)			
Taxable supplies (1/3)	23,333		(23,333)
Exempt supplies (2/3)		46,667	(46,667)
Remaining residual tax:			
58% as above	11,600	8,400	(20,000)
	44,933	70,067	

The difference in the amount of input tax that may be reclaimed is £17,267 (£62,200 − £44,933).

12.8.6   Transfers of going concerns

To determine 'use' for the purposes of the standard-method override, a further consideration applies to someone who transfers a business which is treated as the transfer of a going concern for VAT purposes. When apportioning residual tax on the basis of use, the transferor must take account of the use which the transferee or any successor will make of the underlying costs.

For these purposes a successor is anyone to whom a business is transferred as a going concern and tax is not due on the assets because the transfer is a tax-free transfer for VAT purposes: see the VAT Regulations 1995 (SI 1995/2518), reg. 107D.

Law: VAT Regulations 1995 (SI 1995/2518), reg. 107A(1) and 107B(1)

12.8.7   Necessary adjustments

An adjustment to input tax recovery is due when a 'substantial' difference arises. This is when input tax recovery computed as normal is substantially higher than that computed on the basis of use made or to be made of the underlying costs. A difference is considered 'substantial' when, as defined in the VAT Regulations 1995 (SI 1995/2518), reg. 107C, it is as follows:

- more than £50,000; or
- more than 50 per cent of the residual tax and more than £25,000.

In the example above, an adjustment was not necessary because the difference was £17,267 (i.e. less than £25,000 and less than 50 per cent of the residual tax). If the difference had been £47,000 an adjustment would have been necessary because the difference would have been more than 50 per cent of the residual tax and greater than £25,000.

12.8.8   When to make the adjustment

Any adjustment due because of the standard method override must be made:

- on the final return if the person concerned is deregistering; or
- at the same time as the normal partial exemption 'annual' adjustment; this is on the return for the first period following the end of the 'year' to which the annual adjustment relates.

12.8.9   De minimis limits

The partial exemption *de minimis* limits apply as normal (see **12.11** below). However, if an adjustment is due because of the standard method override it follows that the input tax attributable to exempt supplies exceeds the *de minimis* limits.

12.9   Special methods

12.9.1   Authorisation

Special methods are devised to deal with situations where the standard method does not give a fair and reasonable attribution of input tax to supplies made. HMRC may either authorise or impose a special method.

> **Planning point**
>
> Any special method will have in common with the standard method the fact that the first step is to identify input tax wholly attributable to the making of taxable supplies and input tax wholly attributable to exempt supplies. That is to say, special methods have to do with how residual input tax is apportioned, rather than altering the fundamental principles of partial exemption.

Application to HMRC to use a special method must be made in writing and agreed in writing before the method is put into practice. It is essential that any agreement received from HMRC be in writing. In a major case involving this topic it was said 'every agreement of that nature ... should be put in writing and signed by or on behalf of the parties thereto' (*C & E Commrs v CH Beazer (Holdings) plc* (1989) 4 BVC 121).

Any special method cannot deprive the taxpayer of the right to deduct a proportion of the residual input tax. In *Ampleforth Abbey Trust* [1999] BVC 2,083, the trust agreed to use a method by which input tax relating to taxable supplies was reclaimed but some residual input tax was not reclaimed. The VAT and Duties Tribunal decided that this was not a correct special method. The lack of consideration meant that although the agreement with HMRC had been made in writing, there was no binding contract preventing Ampleforth Abbey Trust from correcting the situation.

> ### ⚠ *Warning!*
>
> Authorisation to use a special method is unlikely to be forthcoming unless it can be checked and verified by reference to the business and the business records. It would be ill-advised to suggest a special scheme on the basis of a one-off sample. The aim is to devise a method that reflects the pattern of business and can be demonstrated to do so.

There are trade associations that have agreed special methods which may be used by their members (see **12.9.3**).

Law: VAT Regulations 1995 (SI 1995/2518), reg. 102

12.9.2   Normal features of a special method

Special methods are mainly concerned with apportioning the residual input tax. A special method is not normally agreed by HMRC, unless it includes the direct attribution of input tax used exclusively in making taxable or exempt supplies.

> ### *Planning point*
>
> In order to apportion residual input tax the trader is allowed to devise any 'fair and reasonable' method. If HMRC fail to agree that the method gives this 'fair and reasonable' result, the trader has the right of appeal to the tribunal.

As with the standard method, provisional calculations are carried out period-by-period with a final 'annual' adjustment. The annual adjustment periods are the same as for the standard method unless other arrangements are authorised by HMRC.

It is normal practice for special methods to be authorised for use from a current date (that is to say, effective from the beginning of the partial exemption year in force at the time of application) or a future date. The relevant regulation appears to give HMRC the discretion to authorise a special method retrospectively, but this is not usually done.

> ### *Planning point*
>
> Prior to a trader ceasing to use a special method, agreement with HMRC must be obtained. A trader should not unilaterally stop using a special method. A date of cessation should be agreed with HMRC and it is advised that the agreement be made in writing.

12.9.3 Apportioning residual input tax

The heart of any partial exemption special method is the method by which residual input tax is divided between exempt and taxable supplies.

There is no set formula for devising a method for the apportionment of this residual input tax. The trader may devise any suitable means of obtaining a 'fair and reasonable' result. In *Notice 706*, para. 21, HMRC suggest a number of special methods. This list should be taken to be an indication of special methods, not a definitive guide.

> **Planning point**
>
> When agreeing the special method with HMRC and during any subsequent assurance visit, it is essential that the apportionment of residual input tax is readily checkable.

> **⚠ Warning!**
>
> Calculation of the recovery rate must be made to two decimal places – unlike the standard method that usually permits rounding up to the nearest whole percentage point.

Possible apportionment methods include:

- a ratio of the number of taxable transactions to the total number of transactions;
- a ratio of the area of a building used for making taxable transactions to the total area of the building;
- a ratio of the input tax only used or to be used in making taxable supplies to the total input tax for taxable and exempt supplies;
- the value of any goods and services used or to be used in making taxable supplies to the total value of taxable and exempt supplies;
- the ratio of the numbers of staff used in making taxable and exempt supplies;
- a ratio of time spent exclusively on taxable activities to all time spent;
- a cost-centred or department-based ratio; and
- agreements with trade bodies.

There are a number of trade associations that have reached general agreement with HMRC that their members are allowed to use certain special methods. It is still advisable that each trader should write to their local VAT office and get local, written approval prior to using the method.

The following trade associations have made their agreements generally available. These are the:

- Brewers' Society;
- Building Societies Association;

- Association of British Factors and Discounters;
- Finance Houses Association Ltd;
- Association of British Insurers; and
- Association of Investment Trust Companies.

Details of these agreements are published by HMRC.

> **Planning point**
>
> Businesses in these sectors may choose to use the agreed method but are not obliged to do so.

> **Planning point**
>
> Not all trade agreements are published. Members of trade bodies who believe they may be affected should contact their trade association.

Other guidance: VAT Notice 700/57 and HMRC Guidance Manual Vol. V1-15, Ch. 3, s. 5.

12.9.4 Change in circumstances

The amount of input tax that may be fairly and correctly reclaimed may be affected by any change in business or circumstances.

> **Planning point**
>
> Following any change in business or circumstances, traders should give consideration to whether any authorised special method still gives a fair and reasonable result. Any special method should be reviewed and HMRC should be consulted about the continued use of the special method.

HMRC have the power to issue a written direction that a special method must be discontinued if it is considered that it fails or has failed to give a fair and reasonable attribution of input tax. The direction will be that the special method is discontinued from a future date and the standard method is used unless a different special method receives authorisation.

12.9.5 Power to direct the use of a special method

The overriding consideration of any partial exemption method is that a 'fair and reasonable' method for the attribution of input tax be used. If HMRC consider that a fair and reasonable result is not being obtained by using the standard method, they have the power to direct the use of a special method. Although the result of an imposed special method is often that the amount of input tax reclaimed is lessened, this is not the aim of the direction. The purpose is to obtain an equitable result.

HMRC usually attempt to reach an agreement with the trader regarding any proposed change in method before issuing a formal direction.

In one unsuccessful appeal against the imposition of a special method, Customs showed that they had entered into protracted negotiations with the trader before issuing the direction to use the special method. They:

- carefully considered all proposals put to them;
- invited the trader to suggest other methods;
- held lengthy negotiations;
- gave a final six-month warning before the direction was made;
- did not have regard to any irrelevant matter; and
- did not disregard any relevant matter.

(*BMW (GB) Ltd* [1997] BVC 4,090)

It is necessary to review any special method regularly. One reason for this is to ensure that a tried and tested method continues to give a 'fair and reasonable' attribution of input tax. In cases of dispute, a better result may be achieved by negotiation with HMRC rather than waiting for the imposition of a special method.

Law: VAT Regulations 1995 (SI 1995/2518), reg. 102

12.9.6 Obligations and rights

In situations where HMRC attempt to impose a special method traders have some rights, duties and expectations.

1. There is no retrospection. The direction must be from a current or future date.

2. To be effective the direction must be clear and unambiguous. This was decided by the Court of Session in Scotland in the case of *Kwik-Fit (GB) Ltd v C & E Commrs* [1998] BVC 48.

3. The trader has the right of appeal to the VAT and Duties Tribunal.

4. The method must be used until HMRC agree or direct the termination of its use.

12.9.7 The special method override notice

If a special method is in force at any given time and is regarded by HMRC or by the business as unfair or inappropriate, either party may issue a notice on the other to this effect, which allows for correction of any under- or over-recovery of VAT until a suitable replacement agreement can be reached.

HMRC state that they will not issue such a notice unless:

- they have clear evidence that the method in force does not fairly and reasonably reflect the principle of use (of the costs on which the VAT has been incurred),
- they are satisfied that agreeing a replacement method will not be quick and either party will in the interim lose out; and
- they have decided that directing use of a special method is not an appropriate step to take.

12.9.8   Checklist for special methods

Prior to using a special method, the following questions should be asked.

1. Is there a facility for the direct attribution of input tax to exempt and taxable supplies?

2. Is a 'fair and reasonable' attribution of input tax – including residual input tax – to supplies obtained by the special method?

3. Can the method and its results be verified?

4. Has written authorisation from HMRC been obtained?

5. Has the start date been agreed with HMRC?

6. Is there a suitable special method already agreed between HMRC and an appropriate trade body?

On an ongoing basis, the following points should be borne in mind.

1. Is there a regular review to ensure that it is continuing to give a fair and reasonable result?

2. Have there been any changes in circumstances or business that may have an effect on the appropriateness of the special method?

12.10   Attributing input tax in particular circumstances

12.10.1 Particular circumstances

Some everyday situations and common business decisions give rise to particular problems when dealing with the attribution of input tax.

12.10.2 Acquiring a business as a going concern – the costs involved

When acquiring a business as a going concern, input tax incurred on the costs should be attributed according to the use to be made of the acquired assets.

> ### *Planning point*
>
> Hence if the assets are intended to be used exclusively in the making of taxable supplies, the input tax relating to the costs are recoverable. However, the converse is true: if the supplies to be made are exempt then the input tax must be considered as directly attributable to these. Sometimes the assets are to be used to generate a mixture of exempt and taxable supplies. In these cases the input tax is non-attributable and should be considered as residual input tax.

The Court of Appeal upheld the view that where the assets of a business are to be used in making taxable supplies, the input tax is fully recoverable (*C & E Commrs v UBAF Bank Ltd* [1996] BVC 174).

12.10.3 Disposing of a business as a going concern

Input tax incurred in connection with transferring a business as a going concern was considered in *Abbey National plc v C & E Commrs* (Case C-408/98) [2001] BVC 581. The court ruled that when an entire business making taxable and exempt supplies is transferred, the disposal costs are a general overhead and the input tax is attributable to taxable and exempt supplies.

> ### *Planning point*
>
> There may be occasions when the input tax on disposal costs is wholly attributable to taxable or exempt supplies. The court considered that this could happen if only part of a business is transferred. If the part transferred makes only exempt or taxable supplies and there is a 'direct and immediate' link between the disposal costs and relevant supplies, the input tax should be analysed accordingly.

12.10.4 Property developers

Property developers can sometimes have particular problems with analysing input tax for partial exemption purposes.

Other guidance: VAT Information Sheet 8/01

12.10.5 Pre-registration input tax

The input tax incurred on pre-registration expenses that are linked exclusively or partly to exempt supplies is not recoverable. Pre-registration residual input tax is not allowed by HMRC to be included in the partial exemption calculations for the first return.

Douros (t/a Olympic Financial Services) [1995] BVC 1,132 attempted to reclaim the input tax on pre-registration supplies that were used in the making of predominantly exempt supplies on the grounds that the exempt input tax was below the *de minimis* limits. The tribunal upheld the right of Customs to use their discretion not to allow this repayment.

12.10.6 Self-supply and reverse charges

Input tax generated under the self-supply and reverse charges procedures cannot be attributed to those supplies.

Law: VAT Regulations 1995 (SI 1995/2518), reg. 104

12.10.7 Road fuel

The correct, if impractical, arrangement is that input tax in respect of private motoring is fully deductible when the full scale charge is paid, whereas input tax in respect of business motoring should be attributed to taxable or to exempt supplies in the normal way. HMRC appreciate the difficulties in doing this and are agreeable to an alternative.

If a business is unable to separate business and private motoring, then the motoring scale charge may be reduced to equal the percentage of input tax recoverable under their particular partial exemption method.

12.11 De minimis exempt input tax

Input tax attributable to exempt supplies is not normally recoverable. The exception is when it is within certain limits (or it relates to specified exempt supplies). These limits are commonly referred to as the *de minimis* limits.

12.11.1 Simplified de minimis limits on and after 1 April 2010

On 1 April 2010, new *de minimis* limits were introduced to simplify partial exemption. The change was introduced to enable some businesses to treat all their input tax as fully recoverable without the need to undertake the full partial exemption calculation that was required under the old rules. Where a business can pass either the original *de minimis* limit, test one or test two, it can treat itself as *de minimis* and not undertake a partial exemption calculation. These tests are:

Test One: The total input tax incurred is no more than £625 per month on average and the value of exempt supplies is no more than 50 per cent of the value of all supplies.

Test Two: The total input tax incurred, less the input tax directly attributable to taxable supplies, is no more than £625 per month on average and the value of exempt supplies is no more than 50 per cent of the value of all supplies.

If a business fails to meet these *de minimis* limits, it must use the original *de minimis* tests shown in **12.11.2**.

Example 12.8

Ranjit is partially exempt and has a VAT year running from 1 April 2010 to 31 March 2011. Ranjit acts as a delivery driver with his own van. His exempt activity arises from his activity as a day trader buying and selling shares using his home computer. He has incurred a total of £8,400 VAT in the year. This is £700 a month on average. He has failed to meet test 1.

Included in these costs was VAT of £4,000 that related wholly to the purchase of a van that Ranjit used in his taxable business only. Thus, Ranjit has £4,400 that relates to exempt activities and his overheads. This is less than £625 a month on average and thus Ranjit meets test 2. Ranjit can reclaim all the VAT he has incurred. If Ranjit had failed test 2 he would have had to undertake a full partial exemption calculation to determine if he met the *de minimis* limit described in **12.11.2** below.

The situation in example 12.8 describes the annual test undertaken by Ranjit. The partial exemption rules, until 1 April 2009, required a quarterly test (if quarterly returns were prepared) and then a final annual adjustment. This required four or five partial exempt calculations or, using the new rules, five attempts to meet the new *de minimis* tests (depending on when it was chosen to undertake the annual adjustment). To further simplify matters, HMRC has introduced, from 1 April 2009 a provision that will allow a business that met the *de minimis* test the previous year to only undertake an annual check of its *de minimis* position. Thus, a business that was fully taxable in the year ending 31 March 2008 would only have to consider their partial exemption position at the end of the next VAT year, that is 31 March 2010. Where, however, a business expects to incur £1 million in input tax in that year, it must apply the *de minimis* rules each VAT period and is ineligible to use the annual test.

12.11.2 Original de minimis limits

Where tests one and test two are failed, and for partial exemption periods ending before 1 April 2009, a different *de minimis* rule applied. Input tax attributable to exempt supplies may be reclaimed if it is within the following limits:

- not more than £625 per month on average; and
- not more than 50 per cent of all the input tax for the period concerned.

The relevant tax is not reclaimable unless it is within both these limits. The input tax that must be taken into account is that attributed to exempt supplies in accordance with the following:

- the operated standard or special method used;
- as applicable, the standard method override;
- the method for dealing with foreign supplies that would be exempt if made in the UK but excluding tax which may be reclaimed because it relates to specified supplies (see **13.13**);
- the method for dealing with investment gold; and
- the initial interval of the capital goods scheme.

Law: VAT Regulations 1995 (SI 1995/2518), reg. 106 and 106A(2)

12.11.3 Applying the de minimis limits

The *de minimis* limits are firstly applied each VAT period and then to the whole tax year when the annual adjustment is computed (unless the business is eligible to just use the annual test as described in **12.11.1**). The final test is that done as part of the annual adjustment. This process may mean that some exempt input tax is reclaimed when considering each period separately but must be repaid when making the annual adjustment. The reverse can also occur.

Example 12.9

Big Wig is partly exempt and uses the standard method. He is on quarterly returns. After apportioning the residual tax, the input tax attributable to taxable and exempt supplies in the first three periods of the tax year is as follows.

Input tax attributable to:	Taxable supplies	Exempt supplies	Exempt input tax (per month on average)	% of total
	£	£	£	
Period 1	3,000	2,000	667	40.0%
Period 2	2,500	1,800	600	41.9%
Period 3	1,400	1,500	500	51.7%

Period 1

Exempt input tax may not be reclaimed. The average is more than £625 per month.

Period 2

Exempt input tax may be reclaimed. The average is less than £625 per month and less than half the total (41.9 per cent).

Period 3

Exempt input tax may not be reclaimed. The average is less than £625 per month but it is more than half (51.7 per cent) of the total input tax.

12.12 Change of plans

12.12.1 Overview

A partly exempt trader may plan to make certain supplies and attribute the input tax accordingly. However, plans can and do change.

A common example is a speculative builder who has bought bare land with the intention of building and selling new houses. However, having obtained planning permission, he instead sells the site on to another developer without opting to tax. Instead of making taxable supplies of new dwellings, he in fact makes an exempt supply of bare land.

It also necessary to consider reverse situations. For example, the builder may have constructed a new house for letting. Input tax is not reclaimed because of intended exempt supplies of rental income. Before a tenant is found the builder receives an excellent offer for the house and decides to sell it. Thus the builder makes a zero-rated supply rather than using the dwelling to generate exempt supplies.

Changes like this trigger the requirement to make adjustments.

Law: VAT Regulations 1995 (SI 1995/2518), reg. 108 and 109

12.12.2 When reg. 108 or 109 apply

Regulation 108 or 109 is triggered by the following circumstances:

(a) input has been attributed to taxable, exempt or taxable and exempt supplies on the grounds that certain supplies will be made; and

(b) in the event the expected supplies are not made or are preceded by different supplies which would have required the input tax to be allocated differently.

12.12.3 Affected period

Regulation 108 or 109 applies for a period of six years. The six years begin on the first day of the VAT period in which the relevant input tax was attributed to the planned supplies.

> ### Example 12.10
>
> During the period 1 July to 30 September 2003, Fred, a farmer, correctly attributed input tax on planning costs to intended taxable supplies of holiday accommodation. In December 2006, before he has made any supplies, he decides instead to let the property on a five-year tenancy, making exempt supplies. He must consider the application of these rules. Had he not let the property until on or after 1 July 2009, there could be no requirement to make any adjustment.

12.12.4 Regulation 108

In essence, reg. 108 is an anti-avoidance measure. It requires input tax to be repaid when:

- an exempt supply precedes the taxable supply or supplies to which the input tax was attributed; or
- input tax was originally attributed to both taxable and exempt supplies but in the event there were not any taxable supplies to which the input should be attributed.

12.12.5 Regulation 109

Regulation 109 permits a trader to recover more input tax. A claim may be made when:

- a taxable supply precedes the exempt supply or supplies to which the input tax was attributed; or
- input tax was originally attributed to both taxable and exempt supplies but in the event there were not any exempt supplies to which the input should be attributed.

12.12.6 Calculating the adjustment

Any adjustment due under reg. 108 or 109 should be calculated by revisiting the workings for the partly exempt year/longer period in which the input tax was incurred. The relevant input tax must be re-attributed in accordance with the actual supplies and the calculations for partial exemption year/longer period reworked. In *C & E Commrs v Briararch Ltd* [1992] BVC 118, Hutchinson J said at para. 125F:

> 'The requirement is that the apportionment should be made in accordance with the method used when the original input tax reclaimed was reclaimed.'

The necessary adjustment is the difference between that which was reclaimed for the partial exemption year in question and the input tax that may be reclaimed after reworking the calculations.

> **Planning point**
>
> It follows from this that the change of intention may not give rise to any need to repay or reclaim additional tax. If, in the example of Fred above, his exempt input tax was still below the *de minimis* limits for the VAT year ending 31 March 2004, he would have no need to repay the input tax incurred on the planning costs.

12.12.7 Declaring the adjustment

A repayment due under reg. 108 must be made on the return for the period in which the change which triggers the adjustment takes place. To reclaim more input tax under reg. 109 it is necessary to write with details to the area VAT office dealing with written enquiries. The tax may not be recovered until the claim is agreed and a refund authorised!

12.13   Supplies made outside the UK

12.13.1 Introduction

Some input tax incurred in respect of supplies made outside the UK is recoverable. It is recoverable if the supplies made outside the UK are as follows:

* supplies which would be taxable supplies if made in the UK (VATA 1994, s. 26(2)(b));
* certain supplies which would be exempt if made in the UK (VAT (Input Tax) (Specified Supplies) Order 1999 (SI 1999/3121)); or
* investment gold.

12.13.2 Exempt supplies made outside the UK

Input tax is recoverable when certain exempt services are supplied as follows:

* to a person belonging outside the EU;
* directly linked to the export of goods to places outside the EU; or
* intermediary services associated with (a) and (b). The intermediary services must be as defined by item 4 or item 5 to Grps. 2 and 5 respectively of Sch. 9 to VATA 1994.

The exempt supplies for which input tax is recoverable when these conditions are met are as follows:

- insurance within VATA 1994, Sch. 9, Grp. 2; or
- financial services within VATA 1994, Sch. 9, Grp. 5, items 1–6.

12.13.3 Quantifying how much input tax may be reclaimed

The tax which may be recovered in respect of taxable supplies and/or the specified exempt supplies which are made outside the UK must be quantified in a particular way (VAT Regulations 1995 (SI 1995/2518), reg. 103). Input tax is recoverable on the basis of how the supplies upon which the input tax was incurred were used in connection with the supplies made outside the UK.

It is necessary to determine to what extent the costs upon which the input tax was incurred were used in making the relevant supplies. There is no statutory method for doing this. Any calculation may be used so long as the results are 'fair and reasonable'.

In *C & E Commrs v Liverpool Institute for Performing Arts* [2001] BVC 333, the House of Lords considered reg. 103. It held that reg. 103 provides a method for determining the tax incurred in connection with supplies made outside the UK and for which input tax is recoverable.

The impact of the case was explained in *Business Brief 12/01* (11 September 2001).

12.13.4 Investment gold

Some input tax incurred in connection with some supplies of investment gold may be reclaimed (VAT Regulations 1995 (SI 1995/2518), reg. 103A). The exempt supplies for which input tax may be reclaimed are as follows:

- supply of investment gold (VATA 1994, Sch. 9, Grp. 15, item 1); and
- grant, assignment or surrender of any right, interest, or claim in, over or to investment gold if the right, interest or claim is or confers a right to the transfer of the possession of investment gold (VATA 1994, Sch. 9, Grp. 15, item 2).

The input tax relating to these exempt supplies that may be reclaimed is that incurred on:

- purchases of investment gold upon which tax is charged, usually because the vendor elected to waive the exemption;
- purchases of gold which the purchaser will transform into investment gold; and
- costs incurred to transform gold into investment gold.

> **Planning point**
>
> The recoverable input tax must be calculated on the basis of use. There is no statutory method for doing this. Again, any calculation which produces a fair and reasonable result may be used.

12.13.5 Interaction with UK standard method or agreed special method

Regulations 103 and 103A must be applied before operating the standard method or, as appropriate, a special partial exemption method. The steps to be taken are as follows:

- quantify how much input tax may be recovered in respect of the taxable and/or specified exempt supplies made outside UK;
- quantify how much input tax may be recovered in respect of the exempt supplies of investment gold; and
- the remaining input tax should be included in the standard method or the approved special method calculations.

12.14 Non-business considerations

12.14.1 Associated input tax

Input tax associated with non-business activities must be eliminated before applying any partial exemption method.

There is no statutory method for dealing with this.

As with straightforward partial exemption, the overall aim must be to achieve a fair and reasonable allocation of input tax. Discussions with HMRC may be needed in order to agree an acceptable method. HMRC do not have the right to impose a method; neither does the trader have the right to arbitrarily use any method. Both sides must endeavour to reach an agreement.

> **Planning point**
>
> Although there is no right to choose an arbitrary method, there is also no requirement to seek HMRC's approval for the method used. In some cases it can be more appropriate to decide on a suitable and fair method and to use it unilaterally, allowing HMRC to review it for reasonableness on a VAT visit.

12.14.2 Attribution

Acceptable schemes devised to deal with the attribution of input tax associated with non-business activities normally have the characteristics of a partial exemption method. HMRC prefer that a process of direct attribution is used to eliminate input tax on costs associated with non-business activities.

Agreed schemes will normally analyse input tax into three parts.

1.   Input tax exclusively attributable to non-business activities.

2.   Input tax exclusively attributable to business activities.

3.   A 'remainder' which is not exclusively linked to either category.

The 'remainder' must be apportioned between business and non-business activities.

There is no statutory method laid down for carrying out this apportionment.

The overriding consideration is that the resulting attribution should be fair and reasonable.

> **Planning point**
>
> Although traders are free to devise their own system, HMRC appear to like methods carried out on a receipts-based ratio. Of course, this is easy to quantify. However, it often does not reflect the balance of business to non-business activities very adequately and should be resisted if it has a disadvantageous result.

12.14.3 Seasonal variations

HMRC prefer that any scheme designed to cope with an ongoing need to attribute input tax to non-business supplies incorporates an 'annual adjustment' in order that any seasonal variations are evened out.

> **Planning point**
>
> For such annual adjustments, law does not fix the year end and the timing of the declaration. Therefore, it can be advisable to agree the timing of these adjustments with HMRC, although, again, a sensible judgment (e.g. partial exemption year or accounts year) can successfully be made without reference to them.

12.14.4 Partly exempt trader having non-business activities

Such traders must eliminate all input tax relating to the non-business activities (including the part of the remainder allocated to non-business activities) before dealing with partly exempt matters.

Subsequently, input tax attributed to business activities (including the part of the remainder allocated to business activities) must be analysed according to the trader's partial exemption method. The partial exemption method is worked through in the normal way.

The overriding consideration is that the method must arrive at a fair and reasonable attribution.

12.15 Interaction with the capital goods scheme

12.15.1 General

The capital goods scheme was introduced with effect from 1 April 1990. It is designed to adjust the input tax recovery to reflect the changes in use made of certain assets over several years. In principle it is merely an extension of the partial exemption rules, where changes in the relative proportions of exempt and taxable use differ over a number of years. In respect of goods covered by the scheme, the initial input tax claim made in the year of acquisition of the item may be adjusted over a period of time (broadly, ten years) if there is any change in the degree of taxable/exempt use. Further details may be found in **12.18**.

12.16 Special circumstances

12.16.1 Groups of companies

Normal rules of VAT group registrations apply to partly exempt VAT groups. The group is treated as a single person making supplies through its representative member. It is usual for supplies between members of the group to be ignored, although HMRC do have powers to direct otherwise. Supplies made to and received from outside the group are usually the relevant considerations (VATA 1994, s. 43).

Input tax recovery is determined by the way in which supplies to the group are used to generate supplies outside the group. This is significant when dealing with partly exempt groups.

There will only be one partial exemption method. This will be either the standard method or an agreed special method. The method is applied to the group as a whole.

It is not possible to apply the *de minimis* tests on a company-by-company basis and therefore gain an input tax advantage. The VAT group is one single entity for partial exemption purposes and therefore the *de minimis* tests are applied to the group as one unit.

The partial exemption method in use determines the way in which input tax incurred by members of the group is attributed to supplies made to persons outside the group.

It is possible that the transfer of a going concern to a VAT group which is partly exempt may trigger an anti-avoidance measure.

When the measure applies, the receiving VAT group triggers a self-supply charge and must account for output tax on the incoming business. There is therefore an output tax charge and input tax credit as with other self-supplies (VATA 1994, s. 44).

12.16.2 Checklist for VAT groups

Planning point

1. It is essential that the structure of the VAT group is arranged to maximise input tax recovery.
2. Companies that only make exempt supplies may be able to recover some or all of the input tax when grouped with a company making taxable supplies.
3. If a company only makes exempt supplies to other group members, it is generally best to be included in the group.
4. It may be possible to have a group structure that allows the group to reclaim exempt input tax up to the maximum allowed by the *de minimis* regulations.
5. Holding companies having no trading activities and not providing management services to their subsidiaries are usually best included in a VAT group.
6. Any change to the group may have an effect on an agreed special method applied by the group. It is possible that HMRC may take the view that a change significantly affects the method. Therefore any change should trigger a review.

12.16.3 Divisional registrations

A divisional registration is when one legal entity is allowed to register the divisions of its business separately.

A partly exempt business is not allowed to carry out this divisional registration unless the exempt input tax for the whole business is below the *de minimis* limit.

Planning point

It is necessary to consider all divisions of a business. If only one division is making exempt supplies the whole business is considered to be partly exempt and *de minimis* limits must be considered. The position should be reviewed regularly.

12.16.4 Educational establishments

All VAT-registered educational establishments are under the same rules as any partly exempt business. The income of these establishments raises particular problems because much of it may be outside the scope of VAT. Frequently it is found that they receive grants and donations.

HMRC will view every situation on its own merits, there being no strict requirement for uniformity.

As with all partial exemption situations the overall effect should be that a fair and reasonable deduction of input tax is achieved. It is probable that this may best be achieved by consideration of a special method rather than the standard method.

12.16.5 Local authorities

Local authorities are governed by VATA 1994, s. 33 and are subject to special rules regarding the recovery of input tax.

Exempt input tax is recoverable when it is 'insignificant'. This is defined with reference to the partial exemption *de minimis* limits and a further criterion unique to local authorities. HMRC have developed a special partial exemption method for use by local authorities.

Any separate trading company set up by a local authority would be governed by normal partial exemption rules.

12.17 Partial exemption checklist

Table 12.1

1.	As early as possible; ideally prior to any afforded supplies being made:	Identify all exempt supplies and other non-business activities.
2.	As soon as such supplies are planned:	Arrange an accounting system that can enable input tax to be analysed between taxable and exempt supplies and non-business activities.
3.	Period-by-period:	Complete the calculations quantifying 'exempt input tax'.
4.	Period-by-period:	Decide if the *de minimis* limits enable the 'exempt input tax' to be reclaimed.
5.	Each tax year or longer period:	Review the *de minimis* situation.
6.	Each tax year or longer period:	Prepare the annual adjustment.

7.	At the annual adjustment:	If using the standard method, consider if the anti-avoidance measure bites.
8.	Ongoing:	Consider if the standard method provides a fair and reasonable recovery level or if a special method would be more suitable.
		If necessary devise and agree with Customs a special method.
9.	Ongoing:	Ensure that any companies are in the optimum VAT groups or non-VAT group position, e.g. to enable the *de minimis* limits to be utilised to maximise the recovery of exempt input tax. Plan for the registered person to comprise the optimum mix of taxable and exempt supplies within each tax year.
10.	Before any capital expenditure:	Plan capital expenditure not subject to capital goods scheme adjustments to ensure the most advantageous recovery of input tax.

12.18   Capital goods scheme

12.18.1 Introduction

The capital goods scheme (CGS) was introduced by HMRC to deal with the very real problem of input tax incurred on certain capital assets which are capable of being consumed to make a mixture of taxable and exempt supplies over a period of years. There can be variations over those years in the extent to which goods are used in making taxable and exempt supplies.

This chapter explains the CGS, which came into force on 1 April 1990. Before the introduction of the scheme, under the normal rules recovery of input tax on all capital goods was usually determined once and for all by the first use of the goods. Previously businesses could acquire large capital assets, recover the input tax on the grounds that they made taxable supplies, and then change the use of those assets to making exempt supplies whilst retaining all of the VAT originally incurred. Conversely, if no VAT has been claimed at the outset on account of fully exempt use, some deduction should later be available if taxable use takes place.

When a capital item within CGS is acquired, the normal rules for claiming input tax apply:

*   if it is used wholly in making taxable supplies, input tax is recoverable in full;
*   if it is used wholly in making exempt supplies, none of the input tax is recoverable; and

- if it is used for making taxable and exempt supplies, a proportion of the input tax may be claimed under the partial exemption rules.

Where, subsequently, in the adjustment period for that item there is a change in the extent of taxable use, an input tax adjustment has to be made to take account of this. If the taxable use increases, a further amount of input tax can be claimed and, if it decreases, some of the input tax already claimed must be repaid.

12.19   Legal basis of the scheme

12.19.1   EU law

The scheme is mandatory under art. 187 of EU Directive 2006/112.

12.19.2   UK law

The detailed UK legislation relating to the scheme can be found in the VAT Regulations 1995 (SI 1995/2518), Pt. XV. This legislation effectively implements the European provisions in the UK and provides a mechanism for adjustments to be made to the initial amount of claimed input tax to reflect those variations over a longer period usage rather than the annual position which previously existed.

The scheme applies only to specific items, whether new or second-hand, acquired and brought into use on or after 1 April 1990 and used for exempt or non-taxable purposes, or subsequently the subject of an exempt or non-taxable disposal during the relevant period.

CGS does not apply to items purchased for resale or as stock-in-trade.

VAT Notice 706/2 – issued in January 2002 – deals with the scheme and includes several worked examples. VAT *Information Sheet* 4/02 – issued in April 2002 – explains how the partial exemption standard method override, announced in the Budget on 17 April 2002, affects businesses using the standard method to determine the VAT they can deduct. It also describes how the standard method override can affect businesses that have to adjust input tax under the CGS provisions.

Law: VAT Regulations 1995 (SI 1995/2518), Pt. XV

Other guidance: VAT Notice 706/2

12.20   Capital items involved in the scheme

12.20.1 Computer equipment, ships, boats, aircraft and land

Capital items to which CGS applies are only certain items of computer equipment, ships, boats, aircraft and interests in land. Only items which are used by the owner in the course or furtherance of a business carried on by him and for the purposes of that business, otherwise than solely for the purpose of selling that item, are included.

The scheme applies specifically to the following (all values are VAT exclusive).

(1)   Computers and individual items of computer hardware with a VAT exclusive value of £50,000 or more per unit supplied to or acquired or imported by the owner. Computer means a single item of equipment and not various units making up a network. Also excluded is equipment such as computerised telephone systems or computer controlled factory equipment (as their primary function is not as a computer);

(2)   From 1 January 2011 capital expenditure on aircraft, ships, boats and other vessels with a VAT exclusive value of £50,000 or more. The adjustment applies to the VAT incurred on acquisition as well as VAT incurred on manufacture, refurbishment, fitting out, alteration or extension; and

(3)   Land and buildings with a VAT exclusive value of £250,000 that were subject to VAT at the standard or reduced-rate being either:

   (a)   an interest in land, building, part of a building or a civil engineering work;
   (b)   land, buildings, parts of buildings and civil engineering works that the owner constructs;
   (c)   alterations, extensions, annexes to buildings that increase the floor space by more than ten per cent (for input tax incurred post 1 January 2011 the definition has been simplified by removing the floor space element, so any extensions, alteration or annex to a building in excess of £250,000 is now caught);
   (d)   for input tax incurred on or after 1 January 2011 capital expenditure on alterations, extensions and annexes to civil engineering works;
   (e)   capital expenditure on services and goods affixed to a building that is or has been refurbished or fitted out (from 1 January 2011 the goods no longer need to be affixed to a structure, they just need to be capitalised to be included within the CGS); and
   (f)   for input tax incurred on or after 1 January 2011 the CGS has been extended to refurbishments of civil engineering works.

Civil engineering works include items such as roads, bridges, pipelines, sports facilities, etc.

> ### ⚠ Warning!
>
> Any rent payable or paid more than 12 months in advance, or invoiced for a period of more than 12 months, must be included in determining the value of the property for the purposes of the scheme.

Capital expenditure is any expenditure that is capitalised for accounting purposes. HMRC will not normally challenge the capitalisation policy of a business unless it believes there is avoidance. As charities do not normally capitalise expenditure, expenditure included in the CGS will be expenditure that would normally be capitalised. Included in this valuation, where relevant, is any non-business expenditure incurred on the item.

It is only necessary to include VAT in the CGS adjustment if it is related to the land, building, computer, etc. It is not necessary to include associated expenditure such as legal or real estate agent fees. It should be noted that rent or the service charge paid or payable more than 12 months in advance are to be included in the value for the CGS. Also rent or service charges invoiced for a period of more than 12 months are to be included when calculating the value of the capital item.

> ### Planning Point
>
> A business with non-business activities (such as a charity with a building or computer or a person using an asset such as a boat for business and non-business purposes) can hold an asset or part of an asset outside the CGS system. Where this option is made the asset is never included as part of the business activities and is only available for private or non-business use. VAT relating to the part excluded from the VAT and CGS system is not deductible and this includes costs incurred in running or maintaining the asset. HMRC do not need to be informed of the option being exercised but this should be recorded in board minutes or some other suitable place (e.g. letter to the accountant, internal memorandums, etc.).

12.20.2 Types of computers and computer equipment covered by CGS

In practice the scheme mainly covers mini-computers and mainframe computers. This is because the minimum value of £50,000 applies to individual items of computer equipment, not to complete systems or networks.

Computer systems are generally made up of a number of separate pieces of equipment linked together (e.g. disk drives, VDUs, printers, etc.).

A computer or item of equipment for use in a business is covered by the scheme only if it is worth £50,000 or more on its own. For example, if one computer printer is valued at £50,000 or more it would be covered by the scheme, but if a whole system was made up of a number of items of equipment each individually valued at less than £50,000 it would not. Any delivery or installation costs should be included unless invoiced separately. If imported, the value for VAT at importation (including import duty) should be used.

The scheme does *not* apply to:

- any item acquired before 1 April 1990;
- any item of value less than £50,000;
- any item acquired for resale or sold before it is used;
- computer software;
- computers or computer equipment manufactured by the business itself; and
- computerised equipment, e.g. a computer-controlled blast furnace, a computerised telephone exchange, a lift system, etc. (but if computerised equipment is installed as a fixture in a new building covered by the scheme it would be treated as part of the building).

Planning Point

It is necessary to include in the CGS value the delivery and installation costs unless these are supplied separately. It may make calculations simpler if these items are supplied separately. Where, however, it is expected that taxable use will increase over a period of time the delivery and installation costs should be included in the purchase contract to enable a greater proportion of the VAT incurred to be claimed under the CGS. Also, if import duty is charged on the import of a computer (duty is rarely charged on computer equipment) this is a further cost that is to be included in the CGS value.

12.20.3 Types of land, buildings and civil engineering covered by the scheme

Supplies of land and buildings may be exempt from VAT, zero-rated or standard-rated. The scheme can only apply where VAT is charged on the acquisition/construction of the land or building at the standard rate (including where the supplier has exercised his option to tax the land or building). Note where land and buildings are referred to, this generally includes civil engineering works.

Examples of acquisitions that are covered by the scheme where the tax-exclusive value of the supply is £250,000 or more include:

- the freehold of a building which a business either occupies for its own business or leases to someone else;
- an extension or annexe which a business constructs, or an alteration which it makes to a building in which it has an interest; and

- land or buildings which a business acquires on a lease where it pays a premium of £250,000 or more (including rents or service charges invoiced, paid or payable from more than 12 months in advance).

The scheme does *not* apply to:

- any acquisition of a value of less than £250,000;
- any land or building acquired for resale or sold before it is used;
- the acquisition of a lease of land or a building where the premium is less than £250,000 (or where no premium is paid, i.e. involving rent only); and
- the freehold of a piece of bare land purchased for possible future development, e.g. acquired for its 'land bank' and not used before development or sale.

'Goods affixed' literally means what it says. Goods should only be included in the value if they become part of the fabric of the building. Generally these are items that are sold with the property and are not portable or easily removed. Goods affixed is no longer a requirement from 1 January 2011, the value of the goods (and services) need to be included in the CGS where they are capitalised by the business in their accounts.

'Goods affixed' does not include items secured for safety or security reasons or computers or computer equipment. These may be subject to the CGS in their own right.

Common inclusions are:

- materials to build;
- internal and external walls;
- roofs and ceilings;
- floors and hard flooring;
- permanent partitioning;
- windows;
- lifts;
- 'built-in' storage such as cupboards or shelving;
- air conditioning;
- lighting; and
- decorative features.

Common exclusions are:

- office furniture;
- storage unless it is 'built-in';
- carpets;
- computers and computer equipment; and
- factory and office machinery.

Items that should be included in the value of constructed buildings or civil engineering works include:

- the interest in the land (if the supply was taxable, other than zero-rated);

- services such as security equipment hire, haulage and professional and managerial services such as architects and surveyors;
- demolition;
- items and services used in construction;
- landscaping; and
- fitting out including the value of the fixtures.

Where land is bought and a building is subsequently built on the land, this is not two capital items. It is one capital item and the value of the land and building construction needs to be combined to see if the £250,000 threshold has been breached.

These lists are not exhaustive.

Changes made to the definitions of CGS items from 1 January 2011 (but are relevant prior to that date) include:

- removal of the requirement that an alteration, extension or an annex must create additional floor area of 10 per cent or more (so it is only necessary to consider if there has been capital expenditure);
- removal the requirement for goods used for a refurbishment to be affixed to a building (again so it is only necessary to consider if there has been capital expenditure);
- removal of the self-supply charges arising before 1 March 1997 from the capital goods scheme;
- include the refurbishment, fitting out, alteration or extension of a civil engineering work within the capital goods scheme; and,
- the requirement to include non-business expenditure in the value for the CGS.

An extra-statutory concession by HMRC (*Business Brief 02/00*), which allows businesses to use 'an alternative means of valuing refurbishment or fitting out work' for the purposes of CGS, took effect from 1 January 2000.

Previously, when calculating the value of refurbishment or fitting-out work, businesses could only include the value of capital expenditure on services and 'goods affixed to the building', such as suspended ceilings and installed lighting. The value did not include the value of goods which did not become affixed to the building, e.g. office furniture.

Under the concession, businesses no longer need to separate out the value of goods which are not affixed to the building from the total value of capital expenditure on refurbishment or fitting out, and can choose whether to include some or all of the goods affixed. The concession applies where the adjustment period started after 31 December 2000.

For adjustment periods starting before that date, businesses wishing to include goods affixed should seek approval from their local VAT office. Businesses must keep a record of the concessionary value of the capital expenditure, including full details of the supplies on which the value was determined. The concessionary value must be used in calculating adjustments to the claimed input tax for the whole of the adjustment period.

If HMRC consider that this concession is being used to avoid tax then they may withdraw or restrict its use. Businesses should be aware that by electing to use an enhanced value, an item may fall within CGS by virtue of exceeding the scheme threshold, where under the normal legal value it would not.

Where a refurbishment is in phases it needs to be considered if there is one or more than one CGS item. Generally there is more than one refurbishment CGS item where there are separate contracts for each phase of the works or there is a contract where the phases are separate options that may or may not be proceeded with, and each phase of work is completed before work on the next phase commences. Where there are rolling refurbishments the original refurbishment must be treated as destroyed if there is nothing left of it following a subsequent refurbishment and any CGS adjustments come to an end for that original refurbishment. If any element of the original refurbishment remains, the CGS adjustments continue.

12.21 Review periods

In the first instance, input tax on items involved is recovered in the normal way. This initial recovery is then subject to review in subsequent years.

In the case of boats, ships, aircraft and computer equipment, the review takes place over the 'intervals' defined at **12.22** below, giving a total review period of, broadly, five years.

In the case of land and buildings the review takes place in the 'intervals' defined at **12.22** below, giving a total review period of, broadly, ten years (less where the interest expires in less than ten years).

12.22 Intervals

12.22.1 Definition

These are defined in the VAT Regulations 1995 (SI 1995/2518). The first interval can actually be defined in six separate ways, but will not normally exceed one year. Subsequent intervals will normally equate to the tax year.

> ⚠ **Warning!**
>
> The rules for determining the intervals include provisions to counter VAT avoidance schemes which operated by collapsing the period of adjustment by using the TOGC provisions or the VAT grouping rules. The new rules counter such shortening of the review period and also require that, following such a movement of a capital asset, agreement is reached with HMRC for the calculation of the remaining adjustments.

> ### *Planning Point*
>
> Where the period of adjustment had not started before 1 January 2011 it is possible to align the periods of adjustment with the owner's interest in the asset. This provides greater ease of use and a more accurate reflection of the use of the asset.

12.22.2 Aligning the period of adjustment with your interest in the asset

On occasion the period an asset is held is less than the normal adjustment period under the CGS. Prior to 1 January 2011 the adjustment period for, say, a lease of a building for seven years, would be dealt with under the CGS by having five adjustment periods. From 1 January 2011 the adjustment period is aligned with the interest held in the asset.

Where the number of intervals in the normal CGS adjustment exceed the number of complete years of the interest in the asset, the period of adjustment is reduced to the number of intervals equal to the complete years plus one (with a minimum of three adjustment periods). For example, a business acquires a lease for seven years, the normal adjustment period is ten years. As this ten year period exceeds the seven year interest by more than one, the adjustment periods are reduced to the number of complete years plus one, that is eight.

12.22.3 The first interval

The start of the capital goods scheme has been defined by its purchase, acquisition, import or on VAT registration prior to 1 January 2011. This has been changed for assets where the period of adjustment under the old rules has not started before 1 January 2011. For the start of the capital goods scheme, which did not have a period of adjustment starting before 1 January 2011, the first adjustment period is the first use of the asset. The old rules for determining when the first interval commences are:

- the date of purchase, importation, acquisition (or self supply of the item);
- the date the owner first uses the item where the item is constructed, altered, extended, refurbished or fitted out; or
- the date of registration (or inclusion into an existing VAT group) where the owner is not a registered person when he first uses the item.

'Use' includes any use in the business. For buildings, it usually consists of the granting of a lease or physical occupation. 'First use' will be the time that any part of the constructed, altered, extended, refurbished or fitted-out building is used.

Where the owner is not registered when he first uses an item as a capital item:

- if he subsequently becomes a registered person, the first interval commences on his effective date of registration and ends on the following 31 March, 30 April or 31 May depending upon the VAT period allocated to him; and
- if he is subsequently treated as a member of a group for VAT purposes, the first interval corresponds with, or is that part still remaining of, the then-current tax year of the group.

The first interval ends on the day before the start of the next partial exemption tax year (see **12.7.2**).

> **Planning point**
>
> If there is no change of use between the first and the second interval and the length of the two intervals combined is less than 12 months, the two intervals are rolled together and treated as the first interval.

12.22.4 Subsequent intervals

Subject to the rules relating to the transfer of a business as a going concern and the rules relating to groups of companies, each subsequent interval after the first interval corresponds with a longer period applicable to the owner or, if no longer period applies, a tax year. In either case this will normally run to the following 31 March, 30 April or 31 May depending upon the owner's VAT periods.

12.23 Operation of the scheme

12.23.1 Adjustments

The taxpayer is required to adjust the input tax claimed in respect of the appropriate items if the use for taxable purposes and/or his partial exemption position alters.

Put simply, input tax is recovered in the initial period on the basis of the expected use of the item for taxable purposes. Beginning with the first interval after the item is first acquired or used, annual adjustments will be due if the extent for which it is used for taxable purposes alters. In each of the following intervals a further adjustment may be due.

Regulation 116(1) provides that the attribution of the total input tax for a capital item for each subsequent interval shall, for the purposes of the CGS, be carried out on the same basis as used for the partial exemption provisions. Under reg. 116(2)HMRC can allow or direct another method by which taxable use in any subsequent period is to be ascertained.

> **Planning point**
>
> If the partial exemption method in force will give rise to an inappropriate result for the capital item concerned, a special method incorporating provisions particular to the item should be considered.

Taxable use, which is the basis for any adjustment, must be determined as a percentage. The difference between the recovery percentage applicable during the first interval and that applying to subsequent intervals is described as the 'adjustment percentage'.

The taxpayer is required to make an adjustment using the 'adjustment percentage' if the taxable use has altered.

12.23.2 Valuation of the asset

Capital expenditure will normally be determined in accordance to a business's capitalisation policy and accounts treatment. Exceptions are made where avoidance is suspected or for charities that do not capitalise expenditure as they do not have unfettered rights of the property.

The method of valuing assets has been altered to include the value of non-business expenditure (with effect from 1 January 2011); prior to this date the non-business expenditure did not need to be included. This will mainly impact upon the charity sector.

A business does, however, have the option of excluding all or part of the asset and hold that part or all of the asset privately. Where this election is made (which if an internal accounting election or a board minute, HMRC do not need to be notified) the excluded element will never form part of the business assets (and consequently no VAT needs to be accounted for on that asset or part of the asset when it is disposed of). HMRC have provided the following example in Information Leaflet 06/11 of how to value an asset that has business and non-business expenditure:

> **Example 12.11**
>
> A business purchases a building for £1 million and incurs £200,000 VAT. The building is to be used for 60 per cent business purposes and 40 per cent non-business purposes (e.g. charitable use). Prior to 1 January 2011, £600,000 (60 per cent of £1 million) determined the value for CGS purposes. Under the new rules that took effect from 1 January 2011, all of the expenditure on the building (£1 million) is used for its valuation. As the CGS threshold for buildings remains at £250,000, the building falls to be a CGS asset in both scenarios. As would be expected, prior to 1 January 2011 the VAT incurred on the business element (the £600,000) is subject to adjustment. From 1 January 2011, the VAT on the full cost of £1 million is subject to adjustment.

This change in the amount of VAT that is regarded as being part of the capital goods scheme has an obvious impact upon the capital goods scheme adjustment calculation. Where expenditure is incurred both before and after 1 January 2011, it is necessary to consider the VAT incurred before 1 January 2011 in the light of changes to the taxable and exempt activities. From 1 January 2011, it is necessary to consider changes in business use and also taxable and exempt activities.

Planning point

Many charities and other non-business users of assets may have believed that the asset was valued using the total expenditure (including its non-business element) in the past. Check the valuation of assets by excluding the non-business element to confirm whether the asset should be within the capital goods scheme or not, prior to 1 January 2011.

Example 12.12

A property was acquired by a charity post 1 January 2011 for £1 million plus £200,000 VAT. The property was initially used 50% for business purposes and 50 per cent for non-business purposes. The business is 75 per cent taxable and 25 per cent exempt. The amount of VAT that can be reclaimed initially is:

£200,000 x 50 per cent x 75% = £75,000;

that is a recovery rate of 37.5 per cent

In the first adjustment period business use increased to 65 per cent, but exempt activity also increased to 35 per cent. Thus, the recovery rate is now;

65 per cent x 65 per cent = 42.25 per cent.

The adjustment will, therefore, be (42.25 per cent - 37. 5 per cent) x £200,000/10 = £950.

Non-business use can now also be included in special partial exemption methods and any non-business use must be included in any special method agreement. Where a business with a non-business method agreement becomes partially exempt the override provisions will apply until a special partial exemption method can be agreed that includes the non-business activities.

As this is partly a non-business use the charity can opt to hold the non-business element outside the VAT and CGS system meaning no adjustments relate to that part of the asset but no input tax can be claimed.

12.23.3 Part disposals

Prior to 1 January 2011, adjustments only ceased when the asset was disposed of in full (or the five or ten year adjustment periods have been utilised). Thus, if part of an asset was destroyed or disposed of adjustments had to continue even though part of the asset was no longer in possession of the business. From 1 January 2011, a final adjustment is made in respect of the part disposal and adjustments are only required on that part of the asset still in existence or owned.

12.23.4 Period of ownership

If the period of ownership of the asset is intended to be less than the number of adjustment periods (that is ten years for properties other than leases of less than ten years and five years for these short leases and computers, aircraft, ships and boats) the number of adjustment periods will be reduced. Where the number of adjustment intervals exceeds the number of complete years the owner has an interest in the asset by more than one, the period of adjustment is reduced to the number of complete years plus one, down to a minimum of three intervals. Thus, a property acquired for six years will have seven adjustment interests (and will have adjustments of one-seventh of the VAT rather than one-tenth of the VAT incurred). The extra interval is added to deal with residual interests. Three is the minimum number of adjustment intervals as it is not intended to include assets owned for less than two years in the capital goods scheme.

12.23.5 Ownership

HMRC have confirmed that the following are treated as owner of the asset and liable to make the necessary adjustments:

- The transferee on a transfer of a going concern and the transferee is treated as having done everything that the transferor had done in respect of the asset; and
- The representative member in a VAT group. The person responsible for capital goods scheme adjustments is person treated as the owner at the time immediately prior to the end of the interval.

12.23.6 VAT incurred before registration

A concession existed for a business not registered for VAT that had opted to tax a property and subsequently registering for VAT. Such a business was only entitled to recover VAT incurred up to four years (for goods) and six months (for services) prior to registration. There was no ability to reclaim any of the VAT incurred prior to this. The concession allowed a business that acquired a capital goods scheme asset when it was not registered for VAT to reclaim VAT under a capital goods type calculation on opting to tax and registering for VAT. This concession has now been legislated for. Persons registering on or after 1 January 2011 do not need to rely on the concession. The new provisions provide the following:

(1) Expenditure incurred by the unregistered business counts towards the capital goods scheme threshold.

(2)   One adjustment interval is removed for each complete year that has elapsed from the date of first use of the asset and the date of registration (so if a building was bought by the business some 15 months prior to registration there will be only nine adjustment periods).

(3)   As the VAT is incurred when the business was unregistered the baseline recovery percentage is nil.

(4)   The first interval runs from the date of first use to the day before the start of the business's first tax year (that is ending on the same day as the end of the registration period); this may be several years.

(5)   Where there has been taxable use since VAT registration a VAT credit can be claimed in relation to the period from the date of registration to the end of the registration period.

(6)   Pre-registration use is accounted for by the reduction in the number of adjustment periods so this does not need to be taken into account again.

HMRC has provided the following example taken from *Information sheet 06/11* that explains how the adjustment method works:

Example 12.13

A business purchased a building while it was unregistered for £250,000 and incurred VAT of £50,000. It first used the building on 1 October 2009. On 1 January 2011, it registers for VAT and its first tax year starts on 1 April 2011. It uses the building entirely for making taxable supplies after it registers for VAT.

The CGS period of adjustment for the building is ten intervals and the baseline recovery percentage is nil. However, as one whole year has elapsed between first use of the building and the date the business registered for VAT, the CGS period of adjustment is reduced by one to nine intervals. The first interval runs from 1 October 2009 to the day before the business's first VAT tax year which, in this example, is 31 March 2011. As the legislation treats this interval as a subsequent interval, the business needs to establish the recovery percentage for its first interval.

As the business only makes taxable supplies in the first interval, it is entitled to recover 100 per cent of 50,000/10 = £5,000 in relation to the first interval. The definition of the first interval covers all the way back from first use but this simply sets the CGS running. As exempt pre-registration use is reflected by the number of intervals being reduced (in this case from ten to nine) that use does not need to be taken into account again in the first interval adjustment. So, it is only the use while registered that is taken into account.

Assuming the building is used entirely for taxable purposes in subsequent intervals, the business will also be entitled to recover 100 per cent of 50,000/10 = £5,000 in respect of the remaining eight intervals (as the period of adjustment has been reduced to nine to reflect use of the asset when the business was unregistered).

12.24 Accounting for adjustments

12.24.1 Example of calculating input tax

Any necessary adjustment must be made via an adjustment in the VAT account for the second period after the end of the tax year. In other words, the period after the one in which a partial exemption annual adjustment is normally made.

You can, however, choose to make the annual adjustment in the last tax period of your tax year if you have also chosen to make to your partial exemption adjustment in that period. If you choose to do this you must apply the time of adjustment consistently.

You can, however, choose to make the annual adjustment in the last tax period of your tax year if you have also chosen to make to your partial exemption adjustment in that period. If you choose to do this you must apply the time of adjustment consistently.

The following example is taken from *VAT Notice 706/2* and illustrates the working of the scheme.

This example considers a constructed building which was first occupied for use by a partly exempt business on 1 August 1997. At the first interval £800,000 input tax was incurred on the capital item of which 75 per cent was recovered using the business's partial exemption reclaimable percentage. Additional amounts of input tax were incurred in subsequent intervals in completing the construction as below:

Table 12.2

Dates	Interval	Input tax incurred on building	Partial exempt percentage	Input tax claimed on building
1/8/97 to 31/3/98	1	£8,000,000	75%	£6,000,000
1/4/98 to 31/3/99	2	£4,000,000	90%	£3,600,000
1/4/99 to 31/3/00	3	£3,000,000	75%	£2,250,000
1/4/00 to 31/3/01	4	£2,500,000	72%	£1,800,000
1/4/01 to 31/3/02	5	£0	80%	£0
1/4/02 to 31/3/03	6	£0	84%	£0
1/4/03 to 31/3/04	7	£0	88%	£0
1/4/04 to 31/3/05	8	£0	74%	£0
1/4/05 to 31/3/06	9	£0	72%	£0
1/4/06 to 31/3/07	10	£0	70%	£0
Total £17,500,000 Average 78% over 10 intervals				

Note: Work out the amount of adjustment for an interval, divide the total input tax incurred on the capital item by the total number of intervals in the adjustment period (either five or ten). You then multiply by the adjustment percentage:

$$\frac{\text{Total input tax on the capital item}}{\text{Number of intervals in the adjustment period}} \times \text{the adjustment percentage}$$

12.24.2 Combined adjustments

This approach involves rolling together the adjustment calculations for the remaining intervals.

Each time an additional amount of input tax is incurred the overall initial recovery percentage (the 'baseline') should be re-evaluated and used to measure against for future intervals. The baseline can be calculated by determining what percentage of input tax has been reclaimed over the expired intervals, using the formula (figures in the table are in thousands):

$$\frac{\text{Input tax reclaimed}}{\text{Input tax incurred}} \times 100\% = \text{Average reclaimable }\%$$

Table 12.3

Interval	Input tax incurred	PE %	Input tax reclaimed	CGS baseline %	Input tax to be adjusted	CGS adjustment %	CGS adjustment Amount
1	£8,000	75	£6,000	75	n/a	0	0
2	£4,000	90	£3,600	75	£8,000	15	£120
3	£3,000	75	£2,250	80	£12,000	(5)	(£60)
4	£2,500	72	£1,800	79	£15,000	(7)	(£105)
5	£0	80	£0	78	£17,500	2	£35
6	£0	84	£0	78	£17,500	6	£105
7	£0	88	£0	78	£17,500	10	£175
8	£0	74	£0	78	£17,500	(4)	(£70)
9	£0	72	£0	78	£17,500	(6)	(£105)
10	£0	70	£0	78	£17,500	(8)	(£140)
Totals	£17,500		£13,650				(£45)

At the end of interval 2 the business had reclaimed:

$$\frac{£9,600}{£12,000} \times 100 = 80\%$$

This becomes the CGS baseline percentage for interval 3.

At the end of interval 3 the business had reclaimed:

$$\frac{£11,850}{£15,000} \times 100 = 79\%$$

This becomes the CGS baseline percentage for interval 4.

Note: You should round special method percentages to two decimal places.

This method produces a net adjustment figure of £45,000 due to HMRC over the ten-year adjustment period.

When deducted from the input tax initially reclaimed of £13,650,000 (over four years), the business's total amount of input tax reclaimed is £13,605,000.

Against total input tax incurred of £17,500,000 this is a reclaimable percentage of 77.74 per cent.

12.24.3 Parallel adjustments

This approach involves carrying out separate but simultaneous adjustments for the remaining intervals of the capital goods scheme adjustment period (figures in table are in thousands).

Table 12.4

Interval	Input tax incurred	PE %	Input tax reclaimed	Adj. of interval 1 input tax incurred*		Adj. of interval 2 input tax incurred*	
				%	Amount	%	Amount
1	£8,000	75	£6,000	n/a	n/a	n/a	n/a
2	£4,000	90	£3,600	15	£120	n/a	n/a
3	£3,000	75	£2,250	0	0	(15)	(£60)
4	£2,500	72	£1,800	(3)	(£24)	(18)	(£72)
5	£0	80	£0	5	£40	(10)	(£40)
6	£0	84	£0	9	£72	(6)	(£24)
7	£0	88	£0	13	£104	(2)	(£8)
8	£0	74	£0	(1)	(£8)	(16)	(£64)
9	£0	72	£0	(3)	(£24)	(18)	(£72)
10	£0	70	£0	(5)	(£40)	(20)	(£80)
Totals	£17,500		£13,650		£240		(£420)

* Figure is divided by the amount of intervals in the adjustment period. In this case divided by ten.

Table 12.5

Interval	Adj. of interval 3 input tax incurred*		Adj. of interval 4 input tax incurred*		Totals
	%	Amount	%	Amount	
1	n/a	n/a	n/a	n/a	£0
2	n/a	n/a	n/a	n/a	£120
3	n/a	n/a	n/a	n/a	(£60)
4	(3)	(£9)	n/a	n/a	(£105)
5	5	£15	8	£20	£35
6	9	£27	12	£30	£105
7	13	£39	16	£40	£175
8	(1)	(£3)	2	(£5)	(£70)
9	(3)	(£9)	0	£0	(£105)
10	(5)	(£15)	(2)	(£5)	(£140)
Totals		£45		£90	(45)

* Figure is divided by the amount of intervals in the adjustment period. In this case divided by ten.

This method produces a net adjustment figure of £45,000 due to HMRC over the ten-year adjustment period.

When deducted from the input tax initially reclaimed of £13,650,000 (over four years), the business's total amount of input tax reclaimed is £13,605,000.

Against total input tax incurred of £17,500,000 this is a reclaimable percentage of 77.74 per cent.

12.24.4 Taxable use in subsequent intervals

The extent of taxable use in subsequent intervals is measured as follows.

1. If the capital item is used for making taxable supplies only then the percentage of taxable use is 100 per cent.

2. If the capital item is used for making exempt supplies only then the percentage of taxable use is 0 per cent.

3. If the capital item is used for both taxable and non-taxable supplies, the amount of taxable use is the recoverable percentage of residual input tax in the partial exemption annual adjustment (see *VAT Notice 706* and **Chapter 12**).

4.   If different percentages are calculated for different parts of the business, the percentage used should be from the part of the business where the capital item is used.

Other guidance: VAT Notice 706, s. 13

12.25   Disposal of capital item

Where an item is sold as a taxable supply the scheme calculation is done on the basis that the taxable use for the remaining intervals is 100 per cent. If the item is sold without the occurrence of a taxable supply, the scheme calculation is done on the basis that the use is nil. However, it must be stressed that the 100 per cent use only applies to complete intervals; if the item is sold part-way through an interval the taxable use percentage must be calculated in accordance with the use.

> **Planning point**
>
> Where the item is irretrievably lost, stolen or totally destroyed, or a lease of less than ten years expires, no further adjustments are required for the remaining complete intervals.

12.26   Input tax capping

The legislation restricts recovery of input tax on the sale of an asset to a sum equivalent to the output tax charged on the sale. In practice, 'capping' is likely to apply in the case of fast-depreciating items of computer equipment rather than property which is likely to hold its value.

The scheme was amended from 3 July 1997 with the result that the amount of input tax recovered during the life of the capital asset, including the final adjustment, must be compared with the output tax due on disposal. This test is referred to as 'the disposal test'.

If the input tax figure exceeds the output tax the final adjustment must ensure that the two figures agree, resulting – where appropriate – in a payment of tax to HMRC. There is no recovery where the output tax due exceeds the total input tax. This change means that, in principle, any disposal at a loss because of depreciation or market conditions will result in a liability to extra tax.

Law: VAT Regulations 1995 (SI 1995/2518), reg. 115(3)

> **Planning point**
>
> However, HMRC have been given the power to disapply this provision and have indicated that they will only impose it where the value of the asset has been artificially reduced and not to bona fide commercial transactions.

12.27 Interaction of the CGS with the partial exemption standard method override

The CGS and the partial exemption regulations are intertwined where:

- taxable use of a capital item is normally derived from the partial exemption annual adjustment computations (VAT Regulations 1995 (SI 1995/2518), reg. 116(1));
- the CGS adjustments are ignored for the purpose of the partial exemption *de minimis* limits (reg. 106(2)(b)); and
- usually an 'interval' for the purposes of the CGS is the same as the partial exemption tax year (VAT Regulations 1995 (SI 1995/2518), reg. 114).

VAT *Information Sheet* 4/02 (April 2002) explains how the standard method override, announced in the Budget on 17 April 2002, affects businesses using the partial exemption standard method to determine the VAT they can deduct. It also describes changes to the definition of 'exempt input tax' that can affect businesses that first become partly exempt.

The standard method override is targeted primarily at aggressive VAT avoidance by large businesses that use the standard method to deduct exempt input tax. Fully taxable businesses and partly exempt businesses using a special method are not affected by any of these changes. Nor are the vast majority of businesses for whom the standard method produces a fair and reasonable deduction of VAT. Other than avoiders, very few businesses will be required to make an adjustment, and those that are will be as likely to benefit as to lose.

However, if a business incurs input tax on a CGS item within a period covered by the override, then it must include that input tax in considering whether the override applies and, if so, consider the use or intended use of the capital item in determining if there is a substantial difference.

The override applies only where input tax incurred within a tax year or longer period (being a subsequent interval for the CGS):

- exceeds the override threshold; and
- there is a substantial difference between the outcome of the standard method and the use of tax-bearing costs incurred in the tax year or longer period.

> ⚠ **Warning!**
>
> CGS adjustments must not be counted as input tax when determining whether the override applies. However, the basis of adjustments in subsequent intervals may be affected if the override applies to a tax year or longer period that is a subsequent CGS interval.

12.28 Record-keeping

For the most part, the accounting records required to cope with the application of VAT to computers, land and property transactions are no different to those required for any other kind of business.

However, businesses acquiring and bringing into taxable use capital goods are required to keep separate records showing how adjustments to input tax recovery have been calculated. As these may be required for the following ten years in relation to land and buildings transactions, clearly sufficient records must be retained to allow businesses to carry out the annual adjustment calculation or to justify that no annual adjustment is necessary.

> **Planning point**
>
> Although current law requires records to be retained for six years only, HMRC recommend that records should be kept long enough to show how a business has calculated each adjustment.

> ⚠ **Warning!**
>
> A frequently overlooked point is that, when a property is acquired by means of a TOGC, if it was subject to CGS in the hands of the vendor, then the purchaser inherits the remaining CGS annual adjustment liabilities. When a property is acquired under a TOGC, the purchaser should make the necessary arrangements to have the appropriate accounting records relating to that property transferred to him, to ensure that he properly discharges his inherited liabilities under the CGS.

12.29 Completing VAT returns

Where an adjustment is required, it should be included in the return for the second VAT period following the interval to which the adjustment relates or in which the supply as a result of sale, or deemed supply as a result of deregistration, takes place. This is the period after the one in which the partial exemption annual adjustment is made for the year. The adjustment should be included in box 4 of the VAT return.

> ### Example 12.14
>
> A business prepares VAT returns for the quarters ended 31 March, 30 June, 30 September and 31 December.
>
> The 'tax year' of the business is the year ended 31 March. Any partial exemption annual adjustment must be made in the return for the quarter to 30 June and any CGS adjustment in the return for the quarter to 30 September.
>
> Where an interval has come to an end because:

- the owner of the capital item has ceased to be a member of a VAT group; or
- the owner (who remains a taxable person) has transferred part of his business as a going concern,

the adjustment for that interval must be included in the return for the group or transferor (as the case may be) for the second VAT period after the end of the tax year of the group/transferor in which the interval in question fell.

HMRC may allow any adjustment to be made in a later return but only if it is a return for a VAT period commencing within three years of the end of the period when the adjustment should have been made.

If VAT registration has been cancelled, the adjustment should be entered on the final VAT return for the period ending with the effective date of deregistration.

12.30 Business transfers

Where a business is transferred as a going concern and the supply, including capital items to which the CGS applies, falls outside the scope of VAT by virtue of the VAT (Special Provisions) Order 1995 (SI 1995/1268), art. 5, the new owner takes over the responsibility for continuing the adjustments due under the scheme.

The timing of the intervals may change and will depend on whether or not the transferee takes over the transferor's VAT registration number. Where he does so, the adjustment interval for any capital item continues without a break, and the transferee assumes responsibility for any adjustments as if he had owned the capital item throughout the interval in which the transfer occurs.

Where the transferee does not take over the transferor's VAT number, the adjustment interval for each capital item ends on the day of transfer. The transferor must make any adjustment for that interval in the normal way in his VAT return for the second period after the end of his tax year (unless the registration ceases, when it must be made in his final tax return). The transferee's first interval runs from the date of transfer to the first anniversary of the date of transfer.

12.31 Interaction of CGS with VAT grouping

12.31.1 Introduction

The CGS provisions should always be considered when a VAT group is formed or disbanded or there is a change in the membership of a VAT group.

Computers, land and buildings which are subject to the provisions of the scheme are known as 'capital items'. The purpose of the scheme is to provide adjustments, over a fixed period, to the input tax incurred on capital items where there is a change in the extent to which they are used to make taxable supplies.

If a company which owns a 'capital item' joins or leaves a VAT group, there may be a change in the way in which the item is used in the business, and adjustments under the scheme may be necessary. For example, a leasing company has a computer (a 'capital item') which is used for the taxable leasing activities of the business. The company joins a VAT group and the computer is leased to another group member which uses it, in turn, to make exempt supplies outside the group. The representative member would then be required to make the necessary adjustments under the CGS to take account of this change in use of the item.

If a company owns a 'capital item' and it joins or leaves a VAT group, this can also have an effect on the time when adjustments have to be made under the scheme. Normally the CGS adjustment intervals are the same as a company's VAT tax year. However, these intervals can change if it joins or leaves a VAT group. For example, if it joins a VAT group, the interval then applying to its capital item ends on the day before it joins the group, and any adjustment required must be made on the final return of its old registration.

The representative member will take over responsibility for making future adjustments under the scheme, and all remaining intervals will run for 12 months from the date the company joined the VAT group. These intervals will remain fixed until the adjustment period for the capital item has expired — even if it subsequently leaves the group or joins another VAT group.

12.31.2 Interaction with reverse charge liability on VAT grouping

Under VATA 1994, s. 44(4), the reverse charge on chargeable assets imposed when a business is transferred as a going concern to a member of a VAT group does not apply to assets coming within the CGS.

12.31.3 Partly exempt VAT group

Another situation in which a business may find itself incurring additional irrecoverable VAT on a TOGC transaction arises where the purchaser is a member of a partly exempt VAT group. In those circumstances, the transfer may give rise to a self-supply by the representative member of the group. The provisions are meant to counter avoidance, but they seem somewhat inequitable, when a partly exempt business which is not part of a group does not suffer the same consequences.

Some comfort is to be derived from the fact that the requirements to account for a self-supply are limited to assets which have been owned by the vendor for less than three years, items which were standard-rated when supplied and those which were not treated as capital goods. Goodwill is also to be ignored in calculating the self-supply charge. If the transferor was not in a position to recover all the input tax when the assets were acquired, the output tax on the deemed supply may be reduced accordingly, so being aware of the vendor's recovery rate is essential where these provisions are likely to come into play.

12.32 Effect of CGS for fully taxable businesses

The majority of supplies made by many businesses are taxable. As a result it seems a reasonable assumption that the CGS will not apply. This may be true in respect of purchases of computer equipment used for the taxable activities of the business. The same assumption is not true for land and buildings.

> ### ⚠ *Warning!*
>
> A trader such as a solicitor could be affected by the CGS with significant cost implications, as illustrated in the following examples. In both of these examples it is assumed that the anti-avoidance test on disposal does not apply.

> ### *Example 12.15*
>
> A solicitor purchases a new office block for £1 million plus £175,000 VAT on 1 April 2000. The solicitor's practice, which is fully taxable, occupies the office block and reclaims in full the VAT paid on the acquisition.
>
> On 1 April 2004 the solicitor sells the office block but does not charge VAT as the building is no longer new, being over three years old. The consequence of the sale is that the exempt disposal triggers an adjustment under the CGS. As a result the solicitor must repay £87,500 to HMRC, being half the input tax originally recovered.

> ### *Example 12.16*
>
> Facts of purchase of new office block as above.
>
> On 1 April 2001 the solicitor lets 25 per cent of the office space 'exempt' for five years.
>
> The consequence of the letting is that for each of the five remaining adjustment periods from 1 April 2001 the solicitor must repay £4,375 to HMRC. This amounts to a total repayment over the periods of £21,875. This is calculated as 25 per cent of the input tax originally recovered which is time apportioned to each of the five years remaining in the adjustment period.
>
> If the requirement for repayment of the tax is not identified at the time, there is a potential liability for a misdeclaration penalty and interest.

> ### *Planning point*
>
> The solicitor could avoid the difficulties that the above examples illustrate by electing to waive exemption in respect of the property (opting to tax). The exempt supplies would become taxable and the CGS adjustments would not be triggered. It is necessary to identify the problem at the time of making the decision to sell or let. An election to waive exemption cannot be retrospective.

12.33 Local authorities

It should be noted that CGS deals with input tax and therefore does not, strictly speaking, deal with a change in use of non-business input tax since, by definition, input tax excludes VAT on non-business use. Nevertheless, HMRC take the view that CGS must be applied and non-business activities should be regarded as taxable activities (*VAT Notice 749*, para. 3).

Therefore, during the scheme period annual adjustments are calculated and VAT may have to be paid to HMRC or repaid to the local authority.

If a capital item changes its use from taxable to exempt use then, provided it remains *de minimis*, no CGS adjustment need be made. However, if the authority exceeds the 5 per cent *de minimis* limit and becomes partly exempt, the appropriate calculation must be made and VAT repaid to HMRC.

Should the opposite happen and taxable (and non-business) use increases, again an appropriate calculation would need to be made. If at the time of acquisition the local authority was *de minimis* and able to recover all of its VAT, then there would be no need to adjust input tax. If, however, it had been partly exempt at the time of acquisition and input tax was restricted, then the appropriate adjustment should be made, reclaiming previously restricted input tax.

Local authorities are subject to the same regulations as apply to ordinary businesses when it comes to keeping, maintaining and making available records. The same applies to visits from HMRC officers. Larger authorities will be subject to regular VAT assurance visits from local VAT offices, mainly because of the VAT complexity of their affairs.

12.34   Interaction with direct tax

Capital allowances are claimed for direct tax when capital items are purchased. A cost base is established and a percentage of that cost is allowed as a deduction from income each year. In direct tax, the cost of a capital item is spread over a period of years rather than being a full deduction in the year of acquisition. A problem faced with direct tax is that the capital items scheme will adjust the cost base as the cost of the item varies depending upon the amount of VAT that is claimable. It would be extremely difficult to adjust the capital allowance claimed in previous years, so a pragmatic solution has been adopted. Any previous capital allowance computations are not distorted when a VAT liability or extra VAT can be claimed under the capital items scheme. Any extra VAT that is claimed under the capital items scheme is taken into account in the capital allowances computation for the period in which the repayment is made by HMRC. Where additional VAT is payable, this is treated as extra qualifying expenditure in the period when the VAT becomes payable.

12.35   Case law

12.35.1 *Verbond van Nederlandse Ondernemingen v Inspecteur der Invoerrechten en Accijnzen*

In *Verbond van Nederlandse Ondernemingen v Inspecteur der Invoerrechten en Accijnzen* (Case 51/76) [1977] ECR 113, 'capital goods' were defined as 'goods used for the purposes of some business activity and distinguishable by their durable nature and their value and such that the acquisition costs are not normally treated as current expenditure but written off over several years'.

12.35.2 *C & E Commrs v Trustees for R & R Pension Fund*

C & E Commrs v Trustees for R & R Pension Fund [1996] BVC 348 was the first case dealing with the interaction of VATA 1994, Sch. 10, para. 3(9) with CGS. The trustees constructed a commercial building and reclaimed input tax. Without waiving exemption they granted a 15-year lease which resulted in the payment of a 'developer's' self-supply charge. Subsequently they applied for permission to waive exemption and proposed to reclaim 99.1 per cent of the self-supply input tax on the basis that the period of the exempt lease was then 16 months compared to an expected life of the building of 150 years. Customs refused to allow the election on the grounds that it did not produce a fair and reasonable attribution of the input tax.

Customs contended that they could not allow any revised initial attribution of input tax because the building was a capital item within CGS and if the building continued to be used for taxable purposes, 86.67 per cent of the relevant input tax would be recovered within ten years.

The trustees appealed, contending that the application of CGS did not amount to a 'fair and reasonable' attribution of input tax under VATA 1994, Sch. 10, para. 3(9) since they would have to wait for several years to recover most of the input tax.

The QB rejected this contention and upheld Customs' ruling that they were under no obligation to accept or agree as fair and reasonable, any attribution of input tax that was different from that which the law provided under the CGS in order to put them in a position to give permission to elect.

12.35.3 *C & E Commrs v University of Wales College of Cardiff*

The issue in *C & E Commrs v University of Wales College of Cardiff* [1995] BVC 211 concerned the correct method of apportioning input tax between exempt and taxable supplies.

Input tax was incurred by the University from 1 April 1989 onwards (following the decision in *EC Commission v United Kingdom* (Case 416/85) (1988) 3 BVC 378) because the University did not qualify for any of the transitional reliefs. The CGS allowed for a measure of relief for input tax incurred after 1 April 1990 (when the scheme was introduced).

In order to obtain relief for the year ended 31 March 1990, the University sought and received Customs' approval of a lease and lease-back arrangement under which the University would be able to recover input tax on the construction works directly attributable to the supplies under the lease granted by it. The University granted leases of both buildings to a wholly owned subsidiary and waived exemption. It claimed relief for a proportion of the pre-April 1990 input tax based on a time-apportionment calculation relating to the use to which each building had been put. On that basis 93 per cent of the input tax on one building and 97 per cent on the other was attributed to taxable use, i.e. to the taxable leases granted to the subsidiary.

Customs rejected the claim. They contended that since 51 per cent of the University's income for the year ended July 1990 had been standard-rated, only 51 per cent of the input tax on the construction was attributed to taxable supplies.

The University appealed. The tribunal upheld the appeal. It held that the attribution made by Customs was in effect provisional under reg. 30 (now reg. 101), but that there was no regulation that could operate to transform the college's provisional right to deduct input tax into an absolute one. While that method might have been fair and reasonable in the light of what was known at the time of the original supplies, as events developed, the use to which the buildings were put no longer conformed to the basis adopted in making the provisional attribution. Thus a final attribution of input tax on a fair and reasonable basis that took account of the uses of both buildings should have been made. The tribunal considered that its conclusion was consistent with the interpretation of art. 167 and 187 of Directive 2006/112.

Customs appealed. Carnwath J held that the effect of the University's contentions would be that adjustments to recover input tax could be made without any time limit as long as the building existed. Such a result would lead to an unacceptable degree of uncertainty, and was contrary to the spirit of Directive 2006/112 which contemplated a capital goods adjustment period of not more than ten years.

12.35.4 *Higher Education Statistics Agency Ltd v C & E Commissioners*

In *Higher Education Statistics Agency Ltd v C & E Commrs* [2000] BVC 150, the company, which was a registered charity, purchased a rented property at auction. The vendor had elected to waive exemption in respect of the property, and it was accepted that the letting of the property constituted a business.

Following the exchange of contracts, the charity elected to waive exemption in respect of the property. Customs issued a ruling that tax was chargeable on the transfer. (The effect of the ruling was that, by virtue of the transfer, the property became a 'capital item' within the CGS, so that if the property were to be used for exempt or non-business purposes within the following ten years, there would be a charge to tax by means of an adjustment to the initial deduction of input tax.)

The charity appealed, contending that the effect of art. 5 of the VAT (Special Provisions Order) 1995 (SI 1995/1268) was that the transfer should not be treated as a supply.

The tribunal rejected this contention and dismissed the appeal. The effect of art. 5(2) was that the transfer was to be treated as a supply, unless the transferee had elected to waive exemption 'no later than the relevant date'. The effect of art. 5(3) was that the relevant date was the date of the contract, rather than the date of completion. The tribunal observed that conveyancing solicitors were generally aware of Customs' view that 'where it is intended that the transfer of otherwise taxable property is to be regarded as the transfer of a going concern, then the purchaser must elect prior to the tax point relating to the transfer'. The tribunal also held that the relevant legislation was not inconsistent with Directive 2006/112, since art. 19 of the Directive provides that 'Member States may, in cases where the recipient is not wholly liable to tax, take the measures necessary to prevent distortion of competition'.

The charity appealed to the QB, which upheld the tribunal decision. Moses J held that 'the relevant date is the date when the deposit was paid'. Since the charity had not made an election on or before that date, it was liable to pay output tax on the purchase.

12.35.5 *Centralan Property Ltd v C & E Commrs*

The tribunal dismissed the case of *Centralan Property Ltd v C & E Commrs* [2003] BVC 187 wherein a university, by its own admission, entered into a planning scheme to avoid paying over a fairly substantial amount of VAT due under the CGS. The planning scheme took advantage of the now-defunct legislation whereby an election to waive exemption between two connected parties was declared ineffective.

Customs successfully argued that the exempt use of an item should be determined by the exempt supplies made. In this case an exempt grant of a 999-year lease, followed by the sale of a freehold reversion in the same period constituted the taxpayer's entire use of the capital item. This exempt use would then be carried forward when adjusting the input tax recovery in future periods.

12.36   Partial exemption Checklist

12.36.1 Partly-exempt businesses

Is the business partly exempt by making exempt and taxable (standard- and/or reduced- and/or zero-rated) supplies?

Note: A fully-taxable business can recover all allowable input tax. A partly-exempt business may not be able to recover all the input tax related to exempt supplies, for example certain sports clubs.

Can the business be treated as 'fully taxable' when making both taxable and exempt supplies where the input tax relating to the exempt supplies is *de minimis*?

Has the business completed partial exemption calculations for each return period?

12.36.2 Partial exemption calculations

Note: If the business is not fully taxable, partial exemption calculations must be carried out for the prescribed accounting periods in order to check the input tax recovery.

Is the business calculating the following for each period: [*SI 1985/886*]

(a)   the amount of input tax wholly attributable to its taxable supplies; and

(b)   the amount of input tax wholly attributable to exempt supplies?

Note: One-off supplies incidental to the main business activities and certain other supplies may fall to be excluded from the taxable or exempt supplies.

Is the business apportioning any input tax which does not fully relate to its taxable or exempt supplies by either:

(a)   the standard method of apportionment of the non-attributable input tax to relate to:

   (i)   taxable supplies being:
   input tax × taxable supplies/total supplies;
   (ii)   exempt supplies being:
   input tax × exempt supplies/total supplies;

Note: If the business makes supplies outside the UK these are to be excluded from taxable supplies even if such supplies would be taxable in the UK.

or

(b)   a special method of apportionment of the non-attributable input tax more suited to the business?

Note: HMRC's approval must be obtained.

Planning point

Special methods can increase input tax recovery and may make exempt input tax *de minimis* leading to full VAT recovery.

Is the business claiming in full the amounts of input tax relating to its taxable supplies (wholly attributable and as apportioned)?

If there is a group registration:

(a)   has the partial exemption calculation been made for the whole group registration;

(b)   have the rules regarding certain excluded exempt supplies been applied separately to each group member; and

(c)   has input tax been claimed only to the extent it relates to taxable supplies by a group member to persons outside the group?

Notes: If the input tax exceeds £50,000, or £25,000 in the case of groups, has the standard method override been applied?

HMRC will review very thoroughly any method which deals with VAT recovery by reference to floor area calculations.

12.36.3 De minimis limits

(a) Is the business recovering in full the amounts of input tax relating to its exempt supplies (wholly attributable and as apportioned) if the total is below the *de minimis* limit for the return period?

(b) If the amounts of input tax relating to exempt supplies are above the *de minimis* limit, are the restrictions to the recovery of the input tax being made to the amount claimed on the VAT return?

(c) Are annual adjustments being made to the VAT reclaimed during the business's VAT year (ending 31 March, 30 April or 31 May, unless an alternative has been agreed in writing with HMRC) on the subsequent period's return?

12.36.4 Capital goods scheme

If the business is partly exempt, are there items that the CGS applies to:

(a) land and buildings (value exceeding £250,000 VAT exclusive) acquired either as:

    (i) taxable purchases;
    (ii) self-supplied;

(b) works to buildings carried out by the business increasing the floor space by more than 10 per cent;

(c) works to buildings of refurbishment or renovation exceeding £250,000; and

(d) computers and individual items of hardware (value exceeding £50,000 VAT exclusive)?

If there are CGS items is the business making annual adjustments according to the extent of exempt use?

Is the business making the required adjustments:

(a) over a ten-year period for land and buildings (with an interest to run more than ten years); and

(b) over a five-year period for computers and land and buildings where the interest has less than ten years to run?

Has the business disposed of a CGS item?

If so:

(a) did this form part of a TOGC – if so, obtain guidance as to the adjustments required; and

(b) on disposals since 2 July 1997, does the total amount of input tax deductible exceed the output tax chargeable?

Note: HMRC require the excessive input tax to be repaid unless there are genuine reasons for the loss on the sale.

Buying a Business

13.1 Introduction

13.1.1 Buying or selling a business: overview

The purchase of an established business is an event that requires careful consideration for VAT as well as other taxes. It has been observed that the number of possible ways of carrying out such a basic transaction approximates to the number of different businesses there are, multiplied by the number of professional advisers who might be involved. Each different way of undertaking the transaction needs to be examined for its VAT implications. A complimentary chapter to this is **Chapter 14, Selling a business**.

13.2 Buying a business

13.2.1 Basic options on business purchase

It is clear from the commercial realities of the sale and purchase of a business that there are a number of possible basic outcomes for what appears to be a fairly simple transaction. These can be multiplied for some of the extra terms and conditions (such as additional, post-transfer performance-related payments) which are often required in order to reach a satisfactory deal.

This section sets out to cover the basic features of business purchases and their implications, but cannot possibly deal with every nuance (and there are plenty) which can arise on a particular transaction.

> ### ⚠ *Warning!*
>
> This section should provide a useful guide, but every transaction needs to be examined from the ground up in terms of basic VAT principles.

Watch out, in particular, for *side deals* which may arise between parties interested or involved in the purchase/sale but who are not necessarily the main players. Watch also for the complications when some of the assets relating to the business (such as land) are in different entities, or acquired or retained in different entities, rather than the whole business being transferred as a job lot. The potential variations here are too great to cover, although some are mentioned. For example, a business that is being bought as a going concern will benefit from the VAT relief that permits no VAT to be charged on the transaction. Any *side deal* will not benefit from this relief.

13.2.2 Buying the business assets

The basic question on the purchase of business assets is, of course, whether VAT is properly chargeable on the transaction. This has obvious consequences if the business is exempt from VAT. If VAT is charged on some or all of the assets purchased, the purchaser will suffer what may be a considerable VAT cost and be unable to recover any of the VAT charged. In addition, the purchaser will have to pay Stamp Duty Land Tax on any chargeable assets on the VAT inclusive value, increasing this cost.

Where VAT is charged, the purchaser may wish to reduce the amount payable as in the case of a taxable business, the charging of VAT (if properly due) is of less importance (other than the impact on the SDLT charge), as the VAT charged can generally be recovered by the purchaser. The purchaser should also ensure that he is liable to pay any VAT that is due in addition to the agreed price, especially where the purchaser cannot reclaim this VAT. The contract will usually have a clause requiring VAT to be added to any agreed price. Where there is no such agreement, the VAT will be a part of the agreed price and the purchaser will not suffer an increase in cost due to VAT being charged. In addition, the purchaser should ensure a clause is entered in the contract to ensure that a proper tax invoice is provided at settlement in order that he can claim back the VAT that he is charged.

A further point the purchaser may wish to consider is obtaining the agreement of the vendor to delay the payment of VAT until he has been able to recover the VAT from HMRC on his VAT return. This is to reduce the VAT cash flow impact upon the business. The vendor may agree to a delay in the receipt of the VAT, but will usually want the VAT before he becomes liable to pay the VAT amount. To ensure no-one is 'out-of-pocket' for the VAT element the purchaser should endeavour to submit his return as early as possible to ensure early repayment of the VAT element.

As the VAT charge on the sale of a business is likely to be a large amount it may cause there to be a repayment of VAT on that return. HMRC may wish to review the return before making payment. The business can mitigate any delay by sending to HMRC a copy of the contract, the purchase invoice and other relevant details.

It is possible that at a stage before the actual purchase, that the purchaser will express an interest by purchasing an option. This may be an option to buy shares in the company, an option to buy the business or other assets. Purchasing an option usually means that the purchaser has first call on the company (or business) so securing his right to buy, but without finally committing the purchaser to the purchase. The VAT liability of the option takes the same liability as the underlying asset. Thus, if the option is for shares, the supply of the option is exempt. Where it is an option to purchase the business, the supply will be taxable, even if the later supply of the business is treated as not being a supply due to the provisions of the Transfer Of a Going Concern rules.

> **Planning point**
>
> Ensure you know what you are buying or selling; what is being sold will determine the VAT liability. In addition, ensure you know what the consideration is, and is it VAT inclusive or exclusive.

13.2.3 Purchase of the whole business

A common transaction in business reorganisations is the sale of all of the assets of a business (with or without associated liabilities) to one entity. Provided that the purchaser is going to carry on the same business using the assets, and all of the other necessary conditions are met the transfer is likely to be 'desupplied' as a Transfer Of a Going Concern (TOGC, see **13.3.1**), so that no VAT is chargeable regardless of the nature or VAT liability of the underlying assets.

Where TOGC treatment applies, there is simply no VAT on the transaction itself. There are, however, consequences for the purchaser in taking over some past VAT treatments from the vendor, matters to be addressed about the retention of business records and questions about the vendor's input tax recovery on costs relating to the transaction. If the purchaser is a member of a VAT group, there may also be a VAT charge on the deemed supply of the assets to the business.

TOGCs are common and usually the easiest way of dealing with a transfer of a business for VAT purposes. It is, however, where the facts (and future facts) are often difficult to determine and care needs to be taken.

> **Planning point**
>
> As a general rule:
>
> - the purchaser should ensure that the contract requires the vendor to produce a proper tax invoice at settlement;
> - the purchaser should ensure that it does not have to pay VAT to the vendor without being assured that it is properly due and therefore recoverable;
> - the purchaser should agree with the vendor the date when the VAT payable, if any, is due to be paid – the purchaser should endeavour to delay this date until he can make a recovery from HMRC and he should laso attempt to facilitate early repayment by submitting an early VAT return and providing HMRC with details of the transaction at an early stage; and
> - where there is any doubt regarding VAT liabilities or other matters, both purchaser and vendor should obtain a ruling or clearance from HMRC.

Consideration also needs to be given to the possibility of transferring the transferor's existing VAT number to the transferee, although this is usually unnecessary and also inadvisable. This is considered further at **14.1.9**.

13.2.4 Partial purchase of assets

Matters get more complicated where less than the entire assets of the business are purchased. TOGC treatment can still apply but only if the assets sold represent a part of the business capable of separate operation. It is a question of fact whether this condition is met. A further question of fact is the nature of the business, which must be established in order to determine whether the transferee uses the assets to carry on the same kind of business (whether or not as part of a larger business activity) as that previously carried on by the transferor.

As a general rule, when only some of the business assets are transferred, a VAT-registered transferor will remain registered for VAT, in which case the option of transferring the VAT registration number is not available.

13.2.5 Piecemeal purchase of assets

Where assets are purchased piecemeal and cannot be operated as a separate business, rather than with the intention of transferring the business as a whole, there is normally no special VAT treatment and VAT will be chargeable according to the VAT liability of the supplies made.

> **Planning point**
>
> A difficulty that can arise is similar to that where there is a partial purchase of a business, is that it can be difficult to tell whether the TOGC provisions apply.

An example arose in the case of *C Cohen (Furriers) Ltd* (1990) 5 BVC 1,363. A company carrying on a business as furriers bought stock from an ailing rival. Because of financial difficulties the rival made its staff redundant. Three days after buying the stock the appellant took over the rival's premises, and also employed some of its former staff. HMRC denied the appellant's claim for input tax on the stock purchase, claiming that the combination of transactions amounted to a transfer of a going concern so that VAT was not properly chargeable on the sale of stock.

The tribunal allowed the appeal, holding that on the evidence before it there was no consensus between the parties that the business should be transferred and the transaction was a mere sale of stock on which VAT was properly chargeable.

> ⚠ *Warning!*
> Where it is not clear-cut whether or not a transaction qualifies as a VAT-free business transfer, there is a potential risk for both parties. It is advisable not to make assumptions and to take appropriate advice before proceeding with the deal.

13.2.6   Transfer of VAT registration number

If a business is transferred as a going concern, and the vendor ceases to be registered for VAT as a result, it is possible to transfer the VAT registration number to the new owner with the assets. This procedure requires the agreement of both parties, evidenced by their completion and signature of form VAT 68. The form includes detailed confirmation by the parties of their acceptance of the consequences that go with transferring the registration number.

Where a VAT registration number is transferred, the transferee takes over the liability of the transferor:

- to submit returns and payments for periods before the transfer (including the return covering the period of transfer), to the extent that this has not already been done by the transferor; and
- to account for tax previously reclaimed as input tax which becomes the subject of a bad-debt relief claim by the supplier.

The transferee also takes over:

- any right of the transferor to input tax credit; and
- any right of the transferor to claim bad-debt relief.

Any right of either the transferor or the transferee to a net repayment on a repayment return may be satisfied by HMRC making payment of the appropriate amount to either of them.

It has been held that the liability to meet the transferor's past liabilities extends only to VAT due on returns submitted but not yet paid, or on returns which had not been submitted at the time of the transfer, not to any liability to pay to HMRC amounts underdeclared by the transferor in completing returns previously submitted (*Pets Place (UK) Ltd* [1997] BVC 2,164).

> *Planning point*
> The potentially adverse consequences of retaining the existing VAT number of a business mean that it is best done only in cases where there is a close connection between the transferor and the transferee, such as a sole trader taking in a partner, or a sole trader or partnership incorporating. Even in cases such as these, it can be beneficial on occasion to take the opportunity of having the former number cancelled (if there is a history of late returns, for example), if the benefits outweigh any disadvantages.

13.2.7   Ongoing payments

Additional consideration

It is not unusual for agreements to provide for the payment of additional consideration dependent on the performance of the activity concerned, sometimes over a period of years.

If the main transaction fell within the TOGC provisions, and nothing further has to be done for the additional payments, then they will normally not be treated as consideration for supplies and there is no VAT consequence.

> **Planning point**
>
> If there is some ongoing activity on the part of the transferor, separate and distinct from the transfer of the assets of the business, there is likely to be a further supply made which may well be subject to VAT.

Often there is a non-competition agreement which can, in principle, give rise to supplies. If the parties do not wish for this to have VAT consequences the parties should:

- ensure that the additional consideration is not specifically linked with the non-competition agreement in the contracts;
- ensure that the agreements demonstrate that the non-competition agreement is merely ancillary to the main agreement for the transfer of the assets; and
- agree the position with HMRC.

Where the transfer was not within the TOGC provisions, any further consideration will follow the liability of the supplies of assets (and of any additional services provided in return for the additional consideration).

> **Planning point**
>
> These additional payments will probably be within the special tax point provisions for retention payments. This point should be agreed with HMRC if there is any doubt. Liability will then arise when the additional payments are received, or tax invoices issued in respect of them.

13.2.8   Points for the purchaser to consider

The main matters of principle which will be of particular concern to the purchaser are:

- whether the transfer involves a transfer of a business as a going concern, or the making of supplies (or, on occasion, both);

- if there are supplies, whether VAT is due on these;
- whether the agreements allow for VAT to be added to the consideration only where appropriate (the purchaser will not wish to pay any VAT which is not properly due as this will not in principle be recoverable as input tax);
- whether the agreement provides for the provision of a proper tax invoice so that the purchaser can reclaim the VAT incurred;
- a provision concerning the date when any VAT payable has to be paid to the vendor;
- in the case of a TOGC, whether the purchaser will face a deemed supply under the provisions relating to groups (see **Chapter 4**);
- is any tax charged recoverable by the purchaser, or is it a cost of the transaction;
- what are the effects of the above in terms of taking over liabilities of the vendor (such as future CGS adjustments, making the necessary option to tax elections, etc.);
- are the resultant business structures suitable for the purchaser's ongoing operation of the business(es) concerned;
- are there any better ways of approaching the transactions; and
- have all uncertainties been fully addressed in the agreements, in negotiations with HMRC; or both?

Of course, as for the vendor, all of these matters need to be considered in conjunction with the commercial and direct tax implications of the transactions and possible variations.

13.2.9   Buying shares

The acquisition of a business by the purchase of shares is, in many ways, far simpler for VAT than the purchase of the underlying assets. The person carrying on the business (i.e. the company sold) remains the same after the transaction as before it, so there is no change of VAT entity, unless the purchaser subsequently transfers the undertaking to some other vehicle.

The main issue for the purchaser to consider is 'what is being bought'? Any VAT liabilities and obligations of the company that is purchased will also be purchased. The distinct advantage, for VAT, of buying assets is that the purchaser has a 'clean slate' for VAT when assets are purchased, but when shares are purchased the whole VAT history of the company is acquired. There can, of course, be advantages to this as well as disadvantages. For example, any agreements with HMRC will continue when shares are purchased, but these would need to be renegotiated with HMRC when assets are purchased.

It would be prudent for the purchaser to undertake a due diligence exercise on the target company. This should not be restricted to just ensuring it has paid the VAT shown on its VAT returns. The due diligence should encompass reviewing past returns, reviewing any agreements with HMRC confirming VAT liabilities of supplies made and the partial exemption position of the entity. Other matters may be considered such as the impact of any anti-avoidance legislation on the company, whether there are any problems with past property transactions, VAT grouping issues or international transactions. Due diligence for VAT is frequently given a low priority and whilst most companies purchased will not reveal significant problems, the identification of just one matter may be material or be sufficient to break a deal. If the company has been lax with its compliance, or failed to take due risk-management action to deal with uncertain areas, this is likely to come to light in the due diligence process and may well impact the price ultimately agreed for the company. It may also result in a requirement for indemnities from the former owners (in which case it may be expected that the purchasers will take action to flush out any actual liabilities, by agreeing the position with HMRC, while the indemnities are in force and the former owners are around to pay up under them).

Planning point

The main comment to make is that there is nothing to beat first principles. When the transactions go beyond the simple models described here, it is absolutely necessary to go back to that basic model for VAT planning more generally, the Four As (ascertainment, analysis, alternatives, action) and arrive at a bespoke plan for the particular circumstances of the case, including (by cooperation with other advisers) the non-VAT aspects of it.

Corporate purchaser

Costs incurred by a corporate purchaser of shares will usually (unless the purchaser is a purely passive holding company) be input tax in the purchaser's hands. Since it will not be directly linked as a cost component to any particular supply by the purchaser, it will generally be treated as residual input tax in the purchaser's hands and recoverable according to its partial exemption method.

Planning point

In some instances it may be possible to establish a direct link with taxable supplies by the purchaser, such as supplies of management services to the acquired company (or other supplies, particularly where the acquisition is specifically made to protect the purchaser's market with the company being purchased), in which case the input tax will be wholly recoverable. This is very much a matter for negotiation and should not be relied upon for planning purposes. This matter, however, is currently subject to review and the UK's position has been questioned by the European Commission – see **Chapter 4**.

Private purchaser(s)

Where the purchasers are private individuals, their purchase will normally be a non-business activity unless they are to hold the shares as assets of a business carried on by them in which case they will not be able to recover any input tax incurred on their costs.

> **Planning point**
>
> These individuals will wish to ensure that their advisers take maximum advantage of any exemption available for supplies of arranging the transaction.

Side transfers of assets

When planning the transaction it is necessary to bear in mind that there may be more to it than the mere sale of shares. Related transactions, such as the separate purchase of property occupied by the company, need to be considered as well.

Management buyouts

A management buyout is not, in the VAT sense, a particular type of transaction but a generic term for the underlying reason for various kinds of transactions which result in the business being owned by its former (and continuing) management, probably in conjunction with external venture capitalists.

> **Planning point**
>
> The details of (indeed, the overall approach to) management buyouts vary considerably from case to case, and the most that can be said is that each case needs to be looked at from first principles on the basis of its own facts. In essence, what needs to be considered is; is there a purchase of shares, a purchase of assets and if so, is it a TOGC?

A reasonably common approach is for the management team to establish a NewCo to act as the vehicle for the buyout, to arrange for funds to be injected by a combination of share issues to the management team and to the venture capitalist, plus loan capital (perhaps a combination of bank borrowings and the issue of loan stock), then for the NewCo to purchase either the assets of the target business or the shares in the company. This may have been preceded by a transfer of assets into another NewCo owned by the vendor. Once the buyout is complete, it may be desired to tidy things up by transferring assets acquired within a company into the Newco. Any number of other variations are possible.

It will be seen that, where this sort of approach is taken, there is likely to be an issue of shares in a newly formed company, other financial transactions, a purchase and sale of assets or shares, and possibly some subsequent reorganisational transactions, each potentially leading to input tax restrictions. Each aspect needs to be considered on its own merits.

As with a sale of assets, there may well be some form of earn-out arrangement involving the payment of additional consideration based on results achieved by the company sold. These will normally be additional consideration for the shares or a TOGC and may well have no particular VAT implications.

> **Planning point**
>
> Care is needed to ensure that if, in reality, they are consideration for some ongoing supply, this is recognised from the outset.

As with the purchase of assets, another form of ongoing payment arises where one or more shareholders or former managers of the company also take on consultancies with the transferee and receive fees for this. In principle these will generally be subject to VAT, requiring the consultants (or the entities through which they act) to become or remain registered for VAT (subject to VAT registration turnover limits, etc.).

> **Planning point**
>
> The charging of VAT and when it is to be charged is something else which needs to be considered in drawing up the agreements.

On a share sale the purchaser takes over the company which has previously carried on the business and is, therefore, exposed to any historic liabilities. As a consequence, an examination of the historic VAT position of the company being taken over will form an important part of the due diligence exercise preceding finalisation of the deal, see section **13.2.9** above.

If the company sold is a member of a VAT group, action will be needed to remove it from the group and regard needs to be had to any consequences of this including the possible application of anti-avoidance provisions.

The question also arises (especially in the case of a corporate purchaser) of the possible inclusion of the newly acquired company in a VAT group.

> **Planning point**
>
> Appropriate applications should be lodged with HMRC on a timely basis, bearing in mind that most matters regarding group registration cannot be effected retrospectively (but quite often not in advance either).

13.3   Transfer of a going concern

13.3.1   Overview

The TOGC provisions are a common area for VAT disputes. This is partly because they depend to a large extent on questions of fact which can be difficult to determine, partly because of some quite complex special conditions which apply and partly because of the circumstances in which they come under the HMRC microscope. There are often uncertainties in a TOGC, or a transaction that purports to be a TOGC. It can be frustrating as well as expensive for a purchaser to find that his input tax credit on an acquisition has been denied as HMRC regard it as a TOGC. The purchaser may then be in the difficult position of trying to obtain a refund from a vendor that no longer exists or cannot be found. Where HMRC believe that a transaction is a TOGC they will often permit the purchaser to reclaim the amount charged as VAT as if it were input tax where the vendor has accounted for output tax on the transaction. Thus, if HMRC do not permit the amount charged as VAT to be reclaimed it can be assumed that any recovery from the vendor is going to be difficult.

> **Planning point**
>
> There are often sufficient uncertainties over the true facts that the case can reasonably be argued either way and, naturally, HMRC tend to regard it in the way most favourable to them.

There are some basic rules that apply whenever there is, on general principles, a transfer of a business as a going concern. There are further special rules (such as non-supply treatment of the transfer itself) which only apply if certain special conditions are met as well.

Law: VATA 1994, ss. 44 and 49; Value Added Tax (Special Provisions) Order 1995 (SI 1995/1268), art. 5

Other guidance: VAT Notice 700/7

13.3.2   Consequences: basic

The basic consequences of a TOGC are set out in VATA 1994, s. 49 and apply whenever a business carried on by a taxable person is transferred to another person as a going concern. It should be noted that the term 'taxable person' is specially defined for the purposes of VATA 1994 and does not therefore carry the more general EU meaning of anyone who is carrying on a business. Instead it means a person who is, or is required to be, registered under the Act.

13.3.3   Application of turnover limits

In applying the turnover limits to determine whether the transferee is liable to be registered, the transferee is deemed to have been carrying on the business before as well as after the transfer. In other words, the transferor's turnover counts as that of the transferee in determining whether the transferee must register.

> ### *Planning point*
>
> It should be noted that, because of the restricted meaning of taxable person mentioned above, the transferee will not take over the turnover history if the transferor was neither registered nor required to be registered. This will be important from a planning viewpoint when considering the registration strategy of someone who would prefer to defer, or avoid, registration (see also **Chapter 3**).

13.3.4 Retention of business records

There is a general requirement under VATA 1994, Sch. 11, para. 6 that a taxable person should keep the records required by regulations and retain them for a period of six years. This provision applies equally in the circumstances of a TOGC. Prior to 2007 the obligation to retain the records following the transfer shifted to the transferee.

If the transferor is to be deregistered, it is open to the parties to apply for the transfer of the VAT registration number to the transferee, provided that they accept the conditions which apply to such a transfer. In such a case, the retention of the records becomes the responsibility of the transferee.

13.3.5 Consequences: special property conditions

Further consequences apply in respect to properties. To the extent that the assets concerned consist of taxable land and buildings (either new commercial buildings or opted land and buildings) the non-supply treatment will not apply (and VAT will need to be charged on the value of the property) unless the transferee exercises and notifies of the option for taxation to HMRC and making the necessary declaration to the transferor (**13.3.15** and **17.10.3**)

13.3.6 Other consequences

There are other consequences that apply when there has been a desupplied TOGC because the special conditions are met.

1. The transferee takes over the transferor's obligation to make adjustments under the CGS (VAT Regulations 1995 (SI 1995/2518), reg. 14(7)).

2. Special rules apply in respect of future sales of second-hand goods and used motor cars, to ensure that the transferee's base cost is restricted to that of the transferor (or, in the case of a series of TOGCs, that of the original transferor).

3. There are also special anti-avoidance rules to ensure that tax is due on the future free supply of goods or services included in the TOGC where the transferor (or,

in the case of a series of TOGCs, some earlier transferor) has obtained an input tax deduction in respect of the items concerned.

4.   If the purchaser is a partly exempt group, it may be deemed to make a supply of assets included in the transfer that the vendor acquired in the previous three years. The partially exempt purchaser/transferee must account for output tax on all assets that the transferor acquired in the past three years and only claim input tax credits in accordance to its partial exemption scheme.

For each of these conditions, the transferee must obtain the relevant information from the transferor and obtain a relevant warranty regarding the required information.

13.3.7   Whether basic conditions are met

The basic conditions are met when a taxable person transfers a business as a going concern. A taxable person is a person who is registered for VAT, or is required to be registered.

The other conditions are:

- that the transfer should be a transfer of a business rather than a mere transfer of assets; and
- that the business should be transferred as a going concern.

These two points were considered together by Widgery J in an often repeated extract from his judgment in an employment law case, *Kenmir Ltd v Frizzell* [1968] 1 All ER 414:

'We think that the principles applied in these two cases govern the present case also. In deciding whether a transaction amounted to the transfer of a business regard must be had to its substance rather than its form, and consideration must be given to the whole of the circumstances, weighing the factors which point in one direction against those which point in another. In the end, the vital consideration is whether the effect of the transaction was to put the transferee in possession of a going concern, the activities of which he could carry on without interruption. Many factors may be relevant to this decision though few will be conclusive in themselves. Thus, if the new employer carries on business in the same manner as before, this will point to the existence of a transfer, but the converse is not necessarily true because a transfer may be complete even though the transferee does not choose to avail himself of all the rights which he acquires thereunder. Similarly, an express assignment of goodwill is strong evidence of a transfer of the business, but the absence of such an assignment is not conclusive if the transferee has effectively deprived himself of the power to compete. The absence of an assignment of premises, stock-in-trade or outstanding contracts will likewise not be conclusive, if the particular circumstances of the transferee nevertheless enable him to carry on substantially the same business as before.'

Perhaps the most important point highlighted by this extract, is that we are dealing with a complex question of fact so each case will depend very much on its own facts and circumstances. This may be determined by the parties to the transaction, by

HMRC if they review the transaction or by a tribunal on the evidence before it. There are many factors which can be relevant but few, if any, which will be conclusive on their own. The various facts and circumstances must be taken together and weighed, rather than there being any single test. This is actually a judicial way of saying that the whole thing is a matter of opinion, so do not expect certainty as you will be disappointed (whoever said that the only certainties were death and taxes surely only meant the existence of these things not the manner of them or, in the case of the latter, the amount).

> ### Planning point
>
> Employment law cases are a useful guide to what is considered to be a transfer of a going concern. Whilst staff are not chattels to be transferred, where there is continuity of a business as opposed to the sale of assets, there are employment law protections offered to staff to ensure that they can continue in their employment. The contract should contain a clause regarding the continuity of the business to emphasise that this is a TOGC. Where there is any doubt a ruling should be obtained from HMRC.

13.3.8   Whether there is a transfer of a business

The simultaneous sale of the entire assets of a business combined with a transfer of staff is clearly likely to be seen as a transfer of the business itself. Although even this is not a certainty, especially if it was clear to all concerned that the purchaser wished to carry on an entirely different business using similar assets and staff, or made some legal undertaking not to carry on the pre-existing business.

Anything below such a total transfer rapidly enters the realms of uncertainty.

Important deciding factors will be the nature and extent of assets transferred. Assets whose explicit or implicit transfer points particularly towards a transfer of a business include:

- goodwill (including the use of the business name);
- customer lists;
- intellectual property specific to the business; and
- staff, premises, fixed assets, trading stocks, etc..

The existence or non-existence of a consensus between buyer and seller that what is being transferred is a business can be highly significant, as found in *Westpark Interiors Ltd* (1983) 1 BVC 1,206, but is still not conclusive in itself and must be judged in the light of the surrounding facts. Such a consensus might be evidenced in the contractual documents or inferred from the manner in which the assets are held out for sale.

Consensus was important in the case of *C Cohen (Furriers) Ltd* referred to earlier, where an unplanned and piecemeal series of acquisitions of various assets might have been seen as amounting, in effect, to the transfer of a going concern (although this could not have been foreseen at the outset) but was held not to do so, partly because there was no consensus between the parties for such a transfer.

> ### *Planning point*
>
> Whilst the matter can be subjective, a good guide as to whether there has been a TOGC is to ask has this transfer (or transfers) put the new owner in possession of a viable business that can stand on its own (rather than in combination with other assets or structures of either the vendor or purchaser)? If yes, it is a TOGC; if not, it is a sale of assets. See also **13.3.13**.

13.3.9 Whether there is a transfer as a going concern

If there is a transfer of a business in the terms described above, it will probably be transferred as a going concern. The vital question, as indicated in *Kenmir Ltd v Frizzell*, is whether the transferee is put in possession of a going concern, the activities of which he could carry on without interruption.

Where there is not a TOGC there will be a sale of individual assets that will be subject to VAT under the normal rules.

13.3.10 Interruption of business

It does not appear to be relevant whether the transferee actually does carry on the activities without post-transfer interruption, provided that this is possible, although this may be one of the factors to take into account in considering whether what was transferred was, in the perception or consensus of the parties, a business. An interruption in the carrying on of the business before the transfer might be relevant, although a two-month break in trading has been held not to preclude a going concern transfer (*Montrose DIY Ltd* (1988) 3 BVC 1,362). The post-transfer interruption is just that and cannot affect what was transferred prior to the interruption.

> ### *Planning point*
>
> To ensure that it is not necessary to incur VAT it is prudent for the purchaser to commence trading as soon as possible, preferably with no break. Even where there are works to be undertaken, such as decoration, a limited business may be carried on to demonstrate continuity.

13.3.11 Insolvent or unprofitable business

It might be thought that an insolvent business could not be regarded as a going concern, but this is not the case. The tribunals have generally taken the view that, simply because a business has failed under its previous management, this does not mean that the same business cannot be revived by the purchasers and already be, in essence, a going concern (this does not seem unreasonable as it is, presumably, precisely the view taken by the purchaser – otherwise there would be no purchase).

Ultimately, the phrase when a taxable person transfers a business as a going concern must be considered in its entirety, and whether it is applicable in a particular case depends on all the facts and evidence in that case as well as the opinion of the tribunal hearing the case (if it goes that far).

> **Planning point**
>
> It would be wise to make sure that evidence of what happens, and of the intentions and consensus (if any) of the parties, is produced and retained, that contracts take account of the possible outcome, and that the position is formally agreed with HMRC (in advance of contracts if possible) in doubtful cases.

13.3.12 Whether special conditions met

The special conditions under which a TOGC may be treated as not involving a supply are set out in the VAT (Special Provisions) Order 1995 (SI 1995/1268), art. 5.

In the normal case where the transferor is a taxable person, non-supply treatment can only apply if the transferee is also a taxable person or immediately becomes one as a result of the transfer. If the transferor is not a taxable person there is no requirement that the transferee be, or become one, for non-supply treatment to apply.

13.3.13 Part of business capable of separate operation

If the transfer is only of part of the business, then non-supply treatment can only apply if that part is capable of separate operation. Presumably, it cannot be said that an entire business has been transferred if it is not capable of separate operation, so there is no such requirement imposed once it has been determined that the transfer is of a whole business. There is no requirement that the part transferred actually be operated separately, as is apparent from the second condition.

It should also be noted that there is no requirement that the assets transferred were operated as a separate business before the transfer.

In determining what can be regarded as being capable of separate operation, it is not essential that it should be so capable without calling in some external resources. For instance, in *Hivemead Ltd* (1984) 2 BVC 205,059 the assets transferred were not capable of carrying out the whole of the production process, but the tribunal took account of the possibility of subcontracting part of the work and held that they were capable of separate operation.

In *Cosalt Coolair Ltd* (1985) 2 BVC 208,072, the tribunal held that the fact that a business depended upon certain central services provided by the vendor (who was bound, under the agreement, to provide all reasonable assistance) did not prevent it from being capable of separate operation. The chairman commented:

> 'The fact that part of a business can only run if integrated into another business which has the facilities to support it does not, in the judgment of the tribunal, necessarily mean that it is incapable of separate operation.'

13.3.14 Use for same kind of business

It has for many years been a given that, for the transaction to be treated as a TOGC, the assets must be used by the transferee to carry on the same kind of business as that carried on by the transferor, whether or not as part of any existing business.

This position has been called into serious question with the ECJ case of *Zita Modes Sàrl v Administration de l'enregistrement et des domaines* (Case C-497/01) [2005] BVC 772, where it was held that the transferee need not pursue the same type of business as that carried on by the transferor prior to the transfer. All that is required is that the transferee intends to carry on a business (not simply liquidating the assets, for example).

This new interpretation has been accepted by HMRC (see *Business Brief 09/05*). Somewhat oddly, however, bearing in mind that the VAT (Special Provisions) Order 1995 (SI 1995/1268) uses the wording 'carrying on the same kind of business' (art. 5(1)(a)(i) and (b)(ii)), HMRC goes on to say that UK legislation is in line with the decision and needs no change. HMRC were considering whether or not their guidance needs to be revised, and have not as yet announced any changes.

In any event, arguably no reliance need any longer be placed on this test in determining whether or not a qualifying TOGC has taken place.

13.3.15 Taxable land

A further condition applies to the extent that the assets transferred include taxable land, buildings, etc. being:

- land, etc.. in respect of which the transferor has exercised the option for taxation; or
- freehold land on which is a new or partly completed commercial building or civil engineering work.

In this case the transfer of the land cannot be treated as a non-supply unless the transferee, before the first potential tax point in respect of the supply (which could be the date of payment of a deposit, if this is received by the transferor's solicitor as agent rather than stakeholder):

- opts for taxation;
- notifies HMRC of this in writing; and
- notifies the vendor that his option to tax will not be disapplied as a result of the connected party anti-avoidance provisions.

If these conditions are not met, the transfer of the land is treated as a supply, while the transfer of the other assets (if the other conditions have been met) continues to be de-supplied.

Planning point

Where the transfer is of a property letting business, the transferee will in any case usually wish to opt for taxation. If the transferee is to occupy the property itself, then it is necessary to consider the effects on future marketability of the property before reaching a decision.

13.3.16 Rulings from HMRC

As is apparent from the above, there are a number of questions to be answered in determining whether the TOGC provisions apply, several of them involving questions of fact and degree. There are also a great many decided cases on the subject but these provide little in the way of firm guidance since each case depends very much upon its own facts, and often on the overall impressions of the tribunal rather than some narrow point of law.

Planning point

HMRC are prepared to give rulings on such transactions and it is prudent to make use of this, taking care to provide all relevant information, as a ruling on partial facts is worthless. In order to obtain a relevant ruling in time (as it will usually take HMRC a month to reply) the application should be made as soon as possible).

⚠ Warning!

TOGCs can only apply to transfers of a business and so would not apply to charitable non-business activities or to non-business relevant residential use as these are not business activities. There may be a case for apportionment where a building is part used for such a qualifying purposes.

Selling a Business

14.1   Selling a business

14.1.1   Basic options on the sale of a business

It is clear from the commercial realities of the sale and purchase of a business that there are a number of possible basic outcomes for what appears to be a fairly simple transaction. These can be multiplied for some of the extra terms and conditions (such as additional, post-transfer performance-related payments) which are often required in order to reach a satisfactory deal.

This section sets out to cover the basic features of business sales, and their implications, but cannot possibly deal with every nuance (and there are plenty) which can arise on a particular transaction. There is also a degree of cross over with the previous chapter, **Chapter 13, Buying a business**.

> ### ⚠ *Warning!*
>
> This section should provide a useful guide, but every transaction needs to be examined from the ground up in terms of basic VAT principles.

Watch out, in particular, for *side deal* which may arise between parties interested or involved in the sale but who are not necessarily the main players. Watch also for the complications when some of the assets relating to the business (such as land) are in different entities, or sold or transferred from different entities, rather than the whole business being transferred as a job lot. The potential variations here are too great to cover, although some are mentioned. For example, a business that is being sold as a going concern will benefit from the VAT relief that permits no VAT to be charged on the transaction. Any *side deal* will not benefit from this relief.

14.1.2   Selling the business assets

The basic question on the sale of business assets is, of course, whether VAT should be charged on the transaction. Where VAT is not charged and it is found that VAT should have been charged it can often be difficult to obtain this VAT from the purchaser. It should be noted that where the business making the sale is exempt from VAT and no VAT was claimed on the acquisition or purchase of the assets now being sold, any supply of the business assets is exempt from VAT under art. 136(a) and (b) of the Principal VAT Directive (Directive 2006/112).

In the case of a taxable business, the charging of VAT (if properly due) is of less importance, as the VAT charged can generally be recovered by the purchaser. There are, however, various other considerations. Most importantly is the determination of the contractual position between the parties and the price to be paid for the assets. This is overlooked surprisingly often, giving rise to an awful lot of disputes between the parties, some of which subsequently come before the VAT tribunals. The vendor will obviously wish to ensure that the contractual arrangements allow the charging of VAT, if due, on top of the agreed consideration

The vendor may sell an option to purchase to a potential buyer. This will take the same liability as the underlying asset. Thus, if the option is for shares, the supply of the option is exempt. Where it is an option to purchase the business, the supply will be taxable, even if the later supply of the business is treated as not being a supply due to the provisions of the Transfer Of a Going Concern rules. An option to buy business assets will have the same VAT liability as the underlying assets (for example exempt for land and buildings unless a new commercial building or the option to tax has been exercised when they will be standard rated).

> ### Planning point
>
> Ensure you know what you are selling; what is being sold will determine the VAT liability. In addition, ensure you know what the consideration is, and if it is described as VAT inclusive or exclusive in the contract.

14.1.3   Sale of whole business

A common transaction in business reorganisations is the sale of the whole of the assets of a business (with or without associated liabilities) to one person (or to a partnership, which counts as one person for VAT purposes). Provided that the purchaser is going to carry on the same business using the assets, and all of the other necessary conditions are met (TOGC, see **13.3.1**), the transfer is likely to be 'desupplied', so that no VAT is chargeable regardless of the nature or VAT liability of the underlying assets.

> ### Planning point
>
> As a general rule:
> * the vendor should ensure that the contracts enable it to charge VAT, if applicable, in addition to the agreed consideration;
> * the contract should determine when the purchaser is to pay the consideration and any VAT that is due; and
> * both parties may wish to have provisions in place for finalising the position, often by obtaining specific clearance from HMRC.

Consideration also needs to be given to the possibility of transferring the transferor's existing VAT number to the transferee, although this is usually unnecessary and also inadvisable. This is considered further at **14.1.9**.

14.1.4   Partial sale of assets

Things get more complicated where what is sold does not amount to the entire assets of the business. TOGC treatment can still apply but only if the assets sold represent a part of the business capable of separate operation. It is a question of fact whether this condition is met. A further question of fact is the nature of the business, which must be established in order to determine whether the transferee uses the assets to carry on the same kind of business (whether or not as part of a larger business activity) as that previously carried on by the transferor.

As a general rule, when only some of the business assets are transferred, a VAT-registered transferor will remain registered for VAT, in which case the option of transferring the VAT registration number is not available.

> **Planning point**
>
> The transferor needs to consider the VAT status of the remaining business after the sale. If the continuing business will be trading with the transferee, the VAT status of the supplies made needs to be considered by both parties.

> ⚠ **Warning!**
>
> It is the vendor's responsibility to determine the VAT liability of the sale. Where there is an error it is the vendor that will be liable to account for the VAT to HMRC and may also incur penalties and interest charges. If there is any reliance on the transferee (for example regarding the future use of the assets) appropriate warranties and indemnities must be obtained. Where there is any doubt as to the VAT liability of the transaction professional advice must be sought and a ruling obtained from HMRC.

14.1.5   Piecemeal sale of assets

Where assets are sold piecemeal and cannot be operated as a separate business, rather than with the intention of transferring the business as a whole, there is normally no special VAT treatment and VAT will be chargeable according to the liability status of the supplies made.

> **Planning point**
>
> A difficulty that can arise is similar to that where there is a partial sale of a business, is that it can be difficult to tell whether the TOGC provisions apply. Consideration should be given to obtaining a ruling from HMRC and also to providing terms in the contract that will allow VAT to be charged if necessary.

An example arose in the case of *C Cohen (Furriers) Ltd* (1990) 5 BVC 1,363. A company carrying on a business as furriers bought stock from an ailing rival. Because of financial difficulties the rival made its staff redundant. Three days after buying the stock the appellant took over the rival's premises, and also employed some of its former staff. HMRC denied the appellant's claim for input tax on the stock purchase, claiming that the combination of transactions amounted to a transfer of a going concern so that VAT was not properly chargeable on the sale of stock.

The tribunal allowed the appeal, holding that on the evidence before it there was no consensus between the parties that the business should be transferred and the transaction was a mere sale of stock on which VAT was properly chargeable.

> **⚠ Warning!**
>
> Where it is not clear-cut whether or not a transaction qualifies as a VAT-free business transfer, there is a potential risk for both parties. It is advisable not to make assumptions and to take appropriate advice before proceeding with the deal.

14.1.6   Assets owned by different entities

Careful analysis is needed where there are multiple entities involved on one side of the transaction or the other.

14.1.7   Merging ownership of assets owned separately

Caution must be exercised where there are two vendors but only one purchaser.

Where, for example, a trader (T) carries on a business in premises rented from an associated party (A) and it is proposed that the business and the property be sold to a third party purchaser (P).

In this case the TOGC provisions probably apply to the transfer of the trading activity.

However, if P also buys the property and occupies it itself, it will not be using it to carry on the same kind of business (property letting) as that previously carried on by A. Consequently, the TOGC provisions will not apply to the sale of the property, which will give rise to an exempt or a taxable supply depending on whether it is a new freehold property or whether A has opted for taxation. This will impact on whether VAT is chargeable on the supply and also on whether A is entitled to recover the input tax associated with the disposal. It will also have consequences for other purposes, such as the operation of the capital goods scheme.

> **Planning point**
>
> If it proves essential for one reason or another to achieve TOGC treatment for both transactions, one possibility would be to structure the initial deal differently, so that the purchaser uses two separate entities for the purchase.

One possibility would be to buy the property into one company and the operating assets into a subsidiary. Both would carry on the taken-over businesses for a while. Subsequently, the operating assets could be hived up into the company which already owned the property.

On this approach, both the sale of the property and the sale of the operating assets are likely to qualify for TOGC treatment, since each of the purchasing companies will continue to use the assets in carrying on the same kind of business as that previously carried on by the transferor. On the subsequent hive-up of the operating assets, the transferee will continue to use the assets for the same kind of business as that carried on by the transferor, while the property-letting activity will disappear and be merged into the main operating activity.

Another possibility would be to merge the assets before transfer. In this situation, the trading company would transfer its business to the property-owning associated company, which would carry on the business for a while. The property-owning associated company would then transfer the merged assets to the purchaser as a going concern.

> **⚠ Warning!**
>
> Variations of this sort should, of course, be approached with caution, and the implications for the specific case (non-VAT issues such as direct tax as well as VAT matters) must be thoroughly analysed. Special care is needed to see whether any anti-avoidance provisions may have an effect (including those covering a VAT group acquiring assets under a TOGC).

14.1.8   Contract terms

It is best to embark on the process of analysing the VAT position at an early stage in the negotiations, particularly where complex structures are likely to be involved. VAT consequences not appreciated until late in the proceedings can be a deal breaker and it may be necessary to settle for a less than optimum VAT position if, by the time VAT is considered, the structure of the deal is too far entrenched for it to be feasible to make alterations to improve the VAT treatment in the time available. The points in section **14.1.3** need to be considered, and a purchaser may also have other requirements that should be included.

Planning point

Early consideration of the VAT contract terms is important, but often forgotten.

Of course, getting the contract terms right can be difficult if the parties are unsure of the appropriate VAT treatment, such as whether the TOGC provisions apply or not.

In some cases this is so critical to the commercial viability of the deal that it is essential to obtain sufficient certainty before finalising the transactions, usually by providing full details of the proposals to HMRC before finalisation and seeking their written agreement to the desired treatment. It is essential in such cases to ensure that full information has been provided, that there is evidence of this and also that the written agreement from HMRC is clear and unambiguous.

Experience has shown that HMRC are highly variable in their willingness to provide speedy rulings on such business transfers, even where they realise the commercial importance of achieving certainty as to the VAT treatment. However, they cannot always meet the deadlines which are important to the parties and are sometimes reluctant to provide an advance ruling at all, on the basis that, until it happens, it is merely theoretical, or, more recently, that as VAT is a self-assessed tax and that the onus is therefore on the taxpayer to make the decision.

Planning point

In many cases the precise VAT treatment is not ultimately crucial, provided that appropriate terms between the parties can be embodied in the contract. In these cases it is not unusual to draft clauses to meet the position in either case, with an agreement between the parties to obtain appropriate rulings. This can enable the transaction to proceed on schedule even though the final VAT result remains unknown for a while. In these cases it is also common for uncertain amounts of VAT to be secured by payment into an escrow account, to be released to one party or the other, with interest, depending on the ruling finally obtained from HMRC.

⚠ Warning!

It will be clear from the above that both buyer(s) and seller(s) need to analyse the proposed transactions carefully before finally committing themselves. They also need to ensure that the contract terms embody the transactions which they have finally settled upon and the VAT consequences of them and that both parties are satisfied with the result.

14.1.9   Transfer of VAT registration number

If a business is transferred as a going concern, and the vendor ceases to be registered for VAT as a result, it is possible to transfer the VAT registration number to the new owner with the assets. This procedure requires the agreement of both parties, evidenced by their completion and signature of form VAT 68. The form includes detailed confirmation by the parties of their acceptance of the consequences that go with transferring the registration number.

Where a VAT registration number is transferred, the transferee takes over the liability of the transferor:

* to submit returns and payments for periods before the transfer (including the return covering the period of transfer), to the extent that this has not already been done by the transferor; and
* to account for tax previously reclaimed as input tax which becomes the subject of a bad-debt relief claim by the supplier.

The transferee also takes over:

* any right of the transferor to input tax credit; and
* any right of the transferor to claim bad-debt relief.

Any right of either the transferor or the transferee to a net repayment on a repayment return may be satisfied by HMRC making payment of the appropriate amount to either of them.

It has been held that the liability to meet the transferor's past liabilities extends only to VAT due on returns submitted but not yet paid, or on returns which had not been submitted at the time of the transfer, not to any liability to pay to HMRC amounts underdeclared by the transferor in completing returns previously submitted (*Pets Place (UK) Ltd* [1997] BVC 2,164).

> **Planning point**
>
> The potentially adverse consequences of retaining the existing VAT number of a business mean that it is best done only in cases where there is a close connection between the transferor and the transferee, such as a sole trader taking in a partner, or a sole trader or partnership incorporating. Even in cases such as these, it can be beneficial on occasion to take the opportunity of having the former number cancelled (if there is a history of late returns, for example), if the benefits outweigh any disadvantages.

14.1.10   Input tax position of vendor

As far as the vendor is concerned, the above remarks have concentrated mainly on the output tax position (albeit with due consideration of the effects of that on input tax recovery), so it may be worth summarising the principles affecting the input tax position. The detailed principles of input tax attribution and the workings of the CGS are covered in **Chapter 12**.

> ### *Planning point*
>
> The vendor's position depends essentially on whether the transaction falls within the TOGC rules. If it does not, then the input tax on inputs attributable to the sale of the assets will be recoverable or not according to the liability of that supply. In the case of assets within the CGS, any final attribution will also be made according to the liability of the supply made.

Where the transaction is within the TOGC rules, the input tax attributable to the transaction (selling costs, etc.) is residual. In the case of a fully taxable vendor, this may be expected to lead to full recovery of the tax. In the case of a partly exempt vendor a proportion will be recoverable in accordance with the partial exemption method in force.

However, there is a further complication in the case of a transfer of a separately identifiable part of a business. In this case, the treatment of the input tax on selling costs depends upon the VAT status of the business activity sold. If it is fully taxable, the input tax is wholly recoverable; if it is wholly exempt, the input tax is non-recoverable; if it makes mixed supplies, the input tax is residual (*Abbey National plc v C & E Commrs* (Case C-408/98) [2001] BVC 581, *Business Brief 8/01* (2 July 2001)).

In the case of items within the CGS transferred as part of a TOGC, the transferor will make any necessary adjustments up to the date of the transfer, and the transferee takes over the liability to do this for the remainder of the adjustment period.

14.1.11 Ongoing payments

Additional consideration

It is not unusual for agreements to provide for the payment of additional consideration dependent on the performance of the activity concerned, sometimes over a period of years.

If the main transaction fell within the TOGC provisions, and nothing further has to be done for the additional payments, then they will normally not be treated as consideration for supplies.

> ### *Planning point*
>
> If there is some ongoing activity on the part of the transferor, separate and distinct from the transfer of the assets of the business, there is likely to be a further supply made which may well be subject to VAT.

Often there is a non-competition agreement which can, in principle, give rise to supplies. VAT may not arise if the parties:

- ensure that the consideration is linked to the main supply of the businesses;
- ensure that the additional consideration is not specifically linked with the non-competition agreement in the contract;
- ensure that the agreements demonstrate that the non-competition agreement is merely ancillary to the main agreement for the transfer of the assets; and
- agree the position with HMRC.

Where the transfer was not within the TOGC provisions, then further consideration for the assets will follow the liability of the supplies of assets (and of any additional services provided in return for the additional consideration). Since there has been an actual supply of the assets this can, on the face of it, give rise to tax point problems since there can be a liability to account for tax on an amount that is not yet known.

Planning point

It seems proper to regard the additional payments as being within the special tax point provisions for retention payments, agreeing this with HMRC if there is any doubt. Liability will then arise when the additional payments are received, or tax invoices issued in respect of them.

Consultancies

Another form of ongoing payment arises where one or more owners or managers of the transferring business also take on consultancies with the transferee and receive fees for this. In principle these will generally be subject to VAT, requiring the consultants (or the entities through which they act) to become or remain registered for VAT (subject to VAT registration turnover limits, etc.).

Occasionally, however, if the provision of this consultancy is an obligation of the vendor (as opposed to the individual concerned), and is provided for in the sale contract, it may amount to part of the TOGC and not be subject to VAT, although this can be a difficult argument to sustain. Where an entity is required to provide services post the transfer, it is usual for that entity to have to account for VAT on these services on any consideration received.

Planning point

The charging of VAT (or otherwise) on these amounts is something else which needs to be considered in drawing up the agreements.

14.1.12 Matters for the vendor to consider

The main matters of principle which will be of particular concern to the vendor are:

- whether the transfer involves a transfer of a business as a going concern or the making of supplies (or, on occasion, both);
- if there are supplies, whether tax is due on these;
- whether the agreements allow for tax to be added to the consideration where appropriate;
- what are the effects of the above on the vendor's input tax recovery (including any CGS adjustments);
- are there any better ways of approaching the transactions; and
- have all uncertainties been fully addressed in the agreements, in negotiations with HMRC; or both?

The vendor also needs to address administrative matters such as the need, on a TOGC, either to hand the business records over to the transferee or to obtain written permission from HMRC to retain them. Of course, all of these matters need to be considered in conjunction with the commercial and direct tax implications of the transactions and possible variations.

14.1.13 Selling shares

The transfer of a business by the purchase and sale of shares is, in many ways, a far simpler matter for VAT than the purchase and sale of the underlying assets. The person carrying on the business (i.e. the company sold) remains the same after the transaction as before it, so there is no change of VAT entity, unless the purchaser subsequently transfers the undertaking to some other vehicle.

However, it raises more questions (to many of which there are currently no satisfactory answers) about the recovery of input tax. The sale of the shares is input taxed not permitting VAT to be reclaimed on the selling costs. The person acquiring the shares will also have incurred costs and the recovery of the VAT incurred may be difficult; if the VAT is incurred in a non-trading holding company, no VAT can be reclaimed. Even if the cost is incurred in a taxable trading entity, HMRC may ascribe the VAT on the costs to the acquisition of shares rather than to taxable supplies.

Often what happens is a combination of share sales and asset sales (the latter sometimes back into the originally owning group) and various related transactions to achieve the finally desired arrangements in terms of financing the newly organised entities at either end of the transactions.

> **Planning point**
>
> The main comment to make is that there is nothing to beat first principles. When the transactions go beyond the simple models described here, it is absolutely necessary to go back to that basic model for VAT planning more generally, the Four As (ascertainment, analysis, alternatives, action) and arrive at a bespoke plan for the particular circumstances of the case, including (by cooperation with other advisers) the non-VAT aspects of it.

A sub-comment is that, when it comes to share sales, perhaps the biggest VAT question which arises concerns the vendor's entitlement to recovery of input tax (this can affect the purchaser as well, where it issues new shares to finance the purchase).

Sale by company

Where a company disposes of the shares in a subsidiary, this gives rise to a supply of those shares. Generally this will be an exempt supply, so, depending on VAT group registration issues, input tax on the parent company's costs attributable to the disposal will in principle be irrecoverable.

However, if the shares are supplied to a person belonging outside the EU, then the supply is outside the scope, but with a right to input tax recovery.

> **Planning point**
>
> Where the purchaser is a multinational organisation it may be possible to arrange for the shares to be sold to one of its non-EU entities, leaving it to the purchaser to transfer them on to a UK entity at a later date if this is desired.

If the vendor is a purely passive holding company (i.e. its only activity is to hold shares in its subsidiaries without taking an active part in their management, deriving its income purely from dividends rather than management charges, intra-group trading, etc.) it may be regarded as not carrying on a business (*Polysar Investments Netherlands BV v Inspecteur der Invoerrechten en Accijnzen, Arnhem* (Case C-60/90) [1993] BVC 88). In this case it will have no entitlement to input tax recovery, unless it forms part of a VAT group.

Sale by private shareholders

Private shareholders selling their company are normally not regarded as carrying on a business activity, so will be unable to recover input tax on any costs which they incur in connection with the disposal.

> **Planning point**
>
> Such private shareholders will therefore wish to ensure that their advisers take maximum advantage of any exemption available for supplies of making arrangements for the transaction.

There may be exceptions in some cases where the shares are held as assets of a sole trader or partnership business, especially if there are close connections between the shareholding and company and the activities of the unincorporated business.

The company being sold may itself incur costs in connection with the transaction. On the face of it these are incurred for the benefit of the shareholders rather than of the company, so VAT arising on them will not be regarded as input tax in the hands of the company.

However, this depends very much on the facts of the case. There are instances where the purpose of the transaction is as much to benefit the company and its business activity as it is to benefit the shareholders (for instance, by giving it access to financial and technical support from a larger group, better access to markets, more professional management, etc.), in which case input tax incurred by the company may well be recoverable; clearly, it is necessary to distinguish between the VAT incurred for private purposes and the VAT incurred by the business for its own business purposes.

Side transfers of assets

When planning the transaction it is necessary to bear in mind that there may be more to it than the mere sale of shares. Related transactions, such as the separate sale of property occupied by the company, need to be considered as well.

14.2 Disposing of a business as a going concern

Input tax incurred in connection with transferring a business as a going concern was considered in *Abbey National plc v C & E Commrs* (Case C-408/98) [2001] BVC 581. The court ruled that when an entire business making taxable and exempt supplies is transferred, the disposal costs are a general overhead and the input tax is attributable to taxable and exempt supplies.

> **Planning point**
>
> There may be occasions when the input tax on disposal costs is wholly attributable to taxable or exempt supplies. The court considered that this could happen if only part of a business is transferred. If the part transferred makes only exempt or taxable supplies and there is a 'direct and immediate' link between the disposal costs and relevant supplies, the input tax should be analysed accordingly.

14.3   Business transfers – Capital Goods and land

Where a business is transferred as a going concern and the supply, including capital items to which the CGS applies, falls outside the scope of VAT by virtue of the VAT (Special Provisions) Order 1995 (SI 1995/1268), art. 5, the new owner takes over the responsibility for continuing the adjustments due under the scheme. The vendor ceases to be responsible for the assets and any subsequent adjustments.

The liability of any disposal of land as set out in the table at **36.1** will not apply where the disposal is regarded as a transfer of all or part of a going concern.

The transfer of a property development can be the transfer of a going concern (TOGC) in certain circumstances. Clearly the transfer of property can occur in the context of the sale of a business and will be an element of a transfer of a going concern. In other circumstances, property will be the subject of the business itself, for example the sale of an uncompleted property development or of a property investment business.

14.4   Transfers of going concerns

If the sale of assets is a TOGC, then the sale of those assets is treated as neither a supply of goods nor of services and is not subject to VAT.

The conditions for TOGC treatment are:

- the assets must be supplied to a person to whom the transferor transfers his business (or a part of the business) as a going concern;
- the assets are to be used by the transferee in carrying on the same kind of business as that carried on by the transferor (whether or not as part of an existing business); and
- where the transferor is a taxable person, the transferee is already, or immediately becomes as a result of the transfer, a taxable person.

As far as land is concerned, however, a supply of assets does not qualify as a TOGC insofar as it consists of a supply of land that would, save for TOGC treatment, be a standard-rated supply as:

- the property is subject to a valid and effective option to tax; or
- it is a freehold sale (or its equivalent) of a new or partly completed commercial building or new or partly completed civil engineering works,

unless the transferee has made and notified an option to tax by the time that the supply would, other than being treated as a TOGC, have been treated to have been made (effectively before completion of the contract). Furthermore, with effect from 18 March 2004, the transferee must provide the transferor with a declaration to the effect that anti-avoidance provisions do not apply to him in respect of the property to be transferred. This is an anti-avoidance provision. The actual declaration takes the form of notifying the transferor that para. (2B), art. 5 of the Value Added Tax (Special Provisions) Order 1995 (SI 1995/1268) does not apply to him in respect of the property transferred.

> ### ⚠ *Warning!*
> This last condition is onerous. It also represents a risk for both parties. The purchaser who fails to give a notification will incur VAT on the purchase, with the consequential increase in SDLT. The vendor who treats the sale as VAT-free without receiving a notification may find that he is assessed for VAT on a later VAT visit, on the basis that the conditions for VAT-free treatment were not met.

HMRC consider the following to be capable of being transferred as a going concern:

- a property which is let to a tenant, where it is sold with the benefit of the existing lease, this is the case even if the property is only partly tenanted;
- the assignment of a lease of a property (which is subject to a sub-lease) if the lease is assigned with the benefit of the sub-lease;
- the disposal of a building that is being let out even though there is an initial rent-free period and the building is sold during that period;
- the sale of a building where leases have been granted but the tenants are not yet in occupation; and
- a property that is intended to be let but for which no tenant has actually entered into a lease agreement, if there is sufficient evidence of intended economic use.

In contrast, HMRC consider the following not to be capable of being transferred as a going concern:

- the sale of a property by a property developer that has built a building and allowed someone to occupy it temporarily (without any right to occupy after any proposed sale) while the building is being marketed;
- the sale of a property where the lease granted is surrendered immediately before the sale; and
- the sale of a property to the existing tenant where the tenant leases the whole property from the vendor.

Other guidance: *VAT Notice 700/9*, (March 2002 edn.)

What HMRC are trying to achieve is to ensure that a viable and continuing business is being transferred rather than an asset.

> ### *Planning point*
> The above examples represent HMRC's views and are not set out in the legislation as such. Indeed, some are arguably questionable. However, it is useful and sometimes instructive to be aware of HMRC's views, especially where the consequent analysis of the transaction is beneficial.

The tribunal has held that where a property developer transferred property to a property investor, the transfer was of the same kind of business and thus a TOGC (*Hallborough Properties Ltd* [1994] BVC 1,377). The tribunal has similarly held that where an uncompleted development has been sold to a purchaser for completion of the development there was a TOGC (*The Golden Oak Partnership* [1992] BVC 704), but when active development had not commenced there was no TOGC (*Gulf Trading and Management Ltd* [2001] BVC 4,053).

Planning point

As tribunal decisions are persuasive rather than binding (other than on the parties), they can be very helpful but it is wise not to place undue reliance on any particular one.

Where a property is transferred as a going concern, any remaining adjustments under the capital goods scheme (CGS) are required to be made by the purchaser after the transfer. Where the purchaser does not take on the VAT registration of the vendor, subsequent intervals under the CGS commence on the anniversary of the transfer.

⚠ **Warning!**

All vendors and purchasers of property, whether by way of a TOGC or as an asset sale, need to be aware of their obligations under the CGS (see **Chapter 12** and HMRC *VAT Notice 706/2*). In summary, vendors who are selling a capital item may have to make a final adjustment under the scheme, whilst purchasers will create a new capital item unless the property is acquired by way of a TOGC, in which case they may inherit a liability to adjustments under the scheme from the previous owner.

⚠ **Warning!**

As the purchaser needs to make the CGS adjustments, he should obtain appropriate records from the vendor to show what adjustments have been made in the past, the original acquisition cost and how much input tax was originally claimed. Furthermore, a warranty should be obtained in respect of the need to undertake adjustments and an indemnity for any consequence loss if the warranty fails.

Other Business Transfers

15.1 Sales of assets, incorporation and partnerships

15.1.1 Introduction

This chapter examines various asset disposal and changes in business structures. Buying and selling businesses are dealt with in **Chapter 13, Buying a business** and **Chapter 14, Selling a business**.

15.1.2 Merging ownership of assets owned separately

Caution must be exercised where there are two vendors but only one purchaser.

Where, for example, a trader (T) carries on a business in premises rented from an associated party (A) and it is proposed that the business and the property be sold to a third party purchaser (P).

In this case the TOGC provisions probably apply only to the transfer of the trading activity. The transfer of the property will probably not be a TOGC as, if the purchaser occupies the premises for the trading activity, there is no continuing activity of property letting. This will give rise to an exempt or a taxable supply depending on whether it is a new freehold property or whether A has opted for taxation. This will impact on whether VAT is chargeable on the supply and also on whether A is entitled to recover the input tax associated with the disposal.P will also have to consider if it can reclaim VAT on the acquisition of the property. It will also have consequences for other purposes, such as the operation of the capital goods scheme.

> **Planning point**
>
> If it proves essential for one reason or another to achieve TOGC treatment for both transactions, one possibility would be to structure the initial deal differently, so that the purchaser uses two separate entities for the purchase.

One possibility would be to buy the property in one company and the operating assets into a second entity. Both would carry on the taken-over businesses for a while. Subsequently, the operating assets could be transferred to the company that already owns the property.

Using this approach, both the sale of the property and the sale of the operating assets are likely to qualify for TOGC treatment, since each of the purchasing companies will continue to use the assets in carrying on the same kind of business as that previously carried on by the transferor. On the subsequent transfer of the operating assets, the transferee will continue to use the assets for the same kind of business as that carried on by the transferor, while the property-letting activity will disappear and be merged into the main operating activity.

Another possibility would be to merge the assets before transfer. In this situation, the trading company would transfer its business to the property-owning associated company, which would carry on the business for a while. The property-owning associated company would then transfer the merged assets to the purchaser as a going concern.

> ⚠ **Warning!**
>
> Variations of this sort should, of course, be approached with caution, and the implications for the specific case (non-VAT issues such as direct tax as well as VAT matters) must be thoroughly analysed. Special care is needed to see whether any anti-avoidance provisions may have an effect (including those covering a VAT group acquiring assets under a TOGC).

15.1.3 Splitting ownership of assets within single ownership

Similar considerations arise if a single operating company, T, owns the property and other business assets but the purchasers wish to divide them between two entities; the property purchaser, PP, and the business purchaser, PT.

In this case, T's sale of the trading assets to PT is likely to amount to a TOGC, and be treated as not giving rise to a supply.

T's sale of the property to PP cannot be a TOGC, as PP is to use the asset to carry on a property letting business and T, as an owner-occupier, has carried on no such business. The VAT treatment of the property sale and consequences for input tax recovery in T, therefore needs to be analysed carefully. If an exempt supply of the property is likely to give rise to a substantial CGS claw-back of input tax T may well wish to opt for taxation, which will need to be reflected in the agreements. PP will need to look carefully at the implications of this from its point of view, and may also wish to opt for taxation. Of course, this presupposes that the main business is taxable. If it is exempt then it may be impossible to agree a deal structured on these lines.

It should also be noted that a different outcome arises where T not only occupies the premises for its own business, but lets a part out to a third party. In these circumstances, the sale of the property to PP could be treated as a TOGC (assuming other conditions are met, such as all parties having opted to tax); it would not be a TOGC if these conditions were not met. This shows that a variety of VAT outcomes are possible from what is essentially, for business purposes, the same or similar transactions.

> **Planning point**
>
> Ensure that you know what it is you are selling, from which entity or entities and to which entity or entities, that the various conditions for the desired VAT outcome are met (and that you know what VAT outcome you want) and that the necessary paperwork is completed and submitted to HMRC on time.

15.1.4   Fragmented disposal

The classic and simplest transaction, of a simple sale of the whole of the business assets by one person to another, may be departed from for other reasons, such as direct taxation considerations. Again, this most commonly concerns the property assets of the business.

A typical example is where, immediately prior to the sale, the property is sold to another group company which has unused capital losses, so that these can be utilised against any gain arising on the sale, with conveyance of the property directly from the original owner to the purchaser. This is described below.

In this case, the VAT treatment depends on whether Groupco 1 and Groupco 2 are in the same VAT group. If they are, then the intra-group supply of the property should be ignored, while the supplies to the purchaser of both the business assets generally and the property will be seen as made by the representative member (which is also deemed to have carried on the business now being transferred). The supplies to the purchaser should, therefore, be seen as desupplied under the TOGC provisions, provided the other conditions for this are met (although it will be prudent to confirm this with HMRC).

The position is different if Groupco 1 and Groupco 2 are not in the same VAT group. In this case the transfer of the main business assets may well qualify for TOGC treatment. However, the supply path for the property transactions follows the sale route from Groupco 1 to Groupco 2, then on to the purchaser. As Groupco 2 will not have used the property to carry on the same type of business as Groupco 1, neither the supply to Groupco 2 nor the onward supply to the final purchaser can fall within the TOGC provisions. In addition, onward sales of a property or asset will not qualify for a TOGC where the intermediate company or entity has not traded the asset or business (see *Kwik Save Group plc* [1996] BVC 4,004).

The status of these supplies, and the implications of them, need to be examined and taken into account before contracts are finalised.

15.1.5 Incorporating a business

The incorporation of a non-corporate business can be a special area for direct tax purposes. For VAT it is really no more than a variant of the sale of a business (or of the assets of a business).

Typically, a company is formed and the business assets are transferred to it, either in return for shares or by way of gift. In either case there is, in principle, a supply of the assets by the non-corporate entity (usually a sole trader or a partnership) to the newly formed company.

The same VAT analysis must be applied as on any other disposal of the business assets. As usual, this may be complicated by the retention of part of the assets in, or the transfer of part of the assets to, some different entity. Also, all the usual special rules for TOGC treatment apply as much to the incorporation of a business as to any other transfer of business assets.

> **Planning point**
>
> This is one of the rare occasions when the transfer of the registration number is unlikely to have any particular downside, given that the ownership of the company and that of the pre-existing business entity tend to be in the same, or similar, hands.

15.1.6 Partnership changes

A change in the members of a partnership requires notification to HMRC and an amendment to the VAT register. However, it does not involve any change of VAT entity, so there is no question of there being a supply as a result (HMRC generally accept that the sale by a partner of an interest in a partnership is not done in the course of a business and so does not involve a supply).

Interestingly, this raises the possibility (rarely used) of transferring a business without there being a supply for VAT purposes, as set out in the following example.

> **Example 15.1**
>
> A and B are in partnership. C and D would like to take over the partnership business. Instead of a straight sale they decide (for reasons best known to themselves) to take a different approach, as follows:
>
> 1. C and D are admitted to partnership with A and B, contributing some nominal amount of capital and obtaining an equally nominal partnership share.
>
> 2. A and B then sell their partnership shares to C and D, this being a transaction carried out outside the partnership itself and in a personal capacity.

3. The end result is that the partnership assets and business are now owned by C and D, without any supply having taken place.

Both sets of partnership changes must be notified to HMRC for amendments to be made to the VAT register.

Planning point

Although this provides a relatively straightforward way of effecting a business transfer for VAT purposes, without needing to agonise about the minutiae of TOGC treatment, etc., the effects for other tax purposes and the commercial implications of the short period when all of the partners, original and new, share joint and several liability need to be considered carefully.

Arguably, the same effect could be achieved by having the original partners simply sell their partnership shares (not necessarily in the exact proportions originally held) to the new partners, without there being a change of entity or a supply by the partnership (as opposed to the individual partners). There would simply be a simultaneous retirement from partnership of A and B and entering partnership of C and D. However, it seems less likely that HMRC would accept this approach without detailed scrutiny, although it may still qualify as a TOGC.

15.1.7   Property letting businesses

Before the changes to the VAT regime for property transactions in 1989, and the introduction of the option for taxation, property letting businesses tended to be exempt from VAT and their treatment on a transfer of a business was largely ignored. Since those changes they have posed considerable difficulties.

If a fully let property is sold to a new landlord, that is fairly clearly within the TOGC rules. The difficulties arise with such things as partly let buildings and buildings sold by developers with prospective tenants having signed agreements for lease, but the leases yet to be entered into (and the rental flow yet to commence).

HMRC set out their views on which transactions relating to property letting businesses fall within the TOGC rules and which do not in *VAT Notice 700/9*, s. 7.

Planning point

The first planning point is to be aware of HMRC's view, while the obvious second point is to decide what action to take in the circumstances of the particular case. It seems that people are generally able to come up with work-arounds of one kind or another, since there has yet to be litigation on this particular point.

15.1.8   Contract terms

It is best to embark on the process of analysing the VAT position at an early stage in the negotiations, particularly where complex structures are likely to be involved. VAT consequences not appreciated until late in the proceedings can be a deal breaker and it may be necessary to settle for a less than optimum VAT position if, by the time VAT is considered, the structure of the deal is too far entrenched for it to be feasible to make alterations to improve the VAT treatment in the time available.

> **Planning point**
>
> Early consideration of the VAT contract terms is important, but often forgotten.

Of course, getting the contract terms right can be difficult if the parties are unsure of the appropriate VAT treatment, such as whether the TOGC provisions apply or not.

In some cases this is so critical to the commercial viability of the deal that it is essential to obtain sufficient certainty before finalising the transactions, usually by providing full details of the proposals to HMRC before finalisation and seeking their written agreement to the desired treatment. It is essential in such cases to ensure that full information has been provided, that there is evidence of this and also that the written agreement from HMRC is clear and unambiguous.

Experience has shown that HMRC are highly variable in their willingness to provide speedy rulings on such business transfers, even where they realise the commercial importance of achieving certainty as to the VAT treatment. However, they cannot always meet the deadlines which are important to the parties and are sometimes reluctant to provide an advance ruling at all, on the basis that, until it happens, it is merely theoretical, or, more recently, that as VAT is a self-assessed tax and that the onus is therefore on the taxpayer to make the decision.

> **Planning point**
>
> In many cases the precise VAT treatment is not ultimately crucial, provided that appropriate terms between the parties can be embodied in the contract. In these cases it is not unusual to draft clauses to meet the position in either case, with an agreement between the parties to obtain appropriate rulings. This can enable the transaction to proceed on schedule even though the final VAT result remains unknown for a while. In these cases it is also common for uncertain amounts of VAT to be secured by payment into an escrow account, to be released to one party or the other, with interest, depending on the ruling finally obtained from HMRC.

⚠ *Warning!*

It will be clear from the above that both buyer(s) and seller(s) need to analyse the proposed transactions carefully before finally committing themselves. They also need to ensure that the contract terms embody the transactions which they have finally settled upon and the VAT consequences of them and that both parties are satisfied with the result.

Raising Business Finance

16.1 Input tax implications

16.1.1 Introduction

Costs can be incurred when obtaining business finance. For a fully taxable business this can mean an unexpected loss of input tax. The business will normally be able to reclaim all the VAT that it incurs, but where it raises finance there are circumstances where VAT costs will be incurred.

16.1.2 New share issues

Finance can also be raised through an issue of shares. HMRC had, for many years, prevented businesses from reclaiming input tax credits on costs associated with the issue of shares; this has ultimately proved to be an incorrect position. The position changed following the decision in *Kretztechnik AG v Finanzamt Linz* (Case C-465/03) [2006] BVC 66. The company, *Kretztechnik*, made an issue of shares. It reclaimed the VAT incurred but the Australian tax authority rejected the claim in the belief that *Kretztechnik* had made an exempt supply (the issue of shares). *Kretztechnik* appealed (ultimately to the European Court of Justice) on the basis that the issue of shares was not a taxable supply. The VAT incurred, therefore, should be treated as part of the general overheads of the business. The ECJ agreed with this view.

Any VAT incurred can be reclaimed in line with the share issuing company's partial exemption scheme; the costs are treated as overhead or residual expenses. Thus, a fully taxable company can reclaim all the VAT incurred despite issuing shares. An exempt company can reclaim no VAT, and a partially exempt company will only be able to reclaim a proportion of the VAT incurred on fees.

> **Planning point**
>
> VAT incurred on supplies made to an entity issuing shares is deductible as an overhead expense. This applies whether the shares are issued solely to raise finance, to place the company on a stock exchange or for any other purpose.

16.1.3 Who can deduct the input tax incurred?

A further complication arises on acquisition costs. Are the costs of acquiring another company deductible? This matter has recently been examined in the Upper Tribunal decision of *R & C Commrs v BAA* [2011] BVC 1,664 (and the cross appeal of *BAA v R&C Commrs* [2011] UKUT 258 (TCC)). An attempt was made by the company that acquired the British Airports Authority (BAA) to reclaim the VAT it had incurred on its acquisition costs. Although BAA was unsuccessful in their appeal to the Upper Tribunal it has raised the question as to whether the VAT incurred was deductible input tax.

The acquiring entities created a new company, Airport Development and Investment Limited (ADIL), to acquire BAA. Subsequent to acquiring BAA, ADIL joined the BAA VAT group and changed its name to BAA Limited. The new company provided management services to the group, but it did not charge a fee. The First-Tier Tribunal decided that the acquisition costs (investment bank costs, legal fees and professional advisers) were mainly concerned with the takeover. Acquiring the BAA shares was not 'an end in itself'. It was to enable ADIL to acquire the airports. There was sufficient nexus between the acquisition costs and the supplies that would be made by the BAA group after the acquisition to permit the input tax to be deducted. As the supplies made by BAA were taxable, the VAT incurred was deductible.

The taxpayer raised this argument again in its appeal to the Upper Tribunal and further argued that it had incurred the VAT as preparatory costs to make taxable supplies of management services (or the supplies it would be treated as making after it joined the VAT group). HMRC countered that ADIL was a passive holding company as it had not made any charges for its supplies. All it had done was incur the costs to enable it to acquire the BAA shares. ADIL had not undertaken any economic activity nor had there been any intention to make taxable supplies. Furthermore, there was no link between the pre-acquisition costs and any taxable supply as no management charges had been made.

In what may have been a surprise finding (certainly to HMRC), the Upper Tribunal confirmed the First-Tier Tribunal's finding that ADIL had an economic activity as the purpose of acquiring shares was the first step of an investment in the airports and it involved the management of the group. At first glance, this would appear to give BAA (as ADIL had now become) cause to reclaim the VAT incurred. Unfortunately, for BAA, the Upper Tribunal also held that there was no 'direct and immediate link' between the costs incurred and any taxable supplies made by ADIL, neither before it joined the VAT group nor any supplies made subsequent to grouping. It had been fatal to ADIL/BAA's arguments that they had not made any taxable supplies either when it incurred the VAT or after the takeover had been completed. It was apparent that ADIL had only formed an intention to make taxable supplies subsequent to the acquisition; thus, the costs could not be seen as relating to any taxable supplies that were to be made as there was no such intention at the time the costs were incurred.

The Upper Tribunal also found that the input tax could not be reclaimed as a consequence of grouping. The acquisition costs were not a component of any taxable supplies that would have been made subsequent to grouping.

Planning point

A business that acquires another business may (see Warning! below) be able to reclaim the VAT incurred on acquisition costs where it can clearly demonstrate that there is an intention to make and charge for taxable supplies of management services to the target entity subsequent to the acquisition. This intention should be documented. In addition, the position will be improved if the acquiring entity makes taxable supplies in addition to these management services to the acquired entity. The costs incurred may be regarded as part of the general overheads of a management company and deductible in line with its partial exemption position.

⚠ Warning!

The Upper Tribunal made its decision based upon the facts as determined by the Lower-Tier Tribunal. Where the facts differ, the VAT position may also differ. Furthermore, HMRC may not accept these conclusions and could seek to challenge any such input tax recovery and seek to establish different facts, particularly in respect to economic activity being established by the acquiring entity.

16.1.4   Subsequent share issues

The sale, supply or trading in existing shares (as opposed to issuing new shares) is an exempt supply and any VAT incurred that relates to this activity is not deductible unless a relief is available (such as selling the shares to an overseas customer). Thus, where existing shares are issued an exempt supply will be made. Any VAT incurred on the issue costs will be irrecoverable.

Planning point

Advisors and professional entities that provide services in respect of the supply of the shares may be acting as an intermediary and be able to treat their supplies as exempt. Exempt should be available where the intermediary assists in arranging the supply of the shares and introducing the purchaser of the shares to the company (a broker). Most professional services, however, will be taxable and the VAT will be irrecoverable as relating to the exempt supply of shares.

16.1.5   Bank loans

A business that wished to raise finance through a bank loan is usually able to reclaim all the VAT that it incurs. The expenditure is seen as relating to the economic activity (or the business) of the business. The one exception to this is where a bank undertakes due diligence and commissions reports or incurs other costs. The bank is unable to reclaim the VAT incurred on these costs as the bank is making an exempt supply of finance (the loan to the business). Banks will frequently require the business seeking the loan to pay the bank's costs. This does not mean that the business can claim the VAT incurred; although the business has paid for the costs incurred, the supply has been made to the bank and not the business. The only entity that can reclaim the VAT is the bank, and it is prevented from doing so as it has made an exempt supply.

Planning point

VAT incurred on supplies made to an entity raising bank finance is deductible.

⚠ *Warning!*

VAT on supplies made to a business can be reclaimed. Paying the costs of a third party does not give an entitlement to reclaim the VAT on that cost.

Property Transactions for your Business

17.1   Property transactions

17.1.1   Introduction

Transactions relating to investment properties and residential properties are included in **Chapter 18, Investment properties** and **Chapter 36, Residential properties**.

The place of supply of services related to land is deemed to be where the land is located. When the land is in another EU member state, the supplies are made there. The supplier, or when the reverse charge rule applies, the recipient, must account for tax in the member state concerned. This chapter looks at the property transactions that may impact upon a business.

When the land is outside the EU, supplies of the relevant services are outside the scope of EU VAT, but may be subject to local taxes.

> ⚠ ***Warning!***
>
> The danger with advising clients regarding the VAT implications of construction services is that a client does not necessarily give all the relevant facts and it is therefore important to know what questions to ask in order to obtain the full picture. Advice given over the telephone by HMRC is not necessarily binding, although staff in the National Telephone Advice Service should be asked to provide a reference number in respect of the particular query.

17.1.2   Services relating to land

Services relating to land include:

- the supply of hotel accommodation;
- the provision of a site for a stand at an exhibition where the exhibitor obtains the right to a defined area of the exhibition hall;
- services supplied in the course of construction, conversion, enlargement, reconstruction, alteration, demolition, repair or maintenance (including painting and decorating) of any building or civil engineering work;
- the supply of plant or machinery, together with an operator, for work on a construction site;
- services of estate agents, auctioneers, architects, solicitors, surveyors, engineers and similar professional people relating to land, buildings or civil engineering works. This includes the management, conveyancing, survey or valuation of property by a solicitor, surveyor or loss adjuster;

- services connected with oil/gas/mineral exploration or exploitation relating to specific sites of land or the seabed;
- the surveying (such as seismic, geological or geomagnetic) of land or seabed, including associated data processing services to collate the required information;
- legal services such as conveyancing or dealing with applications for planning permission;
- packages of property management services which may include rent collection, arranging repairs and the maintenance of financial accounts; and
- the supply of warehouse space.

As can be seen, this is a much wider definition of land than the previous definition (See *Notice 741A*, 6.4.).

Example 17.1

Solicitors, Ball and Chain act for a UK client, Mug, buying a holiday home in Dublin. Ball and Chain's services are deemed to be supplied in Ireland because that it is where the property is. Ball and Chain must register for VAT in Ireland if they exceed the Irish VAT registration threshold.

Mug persuades the builder who has done work for him in the UK to take on the task of renovating the Dublin holiday home. The builder goes ahead with the work. The builder must register for Irish VAT. Like the solicitor, the builder is working on property located in Ireland.

17.1.3 Services merely having a connection with land

There are certain services that are considered not to relate to land although there may be an incidental land element. HMRC give their views of services that are not connected with land as follows:

'• Repair and maintenance of machinery which is not installed as a fixture. This is work on goods.
- The hiring out of civil engineering plant on its own, which is the hire of goods; or the secondment of staff to a building site, which is a supply of staff.
- The legal administration of a deceased person's estate which happens to include property. These are lawyers' services.
- Advice or information relating to land prices or property markets as they do not relate to specific sites.
- Feasibility studies assessing the potential of particular businesses or business potential in a geographic area. Such services do not relate to a specific property or site.
- Provision of a recording studio where technicians are included as part of the supply. These are engineering services.
- Services of an accountant in simply calculating a tax return from figures provided by a client, even where those figures relate to rental income.'

Law: VAT Notice 741, s. 6.5.1

17.2   Property and VAT liability

Most property transactions are exempt from VAT. There are, however, a number of exclusions from the exemption. A list of these exclusions is given at **17.14.9**. Where an item is excluded from the exemption it will be standard rated. Items included in this exclusion are items such as; admission fees, holiday lettings, camping fees, rights to take game or fish, hairdresser rentals and storage fees. Where a property supply is exempt from VAT it is usually possible to opt to tax the transaction. This allows VAT to be charged on the supply, but allows input tax related to the supply to be reclaimed. Thus, opting to tax is usually seen as an advantage. There is complex anti-avoidance legislation concerning the option to tax.

The supply of new commercial property and new civil engineering works is standard-rated. Buildings and civil engineering works are regarded as remaining new for three years.

The supply of construction services is taxable and may be subject to the standard rate of VAT, the reduced rate of VAT or the zero rate. The VAT liability of a particular supply will be standard-rated by default, unless it is specifically included within Sch. 8 (zero rate) or Sch. 7A (reduced rate) to VATA 1994.

Supplies of land and buildings may also be zero-rated (if the first sale of a residential property or first long lease of such a property). Residential property that is not new (and short leases) are exempt from VAT but without the option to tax. Residential properties are dealt with in **Chapter 36**. Supplies in connection with residential and charitable buildings are dealt with in a subsequent chapter (and these benefit from significant zero-rate reliefs).

17.3   Construction services

Tax Point/time of supply

The tax point or time of supply determines when the supplier has to account for VAT on the supply and also the time when input tax credits can be claimed. Any claim for an input tax credit, however, needs to be supported by a tax invoice.

17.3.1   Single payment contract

In general, the normal tax point rules will apply to supplies of construction services, although there is a specific anti-avoidance provision in relation to certain supplies.

Where a service is performed and there will be a single payment in relation to the contract, the basic tax point for the services is the time when the services are performed. This is normally taken to be the date when all the work except any outstanding invoicing has been completed.

However, an actual tax point will be created when the supplier issues a VAT invoice or receives payment in respect of the supply before the basic tax point arises. The tax point will then be the date of issue of the invoice or the date payment is received. In addition, an actual tax point is created if the supplier issues a VAT invoice within 14 days after the basic tax point, unless HMRC have agreed to an extension of the 14-day rule.

17.3.2 Continuous supplies of services

Where a contract provides for periodic payments to the supplier (e.g. stage payments) a tax point will arise at the earliest of the following dates:

(a)   the date a payment is received by the supplier;
(b)   the date that the supplier issues a VAT invoice;
(c)   where the parties are 'connected', no more than 12 months after the previous tax point under new legislative provisions introduced from 1 October 2003; or
(d)   the day on which the services are performed where the building in question is to be occupied by a person who cannot recover all of the VAT that is incurred and the contractor is connected with either the occupier or has been financed by the occupier/someone connected to the occupier to carry out the construction services.

Other guidance: VAT Notice 708, s. 24

17.3.3 Retention payments

If the anti-avoidance provisions described at (c) or (d) above apply, the tax point will follow the relevant tax point provisions.

In all other cases, the tax point in respect of a retention will arise on the date a payment is received by the supplier or the date that the supplier issues a VAT invoice, whichever is earlier.

> ### *Planning point*
>
> There are two distinct ways in which retentions are invoiced. Sometimes, the VAT is added to the gross contract value before the retention is deducted, sometimes it is added to the net payment due and then to the retention at the time it is released. Contractors should be careful not to account twice for the VAT on retentions. The danger of this is increased where the transaction is self-billed by the customer.

17.4   Self-supply of construction services

Where a business undertakes certain construction services, VAT must be accounted for under the self-supply rules.

Where a person, in the course or furtherance of a business carried on by him or her, for the purpose of that business and otherwise than for a consideration performs any of the following services:

(a)   the construction of a building;
(b)   the extension or other alteration of, or the construction of an annexe to, any building such that additional floor area of not less than 10 per cent of the floor area of the original building is created;
(c)   the construction of any civil engineering work; or
(d)   in connection with any such services as are described in (a), (b) or (c) above, the carrying out of any demolition work contemporaneously with or preparatory thereto,

then VAT must be accounted for on the open market value of the services performed, where the value of the services is at least £100,000 and the services would have been subject to VAT if supplied by a third party (VAT (Self-Supply of Construction Services) Order 1989 (SI 1989/472)).

Planning point

The practical implications of this self-supply order are that input tax on the purchases of any goods and services in respect of the building works is fully recoverable (subject to the normal rules) as it is treated as relating to the onward taxable self-supply. VAT output tax must be accounted for on the open-market value of services performed and this output tax can be recovered as input tax in the same period, to the extent that it is attributable to the making of taxable supplies.

⚠ *Warning!*

Where a business is fully taxable and the building is going to be used solely for the purposes of making taxable supplies, the input tax on the self-supplies is fully recoverable and the self-supply charge has no overall effect, apart from inflating both the output tax and input tax amounts. However, where a business is either fully exempt or partly exempt, the VAT incurred on the self-supply charge will either be wholly irrecoverable or partly irrecoverable.

17.5   Problem areas

The main difficulty with the supply of construction services and VAT is actually establishing the VAT liability of the supplies in question. Where the recipient of the services is registered for VAT and is able to recover all their input tax, the charging of

VAT by the contractor has not been particularly significant in the past, since the VAT has been treated as fully recoverable and only affected the cash flow of the business. This remains the case on some occasions, but is an increasingly risky position to take in light of recent developments (see Warning! below).

⚠ *Warning!*

Wrongly charged VAT is not in law deductible as input tax. Whilst, in the past, this point has rarely been taken by HMRC, it appears to be the case that challenges to such claims are becoming more widespread. Best practice, therefore, is to ensure that all contractors and subcontractors charge VAT at the correct rate regardless of the VAT position of the customer.

Planning point

Where the recipient of the supplies is either not registered for VAT or is unable to recover all the VAT that is incurred, the charging of VAT and the rate of VAT is always significant. In these circumstances it is important that the person commissioning the building work has some understanding of the different VAT liabilities that can apply to construction services and it may be possible to plan in advance to mitigate the VAT. For example, the VAT consequences may tilt the balance when considering whether or not to demolish an existing building completely before constructing a new dwelling or whether some of the existing building should be retained.

⚠ *Warning!*

The VAT consequences of a particular transaction should be considered at an early stage so that a VAT charge does not become an unpleasant surprise later.

It is important to remember that only specific parts of some of HMRC's Notices have the force of law, the remainder being HMRC's interpretation of the law.

Planning point

It is always therefore prudent to refer directly to the law when trying to establish the VAT liability of a particular supply. If it is still not possible to resolve a query categorically from reference to the law, it may be necessary to seek professional advice from a VAT adviser or seek a written ruling from HMRC.

⚠ *Warning!*

When certain supplies do qualify for zero-rating or the reduced rate of VAT, it is important to ensure that the rate of VAT that has been applied can be substantiated and that all relevant documentation is available. For example, proof that a house has been empty for three years or proof that a building is a listed building. Failure to do this could result in an unwelcome assessment at a later date following a routine VAT visit.

Planning point

The professional services rendered by an architect or surveyor in their own right are always subject to standard-rated VAT, but it may be possible to arrange for the services to be supplied through a management contract or a design and build contract in order to minimise the VAT.

17.6   Questions to ask

17.6.1   General

It is not always easy to establish the VAT liability that would apply to certain supplies of construction services; it may be necessary to ask a contractor or client for further information before being able to advise on the VAT.

Planning point

To assist in this process, the list below is a selection of questions that can be asked in order to establish the full facts behind a particular project. Please note that this list is not exhaustive, but asking these questions should certainly give a good starting point for establishing the liability.

17.6.2   New build

Questions to ask:

1.   Is the building going to be constructed from scratch?
2.   Will the new building make use of any existing structures?
3.   Will the new building be designed for use as a dwelling?
4.   Will the new building be designed for use as a number of dwellings?
5.   Will the building be used as a relevant residential purpose building?
6.   Will the building be used as a relevant charitable purpose building?
7.   Are the four criteria within the definition of 'dwelling' satisfied?
8.   Is it necessary to receive a certificate from the customer?
9.   Will the supply include the demolition of an existing structure?
10.   Will the supply be a design and build project or through a management contract?

17.6.3 Work to an existing property

Questions to ask:

1. What is the use of the existing property?

2. What is the extent of the work that will be done to the existing property?

3. Will the work constitute the construction of a new qualifying building?

4. Will the construction constitute a self-contained annexe to a relevant charitable building?

5. What will be the use after the work is completed?

6. Is it necessary to receive a certificate from the customer?

7. Is the property a listed building?

8. Have the works required listed building consent?

9. Will the work result in a changed number of dwellings?

10. Will the work constitute a conversion from one or more single-household dwellings into one or more multiple-occupancy dwellings?

11. Will the work constitute a special residential conversion?

12. Does the work relate to the renovation or alteration of a qualifying building that has been empty for at least three years?

13. Can evidence be obtained to prove that the building has been empty for three years?

17.7 Sales, letting and leasing of property

17.7.1 VAT in the context of property transactions

Property transactions affect everyone, from the individual who is not in business, to large multinational companies and government. VAT is likely to impact on all such transactions. However, because the persons involved and their objectives in relation to property transactions vary, there are a wide variety of possible situations. The first matter to consider is whether the transaction is one related to property. If it is not a property transaction it cannot benefit from exemption or any other relief related to land. Thus, is the supply a supply of facilities (which is taxable) or an interest in land which is exempt (with the option to tax)? It is vital to understand the nature of the supply made first, before trying to determine the nature of the supply before determining its liability.

This chapter is structured to reflect the different VAT concerns of various types of property users, other than residential construction services (covered in **Chapter 36**). In essence, these are:

- those who sell property, whether on an occasional basis or otherwise; and
- landlords and their tenants and other persons who hold property for own use.

There are a number of ancillary issues that also apply which cannot conveniently be categorised by use. These include:

- the option to tax, which might equally be exercised by a landlord, owner or other user as well as by a developer or contractor; and
- ancillary services, e.g. the services of estate agents, conveyancers, etc. who supply services relating to land.

Finally, since all VAT-registered persons have to decide what VAT they can deduct and must comply with the accounting and administrative requirements, there are brief notes on each of these aspects.

17.7.2   The relevant legislation

The tables below broadly summarise the VAT liability of property transactions in the UK. While they summarise the rules in general terms, it is important to note that where there is a relief there are conditions that have to be met in order for it to apply.

> ⚠ **Warning!**
>
> A further feature of the legislation dealing with property is the numerous definitions. In some cases, the same term is defined in three or four parts in slightly different terms (e.g. the definition of the term 'dwelling'). It is easy to overlook the fact that there are these regrettable differences and the tendency is to use one term to fit all.

Where a supply of goods or services is taxable at the standard, zero or reduced rate, the supplier will have the normal right to recover any VAT. However, there is an exception in relation to VAT on certain materials used in the construction of non-commercial buildings. The tables are intended to assist readers to navigate around the chapter and are not intended to stand alone.

Table 17.1 Sales, letting and leasing of land and buildings

	Type of property		
Type of supply	**Dwellings and relevant residential**	**Relevant charitable**	**Other (see note (a) below)**
Sales of bare freehold land.	Exempt	Exempt	Exempt
Sale of freehold in land and buildings:			
• new, and	Zero-rated	Zero-rated	Standard-rated
• other.	Exempt	Exempt	Exempt

		Type of property	
Type of supply	**Dwellings and relevant residential**	**Relevant charitable**	**Other (see note (a) below)**
Grant or disposal of leasehold interest in land and buildings exceeding 21 years (not less than 20 years in Scotland):			
● first grant or disposal by person constructing, and	Zero-rated	Zero-rated	Exempt
● other grants or disposals.	Exempt	Exempt	Exempt
Letting and leasing of land and buildings including licences as follows:			
● leases other than those referred to above;	Exempt	Exempt	Exempt
● fishing or gaming, hotel or holiday accommodation, caravan parking, camping and other parking;	Standard-rated	Standard-rated	Standard-rated
● admission to theatre, sports and other events, and	Not applicable	Standard-rated	Standard-rated

		Type of property	
Type of supply	**Dwellings and relevant residential**	**Relevant charitable**	**Other (see note (a) below)**
● rights to remove timber.	Standard-rated	Standard-rated	Standard-rated
Sale of building materials:			
● by person constructing a building;	Zero-rated if part of zero-rated construction	Zero-rated if part of zero-rated construction	Standard-rated
● to a DIY builder, and	Zero-rated (new)	Not applicable	Not applicable
● other.	Standard-rated	Standard-rated	Not applicable
Assignments and surrenders/cancellations of leases:			
● assignment of lease or licence;	Exempt	Exempt	Exempt unless the assignor of the lease or licence has opted to tax
● inducement to enter into lease:			

Type of supply	Type of property		
	Dwellings and relevant residential	**Relevant charitable**	**Other (see note (a) below)**
– premium; – rent-free period, and – works done;	Standard-rated if the tenant is required to do something for the landlord; otherwise outside the scope of VAT	Standard-rated if the tenant is required to do something for the landlord; otherwise outside the scope of VAT	Standard-rated if the tenant is required to do something for the landlord; otherwise outside the scope of VAT
• surrender of lease to landlord:			
– landlord pays tenant, and	Exempt	Exempt	Exempt unless the tenant has opted to tax
– tenant pays landlord (i.e. reverse surrender).	Exempt	Exempt	Exempt unless the landlord has opted to tax

Table 17.2 Other services

Type of supply	Type of property		
	Dwellings and relevant residential	**Relevant charitable**	**Other**
Other services (see Note (e) below):			
• architects, surveyors or persons acting in a consulting or supervisory capacity;	Standard-rated	Standard-rated	Standard-rated
• conveyancing and similar services;	Standard-rated	Standard-rated	Standard-rated
• management and accounting services;	Standard-rated	Standard-rated	Standard-rated
• general legal advice about land, and	Standard-rated	Standard-rated	Standard-rated
• design and build contracts.	Follows liability of construction services if lump sum contract	Follows liability of construction services if lump sum contract	Standard-rated

Notes to tables

(1) Where a supply that is listed in the 'Other' column in Table 17.1 above is exempt, the landlord, owner or other person making the supply will usually have the right to waive exemption, but there are exceptions.

(2) VAT law has a number of cases dealing with what are 'buildings'.

(3) The tables show the general rule, but there are exceptions.

(4) There are also exceptions in respect of mixed-use buildings.

(5) While civil engineering, demolition work and various professional services are normally standard-rated, they may in some circumstances (described below) be regarded as ancillary to another service. In such cases, they will follow the liability of the other service, e.g. an architect's service as part of a 'design and build' contract.

⚠ *Warning!*

The tables above should not be taken as a comprehensive guide to the VAT law on property but as a map intended to allow readers of this chapter to find the appropriate section or sections dealing with a particular issue that they wish to address.

17.7.3 Derogations from the general rules on rates

Sales, letting and leases of property are generally exempt although there are some standard-rated exceptions. However, within EU VAT law there are three further provisions allowing member states an option to depart from the normal rules. These are as follows.

1. Member states can either exclude from exemption or allow taxpayers an option to exclude from exemption the letting and leasing of land (Directive 2006/112, art. 135(2)). The UK has taken advantage of both provisions (see for example the exclusions in VATA 1994, Sch. 9, Grp. 1, item 1 and Sch. 10).

2. Member states can apply a reduced rate of tax to the 'supply, construction, renovation and alteration of housing provided as part of social policy' (Directive 2006/112, art. 93 and Annex III, point (9)). The UK has applied these provisions (see VATA 1994, Sch. 7A, Grp. 6 and 7).

3. Member states who had zero-rates when the Sixth VAT Directive came into force were permitted to retain them (Directive 2006/112, art. 28). The UK retained the zero-rate insofar as it covered certain supplies of goods and services in relation to non-commercial buildings.

Article 132(2)(b) and (d)contain two exclusions from exemption in respect of permanently installed equipment and machinery and the hire of safes. The UK legislation contains no specific legislation dealing with either exclusion. However, in respect of the hire of safes, it appears that because the exemption is framed by reference to English land law, the hire of safes may effectively be excluded in any event. In relation to permanently installed equipment and machinery, there has been a UK case that suggests that the exclusion has not been implemented in UK law but can be applied in some circumstances by the taxpayer (*Aquarium Entertainments Ltd* [1995] BVC 728).

Both the zero-rate and the reduced rate apply only to:

- 'dwellings';
- buildings that are used or are to be used for a 'relevant residential purpose';
- buildings that are used or are to be used for a 'relevant charitable purpose'; and
- 'protected buildings'.

The meaning of these terms is described in **17.14**.

17.8   Sales of land

17.8.1   Summary

A person who owns land or holds land under a lease may dispose of the interest held. Provided that the disposal is made in the course of a business and is for consideration, there will be a supply. In certain circumstances where land is transferred for no consideration it is nevertheless deemed to be a supply for consideration. While, as for other interests in land, the general rule is that the supply of land is exempt, there are exceptions. Further, land may be disposed of in a number of different ways. This, together with the liability of each, is set out in **Table 17.3**.

> **Planning point**
>
> An important exception is that the disposal of land together with any buildings thereon as part of the transfer of a going concern will not be regarded as a supply and will therefore not be subject to VAT if certain conditions are met. These are considered in **17.8.3**.

> **Planning point**
>
> When disposing of land it is also necessary to consider the effect of the option to tax (see **17.9**) and the impact of the disposal on input tax previously recovered in relation to the land (in particular see **Chapter 12** regarding adjustments under the capital items scheme).

17.8.2   Disposals of land

Table 17.3 Disposals

Note: In all cases below where there is a reference to the option to tax, it should be borne in mind that the option may be disapplied in certain circumstances. Accordingly, references to the option to tax mean an option that has been made and is effective. (See **17.9** for commentary on the option to tax.)

Nature of transaction	Condition	Liability and legislative reference
Sale of building land or grant of a long lease in bare land.	–	Exempt (VATA 1994, Sch. 9, Grp. 1, item 1) but subject to the option to tax. The option does not apply to a residential caravan pitch or moorings for a residential houseboat.
The sale of the freehold in a new or uncompleted commercial building.	A building is taken to be new if it was completed less than three years before the sale (VATA 1994, Sch. 9, Grp. 1, Note (4)). A building is completed when an architect issues a certificate of completion or it is fully used, whichever happens first (VATA 1994, Sch. 9, Grp. 1, Note (2)).	Standard-rated (VATA 1994, Sch. 9, Grp. 1, item 1(a)(ii)).
The sale of new or uncompleted civil engineering works.	A civil engineering work is taken to be new if it was completed less than three years before the sale (VATA 1994, Sch. 9, Grp. 1, Note (4)). A civil engineering work is completed when an engineer issues a certificate of completion or it is fully used, whichever happens first (VATA 1994, Sch. 9, Grp. 1, Note (2)).	Standard-rated (VATA 1994, Sch. 9, Grp. 1, item 1(a)(iii) and (iv)).

Note: In all cases below where there is a reference to the option to tax, it should be borne in mind that the option may be disapplied in certain circumstances. Accordingly, references to the option to tax mean an option that has been made and is effective. (See **17.9** for commentary on the option to tax.)

Nature of transaction	Condition	Liability and legislative reference
First grant of a major interest in land and buildings (see **17.14.2** for definition of a major interest) by the person constructing the buildings: a non-commercial building.	See **17.14** for definition of dwelling, relevant residential and relevant charitable use.	Zero-rated (VATA 1994, Sch. 8, Grp. 5, item 1(a)(i) and (ii)).
	Construction in relation to 'the person constructing' does not include conversion, reconstruction, or alteration of existing buildings.	(VATA 1994, Sch. 8, Grp. 5, Notes (16) and (17)).
Any other grant of a major interest in a non-commercial building described above.	–	Exempt (VATA 1994, Sch. 9, Grp. 1, item 1).
First grant of a major interest in land and buildings (see **17.14.2** for definition of a major interest) by the person substantially reconstructing any protected building, as defined.	The building must be either designed as a dwelling or dwellings or intended solely for a relevant residential or relevant charitable purpose.	Zero-rated (VATA 1994, Sch. 8, Grp. 6)).
	Must be either a 'listed building' or a 'scheduled monument' (see **17.14.4**).	(VATA 1994, Sch. 8, Grp. 6, Note (4)).
	The term 'substantially reconstructed' requires that 60 per cent of the works carried out (other than the services of architects, surveyors, consultants and those acting in a supervisory capacity) must be zero-rated construction work. The work must incorporate only the original building and external features of historic interest.	

Note: In all cases below where there is a reference to the option to tax, it should be borne in mind that the option may be disapplied in certain circumstances. Accordingly, references to the option to tax mean an option that has been made and is effective. (See **17.9** for commentary on the option to tax.)

Nature of transaction	Condition	Liability and legislative reference
Any other grant of a major interest in a protected building, described above.	–	Exempt (VATA 1994, Sch. 9, Grp. 1, item 1).
The grant of any interest in a non-commercial building; other than those considered above.	The option to tax cannot apply where the purchaser of the land has made known his intention to use the building for residential purposes.	Exempt (VATA 1994, Sch. 9, Grp. 1, item 1).
	The vendor and the purchaser can agree to apply the option to tax even though the land is to be used for residential purposes where it is the purchaser's intention to carry out construction and grant a major interest in the buildings.	Standard-rated (VATA 1994, Sch. 10, para. 3).
The grant of any interest in a commercial building other than those considered above.	–	Exempt (VATA 1994, Sch. 9, Grp. 1) but subject to the option to tax.
The assignment of a lease.	–	Exempt (VATA 1994, Sch. 9, Grp. 1) but subject to the option to tax.
An option to acquire any of the rights that are themselves standard-rated.	–	Standard-rated (VATA 1994, Sch. 9, Grp. 1, item 1(n)).

Note: The sale of a reversionary interest in land follows the same liability as for freehold sales.

17.8.3   Transfers of going concerns

The liability of any disposal of land as set out in **Table 17.3** will not apply where the disposal is regarded as a transfer of all or part of a going concern.

The transfer of a property development can be the transfer of a going concern (TOGC) in certain circumstances. Clearly the transfer of property can occur in the context of the sale of a business and will be an element of a transfer of a going concern. In other circumstances, property will be the subject of the business itself, for example the sale of an uncompleted property development or of a property investment business.

If the sale of assets is a TOGC, then the sale of those assets is treated as neither a supply of goods nor of services and is not subject to VAT.

The conditions for TOGC treatment are:

- the assets must be supplied to a person to whom the transferor transfers his business (or a part of the business) as a going concern;
- the assets are to be used by the transferee in carrying on the same kind of business as that carried on by the transferor (whether or not as part of an existing business); and
- where the transferor is a taxable person, the transferee is already, or immediately becomes as a result of the transfer, a taxable person.

As far as land is concerned, however, a supply of assets does not qualify as a TOGC insofar as it consists of a supply of land that would, save for TOGC treatment, be a standard-rated supply as:

- the property is subject to a valid and effective option to tax; or
- it is a freehold sale (or its equivalent) of a new or partly completed commercial building or new or partly completed civil engineering works,

unless the transferee has made and notified an option to tax by the time that the supply would, other than being treated as a TOGC, have been treated to have been made (effectively before completion of the contract). Furthermore, with effect from 18 March 2004, the transferee must provide the transferor with a declaration to the effect that anti-avoidance provisions do not apply to him in respect of the property to be transferred. This is an anti-avoidance provision. The actual declaration takes the form of notifying the transferor that para. (2B), art. 5 of the Value Added Tax (Special Provisions) Order 1995 (SI 1995/1268) does not apply to him in respect of the property transferred.

⚠ *Warning!*

This last condition is onerous. It also represents a risk for both parties. The purchaser who fails to give a notification will incur VAT on the purchase, with the consequential increase in SDLT. The vendor who treats the sale as VAT-free without receiving a notification may find that he is assessed for VAT on a later VAT visit, on the basis that the conditions for VAT-free treatment were not met.

HMRC consider the following to be capable of being transferred as a going concern:

- a property which is let to a tenant, where it is sold with the benefit of the existing lease, this is the case even if the property is only partly tenanted;
- the assignment of a lease of a property (which is subject to a sub-lease) if the lease is assigned with the benefit of the sub-lease;

- the disposal of a building that is being let out even though there is an initial rent-free period and the building is sold during that period;
- the sale of a building where leases have been granted but the tenants are not yet in occupation; and
- a property that is intended to be let but for which no tenant has actually entered into a lease agreement, if there is sufficient evidence of intended economic use.

In contrast, HMRC consider the following not to be capable of being transferred as a going concern:

- the sale of a property by a property developer that has built a building and allowed someone to occupy it temporarily (without any right to occupy after any proposed sale) while the building is being marketed;
- the sale of a property where the lease granted is surrendered immediately before the sale; and
- the sale of a property to the existing tenant where the tenant leases the whole property from the vendor.

Other guidance: *VAT Notice 700/9*, (March 2002 edn.)

What HMRC are trying to achieve is to ensure that a viable and continuing business is being transferred rather than an asset.

Planning point

The above examples represent HMRC's views and are not set out in the legislation as such. Indeed, some are arguably questionable. However, it is useful and sometimes instructive to be aware of HMRC's views, especially where the consequent analysis of the transaction is beneficial.

The tribunal has held that where a property developer transferred property to a property investor, the transfer was of the same kind of business and thus a TOGC (*Hallborough Properties Ltd* [1994] BVC 1,377). The tribunal has similarly held that where an uncompleted development has been sold to a purchaser for completion of the development there was a TOGC (*The Golden Oak Partnership* [1992] BVC 704), but when active development had not commenced there was no TOGC (*Gulf Trading and Management Ltd* [2001] BVC 4,053).

Planning point

As tribunal decisions are persuasive rather than binding (other than on the parties), they can be very helpful but it is wise not to place undue reliance on any particular one.

Where a property is transferred as a going concern, any remaining adjustments under the capital goods scheme (CGS) are required to be made by the purchaser after the transfer. Where the purchaser does not take on the VAT registration of the vendor, subsequent intervals under the CGS commence on the anniversary of the transfer.

> ### ⚠ *Warning!*
>
> All vendors and purchasers of property, whether by way of a TOGC or as an asset sale, need to be aware of their obligations under the CGS (see **Chapter 12** and HMRC *VAT Notice 706/2*). In summary, vendors who are selling a capital item may have to make a final adjustment under the scheme, whilst purchasers will create a new capital item unless the property is acquired by way of a TOGC, in which case they may inherit a liability to adjustments under the scheme from the previous owner.

> ### ⚠ *Warning!*
>
> As the purchaser needs to make the CGS adjustments, he should obtain appropriate records from the vendor to show what adjustments have been made in the past, the original acquisition cost and how much input tax was originally claimed. Furthermore, a warranty should be obtained in respect of the need to undertake adjustments and an indemnity for any consequence loss if the warranty fails.

17.9   The option to tax

17.9.1   Introduction

A person who sells or grants a lease in a commercial building, where that sale or grant would otherwise be exempt from VAT, is entitled to elect to opt to tax the sale or grant subject to certain conditions.

> ### *Planning point*
>
> The main purpose of exercising the option to tax is to allow the person making the sale or grant to recover any VAT incurred in relation to the land. However, opting to tax will result in higher costs to the purchaser or tenant if he is unable to recover the VAT charged. Since SDLT is chargeable on VAT, there will in many cases also be an additional cost for the purchaser for this reason too.

The option to tax does not apply to certain grants of land and buildings to be used for relevant residential or charitable purposes and is ineffective in relation to certain supplies where the end-user is significantly exempt or otherwise non-taxable.

Once the option has been made it can only be revoked in very limited circumstances.

Planning point

In general terms, a person can opt to tax any land without any reference to HMRC, other than the formal act of notification. However, where the person has made or will have made any exempt supply of the land or buildings prior to the option becoming effective, he must obtain permission from HMRC prior to making the election.

The detail concerning the option to tax is included in **Chapter 18, Investment Properties**.

17.10 Landlords, owners and occupiers of property

17.10.1 Introduction

This section deals with persons who occupy land under a lease or similar arrangement. The disposal of any interest in land is dealt within **17.8**. The ownership of an investment property, the supply of a lease or letting is dealt with in **Chapter 18, Investment Properties** and this details the liability of leases and licences over land.

17.10.2 Basic rules

The basic rule is that the sale, letting and leasing of land are exempt (VATA 1994, Sch. 9, Grp. 1, item 1 and the Directive 2006/112, art. 135(2) and 135(1)(h)). However, there are four significant exceptions to this rule.

1. Freehold sales of new commercial buildings are taxable.

2. Certain licences and rights to exploit land are specifically excluded from exemption and are therefore taxable.

3. A taxpayer may in certain circumstances elect to tax what would otherwise be an exempt lease or letting of land. The option is considered in detail in **17.19.1**.

4. Certain 'major interests' in dwellings and land used or to be used for a relevant residential or charitable purpose will be zero-rated. The term 'major interest' is defined at **17.14.2**.

HMRC provide the following explanation of what they consider to be an interest in land. They advise that an interest in land can be:

*   a legal interest, i.e. the formal ownership of an interest in or right over land such as a freehold or leasehold interest in it; or
*   a beneficial (or equitable) interest, i.e. the right to receive the benefit of supplies of it (e.g. the sales proceeds or rental income).

A beneficial interest may be held and transferred separately from the legal interest.

Rights over land include:

- rights of entry which allow an authorised person or authority to enter land (e.g. they might allow someone to come on to land to perform a specific task);
- easements which grant the owner of neighbouring land the right to make their property better or more convenient, such as a right of way or right of light;
- wayleaves, i.e. a right of way to transport minerals extracted from land over another's land, or to lay pipes or cables over or under another's land; and
- *profits a prendre*, i.e. rights to take produce from another's land, such as to extract minerals.

Planning point

However, as the case of *Finanzamt Ülzen v Armbrecht* (Case C-291/92) [1996] BVC 50 demonstrates, VAT law has to be interpreted in a manner consistent with Directive 2006/112 and principles of European law. In *Armbrecht*, the ECJ considered that German land law similar to English land law, which provided that buildings are to be regarded as a part of the land on which they stand, did not prevent the taxpayer from allocating part of the land to business purposes and part of the land to residential use so that the disposal of the residential part was not subject to VAT.

17.10.3 Business occupiers

Land may be held for own occupation rather than for sale, letting or leasing. A taxpayer who owns or occupies land for own occupation will, in regard to that occupation, be primarily concerned with whether or not the person who supplies him with the land (whether a vendor or a landlord) does not charge VAT if it is not appropriate to do so and, if VAT is payable, whether it is recoverable.

However, the taxpayer may also be a landlord and, to the extent that he is a landlord, the taxpayer will be in exactly the same position as any other landlord and will need to be aware of the matters discussed in the rest of this section.

17.10.4 Inducements

It is fairly common for landlords to provide inducements to tenants in order to enter into leases. Two common forms of inducement are reverse premiums and rent-free periods. The liability of inducements is complex and has been the subject of a number of judicial decisions.

Inducement to enter into a lease (reverse premiums)

After a considerable period of uncertainty triggered by the ECJ case of *C & E Commrs v Mirror Group plc* (Case C-109/98) [2002] BVC 16, it is now unequivocally agreed that reverse premiums are not consideration for any supply made by the incoming tenant to the landlord, unless the tenant is undertaking in exchange to do more than just enter into and be bound by the terms of the lease. HMRC's confirmation that they accept this position can be found in *Business Brief* 12/05 (15 June 2005), which reverses their earlier policy immediately following the decision in *Mirror Group*.

> ### ⚠ *Warning!*
>
> However, the payment of an inducement by a landlord to a tenant to enter into a lease is payment for a supply where the tenant undertakes to do more than simply take up the lease, for example carrying out building work to the premises for the landlord or becoming 'anchor tenant' in a multi-tenanted property.

The *Mirror Group* case involved a payment from the landlord to the tenant to become an anchor tenant, which the ECJ held amounted to advertising services which were taxable.

Other inducements (rent-free periods)

Where a landlord provides an incoming tenant with a rent-free period, this will not constitute consideration for a supply unless the incoming tenant agrees to do something in return. If the tenant agrees to do something in return for the rent-free period, such as refurbishing, maintaining or upgrading the building, then the value of the rent foregone in the rent-free period will represent consideration for a supply by the tenant to the landlord (see *Ridgeons Bulk v C & E Commrs* [1994] BVC 77 and *Neville Russell (a firm)* (1987) 3 BVC 611).

17.10.5 Change of use

Change of use of relevant residential or relevant charitable buildings

There are two provisions that deal with a change in use of a building that has been zero-rated either because it was to be used as a dwelling or dwellings or for relevant residential purposes, or because it was to be used for a relevant charitable purpose. The first provision deals with what occurs when the person makes a grant, e.g. leases the building to a third party and the land subject to the grant is not intended for a qualifying use. The second deals with the situation where the person who obtained zero-rating uses the premises for commercial purposes himself.

478

> **Planning point**
>
> In March 2007, HMRC produced *Revenue & Customs Brief 29/07* in which they announced that they would no longer enforce the VAT liability arising on change of use where zero-rating had been obtained under the concession applicable where less than ten per cent of use is for business purposes. In addition, they indicate that they may not do so in other cases. Somewhat curiously, however, they leave the position open, asking charities affected to contact them for further advice. The law itself has not been changed, and the paragraphs below reflect the legal position. Any charity finding itself in this position, however, should make reference to HMRC's statement in the first instance.

Grant of interest in land within ten years of receipt of zero-rated supply

This provision applies where a taxpayer:

- has received a zero-rated supply (whether of construction or the grant of an interest in a building);
- within ten years of the day on which that building was completed, grants an interest in part of the building that was zero-rated; and
- the supply granted is not intended for use for a relevant residential purpose or relevant charitable purpose.

Where the provision applies, the taxpayer must charge VAT on the grant at the standard rate.

Law: VATA 1994, Sch. 10, para. 1(1)–(3)

Taxpayer commencing to use the land otherwise than for a qualifying purpose supply

This provision applies where a taxpayer:

- has received a zero-rated supply (whether of construction or the grant of an interest in a building); and
- within ten years of the day on which that building was completed, starts to use the building otherwise than for a relevant residential purpose or relevant charitable purpose.

Where the provision applies, that taxpayer is regarded as making a supply to him- or herself of the building, which is not zero-rated and is therefore subject to the standard rate of VAT. The value of the supply is determined by the formula $A \times (10 - B)/10$ where:

- A is the amount that yields an amount of VAT chargeable on it equal to that which would have been chargeable on the zero-rated supplies received had so much of the building not been intended for use solely for a relevant residential or relevant charitable purpose; and
- B is the number of whole years since the day the building was completed.

The VAT chargeable on the self-supply will be deductible if the new use to which the building is put is taxable, or will be partly deductible if it is used partly for taxable supplies and partly for exempt supplies.

> **Planning point**
>
> Despite some suggestions to the contrary, especially on the certificate, this provision does not apply where the original zero-rating of work was granted because it constituted approved alterations to a protected building.

Law: VATA 1994, Sch. 10, para. 1(1) and (4)–(6)

17.11 Recovery of VAT incurred

17.11.1 Recap – general rules

Input tax can be recovered where it relates to the making of any taxable supplies. Only certain interests in land are automatically taxable. Where the grant of an interest in land is taxable (whether at the standard or zero-rate), the input tax referable to that grant will be deductible. It should be noted that certain input tax cannot be claimed on certain items installed in a new non-commerical building – see **Chapter 36, Residential properties**.

VAT will also be deductible where the grant would normally be exempt but the taxpayer has exercised the option to tax and that option is effective. The general rule is that input tax relating to the grant of an interest in land can be recovered even if it was incurred prior to an option to tax being exercised in respect of that land.

However, where the input tax is incurred and an interest in the land is granted prior to the option being made, the taxpayer will be unable to exercise the option to tax without prior permission of HMRC, who will not grant permission unless they can agree with the taxpayer a fair and reasonable method of attributing the tax to the exempt supplies first made and the subsequent taxable supplies.

> **⚠ Warning!**
>
> Permission to opt may still be required where exempt supplies have taken place even if no additional VAT is to be claimed.

17.11.2 Provisional deduction of input tax

There may be occasions when a developer makes purchases and does not know at that time which type of supply they will be used for. In such a case, the partial exemption provisions will be of relevance (see **Chapter 12**).

17.11.3 Capital items

From 1 April 1990 input tax incurred on land and buildings costing more than £250,000 is required to be adjusted over a period of ten years (or a lesser period if the interest held does not equal or exceed ten years) (VAT Regulations 1995 (SI 1995/2518), reg. 113).

The regulations apply to input tax incurred on the following:

- the acquisition of land and/or buildings;
- a developer's self-supply under the provisions outlined in **17.4**;
- a self-supply following a change in use of a qualifying building; and
- a self-supply of construction services where a building is extended by more than ten per cent.

A full discussion of this subject appears in **Chapter 12**.

17.11.4 Service charges

The VAT liability of a service charge will normally follow the VAT liability of the rent charge. This is because the service charge is seen, in the UK, as being further consideration for the rent. Thus, an exempt rent will have an exempt service charge. Where the landlord has opted to tax, the service charge will also be subject to VAT. This can result in a loss of input tax where a landlord has not opted to tax and the tenants who are fully taxable can reclaim the VAT on their costs. The landlord cannot reclaim VAT on the costs that they incur and the recharge through the service charge will include this irrecoverable VAT. The tenant, however, cannot reclaim the VAT that is included in the charge as the VAT element is a component of an exempt supply, no VAT has actually been charged to the tenant. This is called the cascading of VAT. It cascades through the VAT system and accumulates, rather than being available as a credit.

It has been argued in a recent VAT Tribunal *Field Fisher Waterhouse LLP* [2011] TC 01371 that the service charge is not linked to the supply of the land. Thus, the service charge should be subject to VAT even where the underlying rent is exempt. The appellants argued that their view was supported by the ECJ Judgement *RLRE Tellmer Property sro v Finanční ředitelství v Ústí nad Labem* (Case C-572/07) [2010] BVC 802 (*Tellmer*). *Tellmer* owned apartment blocks, charging tenants exempt rent. It also separately invoiced tenants for the cleaning of common parts. The tax authority regarded the cleaning services as separate taxable supplies and required VAT to be charged. *Tellmer* appealed and the case was referred to the ECJ. The ECJ was asked whether the letting of an apartment and the cleaning of common parts were separate supplies, and if they were not separate supplies was VAT to be charged on cleaning as a cleaning service is taxable. The ECJ held that in these circumstances the supplies could not be regarded as a single letting transaction. The cleaning service was supplied separately.

Field Fisher Waterhouse had been charged an exempt rent. It wished to recover the VAT on the service charge that it had incurred. In addition to the *Tellmer* decision, it argued that the service charge could not be related to the area it rented as the charge also applied to common areas and would be used by persons that were not even tenants of the building. HMRC did not believe that *Tellmer* supported the appellant's arguments. HMRC argued that the ECJ had only considered the single or multiple supply issue. This was not relevant to these circumstances as the service charge was part of the rent . In *Tellmer* the tenant could appoint a third party to provide the cleaning service and had chosen the landlord to provide this service. *Field Fisher Waterhouse* was not in this position as the rent agreement clearly stated that the service charge was part of the rent and did not allow a third party to be appointed.

HMRC agree that where the lease agreement permits a third party to provide a service, such as cleaning, that this is a separate supply. VAT would be charged on this supply (if appropriate) and the input tax could be claimed by the tenant according to the normal rules. The Lower-Tier Tribunal has, however, referred this case to the European Court of Justice to determine if such supplies are separate to the main supply of letting or merely ancillary and part of the same single supply of letting. In addition, the ECJ has been asked if it is necessary for the supplies to be supplied by a third party for the service charge or cleaning charge to be regarded as a separate supply.

Planning Point

A service charge is regarded as a separate supply where a third party from the landlord can make the supply. The service charge will then take the VAT liability of the supply made (usual standard rated unless a zero-rate, reduced-rate or exemption relief applies). Where a separate service charge is supplied the tenant can reclaim any VAT charged according to the normal rules and his partial exemption position.

Where a service charge is reserved in the rent agreement as part of the rent, the service charge will have the same liability as the rent. Whether any VAT can be reclaimed on the costs that make up the cost of the service charge (for example contractors to the landlord) will depend upon the ability of the landlord to reclaim VAT and not be determined by the tenant's VAT position (with the proviso that the ECJ decision in *Field Fisher Waterhouse* may change this).

17.12 Other services relating to land

17.12.1 Summary

Most other services relating to land will be taxable. These will include:

- architects' services;
- estate agency services;
- legal and conveyancing services;
- supervisory and management services; and
- water, fuel and power.

Law: VATA 1994, Sch. 8, Grp.. 5, item 2

17.12.2 Architects' and similar services

The services of architects, surveyors, consultants and persons who act in a supervisory capacity are always excluded from the zero and reduced rates and so are standard-rated.

An exception to this is where a person enters into a 'design and build' contract. This describes the position where the architect, etc. is appointed by the main contractor, rather than the owner of the property. In such cases, although the architect's services to the main contractor remain standard-rated, it is accepted that, once they have been incorporated into a much greater supply to be made by the main contractor, they are ancillary to the main supply and so will be zero-rated or subject to the reduced rate depending what the main supply is.

17.12.3 Water, fuel and power

Landlords may supply water, fuel or power to tenants. Where they do so, the liability will depend on whether, on a proper construction of the arrangements, there are separate supplies or not. If the supplies are not regarded as separate from the grant of any tenancy, the payments made by tenants for such supplies will be treated as part of the rent and will be exempt. In some non-commercial buildings, the supplies will be subject to the zero-rate (water) or the reduced rate (fuel and power).

Other guidance: VAT Notice 742, para. 11.7

17.12.4 Land outside the UK

This chapter is not intended to deal with land outside the UK nor with services relating to land outside the UK. However, since UK businesses may provide some services that appear to relate to land outside the UK, it is appropriate to mention what services relating to land are.

Clearly, services such as those of architects, surveyors, conveyancers and estate agents will not be within the UK VAT net where the service is provided in relation to specific land that is located outside the UK, even if the work (e.g. drawing up plans) is done inside the UK. There may, however, be a liability to register for VAT overseas. Other services that may have some connection with land will not be regarded as a service relating to land, e.g. keeping the accounting records relating to land wherever located. For such services, the casual connection with land makes no difference to the nature of the service.

17.12.5 Sports Fees

Entry fees charged by a sports club (which is an eligible body as defined by item 3 Group 10 Schedule 9 VAT Act 1994) to members are exempt from VAT. It was held in the First Tier Tribunal *The Bridport and West Dorset Golf Club Ltd* [2011] TC 01214 that all fees should be exempt, whether charged to members of the public. HMRC appealed this decision and the Upper Tribunal has referred the matter to the European Court of Justice.

Planning Point

Although HMRC will not pay any claims made as it treats the First Tier Tribunal decision as relating to the appellant only, it is suggested that protective claims should be made so that sports clubs can protect their position in the event that the European Court finds in favour of the Bridport and West Dorset Golf Club. Due to the four year capping provisions an early claim is recommended. All sports clubs should make claims not just golf clubs. It should be noted, however, that by making such a claim to reduce output tax that there will be a commensurate reduction in input tax that can be claimed. Thus, some clubs with large amounts of input tax may wish not to claim.

17.13 Administrative and accounting issues

17.13.1 Tax points

Major interests in land

The grant, assignment or surrender of a major interest in land is a supply of goods.

The general rule is that the tax point in respect of a supply of goods is the date when the goods are made available to the purchaser, or the date when a tax invoice is issued or the seller receives payment in respect of the interest, whichever is the earliest.

The time of supply of a major interest in land is therefore on conveyance, unless a tax invoice has already been issued or payment has been received.

If a tax invoice issued within 14 days following the date upon which the interest granted is made available to the grantee or payment is received, the tax point is the date of the invoice.

> ### Planning point
>
> The fact that normal tax point rules apply does mean that the parties to a land transaction, and the vendor in particular, can have some control over the date on which VAT becomes due, by advancing or retarding the invoice date. This can sometimes be useful in order to move the transaction into a more preferential VAT period of either vendor or purchaser or both.

Where payment precedes conveyance or the issue of a tax invoice, the tax point is the date of payment to the extent of that payment. The supplier need not receive total control of the monies paid for payment to be effected (see *C & E Commrs v Faith Construction* (1989) 4 BVC 111).

A tax invoice cannot be issued in respect of a zero-rated supply and so the tax point is then the date on which the interest is made available, or the date of payment for it, whichever is the earlier.

Special rules apply when a major interest is a lease or tenancy and the whole or any part of the consideration is payable periodically or from time to time. In this event, the tax point is the earlier of:

- the date on which an invoice is issued; or
- the date when any payment is received by the supplier in respect of the grant.

Special rules also apply:

- when land is compulsorily purchased and the amount of payment to be received is not known at the time of the compulsory purchase; and
- when a vendor grants or assigns the freehold and at the time of the grant or assignment the consideration is unascertainable.

However, in the case of unascertainable consideration, there are specific anti-avoidance rules which effectively mean that the periodic tax point can only be applied where the vendor has opted to tax and the option to tax is not disapplied (VAT Regulations 1995 (SI 1995/2518), reg. 84).

Law: VATA 1994, s. 6, Sch. 4, para. 4; VAT Regulations 1995 (SI 1995/2518), reg. 20, reg. 85

Other interests in land

All other interests in land are treated as supplies of services. Rent is normally payable periodically, and so it is treated as a continuous supply that is successively and separately supplied each time a payment is received by the supplier or a tax invoice is issued, whichever is the earlier.

17.13.2 Zero-rating certificates

In order to qualify for certain reliefs mentioned above, such as zero-rating the construction or sale of relevant residential and charitable buildings, or reduced-rating renovation and conversion of relevant residential buildings, the person who intends to use the building must provide his supplier with a certificate stating that the building will be used for a 'relevant residential' or 'relevant charitable' purpose. There are two distinct prescribed certificates: one covering construction, renovation and conversion services and the other covering sales or long leases of new buildings.

Other guidance: VAT Notice 708, s. 16

17.13.3 Value of supplies of land

The UK provisions relating to the value of the consideration in respect of supplies of goods and services in the legislation.

The basic principle is that, where the consideration is purely money, the amount received is inclusive of VAT. In other words, the value of the supply is the consideration passing minus the VAT payable to HMRC.

Where there is no monetary consideration, or the consideration does not consist wholly of money, the value of the supply is that amount in money that with the addition of VAT is equivalent to the consideration (VATA 1994, s. 19(3)).

This provision is extremely important since it applies to, *inter alia*, property exchanges such as land-for-land swaps and barter deals generally.

Law: VATA 1994, s. 19 and Sch. 6

Connected persons

Where there is a supply for consideration in money between 'connected persons' and the recipient of the supply cannot recover all his input tax, HMRC have the power to direct in writing that the open-market value be used as the value of the supply. The term 'connected persons' is defined by reference to ICTA 1988, s. 839. Connected persons for these purposes include the following.

1. In relation to an individual, certain close relatives.

2. In relation to a trustee, the settlor, persons connected with the settlor, and any body corporate connected with the settlement.

3. In relation to a business partner (except for bona fide commercial arrangements), any partner, partner's spouse and certain close relatives.

4. In relation to a company (as defined), companies under common control (as defined).

> **Planning point**
>
> A direction may not be made more than three years after the supply in question. Directions can also apply to future supplies.

17.13.4 Record-keeping

Persons involved with land transactions have the same general record-keeping obligations as all other VAT-registered traders. However, the obligations of the CGS require landowners to keep specific records to facilitate adjustments under the scheme. In addition, vendors of property subject to the scheme will need to pass sufficient information to purchasers to enable them to carry out any remaining adjustments.

It is also advisable for traders to keep accurate records of the exercise and notification of the option to tax on properties that they have opted to tax.

17.13.5 Tax planning and avoidance

As land and property transactions frequently involve large values, there is a clear financial motivation for businesses to ensure that any VAT costs associated with such transactions are kept to the minimum payable under the law. The use of buildings, either for occupation by a partly exempt business or for economic use where the option to tax is not permitted or is disapplied, means that where acquisition or construction costs bear VAT, that VAT will be irrecoverable either wholly or in part.

There can be a range of tax planning undertaken with regards to land and property. The use of the option to tax, for example, which facilitates recovery of input tax where, if the option to tax had not been exercised, input tax would be irrecoverable, could be regarded as tax planning. Similarly there is the use of VAT grouping so that supplies made intra-VAT group are disregarded. The ability to transfer property businesses and parts of property businesses as TOGC may be used as part of tax planning arrangements. However, in each of these 'planning' methods, the planning is available because of the operation of the legal provisions and the scheme of VAT.

> ⚠ **Warning!**
>
> There is considerable difficulty in determining where the boundaries lie between acceptable tax planning using the methods described above, and what HMRC consider to be unacceptable tax avoidance. What is clear, however, is that HMRC are expending considerable resources in challenging arrangements which they perceive as being unacceptable tax avoidance.

The UK Government has made several changes to the law regarding the option to tax, introducing the so-called disapplication provisions. Nonetheless, taxpayers may still undertake transactions that they consider enable them to properly deduct the input tax incurred.

The provisions regarding disclosure of VAT avoidance schemes (described fully in **Chapter 32**) also need to be considered in the context of any planning in this area.

> **Planning point**
>
> The high values involved in property transactions mean that efforts to reduce VAT costs are often considered by those undertaking them. By the same token, businesses should be on notice that any structures relating to land and property transactions may be subject to close scrutiny, and that if HMRC suspect 'avoidance' then a challenge to input tax recovery is likely to result.

17.14 Definitions

17.14.1 Dwelling

A dwelling is:

'(2) A building is **designed as a dwelling** or a number of dwellings where in relation to each dwelling the following conditions are satisfied–

(a) the dwelling consists of a self-contained living accommodation;

(b) there is no provision for direct internal access from the dwelling to any other dwelling or part of a dwelling;

(c) the separate use, or disposal of the dwelling is not prohibited by the terms of any covenant, statutory planning consent or similar provision; and

(d) statutory planning consent has been granted in respect of that dwelling and its construction or conversion has been carried out in accordance with that consent.'

Law: VATA 1994, Sch. 8, Grp. 5 Note (2),

17.14.2 Major interest

A major interest can comprise either the sale of the freehold (or equivalent) or a leasehold interest exceeding 21 years (or, in Scotland, of not less than 20 years). For details regarding grants of a leasehold interest that is a major interest see **17.13**.

Law: VATA 1994, s. 96(1)

17.14.3 Seasonal caravan pitches

The supply of a caravan pitch is usually standard rated as a holiday letting. An extra statutory concession has existed to treat the supply as exempt where the caravan pitch is used for residential rather than holiday purposes. This is being put on a statutory footing by Value Added Tax (Land Exemption) Order 2012 (SI 2012/58), that amends VATA 1994, Sch. 9, Grp. 1, Note (14)so that nonresidential pitches on any site or pitches on holiday sites (other than pitches for employees) are excluded from the exemption. A nonresidential pitch is defined as a pitch provided for less than a year or, where it is provided for more than a year, there is an occupational restriction that restricts occupation throughout the period of the provision of the pitch (so that if restriction for occupation of less than a year was being ignored the supply remains standard rated).

17.14.4 Non-business use by charity

The definition of business is wide and includes any trade, profession or vocation. However, whilst the test is restrictive, it is possible for charities to occupy premises for non-business purposes. Typically this may arise when the charity is grant funded and does not charge the users for the provision of any services that the charity provides. However, there can also be other circumstances (see *Cardiff Community Housing Association Ltd* [2001] BVC 2,112). In *C & E Commrs v Yarburgh Children's Trust* [2002] BVC 141 the grant of a lease to a playgroup did not constitute a business activity on the facts of that case.

17.14.5 Protected building

'Protected building' means a building which is designed to remain as or become a dwelling or number of dwellings or is intended for use solely for a relevant residential purpose or a relevant charitable purpose after the reconstruction or alteration, and which, in either case, is:

'(a) a listed building, within the meaning of–

  (i)   the Planning (Listed Buildings and Conservation Areas) Act 1990; or
  (ii) the Planning (Listed Buildings and Conservation Areas) (Scotland) Act 1997; or
  (iii) the Planning (Northern Ireland) Order 1991; or

(b)   a scheduled monument, within the meaning of –

(i)   the Ancient Monuments and Archaeological Areas Act 1979; or
(ii)   the Historic Monuments and Archaeological Objects (Northern Ireland) Order 1997.'

(VATA 1994, Sch. 8, Grp. 6, Note (1).)

17.14.6 Relevant charitable use

According to VATA 1994, Sch. 8, Grp. 5, Note (6):

'**Use for a relevant charitable purpose** means use by a charity in either of the following ways, namely –

(a)   otherwise than in the course or furtherance of a business;
(b)   use as a village hall or similarly in providing social or recreational facilities for a local community.'

Extra-statutory concession

Both for non-business use and for use as a village hall or similarly, HMRC operate an Extra-Statutory Concession ESC 3.29 which means that HMRC accept that where a building is either used 90 per cent of the time or has 90 per cent of floor space used for a relevant charitable purpose then the entire building is treated as used for a relevant charitable purpose.

Removal of the concession

Revenue & Customs Brief 39/2009 and *VAT Information Sheet* 8/2009 announced the removal of the above concession (ESC 3.29) on 1 July 2010. There is a transitional period from 1 July 2009 in which charities have a choice of using either ESC 3.29 or a new interpretation of 'solely' to determine whether they can take advantage of the zero-rate.

HMRC now recognize that the term 'solely' as used in the phrase 'solely for a relevant residential or relevant charitable purpose' can incorporate an appropriate *de minimis* margin. HMRC will accept that this statutory condition is satisfied if the relevant use of the building by the charity is 95 per cent or more.

Any method can be used to determine the qualifying use of the building so long as it is fair and reasonable.

If a building is zero-rated as a result of applying this new interpretation, there will be a change of use charge if it ceases to be eligible within ten years of the completion of the building.

17.14.7 Relevant residential use

'Relevant residential use' is use as:

'(a) a home or other institution providing residential accommodation for children;

(b) a home or other institution providing residential accommodation with personal care for persons in need of personal care by reason of old age, disablement, past or present dependence on alcohol or drugs or past or present mental disorder;

(c) a hospice;

(d) residential accommodation for students or school pupils;

(e) residential accommodation for members of any of the armed forces;

(f) a monastery, nunnery or similar establishment; or

(g) an institution which is the sole or main residence of at least 90 per cent of its residents,

(h) except use as a hospital, prison or similar institution or an hotel, inn or similar establishment.'

Law: VATA 1994, Sch. 8, Grp. 5, Note (4)

The same definition applies to:

- 'Protected buildings' (by virtue of VATA 1994, Sch. 8, Grp. 6, Note (2));
- 'Residential conversions' (by use of identical wording in VATA 1994, Sch. 7A, Grp. 6, Note 6); and
- 'Residential renovations and alterations' (by use of identical wording in VATA 1994, Sch. 7A, Grp. 7, Note 4, which applies the definition for 'residential conversions' to 'residential renovations and alterations').

17.14.8 Use as a village hall or similarly

This test is also restrictive (see *Jubilee Hall Recreation Centre Ltd v C & E Commrs; C & E Commrs v St Dunstans Educational Foundation* [1999] BVC 184). However, decisions post *Jubilee Hall* have confirmed that the relief is available when the conditions are met (*Ledbury Amateur Dramatic Society* [2001] BVC 4,051 and *Southwick Community Association* [2002] BVC 4,058). What appears to be material is whether the facilities are operated in a similar manner to a village hall, and that the facilities are for the use of the local community.

17.14.9 Exclusions from exemption

Table 17.4

Nature of transaction	Conditions	Liability and legislative reference
Commercial land and buildings		
Grant of a right to take game or fish.	Other than a grant made at the same time as that of the freehold (or equivalent interest) of the same land to the grantee.	Standard-rated (VATA 1994, Sch. 9, Grp. 1, item 1(c)).
		An apportionment is required where a grant to take fish is supplied with a grant of an interest or right to occupy land to determine the extent of each supply (VATA 1994, Sch. 9, Grp. 1, Note (8)).
The provision in a hotel, inn, boarding house or similar establishment of sleeping accommodation or of accommodation in rooms which are provided in conjunction with sleeping accommodation or for the purpose of a supply of catering.	The term `similar establishment' includes premises where furnished sleeping accommodation is provided whether or not with board or facilities for the preparation of food that are used by or held out as being suitable for use by visitors or travellers.	Standard-rated (VATA 1994, Sch. 9, Grp. 1, item 1(d)).But see VATA 1994, Sch. 6, para. 9, which provides for a reduction in the value of the supply where the supply is for more than four weeks.
Grant of any interest in, right over or licence to occupy holiday accommodation.	Holiday accommodation includes any accommodation in a building, hut (including a beach hut or chalet), caravan, houseboat or tent which is advertised or held out as holiday accommodation or as suitable for holiday or leisure use.	Standard-rated (VATA 1994, Sch. 9, Grp. 1, item 1(e) and Note (13)).
	Freehold sales of holiday accommodation or grants of a lease for a premium.	Exempt (VATA 1994, Sch. 9, Grp. 1, Note (12)).
Provision of seasonal pitches for caravans, and the grant of facilities at caravan parks.	A seasonal pitch is one where occupancy is for less than a year or, if for more than a year, occupation is prohibited for part of the year by planning consent or covenant.	Standard-rated (VATA 1994, Sch. 9, Grp. 1, item 1(f) and Note (14)).

Nature of transaction	Conditions	Liability and legislative reference
Provision of pitches for tents or of camping facilities.	–	Standard-rated (VATA 1994, Sch. 9, Grp. 1, item 1(g)).
Car parking facilities.	Except where supplied as part of another exempt supply, e.g. parking supplied with residential accommodation.	Standard-rated (VATA 1994, Sch. 9, Grp. 1, item 1(g), item 1(h)).
Grant of a right to fell and remove standing timber.	–	Standard-rated (VATA 1994, Sch. 9, Grp. 1, item 1(j)).
Grant of facilities for the housing or storage of aircraft, or mooring or storage of boats and other vessels.	But not mooring of a residential houseboat.	Standard-rated (VATA 1994, Sch. 9, Grp. 1, item 1(k)).
	Mooring includes anchoring or berthing.	(VATA 1994, Sch. 9, Grp. 1, Note (15)).
Grant of a right to occupy a box or other accommodation at a sports ground, theatre, concert hall or other place of entertainment.	But there may be a separate exemption in some cases for certain non-profit making bodies.	Standard-rated (VATA 1994, Sch. 9, Grp. 1, item 1(l)).
Grant of facilities for playing any sport or participating in any physical recreation.	–	Standard-rated (VATA 1994, Sch. 9, Grp. 1, item 1(m)).
	Exception: Where grant is for a continuous period exceeding 24 hours or a series of ten periods to a grantee who is a club, an association or an organisation representing affiliated clubs or constituent associations and certain other conditions are satisfied namely:	Exempt (VATA 1994, Sch. 9, Grp. 1, Note (16)). Members clubs can also exempt supplies to members (such as green fees and other entry fees), but HMRC require VAT at the standard rate to be charged to non-members. This has been challenged in the VAT Tribunals, with the First Tier Tribunal holding that all fees for taking part in sport, to members or otherwise, should be exempt. HMRC has appealed this decision and the Upper Tribunal has referred the question to the ECJ *The Bridport and West Dorset Golf Club Ltd* [2011] TC 01214

Nature of transaction	Conditions	Liability and legislative reference
	– each period is in respect of the same activity at the same place;	
	– the interval between each period is between one and 14 days, and	
	– consideration is payable by reference to the whole series and is evidenced by written agreement.	
	The grantee has exclusive use.	
Grant of storage facilities	Taxable when supplied to an end consumer	Not yet enacted, effective 1 October 2012
Grant of a chair rent facility in a hairdressers	Taxable unless a whole room is provided with exclusive occupation	Not yet enacted, effective 1 October 2012

17.15 Property acquisitions

On the purchase by the business of a freehold/leasehold interest in property, is VAT to be charged by the vendor?

If VAT is chargeable is the business satisfied that this is correct? Either:

(a)   the property is a commercial building less than three years old; or

(b)   an option to tax has been submitted.

> **Planning point**
>
> Has a copy of the vendor's option to tax and the acknowledgement from HMRC been requested?

On the purchase of taxable business property, has the business determined that allowable input tax may be recoverable (taking into account partial exemption and CGS requirements)?

Note: VAT incorrectly charged may prove to be irrecoverable.

(a)   If no VAT is to be charged by the vendor, is the purchaser satisfied that the property is VAT exempt:

(i)   not under an option to tax;

(ii)   commercial property over three years old?

(b)   Is the property outside the scope of VAT as an asset included in a transfer of a business which meets the conditions of a TOGC for VAT purposes?

(c)   If VAT at the zero rate is to be applied is the property a 'new' dwelling or building for relevant charitable or residential use for sale by the constructor?

(d)   Does the property contract include clauses showing the appropriate VAT treatment and necessary warranties and indemnities?

(e)   Does the business require VAT registration to be in effect on the completion date as in the case of a TOGC?

(f)   Has form VAT 1 been completed and submitted to HMRC if a new registration is required (whether compulsorily or voluntary) within the relevant time?

(g)   If under a TOGC has the business:

  (i)   notified the option to tax to HMRC by the completion date;

  (ii)   confirmed to the vendor that the election to waive exemption will not be disapplied?

Investment

18.1 Property letting businesses

Before the changes to the VAT regime for property transactions in 1989, and the introduction of the option for taxation, property letting businesses tended to be exempt from VAT and their treatment on a transfer of a business was largely ignored. Since those changes they have posed considerable difficulties.

If a fully let property is sold to a new landlord, that is fairly clearly within the TOGC rules. The difficulties arise with such things as partly let buildings and buildings sold by developers with prospective tenants having signed agreements for lease, but the leases yet to be entered into (and the rental flow yet to commence).

HMRC set out their views on which transactions relating to property letting businesses fall within the TOGC rules and which do not in *VAT Notice 700/9*, s. 7.

> **Planning point**
>
> The first planning point is to be aware of HMRC's view, while the obvious second point is to decide what action to take in the circumstances of the particular case. It seems that people are generally able to come up with work-arounds of one kind or another, since there has yet to be litigation on this particular point.

18.2 Contract terms

It is best to embark on the process of analysing the VAT position at an early stage in the negotiations, particularly where complex structures are likely to be involved. VAT consequences not appreciated until late in the proceedings can be a deal breaker and it may be necessary to settle for a less than optimum VAT position if, by the time VAT is considered, the structure of the deal is too far entrenched for it to be feasible to make alterations to improve the VAT treatment in the time available.

Of course, getting the contract terms right can be difficult if the parties are unsure of the appropriate VAT treatment, such as whether the TOGC provisions apply or not.

In some cases this is so critical to the commercial viability of the deal that it is essential to obtain sufficient certainty before finalising the transactions, usually by providing full details of the proposals to HMRC before finalisation and seeking their written agreement to the desired treatment. It is essential in such cases to ensure that full information has been provided, that there is evidence of this and also that the written agreement from HMRC is clear and unambiguous.

Experience has shown that HMRC are highly variable in their willingness to provide speedy rulings on such business transfers, even where they realise the commercial importance of achieving certainty as to the VAT treatment. However, they cannot always meet the deadlines which are important to the parties and are sometimes reluctant to provide an advance ruling at all, on the basis that, until it happens, it is merely theoretical, or, more recently, that as VAT is a self-assessed tax and that the onus is therefore on the taxpayer to make the decision.

Planning point

In many cases the precise VAT treatment is not ultimately crucial, provided that appropriate terms between the parties can be embodied in the contract. In these cases it is not unusual to draft clauses to meet the position in either case, with an agreement between the parties to obtain appropriate rulings. This can enable the transaction to proceed on schedule even though the final VAT result remains unknown for a while. In these cases it is also common for uncertain amounts of VAT to be secured by payment into an escrow account, to be released to one party or the other, with interest, depending on the ruling finally obtained from HMRC.

⚠ Warning!

It will be clear from the above that both buyer(s) and seller(s) need to analyse the proposed transactions carefully before finally committing themselves. They also need to ensure that the contract terms embody the transactions which they have finally settled upon and the VAT consequences of them and that both parties are satisfied with the result.

18.3   The relevant legislation

The tables below broadly summarise the VAT liability of property transactions in the UK. While they summarise the rules in general terms, it is important to note that where there is a relief there are conditions that have to be met in order for it to apply.

⚠ Warning!

A further feature of the legislation dealing with property is the numerous definitions. In some cases, the same term is defined in three or four parts in slightly different terms (e.g. the definition of the term 'dwelling'). It is easy to overlook the fact that there are these regrettable differences and the tendency is to use one term to fit all.

Where a supply of goods or services is taxable at the standard, zero or reduced rate, the supplier will have the normal right to recover any VAT. However, there is an exception in relation to VAT on certain materials used in the construction of non-commercial buildings. The tables are intended to assist readers to navigate around the chapter and are not intended to stand alone.

Table 18.1 Sales, letting and leasing of land and buildings

Type of supply	Type of property		
	Dwellings and relevant residential	Relevant charitable	Other (see note (a) below)
Sales of bare freehold land.	Exempt	Exempt	Exempt
Sale of freehold in land and buildings:			
• new, and	Zero-rated	Zero-rated	Standard-rated
• other.	Exempt	Exempt	Exempt
Grant or disposal of leasehold interest in land and buildings exceeding 21 years (not less than 20 years in Scotland):			
• first grant or disposal by person constructing, and	Zero-rated	Zero-rated	Exempt
• other grants or disposals.	Exempt	Exempt	Exempt
Letting and leasing of land and buildings including licences as follows:			
• leases other than those referred to above;	Exempt	Exempt	Exempt
• fishing or gaming, hotel or holiday accommodation, caravan parking, camping and other parking;	Standard-rated	Standard-rated	Standard-rated
• admission to theatre, sports and other events, and	Not applicable	Standard-rated	Standard-rated
• rights to remove timber.	Standard-rated	Standard-rated	Standard-rated
Sale of building materials:			
• by person constructing a building;	Zero-rated if part of zero-rated construction	Zero-rated if part of zero-rated construction	Standard-rated
• to a DIY builder, and	Zero-rated (new)	Not applicable	Not applicable
• other.	Standard-rated	Standard-rated	Not applicable

	Type of property		
Type of supply	**Dwellings and relevant residential**	**Relevant charitable**	**Other (see note (a) below)**
Assignments and surrenders/cancellations of leases:			
• assignment of lease or licence;	Exempt	Exempt	Exempt unless the assignor of the lease or licence has opted to tax
• inducement to enter into lease:			
– premium; – rent-free period, and – works done;	Standard-rated if the tenant is required to do something for the landlord; otherwise outside the scope of VAT	Standard-rated if the tenant is required to do something for the landlord; otherwise outside the scope of VAT	Standard-rated if the tenant is required to do something for the landlord; otherwise outside the scope of VAT
• surrender of lease to landlord:			
– landlord pays tenant, and	Exempt	Exempt	Exempt unless the tenant has opted to tax
– tenant pays landlord (i.e. reverse surrender).	Exempt	Exempt	Exempt unless the landlord has opted to tax

Table 18.2 Other services

	Type of property		
Type of supply	**Dwellings and relevant residential**	**Relevant charitable**	**Other**
Other services (see Note (e) below):			
• architects, surveyors or persons acting in a consulting or supervisory capacity;	Standard-rated	Standard-rated	Standard-rated
• conveyancing and similar services;	Standard-rated	Standard-rated	Standard-rated
• management and accounting services;	management and accounting services;	Standard-rated	Standard-rated
• general legal advice about land, and	Standard-rated	Standard-rated	Standard-rated
• design and build contracts.	Follows liability of construction services if lump sum contract	Follows liability of construction services if lump sum contract	Standard-rated

Notes to tables

(1)   Where a supply that is listed in the 'Other' column in Table 18.1 above is exempt, the landlord, owner or other person making the supply will usually have the right to waive exemption, but there are exceptions.

(2)   VAT law has a number of cases dealing with what are 'buildings'.

(3)   The tables show the general rule, but there are exceptions.

(4)   There are also exceptions in respect of mixed-use buildings.

(5)   While civil engineering, demolition work and various professional services are normally standard-rated, they may in some circumstances (described below) be regarded as ancillary to another service. In such cases, they will follow the liability of the other service, e.g. an architect's service as part of a 'design and build' contract.

⚠ *Warning!*

The tables above should not be taken as a comprehensive guide to the VAT law on property but as a map intended to allow readers of this chapter to find the appropriate section or sections dealing with a particular issue that they wish to address.

18.4   The option to tax

18.4.1   Introduction

A person who sells or grants a lease in a commercial building, where that sale or grant would otherwise be exempt from VAT, is entitled to elect to opt to tax the sale or grant subject to certain conditions.

Planning point

The main purpose of exercising the option to tax is to allow the person making the sale or grant to recover any VAT incurred in relation to the land. However, opting to tax will result in higher costs to the purchaser or tenant if he is unable to recover the VAT charged. Since SDLT is chargeable on VAT, there will in many cases also be an additional cost for the purchaser for this reason too.

The option to tax does not apply to certain grants of land and buildings to be used for relevant residential or charitable purposes (see **18.4.2**) and is ineffective in relation to certain supplies where the end-user is significantly exempt or otherwise non-taxable (see **18.4.3**).

Once the option has been made it can only be revoked in very limited circumstances.

> ### *Planning point*
>
> In general terms, a person can opt to tax any land without any reference to HMRC, other than the formal act of notification. However, where the person has made or will have made any exempt supply of the land or buildings prior to the option becoming effective, he must obtain permission from HMRC prior to making the election.

18.4.2 Scope of option

A supplier can generally waive exemption on any land. However, the option will be ineffective (being specifically disapplied by the legislation) if the grant comprises any of the following.

1. A building or any part of a building which is intended for use as a dwelling, a relevant residential use or a relevant charitable use (other than use as an office), subject to certification in certain cases (see below).

2. A pitch for a residential caravan park.

3. Facilities for the mooring of a residential houseboat.

4. The grant of land to a registered housing association which has given to the grantor a certificate stating that the land is to be used (after any necessary demolition work) for the construction of a dwelling or dwellings or solely for a relevant residential purpose (see below).

5. The grant of land to a do-it-yourself house builder who intends to use the building he constructs as a dwelling.

Where a building is a dwelling or relevant residential building at the time of the grant, the option to tax is automatically disapplied. However, where the building is not a residential property, but the grant is made to a person who intends either to convert it to a dwelling or relevant residential building or to make an onward grant to someone else who will do so, disapplication is contingent on the issue by the grantee of a certificate (form VAT1614D). The same is true of land sold to a housing association. In both cases, the timing of the issue of the certificate is critical. The legislation provides that, if the certificate is issued by the grantee on the grantor at a point before the value of the transaction is legally fixed, the grantor has no choice but to accept it if proceeding with the grant. If the certificate is issued after that point, the grantor has discretion as to whether or not to accept it and allow the option to tax to be disapplied.

> ### *Planning point*
>
> The purpose of this provision, which was introduced in its current form on 1 June 2008, appears to be to allow the grantor to take account of the effect of an exempt sale in the pricing of the grant, or to back out of the deal altogether if the financial consequence of an exempt transaction is unacceptable.

Planning point

HMRC give examples of the date on which the price of a grant is fixed as exchange of contracts, letters or missives, or the signing of heads of agreement. There is potentially fertile ground for dispute here, but, provided both parties are well advised, it should be possible easily to avoid problems in this area.

Where an option to tax is exercised it will apply to the whole property. Where some of the property, however, is residential or the option is ineffective for some other reason the option will not apply to that part. Thus, a property with a pub downstairs but residential accommodation upstairs will require an apportionment of the rent with the commercial element being subject to VAT (when the option to tax has been exercised) and the residential part being exempt. Where the residential part is used for storage and not for residential purposes the whole rent is subject to VAT. Where the rent is to be apportioned there may be some discussion concerning the value to be attributed to the rents; it may be necessary to obtain a surveyor's or valuer's opinion regarding this. It seems clear, however, that it is not possible to attribute a nil rent to the residential part. In *Enterprise Inns plc & Anor v R & C Commers* [2012] BVC 1,768 the Upper Tribunal confirmed the First Tier Tribunal's decision that rents needed to be charged in respect of the residential portion of the property. The pub owners had argued that the rents were based upon the commercial turnover of the pub and that the accommodation was provided free. The Tribunals disagreed. Prior to submitting the appeal the pub companies had apportioned rent 90/10 commercial/residential.

Law: VATA 1994, Sch. 10, para. 2

Planning point

The fact that the option is ineffective does not mean to say that the option does not exist. For example, assume an owner of a property rented a flat above a shop to an individual; the rental would be exempt even if the option had been exercised. However, if the owner subsequently converted the flat to offices, the option would then apply and the rental of the offices would be taxable.

Planning point

It can be helpful to think in these terms when considering the disapplication of the option to tax: whilst the option is exercised on a property-by-property basis, it is disapplied on a grant-by-grant basis.

A supplier can exercise the option in relation to any land or buildings without reference to the tenant or purchaser of that land, although it may not always be effective.

The relevant legislation provides that the option has effect in relation to any land specified, or to any land of a description specified, in the notification. As a matter of English land law, land includes any building on it. For practical purposes, most options are made on a building-by-building basis. (However, see **18.4.4** for the rules that apply when a building is demolished.)

Where an option to tax is made regarding a building (or planned building) it has effect in relation to the whole of the building and all the land within its curtilage. Complexes consisting of separate units grouped around a fully enclosed concourse are taken to be a single building, as are any buildings linked by internal access or covered walkway.

Planning point

Curtilage is not a defined term, but in land law it is taken to be the land immediately surrounding the building, land that is required for its proper use. It will include courtyards and surrounding paving. The size of the curtilage will depend upon the nature and situation of the building concerned. It will vary from building to building. It is always advisable to submit a map or plan with any election to clearly show the area that is subject to the election.

⚠ Warning!

Buildings that may be regarded as completely separate can be treated as linked buildings for the option to tax; atriums, walkways and passageways (even with security locks) will mean that the buildings will be joined together for the option to tax and treated as a single building. HMRC have treated a building on a racecourse to be linked to another due to connecting electricity cables. Where there is any form of link, it is advisable to seek HMRC's views as to whether the properties are linked or not. HMRC have stated that two buildings linked by a single exterior fire escape will not be treated as a single building. Also, two buildings linked by an underground car park will also not be treated as a single building.

The option to tax can now be exercised in relation to discrete parcels of agricultural land without there being any effect on any adjoining similar land. However, when notifying an option to tax to HMRC, a map or plan detailing the land that will be subject to the option should be included.

Law: VATA 1994, Sch. 10, paras. 2–3

Other guidance: VAT Notice 742A, s. 4.2

18.4.3　Disapplication of option to tax: connected parties

In addition to the circumstances set out at points 1–5 in **18.4.2**, the option to tax is also disapplied in the context of certain connected-party transactions.

These disapplication provisions should not commonly arise on transactions between parties acting at arm's length. However, given the potential significance of the VAT effect and subsequent VAT cost, they are considered fully below.

> ## Planning point
>
> It can be useful at the outset to make clear that, for these provisions to apply, three triggers have to be present; if any of the three is absent, there will be no need to consider the disapplication of the option to tax. The three triggers are:

(1) The property is a capital item for VAT purposes (broadly, was acquired, constructed, extended or refurbished within the last ten years at a cost of more than £250,000, plus VAT).

(2) The grant is between connected parties.

(3) The intention is that the property will be occupied for less than 80 per cent taxable purposes.

Often, looking at it in these terms, it is possible quickly to eliminate the need to consider the matter further.

An election which has been made is disapplied in relation to any supply made on or after 19 March 1997 if the following conditions are fulfilled:

- the supply arises from a grant made by a person ('the grantor') who was a 'developer' of the land; and
- at the time of the grant, it was the intention or expectation of the grantor, or a person responsible for financing the development of the land, that it would become or continue to be 'exempt land', whether immediately or not.

Where a grant is regarded as giving rise to successive supplies (e.g. the rentals payable under a lease agreement), the question of whether or not the provisions of this and the following provisions apply is to be determined by reference to the time that the supplies are made rather than the time when the original grant is made.

> ## ⚠ Warning!
>
> For VAT purposes, each lease payment or invoice that creates a tax point is regarded as being a further grant of an interest, although in land law the only grant made is the initial granting of the lease. The VAT legislation often refers to grant and this must be interpreted in its VAT context rather than according to land law.

A person is a 'developer' of land for this purpose if the land, or a building or part of a building on that land, is a capital item in relation to that person and the grant was made during the adjustment period defined by the regulations relating to capital goods.

A person is regarded as being responsible for financing the grantor's development of the land for exempt use if:

- that person has provided finance for the grantor's development of the land; or
- that person has entered into any agreement, arrangement or understanding (whether or not legally enforceable) to provide finance for the grantor's development of the land.

The provision of finance for the grantor's development of the land includes any one or more of the following:

- the provision of funds directly or indirectly for meeting the whole, or any part of, the cost of the grantor's development of the land;
- procuring, whether directly or indirectly, the provision of such funds by another person;
- the provision of funds, whether directly or indirectly, for discharging, in whole or in part, any liability that has been, or may be, incurred by any person for, or in connection with, the raising of funds to meet the cost of the grantor's development of the land; and
- the procurement, whether directly or indirectly, that any such liability is or will be discharged, in whole or in part, by another person.

References above to the provision of funds include:

- lending funds;
- the provision of a guarantee or other security for a loan;
- the provision of any consideration for the issue of shares or other securities, these being issued wholly or partly for raising those funds for the development; or
- any other transfers of assets or value as a consequence of which any of those funds are made available for that purpose.

Planning point

HMRC's guidance to officers asserts that the above provisions are not intended to apply to a situation where a financier, such as a bank, agrees to fund a development and then, in a wholly unrelated transaction, agrees to lease part of a development for its own use. However, if a bank entered into an agreement to lease a building or part of a building and paid a premium under that lease which was used to pay for construction or other works in respect of that land, the premium would be regarded as funding the development.

⚠ Warning!

These provisions will apply to normal commercial transactions (as detailed in the planning point above) as well as to an avoidance transaction and, as can also be seen from the planning point above, the parties do not even have to be connected or related in any way. There needs to be no intent to avoid, nor any VAT planning for these provisions to come into effect.

References to the grantor's development of the land include:

- the acquisition of land or a building or part of a building on the land which is a capital item; and
- the construction or reconstruction and the carrying out of any other works in respect of the land if they fall to be treated as a capital item.

Land is 'exempt land' if, at any time within the CGS adjustment period:

- the grantor;
- a person responsible for financing the grantor's development of the land for exempt use; or
- a person who is regarded as connected with the grantor under ICTA 1988, s. 839 or with a person responsible for financing the grantor's development of the land for exempt use,

is in occupation of the land without being in occupation of it for less than 80 per cent eligible purposes.

Planning point

The 80 per cent test applies from 1 June 2008, when all previous versions of this provision were replaced by a statutory percentage, removing the uncertainty as to exactly what level of non-taxable activity triggered the application of these provisions.

A person's occupation of any land is regarded as being occupation for eligible purposes only where the person is a taxable person at that time, and to the extent that he occupies the land for the purpose of making supplies in the course or furtherance of a business, and the supplies are of such a description that any input tax of his or hers which was wholly attributable to those supplies would be input tax for which that person would be entitled to a credit. Thus, a grant (but remembering the VAT definition of grant) may be made to a taxable person that later uses the property for an ineligible purpose without the anti-avoidance provisions coming into effect. Conversely, the provisions cannot be undone where an occupier's use changes from ineligible to eligible after the grant.

A body to which VATA 1994, s. 33 applies (i.e. a local authority or similar body) is regarded as being in occupation of the land for eligible purposes to the extent that it occupies the land for purposes other than those of a business carried on by that body (i.e. for the purposes of carrying out its statutory duties.) Similarly, a government department that is able to recover VAT that it incurs under VATA 1994, s. 41 is regarded as being in occupation of the land for eligible purposes.

A person is regarded as being in occupation of land for the purposes for which he proposes to use it for as long as it is held by that person in order to be put to that intended purpose, and is not land of which he is in occupation for any other purpose and is taken to be in occupation whether in occupation alone or with other persons, and whether occupation is of all of the land or only part of it.

The occupation of land by a person who is not a taxable person but whose supplies are treated as supplies made by another person who is a taxable person (e.g. a member of a VAT group and the representative member of that group), is determined as if both persons were a single taxable person.

It should be noted that from 1 March 2011, an option to tax will no longer be disapplied where the grantor or persons connected with the grantor only occupy minor parts of buildings (no more than two per cent) even when the other conditions of the anti-avoidance rule are met.

A person will not be treated as being in occupation of the property if they meet the two percent occupation rule; this includes that:

- there is no intention or expectation that the two percent threshold will be exceeded during the period of the grantor's capital goods scheme adjustment periods. A forward look is required to determine the intention, and evidence of this should be retained;
- the occupation of the grantor and all persons connected with the granted are aggregated when determining the two percent rule;
- the proportion of the building occupied is calculated in relation to the whole of the single building and not the part that is subject to the grant:
  - where the grantor only has an interest in part of the building it is that interest which is considered when calculating the two percent occupation;
  - where a number of buildings are included in the same grant, the two percent rule is calculated on a building by building basis;

Other points to consider are that:

- the two percent rule cannot be used for occupation of land that is not a building although incidental land within the curtilage of the building or a car park space can be disregarded;
- the RICS 'Code of Measuring Practice' is to be used when calculating the two percent usage; and
- HMRC require evidence of the calculation where the area occupied is close to two percent (say over 1.5 per cent).

It should also be noted that the treatment of Automatic Teller Machines (ATMs) has also been amended. From 1 March 2011, occupation of any building which is solely by way of ATMs will not be treated as occupation for the purposes of the anti-avoidance test.

Law: VATA 1994, Sch. 10, para. 3A

Other guidance: *VAT Notice 742A, s. 13*

18.4.4   Revocability of option to tax

An option to tax which has been made may be revoked if either of the following apply.

1.   The option to tax was exercised less than six months from the time it is to be revoked, and:

   (a)   no output tax has become chargeable as a result of the exercise of the option,

   (b)   the land subject to the election has not been transferred subject to a grant which has been free of VAT as being a TOGC,

   (c)   no use of the land, including by way of own occupation, has been made since the making of the option to tax; and

   (d)   no input tax claim has been made by virtue of the election that will not become repayable to HMRC under the normal VAT rules on revocation.

2.   The option to tax has been in effect for more than 20 years, and

   (a)   the property is not at the time a capital item for the purposes of the capital goods scheme,

   (b)   no supply at undervalue has been made of the relevant property or building in the ten years preceding revocation,

   (c)   no grant of the property has been made prior to revocation that will give rise to a supply after revocation of significantly greater value than equivalent supplies made prior to revocation; and

   (d)   no input tax incurred prior to revocation relates to expenditure on the property that will relate to use of the property more than 12 months after revocation.

A option to tax may also be revoked 20 years or longer after its exercise, without reference to the conditions above, if neither the taxpayer nor any person connected to the taxpayer has any interest in the property at the time of revocation.

Notification of a six-month revocation must be made on form VAT1614C. If all the conditions except the last are fulfilled, it remains possible to request permission to revoke the option, also using form VAT1614C.

Notification of a 20-year revocation must be made on form VAT1614J.

A third type of revocation was introduced as part of the changes of 1 June 2008, namely an automatic deemed revocation of any option to tax occurring six years after the taxpayer ceases to have any interest in the property concerned. This is arguably largely academic, since most businesses will cease to be concerned with any property disposed of that long ago. Its effect will only be felt in the very occasional situation of re-acquisition of property. If a person disposes of an interest in a property, having opted to tax, and re-acquires the same or a different interest ten years later, the original option will no longer be effective. Previously, it would continue to have been in force until revoked (not possible until 20 years after exercise).

If an option to tax has been exercised over a building which is subsequently destroyed or demolished, HMRC formerly took the view that the option to tax lapsed in relation to that land, and the person who opted in respect of the previous building was no longer bound by that option. This changed with effect from 1 June 2008 and any option to tax notified in respect of a building automatically has effect in relation to the land on which the building stands even after the building is demolished. However, in order to allow taxpayers to continue to take advantage of their previous position (in the rare case where this will be advantageous), there are two specific provisions under the new arrangements. Where an option to tax was made on a building prior to 1 June 2008, a taxpayer may treat that option as revoked on demolition of the property at any future date (HMRC *VAT Notice 742A*, para. 2.4). Where an option to tax exists on land, and a building is constructed on that land, it is possible for the taxpayer to exclude the building from the option; this must be done by submitting form VAT1614F, and cannot be done later than the earliest of the first grant, the first use and the completion of construction of the building.

18.4.5   How the option to tax is exercised

An option to tax could not be effective before 1 August 1989. An option to tax takes effect from the beginning of the day on which it is exercised or any later day that is specified within the notification to exercise the option. It is not possible to exercise the option to tax retrospectively.

Notification of an option to tax must be given to HMRC within 30 days beginning with the day on which the option is made, or such longer period as HMRC may allow.

Notification itself is a simple process. The person exercising the option need only write a letter to the Central Option to Tax unit at the VAT office in Glasgow, giving his or her name and address, stating unambiguously the land or buildings over which he wishes to exercise the option, and giving HMRC such other information as they may require. The option is ineffective unless notified within the period allowed. A taxpayer may not be bound by an erroneous notification if the taxpayer has not in fact opted to tax (*Blythe Limited Partnership* [1999] BVC 2,224).

Planning point

The notification may be made using HMRC's official form, VAT 1614, or by any other means, including by email. However, use of the form is broadly recommended, as it presents the information in a manner unambiguously acceptable to HMRC and contains a very useful reminder of the need in certain cases to obtain permission before an option can be validly made.

⚠ Warning!

There are certain circumstances, as set out below, in which the option to tax is not effective unless HMRC have given their permission to its exercise. This is the case where exempt supplies of the relevant property have been made and the conditions for automatic permission are not met. This provision is often neglected (usually by reason of ignorance), to the point where, since 1 June 2008, it has become possible to apply after the event for permission where it was not requested on a timely basis.

If it is proposed to exercise an option to tax on any property in respect of which the grantor of any interest has already made or will make, prior to the date upon which the exercise becomes effective, any exempt supply, the option to tax can only be exercised if one of the following two conditions is met.

1. Any of the four conditions for automatic permission specified in the relevant HMRC notice have been met. These conditions are:

    (a) it is a mixed-use development and the only exempt supplies (sales, leasing or lettings) have been in relation to the dwellings;

    (b) that the person opting to tax is not seeking to recover any VAT on inputs received prior to the date the option has effect, the only consideration received up to the option date for exempt supplies has been rent, and the only input tax for which credit is sought after the option takes effect is on day-to-day overheads;

    (c) where the person opting is seeking to recover input tax incurred prior to the date of the option, only if this input tax relates solely to tax charged by tenants on a surrender of a lease, the building has since been unoccupied, and there will be no subsequent exempt supplies of the property; and

    (d) the exempt supplies have been incidental to the main use of the property, such as the siting of an advertising hoarding within the curtilage of a building.

With effect from 1 May 2009 an automatic condition was introduced which HMRC consider will give more businesses the ability to opt to tax without first requiring permission from HMRC. The condition (copied below from *VAT Information Sheet* 06/09) should be read in conjunction with the new automatic condition rules.

'Automatic permission condition

You may opt to tax if you satisfy the first (outputs) requirement and (if applicable) the second (inputs) requirements.

Definitions

For the purposes of this condition:
- 'property' includes land, buildings and civil engineering works;
- the question of whether a person is connected with another person is to be decided in accordance with section 839 of the Taxes Act 1988;
- 'permissible exempt supplies' means the following exempt supplies arising from a grant in relation to the land:

    (a) supplies for which the consideration solely represents legal and/or valuation costs reimbursed under the agreement for the grant; or

    (b) supplies where:

        (i) the consideration is provided by way of regular rents and/or service charges;

        (ii) the consideration relates to a period of occupation of the property and that period ends no later than 12 months from the date on which the option first takes effect; and

(iii) no opted supply, other than an opted supply relating solely to the same period of occupation as an exempt supply under point (ii) above, will be reduced in value as a result of the consideration payable for these exempt supplies.

First (*outputs*) requirements

You do not intend or expect that any supply which will be taxable as a result of you making your option to tax will either:

- be made to a person connected with you; or
- arise from an agreement under which you or another person has made or will make an exempt supply in respect of a right to occupy the property, where the right begins or continues after the date on which the option takes effect.

Application of the first (outputs) requirement

You may disregard paragraph 1 of the requirement if the person connected with you is expected to be entitled to credit or refund of a least 80 per cent of the VAT chargeable on the supply.

For the purposes of paragraph 2 of the requirement you may ignore permissible exempt supplies.

Second (inputs) requirement

- This requirement applies if you have been or expect to be entitled to credit for any part of the input tax incurred on your capital expenditure on the property as being wholly or partly attributable to supplies that are taxable supplies by virtue of your option to tax.
- Where the requirement applies you must not intend or expect to use any part of the capital expenditure for either of the following purposes:

    (a) making exempt supplies which do not confer a right to credit for input tax pursuant to section 26(2)(c) of the Value Added Tax Act 1994; or
    (b) for private or non-business purposes, other than purposes giving rise to a right to a refund of VAT on the supplies under sections 33, 33A or 41(3) or the Value Added Tax Act 1994.

Application of the second (inputs) requirement

- For the purposes of the requirement, your capital expenditure is your expenditure on goods or services used in connection with the acquisition of, building works on, construction works on or the fitting out of, the property. Capital expenditure does not include expenditure on routine repairs and maintenance.
- For the purposes of the requirement, 'entitled or credit' includes a deduction or credit arising as a result of the applicable of Regulation 109 or Part XV of the VAT Regulations 1995 (SI 1995/2518).
- You may disregard paragraph 2a of the requirement if any of paragraphs a), b) or c) below apply:

    (a) all the exempt supplies concerned are supplies which fulfil any of the following description:

(i)   supplies within paragraphs 5 to 11, Sch. 10, Value Added Tax Act 1994, and made to a person who is not connected to you;

(ii)   permissible exempt supplies;

(iii)   supplies within Group 5 of Schedule 9 to the Value Added Tax Act 1994 which are incidental to one or more of your business activities;

(b)   you make exempt supplies, but intend or expect the input tax incurred on your capital expenditure on the property that is attributable to those exempt supplies, including any subsequent adjustments to initial input tax deduction, will not exceed £5,000;

(c)   you expect to be entitled to full credit for all the input tax incurred on your capital expenditure on the property as a result of the application of section 33(2) of the Value Added Tax Act 1994.'

2.   An appropriate application has been made to HMRC using form VAT1614H. Consent will only be given if HMRC are satisfied that there will be a fair and reasonable attribution of any input tax incurred prior to the exercise of the option which the person opting wishes to claim once the option becomes effective.

Planning point

Whilst the use of form VAT1614H is not compulsory, it ensures that all the information required by HMRC is provided. In addition, HMRC find it simpler to use this form rather than trying to extract the necessary information from a letter.

Planning point

Since 1 June 2008, the option to tax, once approved by HMRC, will be treated as effective from the date of application, rather than a date after the grant of HMRC's permission.

If the person exercising the option to tax is already registered for VAT, he must inform his or her local VAT office of his VAT registration number. For the option to tax to have any immediate practical effect, the person exercising it must be registered for VAT. It is possible that the exercise of the option will mean that the person exercising it breaches the VAT registration threshold. If this is the case, registration is obligatory. In other cases, voluntary registration is necessary for the option to be effective.

⚠ Warning!

When a person who is not already registered for VAT wishes to opt to tax, the person should first consider the effect of registering for VAT on his other business activities. Although the value of any supplies of capital assets is normally ignored in determining whether or not a person must be registered for VAT, sales of opted land and buildings that are capital assets cannot be excluded.

> ### *Planning point*
>
> If land that is subject to the option to tax is acquired or occupied by another party, the option to tax does not apply to the person acquiring or occupying the property (unless that person had previously opted to tax it) and a fresh option needs to be made by the person acquiring the land if he wishes to charge tax. For example, a tenant of opted land can choose whether or not to opt in respect of any onward supply of a sub-lease. (If the tenant does not opt, he may not be able to recover the VAT that he has been charged by the landlord.) If the tenant then purchases the land from the landlord, the option continues to apply to the greater interest in land that he now has.

18.4.6 Associated companies and connected persons

When an option to tax is exercised by a body corporate, the legislation provides that a 'relevant associate' of the body corporate is also bound by the exercise of the option.

A 'relevant associate' means a body corporate which:

- was treated as a member of the same VAT group as the body corporate which exercised the option at the time when the option first took effect;
- has been treated as a member of the same VAT group at any later time when the body corporate by which the option was exercised had an interest in, right over or licence to occupy the building or land (or any part of it); or
- has been treated as a member of the same VAT group as a body corporate within the points above or within this paragraph at a time when the body corporate had an interest in, right over or licence to occupy the building or land (or any part of it).

A body corporate ceases to be a 'relevant associate' if the conditions above no longer apply. It is also possible, since 1 June 2008, to apply for permission to cease to be a 'relevant associate', provided that certain other conditions are fulfilled. This is done by way of form VAT 1614B.

Other guidance: VAT Notice 742A, para. 6.3

18.4.7 Real estate elections

Since 1 June 2008, it has been possible to make a real estate election (REE). In essence, this is intended as a means of saving taxpayers from having to notify a separate option to tax on each property in which they acquire an interest. A real estate election, which is permanently irrevocable, is effectively an option to tax that covers any property in which the taxpayer subsequently acquires an interest. Each such property is regarded as subject to an election with effect from the date of its acquisition. The election is notified using form VAT1614E. If the taxpayer acquires a property in respect of which an option is not desired, it is possible to notify HMRC accordingly, using form VAT1614F.

> **Planning point**
>
> The detailed rules applicable to REEs are such that it is thought that few taxpayers will want to take advantage of their existence. However, it is possible to see a number of situations where it could be particularly advantageous. This will be the case for anyone acquiring interests in property so frequently that the submission of multiple options to tax becomes a compliance burden. An example might be a hirer of advertising hoardings.

Other guidance: VAT Notice 742A, s. 14

18.4.8   Effect of option to tax on existing contract

When an option to tax is exercised after the making of a contract or lease but before a supply has been made, VAT is automatically added to the consideration unless there is a contrary provision in the lease. (This could be something quite general, such as a provision or covenant that the landlord would bear all the taxes referable or relating to the property.) Where, however, a contract or lease is made after an option has been exercised, this provision does not operate, and there must be an express provision allowing VAT to be charged (VATA 1994, s. 89).

> **⚠ Warning!**
>
> Before exercising an option to tax, a landlord should always ensure that he has the right to add VAT to the rent. Otherwise, he will have to account for the VAT out of the rent at the VAT fraction (currently 7/47) and still be required to give a VAT-registered tenant a VAT invoice.

> **Planning point**
>
> All new leases should contain a VAT clause making the position clear, i.e. whenever the lease gives rise to a supply of goods or services by the landlord, the tenant will have to pay any VAT in addition to the basic amount otherwise payable by the tenant.

18.5   Landlords, owners and occupiers of property

18.5.1   Introduction

This section deals with persons who either own land or occupy land under a lease or similar arrangement and who supply interests in the land so held to tenants or licensees. The disposal of any interest in land is dealt within **17.8**.

18.5.2 Basic rules

The basic rule is that the sale, letting and leasing of land are exempt (VATA 1994, Sch. 9, Grp. 1, item 1 and the Directive 2006/112, art. 135(2) and 135(1)(h)). However, there are four significant exceptions to this rule.

1.   Freehold sales of new commercial buildings are taxable.

2.   Certain licences and rights to exploit land are specifically excluded from exemption and are therefore taxable.

3.   A taxpayer may in certain circumstances elect to tax what would otherwise be an exempt lease or letting of land. The option is considered in detail in **18.4.1**.

4.   Certain 'major interests' in dwellings and land used or to be used for a relevant residential or charitable purpose will be zero-rated. The term 'major interest' is defined at **17.14.2**.

HMRC provide the following explanation of what they consider to be an interest in land. They advise that an interest in land can be:

- a legal interest, i.e. the formal ownership of an interest in or right over land such as a freehold or leasehold interest in it; or
- a beneficial (or equitable) interest, i.e. the right to receive the benefit of supplies of it (e.g. the sales proceeds or rental income).

A beneficial interest may be held and transferred separately from the legal interest.

Rights over land include:

- rights of entry which allow an authorised person or authority to enter land (e.g. they might allow someone to come on to land to perform a specific task);
- easements which grant the owner of neighbouring land the right to make their property better or more convenient, such as a right of way or right of light;
- wayleaves, i.e. a right of way to transport minerals extracted from land over another's land, or to lay pipes or cables over or under another's land; and
- *profits a prendre*, i.e. rights to take produce from another's land, such as to extract minerals.

Planning point

However, as the case of *Finanzamt Ülzen v Armbrecht* (Case C-291/92) [1996] BVC 50 demonstrates, VAT law has to be interpreted in a manner consistent with Directive 2006/112 and principles of European law. In *Armbrecht*, the ECJ considered that German land law similar to English land law, which provided that buildings are to be regarded as a part of the land on which they stand, did not prevent the taxpayer from allocating part of the land to business purposes and part of the land to residential use so that the disposal of the residential part was not subject to VAT.

18.5.3 Landlords

Landlords supply interests in land. A transaction with a tenant may comprise more than one interest as well as other services. Thus, a landlord might rent a flat and a garage to a tenant and, in addition, supply other services for which a service charge is made. In some cases, although there are apparently separate things done and there may be separate considerations, there will nevertheless be only one supply (see *Card Protection Plan Ltd v C & E Commrs* [2001] BVC 158).

It is not within the scope of this chapter to discuss how to determine whether each of the different interests or services provided are to be regarded as separate supplies taxable at the rate applicable to the particular supply made. It is sufficient to point out that before he can decide what the VAT liability of any supply is, the landlord must first determine whether he has one supply or more than one supply. Thus, it is possible that the rent for the flat plus the service charge should be regarded as consideration for a single exempt supply of a residential property, while the rent for a garage may be consideration for a separate standard-rated supply.

HMRC consider that where a landlord provides services to tenants connected with the external fabric or common areas of the property, the service charge follows the same liability as the underlying lease, provided that the services are paid for by all occupants through a common service charge.

Other guidance: VAT Notice 742, para. 11.2

18.5.4 Liability of leases and licences over land

Table 18.3 below sets out the liability of the grant of an interest in land (other than disposals, which are dealt with in **17.8** above). As noted above, it is interests in land and licences to occupy land that are exempt.

A licence is an authority to do something that would otherwise be a trespass. HMRC consider that a licence to occupy land is created when the following criteria are met.

1. The licence is granted in return for a consideration paid by the licensee.

2. The licence to occupy must relate to a specified piece of land, even if the licence allows the licensor to change the exact area occupied, for example to move a licensee from the third to the fourth floor.

3. The licence is for the occupation of the land by the licensee.

4. Another person's right to enter the specified land does not impinge upon the occupational rights of the licensee, and either:

    (a) the licence allows the licensee to physically enjoy the land for the purposes of the grant, for example to hold a party in a hall; or

(b)   the licence allows the licensee to exploit the land economically for the purposes of its business, for example to run a nightclub.

(*VAT Notice 742*, para. 2.5.)

A licence over land that falls short of a licence to occupy land, e.g. allowing the public admission to premises or events, such as historic houses and spectator sports events, is standard-rated. Whilst a license creates rights over land, it is not to the exclusion of others; consequently, the granting of a licence is not an interest in land.

> ⚠ **Warning!**
>
> HMRC announced in the Budget 2012 their intention to extend compulsory taxation to the supply of self storage. HMRC regard the position of a removal company supplying storage facilities in a non-defined space (taxable) and the supply of a clearly defined lockable space (exempt before the changes introduced by the 2012 budget) as anomalous and tax avoidance. HMRC also believed it anomalous that some suppliers opted to tax so that some self-storage was taxable and other supplies were not. HMRC also believed that some suppliers opted to tax to recover VAT on costs but use avoidance mechanisms to avoid paying VAT on their supplies of storage.
>
> The legislation takes effect from 1 October 2012. Anti-forestalling legislation applies to supplies made on or after 21 March 2012. The anti-forestalling measures apply to pre-change supplies that take place on or after 21 March 2012 and is a supply linked to a period on or after 1 October 2012. An amount equivalent to the 20 per cent VAT charge will be applied to the use of self-storage facilities on or after 1 October even if the supply was made on or after 21 March but before 1 October 2012.
>
> The legislation will not tax the supply of premises other than the provision of storage facilities to the end user. Thus, self storage in purpose built facilities, warehouses and distribution centres, moveable containers, railway arches and spare rooms will be taxed where the space is supplied for the purpose of storing someone else's goods. The sale of a building, the rent of a property that has some storage facilities which is ancillary to the main supply or the rent of space to a charity for storage for non-business purposes will not be taxed. HMRC seem to have succeeded in introducing new dividing lines and will be creating new anomalies. For example a partially exempt company could use a subsidiary to construct and supply self storage to the main partially exempt company. VAT would be recovered by the subsidiary and the charge to the main company would be taxable. This would be irrecoverable VAT, but would probably be minor compared to the cost of the VAT on the construction costs. HMRC are, therefore, to introduce an anti-avoidance measure to this anti-avoidance proposal! The supply of self storage in these circumstances will continue to be exempt.

> ⚠ **Warning!**
>
> HMRC announced in the Budget 2012 their intention to extend compulsory taxation to the supply of hairdresser chair rents. There is a period of consultation to 4 May 2012 and new legislation is due to be introduced towards the end of 2012. HMRC regard the supply of a specific area for a hairdresser to supply their trade for an exempt rent as anomalous from the position where a hairdresser receives a taxable

supply of a non-exclusive area (the hairdresser may use any chair in the salon rather than being rented a specific area to work from) or is just supplied facilities. There has been considerable litigation on this matter and HMRC have lost cases, as well as won them. In order to 'simplify and clarify' HMRC proposes to compulsorily tax chair rents and in the process raise a miserly £5 million pounds. The legislation will specifically add a new part and note to the land group of the VAT Act. This will except the grant of facilities within a salon, shop or other establishment to a person supplying hairdressing services. The rent of a room, floor or building will continue to be exempt with the option to tax. HMRC have excluded the grant of facilities. It is questioned, therefore, if this removes the grant of land to a hairdresser in a salon from the exemption.

⚠ *Warning!*

HMRC announced in Budget 2012 their intention to extend compulsory taxation to the supply of self storage. There is a period of consultation to 4 May 2012 and new legislation is due to be introduced towards the end of 2012. HMRC regard the position of a removal company supplying storage facilities in a non-defined space (taxable) and the supply of a clearly defined lockable space (exempt before the changes proposed by Budget 2012) as anomalous and tax avoidance. HMRC believed it anomalous that some suppliers opted to tax so that some self-storage was taxable and other supplies were not and that some suppliers opted to tax to recover VAT on costs but use avoidance mechanisms to avoid paying VAT on their supplies of storage.

The proposed legislation will not tax the supply of premises other than the provision of storage facilities to the end user. Thus, self storage in purpose built facilities, warehouses and distribution centres, moveable containers, railway arches and spare rooms will be taxed where the space is supplied for the purpose of storing someone else's goods. The sale of a building or the rent of a property that has some storage facilities which is ancillary to the main supply or the rent of space to a charity for storage for non-business purposes will not be taxed. HMRC seem to have succeeded in introducing new dividing lines and will be creating new anomalies. For example, a partially exempt company could use a subsidiary to construct and supply self storage to the main partially exempt company. VAT would be recovered by the subsidiary and the charge to the main company would be taxable. This would be irrecoverable VAT, but would probably be minor compared to the cost of the VAT on the construction costs. HMRC are, therefore, to introduce an anti-avoidance measure to this anti-avoidance proposal! The supply of self storage in these circumstances will continue to be exempt.

⚠ *Warning!*

HMRC announced in Budget 2012 their intention to extend compulsory taxation to the supply of hairdresser chair rents. There is a period of consultation to 4 May 2012 and new legislation is due to be introduced towards the end of 2012. HMRC regard the supply of a specific area for a hairdresser to supply trade for an exempt rent as anomalous from the position where a hairdresser receives a taxable supply of a non-exclusive area (the hairdresser may use any chair in the salon rather than being rented a specific area to work from) or is just supplied facilities. There has been considerable litigation on this matter and HMRC have lost cases as well as won them. In order to 'simplify and clarify' HMRC proposes to compulsorily tax chair rents and in the process raise a miserly £5m. The legislation will specifically add a new part and note to the land group of VATA 1994. This will exempt the grant of facilities within a salon, shop or other establishment to a person supplying hairdressing services. The rent of a room, floor or building will continue to be exempt with the option to tax. HMRC have excluded the grant of facilities. It is questioned, therefore, if this removes the grant of land to a hairdresser in a salon from the exemption.

Table 18.3 Liability of grant of interests in land

Nature of transaction	Conditions	Liability and legislative reference
Non-commercial buildings		
First grant of a lease which is a major interest in land (see **17.14.2** for definition of a major interest) by the person constructing the building:		
• a new dwelling or new dwellings;	See **17.14.1** for definition of dwelling.	Zero-rated (VATA 1994, Sch. 8, Grp. 5, item 1(a) (i)).
• a building to be used for relevant residential use or relevant charitable use, and	See **17.14.4** and **17.14.6** for definition of relevant residential and relevant charitable use.	Zero-rated (VATA 1994, Sch. 8, Grp. 5, item 1(a) (ii)).
• an enlargement or extension of an existing non-commercial building.	The enlargement or extension is only zero-rated to the extent that it creates an additional dwelling or dwellings.	Zero-rated (VATA 1994, Sch. 8, Grp. 5, Notes (16) and (17), item 1(a)).
	In each of the above cases, construction in relation to 'the person constructing' does not include conversion, reconstruction, or alteration of existing buildings.	
The grant of any other lease of a non-commercial building.	–	Exempt (VATA 1994, Sch. 9, Grp. 1, item 1).

Nature of transaction	Conditions	Liability and legislative reference
First grant of a major interest in land by the person substantially reconstructing any protected building, as defined (see **17.14.2** for definition of a major interest and **17.14.5** for definition of a 'protected building').	The term 'substantially reconstructed' requires that 60 per cent of the works carried out (other than the services of architects, surveyors, consultants and those acting in a supervisory capacity) must be zero-rated construction work (see **Table 18.2**). The work must incorporate only the original building and external features of historic interest.	(VATA 1994, Sch. 8, Grp. 6, Note (4)).
	Must be either a 'listed building' or a 'scheduled monument' (see **17.14.5**).	Zero-rated (VATA 1994, Sch. 8, Grp. 6, item 1).
Any grant, other than the first grant of a major interest in a protected building, described above.	–	Exempt (VATA 1994, Sch. 9, Grp. 1, item 1).
Lease or licence of a site in a residential caravan park.	–	Exempt (VATA 1994, Sch. 9, Grp. 1, item 1) but see below for an exception where occupation is not permitted throughout the year.
Commercial land and buildings		
Grant of lease in a commercial building.	–	Exempt (VATA 1994, Sch. 9, Grp. 1, item 1) but subject to the option to tax (see **18.4.1**).
An option to acquire any of the rights that are themselves standard-rated.	–	Standard-rated (VATA 1994, Sch. 9, Grp. 1, item 1(n)).
Surrenders and assignments		
The surrender or 'reverse' surrender of an interest in land. A reverse surrender occurs when the surrendering party pays the counterparty to accept the surrender.	–	Exempt (VATA 1994, Sch. 9, Grp. 1, Notes (1), (1A)) but subject to the option to tax.
The assignment of a lease.	–	Exempt (VATA 1994, Sch. 9, Grp. 1) but subject to the option to tax.

Nature of transaction	Conditions	Liability and legislative reference
Reverse assignment of a lease (that is where a person assigning a lease makes a payment to a prospective tenant to accept the assignment).	–	Standard-rated (*C & E Commrs v Cantor Fitzgerald International* (Case C-108/99) [2002] BVC 9).

18.5.5 Option to tax

The liability of a supply of property involving a lease interest can be affected by whether the landlord or tenant has opted to tax their interest. The option to tax is considered in detail in **18.4.1**. The option to tax usually has the effect of converting what would have been an exempt supply into one that is standard-rated but this is subject to exceptions described in **18.4.1** above.

Other guidance: VAT Notice 742A

18.5.6 Capital items scheme

The capital goods scheme (CGS) can affect the transfer of leasehold interests in the same way as it affects freehold sales. If the leasehold interest is within the CGS when the interest is surrendered or assigned, adjustments may be required. For details of the CGS see **Chapter 12**.

Other guidance: VAT Notice 706/3

18.5.7 Supplementary notes and other exceptions

Dwellings

The definition of dwelling for VAT purposes is set out at **17.14.1**. Although the term dwelling is described in the VAT legislation, there have still been disputes as to whether certain properties, specifically bedsits, constitute dwellings or not, and there have been apparently conflicting decisions which lead to some uncertainty (*Look Ahead Housing Association* [2001] BVC 2,107 and *Amicus Group Ltd* [2003] BVC 4,005).

Relevant residential purpose

The definition of relevant residential use is provided in **17.14.7**, but essentially it involves certain properties where the building is used by residents for lodging, sleeping or overnight accommodation. Prior to 1998, HMRC held the view that the property must be the sole or main residence of the residents. However, following the Tribunal's decision in *Urdd Gobaith Cymru* [1997] BVC 2,394, HMRC revised their policy (*Business Brief 6/98*). There are specific exclusions such as hotels, hospitals and prisons.

Mixed use

A single parcel of land or a single building may be used for more than one purpose. A building may be used partly as a residential building and partly as commercial office accommodation, for example. Where a building is for mixed use, the liability of the supplies will depend on the particular use of the building. Thus, the letting of a shop will be exempt but with the option to tax, whilst the letting of a residence above the shop to the same tenant will be exempt.

> ### ⚠ Warning!
>
> If the option has not been exercised, there will not be a problem since the whole rental will be exempt. However, if the option to tax has been exercised and the lease does not specify the rent payable for each part of the building, an apportionment may have to be made between the exempt letting of residential accommodation and the standard-rated letting of the shop.

As noted, it is not mixed use when, say, the use of a parking space attaches to the letting of a residential property but there may be two supplies where tenants have the option but not the obligation to lease a parking space from the landlord.

Caravans

Zero-rating also applies to caravans that are too large to be towed on the roads. Where these caravans have an unladen weight that exceeds 2,030kg, are less than 7 metres in length and 2.55 metres wide, the supply of the caravan can be zero-rated. This is because it is regarded as a residential unit rather than a caravan used for holidays. Zero-rating also applies to houseboats. Zero-rating applies even when these caravans are used for holiday purposes. HMRC has proposed in the 2012 budget that because other holiday accommodation is taxed they will tax certain supplies of caravans. From 1 October 2012 HMRC propose that the size and weight test will be replaced by British Standard 3632. BS 3632 is a standard that indicates that the caravan is designed and manufactured for continuous year round use and is suitable for residential accommodation. A caravan that is sold that meets this standard will be zero-rated even if it is intended to be used for holiday lettings.

The grant of a licence to occupy a caravan site or pitch is exempt as long as the site is not a seasonal pitch. A seasonal pitch is defined as one that is provided for less than a year or there are restrictions that prevent the caravan owner living on site for the year.

It should also be noted that an extra statutory concession permits pitches that were for gypsies, travellers or were on sites that were not advertised nor held out for holiday use can also be treated as exempt from VAT when the pitches are used as a principal private residence. This concession is being put on a statutory basis following the 2012 budget.

18.5.8   Inducements

It is fairly common for landlords to provide inducements to tenants in order to enter into leases. Two common forms of inducement are reverse premiums and rent-free periods. The liability of inducements is complex and has been the subject of a number of judicial decisions.

Inducement to enter into a lease (reverse premiums)

After a considerable period of uncertainty triggered by the ECJ case of *C & E Commrs v Mirror Group plc* (Case C-109/98) [2002] BVC 16, it is now unequivocally agreed that reverse premiums are not consideration for any supply made by the incoming tenant to the landlord, unless the tenant is undertaking in exchange to do more than just enter into and be bound by the terms of the lease. HMRC's confirmation that they accept this position can be found in *Business Brief* 12/05 (15 June 2005), which reverses their earlier policy immediately following the decision in *Mirror Group*.

> ### ⚠ *Warning!*
>
> However, the payment of an inducement by a landlord to a tenant to enter into a lease is payment for a supply where the tenant undertakes to do more than simply take up the lease, for example carrying out building work to the premises for the landlord or becoming 'anchor tenant' in a multi-tenanted property.

The *Mirror Group* case involved a payment from the landlord to the tenant to become an anchor tenant, which the ECJ held amounted to advertising services which were taxable.

Other inducements (rent-free periods)

Where a landlord provides an incoming tenant with a rent-free period, this will not constitute consideration for a supply unless the incoming tenant agrees to do something in return. If the tenant agrees to do something in return for the rent-free period, such as refurbishing, maintaining or upgrading the building, then the value of the rent foregone in the rent-free period will represent consideration for a supply by the tenant to the landlord (see *Ridgeons Bulk v C & E Commrs* [1994] BVC 77 and *Neville Russell (a firm)* (1987) 3 BVC 611).

18.5.9 Change of use

Change of use of relevant residential or relevant charitable buildings

There are two provisions that deal with a change in use of a building that has been zero-rated either because it was to be used as a dwelling or dwellings or for relevant residential purposes, or because it was to be used for a relevant charitable purpose. The first provision deals with what occurs when the person makes a grant, e.g. leases the building to a third party and the land subject to the grant is not intended for a qualifying use. The second deals with the situation where the person who obtained zero-rating uses the premises for commercial purposes himself.

> ### *Planning point*
>
> In March 2007, HMRC produced *Revenue & Customs Brief 29/07* in which they announced that they would no longer enforce the VAT liability arising on change of use where zero-rating had been obtained under the concession applicable where less than ten per cent of use is for business purposes. In addition, they indicate that they may not do so in other cases. Somewhat curiously, however, they leave the position open, asking charities affected to contact them for further advice. The law itself has not been changed, and the paragraphs below reflect the legal position. Any charity finding itself in this position, however, should make reference to HMRC's statement in the first instance.

Grant of interest in land within ten years of receipt of zero-rated supply

This provision applies where a taxpayer:

- has received a zero-rated supply (whether of construction or the grant of an interest in a building);
- within ten years of the day on which that building was completed, grants an interest in part of the building that was zero-rated; and
- the supply granted is not intended for use for a relevant residential purpose or relevant charitable purpose.

Where the provision applies, the taxpayer must charge VAT on the grant at the standard rate.

Law: VATA 1994, Sch. 10, para. 1(1)–(3)

Taxpayer commencing to use the land otherwise than for a qualifying purpose supply

This provision applies where a taxpayer:

- has received a zero-rated supply (whether of construction or the grant of an interest in a building); and

- within ten years of the day on which that building was completed, starts to use the building otherwise than for a relevant residential purpose or relevant charitable purpose.

Where the provision applies, that taxpayer is regarded as making a supply to him- or herself of the building, which is not zero-rated and is therefore subject to the standard rate of VAT. The value of the supply is determined by the formula $A \times (10 - B)/10$ where:

- A is the amount that yields an amount of VAT chargeable on it equal to that which would have been chargeable on the zero-rated supplies received had so much of the building not been intended for use solely for a relevant residential or relevant charitable purpose; and
- B is the number of whole years since the day the building was completed.

The VAT chargeable on the self-supply will be deductible if the new use to which the building is put is taxable, or will be partly deductible if it is used partly for taxable supplies and partly for exempt supplies.

> **Planning point**
>
> Despite some suggestions to the contrary, especially on the certificate, this provision does not apply where the original zero-rating of work was granted because it constituted approved alterations to a protected building.

Law: VATA 1994, Sch. 10, para. 1(1) and (4)–(6)

18.6 Recovery of VAT incurred

18.6.1 Service charges

The VAT liability of a service charge will normally follow the VAT liability of the rent charge. This is because the service charge is seen, in the UK, as being further consideration for the rent. Thus, an exempt rent will have an exempt service charge. Where the landlord has opted to tax, the service charge will also be subject to VAT. This can result in a loss of input tax where a landlord has not opted to tax and the tenants who are fully taxable can reclaim the VAT on their costs. The landlord cannot reclaim VAT on the costs that they incur and the recharge through the service charge will include this irrecoverable VAT. The tenant, however, cannot reclaim the VAT that is included in the charge as the VAT element is a component of an exempt supply, no VAT has actually been charged to the tenant. This is called the cascading of VAT. It cascades through the VAT system and accumulates, rather than being available as a credit.

It has been argued in a recent VAT Tribunal *Field Fisher Waterhouse LLP* [2011] TC 01371 that the service charge is not linked to the supply of the land. Thus, the service charge should be subject to VAT even where the underlying rent is exempt. The appellants argued that their view was supported by the ECJ Judgement *RLRE*

Tellmer Property sro v Finan[[ampccaron]]ní [[amprcaron]]editelství v Ústi nad Labem (Case C-572/07) [2010] BVC 802 (*Tellmer*). *Tellmer* owned apartment blocks, charging tenants exempt rent. It also separately invoiced tenants for the cleaning of common parts. The tax authority regarded the cleaning services as separate taxable supplies and required VAT to be charged. *Tellmer* appealed and the case was referred to the ECJ. The ECJ was asked whether the letting of an apartment and the cleaning of common parts were separate supplies, and if they were not separate supplies was VAT to be charged on cleaning as a cleaning service is taxable. The ECJ held that in these circumstances the supplies could not be regarded as a single letting transaction. The cleaning service was supplied separately.

Field Fisher Waterhouse had been charged an exempt rent. It wished to recover the VAT on the service charge that it had incurred. In addition to the *Tellmer* decision, it argued that the service charge could not be related to the area it rented as the charge also applied to common areas and would be used by persons that were not even tenants of the building. HMRC did not believe that *Tellmer* supported the appellant's arguments. HMRC argued that the ECJ had only considered the single or multiple supply issue. This was not relevant to these circumstances as the service charge was part of the rent . In *Tellmer* the tenant could appoint a third party to provide the cleaning service and had chosen the landlord to provide this service. *Field Fisher Waterhouse* was not in this position as the rent agreement clearly stated that the service charge was part of the rent and did not allow a third party to be appointed.

HMRC agree that where the lease agreement permits a third party to provide a service, such as cleaning, that this is a separate supply. VAT would be charged on this supply (if appropriate) and the input tax could be claimed by the tenant according to the normal rules. The Lower-Tier Tribunal has, however, referred this case to the European Court of Justice to determine if such supplies are separate to the main supply of letting or merely ancillary and part of the same single supply of letting. In addition, the ECJ has been asked if it is necessary for the supplies to be supplied by a third party for the service charge or cleaning charge to be regarded as a separate supply.

Planning Point

A service charge is regarded as a separate supply where a third party from the landlord can make the supply. The service charge will then take the VAT liability of the supply made (usual standard rated unless a zero-rate, reduced-rate or exemption relief applies). Where a separate service charge is supplied the tenant can reclaim any VAT charged according to the normal rules and his partial exemption position.

Where a service charge is reserved in the rent agreement as part of the rent, the service charge will have the same liability as the rent. Whether any VAT can be reclaimed on the costs that make up the cost of the service charge (for example contractors to the landlord) will depend upon the ability of the landlord to reclaim VAT and not be determined by the tenant's VAT position (with the proviso that the ECJ decision in *Field Fisher Waterhouse* may change this).

18.7 Option to tax checklist

Note: The effect of an option to tax is to charge to the standard rate transactions which otherwise are exempt mainly in order to recover associated allowable input tax.

An option to tax will not be effective in respect of:

(a) buildings:

    (i) a dwelling (residential and domestic property);

    (ii) for residential or charitable use; and

(b) land:

    (i) a supply to an individual to be used for construction of a building (not by way of business) for use as a dwelling;

    (ii) a pitch for a residential caravan;

    (iii) mooring facilities for a residential houseboat.

On a property-by-property basis has the business considered whether an option to tax is required to be submitted?

The option to tax extends to:

(a) commercial buildings:

    (i) the whole of the building specified;

    (ii) linked internally or by covered walkway;

    (iii) complexes consisting of a number of units grouped around an enclosed concourse;

Note: Parades, precincts and complexes divided into separate units are not regarded as a single building for the scope of the option.

(b) land:

    (i) the land specified;

    (ii) the land within the curtilage of a building, forming the grounds;

    (iii) a licence to occupy land: do the business supplies fall to be treated as a licence to occupy land?

> **Planning point**
>
> Is the licence granted in return for a consideration paid by the licensee?
>
> Is the licence for the occupation of land by the licensee?
>
> Is the licence to occupy a specified piece of land?
>
> Are the occupational rights of the licensee not affected by other persons' rights to enter the specified land?
>
> Does the licence allow for the licensee to physically enjoy the land?
>
> Does the licence allow the licensee to economically exploit the land for the purpose of its business?

Note: these are the characteristics of a licence to occupy land published by HMRC in *VAT Notice 742*, s. 2, for guidance.

Is the business required to obtain permission from HMRC to make an option to tax?

HMRC's permission is required where:

(a)   the building has been used to make exempt supplies in the ten years prior to the date the option is to take effect; and

(b)   the business wishes to recover a proportion (as agreed by HMRC) of input tax incurred prior to the election, or input tax to be incurred on future capital expenditure.

Note: If permission is not required an option can be made at any time.

The business must advise HMRC of the making of an option to tax:

(a)   by written notification within 30 days of the date to take effect; and

(b)   specifying the land and buildings covered by the election.

If an option to tax is to be made, the business must:

(a)   submit a letter to HMRC notifying the option to tax and clearly state the specified land and buildings to be covered by the option; and

(b)   record the decision to opt to tax in the business records stating the land and buildings to be covered by the option.

> **Planning point**
>
> NB: there are two separate actions required in making an option to tax – the decision by the business to opt and the notification of the decision to HMRC.

An option to tax made by the business is irrevocable unless:

(a)   a notice to cancel is made within six months of the date the option commenced, provided it has had no effect on output tax or input tax;

(b) more than 20 years have elapsed since the date of the option; or

(c) six years have elapsed from the point at which the business ceased to have an interest in the property.

The option to tax is ineffective on the supplies by the business of:

(a) dwellings or residential accommodation, and (subject to conditions) non-residential buildings intended for conversion to residential use;

(b) buildings used for charitable purposes;

(c) residential caravans and houseboats; and

(d) land supplied to a DIY builder or a housing association.

The option to tax is disapplied on a supply by the business as a developer where:

(a) the property is or will become a capital item for the purposes of the Capital Goods Adjustment Scheme; and

(b) either the business or a person responsible for financing the development is intending or expecting the property to be occupied other than for eligible purposes.

Note: eligible purposes means for the making of taxable supplies or certain use by certain bodies.

Dealing with Protected Buildings

19.1 Approved alterations and substantially reconstructed listed buildings

> ### ⚠ *Warning!*
>
> There are significant changes to the approved alterations relief following the 2012 Budget announcement. Approved alterations will no longer be zero-rated. This chapter reflects the historic provisions (as past transactions are still open for review by HMRC) and the few remaining current opportunities that are available.
>
> This is a significant change to the legislation and is being introduced as it is considered perverse to permit zero-rating for alterations but to tax repairs and maintenance. The change removes zero-rating from building materials and construction services supplied in the course of an approved alteration, once the legislation is introduced. Zero-rating of the first sale or long-lease of a substantially reconstructed protected building will be restricted so that the zero-rating is retained for buildings constructed from a shell, but removed for substantial reconstructions where 60 per cent of the reconstruction costs are approved alterations.
>
> A transitional rule is proposed, where a signed contract was in place before budget day (21 March 2012). Zero-rating will be permitted for approved alterations and substantial reconstructions of protected buildings for works performed up until 20 March 2013.

19.2 Approved alteration rules from 1 October 2012

The zero-rate relief for approved alterations to protected buildings and building materials is withdrawn from 1 October 2012. These supplies are standard rated from this date unless there is some other zero-rate relief or they benefit from the transitional rules. .

It should be noted that the relief is withdrawn for churches and other places of worship. A grant scheme, however, is available for listed places of worship. This scheme is overseen by the Department for Culture, Media and Sport. It makes grants to cover the VAT cost for making repairs and necessary alterations to listed buildings used for public worship. Details of the grant scheme are available at *www.lpwscheme.org.uk*.

Relief may be available where a non-residential building is converted to a dwelling or a relevant residential building for a housing association. There are also a number of 5 per cent reliefs for renovation and conversion works.

Zero-rating will continue to apply to works carried on up until 30 September 2015 where a relevant consent (usually a listed building consent) for the works was applied for prior to 21 March 2012 or a written contract had been entered into before that date.

Where the transitional relief rules do not apply, any payment received after 21 March 2012 but before 1 October 2012 will be subject to VAT at 20 per cent where the works are carried out on or after 1 October 2012.

19.3 Relief for approved alterations prior to 1 October 2012

The reliefs from VAT in relation to listed buildings can be split into two main parts. Firstly, the zero-rate which applies to alterations made to a protected building and secondly, the zero-rate for the sale of a substantially reconstructed protected building.

Zero-rating applies to the supply of services in the course of an 'approved alteration' of a 'protected building', with the usual exception in relation to services provided by an architect, surveyor or any person acting as consultant or in a supervisory capacity. The zero-rating also extends to the supply of building materials in association with the supply of zero-rated services, provided that the materials are incorporated in the building or its site.

Having a tax relief for the alteration of our national heritage rather than for its upkeep and repair, which is standard-rated, may at first glance seem peculiar, but the relief stems from the pre-1984 position when all alterations to buildings were zero-rated. In 1984 the Government introduced VAT at standard rate on alterations but, due to pressure by the heritage lobby, the relief was retained for protected buildings. The VAT (Protected Buildings) Order 1995 (SI 1995/283) substituted a new Grp. 6 to Sch. 8 to VATA 1994 with effect from 1 March 1995.

'Protected building' means a building which is designed to remain as or become a dwelling or number of dwellings, or is intended for use solely for a relevant residential purpose or a relevant charitable purpose after the reconstruction or alteration and which, in either case, is:

'(a) a listed building, within the meaning of–

    (i) the Planning (Listed Buildings and Conservation Areas) Act 1990; or

    (ii) the Planning (Listed Buildings and Conservation Areas) (Scotland) Act 1997; or

    (iii) the Planning (Northern Ireland) Order 1991; or

(b) a scheduled monument, within the meaning of –

    (i) the Ancient Monuments and Archaeological Areas Act 1979; or

    (ii) the Historic Monuments and Archaeological Objects (Northern Ireland) Order 1997.'

(VATA 1994, Sch. 8, Grp. 6, Note (1).)

Law: VATA 1994, Sch. 8, Grp. 6

19.4 What is a protected building?

19.4.1 Definition

A 'protected building' is defined in Note (1) as:

'a building which is designed to remain as or become a dwelling or number of dwellings or is intended for use solely for a relevant residential purpose or a relevant charitable purpose after the reconstruction or alteration and which in either case, is–

(a) a listed building within the meaning of–

    (i) the Planning (Listed Buildings and Conservation Areas) Act 1990; or

    (ii) the Planning (Listed Buildings and Conservation Areas) (Scotland) Act 1997; or

    (iii) the Planning (Northern Ireland) Order 1991;

(b) a scheduled monument, within the meaning of–

    (i) the Ancient Monuments and Archaeological Areas Act 1979; or

    (ii) the Historic Monuments and Archaeological Objects (Northern Ireland) Order 1995.'

Essentially this means that the building must be either grade I or II (or grade I* or II*) listed or a scheduled monument. The relief also covers objects or structures within the curtilage of a listed building which, although not fixed to the building, form part of the land and have done so since before 1 July 1948, such as an outhouse. However, where buildings are not attached to the main listed building, they must be used integrally with the main building to qualify for relief.

Unlisted buildings which are in conservation areas (usually buildings noted by the local authority as being of architectural or other interest) are not included in the relief. Buildings covered by immunity certificates do not qualify for zero-rating under this heading, but see **19.6.1**, regarding zero-rating for 'substantial reconstruction'.

Law: VATA 1994, Sch. 8, Grp. 6, Note (1)

19.4.2 Use of the building

The building must be designed to remain or become a dwelling, relevant residential or relevant charitable building.

> **Planning point**
>
> The relief does not apply to commercial buildings, unless the work involves converting them for use as a dwelling, etc.

Dwellings

The meaning of a 'dwelling' for the purposes of the legislation is as follows:

'a building is **designed to remain as or become a dwelling** or number of dwellings where in relation to each dwelling the following conditions are satisfied–

(a) the dwelling consists of self-contained living accommodation;

(b) there is no provision for direct internal access from the dwelling to any other dwelling or part of a dwelling;

(c) the separate use, or disposal of the dwelling is not prohibited by the terms of any covenant, statutory planning consent or similar provision,

and includes a garage (occupied together with a dwelling) either constructed at the same time as the building or where the building has been substantially reconstructed at the same time as that reconstruction.'

Law: VATA 1994, Sch. 8, Grp. 6, Note (2)

Relevant residential property

The legislation defines use for a relevant residential purpose as meaning use as:

- a home or other institution providing residential accommodation for children;
- a home or other institution providing residential accommodation for persons in need of personal care by reason of old age, disablement, past or present dependence on alcohol or drugs or past or present mental disorder;
- a hospice;
- residential accommodation for students or school pupils;
- residential accommodation for members of any of the armed forces;
- a monastery, nunnery or similar establishment; or
- an institution which is the sole or main residence of at least 90 per cent of its residents.

Specifically excluded from the above are uses as a hospital, a prison or similar institution, or a hotel, inn or similar establishment.

The legislation indicates that the building or part of the building must be designed 'solely' for a relevant residential purpose before zero-rating may be allowed. It has been accepted by HMRC however that a mere office in a residential home for the use of a warden, matron or similar person may be ignored.

Where only part of the building qualifies for zero-rating, a 'reasonable apportionment' must be made between zero-rated work and standard-rated work.

Care homes qualify as relevant residential buildings for VAT purposes and approved alterations to protected care homes are therefore zero-rated, as is the grant of a major interest in a substantially reconstructed nursing/rest home by the person substantially reconstructing it, providing in either case that the recipient of the supply issues a certificate to the supplier that he will be using the building for the qualifying purpose.

> ## ⚠ *Warning!*
>
> On account of this condition, subcontractors involved in the works of approved alterations of such a building have to standard rate their supplies to the main contractor. It is the main contractor contracted to and working directly for the 'person substantially reconstructing' who qualifies for zero-rating upon the production of a certificate. If this person is a developer, however, a certificate cannot be supplied and construction will be standard-rated. The developer would then grant a major interest to the person who will use the building for qualifying purposes and zero-rating applies for this supply, providing the requisite certificate is issued.

In the tribunal case of *Hill Ash Developments* [2001] BVC 2,075, the partnership carried out works to a house and outbuildings which had been purchased by one of the partners for use as a nursing home and sheltered accommodation, and treated these works as zero-rated. The house was a listed building but the listing did not include the outbuildings, for which planning permission had been gained to convert them into an extension for care flats and an administration block for the nursing home, providing a staff room, general office, storage and a kitchen.

The taxpayer argued that this was the conversion of a non-residential building into a dwelling and also qualified for zero-rating as an approved alteration to a listed building. The tribunal found that the use of the administration block was so tied up with the main residential building that it constituted use for relevant residential purposes.

Relevant charitable property

A relevant charitable purpose is defined as:

'use by a charity in either or both of the following ways, namely–

(a) otherwise than in the course of furtherance of a business;
(b) as a village hall or similar in providing social or recreational facilities for a local community.'

In the case of (a) above, HMRC allow for up to 10 per cent business use, including letting of the building. The 'use' may be calculated in any reasonable way, using time available for use or floor area, for example. However, where the whole of a building is to be used for a mixture of qualifying and non-qualifying use, and the non-qualifying use exceeds the 10 per cent limit, there is no provision for apportionment of the supplies. It is only in cases where discrete areas are to be used for different purposes that apportionment applies under VATA 1994, Sch. 8, Grp. 5, Note (10).

For (b) above, the main beneficiaries are churches, most church halls, village halls and community centres.

> ### Planning point
>
> Under (b) there is no restriction on the business use of the building, such as lettings to scout or guide groups and other groups within the local community. Again, the provisions do not cover extensions to existing buildings, other than certain approved alterations to listed buildings. It is important to appreciate that not all charities will benefit from this legislation as many engage in 'business activities', e.g. Oxfam shops.

> ### Planning point
>
> HMRC accept that where a building or part of a building is used for both non-business and business purposes, the business use can be disregarded if the non-qualifying use is minimal. The business use can be disregarded if it constitutes less than 10 per cent of the use of the building. Until 30 June 2010, HMRC permitted four options to calculate the 10 per cent non-business use. The first option for calculation is the standard option and can be used without HMRC's prior permission, but the remaining three options require HMRC's written permission.

Business use can be disregarded if the following conditions are met:

1. the entire building will be used solely for non-business activity for more than 90 per cent of the total time it is available for use;

2. in the case of an identifiable part of a building, if that part will be used solely for non-business activity for more than 90 per cent of the total time that part of the building is available for use;

3. 90 per cent or more of the floor space of the entire building will be used for non-business activity; or

4. 90 per cent or more of the people using the entire building (on a head-count basis) will be engaged solely on non-business activity.

It should be noted that only one of these four methods can be used for any one particular building and that the second method is the only one that allows identifiable parts of the building to be considered rather than the entire building. This concession was applied through Extra-Statutory Concession 3.29. This concession can only be used up until 30 June 2010; after this date a new statutory provision applies. To obtain this relief, the builder has to be given a certificate before the supply takes place. HMRC accept that where a certificate has been issued and a meaningful start to construction has commenced before 1 July 2010, then the concession detailed above can apply.

From 1 July 2010, a new statutory provision applies. A relevant charitable building needs to be used solely for charitable purposes, but the legislation permits some minor non-charitable use, up to 10 per cent of the use being non-charitable. HMRC will consider any fair and reasonable method of determining if the property is used for charitable purposes. It will be acceptable provided that it accurately reflects the use of the building, and its application is not overly burdensome and easy for HMRC to verify. A charity can, if it wishes, use one of the four methods described above, but must bear in mind that these may not provide a fair and reasonable result.

Law: VATA 1994, Sch. 8, Grp. 6, Note (6)

19.4.3   Partially qualifying buildings

In cases where only part of the building qualifies for zero-rating as being a dwelling, relevant residential or relevant charitable, there is provision for the value of the supplies to be apportioned.

Law: VATA 1994, Sch. 8, Grp. 6, Note (5)

19.5   Approved alterations

19.5.1   Introduction

A supply in the course of an 'approved alteration' to a protected building is eligible for zero-rating and includes building materials supplied in the course of the qualifying works within the zero-rating. To qualify for zero-rating, the building must either remain or become a dwelling, although the relief does also apply to certain other residential/charitable buildings.

> **Planning point**
>
> Since 1 April 1989, commercial buildings have not qualified for these reliefs. The services of an architect, surveyor or any person acting as a consultant or in a supervisory capacity, in the same way as for construction of new dwellings and other qualifying buildings, are specifically excluded from zero-rating (as they are for the construction of new houses) and these are chargeable at the standard rate.

Law: VATA 1994, Sch. 8, Grp. 6, items 2 and 3

19.5.2   What is an approved alteration?

The issue of what comprises an 'approved alteration', as opposed to repair or maintenance, has been tested through the courts on many occasions. One issue that can disqualify works from zero-rating is if the works did not require listed building consent (even though it has been given).

In most cases, however, listed building consent is required for works amounting to the alteration of a protected building. The point at issue is usually therefore whether the works amount to an 'alteration' or not. The judicial definition of an 'alteration' for these purposes was originally derived from the case of *C & E Commrs v Viva Gas Appliances* (1983) 1 BVC 588, which held that 'alteration' should be construed as including:

> 'any work upon the fabric of the building except that which is so slight or trivial as to attract the application of the de minimis rule.'

However, more recently, in *The Vicar and Parochial Church Council of St Petroc Minor* [2000] BVC 4,068, the tribunal specifically declined to apply that interpretation, holding that in that case the word 'alteration' was used in a context which no longer appears in VATA 1994 and that the contextual interpretation was of no use now. The tribunal decided that even if the appellants were altering the building – they were having work done to prevent the entry of damp with a view to carrying out repairs to damage caused by damp – it was work of maintenance and therefore excluded from zero-rating.

One of the key issues raised in tribunals where doubt arises in the correct treatment of any works, in order to test whether the work is an 'alteration', is whether the part of the building affected was in need of repair prior to commencement of the work. For example, if a roof is replaced because it leaked prior to the works being carried out, then it will likely be considered a repair even if the work results in an alteration (see *Rhodes* [1997] BVC 4,020 where 65 per cent of the roof area had been in need of repair but the remaining 35 per cent was in good repair and therefore qualified as an alteration).

Use of modern building materials and methods in themselves do not constitute an alteration (see the *St Petroc Minor* [2000] BVC 4,068 case). If the roof needed repair but the work also entails substantial alterations, such as repair of the roof with the new construction of rooms in the loft space, then it is likely that apportionment will apply.

In cases where there is an alteration as a result of repair or maintenance works being carried out, this does not change the treatment of the supply – it remains a standard-rated repair (see *C & E Commrs v Windflower Housing Association* [1995] BVC 329).

It should be noted that there are circumstances in which the repair and maintenance element of work done may be reduced-rated, rather than standard-rated, where the project falls within the reduced-rating relief (see **19.8**).

19.5.3 Conditions for zero-rating

In order to qualify for the relief there are a number of conditions that must be met.

1. Listed building consent must have been required and been granted prior to the works being commenced (see *Brice* [1991] BVC 828) except in the case of

ecclesiastical buildings to which s. 60 of the Planning (Listed Buildings and Conservation Areas) Act 1990 applies where listed building consent is not required. Instead, the church obtains a faculty from the Church Committee (houses occupied by ministers of religion are not included in 'ecclesiastical building' – only the church building itself). The ecclesiastical exemption is restricted to the following churches in England and Wales which have all agreed to abide by the guidelines provided by planning authorities: Church of England, Church in Wales, Roman Catholic Church, Methodist Church, Baptist Union of Great Britain and the Baptist Union of Wales, and the United Reformed Church. Ecclesiastical buildings of all denominations in Scotland and Northern Ireland are included in the exemption, providing the building is still used for religious worship.

There is a similar provision for buildings with a Crown or Duchy interest in which case a qualifying alteration is one which would have required listed building consent.

Approval is required for all alterations to scheduled monuments from the Secretary of State. In rare cases a building may be both a listed and a scheduled monument and in such cases it will be the scheduled monument consent which takes precedence.

2.   The work must be to a qualifying building – one designed to remain or become a dwelling, relevant residential or relevant charitable building.

3.   The work must comprise an alteration, rather than a repair or work of maintenance (see below) in which case standard-rating applies.

4.   The everyday meaning of 'alteration' applies – there must be change in the structure (the fabric) of the building. Works to areas which are not the building itself, such as to boundary walls, etc., do not qualify unless the walls actually touch and are therefore part of the qualifying building.

5.   In the case of 'relevant residential' or 'relevant charitable' buildings, the builder must be provided with a certificate to evidence the qualifying use. A certificate can only be supplied by the person who will be using the building for qualifying use directly to the person supplying services to him or her. Therefore any services supplied by subcontractors to the builder will be standard-rated, but will be zero-rated when charged on by the builder to the owner of the building. The form of certificate required is provided by HMRC in *VAT Notice 708, s. 18*. There is a penalty of 100 per cent of the tax involved for the wrong issue of a certificate.

19.5.4   Building materials

For building materials to qualify for zero-rating they must be supplied by the person making the supply of qualifying services in the course of carrying out those services – the separate purchase of materials or goods does not qualify for zero-rating.

> **Planning point**
>
> So the owner of a listed building, purchasing materials direct, will be charged VAT at 17.5 per cent, but if the VAT-registered builder purchases the materials and supplies these in the course of providing the zero-rated alteration services, the combined services and materials qualify for zero-rating.

The usual exclusions apply to recovery of input tax on white goods, fitted wardrobes, carpets and carpeting materials.

19.5.5 Garages

Works to garages physically attached to and for occupation in conjunction with a listed building may also qualify for the relief.

19.5.6 Apportionment

In cases where some of the works carried out qualify for zero-rating and some do not, there is provision for apportionment of works. For example, although redecoration is considered to be a work of repair/maintenance rather than an alteration, if it is carried out as a result of alterations having been made, it too will qualify for zero-rating.

If the total works carried out comprise both alterations and repairs and maintenance then the redecoration works should be apportioned between zero-rated and standard-rated, usually based on the proportion of works directly qualifying as zero-rated to total works.

19.5.7 Examples

Below are listed some examples drawn from tribunal decisions on the subject of what does or does not constitute an 'alteration'.

Reconstruction of a building

This was specifically ruled as not being an alteration in the case of *C & E Commrs v Morrish* [1998] BVC 378, on the grounds that the work led to a reinstatement of what was there before the fire rather than an alteration of the building which existed prior to the fire. The case concerned a cottage which had been badly damaged by fire and required the rebuilding of exterior walls and reinstatement of the roof.

Rebuilding of external walls

This was held to be an alteration in the case of *Logmoor Ltd* [1997] BVC 4,068 on the grounds that the work incorporated the old hayloft stables as part of the house.

Underpinning of foundations

This was held to be an alteration in the case of *ACT Construction Ltd v C & E Commrs* (1981) 1 BVC 451 on the grounds that it was entirely new work, not work to the existing building.

New drainage system and sewage treatment plant

In the case of *Walsingham College (Yorkshire Properties) Ltd* [1996] BVC 2,240, the tribunal ruled that the work went far beyond mere repair or maintenance but the work was apportioned due to it also relating to three unlisted cottages on the estate. The drainage system is generally held to be part of the fabric of the building to the point where it joins the mains services.

Garden works

Garden works in the grounds of a listed building do not always qualify for zero-rating because the relief is restricted to works of alteration to the fabric of the building itself. However, in *Tinsley* [2002] BVC 4,052, the tribunal allowed zero-rating for works to create a terrace.

The decision relied on s. 1(5) of the Planning (Listed Buildings and Conservation Areas) Act 1990 which provides that any object or structure fixed to the building shall be treated as part of the building. As the terrace was connected to the listed building it therefore qualified as an alteration to it.

There was also a question of whether the works required listed building consent. (VATA 1994, Sch. 8, Grp. 6, Note (6)(c) stipulates that the work must require listed building consent in order to qualify for zero-rating – not simply that it is covered by listed building consent. Often, listed building consent is granted to cover all of the proposed works, whether or not all of the works actually require it.)

It was clear, however, that some work to a trellis fixed to the building did require consent and the tribunal took the analogy to mean that the terrace also required consent if it were connected to the building. The works were also clearly authorised by the consent and the Council had written separately to confirm this.

Erection of railings

This was held to be an alteration to the qualifying building where the railings actually touched the qualifying building (*Powell (t/a Anwick Agricultural Engineers)* [1997] BVC 2,067).

Construction of a boundary wall

In the case of *Mason* [2000] BVC 4,025, where the boundary wall was attached to the listed building by a 'timber boxing arrangement', this was held to be an alteration in part.

Construction of a greenhouse

This was held to be an alteration in the case of *Mann* [1996] BVC 4,273 , because it was attached to the listed building. However, in the same case the construction of a swimming pool and stables were held to be standard-rated as they were separate buildings and excluded from zero-rating.

Construction of a separate garage

This was held not to be an alteration in the case of *Bradfield* [1991] BVC 503, because it was physically separate from the main house and was not therefore work to the listed building.

Removal of asbestos

This was held to be repair and maintenance on the grounds that it did not affect the character of the building in *Gibbs* [1991] BVC 557.

Outbuildings

VATA 1994, Sch. 8, Grp. 6, Note (10) specifically excludes the construction of a building separate from, but in the curtilage of, a protected building from the definition of an 'alteration' and hence from zero-rating.

In *C & E Commrs v Zielinski Baker & Partners Ltd* [2004] BVC 309, the court decided in favour of Customs that alterations to an outbuilding within the curtilage of a listed dwelling could not be construed as alterations to a protected building for the purposes of the zero-rating in circumstances where they were not independent dwellings. The outbuildings, once altered, were to be used in conjunction with the main building which was itself a dwelling.

It is clear from this case that alterations to outbuildings will qualify for zero-rating only if they can be seen as independent dwellings in their own right or are physically attached to the main building in conjunction with which they will be used (and all the other conditions are met).

Swimming pool

In *C & E Commrs v Arbib* [1995] BVC 201, the appellant constructed an indoor swimming pool in the grounds of the listed building, which was connected to it by a covered walkway. The High Court upheld the tribunal's decision that zero-rating applied because the swimming pool was part of and integral to the protected building. However, in the case of *Heijn* [1998] BVC 4,121, the swimming pool was held to be a separate standard-rated construction because it was some distance from the house and not used integrally with it.

Thatching

Replacement of straw thatch with reed thatch on two cottages was held to be an alteration in the case of *Dodson Bros (Thatchers) Ltd* [1996] BVC 2,583, as the roofs were not in need of repair prior to commencement of the work.

Replacement of a clay-pot roof with lead

Replacing a clay-pot roof with a lead roof on a church was held to be an alteration in *PCC of St Andrew's Church Eakring* [1998] BVC 2,117, on the grounds that the work was done in accordance with a stipulation of English Heritage in approving the grant, not because it was in need of repair.

Replacement guttering

Replacement guttering laid on to new soles sloping in a different direction and leading to new exit chutes was held to be an alteration in the case of *Parochial Church Council of All Saints Church* [1993] BVC 1,638.

Installation of a new lighting system

Held to be an alteration in the case of *All Saints with St Nicholas Church Icklesham* [2000] BVC 4,039, on the grounds that it was a one-off in the sense of exceptional expenditure and could not be categorised as a repair or maintenance.

Installation of double glazing

Held not to be an alteration in the case of *Moore* [2004] BVC 4,104, the tribunal holding that the simple replacement of windows did not constitute an alteration to the building, since it did not accord with common sense or use of language to consider the internal structure of a window as being part of the fabric of a building.

> **Planning point**
>
> This decision must surely be seen as at least questionable, as the idea that window frames and the glass that they contain not being part of the fabric of a building could be seen as debatable. This case also illustrates the often very fine line between qualifying and non-qualifying works, which can give rise to conflicting tribunal decisions on what are ostensibly similar facts.

19.5.8 Agreeing the treatment with HMRC

It is usual to agree the treatment of works, particularly on large projects, with HMRC prior to commencement. This saves much potential argument at a later date as HMRC can challenge the treatment for up to three years afterwards.

> **Planning point**
>
> The best way of dealing with this is to carry out an analysis of a costed schedule of works or building specification, preparing a spreadsheet of zero-rated alterations, repairs and maintenance works, works which are always standard-rated and works which must be apportioned. This can then be agreed with HMRC and VAT applied on the appropriate proportion of the value of works throughout the term of the contract, with a final adjustment at the end (because the costed schedule will almost certainly be different from the final cost).

⚠ **Warning!**

It is not, however, required that HMRC's approval be sought and in some cases this may be inappropriate. If the issues are uncontentious or the amounts small, it will almost certainly not be necessary and time and effort can be saved by leaving HMRC out of the equation altogether.

19.5.9 HMRC guidance

HMRC *Internal Guidance* (Vol. V1-8A) cites some examples of typical works of alteration in Ch. 3, Annex 5B, and those of repair or maintenance in Ch. 3, Annex 5C.

Typical works of repair or maintenance are said to include:

- treatment for woodworm, dry/wet rot, etc.;
- cracked and peeling walls filled and repainted;
- fire-damaged buildings restored;
- internal works to the mechanism of church organs, bell frames and the mechanical systems for ringing bells;
- rethatching of thatched roofs and other roofing work in general;
- installation of damp-proof course or membrane;
- stripping-out and rewiring old electrical circuits;
- replacing rotten or damaged window frames and doors;
- repointing frost-damaged brickwork;
- redecorating;
- repairing or replacing old or damaged plumbing;
- replacing rotten or broken roof timbers; and
- replacing broken roof tiles.

Typical works of alteration are said to include the following.

1. General:

    (a) new floors constructed at a different level;
    (b) installation of first-time central heating system;
    (c) additions to electrical, heating and plumbing systems installed within the fabric of a building;
    (d) converting the internal layout of a building to provide for rooms to be used for specific purposes (e.g. creating/removing bathrooms or kitchens);
    (e) making new doorways and windows in walls where none existed before;
    (f) erection/removal of walls of a building (includes substantially altering the structure of a wall);
    (g) extension/enlargement to the protected building;
    (h) underpinning;
    (i) the enlargement of window apertures; and
    (j) bricking-up of windows and doors or providing apertures for new windows and doors.

2.   Qualifying work on churches may include:

(a)   changing plain to stained-glass windows and vice versa;

(b)   installation of first-time lightning conductor;

(c)   installation of floodlights fixed to the structure of the church;

(d)   installation of a new bell frame which occupies a different position from the existing frame;

(e)   installation of a new bell frame which differs in size or design from the existing bell frame; and

(f)   alterations to an existing bell frame to carry extra bell(s).

19.6   Substantially reconstructed protected buildings

19.6.1   Substantially reconstructed protected buildings from 1 October 2012

Zero-rating no longer applies to the first grant of a major interest in a substantially reconstructed protected building where the zero-rating relies upon the 3/5ths rule. The relief remains in place where there is a first grant of a major interest in a protected building substantially reconstructed from a shell. The relief as described below remains extant.

Thus, it remains permissible to zero-rate the first grant of a listed building that has been substantially reconstructed that is gutted and where no more remains of the original building (that is to say, the building as it was before the reconstruction began) than the external walls, together with other external features of architectural or historic interest. The rules remain extant as detailed in **19.6.2** and onwards for this type of reconstruction.

It should be noted that the relief is withdrawn for churches and other places of worship. A grant scheme, however, is available for listed places of worship. This scheme is overseen by the Department for Culture, Media and Sport. It makes grants to cover the VAT cost for making repairs and necessary alterations to listed buildings used for public worship. Details of the grant scheme are available at *www.lpwscheme.org.uk*.

Relief may be available where a non-residential building is converted to a dwelling or a relevant residential building for a housing association. There are also a number of 5 per cent reliefs for renovation and conversion works.

Zero-rating will continue to apply to works that relied upon the 3/5ths rule that are carried on up until 30 September 2015 where a relevant consent (usually a listed building consent) for the works was applied for prior to 21 March 2012 or a written contract had been entered into before that date. In addition, where 10 per cent of the work of a substantial reconstruction was completed (measured by cost) was completed prior to 21 March 2012 all the works completed before 30 September 2015 will be zero-rated.

Where the transitional relief rules do not apply, any payment received after 21 March 2012 but before 1 October 2012 will be subject to VAT at 20 per cent where the works are carried out on or after 1 October 2012.

19.6.2   Substantially reconstructed protected buildings prior to 1 October 2012

The grant of a major interest in a protected building (freehold sale or lease of over 21 years) by a person 'substantially reconstructing' it is zero-rated for VAT (VATA 1994, Sch. 8, Grp. 6, item 1) where this was carried out prior to 1 October 2012 although this relief remains extant where there is a gutting of the building.

If the transaction does not qualify for zero-rating, the sale or lease of the property will be exempt from VAT. The importance of this is that a zero-rated transaction is a taxable supply and attracts the right to recover VAT incurred, whereas an exempt transaction is not a taxable supply and there is no right to recover VAT input tax incurred.

Only the 'first grant of a major interest' (i.e. freehold sale or lease in excess of 21 years) in the qualifying categories of dwellings, relevant residential and relevant charitable buildings is zero-rated. Any future grants are exempt from VAT. For these purposes therefore, any subsequent rent received is exempt from VAT, and ongoing input tax is therefore not recoverable, subject to the partial exemption rules.

Planning point

Where a lease contains break clauses, which may be exercised prior to the expiry of 21 years, this does not invalidate the zero-rating from applying. To be a major interest, however, the grant must be of the legal interest, not the beneficial or equitable interest.

Planning point

If, due to an oversight, the term of the lease granted is less than the required 'over 21 years' for zero-rating to apply, this can be subsequently corrected by obtaining a Deed of Rectification (see *Isaac* [1997] BVC 2,175).

19.6.3   Substantial reconstruction

There is no precise definition of what amounts to 'substantial reconstruction' of a building. A two-stage approach is required by HMRC and this is supported by the early tribunal case of *Barraclough* (1987) 3 BVC 644 and the much more recent one of *Southlong East Midlands Ltd* [2005] BVC 2,387.

Before applying the tests set out below, it is necessary to first decide whether the building has been 'reconstructed'. There is no legal definition of 'reconstructed' for these purposes and therefore the ordinary definition should be used. The dictionary defines 'reconstruction' as 'having been rebuilt, re-formed or reconstructed'. HMRC say that a good indication is if there is a radical change of use or a marked increase in the number of units of living accommodation due to the work being carried out.

Once the issue of 'reconstructed' has been decided, VATA 1994, Sch. 8, Grp. 6, Note (4) to the Group provides the following tests as to whether the building has been 'substantially' reconstructed, either of which require to be met.

1.   That at least 60 per cent of the works carried out to effect the reconstruction, measured by reference to cost, qualify for zero-rating as an 'approved alteration' or as building materials supplied in the course of an approved alteration. It is this relief that is withdrawn from 1 October 2012.

2.   Alternatively, that the reconstructed building is gutted and that no more remains of the original building (that is to say, the building as it was before the reconstruction began) than the external walls, together with other external features of architectural or historic interest.

In carrying out the first test, services excluded from zero-rating, such as those of an architect or engineer which are always standard-rated, are excluded from the calculation of the 60 per cent.

Also, in applying this test it is not necessary for the person constructing to have employed a VAT-registered contractor so that the works are actually received as zero-rated services. It is sufficient that the works themselves would have qualified for zero-rating if they had been carried out by a VAT-registered person. Therefore a developer carrying out the works using in-house labour is not prevented from taking advantage of the 'substantial reconstruction' zero-rating upon disposal of the building, and thereby recovering VAT in full on the project.

Planning point

With regard to the second test, there is no requirement under the VAT legislation that listed building consent, etc., be obtained for the work (although if it is not, the work will no doubt flout planning and other regulations). It is simply necessary that the building be gutted, with only the external walls and any other parts of architectural interest remaining.

> ## *Planning point*
>
> Where a building has been fire damaged and is reinstated to look as it was before the damage was caused, the work is unlikely to qualify for zero-rating as an alteration (see *C & E Commrs v Morrish* [1998] BVC 378) and the first test outlined above will therefore not be met. However, the grant of a major interest in the building could still qualify for zero-rating if the second test is met, and it may therefore be possible to structure a lease of over 21 years or the freehold sale of the building into arrangements in order to secure recovery of the VAT incurred on the works.

19.6.4   Conditions for zero-rating

There are a number of conditions imposed on this zero-rating and these are listed below.

1.   The building must be a 'protected building' (see **19.4.1**). In addition, by extra-statutory concession, any building which is subject to an immunity certificate issued on or before 16 April 1996 is included in this relief if the major interest is to be granted to a person for non-business charitable use. Immunity certificates are issued by the Secretary of State for National Heritage and prevent the building being listed for a period of at least five years, thus allowing work to be done outside the constraints of the planning controls for listed buildings.

2.   The person granting the major interest must qualify as the 'person substantially reconstructing' the building. This will normally be the person carrying out the building work or commissioning it. Furthermore, HMRC have limited the status of 'person substantially reconstructing' by restricting it to the first supply in the newly constructed building. This interpretation denies zero-rating to a person constructing who grants a major interest of, for example, a freehold sale, after having granted a lease of over 21 years. This change was made from 1 March 1995 subsequent to the *C & E Commrs v Link Housing Association Ltd* [1992] BVC 113 case.

3.   In the case of a grant of a major interest by virtue of a lease over 21 years the zero-rating applies only to the premium or first rent received (VATA 1994, Sch. 8, Grp. 5, Note (14)) and subsequent payments, e.g. future rent and service charges, are exempt and are not zero-rated. This can have an effect on the recovery of related input tax, but VAT incurred in the course of construction of the building is generally seen as being attributable to the first rent only.

4.   The building must be of a type which may be zero-rated, i.e. a dwelling, relevant residential or relevant charitable building.

5.   There must be no planning or other restriction preventing the person acquiring or leasing the building from residing in the building throughout the year or preventing use of the building as his principal private residence. This generally prevents holiday accommodation from being included within the zero-rating.

6. If the 'major interest' is a lease or tenancy, then in cases where a premium is payable, the zero-rating applies to the premium only. In cases where a premium does not apply, the zero-rating applies to the first payment of rent only.

7. The person 'substantially reconstructing' must receive a certificate from the purchaser confirming that the building is to be put to qualifying use directly by the purchaser unless it is a dwelling, i.e. in cases where the qualifying use is 'relevant residential' or 'relevant charitable'. The certificate should normally be provided before the construction commences; however, by concession HMRC do allow the retrospective issue of a certificate for these purposes. The certificate must be produced to HMRC on demand by the constructor to support the zero-rating of his services. There is a penalty of 100 per cent of the tax involved for the wrong issue of a certificate (VATA 1994, s. 62).

Planning point

It is often useful to obtain clearance from HMRC in order to save any arguments at a later date. As the treatment as 'substantial reconstruction' often rests upon the 60 per cent rule, it is useful to work from a costed schedule of works/bill of quantities in determining whether the 60 per cent test is passed. This can then be submitted to HMRC and the agreed percentage applied to interim payments, with the usual adjustment for differences which inevitably occur at the end of the contract.

19.7 Churches

19.7.1 Eligible buildings

Where the protected building is an ecclesiastical building to which s. 60 of the Planning (Listed Buildings and Conservation Areas) Act 1990 applies, listed building consent is not required. Instead a faculty is obtained from the church committee (but this does not include buildings used as a house by a minister of religion, only the church building itself). The ecclesiastical exemption is restricted to the following churches in England and Wales which have all agreed to abide by the guidelines provided by planning authorities: Church of England, Church in Wales, Roman Catholic Church, Methodist Church, Baptist Union of Great Britain and the Baptist Union of Wales, and the United Reformed Church. Ecclesiastical buildings of all denominations in Scotland and Northern Ireland are included in the exemption, providing the building is still used for religious worship.

Otherwise the guidance set out above as to what qualifies as an 'approved alteration' applies to church buildings in the same way as for dwellings and other qualifying buildings.

The changes in the rules for protected buildings detailed above apply as much to churches as to other listed or protected buildings. As the VAT relief is no longer available there is a relief through a grant scheme, details of which are available at *www.lpwscheme.org.uk*.

19.7.2 Church bells

Customs issued a liability note in December 1995, setting out their understanding of how the relief for alterations to listed buildings applies to the issue of church bells. In this they confirm that the bell frame constitutes part of the 'fabric' of the building but does not include fittings such as bells and ringing fittings. The hanging of a new or additional bell on to an existing frame which is not altered at the same time is therefore a standard-rated supply. In addition they list the following services as qualifying for zero-rating and standard-rating accordingly.

1. Works that qualify for zero-rating include:

    (a) a new bell frame which occupies a different position from the existing frame;
    (b) a new bell frame which differs in size or design from the existing bell frame;
    (c) alterations to an existing bell frame to carry extra bells;
    (d) new or additional bells, other than recast, repaired, remodelled or retuned bells, installed at the same time as a zero-rated bell frame or zero-rated alteration to an existing bell frame;
    (e) a completely new set of ringing fittings needed to operate bells, supplied in conjunction with, and at the same time as, the provision of a zero-rated bell frame; and
    (f) goods and services supplied by the installing contractor as part of the above operations.

2. Works that qualify for standard-rating include:

    (a) a new bell frame which replicates one in poor condition;
    (b) the supply of any bells and/or bell fittings that do not qualify in (d) and (e) above;
    (c) recasts, repairs, tuning, remodelling or any other work to existing bells;
    (d) repairs to existing bell frames and ringing fittings;
    (e) spare parts and other goods provided in conjunction with zero-rated work but not installed; and
    (f) incidental alterations to an existing bell frame in conjunction with the provision of new bells or fittings.

19.7.3 Church organs

For the purposes of these guidelines, a church must be used for a current religious purpose and wholly for non-business activities. A definition of non-business can be found in *VAT Notice 701/1*.

There are two areas where relief from VAT is available for the supply and installation of a new electronic or pipe organ. Firstly, if the church is being newly constructed, and secondly, where the new organ is fitted as part of an approved alteration to a listed church.

In either case, in order for zero-rating to apply:

- a 'qualifying use' certificate must be provided to the supplier by the church;
- both the supply and the service of installation of the organ must be by the same person and be made to the church and not to a developer; and
- the organ must be incorporated into the fabric of the building as a fitting. In other words it must be built into the building so that it cannot easily be removed without doing serious damage; it will not be a fitting if it is mounted on a freestanding platform, fitted on castors, simply plugged in to an electricity socket or designed to be moved.

In most cases work to an existing organ will be standard-rated, except where the organ is in a listed church and the work to the organ is in the course of an approved alteration to the church, where zero-rating is allowed provided that the organ is a fitting as defined above, the church gives a qualifying use certificate to the supplier; and there is an alteration to the structure of the church. The organ itself is not part of the 'fabric of the building' and it should be noted that in order to qualify for zero-rating the works must require alteration to the fabric of the building.

19.7.4   Grants for repairs and maintenance of churches

In addition to the zero-rating for approved alterations there is also a grant available for churches in respect of repairs and other works, to fund the difference between the VAT chargeable at 17.5 per cent (15 per cent from 1 December 2008 to 31 December 2009) and 5 per cent VAT. It was introduced with effect from 1 April 2001 and applies to all works of repair or maintenance carried out on or after that date.

The scheme is administered by the Department of Culture, Media and Sport, and documentation relating to the scheme can be obtained via their hotline on 0845 601 5945, at their website *www.lpwscheme.org.uk* or by writing to Listed Places of Worship Grants Scheme, PO Box 609, Newport, NP10 8QD.

Customs estimated at the time of its introduction that the scheme could be worth £30 million a year to qualifying places of worship.

19.8   Interaction with the reduced rate

Construction services may in certain circumstances be subject to VAT at the reduced rate (five per cent).

Broadly speaking, qualifying projects will involve the change of use of a property, the change of a number of dwellings within a building or part of a building, or the renovation of a dwelling which has not been occupied residentially for at least three years. Full details appear in **Chapter 17**.

If the property to which the reduced-rate project applies is a protected building, the work carried out will qualify in part for zero-rating (subject to the conditions set out in this chapter) and in part for reduced-rating (as regards the remainder).

In this way, certain works of repair and maintenance on listed buildings may be subject to the reduced rate rather than the standard rate.

19.9   Change in use

If, within 10 years of completion of a relevant residential or relevant charitable purpose building it is sold or leased or the building is no longer intended for use solely for a 'relevant residential purpose' or 'relevant charitable purpose', VAT at the standard rate must be accounted for.

If the building (or part of the building) is sold or leased, VAT is accounted for on the value of the original supply relating to those parts of the building that originally benefited from zero-rating. Input tax can, however, be reclaimed where appropriate (where a taxable supply has been made, but not where an exempt supply has been made). The input tax incurred on the change of use adjustment may also be subject to a capital goods scheme adjustment.

Also, where, within 10 years of completion of the building, it is no longer used solely for a 'relevant residential purpose' or 'relevant charitable purpose', VAT must be accounted for. VAT must be accounted for on the building (or part of the building) that had been originally saved on those parts of the building where the change of use takes place. Adjustments are not made where there are changes in the value of the property or for changes in the standard rate of VAT.

An adjustment is made for the amount of qualifying use that has taken place over the period of use of the building. The value of the adjustment has to be reduced by 10 per cent a year. Thus, if there is a change of use in the first year following completion, 100 per cent of the value must be accounted for. If the change of use occurs six years after completion of the building then a 40 per cent charge applies.

> ### *Example 19.1*
>
> If a new relevant residential property is built for a cost of £1m, this will be zero-rated as it is a relevant residential property. After 4½ years there is a change in use of the building (to, say office lettings) and it is no longer a relevant residential use. This requires a 60 per cent charge as this is in the fourth year. The VAT payable if the original supply had been standard-rated = £1m x 20 per cent = £200,000. The amount of VAT due = £200,000 x 60 per cent = £120,000.

The VAT due is declared on the VAT return as output tax in the period in which the change of use occurred. An input tax credit is available to the extent that it relates to taxable supplies. In this instance, no input tax credit would be available unless there was an option to tax.

In addition, it may be necessary to make capital goods adjustments to the input tax amount if the tax exclusive amount that produces the output tax due and the consequent the input tax available for credit, is £250,000 or more, and the building is used to make exempt supplies.

The standard rate of VAT in force when you changed the use of the building may be different to the standard rate of VAT in force when you received the original zero-rated supply. The VAT to be accounted for is the rate of VAT that was in force when the original supply was made.

HMRC has announced a change in the way change in use adjustments are to be calculated for relevant residential and relevant charitable buildings in *Business Brief* 05/11. This change only affects buildings that are completed on or after 1 March 2011. Furthermore, the change only applies to changes in use that occur on or after 1 March 2011.

Owners of buildings completed before this date, or where changes occurred before this date, must use the older provisions outlined above. The new provisions replace the two adjustment mechanisms with a single adjustment. This single adjustment applies to both sets of circumstances where a change in use occurs. This new adjustment applies a standard rated self-supply charge to the value of the original supply, but adjusts this value according to:

- the proportion of the building affected by the change in use; and
- the number of complete months that the building had been used solely for a qualifying purpose prior to the change in use.

When considering a change in use it is important to remember that the determining factor is the occupational use of the building. Although HMRC usually considers the economic use of property for the change in use self-supply charge, it is the occupational use that is important. This can create some seemingly bizarre scenarios. There may be what would normally be a business use by the owner but the occupation is still non-business. For example, a charity may let a part of its building to another charity. As long as the second charity uses the property for a non-business purpose the first charity will not need to apply the self-supply charge for a change in use. Despite the fact that receiving a rent would be a business activity, the occupation of the building is still non-business. Similarly, a lease and lease back would not be regarded as incurring a change in use self-supply charge. Again, the occupation continues to be non-business or for a relevant residential purpose.

> ### *Planning point*
>
> If the change in use has occurred due to a grant being made in relation to the property, or any other taxable supply that is made, then this VAT must still be accounted for in addition to the VAT on the self-supply charge. The self-supply charge is separate from, and in addition to, any other VAT due on other supplies made.

> ### *Planning point*
>
> As the change in use adjustment is a self supply charge, output tax has to be accounted for; but input tax can also be reclaimed if the change in use creates a taxable supply. For example, if the change in use is the taxable letting of a part of the building (following an option to tax being made), then although output tax is charged on the supply a corresponding input tax credit can be claimed.

> ### *Example 19.2*
>
> In February 2011, a charity builds a new building. The cost is £10m. No VAT is incurred as the property is to be used entirely for a non-business purpose by the charity. The building consists of four storeys and an underground car park. The car park is the same size as a normal floor in the buildings. Two years later, the charity leases out the ground floor to a bank. As the ground floor is the most valuable floor of the building, the charity obtains a rent of £450,000 per annum. It does not opt to tax, a condition insisted on by the bank.
>
> The charity is also concerned about its carbon footprint and gets rid of all its cars. It operates the car park as a pay and display car park, and obtains £50,000 per annum in parking fees. The value of the self-supply is calculated as follows:
>
> (1) Value of buildings: £10m.
>
> (2) VAT rate: 20 per cent.
>
> (3) Property no longer used as intended: two floors out of five = 40 per cent.
>
> (4) Months no longer used for a qualifying purposes: 96 out of 120 months = 80 per cent.
>
> VAT due on self-supply charge = £10m x 20 per cent x 40 per cent x 80 per cent = £64,000.

The amount of input tax that can be claimed will depend upon the partial exemption scheme agreed with HMRC. If the standard method is used and the supplies mentioned in this example are the only business supplies, then only 10 per cent of the VAT on the self-supply charge can be reclaimed, that is £6,400. If an area or floor space scheme has been agreed with HMRC, then 50 per cent of the VAT incurred can be reclaimed, that is £32,000. VAT of £10,000 also needs to be accounted for on parking fees received.

It should be noted that the TOGC provisions do not apply to relevant residential use or relevant charitable use buildings. This is because the TOGC provisions only apply to transfers of a business and, therefore, are not relevant to residential or charitable non-business activities. A change of use self-supply charge will apply if there is a TOGC and the entire interest in the building is transferred with the business, as the property must, by definition, be used for a non-qualifying purpose. Similarly, part transfers will incur a charge on the basis of a change in use.

Doing Business in Goods in the EU

20.1   Introduction

It is very important to distinguish between trade in goods within the European Union (EU) and the import and export of goods from and to locations outside the EU as the systems requirements and methods of accounting for VAT are entirely different. It is also necessary to distinguish between the cross border trade in goods and services. This chapter is concerned with goods within the EU. (See **Chapter 21** for a discussion of cross-border EU transactions in services).

There is what might be called a 'tariff wall' surrounding the member states of the EU. Goods imported from countries outside the EU (called third countries) may breach the tariff wall into any member state. However, at that point, the goods are liable to import VAT (where the goods attract a positive rate of VAT in that member state) and are also potentially chargeable to customs duty, excise duty and other tariffs. An import entry is required at that point.

After payment of customs duty, the goods are said to be 'in free circulation' and can move freely within the EU without further payment of the duty but not without further payment of VAT.

Import VAT is paid either in cash or under the duty deferment system and subject to the normal rules, reclaimed later on the importer's VAT returns.

The most significant characteristics of intra-EU trade are as follows.

1.   There are no physical and fiscal barriers between the EU member states, i.e. there is no requirement for the completion of import or export declarations or payment of import VAT either in cash or under the duty deferment system.

2.   Goods are not imported or exported in intra-EU trade. Goods brought into the UK from other member states are 'acquisitions'. Goods supplied from the UK to another member state are EC sales.

3.   The acquisition of goods rather than the import of them is the taxable event, and creates the need to account for acquisition VAT.

4.   There is a liability for UK businesses which are not VAT registered to register if the value of goods acquired from other member states exceeds the VAT threshold (currently £70,000).

5.   A UK business that makes supplies in another member state and exceeds the VAT threshold operated in that country may have to register there. This also applies to businesses from other member states that make supplies in the UK.

Hence a business could be registered for VAT or its equivalent in several member states.

6. Responsibility for providing trade statistics, which were once provided by the import and export declarations, falls to the businesses actually dispatching and acquiring the goods. Statistical information is gathered by means of two boxes on the VAT return (boxes 8 and 9), European Sales Listings (ESLs) for supplies of goods to other VAT-registered businesses in other member states and Supplementary Statistical Declarations (SSDs) commonly known as 'Intrastat'.

Other guidance: *VAT Notice 702, 703,* and *725*

20.2 Intra-EU trade

20.2.1 General principles

The single market was introduced with effect from 1 January 1993 and applies across all member states of the EU (see below for a list of member states). The effect of the single market is to remove the need to account for VAT when goods cross a border between two EU member states.

The single market creates its own VAT compliance requirements as follows, where:

- VAT need not be accounted for on goods supplied by a VAT-registered person in one EU member state to a VAT-registered person in another member state, provided certain conditions are met;
- VAT must be accounted for on goods acquired by a VAT-registered person in one EU member state from a VAT-registered person in another member state;
- special rules apply where persons are involved in 'triangular' or other 'chain' transactions where the invoice route and the delivery route do not coincide;
- special rules apply to persons supplying and installing goods in another member state;
- special rules apply to persons who move their own goods to their branch or premises in another member state;
- special 'distance selling' rules apply in respect of sales to persons not VAT registered in another member state;
- special rules apply to goods subject to excise duty;
- special rules apply to second-hand goods, works of art, antiques and collectors items;
- special rules apply where new means of transport are purchased from suppliers in other EU member states;
- special rules apply to supplies to diplomatic missions, international organisations, NATO forces, etc. in other EU countries;
- businesses selling goods to a VAT-registered customer in another member state must complete EC Sales Lists; and

- businesses involved in cross-border transactions that involve movements of goods have obligations under the Intrastat system.

20.2.2   Place where VAT is due

When goods are dispatched or transported from one member state to another the place where VAT becomes due is the member state in which the 'dispatch or transport ends'. For this to apply the recipient must be a VAT-registered business and the necessary conditions met unless one of the exceptions applies (see **20.5** to **20.7**).

If the goods are not dispatched or transported, VAT becomes due in the place where the goods are located when the supply takes place.

There is another variation for 'distance selling' (e.g. mail order) of goods not liable to excise duty. The place where VAT is due for limited supplies of relevant goods sold in this way is the member state from which the goods are dispatched (see **20.7.3**).

Example 20.1

Wizard is a UK business selling magic wands. It has a retail and wholesale customer base. It is also developing internet selling.

An order is received from a German VAT-registered business. Wizard dispatches the required number of wands to Germany quoting the German VAT registration number on the invoice. The place where VAT is due is where the journey ends – Germany.

A French holiday maker visits Wizard's shop in Scotland and buys a wand. The place of supply is Scotland because this is where the goods are when the supply takes place.

Via the internet Wizard received an order from a private individual in Holland. The wand is posted to Holland by Wizard. The place of supply is Scotland unless Wizard's sales to Holland have exceeded the relevant limit in Holland and Wizard is already registered there for VAT (see **20.9.3**).

20.3   EU states and VAT registration numbers

20.3.1   The format of EU VAT numbers

Table 20.1

Member state	Country code	Format of VAT number	Number of characters	Notes
Austria	AT	U12345678	9	The first character will always be U.
Belgium	BE	0123456789	10	9 digits before 1 April 2005, 9 digit numbers prefixed with 0
Bulgaria	BG	0123456789 or 012345678	9 or 10	
Cyprus	CY	12345678X	9	The last character will be an alpha character.
Czech Republic	CZ	12345678 or 123456789 or 1234567890	8, 9 or 10	Where 11, 12 or 13 numbers are quoted, delete the first three as these are tax codes
Denmark	DK	12345678	8	
Estonia	EE	123456789	9	
Finland	FI	12345678	8	
France	FR	12345678901 or X1123456789 or 1X123456789 or XX123456789	11	May include an alpha character(s), either first, second, or first and second. All alpha characters except I and O are valid.
Germany	DE	123456789	9	Do not use the 10 digit number that is sometimes quoted as this is a different registration number
Greece	EL	012345678	9	
Hungary	HU	12345678	8	
Ireland	IE	1234567X or 1X34567X	8	Includes one or two alpha characters, either last or second and last.
Italy	IT	12345678901	11	
Latvia	LV	12345678901	11	
Lithuania	LT	123456789 or 123456789012	9 or 12	
Luxembourg	LU	12345678	8	
Malta	MT	12345678	8	

Netherlands	NL	123456789B01	12	The three-digit suffix will always be in the range B01 to B99.
Poland	PL	1234567890	10	
Portugal	PT	123456789	9	
Romania	RO	1234567890	2 to 10 digits	Zeros will precede the number if less than 10 digits.
Slovak Republic	SK	1234567890	10	
Slovenia	SI	12345678	8	
Spain	ES	X12345678 or 12345678X or X1234567X	9	Includes one or two alpha characters, either first or last, or first and last.
Sweden	SE	123456789012	12	
United Kingdom	GB	123 4567 89	9	

20.3.2 Countries/territories outside the EC VAT area

The countries and territories outside the EC VAT area are:

- the Aland Islands;
- Andorra;
- the Canary Islands, Ceuta and Melilla;
- the Channel Islands;
- the overseas departments of France (i.e. Guadeloupe, Martinique, St Pierre and Miquelon and French Guiana);
- Gibraltar;
- Mount Athos;
- San Marino,
- the Vatican City; and
- other countries in geographical Europe that do not appear in the table at **20.3.1**.

Planning point

Goods sent to these countries will be considered to be exports to third countries and will benefit from zero-rating according to the normal rules (see **Chapter 22 Exports**).

⚠ Warning!

Although not full members of the EU, the Isle of Man and Monaco are treated, for VAT purposes, as if they were part of the UK and France respectively, which is highly important when considering the VAT consequences of dealing with either territory.

20.3.3 Validating overseas VAT numbers

One of the conditions for zero-rating supplies of goods to a VAT-registered business in another EU member state is that the supplier holds a valid EU VAT registration number for the customer. UK suppliers would be strongly advised to check the validity of the VAT registration number given by a customer in another member state if they are in any doubt at all about its validity.

This can be done by contacting the National Advice Service on 0845 010 9000. HMRC may be able to verify that the address for the VAT number is also valid.

There is also an electronic system for validating other VAT numbers via the Europa website (*http://ec.europa.eu/taxation_customs/vies/vieshome.do*).

As a statement of practice, HMRC have said that provided the UK supplier has taken all reasonable steps to ensure that the customer is registered for VAT in the EU, such as checking with the VAT office as above (and provided all other conditions have been complied with), they will not require the supplier to account for VAT in the UK on the supply if the VAT number subsequently proves to be invalid.

HMRC have stated that they will not regard UK suppliers as having taken reasonable steps if, for example:

- the VAT number quoted on the supplier's invoice does not conform to the publicised format for VAT numbers in the customer's member state;
- the supplier continues to use an EU VAT number which HMRC have previously advised is invalid; or
- the supplier uses a VAT number which he knows does not belong to his customer.

20.4 Acquisitions

20.4.1 Introduction

'Acquisitions' is the term given to the receipt of goods by a person in one member state of the EU from a VAT-registered supplier in another member state. In certain circumstances it can be applied when a business transfers its own goods from one member state to another.

Example 20.2

Henry is a UK VAT-registered retailer. He orders stock from Fritz, a German wholesaler registered for VAT in Germany. The goods are dispatched from Germany to the UK. This is an acquisition in the UK by Henry.

Henry obtains an order from Jacques, a French trader established in France and registered for VAT (known there as TVA). Henry can order goods from Fritz and arrange for Fritz to deliver the goods directly to Jacques. This is 'triangulation' (see **20.6**).

Law: VATA 1994, s. 11

Other guidance: *VAT Notice 725*

20.4.2 Buying goods from VAT-registered suppliers

Subject to complying with certain conditions a VAT-registered buyer is obliged to account for VAT when buying goods from a VAT-registered business belonging in another EU member state. Under this system the seller does not charge VAT but VAT must be accounted for by the buyer. This occurs when the following conditions apply:

* the seller's invoice is endorsed with the buyer's VAT registration number prefixed with the two-digit country code; and
* the goods are transported from the EU member state in which the seller belongs to the member state in which the buyer belongs.

In these circumstances the buyer has made an intra-EU 'acquisition' and must account for VAT. The VAT due is calculated according to the tax rates applying in the country in which the buyer belongs. The buyer must account for this VAT in the following way:

1. The buyer is liable to pay the tax, the 'acquisition' tax, to the relevant tax authority. The tax due is normally included in the buyer's VAT return. In the UK it is added to the VAT due on sales and the total entered on the VAT returns.

2. The 'acquisition' tax may be reclaimed by the buyer according to the normal rules. In the UK it is included with other input tax before entering the reclaimable amount on the form.

> **Planning point**
>
> Partly exempt businesses must pay 'acquisition' tax in full. They may not recover it in full unless the goods concerned are used exclusively in connection with making taxable supplies. The 'acquisition' tax is not recoverable, or only partially recoverable, when used in connection with making exempt supplies. Likewise 'acquisition tax' is not fully recoverable when the goods are used in connection with non-business activities.

20.4.3 Purchases involving persons who are not VAT registered

When a buyer is not VAT registered but the seller is, the seller accounts for VAT. The seller charges VAT according to the rates applicable in his EU state (see specific exceptions at **20.5**).

'Acquisition' tax is not due in the UK on goods acquired from another EU state from a business that is not VAT registered (VATA 1994, s. 10(3)). Other EU states may deal with these transactions differently.

> **Planning point**
>
> UK non-registered businesses buying goods from other EU states must consider these purchases for VAT registration purposes. When relevant purchases exceed a certain amount the business concerned must register for VAT (see **20.12.2**).

> **⚠ Warning!**
>
> A business which incurs 'foreign' VAT before registration may not recover this tax. It is not within the scope of the regulations applying to UK VAT incurred before registration (see **3.9**).

20.4.4 Special circumstances

VAT on an acquisition is always due in the Member State where the goods are received. There is, however, a 'fallback' provision that applies where the VAT registration number quoted to the supplier to secure zero-rating has been issued in a different Member State from the State of acquisition. In these circumstances, VAT must be accounted for in the Member State of registration and the customer must also account for acquisition VAT in the Member State to which the goods have been sent. HMRC will permit the customer to not account for the acquisition VAT if he can demonstrate that acquisition VAT has been accounted in the Member State to which the goods were dispatched where this is different. A refund of any UK acquisition VAT accounted is available but only where a full input tax credit for that acquisition has not or cannot be claimed.

It has been confirmed in the ECJ decisions in the joined cases of *Staatssecretaris van Financiën v X (C-536/08); Staatssecretaris van Financiën v fiscale eenheid Facet BV/Facet Trading BV (C-539/08)* that there is no right to deduct input VAT accounted for under the fall back provisions unless it can be demonstrated that acquisition VAT has been accounted for in the Member State of arrival. The ECJ decision has effected the concession given to persons acquiring yachts that had been announced in *Business Brief* 12/97. This had permitted VAT registered business to reclaim acquisition VAT for yachts that had been acquired from another Member State and delivered to another Member State. This will no longer be p ermitted from 1 June 2011. Persons that entered into contracts for the delivery of yachts prior to 1 June 2011 will remain permitted to reclaim input tax for deliveries after this date if evidence of the contact is retained.

> ### ⚠ *Warning!*
> There are as always several exceptions and relaxations of the general rules above. These are covered at **20.7**.

20.5   EC sales

20.5.1   Introduction

EC sales (strictly 'supplies for intra-Community acquisition') are sales of goods by a VAT-registered supplier in one member state to a customer in another member state, where the goods move from the supplier's EU member state to where the customer is.

The following details of sales to customers in other member states are based upon the supplier being established and VAT registered in the UK. However, the same principles may be applied when the supplier is established in another member state although the time limits and the type of commercial evidence of removal may be different.

Other guidance: VAT Notice 725

20.5.2   Supplies to VAT-registered customers

Supplies to VAT-registered traders in other EU member states are zero-rated provided the following conditions are met:

- the customer's VAT registration number (with the two-digit country code prefix), is shown on the VAT invoice;
- the goods are removed from the UK to a destination in another member state,
- within three months of the time of supply, the supplier obtains and holds valid commercial documentary evidence that the goods have been removed from the UK (see **20.9** for details of acceptable commercial evidence); and
- a reference appears on the sales invoice to the effect of 'This is an intra-Community supply' or some equivalent to that (see HMRC *VAT Information Sheet* 10/07).

From the customer's point of view the supply is treated as an acquisition in the customer's country.

Example 20.3

GoodsRUs plc sell furniture. They supply goods to the value of £3,000 to each of certain customers in France and Germany. Their supplies to France and Germany have not exceeded the 'distance selling' threshold and therefore they have not registered and do not have to register for VAT in either of these member states (see **20.7.3**).

Jean in France is a TVA registered business. He orders several sofas and supplies GoodsRUs with his TVA number. The furniture is sent to him and correct documentation is obtained to show that the sofas have left the UK. The invoice sent shows Jean's TVA number and the goods are zero-rated. Jean deals with the TVA implications in France.

Hans in Germany is a business registered for VAT who orders some tables. However, he does not supply GoodsRUs with his VAT registration number. The correct documentation is obtained that the furniture has left the UK. However, because GoodsRUs cannot endorse the invoice with Hans's VAT number the goods are standard-rated.

⚠ *Warning!*

Simple failure to quote the customer's VAT registration number on the face of the supplier's sales invoice could in extreme circumstances result in the denial of zero-rating for the EC sales affected. Best practice is to ensure that it appears without fail, and that VAT is always charged where it does not. In addition, it is now a requirement where a reverse charge will be applicable to state on the invoice that this is the case; a legend such as 'The supply is subject to VAT under the reverse charge provisions' will suffice.

20.5.3 Supplies to unregistered customers

Generally, suppliers must charge and account for UK VAT at UK rates on supplies of goods to customers who are not registered for VAT in another EU member state. These supplies are treated as being taxable in the UK.

Example 20.4

GoodsRUs receive their first order for goods from Slovenia. Renata places an order for some chairs. She is not registered for VAT. Since no VAT number is available the invoice cannot be endorsed with a Slovenian VAT number and the furniture must be standard-rated although proof of the goods leaving the UK is available.

However, there are some situations which may cause particular difficulties or obligations. Suppliers may have an obligation to register for VAT in the member state of the customer when the sales into that State reach a certain level. This is known as distance selling and is covered at **20.7.3**.

Planning point

Subject to the distance selling provisions, sales of goods by UK traders to unregistered customers in other EU member states are treated in all respects as if they were sales to UK customers. That is to say, UK VAT is chargeable and the sales are not reported in box 8 of the VAT return.

20.5.4   Special circumstances

Planning point

There are as always several exceptions and relaxations of the general rules above. These are covered later at **20.7**.

20.6   Triangulation

20.6.1   What is triangulation?

Triangulation is the term used to describe a sale of goods involving three parties in different EU states. It is when, instead of the goods moving from one party to the next, they are delivered directly from the first party in the chain to the last.

With regard to EU trade, triangulation occurs when goods move directly from a supplier in one member state to the final destination in another member state on the instructions of an intermediate business located in yet another member state.

In its simplest form, triangulation can be illustrated by the following example.

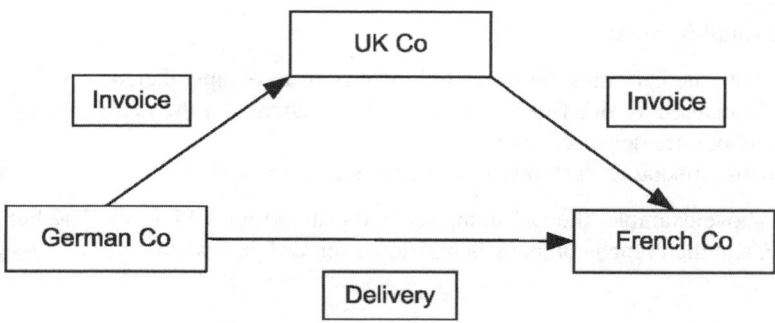

In the above situation, a UK company receives an order from a French customer, which it meets by consigning the goods directly from its own supplier in Germany. For VAT purposes there are two supplies taking place. These are as follows:

- between the German company and the UK company; and
- between the UK company and its French customer.

However, there is a single movement of the goods – from Germany to France.

In this example, the UK company in theory has a liability to register for VAT in France in order to account for VAT:

- on its acquisition of the goods; and
- on the onward supply of the goods in that country.

The purpose of the simplification arrangements is to remove this liability, which would be onerous for the many businesses involved in such transactions.

⚠ *Warning!*

The simplification arrangements for triangulation only work where all three parties belong in the EU. If the intermediate supplier is in the US, for example, they are of no assistance. In this circumstance, the US trader will be obliged to register for VAT somewhere in the EU to avoid an irrecoverable VAT cost on the transaction. In addition, the simplification only works where three parties are involved. Where four parties are involved the triangulation method cannot be used.

20.6.2 Simplification

To avoid intermediaries having to register in the country where the goods are delivered, simplification measures have been introduced. In the above example, simplification avoids the need for the UK company to register in France.

Under simplification, the intermediate supplier opts to have its customer account for the VAT in the country where the goods are delivered. The customer accounts for VAT under the normal rules applying to intra-EU purchases (see **20.4**).

To use simplification:

- the intermediary must be registered for VAT in an EU member state and must not be registered, or otherwise required to be registered, in the member state where the goods are delivered; and
- the intermediary's customer must be registered for VAT.

In the above example, the UK company is registered for VAT in the UK but not in France, and the French company is registered for VAT in France.

20.6.3 Intermediate supplier in the UK

An intermediate supplier in the UK can use its UK VAT registration number to secure zero-rating of the goods from its EU supplier. If the intermediate supplier in the UK opts to have its customer account for the VAT due on its behalf, the UK intermediary must issue the customer with a tax invoice endorsed 'VAT: EC Article 28 Simplification invoice'.

The intermediary must also include this supply on its EC Sales List, identifying the transaction as a triangular supply.

Intermediate suppliers should not give details of transactions with either their supplier or customer – in triangular trade – on their VAT returns or Intrastat supplementary declarations. In the above example, using simplification will:

- allow the UK company not to report this transaction on either its VAT return (in box 8) or on its supplementary declarations;
- endorse its invoice as described above; and
- include the supply on its EC Sales List, identifying it as a triangular transaction.

20.6.4   Intermediate suppliers in another EU member state making supplies in the UK

Intermediate suppliers in another member state may use simplification to avoid registering for VAT in the UK.

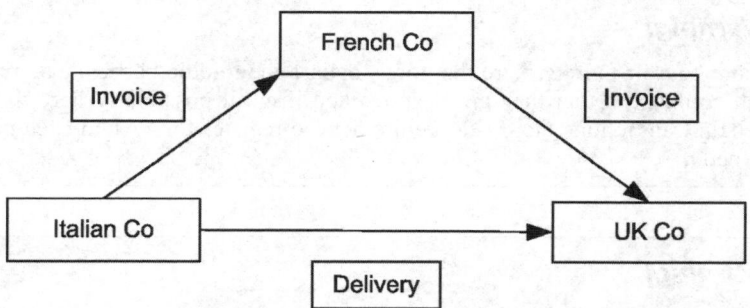

In the above example, the French company can avoid registering for VAT in the UK by doing the following.

1.   By issuing the UK customer with a tax invoice endorsed with 'VAT: EC Article 28 Simplification Invoice'. The invoice must be issued within 15 days of the date on which its supply would otherwise have taken place under normal UK tax-point rules for supplies of goods.

2.   By notifying HMRC of its intention to use the simplification procedure. The address to send notification to is:

HM Revenue & Customs
Non-Established Taxable Persons Unit (NETPU)
Ruby House
8 Ruby Place
Aberdeen AB10 1ZP

The following information must be given:

(a)   name, address and EC VAT number;

(b)   name, address and VAT registration number of the UK customer (separate notifications are required for each customer no later than the date of issue of the first invoice to that customer); and

(c)   the date the goods were delivered or intended to be delivered to the UK customer.

3.   By sending the UK customer a copy of the notification advising them that the simplification arrangements are being used and that the UK customer must therefore account for the tax. The notification must be sent no later than the date of issue of the first invoice to the UK customer.

The UK customer must include these transactions on its VAT returns (in box 9) and, if applicable, on its Intrastat supplementary declarations.

20.6.5   Chains of four or more

There is no simplification available for chain transactions involving four or more parties. Normal VAT rules and procedures apply.

> ⚠ **Warning!**
>
> Chains of four or more (where the goods bypass the middle parties) can give rise to such complexity that they are best avoided if at all possible. Where there are such chain transactions there is a requirement to register for VAT in each country concerned.

> ⚠ **Warning!**
>
> There are no simplification procedures if there is a 'leg' of the transaction outside the EU.

20.7   Intra-EU trade — special circumstances

20.7.1   Supply and install contracts

Goods sent to another member state to be installed or assembled there are not treated as a transfer of own goods. The supply of these goods takes place in the member state in which the goods are installed or assembled and the supplier of the goods may have a liability to register in this state.

To avoid the additional burden of having to register in another member state, most member states have agreed to a simplified procedure for suppliers of installed and/or assembled goods.

Using the simplified procedure, the supply of installed goods is treated as a taxable acquisition in the customer's country.

Under simplification, a business that is registered for VAT in member state A, that supplies and installs goods in member state B, need not register in member state B provided:

(a)   it is not otherwise registered or liable to be registered in country B;
(b)   its customer is registered for VAT in country B; and
(c)   country B allows this form of simplification.

> ### Example 20.5
>
> Vimera Ltd is a UK provider of laboratory units. It supplies and installs laboratory units in Germany. Vimera Ltd may avoid registering for VAT in Germany provided:

- Vimera Ltd is not otherwise registered for VAT in Germany; and
- its German customer is registered for VAT in Germany.

Supply and installation in the UK by a supplier in another EU member state

To use the simplification method in relation to goods supplied and installed in the UK, a supplier in another EU member state must do the following.

1.   Issue a tax invoice to the UK customer with the endorsement 'Section 14(2) VATA Invoice' (the invoice must be issued with 15 days of the date on which the supply would have taken place under normal UK tax point rules).

2.   Advise HMRC that the simplification arrangement is being used. The address to send notification to is:
     HM Revenue & Customs
     Non-Established Taxable Persons Unit (NETPU)
     Ruby House
     8 Ruby Place
     Aberdeen AB10 1ZP

     The following information must be given:

     (a)   name, address and EC VAT number;
     (b)   name, address and VAT registration of the UK customer; and
     (c)   the date on which the installation or assembly of the goods began or will begin.

3. Send the UK customer a copy of the notification advising him that the simplification arrangements are being used and that the UK customer must therefore account for the tax. The notification must be sent no later than the date of issue of the first invoice to the UK customer.

A UK customer who receives such a notification from a supplier in another EU member state has the following two obligations.

1. The customer must account for acquisition tax. The tax point for these acquisitions is the date of issue of the relevant invoice by the supplier. The customer will also be able to claim credit for a corresponding amount of input tax, subject to the normal rules.

2. The customer must include the value of the goods to be installed on:

    (a) its VAT return; and
    (b) if applicable, on any Intrastat supplementary declarations.

> **Planning point**
>
> When a business transfers own goods to another EU state, it is necessary to consider whether the business has an obligation to register for VAT in that EU state (see **20.7.2**).

Law: VATA 1994, s. 14(2); Sch. 4, para. 6(1); VAT Regulations 1995 (SI 1995/2518), reg. 42.

20.7.2 Transfer of own goods from one EU member state to another

> **Planning point**
>
> The rules for accounting for acquisition VAT as shown above, relate not only to 'normal' trade in goods between VAT-registered businesses in different EU member states but also to the situations listed below. In these cases, businesses may find that they have a liability to register for VAT in an EU member state to which they send their goods.

Transfer of own goods between member states

If goods are transferred within the same legal entity to another member state for business purposes, there is a deemed supply of goods for VAT purposes. This includes stock for resale and business assets.

There may be a requirement to register for VAT in the member state of destination of the goods in order to account for VAT on the acquisition of the goods and, if necessary, to account for VAT on any onward supply. Registering for VAT will also enable a business to use its VAT registration number in the other member state to secure zero-rating of the goods when they leave the UK.

Example 20.6

A VAT-registered business in the UK transferring goods to its Italian branch is deemed to be making a supply of goods. The UK business may be required to register for VAT in Italy to account for acquisition tax on receipt of the goods.

If the business registers for VAT in Italy, the Italian VAT number may be used to transfer subsequent goods from the UK to the Italian branch at the zero rate. The Italian branch will account for acquisition tax on receipt of the goods. Any onward supplies of the goods within Italy will be subject to Italian VAT.

Following the decision in 1999 in *Centrax Ltd* [1999] BVC 2,057, HMRC clarified their policy on the VAT treatment of the transfers of own goods from the UK to another EU member state. The case concerned the VAT treatment of parts moved by Centrax from the UK to be used to repair gas turbine generators they had previously supplied and installed in Italy.

HMRC agreed that Centrax could, exceptionally, zero-rate transfers of their own goods from the UK to Italy using their VAT registration number in Italy, even though they were not registered in Italy at the time the transfers took place.

HMRC's policy is set out below on the VAT treatment of the transfer of own goods from the UK to another EU member state for the purposes of either making a supply of installed or assembled goods or a supply of repair services.

Where goods are transferred from the UK to another EU member state to supply installed or assembled goods there, the movement is not a deemed supply of goods.

Where goods are transferred from the UK to another EU member state in order to supply a service of repair, the movement is a deemed supply of goods. To zero-rate the deemed supply, the transferor should have a VAT registration number in the member state to which the goods are transferred. Where no such VAT registration number is obtained, UK VAT is chargeable on the deemed supply. Where HMRC are satisfied that another EU member state does not allow retrospective registrations, they may, exceptionally, be prepared to allow the deemed supply of the transfer of own goods to be zero-rated. This must be against a current registration number held by the UK business in the EU member state to which the goods were transferred. The transferor would be required to provide written evidence from the relevant tax authorities, confirming that retrospective VAT registration is not possible in their country.

If such goods are invoiced to a VAT-registered customer in the member state of receipt, they will of course become subject.

> ### Planning point
>
> It must not be forgotten that the UK is a 'member state' and therefore the transfer of own goods to the UK from a different member state may cause a business to register in the UK.

Consignment stocks, goods on sale or return, approval or similar terms and 'call-off' stocks

> ### ⚠ Warning!
>
> Different EU states have different rules and regulations regarding consignment stocks, goods on sale or return, and call-off stocks. UK businesses are advised to check the situation in the relevant EU member state.

'Consignment stocks' are situations when a business transfers goods to another EU member state to create a stock under its control, from which supplies will subsequently be made by that business or, on its behalf, in that member state.

'Call-off stocks' are goods moved to another EU member state for the customer to maintain a stock for 'call-off' as and when required.

Call-off stocks received in the UK: if a UK business receives call-off stocks from a supplier in another EU member state, it should account for VAT on the acquisition on the basis of the movement of the goods even though title may not pass until the goods are called off. These arrangements only apply when the goods are intended for use by the UK customer for its own business, or to make onward supplies to its own customers. Stocks dispatched to the UK by an EU supplier for onward supply at a later date, or for call-off by more than one customer, should be treated as consignment goods. This creates a liability for the overseas supplier to be registered for VAT in the UK.

Call-off goods delivered to storage facilities operated by the supplier rather than the customer should also usually be treated as consignment stocks.

20.7.3 Distance sales

Distance selling is a situation where a VAT-registered business in one EU member state supplies and delivers goods to customers in another member state who are not VAT registered. These customers will include private individuals, public bodies and charities. It will also include businesses and organisations that are not and should not be registered for VAT.

Goods are taxed under the origin principle, that is, VAT is charged at the rate applicable in the EU member state of dispatch unless and until the value of supplies into any particular member state exceed certain *de minimis* limits. At that point, the supplier is required to register for VAT in that member state and charge VAT to customers at the rate applicable there.

The reason for these arrangements is that a person in an EU member state with a high rate of VAT, for example Sweden, and who is not normally able to recover VAT (for example a private individual), may be tempted to buy goods on mail order terms from a member state which has a lower rate of VAT. The distance selling arrangements, therefore, cut down or eradicate any advantage there may be to cross-border shopping for goods for a tax advantage.

Each EU member state has adopted a threshold of either €100,000 or €35,000 per calendar year above which a business in another member state supplying goods on mail order or delivered terms or under these distance selling arrangements must register for VAT there.

Member states applying the €35,000 limit are:

- Austria
- Belgium;
- Bulgaria (70,000 BGN);
- Cyprus;
- Czech Republic (1,140,000 CZK);
- Denmark (280,000 DKK);
- Estonia;
- Finland;
- Greece;
- Hungary (HUF 8,800,000);
- Ireland;
- Italy;
- Latvia (24,000 LVL);
- Lithuania (125,000 LTL);
- Malta;
- Poland (160,000 PLN);
- Portugal;
- Romania (118,000 RON);
- Slovakia;
- Slovenia;
- Spain; and
- Sweden (320,000 SEK).

EU member states applying the €100,000 limit are:

- UK (GBP 70,000);
- Austria;
- France;

575

- Germany;
- Luxembourg; and
- Netherlands.

> **⚠ Warning!**
>
> A UK business would be advised to keep a very accurate record of distance sales to other EU member states and to monitor it regularly because penalties apply for late registrations.

A UK business registered in another member state may choose to have a fiscal representative in that member state, but this is no longer a requirement.

A UK business can opt to register for VAT in another EU member state on a voluntary basis even though distance sales into that country have not exceeded the distance-selling threshold. In these cases, UK businesses must notify HMRC at least 30 days before the date of the first supply which follows the decision to opt for registration. The notification must be in writing and must state the names of the member states concerned. The UK business must then provide HMRC with documentary evidence that they have notified the tax authorities in the other member states within 30 days of the first supply there.

Once this option has been taken, it must stand for two years. That is, businesses cannot change their minds and move the place of supply back to the UK within that period. The registrations in other member states can, however, be cancelled after that time.

20.7.4 The fallback position

The fallback position is where a business provides its VAT number to obtain a supply that is zero rated even though the goods do not arrive in that country. For example, a UK customer may order goods from a French supplier and have these goods delivered to Germany. This is not triangulation as only two parties are involved (the French supplier and the UK customer). The French supplier could zero-rate the supply if the UK customer gave its UK VAT registration number. HMRC had (until late 2011) allowed the UK customer to account for acquisition VAT and then reclaim this acquisition VAT as input tax. Following the decision in the ECJ of the joined cases of *X* (Case C-536/08) and *Facet Holding BV* (Case C-539/08) the position has markedly changed. Whilst the UK supplier will still be required to account for acquisition VAT as it has provided its VAT number, it will no longer be able to reclaim the input tax credit. For the supply to be VAT 'free' it will be necessary for a third party to be involved (say a German entity in this example) so that the supply can be treated as supplied under the triangulation rules, or the UK entity will need to create a German subsidiary to receive the supply and this German entity can register for VAT and supply its own German VAT registration number. This will have a particular impact upon the yachting trade as HMRC had previously allowed acquisition VAT to be accounted for and credits to be claimed where yachts were acquired from a supplier in another member state but not brought to the UK. The claim for input tax will no longer be permitted.

20.7.5 Goods subject to excise duty

Goods which are subject to excise duty are always taxed for VAT and excise duty purposes in the EU member state of destination.

> ### ⚠ *Warning!*
>
> If the supplier arranges for the delivery to a non-VAT-registered person in another EU member state, he may be liable to register in that member state.

Supplies of goods subject to excise duty to a VAT-registered customer in another EU member state to be used for business purposes are taxable on the customer in that member state. The customer should account for acquisition VAT on his own VAT return.

For sales to non-registered persons for non-private purposes, there are special arrangements for supplies of these goods. They also apply to purchases by businesses trading below the VAT registration threshold in their own EU member state or by non-registered legal persons such as associations and unincorporated bodies, etc. whose activities are not regarded as 'business' activities for VAT purposes. These supplies can be zero-rated from the UK if the following conditions are met.

1. Before the goods are dispatched, the customer:

    (a) makes a declaration to the tax authorities in the EU member state of destination; and

    (b) guarantees that before the goods are dispatched, the excise duty will be paid.

2. The goods are removed from the UK to another EU member state by, or on behalf of, the customer.

Goods must travel with an accompanying administrative document (AAD). The supplier must obtain and retain copy one of the AAD and receipted copy three of the AAD certified by the consignee or fiscal authority of the member state of destination. This must all be completed within 15 days of the end of the month in which the goods are removed.

The movement of goods must be completed and a receipt issued within four months of the time of supply.

If a person occasionally imports excise goods by way of business, HMRC must be notified on a consignment-by-consignment basis and will issue a Form 1165 for each consignment. See *Notice 204*.

> ### Planning point
>
> The only situation whereby excise goods can enter the UK without payment of UK VAT is when an individual collects them personally from outside the UK and brings them back for his own use.

20.7.6 Second-hand goods, works of art, antiques and collectors' items

On 1 January 1995, the margin scheme of accounting for VAT became available throughout the EU and now covers virtually all second-hand goods, works of art, collectors' items and antiques. From the same date, goods sold under the EU-wide scheme became taxable in the member state of origin rather than of destination and are also not subject to the normal distance selling rules.

Margin scheme goods moved from one EU member state to another do not give rise to a deemed acquisition in the other member state, and a business will not normally be required to register for VAT in another EU member state by virtue of the movement.

The practical effect of this is that if a UK business acquires second-hand goods from a VAT-registered business in another EU member state, the supplier should account for VAT on the margin at the rate applicable in his or her own member state. There is, therefore, then no requirement for the UK acquirer of the goods to account for acquisition VAT on receipt of them.

Information on the conditions of the scheme and of qualifying goods appears in **Chapter 7**.

Other guidance: VAT *Notice 718*

20.7.7 New means of transport

New means of transport are taxed in the EU member state of destination whether or not the supplies are to a private individual or sold to VAT-registered businesses in different EU member states in the course or furtherance of the business. This cuts down any advantage there may be to cross-border shopping for a new car in another EU member state.

'New means of transport' are designed for the transport of passengers and one of the following.

1. Any ship exceeding 7.5m in length.

2. Any aircraft of which the take-off weight exceeds 1,550kg.

3. Any motorised land vehicle which:

    (a) has an engine with a displacement or cylinder capacity exceeding $48cm^3$; or

    (b) is constructed or adapted to be electrically propelled using more than 7.2kw.

The ship, aircraft or motorised land vehicle is not 'new' if any of the following conditions apply.

1. The period that has elapsed since its first entry into service is:

    (a) in the case of a ship or aircraft, a period of more than three months; or
    (b) in the case of a land vehicle, a period of more than six months.

2. It has, since its first entry into service, travelled under its own power:

    (a) in the case of a ship, for more than 100 hours;
    (b) in the case of an aircraft, for more than 40 hours; or
    (c) in the case of a land vehicle, for more than 6,000km.

Supplies to VAT-registered customers

If a new means of transport is supplied to a customer who is registered for VAT in another member state, the supply may be zero-rated if the conditions for zero-rating are met.

1. The customer's VAT registration number (with the two-digit country code prefix) is shown on the VAT invoice.

2. The goods are removed from the UK to a destination in another member state.

3. Within three months of the time of supply, the supplier obtains and holds valid commercial documentary evidence that the new means of transport has been removed from the UK.

If the means of transport is a motorised land vehicle, it may not be used on UK roads unless it is registered and licensed. To do this, the supplier and purchaser must complete and sign Form 411A and send it to the nearest Vehicle Registration Office (VRO). A special registration mark will be issued by the VRO which will identify the vehicle as being intended for removal from the UK to another member state.

Supplies to customers who are not registered for VAT

Supplies of new means of transport to customers who are not registered for VAT may be zero-rated provided:

- commercial documentary evidence is obtained to show that the new means of transport is removed from the UK to another member state within two months of the time of supply; and
- the supplier and the customer complete Form VAT 411 and send the top copy of the form to:

HM Revenue & Customs
Central Processing Unit
Postal Depot
Charlton Green
Dover
Kent CT16 1EH

The top copy must be sent within six weeks of the end of the calendar quarter in which the supply was made. For example, if a vehicle is supplied on 23 July 2005, the top copy of Form VAT 411 must be sent to the Central Processing Unit by 14 November 2005. The first carbon copy is retained by the customer, the second by the supplier and the third copy is required when the vehicle is registered.

If it is not possible for the new means of transport to be removed from the UK within two months of the time of supply, the customer must inform HMRC immediately by writing to the above address.

Accounting for VAT on the acquisition of a new means of transport

The Form VAT 411 is the customer's declaration that he will take the new means of transport to another member state and pay VAT in respect of the acquisition in that member state. This applies irrespective of whether the customer is VAT registered in that other member state. However, the method of accounting may differ. Further details of the accounting requirements in each of the other member states can be obtained from HMRC.

A UK VAT-registered person who buys a new means of transport VAT-free from a supplier in another member state must account for acquisition tax on the VAT return for the period in which the new means of transport is acquired.

⚠ *Warning!*

If the new means of transport is a motor car, in most cases input tax deduction will not be available. It is very important to ensure that, in such cases, acquisition tax is brought to account in box 2 of the VAT return but no corresponding entry is made in box 4. If a computerised accounting system is used, an automatic entry in box 4 may be created for all acquisitions; a manual adjustment may therefore be required to reverse this entry.

A person who is not VAT registered and acquires a new means of transport from a supplier in another member state, must notify HMRC within seven days of the later of:

- the acquisition of the new means of transport; or
- the arrival of the new means of transport in the UK.

The notification should be sent, along with the original purchase invoice and any foreign registration documents, to the Central Processing Unit at the above address. HMRC will calculate the VAT due and will issue a written demand for the VAT which must be paid within 30 days of the date of issue. Evidence that the VAT has been paid should be kept by the owner of the new means of transport for six years. (VATA 1994, s. 95; Value Added Tax Regulations 1995 (SI 1995/2518), reg. 148, 155.)

Other guidance: *VAT Notice 728*

20.7.8   Supplies to diplomatic missions, international organisations, NATO forces, etc. in other EU countries

Under current provisional arrangements, deliveries of such goods will not create an acquisition for a UK business in another EU member state. Such supplies can be zero-rated provided that the following conditions are complied with:

- the goods are either for the personal use of entitled persons or the official use of entitled bodies;
- the supplier obtains documentation from the customer as laid down by their host authority for claiming exemption;
- the goods must be removed from the UK; and
- the supplier keeps proof of VAT removal, such as airway bills or bills of lading, etc.

Zero-rated transactions as above fall under the Directive 2006/112, art. 151(1) and are not regarded as distance sales and they do not count towards the distance selling threshold.

These arrangements do not apply to new means of transport, which are dealt with under different rules.

20.8   Intra-EU trade – other matters

20.8.1   Tax points

The rules for determining the time of acquisition, the tax point at which acquisition VAT should be accounted for, is treated as taking place at the same time as the corresponding supply of the goods in the EU member state of dispatch. The tax point for acquisitions is, therefore, the earlier of:

- the 15th day of the month following the one in which the goods were dispatched; or
- the date the supplier issues the invoice.

Unlike the rules for supplies of goods within an EU member state, full or part payment for the goods does not create a tax point for the acquisition and the acquirer need not account for acquisition VAT when part payment is made to the EU supplier. However, a part payment does create the need to generate an invoice and, if the supplier generates that invoice, the UK acquirer should account for acquisition VAT in respect of that amount provided the date of issue of the invoice is earlier than the 15th day of the month following the one in which the goods were dispatched.

> **Planning point**
>
> Acquisition VAT is entered onto the acquirer's VAT return in boxes 2 and 4 at the tax point above. However, as Intrastat declarations are calendar-monthly rather than quarterly, this may give rise to a timing difference. The reference period for inclusion of the statistics on the Intrastat form is different.

20.8.2   Tax value of acquisitions

Generally the tax value of an acquisition is the 'consideration in cash or in kind'. The consideration includes any payment made to the supplier for making the supplies such as the cost of packing, transport and insurance for which they are responsible under the contract.

Generally speaking, the value for VAT is the contract price shown on the invoice, whatever that contract price is. For example, a supplier may supply goods on terms such as ex-works (EXW), FOB, CIF or DDU. These are all standard shipping terms. For example, EXW means that the responsibility for the goods passes to the customer at the supplier's factory gate. FOB means that the responsibility for the goods passes to the customer after the goods have passed over the ship's rail. CIF means cost, insurance and freight. Therefore, if the supplier's invoice states that the terms are EXW, then generally this will be the value for VAT. The value must not be built up by any costs paid by the customer in bringing the goods to the UK, for example insurance and freight as would be the case for goods imported from outside the EU.

If the consideration is wholly in money, the tax value is based on that amount exclusive of any tax. If the customer is offered a discount and he pays the discounted amount, the tax value is based on that discounted amount.

The treatment of conditional discounts or contingent discounts which depend upon some future event taking place is different. In these cases, the tax value is based on the full amount paid. If the acquirer later earns the discount, the tax value is then reduced and the adjustment subsequently made.

If the consideration for the acquisition of goods is not wholly in money, for example as would be the case in a barter transaction, or if the consideration is partly in money and partly something else, for example as in a part-exchange deal, the tax value is the monetary equivalent of the whole consideration.

If there is no consideration on the acquisition of goods, for example when a business in one EU member state transfers its own goods to another, the value is what it would cost the business to purchase the goods in question at the time of acquisition, i.e. the open market value. If the open market value cannot be established, then the value is calculated on what it would cost to produce the goods at that time.

20.8.3   Converting foreign invoices: exchange rates

When a UK acquirer of goods receives a VAT invoice from a VAT-registered business in another EU member state it should not show a VAT charge in that member state. Instead, the invoice is converted to sterling, the VAT is calculated at 20 per cent (15 per cent from 1 December 2008 to 31 December 2009 and 17.5 per cent from 1 January 2010 to 3 January 2011) or 5 per cent (if the goods are subject to VAT in the UK) and the amount of VAT is shown in boxes 2 and 4 of the VAT return.

The allowable rates of exchange are as follows:

- the UK market selling rate at the time of acquisition (the rates published in national newspapers will be acceptable as evidence of the rates at the relevant time); and
- the period rates of exchange as published by HMRC.

Any other basis, for example, the use of an in-house rate, must be approved by HMRC in advance. If, however, by concession an acquirer was using a rate authorised in writing by Customs before 1 January 1993, the acquirer can continue to use this rate unless the rate used wholly derives from currency markets other than the UK. The continued use of concessionary rates is subject to review by HMRC.

20.9 Intra-EU trade – VAT reporting

20.9.1 Accounting and record-keeping requirements

> **Example 20.7**
>
> Joe is a UK-registered trader who buys goods from the Netherlands and has them sent to the UK for onward sale. The local VAT office contacted him about a control visit.
>
> This was not to be a 'normal' VAT control visit.
>
> Joe expected this to be the usual routine inspection of his books and records. To Joe's amazement, the visiting VAT officer produced a schedule showing the value of goods the business had acquired from the Netherlands on a quarter-by-quarter basis. This schedule had been obtained by HMRC via the Netherlands tax authorities.
>
> The VAT officer proceeded to carry out a detailed check that Joe had correctly accounted for VAT on the goods that had been acquired from the Netherlands and subsequently sold.
>
> Joe had dealt with the VAT situation correctly, with the exception of a couple of very minor errors, but was very relieved when the visit was over. Joe had no idea that there was likely to be any communication between the tax authorities in the Netherlands and the tax authority in the UK. As far as he was concerned, he had dealings with the UK VAT authorities that were entirely removed from any dealings in the Netherlands. The local VAT office gave him no warning that they were going to concentrate on record keeping regarding acquisitions from another member state. There was no warning given that the tax authorities of another member state were permitted to pass on information to UK HMRC.

Importance of EC Sales Lists

Part of the mechanism for the exchange of information is in the Intrastat information and the EC Sales Lists that relevant traders must submit.

Two cases that appealed to the VAT and Duties Tribunal tried to depend on a 'reasonable excuse' defence in order to be excused the penalties imposed by the commissioners.

In *Beaches Ltd* [2000] BVC 4,068, the Appellant claimed that the forms had not been returned because they had never been received from Customs. The Tribunal upheld the penalties of £50 and £770. It was found that the firm was fully informed about its obligations regarding EC Sales Lists. It had apparently failed to inform Customs of changes of address and therefore the returns were apparently sent to the wrong address. The Tribunal found that in sending the returns to the last or usual place of business, Customs had acted correctly and the documents were deemed to have been correctly served. The Tribunal also reaffirmed that neither the reliance on another (the firm's bookkeeper), nor lack of money, could be accepted as a reason to be excused from the penalties.

The second Appellants failed to turn up to the Tribunal and the only excuse proffered was that stated in the Notice of Appeal. The Tribunal did not accept that their problems with a computer were enough to excuse the imposition of two penalties of £500 and £980 respectively (*CJW Manufacturing Ltd* [2000] BVC 4,059).

> ### Planning point
>
> 1. Make certain that EC Sales Lists are submitted correctly and on time.
>
> 2. Check that traders who acquire goods from other member states account for VAT correctly and at the correct time.
>
> 3. Ensure that traders are aware that there may be an exchange of information between HMRC and tax authorities in other member states.

20.9.2 Reporting and information requirements

There are two boxes, 8 and 9, on VAT returns in order to declare statistical information. In addition, there are two other returns which certain businesses have to complete. Businesses in the UK who supply goods to VAT-registered traders in another EU member state have to submit lists of these supplies (EC Sales Lists – ESLs). An additional form, Intrastat, is used to declare movements and supplies of goods to other member states.

20.9.3 The VAT return

Acquisition VAT (see **20.4**) is declared in box 2 of the return, and recovered in box 4 to the extent that the goods are used in the course of furtherance of the business and to the extent that they are attributable to making taxable supplies.

Boxes 8 and 9 of the return relate to intra-EU trade in goods only and they should only be completed if goods have been supplied to or acquired from another EU member state. The amounts shown in these boxes must refer to the supply or acquisition of goods and any directly related services such as freight and insurance charges associated with the acquisitions and dispatches and included in the contract price of them. Any other services should not be included.

Box 8 should show the total value of all supplies of goods to VAT-registered businesses in other EU member states and the value of any goods dispatched or moved from the UK to another EU member state even if no actual sale is involved, i.e. 'deemed supplies'.

Also include:

- supplies of new means of transport to registered or unregistered customers in another EU member state;
- supplies of goods dispatched from the UK for installation or assembly in another EU member state; and
- distance sales to unregistered customers in another EU member state where such supplies have exceeded the distance selling threshold and the UK business is registered for VAT in that member state.

But exclude:

- movements of goods for process or repair;
- charges for repairing goods for a customer in another EU member state; and
- distance sales below the limit for VAT registration in another EU member state and where UK VAT is charged.

Box 9 should show a total value of all acquisitions of goods from VAT-registered business in other EU member states.

Planning point

It is not an uncommon error for UK suppliers of goods to unregistered customers in other EU member states to include these in box 8 of the return. This is incorrect as such sales are subjected to VAT and treated for all other purposes in exactly the same way as domestic sales (until such time as the distance selling threshold is breached in any particular country of destination and VAT registration there has been put in place).

20.9.4   EC sales lists (ESLs)

UK VAT-registered businesses that make supplies of goods to VAT-registered businesses in other EU member states are required to provide lists of the supplies to HMRC in the form of an ESL. The purpose of the ESL is to control the taxation on movements of goods within the EU. ESLs are also required from intermediaries in triangular transactions (see **20.6** above).

With effect from 1 January 2010 ESLs will be required for supplies of services subject to the reverse charge.

The information contained on ESLs (and their equivalent in other EU member states) is captured and recorded on an electronic database known as the VAT Information Exchange System (VIES). The information is exchanged at regular intervals through a system of computer interfaces or 'gateways'.

By accessing VIES, HMRC can:

- verify the validity of a declared EU VAT registration number against a name and address;
- check ESL declarations;
- check details of supplies of zero-rated goods to UK businesses as declared by suppliers in other EU member states; and
- issue follow-up single or multiple transaction verification requests to other EU member states where doubt exists about the validity of a declared or non-declared supply between EU businesses.

Additionally, there is a facility for exchanging information with other EU member states under Directive 77/799 concerning mutual assistance.

The returns are due:

- where services only are supplied, calendar quarterly, with an option for monthly returns;
- supplies of goods and services have not exceeded £35,000 in the four previous quarters ending 31 December (the limit prior to 1 January 2012 was £70,000), calendar quarterly with an option of monthly returns:
- supplies of goods and services in excess of the £35,000 limit (or £70,000 limit previously, monthly, and if branches submit separate ESLs the turnover limit applies to all branches combined;
- where monthly returns are required, both goods and services can be reported monthly using a three to identify supplies of services or report goods monthly and services in the third month (again using the indicator three for services);
- where annual VAT returns are submitted and the total annual taxable turnover does not exceed £145,000 and the annual value of supplies to other Member States is not more than £11,000 and these supplies do not include new means of transport, application can be made to HMRC's helpline for annual ESLs; and
- only goods are supplied and the taxable turnover does not exceed the VAT registration threshold plus £25,500, the annual value of supplies to other Member States is not more than £11,000 and these supplies do not include new means of transport, application can be made to the HMRC helpline for a simplified ESL and the date of submission can be agreed with HMRC.

Paper ESLs are to be submitted within 14 days of the end of the reporting period. Electronic ESLs can be submitted within 21 days of the end of the reporting period. VAT periods can be changed to coincide with ESL quarterly return periods on request to the HMRC helpline.

The option to submit quarterly ESLs for goods ends at the end of any month when the quarterly total value of supplies exceeds the threshold for the current and the four previous quarters.

Nil returns

If there are no sales to VAT-registered businesses made in a particular quarter, nil returns are not required.

Forms

The official forms are:

- form VAT 101 (EC sales list);
- form VAT 101A (EC sales list (continuation sheet)); and
- form VAT 101B (EC sales list (correction sheet)).

ESLs can be submitted to HMRC by way of Electronic Data Interchange (EDI) via a value added network or port community, magnetic tape or diskette but HMRC must be informed in advance.

Plain paper returns are permitted, provided this is agreed with HMRC in advance and provided that HMRC's requirements for typeface, font sizes and weights of paper, etc. can be complied with.

HMRC must be advised:

- of all errors exceeding £100 or two per cent of the declared total value of supplies to a customer, whichever is the greater;
- if an incorrect VAT registration number is quoted; and
- where supplies to a customer were incorrectly stated as being part of a triangular transaction.

Form VAT 101B must be used to correct the errors described above.

Branches within a company or individual companies within a VAT group registration can also apply to submit individual ESLs. Divisions of a company which are separately registered for VAT must submit separate ESLs.

> ⚠ **Warning!**
>
> Where an agent completes and submits ESLs on behalf of its principal, the principal remains legally responsible for the accuracy of the form and for ensuring that the time limits for completion are complied with.

20.9.5 Intrastats or supplementary declarations (SDs)

VAT-registered businesses with intra-EU trade above a certain threshold must supply further information on their trade in goods with other EU member states each month. These are called supplementary declarations or Intrastat returns. For Intrastat purposes, goods received from another EU member state into the UK are called 'arrivals' and goods delivered to another member state from the UK are called 'dispatches'.

The thresholds are changed from time to time, and are currently £250,000 for dispatches and £600,000 for acquisitions.

VAT-registered businesses where the EU value of dispatches of goods to other EU member states, or of arrivals of goods from other member states exceeding the threshold described, must submit the appropriate SD.

Once the threshold has been exceeded, a business must continue to submit SDs until the end of the calendar year. Obligations to continue submitting SDs in the following year will depend on whether trade during the current year exceeds the threshold set for the following year. The threshold applies on a calendar-year basis, i.e. January to December.

Planning point

Unlike the UK VAT registration limit, this does not apply on a rolling 12-month basis. Any business starts the year on 1 January with a nil base and must only complete Intrastat returns from the beginning of the month in which the threshold applicable to that year is exceeded.

At the end of each year, the obligations of a business may change. This will depend on whether or not EU trade for the calendar year just ending has exceeded the threshold set for the following year. If it has exceeded the new threshold, a business must supply SDs throughout the following calendar year.

Any change in the threshold does not affect an obligation to continue submitting SDs for the current year. Thus, if the value of EU trade in any calendar year falls below the threshold, a business must continue to supply SDs to the end of the calendar year. The obligation then ceases unless the value of EU trade exceeds the revised threshold for the next year.

Businesses not required to provide SDs at the start of the year still need to monitor their trade. If at the end of a particular month the cumulative value of EU trade from 1 January for either arrivals or dispatches exceeds the threshold, businesses must submit SDs for the rest of the calendar year, including the month in which the threshold is reached.

These rules apply equally to businesses whose EU trade expands to exceed the threshold and to businesses which start to undertake EU trade for the first time. It is the responsibility of a business and not of HMRC to monitor EU trade to determine when to submit SDs.

Arrivals and dispatches require separate forms (numbered C1500 and C1501 respectively), each of which has its own continuation sheet. Forms C1500 and C1501 have instructions printed on their reverse. Supplies of the forms can be obtained from the National Advice Service or HMRC website.

HMRC encourage the use of EDI methods for the transmission of Intrastat data. By taking advantage of EDI, businesses can often achieve practical and financial benefits, especially where declarations are lengthy. The information is transferred quickly and efficiently, eliminating queries that can occur from paper declarations. Problems which arise are spotted earlier and are resolved more easily.

Complete and accurate declarations must be received no later than the end of the month following the 'reference period' to which they relate. The reference period is normally a calendar month.

Planning point

Until quite recently, the time limit for submission of Intrastat returns was ten working days from the end of the month. The change to one month was not widely publicised and it is thought that many businesses will be unaware of this valuable relaxation.

Full details of the information required on Intrastat declarations and the manner in which different sets of circumstances are handled can be found in *VAT Notice 60*.

Penalties

Penalties can be incurred where SDs are persistently late, missing or inaccurate. Although the regime is a criminal one and could result in proceedings in a Magistrates' Court, HMRC normally prefer to avoid any proceedings. This involves the offer of an administrative fine in lieu of any court proceedings.

Payment of a compound penalty does not absolve a business from its legal obligation to submit the SDs for the periods covered by the penalty.

Other guidance: VAT Notice 60

20.10   Registration of overseas persons

20.10.1 Registration in respect of distance sales

A person who makes supplies of specified description which involve the removal of the goods into the UK from another EU member state may be required to be registered in the UK. Such supplies are known as 'distance sales', although the phrase does not appear in the legislation. VATA 1994, Sch. 2 provides for registration for such persons. (Persons established in the UK may be liable to be registered in other EU member states in similar circumstances.)

Distance sales are defined as follows, where:

- the removal of the goods to the UK is under direction of the supplier;
- the supply does not involve the assembly or installation of the goods;

- the goods are acquired in the UK by a non-taxable person;
- the person supplying the goods is established in another member state;
- the supplies are made in the course of that person's business;
- deemed supplies are excluded where the goods are treated as being supplied for private or non-business use;
- goods removed from a place in one EU member state to a place in another EU member state are also excluded where that removal is in the course of the supplier's business; and
- sales of new means of transport are also excluded.

Where a person makes distance sales, a range of options must be considered as follows.

1. If a person is already registered in the UK under VATA 1994, Sch. 1, then any distance sales made into the UK are deemed to be made in the UK (VATA 1994, s. 7(4)).

2. If a person is not registered in the UK but makes distance sales of goods subject to excise duty, such as tobacco and alcohol, then he is liable to register, whatever the value of goods removed (Sch. 2, para. 1(3)).

3. If a person is not registered in the UK, and makes distance sales of goods not subject to excise duty, then he is liable to register once the cumulative value of those supplies in a calendar year exceeds the prescribed limit (Sch. 2, para. 1(1)). VAT charged in another EU member state on such supplies shall not be treated as part of the value of those supplies made.

4. If a person is not registered in the UK, but makes distance sales of goods not subject to excise duty, and he has opted in his home member state to treat those supplies as being made in the UK, then the person is liable to register in the UK, whatever the value of goods removed (Sch. 2, para. 1(2)).

5. A person not liable to be registered under Sch. 2 may request to be so registered. He must satisfy HMRC that:

   (a) he intends to make distance sales of goods subject to excise duty;
   (b) he intends to opt that his distance sales will be treated as being made in the UK; or
   (c) he intends to make supplies to which such an option has already been made (Sch. 2, para. 4).

Example 20.8

Anita is a person established in Italy who sells goods of value £75,000 to non-business customers in the UK, and who charges Italian VAT at the rate of 20 per cent. She accounts for £15,000 VAT in Italy, and her total income is therefore £90,000. Anita's taxable turnover for the purposes of para. 1(1) is £75,000, and she is therefore not obliged to register for VAT in the UK.

Subject to the discretion of HMRC, and subject to such conditions as they may impose, the person making distance selling supplies into the UK but under the registration threshold may be registered in the UK. HMRC would expect to see written evidence of the option to make distance sales and written evidence of the option to tax supplies in the UK. A person who makes such an option shall be registered for a minimum of two years, running from 1 January after he is registered (Sch. 2, para. 7(3)).

Such a person is also required to notify HMRC within 30 days of making the option to treat his distance sales as being made in the UK, or that he has made a supply in the UK (Sch. 2, para. 5).

The registration limit for distance sales is £70,000 and is based upon the calendar year, running from 1 January each year. This limit has not changed since 1993.

Liability to registration under this section must be on form VAT 1A. The application must be submitted to:

HM Revenue & Customs
Non-Established Taxable Persons Unit (NETPU)
Ruby House
8 Ruby Place
Aberdeen AB10 1ZP

Law: VAT Regulations 1995 (SI 1995/2518), Sch. 1, form No. 6

Changes to registration particulars

A person registered in respect of distance sales is required to notify any change in the name, constitution or ownership of his business, or any event which requires a change in the register. Such notification must be within 30 days of the change occurring.

A person registered under this section is required to notify when he ceases to be registrable.

Deregistration

A person who ceases to be liable to be registered under this section may be deregistered. This shall take effect from a date agreed with HMRC.

Where a person was not liable to be registered, but chose to be registered, he shall cease to be registrable if he no longer intends to make an option to treat distance sales as being made in the UK, or he no longer intends to make such supplies as would be so opted. If such a person has contravened a condition of his registration, the registration may be cancelled from the date that the condition was contravened.

A distance selling registration can be cancelled if distance sales are expected to be less than £70,000 in the current year.

Penalties in respect of distance sales registration

The penalties for failing to register for distance sales are the same as for failing to register (see **3.2.9** and **3.2.10**). In addition, there are penalties for breach of regulatory provisions.

20.10.2 Registration in respect of acquisitions

Subject to certain minor exceptions, a UK business or organisation which purchases goods from a registered person in another EU member state, for removal into the UK, makes a taxable acquisition.

> **Planning point**
>
> An organisation which is not a taxable person in respect of its ordinary activities may find that it is liable to register under this section. Such an omission is understandable, given that, to a layman, an acquisition is not the same as a supply. This may leave the organisation liable to a penalty for failure to notify its liability for registration.

Having established that a person is making acquisitions which are taxable in the UK, a person is liable to be registered in respect of his taxable acquisitions when:

- at the end of any month, beginning at the start of January that year, the value of his taxable acquisitions has exceeded the specified limit ('historic turnover' rule); or
- at any time, the person expects that the value of his taxable acquisitions for the next 30 days will exceed the specified limit ('future turnover' rule).

The specified limit is the same as that for registration in respect of UK taxable supplies. Thus, with effect from 1 April 2012, the specified limit is £77,000.

In ascertaining the value of taxable acquisitions, the amount of any VAT charged on the transaction in another EU member state shall be excluded; also excluded shall be the last acquisition or supply of goods before removal from fiscal warehousing, under VATA 1994, s. 18.

A person shall not be liable to be registered if the value of the taxable acquisitions made in the previous full calendar year was below the specified limit and HMRC are satisfied that the value of the taxable acquisitions in the following year will not exceed that limit. However, this rule does not apply where a person expects to make taxable acquisitions exceeding the specified limit in the immediately-succeeding 30 days.

Example 20.9

David made taxable acquisitions of £45,000 in 2007. He makes taxable acquisitions of a similar value during 2008. However, on 1 May 2009, he secures a contract which involves taxable acquisitions worth £75,000 during May. He then expects his taxable acquisitions to return to below £50,000 in 2010.

David is liable to registration in respect of his acquisitions under para. 2(2).

A person liable to registration in respect of his taxable acquisitions is required to notify his liability within 30 days of the end of the month when he exceeded the specified limit. The person will be registered with effect from the end of the next month.

Where a person is registered under the future turnover rule, he must notify HMRC within the 30-day period. The person will be registered from the beginning of that 30-day period.

Planning point

In cases such as that highlighted by the example above, advance planning is required if at all possible. In order to obtain the goods VAT-free in the country of origin, it is necessary to quote a UK VAT number. Since it can take a number of weeks to go through the registration process, an early start is advisable.

Where a person makes taxable acquisitions but is not obliged to be registered, he may apply to be registered. The person is required to satisfy HMRC that he intends to make such acquisitions; written orders would normally suffice. HMRC may register such a person from an agreed date, although they may impose conditions on the registration. In particular, he is required to notify HMRC within 30 days of the first taxable acquisition he makes after registration. If registered, he is required to remain registered for a minimum of two years, from 1 January after the effective date of registration.

Liability to registration under this section must be notified on form VAT 1B, VAT Regulations 1995 (SI 1995/2518), Sch. 1, form 7. The application must be submitted to the Aberdeen VAT Office (see **20.10.1**).

Law: VATA 1994, Sch. 3, para. 2

Changes to registration particulars

A person registered in respect of acquisitions is required to notify any change in the name, constitution or ownership of his business, or any event which requires a change in the register. Such notification must be within 30 days of the change occurring.

A person registered under this section is required to notify when he ceases to be registrable.

Deregistration

A person who ceases to be liable to be registered under this section may be deregistered and is required to notify HMRC within 30 days of ceasing to be registrable. The deregistration shall take effect from the date he ceased to be so liable, or from a date agreed with HMRC.

Where a person was registered under this section, but was not required to be registered, the registration may be cancelled with effect from the date on which he was so registered.

Where a person who was not liable to be registered, but who was registered with the intention to make taxable acquisitions, either does not make such acquisitions or contravenes the conditions imposed by HMRC, his registration shall be cancelled. The registration may be cancelled from the date he expected to make an acquisition, although he did not do so, or from the date he contravened a condition imposed upon him, or from such later date as may be agreed.

Where a person was not registrable or makes no taxable acquisitions or contravenes the conditions imposed upon him, he will not be required to be registered for the two-year minimum normally applicable to voluntary registrations and will be deregistered by HMRC.

A person may cancel their registration for acquisitions if they expect their sales to fall below the registration limit, currently £77,000.

Penalties in respect of acquisitions registration

The penalties for failing to register in respect of acquisitions are the same as for failing to register (see **3.2.9** and **3.2.10**). In addition, there are penalties for breach of regulatory provisions.

20.10.3 Registration in respect of disposal of assets

This section was added with effect from 20 March 2000. It was designed as a measure to counter certain VAT avoidance schemes which took advantage of the fact that any disposal of assets is disregarded when ascertaining whether a person should be registered for VAT.

A UK person could not benefit from the scheme on the basis that he could not recover input tax. However, a person outside the UK could recover input tax through the Eighth or Thirteenth VAT Directives. He could then dispose of those goods VAT-free in the UK. This section creates a liability to register in this circumstance.

The legislation is based around the concept of a person making 'relevant supplies', being:

- taxable supplies of goods which were assets of the business; and
- supplies where the person, or a predecessor of the person, recovered VAT on the purchase of those goods, or of anything comprised in them.

This wording is designed to be relevant where one person makes the claim for repayment of goods and his business is sold as a going concern to another person before sale of those goods. It is also designed to be relevant where the goods purchased are made into different goods before resale.

There is no minimum value of supplies made or to be made before the person is liable to be registered. He is liable to be registered:

- if he has made any such supplies, in which case, the person is required to notify HMRC that he has made such supplies; and he will be registered from that date; or
- he intends to make such supplies within the next 30 days, in which case the person is required to notify HMRC before making such supplies, and he will be registered from the beginning of the 30-day period.

Where the person can satisfy HMRC that the relevant supplies would be zero-rated, then he may be exempted from registration under this section, if they think fit. HMRC may reject any request for exemption, either at the time the application is made or at any later time (VATA 1994, Sch. 3A, para. 7(1) and (4)).

Changes to registration particulars

Where a person is registered under this section and he then ceases to have the intention of making relevant supplies, he is required to notify HMRC within 30 days of such intention.

A person registered in respect of such supplies is required to notify any change in the name, constitution or ownership of his business, or any event which requires a change in the register. Such notification must be within 30 days of the change occurring.

A person who is exempted from registration is required to notify HMRC of any material change in the nature of the supplies he makes, or any material change in the proportion of zero-rated supplies that he makes.

Deregistration

A person may only be deregistered under this section where he satisfies HMRC that he has ceased to be liable to be so registered.

Penalties in respect of registration in relation to disposal of assets

The penalties for failing to register in respect of the disposal of assets are the same as for failing to register (see **3.2.9** and **3.2.10**). In addition, there are penalties for breach of regulatory provisions.

20.10.4 Non-established taxable persons

An NETP is a person who:

- is not normally resident in the UK;
- does not have a business establishment in the UK; or
- in the case of a limited company, is not incorporated in the UK.

An NETP may be liable to be registered for VAT under any of the above sections:

- if he makes taxable supplies;
- if he makes distance sales;
- if he makes taxable acquisitions; or
- if he makes a disposal of assets.

The person may also be registered on a voluntary basis, under any of the first three sections.

Prior to 1 January 2002, HMRC could direct that any NETP appoint a VAT representative. From that date the rules were relaxed, as they were throughout the EU, such that if the NETP is established either in the EU or in any state which has a 'mutual assistance' agreement with the UK, then HMRC cannot direct such a person to appoint a VAT representative. An NETP can, of course, choose to appoint a VAT representative.

An NETP, preferring not to appoint a VAT representative, can handle his own VAT affairs, including registration and related matters. The NETP's VAT affairs will be controlled from the Aberdeen VAT Office.

An NETP registering for VAT is required to complete the relevant form. If he appoints a VAT representative, he is required to complete form VAT 1TR, (see the VAT Regulations 1995 (SI 1995/2518), Sch. 1, form 8).

An NETP can also appoint an agent to fulfil his responsibilities as regards UK VAT without taking on the obligations of a VAT representative. In these circumstances, the NETP is required to sign a form of authority appointing the agent. A copy of this must accompany any registration application where the agent's address is used as the NETP's UK address for VAT purposes (where the NETP has no other place of establishment in the UK, for example).

> ## ⚠ *Warning!*
> Becoming a VAT representative involves taking on joint and several liability for VAT debts. It should therefore be avoided in favour of becoming an agent wherever possible.

Other guidance: HMRC *VAT Notice 700/1, s. 8*

20.10.5 Registration in other states

A UK-based organisation making supplies in the course of its business must be aware of the possibility of registration outside the UK. For example, if a person makes sales of goods to private persons in another EU member state, he may be required to be registered under the distance sales provisions in that state. Alternatively, a UK business may provide specified services which are determined as supplied where they are performed, or where the customer is based, and may therefore be liable to be registered in another state, see VATA 1994, s. 7A and Sch. 4A.

Registration outside the UK is beyond the scope of this publication.

20.11 Land outside the UK

This chapter is not intended to deal with land outside the UK nor with services relating to land outside the UK. However, since UK businesses may provide some services that appear to relate to land outside the UK, it is appropriate to mention what services relating to land are.

Clearly, services such as those of architects, surveyors, conveyancers and estate agents will not be within the UK VAT net where the service is provided in relation to specific land that is located outside the UK, even if the work (e.g. drawing up plans) is done inside the UK. There may, however, be a liability to register for VAT overseas. Other services that may have some connection with land will not be regarded as a service relating to land, e.g. keeping the accounting records relating to land wherever located. For such services, the casual connection with land makes no difference to the nature of the service.

20.12 European Union Checklist

20.12.1 The internal market

Is the supply between taxable businesses in different EU member states? [*Table20.2*]

The place of supply of goods is either:

(a) the place where goods are despatched from; or
(b) if not despatched, the place where the goods are when supply takes place.

The place of supply of services is where the supplier has a business establishment unless the supply is deemed elsewhere under VATA 1994, s. 7A and Sch. 4A, including:

Note: The customer may be subject to the reverse charge provisions.

(a) Is the supply of services connected with land, including:

    (i) the disposal of an interest or right;
    (ii) construction industry services;
    (iii) professional services?

If so, the supply is where the land is situated.

(b) Is the supply of physical services, including:

    (i) performances – cultural, artistic, sporting, scientific, educational, entertainment (and ancillary services);
    (ii) to be attended – conferences, meetings, exhibitions (and ancillary services);
    (iii) work on goods and valuation work;
    (iv) transportation ancillary services?

If so, the supply is where the service is physically carried out.

> **Planning point**
>
> Several EU member states allow suppliers to place the onus of accounting for VAT on the recipient under the reverse charge – specific advice should be obtained.

Note: Since 31 May 1998 veterinary services are supplied where the business is based.

(c) Is the supply that of services (excluding land) to businesses including:

    (i) advertising;
    (ii) consultants, engineers, lawyers, accountants, data, information;
    (iii) banking, financial, insurance;
    (iv) staff;

or is the supply of intellectual property, including:

    (v)   copyrights, patents, licences, trade marks;

    (vi) restrictive agreements?

If so, the supply is where the customer is based.

(d)   Is the supply that of the letting or hire of goods by a UK supplier? If so, the place of supply is outside the UK where either:

    (i)   an EU customer (other than the UK) is using the goods:

for business purposes anywhere

for non-business purposes outside the EU;

    (ii)   a non-EU customer is using the goods for any purpose outside the UK; or

    (iii) a UK customer is using the goods for any purpose outside the EU.

(e)   Is the supply that of an intermediary arranging the services included in (c) above, including:

    (i)   advertising agent;

    (ii)   insurance broking;

    (iii) copyright agents?

If so, the supply is where the customer is based.

Is the supply that of freight or passenger transport services taking place either:

    (i)   between EU member states?

If so, the place of supply is where the customer is based; or

    (ii)   across EU member states and into other countries?

If so, the place of supply is in each country in which transportation takes place.

(g)   Is the supply that of the hire of a means of transport, including:

    (i)   road vehicles;

    (ii)   aircraft;

    (iii) boats, ships, yachts?

        If so, then the place of supply is in the UK if:

- the lessor belongs in the UK and the use and enjoyment of the transport is in the EU
- the lessor belongs outside the UK and the use and enjoyment of the transport is in the UK.

        If not, then the place of supply is outside the UK provided the transport is used outside the EU for the whole duration of hire.

(h)   Is the supply that of telecommunications services including:

    (i)   telephone services;

    (ii)   facsimile and messaging services;

    (iii) electronic mail;

    (iv) access to the internet;

    (v)   satellite transmission services?

If so, then the place of supply is the country where the recipient actually has the effective use and enjoyment of the services.

Has the business checked whether there are registration requirements in other EU countries if:

(a)   there are any supplies made in that country; and

(b)   under the Place of Supply of Services rules the supplies are to be treated as made in another EU country (outside the UK)?

20.12.2   Goods and related services

Is the business involved in the supply of goods to or from other EU member states?

Goods leaving the UK

A UK VAT-registered business making supplies of standard-rated goods to either:

(a)   a customer not registered for VAT in another EU member state is liable to charge UK VAT, subject to the distance selling rules, or

> ### *Planning point*
>
> Are the goods excepted from the distance selling rules, including installed/assembled goods, new means of transport and supplies to certain bodies and organisations?

(b)   a customer VAT registered in an EU member state (other than the UK) is not required to charge UK VAT provided for each supply:

   (i)   the customer's EU VAT registration number is obtained;

   (ii)   this number is shown on the supplier's sales invoice;

   (iii) the goods are sent out of the UK to another EU member state;

   (iv)   the supplier holds commercial documentary evidence of removal from the UK.

Note: If all the conditions are met the supply can be zero-rated and the customer acquiring the goods is liable to VAT under the acquisition rules.

Triangulation

Note: Supplies of goods between VAT-registered businesses in three different EU member states are known as triangular transactions if the goods do not physically pass from one country to the next.

Has the business identified its triangular transactions:

(a)   a supplier, customer and intermediary each in different EU member states; and

(b)   goods which are to be moved directly from the country of supply to the customer's country?

If so, is the simplified VAT treatment being applied so that the end customer accounts for VAT?

Do the sales invoices of transactions in which the business is an intermediary show the endorsement 'VAT: EC Article 28 simplification invoice'?

> **Planning point**
>
> Triangular sales do not require to be included on a VAT return.

EC sales lists and Dispatches Intrastats

(a)   Is the business making supplies of zero-rated goods to other EU member states? If so, the business will be required to complete EC sales lists (form VAT 101) to show for each customer:

   (i)   the EU VAT registration number;
   (ii)   the total value of goods and related services;
   (iii)   whether the goods were for processing;
   (iv)   whether the business acted as an intermediary in a triangular transaction.

> **Planning point**
>
> The EC sales lists are to be submitted:
>
> - for each calendar quarter (or monthly if requested);
> - to HMRC within six weeks;
> - only if there are entries, a nil return is not required; and
> - annually if there is a low turnover.

(b)   Is the business required to provide Intrastat information on goods moving from the UK to another EU member state?

   (i)   is the value of supplies in excess of the limit for the calendar year (or at some point during the year)? [*Table 20.3*]
   (ii)   do the supplies include goods:
   - sold
   - for process or repair
   - on long-term hire, loan or lease
   - to be installed or used in construction?
   (iii)   the supplies should exclude:
   - temporary movements
   - commercial samples.
   If so, the Intrastat form (C1501) in respect of despatches of goods has to be submitted:
   - monthly
   - to HMRC by the end of the following month
   - by electronic means under arrangement with HMRC.

Planning point

Intrastat Declarations should be cross-referenced to EC sales lists as these will be required when HMRC conduct an Intrastat visit.

Distance selling

Is the VAT-registered business making supplies of goods to non-VAT registered customers in other EU member states including:

(a)   individuals;
(b)   charities;
(c)   low-turnover businesses;
(d)   exempt businesses; or
(e)   government and public bodies?

Is the business responsible for the delivery of the goods?

Note: This is referred to as 'distance selling' and includes, in particular, mail order goods.

If distance selling of standard-rated goods takes place from the UK by a VAT-registered business, then for each EU member state in which supplies are made, has the business checked whether the value has exceeded that country's calendar-year threshold for distance selling?

(a)   If it is not exceeded then UK VAT is chargeable.
(b)   If it is exceeded then there is a liability to register and account for EU VAT in that other country, and to appoint a tax representative in that country, if required, to act on behalf of the business.

Goods into the UK

A UK VAT-registered business receiving supplies from an EU VAT-registered business:

(a)   if no EU VAT has been charged (because the UK VAT registration number was provided to the supplier) the business must account for VAT on the next return under the acquisition rules and reclaim any allowable input tax; or
(b)   if EU VAT has been charged then an Eighth Directive VAT refund claim may be submitted to the country of supply.

Note: There are proposals to replace the Eighth Directive VAT refund claim system.

A UK non-VAT-registered business receiving supplies of goods, known as acquisitions, may have a liability to register. The business should check if the threshold is or will be exceeded:

(a)   at the end of any month in a calendar year; or
(b)   in a coming 30-day period.

Arrivals Intrastat

Is the business required to provide Intrastat information on goods moving into the UK from another EU member state?

(a) Is the value of supplies in excess of the limit for the calendar year (or at some time during the year)? [*Table20.3*]

(b) Do the supplies include goods purchased otherwise than by way of trade?

(c) The supplies should exclude movements not regarded as by way of trade. If so, the Intrastat form (C1500) in respect of acquisitions of goods has to be submitted. The requirements are as for despatches.

20.12.3 Table 20.2– European Union territories

The VAT territory of the EU consists of the 27 member states as follows:Previous registration limits

1.	Austria AT
2.	Belgium BE
3.	Bulgaria BG
4.	Cyprus CY
5.	Czech Republic CZ
6.	Denmark: DK
	• excluding Greenland.
7.	Estonia EE
8.	Finland FI
9.	France: FR
	• including Monaco;
	• excluding the overseas départements.
10.	Germany: DE
	• including Jungholz and Mittelberg;
	• excluding the Isle of Heligoland and Busingen.
11.	Greece: EL
	• excluding Mount Athos (Agion Poros).
12.	Hungary HU
13.	Republic of Ireland IE
14.	Italy: IT
	• excluding Livigno, Campione d'Italia and Italian waters of Lake Lugano.
15.	Latvia LV
16.	Lithuania LT

17.	Luxembourg LU
18.	Malta MT
19.	Netherlands NL
20.	Poland PL
21.	Portugal: PT
	• including Azores and Madeira.
22.	Romania RO
23.	Slovak Republic SK
24.	Slovenia SI
25.	Spain: ES
	• including Balearic Islands;
	• excluding the Canary Islands, Ceuta and Melilla.
26.	Sweden: SE
27.	United Kingdom: UK
	• including Isle of Man;
	• excluding Channel Islands and Gibraltar.

The VAT territory of the EU does not include Andorra, Liechtenstein and San Marino.

Strictly, Monaco and the Isle of Man are not within the EU, but they are treated as such for VAT purposes.

20.12.4 Table 20.3 – Intrastat thresholds

Thresholds for the requirement to prepare Intrastat returns are shown below:

	Dispatches £	Acquisitions £
1993	135,000	135,000
1994	140,000	140,000
1995	150,000	150,000
1996	160,000	160,000
1997	195,000	195,000
1998	225,000	225,000
1999	230,000	230,000
2000	233,000	233,000
2001	233,000	233,000
2002	233,000	233,000

	Dispatches	*Acquisitions*
2003	233,000	233,000
2004	221,000	221,000
2005	221,000	221,000
2006	225,000	225,000
2007	260,000	260,000
2008	260,000	260,000
2009	270,000	270,000
2010	250,000	600,000
2011	250,000	600,000
2012	250,000	600,000

Supplying or Receiving Services within the EU

21.1   Introduction

21.1.1 Determining liability

It should never be assumed that services provided from the UK to someone in another country are automatically zero-rated or outside the scope of UK VAT. They may not be, and such services may still give rise to a need to register for VAT in other member states and suffer any penalties that might arise there for late registration. It is axiomatic that a supply will be taxed somewhere.

> **Planning point**
>
> In order to determine the liability of any service being supplied it is vital to know:
>
> - the exact nature of the service;
> - to whom it is being supplied;
> - by whom;
> - from where; and
> - the place of 'belonging' of the supplier and, usually, also the recipient.
>
> Depending on the type of service being supplied, it may also be important to know where the effective use or enjoyment of that service is. Another vital factor for VATA 1994, Sch. 5 services is whether the recipient is receiving the supply for business or private purposes.

Other guidance: VAT Notice 741, VAT Information Sheet 10/07

21.2   Place of Supply from 1 January 2010

21.2.1 Cross-border VAT changes

Introduction

With effect from 1 January 2010 the EC VAT Package will be phased in with three key legislative proposals:

- a directive amending the place of supply of services rules and introducing the VAT One-Stop Scheme [Directive 2008/8/EC];
- a directive on a revised EC VAT Refund Scheme [Directive 2008/9/EC];

- an amending Regulation on VAT Administrative Cooperation [Regulation 143/2008].

With effect from 1 January 2010 there will be changes to EC Sales Lists.

Place of supply of services

From 1 January 2010 there will be a revised main rule (general rule) for the place of supply of B to B (business to business) services which will be deemed to be taxable where the customer rather than the supplier is located (i.e. the place of consumption).

For B to C (business to customer) services, the general rule will remain and supplies will be taxable where the supplier is located.

There will be some exceptions to the general rule, as now; for example property, deemed to be where located, with the aim achieving taxation in the place of consumption.

EC Sales will be required for taxable supplies of services subject to the reverse charge. There will be compulsory reverse charge services for B to B services subject to the general rule.

The UK will apply the reverse charge to a wide variety of services although it will not apply to services of a description within Schedule 9 (VAT Exemption) or to opted properties.

Planning point

If businesses have not already, they must consider the implications of these changes to their accounting and VAT liabilities. The liability of transactions that may have been undertaken for many years will have changed on 1 January 2010.

21.2.2 Exceptions and specific rules

The exception relating to land will specifically refer to hotels where in practice there is no change to current rules. Land related services are not restricted to letting or sale of property or construction services. It also includes supplies such as architects, real estate agents, etc. These are regarded as supplied where the land is; this was the position before the introduction of the VAT Package.

There is also an exception for cultural, artistic and similar services which will be deemed to be liable to VAT where the activity takes place – again this is not a change from the treatment prior to the introduction of the VAT Package.

There will be a new exception for the supply of restaurant and catering services. These are supplied where the service is performed. It is, after all, only sensible to regard a restaurant meal in Paris to be considered to be supplied in France. Restaurant and catering services on board ships, trains and planes are treated as being supplied at the point of departure. Thus, a meal provided on a flight from France to Poland is treated as being supplied in France, even if the meal is served whilst the airplane is over Germany.

There will be a new exception for short-term hire of means of transport which will be subject to VAT where the vehicle is put at the disposal of the customer. Short-term is defined as a period not exceeding 30 days (90 days for a vessel).

21.2.3 Other new place of supply rules

With effect from 1 January 2011 cultural, artistic, sporting, scientific, educational and entertainment services and B to C supplies will remain taxable where the activity takes place. The general rule will apply to B to B services apart from admission to an event or services ancillary to admission to an event which will be taxable where the event takes place.

The long-term hire of means of transport will, from 1 January 2013, be subject to VAT where the customer is located when the vehicle, i.e. the car and other means of transport is hired for more than 30 days or where a pleasure boat is put at the disposal of the customer, as long as the supplier has an establishment or fixed establishment in that place when hired for more than 90 days. The use and enjoyment provisions will remain in respect of the hire of means of transport.

Finally, from 1 January 2015 the taxation of B to C supplies of telecommunications, broadcasting and E-services is expected to change.

21.2.4 Changes to EC Sales Lists (ESLs)

From 1 January 2010 the VAT Package Legislation 2008/8/EC extends the requirement for EC Sales Lists (ESLs) to reverse charge taxable supplies of services. Prior to 1 January 2010 ESLs were only required for goods.

With effect from 1 January 2010, Directive 2008/117/EC has introduced the following further changes to the ESL to tackle VAT fraud:

- monthly ESL reporting periods for goods subject to a threshold;
- monthly ESL reporting period for services but with option for member states to allow quarterly reporting periods (which UK will exercise);
- reduced timeframe for businesses to submit ESLs to tax authority and for tax authority to exchange the data with customer tax authority; and
- time of supply changes for cross-border supplies of services.

HMRC state on their website that the thresholds for various types of supplies are:

How often do you need to submit your ESL?			
Your business is supplying:	**Your customer is:**	**The value of your supplies to those customers:**	**You need to submit EC Sales Lists every:**
Goods	a VAT-registered business in another EU country	is over the threshold of £70,000 in the current or four previous quarters	month
Goods	a VAT-registered business in another EU country	is under the threshold of £70,000 in the current or four previous quarters	quarter
Services that are subject to the reverse charge in the customer's country	a VAT-registered business in another EU country	N/A	quarter (but you can choose to submit them every month)
Goods and services where you are required to submit monthly lists for your goods	a VAT-registered business in another EU country	N/A	• month (for all supplies), or • month (for goods) and quarter (for services)

If you make annual VAT Returns, you can contact HMRC to apply for approval to submit your ESL once a year provided all of the following conditions are met:

(1)   Your total annual taxable turnover does not exceed £145,000.

(2)   The annual value of supplies to other EU countries is not more than £11,000.

(3)   Sales do not include New Means of Transport.

An ESL needs to be completed if:

- box 8 of your VAT Return has been completed – HMRC will automatically send the business an ESL to complete;
- any goods have been supplied to a VAT-registered business in another EU country (the exception being samples). An ESL needs to be completed even if the supply is not invoiced (for example, transfers to an associated VAT-registered branch, office or subsidiary company;
- you have given a VAT-registered customer in another EU country a credit note for goods;
- you have sold goods to a VAT-registered customer in another EU country (outside the UK) but didn't actually handle the items (by triangulation); or
- services have been supplied to VAT-registered EU businesses, where the place of supply is the customer's country and the supply is subject to the reverse charge in that country.

Reporting cross-border supplies of services

When deciding whether an ESL is required for a cross-border supply of services a business will need to determine whether or not the reverse charge applies and the time of supply.

To determine whether the reverse charge applies in the customer's member state, the customer should be checked to ensure they have a VAT registration number and the supply is for a business purpose. If so the supply is subject to the reverse charge.

The time of supply will normally be determined in the customer's member state, the earlier of date of completion or date of payment.

HMRC are aware of difficulties in determining the time of supply solely for completing ESLs for services. UK businesses may use the invoice date where this broadly equates to the date of completion.

Information required on ESL

The ESL which is currently used for reporting intra-EC supplies of goods will be used for reporting intra-EC supplies of services.

There will some minor changes to the form to make it suitable for scanning.

The information that must be entered on the form is the:

- customer's country code;
- customer's VAT registration number;
- total value of supplies in Sterling;
- code 3 in the indicator box code if it is a supply of services; and
- code 2 if it is a triangular supply of goods. No code means a simple cross-border supply of goods.

Time limits for submitting ESLs to HMRC

From 1 January 2010 the new time limits will be:

- for paper ESLs, 14 days from the end of the month or quarterly reporting period; and
- for electronic ESLs, 21 days from the end of the monthly or quarterly reporting period.

Previously the time limit was six weeks.

HMRC will collate, process and collect the ESL data to forward to other member states/tax authorities by the end of the same month. In determining whether a customer is in business the normal evidence of business status will be the provision of the VAT registration number.

EU level discussions continue to consider whether other evidence may be acceptable.

The validity of the customer's VAT registration number can be checked on the Europa website. The system will be enhanced to show business name and address, as well as the validity of the VAT registration number.

HMRC recognise that some businesses would have problems preparing their systems by early 2010. HMRC have confirmed that as long as businesses can demonstrate that steps are being taken to comply with the new legislation at the earliest opportunity HMRC will not levy penalties; this period of a 'light touch' has now expired.

Time of supply for cross-border services

The objective of the VAT authorities across the EU is to rely on the time at which a supplier will enter a transaction on their ESL with the time the customer will declare VAT on the same supply as a reverse charge.

The tax point rules for cross-border supplies of services subject to the reverse charge will be:

- for single supplies the tax point will be the earliest of the date of performance or payment;
- for continuous supplies 31 December if no billing period or payment in previous 12 months or if invoice is issued; and
- for reverse charge purposes it is up to the customer to determine the date of completion.

Planning point

HMRC will accept any methodology that achieves broadly the right result. HMRC expect existing business systems to contain information that can be used to achieve this; the most popular approach will be the date of invoice.

VAT refunds across the EC

From 1 January 2010 a new electronic claims procedure for businesses will apply. This is intended to give claimants quicker refunds and greater legal certainty.

The taxpayer is entitled to interest if the tax authority delays payment of the refund claim.

There are also clear appeal procedures in the member state of refund if the claim is rejected.

Members states will have a time scale for decisions which is four months, unless additional information is required then a maximum of eight months.

Each member state can request additional information and original invoices.

If the claim is delayed interest will be paid by the member state of refund.

The portal structure for electronic processing of claims is expected to comprise two sections:

(1) claimant identifier; and

(2) individual claims.

Claims from VAT groups can be made by the representative member.

If partial exemption calculations apply to the VAT to be claimed this will be carried out under the rules of the member state of establishment.

21.3   Belonging

21.3.1 Where the supplier belongs

In order to decide where the supply takes place, it is sometimes important to determine where someone 'belongs'.

A supplier belongs in a country if:

- he has a business establishment there or some other fixed establishment and no such establishment elsewhere; or
- he has no such establishment (there or elsewhere) but his usual place of residence is there; or
- he has such establishments – both in that country and elsewhere – and the establishment of the supply which he is most directly concerned with is there.

A supplier belongs in the place where he has his business establishment or some other fixed establishment from which he makes that supply, i.e. an office, showroom or factory. If the supplier has a business or other fixed establishment in more than one country, the supplies of services made from each establishment have to be viewed separately. For each supply of services, the supplier will be regarded as belonging in the country where the establishment most directly concerned with that particular supply is located.

If the supplier has no business or other establishment in any country, and the business is a limited company or other corporate body, the company belongs where it is legally constituted. Otherwise, the supplier belongs where he has his usual place of residence.

If the supplier does not have any business or other fixed establishment in a country, the temporary presence there of a director or other employee for the purpose of making the supply of services does not necessarily mean that the supplier belongs in that country.

> **Example 21.1**
>
> A UK car-leasing company, Bangers4All, had its base in London. It decided to open and staff a depot in Strasbourg. This depot secured a lucrative contract to supply vehicles to users in Brussels. The negotiations for this deal, including drawing up and administering the contract, were carried out by the staff in Strasbourg. The arrangements were submitted for vetting to the Bangers4All London headquarters. The place of supply was Strasbourg, not London, because the Strasbourg office was the one most directly concerned with making the supply.

A business establishment for the above purpose includes a branch or agency.

Law: VATA 1994, s. 9(2)

21.3.2 Fixed establishment

The term 'fixed establishment' is not defined in law. However, following the test set out by the ECJ in the Berkholz case (*Berkholz v Finanzamt* (Case 168/84) (1985) 2 BVC 200,178), the term is generally interpreted to mean an establishment (including the business establishment) from which business activities are carried out and which has both the human and technical resources necessary for making or receiving the supplies of services in question.

The Berkholz principle was followed in *ARO Lease BV v Inspecteur der Belastingdienst Grote Ondernemingen, Amsterdam* (Case C-190/95) [1997] BVC 547 when the ECJ decided that in order for there to be a fixed establishment, there had to be a degree of permanence and a human resources structure that was sufficient to supply the services in question on an independent basis.

The case of *Singer & Friedlander Ltd* (1989) 4 BVC 512 concerned a UK company registered in the Isle of Man. The directors of the company were mostly resident in the US. The tribunal held that the presence of resident directors in the US and the holding of intermittent board meetings at various addresses in the US were insufficient to create a business establishment there.

The tribunal also considered whether the company had a 'fixed establishment' in the US. It found that there was no defined place such as an office in the US and therefore no fixed establishment. The tribunal held that the registered office in the Isle of Man was a fixed establishment. Therefore the company belonged in the UK for VAT purposes and the services supplied were subject to VAT.

21.3.3 Where the recipient belongs

For the recipient of a supply of services, there are similar rules. The recipient of a service belongs where he has his business establishment. If there is a business establishment in more than one country it is necessary to determine in which establishment the acquired service is most directly used or to be used in order to decide the place of 'belonging'.

In the case of a company that has no business establishment as such, the company belongs in the country of incorporation.

For where an individual belongs, see **21.3.4**.

There have been several cases where the tribunal has found that the registered office of a limited company in the UK amounts to 'some other fixed establishment' for the purposes of receiving services, even if no business activities are carried out there, but are carried out from other addresses overseas.

This was the case in Binder Hamlyn (*Binder Hamlyn* (1983) 1 BVC 1,190) which concerned a company, Jamaica Sugar Estates Ltd, registered in Scotland but trading in Jamaica. Binder Hamlyn charged Jamaica Sugar no VAT on its fees on the grounds that the company had no business establishment or fixed establishment in the UK. Jamaica Sugar held its AGMs in Glasgow and the company had its registered office at the appellant's office. The share register was maintained in Glasgow. It was decided that this amounted to rather more than an accommodation address and was 'some other fixed establishment' meaning that the fees were standard-rated.

In the case of Omnicom UK plc (*Omnicom UK plc* [1995] BVC 1,198), the appellant supplied advertising services through its UK subsidiary, a London-based advertising agency, to the Spanish Tourist Board. It contended that the services were used at the Board's head office in Spain and not at its London office. The service amounted to publicising Spain as a tourist destination. In this respect, although the Board's office in London helped to supervise the campaigns, it had no authority to make contracts on behalf of the Board. The advertising campaigns were approved and controlled from the head office in Spain. The tribunal concluded that it was the latter that was the establishment with which the agency services were most directly concerned and by which they were most directly used.

Law: VATA 1994, s. 9(3)–(4)

21.3.4 Where an individual belongs

An individual with no business establishment belongs at his 'usual place of residence' which is broadly similar to the residence concept for income tax purposes.

The 'usual place of residence' of a private individual is not defined in the law. It is usually interpreted as meaning the one country where the individual spends most of his time for the period in question. It is likely to be the country where the individual has set up his home, lives with their family and is in full-time employment.

The term 'usual place of residence' was considered in the case of *USAA Ltd* [1993] BVC 1,612 concerning US Forces personnel living in England. The tribunal did not rule out the possibility that a person might have more than one usual place of residency. It found that such personnel living in England, on a three-year term of duty, had their usual place of residence in the UK. During the tour of duty, if they had a permanent address in the form of a home in the US, it was let. If they returned for training to the US, their families remained in the UK. The US personnel could not, therefore, be regarded as having their 'usual place of residence' in the US.

Law: VATA 1994, s. 9(3)–(4)

21.4   Services relating to land and property

21.4.1 Introduction

The place of supply of services related to land is deemed to be where the land is located. When the land is in another EU member state, the supplies are made there. The supplier, or when the reverse charge rule applies, the recipient, must account for tax in the member state concerned.

When the land is outside the EU, supplies of the relevant services are outside the scope of VAT.

Services relating to land include:

* the supply of hotel accommodation;
* the provision of a site for a stand at an exhibition where the exhibitor obtains the right to a defined area of the exhibition hall;
* services supplied in the course of construction, conversion, enlargement, reconstruction, alteration, demolition, repair or maintenance (including painting and decorating) of any building or civil engineering work;
* the supply of plant or machinery, together with an operator, for work on a construction site;
* services of estate agents, auctioneers, architects, solicitors, surveyors, engineers and similar professional people relating to land, buildings or civil engineering works. This includes the management, conveyancing, survey or valuation of property by a solicitor, surveyor or loss adjuster;
* services connected with oil/gas/mineral exploration or exploitation relating to specific sites of land or the seabed;
* the surveying (such as seismic, geological or geomagnetic) of land or seabed, including associated data processing services to collate the required information;

- legal services such as conveyancing or dealing with applications for planning permission;
- packages of property management services which may include rent collection, arranging repairs and the maintenance of financial accounts; and
- the supply of warehouse space.

As can be seen, this is a much wider definition of land than the previous definition (See *Notice 741A*, 6.4)

Example 21.2

Solicitors, Ball and Chain act for a UK client, Mug, buying a holiday home in Dublin. Ball and Chain's services are deemed to be supplied in Ireland because that it is where the property is. Ball and Chain must register for VAT in Ireland if they exceed the Irish VAT registration threshold.

Mug persuades the builder who has done work for him in the UK to take on the task of renovating the Dublin holiday home. The builder goes ahead with the work. The builder must register for Irish VAT. Like the solicitor, the builder is working on property located in Ireland.

21.4.2 Services merely having a connection with land

There are certain services that are considered not to relate to land although there may be an incidental land element. HMRC give their views of services that are not connected with land as follows:

- '• Repair and maintenance of machinery which is not installed as a fixture. This is work on goods.
- The hiring out of civil engineering plant on its own, which is the hire of goods; or the secondment of staff to a building site, which is a supply of staff.
- The legal administration of a deceased person's estate which happens to include property. These are lawyers' services.
- Advice or information relating to land prices or property markets as they do not relate to specific sites.
- Feasibility studies assessing the potential of particular businesses or business potential in a geographic area. Such services do not relate to a specific property or site.
- Provision of a recording studio where technicians are included as part of the supply. These are engineering services.
- Services of an accountant in simply calculating a tax return from figures provided by a client, even where those figures relate to rental income.'

Law: VAT Notice 741, s. 6.5.1

21.5   Passenger transport

21.5.1 Passenger transport

The place of supply of passenger transport, is where it takes place. Where a journey involves travel through more than one member state then the supply of transport is made in each member state to the extent that the transport takes place there.

Journeys that begin and end in one country are regarded as taking place in that country alone even if they enter and leave another country or member state, as long as there is no stop in that other member state or country.

21.5.2 Land passenger transport pre 1 January 2010

The transport of passengers is treated as supplied in the country in which the transportation takes place to the extent that it takes place in that country. Therefore, any journey which takes in several countries must be looked at on a section by section basis.

> ### ⚠ *Warning!*
>
> If a land journey involves travel through other member state(s), the supplier may be required to account for VAT in that member state(s) on that section of the journey.

21.5.3 Sea and air passenger transport pre 1 January 2010

When air or sea transport make a non-landing trip, even from one port in the originating country to another port in the same country, the aircraft or ship may during the journey travel outside the territorial jurisdiction of the country in which it starts (and finishes). Such journeys are treated as supplied in the originating country when:

(a)   it takes place in the course of a journey between two points in that country, whether or not as part of a longer journey involving travel to or from another country; and

(b)   the means of transport used does not put in or land in another country in the course of the journey between those two points.

If the ship or aircraft lands in another country the result is that the supplier may be required to account for VAT in that member state on that section of the journey.

> ### *Example 21.3*
>
> Seb Co Ltd owns and operates several aircraft. It offers passengers the option of two pleasure trips by air. The first aircraft will take off from Gatwick and will fly over France and across Paris to give passengers the opportunity to view Paris from a great height. It will then return to Cardiff. The second aircraft will leave Gatwick, land at Orly airport and allow punters the chance of visiting Paris before returning to Orly airport and thence to Cardiff.
>
> For the first trip the journey is treated as being wholly in the UK even though part of the journey takes place in French air space. For the second trip because the aircraft lands at Orly, part of the trip will be considered to take place in the UK and part in France.

21.5.4 Pleasure cruises, etc. pre 1 January 2010

A pleasure cruise is treated as the transport of passengers.

Any goods or services provided as part of a pleasure cruise are treated as being supplied in the same place as the passenger transport. Likewise, the transportation of luggage or motor vehicles when accompanied by passengers is also treated as being supplied in the same place as the passenger transport.

The Peninsular and Oriental Steam Navigation Co case (*The Peninsular & Oriental Steam Navigation Co (No. 2)* [1996] BVC 2,435) concerned cruises sold at an inclusive price. Charges covered accommodation, entertainment, food and transport. Customs argued that there was a multiple supply and that even if it were a single supply it was that of a holiday cruise and not transport within the zero-rating provisions. The VAT & Duties Tribunals ruled as follows:

> 'Cruising implied a leisurely journey upon the sea and the transport of passengers was the taking of passengers from A to B and elsewhere, including back to A. The cruises supplied by the appellant constituted the transport of passengers which, being a single supply, was a zero-rated supply of services.'

21.5.5 Tour operators margin scheme

The place of supply is varied when the passenger transport is within the scope of the tour operators margins scheme (TOMS), see **Chapter 7**.

21.6 Freight transport and related ancillary services

21.6.1 General

There is a difference in treatment between B2B and B2C services. B2B services are treated under the general rule (through the reverse charge); the treatment of B2C supplies is more complex.

21.6.2 B2C freight services

The definition of the place of supply of these services is described in *VAT Notice 744A*, para. 11.1.

Supply of B2C freight service	Place of Supply is:
Domestic freight in one member state	Where the transport takes place
International freight,	Where the transport takes place
(a) between the EU and non-EU countries, or (b) wholly outside the EU	
Freight from one member state to another	The member state where the transportation begins
Ancillary services relating to domestic or international freight	Where physically performed
Making arrangement for domestic or international freight service	Where the transport takes place
Making arrangement for intra-EU freight service	The member state where the transportation begins
Making arrangement for ancillary freight service	Where the ancillary services are physically performed

Intermediary services are normally regarded as being supplied in the place that the transportation begins. Where, however, it is supplied to a VAT registered person from another member state that provides a valid VAT number, the supply is zero-rated and subject to the reverse charge.

21.6.3 General pre 1 January 2010

The place of supply of freight transport is normally in the country in which the transportation takes place.

There are two main exceptions to this:

* international freight transport; and
* intra-EU freight transport

21.6.4 International freight transport pre 1 January 2010

'International' freight transport involves goods being taken to or from the EU.

The place of supply of international freight transport between the EU and third countries is in the country where the transportation takes place. Various sections of the journey may be taxed differently. Sections outside the EU are outside the scope of VAT. Sections of the journey that take place in each EU state will be taxed according to their VAT laws. Parts of the journey that take place in the UK will normally be zero rated.

21.6.5 Intra-EU freight transport pre 1 January 2010

Intra-EU transport is the movement of goods from one member state:

- which takes place entirely within the EU when it is part of a single movement of goods from one member state to another; and
- from one member state to another when a journey goes through a non-EU country, for example the transport of goods from London to Rome via Switzerland.

The place of supply is normally where the journey commences.

However, when the supply of intra-EU freight transport, related ancillary services or intermediary services, is to a customer who receives the supplies under a valid VAT-registration number in another member state, the place of supply is where the customer is registered.

If a supplier supplies intra-EU transport, related ancillary services or an intermediary service of arranging such supplies to either a private individual or a customer in another member state who has not given a valid EU VAT-registration number, then the place of the supply of the service is where the journey commences. VAT will be due in the relevant member state, and if the supplier is not already registered there, this may create an obligation to do so.

Example 21.4

Dingy is a specialist boat moving company based in the UK. It has received an order to take two yachts from the UK to France. One yacht is owned by a UK resident and the other by a French business. The two yachts are taken from the UK to France on the same lorry and trailer.

The UK resident is a private individual who wants his yacht moved to near his new home in the Loire. Dingy must charge UK VAT on this service as the journey begins in the UK albeit the customer has a French address.

The French company provides Dingy with its TVA number. Due to this the place of supply changes to France. Dingy does not account for UK VAT. Instead, the French company accounts for TVA under the 'reverse charge' rules.

21.6.6   Ancillary and intermediary transport services pre 1 January 2010

The place of supply of ancillary transport services, and of intermediary services of arranging an ancillary transport service, is where they are physically performed. The place of supply of intermediary services of arranging intra-EU freight transport is where the transport of the goods begins. However, when these services are supplied to a customer registered for VAT in another member state, the place of supply is the member state of the customer, provided that the customer provides the supplier with a valid VAT number. The customer accounts for VAT under the reverse-charge procedure.

'Ancillary transport services' are defined in the preamble of the VAT (Place of Supply of Services) Order 1992 as 'loading, unloading, handling and similar services'. HMRC take the term to include stowing, opening for inspection, cargo security services, preparing or amending bills of lading, airwaybills, and certificates of shipment, packing necessary for transportation and storage in connection with transportation.

'Intermediary services' means the services of those who arrange freight transport or ancillary services for others; such intermediaries are often referred to as agents or brokers.

21.7   Other intermediary services pre 1 January 2010

The place of supply of the services of an intermediary is normally the same as the place of supply of the main service. There are exceptions according to the type of service provided and, in some circumstances, whether or not the recipient is registered for VAT in another EU state. The exceptions are:

- intra-community transport of goods and ancillary transport services (see **21.5.3**); and
- services deemed to be supplied where received (see **21.8**).

21.8   Services taxed where physically performed

21.8.1 Place of supply

The place of supply of certain services is the location where the services concerned are carried out or performed. As a result the supplier of the service is deemed to be making supplies at the location where the services are performed. If this is another EU member state, the services are liable to tax in the state concerned and the supplier may be obliged to register for VAT in the state concerned. When these services are performed outside the EU they are not liable to VAT.

The services to which this rule applies are:

- cultural, artistic, sporting, scientific, educational or entertainment services;
- services relating to exhibitions, conferences or meetings;
- services ancillary to the above; and
- the valuation of, or work on, moveable goods.

Jürgen Dudda (*Dudda v Finanzamt Bergisch Gladbach* (Case C-327/94) [1997] BVC 3) supplied sound-engineering services (the provision of optimum sound levels and sound quality) for concerts and similar events. His business was established in Germany but most of the events at which he provided services took place outside Germany. The ECJ ruled that the services were supplied at the location where the concert took place. It said as follows:

'... the place of the supply of services relating ... to artistic and entertainment activities and ancillary services was the place where those services were physically carried out.'

Example 21.5

A UK VAT registered training supplier is contracted to provide training to an American company. Some of the training is given at the American company's UK establishment, some in Berlin and the rest at the American HQ in Seattle.

The consequences of this are:

- training performed at the UK establishment is liable to tax in the UK;
- training provided in Berlin is liable to VAT in Germany and the supplier may have to register there,
- training performed in Seattle is outside the scope of VAT as its 'place of supply' is America.

Other guidance: VAT Notice 741A, s. 8

The rules have again changed markedly from 1 January 2010. They are also due to change on 1 January 2011. The following is a brief summary of the changes:

Valuation and work on moveable goods and ancillary transport services: B2B are subject to the general rule from 1 January 2010. B2C services are treated as supplied where they are physically performed.

Services relating to cultural, artistic, sporting, scientific, entertainment and similar activities including the ancillary services of organisers: B2C & B2B services are supplied where physically carried out from 1 January 2010. B2B services from 1 January 2011 are subject to the general rule.

Admission services to cultural, artistic, sporting, scientific, entertainment and similar activities including the ancillary services of organisers: B2B services are treated as where the services are carried out from 1 January 2010, but where the event takes place from 1 January 2011. B2C services do not change and the supply is where physically carried out.

Examples of activities that are carried out where performed include the activities of sportspersons, entertainers, technicians carrying out tests or preparing equipment, services related to conferences, meetings, exhibitions, etc. Activities that are not supplied where performed will include product endorsements or publicity appearances (these are Schedule 5 advertising services), written translation services (again a Schedule 5 service), hire of goods even if used at an exhibition or concert (subject to the general rule).

21.8.2 Valuation of, or work on, moveable goods

The place of supply for services of valuation of, or work carried out on, moveable goods is subject to the general rule from 1 January 2010 for B2B transactions. Prior to that date and for all B2C transactions both pre- and post 1 January 2010, the supply is, and was, where the services are performed. For B2B customers, the supply is subject to the reverse charge as long as the normal conditions are met (that the customer supplies a valid VAT number and the invoice is endorsed and that it is subject to the reverse charge).

Examples of the work to which the rules apply (taken from *Notice 741*, s. 8.5.2) are:

- processing, manufacturing or assembling;
- repairs, cleaning or restoration;
- alterations, calibrations, insulating, lacquering, painting, polishing, resetting (of jewellery), sharpening, varnishing, waterproofing; and
- nominations to stallions/covering (that is, attempting to secure the pregnancy of mares).

Example 21.6

A Rotterdam jeweller sends jewellery to London for resetting and polishing. The work is done in London by Smoothstone. Smoothstone is VAT registered. When the work is completed the jewellery is sent back to Rotterdam. Smoothstone does not charge UK VAT because:

- the Rotterdam jeweller provides a Dutch VAT number;
- Smoothstone quotes the Dutch Number on its invoice to the Rotterdam jeweller;
- Smoothstone has proof that after the work the jewellery was returned to Rotterdam; and
- the Rotterdam jeweller accounts for Dutch VAT under the 'reverse charge' procedure.

21.9   Intellectual, professional, financial services, etc.

21.9.1 The services concerned

> ### *Planning point*
>
> When dealing with the following type of service it is necessary to be sure of:
>
> - the nature of the services concerned;
> - where the customer belongs (see **21.2**),
> - for intra-EU work, the status of the customer.

The nature of the services is relevant because the following rules only apply to certain services, viz.:

- transfers and assignments of copyrights, patents, licences, trademarks and similar rights;
- advertising services;
- services of consultants, engineers, consultancy bureaux, lawyers, accountants and other similar services, data processing and provision of information (but excluding any services relating to land);
- acceptance of any obligation to refrain from pursuing or exercising, in whole or in part, any business activity or rights as defined in the first bullet point;
- banking, financial and insurance services (including reinsurance but not the provision of safe deposit facilities);
- the supply of staff; and
- services rendered by one person to another person of procuring any of the above services.

Law: VATA 1994, s. 7A and Sch. 4A, para. 16(2)

Other guidance: VAT Notice 741, s. 11

21.9.2 Customer belongs outside EU

When any of the above services are supplied to a customer belonging outside the EU the place of supply is deemed to be where the customer belongs. This takes such services outside the scope of VAT as they are deemed to be provided outside the EU.

> ### *Planning point*
>
> A UK-based supplier of such services will never have any VAT obligations where the customer belongs outside the EU. No UK VAT is chargeable and no overseas obligations arise.

21.9.3 Customer belongs in EU

The status of the customer is relevant when any of the above services are supplied to someone belonging in another EU state. The place of supply varies according to whether the supplier is dealing with a business customer or non-business customer. The difference is as follows:

(1) Supplies of the above to a customer for the purpose of a business established in another EU state are deemed to be provided where the customer's business belongs. They are taxable in the State in which the customer belongs (under the reverse charge procedure) not in the State in which the supplier of the services belongs.

(2) Supplies of the above to non-business customers belonging in another EU State are taxable in the State where the supplier is established. They are not taxable where the customer belongs.

Planning point

A UK-based supplier of such services will never have any VAT obligations if the customer belongs within a member state of the EU other than the UK and receives the services for the purpose of a business carried on there. No UK VAT is chargeable and no overseas obligations arise.

Planning point

It should also be noted that the criterion for no UK VAT being chargeable is that the customer is in business, not that they are VAT-registered in their member state of belonging (as is required for transactions in goods). It is not, therefore, necessary to hold the customer's VAT number in order to relieve the supply of VAT, since the customer need not be VAT-registered for the relief to apply.

Warning!

A UK-based supplier of such services to customers in the EU who are not in business in another member state must treat such supplies in the same way as identical supplies to UK customers.

Example 21.7

Rambini is an American on holiday in the UK. Whilst exploring the narrow roads of Cornwall he manages to damage the car of Pierre, a French citizen also on holiday in the UK. Not worrying too much about it, Rambini continues on his merry way only to be confronted by lorry owned by Van Tulip, a Dutch firm, delivering flowers to Popsies Florists. He is reckless enough to inflict damage on this vehicle.

UK lawyers are instructed to act for:

- Rambini;
- Pierre; and
- Van Tulip.

The VAT situation is as follows:

- Rambini is a USA citizen and the fees are outside the scope of VAT.
- Pierre is an EU citizen but the supply is for non-business purposes and therefore the fees are subject to UK VAT.
- The supply to Van Tulip is to an EU business established in another EU State and therefore is taxable where Van Tulip belongs (Netherlands) under the reverse charge procedure.

21.10   Hire of goods other than means of transport

The hire of goods for a B2B transaction is where the customer belongs and is subject to the reverse charge. A B2C service is supplied where the supplier belongs except for supplies to a non-business person that belongs outside the EU. In this case, the supply is where the customer belongs. This is then modified by a 'use and enjoyment' rule. Where the use and enjoyment is outside the EU but would otherwise be regarded as being supplied in the UK, the supply is treated as being supplied outside the EU and thus, outside the scope of EU VAT.

Conversely, where the supply is made to a person that is outside the EU the supply would normally be outside the scope of VAT. If that person, however, brings the equipment to the UK and use it in the UK, the hire charge is subject to UK VAT.

Planning point

Computer Hire plc hires computer equipment to Joe. Joe takes the equipment overseas and informs Computer Hire of this. Whilst the equipment was in the, UK Computer Hire charged UK VAT on the supply. When the goods were taken overseas, UK VAT no longer needed to be charged. Computer Hire would require proof that the goods were used and enjoyed overseas.

21.10.1 The normal rules pre 1 January 2010

Planning point

When dealing with the hire of goods (other than means of transport) it is necessary to be sure that:

- according to the normal rules, the service is supplied in the UK or is deemed to be supplied in the UK;
- according to the normal rules, the service is supplied outside the EU or is deemed to be supplied outside the EU; and
- where the items concerned are effectively used and enjoyed.

Within the EU the hire of goods (other rather a means of transport) is liable to tax according to the same rules that apply to intellectual services (see **21.9**). On this basis the place of supplier may be where the hirer belongs or, according to circumstances, where the person hiring the goods belongs.

21.10.2 UK variations pre 1 January 2010

When under the normal rules it is established that the services concerned are supplied in the UK or outside the EU it is necessary to consider the UK variation to the place of supply rules. According to circumstances this changes matters as follows:

(1) Where the place of supply is the UK according to the normal rules, hire charges are deemed to be supplied outside the EU in respect of any use of the items occurring outside the EU.

(2) Where the place of supply is outside the EU according to the normal rules, hire charges are deemed to be supplied in the UK in respect of any use of the items occurring in the UK.

These changes to the place of supply rules only apply to the extent that the goods are used outside the EU or within the UK. It is therefore necessary to apportion charges in some circumstances.

21.11 Hire of means of transport

21.11.1 Definition

Planning point

It is necessary to distinguish between the hire of a means of transport and the supply of passenger transport.

'Passenger transport services are supplied when a vehicle, ship or aircraft is provided together with a driver or crew, for the carriage of passengers...

If you hire a vehicle, ship or aircraft without a driver or crew, then you do not supply passenger transport services, but a means of transport...'

Other guidance: *Notice 744A*, Passenger Transport, para. 1.2.

Means of transport includes boats, yachts, barges, aircraft, trucks, vans, touring caravans, trailers, motor bikes, bicycles, railway stock and cars.

21.11.2 Normal rules post 31 December 2009

The rules vary according to whether the hire is a short-term or a long-term hire and whether it is a B2B or B2C transaction. Short-term hire is defined as a contract not exceeding 30 continuous days of hire (except for a vessel when it is 90 days). Contracts for the same vehicle will be treated as a single contract where less than two days separate the contracts.

The place of supply for a B2B long-term hire is where the customer belongs and is subject to the reverse charge. The place of supply for a long-term hire to a consumer is the place of belonging of the supplier (see **21.11.3** for pleasure boat hire from 1 January 2013).

The place of supply for B2B and B2C short-term hire is the place where the transport is put at the disposal of the customer; that is the location where the customer takes physical possession of the means of transport.

21.11.3 Post 31 December 2012

From 1 January 2013, the long-term hire of a pleasure boat to a final consumer or other non-business person is taxed at the place of belonging of the supplier's business.

21.11.4 Normal rules pre 1 January 2010

Within the EU the hire of a means of transport is liable to tax in the country where the supplier belongs.

In *Cookies World VertriebsgmbH iL v Finanzlandesdirektion für Tirol* (Case C-155/01) [2005] BVC 208 an Austrian business leased a car from a German firm. The car was used in Austria for purposes of its business. The ECJ ruled that:

> '... the place where the supplier of the leased vehicle had established his business or has a fixed place of business was in Germany and the place of supply of the vehicle-leasing services was deemed to be in that state. Therefore the VAT on the leasing of the vehicle had to be paid in Germany ...'

21.11.5 UK variations pre January 2010

When under the normal rules it is established that the services concerned are supplied in the UK or outside the EU it is necessary to consider the UK variation to the place of supply rules. According to circumstances this changes matters as follows:

(1)   Where the place of supply is the UK according to the normal rules, hire charges are deemed to be supplied outside the EU in respect of any use of the items occurring outside the EU.

(2)   Where the place of supply is outside the EU according to the normal rules, hire charges are deemed to be supplied in the UK in respect of any use of the items occurring in the UK.

These changes to the place of supply rules only apply to the extent that the goods are used outside the EU or within the UK. It is therefore necessary to apportion charges in some circumstances.

Other guidance: VAT (Place of Supply of Services) Order 1992 (SI 1992/3121), art. 17

21.12   Electronic services

For details of these services and the VAT rules, see **Chapter 26**.

21.13   Telecommunications services

The definition of telecommunication services includes the sending or receiving of material by electronic or similar communication systems via cable, radio waves, microwaves, satellite or copper wire. Also covered are telephony, which are systems for the transmission of speech and other sounds and telegraphy (systems involving any process that provides reproduction at a distance of a written, printed or pictorial matter). Also covered is the right to use such facilities.

The services include:

*   telephone calls, calls delivered by cellular phones, paging, the transmission element of EDI, teleconferencing and call-back services;
*   switching, completion of another provider's calls, the provision of leased lines and circuits or global networks;
*   telex, facsimile, multi-messaging;
*   email and access to the internet; and
*   satellite transmission services covering transponder rental/hire and both space segments and earth segments, which includes up-links and down-links via land earth stations, coastal stations, outside broadcasting units or similar.

The provision does not cover the content of a transmission – the treatment depends on the nature of the actual services. The provision of information, digital items (such as pictures, avatars, etc.) and music are treated as electronic services.

21.13.1 Rules post 31 December 2009

The provision of telecommunications services for a B2B transaction is where the customer belongs and is subject to the reverse charge. A B2C service is supplied where the supplier belongs except for supplies to a non-business person that belongs outside the EU. In this case, the supply is where the customer belongs. This is then modified by a 'use and enjoyment' rule. Where the use and enjoyment is outside the EU but would otherwise be regarded as being supplied in the UK, the supply is treated as being supplied outside the EU and thus, outside the scope of EU VAT.

Conversely, where the supply is made to a person that is outside the EU the supply would normally be outside the scope of VAT. If that person, however, brings the equipment to the UK and uses it in the UK, the hire charge is subject to UK VAT.

Planning point

Mobile Phone plc hires a mobile phone to Joe. Joe takes the phone overseas and informs Mobile Phone plc of this. Whilst the phone was in the UK, Mobile Phone plc charged UK VAT on the supply. When the phone was taken overseas, UK VAT no loner needed to be charged. Mobile Phone plc would require proof that the goods were used and enjoyed overseas, but could obtain this from the phone records and roaming records when he phone was used.

21.13.2 Rules pre 1 January 2010

Telecommunications services fall to be taxed where the customer belongs. Additional provisions relating to where the effective use and enjoyment of the services occurred further adjusted the VAT treatment in certain situations.

The place of supply is where the customer belongs when telecommunications services are received by:

- any person who belongs outside the EU; or
- a person who belongs in a different EU member state from the supplier and who receives the supply for business purposes.

Therefore, UK businesses must apply the reverse charge provisions on telecommunications services received from a provider who belongs outside the UK. Services supplied by a UK provider either to customers outside the EU or to customers in other EU member states who received them for business purposes are outside the scope of UK VAT.

If these services are received in the UK but used outside the EU, or received outside the EU but used in the UK, the place of supply is determined by where the effective use and enjoyment occurs. Effective use and enjoyment takes place where the recipient actually consumes services; this is irrespective of contract, payment or beneficial interest. This provision eradicates any distortion there might be for telecommunications services that are actually consumed outside the EU, which would, therefore, otherwise be subject to UK VAT. They also impose EU VAT on services if they are consumed in a EU member state.

Therefore, where the place of supply of telecommunications services would be the UK, because either the provider or the recipient belong here, but the services are effectively used and enjoyed outside the EU, the place of supply is where the services are used and, in such a case, the supplies would be outside the scope of UK VAT.

Where the supply of telecommunication services would be outside the EU, either because the provider or the recipient belong there, but the services are effectively used and enjoyed in the UK, the place of supply is the UK.

Consideration is only given to the effective use and enjoyment provisions when the EU VAT position would otherwise be distortive. Therefore, the place of supply of telecommunication services is not determined by these provisions when:

- the place of supply of the services is the UK and the services are effectively used and enjoyed in another EU member state;
- the place of supply of the services is another EU member state and the services are effectively used and enjoyed in the UK; or
- the administrative measure for travellers applies.

With regard to the last point, it follows that telecommunication services are subject to UK VAT when used in the UK by non-EU visitors, for example, by way of public pay-phones, fax shops and charges for calls made from hotel rooms. As an administrative measure, UK HMRC will not seek to tax elements of telecommunications services used in the UK which are:

- simply an incidental part of an established telephone contract or account held by a customer who belongs outside the EU;
- used by a non-EU temporary visitor; and where
- HMRC are satisfied that those conditions are not being abused.

If a non-EU provider supplies telecommunication services which are used and enjoyed in the UK, UK VAT will not be required provided that HMRC are satisfied that VAT has been accounted for in another EU member state.

21.14 Radio and television broadcasting

The provision of telecommunications services for a B2B transaction is where the customer belongs and is subject to the reverse charge. A B2C service is supplied where the supplier belongs except for supplies to a non-business person that belongs outside the EU. In this case, the supply is where the customer belongs. This is then modified by a 'use and enjoyment' rule. Where the use and enjoyment is outside the EU but would otherwise be regarded as being supplied in the UK, the supply is treated as being supplied outside the EU and thus, outside the scope of EU VAT.

Conversely, where the supply is made to a person that is outside the EU the supply would normally be outside the scope of VAT. If that person, however, brings the equipment to the UK and uses it in the UK, the hire charge is subject to UK VAT.

Prior to 1 January 2010, these services fall under VATA 1994, Sch. 5. The same use and enjoyment provisions apply to them as apply to telecommunications services as described above.

21.15   Tour operators margin scheme supplies

Under basic EU rules passenger transport is supposed to be taxed in the State where it takes place and hotel accommodation in the country in which the hotel is situated (see above) These principles may necessitate affected businesses registering for VAT in several member states.

Services within the scope of TOMS incur VAT in one, instead of in many, EU States. The place of supply is the State where the business to which TOMS applies belongs.

Although TOMS doesn't completely eliminate the need for a tour operator to register in more than one EU country, it does significantly curtail the problem. TOMS is intended to tax 'travel facilities' within the EU, any that are enjoyed outside the EU are exempted from tax.

This subject is covered in **Chapter 7**.

Other guidance: VAT Notice 709/3

21.16   The reverse charge

21.16.1 Introduction

The reverse charge is a method of accounting for VAT on the 'import' of services from another member state or from a supplier outside the EU (VATA 1994, Sch. 5).

From 1 January 2010, a revised main rule (general rule) relating to the place of supply of services will be where the customer is located (i.e. place of consumption). A supplier that does not charge VAT as the VAT is accounted for under the reverse charge must endorse the invoice with the legend 'VAT is accounted for under the reverse charge for this supply'. The customer's VAT number should also be shown.

The recipient of the supply effectively accounts for output VAT as if he had made the supply, and then recovers a certain amount of input VAT as though he had supplied the service to himself. The output tax is shown in box 1 of Form VAT 100 (the return) and the input VAT is recovered in box 4.

However, the main point is that the recipient can only recover input tax in box 4 to the extent that he is normally allowed. The net effect of the reverse charge is 'nil' to a fully taxable business. It will affect the import of services used for certain types of non-business purpose, in which case input tax cannot be recovered at all, and import of services by partly-exempt business, who can only usually recover a proportion of input tax incurred. If the imported service is wholly attributable to a subsequent exempt supply then it cannot be recovered at all in box 4.

The effect of the reverse charge is to eliminate any advantage there may be for a business in one member state which cannot recover all its input tax to cross-border shop for services either in another member state, where the rate of VAT is lower or outside the EU.

Where a UK supplier of services to a business located in another member state is relying on the reverse charge provisions to ensure that the customer accounts for VAT (and the UK supplier is relieved of any responsibility to register in the member state of supply, it has, since 1 October 2007 been a requirement for the invoice to make reference to this fact. A statement must appear on the face of the invoice along the lines of 'This is a reverse chargeable supply'. Further guidance on this provision can be found in HMRC VAT *Information Sheet* 10/07.

21.16.2 Services covered

The reverse charge will be compulsory for business to business services subject to the general rule. A number of exceptions apply in the same way as prior to 1 January 2010 including new exceptions for the supply of restaurant and catering services and a new exception for short-term hire of means of transport, which will be liable to VAT where the vehicle is put at the disposal of the customer .

Until 1 January 2010, the reverse charge principle of accounting for UK VAT relates to services received by UK VAT-registered persons which, although provided by suppliers who belonged overseas, were UK supplies by virtue of the VAT (Place of Supply of Services) Order 1992 (SI 1992/3121). Paragraphs 9–10 of VATA 1994, former Sch. 5 include:

- intra-EU freight transport and associated services;
- some land-related services; and
- services characterised by physical performance such as those in the fields of art, entertainment and sport.

With regard to the last point above, without this reverse-charge provision, businesses in other member states which make supplies in the UK, for example, a conductor conducting an orchestra in the UK, would have to be registered for UK VAT. The effect of this is that registration can be avoided if the recipient of the service in the UK accounts for VAT under the reverse-charge procedure. In some countries this is known as the tax liability shift mechanism.

21.16.3 Receipt of services

UK recipients of services, from either suppliers in other member states or from suppliers outside the EU, must account for VAT under the reverse charge if:

- they are received for the purpose of any business carried on by them in the UK; or
- the services would be standard-rated if supplied in the UK to a UK customer.

Some services would be zero-rated or exempt if supplied in the UK, for example, the underwriting of securities or the surveying of a ship, and these can be excluded from the reverse charge.

Planning point

There always seems to be a feeling among UK businesses that a service provided, for example by a lawyer in the US, cannot possibly be subject to VAT. This is, of course, incorrect. It can and VAT must be accounted for in respect of it – under the reverse charge.

The value of the services received either from other member states or outside the EU for use in the business, must be added to the value of taxable supplies in determining whether a business is registrable for VAT purposes.

⚠ Warning!

For some UK businesses this means that the value of reverse-charge services alone would push them over the registration limits. The normal penalty for late registration applies.

Planning point

A supplier who belongs outside the UK and whose customers account for VAT by means of the reverse charge can reclaim VAT on purchases made in the UK under Directive 79/1072, the Eighth VAT Directive mutual-recovery procedure.

> ### *Planning point*
>
> Overseas suppliers of reverse charge services can register for VAT in the UK if they wish to do so, and then charge domestic VAT on their supplies in the normal way. This might be advantageous to reclaim input tax which is often repaid more quickly when claimed on a VAT return.

21.17 The pre 1 January 2010 rules

21.17.1 General

Directive, 2006/112, forms the basis for all domestic VAT law within the EU. The main place of supply rules for services are contained within art. 43 of Directive 2006/112. The starting point for addressing any supply of services, whether cross-border or not, is the basic place of supply rule.

Article 43 of Directive 2006/112 states:

> 'The place of supply of services shall be deemed to be the place where the supplier has established his business or has a fixed establishment from which the service is supplied, or in the absence of such a place of business or fixed establishment, the place where he has his permanent address or usually resides.'

A Dutch firm leased cars to clients based in Belgium. These agreements were drawn up at the lessor's office at 's-Hertogenbosch, in the Netherlands. The ECJ ruled that the services were supplied in the Netherlands. The ruling was as follows:

> '... services could not be deemed to be supplied at an establishment other than the main place of business unless that establishment had a minimum degree of stability derived from the permanent presence of both the human and technical resources necessary for the provision of the services ARO Lease BV v Inspecteur der Belastingdienst Grote Ondernemingen, Amsterdam (Case C-190/95) [1997] BVC 547.'

In another case involving the place of supply, Linthorst, Pouwels and Scheres (a partnership) ran a general veterinary practice at Ell in the Netherlands. Some of its clients were Belgian farmers. The partnership had no fixed establishment in Belgium but carried out work there when visiting its Belgian clients. The ECJ ruled that the work for Belgian clients was taxable in the Netherlands. Its reasons were as follows:

> '... the place where the services principally and habitually carried out by a veterinary surgeon should be deemed to be supplied was the place where the supplier had established his business or had a fixed establishment from which the services were supplied or, in the absence of such a place of business or fixed establishment, the place where he had his permanent address or usually resided ... Maatschap MJM Linthorst, KGP Pouwels and J Scheres cs v Inspecteur der Belastingdienst/Ondernemingen Roermond (Case C-167/95) [1997] BVC 480.'

Article 43 is reflected in the UK legislation in VATA 1994, s. 7(10) as follows:

'A supply of services shall be treated as made–

(a)　in the United Kingdom if the supplier belongs in the United Kingdom; and

(b)　in another country (and not in the United Kingdom) if the supplier belongs in that other country.'

Planning point

Although this is the default position for supplies of services, so many, in fact, fall within the exceptions below that it covers only a minority of services.

21.17.2　Exceptions to the basic rule

For UK purposes, most of the rules for determining the place of supply for services from 1 January 2010 are set out in VATA 1994, s. 7A and Sch. 4A.

Situations that do not follow the basic rule and are covered in this section are:

- services relating to land and property;
- passenger transport;
- freight transport, related services and related intermediary services;
- some intermediary services;
- services supplied where physically performed:

  (a)　cultural, artistic, sporting, scientific, educational or entertainment services;
  (b)　services relating to exhibitions, conferences or meetings; and
  (c)　services ancillary to the above;
- valuation of, or work on, moveable goods;
- intellectual, professional, financial services, etc.;
- hire of goods other than means of transport;
- hire of means of transport;
- electronic services;
- telecommunications services; and
- tour operators margin scheme (TOMS) supplies.

Planning point

- Determine the nature of the relevant supplies.
- Determine the place of supply of the services.
- If provided in another EU state, determine who accounts for tax on the supply – for example it may be the recipient through a reverse charge system.
- If the supplier should account for tax, ascertain if it is necessary to register for VAT in that state.
- If the place of supply is outside the EU, services are not normally liable to tax.

21.18 VAT incurred in another EU member state

21.18.1 Claiming a VAT refund

When a UK business incurs VAT from another EU member state, the claim for refund cannot be made on the UK VAT return. It is necessary for a separate claim to be made. Since 1 January 2010, refunds of VAT paid in other EU countries must now be claimed electronically on a standardised form. Claims are to be made through the UK Government Gateway or HMRC VAT Online services. Prior to 2010, the claim would have been a paper based claim and made direct to the tax authority of the EU country where the VAT had been incurred.

There is no limit to the maximum amount you can claim, but each EU country has set a minimum amount that they will refund; this is usually quite low. A common minimum is 25 for a full year's claim or 200 for a claim for part of a year.

The claim must be made no later than nine months after the end of the calendar year when the VAT was incurred. This is usually the date on the invoice and not the date you paid the supplier. A claim cannot be for more than a calendar year or for a period of less than three months (unless that is all that is left in the calendar year).

Each EU country will only repay VAT for VAT that is input tax in that country. Thus, France will not repay VAT incurred on hotel costs, as the French authorities do not repay this VAT to French VAT registered businesses. Most business type costs, however, can be reclaimed, such as conference costs.

Example 21.8

Joe incurs VAT on conference costs in France. He has incurred VAT on a hotel bill for his accommodation, which cannot be claimed. Joe also has an invoice for attending the conference for 200. The date on the invoice is October 2009. This forms part of the claim for the year ending 31 December 2009. The claim for the VAT incurred must be submitted by 30 September 2010 at the latest.

Details are given at **9.8** on how to make the claim.

21.19 Checklist for international suppies

The following brief checklist will assist in determining how to treat international supplies.

21.20 Services

Is the business involved in making supplies of international services to customers outside the UK?

Check the place of supply rules and if the supply takes place:

(a)   in the UK then UK VAT is chargeable; or

(b)   if outside the UK the zero rate is chargeable:

    (i)   to customers outside the EU;

    (ii)   to EU customers upon receipt of evidence of business status. Supplies to non-business customers in the EU cannot be zero-rated.

Has an ESL been completed where required (from 1 January 2010)?

Has UK VAT been charged on supplies treated as taking place outside the UK when made to non-business customers in the EU, including individuals and charities?

Is the VAT-registered business involved in receiving services from outside the UK?

(a)   A supply for business purposes should be zero-rated by an EU VAT-registered business on the production of evidence of business status.

Note: The UK VAT registration number is the best evidence, or provide alternative commercial documentation.

(b)   The 'reverse charge' procedure must be applied to account for UK VAT on the supply and to recover the allowable input tax.

Are supplies of services made by an overseas business to non-VAT registered persons in the EU? If so, is VAT being properly accounted for in the EU?

Planning point

Reverse charge supplies should be analysed carefully to ensure the correct partial exemption recovery can be applied. In particular, should these reverse charge supplies be treated as a separate item under a special method?

Exports

22.1 Exports

22.1.1 Introduction

For VAT, an export only occurs where goods are supplied to a place outside the EU. Supplies to a place in another member state are dispatches. The treatment of dispatches is detailed in **Chapter 20, Doing business in goods in the EU**. When goods are exported the supply is zero-rated, the status of the customer is not important. A key criteria to obtain zero-rating, however, is obtaining and retaining proof of export. The VAT liability of goods is determined by the movement and location of the goods.

22.1.2 Goods not services

It is also important to note that exports only concerns goods. Services are treated differently. The basic position for services for many years was that they were supplied where the supplier is based. Consequently there is no general relief for services that were supplied to persons based overseas. This has changed significantly over recent yeas and certain services are treated as supplied where the customer belongs, the VAT liability can change depending on what is supplied, where the customer is located and what type of customer is supplied (a business or final consumer). This is examined in **Chapter 21, Supplying and receiving services within the EU**. This chapter concerns the supply of goods from the UK to a place outside the EU.

22.1.3 Direct exports

> **Planning point**
>
> It is important to confirm that the goods are removed to a country or territory that does not belong to the EU for VAT purposes, e.g. goods sent to the Isle of Man are not exports, those sent to the Channel Islands are exports. The countries of the EU are detailed at Table 20.2 at **20.12.3**.

An export of goods from the UK involves the supply of goods to a place outside the EU. Supplies of goods for export may be zero-rated provided certain conditions are fulfilled. The sale of goods to customers in another EU member state is an EU sale, not an export.

A direct export is where the goods are under the control of the UK owner or supplier and are exported outside the EU by the owner, supplier or other person acting on his behalf, e.g. a shipping agent.

Other guidance: VAT Notice 703

22.1.4   Indirect exports

These are supplies to overseas persons who arrange for the goods to be exported to a place outside the EU member states. An overseas person is defined as:

- a person not resident in the UK;
- a trader who has no business establishment in the UK from which taxable supplies are made; or
- an overseas authority.

Other guidance: VAT Notice 703

22.1.5   Essential export administration

In order to zero rate supplies for export, the exporter must:

- ensure that the goods are exported from the UK within three months of the date of supply;
- obtain and keep valid, official or commercial evidence of export within three months of exportation (see **22.2**);
- not deliver or post the goods to a UK customer's address in the UK, even if it is claimed that they are for subsequent export;
- not allow the goods to be collected by or on behalf of a UK customer, even if it is claimed that they are for subsequent export.
- keep records of export transactions and make them available to visiting HMRC officers; and
- comply with any other requirements set by HMRC in the relevant legislation and regulations.

> ### *Planning point*
>
> In addition to the usual requirements, there are certain goods that are controlled goods. In such instances it is essential that the relevant export licence be obtained prior to moving the goods.

Interest may become chargeable if correct documentation is not available within the time limits (see **22.2.4**).

> ## ⚠ *Warning!*
> If it cannot be proven that the goods were exported to a destination outside the EU, VAT must be accounted for as if the goods had remained in the UK and were sold to someone in the UK.

22.1.6   Rate of VAT chargeable on exports

Subject to the timely obtaining of satisfactory evidence and the physical removal of the goods from the EU, exports can be zero-rated, regardless of the liability within the UK of the goods.

This applies regardless of the location of the customer, to whom the supply has been invoiced, who may be in the place to which the goods are delivered, in the UK, or elsewhere. In the issue of *Notice 703* (*Exports*, April 2005), HMRC stated that such a supply was not eligible for zero-rating if the customer was VAT registered in the UK. They appear to have withdrawn from this position (which had doubtful validity anyway), however, since this restriction is no longer mentioned in *Notice 703*.

Law: VATA 1994, s. 30(6)

22.1.7   Other types of export

Exports of own goods

If a person makes taxable supplies in the UK and goods are transferred from the UK to another place of business outside the EU, the transfer is not a supply for VAT purposes. However, the transfer should be treated as a direct export and the relevant time limits for obtaining proof of export must be applied.

Retail export scheme

A voluntary scheme is in place that permits retailers to make a VAT refund and therefore zero-rate supplies to certain customers who purchase goods for export to a destination outside the EU within specific time limits.

The scheme is covered at **35.6.2**.

Other guidance: VAT Notice 704

Sailaway boats

Boats may be zero-rated when purchased by an overseas resident and exported under their own power outside the EU.

There is an extra-statutory concession (*Notice 48*; para 8.1) that permits the same relief to be given to a UK resident. One major difference is that an overseas resident has six months in which to export the boat, whereas a UK resident has only two months.

Evidence of export must be produced and, in the case of the UK resident, it must also be shown that the boat will remain outside the EU for at least 12 months.

Other guidance: VAT Notice 703/2 and 703/3

Postal exports

If goods are posted to an address outside the EU they may be zero-rated if they are direct exports.

Evidence of export must be retained. Suitable evidence is a Post Office supplied certificate of posting or the Post Office certificate form, HMRC 132, which shows the name and address of the consignee.

Exports through auctioneers

A supplier selling goods through an auctioneer who is not acting in his own name and who actually exports the goods may zero rate the supply, subject to certain conditions. The main conditions are that the supplier obtains a certificate of export from the auctioneer within one month of the date of the auction. The auctioneer must hold valid evidence to show the export of the goods.

If a supplier sells goods through an auctioneer who is acting in his own name, the goods are treated as being supplied to the auctioneer and so cannot be zero-rated by the supplier as an export. Only the auctioneer's own onward supply and removal of the goods from the EU will qualify for zero-rating.

> ### ⚠ Warning!
> Suppliers of goods in these circumstances are, therefore, advised to check the status of the auctioneer in advance of selling the goods in order to comply with the requirements correctly. The VAT tribunal case of *Bashir Mohamed Ltd* [2001] BVC 4,033 shows the dangers of not giving due thought to this point.

Goods exported by charities

Goods exported by a charity to a place outside the EU may be zero-rated. The export is deemed to be a supply carried out in the course or furtherance of a business.

If a charity exports goods for its own use overseas (e.g. for famine relief), it is deemed to be in business in respect of those exports and may register for VAT, thus being able to zero rate the deemed supply. Associated handling charges, etc. may be subject to input tax that may be reclaimed.

Law: VATA 1994, s. 30(5)

Goods exported after being temporarily imported for repair, etc.

Zero-rating is available for these goods (including motor vehicles and light aircraft) provided evidence is obtained that the customer is an overseas person and that the goods are subsequently re-exported.

> ### ⚠ Warning!
>
> This is a complex and highly regulated system. Further advice should be sought.

Other guidance: Notice 221 Inward processing relief

Goods supplied to visiting forces, diplomats, etc.

Such supplies may be zero-rated subject to complying with the necessary conditions that are explained in.

> ### ⚠ Warning!
>
> There are different rules that apply when the representatives of the foreign government are located in the UK or another EU state. Current conditions should be checked in each case.

Other guidance: Notice 431

22.1.8   Place of supply

The place of supply of exports is normally the UK.

Moving goods from one part of the UK to another part of the UK is not an export, even if the journey is through international waters or via a non-EU country.

Law: VATA 1994, s. 7

22.1.9   Penalties

From 27 November 2003, a civil penalty regime has been applied to persons failing to comply with import/export regulations or evading relevant taxes and duties.

In addition to evasion, infringements penalised include:

- occasional error involving at least £10,000 duty and/or VAT;
- persistent failure to comply with regulatory obligations; and
- failure to correct deficiencies in systems, operations or physical security.

22.1.10 Appeals

Appeals against the amount of VAT due or penalties incurred may be made to the VAT and Duties Tribunals. See **Chapter 37**.

22.2 Evidence of goods leaving the UK

22.2.1 Introduction

It does not matter whether the goods are removed to another member state or exported to a third country, proof of the goods leaving the UK is required. However, the types of evidence acceptable to support zero-rating.

22.2.2 Export evidence

Where exports are concerned, HMRC have the power to specify exactly what forms of evidence will suffice to substantiate zero-rating. In this respect, their publication *VAT Notice 703* has the force of law.

Official evidence is normally a Single Administrative Document (Form C88). Commercial evidence includes airway bills and bills of lading etc.

The various categories of evidence needed in various circumstances are as follows.

1. For shipments by air and sea freight, the required evidence is the airway bill or shipped bill of lading.

2. Export by overseas traders, the normal evidence will consist of airway bills and bills of lading, etc. However, if these are not available, the overseas trader should be requested to obtain and forward their certificate of export issued by HMRC on the appropriate export declaration form, i.e. a Single Administrative Document (Form C88) stamped by HMRC.

3. Aggregation: the freight forwarder will have the primary commercial evidence to support zero-rating, such as airway bills and bills of lading, they will cover more than one supply and more than one supplier. Agents should, therefore, produce an individual certificate giving the level of detail that would be available on a normal airway bill or bill of lading. Export houses should also produce a certificate containing a similar amount of information.

Photocopy certificates of shipment, shipping bills or airway bills are not normally acceptable as evidence of export. HMRC may, however, accept authenticated copies in certain circumstances.

If an exporter loses the official or commercial evidence of export, duplicate evidence must be obtained and the replacements must be clearly marked as duplicates and be authenticated and dated by an official of the issuing company.

There are more detailed rules regarding the required proof of export for the procedures listed below, namely:

- merchandise in baggage;
- road vehicles via a 'roll-on, roll-off' ferry;
- groupage or consolidation transactions;
- goods exported by post;
- goods exported by courier and fast parcel services;
- goods exported by rail and through packers and approved depositories; and
- exports of liquid and natural petroleum gases.

Other guidance: VAT Notice 703

22.2.3   Evidence of removal

Where EC sales are concerned, HMRC do not have the power to specify particular forms of evidence. It follows that a wider range of documentation may qualify as proof. This includes, but is not limited to, the evidence that may be used in respect of exports.

In HMRC's public guidance, they stipulate that the documents held must amount to 'clear evidence' that the goods have been removed from the UK, but otherwise may take a variety of different forms, including commercial documentation relating to order, dispatch, payment or insurance or 'any other documents relevant to the removal'.

Other guidance: VAT Notice 725, para 5.1

22.2.4   Time limits for producing evidence of removal from UK

Planning point

It is only when the proof of export is available that the goods may be zero-rated. If the evidence is not available within the time limits, VAT must be accounted for on the supply. See the experience of Musashi at **22.2.5**.

Table 22.1

Type of removal	Time limit
Direct exports or removals; goods transferred under the control of the supplier.	3 months
Indirect exports or removals; goods transferred by someone other than the supplier, perhaps a customer purchasing and exporting goods.	3 months
Groupage or consolidation shipments. This is common commercial practice for many types of shipment.	3 months
After processing or incorporation into different goods. This would include repairs and renovations as well as where the goods are incorporated into a larger item, e.g. widgets incorporated into an engine,	6 months

22.2.5   Interest due when time limits are not met

The Court of Appeal upheld a decision of the High Court that means a firm is liable to pay interest to HMRC even though there was no tax payable.

The case involved the documentation needed in order to zero rate supplies to another member state correctly. Musashi Autoparts Europe Ltd manufactures and supplies component parts for motor vehicles from premises in Wales. They are registered for VAT and have important customers based in other member states. On visits to the firm in 1999, Customs officers decided that the correct documentation was not available to show that certain goods had been removed from the UK. These goods had been zero-rated and Customs assessed the firm for £800,626 under VATA 1994, s. 73(1). Interest was also charged on the unpaid tax of £55,084.09. At a later date, Musashi provided the necessary evidence that the goods had been removed from the UK and subsequently Customs withdrew the assessment. However, Customs claimed that the interest was still due. The firm appealed to the VAT and Duties Tribunal. The Tribunal agreed with the firm. The assessment was reduced to nil and there was no liability for tax, therefore there could be no liability for interest.

Customs appealed to the High Court where a different conclusion was reached. The Court of Appeal heard the case and the decision went against the trader.

A trader supplying goods to another business in a different member state has three months from the date of the supply in which to obtain the correct evidence that the goods have left the UK in order to zero rate the supply (Value Added Tax Regulations 1995 (SI 1995/2518), reg. 134). If the evidence is not available after three months and the goods would normally be standard-rated in the UK, the trader must account for VAT accordingly (Value Added Tax Regulations 1995 (SI 1995/2518), reg. 40(1)). The amount of VAT must be included in box 1 of the relevant return and paid to HMRC. If the evidence is subsequently obtained, the trader should make an adjustment to their VAT account for the period in which the conditions are met, and zero rate the supply.

Musashi were submitting monthly VAT returns. Customs found that evidence of goods leaving the UK was not available for periods from 07/98 to 05/99, and hence goods that should have been standard-rated during these periods had been zero-rated. Therefore an assessment was raised. The courts accepted that, in these circumstances, Customs were entitled to make an assessment for the VAT that should have been paid. They were also entitled to levy interest from the date it should have been paid.

Chadwick LJ emphasised that there was nothing in the notices or regulations that indicated that the obligation to account for VAT was rescinded or otherwise extinguished when the trader, having had to account for VAT at the standard rate, obtained the necessary evidence and could subsequently adjust their VAT account. It does not make any difference if, at the time the necessary evidence is forthcoming, the trader has paid the assessment. If he has not paid, he remains liable to pay notwithstanding he can recoup the amount for which he is liable, indirectly, by paying less VAT for a subsequent period. Interest may be levied for the time the money is owed.

In this case, Musashi should have accounted for tax three months after supplying the goods, because the correct documentation was not in place. They did not do so. In effect they had the use of the VAT that they should have accounted for. Hence they were liable for the interest charged (*Musashi Autoparts v Customs and Excise Commrs* [2003] BVC 526).

⚠ *Warning!*

In the light of their case, it appears that HMRC's long-standing policy of allowing time for traders to obtain evidence before issuing an assessment (or of issuing a protective assessment and withdrawing it after the evidence has been obtained) is to be abandoned in favour of an approach whose only benefit to them is the interest that they will be able to collect. This is confirmed by further tribunal cases on the same point, lost by the appellants.

22.3   Exports Checklist

Goods

The business is not required to charge VAT on standard-rated goods for export outside the EU provided certain conditions are met including:

(a)   the goods are removed from the UK within certain time limits:

    (i)   three months for direct exports under the control of the exporter;

    (ii)   one month for indirect exports to be exported by another party, such as freight forwarder; and

(b) documentary proof of export and records of the transaction are received within certain time limits after removal of the goods.

Note: The export procedures must be carefully followed to avoid the risk of forfeiture of the goods. It is recommended that the exporter seeks further guidance and the services of a freight forwarder, if required.

Supplies which may qualify for zero-rating provided all the conditions are met include:

(a) supplies of goods generally including:

      (i) motor vehicles;
      (ii) sailaway boats;
      (iii) retail export scheme;
      (iv) freight containers;

(b) supplies for:

      (i) flights outside the EU;
      (ii) the stores of ships, aircraft and hovercraft; and

(c) supplies by:

      (i) charities;
      (ii) authorities and bodies managing the project.

Services

If the VAT-registered business makes supplies of certain standard-rated services to customers outside the EU check that:

(a) if the place of supply is outside the UK, no VAT is charged; and

(b) if the place of supply is in the UK, VAT is charged.

Imports (from outside the EU)

23.1   Imports

23.1.1 General

Goods are only imported for VAT purposes when they come from a source outside the EU. Goods are imported when they are physically brought to the UK from outside the EU. The date of importation is as follows.

1.   In the case of goods imported by sea, when the ship carrying the goods enters a UK port.

2.   In the case of goods imported by air, at the earlier of the following:

(a)   when the aircraft lands; or
(b)   when the goods are unloaded.

3.   In the case of goods delivered by pipeline, when the goods are brought within the limits of a port or other approved place.

Law: CEMA 1979, s. 5

23.1.2 VAT payable and input tax deduction

The VAT payable at import is due at the same rate as a supply in the UK. Thus, all the usual zero-rate, reduced rate and exemption reliefs apply. The VAT due is payable along with any duty and other tariffs before the goods are released into 'free circulation'. Free circulation means the goods are free to move within the EU without any further customs restrictions or duties. The VAT rules and regulations in respect of intra-community movement of goods still apply. Goods may be released without the payment of the VAT and Duty due where the VAT and Duty deferment regime is utilised, see **Chapter 23**.

Any VAT that is paid on import, either at the point of entry or through the duty deferment regime can be reclaimed on the VAT return subject to the normal rules. The usual document to evidence the claim for input tax is the form C79 that is provided by HMRC. HMRC retain copies of these documents for several years and copies can be obtained if necessary.

23.1.3 Duty suspension regime

If goods are placed in a duty suspension regime, in either the UK or elsewhere in the EU, then no VAT is due until the goods are released from all customs procedures and controls into free circulation in the UK.

The most common types of duty suspension regime are:

- a warehouse;
- a free zone;
- inward processing relief arrangements;
- temporary importation arrangements; or
- transit arrangements.

23.1.4 Essential administration at importation

When goods enter the UK at a customs-controlled area, for example a port, airport or inland clearance depot, there is an obligation to report their arrival to HMRC. An entry is then lodged with HMRC.

After an entry is lodged and all duties and taxes paid, the goods will be released and will be in free circulation in the UK and thus in the EU.

Standard documentation

The standard entry documentation used throughout the EU is completion of form C88 (single administrative document (SAD)).

This gives details of, amongst other matters:

- the goods being imported;
- the value for customs and VAT purposes; and
- the name of the importer.

It is submitted through completion of and physical submission of the paper version of the eight-part form or, alternatively, may be dealt with electronically at many ports. Submission is then via computer direct from the importer to HMRC.

Alternative documentation

There are some simplified methods that may be used in place of the basic procedure.

These include the following.

1. *Bulked entry*: a person who is importing several consignments for different destinations or consignees may make one declaration for all the consignments.

2. *Period entry*: regular importers who use electronic methods of accounting and stock control may use a simplified SAD at the point of entry. Detailed information is then periodically provided to HMRC on computer media after importation.

3. *Simplified procedure for import clearance (SPIC)*: certain low-value goods may be entered using a single form for up to six consignments. The entry form is C1451.

4. *ATA Carnet*: this is issued by a chamber of commerce and may be used for a single alternative to HMRC's normal entry procedures for some temporary imports.

5. *Postal imports*: if goods valued at less than £2,000 are imported, a VAT-registered person may account for the VAT on the normal VAT return. A customs declaration should accompany all such goods. In cases where Datapost packets are used, the Post Office collects the VAT at the time of delivery. When consignments exceed £2,000, a declaration must be made and returned to HMRC at the time of importation.

Planning point

Full details of the various entry procedures may be found in vol. 3 of *Integrated Tariff of the United Kingdom* (commonly referred to as 'The Tariff'). This is available by annual subscription and also in some public libraries and some HMRC offices.

A simplified guide to importing is available on HMRC's website.

23.1.5 Identity of importer

CEMA 1979, s. 1(1) defines the importer of goods from the time of importation until when they are delivered out of charge as: 'including any owner or other person for the time being possessed of or beneficially interested in the goods'. This does indicate some possibility of choice in the selection of the identity of the importer.

Practically, the identity of the importer is usually taken to be the person named on the SAD or other entry documentation.

⚠ Warning!

Ensure that the person identified as the importer is the person who wishes to reclaim any associated import VAT as the importer is the only person eligible to make the reclaim. Do not list the importer as an overseas, non-registered entity.

23.1.6 Value of imported goods for VAT purposes

The value of imported goods for VAT purposes is their customs value plus the following, if not already included in the price:

*   customs duties, excise duties and other charges; and

- all incidental expenses such as commission, insurance packing and transport to the final known destination in the EU at the time of import (transport costs include loading and storage charges, and the supply of such transport services to a UK importer is zero-rated for VAT purposes).

The valuation of goods for customs duty purposes is a complex subject. While the starting point is always the commercial price (plus carriage, insurance and freight if not otherwise included), different rules will apply if there is a relationship between the buyer and seller that has an influence on the price. Royalties and licence fees should be excluded when valuing imported goods, as these are taxable under the reverse-charge arrangements (see **Chapter 21**).

HMRC give details of their interpretation of these matters in *VAT Notice 252*.

> ### Planning point
>
> In 90 per cent of cases, the above method is suitable for determining the value for importation. However, other methods may be used. These are explained in detail in *VAT Notice 252*.

Certain works of art

From 1 July 1999, there is a reduced value for importations of works of art, etc. This is currently 25 per cent of the full value and gives an effective rate of VAT of 5 per cent (where the value of the item imported is £100, the calculation of the VAT due is £100 X 25% X 20% = £5). However, there is an anti-avoidance measure whereby works of art are given their full value if exported from the UK and reimported within 12 months. Thus they are subject to the standard rate of VAT. On 15 April 2002, Customs (as they then were) said that they will apply a concession by which the reduced value will be given to such imports unless the importer has arranged the export and reimportation in order to take advantage of the five per cent rate.

Other guidance: VAT Notice 702 VAT – Imports, para. 3.4

23.1.7 Rate of VAT chargeable on imports

The rate of VAT chargeable on imports is that applicable to the goods concerned under UK legislation. That is to say, it is the same rate which would apply to a domestic supply made in the UK by a VAT-registered trader. Accordingly, books, children's car seats and laptop computers, for example, would be chargeable to import VAT at 0 per cent, 5 per cent and 20 per cent (15 per cent from 1 December 2008 to 31 December 2009; 17.5 per cent from 1 January 2010 but before 4 January 2011) respectively.

It must be remembered that many goods bought in the UK are only liable to the zero rate or reduced rate when supplied in conjunction with services or because of the status of the recipient. It is usually the case that the necessary conditions are not met when dealing with imported goods.

Some goods are exempt from VAT when supplied in the UK. This is mostly when supplied with a service. There are not many instances of goods being exempt from VAT when supplied separately. At importation, goods are more often exempt because of specific customs relief than because they are within the scope of the exemption schedule (Sch. 9) to VATA 1994.

Example 23.1

Fred has difficulty in going up the stairs in his house because he is disabled. He researches the supply of stair lifts and is overjoyed to discover that there is a source in America where he can purchase a stairlift and pay 20 per cent less than the same article in the UK. He knows of a good builder who will install the stair lift in the house. Therefore, Fred buys and imports a lift kit.

At importation he has to pay both duty and standard rate VAT on the stairlift. He cannot reclaim this VAT and therefore the purchase is not as good a deal as he had expected. If the same article had been supplied and installed by the builder, it would have benefited from zero per cent VAT. Fred could have achieved his aim by asking the builder to import and install the stair lift. The builder could have reclaimed the VAT and zero-rated the onward supply to Fred.

23.1.8 Payment of import VAT

The SAD (form C88) is used to declare imported goods to HMRC. The SAD document contains information on the goods imported as well as information on the importer.

Import VAT will be paid:

- outright at importation or under the period entry system;
- under VAT and duty deferment arrangements; or
- on release of the goods from a duty-suspension scheme.

23.1.9 VAT and duty deferment

This scheme allows a VAT-registered importer or an importer's agent to clear imported goods through customs without paying the VAT and customs duties and any excise duties at the time of importation. Generally, deferment gives an average of 30 days' credit, as the charges are deferred until the 15th day of the month following the month in which the goods were imported.

Example 23.2

Cassandra imports a consignment of widgets on 2 April. She imports another batch on 29 April. Charges on both imports are due on 15 May.

HMRC require a guarantee from a bank or from an insurance company before they grant approval to use the deferment scheme. The level of the guarantee depends on the value of the estimated monthly imports.

The following forms must be completed in order to apply for VAT and duty deferment:

- form C1200: application form;
- form C1201: guarantee form;
- form C1202: direct debit mandate; and
- form C1207N: agent's authority.

Copies of these forms can be obtained from HMRC's website or the address below:

Central Deferment Office
6th Floor NW
Alexander House
21 Victoria Avenue
Southend on Sea Essex SS99 1AA
Tel: 01702 367425/367431/367450 or 367429

The completed forms should be returned to the above address. An application for a deferment number cannot be made until a person is registered for VAT.

A certificate of approval (form C1203) noting the deferment approval number will be issued by the deferment office if the application has been approved. The deferment approval number must be quoted on each request for deferment.

Subsequent payments to HMRC by users of this scheme should be made via the BACS system.

Other guidance: Notice 101

23.1.10 Simplified import VAT accounting (SIVA)

Certain importers are allowed a system using lesser security. Those authorised under SIVA have a reduced or nil guarantee level in respect of VAT and may limit their guarantee to the duty element of importation liabilities only. This is often a small proportion of the total tax liabilities and, in some cases, is non-existent where the goods concerned have a nil rate of customs duty.

HMRC will only approve traders to use SIVA if the trader has:

- been VAT registered for three years;
- a good VAT compliance record;
- a good payment history;
- financial means to meet any amount deferred;

656

- a clean offence record (serious offences will result in automatic expulsion);
- a 12-month record of international trade operations; and
- a good compliance record for international trade.

Permission must be sought from HMRC before using this scheme. Details are available direct from the HMRC's website and the specific SIVA section.

Planning point

For businesses eligible to apply, SIVA removes the biggest cost of a deferment account, namely the bank charges connected with the guarantee. Traders whose main reason for not holding a deferment account was this cost should undoubtedly reconsider their position in the light of this relaxation. The cash flow advantage of a deferment account is significant for regular importers, who otherwise need to pay VAT and duty at the time of each importation.

23.1.11 Reclaiming import VAT

Input tax paid on goods imported for business purposes may be reclaimed according to the normal rules (VATA 1994, s. 24 (1)).

Care must be taken that the correct documentary evidence is obtained. The usual evidence required is the import VAT certificate, form C79, that is issued monthly.

In cases where an agent pays the VAT on the importer's behalf, the agent cannot reclaim the VAT from HMRC as input tax. It must be recovered from the importer as a disbursement.

Copies of certificates that are lost can be obtained from the address below:

HM Revenue & Customs
VAT Central Unit, Microfilm Section
8th Floor
Alexander House
21 Victoria Avenue
Southend on Sea
Essex SS99 1AA
Fax: 01702 367385

Requests must be made in writing on business headed notepaper quoting the VAT registration number of the business and the month for which replacements are required. HMRC keep records of certificates for six years.

> ### *Planning point*
>
> The invoice issued by the agent to the importer to achieve this may not be used by the importer as evidence for his or her input tax recovery. Except in the circumstances set out, the only acceptable evidence is the form C79. It is however advisable to cross-check the invoices against the certificate to ensure that entries have not been missed.

Evidence for the recovery of input tax in the case of specific forms of import procedure are as follows.

Import procedure	Evidence for input tax deduction
Air/maritime imports:	
Single administration document (SAD) – manually processed	Monthly VAT certificate
SAD – trader input/computer processed	Monthly VAT certificate
SAD – HMRC input/computer processed	Monthly VAT certificate
Bulked entries – SAD	HMRC-authenticated invoices
Registered consignees	HMRC-authenticated invoices
Period entry – SAD (simplified)	Trader-produced computer schedule PE33 (not authenticated by HMRC) VAT adjustment schedule
Period entry – adjustment schedules only	Monthly VAT certificate
Transit shed register – imports not exceeding £600 (non-DTI)	HMRC-authenticated commercial invoice or locally produced forms certified by HMRC. The concession allowing use of copies of agents' disbursement invoices in certain circumstances will continue.
Postal imports:	
Exceeding £2,000 – SAD	Authenticated copy of SAD
Not exceeding £2,000 – HMRC declaration (form C1 (green label) or form C2/CP3)	No input tax evidence issued
Post entry correction	Monthly VAT certificates
Removals from warehouse:	
Excise warehouse or customs warehouse	Monthly VAT certificate
Hydrocarbon oils	Monthly VAT certificate

> ### Planning point
>
> The tax point is the date upon which the VAT became chargeable (i.e. date of importation), not the date of the C79 certificate — that may be issued up to a month later.

23.1.12 TURN (Traders unique reference number)

Importers registered for VAT should apply to HMRC for a unique reference number (TURN) in order to ensure that they receive the evidence required to reclaim VAT on imports. Systems are in place to assign non-VAT registered traders and private importers with relevant pseudo or dummy TURNs.

The TURN team is based in Carmarthen and may be contacted at:

Ty Myrddin
Old Station Road
Carmarthen
SA31 1BT
Tel: 01267 244049/244050/244051/244075
Fax: 01267 244068

Other guidance: Notice 533

23.1.13 Duty suspension schemes

Subject to conditions, goods imported from outside the EU may be placed into one of the various customs suspension regimes. Import duties or VAT are not due until the goods are removed or released from the relevant suspension scheme. The suspension schemes are as follows.

1. Temporary storage (although not strictly a suspension regime, all goods arriving from outside the EU are regarded as having temporary storage status until cleared of customs control).

2. Warehousing.

3. Inward processing relief.

4. Free zones.

5. External and internal community-transit arrangements.

6. Goods admitted to territorial waters:

   (a) in order to be incorporated into drilling or production platforms for the purposes of the construction, repair, maintenance, alteration or fitting-out of such platforms, or to link such drilling or production platforms to the mainland; and

   (b) with the fuelling and provisioning of drilling or production platforms.

VAT becomes chargeable when goods are removed from one of these regimes. The appropriate customs procedure (customs entry, security, etc.) applies even when VAT is the only import charge.

Other guidance: a variety of HMRC notices cover these reliefs and can be found on HMRC's website (*www.hmrc.gov.uk*).

23.1.14 Warehousing

This duty suspension scheme is only available when goods are stored in approved warehouses or storage facilities. Approval is granted by HMRC and normally specifies the type of goods that can be stored in the warehouse or premises concerned. The warehouse or premises may be designated a customs warehouse, an excise warehouse or both.

Some of the advantages of using the warehouse suspension scheme are:

- VAT and duty are not payable until the goods are removed/released into free circulation;
- official examinations of imported goods can take place at the approved warehouse;
- goods may be re-exported without payment of VAT; and
- faulty goods can be returned without payment of import duties or VAT.

These facilities are available for imported goods liable to VAT only.

> **Planning point**
>
> As different warehouses will serve different needs, it is essential to confirm in advance that the intended warehouse is approved for the goods concerned.

23.1.15 Inward processing relief

Subject to conditions, duties and VAT are not payable when goods are imported for process or repair before re-exportation. Since 1 January 2003, this relief is available for goods subject to import VAT only. VAT is only due if, or when, the goods are entered for free circulation.

> **Planning point**
>
> The scheme may not be used without first obtaining approval from HMRC. Applications should be submitted and agreed before the goods are imported.

23.1.16 Free zones

There are free zones in the Isle of Man, Liverpool, Prestwick, Southampton, Tilbury and Sheerness. Contrary to customs warehouses, goods may be processed within the free-zone area. By concession, the release from the free zone is a zero-rated supply if the customer undertakes to clear the goods into free circulation (*Notice 48*, ESC 3.14).

Other guidance: Notice 334

23.1.17 Other import reliefs

These are the main areas where relief is available. Each has its own conditions and care and further advice should be sought.

1. Certain visual and audio material produced by the UN. (VAT (Imported Goods) Relief Order 1984 (SI 1984/746), Sch. 1).

2. Goods described in the VAT (Imported Goods) Relief Order 1984 (SI 1984/746), Sch. 2, including:

   (a) capital goods/equipment when business transferred to UK;
   (b) certain goods for the promotion of trade;
   (c) goods for testing;
   (d) according to circumstances, certain health products, e.g. human blood;
   (e) certain goods imported by charities – mainly to do disaster relief;
   (f) certain printed matter, e.g. government publications;
   (g) various articles sent for miscellaneous purposes; and
   (h) certain works of art and collectors' pieces.

3. Personal effects permanently imported into the UK.

4. Goods brought into the country by diplomats, international organisations and visiting forces.

5. Reimported goods.

6. Duty-free allowances given to travellers.

7. Small non-commercial consignments between private individuals with a value of less than £36 (45), provided that it is not part of a larger consignment.

8. Certain gold and gold-coin importations by a central bank from a non-EU country.

9. Aircraft ground and security equipment. Imported by an aircraft of a country that is signatory to the convention on International Civil Aviation (Chicago Convention).

HMRC information

Customs *Notices* concerning goods imported free of duty and VAT include:

- 236 Returned goods;
- 317 Imports by charities;
- 340 Scientific instruments;
- 341 Donated medical equipment;
- 342 Miscellaneous documents;
- 343 Capital goods;
- 350 Private gifts;
- 361 Museum and gallery exhibits;
- 364 Decorations and awards;
- 365 Animals for scientific research;
- 366 Biological and chemical substances;
- 367 Commercial samples;
- 368 Inherited goods;
- 369 Blood grouping and certain therapeutic substances;
- 371 Goods for disabled people;
- 373 Visual and auditory goods; and
- 374 Goods for test.

23.1.18 Place of supply

The place of supply varies according to whether the goods are imported by the customer or by the supplier/vendor. When the customer is the importer, the place of supply is outside the UK. Goods are supplied in the UK if imported by the supplier/vendor. This complies with EU law.

It should be remembered that whoever imports the goods, VAT and possibly duty are due at importation.

⚠ **Warning!**

Subject to the normal rules, import VAT is recoverable by the importer. This creates a potential trap when the importer is the supplier/vendor. As the goods are deemed to be supplied in the UK, the import VAT will not be recoverable unless the supplier/vendor is registered for VAT in the UK.

Law: VATA 1994, s. 7(6)

23.1.19 Penalties

From 27 November 2003, a civil penalty regime is applied to persons failing to comply with import regulations or evading relevant taxes and duties.

In addition to evasion, infringements penalised include:

- occasional error involving at least £10,000 duty and/or VAT;
- persistent failure to comply with regulatory obligations; and
- failure to correct deficiencies in systems, operations or physical security.

See **Chapter 31**.

23.1.20 Appeals

Appeals against the amount of VAT due or any penalty imposed may be made to the VAT and Duties Tribunal. See **Chapter 37**.

23.1.21 Low import threshold

Article 23 of Council Directive 2009/132 (the VAT Directive) permits goods with a value of less than 10 (currently £9) to be imported VAT-free. The Directive also permits Member States to increase the limit to a maximum of 22 (currently £20). The UK limit has been £18 for many years (see the Value Added Tax (Imported Goods) Relief Order 1984 (SI 1984/746).

The 2011 budget announced that legislation is to be introduced to reduce the level at which the low value consignment relief (LVCR) applies. From 1 November 2011, the limit will be reduced from £18 to £15. Imports of goods from outside the EU below this threshold are VAT-free. The Government entered discussions with the European Commission to further limit the scope of LVCR and may seek a derogation from EU legislation. This is to restrict the VAT-free import of consumer goods from outside the EU (often the Channel Islands) such as CDs and DVDs. The government believes that the large scale selling of these items is causing a distortion to trade as UK suppliers have to charge VAT and the sale of these goods from offshore has been greatly facilitated in recent years by the use of the internet. As a consequence from 1 April 2012 the low value concession was withdrawn for the mail order trade from the Channel Islands. Mail order supplies from the Channel Islands are now subject to UK VAT at 20 per cent.

23.2   Imports – Goods and Services

Goods

The business must account for VAT on the importation of goods either:

(a)   by direct and immediate payment at the customs entry to release the goods; or
(b)   by payment deferment arrangements to HMRC.

Note: Imported antiques are liable at 17.5 per cent on a reduced value; the effective rate is 5 per cent.

The relief for import VAT paid is claimed on the VAT return upon receipt of form VAT C79.

The charge to VAT may be suspended or relieved under customs arrangements including:

(a)   customs or fiscal warehousing;
(b)   temporary storage or importation;
(c)   inward processing; and
(d)   free zones.

Note: The import entry procedures must be carefully followed. It is recommended that the importer seeks further guidance and the services of an import agent, if required.

There is what might be called a 'tariff wall' surrounding the member states of the EU. Goods imported from countries outside the EU (called third countries) may breach the tariff wall into any member state. However, at that point, the goods are liable to import VAT (where the goods attract a positive rate of VAT in that member state) and are also potentially chargeable to customs duty, excise duty and other tariffs. An import entry is required at that point.

After payment of customs duty, the goods are said to be 'in free circulation' and can move freely within the EU without further payment of the duty but not without further payment of VAT.

Import VAT is paid either in cash or under the duty deferment system and subject to the normal rules, reclaimed later on the importer's VAT returns.

Services

If the VAT-registered business receives certain services from outside the EU:

(a)   the reverse charge procedure is to be applied on the next VAT return; and
(b)   the claim for allowable input tax is to be made on the same return.

Supplying or Receiving Services to or from a Place Outside the EU

24.1 Introduction

The place of supply rules that apply for services supplied to and from the EU also apply for services supplied to and from a place outside the EU with one exception. This exception is that a supply to a final consumer outside the EU can be supplied without VAT whereas a supply into the EU to a final consumer would be subject to UK VAT.

The place of supply rules and the rules in respect of belonging and fixed establishment are the same as for supplies of services received or supplied from or to the EU. Thus, these rules and the old rules that applied before 1 January 2010 are not replicated here but are in **Chapter 21**.

It should be noted that where a supply is regarded as not being in the UK or EU that it may be regarded as being located and taxed in another jurisdiction. Whenever supplies are made to persons that are overseas or have some form of connection overseas the supplier should confirm whether or not there is any local taxation due.

24.1.1 Place of supply

From 1 January 2010 the revised main rule (general rule) for the place of supply of all supplies to a place outside the EU, is deemed to be taxable where the customer rather than the supplier is located (i.e. the place of consumption).

This applies to B2B as well as B2B supplies.

There will be some exceptions to the general rule, as now; for example property, is deemed to be where located, with the aim achieving taxation in the place of consumption.

A reverse charge applies to a wide variety of services but not to services detailed in Schedule 9 (VAT Exemption) or to opted properties.

24.1.2 Exceptions and specific rules

The exception relating to land will specifically refer to hotels where in practice there is no change to current rules. Land related services are not restricted to letting or sale of property or construction services. It also includes supplies such as architects, real estate agents, etc. These are regarded as supplied where the land is; this was the position before the introduction of the VAT Package.

There is also an exception for cultural, artistic and similar services which will be deemed to be liable to VAT where the activity takes place – again this is not a change from the treatment prior to the introduction of the VAT Package.

There will be a new exception for the supply of restaurant and catering services. These are supplied where the service is performed. It is, after all, only sensible to regard a restaurant meal in Paris to be considered to be supplied in France. Restaurant and catering services on board ships, trains and planes are treated as being supplied at the point of departure. Thus, a meal provided on a flight from France to Poland is treated as being supplied in France, even if the meal is served whilst the aeroplane is over Germany.

There will be a new exception for short-term hire of means of transport which will be subject to VAT where the vehicle is put at the disposal of the customer. Short-term is defined as a period not exceeding 30 days (90 days for a vessel).

With effect from 1 January 2011 cultural, artistic, sporting, scientific, educational and entertainment services supplies are taxable where the activity takes place. Admission fees for an event or services ancillary to admission to an event which will be taxable where the event takes place.

The long-term hire of means of transport will, from 1 January 2013, be subject to VAT where the customer is located when the vehicle, i.e. the car and other means of transport is hired for more than 30 days or where a pleasure boat is put at the disposal of the customer, as long as the supplier has an establishment or fixed establishment in that place when hired for more than 90 days. The use and enjoyment provisions will remain in respect of the hire of means of transport.

Finally, from 1 January 2015 the taxation of B to C supplies of telecommunications, broadcasting and e-services is expected to change.

24.1.3 Land

The place of supply of services related to land is where the land is located and where the land is outside the EU it is outside the scope of VAT.

Services relating to land include:

- the supply of hotel accommodation;
- the provision of a site for a stand at an exhibition where the exhibitor obtains the right to a defined area of the exhibition hall;

- services supplied in the course of construction, conversion, enlargement, reconstruction, alteration, demolition, repair or maintenance (including painting and decorating) of any building or civil engineering work;
- the supply of plant or machinery, together with an operator, for work on a construction site;
- services of estate agents, auctioneers, architects, solicitors, surveyors, engineers and similar professional people relating to land, buildings or civil engineering works. This includes the management, conveyancing, survey or valuation of property by a solicitor, surveyor or loss adjuster;
- services connected with oil/gas/mineral exploration or exploitation relating to specific sites of land or the seabed;
- the surveying (such as seismic, geological or geomagnetic) of land or seabed, including associated data processing services to collate the required information;
- legal services such as conveyancing or dealing with applications for planning permission;
- packages of property management services which may include rent collection, arranging repairs and the maintenance of financial accounts; and
- the supply of warehouse space.

Services that are considered not to relate to land include:

- Repair and maintenance of machinery which is not installed as a fixture. This is work on goods.
- The hiring out of a civil engineering plant on its own, which is the hire of goods; or the secondment of staff to a building site, which is a supply of staff.
- The legal administration of a deceased person's estate which happens to include property. These are lawyers' services.
- Advice or information relating to land prices or property markets as they do not relate to specific sites.
- Feasibility studies assessing the potential of particular businesses or business potential in a geographic area. Such services do not relate to a specific property or site.
- Provision of a recording studio where technicians are included as part of the supply. These are engineering services.
- Services of an accountant in simply calculating a tax return from figures provided by a client, even where those figures relate to rental income.'

24.1.4 Transport

The place of supply of passenger transport, is where it takes place. Where a journey involves travel through more than one member state then the supply of transport is made in each member state to the extent that the transport takes place there.

Journeys that begin and end in one country are regarded as taking place in that country alone even if they enter and leave another country or member state, as long as there is no stop in that other member state or country.

Freight services are taxed according to the general rule for B2B supplies and where the transport takes place for transport outside the EU or wholly outside the EU for B2C services.

The hire of means of transport is treated as being in the place where the customer belongs.

24.1.5 Services supplied where they are performed

Services supplied where performed are:

- cultural, artistic, sporting, scientific, educational or entertainment services;
- services relating to exhibitions, conferences or meetings;
- services ancillary to the above; and
- the valuation of, or work on, moveable goods.

24.1.6 Intellectual services

Intellectual services are regarded as being supplied where the customer belongs (and is outside the scope of EU VAT). These services include:

- transfers and assignments of copyrights, patents, licences, trademarks and similar rights;
- advertising services;
- services of consultants, engineers, consultancy bureaux, lawyers, accountants and other similar services, data processing and provision of information (but excluding any services relating to land);
- acceptance of any obligation to refrain from pursuing or exercising, in whole or in part, any business activity or rights as defined in the first bullet point;
- banking, financial and insurance services (including reinsurance but not the provision of safe deposit facilities);
- the supply of staff; and
- services rendered by one person to another person of procuring any of the above services.

24.2   The reverse charge

24.2.1 Introduction

The reverse charge is a method of accounting for VAT on the 'import' of services from a supplier outside the EU (VATA 1994, Sch. 5).

From 1 January 2010, a revised main rule (general rule) relating to the place of supply of services will be where the customer is located (i.e. place of consumption).

The recipient of the supply effectively accounts for output VAT as if he had made the supply, and then recovers a certain amount of input VAT as though he had supplied the service to himself. The output tax is shown in box 1 of Form VAT 100 (the return) and the input VAT is recovered in box 4.

However, the main point is that the recipient can only recover input tax in box 4 to the extent that he is normally allowed. The net effect of the reverse charge is 'nil' to a fully taxable business. It will affect the import of services used for certain types of non-business purpose, in which case input tax cannot be recovered at all, and import of services by partly-exempt business, who can only usually recover a proportion of input tax incurred. If the imported service is wholly attributable to a subsequent exempt supply then it cannot be recovered at all in box 4.

The effect of the reverse charge is to eliminate any advantage there may be for a business in one member state which cannot recover all its input tax to cross-border shop for services either in another member state, where the rate of VAT is lower or outside the EU.

Where a UK supplier of services to a business located in another member state is relying on the reverse charge provisions to ensure that the customer accounts for VAT (and the UK supplier is relieved of any responsibility to register in the member state of supply, it has, since 1 October 2007 been a requirement for the invoice to make reference to this fact. A statement must appear on the face of the invoice along the lines of 'This is a reverse chargeable supply'. Further guidance on this provision can be found in HMRC VAT *Information Sheet* 10/07.

24.2.2 Services covered

The reverse charge will be compulsory for business to business services subject to the general rule.

24.2.3 Receipt of services

UK recipients of services, from suppliers outside the EU, must account for VAT under the reverse charge if:

- they are received for the purpose of any business carried on by them in the UK; or
- the services would be standard-rated if supplied in the UK to a UK customer.

Some services would be zero-rated or exempt if supplied in the UK, for example, the underwriting of securities or the surveying of a ship, and these can be excluded from the reverse charge.

Planning point

There always seems to be a feeling among UK businesses that a service provided, for example by a lawyer in the US, cannot possibly be subject to VAT. This is, of course, incorrect. It can and VAT must be accounted for in respect of it – under the reverse charge.

The value of the services received either from other member states or outside the EU for use in the business, must be added to the value of taxable supplies in determining whether a business is registrable for VAT purposes.

⚠ Warning!

For some UK businesses this means that the value of reverse-charge services alone would push them over the registration limits. The normal penalty for late registration applies.

Planning point

A supplier who belongs outside the UK and whose customers account for VAT by means of the reverse charge can reclaim VAT on purchases made in the UK under Directive 79/1072, the Eighth VAT Directive mutual-recovery procedure.

Planning point

Overseas suppliers of reverse charge services can register for VAT in the UK if they wish to do so, and then charge domestic VAT on their supplies in the normal way. This might be advantageous to reclaim input tax which is often repaid more quickly when claimed on a VAT return.

24.2.4 Interaction with reverse charge liability on VAT grouping

Under VATA 1994, s. 44(4), the reverse charge on chargeable assets imposed when a business is transferred as a going concern to a member of a VAT group does not apply to assets coming within the CGS.

Overseas Suppliers

25.1 General rule

25.1.1 Activities in the UK

Suppliers that are based overseas will not normally have to account for VAT within the UK. An overseas supplier is a person that is based outside the EU and has no place of belonging or fixed establishment in the UK or the EU. There are, however, a few exceptions to this general rule of not accounting for VAT. Where these exceptions require the overseas person to account for VAT this is on the assumption that the supplies made exceed the VAT registration threshold. It should be noted that from 1 December 2012 the VAT registration threshold is removed for overseas traders. Thus, if a person established outside the EU makes any taxable supplies at all, it will be required to register for VAT and account for VAT on the supplies made.

25.1.2 Goods

Where the overseas supplier has goods in the UK and these are supplied to another person for consideration then a supply is made in the UK and VAT is due. It is likely that the person making the supply would want to be registered so that they can reclaim any VAT on costs that they have incurred including the purchase, import or acquisition of the goods that are being supplied.

25.1.3 Services

Where services that are treated as being supplied in the UK are supplied the overseas person will be required to register for VAT and account for VAT on the supply. Supplies that may be regarded as being supplied in the UK will be all the supplies that are not charged to tax under the reverse charge. For example, a performer (sporting or artistic) that holds a performance in the UK will be required to account for VAT as the service is treated as being supplied where it is performed. See **Chapter 21, Supplying or receiving services within the EU** regarding the place of supply rules.

25.1.4 Electronic services

Special rules apply for the provision of electronic services such as web hosting or email systems to UK and/or EU customers. See **Chapter 26, Electronic supplies** for information regarding how these supplies are treated for VAT.

25.1.5 VAT registration

A business that makes supplies in the UK but does not have any place of establishment in the UK must register with an office that is dedicated to Non-Established Taxable Persons (NETP) in Aberdeen. This office does not accept online applications and the VAT 1 must be downloaded from the website, completed manually and posted to:

The Non Established Taxable Persons Unit (NETPU)
HM Revenue & Customs
Ruby House
8 Ruby Place
Aberdeen
AB10 1ZP

HMRC are making progress to enable electronic registration for overseas businesses.

> ### *Planning point*
>
> A supplier who belongs outside the UK and whose customers account for VAT by means of the reverse charge can reclaim VAT on purchases made in the UK under the Directive 86/560 13th VAT Directive VAT recovery procedure – see **25.2.1** below.

> ### *Planning point*
>
> Overseas suppliers of reverse charge services can register for VAT in the UK if they wish to do so (at the NETPU detailed above), and then charge domestic VAT on their supplies in the normal way. This might be advantageous to reclaim input tax which is often repaid more quickly when claimed on a VAT return rather than through the 13th Directive mechanism.

25.2 VAT incurred in the UK by non-EU businesses

25.2.1 Introduction

Businesses established outside the EU may incur VAT in the UK by, for example, visiting the UK to attend a conference or trade show or receiving services from a UK business which do not qualify for relief from VAT. Directive 86/560, the EC 13th VAT Directive, provides the mechanism for these businesses to recover the VAT charged.

If an overseas business has to be charged UK VAT, it is possible to arrange to assist them in making a claim for its recovery. If a person other than the business incurring the expense makes the claim, a Power of Attorney or letter of authority will be required to authorise HMRC to deal with that person and make repayment to them. Claims can be made direct by the overseas business or there are a number of agencies which provide this service, usually on a commission basis.

It is likely that an inspection will be made to check that the output tax has been correctly charged and accounted for prior to payment of the claim being made.

'Draft letter of authority

I [name and address of claimant] hereby appoint [name and address of agent] to act on my behalf in connection with any claims I make to HMRC under the Value Added Tax (Repayment of Community Traders) Regulations 1980 as from time to time amended or replaced. Any repayment of VAT to which I am entitled pursuant to any such claim made on my behalf by my above named agent shall be paid to [name and address of payee].

Date

Signed [by the claimant]'

25.2.2 Can I make a claim?

A business that is established outside the EU is entitled to recover VAT paid in the following circumstances.

1. Provided that the claimant is not registered or liable to be registered for VAT in the UK.

2. Provided that the claimant does not have a place of business or residence in the EU.

3. Provided that the claimant has made no taxable supplies in the UK other than:

    (a) international freight transport (and ancillary services); and
    (b) services where the VAT due is accountable by the recipient under a reverse charge in the UK (see VATA 1994, Sch. 5 for a list of these services).

However, if the country in which the business is established has a system of turnover taxes and a system of refunds, and does not allow reciprocal refunds to UK businesses, HMRC will not normally allow the refund to be paid.

Not all VAT is recoverable. The VAT must be incurred in the course or furtherance of the business. See also the list of items specifically excluded at **9.2.3**.

25.2.3 Non-deductible input tax

VAT cannot be reclaimed on the following items:

- immovable property;
- a supply that is not for the purpose of the business;
- the part of a supply that is used for non-business or exempt purposes;
- supplies that the taxable person intends to use for a supply in the Member State where the claim is being made;
- a supply that has been exported or is intended to be exported;
- supplies that relate to Tour Operator Margin Scheme costs; and
- VAT on expenditure that is non-deductible for UK taxpayers such as VAT on cars, business entertainment, etc.

25.2.4 How to make a claim

Certificates of status

A certificate is required from the official authority in the relevant country confirming registration for business purposes in that country. This certificate must include the name and address of the business, the name and address and official stamp of the issuing authority, details of any trading name, the business registration number (if any) and details of the nature of the business.

Form

Copies of the form (VAT 65A) for making a claim are available from:

HMRC
VAT Overseas Repayments, 8th/13th Directive
Custom House
PO Box 34
Foyle House
Duncreggan Road
Londonderry
Northern Ireland BT48 7AE.
Phone: (+44)(0) 28 7130 5100
Fax: (+44)(0) 28 7130 5101
Email: enq.oru.ni@hmrc.gsi.gov.uk

Tax invoices

The claim must be accompanied by the original tax invoices detailing the VAT incurred regarding evidence for input tax claims. If the originals are not available as a result of being lost, copies may be acceptable and a letter explaining the reason for the originals not being available should be sent with the claim.

Time limits

A claim must be made within six months of the end of a prescribed year, which runs from 1 July to 30 June the following calendar year. The claim should be paid within six months of receipt of a satisfactory claim. Note that this is different for a claim being made by a UK business for VAT incurred in other EU member states.

25.2.5 VAT refunds across the EC

From 1 January 2010 a new electronic claims procedure for businesses will apply. This is intended to give claimants quicker refunds and greater legal certainty.

The taxpayer is entitled to interest if the tax authority delays payment of the refund claim. There are also clear appeal procedures in the member state of refund if the claim is rejected.

Member states will have a time scale for decisions which is four months, unless additional information is required then a maximum of eight months. Each member state can request additional information and original invoices. If the claim is delayed interest will be paid by the member state of refund.

The portal structure for electronic processing of claims is expected to comprise two sections:

(a)   claimant identifier; and
(b)   individual claims.

Claims from VAT groups can be made by the representative member.

If partial exemption calculations apply to the VAT to be claimed this will be carried out under the rules of the member state of establishment.

Electronic Supplies

26.1   Introduction

This chapter seeks to explore the VAT rules applying to electronically supplied services, which were introduced on 1 July 2003, covering such topics as:

* what an electronically supplied service is;
* the business status of a customer;
* broadcasting services;
* the special scheme for non-EU businesses;
* the VAT liability of the place of supply of electronic or digitised publications;
* use and enjoyment rules and harmonisation of VAT invoices; and
* the transmission of invoices by email.

See **20.9.4** for updated information on EC Sales lists (ESLs).

This chapter does not consider telecommunications (see **21.13**) or exports or imports of goods (see **Chapters 22 and 23**). It examines the VAT position of services that are supplied over the internet. It is difficult to determine the place of supply of those services and, with the disparity of VAT rates across the EU (from 15 per cent to 25 per cent for the standard rate alone!) accounting for VAT in the correct jurisdiction becomes a challenge. Most EU legislation was written at a time when computers were still in their infancy, long before supplies were being made over the internet. All the problems stem from the fact that deliveries of services over the internet are not specifically tied to any particular location.

A company can engage in any commerce without having a physical presence in a country where it generates profits and, given the anonymity which runs hand-in-hand with the internet, it is difficult to identify the parties to any particular transaction. Prior to the introduction of the new legislation, wide disparity grew between EU and non-EU suppliers. EU suppliers were deemed liable to charge VAT on their e-commerce transactions at the VAT rate in force in the member state in which they had established their business, whereas non-EU suppliers were not.

Advances in modern technology, particularly in the field of music where individual tracks on the latest CD can be downloaded at minimal cost to the consumer, typify the supplies which can be made electronically and the problems in establishing where VAT should be accounted for. The consumer can download the track on to a PC, transfer it to an MP3 player and listen to the track downloaded at the touch of several buttons. All this proceeds digitally without the need for human intervention or traditional CDs or cassettes, which effectively become redundant.

The EU and the OECD have agreed that the supply of such products electronically shall be treated as services, therefore relieving those services of any import duty when imported into the EU. Additionally, the services should be deemed liable to VAT in the EU member state in which they are consumed, although this can still cause issues with regard to downloaded music, for example, which may be electronically provided to a consumer on a PC in the UK whereupon that person immediately sends the product electronically to another consumer outside the EU who downloads the track onto an MP3 player and is therefore using the music outside the EU.

The supply of digitised products, of course, does not just relate to music but also encompasses music song sheets, books, magazines, videos, etc., all of which can also be treated as digitised products over the internet, thereby changing their format from a supply of goods to a supply of services 'published' over the internet.

The EU has effectively decreed that the supply of digitised products between businesses established in different member states should be subject to the reverse charge, therefore giving the business no particular advantage in being VAT registered in any particular country. However, the reverse charge mechanism does not apply if the services are supplied to non-VAT registered entities. The supplier must account for VAT in the member state in which he is VAT registered in respect of all digitised products supplied to non-VAT registered entities based in the EU.

The new legislation introduced by VAT Directive 2002/38 and applied from 1 July 2003, was introduced in an attempt to eliminate a competitive distortion by subjecting non-EU suppliers of e-commerce products to the same VAT rules and regulations as EU suppliers. The EU considers that the framework for the legislation takes into account a number of elements designed to make the operation of the tax as simple as possible and to ensure that it is not destructive or onerous for a supplier of digital services.

The EU has introduced a single place of registration for non-EU businesses with the option of discharging their VAT obligations through this single administration. The non-EU businesses will collect tax from their European customers at rates ranging between 15 per cent and 25 per cent depending on where they are located, while European companies will charge tax according to the rate where they are established.

Planning point

Non-EU businesses should consider registering for VAT through a branch or agency in a jurisdiction with a low VAT rate.

The EU considers that the OECD principles on taxation on e-commerce have been met; it was agreed in 1998 by the OECD in a conference in Ottawa that the taxation of e-commerce should result in the taxation of such services in the jurisdiction where consumption takes place.

Electronically supplied services or digitised products are deemed to be:

- website supply, web hosting, distance maintenance of programs and equipment;
- supply of software and updating thereof;
- supply of images, text and information and making databases available;
- supply of music, films and games, including games of chance and gambling games, and political, cultural, artistic, sporting, scientific and entertainment broadcasts and events; and
- supply of distance teaching.

Law: VATA 1994, s. 7A and Sch. 4A, para. 8, 9, 15 and 16(2)(i)–(k)

Other guidance: HMRC VAT Information Sheets 01/03, 04/03 and 05/03

26.2   What is an electronically supplied service?

Article 9 of the Sixth VAT Directive has been amended by VAT Directive 2002/38. Paragraph 7C of Sch. 5 to VATA 1994 implements the change into UK law.

Annex II to Directive 2006/112 provides an illustrative list of the services capable of being electronically supplied and an EU VAT Committee guideline has been issued, entitled *Electronically-supplied Services: Guide to Interpretation*, which sets out the guidance as to what is meant by an electronically supplied service.

The guidance indicates that determining an electronically supplied service is a two-step test: in the first instance it is delivered over the internet or an electronic network and, secondly, the nature of the service in question is heavily dependent and reliant upon information technology for its supply.

The EU VAT Committee guideline supplies tables of what is included in an electronically supplied service and includes:

- website supply;
- web hosting and distance maintenance of programs and equipment;
- software and updating thereof;
- images, texts and information;
- making databases available;
- music, films, broadcasts and events;
- games including games of chance and gambling games;
- distance teaching;
- online auction services; and
- internet service packages.

The guideline gives examples of transactions not considered to be a supply of an electronically supplied service and includes services that rely on substantial human intervention; services that are not delivered over the internet; radio and television broadcasting services which are covered by art. 9(2)(e) (now art. 56(1)(a) of Directive 2006/112); and telecommunication services.

Some of the more common examples of services deemed to be electronically supplied services are:

- website hosting and webpage hosting;
- accessing or downloading software plus updates;
- accessing or downloading photographic or pictorial images;
- the digitised contents of books and other electronic publications;
- online news, traffic information and weather reports;
- the provision of advertising space;
- use of search engines and internet directories;
- accessing or downloading music on to PCs or mobile phones;
- accessing or downloading of jingles, excerpts, ringtones or other sounds;
- accessing or downloading of films, downloading games onto PCs, mobile phones, etc.;
- accessing automated online games which are dependent on the internet; and
- online auction services.

26.3 Electronically supplied services – place of supply

The E-Commerce Directive (Dir. 2002/38), implemented on 1 July 2003, covers a wide range of services supplied over the internet electronically; primarily:

- the supply of websites for web hosting services;
- downloaded software, including updates of software;
- downloaded images, text or information, including making databases available;
- digitised books or other electronic publications;
- downloaded music, films or games;
- electronic auctions; and
- internet service packages.

The Directive also includes radio and TV broadcasting services regardless of whether these are supplied by landline, satellite, etc., including subscription for satellite or cable television.

With effect from 1 July 2003, the place of supply of electronically supplied services depends on where the customer belongs, if that is in an EU member state other than the one in which the supplier is established, whether or not the customer is in business.

Where the supplier is established in the UK, supplies of electronically supplied services are therefore subject to VAT when supplied to:

- a customer belonging in the UK; or
- a customer belonging in another member state of the EU who is receiving the services other than for a business purpose.

The UK supplier will not have to account for UK VAT when supplying:

- a customer who belongs in an EU member state other than the supplier and who receives the supply for the purposes of his business there; or
- a customer who belongs outside the EU altogether.

Businesses receiving electronically supplied services are required to account for VAT in their EU member state under the reverse charge procedure. The recipient business will, therefore, be in no worse position had it received the services from a supplier in its own member state and will be able to recover the VAT on the services received in full, subject to partial exemption status and the recovery method adopted.

Planning point

Using the reverse charge to account for VAT means no payment of VAT is actually made and the customer will, therefore, benefit from cash flow. The customer should ensure reverse charge invoices are properly annotated to assist VAT recovery where possible under partial exemption rules.

⚠ Warning!

It must be remembered that, if the customer belongs in the same EU member state as the supplier, or the customer belongs in a different EU member state to the supplier and receives the supply other than for business purposes, the place of supply remains in the country where the supplier belongs. Therefore, if a UK supplier were to supply an individual in France or Estonia or Bulgaria, for example, the UK supplier would be required to account for VAT at 20 per cent (15 per cent from 1 December 2008 to 31 December 2009; 17.5 per cent from 1 January 2010 to 3 January 2011 and prior to 1 December 2008). References to the 20 per cent rate in this chapter should be treated as one of the earlier standard rates if the transaction took place in the appropriate period.

To determine whether or not their customers receive the supply for business purposes, suppliers are required to obtain commercial evidence to support any claim that their customers are in business in the EU member state in which the customers belong.

26.4 Use and enjoyment rules

The effect of the legislation is to ensure that VAT is accounted for in the UK member state or jurisdiction of consumption of the services. Private individuals and non-business organisations are deemed to consume the services where they download the products. The EU considers that most non-business customers use and enjoy the services in the same member state or country to which they belong.

If the business customer actually consumes the electronically supplied services in a different place from the contract, payment or beneficial interest, additional rules will apply where the VAT position would otherwise be distorted. Where a UK supplier provides electronically supplied services, the use and enjoyment rules will apply in two instances where:

- the supply is to another business and the place of supply would be the UK because the supplier or customer belongs in the UK but the services are used and enjoyed outside the EU; or
- the supply would be outside the EU because the supplier or the customer belongs outside the EU but the services were effectively used and enjoyed in the UK.

For example, a UK supplier supplying electronic services to a non-EU customer for their business purposes is required to determine whether or not the services are to be used for the business purposes of the non-EU customer and if so, in which EU member state they are to be enjoyed.

If their use and enjoyment is in the UK, then the services are supplied in the UK by the UK supplier and the supplier accounts for 17.5 per cent VAT (15 per cent from 1 December 2008 to 31 December 2009 and 20 per cent from 4 January 2011).

If the services are to be used in another EU member state, the supplier is making supplies outside the scope of UK VAT, but may be required to account for VAT in the EU member state of use.

Where a UK supplier provides electronically supplied services to a customer that belongs inside the EU but outside the UK and the services are received for business purposes, these supplies are outside the scope of UK and EU VAT if the supply is used and enjoyed outside the EU.

Where the supplier is established outside the EU he must determine whether the customer belongs in the EU and whether the customer has received the services for business purposes.

If the customer is outside the EU and receives the services for business purposes to be used and enjoyed in the EU, the non-EU supplier must account for VAT in the member state of use and enjoyment of the services, subject to the provision by the customer of a VAT number against which the customer can account for VAT under the reverse charge.

Where the non-EU supplier supplies a UK customer for non-business purposes and those services are supplied in the UK, the non-EU supplier should account for VAT due in the UK and may adopt the special scheme subject to the requirements of that scheme to account for VAT.

The overriding use and enjoyment rules do not apply where the supply is to a private individual or non-business organisation or where the place of supply is deemed to be the UK, because either:

- the supplier or the customer belongs in the UK and the product was effectively used and enjoyed in another EU member state; or
- where the place of supply is in another EU member state, because either the supplier or customer belongs there but the supply was effectively used and enjoyed in the UK.

26.5   Accounting for VAT

26.5.1   Introduction

UK businesses should account for VAT in the normal way on electronically supplied services, depending on the place of supply rules and the effective use and enjoyment of the services supplied. A business established in the UK will treat a supply to:

- customers in the UK (both business and non-business customers) as subject to VAT at the standard rate;
- a VAT registered business in the EU as exempt with credit (effectively zero-rated) and the customer will need to account for VAT at the rate of their place of establishment;
- a non-VAT registered customer in the EU as subject to VAT; and
- a customer (business or non-business) established outside of the EU as exempt with credit (effectively zero-rated).

UK customers should account for VAT using the reverse charge procedure where the services are received for business purposes from an overseas supplier. An exception is where the services are used and enjoyed outside the EU or where a UK VAT-registered branch of an international business uses and enjoys services in the UK which have been supplied by an overseas supplier to a non-EU establishment of the business.

Non-EU suppliers of electronically supplied services providing services to private individuals or non-business organisations in the EU are in principle required to register and account for VAT in every EU member state where the supply of the services takes place or where they are used and enjoyed unless they adopt the simplified accounting scheme. This simplified scheme for electronically supplied services permits the non-EU supplier to register electronically in an EU member state of choice and account for VAT via an electronic VAT return. VAT must be accounted for at the rate applicable in each EU member state. The return is submitted to the authority in the EU member state of registration together with payment and that authority will distribute the VAT to the EU member states where the services have been consumed. Although this scheme allows the overseas entity to account for the output tax due, it will still need to submit a 13th Directive claim in order to reclaim any VAT incurred in the EU.

This special scheme does not apply to non-EU businesses already registered for VAT in any EU member state or to non-EU businesses supplying broadcasting services or other services. If non-EU businesses choose not to use the special scheme they will be required to determine their VAT registration in each relevant EU member state. Thus, to avoid using this 'simplified scheme' an overseas entity may decide to choose to create an establishment in a member state with a low rate of VAT. The lowest permitted standard-rate that can be applied in the EU is 15 per cent. This rate (at September 2012) is only applied in Luxembourg. Other low rates in the EU are Cyprus at 17 per cent, Malta at 18 per cent and Germany at 19 per cent. The Azores and Madeira had previously had a low rate of VAT, but this is no longer the case (it is currently 22 per cent).

Planning point

If non-EU suppliers obtain VAT registration, the same VAT rules relating to EU VAT-registered businesses in those areas should apply.

⚠ Warning!

If a business is not already registered for VAT in the UK but receives broadcasting or electronically supplied services from a supplier outside the UK, the reverse charge must be calculated and the resulting value of the reverse charge added to any other taxable supplies made in the UK to determine whether or not UK VAT registration is applicable.

26.5.2 Evidence of customer location and status

Under the new EU place of supply rules, it is important to evidence and identify the status and location of customers in order to determine the place of supply of electronically supplied services.

To determine the place of supply of services, the supplier needs to know where the customer belongs and whether the supplies are received for business or non-business purposes by a business, non-business entity or private individual.

Other guidance: HMRC VAT Information Sheet 05/03

26.5.3 The business status of a customer

Normally where supplies of services are made from one business to another and the recipient business is outside the supplier's EU member state, it is sufficient to determine the customer's status by obtaining a business letterhead, tax fiscal certificate, VAT registration number and country identifier or other alternative evidence. Often the best form of identification of business customers in the EU is their VAT number and country prefix identifier. The VAT number should conform to the format for the registered person's EU member state.

Additional rules have been implemented with regard to verification of business status of customers where electronic services are supplied. Where a relationship has not been established with the business customer, the VAT number should be checked when the VAT involved exceeds £500 in a single transaction, or the cumulative VAT on transactions for electronically supplied services to a single customer in a VAT quarter exceeds £500.

HMRC also indicate that the use of a VAT number should be challenged for businesses that supply downloaded music, games or films of a kind that are normally supplied to private consumers and where a VAT number is quoted that appears to be a supply to a private individual. HMRC also indicate that if a customer claims to be in business but not VAT registered then alternative evidence should be obtained. This can be in the form of other reasonable commercial evidence or records that should normally be available, e.g. contracts, business letterheads, commercial website address, publicity material, certificates from fiscal authorities, etc.

Obtaining and displaying a customer's VAT number is not obligatory but clearly is probably the best and easiest format to display and confirm with HMRC that the services have been supplied for a business purpose.

26.5.4   Location

By the very nature of electronically provided services, it is often not readily apparent where customers are located. Often, under normal business transactions, business suppliers and customers will be aware of their respective locations, but this is not necessarily the case when supplies are made to private individuals and non-business customers.

Acknowledging this concept, the E-Commerce Directive allows businesses supplying electronically supplied services to private individuals to receive and accept a self-declaration by the customer, combined with a reasonable level of verification.

Planning point

HMRC have indicated that where businesses already have in place established practices and procedures to identify and verify the country where the customer belongs this will be acceptable. HMRC do, however, give a list of examples of the methodology used to verify location and if these are not adhered to HMRC should be contacted.

Customers' self-declaration will be acceptable to HMRC where:

- the customer's postal address is provided and it has been previously used to send goods, catalogues, samples, CD-ROMs, invoices, correspondence, etc., and the correspondence has not been returned;
- payment by credit/debit card is accepted and a comparison of the customer's home address and the billing address provides a successful match;
- payment by credit/debit card is accepted, the customer's country of residence is compared with the location of the issuing bank using proprietary software and provides a satisfactory match;
- geo-location or proprietary software is used to verify where the customer belongs; or
- systems are used that are configured to identify where the service is used and enjoyed, e.g. telecommunication suppliers.

> **Planning point**
>
> HMRC have indicated that where a business has adopted the relevant verification procedures, has relied upon the information at that time, but subsequently finds that the customer has made a false declaration, HMRC will not seek to recover VAT from the supplier where it was not charged to the customer.

26.5.5   Invoice wording

Since 1 October 2007, it has been obligatory to note on the face of invoices for certain types of services supplied to business customers in other member states of the EU the reason why VAT has not been charged. Electronic services fall into one of the relevant categories of service. A variety of possible wordings is permitted by HMRC, a typical example of which is 'This is a reverse chargeable supply'.

Other guidance: HMRC VAT Information Sheet 10/07

26.6   Special scheme for non-EU businesses

Effectively, non-EU businesses that supply electronically supplied services to EU customers who are private individuals or non-VAT registered businesses are required to register for VAT in each EU member state in which the supplies are consumed.

The supply by non-EU businesses of electronically supplied services to business organisations in the EU will be subject to the reverse charge being applied by the customer in the EU jurisdiction to which the customer belongs.

The special scheme for non-EU businesses gives them the option to register electronically in a single EU member state of their choice.

VAT on the sale of electronically supplied services to all EU consumers is accounted for on a single quarterly electronic VAT declaration, which will provide details of VAT due in each EU member state. This is submitted with payment to the tax administration in the EU member state of registration, which will then distribute the VAT to the member states where the services are consumed.

Planning point

Given that there is a wide disparity of VAT rates from 15 per cent to 25 per cent, non-EU businesses supplying electronically supplied services to non-businesses in the EU should consider whether to select the special scheme or alternatively opt to register for VAT in an EU member state where VAT is at one of the lower rates, i.e. 15 per cent. Selecting and registering for VAT in a member state with a low rate of VAT means that the non-EU business could account for and pay VAT at the lower rate on all its supplies to non-businesses in the EU, as opposed to supplying its electronic services at the rate prevalent in each member state and predominately above that rate.

The UK VAT legislation under Sch. 1 to VATA 1994 enables businesses which are not registered for VAT in the UK, but who perform their business through a branch or agency in the UK, to be VAT registered in the UK. Once VAT registered, a non-EU business is not able to use the special scheme for accounting for VAT, but would be entitled to charge VAT at the rate of 20 per cent on all of its supplies to non-business EU customers. This would be a terrific saving if all of its customers were based in Sweden or Denmark where the VAT rate is 25 per cent or Hungary where the VAT rate is 27 per cent.

The mechanics for VAT registration and applying to use the special scheme for non-EU businesses are contained in VAT *Information Sheet* 7/03 (14 May 2003). Various later *Information Sheets* contain further guidance on the scheme.

Businesses that register under the special scheme will receive their own unique identification number which begins with the prefix 'EU'. Non-EU businesses can be registered under the special scheme prior to making any supplies of electronically supplied services and once application is made would normally receive their unique identification number within a working week.

Declarations are submitted electronically every calendar quarter and are required to be submitted within 20 days after the end of the quarter to which they relate. Nil declarations are required to be submitted. There is a dedicated website for submitting the declaration, which is password-protected to provide security.

For each EU member state in which the business has supplied electronically supplied services, the declaration must state the total value of the supplies in the period, excluding any VAT, the VAT rate that applies and the total amount of VAT payable.

Clearly non-EU businesses which have little or no other trade in the EU will need to keep abreast of the different VAT rates and changes as they occur to ensure that they continue to charge VAT in the correct country at the correct rate.

Interestingly, the special scheme does not allow for any VAT to be recovered in any EU member state by non-EU businesses and only provides for payment of the VAT due on sales to their EU customers. Given the problem that non-EU businesses face in recovery of VAT on expenses such as marketing, advertising, general business development, etc., particularly with regard to submitting claims to all the different EU member states in the different languages of those jurisdictions, this would have been an ideal time to abolish the 13th VAT Directive and enable VAT claims to be made via the special scheme. However, this is not to be, and non-EU businesses are still lumbered with making the 13th VAT Directive claim, which has been shown from past experience to involve a considerable amount of time, effort and wasted energy when those claims are not paid.

Payments under the special scheme are made at the same time the declaration is submitted. These are required to be made via the business's bank and paid electronically to (in the UK) HMRC's bank account. In the UK, businesses registered for this special scheme are required to submit declarations and payments in sterling. Clearly this could be a disadvantage to businesses supplying their electronic services in other EU countries which use the euro, as exchange rates may not be beneficial. The converse is also true. Conversions from other currencies into sterling are expected to be made using the exchange rates published by the European Central Bank for the last day of the reporting period to which the declaration relates or, if no such rate is published for that day, for the next day for which such a rate is published.

Non-EU businesses which register for the special scheme are required to keep records to enable each jurisdiction to verify that the VAT declaration and admissions made are correct. These records are required to be maintained electronically and must be submitted to either the tax jurisdiction from which the special scheme is operated or the jurisdiction where the customer belongs.

Planning point

Non-EU businesses should consider very carefully their requirement to be VAT registered. Selection of the special scheme of registration may be applicable, but registering for VAT in one EU member state may give them the opportunity to account for VAT in that member state in respect of supplies of electronically supplied services to non-business EU persons, which may have definite advantages over the special scheme.

Dealing with Agents

27.1 Special supplies

27.1.1 Staff supplied by an agency

Until 2009, VAT had been accounted for on the supply of temporary staff supplied by an agency by the value of the commission only. No VAT was charged on the value of the salary paid to, or taxes paid on behalf of, the temporary staff member. The so-called temporary staff concession changed, and from 2009 HMRC required VAT to be accounted for on the value of the commission, salary and taxes where an agency provided staff on a temporary basis. This is because HMRC regarded that the agency supplying the staff was acting as a principal under the Conduct of Employment Agencies and Employment Businesses Regulations 2003 (SI 2003/3319).

The First Tier Tax Tribunal has given a decision that now questions this treatment in particular circumstances. In *Reed Employment Ltd* [2010] TC 01069 it was held that VAT was only due on the value of the commission. HMRC may appeal this decision. In addition, the Tribunal also stated that HMRC could rely on the unjust enrichment principals that would effectively prevent VAT that had been accounted for in earlier periods from being reclaimed.

There are, however, defences to unjust enrichment, particularly if it can be shown that an economic/market price is charged rather than VAT being added to a fee. Thus, there may be opportunities to make backdate claims and, in addition, VAT costs can be reduced in the future.

The Tribunal found that it was not possible to consider the principal/agent position without first considering the economic reality of the transactions and relationships. The arrangement was to be viewed as a whole. In addition, the Tribunal held that Reed did not control the temporary workers. Consequently, Reed could not pass control of the workers to the hirer as it did not have that control to pass. The temporary workers came under the control of the hirer. The Tribunal had held that the obligations of the temporary worker only started once it started employment with the hirer. Thus, Reed was not supplying temporary workers but providing introductory services. As a consequence, the amounts paid by Reed to the temporary worker were made on behalf of the hirer and not part of Reed's supply. VAT was, therefore, due on the commission paid to Reed and any other payments that were made to Reed that did not relate to the relationship between the hirer and the temporary employee. For example, holiday pay and loyalty bonuses were paid to temporary workers by Reed, but these did not relate to any specific payments made by the hirer for the temporary workers' services. Thus, they were part of the consideration for the introductory services.

> **Planning point**
>
> Consider the economic relationship between the parties to determine which elements bear VAT.

If VAT has been accounted for on supplies of temporary staff, consider the relationship and determine if a VAT refund claim can be made and if VAT needs to be charged on salary and tax elements in the future.

The Tribunal stated that, the economic reality had to be considered, as per the European Court's judgment in the joined cases of *R & C Commrs v Loyalty Management UK Ltd; R & C Commrs v Baxi Group Ltd* (Cases C-53/09 and C-55/09) [2011] BVC 1. This required the arrangements between the three parties (Reed, the temporary worker and the hirer) to be viewed objectively as a whole. Because the economic reality was that there was only an introductory service then VAT was only due on the introductory commission and not the value of the 'disbursements' for wages and taxes paid by Reed and passed on to the hirer.

27.1.2 Tripartite supplies

The House of Lords decision in *C & E Commrs v Redrow plc* [1999] BVC 96 determined that more than one party can be the recipient of a supply of services. In this case, Redrow not only paid the estate agent's fees for persons purchasing one of their new houses but were also involved in instructing the estate agent. They were, therefore, entitled to recover the VAT incurred on the estate agent's charges as they contracted for them. It is not enough to simply pay the bill; the person claiming the VAT must be able to show that the supply was made to him. As Redrow had made specific arrangements with the estate agent, in this instance it was seen to be enough to permit Redrow to reclaim the VAT incurred on the estate agent's fees, even though it is also true that the estate agent will have supplied services to the vendor of the house (the person that was buying a house from Redrow).

This decision has a significant advantage as it would appear to permit a person that can reclaim VAT to arrange supplies for a person that cannot reclaim VAT and claim back the VAT incurred, thus creating a significant saving. This has, however, always been a difficult decision to apply and one that has met with some 'pushback' from HMRC. It could have been argued, and probably was, that there was only one supply by the estate agent and that was to the vendor of the house; Redrow did not receive anything but only made the payment for the supply made. The principle that had been established, however, was that if a third party arranged the supply then it could also reclaim the VAT incurred.

This principle has recently suffered a setback in the European Court of Justice in the decisions of *Loyalty Management UK Ltd* (Case C-53/09) and *Baxi Group Ltd* (Case C-55/09). Loyalty Management UK Ltd (LMUK) operated a loyalty scheme, the

Nectar card scheme. A customer using a Nectar card when making purchases could collect points electronically from retailers participating in the scheme. The customer could then redeem the points with a supplier of the redemption goods. The supplier of the redemption goods expected a payment from LMUK for this supply of goods. LMUK argued that the payment was for the service of supplying the redemption goods and it, LMUK, could reclaim the VAT incurred. HMRC argued, successfully, that the payment was not for this service but for the provision of the goods to the customer; it was third party consideration for the redeemed goods. Thus, LMUK could not reclaim the VAT incurred. The only person that could reclaim the VAT was the customer. As the customer was invariably an end consumer there was a VAT cost as no VAT could be reclaimed.

The Baxi case was similar but concerned the supply of boilers to plumbers and the provision of reward goods against points accumulated for every Baxi boiler installed. Baxi was also not able to reclaim VAT on the cost of the loyalty goods provided, but it was able to reclaim VAT on the value of service provided to it by the redemption company. There was a value attributed to this service and VAT on that value was recoverable.

It would appear from these decisions that the use of tripartite arrangements is very restricted if not now 'dead'. This can affected many businesses, particularly those operating reward schemes or where the lease costs of third parties are paid in property transactions.

27.2 Agency

27.2.1 Introduction

Like tripartite transactions there are three entities involved in an agency relationship. There is no legal definition of agency. Agency is characterised as somebody acting for or on behalf of another person or representing that person to a third party. An agent is arranging the transaction (sale or purchase) on behalf of another party; the agent does not take possession of goods or alter the goods or services supplied. A tripartite relationship (see **27.1.2**) does not have anybody acting for another person; it is a relationship between three parties each making or receiving their own supplies. A person describing himself as an agent may not be an agent (e.g. an travel agent may act as a principal in buying and selling the holiday or travel facility, or may act as an agent in arranging the transaction). A lawyer or accountant will normally act as a principal and would not normally describe himself as an agent, but may agree to represent a client in a transaction and arrange supplies for their client.

In agency there are usually three parties involved;

(1) the principal – the supplier of the goods or services;

(2)   the agent – the intermediary that acts for or represents the principal; and

(3)   the customer/recipient – the recipient of the goods or services supplied by the principal.

This describes a selling agency, where the agent is acting for a principal that is going to supply goods or services. The situation could just as easily be reversed: in a buying agency, the agent will represent the customer (who now becomes the principal) to the supplier of the goods or services. It should also be noted that the agent may be a disclosed or an undisclosed agent. Where the agent is a disclosed agent, the customer will know who the principal is. When acting as an undisclosed agent the customer will not know who the principal is and will, for all intents and purposes, believe that he is dealing with the principal when they are actually dealing with an agent.

There is also no legal definition of agent. An agent/principal relationship exists where the parties agree that it exists and the agent has agreed with the principal to act on his behalf. The arrangement may be written, oral or inferred from the relationship between the parties and the way they have acted. The agent is to arrange the transactions only; it is not trading in the goods or services supplied, nor owns the goods, uses the goods or services or alters them. It was held in *C & E Commrs v Johnson* (1980) 1 BVC 338 that agency is the 'relationship which exists between two persons, one of whom expressly or implied consents that the other should represent him or act on his behalf and the other of whom similarly consents to represent the former or so to act'.

Planning Point

Review your relationships with your 'customers' and 'suppliers' to determine if you are acting as an agent or principal. Whether you are acting as an agent or a principal will alter they way you account for VAT.

27.2.2   An Agent's Supplies

An agent is involved in two supplies:

- the agency service to the principal for which it charges a fee or receives a commission; and
- the supply of goods or services from the principal to the customer (where the agent is acting as a selling agent).

The supply made by the agent will normally be subject to VAT at the standard rate (it may not where the principal, the person that the agent supplies his services to, is based overseas). The supply of the goods or services by the principal will bear its own normal VAT liability.

It should be noted that an agent may be a buying or selling agent. The agent may act for the principal in buying goods or services or may act for the principal in selling the principal's goods and services. It is more usual for the agent to be a selling agent and this section deals with agency from the perspective of a selling agent, but the same principles apply to a buying agent.

Example 27.1

Andy's agency acts as an agent for Peter's meat packers. Andy finds customers for Peter and charges Peter five per cent for all sales arranged by him. Andy has organised a consignment of meat to be supplied to Charlie. Charlie agrees to pay £1,000 and pays this to Andy, as the arranging agent. Andy passes this amount on to Peter. No VAT is charged on this amount as the supply of meat is zero-rated. Andy also charges Peter £50 as his commission. This amount is subject to VAT of £10.

Most businesses described as agencies are not treated as agencies for VAT purposes. A real estate agent (estate agent) represents his client (the property vendor) to potential customers. The estate agent does not, however, make a supply of property from his client to the purchaser. The vendor (the principal) will make the sale/make the supply to the purchaser. The estate agent will charge a fee or commission to the principal, but will not be involved in the particular VAT accounting that is described below. A travel agent may represent a travel company or several travel companies, but it does not usually make a supply to the ultimate customer. The travel company will usually make a charge for the travel or holiday direct to the customer. The agent will recover its fee from the travel company; in these circumstances the agent is acting as an intermediary merely introducing the two parties. There are, however, numerous different ways that travel companies and travel agencies manage their fees and commissions. It is possible that the travel agent will act as an agent. If it is acting as an agent (as defined for VAT) then it will need to follow the rules described below.

27.2.3   Disclosed Agents

As the name infers, the role of the agent is disclosed and the name of the principal will be known to the customer. The agent often takes a small part in the transaction merely introducing the principal and customer, but it may take a greater part in the supply by holding stocks or delivering goods. The principal will normally invoice the customer for the supply. The agent's supplies are then limited to the service to the principal. The value of that supply, or the consideration received, is the amount that is subject to VAT, the amount that counts towards the VAT registration threshold and other thresholds. The value of the supply of goods or services from the principal to the customer are not supplies made by the agent when they are invoiced direct to the customer by the principal.

27.2.4   Undisclosed Agents

An entity acting as an undisclosed agent does not usually reveal that they are acting in this capacity. They are authorised to act by the principal and can commit a principal to make supplies and may also be able to enter into contracts with third parties on behalf of the principal. Where the principal remains anonymous it will clearly be necessary for the agent to invoice the customer for any supplies made (or receive the invoices for purchases made on behalf of the principal).

Although the transaction remains between the principal and the customer (or vendor) in legal and commercial terms, the transaction is treated differently for VAT; the treatment differs for goods and services and whether the transaction is within the EU. In most circumstances the supply is treated as being made by the agent. Thus, the agent will account for the VAT due on the supply and will make a charge to the principal. For supplies within the UK VAT is accounted for on the supply of goods by the agent and to the agent in the same VAT period; supplies involving transactions that take place fully or partly outside the UK are dealt with differently (see below). As the nature of the supply has not changed the VAT by the use of an agent, the VAT on the supply to the agent and by the agent is the same. Thus, the input tax and output tax will net off in the VAT period. VAT on the supply of the goods by the agent cannot be accounted for in a different period from the supply of the goods to the agent. The agent can invoice his agency services to the principal in a different period. The VAT liability of the agency services may differ from that of the underlying supply.

Example 27.2

Joe is an agent to Frank. Frank supplies, through his agent Joe, widgets to Winston for £5,000 plus VAT in the VAT period ending 31 March 2013. Frank has to account for £1,000 in output tax and issue an invoice to Joe in the VAT period ending 31 March 2013. Joe can reclaim the £1,000 in input tax in the same VAT period (ending 31 March 2013) but must also account for £1,000 output tax in that same period on the supply of the widgets to Winston. Winston can reclaim the VAT he has been charged according to the normal rules. Joe will also issue an invoice (for, say, £750 plus VAT) to Frank for his commission and charge VAT on this. Joe may issue the invoice and account for the VAT either in the period ending 31 March 2013 or in a later period.

Where the transaction involves an intra-EU supply or a supply from outside the EU the supply must be accounted for differently. It should also be noted that a wholly UK transaction can also be treated in this manner if the agent wishes. In these circumstances, the supply is treated as being made from the principal to the agent and then to the customer. There is no separate supply of agency services. Thus, in the example above, if Frank is based outside the UK and is not VAT registered in the UK, the supply would be seen as being a supply for £4,250 from the principal (Frank) to Joe (that is £5,000 less £750). Joe will then make a supply for £5,000 to Winston. No commission invoice is to be issued. If the goods are imported then the person importing (usually Frank, the agent), will declare the goods at the import value of £4,250; or in the case of an acquisition from the EU, the acquisition will be declared at that value. All the UK costs, such as warehousing and transport will be incurred by Frank, the agent, and he can reclaim the VAT he is charged subject to the normal rules.

The same rules, broadly and in practice, apply for services.

Law: VATA 1994, s. 47(3)

27.2.5 Disbursements

A charge for a disbursement is not a supply for VAT purposes. A disbursement, however, has a limited meaning for VAT, and items described as disbursements for commercial purposes often are not disbursements for VAT. An incidental cost to a supply is regarded as being part of the main supply for VAT. Even if the charge is billed separately the payment for the supply will be treated as further consideration for the main supply. A disbursement for VAT purposes is where an amount is paid to a third party as an agent for the client/principal. The cost, however, must be a cost of the client/principal.

Example 27.3

Sue, a lawyer, has two clients. Sue has to fly from London to Glasgow for client one. Sue's time costs for the job were £2,500 and the flight cost £250. No VAT was incurred on the flight (as it is zero-rated passenger transport). When Sue charges client one she charges £2,500 for her time and £250 for the flight, a total of £2,750. VAT is charged on the full value; 20 per cent of £2,750 = £550, a total invoice of £3,300. This is because the flight is not a disbursement for VAT purposes (even though Sue may describe it as such on her invoice to client one). It is a part of Sue's cost for providing the service of legal services. Her invoice has broken down the cost into time cost and expenses to fully explain the fee to the client. The flight was not a fee incurred for the client, it was a fee incurred to enable Sue to do her job and as such the recharge is further consideration for the legal service and VAT is charged on this even though no VAT was incurred on the cost.

Sue has a second client. Sue has to go to court to represent client two. A court fee of £250 (no VAT) is incurred on behalf of the client to enable the client to go to court. Sue incurs time costs of £2,500 for client two. When Sue charges client two she charges £2,500 plus VAT plus a disbursement for the court fee of £250 with no VAT. The court fee is a disbursement for VAT purposes as the cost is the responsibility of client two and was paid to the court by Sue on behalf of client two. The invoice to client two will be for £2,500 for legal services, VAT of £500 and a non-VAT chargeable disbursement of £250 making a total of £3,250.

Review of Business for VAT Issues

28.1   Regular review

28.1.1   Introduction

Strictly speaking, regular review is a non-subject, as effective VAT planning needs to be a constant process, or continual revolution, as someone once put it.

However, this is a counsel of perfection and unlikely to be achieved in the real world. It is therefore well worth setting up a programme of regular review of the VAT position and possible planning steps, with an eye both to compliance and to obtaining any VAT advantages which are available.

In terms of the general approach to VAT planning, the review process is largely to do with ascertainment of the existing facts and likely developments and, to a lesser extent, with analysis of the technical VAT position. If neither the facts nor the law (or the current interpretation of the law as demonstrated by decisions of the courts or publications by HMRC) have changed, then there is unlikely to be fresh planning work to be carried out.

The review process need not consume a great deal of time or effort, unless it transpires that there is indeed something to be done.

28.1.2   Formal review triggers

It is as well to set some diary dates to give special consideration to VAT, such as the following.

1.   Shortly before the end of each VAT period.

2.   Shortly before the end of the VAT year (31 March, 30 April or 31 May, depending on the business's stagger, unless some other year end has been specifically agreed with HMRC).

3.   Shortly before the end of the financial accounting year.

4.   Prior to audits (whether internal, external or by HMRC).

5.   When soaking in the bath, or listening to music, or just daydreaming. The best ideas often turn up when we are relaxed, rather than sitting seriously at a desk. Presumably, this sort of review does not appear in the diary, but it is important to allow the possibility of it.

It is suggested that all VAT returns should be reviewed prior to submission to ensure that it does not appear unusual. Is it out of line with other returns? Is output tax lower (or higher) than expected, is input tax higher or lower than expected? Is an unusually large payment being made, or a smaller one than normal? If there are such changes and there has been no change to the business pattern, it is suggested that the return should be reviewed to determine why it is different than expected. Furthermore, where there have been unusual activities, such as the purchase of new equipment, or the sale of old equipment, the return should be checked to ensure these have been accounted for correctly. Any transactions, such as these, that are outside the normal range of transactions run the risk of being excluded from the normal accounting where VAT is picked up and accounted for. Reviewing journals and cash books is a fruitful source for locating errors.

In addition, VAT returns should be compared to previous returns and the return for the corresponding four previous years. For example, a quarterly VAT period ending 31 March should be compared to the previous period (ending 31 December) to see if there is a marked change in output tax, input tax or inputs and outputs, as well as any intra-community acquisitions and dispatches). There may be differences, of course due to seasonal variations. This March period should also be compared to previous March periods over the past four or five years to identify any significant changes that cannot be explained by changes in business volume. Completing a graph showing input tax, output tax and net payments over a number of periods can also show trends and identify significant variations.

Checks should also be made to ensure that output tax is 20 per cent of sales and that input tax is 20 per cent of inputs less non-taxable items such as wages, finance costs and non-taxed rents. Where systems permit running an exception report to identify VAT that is not 20 per cent of costs and supplies made is also useful in identifying errors.

Professional advisers might like to add some further times for making enquiries on matters which may have VAT (and other) implications, such as:

- any meeting with the client;
- accounts preparation;
- accounts finalisation;
- tax return preparation; and
- tax return finalisation.

These are all, however, more a safety net than anything else. Once initial planning has been done, proper planning should only arise when there is a change in the law or the circumstances or (preferably) when such a change is spotted before it actually comes over the horizon.

> **Planning point**
>
> Periodic reviews are a good time to look, not only at the future, but also at the past, to see whether developments in case law reveal past overpayments which can be reclaimed. This is particularly important now that repayments are subject to the three-year capping provisions.

28.1.3 Formal review process

The essential aim of the review process is to discover whether anything has changed (or is going to change) either in terms of the business itself or in technical terms which might invalidate previous planning, or change its emphasis.

The planner will therefore need to revisit previous planning (whether or not embodied in formal reports) in the light of whatever information is currently available. This will include such information sources as:

- accounts data and reconciliations between accounting results and VAT returns;
- management accounts and forecasts;
- internal publications;
- information received from colleagues, whether formally or informally;
- results of VAT control visits and resultant correspondence with HMRC; and
- the planner's own technical knowledge, based on initial training and ongoing technical reading.

28.1.4 Ad hoc review triggers

True VAT planning is concerned with handling the changes which occur, either because of changes in the way a business operates or is structured, or because of changes in the legislation and its interpretation. If the original VAT planning was properly done and nothing has changed, then no fresh planning needs to be done.

> **Planning point**
>
> The essential step is to have some means of becoming aware of changes and monitoring these with VAT in mind. The means to be adopted are various and will depend on the size and type of the organisation, and the position of the VAT planners within it (or, where external professional advisers are used, outside it).

28.1.5 Business developments

The planner needs to become aware of the kinds of business developments which are likely to give rise to a need for VAT planning before they occur. The main kinds of developments concerned are those set out at **1.7**. It will be seen that many of these involve transactions of types which will often be initiated and negotiated in conditions of great secrecy.

> **Planning point**
>
> It is essential, if the planner is to find out about these in time for planning to be effective, that the planner wins the ear and the confidence of senior management and that they in turn are aware of the need for successful planning to be done before the transactions and structures are finalised, and of both the possible costs of a failure to plan and the benefits to be obtained from successful planning.
>
> This may well necessitate an ongoing campaign of promoting the VAT function within the organisation. The precise approach to this will depend heavily on the nature and culture of the organisation and on the individuals involved.

28.1.6   Technical developments

In order to be effective the planner needs to maintain technical awareness, particularly with regard to the application of VAT to the particular sectors in which the organisation operates. Possible sources include the following.

1. Documents of current record, such as *CCH VAT News*. These include information such as HMRC's press releases and *Revenue & Customs Briefs*, reports of court cases, statutory instruments, etc.

2. HMRC's *VAT Notices* and *Information Sheets*.

3. *VAT Notes* (issued by HMRC with VAT returns).

4. The legislation itself, as updated for amendments.

5. Lectures and seminars.

6. Circulars, technical publications and publicity material emanating from firms of professional advisers.

7. Trade publications covering the organisation's operating sectors, which often feature heavy coverage of developments receiving little attention elsewhere as being of little general interest.

Up-to-date versions of the legislation and HMRC's publications can be obtained from a reporting service such as the *CCH British Value Added Tax Reporter*, available in looseleaf or electronic format.

28.1.7   On the ground

It is not unusual for one person, or a very small department, to have lead responsibility for VAT planning throughout a very large organisation. In such a case it is essential that there are people on the ground (generally financial accounting staff) who can act as the eyes and ears of the planner.

The planner will need to see that these people have the basic tools, in terms of technical awareness and information, plus the motivation to use them, to spot areas where planning may be desirable and bring these to the planner's attention. It is often useful to be sending information to these people on a regular basis, as well as requesting information from them.

> ### *Planning point*
>
> It will generally be useful to ask them for information on potential planning points when completing, for instance, internal VAT returns or copying external ones to headquarters as the case may be. A possibility would be to add a checklist for actual or impending transactions based on the planning triggers in **1.7**, modified to include additional triggers specifically relevant to the organisation concerned.

Once more, the precise approach to be taken varies considerably between organisations. For instance, a very large organisation may be based on an intrinsically simple business process which simply happens to be taking place at a large number of locations. In this case most matters of importance will in any case be known centrally, and the function of the diverse locations (apart from carrying on properly the business itself) will mainly come down to reporting back to the centre according to some centrally-devised rule book.

In other cases the activities carried on can be extremely diverse, and separate locations may have a great deal of autonomy. In this case there is much to be said for a rolling programme of visits to the different locations, to develop personal contacts and discover exactly what is happening, rather than relying on centrally devised reporting which may bear little relationship to the real business activities (and most of which has, in any case, been devised for non-VAT purposes).

There may in any case be much to be said, in the case of a diverse organisation, for having local responsibility for VAT planning rather than seeking to centralise this. However, this may be impossible either because there is, in any case, a single legal entity involved, or because partial exemption considerations dictate a group treatment (while this remains permissible) resulting in a single VAT entity, in either case resulting in an interaction between the VAT treatment of the various parts of the organisation.

28.1.8   Central

As well as having good contacts with local sites, the VAT planner also needs good contacts (and good relations) with central departments of a large organisation, in order to be aware of major developments affecting the whole organisation before they happen (and probably before contacts at a geographically local level know about them).

How best to approach this once more depends very much upon the organisational culture and the individuals concerned. However, it is unlikely that a great deal can be achieved by sending questionnaires, etc. to people who probably know little about VAT, have little concern with it, and are not already reporting basic VAT information such as internal returns.

28.1.9 Marketing department

The reason why marketing can create VAT problems is that the activities involved in marketing, once they go beyond simply buying in some decent advertising, are fundamentally at odds with the simplistic nature of the mechanics of the VAT legislation. The VAT legislation envisages a simplistic model where, throughout the chain of production and distribution, all that happens is:

- A makes a supply to B;
- B makes a supply to C;
- C (ignoring both A and E) makes a supply to D; and
- D makes a supply to E (whom we presume to be the final consumer, rather than exhausting the alphabet).

Marketing sets its face entirely against this simple model, and employs highly creative minds to break out of it. As a typical example, let us suppose that B in the chain is a manufacturer and owner of a brand. B wishes to promote this brand to its market generally (E), regardless of the identity of intermediaries such as C and D. B can (and does) advertise directly to consumers, via TV ads, newspaper ads and the like. This does not cause any particular problems, even though C and D may benefit from the advertising (especially if they are exclusive dealers). Frequently, though, things become much more complex but still with a direct appeal from B to E. This can involve such things as discounts on additional purchases (the discounts being administered along the chain of supply and so involving C and D), cash backs direct to E, complex voucher schemes or whatever marketing departments come up with next. Alternatively, the marketing or product development department may decide to alter the product subtly to enhance is marketability and sales and this may alter the VAT liability. For example, adding chocolate decoration to a biscuit will convert the product from being zero-rated to taxable.

> ### *Planning point*
>
> If the organisation has a marketing department, it is worth paying special attention to this. Marketing departments probably create more potential VAT problems than any other identifiable parts of organisations other than main boards. Despite this, they have little effect on other tax considerations, so are not generally identified as an area for special attention.

Despite some interesting judgments by the ECJ (which does not have to administer the results of its decisions) there is currently no single model, or certain treatment, for many of these schemes and certainly not for the ones which have yet to be devised.

Indeed, the European Court has itself recognised the impossibility of setting out fixed principles to cover all of the possibilities, in the following remark of the Advocate General in *Kuwait Petroleum (GB) Ltd v C & E Commrs* (Case C-48/97) [1999] BVC 250:

> 'I cannot pretend that it is easy to extract from the case law a completely coherent set of rules which it is possible to apply with total confidence to every promotion scheme devised by the ingenuity of commerce. The court has been asked to give rulings of principle on a wide variety of schemes which, in reality, it has had to judge on an ad hoc basis.'

Planning point

With some marketing schemes, it may be possible to make tweaks to bring them within existing precedents (with tolerable certainty). With others, it may be possible to identify a worst-case position and make sure that they still make commercial sense even if this is the one which is ultimately found to apply. With all of them, an analysis of the VAT position is a necessary part of basic commercial planning and risk management (although the marketing folk may not be convinced of this unless they have been stung before).

The basic conclusion remains that marketing departments deliberately and necessarily set out to work in a way which is contrary to the model on which the mechanics of VAT law are based and this inevitably brings them (or their schemes) into conflict with the VAT authorities. It is therefore essential to be in touch with them and preferably have them onside in addressing the VAT issues likely to arise, even if it is only a matter of ensuring that the marketing is likely to be worthwhile even on a worst-case basis.

28.1.10 Regular review: conclusion

Regular review is essential to keep the VAT planning process in line with current needs. Exactly how it should be approached depends very much on both the nature of the organisation and the individuals involved in running it at various levels. A blueprint that was right for one organisation would be wrong for 95 per cent of others and could be wrong for that organisation overnight following a change of top management.

The basic ideas mentioned in this chapter seem, from experience, to be of reasonably general application. Putting them into practice must be a matter of the bespoke rather than the ready-made.

28.2   Changing a business activity: overview

The VAT position needs to be reviewed in advance of significant changes to the business activities carried on by an entity or entities, and the organisation of these. The kinds of changes which may arise include the following.

1.   Changes to the business itself, such as:

   (a)   new lines of business;
   (b)   new terms of business; and
   (c)   doing business in new jurisdictions.

2.   Changes to the business entities or their constitution, such as:

   (a)   sole trader taking in a partner;
   (b)   change of partners;
   (c)   incorporation of a non-incorporated business;
   (d)   changes to a VAT group treatment; and
   (e)   floating a company.

3.   New financing and other major transactions, including:

   (a)   sale of a subsidiary;
   (b)   sale of capital goods (such as land);
   (c)   sale and leaseback of assets; and
   (d)   issue of fresh shares.

4.   Passive changes, such as:

   (a)   major changes in the perceived liability of transactions following clarification of the existing VAT law in the courts; or
   (b)   changes to the legislation itself.

28.3   Changes to the business itself

28.3.1   New lines of business

If an entity decides to start carrying on entirely new lines of business (even if they are economically close to each other) it is time to take a fresh look at the VAT position.

The start point must be to determine the VAT treatment of the new line, as initially envisaged, and to clear any uncertainties associated with this. The next is to determine the impact (if any) on the VAT treatment of the entity as a whole and its relationships with related entities.

> **Planning point**
>
> Care must be taken to take account of other aspects of the proposed setting up of the new line, such as renting or buying-in of property, staff and other services, either from outside or from related entities.

The chances are that everything will be straightforward and, after analysis (of the VAT position, not the people), everyone will agree that no particular changes are needed although any uncertainties identified ought to be cleared with HMRC, and documented as cleared.

On occasion, there will potentially be real changes to the VAT position. These need to be identified and analysed in detail in the same way as on the establishment of a new business. There is the added complication that, in the case of a change to an existing business, there will often be existing entities and arrangements and these existing arrangements may be difficult or costly to change.

It is a fact of life that the VAT planner (like most other planners) cannot usually start with a clean sheet and it is a matter of achieving the best available position rather than a perfect position, particularly when non-VAT factors are taken into account (as they must be).

> **Planning point**
>
> One of the most important points to be made in a work on VAT planning is that there are occasions when, for the benefit of the client, it is important to pay some attention to non-VAT matters.
>
> This is particularly the case if the VAT planner is the first to advise. Once again, this is a matter of dealing with the interactions between taxes, and of the VAT planner being sufficiently aware to raise this requirement when specialists in other fields have not yet given their input (for instance, a VAT planner might, for one reason or another, suggest whizzing a property, or interests in it, around different companies in a group and then find that the wonderful VAT consequences were far outweighed by disastrous direct tax effects).

The important points here are both related to earlier comments on the setting up of a new business. They should be considered at all times in any tax-planning context as:

- the VAT position needs to be considered afresh in the light of the current entities, activities, VAT treatments, etc.; and
- the VAT position cannot be considered in isolation; it is usually a good idea to look at the general commercial position and the direct tax position first, then see how this all fits with the VAT position.

Potential VAT solutions which do not adversely affect other matters can then be considered.

28.3.2 New terms of business

This is really a matter of starting the VAT analysis once more, from the very start, preferably before any new arrangements come into effect.

An example is a company that has previously sold goods as agent for someone else, and now buys the goods and resells them as principal. Clearly the company's turnover is likely to increase by several orders of magnitude, drastically altering the profile of its VAT returns. If it also makes exempt supplies, this is likely to have a considerable effect on its partial exemption position. It may also affect its eligibility for cash accounting.

Depending on the nature of the goods, it may even affect the liability of its supplies. For instance, if the goods concerned are books, the company will now be making zero-rated supplies, whereas previously it made standard-rated supplies of arranging for the sales.

> **Planning point**
>
> Consideration of the effect on a business (partial exemption position and other special schemes, such as cash accounting) should be made where new terms of business are contemplated.

> **Planning point**
>
> The use of different terms of business inevitably can have effects on the VAT position of the business entity, and certainly should not be ignored. Apart from anything else, no one would bother to bring about such changes unless there was a real effect somewhere.

28.3.3 Doing business in new jurisdictions

It is increasingly common for businesses with activities within their own territories to extend these to other territories (within the EU and outside).

> **Planning point**
>
> The VAT consequences of transactions with an international dimension can vary, although not usually adversely for the home registration. These need to be checked, and all necessary formalities put in place to handle any overseas obligations.

28.4   Passive changes

28.4.1   Changes in liability as a result of case law

Changes resulting from case law can sometimes have a substantial effect on the overall status of the business, and the whole of the VAT planning needs to be reviewed when such changes seem likely.

> ### *Planning point*
>
> As a general rule the possibility of substantial change will emerge following a tribunal decision but may take years to become absolute following appeals. HMRC's interim pronouncements need to be monitored carefully so that the business can react accordingly and make contingency plans where necessary.

> ### *Planning point*
>
> HMRC's capping provisions need to be considered. Alterations to VAT paid or claimable are capped at four years (three years prior to 1 April 2010) and whilst an appeal is progressing through the Courts it will be necessary for a business that wishes to make use of the beneficial, or potentially beneficial, decision to submit the necessary claims or account for VAT in the beneficial manner. As a minimum, the business may want to submit a claim to HMRC that it asks HMRC to hold over until the final decision is reached. The business may also wish to notify HMRC of what it is doing to remove the possibility of penalties and reduce interest charges.

For the most part, adverse changes that run counter to HMRC's existing guidance will only have effect from a current (or future) date announced by HMRC.

Beneficial changes counter to HMRC's previous guidance can usually be relied upon retrospectively by persons whose circumstances are the same as those in the litigation concerned. Repayments should be claimed as early as possible, without waiting for the final outcome, to avoid the eventual repayment being reduced under the four years capping regime (three years prior to 1 April 2010).

> ### *Planning point*
>
> Careful consideration should also be given to whether potential repayments may be affected by the unjust enrichment provisions.
>
> If so, it is worth considering applying a favourable tribunal decision as soon as it is known, and risk having a subsequent tax and interest liability if HMRC's view ultimately prevails, rather than being deprived of the fruits of the decision by the unjust enrichment provisions. These can only apply where a repayment is claimed. If the money has never been handed to HMRC in the first instance there can be no unjust enrichment.

> **Planning point**
>
> Before making major changes to the business structures as a result of the outcome of a case, it is worth considering the likely longevity of the change.

If it results from failure of the UK legislation to comply with EU law, then it is likely to be permanent. In the case of purely UK matters, HMRC may introduce new legislation to restore the position that it regards as correct.

28.4.2   Changes to the legislation

For obvious reasons the business and its advisers need to keep themselves aware of potential changes to the legislation which would affect the VAT position, and formulate appropriate responses in terms of the business structures adopted.

28.5   Claims for overpaid VAT

28.5.1   Introduction

At under 40 years old, VAT is still a relatively new tax on the scene. Also, because it is governed from Europe, the UK has limited room for manoeuvre when it comes to writing the rules. These two factors result in frequent changes to the interpretation of the legal provisions, which often result in the realisation that VAT has consistently been overpaid in the past by some businesses. In such circumstances, claims can be made, subject to the four-year cap (three years prior to 1 April 2009).

> **Planning point**
>
> At the time of writing, claims are still outstanding for the refund of VAT overpaid before the introduction of the capping regime. Litigation is ongoing into the extent of claims, but any new claims will be subject to the four-year cap. As part of a review, it should be considered if any VAT can be claimed for overpaid VAT and recent case law considered to determine if any opportunity arises.

A claim will take the form of an error correction declaration and should be reported to HMRC as such. If the overpayment resulted from official error (including HMRC's failure to implement UK or EU law correctly), interest should also be paid by them. Where an error is discovered this can be corrected on the VAT return where the net value of the errors does not exceed £10,000 or if it exceeds this amount but is below £50,000 it does not exceed 1 per cent of the value shown in box 6 of the VAT return. Other notifications can be made by using VAT form 652 and sending it to the VAT

Error Correction Team, HMRC, Queens Dock, 22 Kings Parade, Liverpool, L74 4AA (Phone 0845 601 0904).

Example 28.1

Paul, whose VAT periods end on 31 March, 30 June, 30 September and 31 December, discovers in January 2012 that he has failed to claim any input tax on his leased car over the last two years, whereas he was entitled to 50 per cent of the VAT incurred. The underclaimed amount is £960. In March 2012, he is informed by his auditors that, as a result of the corruption of data on his computer system, he underdeclared his output tax for period 06/08 by £10,650. The box 6 figure on his 03/12 VAT return is £300,000.

As the errors were both discovered in the same VAT period and amount to a sum no greater than £10,000, Paul is entitled to net them off against each other and make an adjustment in HMRC's favour on the 03/12 VAT return of £9,690.

Paul may also choose to notify HMRC of the errors separately from his VAT return; if he does so, HMRC will charge no interest as none would have been due had he corrected the errors on his VAT return.

Under the provisions of the four-year cap, no voluntary disclosure can be made more than four years after the period in which the original error took place. However, the precise method of calculating this is not totally straightforward. The orthodox time limits for making voluntary disclosures vary according to the nature of the error and the status of the VAT return on which the original error took place.

If the error was an overdeclaration, resulting in too high a sum being actually paid to HMRC, in relation either to output tax or to input tax, the four years run from the date on which the payment due with the return on which the error arose was received by HMRC.

If the error was an overdeclaration, resulting in too small a sum being claimed by the trader on a net repayment VAT return, the four years runs from the last day of the VAT period in which the original error took place.

If the error was an underdeclaration, resulting in too small an amount being paid to HMRC or in too large a repayment being claimed, the four years runs from the last day of the VAT period in which the original error took place.

Planning point

The payment of interest does not always happen automatically and sometimes needs to be specifically claimed.

Planning point

If an error results in a net sum due to HMRC, this will normally be processed routinely by HMRC without any enquiries being made. A very simple description of the errors on form VAT 652 is often the best way of dealing with such situations. If the notification relates to an amount repayable to the taxpayer, HMRC will normally require a much greater amount of information to justify releasing the money requested, and a detailed letter explaining the nature of the error(s) is likely to be appropriate, often accompanied by some documentary evidence of what has happened.

Planning point

If a disclosure is notifying tax due to HMRC, there is no requirement to send payment with the disclosure. Once it has been processed by HMRC a demand, together with interest if applicable, will be issued automatically to the registered person. However, it is permissible to send payment with the notification, which has the effect of stopping interest running; those who follow this method need to be aware that a demand for interest will subsequently be received.

Planning point

If a correction of errors relates to a failure to charge output tax on a standard-rated supply in circumstances where the recipient of the supply would have been able to claim the VAT back as input tax had it been correctly charged at the time, HMRC should not require interest to be paid (see *VAT Notice 700/43, para. 2.3*).

Other guidance: *VAT Notice 700/45*

28.5.2   Unjust enrichment

Where a business has overpaid VAT, HMRC can refuse to repay it if they can show that it would unjustly enrich the taxpayer (VATA 1994, s. 80).

This legislation was originally introduced in 1990. From 4 December 1996, regulations were introduced regarding reimbursement of customers who have borne the original VAT charge (VAT Regulations 1995 (SI 1995/2518), reg. 43A–43G). In such cases, suppliers must undertake to reimburse customers with the full amount of VAT and of any interest received by the supplier from HMRC within 90 days of receiving repayment. There is no provision for the making of a handling or other charge – all of the funds must be repaid to the customer that paid the original VAT charge or the refund received from HMRC must be repaid to them within 14 days of the end of the 90-day period. In such cases it is not in the supplier's interest to make a claim for a refund, unless under pressure from customers to do so, or if it can be utilised as a matter of customer care. Suppliers are required to keep a record of all repayments made.

From 19 March 1997, where the VAT has been borne by someone other than the claimant (as is the case where the customer has been charged and has paid the VAT) the claim is restricted to an amount that compensates the claimant for the loss or damage which he has or may incur as a result of mistaken assumptions regarding the operation of any VAT provisions.

The issue of unjust enrichment has been considered by the European Court in the joined cases of *Société Camateb v Directeur Général des Douanes et Droits Indirects* (Joined cases C-192/95 to C-218/95) [1997] ECR I-165. The court ruled that the tax authority of an EU member state could only refuse to repay a charge which had been wrongly levied if that charge had been borne in its entirety by another person and that reimbursement to the supplier would amount to unjust enrichment. But where only a part of the charge had been passed on, the supplier should be reimbursed to the extent of the part which was not passed on.

However, where prices are set at market level regardless of the impact of VAT, and VAT accounted for out of the charge made, then the taxpayer has a just argument for recovery of overpaid VAT. In the case of *King (t/a The Barbury Shooting School)* [2003] BVC 4,039, they started trading as The Barbury Shooting School in 1987 and set their prices according to what they thought customers would pay. They accounted for VAT on their income, but in January 2002 submitted a refund claim for supplies to individuals on the basis that these supplies were exempt from VAT under VATA 1994, Sch. 9, Grp. 6, item 2. Customs accepted that VAT had been overpaid but challenged the refund claim on grounds of unjust enrichment. In deciding that the appellants had not been enriched let alone unjustly, the tribunal reasoned that having received the repayment they would have been no better off than they would have been had they accounted for VAT correctly in the first place, their prices being set according to what the market would stand.

Law: VATA 1994, s. 80(3)–(3C)

Other guidance: VAT Notice 700/4, s. 145

Deregistration

29.1 Introduction

There comes a time when a business eventually ceases, or its turnover falls, and it will wish to consider deregistering for VAT. Similar principles apply for a business that is continuing that may wish to deregister for VAT. For example, if the customers of the business are VAT registered there may be an advantage to continue with the registration. Where the customers cannot reclaim VAT there will be an advantage in deregistering. On deregistration a VAT charge applies to goods that are still on-hand (where VAT had been reclaimed on their purchase or acquisition) subject to a de minimis limit. No VAT incurred after the date of registration can be claimed, although provision has been made for VAT on expenses that relate to the period of registration to be reclaimed where the invoice for the service arrives subsequent to deregistration. VAT must no longer be charged subsequent to deregistration; to charge VAT when no longer registered is an offence.

29.2 Compulsory deregistration

HMRC make the distinction between a person who is required to be deregistered, and a person who wishes to deregister. Where a person ceases to make taxable supplies, or ceases to have the intention of making taxable supplies, he is required to notify HMRC within 30 days of that date. The person will then be deregistered for VAT either from that date or from a later date agreed with HMRC. If he would be registrable under another Schedule, then his registration will not be cancelled on this basis.

Where a person who makes supplies outside the UK is registered in the UK and he either ceases to make such supplies or he intends to cease making such supplies, the person is required to notify HMRC within 30 days. The person will then be deregistered for VAT either from that date or from a later date agreed with HMRC. If he would be registrable under another Schedule, then his registration will not be cancelled.

The deregistration limit is usually £2,000 less than the registration limit. From 1 April 2012, it is £75,000. The list of historic deregistration thresholds is shown at the end of this chapter. It should be noted that the various schemes use different rules for determining turnover, usually this is the gross income and not the margin upon which VAT is calculated, and the scheme rules need to be considered when determining taxable turnover for deregistration. In addition, where income is received from land and buildings any income that is subject to the option needs to be included when calculating turnover.

Where HMRC consider that a person ought not to have been registered, they can deregister him with effect from the date on which he was originally registered. This may be a significant period later and input tax may also be repayable. See *Tourick (RM) & Co* [1992] BVC 825 for a case involving such a matter.

Where a taxable person dies, becomes bankrupt or incapacitated and his business is carried on by another person, a 'personal representative', that person is required to notify HMRC within 21 days (VAT Regulations 1995 (SI 1995/2518), reg. 9 and 30). A personal representative may be an executor, administrator, receiver or liquidator, depending on the specific circumstances. He is responsible for ensuring that all VAT obligations are fulfilled. The personal representative is only liable for VAT over which he has control.

In addition to a business being sold, ceasing to make supplies or being closed, deregistration is required when there is a change in legal entity (such as from sold trader to partnership or vice versa or an un-incorporated business incorporating), or where an intending trader ceases to have an intention to make taxable supplies. In addition, where a person is already VAT registered and wishes to join the agricultural flat-rate scheme the existing VAT registration will be cancelled. Where there is a change in legal entity (or where the business is transferred to another person, the VAT number can be transferred to the new entity if form VAT 68 is completed. It is often advised not to complete this form as when a new VAT registration number is issued and problems with the old number cease thus, if an error was made when registered with the old VAT number, HMRC cannot require a correction to be made by the entity with the new VAT number. It is highly recommended that a new entity taking over a business does not complete form VAT 68 and does not encumber itself with any outstanding problems or VAT debts of the old business.

Notification can be by letter or by using form VAT 7 and must be made within 21 days of the date of the change that required deregistration.

Where the taxpayer makes a combination of taxable supplies, distance sales, acquisitions and/or relevant supplies, deregistration is not permitted deregistaration is permitted for all these supplies and acquisitions.

See **Chapter 4, VAT Implications of different structures** for the issues concerning groups.

The date of deregistration is usually the date taxable supplies are no longer made, the business is sold, or the date when one of the other circumstances detailed above apply.

The form VAT 7 should be sent to:
HM Revenue & Customs
Imperial House
77 Victoria Street
Grimsby
Lincolnshire
DB31 1DB

714

29.3   Failure to deregister

There is a requirement to notify HMRC, within 30 days, of the requirement to deregister from VAT. This includes:

- a registered person ceasing to make taxable supplies, or of his intention to cease making taxable supplies;
- a registered person who was not required to be registered ceasing to make taxable supplies, or of his intention to cease making taxable supplies; and
- a person who makes no taxable supplies, but who is registered under Sch. 1, para. 10 ceasing to make the specified supplies, or of his intention to cease making the specified supplies or who fails to notify HMRC within 30 days that he has made taxable supplies, or intends to make taxable supplies.

Where there is such a failure, the person can be subject to a daily penalty for breach of regulations (see **Chapter 3**).

> ### *Planning point*
>
> Notwithstanding these provisions, it is highly unusual for HMRC to impose a penalty for failure to notify a liability to deregister. A registration will normally be cancelled from the point at which the position is brought to their attention. However, if input tax has been claimed on VAT returns post-dating the cessation date, they may seek to have this repaid, insisting that a post-deregistration (VAT 427) claim is lodged instead.

29.4   Voluntary deregistration

Where a person can satisfy HMRC that his taxable turnover will be lower than the specified limit during the following 12 months, he may apply to be deregistered. The 'specified limit' is – with effect from 1 April 2012– £75,000. This limit lags behind the registration limit and is usually increased each year in the Budget. Historical limits are available in a supplement to *VAT Notice 700/11* and can also be found at the end of this chapter.

Where taxable supplies are wholly or mainly zero-rated a person can apply for deregistration even if these supplies are in excess of the deregistration threshold. If any standard-rated supplies are made HMRC will only permit this where the input tax claimed exceeds any VAT on output tax.

When considering a person's future turnover, the following are to be excluded from the value of his taxable turnover:

- any capital assets which he expects to sell; and
- supplies of distance sales made in the UK (VATA 1994, s. 7(4)).

Any interest in, right over or licence to occupy land, where that is a taxable supply, is to be included.

Where a person makes an application under this section, HMRC will not be satisfied that the person should be deregistered where the reason his taxable turnover will fall below the specified limit is either:

- that the person will cease to make taxable supplies during that period; or
- that the person will suspend making taxable supplies for 30 days or more.

Example 29.1

Joanna makes taxable supplies over the registration threshold. She is notified on 20 May 2010 that with effect from 1 September 2010 those supplies will become exempt.

On 1 June 2010, she writes to HMRC requesting deregistration, on the basis that her taxable turnover in the next 12 months will be below the specified limit. They refuse that application, under Sch. 1, para. 4(2).

She is, however, required to notify HMRC within 30 days of 1 September, that she has ceased making taxable supplies with effect from that date. This requirement is in Sch. 1, para. 11. Upon making such notification, HMRC deregister her with effect from 1 September 2010.

Planning point

It is not uncommon for a person to seek retrospective deregistration under this section. This may occur where a person realises that he or she is no longer required to be registered and their turnover has been reduced for some months. HMRC, supported by the tribunal, have consistently opposed any backdating of deregistration.

HMRC periodically contact persons trading under the specified limit, inviting them to deregister. This is part of their responsibility to manage the VAT register efficiently.

29.5   Consequences of deregistration

Where a person is deregistered, he is not required to complete and submit VAT returns for any periods later than the deregistration date. Thus, he will not be entitled to recover input tax on purchases, nor will he be permitted to issue VAT invoices after the date of deregistration.

The person will be required to complete and submit a return for the period up to the deregistration date. On this return he is required to account for output tax on any assets held in stock at the date of deregistration, where the output tax due on those assets would exceed £1,000. It is not necessary to include in this calculation any such asset where no VAT was incurred or no VAT was claimed on purchase. Note, however, that any stocks and assets purchased VAT-free as part of a transfer of a business as a going concern at an earlier date must be included.

⚠ **Warning!**

It should be noted that where land or any property is subject to the option to tax, VAT will be due on the value of that property on deregistration unless the option can be revoked.

Example 29.2

A business making clothes is about to close down, as its owner, Rebecca, is retiring. The business owns £25,000 worth of machinery, which the owner wants to sell.

If she sells that machinery prior to closure and deregistration, she can charge output tax on the £25,000, which the purchaser can recover.

If she retains the machinery until after closure, she will be liable for an output tax charge on deregistration but any purchaser will be unable to recover that amount as input tax.

Rebecca is therefore advised to defer her date of deregistration until she has sold the machinery. She will need to apply for deregistration to take effect at a date later than the closure of the business, to ensure that the sale of assets precedes deregistration.

Where a person incurs VAT on certain services after deregistration, he is entitled to recover that VAT as input tax, as long as the services relate to his pre-deregistration supplies. Typically, accountants' and solicitors' fees may be invoiced after deregistration. HMRC may require that sufficient evidence of such services be provided. A claim should be made on form VAT 427, accompanied by the actual invoices.

A person may also make a claim in respect of bad debts, where the invoice was issued prior to deregistration but the debt only went bad later.

Other guidance: *VAT Notice 700/18 (2002 edn.)* para. 5.3

29.6　Breach of regulations (VATA 1994, s. 69)

VATA 1994, s. 69 penalises any breach of regulations. This includes the failure to notify deregistration and failure to register under various regulations (for example, for EU acquisitions, or EU dispatches, etc.).

The penalty is calculated by a daily rate, multiplied by the number of days the failure continues, up to a maximum of 100 days or £50, whichever is greater. The daily rate is determined by the number of failures to comply with the requirement during the previous two years. For the first failure, the daily rate is £5, for the second, the rate is £10, for the third and subsequent failures, the rate is £15.

A penalty will not apply where the person is convicted of an offence or assessed for a civil penalty in relation to the same conduct.

> ### *Example 29.3*
>
> Nick is registered under Sch. 1, para. 10, since he makes supplies outside the UK, but is established in the UK. He begins to make similar, taxable supplies in the UK, but fails to notify HMRC of the change, and fails to declare output tax on his VAT returns.
>
> HMRC decide that a civil evasion penalty for dishonest conduct is appropriate. Thus, a penalty under s. 69 cannot be assessed.
>
> If she retains the machinery until after closure, she will be liable for an output tax charge on deregistration but any purchaser will be unable to recover that amount as input tax.

It should be noted that other s. 69 breaches require that a warning letter be issued (VATA 1994, s. 76(2)). There is no such requirement for penalties in respect of registration or deregistration offences.

The legislation refers to a 'continuing failure'. This means that such a failure is regarded as a single failure on the date when it began, i.e. when the person was required to notify HMRC of the change in particulars. The penalty will continue up until the date when the failure was remedied. Where HMRC assess a person for a failure under this section, such an assessment will indicate the date to which the assessment is calculated. If the failure is not remedied by that date, a subsequent assessment may be issued from that date.

The VAT Regulations 1995 (SI 1995/2518), reg. 5(2) requires that a registered person notify any changes of his business particulars (see 3.2.8). Any failure to do so will render the person liable to a penalty (VATA 1994, s. 69(1)(d)). A penalty cannot be issued under this section unless HMRC first issue a warning letter.

Law: VATA 1994, s. 69

29.7   Post-deregistration expenses

VAT incurred on services received after the date of deregistration can be recovered, provided that the services on which it is incurred are used in respect of the business carried on prior to the deregistration taking place. For example, VAT on an accountant's bill for preparing the accounts and tax computation for the final period of trading will be recoverable. Claims are made on form VAT 427 and must be submitted with the original invoices. HMRC request that claims are made within six months; however, a claim can be made provided it is not more than four years (three years before 1 April 2010) after the date of registration and there is a reasonable explanation for any delay. The form can also be used to claim input tax on goods and services supplied prior to deregistration which has not already been recovered on a VAT return, e.g. if the correct evidence was not held at the time the final return was submitted.

Claims should be submitted to:
HM Revenue and Customs
Accounting Adjustments (VAT 427 team)
3rd Floor South
Queens Dock
Liverpool
L74 4AA

> ### ⚠ *Warning!*
>
> One issue that has thwarted many claims is that the partial exemption *de minimis* limits (see **12.11**) do not apply post deregistration. This means that if VAT is incurred on an exempt supply, such as legal fees on the sale of the business premises, it is not recoverable. If possible, these types of expenses, when below the *de minimis* limits should be incurred prior to deregistration.

VAT incurred on goods purchased after the date of deregistration is not recoverable. Also, purchasing goods prior to the registration cancelled is unlikely to be beneficial as any goods on hand will be subject to a VAT charge on deregistration.

29.8   Deregistration Limits

1 May 1993 – 30 November 1993	£36,000
1 December 1993 – 29 November 1994	£43,000
30 November 1994 – 28 November 1995	£44,000
29 November 1995 – 26 November 1996	£45,000
27 November 1996 – 29 November 1997	£46,000
30 November 1997 – 31 March 1998	£47,000

1 April 1998 – 31 March 1999	£48,000
1 April 1999 – 31 March 2000	£49,000
1 April 2000 – 31 March 2001	£50,000
1 April 2001 – 24 April 2002	£52,000
25 April 2002 – 9 April 2003	£53,000
10 April 2003 – 31 March 2004	£54,000
1 April 2004 – 31 March 2005	£56,000
1 April 2005 – 31 March 2006	£58,000
1 April 2006 – 31 March 2007	£59,000
1 April 2007 – 31 March 2008	£62,000
1 April 2008 – 30 April 2009	£65,000
1 May 2009 – 31 March 2010	£66,000
1 April 2010 – 31 March 2011	£68,000
1 April 2011 – 31 March 2012	£71,000
1 April 2012 to date	£75,000

Administration

30.1 Introduction

In this chapter, a number of administrative issues are drawn together, with some recommendations on how best to approach the issues.

30.2 Rulings

HMRC are willing to provide rulings in respect of liability issues, etc. However, a number of complications can be encountered in the process, to the point that many advisers hesitate to apply for one except in exceptional circumstances.

HMRC generally refuse to answer hypothetical questions, which can be deemed to include any transaction which has not yet taken place. Rulings given are often qualified to the point of being almost worthless. Alternatively, they take the sublimely unhelpful form of a reply along the lines of:

> 'We enclose the relevant public notice; if the relevant transaction falls within the conditions stated, it will qualify for zero-rating.'

More recently, some letters have been framed in terms approximating to:

> 'VAT is a self-assessed tax, and it is therefore your responsibility to make a judgement on the VAT liability of the transaction concerned.'

There is also a tendency for HMRC to insist that they will not be bound by a ruling unless they have been given all relevant facts. Whilst understandable, this provides a valuable get-out clause for future use. It must be conceded that HMRC have had their fingers burnt more than once in the past and must protect themselves, but the pendulum has arguably swung too far the other way.

In August 2003, HMRC published *VAT Notice 700/6* in which they set out the information they will require before issuing a ruling in any given case. Their reasons for imposing conditions are entirely understandable, but it is nonetheless regrettable that the effect is to make the process of obtaining a ruling more time-consuming and lengthy.

The following extract illustrates how cumbersome a process applying for a ruling has now become:

'2.3 How do I get a VAT ruling?

When requesting a ruling on VAT from us, you must write to us, providing the following information:

- your business name and VAT number; (advisers – you should give these details for any business(es) on whose behalf you are writing);
- the full facts and context concerning the transactions or issues in question – see paragraph 2.4 below;
- the intended use of the decision.

    But please note – we do not give general rulings, and will only be bound in respect of the taxpayer who sought the ruling, or on whose behalf the ruling was sought, unless clearly stated otherwise – see paragraph 2.1.1 below; and

- your statement that, to the best of your knowledge and belief, the facts you have given are correct and that the full facts and relevant information have been disclosed.

2.4 What information do I need to give?

For a ruling to be binding, we must be put in possession of the "full facts" and context of the transaction or issues in question by you and/or your adviser at the time the ruling is sought – see also paragraph 3.3. The responsibility for ensuring that this is fulfilled rests with you and your adviser. We are happy to give you a ruling, whether or not you use a tax adviser.

The information that you will need to give depends on the circumstances of the individual case. If you are in any doubt about whether a particular item is relevant you should disclose it.

Please include:

- a clear explanation of the precise point(s) about which you are unclear of the tax consequences;
- where you have received professional advice in respect of the tax question on which you are seeking a ruling, you must tell us the reason for uncertainty;
- if you or your professional advisers have considered alternative tax treatments, you should give a brief indication of the alternative interpretations considered;
- if the point at issue concerns a transaction which has yet to take place, you should provide a copy of the final draft contract, where appropriate, and full details of the other parties involved to the extent that this is possible;
- where a ruling is sought before contracts are finalised, a ruling may still be given, but will not be binding if a contract is produced later and the relevant facts vary significantly from those disclosed (paragraph 3.3 below). You should come back to us to review our ruling where the relevant terms of the contract have changed;
- copies of all of the relevant documents with what **you consider to be** the relevant areas clearly highlighted (or otherwise drawn attention to);
- (so that we can target our resources appropriately) an estimate of the money associated with the decision, for example, the annual value of sales of an item, in respect of which you want a ruling on the liability to tax; and
- any transactions (proposed or actual) related to, consequent upon, or forming part of a series with the transaction in respect of which a ruling is sought, whether or not these transactions are certain to take place.'

In addition, HMRC list certain situations in which they will not give a ruling, including:

- giving rulings on hypothetical transactions or 'what if?' questions;
- approving tax planning arrangements;
- matters that do not involve genuine points of doubt or difficulty; and
- matters that are covered by VAT notices or other published guidance.

Regrettably, when all these factors have been taken into account, it can be seen that the system is not organised in such a way as to make obtaining a ruling of any value straightforward or even, in some cases, possible at all.

> **Planning point**
>
> There are strong reasons for avoiding seeking rulings in as many cases as possible and, for those who are not VAT specialists, relying on advice from a competent adviser instead.

30.3 Claims for overpaid VAT and correcting errors

30.3.1 Error correction

Error correction is discussed in **Chapter 28.**

Other guidance: VAT Notice 700/45

30.4 Repayment supplement

Repayment supplement is an additional sum payable by HMRC to a VAT-registered person where delays arise in meeting a repayment claimed on a VAT return.

HMRC are obliged to pay the supplement, which is calculated at 5 per cent of the refund due, if more than 30 days are taken after receiving the return to make repayment (allowing for reasonable enquiries).

Essentially, the 30-day clock stops running at the point where HMRC first make contact with the trader and restarts when satisfactory responses have been received to any reasonable queries which they raise concerning the repayment.

HMRC are very aware of their responsibilities in regard to the prompt repayment of such VAT claims (something which regrettably cannot be said of refunds requested by voluntary disclosure, which are not subject to this regime). For this reason they take detailed notes of all action taken to verify claims before they are authorised, such as telephone calls, delays in arranging visits to check the records, etc., in order to demonstrate that they are not responsible for any slowness in making repayment.

Repayment supplement is not payable in circumstances where the return is rendered late or, as a result of HMRC's checks, it is established that the amount actually due to be repaid is less than the amount claimed by more than 5 per cent of the correct amount or £250, whichever is the greater.

> **Planning point**
>
> If a repayment supplement is due, it may not necessarily be paid automatically by HMRC. It is therefore advisable for a business making a repayment claim to maintain its own record of events and dates, so as to make a claim for the supplement if it is thought to be due.

30.5   Time-to-pay agreements

From time to time traders find themselves in a position where their full VAT liability cannot be paid. If approached properly at the right time, HMRC's debt management units (DMUs) – now centralised regionally – can be very helpful in agreeing time to pay. Initially, requests for assistance for payment problems must be made through the National Advice Service (0845 010 9000) who will direct the caller to the debt management unit.

> **Planning point**
>
> HMRC have, in the current economic downturn become more lenient with time to pay arrangements. The new Business Payment Support Service are very flexible. HMRC comment "VAT default surcharges will not be charged if the business contacts us before the payment is due and agrees a time to pay arrangement. Entering into the time to pay arrangement will not be treated as a default so it will not extend the 12 month rolling period nor will the default percentage increase because of the time to pay arrangement, provided the terms of the arrangement are adhered to."

As often as possible, some payment, as an earnest of good faith, should be made with the relevant return, voluntary disclosure, etc. A written proposal for set sums to be paid over a given period of time can then be sent to the DMU. HMRC appear to work to a normal 12-week maximum for the discharge of most debts, ensuring that the liability is discharged before the next return and payment are due, but an initial proposal will often request a longer timescale.

Planning point

Under normal economic circumstances HMRC expect to see firm evidence of the fact that there is no other available source of funding, i.e. copies of bank statements and a letter from the bank stating that it is unwilling to make a loan or extend the overdraft facility. Any taxpayer in default should seriously consider all other options before trying to gain long-term funding by way of a time-to-pay agreement with HMRC.

Any proposal should take into account future liabilities and perhaps suggest a longer gap between payments at the time the next return is due. Normally, a compromise is reached that is acceptable to both parties, and the time taken over the necessary exchanges of correspondence can provide a welcome breathing space itself.

Planning point

Although HMRC may enter into such agreements late in the day, when they have begun to enforce the debt, it is far better to take the initiative and start the ball rolling before this point is reached.

Planning point

If the gross debt exceeds £100,000, it will be dealt with by the national debt management office in Northampton, rather than a regional office. Experience current at the time of writing indicates that, assuming full cooperation and ready communication, they can be very flexible in negotiations.

30.6   Bad-debt relief

Bad-debt relief in the context of VAT is effectively a method of government compensation. Output VAT is due on supplies which have been made, regardless of whether or not payment is made for the supply. For any business not on cash accounting, therefore, a VAT liability arises in respect of every supply at a positive rate of VAT. By way of an exception to this basic principle, the government permits any VAT accounted for to be reclaimed from HMRC in the event of non-payment. This prevents the supplier suffering twice, once from non-receipt of the monies due to them and also from the need to account for VAT out of their own resources.

VAT relief is available six months after the due date for payment of the supply concerned. Thus, if terms are payment within 30 days bad-debt relief can be claimed after six months and 30 days. If terms are immediate payment, then bad-debt relief entitlement arises six months from the date of the invoice.

> **Planning point**
>
> In addition to any commercial reason for doing so, this represents a powerful reason to state payment terms on the face of the sales invoice, as this indisputably fixes the date of entitlement to VAT bad debt relief.

> **Planning point**
>
> It should be noted that there is no requirement that the debt be written off in the accounts, nor even provided for, in order for relief to be claimed. What is required is that the amount is transferred to a 'refunds for bad debts account'. This account can be created for VAT purposes only and does not have any effect over the usual accounting treatment for otherwise bad or doubtful debts.

The claim should be made by entering the amount of VAT claimable in box 4 of the VAT return for the period in which the entitlement arose (or such later return as the trader may choose, always accepting that no claim may be made more than three years and six months after the due date for payment).

> **Planning point**
>
> Strictly, a claim for relief can be made if the six months has elapsed by the time of submission of the VAT return on which the claim is made, since the claim is not for VAT as such but for 'relief' (effectively governmental compensation for the loss).

If payment is received subsequent to bad-debt relief having been claimed, then the VAT proportion of the consideration received must again be accounted for as output tax.

Under current legislation, the customer is still required to adjust his claim to input tax, if any, six months after the due date for payment (see **30.7**).

> **Planning point**
>
> A system for making claims should be in place, allocating responsibility to an individual to monitor aged debtors and to ensure that claims are made on a timely basis.

> ## ⚠ *Warning!*
>
> If a customer has paid part of an invoice, bad-debt relief can be claimed on the balance outstanding, calculated by how much VAT is included within the balance, i.e. applying the VAT fraction of 1/6th (or 7/47ths from 1 January 2010 to 3 January 2011 and 3/23rds from 1 December 2008 to 31 December 2009 and 7/47ths prior to 1 December 2008. The fraction claimed will depend upon the period the tax point arose, that is when the invoice was issued in or when the supply was made), assuming the supply to have been standard-rated. If the customer has paid the net amount and left only the VAT amount outstanding, the same rule applies and only the VAT proportion (1/6th or whatever fraction is applicable) of the amount outstanding is claimable as bad debt relief. Thus, if a supply was made for £100 plus £20 VAT and the customer only paid £100 bad debt relief of £3.33 only can be claimed (£20/6). A seeming exception to this is where the customer did not pay a VAT only invoice. Although the net amount has been paid and the VAT element has not been paid the Upper Tier Tribunal has permitted the appellant's appeal to claim the whole amount as bad debt relief and not the VAT fraction element of the VAT amount not paid. (*Simpson & Marwick v R&C Commrs* [2012] BVC 1,533) The Upper Tier Tribunal considered that the bad debt relief provisions justified treating the whole amount of a VAT only invoice as unpaid VAT and eligible for refund. Where the consideration written off is all VAT the refund should be calculated accordingly as it was established case law that the amount of VAT to be collected by the tax authorities is not to exceed the amount that is actually paid by the final consumer.

For smaller businesses, instant bad-debt relief can of course be gained by use of the Cash Accounting Scheme. This is available to any business with an annual turnover of up to £1.35m and once using the scheme a business can go up to £1.6m before having to stop using the scheme.

It is now also possible to claim back bad-debt relief incurred after the transfer of a business as a going concern in respect of pre-transfer supplies, provided that the VAT registration number is transferred. The potential benefit of this should, however, be carefully weighed before the registration number is taken on by the purchaser as this can lead to responsibility for other liabilities incurred prior to the transfer.

When bad-debt relief is claimed and the customer becomes insolvent, the supplier should prove in the insolvency for the full amount of the debt. Under the terms of Extra-Statutory Concession 3.20 and *Notice 48*, an insolvency practitioner is not required to make a bad-debt relief adjustment for any bad debts relating to a supply made prior to the insolvency. However, adjustments are required if the supply was made during the insolvency appointment.

If a taxpayer assigns a debt prior to making a claim for bad-debt relief, then the payments received by the assignee must be taken into account when calculating the amount of the claim. However, if the debt is assigned after the making of a claim, no adjustment is required to the claim unless the debt is assigned to a connected party, in which case an adjustment is required (this adjustment came into force on 11 December 2003).

Law: VATA 1994, s. 36; VAT Regulations 1995 (SI 1995/2518), Part XIX–XIXA

Other guidance: VAT Notice 700/18

30.7   Aged creditors

When the bad-debt relief rules were last changed (affecting supplies made from 1 January 2003 onwards), HMRC lost the trigger which caused a VAT-registered debtor to repay any input tax claimed on the supply in respect of which the creditor was claiming bad-debt relief. A replacement mechanism was needed to ensure that this tax was brought to account. The easiest, most obvious and quite possibly the only way of doing this was to place an obligation on every debtor to repay input tax on any outstanding purchase balance remaining unpaid six months after the due date for payment. Simple such a scheme may be, but it has the effect of placing an obligation on the debtor whether or not the creditor has chosen to make a bad-debt relief claim. Although it is ostensibly the mirror image of bad debt relief, for this reason it is not a measure which restores balance, but one which tips the balance in favour of HMRC quite decisively.

> ### ⚠ *Warning!*
>
> No debtor can afford to be unaware of these rules. Indeed, unless the business is one which consistently pays all creditors on a timely basis, systems should be set up to monitor aged creditors to ensure that input tax is repaid as soon as the deadline arises, i.e. on the VAT return covering the relevant date.

All official announcements of these rules and all published guidance on them appear under the general heading of 'bad-debt relief', which is arguably very unhelpful. By their nature they affect many businesses which have no call to take account of bad debt relief, such as retailers, farmers and other repayment traders. Such businesses are often ignorant of these provisions for entirely understandable reasons.

> ### ⚠ *Warning!*
>
> HMRC are well aware of the lack of appreciation of these rules on the part of many businesses (although perhaps also sadly unaware of their own contribution to this ignorance by treating it as a bad-debt issue) and in some parts of the country have undertaken VAT visits specifically to look at this particular issue. It has also become a regular area for checking on more routine visits.

Of course, if input tax has been repaid correctly to HMRC in the event of a long-outstanding creditor, and payment is subsequently made, the input tax may be claimed a second time.

> ### ⚠ *Warning!*
>
> It is difficult to overemphasise the dangers and adverse impact of this provision. It is especially damaging for struggling businesses, where the very reason for delayed payment is adverse cash flow, which can only be made worse by the requirement to part with actual money to HMRC if the six-month limit is passed. Where possible, such businesses would be advised to agree revised payment dates with their creditors, which has the effect of forestalling the need to make repayment of the input tax.

Law: VATA 1994, s. 26A; VAT Regulations 1995 (SI 1995/2518), Part XIXB

Other guidance: VAT Notice 700/18

30.8   Change of VAT rate – Anti-avoidance

To ease the economic crisis the standard VAT rate was reduced from 17.5 per cent to 15 per cent with effect from 1 December 2008.

The standard rate is to return to 17.5 per cent with effect from 1 January 2010.

The standard rate is also due to increase to 20 per cent from 4 January 2011.

The VAT fraction is:

   15 per cent: 3/23.

   17.5 per cent: 7/47.

   20 per cent: 1/6.

> ### *Planning point*
>
> Pubs, clubs, hotels and other establishments whose busiest night of the year will be affected by the change in VAT rate, i.e. sell drinks at 11.59pm on 31 December 2010 at 15 per cent and 12:01am on 1 January 2010 at 17.5 per cent will be able to determine the VAT rate based upon a 'session'. This means that the 15 per cent VAT rate can be used until the session commencing immediately prior to midnight on the 31 December and ending one or two hours into the New Year is completed. This has been ratified in a Parliamentary question posed mid-2009.

30.8.1   Dealing with the change in rate

VAT is to be accounted for at 20 per cent for all takings received on or after 4 January 2011. Where, in a cash or retail business mainly dealing with non-business customers, goods were taken away before this date, but paid for after this date, VAT can be accounted for at 17.5 per cent. Where a retailer uses an apportionment or direct calculation scheme, it will be necessary to make a calculation up to 3 January 2011 and a further calculation for the period commencing 4 January 2011. Where sales are made through a coin operated machine that does not record when the sales are made, it is necessary to apportion the income received according to typical usage of the machine.

Where the customers are mainly business customers, VAT at 20 per cent needs to be accounted for on all invoices issued on or after 4 January 2011 that are issued within 14 days of the service being completed or goods delivered (or such longer period as agreed with HMRC).

> **Planning point**
>
> Issue invoices for all outstanding sales on 3 January or before to ensure that VAT can be charged at 17.5 per cent (see **30.8.2** regarding avoidance legislation). Where the customer is a business customer that can reclaim VAT this is not an important issue.

Credit notes need to identify the invoice that was issued to ensure that the correct VAT rate is adjusted. An invoice issued at 17.5 per cent needs a credit note for 17.5 per cent even if issued after 4 January 2011; all refunds also need to reflect the VAT originally charged. Similarly, if Bad Debt Relief is claimed, it must be claimed at the same rate as the VAT that was originally charged.

If a deposit is received before 4 January 2011, the deposit will be subject to 17.5 per cent VAT. If the balance is received on or after that date, it will be subject to 20 per cent VAT (although the issue of a tax invoice may override this). The supplier can, if it simplifies accounting, charge 20 per cent of the deposit and the balancing payment.

Continuous supplies that span the date of the rate change can be apportioned for the value supplied before and after the change in rate. A single supply that spans the rate change, however, will be subject to VAT at 20 per cent as it will not be completed until after the change in rate. It is possible to invoice for the value supplied up until the change in rate at 17.5 per cent for work done up to 3 January 2011 if an invoice is issued or payment received before the date of the change in rate. Similar rules apply to stage payments made for work in progress and work completed in the construction industry.

Where a ticket is sold, or a season ticket is sold, before 4 January 2011 the VAT rate for the supply will be 17.5 per cent even if the event does not take place until after 3 January 2011.

VAT will need to be claimed at the appropriate rate on invoices for supplies received. For example, the appropriate VAT fraction needs to be applied to less detailed tax invoices according to the date of issue. Supplies made over a period that provide a schedule with the invoice will be required to issue a new schedule for supplies after 4 January 2011.

The new scale charges that reflect the 20 per cent rate are shown in **Chapter 11.**

30.8.2   Anti-forestalling Legislation

HMRC have issued anti-forestalling legislation effective from 25 November 2008 to combat businesses that try and take advantage of the 15 per cent VAT rate for supplies which predominately take place after 1 January 2010 when the rate rises to 17.5 per cent (Finance Act 2009, Sch. 36). Similar legislation has been introduced in respect of the rate change on 4 January 2011. Effectively, the supplier tries to fix the VAT rate by issuing an invoice or receiving payment before the rate rises. This fixes the VAT due at the lower rate even though the goods or services are not delivered or performed until on or after the date of the rate rises.

The legislation that affects the 2011 change introduces a supplementary charge to VAT on the supply of goods or services (or the grant of the right to receive goods or services) where the customer cannot recover all of the VAT charged on the supply and one of the following conditions is met:

- the supplier and customer are connected parties;
- the supplier issues advance invoices to persons connected with the supplier for future supplies;
- prepayments are received or invoices are issued in advance in excess of £100,000 and this is not normal commercial practice;
- rights or options are supplied to receive goods or services free of charge or at a discount;
- the supplier funds the purchase of the goods or services or grant of rights; or
- a VAT invoice is issued by the supplier where payment is not due for at least six months.

A supplementary charge of 2.5 per cent will apply to transactions that meet these criteria.

Civil Penalties

31.1   Background

Penalties in relation to VAT were introduced in the Finance Act 1972. These provided for criminal offences in relation to regulatory matters as well as fraud and recklessness.

In 1985, the position was reviewed through the Keith Committee. The Keith Committee reported on the ineffectiveness of the previous criminal regime in improving compliance, and proposed two essential changes:

- the decriminalisation of breaches of regulatory provisions; and
- the establishment of a system of civil fraud.

These changes were enacted in the Finance Act 1985. Although there have been a number of changes in respect of the particular penalties, the civil penalty regime today is based largely on the Keith Committee recommendations. In general terms, the civil penalties are designed to encourage taxpayer compliance.

Following their introduction, civil penalties have generally been reduced in severity, following complaints that the penalty rates (for misdeclaration penalty, default surcharge and failure to notify liability to registration) were too high, and that there was no power for the tribunal to mitigate the penalty. What is now VATA 1994, s. 70 was introduced by the Finance Act 1993, having effect in relation to penalties issued on or after 27 July 1993. Further changes to the penalty regime were also introduced with effect from 1 April 2009.

There remains, in the VATA 1994, s. 72, provision for the criminal prosecution of offenders. HMRC may also seek to secure a conviction under the Theft Act 1968 (see *R v Redford* (1988) 3 BVC 410, where the defendant sought to appeal against his conviction under the Theft Act, for offences which could have been prosecuted under VATA 1994). The circumstances under which HMRC will consider action under the criminal regime are described in *Notice 700, para. 27.4*. In addition, taxpayers may be charged with the common law offence of Cheating the Revenue. This offence has been preserved by s. 32(1) Theft Act 1968. It is usually reserved for serious offences where monies have been diverted by dishonest conduct from the Revenue. There is no statutory maximum penalty.

More recently, it has been held that a civil evasion penalty (VATA 1994, s. 60) is a 'criminal charge' for the purposes of art. 6 of the ECHR. See *Han & Yau* [2001] BVC 2,163, upheld on appeal at *C & E Commrs v Han & Yau* [2001] BVC 415. The Court of Appeal held, in *Han & Yau*, that this classification does not make the penalty criminal for all domestic purposes, but merely entitles the defendant to those safeguards provided expressly or by implication by art. 6 of the ECHR and may afford the defendant public funding (this used to be called legal aid) to assist their defence.

The tribunal has been asked whether the principles of *Han & Yau* can be applied to other civil penalties. The decision in *Ali (t/a Shapla Tandoori Restaurant)* [2002] BVC 2,254 addressed this question in relation to:

- default surcharge;
- misdeclaration penalty; and
- failure to notify liability to registration.

In each case, the tribunal held that these penalties did not share the characteristics of a criminal penalty. Indeed, it held that the penalties were regulatory in nature, and VATA 1994 provides both a defence and mitigation in relation to them.

The dishonesty penalty alone requires HMRC and, on appeal, the tribunal, to attribute a state of mind to the taxpayer. The other penalties are strict liability penalties that arise in specified circumstances. As such, there is also a statutory defence.

31.2 Introduction to civil penalties

In practice, the three most important civil penalties, on account of the frequency of their application, are default surcharge, misdeclaration penalty and the belated notification penalty. The others are very infrequently applied indeed, with the possible exception of the civil fraud penalty, but (as noted above) that is restricted to cases of alleged dishonest conduct.

Although not strictly a penalty, default interest is also commonly seen and worth understanding, especially as regards the circumstances in which it is not due (or, more correctly, not applied by HMRC).

Finally, repayment supplement, which is also not a penalty proper but acts like one imposed on, rather than by, HMRC, should not be forgotten and is covered in **Chapter 30**.

31.3 Default surcharge

31.3.1 Introduction

This penalty is directed at the taxpayer who submits or pays his returns after the due date. A corresponding penalty applies for the taxpayer who uses the payments on account scheme.

A 'default' is recorded when:

- HMRC have not received a return; or
- HMRC have received the return but not the full amount shown as due on the return. (It is understood that if the shortfall is minimal, below £20, then no default is recorded.)

Upon a person's first default HMRC serve a 'default liability notice' which specifies a 'surcharge period'. This period runs for one year from the last day of the period covered by the return. Any further default within that period triggers a surcharge at two per cent of the amount outstanding and extends the surcharge period. Further defaults increase the penalty rate to five per cent, ten per cent and a maximum 15 per cent of the amount outstanding.

Where the person submits a nil or repayment return late, he will default, but will not trigger a surcharge.

The minimum penalty is £30. Additionally, by concession, a surcharge will not be assessed at two per cent or five per cent where the assessment would be less than £400. However, the penalty rate will continue to increase.

Further, in the 2002 Budget, the Chancellor announced that no automatic surcharge would be applied for businesses with annual turnover below £150,000 (*Notice REV/C&E 2*). However, no further explanation of this concession has subsequently been announced.

By concession, some taxable persons are excluded from the default surcharge regime:

- taxpayers submitting their first return, unless the business has been transferred to them as a going concern;
- taxpayers classified as repayment traders; or
- local authorities and statutory bodies, registered under VATA 1994, s. 33.

Planning point

A surcharge cannot be assessed where HMRC fail to serve a default liability notice. Subsequent extension notices, which only extend the surcharge period, do not state when the period begins and are therefore not valid. If the notice is dated after a second default, a surcharge cannot be assessed in respect of that period. The leading case in this respect is *C & E Commrs v Medway Draughting and Technical Services Ltd* (1989) 4 BVC 60. The court held that the non-service of a notice made subsequent surcharges invalid but also stated that the non-service of a notice did not constitute a reasonable excuse.

Where a surcharge has been issued in relation to a prescribed accounting period, and the amount of outstanding VAT is subsequently altered, for example by the submission of a voluntary disclosure or the issue of an inspecting officer's assessment, then the surcharge will be altered accordingly.

> ### *Planning point*
>
> If this results in a reduced amount of net tax due, the taxpayer or his adviser should ensure that the surcharge reduction is properly implemented.

> ### ⚠ *Warning!*
>
> Where a taxpayer enters into a 'time to pay' agreement in relation to VAT that he has been unable to pay, defaults will still be recorded against him and surcharges levied on any tax not paid by the due date.

HMRC are expected to notify him that the agreement to pay off his debt in instalments will not prevent or cancel the recording of any defaults or surcharges. In early cases, HMRC (then Customs) failed to mention the taxpayers' continued risk of incurring surcharges. See *Andrews Kent & Stone* [1992] BVC 1,516 where Customs' failure constituted a reasonable excuse for a later surcharge.

> ### *Planning point*
>
> Since a surcharge period runs for 12 months, a taxpayer is required to submit and pay four quarterly returns within the time limit, in order to be no longer liable to surcharge.

The person assessed to a default surcharge will not be liable to the surcharge and will be treated as having not been in default for that period, where:

- he submitted his return and, where appropriate, his payment in time to reach HMRC by the due date (see **31.10.1**); or
- there is a reasonable excuse for the return or the payment not having been so despatched (see **31.11**).

The effect of a reasonable excuse being established is that the penalty rate applicable to later defaults and surcharges will be reduced or cancelled in full.

In *Kaizen Search Ltd* [2011] TC 01037, the Tribunal held that the default surcharge regime can, in exceptional cases, be disproportionate. The matters considered were the gravity of the default (particularly the culpability of the appellant), how long the VAT had been outstanding and the amount of the surcharge relative to the wealth of the appellant. In this instance, the appellant was unsuccessful but this is an indication that such a defence may be possible.

> **Planning point**
>
> Whilst a person may appeal against a surcharge issued under this section, he may not appeal against a default in the absence of a surcharge. Once liability to a surcharge is established, the taxpayer may appeal and bring into account circumstances relating to any material default.

Law: VATA 1994, s. 59

Other guidance: VAT Notice 700/50

31.3.2 Inflated assessments

Where a person fails to submit VAT returns, and HMRC issue estimated assessments in the absence of those returns, and the taxpayer pays the assessment amounts in preference to submitting and paying returns, they may issue assessments in amounts higher than they would otherwise have done. Thus, persistent non-compliance in this area is penalised by increasing liability.

This penalty has a knock-on effect on default surcharges, which are based on the amount of outstanding VAT. Where a person fails to pay an estimated assessment, that amount is treated as outstanding VAT for the purposes of VATA, s. 59, and therefore it is the basis of calculation of the default surcharge.

> **Example 31.1**
>
> Based on assessments increasing by 20 per cent each period.
>
> | VAT period | P12/02 | P03/03 | P06/03 | P09/03 |
> |---|---|---|---|---|
> | Estimated assessment | £10,000 | £12,000 | £14,400 | £17,280 |
> | Default surcharge rate | 10% | 15% | 15% | 15% |
> | Default surcharge amount | £1,000 | £1,800 | £2,160 | £2,592 |

> **Planning point**
>
> The submission of a VAT return in these circumstances will give rise to a recalculation of the default surcharge. There is therefore a double benefit to submitting outstanding returns where the assessments have overstated the tax due.

31.3.3 Default surcharge – payments on account scheme

Where a person is using the payments on account scheme for larger traders, he makes a default when he:

- fails to make an interim payment by the due date, as required by VAT (Payments on Account) Order 1993 (SI 1993/2001);
- fails to submit his return; or
- submits his return but fails to make payment by the due date.

After a first default, the person will receive a surcharge liability notice specifying a surcharge liability period. This period begins on the date of the notice and ends one year after the last day of the period in which the default occurs. The period is extended by any subsequent defaults.

Where the person incurs a default within a surcharge liability period, he is liable to a penalty, beginning at two per cent of the value of defaults in that period. The rate of penalty increases to five per cent, then ten per cent, to a maximum of 15 per cent. The penalty is subject to a minimum of £30.

Although a person may default three times in relation to one quarterly accounting period (two interim payments and one return and balancing payment), the rate of penalty only increases with the number of prescribed accounting periods in which one or more defaults occur.

The value of defaults is calculated as the total of:

- the value of interim payments not received by the due date, even if they are received by the due date of the return; and
- the value of total outstanding VAT, less any payments on account not made by the due.

Example 31.2

Caroline is liable to make two interim payments of £100,000 and a balancing payment of £400,000, giving a total return liability of £600,000.

She pays, respectively, £100,000, £30,000 and £300,000, making a total of £430,000.

The total value of defaults is:

		Paid	Outstanding
First interim payment		£100,000	Nil
Second interim payment		£30,000	£70,000
Total outstanding VAT	Outstanding VAT on return	£600,000 − £430,000 = £170,000	
	Less interim payments not made	£70,000	
	Total outstanding VAT	£100,000	£100,000
Total value of defaults			£170,000

HMRC's explanation of this is in *Notice 700/50* (September 2004), para. 3.4, which is less circuitous than VATA 1994, s. 59A(6).

A surcharge cannot be assessed where HMRC fail to serve a default liability notice. The guidance given above is presumed to relate also to a default surcharge issued under this section.

A default may not arise in relation to a prescribed accounting period where the person has been assessed for a penalty under s. 69, breaches of regulatory provisions.

Where a taxpayer moves into and out of the payments on account scheme, his defaults will remain material for the purpose of the default surcharge. Thus, if his initial defaults occurred before he joined the scheme, the taxpayer's first default under the scheme will trigger a surcharge.

The person assessed to a default surcharge will not be liable to the surcharge and will be treated as having not been in default for that period, where:

- he submitted his return and, where appropriate, his payment in time to reach HMRC by the due date (see **31.10.1**); or
- there is a reasonable excuse for the return or the payment not having been so despatched (see **31.11**).

The effect of a successful defence being established is that the penalty rate applicable to later defaults and surcharges will be reduced or cancelled in full.

Since more than one default may arise in relation to one accounting period, the cancellation of one default may not result in a surcharge being cancelled or reduced. Therefore, a default may or may not be 'material' to a surcharge. Thus where a person seeks to establish a defence, he is also required to establish that the default in question is material for the purposes of the surcharge.

Law: VATA 1994, s. 59A

31.4   Penalties (prior to 1 April 2009)

31.4.1 Misdeclaration penalty

This penalty, along with its sister penalty – the repeated misdeclaration penalty – is intended to encourage businesses to submit accurate VAT returns. Both punish serious misdeclarations. Indeed, the misdeclaration penalty was previously called the serious misdeclaration penalty.

The misdeclaration penalty arises in the following circumstances.

1.   A person submits a VAT return which understates his liability or which overstates the amount of credit due to him, and that understatement is at least £1 million or 30 per cent of the gross amount of VAT for that period, being the sum of the output tax and input tax which should have been entered on the return.

2. A person has received an assessment for any prescribed accounting period and that assessment understates his liability, and he fails – within 30 days – to notify HMRC of that fact; and that understatement is at least £1 million or 30 per cent of the true amount of tax, being the net amount due on the return, either due to or from HMRC.

The rate of penalty is 15 per cent of the VAT that would have been lost or understated.

> ## Example 31.3
>
> Kelly's VAT return shows:
>
> - output tax: £240,000; and
> - input tax: £170,000.
>
> She understates the output tax by £190,000.
>
> The gross amount of tax is therefore: £240,000 + £170,000 + £190,000 = £600,000.
>
> 30 per cent of the gross amount of tax is £600,000 × 0.30 = £180,000.
>
> The understatement, being £190,000, exceeds this amount. Kelly is liable to a penalty under this section.
>
> The penalty is £190,000 × 15 per cent = £28,500.

> ## Example 31.4
>
> Gerry, having failed to submit his VAT return for a given period, receives an assessment for £75,000.
>
> His correct output tax is £325,000.
>
> His correct input tax is £205,000.
>
> His correct net tax is therefore £325,000 – £205,000 = £120,000.
>
> 30 per cent of the true amount of tax is £120,000 × 0.30 = £36,000.
>
> The understatement was £120,000 – £75,000 = £45,000, exceeding £36,000. Gerry is liable to a penalty under this section.
>
> The penalty is £45,000 × 15 per cent = £6,750.

The gross amount of tax expressly includes refunds and repayments apart from input tax such as, for example, bad-debt relief claims.

> ## Warning!
>
> For some reason, this aspect of this penalty is not well known. However, it should always be considered where a VAT return has not been submitted and an assessment received from HMRC, whether or not the assessment has been paid.

Whether the gross amount of tax may be altered has been the subject of some litigation, see *The Currie Group Ltd* [1991] BVC 1,365 and *Bulldog International*

Transport Express Ltd [1991] BVC 762. VATA 1994, s. 63(8) provides that subsequent adjustments must be taken into account in calculating the gross amount of tax. In relation to the true amount of VAT, this is relevant only where a person has failed to submit his return. Any overstatement or understatement on the return for that prescribed accounting period cannot be relevant in addition to a penalty raised under s. 63(1)(b).

HMRC must assess the penalty within two years from the date the amount of VAT due was finally determined, and can assess no more than three years after the end of the prescribed accounting period. Where possible they should attribute the penalty to individual prescribed accounting periods to the best of their judgment.

A person cannot be assessed for a penalty under this section if he is convicted of an offence or assessed to a civil evasion penalty in relation to the same circumstances.

There are statutory defences to the misdeclaration penalty:

- there is a reasonable excuse for his conduct (see **31.11**); or
- the taxpayer provided HMRC with full details of the error (see **31.10.2**).

In addition, *Notice 700/42* provides a range of circumstances in which a penalty would not normally be issued where:

- HMRC discover an error on the most recent VAT return or before the due date for submission of that return;
- the understatement is corrected by an overstatement in the immediately preceding or immediately succeeding VAT return; or
- the penalty amount would be less than £300.

Since the error will necessarily be substantial if a misdeclaration penalty is triggered, HMRC may view this as a lack of care on the part of the taxpayer and may therefore resist a claim of reasonable excuse.

Importantly, it should be noted that a change to the penalty regime resulted in the replacement of misdeclaration penalty with effect from VAT returns due to be filed on or after 1 April 2009. This is part of an exercise undertaken by HMRC to harmonise penalties across the taxes for which they are responsible. The penalty regime with effect from 1 April 2009 is perhaps best explained by reproducing in full the *Revenue & Customs Brief* in which the announcement was made and the new regime explained (see **20.5**).

31.4.2 Repeated misdeclaration penalty

This penalty arises where a person has made a 'material inaccuracy' in a VAT return, this being an error exceeding either £500,000 or 10 per cent of the gross amount of tax for the period.

Before the end of five prescribed accounting periods, HMRC issue a 'penalty liability notice', form VAT 670. This warns the taxpayer that the second and any subsequent 'material inaccuracy' within the next eight prescribed accounting periods will trigger a penalty.

Thus, if the taxpayer makes two or more 'material inaccuracies' within that period, he will be liable to a penalty of 15 per cent of the amount of the second and subsequent material inaccuracy.

Example 31.5

P03/01	P06/01 P09/01 P12/01 P03/02	P06/02 P09/02 P12/02 P03/03 P06/03
Material inaccuracy	Notice issued	Material inaccuracy	Material inaccuracy

A penalty arises in P06/03.

Since the notice (penalty liability notice) was issued in P09/01, the penalty period ends on 30 June 2003. The eight periods include the period in which the notice is issued.

HMRC must assess within two years from the date the amount of VAT due was finally determined and can assess no more than three years after the end of the prescribed accounting period. Where possible they should attribute the penalty to individual prescribed accounting periods to the best of their judgement.

Conduct which results in a conviction under s. 72 or a penalty under s. 60 cannot also provide a 'material inaccuracy' under this section. However, an error subject to a misdeclaration penalty may constitute a 'material inaccuracy' for the purposes of this section; but a penalty cannot be issued under both s. 63 and s. 64 for the same error. Where an error is large enough to trigger a penalty under s. 63, then that penalty will apply in preference to a s. 64 penalty.

It is presumed that HMRC will continue to extend the penalty period in circumstances where a taxpayer continues to make 'material inaccuracies'.

There are statutory defences to the repeated misdeclaration penalty, in that:

- there is a reasonable excuse for his conduct (see **31.11**); or
- the taxpayer provided HMRC with full details of the error (see **31.10.2**);

In addition, *Notice 700/42* provides a range of circumstances in which a penalty would not normally be issued:

- HMRC discover an error on the most recent VAT return or before the due date for submission of that return;
- the understatement is corrected by an overstatement in the immediately preceding or immediately succeeding VAT return; or
- the penalty amount would be below £300.

Since the error will necessarily be substantial if a misdeclaration penalty is triggered, HMRC may view this as a lack of care on the part of the taxpayer and may therefore resist a claim of a reasonable excuse.

> **Planning point**
> Repeated misdeclaration penalty has always been encountered only rarely. It will become entirely a thing of the past when the new penalty regime is introduced.

Law: VATA 1994, s. 64

Other guidance: VAT Notice 700/42

31.5   Penalties for errors effective from 1 April 2009 (replacing the serious misdeclaration penalty and repeated misdeclaration penalty)

'Revenue & Customs Brief 19/08

New penalties for errors in returns and documents

Introduction

This brief explains how the new penalties will affect our customers and their advisers.

HM Revenue & Customs (HMRC) inherited a confusing variety of penalty charging powers. The new penalties are one of the first pieces of cross cutting legislation designed to make the tax system simpler and more consistent. It follows consultation with our customers and other interested parties during the Review of Powers, Deterrents and Safeguards.

The legislation aims to help those who try to comply, and come down hard on those who don't. The clear messages for customers are that:

- if they take reasonable care when completing their returns they will not be penalised;
- if they do not take reasonable care, errors will be penalised and the penalties will be higher if the error is deliberate; and
- disclosing errors to us early will substantially reduce any penalty due.

Taxes affected

The new penalties are for errors on returns and documents initially for VAT, PAYE, National Insurance, Capital Gains Tax, Income Tax, Corporation Tax and the Construction Industry Scheme.

For these taxes, it applies to returns or other documents for tax periods starting on or after 1 April 2008 that are due to be filed on or after 1 April 2009. The legislation is Schedule 24 of Finance Act 2007.

When can a penalty for inaccuracy be charged?

Two conditions must be satisfied before we can charge a penalty.

(1) The document given to HMRC must contain an inaccuracy that leads to:

- an understatement of the person's liability to tax;
- a false or inflated statement of a loss by the person;
- a false or inflated claim to repayment of tax.

(2) The inaccuracy must be careless, deliberate or deliberate and concealed.

A penalty can also be charged where, in the absence of a return, we issue an assessment which is too low and the person does not take reasonable steps to tell us of the under-assessment within 30 days of the date of the assessment.

How is the penalty calculated?

There is no penalty if a person takes reasonable care but submits an incorrect return. However, if the person later discovers the error but does not take reasonable steps to tell us about it, the inaccuracy will be treated as careless.

The penalty percentages are applied to the additional tax due as a result of correcting the error (known as the potential lost revenue). There is a different measure of potential lost revenue where the error results in an overstated loss:

- the penalty is up to 30 per cent of the potential lost revenue if the error is careless;
- the penalty is up to 70 per cent of the potential lost revenue if the error is deliberate;
- the penalty is up to 100 per cent of the potential lost revenue if the error is deliberate and the person conceals it.

The penalty chargeable where tax has been under-assessed because of the customer's failure to send us a return is 30 per cent of the potential lost revenue.

How can penalties be reduced?

There can be a substantial reduction in the level of penalty charged for unprompted disclosure of errors. A disclosure is unprompted if it is made at a time when the person making it has no reason to believe that HMRC has discovered, or is about to discover, the error.

Further reductions can be given based on the quality of the disclosure. The more a person tells, helps or gives access to HMRC the more the penalty may be reduced.

To calculate the reduction for disclosure we will consider three elements of disclosure. To what extent is the customer?

- telling HMRC about their error;
- helping HMRC work out what extra tax is due;

- giving HMRC access to their records to check their figures,

The reductions are made because we want to encourage people to come forward when they think there is a problem with their tax affairs, or they have not met a requirement.

Reasonable care

Each person has a responsibility to take reasonable care. But what is necessary for each person to meet that responsibility has to be viewed in the light of their abilities and circumstances.

For example, we would not expect the same level of knowledge or expertise from a self-employed and unrepresented individual as from a large multinational company. We expect a higher degree of care to be taken over large and complex matters than simple straightforward ones.

Every person is expected to make and keep sufficient records for them to provide a complete and accurate return. A person with simple, straightforward tax affairs needs to keep a simple system of records, which are followed and regularly updated. A person with larger and more complex tax affairs will need to put in place more sophisticated systems and maintain them equally carefully.

We believe it is reasonable to expect a person who encounters a transaction or other event with which they are not familiar to take care to check the correct tax treatment or to seek suitable advice. We expect people to take their tax seriously.

Some penalties may be suspended

Suspension is intended to support those who try to meet their obligations by helping them to avoid penalties for inaccuracies in the future.

Only a penalty for failing to take reasonable care can be considered for suspension. Suspension conditions will be agreed and set and if they are met the penalty will be cancelled. If they are not met the penalty becomes payable. The period of suspension can be for up to two years.

For example, if a careless inaccuracy is due to poor record-keeping one of the conditions of suspension could be that specified improvements are made to the way records are kept. This will help the customer avoid future errors.

We will consider the taxpayer's general compliance behaviour, the level of disclosure and the nature of the inaccuracy before deciding whether to suspend the penalty.

Change in HMRC policy for calculating penalties

HMRC announced a change in policy in the way penalties are to be calculated on 6 April 2011 (see *R&C Brief 15/11*). This affects when penalties will be applied where an error is made that would correct itself in the normal course of events on the following return. For example, where input tax is claimed in a period earlier than the entitlement arose.

Where a return contains an inaccuracy that relates to a timing error that will be automatically reversed in the following tax period, the penalty is calculated on a reduced amount to take account of the timing error. Thus, if there is an error of £10,000 VAT that would have been reclaimed in the following period 2, there is an error of an overclaim of £10,000 in the first period and an underclaim of £10,000 in the next period. Any penalty for the overclaim in the first period is not calculated on the £1,000 but on a reduced amount to take account of the automatic reversal in the next period. As this is a time-based penalty, the penalty is calculated at 5 per cent of the value of the error for each year. If the error is corrected automatically within one quarterly period, the amount of value of the error is ¼ of 5 per cent, that is 1.25 per cent. If HMRC are to apply a 15 per cent penalty (the prompted disclosure penalty) they will apply the charge of 15 per cent x 1.25 per cent to the error. In the above instance of a £10,000 that would be £18.75. HMRC would not impose a penalty for this amount being below its *de minimus* limit.

The change in policy announced by HMRC is that they will apply the reduced penalty where HMRC has "intervened" to correct the inaccuracy before the second return was received. For example, where HMRC visits the taxpayer, notice the error and make the amendment prior to the second return being submitted. When HMRC are satisfied that the inaccuracy would have been automatically corrected in a subsequent return, the taxpayer will incur the reduced penalty based on the delayed tax rules.

Other taxes

The 2008 Finance Bill makes provision to extend the new penalties to cover incorrect returns for the other taxes and duties HMRC administer. We expect the new provisions will apply for periods commencing on or after 1 April 2009 where the return is due to be filed on or after 1 April 2010 – see Budget Notice 96.

More information

Please check the Frequently Asked Questions (FAQs) and the technical guidance in the Compliance Handbook on our internet site.

Issued 1 April 2008'

Law: VATA 1994, s. 63

Other guidance: VAT Notice 700/42

Commencement date

These provisions come into force for any return that is due after 31 March 2009, but specifically on:

- 1 April 2008 in relation to documents in relation of VAT periods commencing on or after 1 April 2008;
- 1 July 2008 in relation to documents relating to 13th Directive claims for years commencing on or after 1 July 2008;
- 1 January 2009 in relation to documents in relation to 8th Directive claims for years commencing on or after 1 January 2009;
- 1 April 2009 in relation to all other claims for repayments of VAT made on or after 1 April 2009 which are not related to a VAT period; and
- 1 April 2009 in any other case

BUT, no penalty is applicable in relation to any VAT period where the return is required to be made before 1 April 2009.

A penalty can be applied to any return statement or declaration or a document that HMRC may rely on in respect to a taxpayer's VAT liability, payments, penalties or any repayment or credit. A penalty will be applied where there is any understatement or inflated claim which is careless or deliberate. Careless is defined as not taking reasonable care. A deliberate error can be concealed or not concealed.

Penalties for incorrect returns

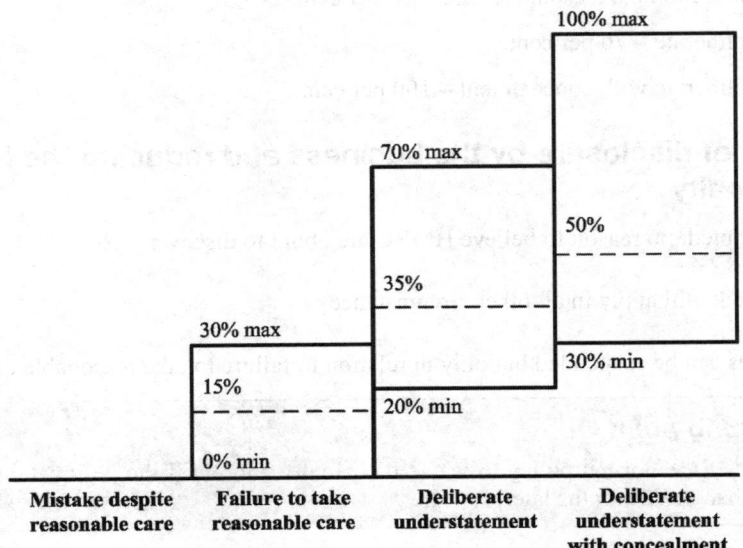

Reasonable care – expectation of HMRC

Records:

- to keep sufficient records to make an accurate return.

Unfamiliar transactions or other events:

- to take care to research the correct tax treatment or to seek suitable advice.

Draw attention to the entry:

- if still unsure, then draw attention to the entry and the uncertainty when sending the return or document to HMRC.

Reasonable care – examples

- a reasonably arguable view of the law that is subsequently not upheld;
- an arithmetical or transposition inaccuracy that is not so large either in absolute terms or relative to overall liability as to produce an obviously odd result or be picked up by a quality check;
- following advice from HMRC when all the details and circumstances were provided.

It is also understood that HMRC will accept the following:

- acting on advice from a competent adviser which proves to be wrong despite the fact that the adviser was given a full set of accurate facts.

The level of penalty will depend on what steps the business has taken.

(1) Reasonable care – 0 per cent.

(2) Failure to take reasonable care – 30 per cent.

(3) Deliberate – 70 per cent.

(4) Deliberate with concealment – 100 per cent.

Level of disclosure by the business and reducing the level of penalty

Unprompted: no reason to believe HMRC are about to discover error.

Prompted: will apply in all other circumstances.

Penalties can be suspended but only in relation to failure to take reasonable care.

> **Planning point**
>
> It is HMRC's normal policy to waive the penalty entirely if the notification is no more than three months late.

Reasonable excuse

Not accepted by law are:

- insufficient funds; and
- reliance on a third party.

Other situations not normally accepted:

- ignorance of the law;

- pressure of work;
- task is too difficult; and
- HMRC did not remind me.

Reasonable excuse

A penalty is NOT due following, for example, the:

- loss of records through: fire, flood, theft;
- serious illness/bereavement;
- computer breakdown;
- loss of key personnel;
- unexpected cash crisis; and
- unavoidable delays beyond taxpayer's control.

31.6   Belated notification penalty

Where a person is required to notify his liability to register for VAT and he has failed to do so, that person is liable to a penalty.

This penalty applies to registration in relation to:

- taxable turnover in the last 12 months;
- expected taxable turnover in the next 30 days;
- the transfer of a business as a going concern;
- distance sales from other EU member states;
- acquisitions received from other EU member states; and
- overseas traders disposing of assets where input tax has been claimed.

The amount of the penalty is based on the penalty rate and the amount of relevant VAT, subject to a minimum of £50.

The penalty rate is 5 per cent where the delay in notification is less than 9 months, 10 per cent where the delay is between 9 and 18 months, and 15 per cent where the delay exceeds 18 months. The period is measured from the date the person was required to have been registered, to the date he notified HMRC or the date they became aware of his liability to registration. The relevant VAT is the net amount of VAT for the same period.

> **Planning point**
>
> It is HMRC's normal policy to waive the penalty entirely if the notification is no more than three months late.

A penalty under this section may be assessed up to 20 years after the event giving rise to the penalty. HMRC may not assess a penalty under this section if the person is convicted of an offence in relation to his conduct or is assessed to a civil evasion penalty in relation to his conduct.

The legislation imposes a continuing obligation on the taxpayer to notify his liability to registration. Thus, when a person was required to notify his registration before the enactment of s. 67 (or its predecessor, FA 1985, s. 15), his liability to notify remained and is therefore liable to a penalty under this section. See *C & E Commrs v Shingleton* (1987) 3 BVC 194.

A person is relieved from a penalty under this section if he can establish a reasonable excuse for his failure to notify his liability to registration (see **30.11**).

Planning point

It is HMRC's normal policy to mitigate the penalty by up to 50 per cent in cases where the person concerned has notified their own liability to be registered, albeit belatedly, rather than its coming to their attention by other means. However, this mitigation is not always applied automatically and may need to be requested.

Law: VATA 1994, s. 67

Other guidance: VAT Notice 700/1, Section 13; *VAT Notice 700/41*

31.7   Conduct involving dishonesty

31.7.1 Civil evasion

This penalty, often referred to as civil evasion, arises where a person does or omits to do any act for the purpose of evading VAT, and his conduct involves dishonesty. The penalty equals the amount of VAT that has been evaded or the amount the person sought to evade.

Evasion of VAT includes the making of a claim to which the person is not entitled:

- to obtain a refund in respect of goods acquired in the UK, where such refund was already made in another EU member state;
- to a VAT credit;
- to a refund under the do-it-yourself builders scheme, the bad-debt relief scheme, or in relation to new means of transport supplied to a person in another EU member state; or
- to a refund to a person outside the UK under the Eighth or Thirteenth VAT Directives.

The procedures by which HMRC investigate the circumstances applicable to a penalty under this section have changed, reflecting case law pertaining to the Human

Rights Act 1998. In particular, since a s. 60 penalty is deemed a 'criminal charge', the taxpayer has rights as defined in art. 6 of the ECHR. A 'new approach' was introduced on 1 April 2002, under which HMRC seek to reach an agreement with the taxpayer as to 'the nature, extent and reason' for the irregularities they identify. A taxpayer is not obliged to follow these procedures, in which case the 'full civil evasion procedures' as set out in *Notice 730* are followed. The new procedures are explained in HMRC *Information Sheet* 1/02.

The amount of VAT evaded is essentially the amount of VAT falsely claimed by way of input tax or any other claim and/or the amount of VAT understated by way of output tax falsely declared. Both approaches to investigation allow for a mitigation of the penalty. Ordinarily the 'new approach' may give rise to mitigation by up to 80 per cent and the conventional (*Notice 730*) approach by up to 75 per cent. However, the legislation allows mitigation up to 100 per cent, somewhat bizarrely, it may be thought, considering that its imposition presupposes dishonest conduct!

HMRC may assess a person to a penalty under this section. Where possible this should be attributed to prescribed accounting periods, but the penalty is not invalid if HMRC are unable to or choose not to attribute in this way (see *C & E Commrs v Bassimeh* [1997] BVC 106). HMRC must assess within two years from the date the amount of VAT due was finally determined, and may assess for any prescribed accounting period within 20 years of the date of the assessment.

A penalty under this section has been issued on a person who failed to register for VAT – see *Stevenson and Telford Building & Design Ltd v C & E Commrs* [1996] BVC 428.

A penalty notice can be made on a partnership, without the necessity of separate notices (see *Akbar (t/a Mumtaz Paan House)* [1998] BVC 2,157). The committing of a dishonest act may be made by an individual or by a taxable person, such as a partnership (see *Islam & Goodwest Ltd* [2003] BVC 4,043). In another case, a penalty notice sent to one partner was held to constitute sufficient notification of the penalty (see *Yarl Wines* [2003] BVC 4,045).

Where a taxpayer paid a centrally issued assessment, knowing it to be substantially below his return liability, and taking no steps to notify HMRC of his higher liability, he was assessed for a penalty under this section (see *Storey* [2003] BVC 4,030).

Planning point

Where HMRC issue a ruling as to the treatment of a particular series of transactions, the deliberate refusal to apply that ruling and a continuation of the practice which conflicts with it, may be regarded as dishonest (see *Taylor (t/a Riverside Sports and Leisure Club)* [2003] BVC 4,100).

Where a person is convicted of an offence under s. 72 in relation to his conduct, that same conduct cannot also trigger a penalty under this section.

Law: VATA 1994, s. 60

31.7.2 Liability of directors and other persons

Where a penalty under VATA 1994, s. 60 is applicable to a corporate body, and the conduct giving rise to the penalty may be attributed to any director or managing officer, HMRC may, under powers in s. 61, assess that person for part or all of the penalty. The legislation is widely drafted to include any person acting or purporting to act as a director. Such a person is a 'named officer' on whom is served a notice stating the amount of penalty being 'the basic penalty', assessed on the corporate body, and the amount of the penalty assessed on the named officer. Where a penalty is assessed under this section, the penalty assessed on the corporate body is reduced by the amount assessed on the named officer.

The tribunal has criticised HMRC where their notification of a penalty under this section was incomplete, see *Nazif* [1996] BVC 2,510. However, a single notice to both the director and the company notifying both penalties does not render either ineffective. See *Nidderdale Building Ltd v C & E Commrs* [1997] BVC 378.

> **Example 31.6**
>
> HMRC assess a company for a penalty of £160,000 under VATA 1994, s. 60.
>
> They attribute 75 per cent to the dishonesty of a director.
>
> They therefore assess the director for £160,000 × 75 per cent = £120,000.
>
> The penalty assessed on the company is therefore reduced to £160,000 − 120,000 = £40,000.
>
> The total of the two assessments remains the same as the basic penalty, i.e. £160,000.

Law: VATA 1994, s. 61

31.8 Other penalties

31.8.1 Failure to submit an electronic VAT return

Penalties will be applied where a business that is required to submit its VAT returns electronically and fails to do so. For accounting periods ending on or after 31 March 2011, a penalty is applied each time a paper return is filed instead of the electronic return. The penalty is geared according to the business's turnover (excluding VAT) for the 12 months prior to the date of the paper return that incurs the penalty.

The penalty amounts are listed in the table below.

Annual VAT-exclusive turnover	Penalty
£22,800,001 and above	£400
£5,600,001 to £22,800,000	£300
£100,001 to £5,600,000	£200
£100,000 and under	£100

31.8.2 Incorrect certificate for zero-rating or reduced-rating

In a number of situations, a person receiving a supply from a taxable person is required to give the supplier a certificate in relation to zero-rating, reduced-rating or exemption:

- under VATA 1994, Sch. 8, Grp. 5, the construction of buildings for relevant residential or charitable use;
- under VATA 1994, Sch. 8, Grp. 6, construction work in relation to protected buildings for relevant residential or charitable use;
- under VATA 1994, Sch. 9, Grp. 1, land or property; or
- under VATA 1994, Sch. 7A, all groups.

A certificate is also provided in relation to the fiscal warehousing regime:

- that certain goods are subject to fiscal warehousing (s. 18B(2)(d));
- that certain services are performed in relation to goods which are subject to fiscal warehousing (s. 18C(1)(c)); or
- that there is an acquisition of goods subject to fiscal warehousing and, in this instance, the certificate is prepared by the acquirer of the goods (s. 18B(1)(d)).

Where such a certificate is incorrect, then the person giving the certificate is liable to a penalty. This applies to the person preparing the certificate, where that person is the acquirer of the goods or services. The amount of the penalty is set at the difference between the amount of VAT chargeable had the certificate been correct and the amount that was actually chargeable. In this respect the penalty is akin to the civil evasion penalty. However, HMRC are not required to demonstrate dishonesty.

Planning point

This penalty is not restricted to VAT-registered persons, since an unregistered person may issue a certificate incorrectly so as to avoid paying otherwise irrecoverable VAT on the supply in question.

Where a person is convicted of an offence under s. 72 in relation to his conduct, that same conduct cannot also trigger a penalty under this section.

> **Planning point**
>
> The recipient of a certificate is expected to take reasonable steps to validate the certificate. In such circumstances, where he has acted in good faith and can demonstrate the checks he has made, he will not be liable to account for additional VAT. See *Notice 708, para. 16.3*. The liability of the person issuing the incorrect certificate is a separate matter.

The sole defence to the penalty is where the taxpayer has a reasonable excuse for his conduct.

Law: VATA 1994, s. 62

31.8.3 Failure to submit EC sales statements

This penalty is directed at the person who is late in submitting his EC sales statement (known as the EC sales list or ESL), as required for a person making supplies of goods to taxable persons in other EU member states, including being an intermediary in triangulation arrangements.

Where a person makes no relevant supplies, he is not required to complete and submit a statement and therefore failure to do so will not trigger a default.

Where a person is in default, that is he has failed to submit his ESL by the due date, HMRC serve a notice, amongst other things, allowing 14 days to submit it. If the person fails to do so, he will be liable to a penalty of £5 per day until he submits his statement. This is subject to a minimum of £50 and a maximum of £500, i.e. 100 days.

In *Moll* [2001] BVC 4,161, it was held that, where the warning notice was issued after the due date of a statement, then no penalty could be assessed in relation to that statement (VATA 1994, s. 66(2)).

The notice also warns the person that subsequent defaults within a 12-month period will trigger a penalty without a further warning. A second default triggers a penalty at £10 per day, subject to a minimum of £50 and a maximum of £1,000, i.e. 100 days. Later defaults trigger a penalty at £15 per day, subject to a minimum of £50 and a maximum of £1,500, i.e. 100 days.

HMRC may assess a penalty at any time after the service of the notice. This will show the amount of the penalty calculated up to a specified date, either on or before the date of the assessment. Later penalties may be assessed. The total value of penalties assessed in respect of one default cannot exceed the maximum allowed, i.e. 100 days at the specified daily rate.

The person assessed to a penalty under this section will not be liable to the surcharge and will be treated as having not been in default for that period, where:

- he submitted his statement in time to reach HMRC by the due date (see **31.10.1**); or
- there is a reasonable excuse for the statement not having been so despatched (see **31.11**).

The effect of a successful defence being established is that the penalty rate applicable to later defaults and surcharges will be reduced or cancelled in full.

A person not in possession of an ESL is expected to obtain a blank ESL for completion. A failure to do so will prevent him establishing a reasonable excuse defence (see *Proops (t/a J P Antiques)* [2000] BVC 4,058).

Law: VATA 1994, s. 66

Other guidance: *VAT Notice 725, s. 14*

31.8.4 Inaccuracy in EC sales statement

This penalty affects the person who persists in submitting inaccurately completed ESLs. The procedure provides for two warning notices preceding any assessment to a penalty, thus giving the person opportunity to improve his reporting systems.

The procedure is as follows.

1. The person submits a statement containing a 'material inaccuracy'.

2. HMRC discover the inaccuracy.

3. HMRC issue the first warning notice (this must be within six months of stage 2).

4. The person submits another statement containing an inaccuracy, within two years of stage 3.

5. HMRC discover the inaccuracy.

6. HMRC issue the second warning notice (this must be within six months of stage 5).

7. The person submits a further statement containing an inaccuracy, within two years of stage 3.

8. This third breach triggers a penalty under the section.

An inaccuracy is considered to be a 'material inaccuracy' if the inclusion or omission of any information is misleading in any material respect. *Notice 725, para. 14.21* suggests that the following items may be so considered:

- errors exceeding £100;
- an incorrect VAT registration number; and
- an incorrect statement relating to a triangulation arrangement.

The penalty is set at £100.

Where a person is convicted of an offence in relation to an ESL, the inaccuracy to which the offence relates is not treated as a material inaccuracy in relation to this section.

There are statutory defences to a penalty issued under this section:

- there is a reasonable excuse for his conduct (see **31.11**); or
- the taxpayer provided HMRC with full details of the error (see **31.10.2**).

Law: VATA 1994, s. 65

Other guidance: *VAT Notice 725, s. 14*

31.8.5 Failure to notify events affecting exemption from registration

Where a person is exempt from registration for VAT, he remains under a duty to notify HMRC in the event of certain changes in the nature of his supplies or alteration in the proportions of taxable supplies. Three classes of persons are affected:

(1)   Persons making zero-rated supplies.

(2)   Persons making zero-rated acquisitions.

(3)   Persons making supplies of zero-rated goods for which input tax repayment has been claimed.

The amount of the penalty is based on failure to register penalty (see **3.2.9**). The penalty rate is determined by consideration if the failure was deliberate and concealed (100 per cent), deliberate, but not concealed (70 per cent) or 30 per cent in any other case. The penalty can be mitigated for disclosure (unprompted or not) and may even be reduced to nil.

31.8.6 Failure to notify goods acquired from EU member states

VATA 1994, s. 10(1)(c) creates a charge to tax for acquisitions of goods subject to excise duty and new means of transport, whether or not the person acquiring the goods is a taxable person. Schedule 11, para. 2(4) provides for regulations relating to such a charge to tax, the notification of such acquisitions and payment of VAT. Regulation 36 imposes a duty upon a person acquiring goods subject to excise duty to notify HMRC immediately on acquisition or arrival, whichever is the sooner. Similarly, reg. 148 imposes a duty upon a person acquiring a new means of transport to notify HMRC within seven days of acquisition or arrival, whichever is the sooner.

For the definition of a new means of transport, see VATA 1994, s. 95; VAT Regulations 1995 (SI 1995/2518), reg. 147.

Where the person fails to notify HMRC as required, or where he fails to pay the VAT amount due, he is liable to a penalty under this section. A person will not be liable to a penalty under this section if he is convicted of an offence in respect of conduct or he is assessed for a civil evasion penalty in respect of it. A penalty under this section may be assessed up to 20 years after the event giving rise to the penalty. The assessment of the VAT, under s. 75, and the assessment of the penalty may be combined in a single document, although the amount of each must be separately identified.

The amount of the penalty is based on the penalty rate and the amount of VAT on the acquisition or the amount of VAT unpaid, to which the failure relates.

The penalty rate is five per cent where the person has failed to notify his acquisition for less than three months, ten per cent for a failure for between three and six months and 15 per cent for any longer period. The minimum penalty is £50.

A person is relieved from a penalty under this section if he can establish a reasonable excuse for his failure to notify his acquisition or the failure to pay the VAT amount due (see **31.11.1**).

Law: VATA 1994, s. 67

31.8.7 Unauthorised issue of VAT invoices

Where a person not authorised under VATA 1994 issues invoices indicating an amount of VAT or an amount attributable to VAT, then that person is liable to a penalty.

The amount of the penalty is based on failure to register penalty (see **3.2.9**). The penalty rate is determined by consideration if the failure was deliberate and concealed (100 per cent), deliberate, but not concealed (70 per cent) or 30 per cent in any other case. The penalty can be mitigated for disclosure (unprompted or not) and may even be reduced to nil.

31.8.8 Breach of walking possession agreement

This penalty arises in a situation where a person has refused to pay an amount of VAT or is unable to do so. HMRC enter into a 'walking possession agreement' with the person, as provided for by the Distress for Customs & Excise Duties and other Indirect Taxes Regulations 1997 (SI 1997/1431), reg. 2(1) and VATA 1994, s. 68(2). This penalty does not apply in Scotland.

Where a walking possession agreement is entered into, the person agrees not to remove or allow to be removed any goods which are the subject of the agreement. If the person does so, he is liable to a penalty under this section.

The penalty is 50 per cent of the amount of VAT due or alleged to be due.

A person is relieved from a penalty under this section if he can establish a reasonable excuse for his failure to comply with the walking possession agreement.

It appears that there is no case law in relation to the penalty under this section, but HMRC have indicated that a reasonable excuse may be established:

- where the goods are stolen, accidentally damaged or destroyed, e.g. by fire;
- the walking possession agreement fails to clearly identify the goods; or
- the taxpayer believes that the walking possession agreement no longer applies, e.g. if he enters into a 'time to pay' agreement or there is a long delay following the issue of the walking possession agreement.

In other respects the general guidance in relation to reasonable excuse applies (see **31.11.1**).

Law: VATA 1994, s. 68

31.8.9 Failure to furnish returns and pay tax

This penalty acts as an alternative to the default surcharge. Where a person is assessed to a default surcharge, he is not liable to such a penalty.

The failure to furnish penalty applies without warning to any failure to submit a VAT return and to any failure to pay the amount of VAT due, in either case by the due date.

The amount of the penalty is based on a daily rate, multiplied by the number of days on which the failure continues. The daily rate is calculated as:

- a percentage of the VAT shown as due on the VAT return; or
- where the return has not been submitted, a percentage of the amount assessed by HMRC in the absence of the return.

The percentage is:

- where there has been no previous failure to furnish, 0.17 per cent;
- where there has been one previous failure to furnish, 0.33 per cent; or
- where there has been more than one previous failure to furnish, 0.5 per cent.

The penalty applies up to a maximum of 100 days.

A penalty may be assessed under this section up to three years after the prescribed accounting period for which the person failed to furnish either the return or the payment.

HMRC may not assess a penalty under this section if the person is convicted of an offence in relation to his conduct or is assessed to a civil evasion penalty in relation to his conduct. In addition, if the person's conduct gives rise to a misdeclaration penalty, then he will not be liable to penalty under this section.

A person is relieved from a penalty under this section if he can establish a reasonable excuse for his failure (see **31.11.1**). Where a reasonable excuse is established there is deemed to have been no failure to furnish for that prescribed accounting period.

Law: VATA 1994, s. 69

31.8.10 Failure to preserve records

Any person required to preserve records for the six years laid down who fails to do so, is liable to a penalty under this heading.

The penalty is set at £500.

A distinction is made between this penalty and a failure to produce records for inspection by HMRC.

A penalty may be assessed under this section up to three years after the prescribed accounting period for which the person failed to furnish either the return or the payment.

HMRC may not assess a penalty under this section if the person is convicted of an offence in relation to his conduct or is assessed to a civil evasion penalty in relation to his conduct. In addition, if the person's conduct gives rise to a misdeclaration penalty, then he will not be liable to penalty under this section.

A person is relieved from a penalty under this section if he can establish a reasonable excuse for his failure to preserve records (see **31.11**).

Law: VATA 1994, s. 69

HMRC have issued eBrief No. 06/2012 dated 13 February 2012 that outlines their new requirements in respect to the retention of tax records that are maintained in electronic format. This is relevant for any electronic, photographic or other process used for the storage, maintenance, transmission, reproduction and communication of any record. These new requirements introduce two changed requirements. Firstly, it is no longer a requirement to retain paper originals of any third party record where an electronic copy of the original record is retained. Secondly, all electronic copies of records must be accessible to an HMRC official in paper or electronic form, in a format that is specified by the HMRC official.

31.8.11 Breach of record-keeping requirements in relation to transactions in gold

HMRC have introduced special accounting arrangements for transactions in gold. In particular, regulations provide for specified records to be maintained and for specified information to be provided to HMRC in respect of those transactions. It is a failure in either maintaining such records or in providing such information that falls foul of this penalty.

The penalty is an amount 'not exceeding 17.5 per cent' of the value of the transactions to which the failure relates. Thus, the penalty has an in-built mitigation, in addition to the provisions of s. 70. *Notice 701/21, para. 9.7* includes specific areas which may constitute grounds for mitigation as:

- the number of breaches;
- the seriousness of breaches;
- cooperation with HMRC;
- compassionate grounds;
- the period of time involved;
- deliberate or reckless behaviour;
- perceived risk to the revenue; and
- degree of care exercised.

An assessment to a penalty under this section has to be made within two years of the time when HMRC receive or obtain evidence of the facts sufficient to justify the making of the assessment. These 'facts' include both the evidence of the person's failure and the determination of the value of the supply.

A penalty may be assessed under this section up to three years after the event giving rise to the penalty.

HMRC may not assess a penalty under this section if the person is convicted of an offence in relation to his conduct or is assessed to a civil evasion penalty in relation to his conduct.

A person is relieved from a penalty under this section if he can establish a reasonable excuse for his failure to comply with these requirements (see **31.11.1**).

Law: VATA 1994, s. 69

31.8.12 Breach of regulatory provisions

VATA 1994, s. 69 provides civil penalties in a range of other circumstances, including some 'catch-all' provisions as:

- any regulations made under the Act, apart from the tribunal rules (s. 69(1)(e));
- any order made by the Treasury under the Act (s. 69(1)(f)); or
- any regulations relating to VAT and made under the European Communities Act 1972 (s. 69(1)(f)).

A batch of provisions relates to registration matters and these include when:

- a taxable person fails to notify his cessation of making taxable supplies or his intention to cease making taxable supplies, as required by Sch. 1, para. 11;
- a person registered in respect of supplies which would be taxable if made in the UK fails to notify his cessation of making such supplies or his intention to cease making such supplies, as required by Sch. 1, para. 12(a);
- a person registered in respect of supplies which would be taxable if made in the UK fails to notify his making of taxable supplies or his intention to make taxable supplies, as required by Sch. 1, para. 12(b);
- a person registered in respect of distance sales made into the UK who fails to notify matters affecting the continuance of his registration, as required by Sch. 2, para. 5;
- a person registered in respect of acquisitions who fails to notify matters affecting the continuance of his registration, as required by Sch. 3, para. 5; or
- a person registered in respect of disposals of assets for which VAT repayment is claimed, who fails to notify his cessation of making such supplies or his intention to cease making such supplies, as required by Sch. 3A, para. 5.

A breach also falls within this section if a VAT representative fails to notify his appointment or his retirement, as required by VAT Regulations 1995 (SI 1995/2518), reg. 10.

A breach also falls within this section where a person fails to comply with the conditions relating to fiscal warehousing, as required by s. 18A.

Where regulatory provisions relate to the maintaining of records and the furnishing of information, see **31.8.13**.

The penalty for breaches under this section is based on a daily rate multiplied by the number of days for which the breach continues, up to a maximum of 100 days and subject to a minimum of £50.

If there has been no previous breach, the daily rate is £5. If there has been one previous breach, the rate is 10 per cent. If there has been more than one previous breach, the rate is £15 per day.

HMRC may not assess a penalty under this section if the person is convicted of an offence in relation to his conduct or is assessed to a civil evasion penalty in relation to his conduct. HMRC also may not assess a breach under this section if they have already assessed a default surcharge or misdeclaration penalty.

A person is relieved from a penalty under this section if he can establish a reasonable excuse for his failure to comply with the requirements (see **31.11**).

Law: VATA 1994, s. 69

31.8.13 Breach of regulatory provisions – maintaining records and furnishing information – for offences before 1 April 2009

A breach falls within this section in relation to a failure to:

- keep such records as are required by regulations;
- furnish information relating to goods or services or to supplies, acquisitions or importations, as HMRC may reasonably require;
- produce, or cause to be produced, documents relating to goods or services or to supplies, acquisitions or importations, as HMRC may reasonably require; or
- as required by Sch. 11, paras. 6(1) or 7.

The tribunal has held that there is no contradiction with HMRC powers under Sch. 11 and the requirements of the Companies Acts. Thus, the claim to deny HMRC access to inspect records on the basis that the directors would become liable under the Companies Act is unreasonable (*Fabco Ltd* [1993] BVC 802). Where records are held by a person's accountant, HMRC powers under Sch. 11 require that the records be made available for their inspection; thus this statutory duty has priority over other business matters (*HEM Construction Ltd* [1995] BVC 1,517 and *HEM Construction Ltd* [1996] BVC 4,094).

The decisions quoted refer to HMRC practice of issuing a formal demand to see a person's records. This demand warns the person that further refusal to allow access will render him liable to a penalty under this section. In reality, the person is already so liable. The penalty for breaches under this section is based on a daily rate, multiplied by the number of days for which the breach continues, up to a maximum of 100 days, and subject to a minimum of £50. If there has been no previous breach the daily rate is £5. If there has been one previous breach the rate is 10 per cent. If there has been more than one previous breach the rate is £15 per day. HMRC may not assess a penalty under this section if the person is convicted of an offence in relation to his conduct or is assessed to a civil evasion penalty in relation to his conduct. HMRC also may not assess a breach under this section if they have already assessed a default surcharge or misdeclaration penalty in relation to the same conduct.

A person is relieved from a penalty under this section if he can establish a reasonable excuse for his failure to comply with the requirements (see **31.11**).

Law: VATA 1994, s. 69

31.8.14 Failure to comply with an information notice

From 1 April 2009, a person who fails to comply with an information notice or deliberately obstructs an officer during an inspection authorized by a Tribunal is liable to a penalty of £300. If the failure continues, the penalty is £60 a day up to a maximum of £3,000. Failure to produce includes destroying or disposing of a document (unless the information has been previously provided) or in the case of a copy document, six months have elapsed since the copy was originally provided. In addition, a person must not conceal a document if he is told it is likely that it will become the subject of an information notice.

Where a person is subject to a penalty and an HMRC officer believes that a substantial amount of tax is at stake, he may apply to the Upper Tribunal for an additional penalty. The Upper Tribunal will determine the amount of penalty based upon the amount of tax likely to be at stake. This is in addition to the standard and daily rate penalties. The penalties are payable within 30 days of notification as if they are tax amounts.

Law: FA 2008, Sch. 36, paras 39-52

31.8.15 Failure to comply with a notice requiring contact details of a debtor

From 1 April 2009, a person who fails to comply with a notice requiring contact details of a debtor is liable to a penalty of £300.

31.8.16 Evasion of import VAT

This penalty arises where a person engages in any conduct for the purpose of evading import VAT and that conduct involves dishonesty. The penalty equals the amount of import VAT that has been evaded or the amount the person sought to evade.

Evading import VAT includes repayment, relief or exemption from import VAT and the cancellation of any withdrawal of any repayment, reliever or repayment, and also deferral or other postponement of his liability to pay import VAT.

Where a person is convicted of a criminal offence or is liable to a penalty under any other provision relating to import VAT in relation to his conduct, he will not be liable to a penalty under this section. Similarly, if he has received and not had withdrawn a demand notice in respect of a penalty under the Companies (Forms) (Amendment) Regulations 2003 (SI 2003/2985) he will not be liable to a penalty under this section.

A person may be assessed up to 20 years after the conduct giving rise to the penalty. A person must be assessed within two years after evidence of facts, sufficient to justify

763

HMRC in giving him a demand notice, comes to their knowledge. A person may be assessed up to three years after his death.

A penalty under this section may be assessed against the directors or officers of a body corporate, to the extent that HMRC consider the conduct of the body corporate was attributable to the dishonesty of that person or persons. The person is then personally liable for that penalty (FA 2003, s. 28).

The penalty may be mitigated or withdrawn in full, by HMRC or, on appeal, by the tribunal. But, in considering the amount of any reduction, what cannot be taken into account is:

- insufficiency of funds on the part of the person liable to pay the import VAT;
- the fact that there has been no significant loss of import VAT; or
- the person liable to the penalty, or a person acting on his behalf, was acting in good faith.

The legislation provides for a procedure under which the demand notice is issued to the person, and under which any review of HMRC's decision is made.

Law: Finance Act 2003, ss. 24 and 30–35

31.8.17 Non-compliance with import regulations

A person is liable to a penalty under this heading if he engages in any conduct by which he contravenes any duty, obligation, requirement or condition relating to import VAT, imposed by or under any of the following legislation:

- CEMA 1979, or other Act or statutory instrument;
- EU customs rules (as laid down in EC VAT Directive 2913/92 dated 12 October 1972) and including those provisions adopted at EU or national level to implement them;
- any directly applicable EU legislation; and
- any relevant international agreements having effect as part of the law of any part of the UK, by virtue of any of the above.

The penalty is set at a maximum of £2,500.

HMRC may not assess a penalty under this section where the person is:

- prosecuted for an offence;
- given (and has not had withdrawn) a demand notice in relation to a penalty under FA 2003, s. 24;
- liable to a penalty under any other provision relating to import VAT; or
- liable to a penalty under the other civil VAT provisions.

A person must be assessed to a penalty under this section within three years of the conduct giving rise to the penalty and within two years of evidence of facts coming to HMRC's knowledge.

A person is relieved from a penalty under this section if he can establish a reasonable excuse for his conduct (see **31.11**). The meaning of reasonable excuse pertaining to this penalty is different to that applicable for other civil breaches.

31.8.18 Failure to comply with a direction or summons

This penalty is issued by the VAT and Duties Tribunal rather than HMRC. Where a person or, indeed, HMRC, fails to comply with a direction or summons issued by the tribunal under its rules, he is liable to a penalty of up to £1,000. The decision is 'issued' in a document produced under reg. 30(1)–(2). In the case of *Wine Warehouses Europe Ltd* [1995] BVC 611 an award under this section was made against HMRC in view of their repeated failure to comply with directions. Where the penalty is issued against a person, the amount is recoverable as VAT.

A person who has received a penalty under this section may appeal to the High Court.

31.8.19 Failure to comply with the duties of a senior accounting officer

From 1 April 2009, a person who is a senior accounting officer will be liable to a penalty of £5,000 if he or she fails to comply with their main duties in respect of accountancy arrangements. Only one penalty can be applied per year for each company. Failing to provide certificates or issuing certificates with a careless mistake is subject to the same penalty.

31.9   Default interest

31.9.1 Overview

Where an amount of tax or money representing tax is assessed under VATA 1994, s. 73, it carries interest under this section. Thus, interest arises in a number of circumstances. Interest is calculated from a 'reckonable date', which may vary depending upon the circumstances of the case.

Default interest is described as a means of 'commercial restitution' whereby the Exchequer is compensated for him being deprived of the amount of VAT for a period of time. Thus, HMRC have indicated that default interest will not be charged in circumstances where there is no loss of tax. However, this is a concession and is not statutory (see *Terracopia* [1995] BVC 1,329).

> ### Planning point
> HMRC almost invariably waive the interest where the underdeclared tax assessed or voluntarily disclosed is output tax which would have been recoverable as input tax by the customer had it been charged at the appropriate time. However, this is not applied automatically and must often be requested.

Where there are adjustments of underdeclarations and overdeclarations of VAT in the same prescribed accounting period, default interest applies to the net amount (*London Borough of Camden* [1993] BVC 1,004). That case was followed when underclaimed input tax was notified before an underdeclaration was identified by HMRC (*SGS Holdings UK Ltd* [1996] BVC 4,056), but was distinguished in a case where underclaimed input tax was notified to HMRC after an underdeclaration was identified (*MacKenzie* [1995] BVC 1,373).

HMRC have published a list of circumstances where default interest will not normally be charged:

- management charges between taxable persons;
- liability errors on supplies to fully taxable persons;
- underdeclarations of output tax on transactions between taxable persons where, if the output tax had been charged and declared correctly by the supplier, it would have been immediately reclaimable as input tax by the customer;
- output tax declared at the right time by the wrong VAT registration;
- input tax claimed by the wrong VAT registration; or
- import VAT claimed by the wrong VAT registration – this includes errors arising out of the use of the wrong deferment number.

They have also provided a list of circumstances where default interest would normally be charged:

- omission from VAT records of sales invoices issued to customers;
- late entry in VAT records of sales invoices issued to customers;
- errors involving operation of cash accounting;
- retail scheme errors;
- partial exemption scheme errors;
- errors in partial exemption calculations;
- arithmetic errors, duplicated input tax claims, omission of input tax credit notes, etc.;
- additional assessments;
- bad-debt relief;
- assessments based on credibility techniques, such as mark-up exercises, parts to labour, etc., where the sales are to unregistered customers;
- discrepancies in annual accounts or cash reconciliations;
- liability errors;

- failure to charge tax;
- own use of goods;
- input tax not deductible; and
- road fuel scale charges.

The current prescribed rate of interest is reported on the HMRC website (*www.hmrc. gov.uk*).

There is no reasonable excuse defence to default interest.

VATA 1994, s. 83(q) provides for a right of appeal against an assessment to interest. A number of appeals made against the imposition of interest have been struck out.

Interest is charged on VAT and not on penalties or other interest. Thus it is applicable in the various circumstances listed below.

31.9.2 Assessments – general

Where HMRC raise an assessment under VATA 1994, s. 73(1), where a person has failed to submit a return or the return is considered incomplete or incorrect, then the assessment carries interest – as long as one of the following is fulfilled:

(1) The assessment relates to a period for which a return has been made or an assessment has already been notified.

(2) The assessment relates to a prescribed accounting period exceeding three months and begins on the date he was, or was required to be, registered.

(3) The assessment relates to a prescribed accounting period and at the beginning of that period the person was exempted from registration but should not have been so exempted.

Interest is calculated from the last date the return was required to be made and is calculated up to the date of payment.

31.9.3 Assessments – excessive repayment

Where HMRC raise an assessment under s. 73(2) or (3) to recover VAT overpaid to a person as:

- a repayment or refund of VAT;
- a VAT credit; or
- a VAT credit wrongly paid to a person whose registration has been cancelled,

interest is calculated from the seventh day after the date HMRC issued a written instruction to direct the payment of the money to the person concerned.

31.9.4 Assessment – failure to account for goods

Where HMRC raise an assessment under s. 73(7) in relation to goods, when the person has failed to account satisfactorily for those goods, the assessment carries interest.

Interest is calculated from the last date the return was required to be made and is calculated up to the date of payment.

31.9.5 Assessment – fiscal warehousing deficiency

Where HMRC identify a deficiency in goods subject to fiscal warehousing, or goods have been removed without payment of VAT, they may raise an assessment under s. 73(7A) or (7B) that carries interest.

Interest is calculated from the last date the return was required to be made and is calculated up to the date of payment.

31.9.6 Assessment – unauthorised invoices

Where an unauthorised person issues an invoice showing an amount of VAT or an amount attributable to VAT, that amount is recoverable from him (Sch. 11, para. 5). The person will be also liable to interest on the amount so shown, from the date of the invoice until payment.

31.9.7 Adjustment – voluntary disclosure

Where a person makes a voluntary disclosure of errors and pays the amount due, interest shall still apply even though no assessment is made. HMRC have indicated that where the net amount shown on a voluntary disclosure is less than £2,000 they will not charge default interest. Where a number of adjustments are made to one prescribed accounting period, such that one or more increases the liability and one or more decreases the liability, interest is only calculated on the net amount.

If an assessment could have been made under s. 73(1), interest is calculated from the last date the return was required to be made and is calculated up to the date of payment. If, however, the assessment could have been made under s. 73(2), then the interest is calculated from the seventh day after the date HMRC issued a written instruction to direct the payment of the money to the person concerned.

Following the decision in *R v IR Commrs, ex parte Wilkinson* [2005] BTC 281, this practice of not charging default interest on small value error notifications (or voluntary disclosures) was not considered lawful by HMRC. Consequently, HMRC's policy of not charging default interest on net errors of £2,000 or less that are notified to HMRC by Voluntary Disclosure was withdrawn with effect from 1 September 2008. From this date, all error notifications requiring an assessment will be subject to a penalty no matter how small the error. Small value errors can, however, be corrected on a later VAT return and will not attract an interest charge.

Errors that are not deliberate errors, which are discovered for return periods beginning on or after 1 April 2008 but with a due date on or after 1 April 2009, can be altered on a later VAT return if:

- the net value of all errors found on previous returns to be adjusted does not exceed £10,000; or
- the net value of all errors found on previous returns to be adjusted is between £10,000 and £50,000 but does not exceed 1 per cent of the total outputs (the box 6 figure) on the VAT return for the period in which the errors are discovered.

Amounts greater than these *de minimis* amounts, or errors of any value that have been made deliberately, must be disclosed to HMRC on form VAT 652 (the Notification of Errors in VAT Returns form) and will attract interest charges. It should be noted that the error value is the net value of all errors. It is necessary to set off all errors discovered and to calculate the net amount owing to HMRC when applying these *de minimis* amounts. It should also be noted that if amounts that could have been declared on a return are notified to HMRC for correction, that the interest charge will still apply. Thus, errors should be disclosed on returns wherever possible.

When an error is notified to HMRC, the interest charge is calculated, separately for each error made, from the date when the VAT notified as an error first became due (usually the date the return which contained the error was due to be paid) to the calculation date shown on the Notice of Assessment or Notification of Errors in Returns form. Where the return which is in error is a repayment claim and it is found that there has been an over claim of VAT, the interest is calculated from seven days after the date the repayment is authorised by HMRC to the calculation date in the Notice of Assessment or Notification of Errors in Returns form. This extra seven days is to take account of the time a repayment may take to reach the taxpayer.

31.9.8 Adjustment – failure to reimburse customers

Where a person who claims back overpaid VAT from HMRC is directed to make reimbursement to his customers and fails to do so, he is liable to an assessment under s. 80(B) and is liable to pay interest on any amount so assessed.

Interest is calculated from the date of the assessment to the date of payment.

31.9.10 Adjustment – statutory interest

If a person makes a claim for statutory interest but is not entitled to that interest, HMRC may assess him for that overpaid interest under s. 78A and for interest due on that amount.

Interest is calculated from the date of the assessment to the date of payment, on a daily basis.

When an assessment is made under s. 73(1) or (2), interest may run for a maximum of three years. Where the period from the reckonable date to the date of payment exceeds three years, the interest is calculated on the last three years of that period. In respect of other assessments to interest, there appears to be no limit on the length of period for which interest may be assessed. The application of this three year restriction was addressed in *Shokar (t/a Manor Fish Bar)* [1999] BVC 4,003.

The rate of interest was originally, from 1 April 1990, prescribed by statutory instrument made under FA 1996, s. 197. More recently it has been announced in HMRC's *Notices* and *Business Briefs*.

Law: VATA 1994, s. 74

Other guidance: *VAT Notice 700/43*

31.10 Defences, mitigation and appeal

In general terms, a taxpayer may challenge the imposition of any penalty – as a matter of principle – or in relation to quantum.

It should be noted that the reasonable excuse defence is applicable to most of the penalties. However, certain penalties cannot be voided in this way and are listed below.

1. Tax evasion penalties under ss. 60–61. There can, of course, be no 'excuse' for dishonest conduct. However, HMRC may mitigate the penalty (see **31.12**).

2. Failure to comply with a direction or summons under VAT Tribunals Rules 1986 (SI 1986/590). There is an appeal to the High Court for a penalty issued by the tribunal – see Sch. 12, para. 10(3).

3. Default surcharge, under s. 74. This effectively attaches itself to an assessment for VAT.

4 Failing to comply with the duties of a senior accounting officer.

HMRC are not obliged to assess a penalty under any section. Section 76(1) provides that they may assess someone liable to a penalty under the various sections referred to. Thus, there is a discretion granted to HMRC not to enforce liability to a penalty. In *C & E Commrs v Steptoe* [1992] BVC 142, this discretion was termed a 'residual administrative discretion'. In *Dollar Land (Feltham) Ltd, Dollar Land (Cumbernauld) Ltd and Dollar Land (Calthorpe House) Ltd v C & E Commrs* [1995] BVC 115, it was held that there was no right of appeal against HMRC's discretion in this respect. However, there remained a right of appeal against the imposition of the penalty.

The bulk of appeals in relation to a reasonable excuse defence have occurred in relation to three penalties:

(1)   Failure to notify liability.

(2)   Misdeclaration penalty.

(3)   Default surcharge.

This reflects the fact that the number of penalties issued in relation to these penalties is also greater.

In relation to failure to notify liability to registration, HMRC have listed a number of circumstances where they consider that a reasonable excuse might be established by:

- compassionate circumstances;
- transfer of a business as a going concern;
- doubt as to the liability of supplies; or
- uncertainty of employment status.

In relation to the misdeclaration penalties, they will consider factors such as the complexity of the case, compassionate circumstances and unforeseeable events that have adversely affected the business.

In relation to the default surcharge, a different list is provided:

- computer breakdown;
- illness;
- loss of key personnel;
- unexpected cash crisis; or
- loss of records.

This reflects the fact that different circumstances are relevant in relation to different penalties.

Other guidance: *Notice 700/41*; *Notice 700/42*; *Notice 700/50*

31.10.1 Timely submission of return and payment

This defence applies only to the default surcharge, including where a taxpayer uses the payments on account scheme.

VATA 1994, s. 59(7) provides that where a default is material to a surcharge, the default will be cancelled and any surcharge reduced or cancelled if:

'(a)   the return or, as the case may be, the VAT shown on the return was despatched at such a time and in such a manner that it was reasonable to expect that it would be received by Customs within the appropriate time limit; or

(b)   there is a reasonable excuse for the return or VAT not having been so despatched.'

Thus, a taxpayer is required to despatch his return in sufficient time to reach HMRC by the stated date. The timely despatch of a return and payment is a matter of fact and therefore the taxpayer will be required to demonstrate that the return and payment were so despatched. For example, an entry in a post book or a firm recollection of posting, have both been accepted by the tribunal as adequate evidence. However, the date entered on a cheque is not adequate evidence.

There is some inconsistency in decisions on whether a return and payment, due at a weekend, were posted in sufficient time when posted on the Friday. See *La Reine (Limoges Porcelain) Ltd* [1993] BVC 1,632; *Halstead Motor Co* [1996] BVC 4,126.

> **Planning point**
>
> Where a taxpayer chooses to pay by electronic means, which allows him to make payment within seven days of the due date of the corresponding return, he is required to initiate payment in sufficient time so that HMRC receive payment within the extended time limit. Any failure will create a default under the regime.

31.10.2 Unprompted disclosure

This defence applies in relation to the following penalties:

- misdeclaration penalty;
- repeated misdeclaration penalty; and
- inaccuracy in ESL.

The legislation provides (VATA 1994, ss. 63(10)(b), 64(5)(b) and 65(3)(b) respectively) that a penalty will not apply when:

> 'at a time when he had no reason to believe that enquiries were being made by the Commissioners into his affairs, so far as they relate to VAT, the person concerned furnished to the Commissioners full information with respect to the inaccuracy [concerned].'

Thus, a distinction is to be made between a genuinely unprompted disclosure and one made under the shadow of an official review. See *Taunton Deane Borough Council* [1991] BVC 518, which decision has been followed in a number of other cases. Further, where an inspection is being carried out at one taxpayer, but errors identified in the returns of an associated taxpayer, the tribunal has held that there should be no distinction between formal and informal enquiries by HMRC (*FR Jenks (Overseas) Ltd* [1993] BVC 1,313).

In addition, litigation has arisen over what constitutes 'full information'. In *Maston (Property Holding) Ltd* [1992] BVC 1,307, notification was provided simply by means of a cheque payment in respect of errors identified by the taxpayer, without a covering letter. However, the tribunal held that 'full information' had been provided and criticised HMRC for failing to seek further clarification of the circumstances.

31.11   Reasonable excuse

31.11.1 Definition of reasonable excuse

Most of the penalties mentioned within this chapter will be cancelled in full if the taxpayer can establish a 'reasonable excuse' defence. There is no definition of reasonable excuse but VATA 1994, s. 71 specifically states that:

'(a) an insufficiency of funds to pay any VAT due is not a reasonable excuse; and

(b)   where reliance is placed on any other person to perform any task, neither the fact of that reliance nor any dilatoriness or inaccuracy on the part of the person relied upon is a reasonable excuse.'

This section considers a number of areas in relation to which a reasonable excuse has been considered. Although a reasonable excuse may be relevant in relation to several of the penalties, some areas considered here will not be relevant to every penalty. For example, an insufficiency of funds is more relevant to the default surcharge than it is to the misdeclaration penalty.

31.11.2 Insufficiency of funds

The High Court reviewed the extent to which the restriction under s. 71(1)(a) applies, in *C & E Commrs v Salevon Ltd* (1989) 4 BVC 199. Thus, there is a distinction to be drawn between the direct cause of insufficiency of funds and the excuse for that insufficiency. The insufficiency of funds, by itself, cannot constitute a reasonable excuse, but the reasons behind that insufficiency can do so. In this case the wrongful act of another was sufficient to constitute a reasonable excuse. That decision was followed in *Steptoe*, where the insufficiency of funds was not caused by the wrongful act of another but by persistent late settlement of invoices.

> **Planning point**
>
> Thus, following these key decisions, the underlying cause of the insufficiency is not restricted to unforeseeable or inescapable events. However, a taxpayer is expected to exercise reasonable foresight and due diligence and to be able to demonstrate that before HMRC and, on appeal, before the tribunal or courts.

31.11.3 Reliance upon another person

In *C & E Commrs v Harris* (the case was heard with *Salevon Ltd*), the court held that where the taxpayer relied upon another person to effect his registration for VAT purposes, and that person gave a positive assurance that registration was not required, then such circumstances must fall within VATA 1994, s. 71(1)(b).

In *Frank Galliers Ltd v C & E Commrs* [1993] BVC 70, the court suggested that it is permissible to go behind the dilatoriness or inaccuracy and see whether there is an explanation for that which itself constitutes a reasonable excuse. Thus, s. 71(1)(b) does not impose more stringent requirements for the establishment of a reasonable excuse in cases where the taxpayer relies upon another person than where no such reliance is placed.

> **Planning point**
>
> Thus, where reliance is placed upon another person, and the circumstances resulting in the penalty arise nevertheless, it is not impossible for a reasonable excuse to be established.

31.11.4 Ignorance of the law

In *Neal v C & E Commrs* (1987) 3 BVC 143, it was held, in relation to a failure to notify liability to registration for VAT, that ignorance relating to primary VAT law cannot constitute a reasonable excuse. However, the decision left open the possibility that, in some circumstances, ignorance of VAT law could constitute a reasonable excuse. In the case of *Nichols* [1993] BVC 1,410 a distinction was made between basic ignorance in relation to registration for VAT and his ignorance of the fact that expenses incurred abroad and charged to his customers would be regarded as part of his turnover for VAT purposes.

Ignorance of law is relevant both to a failure to notify and to the misdeclaration penalty. This issue has been raised in relation to:

- liability of supplies;
- whether supplies are made in the course of a business;
- place of supply;
- time of supply;
- supplies involving agents or subcontractors;
- the existence of a partnership;
- imports;
- bad debts; and
- credit notes.

31.11.5 Compassionate circumstances – default surcharge

It is clear that serious illness, serious injury or bereavement, etc. can constitute a reasonable excuse, particularly in relation to a failure to notify and the default surcharge, since both penalties are triggered by a failure at a specific point in time.

Although there are many cases in which the taxpayer has been successful, the following should be noted.

1.   The timing of the incident must be sufficiently close to the time when the return should be submitted, for example, an injury occurring after the due date will not constitute a reasonable excuse.

2.   If the person responsible for preparing the return is unable to do so, by virtue of sudden absence (or sudden illness of a close relative), this may be sufficient. However, where a condition continues for a substantial period, the taxpayer will be expected to make alternative arrangements.

31.11.6 Compassionate circumstances – failure to notify

Again, there have been many cases in which serious illness, serious injury or bereavement have established a reasonable excuse. There are a number of matters which must be taken in account as:

*   the timing of the incident must be coincident with the failure to notify; and
*   where a failure to notify has continued for a significant period, the incident may only provide a reasonable excuse for part of that period.

31.11.7 Clerical or computer errors

It is not uncommon for either humans or machines to make mistakes.

Typically, the tribunal will look behind a clerical error to see the reason for it. A misdeclaration penalty arises in respect of an error, and thus the existence of an error cannot be the trigger for the penalty and also the grounds for a reasonable excuse. However, the tribunal will expect that a reasonable business person will make adequate checks of the VAT returns he submits.

In relation to computer problems, the question is asked as to how severe the problem is or was to the preparation or submission of the return, as well as the availability of personnel to resolve the problem, including, where relevant, the preparation of a return by alternative means.

31.11.8 Premises matters

Where there is a fire, flood or burglary, and key documents are damaged or destroyed, then a reasonable excuse may be established. Again, the timing of the incident is relevant, and it is incumbent upon the taxpayer to prepare sufficient evidence to substantiate his claims.

31.11.9 Correspondence with HMRC

Many cases have considered whether required documents were despatched, including:

- a VAT return by HMRC to the taxpayer;
- a warning notice under the default surcharge regime by HMRC to the taxpayer;
- an application for registration for VAT by HMRC to the taxpayer; and
- a completed application for registration for VAT by the taxpayer to HMRC.

A person cannot submit a VAT return if HMRC have not sent one to him. However, he is responsible for notifying HMRC of any change of address, and must be aware of the disruption that would cause in any case. Such a person may have difficulty in demonstrating that he did not receive a return form.

Since the default surcharge regime is dependent upon the issue of a warning notice, a subsequent surcharge will be invalid if the notice is not received or is inaccurate. However, this does not constitute a reasonable excuse. See *C & E Commrs v Medway Draughting and Technical Services Ltd; C & E Commrs v Adplates Offset Ltd* (1989) 4 BVC 60.

Where a taxpayer requests a form and it fails to arrive, it is incumbent upon him to pursue the matter, with follow-up telephone calls as necessary. Similarly, if there is no acknowledgement of receipt of an application for registration by HMRC, the taxpayer is expected to contact them to ensure that it has been received.

It has to be said that the line between establishing a reasonable excuse and not doing so is sometimes fine. Further, the tribunal has apparently not been consistent in its decisions, which is a consequence of the large number of penalty appeals that have been heard.

For example, in relation to misdeclaration penalties issued in respect of incorrect bad-debt relief claims, one decision concluded:

'I do not consider that Parliament ... intended that these penalties would be applied in circumstances such as these.'

(*Vision Computer Products Ltd* [1992] BVC 1,400.)

However, a later decision read:

'We cannot accept that the application of the basic provisions for bad-debt relief was so complex as to afford [the Appellant Company] a reasonable excuse.'

(*Ramm Contract Furnishing (Northern) Ltd* [1993] BVC 1,364.)

Planning point

Thus, while there are clearly-established principles by which such appeals are heard, the taxpayer cannot simply rely on a particular set of circumstances to establish a reasonable excuse.

One objective test, coined in *The Clean Car Company Ltd* [1991] BVC 568, has been followed in many subsequent cases:

> 'Was what the taxpayer did a reasonable thing for a responsible trader conscious of and intending to comply with his obligations regarding tax, but having the experience and other relevant attributes of the taxpayer and placed in the situation that the taxpayer found himself in at the relevant time, a reasonable thing to do?'

A similar test was coined in *Appropriate Technology Ltd* [1991] BVC 571:

> 'Would a reasonable conscientious businessman who knew all the facts of the case as I have set them out, and who was alive to and accepted the need to comply with one's responsibilities in regard to the rendering of VAT returns, consider that the Appellant Company, in acting as it did in the circumstances in which it found itself, had acted with due care in the preparation of its VAT returns?'

Planning point

Consequently, in seeking to establish a reasonable excuse defence, the taxpayer has a clear obligation to demonstrate that he has acted reasonably at all relevant times.

Where the circumstances fail to lead to a reasonable excuse being established, HMRC and, on appeal, the tribunal may consider the possibility that the penalty be mitigated (see **31.12**).

31.12 Mitigation

31.12.1 Instances where mitigation is allowed

VATA 1994, s. 70 provides explicitly that mitigation is available in relation to the penalties of:

- civil evasion;
- misdeclaration penalty (pre-1 April 2009);
- repeated misdeclaration penalty (pre 1-April 2009);
- penalties for errors (from 1 April 2009);
- breach of record keeping requirements;
- failure to notify certain avoidance schemes;
- failure to notify liability to registration;
- failure to notify events affecting exemption from registration;

- failure to notify goods acquired from EU member states;
- unauthorised use of VAT invoices; or
- breach of record-keeping requirements in relation to transactions in gold.

> ### Planning point
> Where HMRC have already granted some mitigation, the tribunal may review the level of mitigation, in addition to any other matters in dispute, and may reduce the mitigation, i.e. increase the penalty.

In considering whether mitigation is applicable, neither HMRC nor the tribunal may give any weight to:

- the insufficiency of funds available to the taxpayer, either in paying VAT due or the penalty due;
- the fact that there has been no loss of VAT or no significant loss of VAT, taking the matter on its own or taking note of any other cases; or
- the fact that the taxpayer or any person acting on his behalf has done so in good faith.

There are many instances in which a taxpayer cannot establish a reasonable excuse. However, the circumstances may be sufficient to allow some mitigation.

The tribunal had held that it should consider the level of culpability, bearing in mind any factors not expressly excluded by s. 70(4), and thus introducing the element of proportionality. The tribunal has rejected the claim that only exceptional matters should be taken into account, see *Cohen* [1995] BVC 1,280.

Amongst matters taken into account in cases before the tribunal are:

- cooperation;
- the taxpayer's conduct in general;
- events subsequent to the default;
- the taxpayer's previous experience in business;
- HMRC's conduct;
- the taxpayer's previous history in relation to VAT;
- business pressures;
- the taxpayer's honesty; and
- the taxpayer's competence.

HMRC's internal guidance provides a framework for the degree of mitigation that will be permitted. This is a guideline only and more or less mitigation may be permitted. Theoretically, a penalty can be mitigated to nil, but this is rare. (See *VAT Civil Penalties Manual* (VCP) 11746).

(A) A maximum of 50 per cent is permitted for how the infringement occurred.

1   Compassionate grounds (where the circumstances are insufficient to warrant a reasonable excuse) such as:

- unforeseen serious illness of the person responsible for completing the VAT returns (including third party such as professional advisor); and
- the death of a close relative of the person responsible for completing the VAT returns.

Mitigation from 20 per cent–50 per cent

2 Other unforeseen and relevant events which, nevertheless, you do not consider, provide a reasonable excuse on their own but are supported by evidence, such as:

- computer or software errors;
- flood, fire or other damage to premises;
- theft or break in;
- pressure of work, i.e. exceptional and significant increase in workloads not in keeping with normal work fluctuations;
- staff problems, i.e. where the person responsible for completing the VAT return leaves at short notice; or
- clerical errors particularly in complex circumstances where management controls are in place but have failed to spot the error.

Mitigation from 10 per cent–50 per cent

3 Complexity of liability in relation to the size of the business and frequency of transaction.

Mitigation from 10 per cent–50 per cent

(B) A maximum of 50 per cent is permitted for the degree of co-operation in disclosing and quantifying arrears (belated notification).

(1) A voluntary disclosure of a belated notification of a liability to be registered accompanied by full quantification of the arrears.

Mitigation up to 50 per cent

(2) A voluntary disclosure of a belated notification of a liability to be registered not accompanied by quantification of the arrears.

Mitigation up to 25 per cent

(3) Full quantification of arrears within X number of days of identification of the belated notification of a liability to be registered.

Mitigation up to 25 per cent

(C) A maximum of 50 per cent is permitted for the degree of co-operation in identifying and quantifying the error (misdeclarations).

(1) Full co-operation and quantification.

Mitigation up to 50 per cent

(2) Partial co-operation and quantification.

Mitigation up to 25 per cent

(3)   Alleged full quantification that later turns out to be partial but the reason was unintentional.

Mitigation up to 10 per cent

(4)   Supplying information promptly and answering questions accurately to allow officers to quantify the underdeclaration.

Mitigation up to 10 per cent

Other actions which result in a saving of Departmental time and resources.

Mitigation up to 10 per cent

(D) Other Factors, a maximum of 50 per cent mitigation

(1)   Published guidance is unclear or not up to date.

Mitigation up to 40 per cent

(2)   Evidence of efforts made to seek advice.

Mitigation up to 10 per cent

(3)   Evidence of steps taken to correct systems in order to prevent similar errors in future.

Mitigation from 5 per cent–25 per cent

(4)   Compliance history of trader over the last three registered years has been good.

Mitigation up to 25 per cent

In relation to penalties for failing to notify liability to registration, mitigation has been granted where the taxpayer's turnover grew only gradually, or exceeded the registration threshold only slightly, or only for a few months.

31.12.2 Civil evasion penalties

Under the 'new approach', a penalty may be mitigated in:

- up to 40 per cent for an early and truthful explanation as to why arrears arose and the true extent of those arrears; and
- up to 40 per cent for fully embracing and meeting responsibilities under the procedure, for example, by supplying information promptly – including a full written disclosure – attending meetings and answering questions.

Thus, a penalty may be mitigated by up to 80 per cent.

Mitigation under the 'full civil evasion procedures' may arise in:

- up to 40 per cent for an early and truthful explanation as to why arrears arose and the true extent of those arrears;

- up to 25 per cent for cooperation and in substantiating the true amount of the arrears; and
- up to 10 per cent for attending interviews and producing records and information as required.

Thus, a penalty may be mitigated by up to 75 per cent.

HMRC have stated that additional mitigation may be granted in exceptional cases. Indeed, s. 70 provides for mitigation for a civil evasion penalty of up to 100 per cent. Section 70 does not provide for any mitigation for a penalty issued under s. 61. However, mitigation of the basic penalty under s. 60 would require that the corresponding s. 61 penalty be reduced.

The level of mitigation granted under the civil evasion procedure may be increased by the tribunal, s. 70(2). See *Tanner (a director of Redland Auto Service Centre Ltd)* [1999] BVC 4,007 and *Lee (t/a Euro Impex)* [1998] BVC 4,083.

31.13 Appeals

31.13.1 Introduction

An appeal may be made in relation to two specific areas:

(1)   Whether the person is liable to a penalty.

(2)   The amount of the penalty.

Thus, under the first head, the taxpayer must bring such evidence as relates to the circumstances giving rise to the penalty. Under the second head, he must bring such evidence as relates to the value of relevant transactions or in relation to mitigation.

Example 31.7

1.   HMRC consider that a person should have notified his liability to registration.

2.   They issue an assessment for VAT deemed to be due.

3.   They issue a penalty at the appropriate rate, relating to the delay in notifying his liability.

The taxpayer may challenge his liability to registration, in which case the appeal falls within s. 83(n).

The taxpayer may accept his liability to registration but challenge the quantum of the assessment to the penalty, in which case the appeal falls within s. 83(q).

In relation to an appeal, the VAT Tribunals Rules 1986 (SI 1986/590) provide the legislative basis for procedures, etc. In addition, the appellant may obtain an explanatory leaflet from the tribunal centre entitled *Appeals and Applications to the Tribunal*.

In mitigation appeals and reasonable excuse appeals, the VAT Tribunals Rules 1986 (SI 1986/590) allow the tribunal to issue its decision in a reduced form, without indicating its findings of fact and the reasons for its decision, as long as both parties agree. Many such decisions have been released under this rule.

Planning point

In relation to an appeal, it is essential that full facts are presented to the tribunal. Many penalties are issued against small and medium-sized businesses, lacking the resources of larger businesses. Even so, the same standards must be achieved in convincing the tribunal of the appellant's case.

31.13.2 Civil evasion penalties

A person may appeal against a penalty issued in accordance with VATA 1994, ss. 60 and 61.

This includes:

- any liability to a penalty;
- the amount of a penalty; or
- the making of an assessment in relation to the 20-year limit.

Where a named officer is assessed, there is also an appeal against:

- HMRC's decision that the dishonesty of the corporate body is attributable to the named officer; and
- HMRC's decision to attribute a proportion of the penalty to him.

Ordinarily, in appeals in VAT matters, the burden of proof lies with the appellant taxpayer. But, in accordance with the quasi-criminal status of this penalty, the burden of proof lies with HMRC. Thus, they are required to prove that:

- the person has done or omitted to do an action with the purpose of evading VAT; and
- his conduct involved dishonesty.

In an early decision, *Gandhi Tandoori Restaurant* (1989) 4 BVC 535, it was held that the civil standard of proof was necessary although at the higher end of the scale. This reflects the fact that the consequences of the tribunal finding against the appellant taxpayer would give rise to a potentially significant financial penalty.

Where a s. 61 penalty applies, HMRC have to establish that the dishonest conduct of the corporate body was due to the named officer and the extent to which it was so (see *Tottey* [1995] BVC 979).

31.13.3 Procedures and burden of proof

The VAT Tribunals Rules 1986 (SI 1986/590) set out different procedures in relation to the different penalties.

Category 1 appeals relate solely to penalties issued under ss. 60 and 61 and may include an appeal against the amount of VAT assessed in relation to the same conduct. Where the appeal is a question of mitigation under ss. 60 or 61, it is treated as a category 2 appeal; see below.

Category 2 appeals relate to all other penalties. The official tribunals leaflet (TR1) lists the following penalties under this category:

- default surcharge; appeals in relation to reasonable excuse or in relation to the despatch of the return with payment in sufficient time;
- misdeclaration penalty and repeated misdeclaration penalty;
- failure to notify liability to registration; or
- mitigation of penalties under ss. 60 and 61.

Rule 2 defines an 'evasion penalty appeal' corresponding to category 1 above.

Rule 2 defines a 'mitigation appeal' and a 'reasonable excuse appeal', both falling within category 2 above. A 'reasonable excuse appeal' includes appeals relating to the timely despatch of documents and appeals relating to the unprompted disclosure of errors.

The primary distinction to be made between different types of appeal is that in category 1 appeals the burden of proof lies with HMRC. Thus, they are required to serve a statement of case setting out the matters and facts on which they rely for the issuing of the penalty. Such a statement of case must include full particulars of the alleged dishonesty. The appellant taxpayer has an opportunity to submit a defence to the statement of case, setting out the matters and facts on which he seeks to rely. HMRC then serve a defence (rule 7). At the hearing, HMRC, having the burden of proof, open their case first.

In mitigation appeals and reasonable excuse appeals, HMRC are not required to serve a statement of case. Rule 10 requires only that they serve a copy of the decision. At the hearing, the appellant taxpayer opens his case first.

Avoidance

32.1   Overview

The use of certain VAT avoidance schemes must be disclosed to HMRC. Notification by post should be sent to:

VAT Avoidance Disclosures Unit
Anti-Avoidance Group (Intelligence)
HM Revenue & Customs
1st Floor
22 Kingsway
LONDON
WC2B 6NR

or by email to *vat.avoidance.disclosures.bst@hmrc.gsi.gov.uk*

Notification to any other address is not considered to be a proper notification and can leave the taxpayer liable to penalty.

Under VAT Act 1994, Sch. 11A, para. 6, there is a duty to notify HMRC of certain VAT avoidance schemes. Failure to do so may result in penalties.

There are two types of VAT avoidance scheme: those which involve the 'hallmarks' of avoidance and those schemes which are named and described in the legislation by Statutory Instrument as 'Listed Schemes'.

Law: VATA 1994, Sch. 11A, Value Added Tax (Disclosure of Avoidance Schemes) (Designations) Order 2004 (SI 2004/1934)

Other information: *VAT Notice 700/8*

> **Planning point**
> These are provisions where HMRC's understanding of their operation is important. The notice provides an excellent guide to the attitude of HMRC to the rules and the circumstances in which disclosure should be made. It therefore repays study by anyone potentially affected by the provisions.

> **Planning point**
> It is also important to note that these rules are not intended to connote illegality. They are, for HMRC, merely a means of obtaining information about who is using schemes and what new schemes are being used or marketed. These schemes can be used subject to any other anti-avoidance legislation that may exist or the concept of 'abuse of right'.

> ### ⚠ *Warning!*
> In practice, the number of transactions requiring notification under these rules is relatively small (hundreds rather than thousands per annum nationally). Whilst this is broadly positive, it does mean that consideration of the requirement to make disclosures may not be as automatic as it should be in the minds of those planning or implementing commercial arrangements, and the need to take action may be forgotten.

32.2 Listed schemes

32.2.1 Introduction

Certain schemes are designated for the purposes of tax avoidance, and are described in the VAT legislation.

Where a business's annual turnover exceeds £600,000 per annum notification must be made to HMRC that a VAT return or claim is made which is affected by its use of a listed scheme. This turnover limit applies to the corporate group of the enterprise (not the VAT group or VAT registration of the business) and includes both the taxable and exempt turnover of the entity.

Each listed scheme has a unique reference number. A scheme may be designated by the Treasury for the purposes of notification where it is of a particular description and has been or might be entered into for the purpose of enabling any person to obtain a tax advantage. Schemes are listed where it is considered unlikely that person would enter into a scheme of that description unless the main purpose or one of the main purposes of doing so was the obtaining by any person of a tax advantage.

A person obtains a tax advantage in any period if the excess of output tax accounted for by him over input tax deducted by him:

- is less than it otherwise would be; or
- means that he obtains a VAT credit when he would not otherwise do so; or
- means that he obtains a larger or earlier VAT credit than would otherwise be the case; or
- in a case where he recovers input tax as a recipient of a supply before the supplier accounts for the output tax, the period between the time when the input tax is recovered and the time when the output tax is accounted for is greater than would otherwise be the case.

> **Planning point**
>
> The essence of a listed scheme is that it is a specific known avoidance mechanism, usually widely used. It follows that a liability to notify use of such a scheme can hardly be overlooked accidentally. Anyone who has implemented such an arrangement will be fully aware of the fact. It further follows that businesses with a turnover under £10 million need have no regard to these rules if they have not implemented a listed scheme.

32.2.2 Liability to notify listed schemes

A taxable person must notify the use of a listed scheme when all of the following conditions are met.

1. The total value of VAT-exclusive taxable supplies and exempt supplies exceeded £600,000 in the year immediately prior to:

    (a) the affected VAT return period; or
    (b) any of the VAT return periods that are the subject of an affected claim.

2. The pro rata proportion of £600,000 was exceeded in the VAT return period immediately prior to the affected VAT return period, or any of the VAT return periods that are the subject of an affected claim (where the accounting period is a quarter, the appropriate proportion is £150,000).

HMRC have powers to prevent any artificial separation of business activities, for example to avoid the turnover thresholds, to avoid notification.

Artificial separation of business activities carried on by two or more persons will result in HMRC issuing a directive that the businesses should be treated as one. The person specified within the direction will be treated as a single taxable person carrying on the activities of a business described in the direction with effect from the date of the direction or such later date as is specified. The persons named in the direction cannot be excluded from notifying the use of a scheme. The direction is served by HMRC on each person named in it and remains in force until it is revoked or replaced by a further direction.

To issue a direction, HMRC must be satisfied that:

- taxable or exempt supplies have been made;
- the activities in the course of which those supplies are made form only part of certain activities, the other activities being carried on concurrently or previously or both by one or more other persons; and
- if all the taxable and exempt supplies of the business as described in the direction were taken into account, the turnover would exceed the minimum turnover limits required for notification (VATA 1994, Sch. 11A, para. 8).

If the taxable person is a group undertaking, the conditions must be met by the taxable person plus every other group undertaking, i.e. it will apply to the group as a whole. Group undertaking for these purposes is defined in Companies Act 2006, s. 1161, and is not a VAT group.

Notification must be made to HMRC in the following cases.

1.　Where a taxable person's turnover has exceeded £600,000.

2.　Where a taxable person is using a listed scheme (see below) and either:

　(a)　in a VAT return for a period beginning from 1 August 2004 the amount shown as payable by or to the taxable person is less than or greater than it would be but for the use of a listed scheme to which he is a party;

　(b)　the taxable person makes a claim for the repayment of output tax or an increase in credit for input tax for any period beginning after 31 July 2004 in respect of which he was previously delivered a return and the amount claimed is greater than it would be but for a listed scheme; or

　(c)　the amount of non-deductible VAT incurred in respect of an accounting period starting on or after 1 August 2005 would have been higher but for the listed scheme.

3.　The taxable person has not already notified HMRC as required.

Non-deductible VAT is VAT incurred on a supply of goods or services (including VAT on reverse charges), or VAT on acquisitions or imports that would have been non-deductible as it was input tax for which credit is not permitted or is not input tax, for which no refund is permitted.

Where there is multiple use of schemes, it is required to notify the use of all the schemes being used and where more than one party is involved, all the parties involved therein.

32.2.3 Time limits for notification

Listed schemes must be notified within 30 days from the end of the date of the affected claim or the last day for submission of the affected VAT return, or where HMRC make a direction regarding artificial splitting of the business the last day for submission of the first VAT return made to HMRC following the direction.

Where a scheme gives on-going benefits (such as a payment handling service scheme) it is only necessary to inform HMRC once. Where, however, a scheme is used more than once, each instance needs to be notified to HMRC.

> ### ⚠ *Warning!*
> It is important to note that notification sent to any address other than the VAT Avoidance Disclosures Unit is not proper notification and may therefore give rise to a penalty.

The notification should be prominently headed 'Disclosure of Use of Listed Scheme – Notification under Paragraph 6(2) of Schedule 11A to the VAT ACT 1994'. Details of the business name, address and VAT registration number should be given.

The number of the listed scheme (SI 2004/1929) is all that is required to be notified to HMRC.

HMRC will acknowledge receipt of notifications received and they will consider what action, if any, should be taken in respect of the notification, contacting the taxable person as necessary.

> **Planning point**
>
> HMRC provide examples of all the listed schemes in *VAT Notice 700/8*. Anyone unsure as to whether or not their circumstances are covered will therefore find further assistance in that publication. As stated above, this is an area where an insight into what HMRC think is covered is helpful in making such decisions.

> **Planning point**
>
> Businesses should consider and draw their own conclusions about transactions and determine whether they amount to a listed scheme.

The listed schemes are:

The first grant of a major interest in a building	Scheme 1
Payment handling service	Scheme 2
Value shifting	Scheme 3
Leaseback agreements	Scheme 4
Extended approval period	Scheme 5
Groups: third party suppliers	Scheme 6
Exempt education or vocational training by a non-profit making body	Scheme 7
Taxable education or vocational training by a non-eligible body	Scheme 8
Cross-border face value voucher schemes involving telecommunications	Scheme 9
The surrender or termination of certain taxable leases of buildings where the tenant remains in occupation	Scheme 10

32.2.4 Details of the schemes

First grant of a major interest in a building

This scheme aims to remove the VAT costs of extending, enlarging, repairing, refurbishing or servicing buildings that are zero-rated when sold by developers.

The first grant of a major interest in any building of a description falling within VATA 1994, Sch. 8, Grp. 5, item 1(a) (a zero-rated grant) where the following apply:

1. The grant is made to a person 'connected with' the grantor.

2. The grantor or any body corporate treated as a member of a VAT group of which the grantor is a member attributes to that grant input tax incurred by him:

   (a) in respect of a service charge related to the building; or
   (b) in connection with any extension, enlargement, repair, maintenance or refurbishment of a building other than for remedying defects in the original construction.

The person is 'connected with' another for the above purposes where one of them is an undertaking in relation to which the other is a group undertaking, or both of them are connected to the same trust, and a person is connected to a trust where:

- he is the settlor of the trust;
- he is a trustee or beneficiary of it; or
- he holds any shares in the company in accordance with the terms of the trust or as a person on whose behalf such shares are held. The schemes are aimed to remove the VAT cost of extending, enlarging, repairing, refurbishing or servicing the building by attributing the VAT incurred to a zero-rated major interest grant in the building to a connected person by a person with constructing status.

Payment handling service

Schemes caught include those where a customer paying by credit or debit card will be offered the goods at a lower price with the balance being charged as an exempt card handling fee, even though the total cost is the same as that paid by a person that does not use such a card. This is a scheme comprising or including a retail supply of goods or services together with a linked exempt supply to the same customer of a payment handling service, where the total consideration for the retail supplier and the linked supply is no different or not significantly different from what would be payable for the retail sale alone. Link supply means the supply by the retailer or any other person that:

- relates to the means of payment used for the retail supply; and
- is a supply of a description falling within VATA 1994, Sch. 9, Grp. 5 (Financial Services).

Value shifting

This is a scheme that attempts to shift value from a standard-rate retail supply into linked zero-rated or exempt supplies. The scheme comprises a retail supply of goods or services together with a linked zero-rate or exempt supply to the same customer where:

- the link supply is treated as a separate supply within the terms of any agreement made by the customer;
- part of the total consideration for the retail supply and the linked supply is attributable to the linked supply by the terms of any such agreement; and
- the total consideration for the retail supply and the linked supply is not different or not significantly different from what it would be for the retail supply alone.

Retail supply means a supply by retail upon which VAT is charged at the standard rate. A linked supply means a supply of goods or services made by the retailer or any other person which is zero-rated or exempt.

The customer will pay the same or similar overall price whether or not they accept the linked supply. The separation of the consideration across the two supplies is alleged to be supported by an agreement, signed or agreed by the customer, at the point of sale.

It is not necessary to notify linked supplies that are free or where it is part of a normal promotion scheme (for example a meal deal providing a zero-rated sandwich with taxable crisps or drinks) and the discount applied to the meal deal is spread equally over the various components of the supply.

Leaseback agreement

This type of scheme aims to defer or reduce the VAT costs of a partially exempt entity by acquiring goods through a subsidiary that leases the goods to the partially exempt entity. The partially exempt entity suffers a lower VAT cost by only paying VAT on the lease charge, but the subsidiary can reclaim all the VAT incurred on the acquisition as it is making taxable supplies (of leasing). The use of the scheme must be disclosed where there is the supply of goods or the leasing or letting on hire of goods to a person (the relevant person) and:

- the relevant person uses the goods in his business but is not entitled to a full input tax credit;
- the taxable person that makes the supply to the relevant person is connected with him and is entitled to credit all the input tax arising on the purchase of the goods; and
- the relevant person or a person connected with him has directly or indirectly provided funds for meeting more than 90 per cent of the cost of the goods.

A relevant person means any person who in respect of the relevant supply is not entitled to credit for all the input tax fully attributable to the supplies he makes. The provision of funds includes the making of a loan of funds and the provision of any consideration for the issue of any shares or other securities issued wholly or partly for raising funds.

The grant, assignment or surrender of a major interest in land is not a supply of goods for the purposes of this scheme.

Supplies between unconnected parties do not need to be notified.

Whilst all schemes that fit this criteria must be notified to HMRC, HMRC are particularly interested in schemes that they believe distort values (by introducing elements to devalue the lease) or leases over extended periods. HMRC will probably not take action where the lease can be shown to be on commercial terms.

Extended approval period

This is any scheme comprising or including a retail supply of goods whereby:

- the goods are sent or taken on approval, or sale or return, or similar terms;
- payment for the supplies is required in full by the retailer before the expiry of any approval, return or similar period; and
- for the purpose of accounting for VAT, the retailer treats the goods as supplied after the date on which payment is received in full.

These are schemes that aim to defer accounting for output tax on the supply of retail goods until an adoption period has been completed or title transfers to the customer by arranging for the goods to be sent or taken on approval, or sale or return, or similar terms whereas payment is required in full before such a time.

Groups: third-party suppliers

Any scheme comprising or including supplies made to one or more VAT group members by a specific body in relation to which the benefits condition is not satisfied.

These are schemes that aim to reduce or remove the VAT incurred on bought-in taxable services, including outsourced services by a user that cannot recover all of the input tax charged to it for these services. The user arranges to include a corporate body in its VAT group with an activity of supplying the services. The corporate body is set up so that the majority of the benefits of the activity accrue to a third service provider and its corporate group rather than the user. The aim is that very little VAT is charged to the user as supplies within a VAT group are disregarded, but the third-party provider who in practice manages the activity of providing the service, receives the profits and other benefits from the activity.

Exempt education or vocational training by a non-profit making body

This is any scheme comprising or including the conduct of a 'relevant business' by a non-profit making body where:

- it receives a relevant supply for a connected taxable person who is not an eligible body; and

- in any one prescribed accounting period the value of such relevant supply is equal to or more than 20 per cent of the cost of making the supplies comprised in the relevant business (i.e. more than 20 per cent of the non-profit making bodies costs).

'Relevant business' means a business whose activities consist wholly or mainly of the supply of education or vocational training to persons who are not taxable persons.

Non-profit making body means a body within VATA 1994, Sch. 9, Grp. 6, Note 1(e).

Relevant supply means the supply including the leasing or letting on hire for use in a relevant business of:

- a capital item used in the course or furtherance of the relevant business; and for the purpose of that business otherwise than solely for the purpose of selling the item;
- staff;
- management services;
- administration services; or
- accounting services.

Eligible body has the meaning in VATA 1994, Sch. 9, Grp. 6, Note (1).

Vocational training has the meaning in VATA 1994, Sch. 9, Grp. 6, Note (3) but does not include vocational training with a description falling within VATA 1994, Sch. 9, Grp. 6, item 5, or vocational training where the consideration results in a mere charge to funds provided under Employment and Training Act 1973, s. 2 – Employment and Training Act (Northern Ireland) 1950, s. 1a or Enterprises and New Towns (Scotland) Act 1990, s. 2, or VATA 1994, Sch. 9, Grp. 6, item 5a – vocational training where the consideration is ultimately a charge to funds provided by the Learning and Skills Council for England or the National Council for Education and Training for Wales under Learning and Skills Act 2000 Parts (I) or (II).

These are schemes that aim to allow a business that provides education or training to avoid charging VAT on these supplies by arranging for the supplies to be made through a non-profit making body. The customers for the services are mainly or wholly private individuals. The non-profit making body will receive supplies for one or more key supplies, e.g. property and asset leases, staff management, from the business that originally provided the services or from another person. The non-profit making body and the providers of the services are connected persons. The effect of this is that the profits of the non-profit making body are still available to the other businesses by means of the supplies made to it, despite the non-profit making body being technically unable to make distributions.

Taxable education or vocational training by a non-eligible body

This is any scheme comprising or including the conduct of a relevant business by a non-eligible body connected to an eligible body where:

- the non-eligible body benefits or intends to benefit the eligible body by way of gift, dividend or otherwise; or
- the eligible body makes any supply to the non-eligible body which is a relevant supply and in any one prescribed accounting period the value of all such relevant supplies is equal to or more than 20 per cent of the cost of making the supplies comprising the relevant business.

Eligible body has the meaning in VATA 1994, Sch. 9, Grp. 6, Note (1).

Relevant business means a business whose activities consist wholly or mainly of the taxable supply of education or vocational training.

Vocational training has the meaning in VATA 1994, Sch. 9, Grp. 6, Note (3).

Relevant supply means the supply or leasing or letting on hire for use in the relevant business of:

- a capital item used in the course or furtherance of the relevant business and for the purposes of that business otherwise than solely for the purpose of selling the item;
- staff;
- management services;
- administration services; or
- accounting services.

These are schemes that aim to enable eligible bodies to avoid incurring irrecoverable input VAT. A business which is not an eligible body is established to provide taxable training or education services to persons who are able to recover the tax from those supplies from customs. The typical customers involved would be bodies such as NHS Trusts and local authorities, but can also include normal commercial bodies. The non-eligible body will be connected to an eligible body (probably as its subsidiary), from which it will receive a range of supplies which enable it to carry out the training or education business. It is expected that the non-eligible body will distribute its profits to the connected eligible body, e.g. by way of gift aid.

Cross-border face-value voucher schemes

With effect from 1 August 2005, cross-border face-value voucher schemes involving telecommunications, broadcasting or electronically supplied services are required to be notified to HMRC. These schemes tend to avoid paying any VAT on the provision of the services to final retail customers within the UK.

The surrender or termination of certain taxable uses of buildings where the tenant remains in occupation

The surrender or termination of certain taxable leases of buildings where the tenant remains in occupation of essentially the same area of the building but following the surrender or termination pays no or substantially less VAT on the rent.

A disclosure is only required if the tenant cannot recover VAT in full on the rent and it is intended that they or someone connected to them treats the building as a capital item for the purposes of the capital goods scheme.

This change targets exempt or partially exempt occupiers who have in the past put in place taxable lease structures in order to obtain full VAT recovery on the capital cost of the building and who now try to obtain further VAT benefits by avoiding irrecoverable VAT on the rental payable for the remainder of the lease term.

32.3   Hallmarked schemes

32.3.1 Introduction

A business whose annual turnover exceeds £10 million must notify HMRC if it enters into a scheme for the purpose of securing a tax advantage and the scheme contains one or more of the hallmarks of avoidance and it makes a return or claim which is affected by the use of the hallmarked scheme.

> ⚠ **Warning!**
> Businesses big enough to have to consider the hallmark provisions should not fail to recognise that they must also pay attention to the rules for listed schemes, which apply to any business with a turnover over £600,000 (as defined) with no upper limit.

A scheme, for the purposes of the hallmark rules, includes any arrangement, transaction or series of transactions.

However, it is not a scheme if:

- a Statutory Instrument is utilised which is a concession open to all;
- a new partial exemption method or capital goods scheme method is negotiated;
- the grouping provisions are used to make changes to the VAT group structure; or
- someone is engaged to review and maximise input tax recoveries.

> **Planning point**
> There is no requirement to notify any scheme where a VAT advantage is not the main purpose or one of the main purposes of entering into the scheme, even if it has one of the hallmarks. It is therefore important to take a step-by-step approach, dealing with this issue first, before moving on to the hallmarks. This point is helpfully stressed by HMRC themselves in *VAT Notice 700/8* (para. 6.3, August 2004 edition).

Law: VATA 1994, Sch. 11A, para. 1

32.3.2 Liability to notify a hallmarked scheme

A taxable person is liable to notify HMRC of the use of any hallmarked scheme they have entered into where:

- the total value of the VAT-exclusive taxable supplies and exempt supplies exceed £10 million in the year immediately prior to the affected VAT return period, or any of the VAT return periods that are the subject of an affected claim of the entity or VAT group to which it belongs; or
- the appropriate proportion of £10 million is exceeded in the VAT return period immediately prior to the affected VAT return period or any of the VAT return periods that are the subject of an affected claim (artificial separation of business activities applies equally to hallmarked schemes and the notes under listed schemes should be read in conjunction with this section).

The appropriate proportion means the proportion which the length of the VAT period bears to 12 months, i.e. one-quarter where quarterly VAT returns are prepared and one-twelfth where monthly VAT returns are prepared.

A person has entered into a hallmarked scheme in the following circumstances.

1. The taxable person is a party to a scheme that is not a listed scheme.

2. The main purpose or one of the main purposes of the scheme is to obtain a tax advantage; and

   (a) either in a return for a VAT period beginning on 1 August 2004 or later, the amount of VAT shown as payable by or to the tax person is less than or greater than it would be but for the use of a scheme to which the person is a party; or

   (b) the taxable person makes a claim for the repayment of output tax or an increase in credit for input tax for any VAT period beginning from 1 August 2004 in respect of which he has previously delivered a return and the amount claimed is greater than it would be but for the scheme.

3. The scheme contains one or more of the hallmarks of avoidance.

4. The taxable person has not already notified HMRC as required under these provisions.

5. The taxable person has not been provided with a scheme number by someone who has registered the scheme with HMRC.

A scheme is any planned action entered into and includes any arrangement, transaction or series of transactions.

A tax advantage includes accounting for less VAT than would otherwise be the case, obtaining a VAT repayment that would otherwise not be available or obtaining a larger repayment or an earlier repayment. A tax advantage also includes recovering input tax credits before the supplier has to account for output tax or reducing any irrecoverable VAT even when there is no effect on a VAT return (for example because none of the

VAT being avoided would have been deductible as input tax) or a non-taxable person obtaining non-refundable VAT. However, the disclosure requirement only applies to those taxable persons who are both knowing parties and meet the normal disclosure rules, such as having a turnover in excess of the relevant turnover threshold. For the tax advantage to be a hallmark it is necessary for this to be a main purpose of the scheme. That is not the only purpose, but a main purpose. HMRC state that this can be taken to mean that the transaction ararrangement would not take place if the tax advantage was not available.

32.3.3 Notification of hallmarked schemes

The time limit for notifying HMRC of hallmarked schemes is within 30 days from the end of:

- the last day for submission of the effective VAT return;
- the date the affected claim is made; or
- where HMRC make a direction that the business has been artificially split, the last day for submission of the first VAT return made to HMRC following the direction.

The method of notification is similar to the notification for a listed scheme. In addition the following information must be notified.

1.   A statement as to which hallmark or hallmarks are included or associated with the scheme being notified.

2.   How the scheme gives rise to a tax advantage, including the extent that it is material to the tax advantage.

3.   Sufficient information must be provided to allow HMRC to understand how the tax advantage is obtained including:

    (a)   the sequence of arrangements;
    (b)   an explanation indicating the timing or the intervals between the arrangements made; and
    (c)   the goods or services involved.

4.   How the involvement of any party to the scheme contributes to the obtaining of the tax advantage.

5.   Any provision having the force of law in the UK or elsewhere relied upon as giving rise to the tax advantage.

> **Planning point**
> There is no obligation to quantify the amount or expected amount of the tax advantage, but sufficient information must be given so that HMRC can understand how the tax advantage is obtained.

HMRC will acknowledge the notification received in respect of the scheme and may require additional information to ensure the taxable person meets their statutory obligations.

> **Planning point**
>
> It is important to ensure that a hallmarked scheme is properly notified to HMRC, as failure to do so could mean that the information supplied is not within the time limit for making the notification and the taxable person will be liable to a penalty. HMRC recommend that a summary of the scheme is provided, plus details of the beneficiaries' tax position without the scheme, details of whether the scheme gives a deferral or absolute saving. HMRC also recommend that a diagrammatic representation of the structure is provided to show participants and transaction flows.

> **Planning Point**
>
> Only generic information need be provided, actual addresses need not be identified nor do contracts or plans need to be submitted, but it is necessary to detail the involvement of any party to the scheme and how they contribute (even if they are not specifically named, or named as Company XYZ Ltd.

> **Planning point**
>
> When notification has already been advised to HMRC, e.g. by the promoter of a scheme, and the scheme reference number is known, there is no obligation to notify the use of the scheme.

32.3.4 Voluntary notification and registration of hallmarked schemes

Hallmarked schemes can be voluntarily disclosed to HMRC by any person at any time.

> **Planning point**
>
> A business that devises or markets a scheme may wish to disclose the scheme to relieve its clients of the obligation of having to notify HMRC of the use of the scheme. The notification should make clear that it is a voluntary notification.

The hallmarks of avoidance schemes include:

(a) confidentiality condition agreements;
(b) agreements to share a tax advantage;
(c) contingent fee arrangements;
(d) prepayments between connected parties;

(e)   funding by loans, share subscriptions or subscription in securities;

(f)   off-shore loops;

(g)   property transactions between connected parties; and

(h)   the issue of face-value vouchers.

The presence of one or more of these hallmarks does not mean that disclosure is required unless the other factors (such as obtaining a tax advantage) are present.

Confidentiality condition

This is an agreement between the promoter and user preventing or limiting the disclosure of how a scheme gives rise to a tax advantage.

HMRC consider that a scheme will fall within the confidentially hallmark if:

- a specific condition of confidentiality is imposed that prohibits or limits a person from revealing details of how a particular scheme gives rise to a tax advantage;
- a general confidentiality condition is introduced specifically in order to prohibit or limit a person from revealing details of how a particular scheme gives rise to a tax advantage;
- a client is required to undertake either in writing or verbally not to reveal details of how a particular scheme gives rise to a tax advantage; or
- an adviser specifically draws a client's attention to a pre-existing general confidentiality condition when introducing a scheme to the client in order to prohibit or limit the client from revealing details of how that particular scheme gives rise to a tax advantage.

The sharing of the tax advantage with another party to the scheme or with the promoter

This is commonly an agreement that the tax advantage accruing from the operation of the scheme is to be shared to any extent with another party to it.

A promoter is deemed to be any person if in the course of his trade, profession or business he involves the provision to other persons of services relating to taxation and he is to any extent responsible for the design or the proposed arrangements or he invites persons to enter into contracts for the implementation of the proposed arrangements.

Fees payable to a promoter are wholly or in part contingent on tax savings from the scheme

This is an agreement that payment to a promoter of the scheme be contingent in whole or in part on the tax advantage accruing from the operation of the scheme.

Prepayment between connected parties

This is a payment for a supply of goods or services between interconnected persons before the basic tax point for the supply or, where applicable, the special tax point that applies to goods supplied on sale or return, or where the supply is a continuous supply and the payment is before the goods or services are provided.

A continuous supply is a supply where one or more of the following applies:

- leases treated as supplies of goods – SI 1995/2518, reg. 85;
- supplies of ordinary gas or any form of power, heat, refrigeration or ventilation – SI 1995/2518, reg. 86;
- continuous supplies of services – SI 1995/2518, reg. 90;
- royalties and similar payments – SI 1995/2518, reg. 91; or
- supplies in the construction industry – SI 1995/2518, reg. 93.

Funding by loan share subscription or subscription in securities

The funding in whole or in part of the supply of goods or services between connected persons by means of a loan between connected persons or the subscription of shares in or securities issued by a connected person.

Offshore loops

A supply of relevant services which is used or intended to be used in whole or in part directly or indirectly in making to a person belonging in the UK a supply which is zero-rated, exempt or treated as made in another country and not in the UK by virtue of VATA 1994, s. 7(10) – Place of Supply of Services.

Relevant services are:

- exempt insurance services or exempt financial services which are supplied to a person who belongs outside the EC or directly linked to the export of goods to a place outside the EC or consist of the provision of intermediary insurance services or intermediary financial services; or
- a supply falling within VATA 1994, Sch. 5, paras. 1–8 where the recipient of that supply belongs in a country other than the Isle of Man which is not an EC country.

Property transaction between connected persons

This is a relevant grant where the grantor or grantee of the interest or right is the person who is not entitled to credit for all the input tax wholly attributable to the supply he makes.

Any work of construction, alteration, demolition, repair, maintenance or civil engineering has been or is to be carried out on land and the grant is made to a person connected with the grantor.

Relevant grant means the grant of any interest in the right over land or of any licence to occupy land, or in relation to land in Scotland any personal right to call for or be granted any taxable interest or right other than a grant of a description falling within

VATA 1994, Sch. 8, Grp. 5, Item 1 or intended use solely for residential or charitable purposes or by a person converting a non-residential building to residential use.

Issue of face-value vouchers

This hallmark applies where face-value vouchers are issued for consideration and either the issuer does not expect at least 75 per cent of the vouchers to be redeemed within three years of the vouchers are issued to a connected person outside the VAT group (no matter what the expected redemption rate is).

32.4   Penalties

Failure to make the required notification may result in penalties applying at the rate of:

- £5,000 for failing to disclose a hallmarked scheme; or
- 15 per cent of the VAT saving for failing to disclose a listed scheme.

The VAT saving is the difference between the amount of VAT which but for the scheme would have been shown on relevant VAT returns, or in the case where a repayment claim is made for earlier VAT periods in respect of which returns have been submitted, the difference between the amount claimed and the amount which but for the scheme would have been claimed. The relevant VAT return period begins with that in respect of which a tax advantage first arose and ends with that in which the taxable person duly notified HMRC or, if earlier, the VAT period immediately preceding the notification by HMRC of the penalty assessment.

A penalty will not apply where there is a reasonable excuse for failure to notify or the taxable person is convicted of a criminal offence or a penalty under VATA 1994, s. 60 (VAT Evasion Involving Dishonesty).

There is a right of appeal in respect of the penalty imposed. Reasonable excuse excludes:

- lack of funds;
- the fact that there is no loss to HMRC; and
- actions taken in good faith.

HMRC Powers

33.1   Introduction

In relation to VAT, HMRC have extensive powers. They communicate in a variety of ways with VAT-registered persons and other members of the public. They carry out routine visits to examine businesses and their records, and from time to time, they issue assessments for tax due. This chapter aims to consider these areas, and begins with a consideration of the structure of the department, in order to set the scene for such matters.

33.2   Background of Customs

The Customs side of HMRC (HM Customs & Excise as it was prior to the merger with the Inland Revenue on 18 April 2005) has a long history, most of which has been devoted to the prevention of smuggling and other activities and the regulation of specific activities such as brewing. This has implications for the character of this part of the new department.

In the early days of VAT, many officers came directly from preventive activities at ports and airports. They often tended to have a confrontational attitude to their work, something which is no longer so widely the case as more and more officers have experience of VAT work only.

This background is also the reason why it took Customs a long time to come to terms with the concept of professional representation of taxpayers.

The taxes administered by HM Revenue & Customs (HMRC) for which HM Customs & Excise were formerly responsible are:

- VAT;
- air passenger duties;
- betting, gaming and lottery duties;
- customs duties;
- excise duties;
- insurance premium tax;
- landfill tax;
- climate change levy; and
- aggregates levy.

33.3　Structure of HMRC

33.3.1 Background

Prior to the merger, the department underwent a major reorganisation which is effectively still continuing. The most significant hallmark of this change has been massive centralisation. This has radically altered the nature of the local VAT office.

HMRC is managed by a board of commissioners responsible for the collection, care and management of taxes and duties allocated to it by Parliament. The chairman of the board is accountable to the Chancellor of the Exchequer. Broad policy direction is provided by Treasury ministers who, in turn, are accountable to Parliament.

33.3.2 Regions

The former regions of Customs, known as collections, no longer exist. There are now seven geographical regions:

(1)　North.

(2)　Central.

(3)　South.

(4)　London.

(5)　Scotland.

(6)　Wales.

(7)　Northern Ireland.

33.3.3 Centralised functions

Telephone enquiries, once a function of the local VAT office, are now dealt with by the national enquiry line, 0845 010 9000.

> ### ⚠ *Warning!*
> The staff answering the telephones are insufficiently senior to deal with many enquiries and are dependent on supervisors to assist with all but the most basic questions. The quality of answers is variable to say the least, and a superficial response may be received if the true nature of the enquiry has not been properly appreciated.

Written enquiries are also handled by a single national centre at National Advice Service, Written Enquiries Section, Alexander House, Victoria Avenue, Southend,

Essex, SS99 1BD. Enquires from charities, however, need to be sent to HMRC Charities, St Johns House, Merton Road, Bootle, Merseyside, L69 9BB. Enquires by email should be sent to estn@hmrc.gsi.gov.uk.

Registration, deregistration and variation work is now centralised at HM Revenue & Customs, Deansgate, 62-70 Tettenhall Road, Wolverhampton WV1 4TZ. Group registrations and deregisration of all registrations are dealt with at HM Revenue & Customs, Imperial House, 77 Victoria Street, Grimsby, DN31 1DB. There are no registration sections left in local offices.

Increasingly, other functions are centralised within regions or nationally. Thus, for example, options to tax are all dealt with at the Option to Tax National Unit, HM Revenue & Customs, Portcullis House, 21 India Street, Glasgow, G2 4PZ. Error corrections are handled by a number of regional offices, and all VAT 427 claims must now be sent to Liverpool. Payment problems are to be dealt with by calling the National Advice Service on 0845 010 9000, but the Insolvency help desk is on 0151 703 8450.

> ⚠ **Warning!**
> To the inconvenience of taxpayers, it is currently impossible to know where to send every item of correspondence and it is necessary either to make enquiries every time or expect the local office to forward correspondence to the appropriate place.

33.3.4 Local VAT office

Many functions which have historically been performed by the local VAT office are now carried on centrally, either within regions or nationally. This has transformed the local office from a multidisciplinary unit to little more than a base for visiting officers to which certain other functions, often performed for the whole region, are attached. It is now no longer possible to visit the local office to obtain forms, make payments or get advice.

Such offices may house investigative staff and those involved in large trader control, but both of these functions are administered nationally and no longer come within the local management structure.

33.4 HMRC's VAT powers

33.4.1 Criminal matters

For historical reasons, the former Customs & Excise and its employees are vested with significant powers. An officer, as a common constable, has greater powers than a policeman. Some powers are general to the Customs side of HMRC and are contained within the CEMA 1979; some are specific to VAT and appear within VATA 1994.

HMRC are granted extensive powers by CEMA 1979 to deal with any assigned matter (CEMA 1979, s. 1(1)), of which VAT is one. Further powers are vested in them by VATA 1994, Sch. 11, which deals with administration, collection and enforcement. Detailed provisions made under the authority of VATA 1994 are in the VAT Regulations 1995 (SI 1995/2518).

At any reasonable time, HMRC can enter, without a warrant, premises used in conjunction with the carrying-on of a business if this is reasonably required to check that person's tax position. This, however, is a power of entry and inspection, and not search. Officers do have the power to enter and search under CEMA, but only in respect of prohibited or restricted goods (such as alcohol, tobacco, arms or pornography). The power is not restricted to premises used for making taxable supplies – it applies in respect of any business premises, even if the business is not registered or is providing wholly exempt supplies; it does not apply to property used solely as a dwelling. If HMRC has reasonable cause to believe that taxable supplies of goods are being made, the authorised person can inspect the premises and any goods found on them.

The inspection can be carried out at an agreed time or after seven days' notice has been given to the taxpayer. A notice will be left at the premises if the time of inspection has not been agreed. HMRC can ask a Tribunal to approve an inspection and, if this is the case, it must be stated in the notice. Copies and extracts from documents can be taken and goods inspected can be marked.

Law: FA 2008, paras. 10–17 & 28 and Sch. 36

> ### Planning point
> It is important to distinguish the right to enter and inspect from the right to search. The former may be done without a warrant, the latter only with a warrant for VAT. Thus an officer may inspect the premises and look at anything in open view at any reasonable time, but may not open drawers or cupboards, etc. unless armed with a valid warrant.

If considered necessary for the protection of the revenue, HMRC can take samples from goods in the possession of a supplier to determine how goods have been or ought to be treated for VAT purposes. For example, this may be necessary to check whether a supply is zero-rated, or whether the purity of water is within the standard in VATA 1994, Sch. 8, Grp. 2, item 2(a). The trader should receive compensation if the sample is not returned within a reasonable time and in good condition. Gaming machines can be opened to ensure VAT is being paid on the full amount of the supplies.

If a magistrate is satisfied that there are reasonable grounds for suspecting that a VAT fraud of a serious nature is being, has been or is about to be committed on any premises, he may issue a search warrant, valid for one month from the date of issue. Any person entering the premises under the warrant may take with him such other persons as appear to him to be necessary, remove any documents believed to be connected with the fraud and search anyone found on the premises who is believed to be in possession of such documents. (A female may only be searched by another female.)

A copy of the warrant must be provided for the occupier if he is there or whoever appears to be in charge of the premises at the time or, if there is no one there, a copy must be left on the premises in a prominent place.

Law: VATA 1994, Sch. 11, para. 10(6)

In an apparently serious case, HMRC may use such an order, which has been signed by a Justice of the Peace, to:

- seize and remove certain documents, etc. relating to the supply of goods and search certain persons; and
- require a person to give access to recorded information or to permit them to remove it.

Law: VATA 1994, Sch. 11, para. 10(3); VATA 1994, Sch. 11, paras. 11–12; Police and Criminal Evidence Act (PACE) 1984, ss. 8, 15 and 16

HMRC have the power to specify what records should be kept by a VAT-registered person and for how long. They also have the power to request the production of documents.

Law: VATA 1994, Sch. 11, para. 7(2)(b); VAT Regulations 1995 (SI 1995/2518), reg. 169 and 211(1).

HMRC can also take all or part of the records back to the local office for further examination. An officer is lawfully on a trader's premises when he is there with the occupier's consent or following one of the statutory powers of entry. Once there lawfully, he has a general power of seizure as specified in PACE 1984, s. 19.

Law: PACE 1984 (Application to Customs and Excise) Order 1985 (SI 1985/1800)

Documents that HMRC may reasonably require include a trader's profit and loss account and balance sheet and, in the view of HMRC, any management accounts produced by or on behalf of a trader. Documents relating to the provision of services provided by a barrister, solicitor or tax adviser can also be required under these provisions. *VAT Notice 700/47* (February 1993) is their statement of practice in respect to confidentiality in VAT matters. HMRC state that they are aware that a great deal of information to which they have access is of a confidential nature and they will take great care to ensure that respect for confidentiality is maintained. (See **23.4.4** in respect of the powers of HMRC to require documents to be provided.)

> **Planning point**
>
> Though the *VAT Notice* states that HMRC have the power to request confidential material from advisers, it does state that they will not normally request the tax adviser or the trader to produce a communication relating to confidential opinion or advice.

Where they believe that it is material to a dispute, however, they will not hesitate to request such documentation, using their powers to require information. An example of this is *Burghill Valley Golf Club* [2005] BVC 2,281, where Customs demanded sight of, *inter alia*, external advice from the club's advisers, fee notes and letters of engagement. In maintaining the penalty Customs had imposed on the club for failure to divulge this information, the tribunal upheld Customs' right to require it.

> ⚠ **Warning!**
>
> However, advisers who are involved in setting up tax planning schemes should be aware that following *Halifax* [2001] BVC 2,240, HMRC may request tax adviser's correspondence to establish whether the structure set up has been established with the sole intention of avoiding VAT or whether it has a genuine business purpose.

HMRC have the power to arrest anyone suspected of criminal fraud or using false documents without a warrant. Ministerial assurance was given that this power would be exercised only by specialist investigators and in the most serious cases.

Law: VATA 1994, s. 72(9)

HMRC have the power to prosecute a person who obstructs, hinders, molests or assaults any officer engaged in his duties or who obstructs an officer checking a computer.

Law: CEMA 1979, s. 16; FA 1985, s. 10(4)

> **Planning point**
>
> Two important powers to note that HMRC do not possess are the right to search (as opposed to inspect) premises without a warrant and the right to demand immediate responses to questions asked of a registered person.

33.4.2 Requirement to provide security and produce evidence

HMRC can, as a condition of repaying input tax, require a person to provide documents and evidence to support the claim. In addition, HMRC can, when making a repayment, require a person to provide security for the amount repaid (or an amount that appears appropriate to HMRC) as a condition of that person making or receiving taxable supplies.

These powers are invoked to protect the Revenue where HMRC suspect that the amount may not be properly repayable or, in cases where the persons running the business have been prosecuted or penalised for VAT offences, concerned with VAT registrations that have not paid all the VAT due or failed in other VAT obligations, or if the business is run by undischarged bankrupts or disqualified directors.

Law: VATA 1994, Sch 111, para 4

33.4.3 Requirement to provide security and produce evidence

Where a taxable person:

- receives a taxable supply of relevant goods;
- knowing or having reasonable grounds to suspect that all the VAT payable on that or previous or subsequent supplies of goods or services will not be paid to HMRC; and
- HMRC have serviced a notice on him,

then that person and other persons liable for the amount specified in the notice are jointly and severally liable for the net VAT unpaid on those goods and services.

The relevant goods and equipment includes telephone equipment, such as mobile phones, computers or computer equipment such as chips, computer equipment for leisure, amusement or entertainment and carbon trading credits.

Reasonable grounds to suspect include, but is not limited to, suspecting that the price is low on the acquisition of the goods and services, the price is less than previous such acquisitions or suspicion that VAT may not have been paid on these goods.

The objective of these provisions is to combat the so called 'carousel' frauds where high value but small goods are moved around the VAT system and a taxpayer then becoming uncontactable following a large supply of the goods or services. The supplier will charge VAT, but not account for it. Before these powers were introduced, HMRC may have had a liability to pay the input tax claimed by the recipient of the supply. This provision makes that recipient liable for the VAT unpaid by his supplier or other suppliers or recipients in the chain.

Law: VATA 1994, s. 77A

33.4.4 Furnishing information and production of documents

HMRC may serve a notice on a taxpayer or third party requiring the production of information or documents that are necessary to check a taxpayer's tax position (different powers existed prior to 1 April 2009). This, however, does not preclude an oral request, but this is not enforceable until a written notice is given. A notice may not be given to a third party without the permission of the taxpayer or the Tribunal unless the notice only refers to information and documents that form part of a person's statutory records and accounts, and relate to the taxable business of that person.

The documents and information must be provided within the time period required in the notice. The notice can specify the form or nature of the document (for example, if an original is required). The notice may also specify the place of production, or this can be agreed with the taxpayer. The notice can only demand documents and information about the possession or power of the recipient of the notice, and cannot require documents relating to the conduct of a tax appeal.

It is possible to appeal against the notice at the First-tier Tribunal.

Law: FA 2008, Sch. 36, paras. 29–33

33.4.5 Other powers

HMRC has the power to require a person to provide the contact details of a debtor where that debtor owes money to HMRC. This power can only be exercised where HMRC believes that the third party has such details and that person (a company, local authority or local authority association) obtained these details in the course of carrying on a business.

HMRC has the power to take samples if deemed necessary on the grounds of fraud or mistake.

HMRC may, at any reasonable time, obtain access to, and inspect and check, the operation of a computer used in the business, or any computer that may be required to produce or deliver a document to HMRC. HMRC can also require the operator of the computer to provide reasonable assistance as is required. Where it is believed that a VAT offence is being committed, an application can be made to a Justice of the Peace to permit a person working under the authority of HMRC to have access to, copy, make extracts from or remove recorded information.

33.5   Assessments

HMRC have powers to make assessments which can apply where:

- there has been a failure to make a return;
- documents required for the purposes of VAT have not been kept;
- facilities to verify a person's returns have not been afforded;

- it appears to HMRC that a return is incomplete or incorrect; or
- any refund or repayment of tax has been incorrectly repaid or credited, or any incorrect input tax claim has been made.

HMRC must make any assessment to the best of their judgement. In the leading case on this point, *Van Boeckel v C & E Commrs* (1980) 1 BVC 378, it was held that this means:

> 'the commissioners will fairly consider all material placed before them and, on that material, come to a decision which is one which is reasonable and not arbitrary as to the amount of tax which is due. As long as there is some material on which the commissioners can reasonably act then they are not required to carry out investigations which may or may not result in further material being placed before them.'

In *Spillane v C & E Commrs* (1989) 4 BVC 245, it was held that the tribunal was justified in finding that the VAT officer who made the assessment, when faced with difficulties in getting information about the extent of the appellant's business, was entitled, when making the assessment to the best of his judgment, to use figures towards the top of a possible range, leaving the appellant to show that this was incorrect.

Even where no new information is available, HMRC may otherwise than in circumstances falling within VATA 1994, ss. 73(6)(b) or 75(2)(b), increase the amount of the original assessment if it appears to them to be the amount which ought to have been assessed. A supplementary assessment is made in the amount of the excess on or before the last day on which the original assessment could have been made. Any assessment must state the reason why it has been made.

In most instances it is easy to ascertain whether an assessment raised against a taxpayer is valid or out of time. However, until *Notice 915* was issued in March 2001, the date on which an assessment was made was not obvious, with the result that those assessments which were close to the time limits were often subject to litigation to establish whether or not they were valid.

The majority of case law has suggested that an assessment has been raised when an officer completes the appropriate assessment form and gets an officer of an appropriate level to countersign this. This case law suggests that the assessment process is a two-tier process, the first part being the making of the assessment and the second part being the notification of this assessment to the trader.

This case law has given rise to confusion and difficulty. If an assessment is made when an internal document is signed within HMRC, how is a taxpayer to check its validity? The law also appears to allow the potential for sufficient delays between countersignature and notification, which is arguably inherently unfair. In the case of *Bent (t/a Bay Tree Trading Co)* [2001] BVC 4,118, for example, an assessment, countersigned on 22 October 1999, was not notified to the appellant until 8 February 2000. The tribunal held that the former was the date on which the assessment was made, meaning that it was valid.

> **Planning point**
>
> HMRC's statement of practice confirms, however, that from 1 March 2001 they will treat the assessment as being made when the taxpayer is notified of the assessment. Notification will usually take place by the issue of a form VAT 655 which is generated by HMRC's completion of the form VAT 641.

The statement of practice does however outline another method by which HMRC can notify the taxpayer of an assessment. If HMRC fear that an assessment will be out of time if the ordinary procedure is followed, they can notify the taxpayer via a letter. This notification letter will specifically state the notification date and HMRC hope in these circumstances that a computer-generated form VAT 655 will be issued at a later date confirming the notification date. The notification letter is quite different from a pre-assessment letter. The pre-assessment letter merely requests further information to allow HMRC to decide whether an assessment should be issued in the first place and therefore does not form part of the notification process of the assessment itself.

It is important to note that this was not a change to the law, which (on the basis of the bulk of the case law) continues to hold that the making of an assessment is separate from, and prior to, its notification to the recipient. It was rather a very welcome administrative relaxation which brought a new transparency to the process of issuing assessments.

The normal time limit is extended in the case of assessments to recover VAT lost due to criminal or civil fraud, a failure to register or the unauthorised issue of invoices. The time limit for making such assessments is increased from three to 20 years.

Law: VATA 1994, s. 73

33.6 Publications

33.6.1 HMRC's organs of communication regarding VAT matters

HMRC propagate information by a variety of means. This includes their library of *VAT Notices* (some formerly known as Leaflets), *Information Sheets*, *Revenue & Customs Briefs* and *Press Notices*. Each has its own particular function and all can be accessed via HMRC's website (*www.hmrc.gov.uk*).

33.6.2 Public notices

In the main, HMRC *VAT Notices* merely express the view of HMRC, which may or may not be consistent with the legislation. In a few cases, a Notice may carry the force of law or contain passages which do so. HMRC are empowered under certain parts of VAT legislation to publish documentation which is itself law (tertiary legislation), usually to do with record-keeping requirements or computational issues, such as retail schemes. A full list appears in *VAT Notice 747*, which is specifically devoted to providing comprehensive details of such tertiary legislation.

Planning point

Although HMRC are not beyond arguing against their own published position in litigation, it can broadly be said that the Notices are of most use in establishing what is acceptable to them or what they expect. This is useful in providing reassurance for a particular view or action or highlighting areas where HMRC can be expected to take issue with a given stand. In no sense should the *Notices* be seen as a definitive statement of the legal position.

33.6.3 Information Sheets

Information Sheets are issued from time to time to provide guidance in areas of current interest or new developments, where these are not covered by existing *Notices*. Often, but by no means always, these are superseded by new versions of *VAT Notices*. However, some remain in force for many years.

33.6.4 Revenue & Customs Briefs and Press Notices

Revenue & Customs Briefs are usually HMRC's response to current events, often the outcome of court cases or tribunals. Sometimes, they are effectively statements of practice; sometimes they set out a new and in HMRC's view compulsory change of legal application. Although such statements of policy have often quite wide application, *Revenue & Customs Briefs* are only published on their website. They are not therefore the most effective manner of promulgating policy.

Press Notices are also posted to HMRC's website. These announce newsworthy events, such as senior appointments or high-profile successful prosecutions of drug dealers, etc.

33.6.5 VAT Notes

VAT Notes, the little leaflets distributed with VAT returns, are in fact HMRC's main method of communicating with registered traders.

> **Planning point**
>
> Although these are not widely read, HMRC will regard their delivery to a trader as the point at which they came into possession of the information they contain. If this involves any additional liability, the trader will have some difficulty arguing thereafter that they could not have been expected to make the required change if HMRC later assess for underpaid tax.

33.6.6 HMRC's internal instructions

Under open Government initiatives, the former Customs' internal guidelines have for some years been publicly available. Selected parts have recently become accessible from HMRC's website, but the full version (subject to the removal of sensitive paragraphs) can still only be found in commercially available tax reference products, such as the *CCH British Value Added Tax Reporter* (electronic version).

> **Planning point**
>
> This guidance considerably amplifies the information to be found in *Notices* and also, by virtue of being addressed to officers of the department, provides a real insight into the way in which the department expects its staff to think, respond and act. That said, it is not at all uncommon for an officer to have made no reference to the instructions in dealing with a particular matter. This in turn means that the guidance is not always rigidly followed and that there are occasions on which it can be helpful or necessary to use this publication in correspondence to support a particular argument.

Often, the guidance lists cases which HMRC use to support their view in certain areas, which is also useful, especially when their own use of such cases is selective.

33.7 Extra-Statutory Concessions

Various ESCs are in force too in respect of many taxes within the jurisdiction of HMRC, many of which relate to VAT. A full list is published by them in *Notice 48*.

The provision allowing no scale charges to be paid if no input tax is claimed on road fuel is an extra-statutory concession. So is the assurance that tax will not be demanded from the recipient of an invalid certificate for zero-rating, where reasonable steps have been taken to check the validity of the certificate. Most of the remainder are designed to remove anomalies in the legislation, where the strict application of the law would give rise to inequity of some description.

> **Planning point**
>
> It is, however, worth drawing attention to one which is perhaps more important and far-reaching. This involves the undercharging of VAT by a registered trader.

The VAT due may be remitted (waived) by HMRC where:

- there is no reason to believe that the VAT has been knowingly evaded;
- there is no evidence of negligence;
- the misunderstanding does not concern an aspect of VAT clearly covered in general guidance published by HMRC or in specific instructions to the trader; and
- the VAT due was not charged, could not now reasonably be expected to be charged, and will not be charged.

This concession is arguably not encountered as often as it should be.

A final extra-statutory concession, which deserves consideration as a topic in its own right, is that on misdirection, the so-called Sheldon statement (see **33.8**).

As ESCs are not actually law, HMRC's refusal to apply them in any given case cannot form the basis of a tribunal appeal.

Other guidance: *VAT Notice 48*

33.8   The Sheldon statement

This policy took its name from Robert Sheldon, the Government minister who gave the original assurance in Parliament.

Up until 31 March 2009, HMRC reviewed claims under ESC 3.5 which read:

'If a Customs & Excise officer, with the full facts before him, has given a clear and unequivocal ruling in writing or, knowing the full facts, has misled a trader to his detriment, any assessment of VAT due will be based on the correct ruling from the date the error was brought to the registered person's attention.'

As an ESC, its non-application by HMRC could not be appealed to the VAT tribunal, a situation which many considered unacceptable.

With effect from 1 April 2009, HMRC advise businesses that think they have received incorrect advice from HMRC to review the guidance given in their publication *When You Can Rely on Advice Provided by HMRC*. This is available for review at *www. hmrc.gov.uk*.

33.9   VAT visits

33.9.1 Background

VAT visits or inspections were for many years known as control visits and this terminology is still widely used, even in HMRC, despite the official change of title some years ago to assurance visits.

Most assurance visits are conducted on a routine basis and are arranged specifically to check that the VAT submitted by a trader to HMRC is correct. Previously, most compliant VAT-registered traders could expect a VAT visit every three to five years. A newly-registered business could expect to receive its first VAT visit within three years of its effective date of registration.

However, the number of visits undertaken annually has been drastically reduced in recent years and HMRC are increasingly using risk analysis to decide when a business should be visited. The risk analysis will be based on the trader's perceived compliance (assessed on a previous visit or whether his VAT data is submitted on a timely basis), the complexity of the business, whether the business is operating in a risk area, etc. If analysis shows there is a good chance of loss to the Government of revenue, either by error or dishonesty, then an assurance visit will be organised. These days, the same criteria will be applied to newly-registered businesses in deciding whether a visit is necessary, meaning that it is on occasion several years after registration before the first visit takes place.

Some local offices have at times stretched the analysis further still by sending a pre-visit questionnaire or self-audited checks. These primarily highlight VAT danger areas and allow Customs to decide whether a visit is necessary or not, but also allow them to establish if there has been an underdeclaration of VAT. Assessments would be raised where, for example, it becomes apparent from the questionnaire that fuel scale charges have not been accounted for.

> ### *Planning point*
> Odd though it may seem to suggest it, there is a case to be made for a taxpayer taking professional advice in completing such a document, as careful completion may avoid complications later on.

Visits are also triggered when traders submit VAT returns which show large repayments. HMRC's computer will automatically 'bounce' these claims and send a reference to the local office to arrange a visit to check the veracity of the return submitted. This is often the first contact that a newly-registered person will have with HMRC (when he tries to recover all of his pre-registration and set-up expenses).

Some business centres have changed their policy towards such pre-repayment credibility ('pre-cred') checks and now request that the trader fax the larger invoices relating to his claim to the VAT office. (If there are a number of consecutive claims HMRC may also visit the trader.)

> ### *Planning point*
> In view of this policy, where a trader is aware that a claim he is submitting is unusually large, he may be advised to write to his local office with copies of the larger invoices (the invoices and correspondence should not be sent to the VAT Central Unit with the VAT return). This will often answer HMRC's queries when the pre-cred reference arrives at the local office with the result that the payment will be made without further delays resulting from enquiries made of the trader.

VAT Notice 989 states:

'You can expect that we will:

- confirm whom we will want to see;
- agree a mutually convenient appointment date and time;
- advise the name and contact number of the officer conducting the visit;
- indicate the likely length of the visit;
- give you the opportunity to indicate any matters you are unsure of so that the officer can be prepared; and
- give you the option to have the above details confirmed in writing.'

HMRC usually arrange the visit by telephoning the trader and confirming the details in writing (perhaps using form VAT 455A). This is now done by specialist teams of visit bookers, most of whom have never attended a VAT visit and will not be able to answer less-general questions about the visit. Occasionally they write asking the trader to contact them if they fail to communicate with him by telephone or facsimile. If this fails to contact the trader, HMRC may just turn up on the doorstep to arrange the visit.

It has been HMRC's policy always to visit the principal place of business (except in the most exceptional circumstances). Increasingly, however, they appear to agree to alternatives (usually an adviser's premises), and sometimes agree to not even meet the registered person. Officers appear not to appreciate that this severely diminishes their ability to understand the business and identify irregularities.

Likewise, a request to be shown round the business premises, once a regular facet of most visits, is now less frequently made.

33.9.2 Handling a visit

The visiting officer should be treated with all courtesy, and offering a cup of tea or coffee is a good way to start. It is wise to ensure that they are given space to work where they cannot see or overhear things which are best not accidentally drawn to their attention. As far as possible, it is sensible to retain control of how information is conveyed to them.

Planning point

All questions should be answered but without volunteering any more than is necessary to deal with the specific query. At the same time, information crucial to an understanding of a particular matter should not be knowingly withheld if it is clear that it is needed.

> ⚠ **Warning!**
> Off-the-cuff estimates should, however, be avoided at all costs. HMRC will note them and treat them as definitive. Much time and money may later be expended in trying to prove that the first response was wrong, in the event that, on further reflection or investigation, this is found to be the case (e.g. *Holloway* (1983) 1 BVC 1,199 where the publican underestimated his wastage rate).

Customs must give a trader reasonable time to provide them with information relating to his VAT affairs. This contrasts with the requirement to produce documents upon demand.

Law: VATA 1994, Sch. 11, para. 7(2)(a) and (b)

Enthusiastic officers may assert that the trader must answer all their questions immediately and in full. The trader should politely point out his right for reasonable time. Any areas of dispute can sometimes be clarified if HMRC put their questions in writing. HMRC often ask about the precise pricing policy, mark-up percentages, level of cash drawings and own consumption. Such questions often need considerable research before they can be properly answered.

Visits may last anything from an hour to several days. At the end, however, the officer should not depart without discussing any errors found or contentious issues, so that any correspondence or an assessment does not come as a surprise. Regrettably, this does not always happen.

> **Planning point**
> A VAT visit is not a complete audit and, if an error is picked up which was not spotted on the previous visit, HMRC are still entitled to assess, unless it can be shown that the specific area in question was looked at by the previous officer.

Charities

34.1 Introduction

34.1.1 History to VAT for charities

There is no blanket exemption from VAT for charities. Whilst many reliefs for charities are available in the VAT legislation, the relevant law is complex and often difficult to find, being spread out rather than concentrated in one place. When taking advantage of any of the reliefs, whether with regard to the treatment of income or reliefs for purchasing goods and services free of VAT, it is necessary to ensure that the detailed conditions are fulfilled. In many cases, a charity may find itself able to take advantage of an exemption as far as its income is concerned, but will have to bear VAT as a cost on its expenditure, without the benefit of recovery that many businesses enjoy.

Over the years there have been calls for the VAT legislation to be amended to afford this recovery but so far all Chancellors have refused to take this step, which is estimated to cost charities some £500 million p.a. The aim of this chapter is therefore to try to make the reliefs that are actually available in the law more accessible to charities and to provide some general planning strategies which may mean restructuring the way in which the charity works in order to take advantage of reliefs which may otherwise not be available.

The issue of non-recovery of VAT due to non-business activities or exempt income is also a major area for charities to deal with.

> ⚠ **Warning!**
> If a VAT planning scheme is in the public domain, HMRC will certainly be aware of it. Such schemes should be avoided unless you are certain that they remain valid. Beware of any schemes which purport to claim input tax without a corresponding charge to output tax — unless the corresponding charge is zero-rated. In addition, care needs to be taken of the concept of 'abuse of right' and also the requirement to disclose avoidance schemes (see **Chapter 32**).

> ⚠ **Warning!**
> In recent years, HMRC have made major inroads to combating many VAT planning schemes, and it is vital that a charity ensures that any arrangements entered into are still valid.

34.1.2 What is a charity for VAT purposes?

Most of the reliefs from VAT in this chapter depend upon the body having charitable status, and the first step in VAT planning is therefore to confirm that this status exists where it is required. However, in certain cases it is not necessary for a charity to be registered with the Charity Commissioners in order to take advantage of the reliefs offered, although those which are not registered may have to evidence their non-profit-making status through their objects or memorandum of association. Until 1 April 2012 it was necessary (other than for these exceptions that are mentioned here) for a body to be registered with the Charity Commissioner in order for it to obtain the VAT reliefs that are available to charities.

Certain charities are of course exempt from registration with the Charity Commission, such as universities, churches, charitable friendly societies, etc. When looking at the treatment of income or availability of a VAT relief throughout this section, the relevant status of the body will be set out if there are any special requirements. In looking at what constitutes charitable purposes there are six main areas to consider as:

- welfare;
- education;
- religion;
- health;
- sports; and
- other purposes of a charitable nature beneficial to the community not falling under any of the above.

From 1 April 2012 it is no longer necessary for a body to be registered with the Charity Commissioner for it to be regarded as a charity for VAT purposes. Most entities that are regarded as charitable will remain registered with the Charity Commissioner, but other bodies may also be eligible for the reliefs that are available to charities. From that date the definition of charity as defined in the Charities Act is disapplied for VAT purposes and a new definition is introduced. The new definition requires the body to be:

- a charity under the law of England and Wales, or would be, if they were established in England and Wales;
- be located in the UK or an EU Member State, Iceland or Norway;
- be registered with the Charity Commissioner in their home country if the law of the home country requires; and
- meet the management condition.

The management condition is that the people involved in the charity's finances must be 'fit and proper persons'.

Other guidance: *VAT Notice 701/1*

34.1.3 Introduction to business/non-business

One of the key issues in planning for charities is to determine whether they are in business or not. If the charity is not carrying on a business or an economic activity in European law terms, then it will not be liable to account for VAT on its income. However, the converse of this is that it will also not be able to recover any of the VAT incurred on expenditure — a basic precept of VAT being that VAT on expenditure is only recoverable if it is incurred in the course and furtherance of a taxable business activity. Sometimes, a key planning strategy is to find a taxable business transaction that the charity can carry out, in order that it can recover the VAT it incurs, especially where high capital costs such as building and construction works are involved.

> ### Example 34.1
> A charity looking after the welfare of dogs or cats could be funded wholly by grants and donations, outside the scope of VAT. Its activities may well be to look after unwanted dogs and to place them in a good home. It would therefore not be able to recover the VAT incurred on construction of kennels, vets' fees, etc. However, by making a charge for the dog to the person it is being placed with (in effect selling the dog in a similar fashion to a pet shop or a breeder) it is making a taxable supply, and this means that the VAT on all of these costs may be recovered, in whole or in part. Of course, output tax will also become due on the sale of the animals, which may be less desirable.

34.1.4 Definition of business

There is no definition of business in VAT legislation. The term used in European legislation is economic activity, which appears to have a somewhat broader concept. The meaning of business for VAT purposes has therefore been built up over time in case law.

> ### Planning point
> One issue that should not be confused is that just because a body is a charity does not mean that it is not carrying on a business. A school registered as a charity and charging school fees is in business, whereas a school which provides education free of charge would not be carrying on a business. Similarly a charity which owns and rents out property is in the business of property letting.

34.1.5 Examples from case law

1. Property letting: *C & E Commrs v Morrison's Academy Boarding Houses Association* (1977) 1 BVC 108.

    The Association was a company limited by guarantee and although not a registered charity, was accepted as a charity by the Inland Revenue. It let accommodation to children boarding at the Academy and parents were invoiced separately from the school fees. The activities of the company were carried out without a view to making a profit, and it claimed it was not carrying on a business. The court ruled in favour of Customs, holding that the lack of profit motive was irrelevant. The meaning of the word 'business' was wide enough to encompass any actively pursued occupation or function with reasonable continuity.

2.   Religion: *Church of Scientology of California v C & E Commrs* (1980) 1 BVC 343.

The Church of Scientology was incorporated in California and had the objects of propagating the faith of scientology. From premises in Sussex it provided training and auditing courses and made sales of books, E meters and other equipment. It appealed against Customs' contention that it was making taxable supplies, contending that a body which propagated religious philosophy should not be treated as carrying on a business. The court rejected this contention and ruled in favour of Customs.

3.   Statutory body: *Institute of Chartered Accountants in England and Wales v C & E Commrs* [1999] BVC 215.

The Institute is a recognised supervisory body, issuing certificates authorising or licensing its members to carry on investment business, insolvency and audit work. In this case, Customs argued that the Institute was not in business so it should not account for output tax on its income, nor recover input tax on its expenditure. The tribunal and on appeal the High Court and House of Lords all agreed that the predominant concern of licensing activities was the implementation of the statutory policy of protecting the public interest through self-regulation of the relevant practitioners, and did not amount to the carrying on of a business.

4.   Legal aid and assistance: *Hillingdon Legal Resources Centre Ltd* (1990) 5 BVC 837.

The company was a registered charity and provided legal aid and assistance free of charge to poor people in the borough of Hillingdon. It had recovered all of its input tax and Customs raised an assessment on the basis that the VAT incurred on the services provided free of charge was not recoverable. The tribunal upheld the assessment, holding that the services provided for no consideration were not carried on in the course or furtherance of a business.

5.   Children's day nursery: *C & E Commrs v Yarburgh Children's Trust* and *St Paul's Community Project* (2005) BVC 12.

Both Yarburgh Children's Trust and the organisation running the playgroup, Yarburgh Community Playgroup, were registered charities. A building was constructed by the Trust, with help from Lottery funding, which let it to the Playgroup at a rent that was less than market value. The court determined that under the circumstances, the lease merely provided for the use of the building by the second charity and did not constitute a business activity. Furthermore, in common with *St Paul's*, it determined that the activities of the Playgroup were not by way of a business because it was operated on a voluntary basis and the charges were set merely to meet operating costs, not with a view to making a profit. The building therefore enjoyed the benefit of zero-rating as a charitable, non-business building.

From case law there are a number of guidelines which must be considered in determining whether an organisation is in business or not.

1. Is the activity a serious undertaking earnestly pursued?

2. Is the activity an occupation or function that is actively pursued with reasonable and recognisable continuity?

3. Does the activity have a certain measure of substance in terms of the quarterly or annual value of taxable supplies?

4. Is the activity conducted in a regular manner and on sound and recognised business principles?

5. Is the real nature of the activity predominantly concerned with the making of supplies for a consideration?

6. Are the taxable supplies that are being made of a kind which, subject to differences in detail, are commonly made by those who seek to profit from them?

34.2   Registration

34.2.1 Introduction

Because of the diversity of income streams common to the charity sector, it can be difficult to determine the point at which registration must be effected. On account of the types of activity carried out by charities, much of the core income is likely to be either non-business (grants, donations, bequests, etc.) or exempt from VAT such as health, education, etc. In such cases it is often in respect of non-core activities or of a specific trading activity, such as a shop, that registration arises.

> **Planning point**
> In respect of their taxable activities, charities are subject to the same VAT registration rules as any other body. The provisions in **Chapter 3** should therefore be considered.

34.2.2 Grouping

VAT group registration is available to corporate bodies only, and the benefit of such arrangements is that VAT is not chargeable on supplies between group members.

This can be of particular benefit to charities where because of their non-business and exempt activities, charges between corporate bodies can lead to the internal creation of irrecoverable VAT. However, in view of the joint and several liability inherent in group registrations, and therefore the effective guaranteeing of other members' VAT liabilities, there is a school of thought which says that VAT grouping should not be entertained with charities. However, in cases where there is a definitive financial benefit to the formation of a VAT group (and proper professional advice has been taken on the point) such concerns should be laid to one side.

The provisions for VAT grouping have been extensively used in VAT planning schemes, and HMRC have consequently provided themselves with considerable powers which may be deployed for the protection of the revenue. These powers are contained in VATA 1994, Sch. 9A and *Business Brief* 15/99 sets out how HMRC expect to apply these powers.

In addition, all applications for VAT grouping which involve a partly exempt or non-business corporate body are now reviewed by anti-avoidance teams.

34.2.3 Branches

Branches are usually part of the single legal entity comprising the charity unless they are separately constituted and therefore income from branches will count towards the registration limit of the charity as a whole. In some cases, friends of the charity act in the same way as a branch might and may not be part of the charity itself. Typically, the friends will undertake fundraising activities and donate the net proceeds to the charity. Indications that a branch is part of the single charity rather than separate are:

- the branch uses the charity's registration number and name;
- there is no separate constitution;
- the funds raised belong to the charity — this can often be determined by considering what would happen with cash on hand if the branch closed;
- any legal action resulting from branch activities would be taken against the charity;
- branch funds and their use are controlled centrally;
- the branch benefits financially from being part of the charity; or
- the head office appoints/vetoes appointments as members of the branch committee.

> **Planning point**
> It is often difficult for a charity with a number of branches to complete VAT returns on time due to a delay in receiving information from the branches. It should be possible to agree with HMRC to use estimation in preparing VAT returns in such circumstances, with annual adjustments being made once the correct figures are provided.

34.3   Liability of income

34.3.1 Income streams

The following table sets out the liability of income common to charities, although it is not of course exhaustive. In cases where the liability of an income stream differs according to the individual circumstances, the issues are generally considered in more detail elsewhere in this chapter.

Income stream	Liability	Comments
Accommodation	SR/EX/OS	Exemption applies when supplied as ancillary to welfare – see **34.3.3**; closely related to education – see **34.3.5**; OS applies when supplied for no fee as non-business activity
Admissions	SR/EX	Exempt if part of fundraising activities – see **34.4**
Advertising	SR/ZR/OS	ZR if purchasing third party's time or space – see **34.5.4**; OS if in acknowledgement of a gift – see **34.4**
Affinity cards	OS/SR	See **34.4.6**
Agency fees	SR	
Aids for the disabled	ZR/SR	See **34.3.4**
Auctions	SR/ZR/EX	See **34.4.4**
Bequests	OS	
Bought-in goods	SR/ZR	Usual liability depending upon type of goods
Catering	SR/EX	SR unless ancillary/closely related to a qualifying exempt supply used – see **34.3.3** and **34.3.4** and **34.3.7** if supplied with accommodation
Church income	OS	Fees for services such as weddings, funerals, offerings – but sales of religious items have usual liability, e.g. books ZR, candles SR
Conferences	SR/EX	See **34.5.6**
Disabled, goods/services for the use of	ZR/SR	See **34.3.2** and **34.3.4**
Dividends	OS	
Donated goods	ZR/SR	See **34.4.5**
Donations	OS	See **34.4.1**
Education	EX/SR	See **34.3.5**

Income stream	Liability	Comments
Export within EU	ZR/SR	See **Chapter 22**
Free services	OS	See Various sections
Fuel and power	SR/RR	See **34.5.5**
Fundraising events	EX/SR	See **34.4**
Grants	OS	See **34.4.1**
Hire of equipment, etc.	SR	
Hire of facilities	SR	Unless for premises, then EX with the option to tax
Hostels	SR/EX	EX when ancillary to care – see **34.3.7**
Interest	EX	From banks, building societies, etc.
International services	OS/EX/SR/ZR	Rules are complex and depend upon type of service, type of supply and place of customer – see **Chapter 21** and **24**
Land and property	OS/EX/SR/ZR	See **34.5.7** for ZR charitable use and **Chapter 36**
Legacies	OS	
Management charges	SR	
Meals on wheels	OS/SR	OS when agent for local authority, otherwise SR
Medical equipment	SR/ZR	See **34.5.2** and **34.5.3**
Medical/hospital care	EX	See VATA 1994, Sch. 9, Grp. 7, items 1 and 4; Customs Leaflet 701/31
Motor vehicles (adapted for the disabled)	SR/ZR	See **34.5.1**
Printed matter	OS/SR/ZR	See VATA 1994, Sch. 8, Grp. 3 and Customs leaflet 701/10
Research	SR/ZR/OS/EX	See **34.3.6**
Share dealings	OS	See *Wellcome Trust Ltd v C & E Commrs* (Case C-155/94) [1996] BVC 377
Sponsorship	SR	See **34.4.1**
Sports facilities	EX/SR	See VATA 1994, Sch. 9, Grp. 1 for exemption
Staff, supplies of	SR	
Subscriptions	EX/SR/ZR	See **34.4.2**
Welfare services	EX/OS	See **34.3.3**
Youth clubs	EX	See VATA 1994, Sch. 9, Grp. 6, item 6

Key to table:

EX = exempt from VAT   ZR = zero-rated   OS = outside the scope of VAT

RR = reduced rate   SR = standard-rated

Planning point

Liability is determined by VATA 1994, in which the UK has implemented the European legislation contained in the Sixth VAT Directive (Dir. 77/388). This interpretation is not always on all fours with its European counterpart and in such cases taxpayers can rely directly upon the provisions of the Sixth Directive. Examples of this can be found in the cases of *Yoga for Health Foundation v C & E Commrs* (1984) 2 BVC 200,044, *International Bible Students Association v C & E Commrs* (1987) 3 BVC 205 and *Viewpoint Housing Association* [1996] BVC 2,220.

Planning point

The VAT legislation works by generally providing that any supply made in the course or furtherance of a business activity is standard-rated. Income received where no supply is made, such as grants, etc. is therefore outside the scope of VAT. The legislation then goes on to provide for the zero rates, reduced rates and exemption, and the supply must conform with the strict conditions laid down by the legislation in order to gain any of these treatments. Therefore, although there are a lot of reliefs from VAT available for charities, care should be taken that the detailed conditions are conformed with in determining the correct VAT treatment.

34.3.2 Welfare: non-business concession

Welfare services supplied by charities, including supplies of related goods, are treated by concession as 'non-business' when made consistently below cost to distressed people for the relief of their distress. The use of the concession is subject to the conditions set out below.

1.   Welfare is defined by HMRC as financial and other assistance provided on a non-commercial basis to persons in need which will help or benefit the recipient (see **34.3.3**).

2.   The supply must be to the individual in need (distressed person) and not to a third party. For example, contracts with other charities, local authorities, etc. would always be business even if the service is supplied at below cost.

3.   The service must be available to all distressed persons at all times. If the subsidy is conditional (beyond the conditions set by the charity's objects), e.g. only available:

     (a)   to those of a certain age;
     (b)   to those living in a certain area; or
     (c)   at certain times of the year,

or restricted to those who cannot afford to pay the full rate, it cannot qualify for the non-business concession.

When determining whether or not the service is provided below cost, comparisons should not be made with commercial operators providing a similar service. The correct test is whether the charity is subsidising its cost from other funds by at least 15 per cent. The cost should include all direct costs and expenses incurred in respect of making the supply, but exclude:

- capital expenditure on buildings;
- depreciation;
- creation of financial reserves;
- the value of volunteer labour; and
- goods and services donated by others.

'Accidental' or unplanned subsidy does not count. The charity must set out with the intention of delivering its service at 85 per cent of cost (or less).

Meals on wheels

Meals on wheels provided by a charity direct to distressed persons at below cost qualify for the above concession. Meals on wheels delivered by a charity as the agent of a local authority are part of the local authority's non-business activities. However, meals on wheels provided as principal under contract with the local authority are business supplies and the concession cannot be applied.

34.3.3 Welfare: exemption

Exemption from VAT is available to charities and not-for-profit organisations making supplies to welfare.

Prior to 21 March 2002, in order to qualify for exemption, the welfare service had to be provided on an otherwise-than-for-profit basis. This is no longer the case and any charity providing welfare now qualifies for exemption. Once it has been determined that there is a supply for consideration the following points should be considered in deciding whether exemption applies.

Meaning of welfare

HMRC define welfare as financial and other assistance provided on a non-commercial basis to persons in need that will help or benefit the recipient. The classes of people qualifying are:

- the elderly;
- the sick;
- the distressed (severe pain, anguish, financial straits, etc.);
- the disabled;
- children and young persons in need of protection; and
- those in need of spiritual welfare.

The definition of care is more open to debate. HMRC define it as some form of continuing personal contact in looking after or supervising people.

> ### *Planning point*
> HMRC have been applying this definition of care strictly, looking closely at day-care centres or home-help activities to determine whether or not the service provided is care in a specialised sense, as opposed to support, and that all beneficiaries of a service are in need. HMRC accept that domestic help can constitute care when supplied to persons assessed as having a high level of need.

Spiritual welfare

Providing spiritual welfare needs to be differentiated from general religious activity. The test is whether the service is providing aid or benefit to someone in need of it. Thus, bereavement counselling would qualify but a prayer meeting or bible class would not as that would be aimed at expanding knowledge of spiritual matters. In order to qualify for exemption from VAT, spiritual welfare must be provided on an otherwise-than-for-profit basis.

Residential courses, retreats, etc. must have, as their main objective, providing spiritual welfare to those attending. An organised retreat is likely to meet this test provided there is proactive guidance, whereas merely creating an environment for contemplation and spiritual reflection is not enough. In this context, conferences are usually organised to discuss spiritual welfare rather than practice it.

Ancillary welfare services

Ancillary services are a common area of dispute. Catering and accommodation must be clearly linked to the recipient of the care, e.g. accommodation provided to someone visiting a person receiving care would not qualify for exemption.

Recreational courses are excluded from the exemption to avoid competition with commercial entities (and therefore breach EU legislation). Such courses on which exemption is claimed are closely scrutinised. In general, holiday camps do not qualify even if the motive of the organisers is to promote, say, spiritual welfare as part of the holiday.

> ### *Planning point*
> Be prepared to challenge HMRC where you consider that there are grounds for claiming that the supply is ancillary to a welfare service. The tribunal in *Trustees for the MacMillan Cancer Trust* [1998] BVC 2,320 took the view that the UK's insistence that catering and accommodation must be ancillary to a supply of welfare (rather than a welfare service in its own right) may be *ultra vires* the Directive 2006/112, art. 132(1)(g). Consider using the various interpretations of this article in any argument.

34.3.4 Health and care institutions

The provision of welfare and goods supplied in connection with qualifying services supplied in an institution is exempt from VAT. HMRC have interpreted this widely to mean that the supply of care by all providers is exempt provided they are registered under the relevant legislation (typically the Care Standards Act 2000). This exemption was amended with effect from 1 January 2003 as a result of the decision in *Kingscrest Associates Ltd; Montecello Ltd (t/a Kingcrest Residential Care Homes)* [2003] BVC 2,592, which cast doubt over the scope of the exemption (as the tribunal took the view that only institutions providing care related to medical or surgical treatment can take advantage of this exemption).

Transport supplied or received by a qualifying institution

The exemption also covers the supply of:

• transport provided by a qualifying institution that forms an integral part of its exempt supply of care or treatment; and
• transport, by any provider, of sick or injured persons to or from a place of medical care or treatment in a vehicle specially designed or adapted for the purpose.

In addition, passenger transport provided in a vehicle designed or adapted to carry not less than ten people qualifies for zero-rating, whether it is supplied by a qualifying institution or any other person. This includes vehicles constructed or modified to carry disabled persons where the vehicle was capable of carrying ten or more passengers prior to the modifications.

Domiciliary care services, independent fostering agencies, voluntary fostering agencies and nursing agencies provided by commercial care agencies

Welfare services provided by state-regulated private welfare agencies became exempt from VAT with effect from 1 January 2003, and this exemption will also apply to charities which provide such services whether or not on a commercial basis (not non-business or otherwise than for profit). Customs allowed a period of grace until 31 March 2003 in which state-regulated agencies making supplies to local authorities could, if they chose, continue to charge and account for VAT on their welfare services while they were preparing to implement the VAT exemption from 1 April 2003. The exemption applies to those bodies required to register under the terms of the National Care Standards Commission, the Scottish Commission for the Regulation of Care, the Care Standards Inspectorate for Wales or the Northern Ireland Health and Personal Social Services Regulation and Improvement Authority. In Scotland the exemption also applies to child-care agencies and housing support services.

Under an Extra-Statutory Concession (ESC 3.37) available from 31 January 2003, providers of domiciliary care and other agencies that would in due course be regulated under the national care standards regulations, could, if they wished, exempt the welfare services that they provide pending registration. This ESC was introduced because many local authorities had not introduced the mechanics of a registration system by 31 January 2003. To take advantage of the concession, commercial providers of welfare services must be able to demonstrate a reasonable expectation that they will be required to register at the appropriate time.

Under this exemption it is not necessary for the services to be provided otherwise than for profit – the exemption includes any such agency which is registered with the above authorities, including commercial agencies operating on a for-profits basis.

The exemption applies to all care services provided by registered bodies, including routine domestic tasks, provided to elderly, sick or disabled persons where the recipient of the service cannot perform the task safely or adequately without significant pain or discomfort.

Prior to the implementation of these changes, Customs had introduced a concession pending the Department of Trade and Industry's intended changes to employment legislation, that businesses providing home-care services only had to account for VAT on the profit made on the provision of such services, not on the salary and associated costs of employing home-care workers – see *Business Brief* 3/00 for further details. This concession was withdrawn with effect from 31 January 2003.

Fostering and adoption agencies

Commercial independent fostering agencies and non-charitable voluntary adoption agencies are also covered by the exemption that applies to any service directly related to the care and protection of children and young people, including the placement of children with foster carers and the screening of prospective adopters whether for domestic or inter-country adoption and any allowances received by the agency for the care of a child.

Arrangement services

The VAT treatment of agencies arranging for the provision of such services will not change as a result of the above legislation and they remain standard-rated (for example, a fee for arranging the provision of services by a self-employed home carer) as do introduction fees.

34.3.5 Education exemption

Exemption for the supply of education and closely related services applies when the body providing the service is a university, school, college or other eligible body in accordance with the definitions shown below.

> **Planning point**
>
> Subsidiary companies of educational institutions are not covered by their parent organisation's exemption (for example, trading subsidiaries set up by charity schools). Therefore, unless they qualify for exemption in their own right, supplies of education and research by them would be standard-rated. When a university's, etc., customer for education and/or research can recover its VAT, there may be an advantage in hiving off the supply to a subsidiary as this would allow input tax attributable to the service to be recovered at no additional cost to the customer.

For charities not registered as schools, etc. to qualify for the exemption, any profits made must be applied solely to the continuance or improvement of the qualifying educational activity that generated them.

> **Planning point**
>
> This can cause problems for charities with more than one object, e.g. education and welfare. In such cases, HMRC's view is that where profits subsidise non-educational activities or overheads, the use of profits condition is not met and any supply is standard-rated. Where the charity's customers can recover VAT, HMRC's view is beneficial. On the other hand, by making the supply taxable the charity can recover attributable input tax. Where exemption is preferred, the charity must ensure that profits are ring-fenced and can be shown to be used only for education.

Meaning of education

The supply must be one of education. Education is defined as a course, class or lesson of instruction or study in any subject. It includes lectures, seminars, conferences, recreational and sporting courses. The key word is instruction. Education does not include supervision (e.g. for safety reasons), i.e. where no instruction is offered. Examination services supplied by or to bodies providing exempt education are also exempt. HMRC also accept that the supply of teaching staff from one exempt provider of education to another for the purpose of teaching (but not administration or other duties) is also a supply of education.

Distance learning packages which include proactive teaching, e.g. tutoring and marking services, are generally viewed as a single supply of education services even if they include other elements, e.g. digitised learning material, books, etc.

Law: VATA 1994, Sch. 9, Grp. 6, item 3

Education provided free of charge

Where no consideration is received by the education provider, the service is not a supply for VAT purposes. In general, direct funding by local or central government is not consideration, but this should not be confused with payments by those bodies for tuition, e.g. to universities. Higher education institutions and fee-paying schools are usually deemed to be providing education by way of business.

What does the exemption include?

Exemption extends to goods and services necessary for the delivery of education such as accommodation, catering and classroom materials. It does not include:

- supplies to staff and non-students;
- sale of goods from shops, vending machines, etc. (including uniforms, etc.);
- sale of goods not needed for regular use in class;
- separately charged personal services (e.g. laundry); and
- admission charges.

Closely related supplies

Supplies which are closely related to education also qualify for exemption. The term 'closely related' is defined as those supplies made directly to students of the institution which are ancillary to and necessary for the provision of the educational supply: for example, a charge made for cooking ingredients or for the materials in a design technology project.

Training

A supply of training by a non-charitable body falls outside the exemption for the provision of education relied on by universities, schools and educational charities. However, the supply may still be exempt (or outside the scope) if it is Government funded, that is to say the consideration payable is ultimately a charge to funds provided pursuant to arrangements made under s. 2 of the Employment and Training Act 1973, s. 1A of the Employment and Training (Northern Ireland) Act 1950 or s. 2 of the Enterprise and New Towns (Scotland) Act 1990. This would include training specifically funded by the European Social Fund (ESF) which is therefore exempt regardless of the status of the supplier. However, when a training provider obtains funds directly from the ESF and there is no immediate link between this and the activity undertaken, the payment is outside the scope of the tax.

It should not be assumed that just because training is routed through a subsidiary that it will be taxable.

Note also that the supply is only exempt to the extent that the consideration payable is ultimately a charge to funds made under s. 2 of the Employment and Training Act 1973, s. 1A of the Employment and Training (Northern Ireland) Act 1950 or s. 2 of the Enterprise and New Towns (Scotland) Act 1990. Therefore apportionment is likely to be required in situations where funding is topped up from other sources. At times, particularly with subcontracted training, it will be difficult to establish the extent to which exemption applies. HMRC are instructed to accept any apportionment that seems reasonable on the information available.

34.3.6 Exemption for research supplied by educational institutions

The exemption for the supply of research by an educational establishment is restricted to research supplied to another eligible body. The extent of the exemption in this regard was tested through the European Court in the case of *EC Commission v Germany* (Case C-287/00) [2003] BVC 11 where the court ruled that the supply of research was not exempt in circumstances where it was not supplied to another eligible body but to commercial organisations.

Meaning of research

Research is defined as original investigation undertaken in order to gain knowledge and understanding. It does not include consultancy, collecting or testing data/substances, opinion polls, writing computer programs, etc.

Eligible bodies

Only research supplied both to and by eligible bodies can qualify for exemption. Eligible bodies include:

- schools, universities and colleges;
- educational charities;
- government departments and executive agencies;
- local authorities;
- health authorities; and
- non-profit-making bodies that carry out duties of an essentially public nature similar to those carried out by local authorities and government departments.

The following comments are based on current understanding of HMRC's unpublished views of the treatment of such supplies. These views have only been expressed recently and may be challenged.

> **Planning point**
> Eligible bodies are restricted to UK-based institutions (although UK campuses of foreign universities qualify). Supplies of research to overseas universities, etc. are therefore outside the UK exemption.

34.3.7 Domestic and sleeping accommodation supplied by charities

The liability of supplies of accommodation can be confusing because the accommodation is described in a way which suggests a different VAT treatment to that which should apply, for example hostels, or because the accommodation's liability is influenced by its interaction with other reliefs, e.g. those for education and welfare.

Tenancy agreement

Licences to occupy land are exempt from VAT regardless of the type of organisation making the supply. If the land is to be used for domestic accommodation the landlord cannot elect to waive exemption. The operative word is licence. The tenant should have an interest in the property to qualify for exemption under this category. The accommodation may be long or short let. Good indicators of a licence to occupy land are:

- a tenancy agreement;
- a rent book; and
- the tenant having rights, e.g. to notice.

Generally the tenant will have exclusive use of space; however, shared facilities in a house do not disqualify the supply from this exemption.

Planning point
Short-term housing can sometimes be wrongly described by housing associations as hostel accommodation. This is a hangover from the way this sort of accommodation was funded. As hostels are generally standard-rated it is important that the exact nature of the occupancy is examined.

Type of accommodation

Specifically excluded from the exemption for interests in land is the provision in a hotel, inn, boarding house or similar establishment (hotel, etc.) of:

- sleeping accommodation;
- accommodation in rooms provided in conjunction with sleeping accommodation; and
- accommodation for the purpose of a supply of catering.

Similar establishment includes premises in which there is furnished sleeping accommodation (with or without board or self-catering facilities) which are held out as being suitable for use by visitors or travellers. Note that:

- length of stay is not a determining factor (but see 'Long-stay visitors' below);
- quality is not a prerequisite (see 'Ancillary to welfare'); and
- conversely, being a hotel, etc. does not debar the supply from exemption if they are relieved under 'Ancillary to welfare' or 'Closely related to education'.

It is possible for accommodation which is similar to a hotel to not be taxed if the basis on which it is provided is ancillary to the provision of care.

HMRC accept that the hire of guest rooms to visitors of sheltered housing or nursing homes which are mostly used by relatives, etc. of residents would not be seen as hotel, etc. accommodation unless advertised as such and is therefore exempt.

Ancillary to welfare

For the definition of ancillary to welfare, see **34.3.3**. Note that subsidised accommodation does not necessarily constitute welfare.

> ### Example 34.2
>
> A city council supplied a hostel for down-and-outs. It was run down and extremely unattractive. It did not grant interests in land to its residents who could book in and out any time and be thrown out if their behaviour was antisocial.
>
> Customs did not accept that the council was providing welfare as anyone regardless of need could book in. Despite its condition, the hostel had the features of a hotel, etc. and therefore fell within the ambit of that exclusion from the exemption for interests in land.
>
> Although the tribunal agreed the hostel fell within the definition of a similar establishment, the fact that non-distressed persons could use the hostel did not detract from the objective of the council which was to help those with nowhere else to go and therefore the supply was one of welfare and the accommodation was exempt (*The Lord Mayor and Citizens of the City of Westminster* (1988) 3 BVC 847).

Closely related to education

For the definition of closely related to education, see **34.3.5**. Note that to qualify under this head the supplier of the accommodation must also provide the qualifying education supplies.

Long-stay visitors

Although supplies not qualifying for exemption are standard-rated, VAT charged to long-stay visitors (those staying over four weeks) can be limited to the price of:

(a)   meals, drinks and service charges; and

(b)   facilities other than the right to occupy a room.

The value under (b) must not be less than 20 per cent of the total amount due.

In addition, it is this lower value to which the VAT registration limits apply, so that a hotel, etc. may have income from letting of accommodation amounting to say £70,000 with £10,000 of this relating to meals. If it adopts the 20 per cent rule above for the provision of facilities, the value of taxable supplies is reduced to the £10,000 for meals, plus 20 per cent of the remaining £60,000 (or £12,000) so that its taxable supplies for registration purposes amount to only £22,000 or is under the registration limits.

34.3.8 Cultural services exemption

This exemption was introduced as recently as 1 June 1996 in recognition of the fact that the UK had not implemented the Directive 2006/112, art. 132(1)(n) which exempts certain cultural services supplied by charities, public bodies, etc. (and should have been introduced under the terms of European law from 1 January 1990). Some charities may offer free admission to their premises or event. In such cases, there is no supply and therefore the activity would not fall within the scope of VAT and would be neither exempt nor taxable.

Generally, if an activity falls outside the scope of VAT, there would be no entitlement to recover any VAT incurred which could be attributed to it. However, in response to lobbying by the museum sector, the Government has agreed to allow certain national museums to reclaim any VAT suffered provided that they do not charge for admission.

Categories of admission

Exemption applies to admission to:

- zoos;
- museums;
- galleries;
- art exhibitions; and
- theatrical, musical or choreographic performances of a cultural nature.

It is restricted to circumstances where the supply is made by an 'eligible body' that in this context means any body (other than a public body) which:

- is precluded from distributing and does not distribute, any profit it makes;
- applies any profits made from supplies (of cultural activities as defined) to the continuance or improvement of the facilities made available by means of the supplies; and
- is managed and administered on an essentially voluntary basis.

The term cultural nature must be given its everyday meaning. Although the performance categories may appear to be restricted to the highbrow, HMRC accept that any form of play, opera, musical comedy, classical music, jazz, ballet or dance is accepted.

> **Planning point**
> HMRC appear to exclude popular (and folk) music from their interpretation of culture. However, given that there is a strong argument that popular music represents modern culture and that jazz is allowed, any refusal to exempt such performances is open to challenge. The same arguments could extend to cinema: to what extent does the use of the condition 'certain' in the EU legislation allow the UK to restrict the relief?

Profit from admissions

Note that it is not enough to be a non-profit-making organisation and that any surplus generated from a supply of qualifying services must be applied to the continuance of the activity which generated it.

> ### Planning point
>
> As in the case of welfare and education, the condition that profits must be applied to the activity which generated them is based on HMRC's interpretation of the judgment in *Bell Concord Educational Trust* rather than the relevant article of Directive 2006/112. If this condition causes problems (e.g. HMRC refuse exemption because the charity has more than one type of activity and profits are used to fund overheads), an appeal to the tribunal should be considered.

Management on a voluntary basis

Until 1 June 2004 the UK had not fully implemented all the conditions available for this exemption in EU law. This was because the consultation exercise, which preceded the introduction of the exemption into UK law, suggested that interested parties did not want the exemption because of its impact on VAT recovery. Consequently, the UK legislation was designed to limit the relief as far as possible, and HMRC appeared to be quite practical in allowing organisations to avoid the exemption if they so desired.

However, their approach was not acceptable to charitable bodies, in particular the insistence that no administrator might be paid without prejudicing the exemption. European legislation grants exemption to bodies managed and administered on an essentially voluntary basis. In the case of *C & E Commrs v The Zoological Society of London* (Case C-267/00) [2002] BVC 414, it was held that the correct interpretation of this condition is that exemption is only denied where paid management are significantly involved in the central management decision-making process (as opposed to the mere performance of management or administration under the direction of unpaid officials, e.g. trustees/governors).

From 1 June 2004 the exemption has been mandatorily applied to all qualifying bodies. HMRC's explanation of how they now intend to apply the exemption, including some very generous reliefs in respect of capital projects under way at that date, can be found in *Business Brief* 28/03.

In *Bournemouth Symphony Orchestra v C & E Commrs* [2005] BVC 547, the High Court upheld Customs' contention that a single paid member of the governing board (in this case the Managing Director, who attended board meetings and played a significant part in the decision-making and setting strategy, although he was not a trustee as such) caused the charity to fall outside the exemption. This decision, which was subsequently upheld by the Court of Appeal (leave to appeal to the House of Lords refused) illustrates the narrow divide between qualifying and non-qualifying charities and provides an indicator of how those charities not wanting to be exempt might consider disqualifying themselves.

> **Planning point**
>
> If exemption is not available under this relief, consider using the exemption for fundraising events if the performance is a one-off.

34.3.9 Sports exemption

This exemption was introduced with effect from 1 April 1994, but under the terms of the Directive 2006/112, art. 132(1)(m), which exempts certain services closely linked to sports or physical education supplied by non-profit-making bodies (and should have been introduced under the terms of European law from 1 January 1990). Some charities may offer free admission to their premises or sporting events. In such cases, there is no supply and therefore the activity would not fall within the scope of VAT and would be neither exempt nor taxable. Prior to 1 January 1990, the exemption was available to all non-profit-making bodies, but since that date, due to certain anti-avoidance provisions, the exemption has been restricted to eligible bodies in order to prevent commercial organisations from taking advantage of the exemption. The anti-avoidance measures have produced a very complex set of conditions which must be looked at very carefully to ensure that the exemption applies.

> **⚠ Warning!**
>
> Certain sports charities incur heavy capital VAT costs, especially upon setting up (such as construction of tennis courts or all-weather pitches). Such an organisation may wish to ensure that they fall outside the exemption and charge VAT on the provision of facilities so that they can recover VAT on the capital costs. For example, paying an officer involved in the strategic planning of the charity a bonus based on profits made from the particular activity would break the conditions for the exemption to apply.

Competitions

The exemption applies to the grant of a right by an eligible body established for the purposes of sport or physical recreation to enter a competition in such an activity. If the body is not established for the purposes of sport or physical recreation, then exemption may still apply provided that the entry fees (which must be in money) are allocated wholly towards prizes in the competition.

Note that sports competitions may also qualify for exemption as a fundraising event.

Sporting services

Exemption applies to all charges made by an eligible body to individuals for services closely linked with and essential to sport or physical education in which the individual is taking part. However, where there is a membership scheme, the exemption is limited to the provision of sporting services to members only. For example, a members' golf club would qualify for exemption for membership fees but would have to standard rate green fees. The term of the membership must be for a period of at least three months. This condition was introduced to prevent short-term membership being used to avoid VAT.

The exemption applies to joining fees and life memberships as well as the actual membership fee.

> ### Planning point
> Some sports clubs have a category of membership for non-playing members. By definition these members' subscriptions cannot be for services relating to sport 'in which the individual is taking part'. They are therefore not eligible for exemption and are consequently normally standard-rated.

To qualify for exemption, the supply must be to an individual rather than to an organisation or corporate body, but note that hire of sports facilities for a period in excess of 24 hours or for a series of ten or more periods may qualify for exemption as a grant of an interest in land. HMRC have stipulated that the term 'individual' includes families and informal groups of people where one person makes a block booking on behalf of the group.

Therefore, supplies of corporate memberships do not qualify for exemption. Neither do social memberships as they are not for taking part in sport, and in cases where a membership fee can be identified as having a social element (such as including the right of entry to a function for which non-members would be charged), then apportionment of the membership fee should take place. Supplies to guests, including members of other eligible bodies, are also outside the exemption and must be standard-rated, but see above as the exemption applies to competitions.

> ### Planning point
> In cases where a member joins within three months of the end of the year, exemption can still apply if the grant of membership is made for a period longer than three months. The membership should therefore be granted for the next year at the same time so that exemption may apply.

Qualifying activities

HMRC provide a list of activities they consider to qualify as sports and physical recreation. For example, baton twirling counts as sport or physical recreation whereas chess or draughts do not.

Services closely linked to sports include playing the sport, competing in the sport, refereeing or umpiring a match, judging, coaching or training. It also includes peripheral supplies such as use of lockers, changing rooms, showers and playing equipment and storage of equipment essential to the sporting activity. For example, where boats or aeroplanes are concerned, their mooring or hangarage and use of workshop facilities qualify for exemption.

It includes match fees charged by an eligible body for use of the playing facilities. However, if the match fees include a charge for a supply of catering, apportionment should be applied.

The services of professional sports coaches are not within the terms of the exemption as they are not supplied by an eligible body (unless they are employed by the eligible body). However, coaching may qualify for exemption as a supply of education if provided by a private individual or by an eligible body.

Attendance at an event as a spectator is not within the terms of the exemption.

Other guidance: *VAT Notice 701/45*

Eligible bodies

Particularly in this area the anti-avoidance provisions have caused complexity in the conditions that must be met to qualify for exemption. Eligible bodies include any form of non-profit-making organisation (this means that the organisation must have been established with a purpose, intention or motive which excluded profit making, not just that it has a clause within its constitution which prevents the distribution of profits), provided that:

- their constitution provides that profits will not be distributed, except in the case of winding up, when profits may be distributed to its members, or in any other case to another non-profit-making body;
- profits are used for the continuance or improvement of the qualifying sports supplies; and
- the organisation is not subject to commercial influence.

However, employees' sports clubs are specifically excluded from the exemption.

Unincorporated club

The club is a non-profit-making organisation. All profit and surpluses will be used to maintain or improve the club's facilities. No profit or surplus will be distributed other than to another non-profit-making body or to members on winding-up or dissolution of the club.

Company limited by guarantee

The income and property of the company shall be applied solely towards the promotion of its objects as set forth in the Memorandum and Articles of Association and no portion thereof shall be paid or transferred directly or indirectly by way of dividend, bonus or otherwise howsoever by way of profit, to members of the company and no director of the company shall be paid by salary or fees, or receive any remuneration or other benefit in money or money's worth from the company for discharging his or her duties as such.

If upon winding up or dissolution of the company there remains, after the satisfaction of all its debts and liabilities, any property whatsoever, the same shall not be paid to or distributed among the members of the company, but shall be given or transferred to some other institution or institutions having objects similar to those of the company.

Company limited by shares

HMRC have accepted that the non-distribution condition will be satisfied by the passing of a resolution by the club to amend the Memorandum and Articles of Association as follows:

- delete certain other prejudicial articles; and
- adopt a new article preventing distributions by way of dividend, bonus and any other means.

HMRC have also accepted that the adoption of a suitable article on winding up fulfils the winding-up criterion.

Commercial influence

An organisation is subject to commercial influence if, within the last three years from the date the supply in question takes place, the organisation has:

- paid a wage or salary (including perks or other remuneration) to anyone who was an officer or a shadow officer of the club, or was connected with such an officer, which was calculated by reference to profits or turnover; or
- purchased relevant supplies from anyone who was an officer or a shadow officer of the club, acting as an intermediary between the club and the officer, or anyone connected with such a person.

For the purposes of the above conditions, an officer includes any committee member, director or trustee of the body. A shadow officer is someone in accordance with whose directions or instructions the officers or members are accustomed to act. An intermediary includes anyone who acts between the body and persons associated with it, including other intermediaries, in the making of a relevant supply. A person connected with another person associated with the body has the meaning in s. 839 of ICTA 1988 and includes anyone who is a relative or business partner of an officer, shadow officer or intermediary or connected by virtue of control of a company.

Relevant supplies include the following:

- the grant of an interest in or right over land or licence to occupy any land which at any time in the relevant period was or was expected to become sports land and, in the case of land in Scotland, of any personal right to call for or be granted any such interest or right (except for grants made for a nominal consideration, which HMRC have interpreted to mean no more than £1,000 p.a.);

- a grant of the use of sports land under leases granted, varied or renewed since 1 April 1996 (except for grants made for a nominal consideration which HMRC have interpreted to mean no more than £1,000 p.a.);
- a supply of any services in managing or administering any of its facilities; and
- a supply of any goods or services for a value in excess of market value.

Grants of an interest in land are not relevant supplies if they are made by way of a gift.

However, any of the above supplies made by charities or local authorities are excluded from the definition of relevant supplies.

34.4　Fundraising

34.4.1　Donations, grants and sponsorship

This is a common area of confusion for charities. In order to be treated as outside the scope of VAT, funding such as donations or grants must not be received as consideration for any supply. It is easy to say a donation is not a donation when there is a direct link between the payment and benefit received by the donor. However, fundraising is usually not so black and white that it is easy to determine whether or not there is sufficient benefit to bring a contribution into the scope of VAT as consideration. This section is designed to offer some guidance to the liability of typical gift situations.

Nature of gift

It is common practice to determine liability by reference to what the gift is called. Donations and grants would therefore be outside the scope of VAT, and sponsorship within it (because sponsorship is typically received in return for a supply of advertising). However, terminology can be misleading: local authority grants to charities are often payments to do something. Generally, the existence of a contract suggests that the grant is in fact payment for a supply. However, this is not always the case as there still needs to be the other elements required to create a supply – notably the need for a direct link between the supply and the payment received. For example, a contract from a local authority which provides that the local authority will fund certain activities by the charity to £x amount, requiring that the charity meet certain guidelines and standards in providing such services, would not be consideration unless the charity were seen as making a specific supply on behalf of the local authority.

> **Planning point**
> Gifts may be in kind or goods rather than cash. Such gifts may bypass a charity's accounting systems. If it is a true gift this is not a problem. However, if the gift is in return for a benefit, the tax liability may be missed.

Charities also need to be careful when restructuring their activities to improve efficiency, etc. in cases where that restructuring creates a new entity and the intention is that the two (or more) bodies will work jointly together to meet mutual objectives. In the case of *C & E Commrs v The Church Schools Foundation Ltd* [2002] BVC 114, a charitable schools foundation (CSF) hived off the running of its schools to another charity. It retained and maintained the school properties: the other charity ran the schools. CSF charged the operating charity market rent (plus VAT) for use of the schools which also made a grant to CSF. This money was used to improve the properties, but was not specifically assigned to that purpose by the giver. Customs contended that the grant was consideration for a supply. Although CSF ultimately won the day, the point was not resolved until it reached the Court of Appeal.

Planning point

When restructuring it is essential that any cost sharing/payments made, etc. are fully evaluated in the context of the rules of supply to ensure that unexpected VAT liabilities are not created.

⚠ Warning!

Items that are donated and then sold are subject to VAT at the zero-rate. The word donation can have a wide meaning. In *Gablesfarm Dogs and Cats Home* [2008] BVC 4,049 it was held that this was not limited to the sale of dogs that had been handed in by owners, but also encompassed dogs that had been rescued by the emergency services and dogs acquired that were strays, abandoned or lost. Where the dogs (goods) are acquired without consideration it would appear that the goods are treated as being donated.

It also needs to be considered if the goods supplied in these cases are sold or just given for a donation. Frequently the aim of the dog home would be to re-home the dog and they will re-home the animal in return for a limited donation even if they suggest a minimum donation. The question to be considered is whether this is a supply for consideration (and zero-rated if the goods supplied had been donated) or the re-homing of a dog and the receipt of a donation. In the decision *Three Counties Dog Rescue* [2011] TC 01653 it was held that dogs that were supplied to a new owner in return for a donation were actually being sold and the supply could benefit from the zero-rate relief. The Tribunal found that the amount was not freely given as something was supplied in return (the dog). In this instance it would be very rare for a dog to be allowed to be re-homed without some form of 'donation'. Thus it was held to be consideration for a supply rather than a donation. This treatment was supported by the books and records of the appellant where the payments for dogs were recorded separately from other freely given donations. Additionally, the payments for the dogs did not qualify for gift aid.

Third-party benefits

Check whether or not the gift benefits a third party associated with the donor. Beneficiaries of the charity would not count unless there is a link with the donor.

Example 34.3

Charity X supports homeless people in Y city. Y city council give a grant to X to support its work. The grant would be outside the scope of VAT as there is no benefit to Y. The fact that the beneficiaries are indirectly connected with Y (as their local council) can be ignored.

Example 34.4

Charity X supports homeless people in Y city. Y city council appoints X to run one of its shelters for the homeless and gives it a grant of £50,000. The grant would fall within the scope of VAT because there is a link between the payment and X having to do something which benefits Y, i.e. take over responsibility for running a shelter.

Example 34.5

Charity X provides training to the disabled. It has a contract with the city council under which the council can place trainees on the programme and receive reports, etc. monitoring how the programme is working. The council provides funding equivalent to 50 per cent of the cost of the programme. The link between payment by the council and supply by charity X to the trainees is not direct enough to create a supply.

Planning point

Some charities seek to convert their grants into consideration by entering into a contractual relationship with the local authority. As the local authority can recover all its VAT it is generally happy to agree to this and, by making a taxable supply rather than carrying out a grant-funded, non-business activity, the charity can recover its VAT costs. However, HMRC are on the lookout for these sorts of arrangements and they may be challenged (*see Wolverhampton Citizens Advice Bureau* [2000] BVC 2,198 and *West Central Halifax Partnership* [2000] BVC 2,295 for examples where the appellants were unsuccessful in arguing that their contractual relationship with the local authority created a supply).

Extent of benefit

At flag days and the like, charities give a token (flag, poppy, etc.) in return for a contribution. The gift is not payment for a supply of the token provided that a minimum payment does not have to be made for the token. This rule extends to other acknowledgements:

- including the donor's name on a programme, notice, back of a chair (as in a theatre), etc.; and
- naming a building or university chair after a donor.

More commercial acknowledgements would be construed as benefits with value (i.e. sponsorship):

- displaying the sponsor's logo in any acknowledgement or advertising;
- naming an event after a sponsor;
- free or reduced-price tickets/priority booking rights, etc. to an event; and
- entertainment or hospitality facilities.

> **Planning point**
>
> Sponsorship payments at certain fundraising events may qualify for exemption (see **34.4.3**).

Minimum payment

If a minimum payment is required for a token (e.g. £1 for an enamel badge is common), VAT is due on the minimum payment. Any contribution over the minimum payment would be outside the scope. However, it should be made clear what the minimum payment is and that any payment made over this amount is made purely as a donation.

> **Example 34.6**
>
> In *C & E Commrs v Tron Theatre Ltd* [1994] BVC 14, a seat sponsorship scheme was implemented to obtain additional funds for refurbishment of the theatre, in which members of the public were invited to sponsor a seat in the theatre for payment of £150. They published a brochure which listed the benefits to sponsors as:
>
> - personalised brass plaque displayed on each seat;
> - acknowledgement on a board featured in Tron Theatre's main foyer;
> - limited edition print by Glasgow artist Johnny Taylor specially commissioned by the Tron to commemorate this major appeal; and
> - priority booking for two gala evenings unveiling the new seating and celebrating in grand style.
>
> The benefits would not be supplied for less than £150, although payments above £150 would be accepted. Tron argued that the whole £150 was a donation or, in the alternative, part of the £150 represented by a donation. Tron won this second argument at tribunal. Customs appealed to the Court of Sessions on the ground that the tribunal had erred in law as the £150 was wholly consideration for the above benefits, on the basis that if those benefits were only supplied in return for £150 then all of the £150 had to be the consideration for them. The court found in Customs' favour, holding that all of the £150 was the consideration for the package of benefits supplied by the theatre.

Donor benefits

Strictly, if any benefits accrue to the donor, the entire contribution falls within the scope of VAT. By concession, HMRC may allow charities to treat part of such payments as outside the scope subject to the benefits being available to all (i.e. not just the donors).

> **Planning point**
>
> If possible, any sponsorship or payment for benefits should be separately identified from any gift by the donor at the time any contribution is made. However, if the donor is VAT registered and can recover the VAT on the gift (i.e. the benefits are not business entertainment on which all VAT recovery is blocked), it may be advantageous to tax the entire contribution as this should improve input tax recovery by the charity.

> **Planning point**
>
> Where a charity suffers significant input tax on a service funded by donations, it may benefit the charity to convert part of the donation into a supply by placing a minimum or nominal charge on its service. Although the input tax will exceed the output tax paid on the nominal charge and the activity could not make a profit, there is a valid supply for VAT purposes. Payments over and above the nominal charge would still be outside the scope if given freely.

34.4.2 Membership subscriptions exemption

This section provides guidance to determine whether or not a charity's membership income brings it within the scope of the exemption introduced on 1 December 1999. This exemption replaced the non-business treatment of subscriptions to non-profit-making bodies with aims of a political, religious, patriotic, philosophical, philanthropic or civic nature. It also brings certain subscriptions to those bodies, which were previously treated as taxable, within the scope of the exemption because the benefits available to members were greater than those allowed for non-business treatment.

Law: VATA 1994, Sch. 9, Grp. 9

Other guidance: VAT Notice 701/5, s. 11

Definition of philanthropic

Although not specifically defined in the legislation, the term 'philanthropic' should include all charities together with other bodies which, although not charities, still perform charitable actions. HMRC interpret the term to mean for the benefit of the general community or a particular section of the community. The term was also considered by the tribunal in *Rotary International* [1991] BVC 690, where it was found that the body was philanthropic because it administered and organised the charitable activities of rotary clubs even though it was not directly engaged in these activities itself. Subscription includes any payment which creates a right of membership or similar benefit, regardless of how it is described (e.g. donation).

One-off life membership payments, levies, loans or other non-monetary consideration may all constitute subscriptions. In *The Game Conservancy Trust* [2002] BVC 2,003, the tribunal rejected Customs' contention that the Trust's subscriptions did not qualify for exemption because its purpose was to support the self-interest of its members rather than to benefit the general community. The tribunal found that taking an overall view of the Trust's objects and activities it is promoting and preserving biodiversity in the widest sense throughout the whole game-related sector of the rural ecosystem and therefore was philanthropic in nature.

Limitations on benefits

The benefits have to be referable to the aims of the body and supplied in return for a subscription to qualify for this exemption. Other benefits provided which are either not connected with the aims of the body or supplied for additional payments outside the subscription will not fall within this exemption. If the subscription simply provides for the member to receive an annual report from the board of trustees and to attend the AGM, etc., it will be exempt.

Exceptions

The exemption does not include any subscription that contains the provision of any right of admission to any premises, event or performance to which non-members are admitted for a consideration.

Any organisation contemplating a reduction in charges needs to allow for the fact that input tax, which was recoverable when the subscriptions were taxable, can no longer be claimed (as it will relate to an exempt supply of subscription benefits). This will increase overheads and this new cost should be taken into account when subscriptions are being fixed.

Likely losers are those bodies whose subscribers could recover their VAT and so the tax is not an issue in the pricing of the subscription. The exemption means that the body loses its input tax recovery which, in turn, increases its overhead costs and may force a rise in subscriptions.

In addition, charities which were able to exploit the reliefs associated with carrying on a non-business activity, i.e. it was a relevant charitable purpose with regard to property construction or acquisition, alterations to listed buildings or fuel and power, will lose that right.

The exemption is compulsory where the conditions are met. Therefore bodies that enjoyed the benefits of taxing subscriptions may wish to consider restructuring their operation to fall outside the scope of this exemption (e.g. routing subscriptions through a subsidiary company).

Planning point

The new exemption is seen as a benefit for bodies which were previously non-business but which include the provision of (zero-rated) publications to subscribers. This is because input tax will be recoverable on the cost of making that zero-rated supply. Bodies whose subscriptions were taxed previously will also benefit in cases where their subscribers could not recover any VAT charged, as this tax can either be removed from the subscription charge to reduce subscriptions or, if subscriptions are maintained at current levels, allow the body to retain more income from the charge.

Apportionment of subscriptions

Although the items noted above are excepted from the exemption, there may still be room to apportion membership subscriptions to reflect different benefits supplied at the VAT rates appropriate to each separate supply.

Prior to the House of Lords decision in *Card Protection Plan* [2001] BVC 158, Customs accepted that subscriptions were a mixed supply or package of benefits and therefore income received could be allocated to each benefit on a pro-rata basis. If those benefits had different liabilities, output tax was only chargeable on those benefits attracting a positive rate. Following that decision, the scope to treat supplies as a multiple (as opposed to single) supply has been significantly narrowed; however, an Extra Statutory Concession (ESC 3.35) allows for non-profit-making bodies to allow apportionment of subscriptions to continue as before provided that the ESC is not used for tax avoidance.

If the subscription payment includes consideration for other valuable benefits, which are an aim of the member in themselves, apportionment will be required. For example, if in return for the membership the member gains the benefit of discounts/advance bookings/etc. to see a production that non-members have to pay full price for, then this is a valuable benefit and the subscription should be apportioned.

If the benefit is available free to non-members or at the same price as members, then receipt of it is not a benefit of membership and therefore it should be disregarded in any apportionment exercise. If the member receives a discount, there is a benefit equivalent to the value of the discount.

Planning point

If the member receives a magazine/newsletter, part of the subscription may be apportioned as zero-rated. This will enable the charity to recover some of the VAT on its overheads, together with any VAT on the cost of producing the magazine/newsletter.

> ### *Planning point*
> Anything given away free may constitute a non-business activity and lead to input tax restrictions. Giving away free printed matter is common: if charities do their own printing, VAT on materials purchased (paper, ink, equipment, etc.) would be blocked. Consideration should be given to using the planning illustrated at **34.7.1**.

HMRC may take the view that lobbying or propaganda is non-business as it benefits both members and non-members alike. However, *C & E Commrs v British Field Sports Society* [1998] BVC 82 should be quoted to challenge this view.

Other guidance: *VAT Notice 701/5*, s. 4

Benefits supplied by third parties

In *Friends of the Ironbridge Gorge Museum* [1991] BVC 565, it was decided that where benefits are provided by a third party, they could not be treated as a benefit of membership. In this case, the museum offered reduced admissions to Friends. Friends donated 50 per cent of its income to the museum. Therefore, discounts, etc. offered by others as a consequence of membership should not be valued as a benefit.

Liability of other benefits to members

Typically, charities will offer a range of benefits to members, e.g. literature, admissions, goods and services, attracting a range of liabilities. Each benefit should be identified and its liability confirmed.

Basis of determining liability on benefits

There is no set formula for valuing the different benefits. Generally, a cost-based apportionment is the easiest, i.e.:

(a) identify the direct cost attributable to each benefit;
(b) total all those costs; and
(c) for each benefit: (a)/(b) × income = the income attributable to the benefit.

Note that if a subscriber obtains a discount because payment of subscription is by deed of covenant (allowing the charity to reclaim tax from the Inland Revenue), the deed is non-monetary consideration equal to the amount by which the charge has been reduced. The value of the subscription is the sum of this discount plus the amount paid, i.e. the regular subscription. If the subscriber pays the same amount as non-covenanting subscribers, the value is the subscription paid as the covenanter receives no advantage from completing the covenant.

> ### *Planning point*
> If there is a donational element in the subscription, i.e. the benefits are minimal compared to the subscription paid, HMRC may allow output tax charges to be limited to the value of the minimal benefit. However, when the benefit is a free

---

or discounted admission to a site which attracts an admission charge, e.g. to a wildlife reserve, valuing the benefit may be difficult. In such cases, HMRC allow the benefit to be calculated by reference to the ratio of number of visits made by members to the site:number of members (provided that admissions are recorded).

Planning point

Many charities do not register for VAT because subscription income is below the registration threshold. However, if the only benefit members receive is literature (i.e. zero-rated), it should consider the benefits of voluntary registration.

34.4.3 Fundraising events exemption

This section provides guidance on the VAT liability of fundraising events since the 1 April 2000 changes which have substantially simplified the relief and widened its effect.

Exemption is available to any charity, together with a subsidiary wholly owned company which passes all of its profits back to the charity, and events held jointly by more than one charity or other eligible body provided that the event is organised exclusively for charitable purposes or exclusively for the qualifying body's own benefit, or a combination of those purposes and that benefit.

Events organised by promoters or agents may still qualify for relief. However, any proceeds retained by them are consideration for their services and are subject to VAT.

Planning point

The legislation has been amended with regard to the requirement for subsidiaries to pass their profits to the parent charity: now, all profits (from any source, not just events) must be given over to the charity for an event run by a subsidiary to qualify for relief. Thus, if a charity is trying to improve a subsidiary's balance sheet by letting it retain some profit, any event run by that subsidiary would be outside the scope of the relief. This legislation could of course be used to a charity's advantage if it wanted to run a taxable event, e.g. to recover input tax, by running that event through a subsidiary which does not pass all of its profits to the charity.

Law: VATA 1994, Sch. 9, Grp. 12

Other guidance: Notice CWL4

Purpose of the event

The pre-April 2000 list of qualifying categories of event has been replaced by a simple purpose test. Provided that the event is both organised and promoted as being primarily for the purpose of raising money, it will qualify. Thus the relief now includes participative events and games of skill (e.g. golf days, sponsored walks, etc.) and even events accessible on the internet. However, it does not extend to fundraising holidays or day trips where accommodation is provided otherwise than on an incidental basis (defined as being for no more than a total of two nights) nor any supply made which is covered by the tour operators' margin scheme; nor does it include social events which incidentally make a profit.

As HMRC define an event as an incident with an outcome or a result, activities of a semi-regular or continuous nature, such as the frequent operation of a shop or bar, cannot be regarded as an event. The relief is not intended to exempt from VAT normal trading activities such as hall hire by one charity to another charity.

> ### Planning point
> It is recommended that documentary evidence is kept to show that the event was organised primarily to raise funds for the charity, e.g. minutes of meetings, costings and similar documents. As the event must also be promoted in such a way that those attending the event are aware that its main purpose is to raise funds, any publicity material, tickets, etc. should clearly refer to fundraising, e.g. fundraising for; in aid of; help us to build; help us to raise money for, etc. It is advisable to keep copies of publicity material, tickets, etc. as further evidence of purpose.

Scale of event

The exemption still has to retain elements to ensure that charities, etc. do not compete unfairly with commercial organisations as this is a requirement of European law. However, the new legislation recognises that low-key events are unlikely to have any commercial impact and so relief is available to any charity or branch thereof for any such event or events (e.g. jumble sales, coffee mornings) provided that aggregate gross weekly takings do not exceed £1,000.

Number of qualifying events per year

The old, vague series and regular condition has been replaced and now the allowable frequency of events is specified at a maximum of 15 events of the same type or kind in one location within any financial year (or pro rata if the financial year is longer or shorter than a calendar year) of the charity or other qualifying body. An event is viewed as a singular, self-contained occurrence. Thus, a theatrical performance counts as one event and, if it is repeated over successive evenings, each performance counts towards the 15-event total (i.e. a charity cannot count a programme of self-contained events as a single event). However, a single event which takes place at the same location for more than one day, such as a golf tournament, is accepted as one event.

A location is any definable place. This could be a town or a place within a town, e.g. a theatre, hall, cinema, etc. A charity's website is seen as a single location. The location rule is designed to be generous to charities which may hold a number of different events of different types in different locations but in the same town, or the same event in many different locations, e.g. 20 balls held by a national charity each in different towns in the same financial year would all qualify for relief. However, there is a caveat. The legislation excludes from exemption any event which would be likely to cause distortions of competition such as to place a commercial enterprise carried on by a taxable person at a disadvantage. As stated above, to comply with the terms of the Sixth VAT Directive, the exemption cannot create such distortions and, one assumes, this condition has been introduced so that, if the exemption is exploited to the detriment of businesses, HMRC can take appropriate action. For example, HMRC advise that they will not accept arrangements such as weekly boot sales each held in different but adjacent fields as constituting a separate location without considering whether such an arrangement is potentially distorting competition.

Note also that, if the 15-event limit for events of the same kind in the same location is exceeded in any financial year, exemption is lost for all those events, not just the ones over the allowance.

Planning point

Remember that this event limit is available for each type of event in each location. Therefore, different types of events (e.g. concerts, balls, sports events, etc.) can be mounted or the location changed to maximise the relief. However, note that it is not possible to extend the limit by running joint events: in such circumstances, joint events and any event run by a subsidiary count towards a charity's 15-event allowance.

Qualifying income

The exemption extends to all income directly relating to the event, including admission charges, advertising space in commemorative brochures, goods, etc. sold at events, and sponsorship. Specifically excluded from the exemption are goods and souvenirs sold after the fundraising event has taken place. For example, video and audio recordings of the fundraising event itself and surplus commemorative items such as adult T-shirts, mugs, etc., would all be standard-rated. However, commemorative programmes and children's T-shirts would be eligible for zero-rating under the reliefs for books, etc. and children's clothes respectively, and goods donated for sale may still be sold VAT-free provided the conditions described in **34.4.5** are met.

⚠ Warning!

Exemption blocks input tax recovery. However, depending on scale and frequency, recovery may be possible under the partial exemption *de minimis* rules (see **Chapter 12**). On the basis that fundraising events should raise more income than the cost of putting them on, and some of the costs are likely to be non-VATable, the exemption should be beneficial in most cases.

> **Planning point**
>
> If most income comes from sponsorship from VAT-registered businesses, consider structuring fundraising to fall outside the scope of the exemption to allow recovery of attributable input tax.

> **Planning point**
>
> If the event includes a charity auction, see **34.4.4**. If the event is cultural and does not qualify for this relief, see **34.3.8**.

> **Planning point**
>
> If the event held by a charity meets the criteria for VAT exemption, it will automatically qualify for exemption from income tax and corporation tax under Extra-Statutory Concession (ESC) C4 as long as the profits are applied charitably. However, it is important to note that ESC C4 does not extend to events organised by a charity's subsidiary even though it may qualify for VAT exemption. In practice, this is not an issue as a subsidiary would have to pass its profits to a charity to qualify for the VAT exemption and therefore it would not be liable to corporation tax on them.

The Bath Festivals Trust Limited (*Bath Festivals Trust Ltd* [2009] BVC 4,028) ran and owned the rights to the Bath International Music Festival. Bath City Council funded the trust via various service level agreements between the City Council and the Trust. HMRC contended that the receipts from the City Council were not for supplies of services for consideration but were a form of grant and outside the scope of VAT. The Tribunal concluded that the Trust, in taking over a job previously undertaken by the City Council did amount to services and allowed the Trust's appeal, therefore entitling VAT to be claimed on the Trust's expenditure attributable to the event.

34.4.4 Charity auctions zero rate

Subject to certain conditions, zero-rating relief is available for the sale of donated goods by auction. The conditions are the same as those that apply to the sale (and/or hire) of goods in charity shops (see **34.4.5** for details of these conditions).

However, note the following points specific to charity auctions are:

- auctions run by anybody other than a charity or profits-to-charity person (see **34.4.5** for definition of this term) cannot use the relief unless that body can demonstrate it was acting as agent for the charity; and
- sales involving goods where the proceeds are shared (i.e. between the vendor and the charity) may also fall outside the relief unless the arrangements are properly structured.

> ### ⚠ *Warning!*
> Documenting the relationships between the parties (donors, charity, auctioneer, etc.) is critical if misunderstandings with HMRC are to be avoided. Ensure that publicity material is consistent with the agreed arrangements: it is no good claiming that you are acting as agent for donors if the auction catalogue states that the donations have been made to the auctioning body!

> ### *Planning point*
> If the auction is part of a fund-raising event which qualifies for exemption, opt to treat the auction as a zero-rated activity (as you are entitled to do) to enable recovery of any attributable VAT.

34.4.5 Charity shops

Charity shops are one of the most popular ways of raising funds. Sales (and with effect from 1 April 2000, the hire) of donated goods (new or second-hand) are zero-rated subject to certain conditions and neither the Inland Revenue nor the Charity Commissioners treat the sale of such goods as trading (rather it is viewed as the conversion of donated goods into donated cash).

Conditions

The following conditions need to be satisfied if the sale and, with effect from 1 April 2000, the hire of goods by the shop are to be treated as zero-rated.

The supply must take place as a result of the goods having been made available to:

- two or more specified persons (defined as disabled people or people on means-tested benefits);
- the general public; and
- not as a result of any prior arrangements entered into by any of the parties involved.

It must be the clear intention of the donor and the charity that the goods are to be sold or hired out. Donated goods retained by the charity for its own use or goods donated to the charity for its own use and subsequently sold or hired out in shops would not qualify.

Raffle prizes are excluded.

Donated goods which are used to make other goods for sale are also excluded (e.g. an original picture used to make prints for resale would not qualify).

If a subsidiary is selling or hiring out the goods, it must qualify as a profits-to-charity person.

> **Planning point**
> The sale of assets bought for non-business use is usually a non-business activity and so sales would be VAT free. However, input tax attributable to the sale may be blocked.

A profits-to-charity person

A profits-to-charity person is a taxable person who, in respect of any goods, has agreed in writing (whether or not contained in a deed) to transfer its profits from the supply of hired, sold or exported goods to a charity or whose profits from such supplies are otherwise payable to a charity. Thus a subsidiary passing all its profits to its parent charity through gift aid under a written agreement would qualify.

Bought-in goods

Problems arise when a charity sells bought-in goods as well as donated goods. The sale of bought-in goods is not a charitable activity and proceeds are liable to direct tax, and VAT if applicable.

Disposal of donated goods used for hire

Note that any goods which are hired out must be rehired, sold or exported or otherwise disposed of once a hiring finishes, otherwise relief is lost, i.e. they cannot be hired out merely to secure the relief and then used subsequently by the charity. If this happens, the original zero-rating will be void and VAT will be due on the value of the donated goods and any lettings of them. Use by a charity of donated goods between lettings will also invalidate the relief claimed on them.

Donation of goods

The donation of goods which form part of the assets of a business and on which VAT has been recovered will generally be a taxable supply even if that donation is to a charity. However, zero-rating is available on the donation if the use of the goods by the charity (or profits-to-charity person) qualifies for the zero-rating relief described above, or they are to be exported (the actual export of the donated goods by the charity or profits-to-charity person also qualifies for zero-rating relief).

Donated goods in need of repair

Where donated goods are repaired before being sold on, the parts used for the repair fall outside the relief. However, HMRC allow an apportionment between the donated element and the bought-in element allowing the latter to be supplied at cost. If the repair parts were subject to VAT, the effect is tax neutral.

> **Example 34.7**
> Some bicycles are donated to charity X. They need new brakes, etc. to make them roadworthy. The parts cost £2 + 35p VAT per bicycle. The finished item sells for £10. Output tax would be due on £2 of the sale (35p): the balance would be zero-rated (i.e. £7.65). Charity X could recover the VAT on the parts (35p) and so its net income would be £8.

> **Planning point**
> Although VAT is a major cost to charities, address the impact of other taxes, legal issues, etc. on any tax-efficient structures being considered.

34.4.6 Affinity cards

Charities involved in affinity credit card schemes should consult Customs Business Brief 18/03 and VAT Notice 701/1.

34.5   Utilising reliefs

34.5.1 Goods purchased by a charity for the benefit of the disabled

This section is designed to illustrate the potential for obtaining zero-rating relief on the supply to a charity of goods which it makes available to disabled persons for their domestic or personal use. Made available includes loan, gift, sale, hire or otherwise. In order to qualify for the relief, the goods in question must either fall within one of the categories listed below at 'Qualifying goods' or be designed solely for use by a disabled person.

Law: VATA 1994 Sch. 8, Grp. 12

Other guidance: VAT Notice 701/7

Meaning of disabled persons

'Disabled' means chronically (i.e. long-term) sick or disabled. It excludes those with temporary sickness or injury and the disability must be severe enough to cause inconvenience.

Domestic or personal use

The goods must be made available to specific disabled individuals for their private or exclusive use. It is not sufficient that they are bought for general use, e.g. a mobile exhibition unit used for teaching disabled persons. Note that:

- the charity does not need to know the identity of the user at the time of purchase;
- purchasing goods for loan to a succession of specific individuals for private use qualifies;
- use by more than one disabled person in a residential home qualifies as domestic use; and
- the relief includes any use whilst the disabled person is an in-patient or out-patient in a hospital or resident in a nursing home when the supply is to a charity for use by a disabled person, but not if the supply is to the disabled person direct (with the exception of wheelchairs or invalid carriages and parts and accessories thereof).

Planning point

If the exclusive use test cannot be met, consider whether or not relief is available as a supply of qualifying goods (see **34.5.3** for the way this relief may be applied to qualifying goods of a scientific and medical nature). Qualifying goods include all items qualifying under the relief for purchases for use by disabled individuals, without having to apply the use test.

Qualifying goods

Comprehensive lists of qualifying goods and services appear in *VAT Notices 701/6* and *701/7*, which should be consulted by those affected. It should be noted that many of the reliefs are very specific.

Planning point

The restrictions placed on this catch-all provision by HMRC have been subject to challenge in the tribunal with varying degrees of success. It is clear that the tribunal will consider the merits of each case individually and therefore if HMRC refuse relief, it may be worth considering an appeal.

Planning point

The above reliefs do not apply when the disabled person is an in-patient or out-patient in a hospital or resident in a nursing home, although certain items provided to a disabled person on prescription and dispensed by a registered pharmacist may qualify for zero-rating in these circumstances (see also **34.5.3**).

Parts and accessories

The relief applies also to parts and accessories that have been designed solely for use in or with qualifying goods.

34.5.2 Services purchased by a charity for the benefit of the disabled

There is potential for obtaining zero-rating relief on the supply to a charity of services which it incurs for the benefit of disabled persons. Reference should again be made to *VAT Notices 701/6* and *701/7* for full details.

34.5.3 Medical and scientific equipment relief

This section is designed to assist a qualifying body to evaluate if a purchase of medical and scientific equipment for use by a charity qualifies for relief. This relief is used widely in the university sector to zero rate purchases of research equipment. In addition to outright purchases of relevant goods, hire or lease and repairs and maintenance of relevant goods also qualify for relief.

In order to qualify for relief, the goods must be qualifying goods, purchased by or for donation to an eligible body and must be used for research, training, diagnosis or treatment.

Qualifying goods

Qualifying goods, as shown below, include medical, scientific, computer, video, sterilising, laboratory or refrigeration equipment. HMRC take a strict view of the meaning of these terms, particularly medical and scientific, in that:

- medical is equipment used for the practice of medicine;
- scientific is equipment used for observation, experimentation and measurement;
- computer is VDUs and keyboards; for networks, etc. only those items used for qualifying use are eligible;
- video includes recorders, tapes and cameras;
- sterilising is equipment for sterilising medical and laboratory instruments, e.g. autoclaves;
- laboratory is equipment such as benches, fume cupboards, bunsen burners, etc. but does not extend to complete furnishing of laboratories;
- refrigeration includes ice-making machines;
- ambulances; and
- adapted and other vehicles.

The relief also includes parts or accessories for use in or with relevant goods. HMRC provide a useful alphabetical list of examples of equipment that does (and does not) qualify in *VAT Notice 701/6*.

Research, training, diagnosis and treatment

Only goods used for research, training, diagnosis and treatment qualify for the zero-rating. The way the goods are to be used should be viewed critically. Although goods do not have to be used exclusively for the required purposes (other than computer software which must be used solely for research, etc.), HMRC insist that qualifying use should be substantial, real and continuing, and bought for that purpose.

Research means original systematic investigations undertaken to gain knowledge and understanding of the treatment or a palliation of a physical or mental abnormality in humans or animals. It excludes routine testing, etc.

Training is the process of bringing a person to an agreed standard of proficiency and must include practical application of the relevant area.

Diagnosis is the identification of diseases and examination of systems.

Treatment includes the administration of medicines, physiotherapy and surgery.

Eligible bodies

Eligible bodies include:

- a Strategic Health Authority or Special Health Authority in England;
- Health Authorities, Special Health Authorities and Local Health Boards in Wales;
- a Health Board in Scotland;
- a Health and Social Services Board in Northern Ireland;
- not-for-profit hospitals (to qualify under this heading, the hospital must be prevented from, and must not, distribute its profits, and any surpluses made from hospital or research activities must be used for the furtherance of the body's objectives);
- not-for-profit research institutions (which includes all universities);
- a charitable institution providing care or medical or surgical treatment for handicapped persons;
- the Common Services Agency for the Scottish Health Service, the Northern Ireland Central Services Agency for Health and Social Services or the Isle of Man Health Services Board;
- a charitable institution providing rescue or first-aid services;
- a National Health Service Trust established under Pt 1 of the National Health Service and Community Care Act 1990 or the National Health Service (Scotland) Act 1978; and
- a Primary Care Trust established under s. 16A of the National Health Service Act 1977.

Meaning of charitable institution

In order to qualify for the relief a charitable institution (in the list above) must provide care, medical or surgical treatment in:

- a day centre (excluding day centres which are primarily for recreation or social activities); or

- an institution which is approved, licensed or registered in accordance with any enactment or Northern Ireland legislation, or exempted from such approval, licensing or registration (e.g. the Care Standards Act 2000), and the majority of persons who receive the care, medical or surgical treatment in that establishment must be chronically sick or disabled.

'Chronically sick' means long-term sickness as defined by the medical profession, and 'disabled' excludes the frail elderly who are not disabled, or people whose mobility is temporarily impaired (e.g. a person with a broken limb).

The qualifying goods must be used in the charitable institution in order to qualify for the relief or, if the charitable institution supplies home-care services and the goods are qualifying goods (or parts and accessories) under section **34.5.1**, and are to be used in conjunction with the provision of such care, the relief also applies.

Meaning of care, medical or surgical treatment

'Care, medical or surgical treatment' includes the provision of protection, treatment, supervision, control or guidance to meet medical, physical, personal or domestic needs of an individual and usually involves personal contact between the provider and the individual. Examples include:

- medical or surgical treatment;
- nursing sick or injured patients;
- assistance with daily personal needs such as dressing, bathing, feeding or using the toilet; and
- looking after or supervising vulnerable people, e.g. children or the elderly.

The relief does not include supplies such as catering or laundry, or other supplies where there is no personal contact required.

Charitable funds or voluntary contributions

Goods must be wholly funded from these sources. A charity's own funds are seen as charitable for the purpose of buying goods for its own use. Alternatively, if a charity gave funds to another charity to buy the goods or if voluntary contributions from a company, individual or group of individuals were given to a charity, that would also qualify. Note, however, that contributions from non-charity sources are only voluntary if the donor receives nothing in return. A collection among employees by a commercial company to raise a donation to an eligible body would count as a voluntary contribution. NHS funds are not charitable or donated and any goods bought with such funds will not be zero-rated.

Goods for donation to an eligible body

Purchase of relevant goods for donation to an eligible body (as opposed to giving the funds to the eligible body to buy the goods itself) qualify for relief provided that all the funding to buy them comes from charitable funds (i.e. the goods are bought by a charity) or voluntary contributions. Purchases for donation to any charity (or other body) not listed above as an eligible body do not qualify for zero-rating. If the recipient eligible body is not itself a charity (e.g. it is an NHS hospital), it could not fund the purchase of any of the goods (in whole or part) itself (i.e. by giving money to the donor of the goods to help buy them), as its funds would not be charitable or count as voluntary contributions.

Brief details of the donor and the eligible body to which the goods are supplied should be given on the declaration or certificate requesting zero-rating. For example, 'John Smith' (address) and friends/family of John Smith Senior, John Smith representing XXX Ltd and YYY Ltd, or XXX Ltd and employees.

The goods have to be actually donated, not just loaned, unless the lender is itself an eligible body and is loaning them for use for a qualifying purpose.

It should be noted that the relief also applies to goods purchased from outside the EU, so care should be taken to ensure that the goods are entered correctly for import VAT purposes so that VAT is not charged. For qualifying imports from other EU member states, no acquisition tax should be accounted for.

⚠ *Warning!*

The relief does not include goods which are put in common store, e.g. by a university engaged in a wide range of research. Although store items may be used for qualifying research, as the use was not known at the time they were purchased, relief is not available. The problem may be addressed by using a subsidiary to purchase the goods from the university immediately prior to qualifying use, then selling them back to the university. As the university could confirm qualifying use at this point, the supply to the university by the subsidiary could qualify for relief.

Planning point

If the normal selling price of qualifying goods includes an amount for fixing or connection to mains services and/or testing the equipment on site, the whole supply may be included in the relief. However, where building works, such as removal of walls or reinforcing floors, are necessary in order to install large items of equipment, these will be standard-rated even when carried out by the supplier of the equipment.

Medical substances and products

Zero-rating relief is also available for supplies to a charity (not just eligible bodies) of:

- a medicinal substance directly used for synthesis or testing in the course of medical or veterinary research; and
- medicinal products if used solely by a charity to provide care or medical or surgical treatment for human beings or animals, or in medical or veterinary research.

A medicinal product for these purposes is any substance or article as defined by s. 132 of the Medicines Act 1968 (excluding instruments, apparatus or appliances) for use wholly or mainly:

- by being administered (as defined by s. 130(9) of the Medicines Act 1968);
- by human beings or animals for a medical purpose (as defined by s. 130(2) of the Medicines Act 1968); or
- as an ingredient in the preparation of a substance or article which is to be administered to human beings or animals for a medical purpose.

Certification

Zero-rating relief is subject to issuing a certificate to the supplier in the format recommended in *VAT Notice 701/6*.

34.5.4 Supplies of advertising to charities

The relief for supplies of advertising to charities was severely curtailed following the decision in *C & E Commrs v Royal Society for the Encouragement of the Arts, Manufacture and Commerce* [1997] BVC 215. However, following the charity taxation review, the relief has been widened and simplified, and the rules cited below apply from 1 April 2000.

The relief applies to charities — a term which has no precise definition for VAT law purposes. Most charities will be registered with the Charity Commission or be exempted from such registration. However, this need not be the case; HMRC accepts that a charity is any body which has been established to advance education or religion, to relieve poverty, sickness or infirmity or to carry out certain other activities beneficial to the community.

Law: VATA 1994 Sch. 8, Grp. 15, item 8

Other guidance: *VAT Notice 701/58*

Supply of adverts to charities

The old qualifying purposes of fund-raising or making known the objects of fund-raising have been replaced by a general qualification which is intended to bring within the scope of the relief all charity advertising including recruitment adverts — except those adverts specifically excluded.

A charity could not, of course, place any advert that it was not empowered by its objects to procure. However, most charities are allowed to expend funds recruiting staff so that its primary objects could be met when the advertising is for this purpose.

The relief extends to all forms of media and not just TV, cinema, radio and certain printed media as before. For example, video and internet are now included. However, the supply of advertising has to be to the charity itself. It does not include advertising produced by the charity itself which would include production within a VAT group by another group member, e.g. a subsidiary. Therefore, it is not possible for charities to have the equipment and raw materials they use in creating these advertisements VAT free. Supplies to agencies (as principals) do not qualify although the onward supply by the agent may qualify in its own right. If the agency is acting as an intermediary, the agency's services would be taxable although the advert may qualify for relief.

> **Planning point**
>
> The advert has to show the name or logo of the charity. There is an assumption by HMRC that any advertising will fall within the objects (i.e. powers) of the charity. However, this should not be confused with a requirement that an advert must promote the objects of the charity to qualify, as was the case under the pre-April 2000 rules, e.g. through adding a strapline stating its primary purpose. The relief now allows charities to zero rate any form of advertising to the general public.

Design and production

Provided that it is intended that the advertisement will be placed in purchased advertising time or space, the supply of design or production of the advertisement will qualify for relief. The services covered here are, for example, the design of a poster or the filming or recording of an advertisement to be broadcast.

Goods closely linked to the design and production of a qualifying advert can also be zero-rated, including:

- a finished article like a film or sound track;
- an element to be incorporated in an advert like a photograph or picture, or a script or a sound track; and
- alternative versions of an advertisement produced to see which works best, for example, will all qualify for relief even if it is the intention that only one version will be used.

> **Planning point**
>
> If the charity incurs costs designing or producing an advert and then does not use it, the relief on these costs is not lost provided it was clearly the charity's intention to use these services for an advert that would have qualified for relief. However, if a charity incurs VAT on goods or services not intended to be used for a qualifying advert and then does adopt them for such a use, it is not possible to get retrospective relief.

Excluded items

Although the relief now extends to all forms of media that communicate with the general public, in each case the space or advertising time must be owned by a third party. Thus, the following are excluded from the relief because they do not involve the supply of someone else's advertising time or space, or the advertising is in the form of general marketing and promotion:

- direct mail and telesales;
- anything on a charity's own internet website;
- advertisements where there is no supply of time or space to the charity, for example an advertisement on a charity's own greeting cards;
- exhibition stands and space;
- services of distribution; and
- commemorative items whether or not they bear the charity's logo, for example pens and adult clothing.

Note also that the actual sale of any advertised items cannot be relieved of VAT unless they are relieved under other provisions.

Direct mail (including email) and telesales are excluded because they are not a supply of advertising time or space. The relief is restricted to advertisements aimed at the general public. It does not include marketing and promotions, therefore it excludes marketing and advertising addressed to selected individuals or groups, i.e. people selected by individual home, business or email address whether named or not. These could be individually named people, all those at the same address such as family groups or everyone in a particular building.

Advertisements targeted at general groups, e.g. readers of a trade or religious magazine, are not considered selected, nor are groups of people in particular parts of the country who, for example, are targeted for a general poster campaign in their area. Therefore these adverts qualify for relief.

> ### Planning point
> In practice this will mean that items delivered by post (direct mail packages) will not be covered by this relief, although there may be relief for individual elements of the package under the provisions for printed matter and concessions, e.g. for appeal letters.

> ### Planning point
> The design and preparation of a charity's own website and advertising in, on or through its website whether or not the website is owned, rented or loaned to the charity falls outside the relief because, to qualify, there has to be a supply of someone else's advertising time or space. For the same reason, adverts in a charity's own magazine, notice board, calendar, diary, pencil or shop window, etc. do not qualify either. However, advertising on someone else's website does qualify for relief.

Advertising agencies

If the charity is using an advertising agency, the VAT position depends upon whether the agency is acting as agent or principal for the advertising time and space which qualifies for zero-rating. If acting as a principal, supplies to the charity of advertising time and space by the advertising agency will be zero-rated but the advertising agency will be charged VAT at the standard rate by the supplier. If acting as agent, the supplier's charge for advertising time and space to the charity will be zero-rated, but the advertising agency's charges to the charity will be standard-rated (because they are not supplying the advertising time or space).

> **Planning point**
>
> VAT can be saved on the advertising agency's fees by having the agency act as principal.

Concessions

The existing concessions for certain paper-based products have been extended to cover collection boxes made of any material, preprinted envelopes for planned giving, and lapel stickers, emblems or badges of nominal value when given in return for a donation, whatever the material of the badge. (Preprinted paper or card collecting boxes, letters appealing solely for money for the charity and envelopes used in conjunction with appeal letters and for forwarding donations may also be zero-rated provided they are overprinted with an appeal request related to that contained in the letter.)

When a charity knows that a proportion of their purchases, such as posters or artwork for magazine advertisements, are going to be used in public places as well as in-house (for example in the charity's own magazine or shop window), this should be reflected in the declaration given to the supplier. The VAT liability should be apportioned accordingly.

> **Planning point**
>
> This does not include badges, etc. that are sold at a fixed price. Charities may suggest a price, but if the badge would not be given in cases where the amount given is lower than the suggested amount, then the relief will not apply. The revised law should make it easier for suppliers to determine eligibility for relief: basically, if the customer is a charity, relief is available. However, the obligation and responsibility for determining liability always rests with the supplier and HMRC recommend that a zero-rating certificate is issued. A form of certificate recommended by HMRC is available in *VAT Notice 701/58*.

34.5.5 Fuel and power and the installation of energy-saving materials

This section is designed to assist charities to determine their eligibility to purchase fuel at the reduced rate (currently five per cent) for use in their premises. The relief for the installation of energy-saving materials is addressed at the end of this section. Eligibility for relief on fuel and power is determined by qualifying use.

De minimis quantities

Low consumption qualifies regardless of the use to which the fuel is put. This is defined as:

- deliveries not exceeding one tonne of coal/coke (held out for domestic use);
- any supply of wood, peat or charcoal (not intended for resale);
- piped gas (150 therms/4,397 KWh or less per month);
- liquid gas (supplied in 50kg (or smaller) cylinders (no limit on number if not for resale, or to premises with storage facilities holding less than two tonnes);
- fuel oil, gas oil or kerosene (no more than 2,300 litres per delivery); and
- electricity (1,000 KWh or less per month).

> **Planning point**
> Where these limits are per delivery, ensure that, if there is a series of deliveries in excess of the limit, these are documented by different contracts or delivery notes.

Qualifying use of fuel and power

Qualifying use includes use for relevant residential or relevant charitable purposes. Use does not have to be wholly qualifying. Provided that it is 60 per cent or more qualifying, the reduced rate applies to all fuel and power purchases. If qualifying use is less than 60 per cent, relief is available to the extent that the building is used for a qualifying purpose.

Residential use

Residential use includes:

- dwellings;
- residential accommodation for children, those needing care (the elderly, infirm, alcohol-dependent or those with mental health issues), hospices, student/pupil accommodation, monasteries, nunneries or similar, or any institution which is the main residence of 90 per cent of its residents; and
- caravans, houseboats, and self-catering holiday accommodation.

It does not include hospitals, prisons, hotels or similar.

> **Example 34.8**
> A hospice's premises comprise accommodation for patients, offices and a shop. The accommodation covers 80 per cent of the floor area, i.e. more than 60 per cent. Therefore the premises qualify for full relief.

Charitable use

Charitable use means use by a charity otherwise than in the course or furtherance of a business. It is not sufficient for the charity to be undertaking charitable activities from the building being supplied with the fuel and power: the activity must be non-business.

Note that charitable use in this context is not as wide as it is for construction or property where it extends to village halls and similar establishments (see **34.5.7**). It is possible to mix and match different qualifying uses, thus if a building is 50 per cent residential and 50 per cent charitable it would be 100 per cent qualified use.

Planning point

Qualifying use can be calculated using any fair or reasonable method: it does not have to be by floor area (which in many cases is impractical). Choosing the right method can be critical if usage is borderline 60 per cent. For example, a further-education college has 550 non-fee-paying students (charitable non-business) and 450 fee-paying students (an exempt business supply). Apportionment based on student numbers would give qualifying use of 55 per cent, i.e. below 60 per cent and so only 55 per cent fuel could be reduced rate. However, analysing the numbers into full- and part-time students with part-timers counting as half, the fee payers dropped to 350 full-time equivalents, which boosted the non-business student percentage to 61 per cent, giving full reduced rate.

Reduced rate for the installation of energy-saving materials

With effect from 1 April 2000, the reduced rate applies to supplies made by installers of energy-saving materials when the installation is in a relevant residential or non-business charitable building. However, it is important to note that the reduced rate does not apply to the purchase of energy-saving materials for DIY installation, i.e. materials provided on their own do not qualify for the relief.

The energy-saving materials that qualify for the reduced rate when installed by a contractor are:

- insulation for walls, floors, ceilings, roofs, water tanks, pipes and other plumbing fittings;
- draught stripping for windows and doors;
- central heating system controls, including thermostatic radiator valves;
- hot-water system controls; and
- solar panels.

34.5.6 Educational conferences: liability of the supply of facilities

VAT can add a significant cost to the price of organising a conference, seminar or course if the VAT is irrecoverable because the income from the conference falls to be exempt. This section details the conditions under which conference facilities may be purchased VAT exempt.

Educational content

The conference must have educational content. For a definition of education, see **34.3.5** — it includes seminars, classes and conferences where there is instruction, i.e. as opposed to discussion.

Provider of facilities

The relief on conference facilities stems from the exemption for supplies of incidentals to students receiving education. In order to qualify for exemption on purchase of facilities under this heading, the supplier must be an eligible body (see **34.3.6** for a definition).

If facilities are provided by other than an eligible body then, although this particular relief will not apply, the rent for a room should be exempt from VAT in any case (unless the supplier has elected to waive exemption in respect of the building in which the conference is held) saving a VAT charge on this element. The exemption will extend to basic facilities such as tables and chairs, and to basic refreshments such as tea/coffee and biscuits, as long as no separate charge is made. Where meals are provided these will be treated as a separate standard-rated supply of catering. However, note that rooms provided in hotels and similar buildings in conjunction with sleeping accommodation or used to supply catering are always standard-rated.

Planning point

Where the same room is to be used successively by the same customer for catering and then non-catering (e.g. conference, meeting, etc.) the supply of the room will be standard-rated. However, if the supplier makes the room the subject of two separate hirings, the non-catering use can be exempt. Note that it is not sufficient to merely raise two charges for the single hire of the room.

Use of profits

In the case of a charity which restricts its educational activities to conferences, etc. profits would have to be ring-fenced and used to subsidise or promote future conferences. If conferences are run at cost or a loss, this condition is irrelevant.

Charging for conferences

A condition of the exemption is that the purchaser of the facilities is supplying education, i.e. is receiving consideration for it (even if at a loss). If the conference is free, there is no supply and therefore no relief on the cost of conference facilities. This condition was reinforced in the case of *Glenfall House Trust* [2001] BVC 4,004 when it was held that it was not sufficient for education merely to be provided; there had to be a supply for a consideration for this exemption to be available.

Planning point

If delegates are charged a nominal amount, that is sufficient to create a supply and pass the test even if the cost has to be underwritten from other resources.

Consumption of services

A further condition is that only supplies to students may be exempt. In the context of a conference, this would mean attendees receiving instruction: it would not include presenters, organisers, etc. unless they also received instruction in addition to presenting.

The exemption only extends to facilities used by students. This would include accommodation and catering and conference materials for the use of students. It does not extend to equipment used by presenters (e.g. video and audio equipment, etc.).

It is recommended that clients claiming exemption complete a declaration confirming eligibility.

> ### Planning point
>
> If the conference delegates can recover VAT charged to them and the above exemption is not available, consider running the conference through a subsidiary. The subsidiary would not qualify for exemption on its supply of the conference (it would fail the test at **34.3.5**) and so its charges would be standard-rated allowing it to recover any VAT charged. See **34.7** for more information on using subsidiaries.

> ### Planning point
>
> Suppliers of conference facilities should ensure that charities claiming exemption meet the criteria as it is for the supplier to determine liability. In practice, provided that the supplier has acted in good faith and has taken all reasonable steps to confirm that the client is eligible for exemption, HMRC are unlikely to take action.

34.5.7 Acquisition of property for a relevant charitable purpose

This section is intended to give guidance in one area of property transactions unique to charities: acquiring premises (i.e. land, buildings, etc.) for a relevant charitable purpose (RCP). If the RCP test is met, the charity has the opportunity to acquire premises VAT free.

Use of property

Relevant charitable purpose does not mean any use by a charity; it is restricted. The first test is to consider if the premises are to be used otherwise than in the course or furtherance of a business. Note that the relief is also available for parts of buildings, as long as that part is wholly used for charitable purposes.

> ### Example 34.9
>
> A charity provides welfare services to distressed persons out of rented premises. It has a contract with the local authority (LA) to provide this service. Although the service would be charitable, the service is treated as business and therefore the premises are not used for an RCP (see **34.3.2**).

The tribunal found that a charitable housing association was not in business because it was entirely state and publicly funded and did not operate on a commercial basis; it was therefore entitled to relief on the construction of its new offices (*Cardiff Community Housing Association Ltd* [2001] BVC 2,112).

A High Court held that, when applying the business test to a building for which rent was received by a charity, it is not the intention of the charity landlord which is relevant but the intended use made of it by the tenant, in this case a playgroup charity, as that was the only purpose for which the building was constructed. As the playgroup did not use it for business purposes (even though a charge was made for attending the playgroup – the charge was set to cover costs, not make a profit) the landlord charity could claim relief on the construction on the basis of non-business use (*Yarburgh Children's Trust*).

However, if the end user is not a charity, there would not be any scope to exploit this part of the relief even if the person constructing or acquiring the property was a charity and it allowed the end user to use it for free in pursuance of its objects (*League of Friends of Kingston Hospital* [1996] BVC 2,039). In *Morley Retreat and Conference House* [2001] BVC 4,153, a chapel that was freely available for all to use at no charge was still found by the tribunal to be part of the appellant's accommodation business which it operated in the adjoining buildings and, therefore, its construction was not eligible for zero-rating relief.

Village hall or similar

If the first test cannot be met, consider whether or not the premises are to be used as a village hall or similarly in providing social or recreational facilities for a local community.

Planning point

If premises are not used wholly for an RCP, HMRC will allow the premises to be treated as such providing that non-RCP use does not exceed 10 per cent. *Business Brief* 8/00 sets out the basis on which non-qualifying use can be calculated with a view to establishing whether or not that use exceeds the 10 per cent permitted by concession. Methods available include:

* time-based;
* floor space; and
* head count.

There are conditions attached and, with the exception of a time-based apportionment for whole buildings, HMRC's permission must be obtained before being adopted.

Vendor/landlord

The vendor who constructed or commissioned the construction of the premises must grant to the charity the first major interest (freehold sale or lease of over 21 years) in the premises and the premises themselves must be new (i.e. not an extension, alteration, conversion or reconstruction of an existing building).

Annexes

Annexes used for an RCP can be zero-rated. However, note that the annexe must be capable of functioning independently, the main access to the annexe must not be through the existing building and the main access to the existing building must not be through the annexe.

Certification

Relief is only available if a certificate of qualifying use (i.e. for an RCP) is issued to the vendor/landlord.

As the tribunal made clear in the case of *Yarburgh Children's Trust*, recipients of the supply of a building may issue a certificate even if they do not use the building themselves for a qualifying use provided that they can certify that the building will be so used by its ultimate occupants.

Option to tax by vendor/landlord

For information on the option to tax, see **17.9**. A vendor's/landlord's option to tax will be disapplied and he will not be able to charge the charity VAT if it makes known that the premises are to be used for an RCP. However, use as an office (even for an RCP) is excluded from the disapplication provisions unless office use is merely incidental to the main RCP.

Construction services

Charities are also able to secure certain construction services at the zero rate if they are building premises for an RCP and the other zero-rating conditions are met. See **Chapter 17** and **Chapter 36** for more information on this and the special rules for alterations to listed buildings. In particular, section **36.2.7** regarding relevant charitable buildings and the new definition of such a building needs to be considered.

***

Planning point

Zero-rating is conditional on premises being used for at least ten years for an RCP. If use changes, there may be a VAT charge.

***

34.6   Reducing VAT costs

34.6.1 Asset purchasing

Where VAT is incurred on assets purchased for both business and non-business use, there used to be two approaches for determining the VAT cost:

(1) Option 1: VAT can be apportioned at the time of acquisition to reflect expected business use.

(2) Option 2: VAT may be recovered in full on acquisition, with output tax being accounted for on non-business use in each accounting period; however, this option may not be used in relation to acquisitions of property (this is called *Lennartz* accounting after a VAT decision of the ECJ).

If option 2 is followed (but see below as this type of *Lennartz* accounting is now highly restricted and can really only apply to schemes currently in existence, but not any new acquisitions), HMRC would require records to be kept showing how the asset was used and the non-business use would have to be valued at full cost. The level of record-keeping and calculation of full cost should be negotiated locally with HMRC.

Example 34.10

Charity X acquires new furniture for £100,000 + £17,500 VAT. It intends to use it for 50 per cent taxable/50 per cent non-business use, but expects taxable use to increase to 55 per cent in year 2 and 60 per cent in year 3.

Option 1 would allow £8,750 recovery with no adjustments.

Option 2 would allow £17,500 recovery up front. Each VAT accounting period, charity X would have to charge itself for non-business use. This could be based on depreciation (over five years) of £20,000 p.a.. In year 1, X would pay £1,750 VAT on a cost of £10,000 (50 per cent × £20,000). In year 2 this would fall to £1,575 VAT and in year 3, £1,400. Assuming years 4 and 5 had 60 per cent taxable use, the output tax due would total a further £2,800 making a total tax charge over five years of £7,525, a saving of £1,225 over option 1.

Example 34.11

As in the example above except business use is 60 per cent at the start, then drops to 55 per cent in year 2 and 50 per cent thereafter.

Option 1 would allow £10,500 recovery with no adjustments.

Option 2 would allow £17,500 recovery up front but non-business use charges would total £8,225, a loss of £1,225 VAT on option 1 savings.

Note that these examples assume that HMRC will accept depreciation as the only cost; additional costs may have to be included, e.g. cost of finance, which would increase the output tax charge and so reduce the saving. The examples also assume that HMRC will accept nil cost once the furniture is fully depreciated. It is essential that all aspects of the cost of non-business use are agreed with HMRC before committing to option 2.

Planning point

Option 2 offers a cashflow benefit if non-business use from the time of acquisition is consistent and a VAT saving if business use is likely to increase over the lifetime of the asset. However, if business use is likely to decrease, option 1 should be preferred.

> **Planning point**
>
> The option 2 approach only applies to assets used for business and non-business. It cannot be used to justify full initial recovery for mixed business use, i.e. taxable and exempt use.

Option 2 cannot be used for items on which input tax is blocked, e.g. cars.

The recovery of VAT for charities has become more limited due to the decision in *Vereniging Noordelijke Land-en Tuinbouw Organisatie v Staatssecretaris van Financien* (Case C-515/07) (*VNLTO*). This considered whether or not *Lennartz* accounting can be used by a taxpayer whose activities are non-business activities and, therefore, not within the scope of VAT. The Court's decision made it clear that EU VAT legislation does not permit, and never has permitted, input tax deduction in full where there is no business use.

Following the decision in the *VNLTO* case, it has become apparent that non-business entities, such as charities, cannot recover input tax using the *Lennartz* method. In the past, the non-business entity would have claimed input tax in full on an asset (often a building) where there is no taxable use, or partial business use, and then pay output VAT over a period of use based upon their use of the building. Even if this did not give an absolute cash saving, it would give a cash flow benefit, making large capital items more affordable.

Following this decision, HMRC issued Brief 02/10 detailing how, from 22 January 2010, they believe VAT should now be dealt with. VAT is recoverable by a business to the extent that the input VAT is incurred for a taxable business purpose. The brief states:

> 'If goods are used for both business and private/non-business purposes, there is a choice about how to treat them for VAT purposes, which must be made at the time they are acquired, namely:
>
> - as a wholly non-business or private asset, in which case the VAT is not deductible;
> - as a part business, part non-business asset, in which case the VAT incurred is only deductible to the extent that it relates to the taxable business activities (section 24(5) of the VAT Act 1994); or
> - as a wholly business asset in which case the VAT incurred is treated as input tax and is deductible in full, subject to any partial exemption restriction; however, output tax must then be declared in so far as the goods are used for private/non-business purposes.
>
> *Lennartz* accounting is not therefore available in cases where goods (including services used to create goods) are used wholly for business purposes.'

It goes on to state that *Lennartz* accounting is now restricted to certain limited instances. This includes where the goods are used both for taxable purposes (where input tax is permitted to be deducted under the 'normal' rules) and the goods are also used for private purposes by the business owner and his staff (and possibly and exceptionally for purposes outside the business's enterprise).

874

The impact of this decision means that *Lennartz* type accounting was never permitted. HMRC could have required entities that were currently using this method to repay all input tax claimed (and presumably offset this by the output tax paid). HMRC will, however, by concession permit existing schemes to continue as long as all the necessary output tax is paid on the non-business use for the remaining period of the scheme. HMRC will not permit any further schemes to be commenced, but will exceptionally consider applications from taxpayers that have made binding commitments based upon their expectation to be able to use *Lennartz* type accounting.

34.6.2 Cost sharing

Cost sharing is common in the sector. Typically, one charity will bear the costs and recharge them to other users. Where these costs are VAT bearing, the VAT effect is neutral as the output tax due would be matched with a corresponding recovery of input tax.

Recharges of staff costs, however, can create additional VAT charges. By concession, HMRC have agreed that where staff are seconded from one charity to another on the basis of salary reimbursement, the supply will be outside the scope of VAT provided that:

- the employee has only been involved in the non-business activities of the seconder and will only be used for non-business activities by the secondee; and
- any payment does not exceed the normal remuneration of the employee (pro rata for part-time secondments).

If the secondment is for business activities consider joint contracts of employment or other ways of removing the VAT charge.

Charities also need to consider the VAT implications of any cost sharing arising from restructuring their activities, e.g. hiving part off to another entity (see **34.4.1** for a case where restructuring led to a dispute with Customs which was only resolved in the charity's favour by an appeal to the Court of Appeal).

> **Planning point**
>
> Following the case of *Durham Aged Mineworkers' Homes Association v C & E Commrs* [1994] BVC 145, HMRC accept that charities can recharge certain costs if one acts as buying agent for the other provided that there is some evidence of an agency agreement, the recharged expenses meet the conditions relating to disbursements and each supply is separately quantified.

34.6.3 VAT recovery on overheads

Charities have lobbied for a refund mechanism in respect of the VAT they suffer on their non-taxable activities. However, the only concession to date on this point is the VAT refund available to Britain's main national museums when they allow free admission to the public. This means that, unless a charity makes only taxable supplies, it will not be able to recover all the VAT it incurs. Typically, a charity will make taxable and exempt supplies and be involved in non-business activity necessitating a business/non-business apportionment of overheads and a subsequent partial exemption method.

⚠ *Warning!*

Beware of hidden exempt or non-business activities. Purchases must be used exclusively for a taxable purpose to justify full recovery.

Planning point

Some charities make only taxable supplies but receive subsidies to underwrite the cost, e.g. theatres. As the only supply is taxable, full VAT recovery has been permitted although HMRC is addressing the issue of input tax recovery in such circumstances and may take action in the future to offset any apparent loss of tax due on the value of supplies.

34.6.4 Influencing liability

The liability of many of the supplies made by charities is dictated by the nature of the supplier. Typically, the exemptions for most welfare, education, cultural services and fund-raising events are only available to charities.

Exemptions are desirable when the client for these services cannot recover any VAT charged to it. However, when it can, it would be advantageous to the charity to make the supply taxable. This would allow recovery of associated input tax. It is not possible to treat a supply as taxable by choice if the legislation directs that it is exempt. However, in most cases, exemption does not apply if all the conditions attached to it are not met, for example all profits having to be used solely to support the activity which generated them.

Example 34.12

A charitable research company contracts with the NHS to carry out research. It applies all its profits to the furtherance of that research. Its supply qualifies for exemption (see **34.3.6**). However, the NHS can recover any VAT charged to it for research.

The charity then undertakes consultancy for the NHS. It does not ring-fence its profits from research, using them for its general overheads. As these overheads support the consultancy, which is not an exempt activity, it has broken a condition for the exemption of its research and so that falls to be taxable. The charity can now recover all of its VAT.

It is not possible to opt in and out of the exemption, ie if a condition is broken for one supply, then all supplies which may have fallen within that exemption will fall outside it (including those to non-VAT registered clients). In situations where supplies are made to non-VAT registered clients, it may be better in practice to consider hiving off the contract which the charity wants to be taxable into a wholly owned subsidiary. This allows the charity to exempt supplies to those who cannot recover VAT and tax supplies to those who can (see **34.7.2**).

34.7   Subsidiaries

34.7.1 Using subsidiaries

Subsidiaries are used extensively in tax planning. In the charity sector, they are encouraged by the Charity Commission as a means of avoiding problems with fund-raising and they are generally accepted by the direct tax part of HMRC as a way of sheltering income which would otherwise be taxed had it been earned by the charity. The subsidiary can of course avoid corporation tax by being a profit-for-charity organisation.

The VAT part of HMRC's view is that using subsidiaries to gain a tax advantage is avoidance, particularly if there is no commercial reason for involving the subsidiary other than achieving a VAT saving. Moreover, seeking to avoid VAT in this way is counter to the purpose of the VAT Directive and as such is an abuse of the law. This view has been supported by the VAT & Duties Tribunal in the case of *Halifax plc* which decided that transactions inserted solely for VAT avoidance in a tax-planning arrangement were not economic activities or supplies and therefore they could not achieve that tax-planning objective sought by the appellant. There have been a number of other similar cases and a principle, the 'abuse of right', has been established in VAT law. This basically means that a taxpayer cannot take advantage of a provision if this provision is an overall abuse of the VAT system. Thus, if a provision exists that permits, say, VAT recovery of input tax through the use of a separate company and recharges, but this would be contrary to the general scheme of VAT, then this VAT recovery would not be permitted. It is an abuse of the right to recovery and is not permissible.

It is beyond the scope of this chapter to debate this point. However, any charity considering using subsidiaries for VAT planning needs to be aware of this view and the likelihood of a challenge from HMRC if they perceive that the motive for routing a transaction through a subsidiary or subsidiaries is tax avoidance.

This chapter considers some of the ways subsidiaries have been and are being used. It should not be taken as an endorsement of any of the planning described or the general use of subsidiaries for planning.

Caution

Using subsidiaries can create a raft of non-VAT issues which need addressing, including:

- direct tax;
- accounting;
- regulatory; and
- legal.

See **34.8** for a checklist.

34.7.2 Impact on VAT liability

Certain exemptions are only available to charities. Similar activities carried out by non-charities, for example subsidiaries, would be taxable. Where the client for the services can recover any VAT charged, consider hiving off the activity/contract to a subsidiary.

> **Example 34.13**
>
> A university has a research contract with an eligible body. The eligible body can recover all VAT charged to it. A university cannot opt in and out of the exemption for research. However, if the contract is passed to a wholly owned commercial subsidiary, the supply will be taxable as companies which can distribute their profits cannot qualify for exemption. The subsidiary would be able to recover all of its VAT and covenant its profits tax effectively to the parent charity.

34.7.3 Purchasing intermediaries

Subsidiaries are used as intermediaries between a supplier and charity to improve VAT recovery where the charity would ordinarily buy a range of goods and services which are standard-rated but could be zero-rated if combined and supplied as a single composite service.

> **Example 34.14**
>
> A charity produces its own leaflets and publications for free distribution. It suffers VAT on printing equipment, paper, ink, etc. This VAT is irrecoverable as the free distribution is a non-business activity. If the charity interposes a subsidiary between it and the suppliers of goods used for printing and the charity hires the printing equipment to the subsidiary, the subsidiary could produce and then supply the printed matter to the charity at the zero rate, recovering any VAT charged to it.

34.7.4 Prepayments

When the rate of VAT on any supply is anticipated to increase, the impact can be offset by making a prepayment against the supply. A prepayment crystallises the tax point at the old rate of tax. A prepayment can be made direct to the supplier. However, this can:

- tie up funds;
- require external funding; and
- be difficult to get back if the rate change does not happen.

Alternatively, a prepayment can be made to a subsidiary interposed between the supplier and the charity. The prepayment can then be loaned back by the subsidiary to the charity or repaid if the rate rise does not occur. •

34.7.5 Leasing

VAT on assets bought for exempt purposes is irrecoverable. Buying assets and leasing them to and from a subsidiary (lease and leaseback) offers the opportunity to mitigate the impact of VAT.

The lease and leaseback approach to asset planning has been questioned by Customs in tribunal (*City of Sunderland College Supplies Ltd* [1999] BVC 4,009) in the context of early termination of leases to secure a VAT advantage. It may therefore be safer to consider sale (to the subsidiary) and leaseback. However, this does have direct tax and accounting implications which need to be addressed.

Lease and leaseback can be used for property. However, such arrangements are subject to anti-avoidance legislation and may be considered an abuse of right.

34.7.6 Setting up a subsidiary

Typically, subsidiaries used for planning and/or non-charitable trading are share companies wholly owned by the charity.

Ensure that the charity trust deed (or other governing instrument) permits the charity to set up a subsidiary (i.e. invest in shares).

Ensure that the Memorandum and Articles of Association of the company allow it to:

- distribute profits (so these can be shed to the charity); and
- undertake the trade or activity to carry out the planning.

Generally, off-the-shelf companies can be used. Occasionally it is more practical to set up a company from scratch, e.g. if it needs special features to fulfil its role in the planning.

> **⚠ Warning!**
> Allow enough time to set up a company in any planning timetable. Off-the-shelf companies can be active almost immediately. However, new companies need to be registered with Companies House.

> **Planning point**
> Although share companies are the most common format, companies limited by guarantee or even charitable trusts may be better vehicles (or even the only vehicle if the charity lacks investment powers and these cannot be amended) depending on the nature of the planning intended.

Profit shedding

Generally, it is desirable to pass any profits made by the company to the parent charity. This will allow any tax paid by the company to be recovered by the charity. With effect from 6 April 2000, the Inland Revenue withdrew tax relief for payments made under a deed of covenant, leaving just two routes to consider:

- gift aid; and
- dividends.

However, existing deeds of covenant remain legally binding until their term expires and should not be abandoned. Payments due under such deeds will be relieved from tax under gift aid.

Gift aid

This method is simpler than a deed of covenant and can be used for one-off payments (there is not the long-term commitment of the deed). With effect from 6 April 2000, gift aid became the only method for donating funds tax free. The gift aid scheme has been radically overhauled to make it more attractive and simpler to operate. A key change is that charity subsidiaries are now able to carry gift aid donations to their parent charity up to nine months back from the date of payment and claim tax relief in an earlier accounting period (in the same way in which they were allowed to under the deed of covenant system). In addition, companies will no longer have to deduct basic rate income tax from their gift aid donations.

Dividends

Profits can be passed to the charity through this route. However, changes to the advance corporation tax regime and problems with estimating profits make this the least attractive alternative, best left as a last resort.

34.8   Planning checklist

Passive planning is considered at **34.3.1**, i.e. using the reliefs available in the legislation. Active planning is considered at **34.7.1**, i.e. creating structures using subsidiaries or captive entities to improve the charity's VAT position. If active planning is pursued, it is essential that it is implemented correctly with regard not only to VAT issues but a range of non-VAT issues (checklists are essential).

Opportunities may arise because a charity has identified a particular issue or is concerned about the VAT cost of specific expenditure and wishes to investigate whether or not something can be done about it.

More likely, the charity is unaware that there is an opportunity to mitigate VAT either through active or passive planning. This checklist is designed to help identify areas where planning opportunities may arise by cross-reference to the relevant section in this chapter.

	Question	Answer
1	**Registration**	
1.1	Is the charity registered?	If yes, go to **1.4**
1.2	Does the charity have a liability to register?	See **34.2.1**
1.3	Is the charity making taxable supplies?	Consider voluntary registration (see **34.2.1**)
1.4	Is the charity a corporate entity with trading subsidiaries?	Consider group registration (see **34.2.2**)
1.5	Is the charity trading below the registration threshold?	Consider deregistration
1.6	Does the charity have branches?	Consider **34.2.3**
2	**Activities**	
2.1	Is the charity involved in the provision of welfare?	Consider **34.3.3**
2.2	Is the charity providing education or research?	Consider **34.3.5** and **34.3.6**
2.3	Is the charity providing accommodation?	Consider **34.3.7**
2.4	Is the charity providing cultural services?	Consider **34.3.8**
2.5	Is the charity involved with fund-raising events?	Consider **34.4.3** and **34.4.4**
2.6	Does the charity have any shops?	Consider **34.4.5**
2.7	Is the charity involved in any sponsorship?	Consider **34.4.1** and **34.4.6**
2.8	Does the charity have membership?	Consider **34.4.2**
2.9	Consider the liabilities being applied to income: are they correct?	Consider **34.3.1**
2.10	Are the charity's customers in a position to reclaim VAT?	Consider **34.7.2**
3	**Reliefs**	
3.1	Does the charity buy medical scientific or other 'relevant goods'?	Consider **34.5.3**
3.2	Does the charity advertise?	Consider **34.5.4**
3.3	Does the charity run conferences?	Consider VATA 1994, Sch. 8 and 9
3.4	Is the charity entitled to any other relief under the exempt or zero-rated schedules?	Consider VATA 1994, Sch. 8 and 9

4	**Property**	
4.1	Does the charity own property?	Confirm usage: is it eligible for relief on fuel and power costs?
4.2	Has the charity undertaken any construction work/acquired new premises?	Consider the scope for retrospective zero-rating (see **34.5.7**)
4.3	Is the charity planning any major work/acquiring new property?	Consider 'active planning' (see **34.7.1**)
5	**Other asset purchases**	
5.1	Is the charity planning any significant purchases?	Consider **34.6.1** and 'active planning' (see **34.7.1**)
6	**General expenditure**	
6.1	Is the charity involved in non-business activity/partially exempt?	Consider apportionment method (see **34.6.3**) and scope for 'active planning'
6.2	Has the charity missed an opportunity to claim input tax?	Consider **34.6.4**
6.3	Does the charity share costs with other charities (e.g. staff)?	Consider **34.6.2**

Retailers

35.1   VAT for retailers

35.1.1 Overview

As VAT is essentially a tax on consumption, ensuring that it is correctly collected at the retail stage is vital to securing government revenue. Retail schemes have been a feature of UK VAT since its inception in 1973. They acknowledged the fact that a system based on showing the VAT due on tax invoices did not take into account the realities of the sales-recording methods used by retailers. Any retail scheme is bound to be the best estimate of the VAT that is due; it does not calculate the VAT due exactly. Any retail scheme is a trade off between accuracy and convenience. With increasing use of point of sales machines that enable retailers to accurately calculate the VAT due, HMRC have, over the years, reduced the number of schemes that are available to retailers. Retail schemes are only required where supplies are made at different VAT rates. Where supplies are made with only one rate of VAT, the output VAT can be calculated by applying the appropriate VAT fraction.

A requirement for tax invoices on all retail sales would have imposed a significant burden on business whilst achieving only a limited improvement on control as it would not have been practicable to use invoices given to retail customers as a checking tool, particularly as most customers are not in business but are final consumers. Although developments in point-of-sale equipment might make an invoicing requirement less burdensome today, the problems of cross-checking with customer copies still remain. Therefore the schemes continue to be available and are widely used by retailers.

> ### ⚠ *Warning!*
>
> HMRC may require a retailer to justify the use of a scheme rather than the straight forward use of bar coding or a multi function till. Reasons could include the cost of introducing a bar scanning system, inaccuracies found with bar coding (for instance, in high volume clothing retailers where tags get torn off), or the well-known problems of training staff (especially where there is a high turnover of staff) to accurately use multi-function tills.

The details of the schemes have been modified since their introduction. Currently, the available schemes are as follows.

For retailers with VAT-exclusive annual turnover of not more than £1 million:

- apportionment scheme 1 (*VAT Notice 727/4*); and
- direct calculation scheme 1 (*VAT Notice 727/5*).

For retailers with VAT-exclusive annual turnover of not more than £130 million:

- apportionment scheme 2 (*VAT Notice 727/4*);
- direct calculation scheme 2 (*VAT Notice 727/5*); and
- the point-of-sale scheme (*VAT Notice 727/3*).

In considering eligibility for the different schemes, the retail turnover of the entire business must be taken into account.

In addition, there are specific variations to suit the needs of retail pharmacists, caterers and retail florists (*VAT Notice 727*).

The largest retailers, with VAT-exclusive annual retail turnover exceeding £130 million, cannot use a retail scheme as such. Instead, they must draw up and agree with HMRC a bespoke scheme specific to their own business. This may incorporate the features of the standard schemes for retailers, although the simplified approach of the scheme 1 methods will usually not be acceptable to HMRC. A bespoke scheme will also set out specifically the treatment of the more problematic areas of the scheme, such as setting and amending estimated selling prices.

Planning point

Retailers with a lower annual turnover may also draw up a bespoke scheme. This may be particularly useful if their business does not suit the straightforward application of the standard schemes.

Planning point

Retailers with a lower annual turnover may also find it advantageous to consider the use of the Flat Rate Scheme, see **Chapter 6**.

⚠ Warning!

Services need to be accounted for outside the retail scheme.

A retailer may use the cash and annual accounting schemes if its total annual tax-exclusive turnover is below the relevant limit, currently £1.35 million. These can be alternatives to using a retail scheme or can be used in conjunction with one. The relevant Notices detail how the retail scheme calculations are modified when the other schemes are used.

Instead of using a retail scheme, a retailer whose total annual tax-exclusive turnover is below the current eligibility limit of £150,000 can consider the flat rate scheme where the retailer accounts for VAT by applying the flat rate scheme percentage applicable to the product lines sold.

> ### Planning point
>
> Use of the flat rate scheme may increase the total VAT liability or decrease it, dependent on the precise circumstances of each case, but it undoubtedly makes the process of calculating the overall VAT liability of the business hugely simpler in either event.

For details of the cash accounting, annual accounting or flat rate schemes, see **Chapter 6**.

The VAT rate for standard-rated supplies changed on 4 January 2011 to 20 per cent. It should be noted that the standard-rate before this date was 17.5 per cent and that rate applies to supplies made before then. Also for a period the standard-rate was 15 per cent (1 December 2008 to 31 December 2009). If making retrospective calculations the correct rate must be used.

35.1.2 Legal background to the schemes

The retail schemes are special measures that differ from the requirements of the EU VAT system as set out in the Sixth VAT Directive. When this Directive was introduced in 1978, retention of the retail schemes was justified by the UK Government in the following terms:

> 'The purpose of the UK's special VAT schemes for retailers is to simplify the calculation of output tax by retailers, in that they do not have to record full details and calculate tax on each transaction. It is considered that the special retail schemes do not derogate in principle from the provisions of the sixth directive, but only apply a totality of the considerations received or receivable in determining the tax due at different rates.
>
> (Letter from Customs to the EC Commission, 28 December 1977.)'

VATA 1994, Sch. 11, para. 2(6) provides for regulations to fix the value of supplies by retailers using methods published in Notices by Customs. Regulations 66–75, Pt IX, VAT Regulations 1995 (SI 1995/2518) set out the broad terms of the retail schemes and authorise HMRC to publish the *Retail Scheme Notices*.

- *VAT Notice 727*;
- *VAT Notice 727/2*;
- *VAT Notice 727/3*;
- *VAT Notice 727/4*; and
- *VAT Notice 727/5*.

These were originally issued in March 2002, but have been updated frequently.

Because of the powers to define the schemes given to HMRC by the Regulations, those parts of the *Notices* that specify how the schemes operate have the force of law. Such tertiary legislation is contained in all the *Notices* except *Notice 727/2*. The sections having legal effect in the other Notices are identified in their introductory paragraphs.

35.1.3 Outline of the schemes

The point-of-sale scheme operates by capturing the value of sales made at the different VAT rates at the time of sale. It avoids the need to maintain other records, such as details of estimated selling prices (ESPs), but does require accurate identification of the VAT rates applicable to sales. Often this can be done by using the VAT rates shown on suppliers' invoices.

> ### ⚠ *Warning!*
>
> This approach of using the suppliers' invoices to calculate output tax liability will not work if the retailer processes the goods, for example, by using food in a catering outlet, or combines items supplied to him at different rates into a hamper of mixed food and drink items.

The apportionment schemes calculate the split of takings at the different rates of VAT. Scheme 1 uses the ratios of purchases made at the different rates; scheme 2 marks up the purchases to give ESPs at the different rates and apportions takings using the ratios of those ESPs. The VAT fraction (1/21 for lower-rated goods taxed at 5 per cent and 1/6 for standard-rated goods taxed at 20 per cent is applied to the apportioned takings at each rate to give the retailer's VAT liability.

The direct calculation schemes also use ESPs but only of 'minority goods'; that is, those goods that, grouped by applicable VAT rate, have the lowest sales value. If the minority goods are liable to VAT, the appropriate VAT fraction applied to the ESP gives the VAT liability at that rate. If only standard-rated and zero-rated goods are sold, and the minority goods are zero-rated, deducting the estimated selling price of the zero-rated goods from daily gross takings gives the standard-rated takings. Applying the VAT fraction 1/6 to this figure gives the VAT liability. If sales are made at all three VAT rates, ESPs are worked out for the two groups of goods with the lowest sales values. Deducting the calculated ESPs from takings gives sales at the remaining rate. The appropriate VAT fraction gives the VAT liability. Scheme 2 uses the same calculations but includes a stock adjustment.

> **Example 35.1**
>
> If a retailer is selling a mixture of standard-rated goods, zero-rated goods and reduced-rated goods and is eligible to use the apportionment scheme, he first needs to identify the minority goods. If total sales are £162,100 and the expected selling prices of the goods are: £119,000 standard-rated, £2,100 reduced-rate goods and £40,000 zero-rated goods, then the minority goods are the reduced-rate and zero-rate goods. VAT is calculated by deducting the minority goods from the total sales. That is £162,100 less (£2,100 + £40,000) = £120,000. The VAT fraction of 1/6 is applied to this figure (£120,000 x 1/6) = £20,000. VAT on the reduced-rate goods is £2,100/21 = £100. Total VAT due is £20,000 + £100 = £20,100.

35.1.4 Who can use a retail scheme

Retailers operate in a variety of ways. The traditional model is the shop, whether the local corner shop or a branch of a national or international chain on the high street or at a retail park. There are many shop formats, including boutiques, supermarkets, hypermarkets, convenience stores, catalogue stores, factory outlets, retail warehouses and so on. Then there are outlets that are remote from the customer. Traditional mail order using newspaper advertisements or catalogues has been joined by TV promotions and dedicated TV shopping channels.

Although the internet is often used as an alternative advertising medium, this can also be used for online order placement and as a delivery medium for electronic games, music and other 'digitised' products. Even a relatively small business may have 'multi-channel' operations exploiting several of these formats. For example, a specialist food producer may have a shop, make mail order sales and/or have a website capable of taking customer orders.

The retail schemes can be used by any form of retail business with an annual VAT-exclusive retail turnover that does not exceed £130 million. The business must be unable to account for VAT in the normal way, that is, keep a record of each supply that shows its tax-exclusive value and the VAT due and produce total figures for each period. Thus, the retail schemes are intended to be used either where the customer does not get a receipt, such as the typical public house, or where that receipt shows only the tax-inclusive price of the purchases or does not distinguish sales at different rates of VAT, as in a supermarket till receipt.

Retailers with retail turnover exceeding £130 million must use a bespoke scheme that has been specifically approved by HMRC. Other retailers may use any scheme without prior approval from HMRC, provided that they do not breach the applicable turnover limits. In choosing between schemes, retailers may consider the practicalities of operating them. For example, can they identify goods at different VAT rates at point of sale, or keep the records required to compute ESPs, as well as the resulting VAT liabilities? The schemes may produce different results because of the differing assumptions that they employ. HMRC cannot object to a scheme merely because another produces a greater VAT liability. However, they can deny use of a scheme where:

- normal accounting could be used;
- the scheme does not produce a fair and reasonable result; or
- they consider it necessary for the protection of the revenue.

The schemes must not be used for non-retail sales, for sales to VAT-registered customers, (other than for occasional cash sales of items such as petrol) or for exempt supplies or those outside the scope of VAT. These sales must be accounted for outside the schemes.

> ### Planning point
>
> Some schemes are not suitable for goods produced by the business or for services. If an alternative scheme that provides for these supplies cannot be used, they must also be handled outside the scheme.

35.1.5 Choosing a scheme

A retailer who is eligible to use a retail scheme can choose to use any scheme suitable for his business. HMRC cannot impose a particular scheme on a retailer, although they do have powers to refuse the use of a scheme.

> ### Planning point
>
> In deciding which scheme best suits a retailer, the first consideration is restrictions on their use.

Apportionment scheme 1 and direct calculation scheme 1 may only be used by retailers with tax-exclusive annual retail turnover below £1 million. The other main restrictions are as follows.

Table 35.1

Scheme	Cannot be used for
Apportionment scheme 1	Services, catering, or self-produced goods
Apportionment scheme 2	Services or catering
Direct calculation scheme 1	Services (unless liable to VAT at a different rate to the minority supplies) and catering
Direct calculation scheme 2	Services (unless liable to VAT at a different rate to the minority supplies) and catering

Planning point

Because of the different assumptions that they use, the VAT liabilities that the schemes generate will differ. The retailer may choose to use the scheme that produces the lowest liability. However, ease of use and complexity of record-keeping requirements should also be taken into account.

The point-of-sale scheme may be used for all types of retail sales and does not require additional calculations. Thus, provided that point-of-sale identification of VAT rates is possible, it is the simplest to use. The other schemes need the following additional steps.

Table 35.2

Scheme	Additional requirements
Apportionment scheme 1	Annual adjustment calculation
Apportionment scheme 2	Initial stock take and rolling ESP calculation
Direct calculation scheme 1	ESP calculation
Direct calculation scheme 2	ESP calculation, initial and annual stock takes and annual adjustment

35.1.6 Using a mix of schemes

It is possible to mix schemes but HMRC impose restrictions on how this is done. Although they prefer to have a single scheme used across an entire business they will allow a scheme to be applied separately at different business locations. However, unless this is the point-of-sale scheme, the retailer must agree with them the treatment of stock transferred between locations.

It is also possible to use different schemes within the business. The point-of-sale scheme can be used with either the apportionment or direct calculation schemes. However, it is not possible to use an apportionment scheme and a direct calculation scheme together, nor to mix different versions of these schemes.

Normal accounting can be used in conjunction with any permitted scheme or combination of schemes.

35.1.7 Changing schemes

It is possible to change schemes and it may be necessary to do so if, for example, the business alters so that it becomes ineligible to use its present scheme. Although HMRC may agree to a retrospective change of scheme, they rarely do so.

> ### ⚠ *Warning!*
>
> The administrative and VAT costs of a scheme should be carefully evaluated before opting to use it as the retailer will almost certainly have to use it for at least 12 months.

A retail scheme can be changed with effect from the anniversary of its first use. This may not coincide with a VAT year but it may be possible to agree with HMRC to make a change from the start of a VAT year.

> ### *Planning point*
>
> It is sensible, therefore, to review the operation of the scheme shortly before its anniversary so that, if unsuitable, it can be changed with minimum further delay.

In addition to agreeing to a change of scheme earlier than the anniversary date, HMRC may also require a change to be made at another time, if, for example, they consider that the scheme in use no longer gives a fair and reasonable result.

If the retailer ceases to be eligible to use a scheme he must stop using it from the end of the next VAT accounting period. This should give sufficient time for the necessary changes to be made to operate another scheme.

> ### ⚠ *Warning!*
>
> The turnover limits are strictly applied so retailers whose turnover is approaching the limit for their scheme should monitor it regularly. HMRC may reject returns submitted by a retailer who continues to use a scheme for which they have become ineligible and they can then assess output tax liability based on an eligible scheme.

In exceptional circumstances, which do not include merely that another scheme would produce a lower VAT liability, HMRC may consent to a change of scheme that is retrospective for a maximum of four years. However, as well as showing that there is an exceptional case for a retrospective change, the retailer must have available the information needed to operate the alternative scheme retrospectively, although HMRC may exercise a little flexibility in the requirements.

Whenever a scheme changes, it will be necessary to perform the closing adjustments.

35.1.8 Changes in VAT rates

A change in one of the VAT rates, the introduction of a new rate or a change in the rate applicable to a particular item can have a number of consequences for retailers. The first is the need to adjust prices to take account of the new rates. This may mean altering shelf and packet prices, adjusting EPOS systems and altering vending machines.

Although there is usually some delay between the date when a change is announced and its implementation, a general shift in rates could involve a large amount of work and retailers should have contingency plans for coping with this situation. A retailer who is unable to pass on the effect of a rate increase to customers must still account for the higher rate on VAT returns. If rates fall, customers will be looking for prices also to fall.

> ### ⚠ *Warning!*
>
> As well as affecting the prices of goods, a rate change will affect the operation of the retail schemes. This may cause extra difficulties where the retailer has relied on rate information from his suppliers and no purchases have been made since the rate change. A point-of-sale scheme will need to capture the new prices and rates. Estimated selling prices will have to be adjusted to reflect not only the new rates but other elements such as changing wastage and price reduction factors as customer buying patterns adapt to new rates.

It may also be necessary to adapt schemes to cope with sales at additional VAT rates. If this is the case, HMRC will issue guidance on any necessary amendments to schemes. Where the rate change occurs part way through the retailer's VAT period, the return will have to include figures prepared on both the old and new bases for the relevant parts of the period.

35.1.9 Ceasing to use a retail scheme

A retailer may cease to use a retail scheme for a number of reasons. The business might be better suited to another scheme, or changes to its operations or the scheme rules or VAT rates may mean that a change to another scheme is necessary. Changes to systems or to the way it does business may mean that it has to change to the normal accounting method. Turnover may fall below the VAT registration limit so that the retailer can deregister and the business may be sold or closed.

When a retailer stops using a retail scheme, the point-of-sale scheme, direct calculation scheme 1 and apportionment scheme 2 do not need any closing adjustments to be made, unless apportionment scheme 2 has only ended in one part of the business. The rolling stock calculation must be adjusted for the stock no longer in the scheme. A retailer ceasing to use apportionment scheme 1 or direct calculation scheme 2 must carry out a closing adjustment in the same form as the annual adjustment.

35.1.10 Purchases

Using a retail scheme does not affect the way in which the retailer accounts for other aspects of his VAT affairs. The retailer can recover the input tax on purchases for use in his business where he holds a correctly completed VAT invoice. Some retailers operate 'call-off' arrangements with their suppliers under which the retailer initiates deliveries of goods to stores and processes all relevant paperwork including the production of invoices. These self-billed invoices may be used as evidence of input tax entitlement provided they meet the requirements for a tax invoice.

35.2 Retail schemes

35.2.1 The bases for the different schemes

The retail schemes start from the business takings (or assumed takings in the case of the direct calculation schemes) but use different approaches to apportion takings between sales at the different rates of VAT and, hence, calculate VAT liabilities.

> **Planning point**
>
> For this reason, as well as considering the administrative burden of each scheme that could be used, the retailer should also estimate the liabilities that each scheme produces. Any reduction in VAT liability will probably result in increased profit as prices will generally not be set directly to reflect VAT.

A retailer using the point-of-sale scheme has to keep a record of the value of sales made at different VAT rates. This can be done by physical separation, for example a stationer and bookseller might have one sales point for books, which are zero-rated, and another for stationery and other standard-rated items. Alternatively, the retailer could use a till which records sales at the various VAT rates, or even keep a paper record of sales. The latter might be adequate where the majority of sales are at one rate and only a few sales at other rates need to be recorded. This might be the case, for example, where a babywear shop sold only a limited number of non-zero-rated items.

The direct calculation and apportionment schemes do not need takings at the different VAT rates to be identified. Rather, they use a calculation to determine the VAT liabilities at the different rates.

The direct calculation schemes calculate the value of the retailer's sales liable to VAT by applying anticipated margins to purchases to obtain ESPs of goods at the different rates of VAT. The amount of VAT due on these sales can then be worked out by applying the appropriate VAT fraction. There is a simplified version (direct calculation scheme 1) for use by businesses which have a VAT-exclusive annual retail turnover not exceeding £1 million. Retailers with VAT-exclusive annual retail turnover under £130 million may use direct calculation scheme 2 which includes an annual stock adjustment.

> ### *Planning point*
>
> Retailers with a high mark up on zero-rated or reduced-rated goods may wish to avoid the use of apportionment scheme 1 as this uses prices rather than ESP to apportion the takings. Retailers with a high mark up of these items would benefit from using apportionment method 2 or the direct calculation schemes.

> ### *Planning point*
>
> Direct calculation scheme 2 may be advantageous to a business that has slow moving standard-rated stock. VAT is not accounted for on this stock until sold due to the annual adjustment mechanism. Method 1 requires the VAT to be accounted for in the period when the goods are purchased.

The apportionment schemes also have two versions. Where VAT-exclusive annual retail turnover does not exceed £1 million, takings are apportioned between the different rates of VAT in the ratio of purchases at those rates (apportionment scheme 1). VAT liabilities are computed by applying the appropriate VAT fraction to the computed takings at each rate. Even though there is an annual recalculation based on a full year's purchases, this method will be prone to inaccuracies unless similar margins apply to all sales.

Apportionment scheme 2, for retailers with VAT-exclusive annual retail turnover under £130 million, seeks to achieve a more accurate apportionment of takings by basing it on the ESPs of the different items. This should automatically adjust for differing margins. The VAT liability is again calculated by applying the relevant VAT fraction to the apportioned takings.

The operation of the schemes is considered in more detail below.

35.2.2 Using the point-of-sale scheme

A retailer using the point-of-sale scheme must be able to identify the VAT rate applicable to each sale so that the value of the sale is included in total sales at the relevant rate. If only goods attracting a single rate of VAT are sold, as could be the case with a gentlemen's outfitters, the scheme is straightforward to operate. Where only goods at either the standard or reduced rate are sold, the point-of-sale scheme is the only one that may be used.

Using the standard rate of VAT of 17.5 per cent (20 per cent from 4 January 2011) and the point-of-sale scheme, a retailer might identify his total sales of £216,000 as consisting of £186,000 at the standard rate, £8,000 at the reduced rate and the balance of £22,000 at the zero rate. The VAT liability is as follows.

Standard-rated sales £186,000	VAT fraction 1/6	£31,000
Reduced-rated sales £8,000	VAT fraction 1/21	£381
VAT liability		£31,381

The major difficulty with the point-of-sale scheme is correctly identifying the applicable VAT rate where sales are made at two or more rates. The problem may be resolved if the business can be physically split into different departments each selling only at a single rate of VAT. Otherwise, either the retailer and his staff must be able to identify the applicable rate and ring up the sale accordingly, or the tilling system must be able to make the distinction.

> ### ⚠ *Warning!*
>
> The first approach is likely to prove difficult where many items have to be identified or there are large numbers of staff to be trained. The second approach also has difficulties. Electronic till systems can be expensive and the information recorded on bar-codes, which is intended primarily to track stock movements, may not provide an adequate VAT analysis; in addition, care needs to be taken with bar coding to ensure errors are not made. For example, it may only identify stock down to department level. If departments can be aligned with VAT rates this will work, but it will not be adequate if a department holds stock liable at different rates. There is also the problem of checkout staff using 'convenience' codes when a product bar-code cannot be scanned. These codes may not give the correct VAT identification. If the till system is capable of holding a VAT rate for every product line, it is critical that those inputting new product lines have a sufficient understanding of VAT liability. If they do not, underpayments or overpayments of VAT can easily arise.

> ### ⚠ *Warning!*
>
> When point of sales systems are used, HMRC will check the volume of purchases and compare them to sales. Use of a multi-function till to separate sales at different VAT rates is a useful method of calculating VAT, but only where the till is used accurately. Obviously, scanning bar codes is of great assistance for this, but where a retailer depends upon staff pressing the correct button on a multi-function till, there is the potential for error. HMRC will carefully check sales recorded for each VAT rate and compare this to what they expect the sale should have been. Where a multi-function till is used, staff must be made aware (and reminded frequently) which buttons to press and the importance of doing so.

> **Planning point**
>
> For these reasons, many retailers find the direct calculation or apportionment schemes easier to use in spite of the extra calculations and record keeping involved.

> **Planning point**
>
> Where a multi-function till is used (and there is no bar code scanning) then the use of different coloured price labels for products is useful. Different coloured labels can be used for different VAT rates to coincide with the coloured label on the till. It is then essential to ensure that the correct labels are applied to products in the shop.

35.2.3 Using the direct calculation schemes

The starting point for computing VAT liabilities using direct calculation scheme 1 is to decide which goods – grouped by applicable VAT rate – are the 'minority' goods, that is those which have the lowest aggregate sales. The ESP of these goods is then calculated by applying the appropriate mark-ups to purchase prices.

If sales are made only at the standard and zero rates, the VAT liability is calculated as follows.

1. Standard-rated goods are the 'minority' goods.

    The ESP of the standard-rated goods are calculated by applying expected margins to goods purchased, made or grown for retail sale. This figure is the sales value on which VAT at the standard rate is due and is computed by applying the VAT fraction.

2. Zero-rated goods are the 'minority' goods.

    The ESP of the zero-rated goods is deducted from daily gross takings to give a value for standard-rated sales to which the VAT fraction is applied to work out the VAT liability.

As expected selling prices are rarely fully achieved, the following factors must be taken into account:

*   price changes, such as sales, special offers and promotions;
*   wastage, goods not sold as spoilt;
*   theft and other losses; and
*   bad debts written off.

It is also essential that wholesale sales, goods taken or bought for private use, and stock disposals as part of a sale of part or all of the business, are treated outside of the retail scheme and not included as part of the ESP calculations.

Planning point

Some businesses may find it simpler to calculate ESPs of majority goods as these may represent fewer lines with differing margins. They may compute VAT liabilities in this way provided it gives a 'fair and reasonable' result.

---

3. Sales at more than two rates of VAT (using a standard rate of 20 per cent).

    If sales are made at zero, reduced and standard rates of VAT, direct calculation scheme 1 can be used but it is necessary to work out ESPs for the two lowest sales value VAT categories. If these are, for example, the zero- and reduced-rate goods, the VAT liability calculation is as follows:

    (a) work out daily gross takings for the period   £...

    (b) calculate ESPs of zero-rated goods   £...

    (c) deduct total (b) from total (a)   £...

    (d) calculate ESPs of reduced-rate goods   £...

    (e) multiply total at (d) by 1/21 (VAT at 5 per cent)   £...

    (f) deduct totals at (b) and (d) from (a)   £...

    (g) multiply total (f) by 1/6 (VAT at 20 per cent)   £...

    (h) add the figure at (g) to the figure at (e) to give output tax liability.   £...

    If ESPs are calculated for standard-rated goods, the VAT liability computation is simpler. The VAT liability in respect of standard-rated sales is computed by applying the VAT fraction 1/6 to the estimated selling price figure. The ESPs of reduced-rated goods, if these are the second minority goods, are also calculated and the VAT fraction 1/21 is applied to this amount to work out the VAT liability for reduced-rate sales. The two figures are added to give the total VAT liability for the period.

    Retailers using direct calculation scheme 2 must also make an annual adjustment to allow for stock movements in the year. This adjustment is made on the anniversary of the first use of the scheme and must also be used if part of the retail business is sold, shut down or otherwise leaves the scheme. The adjustment calculation must omit the value of goods included in opening stock or otherwise already used in the scheme calculation which are no longer in stock but have not been sold by retail. The calculation where goods are sold only at the zero and standard rates and the minority goods are zero-rated is as follows:

    (a) work out the ESPs of opening stock of zero-rated goods for retail sale when the scheme is first used   £...

    (b) work out daily gross takings (DGT) for the year   £...

    (c) work out total ESPs of zero-rated goods received, made or grown for retail sale in the year and add the zero-rated stock figure at (a)   £...

    (d) work out the ESPs of closing stock of zero-rated goods for retail sale at the year-end or when the scheme ceases to be used   £...

(e)   deduct total (d) from total (c) to give the ESPs of zero-rated   £...
      goods sold by retail in the year

(f)   deduct total (e) from total (b) to give standard-rated takings for   £...
      the year

(g)   multiply total (f) by 1/6 (VAT at 20 per cent) – the output tax   £...
      payable for the year

(h)   an adjustment is made on the basis of output tax actually paid   £...
      during the year and the calculation shown at (g).

If the tax calculated at (g) is less than the amount paid in the year, too much tax has been accounted for and the difference can be taken off the output tax for the fourth quarter. If (g) exceeds (h), too little tax has been paid and the difference must be added to the fourth quarter output tax.

A further step is needed if goods are also sold at the reduced rate. This involves the calculation of the ESP of reduced-rate goods (if a minority supply, as is probable) and deducting this from the gross takings. The VAT fraction of 1/21 is applied to that (VAT rate 5 per cent). This and other calculations are set out in *Notice 727/5*.

35.2.4 Using the apportionment schemes

Apportionment scheme 1 assumes that the values of sales at the different VAT rates will be in the same proportions as the values of purchases. The calculation for each period is as follows.

1.   Work out daily gross takings for the period.   £...

2.   Add up the cost, including VAT, of all goods received for retail   £...
     sale at the standard rate.

3.   Add up the cost, including VAT, of all goods received for retail   £...
     sale at the reduced rate.

4.   Add up the cost, including VAT, of all goods received for retail   £...
     sale at standard, reduced and zero rates.

5.   Total (1) × 1/6 (VAT at 20 per cent) × total (2)/total (4). This is   £...
     the output tax on standard-rated sales.

6.   Total (1) × 1/21 (VAT at 5 per cent) × total (3)/total (4). This is   £...
     the output tax on reduced-rated sales.

7.   Add (5) and (6) to give total output tax.   £...

At the end of each year the calculation is recalculated using figures for the full year. The resulting liability is compared with the total liability for the separate periods. If the annual figure is greater the difference is due to HMRC; if smaller the difference can be reclaimed.

This scheme cannot be used for goods made or grown by the retailer or for services or catering supplies.

The calculation of output tax liability using apportionment scheme 2 is similar to that for scheme 1 but it apportions daily gross takings by reference to ESPs rather than purchase prices. Although requiring more work, it is potentially more accurate and can be used for goods made or grown by the retailer. An adjustment for the ESPs of opening stock is needed when the scheme is first used. This and other calculations are set out in *Notice 727/4*.

35.3 Daily gross takings

35.3.1 General

Detailed invoice records of each sale are unavailable where retail schemes are used. An essential record for retailers is their daily gross takings (DGT); this is their record of total sales made from which their VAT liability can be calculated. The point-of-sale, apportionment and some of the direct calculation schemes rely on the DGT figure to compute output tax liabilities. Even where the figure is not used to calculate VAT liabilities, retailers must record daily gross takings as HMRC use this as a check on the accuracy of other aspects of their records.

A retailer using any of the retail schemes must keep a record of DGT showing all payments received from cash customers and the full value of credit or non-cash sales. The form this takes will depend upon the retailer's systems. In many cases till rolls, or the equivalent information produced by electronic tills, will be used. Alternatively, copies of sales slips or a manual note of each sale may suffice.

> **Planning point**
>
> Till rolls must be retained by the business. This can create a huge storage problem, but permission can be sought from HMRC to dispose of till rolls after a period (say 12 months).

The cash receipts total may have to be adjusted to produce the DGT figure needed for the retail schemes.

For example, where a retailer sells goods and provides his own credit facilities, the till records may show only the initial cash deposit received from the customer. VAT is due on the full selling price, excluding any disclosed charge for credit, so the difference between this amount and the initial payment must be added to give the DGT figure at the time of the sale. When subsequent instalments are received, they are deducted from cash receipts in calculating DGT because VAT has already been accounted for on the full selling price. Any interest payments are also deducted because these VAT-exempt amounts are dealt with outside the retail scheme. If finance is provided by a finance company the full sales value is included in DGT at the time of the sale of the goods. Any instalments subsequently received by the retailer on behalf of the finance company are excluded from DGT.

35.3.2 Adjustment for debtors

Retailers with a turnover below £1 million who allow customers to pay them periodically, such as newsagents and milkmen, may take account of opening and closing debtors in calculating DGT. The adjustment set out by HMRC is as set out below.

Example 35.2

In the first period of using a retail scheme:

Takings for the period	£30,000
Closing debtors	(£1,500)
Gross takings for retail scheme purposes	£28,500
In the subsequent period:	
Opening debtors	£1,500
Takings for the period	£31,000
Closing debtors	(£1,600)
Gross takings for retail scheme purposes	£30,900

This defers accounting for VAT on sales until payment is received.

35.3.3 Other adjustments

Other amounts which are added to cash takings to give DGT include:

- non-cash receipts, such as cheques, debit and credit card and electronic cash payments and third-party payment vouchers such as Shopacheque;
- gift, record and book tokens that have been exchanged for goods;
- fraudulent refunds which do not represent refunds for actual sales;
- the cash value of any payment in kind for retail sales; and
- the value of any goods taken out of the business for own use.

Deductions from cash takings in the calculation include:

- receipts which cannot be turned into cash such as dishonoured cheques (other than for credit instalments), foreign currency mistaken for sterling, and counterfeit notes;
- refunds to customers for returned goods up to the original purchase price or for overcharges;

- receipts for exempt supplies, such as rents, and other items dealt with outside the retail schemes;
- the value of promotional coupons accepted from customers which cannot be redeemed because they were issued by competing retailers or are refused by promoters, for example, because they are out of date; and
- recording errors such as till breakdowns and training tills that are not zeroed before being returned to use.

HMRC guidance allows DGT to be reduced by amounts charged to credit cards which are then not honoured because, for example, the signature is illegible (clearly much reduced by 'chip and pin'). There is no guidance as to credit-card vouchers which are declined by accepting banks because of 'customer not present' or other irregularities. It is general practice for credit-card vouchers to be honoured provided the retailer has accepted them in good faith and followed the laid-down security procedures. However, this is not usually the case where the customer is not present, for example mail order or internet sales. Thus, if a card is fraudulently used for a web purchase, the retailer will normally have to bear the cost. Arguably, DGT should also be reduced in these circumstances.

HMRC also say that DGT should not be adjusted where till shortages result from theft of cash, fraudulent refunds and voids or poor cash handling by staff. This is certainly the case where cash is taken after a sale has been made. However, it leaves uncertainty about the treatment of excess change being given to customers, whether accidentally or by reason of staff collusion.

If a customer inadvertently receives too much change, DGT should reflect the consideration actually given by the customer for the goods. If there is collusion resulting in too much change being given, it is still the case that the customer has given consideration less than the marked price and DGT should reflect this. The situation is more complex if the excess is so great that the customer effectively gives negative consideration. DGT should reflect at least a sale at nil value. This should not be regarded as a transaction within the business gift rules because a gift is not intended here.

As the retail schemes are based on the 'totality' of consideration provided by customers, it could be argued that DGT should reflect the full loss to the business, that is, takings received for other sales should be reduced. In practice, it is difficult to identify with any certainty causes of differences between recorded sales and total cash banked and between these figures and an estimate of sales based on marking-up purchases.

Where a retailer adjusts the DGT figure, HMRC expect that details of the adjustment and evidence of the reasons for it will be kept. They also expect that if DGT have been reduced because of, say, a dishonoured cheque, they will be increased by the amount of any correcting payment that may be received later.

900

35.3.4 Treatment of certain transactions

HMRC Notices 727/3, 727/4 and 727/5 set out the adjustments that must be made in calculating DGT for their respective schemes. They also deal with the treatment of other transactions such as payphones, refunds, part exchanges and sales promotions. Generally these have to be accounted for outside the scheme.

The basis of the UK retail schemes as set out in the UK Government's 1978 statement, is to 'apply a totality of the considerations received or receivable in determining the tax due at different rates.' There are transactions where it is difficult to determine whether they represent retail sales or not, or to determine the value of the consideration. HMRC give guidance on these in their Notices. Those most likely to be met are discussed below.

35.3.5 Delivery charges

It is standard practice for some types of goods to be delivered direct to the customer. Examples include such daily home deliveries as milk and newspapers, goods bought by mail order or on subscription such as magazines, and bulky items such as furniture which the retailer arranges to have delivered to the customer's home. The general rule is that if there is no separate delivery charge, the price paid is for the delivered goods and is liable to VAT at the rate applicable to the goods.

Thus, the entire subscription for a magazine posted to the customer will be zero-rated and the full price for house-plants also mailed to the customer will be standard-rated. The full amount is included in DGT and is treated as a supply at the relevant rate in the retail scheme, for example, in computing estimated selling prices. This remains the case even if the delivery charge is separately itemised on an invoice, provided that delivery of the goods is an intrinsic part of the supply (that is, the contactual arrangements with the customer require delivery), as will often be the case, especially with mail order.

A separate charge for delivery contracted for separately (e.g. an optional additional payment for delivery of furniture which the customer has an option of collecting) is payment for a standard-rated supply of services. This is normally accounted for outside the retail scheme but may be brought into some of the direct calculation schemes' computations.

> ### ⚠ *Warning!*
>
> Even where the goods are delivered by mail, so that the charge by the Post Office to the retailer is exempt from VAT, the delivery charge to the customer is standard-rated because only the postal carrier may make an exempt supply of postal services. An attempt to regard the retailer as the customer's agent in arranging for goods to be delivered by post and so secure exemption failed (*C & E Commrs v Plantiflor Ltd* [2002] BVC 572).

Other guidance: VAT Notice 700/24

35.3.6 Deposits

A retailer would normally accept a deposit as advance payment for a supply and include it in DGT when received. If the sale does not take place and the deposit is returned to the customer, the amount may be deducted from DGT. If the deposit is not returned, it has not been consideration for a supply and should be removed from DGT.

A deposit may also be taken as security for goods that have been loaned or hired to a customer. It will either be returned when the goods are returned or forfeited in the event of loss or damage to the goods. This is not consideration for supply of the goods and should not be included in DGT until it is applied to a sale.

35.3.7 Discounts for cash or prompt settlement

If customers are offered discounts for cash or prompt settlement, the discounted amount is entered in DGT, whether or not the customer takes the discount. This does not apply where the customer has been offered the opportunity to pay by instalments.

35.3.8 Handling charges for credit and debit cards

It has become common for customers using debit and credit cards to be charged for their use. If a retailer surcharges customers for paying by credit card, the full price paid, including the surcharge, is the consideration for the goods and goes into DGT.

Credit card issuers may charge retailers a commission for their services, usually deducted from the amounts due to the retailer. This amount is consideration for the card company's services to the retailer and may not be deducted from DGT.

A variation on credit card handling charges has been used by major retailers in an attempt to reduce the VAT due on retail sales of goods. The arrangements entered into involved an in-house credit card handling company (not in the retailer's VAT group), which received from the retailer a handling charge for each transaction effected by credit card. This was argued to be an exempt supply, allowing the retailer to account for VAT only on the balance of the consideration received. Notices (often very small) advised customers of the set up. A typical handling charge would be 2.5 per cent of the price of the good.

The lead case on this issue is *Debenhams Retail plc* [2003] BVC 2,543. Although successful in the tribunal in arguing that the scheme was without merit, Customs were defeated on appeal by Debenhams to the High Court. However, this decision was itself overturned by the Court of Appeal. Leave to appeal to the House of Lords was not granted, meaning that the Court of Appeal's decision stands, striking down the arrangements.

35.3.9 Sale or return

Goods sent on 'sale or return' remain the retailer's property until they are purchased by the customer. The amount payable should only be entered in DGT when this happens. The retailer should keep a separate record of goods sent on sale or return. Any deposit received from the customer should be treated as set out above.

35.3.10 Sale of business assets

Sales of assets are not retail supplies and should not be recorded in DGT. However, VAT must be accounted for the supply, but it is accounted for outside the VAT retail scheme.

35.3.11 Shop within shop arrangements

There are several ways in which retailers may allow others to use part of their premises. The retailer may not only allow the concessionaire's products to be sold but provide the sales staff. Depending on their terms, these arrangements may be the grant of an interest in land, that is floor space, which may be an exempt supply or taxable if the retailer has opted to tax the building. In either case, amounts received are excluded from DGT, even if calculated on the basis of sales.

Alternatively, the retailer may be providing a package of selling services to the concessionaire. In either case the concessionaire has to account for VAT on sales that are made to retail customers and must ensure that they receive all information necessary to deal with their retail scheme, retail exports and so on.

In another variation of this arrangement, the retailer acts as undisclosed agent for the concessionaire. In this case the retailer accounts for output tax due on the sale, treating the concessionaire as a supplier of the goods. Any commission due to the retailer may be subsumed in the value of the supply to the customers, or be separately charged to the concessionaire. In this scenario, the sales are included within DGT by the retailer.

35.3.12 Sales promotion schemes

There are many types of sales promotion schemes and their VAT treatment has been a source of difficulty resulting in numerous court cases. Vouchers have been a recurring problem, as have situations where more than one party, for example the retailer and the manufacturer of the goods, has contributed to the costs of the promotion.

The treatment of the main types of promotion financed by the retailer alone is as set out below.

Other guidance: VAT Notice 700/7

Price reductions

According to EU VAT law, the VAT payable on a supply is proportional to the price paid by the final consumer. In other words, if the price is reduced by way of promotional offer, the VAT is correspondingly reduced also. Price reductions may be described in various ways: 'sale bargains'; 'one day offers'; 'matching competitors' prices'; 'we'll pay your VAT' and so on. The effect is the same — VAT is only due on the price that the customer pays and this is the amount that should be included in DGT.

If the customer does something else to obtain the discounted price, this may result in him being regarded as providing non-monetary consideration. In this event, the retailer will have to account for VAT on the aggregate of the cash paid and the value of the additional consideration. Usually, this will mean that the retailer has to treat the supply as having been made at its usual selling price, before discount.

An example of this is where a mail order retailer allows a discount to new customers who provide information about themselves for credit reference purposes or to existing customers who introduce new customers. The customers are regarded as giving additional consideration which the retailer has to account for by treating the sale as taking place at the full catalogue price, plus delivery charges and other costs of getting the goods to the customer.

Some promotions do require the customers to perform some act in order to qualify for discount. Often this is quite trivial and HMRC accept that no additional consideration arises where:

- the customers obtain a discount for using a store card; and
- the customer's first purchase entitles him to a second item or a discount voucher.

'Free' gifts

The same rules apply to retailers as other businesses when dealing with free gifts to customers. If the VAT-exclusive cost of the gift item is not more than £50, the retailer does not have to account for output tax, although input tax can be recovered in the same way as for other business purchases. If the value exceeds £50, the retailer has to treat the goods as though sold at cost and account for output tax accordingly. The rules for the different schemes are set out in the Notices.

Even if a promotion features a 'free' gift it is necessary to review the arrangements to see if non-monetary consideration issues arise. If the customer has given such consideration, the retailer has to treat the 'gift' as supplied for the value of the consideration. This would normally be the advertised selling price of the goods, or the cost to the retailer if they were not normal stock items, together with delivery costs if applicable.

Thus, while gifts costing not more than £50 do not trigger an output tax liability and gifts of a higher value generate a VAT liability based on their cost, there is always an output tax liability where the customer gives non-monetary consideration. It is important to be clear whether goods are given freely or not, as significant differences in output tax liability could arise.

HMRC will treat some acts by customers as insignificant and not giving rise to non-monetary consideration. These include:

- gifts given when purchases exceed a given level; and
- goods given as prizes when customers enter draws or competitions.

The normal gift rules apply to these items.

Buy one get one free, two for one, etc.

If the customer is offered several items at a favourable price, 'two for one', 'three for the price of two', 'buy a shirt and get a free tie' and so on, the bonus goods are not treated as gifts. The customer is regarded as having purchased the total package of goods for the price paid and the retailer must take this amount into DGT.

> ### Planning point
>
> If the goods are subject to different rates of VAT, it may be necessary to determine the proportion of the sales price allocated to each to operate the point-of-sale scheme or to calculate ESPs. If the goods have been specially purchased for the promotion, this allocation may be done by reference to the retailer's purchase prices for the items. However, if these are regular lines and they normally achieve significantly different mark-ups, it may be appropriate to take this into account in the allocation.

Linked goods

Where two items subject to different VAT rates are sold together for a single price, it may not be necessary to apportion the price between the items if the 'linked supplies concession' applies. Where a 'minor' item:

- is not charged separately to the customer;
- costs the retailer no more than 20 per cent of the combined offer; and
- costs the retailer no more than £1, excluding VAT,

the retailer can account for VAT on the minor item at the same rate as applicable to the principal item. This concession is perhaps most frequently used by magazine publishers, in particular in the context of children's titles where small goods are given away with magazines. If the rules above are met, all the consideration is zero-rated even when standard-rated goods are given with the magazine.

Loyalty card schemes

Many loyalty card schemes give customers 'points' when they make purchases. These points may be redeemed in full or part payment for subsequent purchases, or converted into vouchers that can be so redeemed. The redemption goods should be treated as gifts if no further payment is made for them. In practice, these schemes normally involve goods of a cost of less than £50, so no output tax would be due on redemption. Also, redemptions are usually against a basket of shopping rather than any single item, so the redemption has the effect of a discount against the entire basket.

The issue of points or vouchers has no VAT effect. On redemption, the retailer's DGT may be reduced by the redemption value.

If the retailer allows other businesses to issue points that the retailer will redeem, any payment from the other business is consideration for the standard-rated supply of a right to participate in the promotional scheme. Customer redemptions will be treated in the same way as redemptions of points issued by the retailer.

Privileged customer events

Selected customers or groups of customers, such as store cardholders, may be invited to special events, for example a late-night opening, and offered discounts not available generally. HMRC treat these as ordinary discounts so that VAT is due only on the prices actually paid by the customers.

False value trade-ins

Customers may be offered a flat rate or minimum trade-in value if goods are 'traded in' against the purchase of a new item. The usual treatment of a part exchange is the sale by the retailer of the new goods at their full price and a purchase by the retailer of the used items, which may go into the second-hand goods margin scheme.

However, 'false value' trade-ins where the trade-in price is offered irrespective of the condition or value of the used goods are typically only promotional events and the retailer has no use for the trade-in goods. Where it is clear that the trade-in is purely promotional, HMRC will allow the trade-in allowance to be treated as a discount off the new goods. In consequence, only the amount received by the retailer, net of the trade-in, should be included in DGT. Any consideration received on the disposal of the traded-in goods is subject to VAT at the normal rate.

Interest-free credit

If a retailer offers interest-free credit, whether the credit facility is offered by the retailer or a third party, VAT is due on the price actually paid by the customer without any deduction for any interest charge that the retailer might have to pay for the third-party credit.

Voucher schemes

The VAT treatment of vouchers has been the subject of a number of court cases. The treatment of vouchers. however, changed on 10 May 2012. The old way of dealing with vouchers is described first, for transactions that occurred prior to 10 May 2012, and the new voucher treatment is described following the old method.

Prior to 10 May 2012 the basic types of voucher schemes were as follows.

1. Discount vouchers that entitle the customer to obtain future purchases at a reduced price. These are usually issued free, for example coupons dropped in letter boxes, printed in magazines or issued electronically or given with other purchases. When these are redeemed, VAT is due only on the net price paid by the customer. If these are sold and the discount is available at the retailer that sold the voucher then the payment received must be included in the gross takings. If the discount is available from other suppliers then the item has to accounted for outside the retail scheme at the standard-rate

2. Face value vouchers that are issued free. If these are redeemed for goods without further payment, the goods must be treated as gifts. If the vouchers are redeemed as part payment for further goods, VAT is due on the payment given by the customer. That is, the voucher entitles the purchaser to a discount.

3. Face value vouchers that are sold at face value to the public, such as gift vouchers and book or record tokens; these were often described as credit vouchers. No VAT is due on issue. When they are redeemed, the full face value is treated as consideration for the redemption goods. The face value of the vouchers is taken into DGT on redemption.

4. Face value vouchers that have been issued in exchange for loyalty points. If redeemed for goods without further payment, the gift rules apply. If taken in part payment, VAT is due on the amount paid by the customer.

5. Face value vouchers issued at a discount to face value. When the vouchers are redeemed, the retailer accounts for VAT on the discounted value for which the vouchers were sold. However, to do this, the retailer must be able to distinguish discounted vouchers from those sold at face value.

6   Vouchers given with promotional goods. VAT is due on the full consideration received for the promotional goods with no discount or apportionment for the supply of the voucher; the voucher is regarded as a gift. When the voucher is redeemed, the face value of the voucher is ignored when calculating the VAT due on the redeemed goods.

Although there has been a change in the way vouchers are to be treated, the basic rules above are the same for most retailers subject to the following matters. The most significant change for vouchers is that, from 1 May 2012, a face-value voucher that is for a single type of good or service and the VAT treatment is know at the time of issue will be subject to VAT at the appropriate rate at the time of sale. Thus, a book token that can only be redeemed for a zero-rated book will be sold at the zero-rate. A gift token that can only be redeemed for standard-rated goods (such as petrol) is subject to VAT at the time of sale. Where these are redeemed, the retailer has to exclude the value from the value of gross takings.

For VAT, there are three types of face-value voucher: credit vouchers, retailer vouchers and other vouchers. A face-value voucher is a voucher with a cash value recorded on them. They provide a right to receive goods or services to their face-value without requiring further consideration. They can include gift vouchers, book tokens, phone cards, etc.

A credit voucher is a face-value voucher that is issued by a person who cannot redeem that voucher. The issuer of the voucher will reimburse the person that redeems the voucher. No VAT is accounted for on the voucher (although any excess to the face-value is subject to VAT at the time of issue). On redemption the voucher is to be accounted for at its face-value unless the consumer pays less than the face-value. If the reimbursement is no more than this lower amount the retailer can account for VAT on the lower amount paid for by the consumer.

A retailer voucher is a voucher issued by a retailer. On issue no VAT is accounted for (unless the consideration exceeds the face-value) and VAT is accounted for on redemption.

All other kinds of voucher are subject to VAT at the time of their sale. These vouchers are frequently sold by retailers to third parties for onward sale. These are subject to VAT at the time of sale are to be excluded from retail schemes. No VAT is accounted for on redemption. Where it is known that the voucher will be redeemed for zero-rated or reduced-rate goods or services than the VAT accounted for on sale will be at the zero-rate or reduced rate. A composite rate, calculated from retail scheme percentages, can be charged and accounted for on the sale of the voucher to the third party intermediary, if the voucher is redeemed for goods or services at a variety of rates.

Where an intermediate supplier of vouchers is operating a retail scheme the voucher may have different treatments depending upon the scheme used. The voucher sale will be included in the gross takings where a point of sale scheme is used, but outside the scheme where the apportionment method is used. Vouchers redeemed will normally be included in a direct calculation scheme, but when sold it is only necessary to account for VAT on the value in excess of the face-value. Vouchers sold on invoice to other businesses are not included in retail schemes.

35.3.13 Manufacturer promotions

Manufacturers may offer their own sales promotions to retail customers that have no impact on the retailer's VAT position. For example, the customer may be able to claim a 'cash-back' directly from the manufacturer on proof of purchase. This may enable the manufacturer to reduce his taxable amount, but will have no effect on either the retailer's input tax claim or output tax liability.

35.3.14 Jointly funded promotions

Manufacturers may participate with retailers in customer promotions. If the manufacturer makes a payment towards the cost of the promotion, for example towards advertising costs, this is consideration for a supply of taxable advertising services by the retailer to the manufacturer. The retailer would account for this outside the retail scheme and would normally issue a tax invoice to the manufacturer.

> **Planning point**
>
> A manufacturer may also subsidise a promotion by making a payment towards the cost of the promotional benefit to the customer, such as meeting half of the 'saving' made by the customer on purchasing the goods. Payments from the manufacturer are additional consideration for the customer's goods and the retailer brings them into DGT when received.

35.3.15 Manufacturers' coupons

Manufacturers issue money-off coupons to retail customers, often on the packaging of an earlier purchase but also electronically, by post and printed in or distributed with newspapers and magazines. When the retailer accepts a coupon in part payment for goods, the amount paid by the customer is taken into DGT, but the coupon is excluded. When coupons are subsequently redeemed by the manufacturer, the amount received for the goods is added to the retailer's DGT. If the manufacturer pays a separate handling charge, this is consideration for a separate standard-rated supply of services by the retailer.

35.3.16 Manufacturers' promotions aimed at retailers

Manufacturers offer a number of promotional schemes intended to encourage retailers to purchase more of their products. The manufacturer's invoice will show the VAT attributable to a particular promotional purchase. The treatment by the retailer of the commonest promotions is as follows.

1. Dealer loaders where 'reward goods' are provided when either the retailer places a single order of a specified size or achieves a target purchase level over a set period. HMRC accept that the manufacturer will have costed the price of the reward goods into the scheme and no adjustment is needed to the VAT amount shown on the manufacturer's invoices.

2. Retrospective discounts granted when a certain level of purchases has been reached. The manufacturer may issue a credit note. This does not have to contain a VAT credit, but if it does the retailer must adjust his input tax claim accordingly. Alternatively, the manufacturer may satisfy the discount by supplying further goods at no charge. If these goods are at the same rate of VAT as the original

purchases and are supplied to the retailer for business purposes, the manufacturer may issue a 'no charge' invoice without VAT. The retailer has no VAT accounting to perform in these cases.

3. Reward goods given away or taken for personal use by the retailer. If the reward goods are used as business gifts by the retailer, the business gift rules apply and the retailer must account for output tax if the cost to him of the goods exceeded £50. Where the goods were supplied as part of a promotion, such as a dealer loader, where the retailer has paid for some goods and others were 'free', it will be necessary to allocate part of the total payment to the goods used as gifts to determine their cost for the purpose of applying the gift rules. If the retailer takes goods for private use, their cost must be added to DGT. An adjustment to ESPs may also be necessary.

35.3.17 Discrepancies in daily gross takings

Retailers have to account for VAT once the supply to the customer takes place. Sales proceeds that are stolen from the till cannot be deducted from DGT as they are proceeds of sales that have taken place. Where it can be identified, pre-till cash theft – that is cash received from customers but stolen before the sale is recorded – must also be included in DGT. It can be very difficult to establish whether the cause of a shortfall in cash takings is attributable to theft of cash or of stock, which does not require any adjustment to DGT.

HMRC have used retail industry statistics of the various causes of loss to assess the extent of adjustments due in these circumstances. They advise retailers who identify unexplained accounting discrepancies between stock and sales to consider the extent to which this relates to unrecorded sales, such as theft of cash by staff, and to add the value of such unrecorded sales back to DGT. They expect this to be done in the VAT accounting period in which the theft occurred or that the retailer apportions the value across periods on a fair and reasonable basis. Also, in the absence of evidence to the contrary, they expect the adjustments to be in proportion to the usual sales mix and not, for example, to be allocated exclusively to zero-rated sales.

> ### *Planning point*
>
> Because DGT are a key element of the calculation of retailers' VAT liabilities, HMRC will carefully check the accuracy of the records. A simple check is to apply expected margins to the cost price of purchases and compare the resulting figure with recorded takings. Of course, there will be many reasons why anticipated margins are not achieved. These include theft of stock and end-of-range and other sale price promotions. Retailers should keep a note of circumstances where expected margins are not achieved which can be used to reconcile actual and expected gross takings figures.

35.4   Expected selling prices

The direct calculation schemes and apportionment scheme 2 use ESPs rather than actual selling prices to split supplies between the different rates of VAT. There are three typical approaches to setting ESPs. The retailer can:

- apply individual mark-ups to the cost of each line of goods;
- apply the mark-ups to classes of goods, for example fruit and vegetables, rather than to individual lines; or
- use the recommended retail prices of the goods.

The retailer may use another approach if it gives a fair and reasonable result.

HMRC will only allow the class of goods method if the retailer cannot use the line of goods method and:

- the classes of goods used are commercially based, for example, consist of items normally displayed together;
- mark-ups are reviewed quarterly; and
- the variation in mark-up between individual lines in the group does not exceed 10 per cent.

The retail price method must be supported by suppliers' invoices showing tax-inclusive recommended retail prices and distinguishing sales at each VAT rate and total sales at each rate.

> ### *Planning point*
>
> Once chosen, the method must be used consistently so it is important to ensure that the method both gives a reasonable result and is not excessively costly to use. Because of the importance of ESPs in the VAT liability calculation, events that could affect them have to be taken into account.

The retailer has to adjust ESPs at the end of each quarter to allow for the impact of price variations such as the following:

- wastage, sell-by-date reductions and breakages – although some allowance can be made when originally setting ESPs these should be adjusted in light of actual losses, particularly where these are due to unanticipated events such as flood damage, exceptional weather or equipment failure;
- loss of stock from theft, short deliveries to stores, etc.;
- special offers and promotions to the extent that these were not anticipated when setting ESPs; and
- bad debts written off in the period.

These adjustments must also be made on a consistent basis and records kept of how they were arrived at. In some cases, such as stock loss, it may only be possible to estimate their effect. HMRC will usually expect some allowance for cash losses also to have been made in calculating DGT as it is unlikely that only stock losses will have occurred.

Planning point

If the retailer cannot work out these adjustments to ESPs it may be possible to obtain HMRC agreement to using techniques such as sampling to estimate the adjustments or omit adjustments where this will not distort the scheme. If this cannot be done, the retailer will have to consider another scheme which does not rely on ESPs, such as point of sale.

The apportionment and direct calculation schemes assume that goods will be sold at the same rate of tax at which they were bought. This is not always the case. There are special calculations dealing with pharmacists and caterers for whom this change of rate is a particular feature of their business. It can happen in other circumstances, for example fish or meat is zero-rated when offered for human consumption but standard-rated if held out as pet food.

If goods are bought to be resold at a different rate of VAT, the retailer must keep them as separate stock and show them in the records of goods received for resale at the rate at which they will be sold. If their eventual destiny is unknown when the goods are purchased, they can be kept in a common stock recorded at the VAT rate at which they were purchased. When put up for sale at another rate, the goods must be taken out of the scheme records at their original rate and re-entered at the rate at which they will be sold.

35.5   Bespoke retail schemes

35.5.1 Introduction

The retail schemes are inevitably inaccurate in that they can only provide an approximate VAT liability figure compared to that obtained by identifying the liability of each supply on a tax invoice. Also, the information needed to operate them, especially for the determination of ESPs, may not be easy to access and some approximation, such as the use of statistical sampling, may be necessary.

These potential errors become more significant as the size and complexity of the retail business increases. Very large retailers with a VAT-exclusive retail turnover in excess of £130 million cannot use a standard retail scheme and must agree a bespoke retail scheme with HMRC.

> **Planning point**
>
> Retailers using a standard scheme must monitor their turnover as it approaches the £130 million level so that they can have a bespoke scheme in place. If a bespoke scheme has not been agreed when the threshold is breached, HMRC expect it to be applied retrospectively to that date once it has been agreed.

If a scheme is not agreed with HMRC, the retailer must either issue tax invoices or adopt the normal basis of VAT accounting. The normal basis does not require the issue of a VAT invoice for each sale, merely the ability to record the tax-exclusive value of each supply and the VAT due and to produce total figures periodically.

A bespoke scheme may be based on the standard retail schemes, although, because of their inherent inaccuracies, not those designed for the smallest retailers. It may also specify the use of different schemes in different parts of the business. It will differ from the standard schemes in that definitions of DGT, ESPs and other areas of potential difficulty, such as the treatment of stock transfers between parts of the business using different schemes, will be spelt out in detail in the scheme agreement.

A retailer who is required to have a bespoke retail scheme must set out the following details in a written scheme agreement.

1. Those supplies that will be covered by the scheme and those that will be accounted for normally.

2. Details of how supplies are valued, DGT measured and ESPs calculated.

3. The starting date for the scheme. If this is the first time on which a bespoke scheme has to be used, this will be the date on which the retailer became ineligible to use a standard scheme.

4. The date on which the scheme is due to be reviewed. Most schemes will run for two years between reviews.

HMRC will agree to the use of a bespoke scheme if it meets the following conditions.

1. It applies to retail sales only. Non-retail sales and sales to VAT-registered traders cannot be dealt with in a bespoke scheme except for occasional cash sales, such as petrol.

2. The retailer cannot account for sales on the normal basis.

3. The scheme is commercially realistic, that is, it reflects the trading patterns of the business and does not unnecessarily complicate either the retailer's VAT records or HMRC ability to audit them.

4. The scheme gives a fair and reasonable result. This does not necessarily mean a result that is as close as possible to the liability that would arise if a scheme was not used. In deciding whether it is fair and reasonable, the cost of operating the scheme must be balanced against its accuracy.

When they are satisfied that the scheme set out in the agreement meets these conditions and has been drawn up on the basis of full disclosure by the retailer of matters relevant to the scheme, HMRC will sign the agreement. It will also be signed by representatives of the retailer and will then form a contract between them. The scheme will normally only be changed before its expiry date if the retailer's circumstances change to such an extent that it no longer gives a fair and reasonable result, in which case HMRC must be notified immediately in writing.

HMRC are entitled to withdraw their approval to a bespoke scheme if:

- it becomes necessary for the protection of the revenue;
- it does not produce a fair and reasonable result; or
- the retailer could account normally.

In the absence of changes in the retailer's pattern of trade or of failure by the retailer to make full disclosure of relevant matters in the scheme agreement, HMRC should only be able to withdraw approval in exceptional circumstances. Their original agreement to the scheme would signify that they were satisfied that it did not violate the above tests.

If it becomes clear that a scheme is fundamentally flawed, approval may be withdrawn retrospectively.

Planning point

In reviewing a bespoke scheme there are a number of areas to which HMRC will pay particular attention. These are set out in *Notice 727/2*. These issues may arise in applying the standard schemes and any retailer to whose scheme these matters are significant should ensure that they retain the evidence and/or working papers that can support their figures as these are points that are more likely to be reviewed by HMRC.

Some of the issues that have wide significance are set out below.

35.5.2 Using the point-of-sale scheme

Aspects of the scheme that should be identified include:

- product codings, the level at which they apply, frequency of changes and procedures for dealing with errors;
- methods of allocating refunds between VAT rates;
- allocation of staff discounts between VAT codes;
- treatment of sales through non-EPOS and remote tills and till breakdowns; and
- the treatment of issue and redemption of vouchers and of special offers.

35.5.3 Determining daily gross takings

The scheme should set out the method of computing DGT, for example from till rolls, and how till breakdowns and non-standard sales will be dealt with.

In addition, reasons for adjustments to DGT and how these have been dealt with should be specified. These can include:

- payments received for redeeming manufacturer's coupons;
- foreign coins, dishonoured cheques and forged notes;
- exempt and outside-the-scope supplies and non-retail sales;
- refunds, overs and shorts and other till discrepancies;
- deposits and trade-ins; and
- staff discounts.

35.5.4 Setting estimated selling prices

The factors used in setting ESPs should be set out to include:

- how they are calculated and special situations such as mixed-rate products and how direct deliveries to customers are dealt with;
- the level at which the scheme will be operated, department, store, etc. and how transfers between areas are dealt with;
- whether VAT codes will be used at line, product or department level and how errors will be corrected;
- a listing of VAT codes and how often they change; and
- how periodic fluctuations will be dealt with, for example by use of longer periods as the basis of the estimation, or bringing in opening and closing stock figures.

The method should also give reasons for adjusting ESPs and how these are dealt with in either the direct calculation or apportionment schemes. These can include:

- refunds and staff discounts;
- voucher transactions;
- wastage, leakage and theft;
- price changes, sell-by date, multi-saver and other price reductions; and
- acquiring or disposing of a part of the business or unusual quantities of stock.

Planning point

Retailers whose turnover does not exceed £130 million can also use a bespoke scheme. They may wish to do this where their business requires a mix of schemes or other variation not within the standard retail schemes or where they want the certainty of obtaining prior HMRC approval of their method of using the retail schemes.

A voluntary bespoke scheme is prepared in the same way as a compulsory scheme. When the use of bespoke schemes was introduced in 1997 they were required for retailers with turnover exceeding £10 million. Retailers in this group have been able to revert to using the standard schemes since the turnover limit was increased in 2000. However, many continue to use bespoke schemes because the greater detail specified about their operations reduces the risk of HMRC challenging the VAT liabilities declared by the retailer on the grounds of inaccuracies in their method.

Planning point

Setting out in a scheme document the treatment of problem areas, such as those noted above, means that the approach adopted is approved in advance by HMRC.

35.6   Imports and exports

35.6.1 Purchases

Purchases from abroad are dealt with either as acquisitions, if bought from a registered trader in another EU member state, or as imports. Acquisitions require the vendor to have been given the retailer's VAT registration number, so that local VAT does not have to be charged, and the appropriate entries on the retailer's VAT returns in order to correctly account for VAT. If the value of acquisitions is sufficiently high, the retailer may also have to submit UK Supplementary Statistical Declarations (SSDs).

In the case of goods imported from outside the EU, the import formalities may be dealt with by a shipping agent, or the retailer may pay any VAT and duty due on entry or by using the postponed accounting system.

VAT accounted for on acquisition or entry should be recoverable as input tax. The full purchase price of the goods, including costs of shipping, insurance, etc. and duty is entered into the appropriate retail scheme records.

35.6.2 Sales to foreign customers

Sales to foreign customers fall into a number of different categories.

Unregistered customers in the EU

Sales made to retail customers in the UK will always be subject to the appropriate UK VAT rate if the customer is normally resident in the UK or another EU member state. These sales will be dealt with in the retail scheme. If the retailer ships the goods to the customer's home address the sale will also be subject to UK VAT and go into the retail scheme, unless the tax-exclusive value of all such goods shipped to any one EU member state in a calendar year brings the distance selling rules into play.

Distance selling

If the distance selling threshold is breached, the retailer stops accounting for UK VAT on sales of goods that he ships to the other country and, instead, registers for and accounts for VAT on the retail sales in that country. This will trigger other requirements, such as submitting UK SSDs for goods shipped from the UK under the distance selling regime. Goods sold under the distance selling arrangements must be removed from the UK retail scheme records.

The distance selling threshold adopted by Austria, France, Germany, Luxembourg and The Netherlands is €100,000. All the remaining EU member states have adopted a lower limit of €35,000. (The corresponding limit in the UK is £70,000.) Retailers that operate large personal export departments need to monitor the level of shipments to retail customers in other EU member states to check whether registration under these rules is necessary. The distance selling rules do not apply if the retailer is not responsible for shipping the goods. A retailer who ships excise goods to the customer's home state has to account for VAT and duty in that state irrespective of the aggregate value of such shipments.

Law: Value Added Tax Regulations 1995 (SI 1995/2518), reg. 98

Other guidance: VAT Notice 725, s. 15

Sales to VAT-registered EU customers

Goods sold to another business that is VAT registered in another EU member state may be zero-rated if the retailer obtains the customer's VAT registration number and ships the goods to another EU country. The customer's VAT registration number must be shown on the invoice for the sale and the retailer must retain proof that the goods have been shipped abroad. These sales are dealt with outside the retail scheme and may also require submission of EC sales lists and SSDs.

Sales to non-EU customers

Sales of goods to retail customers from outside the EU may be made 'VAT free'. This can happen in different ways. If the retailer ships the goods directly to a place outside the EU, they may be zero-rated as exported goods provided that the retailer meets HMRC requirements with regard to obtaining proof of export. These exports are excluded from the point-of-sale scheme and have specific treatments within the apportionment and direct calculation schemes. Exports to overseas business customers are dealt with in the same way.

Retail exports

The retailer may also operate the retail export scheme. This allows customers from outside the EU to take goods with them or have them delivered to their point of departure from the UK. Having established that the customer is an overseas visitor entitled to use the scheme, the retailer provides the customer with a VAT refund document. This can be HMRC form VAT 407, a version produced by the retailer or a refund company, or a retail export scheme sales invoice approved by HMRC. The document is certified by a HMRC authority when the customer leaves the EU, the details depending on how the customer travels, and is then returned to the retailer. The retailer may then treat the sale as zero-rated in accordance with the rules of the scheme that is being used.

As zero-rating depends on the certified document being returned to the retailer, it is sensible for the VAT to be refunded to the customer only after this has happened. Retailers do not have to operate the retail export scheme, and they may limit it to certain types or values of goods, may charge a handling fee or may engage a refund company to administer the scheme on their behalf.

Other guidance: *VAT Notice 704*

35.6.3 Electronic retailing or 'e-tailing'

Electronic retailing, or e-tailing, has made it easier for a UK retailer to locate and sell to customers in other countries. The e-tailer may simply use a website as an advertising medium and arrange the sale through traditional correspondence or the order may be taken electronically. When the goods are shipped to the customer the VAT treatment is identical to that which applies to other export sales.

Sales to non-registered customers in another EU member state will be dealt with in the retail scheme, until the distance selling rules mean that the sale has to be treated as made in the customer's country. Goods shipped to customers outside the EU can be zero-rated provided that the retailer obtains proof of export.

As well as being an advertising and ordering medium, the internet can be a delivery channel. Software and games can be delivered electronically and so can music and literature. This causes a number of problems. Where UK VAT is applicable, the VAT rate can be affected by the delivery medium. For example, a book is zero-rated but its contents delivered electronically are standard-rated.

A further complication is that the supply may be deemed to take place in a different jurisdiction depending on whether the product is delivered in tangible goods form or as electronic 'digitised' goods. The latter are regarded as supplies of services for which the place of supply rules differ from supplies of goods.

Some retailers have set up operations outside the EU (with the Channel Islands being regarded a prime location). Goods sold that are below the low value importation limit can be imported by the customer VAT-free and Duty-free. Goods with a value of less than £15 can be imported VAT-free by the customer. Goods with a value of less than £135 can also be imported duty free. Where the values exceed these limits, the customer will be held liable to account for the VAT and/or duty. This will be collected by the postal service or courier. The VAT and/or duty advantage is offset to a degree by the cost of delivery. In addition, the Channel Islands are introducing controls on the 'fulfillment houses' that deliver the goods. In addition, the European Commission has asked member states to control this trade to prevent the VAT saving being abused.

These issues are covered in greater detail in **Chapter 26**.

35.7   Pharmacists, caterers and florists

35.7.1 Retail pharmacists

Because of the way that their businesses operate, retail pharmacists, caterers and florists have special requirements for their retail schemes.

Most retailers purchase goods at the same rate of VAT as they will sell them and the retail schemes work on that assumption. However, retail pharmacists buy most prescription products at the standard rate but may sell them at that rate as over-the-counter medicines or zero-rated when dispensed against a private or NHS prescription.

Moreover, some products, such as special food items available on prescription, may be zero-rated when purchased by the pharmacist. Because of the number of standard-rated purchases that are dispensed at the zero rate, carrying out the standard retail scheme calculations will overstate the proportion of standard-rated sales. A further complication is that NHS prescriptions may be dispensed either without charge or for the flat rate NHS prescription charge. Additionally, the pharmacist receives a payment from the NHS at a later date which covers zero-rated prescriptions and, also, payments for other items, such as rota payments, liable at other rates.

A pharmacist using the point-of-sale scheme can identify the correct VAT rate when payment for prescriptions is received either from patients or the NHS and can include these in DGT, but adjustments are needed under the other schemes, except apportionment scheme 2 which cannot be used with the retail chemist adjustment.

A pharmacist using either of the direct calculation schemes or apportionment scheme 1 must make the following adjustment.

Table 35.3

	Action	
1	Calculate DGT including prescription payments received from patients and the NHS.	£...
2	Calculate output tax according to the scheme rules.	£...
3	Total payments received in the period for zero-rated dispensed goods, even if supplied in another period.	£...
4	Estimate the value of goods included at (3) that were zero-rated when received.	£...
5	Take (4) from (3).	£...
6	Multiply (5) by 1/6 (using a VAT rate of 20 per cent) to work out the amount of VAT included in (2) on dispensed goods.	£...
7	Output tax is (2) minus (6).	£...

This is a very complicated scheme that requires accurate records and great care.

Planning point

The estimation at step 4 must give a fair and reasonable value for payments for dispensed goods that were zero-rated on receipt and were included in the total payments received in the period. This must be based on a sample of purchases for a representative period that takes account of seasonal fluctuations, details of which must be kept. The pharmacist must carry out a new estimation in each tax period.

Other guidance: *VAT Notice 727*, s. 9

35.7.2 Caterers

Like pharmacists, caterers also purchase goods, zero-rated food, that they may sell at the standard rate in the course of catering. The point-of-sale scheme will correctly state the VAT position but the other retail schemes will understate the amount of standard-rated sales made by caterers.

Planning point

HMRC prefer caterers to use the point-of-sale scheme, but if satisfied that the caterer is unable to apply it, will allow a caterer with expected tax exclusive annual turnover not exceeding £1 million to use the catering adaptation. The caterer must notify HMRC that the adaptation will be used and keep a record of DGT.

For each tax period the caterer must carry out the following calculation.

Table 35.4

	Action	
1	Calculate DGT according to the relevant scheme rules.	£...
2	Calculate the percentage of total catering sales liable at the standard rate.	£...
3	Apply percentage (2) to DGT.	£...
4	Multiply (3) by 1/6 to give the output tax on catering sales from the period.	£...

The calculation must give a fair and reasonable result. The calculation of the percentage of standard-rated sales must be based on a sample of sales for a representative period that takes account of seasonal fluctuations, details of which, including when and where it was taken, must be kept. The caterer must carry out a new calculation in each tax period.

Other guidance: *VAT Notice 727*, s. 8

Caters must also consider what is meant by 'premises'. The current legislation (VATA 1994, Sch. 8, Grp 1, Note 3(a) states that the supply of food 'for consumption on the premises on which it is supplied' is a taxable supply of catering. In the 2012 Budget it was announced that the definition of premises was to be altered, following consultation, as the borderline between on-premises consumption and off-premises consumption of cold food was blurred and had been subject to much litigation over the years. In an attempt to *simplify* the tax (and extend its base) the definition is to be changed with effect from 1 October 2012. It is intended that premises will include all areas that are set aside for the consumption of food even where they are shared with other caterers or retailers. This will mean that food courts in shopping centres, motorway service stations, seated areas outside cafes, etc. will be regarded as premises. HMRC state that they do not intend to include in the definition of premises benches that are used for resting in a shopping centre, airport departure seating in the definition of premises for catering establishments.

35.7.3 Florists

Through their membership of Interflora and similar organisations, florists may be paid by customers for flowers that are supplied by another florist or supply flowers where payment has been received by another florist. Special rules are required to deal with the arrangements for making settlements between the sending florists, that is those being paid by the customer, and the executing florists, that is those fulfilling the order.

If the florist belongs to an agency that issues invoices for the sales made by the florist, the agency documentation will show the 'self-billed' output tax due from the florist for sales made via the agency. This must be added to any other amount of output tax calculated using a retail scheme.

Sending and executing members must make the following adjustments to their retail schemes.

Table 35.5

Scheme	Sending member action	Executing member action
Point-of-sale	Include payments received in DGT when the order is taken (no further adjustment needed).	Exclude payments received from the agency from DGT and account for any tax due outside the retail scheme.
Apportionment schemes 1 and 2	Identify the value of sales made as sending member from agency documentation and account for VAT outside the scheme.	Identify from agency documentation any tax due and account for it outside the retail scheme.
	Exclude payments received for sending member sales from DGT.	Exclude agency payments from DGT.
		Exclude the value of flowers from purchase records if using apportionment scheme 1.
		If using apportionment scheme 2, adjust ESPs for the value of flowers sent as executing member and accounted for outside the retail scheme.
Direct calculation schemes 1 and 2	Identify the value of sales made as sending member from agency documentation and account for VAT outside the scheme.	Identify from agency documentation any tax due and account for it outside the retail scheme.
	Exclude payments received for sending member sales from DGT.	Exclude agency payments from DGT.
		Adjust ESPs for the value of flowers sent as executing member and accounted for outside the retail scheme.

Other guidance: *VAT Notice 727*, s. 10

35.8   VAT compliance and control issues for retailers

35.8.1 Factors to be considered

VAT-registered traders account for their own tax, so HMRC have wide powers to examine premises, books and records and related matters in order to ensure that the traders' declarations are correct. Retailers are at the end of the chain of registered traders and their VAT returns account for VAT collected from the general public: the final consumers.

This is a vital step in the VAT collection process and HMRC expend considerable resource ensuring correct collection of tax at the retail level. The factors that they consider will include the:

- registration for VAT at the correct time;
- correct accounting for input tax;
- choice of a special scheme that gives a fair and reasonable result;
- correct treatment of transactions outside the special schemes;
- preparation and retention of accurate records;
- reliability of figures declared on returns; and
- timely submission of returns and payment of tax.

35.8.2 VAT registration

Retailers can generate annual turnover of up to £70,000, excluding income such as bank interest which is exempt from VAT, before they have to register for VAT. Once this figure is reached, they have to account for VAT at the appropriate rates on sales to customers. Care must be taken to check both the historic turnover and the expected turnover for the next 30 days to ensure that the turnover threshold is not being breached. They may also recover VAT charged on their purchases and must submit regular VAT returns together with paying over the excess of VAT collected from customers over input tax paid on purchases. Retailers with taxable turnover below £70,000 may voluntarily register for VAT with the same consequences. Usually a retailer is dealing with final consumers who cannot reclaim VAT, so it is advantageous to delay registration until the retailer must register, unless significant costs have been incurred on, say, shop fitting.

A retailer starting up in business may find it helpful to register as an intending trader before any sales have been made. Provided that HMRC are satisfied of the intention to trade, the retailer may register and recover VAT incurred on start-up expenses, shopfitting, purchasing stock and other expenses as they arise. This not only improves cash flow but may increase overall recovery. The usual date for registering is when trading starts. Recovery of VAT on services (such as shop fitting) is then restricted to that incurred within six months before that date, so there is a balance to be drawn between delaying registration so that no VAT needs to be accounted for on sales and the ability to reclaim VAT incurred on set up costs. Intending trader registration from the beginning of the start-up period enables all VAT on services to be recovered even if it arises more than six months before trading starts.

As there are penalties for late registration, retailers need to monitor turnover as it approaches the registration threshold. There are two tests that have to be considered.

Test 1

If there are reasonable grounds for believing that the value of taxable supplies in the next 30 days alone will be more than £70,000, the retailer must inform HMRC before the end of the period and will be registered from its beginning.

Test 2

If at the end of a month the cumulative value of taxable supplies in the 12 months then ending exceeds £70,000, the retailer must notify HMRC within 30 days of the end of the month and will be registered from the end of the following month.

The second test is the one likely to apply to most retailers and there is time after the threshold has been reached for them to make arrangements to account for VAT. If a retailer takes over an existing business as a going concern and the previous owner was either VAT registered or liable to be registered, the historic turnover of the business will be attributed to the retailer in determining if he should be registered for VAT.

If the retailer makes primarily zero-rated supplies, so that input tax would normally exceed output tax, he can apply to be exempted from VAT registration.

Retailers whose turnover is approaching the registration threshold may attempt to avoid registration by splitting (disaggregating) the business so that different parts are carried on by different individuals or partnerships each operating below the registration limit. HMRC may direct that, from the date of their direction, these separate parts be treated as a single entity liable to be VAT registered if avoidance of VAT is a result of the split.

Increasingly, HMRC are arguing in such cases that two apparently separate businesses in different legal entities are in reality operating as a single partnership. Not only is this a simpler procedure than issuing a direction, they can then enforce registration retrospectively to the time when their combined turnover exceeded the registration threshold. They can assess for output tax back to this date and collect a late registration penalty.

Whether their contention succeeds depends on the facts of the case. Where two businesses operate closely together, such as where a wife provides catering in a pub where the husband is licensee and one or both is unregistered, evidence of genuine separation of the businesses should be kept. This could include evidence of separate till, banking, purchasing and staffing arrangements and agreements between the parties relating to use of premises and equipment, payments for fuel and power and so on.

Treatment as a single entity for VAT purposes is not always disadvantageous. Larger retailers may operate as a number of separate companies. Typically, these may be responsible for the different store formats in the group and administrative functions such as property, finance (including customer credit and store cards) logistics and 'head office' functions. Where there is trading between the different companies there may be both administrative and VAT savings from registering the companies as a VAT group. This is possible where they are established or have a fixed establishment in the UK and are under common control. Transactions between VAT group members are effectively ignored for VAT purposes, no VAT liability arises and there is no requirement to issue VAT invoices. One of the companies becomes the 'representative member' and is responsible for submitting a single VAT return showing the VAT position of the whole VAT group. However, the group members become jointly and severally liable for its aggregate VAT liabilities.

It is possible to omit some companies from the group and to form several VAT group registrations from members of a single corporate group. VAT registrations can then be structured to take account of the ease of collating data for VAT returns as well as any VAT savings. Supplies between the different VAT registrations formed in this way are subject to the usual VAT accounting rules. HMRC may refuse an application for group registration if a company is ineligible or 'for the protection of the revenue'. The latter provision is not usually invoked, even if VAT savings result from grouping, provided that they arise from the normal operation of the VAT group rules.

For more details on registration, see **Chapter 3**; and for information on VAT groups, see **Chapter 4**.

35.8.3 VAT on purchases

Once registered for VAT, the retailer can recover VAT on purchases used for business purposes. The essential compliance requirement is that the retailer has a tax invoice addressed to him that shows the required information about the supply. This may be a full or less detailed tax invoice (see **35.8.5** below) or a cash and carry invoice. The latter is an invoice that may be used by cash and carry warehouses selling to registered traders. It takes the form of a till receipt, modified to show the information required to be shown on a VAT invoice, and distinguishes goods at different VAT rates. If goods are identified by product code, the retailer must keep a copy of the codes.

VAT cannot be recovered on purchases for personal or non-business use, or on expenditure attributable to exempt supplies. The latter include bank interest and rent from property not subject to an option to tax. Many retailers will not suffer any loss of input tax as a result of making exempt supplies because of the *de minimis* reliefs. These apply where input tax attributable to exempt supplies is not more than £625 per month on average and not more than 50 per cent of all input tax. In these circumstances all input tax can be recovered.

When first registered for VAT, it is likely that the retailer will have stock and assets on hand which have borne VAT that has not been recovered. The newly registered business can make a claim to recover the VAT on these assets provided it was incurred not more than three years before the registration date. VAT incurred on services supplied to the business in the six months before registration can also be reclaimed.

35.8.4 VAT on sales

From the registration date the retailer must charge VAT on sales. Thus, it will be necessary to consider whether any pricing changes are needed. In practice, goods will probably be sold at a price near to the manufacturer's recommendation, which will have taken VAT into account, so few changes are likely to be needed for goods purchased for resale. Goods that the retailer has grown or made may need a price uplift to cover the VAT now chargeable. In carrying out this exercise the retailer will have to become aware of the VAT rate applicable to different products so that correct pricing decisions can be taken.

Assuming that the retailer does not wish to use either invoice-based or normal VAT accounting and total taxable turnover does not exceed £150,000 (excluding VAT and total business income is below £187,500 including VAT; this increases to £191,500 on 4th January 2011 when the VAT rate increases to 20 per cent), the retailer can choose between using a retail scheme and the flat rate scheme. The latter will often be the easiest to use but, depending on the product mix, the flat rate percentage used to calculate the VAT liability may produce a higher tax liability figure.

> ### *Planning point*
>
> If the retailer's turnover exceeds £150,000, or the flat rate scheme is unsuitable, the retailer needs to decide which of the retail schemes or mix of them to use. A bespoke scheme will probably be unnecessarily complex for a small retailer. The choice between schemes will depend on the retailer's ability to operate them (for example, can VAT rates be identified at point of sale?) or to do the relevant calculations, such as working out estimated selling prices. If considering either apportionment scheme 1 or direct calculation scheme 1 the retailer should consider when the turnover limits of the schemes might be reached. If a change in scheme was likely to be necessary in the near future, it might prove more cost effective to use one of the other schemes from the outset.

35.8.5 Records

A VAT-registered retailer has to keep a till roll or other record of DGT and the records and calculations needed to calculate output tax under the retail scheme being used. VAT-registered customers may request a VAT invoice for their purchases and copies of these must be kept. A VAT invoice for a sale of goods must show:

- a sequential number based on one or more series that uniquely identifies the document;
- the issuer's name, address and VAT registration number;
- the time of supply (tax point);
- the date the invoice is issued (if different to the time of supply);
- the customer's name and address;
- a description of the goods or services supplied;
- the unit price where relevant;
- the total price charged, excluding VAT;
- the rate of any cash discount offered; and
- the total amount of VAT charged, shown in sterling.

A retailer may also issue a modified tax invoice. This shows VAT-inclusive values rather than exclusive VAT values for each supply. For most retail sales, that is those with a value below £250, a less detailed tax invoice can be issued that shows only the following information:

- the retailer's name, address and VAT registration number;
- the time of supply (tax point);
- a description of the goods or services supplied; and
- for each VAT rate, the total amount payable in sterling, including VAT.

Credit-card vouchers may be adapted to show this information.

Other than for occasional cash sales, sales to VAT-registered customers should be dealt with outside the retail scheme, as should other non-retail supplies such as rental income.

Retailers do not normally have to issue an invoice at all, unless a customer requests one, unless the transaction exceeds £250. Where the transaction exceeds this value the retailer must issue a proper tax invoice.

> **Planning point**
>
> Purchase invoices should be kept in such a way that they can readily be traced to the VAT account and return. Purchases of retail stock that go into the retail scheme calculations should be distinguished from purchases of fixed assets, overhead expenses, expenditure on non-retail activities and other expenditure that should not be included in the retail scheme calculations.

The retailer must maintain a VAT account that shows for each VAT accounting period the 'tax payable portion' and the 'tax allowable portion' of the retailer's VAT affairs. VAT returns must usually be submitted quarterly, although a retailer who is regularly in a repayment situation, such as a grocer or other trader selling mostly zero-rated goods, can apply to submit returns monthly. HMRC may require VAT returns to be submitted monthly; this is normally required only where the retailer has a poor compliance record.

Retailers may keep their records on computer and preserve records in this way or on microfilm, microfiche, etc. Stored data must be readily convertible into printed form if required by HMRC. They may also have access to any computer on which VAT-relevant information is stored to check its operation and the stored information. It is advisable to invite HMRC to review any new computer system to ensure that records stored on it will meet their requirements.

Any VAT liability must be paid to HMRC by the due date for submission of the VAT return, which is the last day of the month following the VAT return period. An extra seven days to submit returns and pay the tax due may be allowed to traders paying by BACS and similar means. If the retailer adopts annual accounting, only one VAT return has to be submitted each year but payments on account of the VAT liability are spread over the year. Retailers with an annual turnover in excess of £2 million may be required to make monthly payments on account of their VAT liabilities.

35.8.6 Records relating to non-retail sales

The use of a retail scheme does not alter the VAT accounting requirements for non-retail supplies made by the retailer. The retailer must issue tax invoices according to the normal rules and keep any other records needed for the particular transactions, such as proof of export or working papers calculating VAT recoveries on partly exempt recoveries. The retailer must keep non-retail purchases out of his retail scheme workings.

35.8.7 VAT control of retailers

As with other VAT-registered businesses, the amount of effort that HMRC will devote to checking the VAT affairs of a retailer depends on:

- the size of the business;
- its complexity; and
- their assessment of the revenue risk that it presents.

As largely cash businesses with unregistered customers, retailers do pose a greater risk than, say, a business that trades only with other registered businesses. However, a soundly run retail business should not be subjected to particularly onerous VAT control.

Small retailers may find that they only receive occasional VAT control visits. Large retailers may be subject to almost continuous control of some aspect of their business and specialists in accounting, computer systems, etc., may be involved. In either case, the officers will be seeking assurance of the reliability of the VAT accounting. Their general approach will be to obtain an understanding of the business by discussing its operations, visiting premises, etc. and to verify that the VAT return information is credible in the light of the information they have about its operations and their knowledge of the retail industry.

> ## Planning point
>
> Some officers, usually those dealing with the largest retailers, have considerable industry knowledge and they are able to share this with less experienced colleagues. The retailer should be aware that he has the greatest knowledge of how his own business functions and sharing this information with the control officers may help to avoid misunderstandings and possibly lengthy disputes about VAT liability.

Some aspects of the retailer's VAT affairs, such as registration, choice and changes of retail schemes and adjustments arising on acquiring and disposing of parts of the retail business will only arise occasionally. Recurring control issues will centre on the completeness and credibility of the VAT records.

> ## Planning point
>
> A basic credibility test is reconciling reported sales, DGT, with expected sales arrived at by marking up purchases. There will inevitably be differences and the retailer should retain evidence of the reasons for these, not just accounting records but other relevant information such as records of special sale events. Records of the consequent adjustments made to ESPs and other aspects of the retail scheme workings should also be kept. Shrinkage and unexplained losses generally are a particular problem area because of the need to distinguish between loss of stock, which does not affect the VAT liability, and loss of unrecorded sales proceeds, which may. The retailer should consider what evidence is available as to the causes of loss, which may include details of security measures, audit tests and even details of staff dismissed for theft.

As well as examining the retailer's records, control officers may also carry out additional credibility checking, such as cross-checking the retailer's purchase records with information held by suppliers.

If the control officer is not satisfied with the reported VAT liabilities, he has power to raise assessments in respect of tax liabilities that appear to have been understated or refunds that have been overclaimed. Assessments may be retrospective for up to three years, 20 years in the case of fraud, so substantial amounts could be at stake if the retailer cannot demonstrate the accuracy and reliability of his records.

In addition, interest and possibly penalties will be added to the assessments. For further details, see **Chapter 31**.

> ⚠ *Warning!*
>
> HMRC will, as part of their assurance visits, carefully monitor the use of retail schemes to ensure that they are not being manipulated. In addition, they will *test* the scheme at its weak points to ensure that the correct amount of VAT is being accounted for. A significant area of weakness in a point of sale scheme would be the incorrect coding of sales, either through incorrect bar coding or through incorrect use of a till. Where HMRC identify an error they will raise an assessment. It is then very difficult to challenge the assessment from the business records as HMRC will have already shown that the records are unreliable. Hence, the need to ensure coding is accurate and frequently reviewed. Similarly, the use of ESPs is open to challenge and a rigours methodology needs to be adopted to ensure that the ESP used is correct. Care needs to be taken to ensure that the ESP is calculated correctly and that all adjustments (such as vouchers, sales, wastage) are accurately calculated and documented to ensure any visiting officer can understand how the ESP has been calculated.

> ⚠ *Warning!*
>
> Retailers are sometimes recommended to use margin schemes or the global accounting scheme. This can be an appropriate method, but only where goods are purchased without an invoice. It is intended that these schemes are only used where the goods are usually acquired from a non-registered person.

35.8.8 Penalties

Penalties may be imposed for a wide range of compliance failures and reporting errors including the following.

1. Late registration – a penalty ranging between 30 per cent and 100 per cent of the tax that would subsequently have been paid if registration had taken place at the correct time.

2. Default surcharge – a penalty for repeated failures to meet deadlines for submission of VAT returns and payment of tax that increases from 2 per cent to 15 per cent of the tax due.

3. Failure to take reasonable care – 30 per cent maximum of the tax underdeclared.

4. Deliberate understatement – 70 per cent maximum of the tax underdeclared.

5   Deliberate and concealed – 100 per cent of the tax underdeclared.

The penalties can be reduced where there has been disclosure; greater reductions are offered for unprompted disclosure.

These penalties, which are covered in detail in **Chapter 31**, may be reduced or avoided if the retailer demonstrates to HMRC, or to a VAT and Duties Tribunal on appeal, that there was a reasonable excuse for the failure. Some can also be mitigated.

35.8.9 Compliance checks

As retailers deal with the final consumer and the businesses are by their nature cash businesses, HMRC take considerable care to check records and ensure that all the VAT due has been accounted for. The following is a brief description of some of the type checks that may be undertaken by HMRC.

Planning point

A business can conduct similar compliance checks to ensure that they are accounting for all the VAT due, identify problem areas (such as theft or loss) and to enable them to provide explanations for any perceived shortfalls.

One of the first checks that HMRC will undertake is a comparison between the annual accounts and the VAT returns. Is the sales figure on the returns the same (after adjusting for accruals) as the accounts? Are stock purchases and stock levels similar to input tax claimed (if sales have been suppressed, then purchases, particularly of zero-rated items may also have been suppressed). Are the ratios appropriate for this type of business? If high margin goods are being sold, is this reflected in the accounts? Is stock being turned over; if not, does this mean sales and purchases have been suppressed? Are profit margins similar to other similar businesses? If not, why not?

What wastage figures are being recorded? Is the level of wastage appropriate to the level of sales? Are some sales being disguised as wastage?

A bank reconciliation or cash reconciliation in a small business can demonstrate if cash is *leaking* from a business. Checking the cash book for unrecorded cash sales is a frequent check undertaken by HMRC.

What does the taxpayer understand by the term daily gross takings (DGT)? Are the correct figures being included in the DGT figure, and are there any deductions? Is the cash in the till reconciled to the till's Z total each day? If a multi-function till is used, what checks are made to ensure that the correct buttons are pressed?

Where goods are scanned, what efforts have been made to ensure that the VAT liabilities of the products are correct? Is the product code list checked regularly to ensure that the codes identify goods of different VAT rates correctly?

In businesses that sell goods in containers (such as take away restaurants) can the volume of sales be equated to the volume of containers purchased?

It is possible to mark up purchases (adjusting for stock changes and wastage) to calculate the expected selling price of goods. This is extremely effective in retailers that have a few main lines of goods sold (such as pubs). It is possible to make a rough calculation of the VAT that should have been accounted for in less than an hour in a pub or similar business.

HMRC will also observe transactions to determine if the correct amount of VAT has been declared. They may spend some time observing the number of customers entering or leaving the premises or may just watch a few transactions being processed on a till to see if errors are made.

35.8.10 Disputes and appeals

Where HMRC are not satisfied with the compliance position they may raise assessments together with interest and penalties where appropriate. Although the retailer has a right of appeal to a VAT and Duties Tribunal against these matters, there are other approaches that may prove both cost effective and place less of a strain on the business.

> **Planning point**
>
> The first approach is to try not to be the subject of an assessment. It will usually be fairly obvious when a control officer is not satisfied with information that he has. In these circumstances it is worth discussing the problems further in the hope that further explanation of how the business operates and the particular issue was handled may resolve the matter. Some control officers will advise the business when they are considering raising assessments and invite further information before they do so.

If an assessment has been issued, the retailer may appeal to the VAT and Duties Tribunal. There is an element of legal formality to this and it should be noted that there are strict time limits for lodging appeals. Before taking this step, the retailer can invoke the 'local review' process. This asks HMRC to have the case reviewed by another officer and enables the retailer to put forward further relevant information. In applying for a local review, the retailer should ask for an extension of time to appeal to the tribunal so that his rights there are not lost.

If local review does not resolve the issue, the retailer can lodge an appeal with the VAT and Duties Tribunal. There are procedures for progressing an appeal and time limits that the tribunal expects will be complied with. Professional assistance may be advisable but is not essential as the retailer may present his own case.

The tribunal has a legally qualified Chairman who may be supported by tribunal members with experience in retailing, accounting or other relevant matters. The tribunal will examine both the facts of the case and relevant legal issues. A retailer who wins his appeal may recover costs from HMRC and they may recover their costs from the retailer if they succeed, although in many cases they will not do so. While a case is under appeal, negotiations with HMRC can continue and these may result in a settlement being reached before the tribunal hears the case. The retailer may also claim costs relating to these negotiations if the appeal is settled by agreement in his favour.

The decision of the VAT and Duties Tribunal may be appealed by the losing side to the UK High Courts or the matter may be referred to the European Court of Justice if the dispute is over the interpretation of EU law in relation to VAT.

Chapter 37 considers the appeal process in detail.

35.8.11 Unjust enrichment

The VAT due on a retail sale is normally passed to the customer, being included in the selling price. For this reason, HMRC will refuse to refund VAT overpaid to them by a retailer, even if the tribunal has found in the retailer's favour in a liability dispute, unless the refunds will be passed on to customers who originally paid the VAT. The retailer may obtain a refund if it can be demonstrated that the VAT was not passed on, perhaps by showing that retail prices were set without taking VAT into account.

A retailer may want to pursue an appeal in order to confirm a reduced VAT liability for future sales. If the issue is VAT overpaid in the past, not only will refunds be limited to a three-year period, but HMRC may invoke the principle of unjust enrichment to deny them altogether. The retailer may face not only the cost of the appeal on the technical issue but of a further appeal on whether he was unjustly enriched.

35.9   Second-hand goods

35.9.1 Introduction

Many retailers accept goods as 'trade-ins' for new items and then sell the second-hand goods to retail customers. Others, such as antique dealers, trade exclusively in second-hand items. Sales of second-hand goods have their own special margin scheme, which is set out in *VAT Notice 718*, and are excluded from the retail schemes.

The margin schemes are covered in detail in **Chapter 7**.

35.10 Cases on retail VAT matters

This section provides a brief summary of some of the leading cases relating to the VAT treatment of retailers.

Table 35.6

Topic	Case	Summary
Daily gross takings record	*Courage Ltd* [1993] BVC 503	The company declared its DGT by reference to cash in the tills of its public houses. The tribunal held that it should have used figures taken from till rolls.
Powers for retail schemes	*Piercy (t/a Shared Earth)* [1995] BVC 1,178	The tribunal rejected an argument that the retail schemes were invalid because they differed from those mentioned in the 1978 derogation.
Retrospective change of retail scheme	*Waring* [1999] BVC 4,045 and various other cases.	The tribunal upheld the discretion of Customs to refuse to agree to a retrospective change of retail scheme unless there were exceptional circumstances. A small difference (4.5 per cent) in the amount of the retailer's VAT liability was not an exceptional circumstance. HMRC will allow a retrospective change where the business has been misdirected by HMRC or where the change will result in a more "accurate" liability and the difference is significant.
Effect of an agreed retail scheme	*Tesco plc* [1996] BVC 2,003	An agreed retail scheme represents a binding contract from which neither party can resile. (Note the case pre-dated the current bespoke schemes which allow Customs to withdraw agreement to a scheme retrospectively if it is fundamentally flawed.)
Discounts	*Freemans plc v C & E Commrs* (Case C-86/99) [2001] BVC 365	Discounts allowed to mail order agents in respect of their own purchases reduced DGT.

Topic	Case	Summary
Stock deficiencies	*WH Smith Ltd* [2000] BVC 2,237	The tribunal upheld the right of Customs to treat stock deficiencies as attributable to cash thefts by employees on the basis of trade statistics where the company did not produce evidence to the contrary.
Interest-free credit	*C & E Commrs v Primback Ltd* (Case C-34/99)[2001] BVC 315	A retailer providing 'interest-free credit' to customers could not reduce DGT by the amount paid to a third-party finance company for the provision of credit facilities.
Delivery charges	*C & E Commrs v Plantiflor Ltd* [2002] BVC 572	A retailer was not acting as the customer's agent in arranging delivery of goods by post. The separate 'postage" charge was for a taxable supply of services by the retailer and not an exempt postal charge.
Sales to VAT-registered customers	*Oxford, Swindon and Gloucester Co-operative Society Ltd v C & E Commrs* [1995] BVC 183	Sales to VAT-registered customers had to be dealt with outside the retail schemes.
Part exchange	*C & E Commrs v Bugeja* [2002] BVC 71	A retailer sold videos for £20. If one was part exchanged, a new video was supplied for £10. The consideration for the second video was £20, being the £10 cash paid by the customer plus the value of the returned video which both the retailer and the customer had treated as being £10.

Topic	Case	Summary
Introductory gifts	*Empire Stores v C & E Commrs* (Case C-33/93) [1994] BVC 253	A mail order company offered gifts to new customers and also to existing customers who introduced new customers, when a first order was placed. The court ruled that the 'gifts' were provided in consideration for the service of introducing a new customer, that is, they were made for consideration. The value of the supply was the cost of the goods to the retailer, that is, their subjective value to the retailer.
Introductory gifts and delivery charges	*Bertelsmann AG v Finanzamt Wiedenbrück* (Case C-380/99) [2001] BVC 403	In circumstances similar to those of *Empire Stores* the court ruled that the value of the supply had to include the costs of the incidental supply of delivering the gift goods to the customer.
Free meals for coach drivers	*Granada Group plc* [1991] BVC 524	Free meals and gift stamps given to coach drivers who brought passengers to a motorway service station were supplied for consideration which was the introduction of customers by the driver.
Free meals for coach drivers	*C & E Commrs v Westmorland Motorway Services Ltd* [1998] BVC 154	In similar circumstances to *Granada Group*, the subjective value to the caterer of the free meal was its published menu price.

Topic	Case	Summary
Discount vouchers	*Boots Co plc v C & E Commrs* (Case 126/88) (1990) 5 BVC 21	Vouchers were given with purchases which could be redeemed against the subsequent purchase of other goods. The vouchers were a price discount that reduced the price of the second purchase.
Vouchers given in loyalty card scheme	*Tesco plc v C & E Commrs* [2004] BVC 3	'Points' were issued to customers when they made a purchase and the vouchers into which they were converted were not supplied for consideration. The redemption value was not deductible from the value of the initial supply but was a discount from the price of the subsequent purchase.
Vouchers sold at a discount	*Argos Distributors Ltd v C & E Commrs* (Case C-288/94) [1997] BVC 64	The retailer sold face-value vouchers to other traders at a discount to face value. The amount to be taken into DGT when the vouchers were redeemed was the price for which they were sold, not their face value.
'Gift' vouchers given with other purchases	*Kuwait Petroleum (GB) Ltd v C & E Commrs* [2002] BVC 71	The retailer gave vouchers with petrol sales which could be exchanged for goods without further payment. No part of the price paid when the petrol was purchased could be attributed to the vouchers. Thus, the redemption goods were provided for no consideration and were treated as gifts.

Topic	Case	Summary
Sales made through unregistered distributors	*Direct Cosmetics Ltd v C & E Commrs* (Case 138/86) (1988) 3 BVC 354	Directions that retailers had to account for VAT on the final retail-selling price where goods were sold to the public through unregistered distributors were upheld, even though there was no deliberate intention to avoid tax.
Unjust enrichment	*Marks & Spencer plc v C & E Commrs* [2004] BVC 151	The court upheld the decision of Customs to withhold a repayment claimed by the retailer on the grounds that it would be unjustly enriched. The evidence was that the burden of the VAT had been passed on to customers.
Credit card transactions	*Debenhams Retail plc* [2003] BVC 2,543	Fees charged by a retailer for the use of a credit or debit card are not exempt when the total amount charged to the card holder is no different from the amount charged to a person paying cash for the same goods.

Residential properties including relevant residential, relevant charitable and housing association properties

36.1 The relevant legislation

The tables below broadly summarise the VAT liability of residential property transactions in the UK. While they summarise the rules in general terms, it is important to note that where there is a relief there are conditions that have to be met in order for it to apply.

> ⚠ **Warning!**
>
> A further feature of the legislation dealing with property is the numerous definitions. In some cases, the same term is defined in three or four parts in slightly different terms (e.g. the definition of the term 'dwelling'). It is easy to overlook the fact that there are these regrettable differences and the tendency is to use one term to fit all.

Where a supply of goods or services is taxable at the standard, zero or reduced rate, the supplier will have the normal right to recover any VAT. However, there is an exception which is considered below at **36.2.15** in relation to VAT on certain materials used in the construction of non-commercial buildings. The tables are intended to assist readers to navigate around the chapter and are not intended to stand alone.

Table 36.1 Sales, letting and leasing of residential buildings

Type of supply	Type of property		
	Dwellings and relevant residential	Relevant charitable	Other (see note (a) below)
Sales of bare freehold land.	Exempt	Exempt	Exempt
Sale of freehold in land and buildings:			
• new, and	Zero-rated	Zero-rated	Standard-rated
• other.	Exempt	Exempt	Exempt
Grant or disposal of leasehold interest in land and buildings exceeding 21 years (not less than 20 years in Scotland):			
• first grant or disposal by person constructing, and	Zero-rated	Zero-rated	Exempt
• other grants or disposals.	Exempt	Exempt	Exempt

Type of supply	Dwellings and relevant residential	Relevant charitable	Other (see note (a) below)
Letting and leasing of land and buildings including licences as follows:			
• leases other than those referred to above;	Exempt	Exempt	Exempt
• fishing or gaming, hotel or holiday accommodation, caravan parking, camping and other parking;	Standard-rated	Standard-rated	Standard-rated
• admission to theatre, sports and other events, and	Not applicable	Standard-rated	Standard-rated

		Type of property	
Type of supply	**Dwellings and relevant residential**	**Relevant charitable**	**Other (see note (a) below)**
• rights to remove timber.	Standard-rated	Standard-rated	Standard-rated
Sale of building materials:			
• by person constructing a building;	Zero-rated if part of zero-rated construction	Zero-rated if part of zero-rated construction	Standard-rated
• to a DIY builder, and	Zero-rated (new)	Not applicable	Not applicable
• other.	Standard-rated	Standard-rated	Not applicable
Assignments and surrenders/cancellations of leases:			
• assignment of lease or licence;	Exempt	Exempt	Exempt unless the assignor of the lease or licence has opted to tax
• inducement to enter into lease: – premium; – rent-free period, and – works done;	Standard-rated if the tenant is required to do something for the landlord; otherwise outside the scope of VAT	Standard-rated if the tenant is required to do something for the landlord; otherwise outside the scope of VAT	Standard-rated if the tenant is required to do something for the landlord; otherwise outside the scope of VAT
• surrender of lease to landlord: – landlord pays tenant, and	Exempt	Exempt	Exempt unless the tenant has opted to tax
– tenant pays landlord (i.e. reverse surrender).	Exempt	Exempt	Exempt unless the landlord has opted to tax

Notes to tables

(1)   Where a supply that is listed in the 'Other' column in Table 36.1 above is exempt, the landlord, owner or other person making the supply will usually have the right to waive exemption, but there are exceptions.

(2)   VAT law has a number of cases dealing with what are 'buildings'.

(3)   The tables show the general rule, but there are exceptions.

(4)   There are also exceptions in respect of mixed-use buildings.

(5)   While civil engineering, demolition work and various professional services are normally standard-rated, they may in some circumstances (described below) be regarded as ancillary to another service. In such cases, they will follow the liability of the other service, e.g. an architect's service as part of a 'design and build' contract.

(6)   Most professional services will be standard rated.

(7)   A design and build contract will have the same liability as the construction service for a single lump sum design and build contract.

Planning point

The VAT incurred on professional services for a residential property will be non-deductible if the residential property is leased on an exempt lease. This cost can be avoided by entering into a single design and build contract which will be zero-rated. The main contractor will incur the professional fees and will be able to reclaim the VAT incurred as the contractor is making a zero-rated supply.

⚠ Warning!

The tables above should not be taken as a comprehensive guide to the VAT law on property but as a map intended to allow readers of this chapter to find the appropriate section or sections dealing with a particular issue that they wish to address.

36.2   Zero-rated construction services

36.2.1   Construction services

The supplies that qualify for VAT zero-rating are detailed within VATA 1994, Sch. 8.

In simple terms, there is provision for the VAT zero-rating of the supply of construction services where this relates to the construction of a new dwelling (house, bungalow, etc.), a number of dwellings (e.g. block of flats), a relevant residential building or a relevant charitable building.

> ### ⚠ *Warning!*
>
> There are restrictions if the building of the new property makes use of any parts of an existing property, so it is important to consider the VAT implications at an early stage when plans are being drawn up, as it is possible that a minor alteration to terms of planning consent or to the plans could make the difference between the supply of services being subject to standard-rate VAT or qualifying for zero-rating. Where any parts of an existing building are being retained (possibly due to planning consent requirements) it is advisable to obtain agreement from HMRC that the services are zero-rated.

36.2.2   Extent of zero-rating

The services that will qualify for VAT zero-rating are usually those provided in relation to the new construction of a qualifying building on bare land, although it is possible to make use of some parts of an existing building (see **36.2.4**) and there are special provisions for the construction of a self-contained annexe to a relevant charitable building (see **36.2.3**).

The construction of a building does not include the conversion, reconstruction or alteration of an existing building; any enlargement of, or extension to, an existing building except to the extent the enlargement or extension creates an additional dwelling or dwellings; or the construction of an annexe to an existing building (unless it qualifies as a self-contained annexe for a relevant charitable purpose building).

Law: VATA 1994, Sch. 8, Grp. 5, Note (16)

36.2.3   Self-contained annexe for a relevant charitable purpose building

The construction of an annexe to an existing building will not usually qualify for VAT zero-rating; however, where a self-contained annexe is constructed for use solely for a relevant charitable purpose, then VAT zero-rating can apply. The conditions that must be met are that the annexe must be capable of functioning independently from the existing building, and the main access to the annexe is not through the existing building, and the main access to the existing building is not via the annexe.

Law: VATA 1994, Sch. 8, Grp. 5, Note (17)

Planning point

With effect from 1 June 2002 it is possible for construction services supplied in relation to a self-contained annexe to be apportioned so that the zero rate can apply to any discrete part of the annexe that will be used for a relevant charitable purpose. Previously, the construction services supplied in relation to a self-contained annexe could only be zero-rated if the whole of the annexe was used for a relevant charitable purpose.

⚠ **Warning!**

HMRC exhibit a real reluctance to grant zero-rating under these provisions, so much caution is required in this area.

36.2.4 Building ceases to be an existing building

This is another area where an awareness of the VAT implications at an early stage could allow for a certain amount of planning in order to mitigate VAT.

A building will only cease to be an existing building when it is either demolished completely to ground level or the parts remaining above ground level consist of no more than a single façade – a double façade on a corner site – where (and only where) the retention was as a condition or requirement of the statutory planning consent or similar permission.

Law: VATA 1994, Sch. 8, Grp. 5, Note (18)

⚠ **Warning!**

If an existing building has been demolished to ground level apart from a single façade, the building on to that façade of a new house (for example) will only qualify for VAT zero-rating if the reason the façade was retained was as a requirement of the planning consent.

⚠ **Warning!**

A roof is required for a structure to be a building. In *Wheeled Sports 4 Hereford Ltd* [2011] TC 01059 it was held that a skate park was not a building, as the construction did not have a roof.

36.2.5 Dwelling or number of dwellings

In practical terms this will be a self-contained house or bungalow or a block of flats, but the actual definition of a dwelling or number of dwellings is contained in VAT law.

> ### Planning point
>
> It is vital to ensure that the four conditions listed below are met in order for construction services to qualify for VAT zero-rating.

A building is designed as a dwelling or number of dwellings where in relation to each dwelling the following conditions are satisfied:

(a)   the dwelling consists of self-contained living accommodation;

(b)   there is no provision for direct internal access from the dwelling to any other dwelling or part of a dwelling;

(c)   the separate use or disposal of the dwelling is not prohibited by the term of any covenant, statutory planning consent or similar provision; and

(d)   statutory planning consent has been granted in respect of that dwelling, and its construction or conversion has been carried out in accordance with that consent.

> ### Planning point
>
> It is sometimes the case that a homeowner will construct an additional unit in the grounds of their home, perhaps for the purpose of housing an elderly relative. The construction services supplied in relation to such a unit will usually fall foul of condition (c) above and be subject to standard-rated VAT, as planning consent normally restricts the use of the unit to use in conjunction with the main house and the separate disposal of the unit is often prohibited.

> ### ⚠ Warning
>
> For a building to benefit from zero-rating it must be a separate dwelling as detailed above. There have been a number of instances where planning authorities have classified extra care accommodation and these have been incorrectly treated as separate buildings for VAT. HMRC has issued *Revenue & Customs Brief* 47/11 to make it clear that the classification for planning purposes is not determinative of the nature of the building. The extra care accommodation must be a separate dwelling as defined in VATA 1994 for it to benefit from zero-rating.

The relevant legislation is VATA 1994, Sch. 8, Grp. 5, Note (2).

There have been numerous cases where it is considered if a building is a dwelling or not. Buildings that will not generally be regarded as a dwelling are those that share facilities or are no more than additions to a home (such as a granny flat). For example, in the decision *University of Bath* [1996] BVC 2,909 it was held that the units built were not dwellings as they shared toilet and cooking facilities. They did not, therefore, have the features of a dwelling, even though people could reside there. Even where there are basic facilities, the property may be regarded as a dwelling. In *Oldrings Development Kingsclere Ltd* [2003] BVC 4,025 a property built in the grounds of a large house was regarded as a separate dwelling (it presumably had permission for separate occupation and disposal). The building only had one large room with a small room for a WC and washbasin. It had its own supplies of hot water and electricity. The Tribunal held that this was a dwelling despite the fact that it was mainly used as an artist's studio.

36.2.6   Relevant residential purpose

In practical terms, a building that is intended for a relevant residential purpose will be one that is designed and used for some sort of communal living. The definition in VAT law is that a relevant residential purpose means use as:

(a)   a home or other institution providing residential accommodation for children;

(b)   a home or other institution providing residential accommodation with personal care for persons in need of personal care by reason of old age, disablement, past or present dependency on alcohol or drugs, or past or present mental disorder;

(c)   a hospice;

(d)   residential accommodation for students or school pupils;

(e)   residential accommodation for members of any armed forces;

(f)   a monastery, nunnery or similar establishment; or

(g)   an institution which is the sole or main residence of at least 90 per cent of its residents,

except use as a hospital, prison or similar institution, or a hotel, inn or similar establishment.

Where a number of buildings are constructed at the same time and are intended to be used together as a unit, solely for a relevant residential purpose (for example separate buildings for accommodation, laundry, dining room, etc.), VAT zero-rating can apply to each of those buildings.

It should be noted that with respect to point (d) above there is no requirement for any minimum length of stay and provided that the accommodation is for lodging, sleeping or overnight accommodation, then VAT zero-rating can apply to the construction services.

There is a requirement for the building contractor to receive a certificate from the person commissioning the building work, confirming that the building is intended solely for a relevant residential purpose (VATA 1994, Sch. 8, Grp. 5, Note (4)).

36.2.7 Relevant charitable use

Use for a relevant charitable purpose means use by a charity in either or both of the following ways.

1. Otherwise than in the course or furtherance of the business.

2. As a village hall or similarly in providing social or recreational facilities for the local community.

Remember that an annexe that is intended to be used by a charity solely for a relevant charitable purpose and which is capable of functioning independently of an existing building will qualify for zero-rating.

> **Planning point**
>
> In order to secure VAT zero-rating a charity will have to issue the building contractor with a certificate confirming that the building will be used for a 'relevant charitable purpose'.

In order for zero-rating to apply to the construction of the building or to an identifiable part of the building it must be used either for a non-business purpose or used as a village hall or similarly. A detailed definition of 'non-business' appears in **Chapter 34**.

Planning point – this method expired on 30 June 2010

HMRC accept that where a building or part of a building is used for both non-business and business purposes, the business use can be disregarded if the non-qualifying use is minimal. The business use can be disregarded if it constitutes less than 10 per cent of the use of the building and this can be calculated in four separate ways. The first option for calculation is the standard option and can be used without HMRC's prior permission, but the remaining three options required HMRC's written permission.

Business use can be disregarded under the old provisions if the following conditions are met:

(a) the entire building will be used solely for non-business activity for more than 90 per cent of the total time it is available for use;

(b) in the case of an identifiable part of a building, if that part will be used solely for non-business activity for more than 90 per cent of the total time that part of the building is available for use;

(c) 90 per cent or more of the floor space of the entire building will be used for non-business activity; or

(d) 90 per cent or more of the people using the entire building (on a head-count basis) will be engaged solely on non-business activity.

It should be noted that only one of these four methods can be used for any one particular building and that the second method (b) is the only one that allows identifiable parts of the building to be considered rather than the entire building. This concession was applied through extra statutory concession 3.29. It can only be used up until 30 June 2010. ; To obtain this relief, the builder has to be given a certificate before the supply takes place. HMRC accept that where a certificate has been issued and a meaningful start to construction commenced before 1 July 2010, then the concession can apply.

This method was advantageous where use changed. HMRC accepted that where there was a clear intention for the business use to be less than 10% at the outset of the use of the building, that the zero-rate relief was available. This generous provision no longer applies.

> ### ⚠ *Warning!*
>
> It is crucial to recognise that this relief only applies where the charity's use of the building is as defined . above. A building used by a charity for business purposes exceeding the ten per cent concessionary level or five per cent statutory level will not be eligible for relief. It is critical that both the charity and the contractor a) appreciate that charities can easily undertake activities which are by way of business (in the VAT definition) and b) understand enough about the charity's activities to reach a valid conclusion as to the availability of relief. See **Chapter 34** for a fuller analysis of these issues.

> ### *Planning point*
>
> It should not be forgotten that the relief applies to a building or part of a building. If a discrete part of a building is to be used entirely for non-business purposes, zero-rating applies to the construction of that part, meaning that an apportionment should be applied to the overall consideration.

Law: VATA 1994, Sch. 8, Grp. 5, Note (6)

From 1 July 2010, a new statutory provision applies. A relevant charitable building needs to be used solely for charitable purposes, but the legislation permits some minor non-charitable use, up to 5 per cent of the use being non-charitable. HMRC will consider any fair and reasonable method of determining if the property is used for charitable purposes. It will be acceptable provided that it accurately reflects the use of the building and its application is not overly burdensome and easy for HMRC to verify. A charity can, if it wishes, use one of the four methods described above, but must bear in mind that these may not provide a fair and reasonable result. Where there is a change in use and the business use exceeds 5% then a charge will be incurred.

Revenue & Customs

Revenue & Customs Brief 39/2009 and *VAT Information Sheet* 8/2009 announce the removal of the above concession (ESC 3.29) on 1 July 2010. There is a transitional period from 1 July 2009 in which charities have a choice of using either ESC 3.29 or a new interpretation of 'solely' to determine whether they can take advantage of the zero-rate.

HMRC now recognize that the term 'solely' as used in the phrase 'solely for a relevant residential or relevant charitable purpose' can incorporate an appropriate *de minimis* margin. HMRC will accept that this statutory condition is satisfied if the relevant use of the building by the charity is 95 per cent or more.

Any method can be used to determine the qualifying use of the building so long as it is fair and reasonable.

If a building is zero-rated as a result of applying this new interpretation, there will be a change of use charge if it ceases to be eligible within ten years of the completion of the building.

36.2.8 Certificates for relevant residential and relevant charitable purposes

Where construction services are to be zero-rated in relation to the construction of either a relevant residential or relevant charitable purpose building, the contractor must receive a certificate from the customer confirming that the building work is eligible for zero-rating.

⚠ *Warning!*

Although it is the customer's responsibility to issue the certificate, the contractor is responsible for determining the VAT liability of the supplies and should take reasonable steps to check the validity of the certificate. If a contractor takes reasonable steps to check the validity of a certificate and makes zero-rated supplies in good faith but fails to identify an incorrect certificate, HMRC will not seek to recover the VAT due from him.

The certificate that must be issued by the customer to the builder is reproduced below. It can be found in *VAT Notice 708*, s. 18 and has the force of law.

Certificate for zero-rated and reduced-rated building work

1. Address of the building:

2. Name and address of organisation receiving the building works:
    VAT registration number (if registered):
    Charity registration (if registered):

3. Date of completion (or estimated date of completion) of the work:
    Value (or estimated value) of the supply: £
    Name, address and VAT registration number of building contractor:

Certificate for zero-rated and reduced-rated building work

4. I have read the relevant parts of Notice 708 *Buildings and construction* and certify that this organisation (in conjunction with any other organisation applicable) will use the building, or part of the building, for which zero-rating is being sought **solely** for (tick as appropriate):

    - a relevant charitable purpose, namely by a charity in either or both of the following ways:

    (a) otherwise than in the course or furtherance of business, or

    (b) as a village hall or similarly in providing social or recreational facilities for a local community.

    - a relevant residential purpose, namely as:

    (a) a home or other institution providing residential accommodation for children

    (b) a home or other institution providing residential accommodation with personal care for persons in need of personal care by reason of old age, disablement, past or present dependence on alcohol or drugs or past or present mental disorder

    (c) a hospice

    (d) residential accommodation for students or school pupils

    (e) residential accommodation for members of any of the armed forces

    (f) a monastery, nunnery or similar established or

    (g) an institution which is the sole or main establishment of at least 90 per cent of its residents:

    and will not be used as a hospital, prison, or similar institution or a hotel, inn or similar establishment.

5. I certify that:

    - the information given is complete and accurate; and

    - if the building, or part of the building, for which zero-rated supplies have been obtained, is let or otherwise used for a purpose which is not solely for a relevant residential purpose or relevant charitable purpose within a period of ten years from the date of its completion, a taxable supply will have been made, and this organisation will account for tax at the standard rate.

    Name (print):   Position held:

    Signed: Date:

Certificate for zero-rated and reduced-rated building work

General warning

1. Customs reserves the right to alter the format of the certificate through the publication of a new notice.

You must ensure that the certificate used is current at the time of issue.

Warnings for the issuer

2. You may be liable to a penalty if you issue a false certificate.

3. You are responsible for the information provided on the completed certificate.

Warnings for the developer

4. You must take all reasonable steps to check the validity of the declaration given to you on this certificate.

5. You must check that you meet all the conditions for zero-rating or reduced-rating your supply – see VAT Notice 708 *Buildings and construction*.

36.2.9   In the course of construction

A building is ordinarily deemed to be completed when it has been finished according to the original plans.

In cases of doubt, the building can be regarded as still under construction up to the date of the certificate of completion, or when contracts have been completed and all building regulations complied with. In addition, the date when the building is first occupied or ready to be occupied may be an indication if any of the above indicators cannot be relied upon.

> ### *Planning point*
>
> Once the building has been completed in accordance with the original plans, any further works done to the building, such as the addition of a conservatory, will be standard-rated. If, however, the original plans do include a conservatory, the building will not be complete until the conservatory is completed.

> ### *Planning point*
>
> When an individual or organisation wishes to have a building constructed in a series of separate phases (perhaps because of financial constraints), it is worth considering applying to HMRC to have the development treated as a phased project. Provided that the original plans and planning consent cover the whole building and the construction of that building would qualify for VAT zero-rating, then the breaking down of the development into separate phases should still allow VAT zero-rating on each separate phase.

36.2.10   Demolition services

Demolition services, when supplied as part of a single project for the construction of a new dwelling or other qualifying building or work, also qualify for VAT zero-rating. However, where demolition services are supplied independently of any zero-rated construction service, these will always be subject to VAT at the standard rate.

36.2.11   Subcontractors

Where a subcontractor provides services in relation to the construction of a new dwelling or number of dwellings, or in relation to an approved alteration to a protected building which is designed as or will become a dwelling or number of dwellings (see below and **Chapter 19**), the services will qualify for VAT zero-rating.

Planning point

However, where a subcontractor works on any other building (commercial, relevant residential or relevant charitable buildings), invoicing another contractor, their services will be liable to standard-rated VAT. In circumstances where a relevant residential or relevant charitable building is being constructed, it is the person commissioning the main contractor or directly engaging the individual contractor (e.g. the charity) that will issue the eligibility certificate to those contractors.

The main contractor is not able to issue any certificates to the subcontractors, so the subcontractors will have to charge standard-rated VAT. Provided that the main contractor is making an onward zero-rated supply, any VAT incurred in relation to subcontractor's services will be recoverable as input tax.

36.2.12 Extent of zero-rating and standard-rated services

The services that qualify for zero-rating in the course of construction of a qualifying building will be those services which are directly relevant to the beginning or ending of the construction work and which are usually carried out prior to completion and first occupation. Paragraph 9.1 of *VAT Notice 708* details those supplies that they consider can be zero-rated and these include:

- demolition work carried out as part of a single project for the construction of dwellings or qualifying buildings;
- site clearance;
- earth moving;
- necessary civil engineering works done in the course of the construction of dwellings or qualifying buildings (this does not include tennis courts, swimming pools or similar works);
- laying of foundations;
- bricklaying, plastering, carpentry, roofing and plumbing services;
- mechanical and electrical services (including central heating);
- plant hire provided with an operator (other than a machine minder);
- erection and dismantling (but not hire) of scaffolding, formwork or falsework;
- incorporation of 'building materials';
- fitting of kitchen units and worktops, and domestic appliances (but not the appliances themselves, which are standard-rated);
- fitting of carpets (but not the carpets themselves);
- internal and external cleaning ('builders' cleans');
- first-time decoration;
- office partitioning (for non-business charity use);
- construction of vehicle crossings;
- remedial or repair work carried out while a dwelling or qualifying building is under construction; and
- site restoration (but not landscaping or ornamental work).

The following services are always standard-rated:

- site investigations (before the letting of any building contract);
- temporary fencing around a site;
- concrete testing;
- site security;
- catering;
- cleaning of site offices, huts, etc.;
- temporary lighting;
- transport and haulage to and from the site;
- plant hire without operator;
- professional services of architects, engineers, surveyors, solicitors, estate agents, valuers, consultants and other persons supplying supervisory services;
- construction management services; and
- landscaping, including the planting of trees (other than any required by the planning authority and shown on the approved plans), flowers, shrubs and the provision of ornamental works, etc.

36.2.13 Civil engineering works

Supplies in the course of construction of any civil engineering work necessary for the development of a permanent park for residential caravans are zero-rated. This zero-rating applies to bring the same VAT reliefs afforded to the construction of dwellings to the works in the course of construction of the caravan park where people will live permanently.

Similar to the definitions for construction of dwellings, the construction of a civil engineering work does not include the conversion, reconstruction, alteration or enlargement of an existing work. Additionally, the construction of any recreational facilities and non-residential buildings at a residential caravan park does not qualify for VAT zero-rating.

> ### ⚠ *Warning!*
>
> A caravan is not a residential caravan if residence in it throughout the year is prevented by the terms of a covenant, statutory planning consent or similar permission. This zero-rating does not apply in respect of civil engineering works in relation to the construction of a caravan park for use as holiday accommodation, but only in respect of a caravan park that will be used as a permanent park for residential caravans.

The relevant legislation is VATA 1994, Sch. 8, Grp. 5, item 2(b).

36.2.14 Supplies to housing associations

Any supplies made to a relevant housing association in relation to the conversion of a non-residential building/part of a building into a building designed as a dwelling/number of dwellings or intended for use as a relevant residential purpose can be zero-rated.

A 'relevant housing association' is defined within VATA 1994, Sch. 8, Grp. 5, Note (21) and means:

- a registered social landlord within the meaning of Pt 1 of the Housing Act 1996;
- a registered housing association within the meaning of the Housing Associations Act 1985 (Scottish registered housing associations); or
- a registered housing association within the meaning of Pt II of the Housing (Northern Ireland) Order 1992 (SI 1992/1725) (Northern Irish registered housing associations).

The zero-rating does not apply to the services supplied by an architect, surveyor or any person acting as a consultant or in a supervisory capacity. It will apply, however, to the physical services provided in the course of conversion of the non-residential building or non-residential part of a building into a building or part of a building designed as a dwelling or number of dwellings, or to a building or part of a building intended for use solely for a relevant residential purpose.

Note (7) to Grp. 5 of Sch. 8 of VATA 1994 defines 'non-residential' in relation to a building or part of a building to mean:

'(a) neither designed nor adapted for use as a dwelling or number of dwellings nor for a relevant residential purpose, or

(b) if so designed or adapted, was constructed before and has not been used as a dwelling or number of dwellings, or for a relevant residential purpose, since 1 April 1973.'

Be aware that if point (a) above applies, there is no need to consider point (b), as this starts 'if so designed'. See **36.6.1** for the definition of dwelling and **36.6.6** for the definition of relevant residential purpose.

Law: VATA 1994, Sch. 8, Grp. 5, item 3

36.2.15 Building materials

The zero rate applies to the supply of building materials when provided in connection with zero-rated services provided that the materials are incorporated into the building.

'Building materials' is defined by Note (22) to Grp. 5 of Sch. 8 and means, in relation to any description of building, goods of a description ordinarily incorporated by builders in a building of that description (or its site), but does not include the following.

1. Finished or prefabricated furniture, other than furniture designed to be fitted in kitchens.

2. Materials for the construction of fitted furniture, other than kitchen furniture.

3. Electrical or gas appliances, unless the appliance is an appliance which is:

    (a) designed to heat space or water (or both) or to provide ventilation, air cooling, air purification or dust extraction;

    (b) intended for use in a building designed as a number of dwellings and is a door-entry system, a waste disposal unit or a machine for compacting waste;

    (c) a burglar alarm, a fire alarm, or fire safety equipment or designed solely for the purpose of enabling aid to be summoned in an emergency; or

    (d) a lift or hoist.

4. Carpets or carpeting material.

Planning point

It is only the materials listed above which are excluded from zero-rating. The services of installing those goods remain eligible for zero-rating.

HMRC regard goods as being incorporated in the building if they are attached to it or its site and make up a whole with the building.

Section 13 of *VAT Notice 708* (June 2007) provides a comprehensive list of those items believed by HMRC to qualify for zero-rating under this heading.

Planning point

However, the publication reflects the view of HMRC. It follows that it does not have legal force, although it is indicative of where they draw the line. It is legitimate to take a different view in regard to a particular item, and the publication is helpful in showing where this is likely to be controversial in the eyes of HMRC.

General

Including:

- lighting systems (excluding non-fixed bulbs and tubes);
- blinds and shutters; and
- mirrors.

Schools

Including:

- blackboards fixed to or forming part of the walls;
- gymnasium wall bars;
- name boards;
- notice and display boards; and
- mirrors and barres (in ballet schools).

Churches

Including:

- altars;
- church bells;
- organs;
- fonts;
- lecterns;
- pulpits;
- amplification equipment; and
- humidifying plant.

Planning point

When a contractor makes a supply of building goods the VAT liability will depend upon whether they are 'building materials' and whether they are supplied along with zero-rated incorporation services.

The following supplies will be subject to VAT:

- the supply of 'building materials' (or other goods) on their own without incorporating them in a building;
- the supply of 'building materials' incorporated in a building when the services of incorporation do not qualify for zero-rating; and
- goods that are not 'building materials' incorporated in a building (although the services of incorporation may still be zero-rated).

The recent First Tier Tribunal (*John Price* [2011] TC 01287) has held that roller blinds were building materials as defined by VATA 1994, Sch 8, Grp. 5, Note 22. Thus, the appellant was entitled to claim a VAT credit on the purchase of the blinds. HMRC's view is that roller blinds and other window furniture are not building materials and will resist any claims for input tax. Due to the small amount of VAT at stake HMRC was not prepared to appeal this decision, but they maintain their view that such materials are not building materials and an input tax credit is not available.

Law: VATA 1994, Sch. 8, Grp. 5, item 4

36.3 Reduced-rated construction services

36.3.1 Installation of energy-saving materials

The supplies that qualify for the reduced rate of VAT are detailed within Sch. 7A of VATA 1994.

This VAT relief applies to the installation of energy-saving materials in a building that is either used as residential accommodation or for a relevant charitable purpose. The relief is available to all householders regardless of their financial status.

> ### *Planning point*
>
> It should be noted that the reduced rate of VAT applies only to the installation of the energy-saving materials along with the actual materials themselves. Any purchases of energy-saving materials that are to be installed on a DIY basis will still be subject to the standard rate of VAT.

Also note that this reduced rate does not apply for installations of energy-saving materials in a building used for charitable non-business purposes.

> ### *Planning point*
>
> Installation will involve putting the energy-saving materials in place. This will usually involve some process by which the materials are permanently fixed in place, although loft insulation may simply need to be unrolled and positioned in place to be installed.

> ### *Planning point*
>
> Any minor building works (e.g. planing doors or windows, enlarging loft hatches and painting or plastering to make good) will also qualify for the reduced rate, provided that these works are undertaken as part of the installation process.

> ### ⚠ *Warning!*
>
> However, if the installation of the energy-saving materials is incidental to another supply that is being made (e.g. the building of an extension or the replacement of a roof), the whole supply is a single supply of construction services and will not be subject to the 5 per cent rate as the installation of energy-saving materials, although it may be eligible for the reduced rate under one of the other groups.

Law: VATA 1994, Sch. 7A, Grp. 2, items 1 and 2

36.3.2   Grant-funded installation

VATA 1994, Sch. 7A, Grp. 3 allows the VAT reduced rate for certain supplies made to specific individuals that are specifically funded by a grant made under a 'relevant scheme'.

There are detailed notes to this group giving definitions of 'relevant scheme', 'heating appliances', 'qualifying security goods' and 'qualifying person'.

A 'qualifying person' is a person who is either aged 60 or over at the time of supply, or is in receipt of one or more benefits that are listed in Note 6(2) to this group.

36.3.3   Qualifying conversions

There are several notes to this group, but, in simple terms, it allows the reduced rate of VAT to apply to services supplied in relation to a residential conversion and the goods supplied along with those services.

A 'qualifying conversion' can be one of three types of project:

(a)   a changed number of dwellings conversion;
(b)   a house in multiple occupation conversion; or
(c)   a special residential conversion.

Other guidance: VAT Notice 708, s. 7

36.3.4   Changed number of dwellings conversion

VATA 1994, Sch. 7A, Grp. 6, Note 3 to this group gives the definition of 'changed number of dwellings conversion' and, in simple terms, this is a conversion where the number of 'single-household dwellings' in a particular building or part of a building is different after the conversion to that which existed before the conversion.

This will include the conversion from an office or shop into a dwelling, as the number of single-household dwellings before the conversion would have been nil, and it will also cover conversions that reduce the number of single-household dwellings, (e.g. work to reinstate a former single-household dwelling that had previously been converted into flats) provided that there is at least one single-household dwelling after the work is complete.

> ### ⚠ *Warning!*
>
> As this provision applies to a building or part of a building, it follows that the reduced rate does not apply to any part of an otherwise qualifying project, where the number of dwellings before and after does not change. In these circumstances, an apportionment will be required.

Example 36.1

Jim Buildwell has been appointed to provide construction services to a developer who is converting a five-storey building containing five single-storey flats, so that after the work is done it will contain two two-storey apartments and a single flat on the top floor.

Ostensibly, the project qualifies for reduced rating. However, the top floor of the building will contain the same number of dwellings before and after conversion. This 'part of [the] building' does not qualify for the reduced rate.

Jim may reduce rate the work on the first four floors, but must standard rate the work to the top floor. If he can isolate the work on the top floor this may be identified as standard-rated. If he cannot, he will be required to apportion his charges. This is likely to be done, in this case, by way of an 80/20 split (one floor out of five standard-rated).

Law: VATA 1994, Sch. 7A, Grp. 6, Note 3

36.3.5   House in multiple occupation

This application of the reduced rate relates to the conversion of one or more single-household dwellings into one or more multiple-occupancy dwellings. It is important to note that the use of the premises after conversion must not be for a relevant residential purpose (see **36.3.6**)

Law: VATA 1994, Sch. 7A, Grp. 6, Note 5

36.3.6   Special residential conversion

This relief applies to the conversion from a building/buildings and/or part of a building/buildings, or from a dwelling or dwellings (including ancillary outbuildings occupied together with the dwelling(s)), to a relevant residential building, provided that the last use before the conversion was not use for a relevant residential purpose (VATA 1994, Sch. 7A, Grp. 6, Note 7).

Planning point

However, where it is the intention that the premises will be used as an institution (children's home; residential care home; hospice; monastery, nunnery or similar establishment; or an institution which is the sole or main residence of at least 90 per cent of its residents), the premises must form the entirety of an institution.

36.3.7   Renovation and alteration of dwellings

Once again, there are detailed notes to this group but, in simple terms, the reduced rate applies to construction services that relate to the renovation or alteration of a single-household dwelling that has been empty for at least two years (three years prior to 1 January 2008), along with the materials that are supplied as part of the renovation or alteration.

In order for the reduced rate to apply, the work must be carried out in accordance with any statutory planning consent or statutory building control approval that is needed.

> ### Planning point
>
> The services that will qualify for the reduced rate will be those services of renovation or alteration in relation to the fabric of the dwelling and works within the immediate site of the dwelling that relate to the provision of water, power, heat or access to the dwelling; the means of providing drainage or security for the dwelling; and the provision of means of waste disposal from the dwelling.

The reduced rate will not apply to the incorporation or installation of any goods that are not building materials (see **36.4**).

The definition of a 'single-household dwelling' is the same as Note 4 to Grp. 6 of Sch. 7A.

'Alteration' includes extension.

The requirement for the dwelling to have been empty for a period of two years is defined in two separate ways within Note 3 to this group. Firstly, an empty home is one that has not been lived in during a period of three years ending with the commencement of the relevant works.

Secondly, where a dwelling is now inhabited:

- it must not have been lived in for a period of at least two years;
- the person(s) living in the dwelling must be the first person(s) to live in the dwelling following a period when it had been empty for at least two years;
- no works by way of renovation or alteration were carried out to the dwelling during the period of two years ending with the acquisition;
- the supply must be made to the person who owns and lives in the dwelling; and
- the works must be carried out during the period of one year beginning with the day of the acquisition.

> ### *Planning point*
>
> The determination of the VAT liability of a particular supply is down to the person providing the supply, but it is obviously in the customer's interest to provide the supplier with relevant information to substantiate that the works can qualify for the reduced rate.

HMRC have indicated within *VAT Notice 708*, para. 8.3 that they will accept evidence, on the balance of probabilities, which shows that the building has been unoccupied for more than two years.

> ### *Planning point*
>
> The evidence can include data from the electoral roll and council tax information, information from the empty-property officer in local authorities, and other sources of reliable information. HMRC will accept a letter from the empty-property officer certifying that a home has been empty for two years (or will have been empty for two years when the work starts) as the sole document needed as evidence that the property has (or will be) empty for two years. If an empty-property officer is either unsure about the length of time a home has been empty or does not provide any written confirmation, the contractor should seek to support his claim that the property has been empty for three years with alternative documentation.

36.3.8   Dwelling

For the conversion services to be available, it is necessary to consider if the property was residential before the conversion and/or residential after the conversion. A building is non-residential if it is neither adapted nor designed as a dwelling (see **36.6.1**) nor designed nor adapted for relevant residential use. Where a property has been so designed or adapted but has in the past ten years not been used as a dwelling, it will be considered for VAT purposes not to be residential. Buildings that are not considered to be in use as a dwellings include:

- public houses and shops where the landlord's/owner's domestic accommodation is not self contained (for example, the landlord shares the kitchen with the pub);
- bedsit accommodation with shared facilities; or
- crofts.

The case law in this area has been confusing. It is suggested in borderline areas that agreement with HMRC is sought. In *Temple House Developments Ltd* [1998] BVC 2,302 it was held that the property, a public house, had not been designed as a dwelling as it shared cooking and toilet facilities with the pub below. This should be contrasted with *Calum Vale Ltd* [2001] BVC 4,056 where it was held that a similar property was a dwelling. This was because a dwelling was a place where one resided. The decision in *Amicus Group Ltd* [2003] BVC 4,005 followed the dicta of Lord Irving in *Uratemp Ventures Ltd v Collins* HL [2001] 1 All ER 46, that a dwelling should be a place where one lives, regarding it and treating it as a home. It would be a home even if a person did not cook there. This would seem to have conclusively indicated that a dwelling or residential property could have shared facilities.

36.4 Goods installed in new non-commercial buildings

To avoid distortion of competition, a taxable person constructing or effecting works to any non-commercial building (where the sale or lease would be zero-rated may not recover any input tax on goods incorporated in the building unless they are 'building materials'.

The supply of such goods to a developer is always standard-rated. Where such goods are incorporated in a building which is then sold as a zero-rated supply, there is no separate supply of the goods. The provisions ensure that the tax on the goods is reflected in the price of the building by disallowing the VAT charged by the supplier to the developer. Input tax on the related services of installing the goods can be reclaimed, provided that the services are separately identified on the supplier's invoice.

The provision ensures that the developer suffers the same VAT cost on goods which are not 'building materials' as any other person who receives a standard-rated supply of such goods.

In addition to any goods not ordinarily installed by a builder in a dwelling of the type concerned, the legislation specifically precludes recovery of input tax on the following items. See section **36.7** for a checklist of building materials.

1. Prefabricated furniture or materials for the manufacture thereof.

2. Electrical or gas appliances, unless they are:

   (a) designed to heat space or water or to provide ventilation, air cooling, air purification or dust extraction;
   (b) a burglar alarm, fire alarm or fire safety equipment for summoning emergency aid; or
   (c) a lift or hoist.

3. Carpets and carpeting material.

VAT Notice 708 contains lists of items that they consider to be allowable and disallowable for different categories of building.

Planning point

HMRC's notice represents their view and should not therefore be seen as definitive. In cases of doubt or difficulty, sensible judgment or reference to the outcome of relevant tribunal cases may be called for.

36.4.1 Showhouses

HMRC take the view that input tax cannot be reclaimed on goods which have been installed in showhouses, apparently in any circumstances. Arguably, however, input tax should be deductible if the goods are for display purposes only and will be removed for use elsewhere, will be scrapped at the end of their useful life or will be the subject of a separate taxable supply (being sold separately from the dwelling in which they have been displayed, for example).

Other guidance: VAT Notice 708, para. 12.3

36.4.2 Landscaping

Following the tribunal decision in *Rialto Homes plc* [2000] BVC 2,161, HMRC accepted that certain soft landscaping in addition to the laying of turf can be zero-rated when supplied in the course of constructing a non-commercial building (*Business Brief 7/00*). However, HMRC maintain that the following landscaping supplies remain standard-rated:

- work not included on a landscaping scheme approved by a planning authority under the terms of a planning consent condition; and
- work performed after completion.

Other guidance: VAT Notice 708, para. 3.3.4

36.5 DIY developments

Without specific relief, the provisions which permit builders who have granted a major interest in residential properties to zero-rate that supply would cause distortions against private individuals or non-business organisations who are not VAT registered and who build homes or other qualifying buildings for their own occupation.

Do-it-yourself (DIY) builders are therefore permitted to recover VAT paid by them on goods which they have used in constructing a building. Those converting a non-residential building into a dwelling for their own occupation are also entitled to claim such VAT, together with any VAT charged to them at 5 per cent by any contractor carrying out work necessary for the conversion. Repayment of tax is subject to the following restrictions.

1. The VAT must be incurred in respect of the construction of a new dwelling, a building constructed for a qualifying purpose, or the conversion of an existing non-residential building into a dwelling.

2. The house must not be built in the course or furtherance of any business carried on by the claimant, although the claimant can be a charity and not an individual (VATA 1994, s. 35(1)(b)).

3.   The person must be constructing a dwelling lawfully – the work, therefore, must be done under the terms of the planning permission (VATA 1994, s. 35(1)(b)).

4.   The goods incorporated in the house must be the same as those on which VAT can be recovered in normal business circumstances by a registered trader, i.e. they must be 'building materials'.

5.   The claim must be made within three months of completion on the prescribed form and be supported by appropriate documentation (see *VAT Notice 719* and claim pack 431 for the prescribed form).

The DIY refund provisions also apply to a garage that is constructed at the same time as a dwelling and intended to be occupied together with the dwelling.

⚠ *Warning!*

Although the broad intention of the scheme is to put DIY claimants on the same footing as developers, there are some ways in which this is not achieved. In particular, no VAT may be claimed through the scheme on services (other than contractors' reduced-rated services on conversions), such as equipment hire or architects' and surveyors' fees; on consumable items, such as sandpaper; or on tools, even if purchased exclusively for the project.

⚠ *Warning!*

The timescale for making claims is very tight indeed, namely within three months of completion of the project (as defined). Claimants must not neglect their claim, even where there are many other conflicting priorities.

Regulations have been made detailing the evidence that a DIY builder must furnish to HMRC on making a claim. The claim must be made within three months of completion of the building on the prescribed form. There is no provision for interim claims.

Law: VATA 1994, s. 35

Other guidance: VAT Notice 719

36.6   Definitions

36.6.1   Dwelling

A dwelling is:

'(2)   A building is **designed as a dwelling** or a number of dwellings where in relation to each dwelling the following conditions are satisfied–

(a) the dwelling consists of a self-contained living accommodation;

(b) there is no provision for direct internal access from the dwelling to any other dwelling or part of a dwelling;

(c) the separate use, or disposal of the dwelling is not prohibited by the terms of any covenant, statutory planning consent or similar provision; and

(d) statutory planning consent has been granted in respect of that dwelling and its construction or conversion has been carried out in accordance with that consent.'

Law: VATA 1994, Sch. 8, Grp. 5, Note (2)

36.6.2 Major interest

A major interest can comprise either the sale of the freehold (or equivalent) or a leasehold interest exceeding 21 years (or, in Scotland, of not less than 20 years).

Law: VATA 1994, s. 96(1)

36.6.3 Seasonal caravan pitches

The supply of a caravan pitch is usually standard rated as a holiday letting. An extra statutory concession has existed to treat the supply as exempt where the caravan pitch is used for residential rather than holiday purposes. This is being put on a statutory footing by *Value Added Tax (Land Exemption) Order* 2012 (SI 2012/58), that amends VATA 1994, Sch. 9, Grp. 1, Note (14) so that nonresidential pitches on any site or pitches on holiday sites (other than pitches for employees) are excluded from the exemption. A nonresidential pitch is defined as a pitch provided for less than a year or, where it is provided for more than a year, there is an occupational restriction that restricts occupation throughout the period of the provision of the pitch (so that if restriction for occupation of less than a year was being ignored the supply remains standard rated).

36.6.4 Non-business use by charity

The definition of business is wide and includes any trade, profession or vocation. However, whilst the test is restrictive, it is possible for charities to occupy premises for non-business purposes. Typically this may arise when the charity is grant funded and does not charge the users for the provision of any services that the charity provides. However, there can also be other circumstances (see *Cardiff Community Housing Association Ltd* [2001] BVC 2,112). In *C & E Commrs v Yarburgh Children's Trust* [2002] BVC 141 the grant of a lease to a playgroup did not constitute a business activity on the facts of that case.

36.6.5 Relevant charitable use

According to VATA 1994, Sch. 8, Grp. 5, Note (6):

> '**Use for a relevant charitable purpose** means use by a charity in either of the following ways, namely –
>
> (a) otherwise than in the course or furtherance of a business;
> (b) use as a village hall or similarly in providing social or recreational facilities for a local community.'

Extra-statutory concession

Both for non-business use and for use as a village hall or similarly, HMRC operate an Extra-Statutory Concession ESC 3.29 which means that HMRC accept that where a building is either used 90 per cent of the time or has 90 per cent of floor space used for a relevant charitable purpose then the entire building is treated as used for a relevant charitable purpose.

Removal of the concession

Revenue & Customs Brief 39/2009 and *VAT Information Sheet* 8/2009 announced the removal of the above concession (ESC 3.29) on 1 July 2010. There is a transitional period from 1 July 2009 in which charities have a choice of using either ESC 3.29 or a new interpretation of 'solely' to determine whether they can take advantage of the zero-rate.

HMRC now recognize that the term 'solely' as used in the phrase 'solely for a relevant residential or relevant charitable purpose' can incorporate an appropriate *de minimis* margin. HMRC will accept that this statutory condition is satisfied if the relevant use of the building by the charity is 95 per cent or more.

Any method can be used to determine the qualifying use of the building so long as it is fair and reasonable.

If a building is zero-rated as a result of applying this new interpretation, there will be a change of use charge if it ceases to be eligible within ten years of the completion of the building.

36.6.6 Relevant residential use

'Relevant residential use' is use as:

> '(a) a home or other institution providing residential accommodation for children;
> (b) a home or other institution providing residential accommodation with personal care for persons in need of personal care by reason of old age, disablement, past or present dependence on alcohol or drugs or past or present mental disorder;
> (c) a hospice;

(d)   residential accommodation for students or school pupils;

(e)   residential accommodation for members of any of the armed forces;

(f)   a monastery, nunnery or similar establishment; or

(g)   an institution which is the sole or main residence of at least 90 per cent of its residents,

(h)   except use as a hospital, prison or similar institution or an hotel, inn or similar establishment.'

Law: VATA 1994, Sch. 8, Grp. 5, Note (4)

The same definition applies to:

- 'Protected buildings' (by virtue of VATA 1994, Sch. 8, Grp. 6, Note (2));
- 'Residential conversions' (by use of identical wording in VATA 1994, Sch. 7A, Grp. 6, Note 6); and
- 'Residential renovations and alterations' (by use of identical wording in VATA 1994, Sch. 7A, Grp. 7, Note 4, which applies the definition for 'residential conversions' to 'residential renovations and alterations').

36.6.7   Use as a village hall or similarly

This test is also restrictive (see *Jubilee Hall Recreation Centre Ltd v C & E Commrs; C & E Commrs v St Dunstans Educational Foundation* [1999] BVC 184). However, decisions post *Jubilee Hall* have confirmed that the relief is available when the conditions are met (*Ledbury Amateur Dramatic Society* [2001] BVC 4,051 and *Southwick Community Association* [2002] BVC 4,058). What appears to be material is whether the facilities are operated in a similar manner to a village hall, and that the facilities are for the use of the local community.

36.7   Checklists for residential property

Supplies of construction services by a building contractor or subcontractor are zero-rated in the course of construction of:

(a)   new self-contained dwellings;

(b)   the enlargement or extension of an existing building creating a new dwelling, which can be disposed of as separate accommodation;

Note: A 'granny' annexe or similar addition of self-contained flat, extension or annexation to a house will not qualify as a new dwelling if separate disposal is prevented, even where the new structure is entirely separate.

(c)   an annexe built on to an existing building for a relevant charitable purpose;

(d)   new relevant residential buildings;

(e)   new relevant charitable buildings;

(f)   approved alterations to protected buildings;

(g)   conversion for a registered housing association in converting a building from non-residential to residential use; or

(h) civil engineering works required for a permanent residential caravan park development including:
  (i) laying new roads, drives, parking bays and paths, ground works (drainage and sewerage);
  (ii) laying new pitches or bases for the homes; and
  (iii) installing water, gas and electricity supplies.

Subcontractor's services

Supplies by a subcontractor are:

(a) zero-rated in the course of construction of new dwellings; and
(b) standard-rated in the course of other constructions, including qualifying buildings for relevant residential or charitable purposes.

Note: The issue of a zero-rating certificate only applies to supplies by the main contractor.

Dwellings

The building may qualify as a dwelling for zero-rating, where it meets the following conditions:

(a) it must be self-contained;
(b) there must be no direct internal access to another dwelling;
(c) it must be capable of separate lawful use, letting or disposal; and
(d) it must have been built according to the granted statutory planning consent.

New buildings

For the purposes of zero-rating, a new construction does not include converting, reconstruction, altering, enlarging or extending an existing building except in certain circumstances.

If there is an existing building, the construction supplies are in the course of constructing a new dwelling or building when:

(a) the conversion, reconstruction or alteration includes either, the entire demolition of the existing building down to ground level or the retention of a single façade (or a double façade on a corner site) which is required as a condition of statutory planning consent and may include developments such as the demolition of a terrace of houses except for the front façade to be replaced by new houses or the demolition of a derelict barn to be replaced by a new farmhouse;
(b) the enlargement or extension creates a separate disposable dwelling including developments such as building a new house in a space in an existing terrace of houses or building another house with separate access on to an existing house to create two semi-detached properties; or
(c) an annexe built for charitable purposes provided it is capable of functioning independently from the existing building and the only or main access to the annexe is not via the existing building.

VAT liability of services during construction

Zero-rated when construction is commenced includes:

(a)   demolition work if part of a single project;
(b)   site clearance;
(c)   earth moving;
(d)   necessary civil engineering works; and
(e)   laying of foundations.

Standard-rated supplies when construction is commenced includes:

(a)   site investigations before any building contract;
(b)   concrete testing; and
(c)   demolition if under a separate contract.

Zero-rated supplies during construction includes:

(a)   bricklaying, plastering, carpentry, roofing, plumbing;
(b)   mechanical and electrical services such as central heating;
(c)   plant hire provided with a machine operator;
(d)   scaffolding, formwork and framework erection and dismantling; and
(e)   remedial or repair work.

Standard-rated supplies during construction includes:

(a)   temporary fencing around the site;
(b)   site security;
(c)   catering;
(d)   cleaning of site offices;
(e)   temporary lighting; and
(f)   hire of scaffolding, formwork or falsework.

Zero-rated when at or near completion includes:

(a)   fitting of kitchen units and worktops;
(b)   internal and external cleaning, known as 'builders' cleans';
(c)   first-time decoration;
(d)   office partitioning for non-business charity use;
(e)   construction of vehicle crossings;
(f)   site restoration such as clearance, levelling and drainage;
(g)   laying of grass, topsoil; and
(h)   construction of basic paths and patios.

Standard-rated at or near completion includes:

(a)   landscaping and the provision of ornamental works.

Always standard-rated includes:

(a)   architects;
(b)   construction management services;
(c)   consultants;

(d)   engineers;
(e)   estate agents;
(f)   solicitors;
(g)   supervisory services;
(h)   surveyors; and
(i)   valuers.

VAT liability of goods installed during construction

Zero-rated includes:

- air conditioning, ventilation equipment and dust extractors;
- burglar alarms and warden call systems;
- built-in heating appliances;
- communal TV aerials in blocks of flats, etc;
- doors and letterboxes;
- fire alarms and smoke detectors;
- fireplaces and surrounds;
- guttering;
- immersion heaters, boilers, hot- and cold-water tanks;
- lifts and hoists;
- power points and certain light fittings;
- radiators;
- kitchen sinks;
- kitchen work surfaces and fitted cupboards;
- baths and basins;
- lavatory bowls, bidets and cisterns;
- shower units;
- vanity units, fixed rails and holders; and
- airing cupboards.

Standard-rated includes:

- carpets and carpeting materials;
- fitted furniture;
- bookshelves;
- goods supplied which are not incorporated into the construction or are supplied on their own;
- electrical and gas domestic appliances; and
- fitted furniture such as cupboard units.

Built in bedroom wardrobes are zero-rated when constructed on site and utilise spaces in walls for the backs and at least one side of the wardrobe.

Charitable or residential developments

Construction services in the course of constructing a building for qualifying charitable or residential use are zero-rated when:

- the supply is made to the person who intends to use the building for the charitable or residential purpose;

969

- the person to whom the supply is made issues a certificate to the main contractor, providing two copies; and
- the certificate is prepared in accordance with guidance contained in VAT Notice 708, Annexe A, confirming that the organisation is to use the building solely for a qualifying purpose.

VAT will be due on the value of the construction if the certified building is subsequently disposed of or otherwise used for a non-qualifying purpose within a ten-year period of the original supply.

Reduced rate for residential conversions

5 per cent VAT will apply to construction services in the course of conversion and renovation of houses and residential homes when:

(a) non-residential property into a residential property, care home or similar relevant residential property;
(b) single-occupancy residential property into multiple occupancy, e.g. bedsit accommodation and relevant residential building;
(c) renovating a residential property, including a care home, that has not been in use for two years or more;
(d) renovating or altering a multiple-occupancy dwelling that has not been in use for three years or more;
(e) multiple-occupancy dwelling into relevant residential building; and
(f) a 'changed number of dwellings' conversion.

A certificate must be issued to the developer/building contractor in respect of special residential conversions prior to work commencing.

Appeals and Complaints

37.1 Introduction

The purpose of this chapter is to look at all the options available to an aggrieved taxpayer. The avenues of appeal against adverse rulings, assessments or penalties are considered and the procedures relating to tribunal appeals explained in some detail. This aspect is approached from the standpoint of an appellant or an appellant's adviser who wishes to take an appeal himself. Its aim is to provide practical information and guidance. It does not dwell on some of the more esoteric points of law and procedure that can occupy the time of the tribunals. Finally, the options available for lodging a complaint in matters not appropriate to the formal appeal process are outlined. It is, however, important to consider the technicalities of the assessment and appeal process. A surprising number of appeals can be won as HMRC have failed to follow the requirements of the assessment or appeal process. HMRC and the *appeals department* are under great time pressure and can occasionally fail to adhere to the regulations (particularly time-limits), and this can provide the opportunity to request judgment without HMRC's case being heard. Indeed, HMRC have been known to lose papers and have to withdraw from contesting an appeal.

37.2 Internal review by HMRC

The first stage in any appeal against an assessment, decision or penalty is to consider a request for an internal review of the assessment or decision by HMRC. HMRC are not obliged to conduct an internal review but almost invariable do. The review is provided by an independent (meaning not previously involved with the case) specially trained officer. HMRC must complete the review within 45 days (unless a longer period is agreed with the taxpayer)

It is entirely possible for an appeal to be lodged immediately with the VAT tribunal but, before this is done, a number of factors need to be taken into account.

The procedures involved in local reconsideration are simpler than those involved in submitting an appeal to the VAT tribunal. If it is considered that the dispute can be relatively readily resolved, it is advisable to approach the local VAT office, rather than the tribunal, in the first instance. If the appeal is against an assessment raised during a VAT assurance visit, HMRC's procedures require that any reconsideration is carried out by a different officer from the one who carried out the visit, to maintain objectivity. It is important to ensure that this condition is fulfilled, although this should be a matter of course by HMRC. Increasingly, such reviews are being centralised in one office in each region, which does lend greater independence to the procedure. Also, review officers are likely to be more technically aware than was the case in the past. Whilst a review is certainly not a process of confirmation of the original officer's view, it is only human nature for the reconsideration to view things in the same light as the assessing officer; officers inevitably approach matters from the same stand point and have the same background and training. Having said this, the review process has proved very useful as, if taken seriously by HMRC, the reviewing officer can find other important factors that require consideration and it does give the taxpayer or his advisor an opportunity to prevent new facts, provide clarification and question the original officer's views. It also provides an initial attempt at reviewing the facts and circumstances of the case before going to Tribunal. When HMRC informs the taxpayer of a decision (such as an assessment) it will offer the opportunity to have the decision reviewed. It is necessary to reply in writing within 30 days of this offer to the address given in the decision letter.

Planning Point

Ensure that a reply is given in writing regarding the review opportunity within 30 days of the date of HMRC's decision. HMRC will still review the decision, on request, after the 30 day period if there is a reasonable excuse for the delay (illness, other extended absence, etc).

Planning Point

When accepting a review offer it is necessary to provide the business name (or the name of the appellant), the reference number shown on the decision letter, the details of the decision or assessment that is being disputed, an explanation of what is disagreed with and what the correct figures (if relevant) are and how these have been calculated.

HMRC's *Litigation and Settlement Strategy* is at the core of all methods of resolving disputes. This can be found at www.hmrc.gov.uk/practitioners/lss-intro.htm and there is a link to a 45-page draft. HMRC's settlements strategy states that it is to support taxpayers getting their tax commitments right the first time, prevent disputes arising and resolve any disputes that do arise to establish the right tax at the least cost to HMRC and the taxpayer. This policy contains inevitable conflicts. Establishing the right tax will not necessarily be at the least cost. Also, there is a conflict between 'acting in a non-confrontational manner and resolving matters in a cost effective manner', and the other policy aims of maximising revenue flows, not compromising in what are described as 'all or nothing cases' and to act in a manner that best closes the 'tax gap'. Furthermore, HMRC have explicitly stated in this document that they will consider the tax at stake in the current and previous years when considering litigation and settlement; this constrains HMRC's dispute settlement policy as they will also be looking to achieve easy and cost effective revenue raising.

Planning point

A disadvantage of the local reconsideration is that there is no ability to claim costs if the dispute is resolved in the trader's favour. Thus, any professional or other costs incurred must be borne by the trader. If the dispute is particularly complex or it is considered that a great deal of legal argument will be necessary in order to defeat HMRC's contentions. In addition, most First Tier Tribunals do not award costs unless the matter is considered complex. (See **37.8** regarding costs.)

Planning point

If a local reconsideration takes place, the time limits for appealing to the VAT tribunal will automatically be extended by HMRC in their response to the reconsideration, if this is to maintain their original decision. Consequently, in taking this route there is no danger of exceeding the time limits set down for appealing to the tribunal.

A tribunal appeal must be lodged within 30 days of the date of the document containing the appeal decision or assessment.

If HMRC have reviewed their decision and upheld it, then a further 21 days from the date of the decision to uphold the original decision is permitted for appealing to the VAT tribunal. This extension will be formally notified in any letter upholding the decision and, if it is absent, HMRC should be requested to confirm it in writing.

The tribunal has discretion to accept appeals which are made outside the statutory periods. Although the tribunal has a reputation for lenience in such matters, best practice dictates that appeals should be lodged on a timely basis wherever possible. Thus, an early appeal is advisable (but see planning point below); it costs nothing (other than a small amount of the advisor's time) and can easily be withdrawn at a later date.

Planning point

If there is any doubt as to whether an issue is appealable then it is advisable to attempt negotiations with HMRC rather than appeal to the tribunal straight away. A further advantage of negotiating with HMRC is that a registered person does not have to submit outstanding VAT returns or liabilities or indeed the VAT in dispute before negotiations can begin. (This is a condition for an appeal at tribunal to be heard, although it is often waived.) However, it has to be said that an appeal made to tribunal at the same time as negotiations with HMRC does in some instances have the effect of focusing the minds of the officers involved and ensuring that the case is dealt with at the correct level (eg policy headquarters where this is necessary). It is unreasonable to expect a local officer to understand all the complexities of VAT, so getting the matter to a review officer or the technical centres of expertise can often quickly resolve the dispute.

A decision as to which course of action to take is therefore highly dependent upon the circumstances of the individual case.

An appeal can be settled by agreement. This usually happens subsequent to a request being made for a review, but can occur before this point and may occur once the formal appeal process proceeds to the Tribunals or Courts. It may be agreed that the appeal is upheld without any variation, or that the appeal is upheld in part, with some variation of the appeal may be discharged or cancelled. Once there is a settlement it is binding on both parties as if it had been determined by a Tribunal. The appellant can, however, within 30 days give written notice to HMRC that it wishes to repudiate or resile from the settlement.

Planning Point

HMRC are introducing a new Alternative Dispute Resolution process (ADR). This is aimed at small and medium enterprises and is only for limited types of disputes; the objective is to help free up disputes that have got bogged down for some reason. In addition, the current trial is being undertaken in a limited geographical area.

An earlier trial by HMRC where participating cases were selected post internal review but expected to go to Tribunal was successful; 60% of were either fully or partially resolved saving time and costs for both parties and HMRC now wish to extend it. A further trial in North Wales and the North East of England was also successful and has now been extended to the whole of the UK. The current trial extends until 30 November 2012, but it is expected that it will be formally introduced subsequent to this date. Currently, only SMEs are eligible to use the ADR. Whilst HMRC has not defined an SME for this purpose it is assumed that a business with less than 250 employees and either a turnover of less than £50m or a balance sheet of less than £43m will be eligible.

The ADR is not a review process but a facilitation to progress the dispute towards resolution. The ADR uses a trained 'facilitator' (for both VAT and direct tax) to try and reach an agreement and resolve the dispute. The facilitator is an HMRC employee, although they are meant to be independent, and will have had no prior involvement in the case.

To apply to be part of the ADR process application can be made online using the link at *www.hmrc.gov.uk/adr/index.htm*. Where there are circumstances that prevent online application contact the HMRC on 01492 397008 (between 0900 and 1600 Monday to Friday).

Where a case is accepted for ADR the taxpayer will be asked to complete a memorandum of understanding to confirm their commitment and participation in the ADR. Taking part in the ADR does not prevent a taxpayer from using the internal review process or making an appeal to the Tribunal. The facilitator will not be called as a witness by HMRC in any subsequent appeal. Examples given of suitable cases include:

974

- restoring communication – where the facilitator can re-establish communication between the HMRC officers dealing with the case and the taxpayer and enable the dispute to progress by ensuring all the necessary information is available;

  - clarifying facts (particularly, it seems, clarifying HMRC's view of the facts);
  - obtaining more suitable evidence, e.g. obtaining a valuation from a District Valuer;
  - further mediation – the example given by HMRC concerns the facilitator checking the assumptions in the business model used by the taxpayer, and
  - obtaining a better understanding of the arguments, again it seems to be focussed on getting the facilitator to explain HMRC's position to the taxpayer.

HMRC have stated that some cases are not suitable for the ADR process and these include matters that:

- involve matters which cannot be settled within the Litigation and Settlements Strategy;
- require clarification in the wider public interest;
- are part of wider, co-ordinated or a series of appeals, and
- which can only be settled by departing from HMRC's established technical or policy views.

37.3   Tribunal appeals

37.3.1 Introduction

In the event of failure to resolve an issue through local review, or the ADR proves fruitless, an appeal can be made to the tribunal. This must be done within the time limits (30 days from the decision or 21 days from notification on review that it has been upheld).

Originally named the Value Added Tax Tribunal, then the VAT and Duties Tribunal, since its sole function previously was to hear appeals against decisions of HMRC in relation to VAT, its jurisdiction was extended to other indirect taxes which are under the care and management of HMRC (then Customs & Excise). The VAT Appeal system was, with other appeal systems, substantially altered in 2009. This established a two-tier Tribunal system with a First Tier Tribunal and an Upper Tribunal. Most, but not all appeals will go first to the First-Tier Tribunal. The Tribunal system is intended to provide a quick and cost-effective forum for the resolution of disputes between HMRC and the taxpayer. In terms of complexity, the tribunal hears a wide range of appeals ranging from simple default surcharge appeals and assessments, where the taxpayer is often unrepresented, to cases where both parties are represented by Queen's Counsel (QCs) and large sums of tax are at stake.

> ### ⚠ *Warning!*
>
> The jurisdiction and powers of the tribunal are statutory with the rules governing its procedure set out in legislation. It is important that the procedure for appeals is followed correctly and that due regard is paid to the time limits specified since failure to comply could result in the appeal being dismissed.

Furthermore, the tribunal has power to award penalties against parties for failing to comply with its directions.

> ### *Planning point*
>
> Although tribunal proceedings are informal, in the sense that the lawyers are not robed, they are adversarial in format and run on court lines. Nevertheless, it is not necessary for the appellant to be represented by a lawyer and anyone has a right of audience before the tribunal, and will usually be helped by the Tribunal although they cannot present their case for the appellant. However, potential advocates should understand that the tribunal's primary task is to establish the facts of the case according to the evidence produced by the parties and then apply the correct legal principles to those facts. Although there is an appeal to a higher court on a point of law, there is no appeal against findings of fact, unless they are perverse. Accordingly, it is essential for the parties to produce their evidence at the tribunal otherwise a decision may be reached on insufficient evidence which will be impossible to correct on an appeal. There should be a correlation between the complexity of the case and the skills and experience of the advocate undertaking the appeal.

Law: VAT Tribunals Rules 1986 (SI 1986/590)

37.3.2 Constitution of the tribunals

The provisions for appeals to the VAT and Duties Tribunal are set out in the Tribunals, Courts and Enforcement Act 2007 which contains the constitution and procedure of tribunals. There is a senior President presiding over the Tribunals and each Tribunal (there are Tribunals for tax, Health, Education, etc.) consists of its Judges and members. Each Chamber has a Chamber president (the First-tier Tax Chamber and the Finance and Tax Chamber of the Upper Tribunal are the relevant ones here).

37.4   Appealable matters

The jurisdiction of the tribunal in respect of VAT appeals is statutory, being contained in VATA 1994, s. 83. Thus for an appeal to lie to the tribunal, the grounds must fall within one of the heads of appeal in s. 83, listed below. For clarity, the statute is set out in italics.

   '(a)   the registration or cancellation of registration of any person under this Act;'

This covers appeals against refusals of voluntary registration and cancellation of registration (for example if there is a dispute about turnover or, perhaps, whether there is a need to register following a TOGC).

'(b)   *the VAT chargeable on the supply of any goods or services, on the acquisition of goods from another member state or, subject to section 84(9), on the importation of goods from a place outside the member states;'*

This head of appeal relates to an actual supply as opposed to a supply intended to be made in the future. HMRC will apply to strike out any purported appeal if no supply has occurred. It may be necessary for the taxpayer to make a 'sample' supply in order to get the case heard.

'(c)   *the amount of any input tax which may be credited to a person;'*

Appeals relating to the issue of deductibility of input tax, ie whether tax claimed is for the purpose of the business, will fall under this head. However, see below for the tribunal's jurisdiction in certain types of input tax appeal.

'(d)   *any claim for a refund under any regulations made by virtue of section 13(5);'*

This head relates to claims for acquisition tax on goods acquired tax paid in another EU country.

'(da)   *a decision of the Commissioners under section 18A–*

(i)   *as to whether or not a person is to be approved as a fiscal warehouse keeper or the conditions from time to time subject to which he is so approved;*
(ii)   *for the withdrawal of any such approval; or*
(iii)   *for the withdrawal of fiscal warehouse status from any premises;'*

This head of appeal relates to decisions on the approval or withdrawal of approval of persons as fiscal warehouse keepers together with withdrawal of fiscal warehouse status.

'(e)   *the proportion of input tax allowable under section 26;'*

Appeals relating to partial exemption such as the withdrawal or refusal to approve special partial exemption methods fall under this head.

'(f)   *a claim by a taxable person under section 27;'*

This relates to claims for input tax deduction on goods imported by a taxable person belonging to a third party where a double charge to tax would result from refusal of the claim.

'(fa)   *a decision contained in a notification under paragraph (4) of article 12A of the Value Added Tax (Payments on Account) Order 1993 that an election under paragraph (1) of that article shall cease to have effect;'*

This relates to the payment on account provisions where the trader wishes to pay the actual tax due for the preceding month rather than the predetermined amount.

'(g)   *the amount of any refunds under section 35;'*

This relates to appeals against refusal of claims under the DIY construction of buildings scheme.

'(h)   *a claim for a refund under section 36 or section 22 of the 1983 Act;'*

Bad-debt relief appeals fall under this provision, including claims under earlier bad-debt claims regimes.

'(j)   *the amount of any refunds under section 40;'*

This provision relates to refunds claimed by non-taxable persons on supplies of new motor vehicles which are removed to another EU country.

'(k)   *the refusal of an application such as is mentioned in section 43B(1) or (2);'*

This relates to refusals of applications relating to group treatment.

'(ka) *the giving of a notice under section 43C(1) or (3);'*

This head relates to appeals against notices issued by HMRC terminating group treatment.

'(l)   *the requirement of any security under section 48(7) or paragraph 4(1A) or (2) of Schedule 11;'*

Appeals against the requirement by HMRC for a trader to give security as a condition for trading are brought under this head. Note that the jurisdiction of the tribunal on this type of appeal is supervisory, not appellate. The tribunal can only consider the reasonableness of HMRC's decision, examining what evidence they did or did not take into account when it made the decision under appeal. The tribunal may disagree with the decision but can only interfere if HMRC have not acted reasonably. See *C & E Commrs v John Dee Ltd* [1995] BVC 361.

'(m)   *any refusal or cancellation of certification under section 54 or any refusal to cancel such certification;'*

This head relates to the flat rate scheme for farmers.

'(n)   *any liability to a penalty or surcharge by virtue of any of sections 59 to 69A;'*

This head of appeal relates to the liability of a person to be issued with a penalty. It is concerned with the legal basis of the penalty, not the amount of any penalty that has been issued.

'(o)   *a decision of the Commissioners under section 61 (in accordance with section 61(5));'*

This concerns the liability of directors and managing officers of companies to be issued with penalties where the company is liable to a penalty.

'(p) an assessment–

(i) *under section 73(1) or (2) in respect of a period for which the appellant has made a return under this Act; or*

(ii) *under subsections (7), (7A) or (7B) of that section; or*

(iii) *under section 75;*

or the amount of such an assessment;'

This is the head of appeal under which most assessments to VAT are brought to the tribunal. Section 73(7) relates to requirements of taxable persons to account for goods acquired or imported. Sections 73(7A) and (7B) relate to the fiscal warehousing regime and s. 75 relates to assessments on non-taxable persons for failing to notify the acquisition of excise goods or new means of transport.

'(q) *the amount of any penalty, interest or surcharge specified in an assessment under section 76;'*

This relates to the amount of a penalty, therefore any claims for mitigation will be brought under this head.

'(r) *the making of an assessment on the basis set out in section 77(4);'*

Appeals against the making of assessments outside the normal time limits are brought under this provision.

'(s) *any liability of the Commissioners to pay interest under section 78 or the amount of interest so payable;'*

This relates to interest paid in the case of official error – it covers both the liability and the amount of such liability.

'(sa) *an assessment under section 78A(1) or the amount of such an assessment;'*

This relates to overpayments of interest paid in the case of official error.

'(t) *a claim for the repayment of an amount under section 80, an assessment under subsection (4A) of that section or the amount of such an assessment;'*

These heads relate to appeals against decisions to repay (or not) tax overpaid by taxable persons and overpayments of such amounts.

'(ta) *an assessment under section 80B(1) or the amount of such an assessment;'*

These heads relate to appeals against assessments for recovery of overpaid VAT under the unjust enrichment provisions where the taxpayer has not repaid his customers under reimbursement arrangements.

'(u) any direction or supplementary direction made under paragraph 2 of Schedule 1;'

This relates to directions made by HMRC in respect of registration of two or more businesses as a single taxable person.

'(v) any direction under paragraph 1, 1A or 2 of Schedule 6 or under paragraph 2 of Schedule 4 to the 1983 Act; '

This relates to appeals against directions that transactions between connected persons and supplies of goods to non-taxable persons for resale must be at open market value.

'(w) any direction under paragraph 1 of Schedule 7;'

This head relates to appeals against directions that acquisitions between connected persons must be at open market value.

'(wa) any direction or assessment under Schedule 9A;'

Appeals against decisions under the grouping anti-avoidance provisions are brought under this head.

'(x) any refusal to permit the value of supplies to be determined by a method described in a notice published under paragraph 2(6) of Schedule 11;'

This permits appeals against refusals by HMRC to allow the use of a retail scheme.

'(y) any refusal of authorisation or termination of authorisation in connection with the scheme made under paragraph 2(7) of Schedule 11;'

This relates to decisions in respect of the cash accounting scheme.

'(z) any requirements imposed by the Commissioners in a particular case by virtue of paragraph 2B(2) or 3(1) of Schedule 11;'

This relates to the refusal of HMRC to allow the production of invoices by computer or self-billed invoices.

'(za) a direction under paragraph 8 of Schedule 11A;'

This relates to HMRC's use of their powers to aggregate the activities of two or more persons, where artificial separation of business activities to fall below the threshold for reporting avoidance schemes is illegal.

'(zb) any liability for a penalty under paragraph 10(1) of Schedule 11A, any assessment under paragraph 12(1) of that Schedule or the amount of such as assessment;'

This relates to the imposition and amount of any penalty for failure to notify an avoidance scheme.

'(zz) a decision of the Commissioners on a review under regulation 21 of the Money Laundering Regulations 2003.'

This relates to HMRC's powers to refuse registration to, or penalise, money service operators and high-value dealers.

Other appealable matters include:

- where HMRC have refused to allow a taxpayer to use the flat rate scheme, or the percentage used is disputed;
- in respect of a liability arising under VATA 1994, s 77A, for joint and several liability of the tax;
- refusal to grant permission to opt to tax, VATA 1994, Sch. 10, pt 1;
- any direction to keep records VATA 1994, Sch. 11, para 6A;
- any decision by HMRC regarding electronic filing of returns under Finance Act 2002, s 135;
- any information notice under Finance Act 2008, Sch. 36, paras 1 or 2; or a penalty under Sch. 35, paras 39-40A of that Act, for failing to keep records or obstructing an officer;
- a penalty imposed under Finance Act 2009, Sch. 46, paras 4-9, for failing to comply with the duties of a senior accounting officer; and
- a notice under Finance Act 2009, Sch. 49, paras 1-3, in respect of the power to obtain contact details of debtors.

⚠ *Warning!*

Any matter not listed above is not appealable to the tribunal. In order to lodge a valid appeal, therefore, it is necessary to confirm that the issue falls into one of the above categories. If it does not, some other form of redress may be appropriate. (See **Complaints 37.11 – 37.14.**)

See **37.5.3** regarding the prerequisites to an appeal and, in particular, an appeal against a decision by HMRC that relied on a prior decision that is not within the items listed above.

It has often been thought that an appeal cannot be made where the taxpayer has relied on an extra statutory concession. It has been held in *R (oao Greenwich Property Ltd) v C &E Cmmrs ChD* [2001] BTC 261, that it would be 'unfair and so unlawful for Customs not to apply the concession'. The concession would, however, only be enforceable where the taxpayer had legitimately applied the concession, used it correctly and abided by all of its conditions.

Planning Point

Where a matter does fall under these headings the usual remedy is a judicial review see **37.10**. Judicial review can be a long and expensive process. It also has strict time limits and if a taxpayer does not act quickly the opportunity to apply for a judicial review can be lost. Judicial review is usually an appropriate course of action where there is an administrative matter (such as the exercise of a discretion) to be decided. The First Tier Tribunal, however, in *Westward Group Ltd* [2012] TC 01736 has decided that it can hear a matter on the exercise of a discretion to strike out a default surcharge penalty on the grounds of proportionality.

> Whilst HMRC claimed that the Tribunal did not have the grounds to determine an administrative matter, the Tribunal held that it could hear a case on the grounds of proportionality.

Law: VATA 1994, s. 83

37.5 Making a tribunal appeal

37.5.1 Parties to an appeal

Normally, the appellant will be the person who has made the supply although the recipient of a supply may appeal if he has sufficient interest in the case (see *Processed Vegetable Growers Association Ltd* (1973) VATTR 87). Other parties can be joined to the appeal if they can demonstrate sufficient interest (see *Barclays Bank plc (No. 4)* [1992] BVC 938).

Where the appeal is brought by a sole trader he will be shown as the appellant together with the trading name of the business. An appeal by a limited company will be brought in the name of the company. An appeal by the group must be brought by the representative member of the group.

Where the taxable person is a partnership, one or more partners can bring an appeal or can apply to the tribunal for the appeal to be brought in the name of the firm.

Where an appellant dies or becomes insolvent so that the interest or liability passes to the personal representatives or the person appointed as successor (in the case of bankruptcy or other incapacity) the appeal may be carried on in the name of that person or persons. If the successor does not wish to continue proceedings the appeal or application may be dismissed. (Rule 13).). Guidance to making an appeal and the appeal documents can be viewed online at *www.tribunals.gov.uk/Tax/FormsGuidance.htm*

37.5.2 The First Tier Tax Tribunal and Tax Appeals Tribunals

Introduction

VAT appeals will generally be heard by the First Tier Tribunal with the Finance & Tax Chamber of the Upper Tribunal intended to function principally as an appeal tribunal.

The role of the Upper Tribunal is to hear appeals from the First Tier Tribunal essentially taking the place of the Chancery Division of the High Court. There are limited instances of where the Upper Tribunal will be the first hearing of a case and a limited judicial review role.

The First Tier Tribunal has three permanent judges and 34 fee-paid judges. There are also 166 fee-paid non-legal members.

Premises will be in Bedford Square – London, Manchester and Edinburgh. There will be a new administrative centre in Birmingham which will be the entry point for all VAT appeals.

Standard and complex VAT are allocated to London, Manchester and Edinburgh.

The Upper Tribunal will have six permanent judges plus judges of the Chancery Division of High Court, plus three Scottish judges. There will also be 26 fee-paid deputy judges and all the judges of the First Tier Tribunal.

Cases can range from the very simple to the extremely complicated and complex, and there are arrangements in the Tax Chamber of the First Tier Tribunal to deal with streaming cases according to their complexity. There is also a procedural possibility of starting an appeal in the Upper Tribunal for the most complex of cases.

Cases are allocated to one of four categories:

(1) Default paper – cases which can normally be dealt with on paper although either party is at liberty to apply for an oral hearing;

(2) Basic – minimal exchange of documents beforehand and completed after a short hearing;

(3) Standard – detailed case management and referral of documentation beforehand and completed after a hearing, and

(4) Complex – substantial case management in the form of one or more pre-trial reviews.

The First Tier Tribunal may only refer complex cases to the Upper Tribunal. The transfer to the Upper Tier will require the agreement of the First Tier Tribunal and the agreement of both the president of the First Tier Tribunal and the president of the Upper Tribunal.

Appeal documentation can be obtained at *www.justice.gov.uk/tribunals/tax/appeals* and the appeal document can be lodged by emailing *taxappeals@tribunals.gsi.gov. uk*. The Tribunal system can also be contacted through their processing centre at:

First-tier Tribunal (Tax)
HM Courts & Tribunals Service
3rd Floor Temple Court
35 Bull Street
Birmingham
B4 6EQ
Telephone: 0845 223 8080 (8:30am – 5:00pm)

The details of what is required in the notice of appeal is contained in the appeal documents. It requires fairly basic details, such as name and address of the appellant and any representative, the address for the service of documents, the details of the disputed decision and any documents relevant to the decision. When initially making the appeal, this basic information is sufficient but it is necessary to provide a lot more detail prior to actually attending the appeal (see **37.5**).

Basic Cases

- Reasonable excuse cases against penalties and surcharges;
- Appeals against penalties for late filing and late payment;
- Appeals against notices to provide information;
- Application for permission to make a late appeal.

Standard Case Allocation

- Standard case allocation deals with any VAT case that is not basic or complex.

Complex Cases

- Lengthy or complex evidence;
- Lengthy hearing, complex or important principles or issue;
- Large financial sums involved.

Costs

The First Tier Tribunal can award costs if a party or representative acts unreasonably or if there is a wasted cost jurisdiction.

No costs are normally payable in the First Tier Tribunal for default paper, basic or standard cases.

In complex cases it is the default position that the normal (High Court) costs regime will apply, ie that costs will usually follow the event, except where a taxpayer has not made a written request to the Tribunal within 28 days of receiving notice that the case has been allocated a complex case that the proceedings be excluded from the default cost regime. The taxpayer has the right to opt-out of the cost regime in which case he will not recover costs against HMRC if he wins. (See **37.8** in respect of costs.)

Venues

The venue will be primarily determined by the taxpayer's postcode. The Tribunal will determine the location and the time of the hearing. It will give 14 days notice unless there are exceptional circumstances. The parties are usually asked what dates they wish to avoid before the listing is made.

It is rare that there is a dispute between the parties as to the location, but a taxpayer did object to HMRC trying to move a hearing to London. The stated reason for the move by HMRC was to join the case with another one being heard in London. The appellants objected to this. It is believed that the appellants and HMRC thought the taxpayer would have a more sympathetic hearing in Scotland. This was an avoidance case and at the time the Scottish Courts were taking a distinct view from the English Courts (RBS Deutschland Holdings GmbH (VTD 18840)).

Law: Rule 31 The Tribunal Procedure (First-tier Tribunal) (Tax Chamber) Rules 2009 (SI 2009/273)

Time Limits

An appeal must be made within 30 days of the decision that is being appealed against, or within 30 days of the person becoming aware of the decision, if the decision was not addressed to that person. The appeal is made to HMRC to review their decision. Where HMRC is requested or required to make a review, an appeal to the Tribunal may not be made until the end of the review period; it is then necessary to appeal to the Tribunal within 30 days of the notice of the decision from HMRC's review person.

HMRC have 45 days to conduct their review process. An appeal can then be made to the Tribunal at the end of that 45-day period, and there is a 30-day time limit to make this appeal from the end of the 45-day review period.

No appeal can be made when a request is made to HMRC to consider the review out of time until HMRC either decide not to review the matter (and then there are 30 days to appeal to the Tribunal) or, if HMRC do review the matter, the normal time limits described above apply.

Late Appeals

The regulations require the taxpayer to confirm the appeal is in time or give reasons for the lateness.

An out of time application is a basic case, but protocol normally gives HMRC 14 days to object otherwise the issue will be dealt with as a preliminary consensual matter at the substantive appeal hearing.

Hardship Cases

It is necessary for the tax due (if any) to be paid before an appeal is heard where the appeal is in respect of output tax due, penalties, surcharges or interest due, or in respect of the unjust enrichment provisions. A taxpayer does not need to repay input tax in an input tax appeal.

Hardship applications must firstly be made to HMRC providing information from the taxpayer to substantiate why payment of the tax should not be made before the case is heard.

An appeal against a refusal by HMRC to allow hardship is an interlocutory matter in the substantive hearing.

To show hardship, it is necessary to show that the entity making the appeal does not have the money to make the appeal. Thus, if a company is making the appeal, the financial position of the shareholders and directors is irrelevant. It is also necessary to show not only that there are insufficient funds to pay the tax due, but also that the money cannot be raised. The fact that it may be difficult to raise funds or it will mean obtaining a loan or mortgage is not relevant, and this is not hardship.

Where hardship is granted and an appeal is heard without the tax being paid, but then lost, default interest is payable for the period the tax was not paid. Where the hardship appeal is lost, but the appeal is won, HMRC may be liable to pay interest on the amount disputed.

Witnesses

It is expected that only in the more complex cases witnesses will be sworn especially where those cases involve deliberate error, concealment or dishonesty. Witnesses do not always need to appear at the Tribunal. If both sides agree, non-controversial evidence can be given in a statement. HMRC will require the witness to appear if they dispute something or they wish to cross-examine the witness. HMRC will usually wish the witness to appear unless good reasons can be given for the witness not to appear.

The Tribunal or either party to the appeal can summon any person to appear as a witness provided it is a matter that a person can be required to give evidence for in a UK Court of Law. The witness must be given 14 days notice, although it is advisable for a longer period to be given. Expenses for travel costs can be paid.

Law: Rule 16 The Tribunal Procedure (First-tier Tribunal) (Tax Chamber) Rules 2009 (SI 2009/273)

Lead Cases and Standovers

There is a formal procedure for the Tribunal to designate lead cases.

This is possibly more common where a party or Tribunal consider it appropriate to stay a case pending the outcome of another case and a direction may be sought to stand over an appeal until a lead case has been heard.

Law: Rule 18 The Tribunal Procedure (First-tier Tribunal) (Tax Chamber) Rules 2009 (SI 2009/273)

Summary

The above is an outline of how the reformed Tribunals are expected to operate and how they have operated to date. At present there is a degree of uncertainty how the reforms will work in practice, although it is expected that they will be run in a familiar manner to the previous Tribunals.

It will be some time before the Upper Tribunal gets into its stride and quite how it will operate in practice – and how differently from the High Court – will be established over time.

The following sections have been left in this publication as they are still relevant for appeal applications which were made prior to 1 April 2009. In addition, it provides guidance on how the new Tribunal system is expected to run; numerous sections in VATA 1994 have not been disturbed and will apply to appeals under the old as well as the new Tribunal system. In addition, it may be some years before appeals made under the old regulations make their way through the legal system and these provisions are, therefore, still relevant. Appeals that were lodged before 1 April 2009 will be heard by the new Tribunals (usually the Lower Tier, but also the Upper Tier where appropriate). These cases will be heard as if the old provisions applied (for example in relation to direction and costs).

37.5.3 Prerequisites for an appeal

VATA 1994, s. 84 contains provisions relating to appeals including some conditions which must be fulfilled before an appeal can be heard by a tribunal.

An appeal cannot be entertained by a tribunal unless an appellant has made and paid all the returns required to have been made by him. This provision has been affected by the decision of the tribunal in *Coleman* [2000] BVC 2,042 where the tribunal held that the provisions of s. 84(2) were contrary to the EU principles of proportionality. The appellant had a directly enforceable right under the Sixth VAT Directive to have the appeal heard. HMRC's practice following that decision is set out in *Business Brief* 23/99 (17 November 1999). HMRC will not apply for the appeal to be struck out if returns are outstanding in respect of periods not in dispute.

Where an appeal is brought against a decision with respect to matters mentioned in s. 83(b), (n), (p) or (q), it shall not be entertained unless the amount determined to be payable as VAT is paid or deposited.

However, the appeal will be entertained if the appellant can satisfy HMRC or, on appeal, the tribunal that payment of the amount assessed would cause the appellant to suffer hardship. HMRC will expect the appellant to demonstrate that he has attempted to borrow the VAT assessed from his bank or other sources and in the event that the borrowing limit has been reached will expect evidence to be made available to them or the tribunal. Hardship applications to the tribunal are heard in private but an applicant should expect to be cross-examined rigorously on his financial standing. However, unlike in customs appeals there does not appear to be a provision enabling the appeal to be entertained when only part of the assessment can be deposited. At one time amounts of input tax which had been assessed did not need to be deposited, but following *Safegold Fashions Ltd* [1992] BVC 847 and the enactment of what is now s. 73(2) of VATA 1994, the appeal would be brought under s. 83(p) so deposit of the VAT is required.

> ### Planning point
>
> Where the appeal relates to a claim for input tax on an item which is in the nature of a luxury, amusement or entertainment, a tribunal shall not allow the appeal unless it considers that the decision made by HMRC was unreasonable or would have been unreasonable if information given to the tribunal that could not have been brought to the attention of HMRC had been available to be taken into account when the decision was taken. The effect of the provision is to change the jurisdiction of the tribunal from appellate to supervisory. Thus the tribunal on such an appeal may only judge the reasonableness of HMRC's decision and cannot substitute its own determination for that of HMRC.

Where an appeal relates to group treatment in circumstances that HMRC consider that the application must be refused for the protection of the revenue, the tribunal's power is to review the reasonableness of HMRC's decision and it cannot substitute its own decision.

The tribunal's jurisdiction in respect of appeals under s. 83(u) is supervisory.

Where on appeal it is found by the tribunal that the amount deposited by the appellant in order to have the appeal entertained was not payable or the credit due to the appellant has not been paid by HMRC, the amount due will be paid to the appellant, together with interest.

Where a hardship application has been allowed and the appeal against the assessment fails, the tribunal has jurisdiction to award interest to HMRC although the power to award interest is discretionary.

The provisions relating to VAT appeals (which have no statutory review procedure, unlike other indirect tax appeals) may not be used to circumvent the review provisions of s. 14 of the Finance Act 1994 unless the appeal relates to the issue of whether goods imported are entitled to be zero-rated.

Where an appeal is against a decision of HMRC that depended upon a prior decision of HMRC in relation to the appellant, the fact that the prior decision is not itself an appealable matter does not prevent the tribunal allowing the appeal if it would have allowed an appeal against the prior decision. This provision was introduced following the case of *C & E Commrs v J H Corbitt (Numismatists) Ltd* (1980) 1 BVC 330. Although at one time this provision was thought to provide an avenue of appeal against the exercise of extra-statutory concessions by Customs, it was held in *C & E Commrs v Arnold* [1996] BVC 464 that there had to be two decisions in order for the provision to apply. Accordingly, this route cannot be used to challenge the exercise by HMRC of their discretion. Consequently, the only effective challenge to HMRC's decisions relating to the exercise of their discretion to apply an extra-statutory concession is by way of judicial review (see below).

37.5.4 Settling appeals by agreement

VATA 1994, s. 85 sets out the provisions whereby the parties can settle customs, excise and VAT appeals by agreement, without recourse to the tribunal. The agreement can be written or oral with the decision under appeal treated as being upheld without variation, varied in a particular matter, or as discharged or cancelled. The effect of an agreement is that the appeal is treated as if the tribunal had determined it in accordance with the agreed terms. The agreement can also address issues relating to costs.

An appellant has 30 days from the date of the agreement to repudiate or resile from it.

Where the agreement is not in writing the agreement is not treated as a disposal of the appeal unless a notice is given by either party to the other confirming the terms.

A further provision relating to the disposal of appeals is contained in s. 85(4). Thus, where an appellant indicates orally or in writing that he does not wish to pursue the appeal, HMRC may treat their decision as upheld unless they serve a notice within 30 days of the appellant's notification stating that they object to the withdrawal.

The provisions relating to the settling of appeals enable HMRC to enforce assessments once agreements are reached with appellants and their representatives. As stated above, payment of costs can be included within the agreement and advisers should ensure that this aspect is covered and that terms as to costs are included.

Provisions with regard to the enforcement of decisions are contained in VATA 1994, s. 87 which provides that HMRC may register decisions so that the amounts of VAT payable as a result of the decision can be recovered under the High Court enforcement of judgment rules. Similar procedures are available in Scotland and Northern Ireland.

37.5.5 Types of VAT appeal – under the Tribunal Rules pre 1 April 2009

Whilst all appeals have to be through the new Tribunal system, any extant appeals will remain within the old system and subject to the old rules. If the appeal has not yet been heard, it will be heard by the First Tier Tribunal or the Upper Tribunal as appropriate. It is likely that all old appeals will have made there way past the Tribunal stage by now.

Evasion penalty appeal

This is an appeal against an assessment to a penalty imposed under VATA 1994, s. 60 for conduct involving dishonesty. It also embraces decisions under s. 61 where the dishonesty of a company is attributable to an officer of the company. It covers appeals against the underlying tax which it is alleged has been evaded.

Mitigation appeal

This appeal is concerned solely with the amount of any penalty imposed in cases where the tribunal has power to mitigate (reduce) the penalty imposed. If the grounds of appeal disclose an issue on the liability to a penalty, the appeal will not be treated as a mitigation appeal. The notice of appeal (see below) should make it clear that the appeal is one of mitigation only.

Reasonable excuse appeal

In this appeal the grounds on the notice of appeal indicate that the basis of the appeal is that the appellant has a reasonable excuse for incurring a penalty. Again, where the appeal raises issues relating to the liability to a penalty it will not fall under this head but under the following category.

Appeals, other than those referred to above

Prior to the introduction of civil penalties there was only one type of appeal. The procedure for this category of appeal covers issues of liability to tax, including input tax claims as well as the amounts of any assessment issued. It is important to note that if a mitigation appeal or a reasonable excuse appeal involves issues of VAT liability and/or issues as to the amount of any assessment, the procedure for this appeal should be followed, rather than the procedure for the shorter form appeals of mitigation and reasonable excuse.

Planning point

As will be explained below, each appeal has its own pre-tribunal procedure so it is important to identify which appeal is being undertaken.

In the Public Notice issued by the President of the VAT & Duties Tribunals (*VAT – Appeals and Application to the Tribunals: Explanatory Leaflet* (revised August 1995)) reference is made to various categories of appeal for the previous appeal system.

1. Category 1 appeals deal with penalties for tax evasion.

2. Category 2 appeals cover 'general penalties' which include:

    (a) default surcharge (late returns or late payments): appeals can be made on grounds of reasonable excuse;

    (b) penalty for misdeclaration or neglect: both dismissal of the penalty on grounds of reasonable excuse (see (a) above) and mitigation (that is, a reduction in the penalty) can be asked for in the same appeal;

(c) late registration penalty (that is, civil penalty for failure to notify liability to register): the position is the same as for serious misdeclaration penalties (see (b) above), and

(d) reduction of a penalty for tax evasion (dishonest conduct): an appeal can be made by a person seeking mitigation (a reduction) of the penalty; note, however, that appeal against liability to the penalty is a category 1 appeal (see point 1 above).

3. Category 3 appeals include all matters except those solely concerning reasonable excuses or penalties. The tribunal rules do not recognise this categorisation but it is mentioned here for completeness.

Law: VAT Tribunals Rules 1986 (SI 1986/590) ('the Rules').

37.5.6 Method of appealing – under the old appeal system

Rule 3 provides that an appeal shall be brought by a notice of appeal served at the appropriate tribunal centre. This is the tribunal centre for the area in which is situated the address to which the disputed decision was sent. It is possible for an appeal to be transferred to another centre if there are reasons why a transfer is appropriate. For example, the decision may have been sent to the representative member of a VAT group based in London whereas the decision concerns the activities of a group member company based in Manchester. Since most of the personnel involved in the case will be in Manchester, including the HMRC officers, it makes sense to transfer the case to Manchester to save costs.

> **Planning point**
>
> Occasionally, if Leading Counsel is based in London, costs can be saved by transferring the case there.

Law: VAT Tribunals Rules 1986 (SI 1986/590), r. 15

37.5.7 Notice of appeal – old appeal system

The notice of appeal must be signed by the appellant or by the appellant's representative and must state the following information:

- the name and address of the appellant;
- the date (if any) with effect from which the appellant was registered for VAT and the nature of the business;
- the address of the HMRC office from which the disputed decision was sent;
- the date of the document containing the disputed decision and the address to which it was sent; a copy of the dispute decision should be attached, and

- the grounds of appeal – either on the official notice of appeal form (Trib 1) or as a separate document; where the appeal is a reasonable excuse appeal the grounds must give particulars of the excuse relied on.

37.5.8 Grounds of appeal

The grounds of appeal should be drafted with sufficient particularity to identify the issues on which the tribunal will have to adjudicate. Equally, the grounds will need to be sufficiently detailed to inform HMRC of the case they will have to meet.

Planning point

Setting out the grounds fully may cause HMRC, on the review of the case by their headquarters, to reconsider the decision giving rise to the appeal. If the appellant does not specify ('plead' is the technical term) all the grounds, there is a risk that the tribunal will refuse to allow a new ground to be admitted and argued at the hearing or, more likely, will penalise the appellant for any costs thrown away as a result of HMRC needing an adjournment to consider the new point. In the event that the appeal is won on the new point, it is very possible that the tribunal would refuse the appellant's costs.

37.5.9 Time for appealing in VAT appeals – old appeal system

The notice of appeal must be served at the appropriate tribunal centre before the expiration of 30 days after the date of the disputed decision. However, r. 4 provides that if during the 30-day period for appealing HMRC have notified the appellant by letter that the time to appeal against the disputed decision has been extended until the expiration of 21 days from the date set out in the letter, the notice of appeal must be served before the 21-day period has expired.

This procedure is useful in the context of local reviews of the disputed decision where an appellant may not wish to proceed to a full appeal immediately since doing so would bring the requirement to deposit the tax. The 'downside' of using the procedure is that if the review results in the decision being withdrawn, there will be no appeal in place to enable an order of costs to be made in the appellant's favour. Thus the decision to appeal is finely balanced. Of course, the argument against depositing the assessed amount is the fact that interest on the assessment will continue whilst the principal sum remains unpaid. If the appeal is ultimately successful then interest on the amount deposited and costs will be payable by HMRC. On balance, since costs start to 'run' from the date of the disputed decision, not the date of a notice of appeal, it is likely to be more sensible to appeal against a decision without delay if substantial costs are likely to be incurred putting forward arguments in support of the review.

If the r. 4 procedure is followed, the notice of appeal must have attached to it the letter from HMRC extending the time limit for appealing.

HMRC do not have power to extend the time limits for appealing so if the time limit has expired the appellant should apply directly to the tribunal for leave to serve a notice of appeal out of time. If the limit has only been exceeded by a matter of days the tribunal will sometimes allow the application 'of its own motion'. This means that the tribunal considers that the 'out of time' period is so short that in all probability it would allow the application, even if HMRC opposed it.

If the r. 4 procedure is to be adopted, the request must come from the recipient of the disputed decision within the 30-day period commencing after the date of the disputed decision. Once the 30-day period has expired HMRC have no power to extend the period or invoke the procedure. The remedy is to go to the tribunal for leave to appeal out of time and then stand over the appeal until the local review has taken place. It may be possible to agree with HMRC that the tax involved is not deposited. Of course, if HMRC do agree to the entire appeal being stood over it would follow that they would be unable to apply for the appeal to be dismissed for failure to deposit the amount of tax assessed unless they apply to remove the standover.

⚠ *Warning!*

Although tribunals in the past were generous in the latitude they allowed to appellants in the context of late appeals, care needs to be taken to ensure that too much time does not elapse between the expiry of the 30-day period and applying to lodge a notice of appeal out of time.

In the case of *University of Reading* [1998] BVC 2,163 the assessment (for £1.3 million) was issued in 1992 and the notice of appeal was not issued until March 1997. The tribunal dismissed the appeal on the basis that the appellant had failed to give a satisfactory reason for not lodging the appeal in time. In the case of *Wan (t/a Wan's Chinese Takeaway)* [1997] BVC 2,364 the tribunal held that in recent cases judicial authority emphasises the need to carry out a discretionary balancing exercise where the balance of prejudice is only one factor to be taken into account. Previously, tribunals had concentrated on whether HMRC would be prejudiced by late appeals.

⚠ *Warning!*

Although the time delay in that instance was extreme, in the light of the *University of Reading* case, the safest course of action is to lodge the notice of appeal as soon as possible.

37.5.10 Procedure after the notice of appeal has been lodged

Following the service of the notice of appeal at the tribunal centre, the Proper Officer, who is the member of the administrative staff appointed by a chairman to carry out functions under the Rules, will send an acknowledgement to the appellant together with a copy of the notice of appeal and any accompanying documents to HMRC.

The acknowledgement will state the date of service of the notice of appeal. This is the date when the document was received at the tribunal centre. The acknowledgement will also state the date of notification of the appeal to HMRC. The date of notification fixes the time for the start of the period within which HMRC may, depending on the type of appeal, be required to submit a statement of case.

37.5.11 Striking out an appeal and notices of direction

Where HMRC consider that the tribunal does not have jurisdiction to hear an appeal they may serve a notice under applying for the appeal to be struck out. Appeals may also be struck out if an appellant does not comply with directions or fails to co-operate with the Tribunal system or the Tribunal does not believe that the appellant has any reasonable grounds for success.

For example, if the appellant appeals against a ruling by HMRC with regard to the liability of supplies to be made in future, an appeal does not lie since the tribunal can only deal with supplies that have been made. Also, if an appeal is lodged against the exercise of their discretion, HMRC will apply for it to be struck out. If, following a hearing, the application is successful the tribunal will strike out the appeal.

Where the appellant has not paid or deposited the tax assessed, HMRC will contend that the appeal should not be entertained. If the application is successful, following a hearing, the appeal will be dismissed. In practice, if HMRC serve such a notice, the appellant should either pay the assessment or serve a notice at the tribunal applying for the appeal to be heard without payment of the tax on the grounds of hardship.

The tribunal can dismiss an appeal for want of prosecution where the appellant or the person to whom the appellant's interest has devolved (for example his personal representatives) or been assigned, has been guilty of inordinate and inexcusable delay.

Subject to the rules relating to settling appeals by consent, an appeal cannot be struck out or dismissed under this procedure without a hearing. See *Gil Insurance Ltd* [2001] BVC 4,055. Applications for directions can be made orally at the hearing or in writing prior to the hearing. Applications can be made for a variety of matters including to strike out an appeal, to add parties to an appeal, to reinstate an appeal that has been struck out, orders for costs, summon persons to the hearing, a hardship application, etc.

Applications must be accompanied by a copy of the disputed decision unless one has previously been served. All other relevant documentation should also accompany the request for a direction in order to enable the Tribunal to make a decision. If insufficient documentation is provided, the Tribunal will find it hard to agree to make the direction.

Where HMRC serve a notice the tribunal will arrange a hearing of the application. In the event that the parties resolve the issue the hearing will be cancelled, provided the tribunal is notified in writing.

Law: Rules 6 & 8 The Tribunal Procedure (First-tier Tribunal) (Tax Chamber) Rules 2009 (SI 2009/273)

37.5.12 Pleadings, statement of case and other papers for the appeal

The term 'pleadings' is the name given to the series of documents drafted and served by one party to litigation on the other party or parties. The purpose of pleadings is to define and narrow the issues between the parties so that the court (in this case the tribunal) that eventually hears the case is able to concentrate on the issues rather than on extraneous and irrelevant matters. The papers provided to the appeal Tribunal will help the Tribunal come to a decision and can be agreed between the parties which can simplify proceedings.

It is advisable that a thorough statement of case is written up. This enables all parties to see the points that are being argued. It also ensures the appellant has a cogent and organised appeal, and helps the appellant ensure that all the necessary points are covered. Reference may be made in the statement of case to Court decisions that support the appeal. It should be noted that old VAT & Duties Tribunal and the First Tier Tribunal decisions are persuasive only. Upper Tier and other Court's decisions are binding on lower Courts. For example, a House of Lords decision is (very) persuasive to a hearing at the House of Lords, but binding to the Court of Appeal, and the Tribunals. A Court of Appeal decision will be persuasive to the House of Lords, but binding on the Tribunals. A lower court or Tribunal may, of course, be able to distinguish the case before it from the higher Court decision and not be bound.

It is necessary to gather documents in various bundles. It is suggested that there should be a separate binder for the Statement of Case. In another bundle will be any case decisions referred to and a third bundle will have all other documents (the decision appealed against, witness statements, copies of public notices or internal guidance, and any other documents relied upon). Each bundle should have every page numbered and an index provided at the front. It is also advisable to place each bundle in a different coloured folder so that they can be referred to easily in the Tribunal. Where the Statement of Case refers to a case or document, the relevant page and the folder colour should be noted in the Statement. It is suggested that two copies of the bundle are provided to HMRC, three to the Tribunal (in case there are two members plus a chairman), at least two for the appellant, and a spare copy. This is a minimum of eight copies.

It is advisable to agree with HMRC which documents are to be bundled. It is common for both parties to rely on similar documents and cases. To prevent confusion and avoid duplication, it may be possible to agree a common set of bundles. Where possible, the appellants can agree a number of facts with HMRC. This saves time at Tribunal where a common set of facts can be portrayed to the Tribunal. (See **23.6.5** for further details for bundle preparation.)

The following details the different types of appeals and what is required.

Default paper cases

HMRC must send a statement of case to the Tribunal and the appellant so that it is received within 42 days after the notice of appeal has been sent by the Tribunal. HMRC also needs to state whether the case is to be dealt with or without a hearing. The appellant can send a reply to the Tribunal and HMRC within 30 days of HMRC's Statement of Case; it is usually advisable to do this. The reply should provide a response to HMRC's statement of case and any other information that it deems relevant. It should also make a request for a hearing if one is required. If the reply is sent late, a request for an extension must also be enclosed with the reply. It is advisable to contact both HMRC and the Tribunal centre before the time limit expires, requesting an extension. After receipt of the reply or when the time limit for the reply expires, the Tribunal will proceed to determine the case or will call a hearing if either party has requested it (or it decides a hearing is appropriate if neither party has requested it).

Basic cases

HMRC do not need to send a statement of case for a basic appeal. Where HMRC wishes to raise new issues that have not previously been communicated to the appellant, these must be documented and notified to the appellant as soon as is reasonably practical. If it is considered that notice is not reasonable, a direction can be sought that more time be allowed to consider the notification. Sufficient detail needs to be given to allow the appellant to respond at the hearing.

Standard or complex cases

HMRC must send a statement of case to the Tribunal and the appellant so that it is received within 60 days after the notice of appeal has been sent by the Tribunal. HMRC also needs to state whether the case is to be dealt with or without a hearing. The appellant can send a reply to the Tribunal and HMRC and it is usually advisable to do this. Both parties are to provide a list of documents that they will rely on within 42 days of the Statement of Case being delivered. The documents are normally made available for inspection to each party (unless privileged).

Law: Rules 24-27 The Tribunal Procedure (First-tier Tribunal) (Tax Chamber) Rules 2009 SI 2009/273)

Evasion penalty appeal – old Tribunal system

The procedure to be followed by the parties to an evasion penalty appeal after the notice of appeal has been served is more involved than in other appeals. The steps are as follows.

1. Within 42 days of the date of notification, being the date when the tribunal centre sends the notice of appeal to HMRC or the date when any r. 6 application has been withdrawn or dismissed, HMRC must serve their statement of case setting out the fact and matters on which they rely for making the penalty assessment and the assessment for the tax due as a result of the conduct of the appellant.

    The statement of case must contain full particulars of the dishonesty together with the statutory references under which the penalty or tax is assessed.

2. Within 42 days of the date of notification of the statement of case, the appellant must serve a document called a defence, setting out the facts and matters on which he relies for his defence to the assessment.

3. Within 21 days of the date of notification of the defence, HMRC may serve a reply to the defence. They must do so if it is necessary to set out a fact or matter showing illegality or which shows the defence is not maintainable or which, if not set out, might take the appellant by surprise or which raises any fact or matter not arising out of the statement of case.

If the appellant makes admissions of fact in his defence, HMRC are not required to prove that fact at the hearing.

The rules provide that each document (statement of case, defence and reply) must contain a statement in brief, summary form, of the matters and facts on which each party relies but not the evidence by which the party intends to prove the facts. Each document must be set out in numbered paragraphs with each paragraph containing a separate allegation. Points of law may be included or raised in the documents although, as a matter of practice, legal argument is better reserved to the hearing.

Law: VAT Tribunals Rules 1986 (SI 1986/590), r. 7

Procedure in reasonable excuse and mitigation appeals – old Tribunal system

There is no requirement for HMRC to serve a statement of case in these appeals although they are required to serve a copy of the disputed decision on the tribunal if one has not already been lodged. In the event that there is an issue of liability to be determined or an issue as to the quantum of an assessment, the usual appeal procedure should be followed.

In the absence of any r. 6 application, the tribunal will set the case down for hearing as soon as convenient.

37.5.13   Other procedural matters

Amendments

A tribunal may amend any of the appeal documents (other than decisions or directions) to correct errors or defects in them and for the purpose of determining the issues in dispute.

Withdrawal of appeal or application

An appellant or applicant may withdraw his appeal or application at any time by serving a signed notice to that effect on the tribunal centre.

Law: Rule 17 The Tribunal Procedure (First-tier Tribunal) (Tax Chamber) Rules 2009 (SI 2009/273)

Power of the tribunal to extend time and to give directions

The tribunal has power to extend time and examples have already been given showing the kinds of situation in which it will exercise its power.

The tribunal can give directions to assist in the speedy disposal of the appeal. In practice, this power is frequently exercised by means of pre-trial reviews in cases that are likely to be complex or lengthy. The parties are brought together to agree the issues to be argued in the appeal. Time limits are frequently given in relation to preparation of skeleton arguments and bundles of documents, as well as hearing dates. Where a case has been the subject of a large number of 'standovers' allegedly in an effort to settle it, the tribunal may set the case down for a hearing for directions in an endeavour to move matters along or bring them to a head.

> ### *Planning point*
> It should be noted that if either party fails to comply with a direction of the tribunal, the appeal or application may be dismissed.

37.5.14   Disclosure of documents – old Tribunal rules

See **37.5.12** in respect of the Tribunal rules for the new Tribunal rules from 1 April 2009.

A large part of the evidence in any case consists of documents. These may be letters between the parties arguing the appeal out in correspondence, which are probably of little value. On the other hand they may be prime documents recording a contract or agreement between the appellant and a third party which is highly relevant to the issues in the appeal. It is important that the parties are aware of the existence of the documents which the other party is likely to produce and rely on as evidence at the hearing. The tribunal's rules provide a procedure for the parties to follow with regard to disclosure of documents in advance of the hearing.

Disclosure, inspection and production of documents

Each party to an appeal (other than a reasonable excuse or mitigation appeal) and to an application for a hardship direction must serve a list of the documents in his possession, custody and power on which he intends to rely at the hearing.

Law: VAT Tribunals Rules 1986 (SI 1986/590), r. 20

Time limits for service of the list of documents

In an evasion appeal the list must be served within 15 days after the last day for the service by HMRC of any reply.

In any other appeal (other than a reasonable excuse or mitigation appeal) the list must be served within 30 days of the date of notification of the notice of appeal, or the date of notification of the notice of withdrawal of any application under r. 6, or the date on which a direction was released dismissing a r. 6 application. This means that the list of documents need not be issued until it is known that the appeal is a 'live' appeal.

> ### Planning point
>
> Lists of documents are often served late by both parties and are sometimes not served at all. However, failure to serve a list of documents means that the party in default will be unable to produce any document in support of its case at the hearing of the appeal.

Discovery of documents

A party may apply to the tribunal for a direction that the other party serves a list of all the documents which are or have been in his possession relating to any question or issue in the appeal and may order that party to verify the list by means of an affidavit. This is frequently done to 'flush out' documents which may prove evasion by the appellant or which might help to establish tax avoidance motives.

> ### Planning point
>
> It can also be used by appellants to obtain sight of officers' notebooks or even HMRC's internal minutes and advice.

A party is entitled to claim that disclosure of a document on the list is resisted on the ground that its production is subject to privilege. However, the party claiming privilege must provide a statement of the grounds of the claim.

The list of documents (together with the affidavit) must be sent to the other party who is at liberty to inspect and take copies of any document on the list which is not privileged from production. The usual practice is for each party to provide copies of the documents to the other side if requested. Appellants should carefully check HMRC's list of documents to ensure that, firstly, they have seen each document on the list and, secondly, that they have a copy since they will need it when the time comes to prepare the bundle of documents for the hearing (see below).

> ⚠ *Warning!*
>
> Any party disclosing a document on a list must produce it at the hearing if called upon to do so by the other party. Consequently, extreme care must be taken to ensure that the documents disclosed are of assistance to the disclosing party's case – rather than possibly having the opposite effect.

> ⚠ *Warning!*
>
> If there is any doubt about the value of producing a document, it is important to seek professional advice – preferably from the advocate instructed to represent the appellant – before disclosing the document. Should it be decided to produce the document (or any other document which the advocate advises should be disclosed) the party can apply to amend the list of documents to include additions. Provided the other side is given a copy of the document, it is not unusual for documents to be exchanged until quite shortly before the hearing, notwithstanding they do not appear on the original list of documents.

> ⚠ *Warning!*
>
> As can be appreciated, the list of documents needs to be submitted early on in the appeal proceedings when not all the evidence is available. Accordingly, care needs to be taken to ensure that only documents relevant to the appeal are disclosed.

If a document is not disclosed on the list or at least served on the other party to the appeal before the hearing, the party may be prevented from producing it at the hearing or may be required to pay the costs of any adjournment requested by the other party to enable it to study the document. It is not permissible to attempt to ambush the other party by springing surprise documents at the hearing.

37.5.15   Evidence in the tribunal

Subject to the rules on witness statements, the tribunal is entitled to direct or allow evidence of any fact to be given in any manner it may think fit and shall not refuse evidence tendered to it on the grounds only that such evidence would be inadmissible in a court of law (r. 28). Thus the tribunal is not bound by the strict rules of evidence and can and will receive evidence such as hearsay in certain circumstances where the evidence might not be received in a court of law.

The burden (or onus) of proof is normally on the appellant or applicant, except in penalty evasion cases where the burden of proof is on HMRC. The leading case on the burden of proof in ordinary appeals is *Grunwick Processing Laboratories v C & E Commrs* (1987) 3 BVC 29.

However, the standard of proof in all appeals is the civil standard of 'the balance of probabilities' rather than the criminal standard of 'beyond reasonable doubt'. In evasion cases the tribunal will normally need to be satisfied of the appellant's culpability with 'probability of a high degree'.

Witness statements

The general rule in the tribunal is that witnesses give evidence in person at the hearing on oath or by affirmation, r. 28(2). There are circumstances where evidence can be given in the form of written statement, with the witness not present, provided it is served on the other party in advance of the hearing. The procedure is subject to the other party agreeing to the procedure and not serving a notice objecting to the statement being treated as evidence.

14 days notice must be given to the witness that they are required to attend (see **37.5.2** for the time limits for the new Tribunal system since 1 April 2009).

The statement must contain the witness's name and address together with the evidence to be given. The statement must be served at the tribunal centre within the following time limits of:

- in an evasion penalty appeal, before the expiration of 21 days from the date of service of HMRC's reply;
- in the case of a mitigation or reasonable excuse appeal, 21 days from the notification of the notice of appeal, and
- in the case of any other appeal, 21 days after the date of notification of HMRC's statement of case.

The party served with the witness statement has 14 days in which to object to it, in which event the statement cannot be used, although the witness may attend and testify at the hearing.

In practice, this procedure is little used because if the evidence is at all contentious the other party will want to test the evidence under cross-examination at the hearing and will therefore object to the production of the statement. The value of the procedure lies in the ability to use it for proving formal matters such as formation of companies. It has been known for HMRC to use the procedure where an officer was too ill to attend the hearing.

There is a procedure under r. 21A whereby affidavits or depositions made in other legal proceedings may in certain circumstances be used as evidence in an appeal. The tribunal may give directions as to whether the document can be used at the hearing, even where the other party objects to the deposition or affidavit being so used.

The application of the rule was considered in the case of *Bord* [1993] BVC 837 where two statements were served which had previously been part of HMRC's case in the Crown Court against the appellant. The tribunal allowed the statements to be given in evidence, despite objection from the appellant. The tribunal chairman said in the course of the decision:

> 'Whether, in the light of the criticisms levelled on behalf of Mr Bord against the statements and their contents, the statements should be given any weight as evidence, is, in the opinion of this Tribunal, entirely a matter for the Tribunal that hears the appeal.
>
> This Tribunal has a discretion in the matter. It is also directed not to refuse evidence on the grounds only that such evidence would be inadmissible in the court of law (Rule 28(1)): so far as the present circumstances are concerned, this Tribunal can see nothing in Rule 21A that is relevant to cut down the scope of this direction. This Tribunal is aware that the Tribunal that actually hears the appeal will be competent to differentiate between what is strictly admissible and what is inadmissible and will be capable of giving such weight to the inadmissible part as is warranted by its merits. Taking all these factors into account, the Tribunal has concluded that it should allow the Statements of the New Yorker and of the Canadian to be admitted in evidence in this appeal.'

Witness summons and summons to third parties

The tribunal (usually by a chairman or the Registrar) has power to issue a summons to a person to attend a hearing to give evidence or to produce a document where the person or the document is required by a party to the appeal. A summons can also be issued to a person ordering him to allow a document to be inspected when it is necessary for the purpose of the appeal. In any case where the recipient of a summons is required to attend a hearing, or post or produce any document, he must be given sufficient money ('conduct money') to enable him to meet the expenses of complying with the summons.

A summons under this rule can be issued without prior notice or reference to the applicant or any other person and without a hearing. If a hearing is necessary then the only party is the applicant. Thus, the other party to the appeal is not made aware of the fact that it has been judged necessary to apply for a summons.

Law: VAT Tribunals Rules 1986 (SI 1986/590), r. 22; Tribunals Court and Enforcement Act 2007, Sch 5, para 10; The Tribunal Procedure (First-tier Tribunal) (Tax Chamber) Rules 2009 (SI 2009/273), r. 16.

Setting aside a witness summons

Under r. 22(8) the person served with the summons can apply by notice to the tribunal centre to set aside the witness summons served on him. Thus in the decision of *Home or Away Ltd* [2002] BVC 4,066 Customs applied for a witness summons to require the company accountant to attend the tribunal on the hearing of the appeal to give evidence. The accountant applied to the tribunal to set aside the summons on the ground that to give evidence would breach his duty of confidentiality to his client and would also be in breach of the European Convention on Human Rights. The application was rejected by the tribunal on the basis that although recognition is given to confidentiality between tax adviser and client, the circumstances of the particular case overrode that duty. The tribunal found that there had been no breach of the Convention.

37.6   The hearing

37.6.1 Preliminaries

After the pleadings have been concluded the tribunal, through the proper officer, will arrange a hearing date for the appeal. A form will be sent out to the parties inviting them to submit dates for the hearing and also requesting an estimate as to how long the parties think the appeal will last. The tribunal does not operate like the Crown Court or High Court where normally a case once started continues until it finishes.

> **Planning point**
>
> The tribunal operates on an appointments basis so that if, for example, two days are estimated by the parties as being sufficient time in which to dispose of the case but more time is required, a further day will need to be arranged which can be some months ahead. Consequently it is better to err on the generous side when giving estimates.

It is sensible to contact the tribunal centre to discuss the availability of dates so that a date convenient to the parties is agreed. Where Counsel is to be instructed, the clerk to Counsel should be contacted to obtain Counsel's availability.

Once a date has been agreed which is suitable to both parties, the proper officer will issue a hearing notice containing the date, time and place when the hearing will take place. This notice must be issued not less than 14 days before the hearing is due to take place. Once the hearing date is fixed the tribunal will generally be unwilling to vacate it unless there are good reasons.

Hearing dates for applications are normally fixed without reference to the parties although a hearing notice giving the details of the hearing of the application must be sent out. However, if the date fixed is likely to cause difficulty it is advisable to contact the tribunal centre as soon as possible to try to agree a convenient date.

37.6.2 Public or private hearing

Although hearings of appeals are generally heard in public, it is possible, in exceptional circumstances, to apply for evidence to be given in private if sensitive information is to be given which could harm an appellant's business. Where the evidence has been heard in private, the tribunal will still publish its decision but will endeavour to exclude as far as possible the sensitive material.

Law: The Tribunal Procedure (First-tier Tribunal) (Tax Chamber) Rules 2009 (SI 2009/273), r. 32

37.6.3 Representation at the hearing

Any party to the appeal or application (other than HMRC) may conduct the case himself or may be represented by any person whom he may choose. The person selected as the appellant's representative need not be legally qualified.

> ### Planning point
>
> However, in a difficult case where the issues are principally of a legal nature or where there is likely to be a need for lengthy cross-examination, an appellant would be advised to consider instructing Counsel to represent him. Many Counsel are familiar with being instructed by accountants in tribunal cases and will advise the appellant's advisers on the steps to be taken to get the case ready for trial.

In the case of HMRC, they tend to instruct Counsel but otherwise will use members of their Solicitors' Office – who tend to be barristers!

Law: The Tribunal Procedure (First-tier Tribunal) (Tax Chamber) Rules 2009 (SI 2009/273), r. 11

37.6.4 Failure to attend a hearing

Procedures exist for the situation where one or both parties fails to attend the hearing of an appeal or application. Where neither party appears, the tribunal may dismiss the appeal or application, although if one of the parties or a person interested in the appeal serves a notice applying for reinstatement within 14 days of the date of release of the decision or direction, the tribunal may reinstate the matter.

If one of the parties does not appear at the hearing, the tribunal may proceed in the party's absence although the absent party can apply within 14 days of the release of the decision or direction to have it set aside.

There have been instances of appellants not appearing at the hearing whereupon HMRC have applied for the matter to be heard – only to have the appeal allowed without evidence being produced by the appellant!

Law: VAT Tribunals Rules 1986 (SI 1986/590), r. 26; Tribunals Court and Enforcement Act 2007, Sch. 5, para 7; The Tribunal Procedure (First-tier Tribunal) (Tax Chamber) Rules 2009 (SI 2009/273), r. 33.

37.6.5 Preparation for the hearing

Once the hearing date has been set, the person conducting the appeal will need to prepare for the hearing. Suggested actions to be taken are as follows.

1. Confirm that the witnesses are still available and know the time and place of the tribunal centre.

2. Check that all the documents shown on both parties' lists of documents are in your possession.

3. Agree with HMRC's Solicitors' Office that a single bundle of documents will be used – this means that the tribunal does not have to keep swapping over bundles, which is confusing and time wasting. As the appellant will open the case to the tribunal it makes sense for him to take responsibility for preparing the bundle as that will enable the appellant to order the documents to suit the chronology of the opening statement.

4. Number all pages and prepare an index of the documents with page numbers. Use the list of documents as the basis for the index and add any documents on HMRC's list which are not on the appellant's list. Use a ring/spiral binder for each bundle of documents.

5. Prepare sufficient sets of documents for the hearing. Check with the tribunal if lay members are sitting with the chairman as they will each need a set. The tribunal hearing officer will need a set as will any witnesses called to give evidence. HMRC will need two sets and the appellant and his advocate will need one. In an appeal with a chairman and two members it will be necessary to have at least eight sets of documents available. Consideration should be given to sending the documents to the tribunal in advance of the hearing.

6. Consider whether it would be useful to have a stenographer present to take notes. The consent of the tribunal must be requested since to record evidence without consent is a contempt of court. In a case which is complex with substantial sums of money at stake and Leading Counsel instructed, the instruction of a stenographer can save much time and therefore costs as well as providing an

accurate record. Modern recording methods enable the record to be transcribed and delivered to the parties and the tribunal on the evening of the day when the evidence is given. Computerised systems have very sophisticated indexing which further assists recovery of the recorded evidence. Although HMRC may be prepared to contribute to the cost, it will be allowed as an expense on taxation of costs if the appeal is successful.

7. The appellant has the right to open his case. Most Counsel prepare a 'skeleton argument' for use in opening the case. This does not need to be served on HMRC in advance and unless they agree, or the tribunal directs an exchange of 'skeletons', it is better not to do so since HMRC may not reciprocate. A copy of the 'skeleton' needs to be given to the other party and the tribunal members at the hearing. The advantage of using a 'skeleton' – which in practice may be the complete opening statement of the appellant – is that the tribunal does not have to write down all the submissions, which saves time. Furthermore, the tribunal has a full record of the appellant's case. In one case, the appellant's representative was criticised by the tribunal for failing to use a skeleton argument in a matter which involved a complex piece of capital goods scheme legislation – notwithstanding that there is no obligation to use a skeleton argument.

8. Preparation of the opening statement will include further search into previous cases on the same subject matter and issues. These precedents, or 'authorities' as they are known, need to be listed, with their case reference, and served on HMRC and the tribunal. Provided sufficient notice is given, the tribunal staff may provide copies of the authorities to the tribunal. However, it is necessary to check the tribunal centre's current practice as this can vary depending on the centre and whether the hearing is at a permanent centre (London or Manchester) or a temporary centre where there are unlikely to be any law reports or sets of tribunal decisions.

9. If reference is made to an authority that is not on the list there must be sufficient copies for HMRC and the tribunal.

The above points are equally relevant for an application although there are likely to be fewer authorities (or even none at all), not least because most applications are heard in private and the decision is not published.

37.6.6 The hearing itself

Planning point

A tribunal will take great pains to assist an appellant. Indeed, at some reasonable excuse and mitigation hearings, an appellant may generate more sympathy by representing himself than by having a professional advocate. The tribunal cannot conduct an appellant's case for him and an appellant and his adviser needs to consider carefully how best to serve his interests.

Notwithstanding that the tribunal regards itself as an informal forum and representatives need not be legally qualified, complex points of law frequently arise in cases and in evasion cases there can be large amounts of evidence to sift and challenge in cross-examination.

> ### Planning point
> The tribunal will expect a professional advocate to be able to present the case competently and conduct himself in a way which is expected in a court of law.

In England witnesses are permitted to remain in the tribunal while the case is opened and the witnesses are being called. However, in Scotland all witnesses must remain outside the tribunal room. Once a witness has finished his testimony, the party calling him can ask for him to be released from further attendance, and providing the other party does not object the request will normally be granted.

Once a witness has commenced his evidence he may not discuss the case with anyone. Thus, if a lunch adjournment occurs in the course of the witness's evidence, the witness will have to stay apart from the rest of his 'team' during the adjournment.

Once the appeal has been called on by the tribunal clerk, and providing that the tribunal does not invite HMRC to make an opening statement, the appellant will open his case to the tribunal. The chairman and the members should be addressed as either 'sir' or 'madam'.

The bundle of documents should be handed to the tribunal if it does have them in advance of the hearing.

The issue in the case should be explained and then the tribunal should be taken through the formal documents such as the notice of appeal and HMRC's statement of case (if any). It is appropriate to comment on any allegation in the statement of case, stating whether it is agreed or disputed.

The opening statement should contain an outline of the evidence to be given by witnesses together with a description of the documentary evidence. The documents that are especially relevant to the appeal and bear directly on the appeal should be read to the tribunal during the opening statement. The advocate should not be too selective and deliberately miss out parts of the documents which are or may be detrimental to the case since the other party will be quick to point out the omission and make 'capital' out of it. It is better to grasp a difficult issue or damaging piece of evidence and seek to minimise the damage, thereby blunting the attack of the opposing party, rather than leaving the field open for the respondents to capitalise on this.

In the course of opening the appeal, reference should be made to the authorities and the relevant legislation in addition to setting out all the arguments and points in favour of the appeal. It should be borne in mind that the tribunal has to decide the facts according to the evidence produced and since this is the only opportunity open to an appellant for producing evidence, care needs to be taken to ensure that every relevant fact is put before the tribunal to enable it to make the findings of fact which it should record in its decision.

37.6.7 Evidence for the appellant

At the conclusion of the opening statement the appellant will be invited to call or produce the supporting evidence. Normally the appellant will be the first witness called and if he is representing himself and has given his version of events in the course of opening the case, the tribunal chairman may invite the appellant to take the oath and simply confirm that what he told the tribunal in opening is true.

If the appellant is represented, he will go into the witness box, take the oath or affirm and be questioned by his representative.

The process of producing a witness and eliciting evidence is known as 'examination in chief'. Examining a witness carries some fundamental rules, the most difficult of which to observe is that the person carrying out the examination in chief must not 'lead' the witness on a fact which is in dispute.

> **Planning point**
>
> 'Leading' the witness does not mean asking the witness a difficult question but means suggesting to the witness the answer which the examiner wishes to elicit. Thus if the date of 23 December is in issue as being the date by which a VAT return should have been posted, the examiner cannot ask, 'Did you post the return on 23 December?' but should ask, 'When did you post the return?'

> **Planning point**
>
> One way in which the appellant can ensure that all the evidence is produced is to agree with HMRC that each witness will prepare a witness statement and read it out to the tribunal when called to give evidence. The witness can then be cross-examined by HMRC's Counsel. The advantage of this procedure is that important facts are not forgotten, which can easily happen if a witness's memory has faded. It also means that the tribunal does not have to take the evidence down in longhand and has a full record of the testimony when it eventually considers its decision. One disadvantage of using this procedure is that HMRC will want to see the statement in advance which gives them more time to prepare their cross-examination.

Once the witness has given his evidence he will then be cross-examined by HMRC's representative, assuming that there are matters in the evidence which they either want to challenge or points which they wish to bring out as adding weight to their arguments. They may also want to discredit the evidence given by the witness. HMRC, through their advocate, will challenge those parts of the evidence which are likely to be at variance to evidence to be produced by their witnesses and should 'put their case' to the witness which means making it clear with which parts of the evidence they disagree.

At the conclusion of the cross-examination, the appellant or the appellant's advocate may re-examine the witness to clear up any ambiguities that may have arisen in cross-examination. However, the appellant or his advocate is not permitted to ask leading questions in the course of re-examination, nor should they introduce new matters at this stage.

When all of the appellant's witnesses have been called, HMRC may open their case. The format will broadly follow that of the appellant's opening except that they will not need to spend too much time on the pleadings as this will have been covered by the appellant. In the majority of liability appeals HMRC do not call any witnesses unless they have brought in an expert to give evidence on a technical aspect of a case or it is necessary to call the assessing officer to clear up a matter which may have arisen in the course of the appellant's case. However, as has been stated, the burden of proof is on the appellant so it is less incumbent on HMRC to produce evidence than it is on the appellant. In any event, much of the ground will have been covered and in many liability cases the primary facts are not in dispute – merely their legal interpretation of them. Where HMRC do not call evidence they will proceed to make their closing speech, to which the appellant has the right of reply.

In the event that HMRC do call witnesses to give evidence, the appellant is entitled to cross-examine them. This does not mean that the witness should be 'examined crossly', as one commentator has put it, but the witnesses should be treated firmly and courteously when they are subjected to challenges to their evidence.

> ### *Planning point*
>
> Again, as with HMRC's cross-examination, the appellant should challenge evidence which contradicts that given by his witnesses and also 'put their case' to the HMRC's witnesses. In cross-examination, the advocate is permitted to ask leading questions – indeed, can and should suggest what the answer ought to be. After all, the witness might agree with the questioner!

HMRC officers usually will wish to give evidence from notebooks in which case the tribunal chairman will seek to establish when the notes were written and if they were written at a time when the events were fresh in the officer's memory. Provided the answers are satisfactory the officer will be allowed to use his notebook. However, the notebook should be inspected to see if there is anything in it that might indicate that the officer's memory is defective as to the time when the notes were compiled and, if so, an objection can be made. Of course, if there is nothing controversial about the evidence to be given then no objection should be made. Notebooks should always be inspected to see if there is anything untoward which casts doubt on the accuracy of the answers given or the veracity of the witness.

At the conclusion of their evidence, or if they have not called or produced any, HMRC's representative will address the tribunal. It is normally at this stage that HMRC will set out their arguments in full, commenting on the case presented by the appellant and attempting to counter his arguments. If HMRC have not previously addressed the tribunal they will need to take the tribunal through the legislation and their authorities in some detail.

At the conclusion of HMRC's speech, the appellant has the 'last word' and can address the tribunal. This is largely, but is not restricted to, a reply to HMRC's speech. At this stage in the proceedings it is not generally permissible to introduce an entirely new point although from time to time issues arise in a case which neither party has considered as they may have been raised by the tribunal. These will be dealt with in the closing speech. HMRC will certainly object to new points being raised during what is essentially a reply to their points.

> ### ⚠ *Warning!*
>
> Frequently the appellant's closing speech will follow immediately HMRC have concluded their address; consequently there will be no time for preparation. Should the appellant not be professionally represented or represented by a person who is not a professional advocate, it is sensible to ask the tribunal for a short adjournment to consider the points which need to be dealt with in answer to HMRC. It is good practice to have some points already prepared for the closing speech.

37.7   Decisions

37.7.1 Decisions

In reasonable excuse and mitigation appeals, the chairman will often announce the tribunal's decision at the conclusion of the hearing. In practice, the tribunal nearly always reserves its decision but must, within 28 days, or as soon as practicable afterwards, give its decision on a notice. This will also give details of the right to appeal and how to do this.

The notice of decision should also give a written statement of facts and reasons for the decision. Where no such statement is made either party can write, within 14 days of the date of the notice, requesting a written statement of findings of fact and reasons for the decision.

Law: The Tribunal Procedure (First-tier Tribunal) (Tax Chamber) Rules 2009 (SI 2009/273), r. 35

The Tribunal may on its own account, or on application by a person that has a right to appeal the decision to the Upper Tribunal, review its decision. This is to correct errors, amend the reasons of the decision or to set aside the decision.

Law: Tribunals Court and Enforcement Act 2007, Sch. 10, para 9

37.8   Costs and interest

37.8.1 Introduction

There is no public funding (formerly legal aid) generally available to a VAT appeal. Where, however, the matter concerns a penalty case that has been deemed to be criminal in nature (civil evasion type penalties) then funding may be available. In addition, where it is thought to be in the interests of justices for the appellant to be represented, funding may be made available. Applications for funding should be made to the Legal Services Commission, 62-68 Hills Road, Cambridge, CB2 1LA.

The costs of, and incidental to, appeals to the Tribunal are at the discretion of the relevant Tribunal. The First-Tier Tribunal, however, will only award costs where it considers that the party or its representative has acted unreasonably, either in bringing the case, in defending it or in their conduct of the proceedings. The First-Tier Tribunal can also award costs in cases that have been categorized as complex. The Upper-Tribunal can order costs. Both Tribunals will give persons the opportunity to make representations regarding costs.

A person making an application for costs must make a written application to the Tribunal and send a copy to the person against whom it is proposed the order be made. A detailed schedule of costs needs to be provided. The application must be made within 28 days from the date that the Tribunal sends its decision notice (one month for Upper Tribunals).

Subject to the provisos above, the general rule in litigation is that costs follow the event so that the successful party is usually awarded his costs, unless there is good reason why he should not receive an award. Thus in *North East Garages Ltd v C & E Commrs* [1999] BVC 443, the tribunal allowed the company's appeal but refused to award it costs since the company had not told the truth in the course of the case. The decision was affirmed by the High Court on appeal by the company.

In *D S Supplies Ltd* [1996] BVC 4,171 costs were refused to the successful appellant as the company had not made its evidence available to Customs before the hearing.

In *Ness* [1995] BVC 1,367 the tribunal dismissed the appeal but awarded costs to the appellant as he had been misdirected by the VAT officer. In that case the grounds of appeal were plainly based on misdirection, but Customs had not applied to have the appeal struck out prior to the appeal being set down for hearing.

HMRC's practice when they succeed on an appeal is not to seek costs unless the appeal was 'frivolous or vexatious'. They will seek costs following 'tribunal hearings of substantial and complex cases where large sums of money are involved and which are comparable with High Court cases, unless the appeal involves an important general point of law.' Evasion penalty cases are treated as High Court cases by HMRC. They will also claim costs if the appellant fails to attend the hearing. Given the change in the way costs are now awarded, it is more likely that HMRC will seek costs where permitted and this policy may no longer be followed. It is not yet known if HMRC will maintain a policy of not seeking costs at First-Tier Tribunals.

HMRC's policy was set out by the Hon Peter Brooke MP, Minister of State, Treasury as follows:

'The practice of Customs and Excise in seeking costs in unsuccessful appeals heard by the VAT Tribunals was set out by the Right Honourable member for Ashton-under-Lyne, when he was Financial Secretary to Treasury, on 13 November 1978. There has been no change in policy since then, but with the new enforcement powers and rights of appeal, particularly on the grounds of reasonable excuse, enacted in FA 1985, it may be helpful to restate it. As a general rule, Customs and Excise do not seek costs against unsuccessful appellants. They do, however, ask for costs in certain narrowly defined cases so as to provide protection for public funds and the general body of taxpayers. They will therefore seek to continue to ask for costs at those exceptional Tribunal hearings of substantial and complex cases where large sums are involved and which are comparable with High Court cases, unless the appeal involves an important general point of law requiring clarification. They will also continue to consider seeking costs where the appellant has misused the Tribunal procedure – for example in frivolous or vexatious cases, or where the appellant has failed to appear or to be represented at a mutually arranged hearing without sufficient explanation, or where the appellant has first produced at a hearing relevant evidence which ought properly to have been disclosed at an earlier stage and which could have saved public funds had it been produced timeously.

The new penalty provisions and right of appeal to the Value Added Tax Tribunals has made no change to this policy. Customs and Excise, with the agreement of the Council on Tribunals, consider that appeals against penalties imposed under FA 1985 s. 13 on the grounds that a person has evaded VAT and his conduct has involved dishonesty, fall to be considered as being comparable with High Court cases. Where such appeals are unsuccessful, Customs and Excise will normally seek an award of costs.

In all cases, the question whether or not costs should be awarded will, of course, remain entirely within the discretion of the Tribunal concerned and the amount of any such award will be fixed either by that Tribunal, or by the High Court as provided by Tribunal procedure rules.

Customs and Excise, in consultation with the Council on Tribunals, will continue to keep their policy under careful scrutiny.'

The starting point for costs in VAT cases is the disputed decision, not the notice of appeal. See *British Institute of Management* (1980) VATTR 42. In the case of *C & E Commrs v Dave* [2002] BVC 516, Burton J held that only costs incidental to the review were recoverable, not costs incurred in persuading HMRC not to assess the appellant to duty or civil penalties.

37.8.2 Assessment of costs

In a simple case the tribunal will assess the amount to be awarded, but in complex appeals it will order an assessment of costs by a costs judge (see Civil Procedure Rules 1998 (SI 1998/3132)). The amount awarded is unlikely to cover the full costs if the award is made on the standard basis. However, if costs are awarded on an indemnity basis full costs will be recovered. The tribunal will only order costs to be paid on an indemnity basis where there has been bad behaviour on the part of HMRC. Thus in *VSP Marketing Ltd* [1995] BVC 1,206 it appeared to the tribunal that a notice requiring security as a condition of trading had been issued for an unauthorised purpose. Accordingly, costs were awarded on an indemnity basis.

Where costs are ordered to be assessed by a costs judge, the appellant would be well advised to use a costs draughtsman to act on his behalf. The draughtsman will charge according to a percentage of the bill of costs, but he will draft the bill and try to negotiate a settlement of the amount with HMRC. In the event it is not possible to agree the quantum, the draughtsman will conduct the hearing in front of the costs judge.

Any assessment of costs will involve a detailed analysis of the time spent and the work done on the appeal by the various members of the adviser's staff together with their chargeout rates.

⚠ **Warning!**

HMRC normally challenge the grades of the personnel involved and the size of their chargeout rates. They will allege that where more than one member of staff was involved there has been duplication of work. Consequently, it is essential to keep detailed records of which members of staff worked on the case and for how long, to demonstrate that the work was done at the appropriate level of staff. This will enable a robust case on costs to be advanced.

Costs of solicitors, barristers and accountants will generally be allowed – although where both solicitors and accountants are involved there may well be a challenge from HMRC alleging duplication – but claiming the costs of an appellant in person are less straightforward.

Where the appellant is not a limited company, the only costs claimable will be travel expenses. Where the appellant is a limited company it may be possible for costs to be claimed by officers of the company who represented the company for the time spent in the preparation of the appeal (*G A Boyd Building Services Ltd* [1993] BVC 1,340).

37.8.3 Award of interest

Where the tax assessed has been paid by the appellant prior to the appeal being heard, a successful appellant is entitled to an award of interest – VATA 1994, s. 84(8). The rate of interest is not specified in either the Act or the Tribunals Rules. In *Parochial Church Council of St Luke, Great Crosby, Liverpool* (1983) 2 BVC 208,018, the tribunal held that the rate of interest to be awarded, in the absence of agreement between the parties, should be the High Court short-term investment account rate.

In *Margrie Holdings Ltd v C & E Commrs* (1990) 5 BVC 170, a claim was allowed by the tribunal for compound rate interest. However, in *Peoples Bathgate & Livingston Ltd* [1996] BVC 4,335, the same (Edinburgh) tribunal declined to follow *Margrie*, holding:

> 'It appears to the Tribunal that compounding interest unless specifically sanctioned by Statute would be a most unusual course to follow. It is easy to envisage it as perhaps being appropriate when some misconduct or oppression has taken place such as for example when a Trustee defaults with Trust funds – a situation vouched by authority – but we were referred to no case other than *Margrie Holdings* in which compound interest had been apparently allowed and in our view it flies in the face of established authority to allow it in a case which cannot be described as exceptional.'

More recently the tribunal has used the rate prescribed by VATA 1994, s. 78 – interest in the case of official error.

37.9   Appeals from the tribunal

> ### ⚠ *Warning!*
> It is important to note that it is not possible to introduce new evidence at an appeal and consequently it is essential that all relevant evidence is introduced at the tribunal hearing. An appeal is to be on a point of law only, unless no Tribunal could have reasonably come to its decision as to the facts.

An unsuccessful party can appeal to the Upper Tribunal on a point of law. The leading decision on the differentiation between law and fact is *Edwards v Barstow & Harrison* HL (1955) 36 TC 207.

An appeal of the First Tier Tribunal decision can only be made with the permission of the First tier Tribunal. If that is not obtained, an application can be made to the Upper Tribunal for leave to appeal. The time limit for appealing is 56 days from the date of release of the decision to the parties. Although accountants can act for appellants in the tribunal they have no standing in courts of law. Indeed, a company has to be represented by a solicitor whose name must appear on the court record. Consequently, unless the appellant is acting in person, a solicitor will need to be instructed to lodge the notice of appeal.

There is a further appeal from the Upper Tribunal to the Court of Appeal and thence to the House of Lords. At any time a court can refer a case to the European Court of Justice if a point arises on the interpretation of the VAT Directive or other EU law which the court feels unable to decide for itself. The House of Lords as the highest appellate court is required to refer a case to the European Court if a point of EU law is involved.

37.10 Judicial review

The legal process known as judicial review can be used for challenging HMRC's decisions. However, there is a body of case law which establishes that judicial review is not appropriate where there is another domestic remedy available. In *R v VAT Tribunals, ex parte Cohen* (1983) 1 BVC 582, McCullough J said in the course of his judgment:

> 'At a very late stage in the argument a further factor emerged which had certainly not been apparent to me beforehand. There is a statutory right of appeal under the Tribunals and Inquiries Act 1971 which enables questions of law arising from decisions of the value added tax tribunal to be ventilated in this court. Notices of appeal have been given by both companies. There being a statutory appellate procedure to this court on points of law of which the companies have availed themselves, it is beyond argument that, whatever the merits of a possible application for judicial review, no one sitting in this jurisdiction and hearing the substantive application would exercise the discretion of the court by granting judicial review. The remedy, as is known, is discretionary and is not granted where a statutory mechanism of appeal enabling the very point of which complaint is made to be dealt with already exists.'

Accordingly, where a tribunal has given a decision on an appeal the correct route for challenging the decision would seem to be by Notice of Motion unless there is a challenge based on the fact that the tribunal has not dealt fairly with the case. See *R v C & E Commissioners, ex parte Dangol (t/a The Great Katmandu Tandoori)* [2000] BVC 76.

37.11 Making a complaint

The first port of call for a complaint against HMRC in respect of how they have handled a particular matter is HMRC itself. Their complaints handling has improved in recent years, and has recently been centralised regionally. A number of regional units have been established in Ipswich, Cardiff, London, Leeds, Belfast, Edinburgh and Southampton. Each will have specially trained staff who will respond to complaints within ten working days.

On the whole, this should be seen as a positive step, although it is not known how many of the complaints they deal with will concern problems arising from the very centralisation process which has brought them into existence!

If the complaint is not satisfactorily resolved at this level, further opportunities exist, in the shape of the Adjudicator, the taxpayer's MP and the Parliamentary Ombudsman.

37.12 Complaints to the Adjudicator

The Adjudicator acts as an impartial referee in cases where the taxpayer feels dissatisfied with the way HMRC have handled their affairs. This includes how HMRC have exercised their discretionary powers, and the manner in which a person or his property has been searched. Other examples include complaints about excessive delays, mistakes or discourtesy by officers.

The Adjudicator is independent and is not part of HMRC's management structure. However, before a complaint can be considered by the Adjudicator, it must first have been made to HMRC. Any such complaint should be supported with as much relevant information as possible. The services of the Adjudicator are free, but complaints must be made within six months of any review by HMRC.

The Adjudicator will not deal with:

- matters which arose before 1 April 1995;
- matters of VAT law and liability (thus cases which are appealable to a VAT or other independent tribunal are outside the Adjudicator's remit);
- matters relating to a criminal prosecution although he can consider matters which could not be considered by the courts, or
- complaints which have been investigated by the Parliamentary Commissioner.

The address for complaints is:

The Adjudicator's Office
8th Floor
Euston Tower
286 Euston Road
London NW1 3US
Tel: 020 7667 1832
Fax: 020 7667 1830

Before complaining to the Adjudicator, the matter must first have been referred to the HMRC Office dealing with the affairs or the collector responsible for the region. If the matter cannot be settled locally, the complaint must be made to the Adjudicator as soon as possible, but within six months at the latest.

Full details should be submitted in writing, quoting the relevant VAT registration number and the exact nature of the complaint, along with any costs that have been incurred as a result of action taken by HMRC. Applicants are advised to put forward recommendations on how they feel the complaint should be resolved.

If the Adjudicator considers the complaint to be valid, and one that falls within his remit, a full report will be requested from HMRC. The circumstances of the complaint will be fully considered and any recommendations on how the matter should be resolved will be forwarded by the Adjudicator to HMRC and the taxpayer involved.

HMRC have agreed to accept the recommendations of the Adjudicator, unless there are very exceptional circumstances for not doing so. Generally, they will provide some financial compensation to redress any loss as a result of their maladministration, as recommended by the Adjudicator. If for any reason HMRC do not follow the recommendation, the Adjudicator will want to know the full reasons why and will publish details in the annual report, retaining the individual's anonymity.

In the early years of the Adjudicator's responsibility for these matters, the backlog of cases at the Adjudicator's office was a real disincentive to using this complaints procedure, but this deficiency has now been rectified and a relatively timely outcome can be expected.

37.13 Complaints to an MP

> **Planning point**
>
> This can be a most effective step but should be used sparingly. There is nothing which focuses HMRC's mind more than an MP's enquiries.

An effective way in which a VAT-registered person can complain against HMRC is to write to their local Member of Parliament. If the MP decides that the complaint is proper, he can deal with it in different ways.

This can be done on a personal basis, for instance taking the form of a letter to HMRC, which usually has the effect of focusing the minds of the officers involved in the dispute. Alternatively it can take the form of the MP asking a Parliamentary question (if he feels the matter is important enough).

With the complainant's permission, he can also refer the question to the Parliamentary Ombudsman.

37.14 Complaints to the Ombudsman

The Parliamentary Ombudsman (officially known as the Parliamentary Commissioner for Administration) is someone completely independent of the Government who can investigate complaints by members of the public about the way they have been treated by government departments. The Office was set up by the Parliamentary Commissioner Act 1967.

The Ombudsman has power to investigate the actions of most central government departments and certain other bodies, including HMRC and the Department of Work and Pensions, but not those of nationalised industries and similar bodies.

The Ombudsman can only help a taxpayer when asked to do so by a Member of Parliament. One of an MP's traditional duties is to help his constituents if they have complaints about government departments, and Parliament decided that the Ombudsman should be brought in only when an MP considers that this is necessary. The first approach, therefore, is to an MP (this does not have to be the taxpayer's constituency MP) to ask for the grievance to be referred to the Ombudsman. The MP may wish to try to put the matter right by a direct approach to the government department concerned.

The facts should be set out in writing for the MP and submitted together with all correspondence with the department. If the MP decides to refer the matter to the Ombudsman, all papers will be returned in due course through the MP. A complaint can also be made to an MP on behalf of the taxpayer by a Citizens' Advice Bureau or a professional adviser such as a lawyer or accountant. The Ombudsman must, however, always be satisfied that the person with the grievance actually wants the matter investigated. If an MP refuses to refer the matter to the Ombudsman, a direct application to him can be made.

There is no charge for using the Ombudsman's service and it is not necessary to incur legal expenses in submitting a complaint.

For the Ombudsman to be able to take up a complaint, the grievance must be caused by administrative actions taken by HMRC. These actions must affect the taxpayer personally or, in the case of a business, firm, society or similar group, they must affect the specific interests of that company, society or group and its members.

The Ombudsman cannot consider complaints about government policy or legislation in general, these are matters for Parliament itself to consider.

The Ombudsman's job is to look at the way government departments deal with the public, not to act as a sort of court of appeal from their decisions. It is not sufficient to disagree with a decision: the taxpayer must show that there might have been something wrong with the way the decision was taken, for example, that the HMRC officer failed in his duty to give full and fair consideration to representations because he failed to take them all into account.

The Parliamentary Commissioner Act 1967, which established the Ombudsman, does not define maladministration. It includes corruption, bias, harshness, misleading a member of the public as to his rights, using powers for a wrong purpose, unreasonable delay and general inefficiency, eg losing a letter, file or an appeal form.

The law states that the Ombudsman may investigate matters where someone claims to have sustained injustice in consequence of maladministration. But the taxpayer must give the Ombudsman something to go on, some evidence, documentary or otherwise, which suggests that on the face of things, a government department has done its work badly and that he personally has been affected by what he believes to be bad administration, which includes such things as a delay in answering letters, showing bias or unfair discrimination, failure to examine a case properly, or levying distress incorrectly.

For the Ombudsman to be able to consider a complaint, the taxpayer must normally be able to show that he brought it to the attention of an MP within a year of realising that he had a grievance, although in exceptional circumstances the Ombudsman has discretion to allow a longer time. The taxpayer must also be able to show that:

- he is resident in the UK (but he need not have British nationality or citizenship);
- if not resident when making the complaint, he was present in the UK when the actions complained about took place, or
- what he is complaining about concerns rights and obligations arising in the UK.

The Ombudsman has powers similar to those of a High Court judge, but does not operate in a formal way, as in a court of law. The Ombudsman has the power to inspect most government files and papers and can summon anyone to give evidence in an investigation (Parliamentary Commissioner Act 1967, s. 8).

Proceedings, however, are usually informal and are always private. The Ombudsman does not usually see complainants personally and in fact many investigations can be completed simply by examining files. Where necessary, the Ombudsman's investigating officers will obtain further information from the taxpayer.

If a taxpayer incurs expenses (for example, by attending an interview with the Ombudsman), these expenses will normally be paid.

When the investigating officers have collected all the relevant facts about the complaint, the Ombudsman personally considers them and decides whether to uphold the complaint. If the complaint is upheld, the department concerned will be invited to offer a suitable remedy for the injustice caused by maladministration and the Ombudsman will send a full report on the case to the MP who referred the complaint, with a copy supplied for passing to the taxpayer.

In almost all cases, departments readily put right anything the Ombudsman finds wrong; but the Ombudsman has no power to order a department to do so. If, exceptionally, a department is not prepared to provide an appropriate remedy, the Ombudsman can report the matter to Parliament, so that Parliament can decide what further action to take. The Ombudsman may conclude that there has been no maladministration causing injustice and that the complaint cannot be upheld. But whatever the conclusions, there is no appeal against the Ombudsman's findings.

Investigations can be lengthy. The report is officially published by the House of Commons.

Not all actions of government departments are open to investigation by the Ombudsman. If the matter giving rise to the grievance is one for which there is a right of appeal to an independent tribunal, then that right of appeal should be used. The Ombudsman is not meant as an alternative to such statutory appeal procedures.

If the matter is one for which the taxpayer could seek a remedy in the courts, the Ombudsman will only agree to look into it if it is considered unreasonable to expect the taxpayer to go to court over it; but the cost of going to court is not normally regarded on its own as a good reason for not going. If the taxpayer has already taken the matter to court (and the court is empowered to deal with it), the Ombudsman has no discretion to investigate it.

Other matters that the Ombudsman generally cannot investigate include:

- the commencement and conduct of court proceedings, and
- contractual or other commercial dealings between the public and government departments (Parliamentary Commissioner Act 1967, Sch. 3).

The Ombudsman's Office will not answer enquiries from the press or public about particular cases. The Act prohibits the Ombudsman from passing on information obtained in the course of an investigation, except for the purpose of making his reports to MPs and to Parliament.

However, the Office is able to give general advice and to answer enquiries about the Ombudsman's jurisdiction, for example, whether a particular department or a particular type of action is within the scope of the Act. However other enquiries about jurisdiction, especially on matters where the Ombudsman's discretion is involved, cannot be answered without investigating the full circumstances of the case after it has been formally referred to the Ombudsman through an MP.

Case Table

(References are to paragraph numbers)

Legislation Finding List

(References are to paragraph numbers)

Value Added Tax Act 1994 – continued

Official Publications

(References are to paragraph numbers)

Index

(References are to paragraph numbers)

Cap

Paw